SPORT

AS A FORM OF

HUMAN FULFILLMENT

AN ORGANIC PHILOSOPHY OF SPORT HISTORY

Robert G. Osterhoudt, Ph.D.

Professor Emeritus of Liberal Arts and Sciences

Volume I

Trafford Publishing

Order this book online at www.trafford.com
or email orders@trafford.com

Most Trafford titles are also available at major online book retailers.

Note for Librarians: A cataloguing record for this book is available from Library
and Archives Canada at www.collectionscanada.ca/amicus/index-e.html

Printed in Victoria, BC, Canada.

ISBN: 978-1-4120-4659-6
Volume 1

*Our mission is to efficiently provide the world's finest, most comprehensive book publishing
service, enabling every author to experience success. To find out how to publish your book, your
way, and have it available worldwide, visit us online at www.trafford.com*

Trafford rev. 2/10/2010

www.trafford.com

North America & international
toll-free: 1 888 232 4444 (USA & Canada)
phone: 250 383 6864 ♦ fax: 812 355 4082

PREFACE

For good, bad, or nil, this is the sort of thing that one spends a lifetime doing. Better said, it is what I have spent a lifetime doing. It is for me the formal end toward which virtually all else has tended. It is, still at this, only the second aspect of a still larger, a two-aspect, venture. The first of these aspects, <u>The Philosophy of Sport: An Overview</u>, was published in 1991; it primarily concerned philosophical issues and had secondarily to do with historical matters. This, the second, aspect invokes the philosophical agenda of the first but is principally devoted to fleshing out the historical record of that agenda. Although the tangible development of this venture and this manuscript began approximately twenty-five to thirty years ago, its germinal origins can be traced to a pre-adolescent sentiment for sport and for serious study that has significantly deepened and widened in the more than half-century since. The book's governing principle, its motive force, is what I take to be the distinctly human passion for sport, for the humanities, and for genuine education. Its special inspirations were provided by Jacob Bronowski's "The Ascent of Man: A Personal View" and Kenneth Clark's "Civilization: A Personal View" which respectively did for science and the arts what I have here aimed to do for (or, as some are likely to say, to) sport. In the improbable event that I ever acquire any money to speak of, I hope to attempt a sharply abridged film version of the manuscript in the approximate style of Bronowski and Clark.

At bottom, this is a synthetic philosophy of world history (from an organic perspective) having principally to do with sport. It is an organic philosophy of world sport history which attempts to comment on the essential factors (the characteristic and decisive factors, the dominant tendencies) in the origin, development, nature, and purpose of human culture and its sporting attributes. It aims at a systematic and comprehensive account of the basic place of sport in human life, at a dutiful recounting and a reflective interpretation of what sport has been and what it is ultimately for; in the end, it aims at a dutiful recounting and a reflective interpretation of sport as a form of distinctly human fulfillment. As such, it is grounded in the broad vision of philosophy; it is oriented to the basic form and content of history; and it is pointed mainly at the fundamental character and development of sport. The emphasis given in the text to the humanities, to the authentically human, to the intrinsic features of human experience, and, thus, to uniquely human experience as such is a characteristic mark of organic teaching. The text consequently tends to condemn what it argues are the inauthentic practices that currently dominate sport (practices entailing the rawest and most strident forms of military, commercial, and nationalistic partisanship), the significance of which is vastly overstated in established world culture. It likewise tends to acclaim what it argues is the authentic (organic) character of sport, the significance of which is vastly understated in established world culture. There are several other features of the text that I want also to comment on here:

- The perspective of the text ends at the conclusion of the twentieth century; neither events that have occurred since December 31, 2000 nor manuscripts that have been published since that time have been therefore considered or cited, even though this practice tends to slight very recent achievements and to depreciate achievements that were ongoing at the end of the century. In a manuscript in which all aspects are as intimately connected to all other aspects as they are in this case, one cannot very well include matters that occurred shortly before publication.
- All of the available English literature in essay, book, thesis-dissertation, and proceedings forms (as well as much of the accessible literature in other languages in these forms) has been considered. With several notable exceptions (namely, the major journals concerning the history and philosophy of sport and several seminal essays concerning the philosophy of sport), however, the <u>Selected Bibliography</u> includes reference only to the most revealing, book-length, English manuscripts that have aimed in the same broad and synthetic direction as the current text. I have thus neglected to cite manuscripts of truncated historical, geographical, or philosophical gaze, biographies, anecdotal reminiscences, and those concerning specific sports (except several leading texts having to do with the history of the most prominent international sports). Much of great relevance and significance has

been therefore left uncited, most notably the primary source literature in English and other languages. Some of this literature, particularly the other-than-English literature, has been not only uncited but unread. As a young man, I did French and Romanian well enough to plough through exacting text and did Spanish, Italian, German, Russian, Latin, and Attican Greek well enough to make sense of a phrase or two. I no longer do even that well. The literature that has been cited nonetheless refers, in turn, to the best of the literature that has not and there may be another 800-page manuscript in a full accounting of what has become an immense body of distinguished work.

- There has been a serious attempt to discuss both the cultural groundings of sport (the political, economic, social, and intellectual groundings) and sporting phenomena themselves. This organic sense of proportionate attention to general tendency and to specific detail has resulted in a fairly extensive discussion of both the most significant of sweeping influences on sport and the most significant sporting achievements themselves (including the development of particular sports and the achievements of great athletes). Both are considered relevant in essential respects to a searching examination of the concerns at issue here; neither is considered trivial to such an examination.
- The text tends to read in a deductive direction, from wide perspectives to the principal embodiments of these perspectives, embodiments on which all more particular (albeit unmentioned) detail "hangs."
- Modern terms are most often used to refer to pre-modern sports closely resembling modern activities and to refer to pre-modern nations now occupied by modern states.
- The birth and death years, if known, of only the most prominent figures have been cited.
- I have not employed the standard relation of text to endnotes except in the case of referential endnotes. What has otherwise landed in the endnotes I take to be of textual significance. What has landed in the textual endnotes would have nonetheless disrupted too emphatically the continuity of textual account if it had been included in the text itself.
- I have neither uniformly employed the standard practice of endnote citation in terms of providing exactingly detailed accounts of the literary source of all claims. The judgments taken here are a consequence of what I understand is the consensus judgment of the established literature (on the various subjects considered) as this judgment may be plausibly interpreted according to organic standard. A philosophy of (sport) history of the type here attempted is not otherwise plausibly attainable.
- The Contents have been arranged to include a reference to all major subjects; the Index has been reserved for notice of others.
- Standard Roman-English characters (which have been taken to include French diacritical marks) have been employed throughout.
- The division of the two volumes is arbitrary in respect to content; the second volume is to be read continuously with the first. I would have thus preferred publishing the manuscript in a single volume but its dimensions, made necessary in order to limit the number of pages and therefore the cost of production and purchase, and its length required that it be done in two. The available technology of paperback binding was not up to the task of enclosing more than 800 unusually large pages in a single volume.

I am deeply indebted to many magnificent people for the gift of life and for the opportunity to be raised successfully to adulthood, to be educated in subjects of profoundly compelling interest to me, and to work in a profession of such meaningful consequence as I have. The street children of Bombay will not and should not long grieve for me. In The Philosophy of Sport: An Overview, I went on about this in ways that not everyone appreciated. I will therefore limit myself here to a concise expression of unqualified gratitude to my wonderful grandparents, Bessie and Willard Osterhoudt and Helen and Loyal Wilmarth; my unsurpassed parents, Rita and Clarence "Oz" Osterhoudt; my engaging brothers and sister, Bill, Gary, and Nancy; my talented and beautiful wife, Barbara Lynn Hamilton; and my unexcelled children, Kris, Kristi, Nicole, Karin, and Kirk. I have also very much valued my grandchildren, Lee, Joshua (Stephanie), Brittany, Kyle, Kyle, Zachary, Derek, Dylan, Christopher, Ruby Arica, and Mackenzie; aunt, Rosena; uncle, Wayne; nieces, Tammy (Jim), Randi, and Jenny; nephew, Richard (Maggie); mother-in-law, Neva; sisters-in-law, Joann, Marlene, Marta (Curtis), and Terry; brother-in-law, Ed; daughters-in-law, Paula and Leah; sons-in-law, Jordan and Kevin; ex-wife, Kerry; and former parents-in-law, Lois and Hooker Kyle. Especially much too is owed to my many remarkable teachers and coaches at the State College (Pennsylvania) Senior High School, Pennsylvania State University, University of Maryland, and University of Illinois; most memorably, Dr. Yib Bolton, Dr. Benton Bristol, Mr. John Doolittle, Mr. Norman Gordon, Mr. Jackson Horner, Dr. Guy Lewis, Mr. William Long, Dr.

John Lucas, Dr. Chauncey Morehouse, Dr. Richard Nelson, Mrs. Maretta Rice, Dr. Richard Schacht, Mr. Mike Shapiro, and Dr. Earle Zeigler. Professors Lewis, Lucas, and Zeigler, all people of commanding distinction, wisdom, resolve, and good will, had most to do with my education in the history and philosophy of sport, the subjects which formed the central precincts of my professional life; my debt to them is incalculable. I want also to remember most fondly and gratefully:

- Dr. Matt Maetozo, who gave me my first full-time professional position at Lock Haven (Pennsylvania) State College, the best and most rewarding post I have had, and who nurtured me through it with well-measured kindness, a ruthless sense of fair play, firm leadership, and uncommon insight;

- the several other very decent and able folk for whom I have worked in professional capacities; most notably, Dr. John Alexander, Dr. Warren Fraleigh, Dr. Eloise Jaeger, Dr. Gary Krahenbuhl, Dr. Tom McIntyre, Dr. Jim Odenkirk, Dr. Bob Pangrazi, and Dr. Mary Young; Jim Odenkirk, in particular, has been a loyal and deeply respected friend for almost thirty years;

- my friends, colleagues, and students at the several American universities at which I studied and taught for nearly forty years, Pennsylvania State University, University of Maryland, Lock Haven State College, University of Illinois, State University of New York at Brockport, University of Minnesota, and a banking institution in Arizona masquerading as a university, an institution so unworthy of public support that I am ashamed to admit any association whatever with it and an institution that I cannot bring myself to explicitly cite here (despite my respect for its library);

- my friends and colleagues of the Philosophic Society for the Study of Sport/International Association for the Philosophy of Sport and the North American Society for Sport History;

- the director of the finest national Fulbright Commission on the planet (the Hungarian Commission), Dr. Huba Bruckner, whose abundant kindness and exemplary judgment were heaped on Barbara and me with neither reluctance nor limit throughout our memorable fellowship in Budapest;

- my many dear friends in masters track and field for whom I have developed an enormous affection and to whom I am deeply indebted for much of the joy in my sporting and wider life;

- the many kind folk of public and university libraries, national and international scholarly societies, national and international sport federations, and sporting museums/halls of fame, as well as independent scholars, who responded so generously to my many annoying requests for obscure information (particularly for the birth and death years of little-known athletes); most notably, Klaus Amrhein, Susan Bandy, Hakon Bjercke, Gherardo Bonini, Fiona Clark, Richard Cox, Scott Davis, Bob Duenkel, Fei Jian (Colin Fee), Ralph Hickok, Tony Hinchliffe, Chuck Hoey, Ove Karlsson, Bill Mallon, Ludmila Maslakova, Kim Miri, Lisa Mitchell, Susan Rayl, Ed Sears, and Chris Turner; and

- the superb folk of Trafford Publishing whose enduring patience, astute judgment, and eminently good will made the tangible production of the book possible; most notably, Jacqui Ouldali, Cara Hamilton, James Gibson, and Alyx Gilgunn.

Bob Osterhoudt
Sun City, Arizona
September 7, 2004

CONTENTS

Volume I

The musical and movement arts

Sporting Developments

Contemporary modern physical education and closely related activities

Contemporary modern athletics to the First World War

Volume II

INTRODUCTION

The principal subject of this modest manuscript is sport. Few subjects are more widely acclaimed, touch the popular imagination more deeply, yet (until the last approximate half of the twentieth century) have been less earnestly studied than sport. Most of the reflective thought that has been devoted to the subject, moreover, has been of a largely scientific, as distinct from a humanistic, type; most such thought has concerned the biological, psychological, or sociological character and significance of the activity as against its historical or philosophical dimensions. Although (until recently) rarely spoken of in exacting historical or philosophical terms, an authentic understanding, appreciation, and practice of sport nonetheless depend necessarily on accounts that show its origin and development (on historical accounts) as well as on accounts that reveal its essential nature and purpose (on philosophical accounts). Together, historical and philosophical interpretations of sport -- the so-termed humanistic perspectives of sport -- demonstrate the basic place of sport in human life, the basic place of sport in the full relief of human experience as such. These interpretations disclose what sport has been and what it is ultimately for. They reveal the grounding charms of sport in distinctly human terms and they also illumine the wider character of humanity itself (insofar as humanity has expressed itself as persistently as it has in sporting ways). Humanistic interpretations of the type here espoused attempt to demonstrate both that sport forms an integral aspect of human experience and that it is also a fundamental expression of that experience. In the creative flow of human activity, sport has had a conspicuous, if a formally neglected, place and it therefore figures importantly in any pensive examination of genuine human experience.

The purpose of this manuscript is to show, in broad overview, the origin, development, nature, and purpose of sport from its first appearance in the ancient primitive world to its elaborate place in contemporary modern civilization; to give a systematic and comprehensive account of sport as a function of the cultural events that have embodied it throughout its occasion in human affairs; and to do all of this under the interpretive gaze of an organic world view. The result is a synthetic précis of the accomplished historical and philosophical literature's collective judgment concerning sport in the wide context of human culture from the perspective of the organic thesis. The result is an organic philosophy of (world) sport history in which the essential factors (the characteristic and decisive factors, the dominant tendencies) in the origin, development, nature, and purpose of human culture and its sporting attributes are dutifully recounted and reflectively interpreted. According to the organic sense of life and sport, it is only by way of such a result that sport can be plausibly connected to the end of distinctly human fulfillment and that human life itself can be waged in full accord with its own most basic inclinations.

There are three main philosophic interpretations of reality (and of sport as well for that matter), the organic, mechanistic, and skeptical interpretations. These interpretations are distinguished by characteristically differing views of the most basic of philosophical issues; namely, the issue sometimes referred to as that of the whole and the parts, that of the one and the many, or that of form and content. This issue concerns the character of reality's governing principle (reality's fundamental nature and purpose, customarily framed in terms of singular and enduring spirituality, or consciousness), the character of all else (all other-than-reality's-governing-principle, customarily framed in terms of multiple and changing materiality, or physicality), and the relation between reality's governing principle and all else. The characteristically differing views of the organic, mechanistic, and skeptical interpretations in respect to the issue of the whole and the parts evoke, in turn, qualitatively discrete perceptions of humanity, nature, divinity, knowledge, (moral, aesthetic, and socio-political) value, as well as such as history, education, and sport.

The organic thesis, unlike its leading alternatives, argues that the governing principle of reality and all else are necessarily related, that each contributes something essential to the other, that neither may be characterized independently of the other (the doctrine of monism), and that each therefore stands in a balanced, proportionate, harmonious, unified, and continuous relation to the other. This means that spirituality and materiality are not utterly different sorts of things (substances), but different aspects of the same thing;

1

that neither spirituality nor materiality has caused the other (that neither thereby holds primacy over the other); that neither has gained ascendancy over the other (that neither thereby depreciates the other); and that neither is inaccessible to human experience as such (that neither is thereby imposed on, unknowable to, or alienated from human experience). This further means both that reality is a purposeful, as distinct from a purposeless, order (i.e., the world fulfills the discernible and enduring aims of its governing principle) and that reality is a developing, as distinct from a changeless, a determined, a freedomless, order (i.e., the world embodies the sense of change and the sense of moral, aesthetic, and socio-political choice that "all oth-er-than-reality's-governing-principle" entails). The organic thesis thereby reveals a way of feeling, thinking, and experiencing – a way of being – that delivers us to our totality as co-equally spiritual and material creatures; that makes the defining characteristics of humanity (namely, self-conscious reason, or that form of embodied consciousness ultimately capable of explaining itself) the central datum of reality, life, and philosophy; and that thus defines reality, humanity, and philosophy as an active search for itself, not over and against nature and divinity as mere entities to be trampled, mere entities to have power over, but in accord with nature and divinity as the two principal aspects of our experience. Concisely said, the organic thesis satisfies the four basic aims of modern life/modern philosophy (the dominant form of philosophy to and including Hegel) more plausibly than its leading alternatives:

- it conceives of reality as an order in which the governing principle of reality stands in a symbiotic relation to all else (and the aspects of all else stand likewise in a symbiotic relation to one another);
- it conceives of reality as an intelligible, not an arbitrary, order, the basis of which is held within (not without) human experience;
- it conceives of reality as a purposeful, not an accidental, order; and
- it conceives of reality as a changing and free, not an utterly determined, order.

The main alternatives to the organic thesis, the mechanistic and skeptical theses, fall down in at least two of these aims. The mechanistic thesis argues that the relation between the governing principle of reality, reality's fundamental nature and purpose, and all else is discontinuous; that this principle and all else relate to one another but not necessarily; that neither therefore contributes anything essential to the other; that each may be thus characterized independently of the other (the doctrine of dualism/pluralism); and that each therefore stands in an unbalanced, disproportionate, disharmonious, and disunified relation to the other. This means that spirituality and materiality are utterly different sorts of things (substances), that either materiality or spirituality has caused the other (that either thereby holds primacy over the other), that either has gained ascendancy over the other (that either thereby depreciates the other), and that either is inaccessible to human experience (that either is thereby imposed on, unknowable to, and alienated from human experience). The mechanistic thesis has taken two chief forms, materialism and spiritualism.

Materialism holds that the physical realm has brought the spiritual into existence and is therefore the primary, the dominant, feature of reality; it thus explains the spiritual realm as a subjugated consequence of the material. Materialism thereby tends to an imbalanced, a one-sided, view of the physical-spiritual relation which privileges the physical at the expense of the spiritual. It also tends to an arbitrary interpretation of reality in the sense that it is the defining characteristics of nature (namely, unconscious physicality), not the defining characteristics of humanity, which form the central datum of reality, life, and philosophy; humanity, by this view, is none other than a natural fact. Materialism likewise manages only a fallow sense of world purpose (whatever is taken as implicitly inherent in nature) but accounts especially well for change and the freedom entailed by change (the mark of "all other-than-reality's-governing-principle").

Spiritualism, conversely, holds that the spiritual realm has brought the material into existence and is therefore the primary, the dominant, feature of reality; it thus explains the material realm as a subjugated consequence of the spiritual. Spiritualism thereby tends to an imbalanced, a one-sided, view of the spiritual-physical relation which privileges the spiritual at the expense of the physical. It also tends to an arbitrary interpretation of reality in the sense that it is the defining characteristics of divinity (namely, unembodied consciousness), not the defining characteristics of humanity, which form the central datum of reality, life, and philosophy; humanity, by this view, is none other than a divine fact. Spiritualism likewise manages only a fallow sense of change and the freedom entailed by change but accounts especially well for world purpose (whatever is taken as explicitly inherent in divinity), which is the mark of reality's governing principle.

And the skeptical thesis, of which nineteenth-century and twentieth-century post-modernism is the most recent, and arguably the most instructive, form, argues that such issues as the fundamental nature and relation of reality's governing principle and "all other-than-reality's-governing-principle" are about irresolvable matters, matters that either exceed the scope of human experience or are themselves without merit. This view effectively rejects the criteria by which modern life/modern philosophy (to and including Hegel) judged itself. It nonetheless deals memorably well with the matter of change and freedom and gives a compelling account of life from the perspective of inherently human experience (thus evading the arbitrary tendencies of materialism and spiritualism). It does not account, however, so explicitly well as the organic thesis for the balanced relation of our material and spiritual expressions nor for a sense of world purpose.

Only the organic thesis has managed to preserve the integrity of both our spiritual and our bodily aspects, thereby putting right the one-sided bodily excesses of materialism and the one-sided intellectual excesses of spiritualism (effectively, the fragmentary estrangements of dualism/pluralism in its two main forms) and putting right as well the vacuous inclinations of skepticism. There are glimpses of the organic tendency in ancient Greek thought (most notably, in the Periclean anthropology, in the Aristotelian ideal, and in classical architecture and sculpture), in the thought of medieval and early modern Islam (most notably, in Mogul architecture), and in the thought of the European Renaissance (most notably, in the literary triumphs of the early modern Italian humanists and in Italian, Burgundian, and German architecture, sculpture, painting, and music). But it was in the genius of the modern European Enlightenment and its romantic/realist sequel (most notably, in French, German, British/Irish, Russian, American, Scandinavian, Italian, and Spanish philosophy, literature, painting, sculpture, and music) that the organic thesis reached its highest formal development. This philosophically dominated movement was importantly foreseen by Spinoza and by Schelling; it was most aptly elaborated in the metaphysical discourses of Hegel; and it was later emulated most skillfully by Croce.

Hegel claimed that Idea (the system of rational laws, or laws of consciousness, that constitutes reality's governing principle; concisely, the whole) concretely actualizes itself (since it is both formal substance and self-actualizing principle in one) as phenomena (concisely, the parts). By this view, the phenomenal world constitutes the material stage (the concrete, self-actualizing differentiations) in the developmental actualization of Idea (i.e., in the dialectic, the living, historical process of rational evolution, the unfolding of Idea). Accordingly, Idea does not exist prior to, nor does it function as the cause of phenomena; it exists only as it is embodied in phenomena. The system of reason exists only as it is revealed in concrete human experience. Otherwise, if Idea were the infinite cause of finitude for most prominent instance, the spiritual and the material worlds would be qualitatively distinct (the view would fall into the alienation of dualism/pluralism), the spiritual world would be raised over the material (the view would commit the one-sided fallacy of spiritualism by stipulating spirit's domination of the physical world), the cause of our experience would be neither accessible nor intelligible to our experience (this cause would then be arbitrary), and the spiritual cause of our experience would determine that experience utterly (the view would extinguish the freedom inherent in new, emerging development). Only by the Hegelian argument is the ground of human experience, the unifying principle of being and purpose, the Idea, neither empty, or gratuitous (as is the universal ground of materialism and skepticism), nor are the phenomenal appearances of human experience illusory, or chimerical (as are the phenomenal appearances of spiritualism).

Hegel's philosophy of history issues from his metaphysical discourses. History is, accordingly, characterized as the development of the world toward the self-actualization of embodied reason, the development of the world toward its own fulfillment, toward rational self-consciousness. Rational self-consciousness, by this view, unfolds in stages, from primitive forms in which all things appear differentiated (i.e., as essentially unrelated to all other things and to the governing principle of reality itself) to "fully" developed forms in which all things are apprehended as a unity (i.e., as essentially related to all other things and to the governing principle of reality itself). Humanity, as the unique possessor of rational self-consciousness (and the moral, aesthetic, and socio-political freedom entailed by rational consciousness), is thus the central aspect of reality for Hegel and philosophy, as the activity uniquely devoted to apprehending rational self-consciousness, is the highest form of human experience. This experience, according to Hegel, develops by a dialectic process in which events, or theses (i.e., broad, implicitly positive tendencies), give rise to separated opposites (i.e., to the inherently opposing, or negative, aspects of those events), which ultimately give way, in turn, to a synthetic conciliation, a resolution, of such opposition in a higher, explicitly positive unity. These patterns recur cyclically, albeit unevenly, in the direction of fulfilling reality's governing principle (its basic nature and purpose). The stages of this development are both a product (a discrete result of prior stages) and a prophecy (a basis for subsequent stages).

In metaphysico-epistemic terms, the Idea acquiring bare inanimate existence is the physical world; the physical world acquiring animate existence is life; life acquiring personal (bio-psychological) consciousness is Subjective Spirit; Subjective Spirit acquiring interpersonal (social) consciousness is Objective Spirit; and Objective Spirit acquiring consciousness of (humanistic) consciousness itself, acquiring rational self-consciousness is Absolute Spirit. In cultural-historical terms, gentile, civil, and political society signify the respective passage from pre-literate culture, to instrumental civilization, to self-actualizing civilization; effectively, the respective passage from implicitly intrinsic, to implicitly and explicitly extrinsic, to explicitly intrinsic forms of cultural life – in the broadest respect, the passage from thesis, to separated opposites, to synthesis. The conjunction of Absolute Spirit and political society -- the organic thesis in fully elaborated form; i.e., in metaphysico-epistemic and cultural-historical form – constitutes the highest mark of our history. This maturation is embodied most notably in twentieth-century European (most especially, Scandinavian) democratic socialism and in twentieth-century European (most especially, Germanic, French, Russian, and Finnish), American, and Mexican expressionist painting, sculpture, and architecture.

The text that follows works principally off of the wide, humanistic tendencies of Hegel's organic metaphysics and philosophy of history. It thus begins with an account of the development of the physical world and of life in its various forms. It then proceeds to an examination of the origins and development of human culture in the ancient, medieval, and modern periods with special attention to the status of:

- organic, mechanistic, and skeptical orientations in these periods;
- bio-psychological, social, and humanistic consciousness in these periods; and
- gentile, civil, and political society in these periods.

The main aim in all of this, of course, is to illumine the origin, development, nature, and purpose of sport by accounting for its enduring continuity in the full context of human experience per se. Sport has been profoundly affected by the political, economic, social, and intellectual contexts in which it has come to life and developed. These contexts are themselves constitutively run through with organic, mechanistic, and skeptical orientations, with bio-psychological, social, and humanistic forms of consciousness, and with gentile, civil, and political cultural tendencies. Sport cannot be authentically understood, appreciated, or practiced, by the organic view, except for a searching acknowledgment of such contexts, orientations, forms, and tendencies. Sport takes on characteristically different shapes and serves characteristically different purposes in each, not all equally edifying. It is in organic, self-conscious, and political circumstance that sport comes to its highest realization. Sport there:

- acts in full accord with its own basic nature and purpose (it becomes most fully itself);
- becomes a form of distinctly and uniquely human expression, a form of universal and fundamental human expression, not unlike religion and the arts (with which it shares the formal outlines of a common originative and developmental history as well as the formal outlines of a common basic nature and purpose);
- becomes an embodiment of our most compelling ideals, an embodiment by which neither our intellectual nor our bodily aspects are to be either indulged or overcome, but proportionately gratified; and thus
- becomes a form of human fulfillment as such.

GEO-BIOLOGICAL ORIGINS

By the most exacting scientific estimates, the **known universe** was created in a colossal explosion (the so-termed **Big Bang**) approximately 14-18 billion years ago.[1] Our local galaxy, the **Milky Way**,[2] is thought to be roughly one-half the age of the known universe, or 8-9 billion years old.[3] And our local solar system, consisting primarily of one star (the Sun), four inner (solid) planets (of which the Earth is the third-most-distant from the Sun; it is eight light-minutes from the Sun), an asteroid belt, and five outer (gaseous) planets, all of which condensed (by means of gravitational collapse) out of a cloud of interstellar gas and dust, is thought to be approximately one-half the age of the Milky Way, or 4-5 billion years old.[4] It is located in a spiral arm of the Milky Way roughly two-thirds the distance from the galaxy's center to its outer edge and it rotates about the galaxy's center once every several hundred million years.

According to the best scientific evidence on the subject, the **Earth** itself is approximately 4.6 billion years old[5] and it was in its earliest form a spherical mass of gas and molten rock subject to virtually perpetual meteorite, astroidal, and cometary impacts.[6, 7, 8] In the first 50-100 million years of its life, the Earth cooled rapidly (by conduction, convection, and radiation), its core formed, its mantle stabilized (largely through volcanic degassing), and a thin (oceanic) crust, primeval oceans, and a primeval atmosphere developed. The first stable (continental) crusts had formed by c. 3.8 billion years ago (i.e., by the end of the Azoic eon); voluminous continental crusts had formed by c. 3 billion years ago (i.e., in the late Archeozoic eon); most of the current crust had formed by c. 2.5 billion years ago (i.e., in the Archeozoic-Proterozoic boundary); the **continental crusts** had aggregated into three mega-continental masses[9] by c. 2 billion years ago (i.e., in the early Proterozoic eon); these masses drifted independently until c. 800 million years ago (i.e., in the late Proterozoic eon) when they collided to form a single supercontinent (viz., Pangaea I); and this supercontinent, in turn, began to fragment c. 600 million years ago (i.e., at the Pre-Cambrian-Cambrian boundary), its major plates variously diverged, drifted, and again collided to form yet another largely unbroken land mass (viz., Pangaea II) by c. 400 million years ago (i.e., in the early Devonian period). The seven major continental plates (i.e., the African, North American, South American, Antarctic, Australian, Eurasian, and Pacific plates) and the several major micro-continental plates (most notably, the Indian plate) of this mass began to draw "conclusively" away from one another c. 250-200 million years ago (i.e., in the Triassic period).[10, 11] Although **continental drift**[12] continues at meager rates, all of the continents and major micro-continents had reached their approximate current positions by c. 3 million years ago (i.e., in the late Pliocene epoch).

The geo-biological history of the Earth has been especially heavily affected by **climate**.[13] The Earth's primeval atmosphere was formed mainly by the volcanic degassing of the planet and it was mostly comprised of ammonia gas, carbon dioxide, methane gas, and water vapor. It was thus comprised of carbon, hydrogen, nitrogen, and oxygen molecules, the principal constituents of organic matter. Under the major influences of volcanism, cosmic ray radiation, the ultraviolet radiation of the Sun, and lightening,[14] these constituents were variously associated, dissociated, and reordered to form the complex molecular groups of organic substance that constitute life (most significantly, nucleic acids such as RNA and DNA, amino acids, proteins, carbohydrates, and fats).[15] Although the luminosity of the Sun was more diminished in the Earth's early development than later, the internal (radioactive) temperatures of the Earth itself were higher and the concentrations of atmospheric carbon dioxide and water were too higher in the Earth's early development than later. The balance of these factors produced surface temperatures and biochemical conditions highly conducive to life.

Since the primeval **atmosphere** was anoxic, the earliest forms of life were anaerobic, of course. These forms were unicellular marine bacteria that lived by means of fermentation (enzymatic activity) and they developed between c. 4 billion and c. 3.5 billion years ago (i.e., at the Azoic-Archeozoic boundary). From them, evolved primitive forms of **plant life**,[16] marine algae, that lived by means of photosynthesis (which metabolizes carbon dioxide and water and which excretes carbohydrates and molecular oxygen). By c. 2.5 billion years ago (i.e., at the Archeozoic-Proterozoic boundary), these forms of plant life had produced sufficient volumes of molecular oxygen to transform the Earth's atmosphere from an anoxic to an oxygenous state, to begin formation of an ozone layer (which did nonetheless not become "fully" secure until c. one billion years ago), and to thus establish the basis on which aerobic life (which sustains life by means of respiration in which oxygen and organic molecules are metabolized and in which carbon dioxide and water are excreted) was to develop. **Microorganisms** partially dependent on molecular oxygen had developed by c. 2.8 billion years ago (i.e., in the late Archeozoic eon); microorganisms entirely dependent on molecular oxygen had developed by c. 2 billion years ago (i.e., in the early Proterozoic eon).

The earliest forms of **animal life**,[17] unicellular organisms (or protozoa), had developed by c. 1.5 billion years ago (i.e., in the middle Proterozoic eon) and they had evolved from reproduction by asexual mitosis to reproduction by sexual meiosis by c. 900 million years ago (i.e., in the late Proterozoic eon). Yet more complex, multicellular animals (or metazoa) had developed by c. 700 million years ago (i.e., in the late Proterozoic eon). The earliest of these were invertebrates such as corals, jellyfish, and worms. Still more complex forms of invertebrate life (most notably, sponges, mollusks, and crustaceans) developed in the Cambrian period (c. 590 million to c. 505 million years ago); the first fish (the first vertebrates), in the Ordovician period (c. 505 million to c. 438 million years ago); the first land plants (fungi, mosses, grasses, and ferns), in the Silurian period (c. 438 million to c. 408 million years ago) when the first fertile soils also developed; the first insects, spiders, and amphibians (the first land-dwelling vertebrates), in the Devonian period (c. 408 to c. 360 million years ago); the first reptiles (the first class to be freed "entirely" from marine dependence), in the Carboniferous period (c. 360 million to c. 286 million years ago); the first trees, in the Permian period (c. 286 million to c. 248 million years ago); the first mammals (monotremes) and the earliest dinosaurs, in the Triassic period (c. 248 million to c. 213 million years ago); the first birds, in the Jurassic period (c. 213 million to c. 144 million years ago); the first marsupial and placental (most notably, the insectivora and the edentata) mammals and the first flowers, in the Cretaceous period (c. 144 million to c. 65 million years ago) when the atmosphere also came to its approximate, current composition (c. 140 million years ago); the first carnivora, ungulata, and rodentia, in the Paleocene epoch (c. 65 million to c. 55 million years ago); and the first chiroptera, cetacea, and primates, in the Eocene epoch (c. 55 million to c. 38 million years ago).

In the Oligocene epoch (c. 38 million to c. 24 million years ago), the monkey line diverged from the other anthropoidea (i.e., the apes [principally, the orangutan, gorilla, and chimpanzee] and the humans) "leaving" the formation of the hominoidea (c. 30 million years ago), but only in the Old World. In the Miocene epoch (c. 24 million to c. 5 million years ago) developed a common hominoidean ancestor of both the apes and the humans, dryopithecus (c. 20 million years ago),[18] from which the apes and the humans diverged (c. 16 million years ago) to form the pongidae (the apes) and the **hominidae** (the humans). The common hominidean ancestors of modern humans, ramapithecus (c. 14 million years ago)[19] and australopithecus africanus (c. 5 million years ago)[20] are owed respectively to the Miocene epoch and to the Miocene-Pliocene boundary. The earliest form of modern human life, **homo habilis**,[21] developed on the Tertiary-Quaternary boundary (c. 2.5 million years ago) and flourished well into the Pleistocene epoch (to c. one million years ago). Homo habilis likely co-existed with, and may have interbred with,[22] australopithecus africanus (which passed into extinction c. 2 million years ago) and with two other forms of ape-man, australopithecus robustus and australopithecus boisei, both of which have been extinct from c. one million years ago. In what remained of the Pleistocene epoch (c. 2 million to c. 10,000 years ago), homo habilis gave rise to **homo erectus**[23] c. 1.6 million years ago, then passed into extinction c. one million years ago; homo erectus gave rise to the earliest recent humans (archaic humans), **homo sapiens**[24] c. 800,000 years ago, then passed into extinction c. 50,000 years ago; and archaic humans gave rise to **homo sapiens sapiens** (effectively, the most recent humans)[25] c. 150,000 to c. 100,000 years ago, then passed into extinction c. 30,000 years ago. Homo sapiens sapiens had developed in the form of its four major races (i.e., the Mongoloid [eastern Asia and the Americas], Negroid [Africa], Caucasoid [Europe, the Middle East, and western Asia], and Australoid [southeast Asia and Oceania])[26] by c. 10,000 years ago (i.e., by the end of the Pleistocene epoch). It persists among c. 10 million species as the most developed form of known life to our time.

The most recent, major period of **continental glaciation** began in approximately the same period as the appearance of ramapithecus, c. 15 million years ago, and continued through the appearance of australopithecus africanus, homo habilis, and homo erectus. A temporary warming began c. 2-1 million years ago (i.e., at the Tertiary-Quaternary boundary) which allowed the migration of homo erectus from Africa to Asia and Europe; it was likewise in this period that archaic humans first appeared. This warming ended c. 600,000 years ago with the first of four recent (Pleistocene) glacial episodes which went on until c. 540,000 years ago. The second such episode began c. 480,000 years ago and went on until c. 430,000 years ago; the third such episode began c. 240,000 years ago and ended c. 180,000 years ago. The major migrations of archaic humans occurred in the interglacial period between the third episode and the fourth which began c. 120,000 years ago and ended c. 10,000 years ago. Homo sapiens sapiens, then capable of great adaptability, appeared in this period and achieved impressively wide and extensive **migrations** also in this period, perhaps driven significantly by drought conditions. These most recent humans had occupied Africa between c. 150,000 and c. 100,000 years ago; the Middle East and Europe by c. 60,000 years ago; Asia, New Guinea, and Australia by c. 50,000 years ago; Japan and North America by c. 20,000 years ago; Taiwan and central America by c. 12,000 years ago; South America by c. 11,000 years ago; Oceania by c. 10,000 years ago; and the Caribbean by c. 7000 years ago.[27] The modern postglacial period, which may well turn out to be still another interglacial age, follows (i.e., in the Holocene epoch).[28]

These then constitute the major prior and remarkable conditions of human life and human culture, as well, of course, as the fundamental pre-conditions of sport. These are the conditions that have made human life, human culture, and sport possible. Although humans have occupied only the most recent several moments of world time and are therefore in this respect small by comparison, they are nonetheless the most complex and creative creatures known by us to have ever existed and are thus in this respect writ large by comparison. Our sporting inclinations, it shall be argued, are a significant mark of this estimable distinction.

ANCIENT PRIMITIVE CULTURE AND SPORT

The culture of the Pleistocene epoch (effectively, c. 3 million-c. 2 million to c.10,000 years ago), the culture of homo habilis, homo erectus, homo sapiens, and early homo sapiens sapiens, is known as **Paleolithic (Old Stone) Age** culture. It was dominated by foraging, gathering, scavenging, hunting, and fishing activity among relatively small tribes and bands of mostly nomadic persons.

The culture of the Holocene epoch (effectively, c. 10,000 years ago to present), the culture of recent homo sapiens sapiens, developed in two main forms, **Neolithic (New Stone) Age** culture[29] and "civilized" culture. Neolithic culture is marked from the development of organized agriculture; it is distinguished by this, the agricultural revolution, as well as by several other crowning achievements: the animal husbandic revolution, the ceramic revolution, the linguistic revolution, the metallurgical revolution, and the socio-political revolution.

The **agricultural revolution** first developed independently in two regions – that from Kurdistan to Palestine of southwestern Asia and the Middle East in the Old World and that from New Mexico to Guatemala of southwestern North America and northern central America in the New World – at approximately the same time, c. 9000 to c. 7000 B.C.E.[30] This revolution entailed the sowing, cultivating, and harvesting, of seeds previously gathered and consumed as food,[31] and it developed in self-sufficient and "permanent" villages where people lived in artificial shelters and owned and worked the land in common.[32]

In the Old World, the agricultural revolution had been dispersed to (or had developed independently in) Persia, Syria, Anatolia, and Palestine by c. 7000-c. 6000 B.C.E.; to (in) Mesopotamia, Cyprus, and the Balkans by c. 6500-c. 4000 B.C.E.; to (in) central and northern Europe by c. 4000-c. 3000 B.C.E.; to (in) Arabia, northern Africa (mainly, Egypt, Sudan, and Ethiopia), and central Asia by c. 3500-c. 2500 B.C.E.: to (in) India and China by c. 2500-c. 1500 B.C.E.; to (in) east, west, and south Africa and southeast Asia by c. 1500 B.C.E.; to (in) Korea by c. 1300 B.C.E.; and to (in) Japan by c. 900 B.C.E. From southeast Asia, the agricultural revolution was dispersed to the south and the west as well as to the east. To the south and west, it had reached Indonesia and Australia by c. 1000 B.C.E., Ceylon and Madagascar by c. 100 C.E. To the east, it had reached Melanesia by c. 1000 B.C.E., western Polynesia (mainly, the Samoas and Tonga) by c. 500 B.C.E., Micronesia by c. 300 C.E., and eastern Polynesia (mainly, Tahiti, the Marquesas, Hawaii, and New Zealand) by c. 1000 C.E..

In the New World, the agricultural revolution had been dispersed to (or had developed independently in) the whole of central America as well as to (in) Colombia, Venezuela, Ecuador, Peru, and Bolivia by c. 2500 B.C.E.; to (in) eastern, northern, and western North America and to (in) the Caribbean by c. 1000 B.C.E.; and to (in) Brazil, Argentina, and Chile by the dawn of the Common Era. It was too passed to eastern Polynesia (mainly, Tahiti, the Marquesas, and the Cooks) from Ecuador and Peru by c. 700 C.E.

The **animal husbandic revolution** likewise first developed in southwestern Asia, Persia, Syria, Anatolia, and Palestine (in the Old World) and in southwestern North America, central America, and north-central western South America (in the New World) by c. 7000 B.C.E.[33] It was later dispersed to (or developed independently in) the other centers of Neolithic culture. The animal husbandic revolution entailed the domestication of animals – principally, dogs, reindeer, goats, and sheep; later, cows, pigs, oxen, horses, camels, and elephants in the Old World; and alpaca and llama in the New World – for food, drink, clothing (mainly, wool textiles), shelter, tools, weapons, containers, work, transportation, security, and herding.

The **ceramic revolution** first developed in the same Old and New World centers of Neolithic culture that had spawned the agricultural and animal husbandic revolutions, then elsewhere, c. 6000 B.C.E.[34] It entailed the fashioning of basketry and clay pottery for transporting, preparing, and storing food and water.[35]

The **metallurgical revolution** is too owed, in its seminal development, c. 4000 B.C.E., to the same Old and New World centers of Neolithic culture that had given rise to the agricultural, animal husbandic, and ceramic revolutions. It entailed the mining, smelting, and fashioning of gold, silver, copper, lead, tin, bronze, glass, iron, and steel substances/objects for use as tools, containers, wheeled carts, boats, jewelry, and weapons.[36]

The **linguistic revolution** likewise first appeared, c. 3500 B.C.E., in the same regions of the Old and New Worlds that had given rise to the other revolutionary achievements of the Neolithic Age.[37] It entailed the development of "permanent" systems of recording and transmitting human experience that ended an utter dependence on repeated, oral reminiscence and that allowed each generation to progress beyond the experience of all prior generations (not merely to repeat the experience of just prior generations).

And the **socio-political revolution** also first appeared, c. 3000 B.C.E., in the same regions of the Old and New Worlds that had given rise to the other revolutionary achievements of the Neolithic Age.[38] It entailed the gathering of increasingly large numbers of specialized workers and rulers into increasingly large and autonomous population centers; first into bands, tribes, and chiefdoms, then into cities, nations, and empires.[39]

These revolutionary achievements established the groundwork on which the several **major cultural and linguistic groups** (or families) were formalized. Three of these groups (the Indo-European,[40] Ural-Altaic,[41] and Hamito-Semitic[42]) form the fundamental basis of Occidental, or Western, civilization (effectively, the native cultures and languages of Europe, western-central Asia, the Middle East, and northern Africa); three (the Sino-Tibetan,[43] Austroasiatic,[44] and Malayo-Polynesian[45]) form the fundamental basis of Oriental, or Eastern, civilization (effectively, the native cultures and languages of eastern-central Asia and Oceania); three (the Khoisan,[46] Niger-Kordofanian,[47] and Nilo-Saharan[48]) form the fundamental basis of African civilization (effectively, the native cultures and languages of sub-Saharan Africa; that is, of west, central, east, and south Africa); six (the Algonquian-Wakashan,[49] Aztec-Tanoan,[50] Eskimo-Aleut,[51] Hokan-Siouan,[52] Nadene,[53] and Penutian[54]) form the fundamental basis of North and central American civilization; and two (the Andean-Equatorial[55] and Ge-Pano-Carib[56]) form the fundamental basis of South American and Caribbean civilization.[57]

The formalization of these groups constitutes the flowering of **gentile society**, the flowering of that form of cultural development that is characteristic of Paleolithic and Neolithic life.[58] In gentile society, the most primitive types of human consciousness (ordinary sensation and the rudimentary principles of logic) predominate and the fundamental and universal aspects of human experience,[59] science, sport, dance, art, religion, history, philosophy, and education, are interpreted in the form of such consciousness. Gentile society did not readily distinguish its main features; it more so implicitly treated such features as cooperative participants in an organic union of event, as features necessarily connected to one another and to the whole of life.[60] It did not carve up its experience into disparate parts, each distinct in qualitative and institutional terms from each of the others. All activities, features, or parts of life's whole formed an essential element of the mainstream. Science, sport, dance, art, religion, history, philosophy, and education in particular were each necessarily related to each of the others and each was likewise a necessary contributor to the preservation and fulfillment of human life as such. These activities were little, if at all, distinguished from everyday experience; they thus took the form of imitative significations (or "reproductions") of such experience. They functioned primarily as inchoate ways of communicating (transmitting or conveying) mainstream cultural values/practices, either among persons or between persons and natural/divine entities. They were therefore rudimentarily intrinsic to, and continuous with human experience in its broadest and deepest, in its fundamental definition; they were implicitly, but incompletely, self-conscious.[61]

Sport (in at least some, not very strict form, as vigorous bodily expression practiced for "recreational" purposes) has been a part of virtually all cultures, including virtually all gentile cultures.[62] Unsurprisingly, the **sport of gentile society (ancient primitive sport)** assumes the sensorico-logical and imitative/communicative form of gentile society itself and is thus implicitly playful, competitive in a cooperative sense, and physical in an intrinsic sense. It is playful in the sense that it functions as an intrinsic type of human fulfillment, as an end-in-and-for-itself. In this circumstance, the rules of sport are self-legislated; they are respected as positive symbols of our distinctly human nature and they are therefore resolutely and cheerfully adhered to. It is competitive in the sense that it attempts to achieve difficult-to-achieve standards of performance, the ultimate purpose of which is subjective (held within our experience) and having primarily to do with excellence and secondarily to do with winning/losing (the quest to gain victory/evade defeat). The primary competitive end of sport, excellence, to which winning/losing is devoted, takes the shape of mutually inclusive edification, a shape that is shared by all participants, those who come first as well as those who do not. "Opponents" are consequently viewed as cooperative facilitators in a shared project, the mutual pursuit of excellence, the mutual pursuit of fulfillment; opponents constrain one another and thereby assist one another to this end. And it is physical in the sense that it respects skillful movement as its definitive medium, as an inherently compelling feature of human experience, as a fulfilling form of human experience.

Sport's earliest practice apparently coincided with humanity's earliest artistic and religious practices, c. 50,000-c. 25,000 years ago. Ancient primitive sport thus appeared in approximately the same period as (dancing, musical, and visual) art and religion and it grew out of the same approximate conditions as these other activities. It consequently shared the same originative history with such activities. The earliest form of sport (as well as art and religion) took the shape of mimetic games, or imitative projects, in which children pretended to forage, gather, scavenge, hunt, fish, keep domicile, protect from natural enemies, and the like; adults gave communicative interpretations of such activities. The earliest form of sporting activity was therefore drawn from the everyday mainstream of cultural life. Sport, in this circumstance, did consequently not function as an isolated aside to the central concerns of life – neither as a mere preparation for, nor as a mere respite from such concerns – but rather as a creative expression of the mainstream itself.[63] It was likewise very often practiced in the context of "other" activities, most particularly dancing, (visual) artistic, musical, and religious activities. Ancient primitive sport was frequently the subject of dancing, (visual) artistic, and musical experiences and it was also frequently "admixed" with mythic religious ceremonies/rituals, with activities of cosmic significance. These experiences and ceremonies were ancestral and/or animistic[64] in character and had primarily to do with assuring the continuity of life, with such "survival" activities as foraging, gathering, scavenging, hunting, fishing, farming, fertilizing, soldiering, birthing, dying, rearing, initiating, negotiating, gifting, cleansing, healing, dreaming, meditating, creating, renewing, valuing, recreating, working, and territorial acquisition/ preservation.

The sporting activities of ancient primitive culture were astonishingly numerous and astonishingly diverse. Quite likely the most notable forms of ancient primitive sport, either because they had an abiding affect on gentile society itself and/or because they established the germinal practice of activities that later became highly influential in civil society, were the team ball games of the North, central, and South American Indians, the canoeing, diving, swimming, and surfing activities of the Melanesian and Polynesian Pacific Islanders, the kayaking activities of the Inuit, the track and field activities (running, jumping, and throwing) of the proto-Celtic and proto-Greek Europeans, and the skiing and skating activities of the proto-Germanic Europeans. Unsurprisingly, bowling, gymnastics (acrobatics), running, jumping, throwing, rowing, various forms of animal racing (such as camel, dog, horse, reindeer, and yak racing), bat-and-ball games, and combative activities (such as archery, boxing, fencing, and wrestling) were even more widely practiced. Of these, in turn, the team ball games of the New World and the track and field activities of the proto-Celtic and proto-Greek Europeans have been the most prominent. These games and activities also lived more nearly than others of the gentile type on the cusp of the gentile-civil distinction; they resembled more nearly than others of the gentile type the games and activities of civil society.

Team ball games of diverse sorts (variously resembling rugby, football, soccer, basketball, team handball, field hockey, and lacrosse) were played extensively by the native Indian cultures of the New World and they were played typically in association with religious ceremonies. In North America, they were played most significantly by eastern woodland, great basin, plains, southwest, and western coast Indians, perhaps from as early as c. 4000 B.C.E. In central America, they were played most significantly by Olmecan, Teotihuacan, Mayan, Toltecan, and Aztecan peoples, perhaps from as early as c. 2000 B.C.E. And in South America, they were played most significantly by Incan communities, perhaps from as early as c. 1000 B.C.E. The track and field activities of the proto-Celtic (mainly Gaelic) Europeans were embodied principally in the Tailteann Games (or Aenach Tailteann Fair) of Ireland. These Games may have been contested from as early as c. 3000 B.C.E.; they too were held typically in association with religious ceremonies; and they consisted mainly in running, high jumping, long jumping, pole jumping, shot putting, hammer throwing, and javelin throwing, as well as in archery, boxing, wrestling, hurling, handball, and equestrian events. The track and field activities of the proto-Greek Europeans were also first associated with religious ceremonies; they were arguably contested from as early as c. 1800 B.C.E.; they principally included running, jumping, and discus throwing, as well as boxing, wrestling, and chariot racing; and they were the precursors of the celebrated, national and local athletics festivals of ancient Greece proper.

The revolutionary achievements of the Neolithic Age together established the terms of technological specialization,[65] social differentiation,[66] and urbanization[67] which brought an unprecedented measure of security, stability, and surplus to the human circumstance. In the Neolithic Age, human beings established sufficient authority over the natural events which both sustained and threatened them that they no longer needed to wander utterly after naturally occurring patterns of plant and animal life nor after naturally occurring patterns of glacial activity. They established instead "permanent" centers endowed with the surplus resource adequate to sustain a small, but nonetheless enormously powerful ruling and leisured class and with the resource adequate to develop the earliest formal (the earliest institutional) forms of science, sport, art, religion, and education.

ANCIENT CIVILIZATION AND SPORT

It was the genius of the Neolithic revolutions that ended characteristically Paleolithic culture, that then brought the Neolithic equation itself to rest, and that inaugurated the era of civil society in the form of ancient civilization.[68] In the passage from gentile to **civil society**, humanity entered a qualitatively new stage of its development. This stage has flourished from the passing of primitive, or gentile, society to our own time. In civil society, the natural and social sciences predominate. Western civilization has tended to the materialistic emphasis of the natural sciences; Eastern civilization has tended to the spiritualistic emphasis of the social sciences (mainly in the form of religion and politics). In civil society, the fundamental and universal aspects of human experience, science, sport, dance, art, religion, history, philosophy, and education, are interpreted in the form of scientific consciousness. They thus take the shape of representative significations (or portrayals) of the material or spiritual aspect of reality and they function primarily as ways of commemorating (preserving, acclaiming, or celebrating) these aspects. They are, consequently, neither imitative (as in gentile society), except in negation; nor are they imaginative (as in political society), except in anticipation. Civil society both carves its experience into disparate parts and tends to disconnect these parts from one another and from the whole of life.[69] The leisure practices of civil society are therefore extrinsic to, and discontinuous with human experience in its broadest and deepest, in its fundamental, character; they are explicitly, but incompletely, conscious.[70]

Unsurprisingly, the **sport of civil society** assumes the scientific and representative/commemorative form of civil society itself. It portrays/celebrates either the instrumentality of the material world (the dominant tendency of Western civilization) or the instrumentality of the spiritual world (the dominant tendency of Eastern civilization). Western sport is mainly devoted to the production, distribution, and consumption of commodities, power, wealth, fame, and privilege in predominantly mercantile/social, entertainment, recreative, military, and medical terms. Eastern sport is mainly devoted to the production, distribution, and consumption of commodities, power, wealth, fame, and privilege in predominantly ideological/social, entertainment, recreative, military, and medical terms. The sport of civil society is thus explicitly work-like, competitive in an adversarial sense, and physical in an extrinsic sense. It is work-like in the sense that it functions, not as a form of human fulfillment, but as an extrinsic type of human activity, as a means to an end without itself. In this circumstance, the rules of sport are imposed by natural or divine imperative; they are "respected" as negative constraints on our distinctly human nature, as means by which we may be kept from criminal behavior, and they are therefore adhered to only begrudgingly and marginally. The sport of civil society is competitive in the sense that it attempts to achieve difficult-to-achieve standards of performance, the ultimate purpose of which is objective (held without our experience) and having primarily to do with winning/losing (the quest to gain victory/evade defeat). The primary competitive end of sport, winning/losing, defines excellence in its own terms and it takes the shape of mutually exclusive, material or spiritual gain, a shape that is unshared and that is therefore held by one or several, but not by all, participants (it is the sole province of those who win). Opponents are consequently viewed as obstacles to be defeated, impediments to be overcome, in an unshared project, in the project of securing partisan advantage; opponents constrain one another to this end. The sport of civil society is physical in the sense that it values skillful movement as the contrary of intellectual activity and as a means of gaining victory as well as the instrumental consequences entailed by victory.

Civil society first developed in the leading cities, nations, and empires of the ancient Western and Eastern worlds. Of these, the most significant sporting (and cultural) traditions were owed to the Sumerian, Egyptian, Indian, Chinese, Babylonian, Assyrian, Israeli, Persian, Greek, Etruscan, Roman, Mayan, Aztecan, and Incan cultures.[71] The sport of other cultures in Europe, Asia, and the Middle East, as well as the sport of northern Africa, sub-Saharan Africa, Oceania, and the Americas remained primarily imitative until the age of modern European colonization (i.e., the fifteenth to the nineteenth centuries C.E.), then largely took the instrumental form of either established Western or established Eastern tendencies.

11

Sumerian Culture and Sport

The Sumerian culture was of Caucasoid ethnic character, it spoke a language evidently unrelated to others, and it developed in the southern regions of Mesopotamia (between the Tigris and Euphrates Rivers in the southeastern reaches of the modern nation-state of Iraq). It first appeared in c. 3500 B.C.E., developed in the form of rigidly stratified, rival city-states (most notably, Ur, Uruk, and Lagash), and was conquered by the Akkadian Empire (of Hamito-Semitic cultural and linguistic character) under Sargon I in c. 2370 B.C.E.; it was nonetheless variously restored thereafter for brief periods until c. 1700 B.C.E. when Babylonia became the dominant power in the region. It crafted the earliest form of written language, civil government, and trade, an elaborate polytheistic and animistic religion, an accomplished mathematical/astronomical reckoning (most notably, its studies of the circle and its development of solar and lunar calendars), a proficient technologic capacity (most notably, its fashioning of the wheel), a distinctive sculptural style (as embodied most notably in the "Head of Gudea," c. 2150 B.C.E.), and a monumental temple architecture (the ziggurat; most importantly those at Uruk [c. 3500-c. 3000 B.C.E.] and Ur [c. 2100 B.C.E.]).

Although the leisure resource among the Sumerian ruling elite was considerable, their taste for sport was limited largely to military uses of it.[72] The Sumerians nonetheless left artifactual evidence of sporting activity in the form of wrestling statuettes and in the form of boxing reliefs on clay tablet. They also left the earliest documentary evidence of formalized types of civil sporting practices; this in the form of textual references (on clay tablet) to religious ceremonies involving activities resembling boxing and wrestling at the "Temple of Kyfaje," c. 3000 B.C.E.

Egyptian Culture and Sport

The Egyptian culture was of Hamito-Semitic cultural and linguistic character and it developed in the northeast regions of Africa (i.e., in the Nile River Valley of the modern nation-state of Egypt). It fashioned among the earliest instances of written language and civil government, an elaborate polytheistic and animistic religion, a refined mathematical/astronomical and medical reckoning, a skilled technologic capacity (most notably, its crafting of paper, the spindle, and the loom), an accomplished sculptural style (as embodied most notably in its "Palette of Narmer," "King Chephren," "Great Sphinx," "King Mycerinus and His Queen," "Prince Rahotep and His Wife Nofret," "King Sesostris III," "King Akenaten," "Head of Nefertiti," and "King Rameses II"), a novel literary genre dominated by a cult of immortality (as embodied most notably in the Book of the Dead), and a monumental funerary and temple architecture. It first appeared in c. 3200 B.C.E.; matured in the form of a rigidly stratified, centralized state; developed from the unification, under Narmer, of Upper and Lower Egypt, c. 3000 B.C.E.; passed through three main periods (the Old, Middle, and New Kingdoms); and was then variously taken over by Libyans, Ethiopians, Assyrians, Persians, and Macedonians to 30 B.C.E., then fell successively under Roman rule (30 B.C.E. to 385 C.E.), Byzantine/Christian (Coptic) rule (385 C.E. to 641 C.E.), and Arab rule (641 C.E. to present). The **Old Kingdom** is marked from c. 2640 B.C.E. to c. 2130 B.C.E.; it established its capital at Memphis, under Zoser; and it was distinguished by the construction of the great pyramids at Saqqara (Zoser, by the great architect, Imhotep) and Giza (Cheops, Chephren, and Mycerinus). The **Middle Kingdom** is marked from c. 2130 B.C.E. to c. 1650 B.C.E.; it established its capital at Thebes; and it was characterized by the development of extensive trade practices and by construction of the temple complex at Karnak. And the **New Kingdom/Empire** is marked from c. 1550 B.C.E. to c. 1070 B.C.E.; it established its capital most importantly at Tell-el-Amarna, under Akenaten/Nefertiti; and it was distinguished by the construction of the temple complexes at Deir el Bahari, Luxor, and Abu Simbel, by the first hints of monotheism (from Akenaten), and by the expansion of the Empire (mainly under Queen Hatshepsut, Tuthmosis III, and Amenophis III) to Nubia (Sudan), Palestine, Phoenicia (Lebanon), Syria, Mesopotamia (Iraq), and Anatolia (Turkey).

The Egyptian term denoting sport, shmh-ib, meant to amuse, or to enjoy, oneself, to have the heart forget, to divert from the hard edges of life.[73] Evidence of sport in ancient Egypt is extensive and varied, both artifactual and documentary:

- implements, such as balls, bows, arrows, and chariots;
- facilities, such as remnants of archery sites and running tracks;

- visual representations, such as painted images on temple/tomb walls, carved images on stelae, and sculptural images; and
- written accounts, such as epigraphical inscriptions and papyri texts; some of these are Egyptian, others are non-Egyptian (i.e., Babylonian, Hittite, Assyrian, Israeli, and Greek).

Of these, likely the most notable are the running and wrestling reliefs in the tomb complex of Zoser at Saqqara, c. 2600 B.C.E.; the wrestling and ball game-playing reliefs in the tomb complexes of Amenemhet, Baqti III, and Kheti at Beni Hasan, c. 1900 B.C.E.; the archery reliefs (of Amenophis II) in the Temple of Amun (the "Sphinx Stela") at Karnak, c. 1400 B.C.E.; the stick-fighting reliefs in the tomb complexes of Rameses III at Thebes, c. 1150 B.C.E.; and the running reliefs of the "Running Stela" of Taharqa at Memphis, c. 650 B.C.E. This evidence points to a wide practice of sport, from the pre-dynastic epoch (before 3000 B.C.E.) to the C.E., by both genders (although never in mixed contexts) and it points as well to the occasional practice of doing sport unclothed in the Old and Middle, but not in the New, Kingdoms. The most prominently practiced forms of sport in ancient Egypt were activities closely resembling archery, ball games (including either the throwing/catching/juggling or the striking of wood, clay, papyrus, or leather-encased hair, straw, reed, or yarn balls), bowling, boxing, chariot racing, diving, equestrian, fencing (stick-fighting), fishing, hunting, gymnastics (acrobatics), jumping (horizontal and vertical), rowing, running, swimming, weightlifting, wrestling (upright), and sailing/yachting.

The formal physical recreation of ancient Egypt, not unlike the formal physical recreation of the ancient world broadly defined, was customarily reserved for the relatively small upper classes. In most cases, which is to say in the cases of the workers, peasants, and slaves, the nature of one's occupation determined the character of one's experience in physical activity of all types, the dominant type, which was non-recreational, as well as the recreational. Among the upper classes in particular, sport was fairly widely practiced and appreciated. Likely the most memorable forms of ancient Egyptian sport were those associated with royal festivals, the royal/religious dogma governing these festivals, and the cultic rituals dominating them. Principal among the royal festivals of sporting moment was the Heb Sed, or Jubilee, Festival which, from as early as Narmer (c. 3000 B.C.E.), celebrated either pharaonic coronation or royal renewal and which included wrestling contests and a ritual run by the pharaoh himself. In this context, sporting activities assisted in settling quarrels among gods concerning the ruling forces/personalities of the world (as in the rowing match between Horus and Seth); they served as well to establish the validity of pharaonic rule by enhancing the reputations of ruling authorities; and they also functioned as a medium in which pharaohs attempted to demonstrate superiority over their predecessors by way of surpassing achievement. Although some pharaonic ascriptions were symbolic, not literal, and some pharaohs more so demonstrated than authentically competed in sporting pursuits – they made unopposed exhibitions as great warrior-athletes, for instance – many pharaohs were accomplished athletes in the strictest of literal senses and the respect for sport as such among aristocrats of virtually all ages and both genders was, on balance, quite considerable. Pharaohs were characterized as the guarantors of life and were thus taken to possess imposing spiritual and physical gifts; which is to say that they were considered inherently athletic.

The apogee of ancient Egyptian sport occurred in the eighteenth dynasty of the fifteenth and fourteenth centuries B.C.E.; i.e., near the opening stages of the New Kingdom. The leading pharaonic athletes of ancient Egypt were of this time: Tuthmosis III (r. c. 1490-c. 1436 B.C.E.), Amenophis II (r. c. 1436-c. 1412 B.C.E.), Tuthmosis IV (r. c. 1412-c.1402 B.C.E.), Amenophis III (r. c. 1402-c. 1364 B.C.E.), Amenophis IV (Akenaten; r. c. 1364-c. 1347 B.C.E.), Tutankhamen (r. c. 1347-c. 1338 B.C.E.), and Ay (r. c. 1337-c. 1333 B.C.E.). All were acclaimed as remarkably adept archers, charioteers, hunters, rowers, and runners. Rameses II (r. c. 1290-c. 1224 B.C.E.) of the nineteenth dynasty and Rameses III (r. c. 1184-c. 1153 B.C.E.) of the twentieth were also widely celebrated as especially proficient charioteers. And Taharqa (r. c. 690-c. 664 B.C.E.) of the 25th dynasty is said to have run 100 kilometers in nine hours, an apparently daunting feat by ancient standard. It was also in the period of the eighteenth dynasty that the most rigorously formal and competitive athletic contests of ancient Egypt were staged, some of them uniquely "international" in scope, some entailing uniquely elaborate prizes, and some in which a form of sporting record was uniquely at issue. Sport was less widely practiced and was practiced in less edifying ways in all other precincts of ancient Egyptian culture; most notably, in the decline of the intermediate period between the Middle and New Kingdoms (i.e., in the seventeenth century B.C.E. invasion of the Hyksos).

With the advent of written language (as well as the literary traditions entailed by written language), a searching form of mathematics, and distinguished scientific thought came too the need for formal education; that is to say, for formal institutions that give systematic instruction in subjects of such complexity that they cannot be readily learned unaided by most either sufficiently well or sufficiently quickly to make the sort of individual and cultural differences needed and desired. These subjects were nonetheless pursued mainly for practical, social, political, and military purposes; they were not typically pursued out of an intrinsic appreciation for their humanizing possibilities. They were also made available mainly to the upper, sometimes the middle, classes. The education of the lower classes remained (as it had in the primitive case) the informal responsibility of the family and it was therefore limited largely to a training in the rudiments of the family's occupation and in the activities of daily life otherwise defined. Although special instruction in sporting skills was routinely available to the privileged classes, sport was not made a standard part of the formal school curriculum except in the eighteenth and nineteenth dynasties, most significantly in the reigns of Amenophis II, III, and IV. These were the most enlightened periods of ancient Egyptian history in this respect as well as in respect to the culture's proportionate attentions to intellectual and to sporting prowess. This is a conjunction – broad conditions of (organic) enlightenment and earnest provisions for sporting recreation – that variously recurs throughout the human record. It is such a persistent feature of this record, such a persistent feature of our experience, that it may constitute a condition of enlightenment itself.

Indian Culture and Sport

Civil cultures on the Indian sub-continent, Indian cultures, first appeared in c. 2300 B.C.E. in the form of ethnic Australoid communities of the Indus River Valley (i.e., in the modern nation-state of Pakistan); most notably, those at Mohenjo-daro and Harappa. Beginning in c. 1500 B.C.E., however, the Indus River Valley was taken over and the Ganges River Valley (i.e., in the northeastern and north-central reaches of the modern nation-state of India) was developed by invading Indo-European peoples who came to fashion the dominant cultures of the region. Numerous, largely independent, often contending cultures developed on the Indian sub-continent, and its sub-tending regions, over the first several millennia of their existence. They were only rarely unified – most notably, by Asoka (r. c. 273-c. 232 B.C.E.) in the context of the Maurya Empire (322-185 B.C.E.) and in the period of the Gupta Empire (320-647 C.E.) – and they were variously self-governing and dominated, in significant measure, by the Persians (c. 513 B.C.E.), by Alexander the Great (327-325 B.C.E.), by the Sassanids (c. 240 C.E.), and, at the end of their ancient form, by the Islamic Arabs (c. 711 C.E.). They nonetheless fashioned:

- among the most inflexible and divisive systems of social class differentiation, the caste system, of the ancient world;
- the earliest (c. 1400 B.C.E.) form of impersonalistic religious orientation (**Hinduism**) and texts (the Vedas, c. 1000 B.C.E., as well as interpretive commentaries on these texts; most notably, the empirical-tending Brahmanas of the ninth century B.C.E., the mystic-tending Upanishads and Bhagavad-Gita of the eighth century B.C.E., and the epic poems, "Mahabharata" and "Ramayana," of the fifth and first centuries B.C.E. respectively);[74]
- a rich aesthetic tradition embodied mainly by the meditative reserve of Hindu and Buddhist images (most significantly, the Buddhist sculptures of the second to the fifth centuries C.E. from the Gandhara region [the northern reaches of the modern nation-state of Pakistan and the eastern reaches of the modern nation-state of Afghanistan] and the Hindu and Buddhist architecture and sculpture of the Gupta and post-Gupta periods); and
- a unique form of musical composition based on a 22-tone scale.

Hinduism, in turn, had a profound affect on the subsequent development of two other major, impersonalistic world religious traditions of Indic origin:

- **Buddhism**, from Buddha, or Siddhartha Gautama (c. 563-c. 483 B.C.E.), whose teachings are collected mainly in the Theravada[75] and
- **Jainism**, principally from Vardhamana, Mahavira, or Jina (c. 540-c. 468 B.C.E.).[76]

The governing principles of ancient Indian life, Hindu, (Hinayana) Buddhist, and Jainist principles, tended to otherworldly and impersonalistic forms of religious sentiment, to an emphasis on the future stage of time, and to caste allegiances, all of which disinclined the culture to a high regard for vigorous activities of a recreative sort.[77] Its renunciation of the material world, including the bodily aspect of human experience, augured badly for such as sport. Although reserved largely for the upper castes and serving primarily religious objectives, ancient Indian education and sport nonetheless included practical-vocational aims defined mainly by the occupational tiers of the caste system. The physical dimension of life was largely determined by the vocational duties of one's caste and tended to be more prominent and less formal in the lower castes than in the upper. The most significant such case for sport was in respect to the warrior caste, the Kshatriyas. The sport of ancient India was confined almost entirely to the Kshatriyas and was limited to skills of martial significance; most notably, to activities such as (or resembling) archery, ball games, boxing, bull fighting, chariot racing, diving, fencing, gymnastics (acrobatics), jumping, polo, swimming, javelin throwing, and wrestling. These activities date from the city-states of Mohenjo-daro and Harappa, c. 2000 B.C.E., where acrobatics, bull fighting, and swimming were most prominently practiced. Although very little sport penetrated ancient Indian life, chariot racing is nonetheless referred to in the Vedas; archery, boxing, and fencing are spoken of in the "Mahabharata;" and hatha-yoga developed out of accounts of spiritual discipline in the Upanishads. Of these activities, only hatha-yoga (and dancing) were at all widely practiced outside of military contexts or by other-than-military persons (including women); and both hatha-yoga and dancing were of broad religious significance. Hatha-yoga, which dates from the second century B.C.E. and which is a uniquely Hindu system of posture and respiration exercises, was practiced as a means of achieving harmony, as a means of freeing the eternal (the spiritual) element from implication in the material (the bodily) world.

Chinese Culture and Sport

Ancient Chinese civilization was of Sino-Tibetan cultural and linguistic character and it developed in central east Asia (i.e., in the approximate region now occupied by the modern nation-state of the People's Republic of China). It first appeared in c. 2200 B.C.E. and it was distinguished by five major dynastic periods: Xia, c. 2200-c. 1766 B.C.E.; Shang, c. 1766-c. 1027 B.C.E.; Zhou, c. 1027-c. 249 B.C.E.; Qin, c. 247-c. 206 B.C.E.; and Han, c. 206 B.C.E.-c. 220 C.E. It was governed throughout by a past-orientation, by strong class identities, and by a family-centered form of ancestral authority which itself variously took either the shape of numerous, loosely connected, often warring feudal states or the shape of a centralized bureaucratic power. The Chinese developed a unique calendar and musical canon (based on a five-tone scale); invented paper (c. 100 B.C.E.); crafted a novel sculptural and architectural style (most significantly in the form of Shang bronzes, martial Qin terra-cotta figures, and the "Great Wall" [construction of which began in the third century B.C.E. and variously continued into the fifteenth century C.E.]); consolidated their prerogative (most notably, under Emperor Shi Huang Di, r. 221-210 B.C.E.) and expanded their influence (most notably, under Emperor Wu Ti, r. 140-87 B.C.E.) to northern, southern, and western Asia; and fashioned the basis of two highly influential religious traditions (Taoism and Confucianism) as well as greatly extended the influence of another (Buddhism):

- **Taoism**, from Lao-tze (c. 604-c. 510 B.C.E.), whose teachings are collected mainly in the Tao-te ching (Classic of the Way and Its Virtue);[78]
- **Confucianism**, from Confucius (551-479 B.C.E.), whose teachings are collected mainly in the Analects, and from Mencius (c. 372-c. 298 B.C.E.), whose teachings are collected mainly in the Book of Mencius;[79] and
- **Buddhism**, which came to China from India in the first century C.E.[80]

The ancient Chinese perception of sport was mixed.[81] The contemplative, impersonalistic, and ascetic tendencies of Taoism and Buddhism and the static tendencies of a past-oriented form of cultural life were not conducive to individuated expressions of physicality. The thisworldly emphasis of Confucianism and the necessarily high regard for military activity were, conversely, favorably disposed to vigorous forms of physical exertion such as sport. The education and the sport of ancient China were reserved largely for the upper classes and were devoted largely to maintaining the established, inflexible social order. Only in the first approximately three centuries of the Zhou Dynasty (i.e., the eleventh to the eighth centuries B.C.E.) were education and sport made widely available to all social classes and to both genders (in the form of a national, public system) and were education and sport devoted to the balanced development of both physical-aesthetic and intellectual-spiritual dimensions of human experience. This epoch marked the "Golden Age of Ancient Chinese Education" in virtue of its devotion to so bringing "all subjects to all people," in virtue of its devotion to universal subject and universal franchise; this is a tendency that Confucius later, albeit unsuccessfully, argued ought to be resurrected as a matter of public policy. Sport otherwise, however, served rather narrower, practical purposes; mainly, purposes of a military, medical, or religious sort.

Military sport (wu shu) in ancient China dated from at least 1500 B.C.E., perhaps from as early as 2100 B.C.E. Most of the Asian martial, or fighting, arts had their incipient origins in these practices. These arts

15

began as hunting skills and utilitarian forms of combat and have more recently developed into exercise modalities, aesthetic forms of physical culture, or sports in the strict sense. The earliest, formal activities of this type were boxing (chung-kuo ch'uan) from c. 1100 B.C.E., wrestling (shuai-chiao) from c. 700 B.C.E., and weapons activities (sword, halberd, hook, staff, dagger, spear, ball and chain, truncheon, bar, sickle, and knife) from c. 700 B.C.E. Sport was especially widely practiced in the periods of the Shang and Zhou Dynasties, less so in the Xia (which had not yet established a sufficient social infrastructure for such activities), the Qin (which forbade the practice of martial arts), and the Han (which was governed mainly by the non-combative aspects of Confucianism). Sport was even the occasional subject of artistic artifacts from as early as the period of the Shang. A team, combative game resembling rugby football (tsu-chu) was formally played in religious and military celebrations from c. 1300 B.C.E.; even some emperors (including Wu Ti) apparently played the game. Archery (lishe) from horseback and from foot was formally practiced as early as 1000 B.C.E.; it was taught by Confucius (who included it in his system of education); and prowess in it was even an occasional basis for choosing the leadership of feudal communities. A game resembling association football, or soccer (taju), was formally organized from the eighth century B.C.E. And another resembling badminton was played from the first century B.C.E. Many other forms of sporting activity were also formally practiced in the approximately two and one-half millennia marking ancient Chinese culture. The most prominent of these were: animal fighting, chariot racing, diving, fencing, golf (chiuwan), gymnastics (acrobatics), horse riding, hunting, ice skating, high jumping (yueju), long jumping (yongyue), pole vaulting, polo (jiju), rowing, running, swimming, throwing, and weightlifting. A system of light, calisthenic and breathing exercise, of medical gymnastics, intended to prevent disease and otherwise promote good health (kong fu) was too developed in the eleventh century B.C.E. (near the end of the Shang Dynasty) and prospered among both men and women throughout the remaining centuries of ancient Chinese history.

Babylonian and Assyrian Culture and Sport

The Babylonian civilization was of Hamito-Semitic cultural and linguistic character and it developed in the southern regions of Mesopotamia (i.e., in the southeastern reaches of the modern nation-state of Iraq). It first appeared in c. 1800 B.C.E. and it unfolded in two main stages: the **First Babylonian Empire**, c. 1800-c. 1100 B.C.E., and the **Second, or New, Babylonian, or Chaldean, Empire**, c. 625-538 B.C.E. It was, in its earlier stage, variously independent and dominated by Assyrians (from central Iraq), Hittites (from Turkey), Kassites (from Persia/Iran), and Elamites (from Persia/Iran). It was, in its second stage, the dominant political influence over Persia/Iran, Mesopotamia (Iraq), Syria, Phoenicia (Lebanon), and Palestine until conquered by the Persians in 538 B.C.E. It had its center throughout at Babylon; it arranged itself in a rigidly stratified and centralized state; it developed ingenious technologies in engineering (weights and measures), medicine, agriculture, mining, metallurgy, law (Code of Hammurabi, 1728-1686 B.C.E.), and trade (money, loans, interest, rentals, and contracts); and it fashioned an epic literature (most notably, The Epic of the Creation of the World, effectively the odyssey of Utnapishtim, c. 2000 B.C.E.; and the Epic of Gilgamesh, c. 1200 B.C.E.), an elaborate polytheistic and animistic religion, and a vibrant form of decorative and architectural art (most notably, the "Ishtar Gate" and the "Tower of Babel," both constructed in the rule of Nebuchadnezzar II, 604-562 B.C.E.).

The Assyrian civilization was also of Hamito-Semitic cultural and linguistic character and it developed in the central regions of Mesopotamia (i.e., in the central reaches of the modern nation-state of Iraq). Its first civil appearance coincided roughly with that of Babylonian culture, c. 1800 B.C.E., and it unfolded in three main stages: the Old Assyrian Empire, c. 1800-c. 1375 B.C.E., the Middle Assyrian Empire, c. 1375-c. 1050 B.C.E., and the New Assyrian Empire, c. 909-c. 608 B.C.E. The **Old Assyrian Empire** briefly dominated the Babylonians and was then itself largely dominated by Hurrians (of Caucasoid ethnic character, who spoke a language evidently unrelated to others; from Turkey), Hittites (from Turkey), Mitannians (from northern Syria and Iraq), and Aramaeans (from Syria). Assyria became the dominant political entity in the region in the period of the **Middle Assyrian Empire**, most significantly in the reign of Tiglathpileser I (r. c.1112-c. 1074 B.C.E.). And it came to dominate extensive territories – Syria, Palestine, Phoenicia (Lebanon), Media (Persia/Iran), Egypt, Urartu (Armenia), Elam (Persia/Iran), and Babylon, as well as the Hittites (from Turkey) and the Cimmerians (from the Caucasus) – in the **New Assyrian Empire**, most significantly in the reigns of Assurnasirpal II (r. c. 883-c. 859 B.C.E.), Sargon II (r. c. 722-c.705 B.C.E.), Sennacherib (r. c. 704-c. 681 B.C.E.), and Assurbanipal (r. c. 668-c. 633 B.C.E.). It declined throughout the last quarter of the seventh century B.C.E. and was conquered by Media and Babylonia in 608 B.C.E. It had its center throughout at Assur and Nineveh; it arranged itself in a rigidly stratified and centralized state; it developed ingenious military technologies (cavalry); it established the first great library (at Nineveh in 639 B.C.E.); it fashioned an elaborate polytheistic and animistic religion; and it crafted a robust form of illustrative and architectural art (most notably, the elaborate reliefs from the "Palace of Assurnasirpal II" in Nimrud and from the "Palace of Assurbanipal" in Nineveh and the gate sculptures from the "Palace of Sargon II" in Khorsabad).

Although the Babylonian and Assyrian circumstances were exceedingly prosperous, technologically advanced, well-endowed with leisure circumstance, and given to fluid aesthetic orientations, broad characteristics that are typically associated with a deep affection for sport, their utter devotion to practical pursuits (mainly pursuits of a mercantile sort in the Babylonian case and pursuits of a military sort in the Assyrian) sharply truncated the attentions each gave to sport.[82] The resource of these cultures was invested and re-invested principally in mercantile and military projects. While leisure is therefore an apparently necessary condition of civil sport, it is clear from the Babylonian and Assyrian cases that it is not alone a sufficient condition. Sport in these cultures, predictably, was made available only to those who performed mercantile and military activities and it was expected to serve strictly mercantile and military ends. There was little thought of sport as a distinctly human event, as an individual or cultural expression enhancing our uniquely human sense of ourselves. Although sparsely practiced and practiced for altogether utilitarian, albeit important, purposes, sport was nonetheless not an utterly fatuous aspect of Babylonian and Assyrian culture. The most widely practiced forms of sport in these cultures were archery, boxing, equestrian activities, gymnastics (acrobatics), running, swimming, and wrestling. The wrestling match of Gilgamesh and Enkidu and the wrestling prowess of Gilgamesh more broadly drawn are among the most enduring metaphors of ancient Mesopotamian literature.

This basic pattern, principally in its military type, was also significantly repeated in **Hittite culture**, the dominant form of human civilization in Anatolia (the region now occupied by the modern nation-state of Turkey) from c. 1800 B.C.E. to c. 1200 B.C.E. Ancient Hittite civilization was nonetheless of Indo-European cultural and linguistic character; it established a strong monarchial authority and an able warrior class; it developed the earliest form of money (c. 900 B.C.E.); and it fashioned a monumental style of sculpture (most notably, the "Lion Gate" at Bogazkoy). It unfolded in two main stages: the Old Hittite Kingdom, c. 1640-c. 1380 B.C.E., and the New Hittite Kingdom, c. 1380-c. 1200 B.C.E. By the end of the New Hittite Kingdom, it had extended its domination over Lebanon, Syria, and Iraq as well as over Anatolia. After c. 1200 B.C.E., however, it was itself variously dominated by Egyptians, Phrygians (of Indo-European cultural and linguistic character; from Turkey), and Assyrians until it fell into oblivion in c. 700 B.C.E. The sport of the Hittites resembled that of the Assyrians, was of largely military (and religious) significance, and most importantly included archery, boxing, gymnastics (acrobatics), (weight) throwing, weightlifting, wrestling, and running contests in which the most prominent men of the realm competed for the honorary office of "holder of the reins of the royal chariot."

Israeli Culture and Sport

Ancient Israeli civilization was of Hamito-Semitic cultural and linguistic character and it developed in the near Middle East (i.e., mainly in Canaan, or Palestine). Although the earliest parables of Israeli culture (the covenant of Abraham) are attributed to the 23rd century B.C.E. and Israeli tribes under Moses and Joshua are thought to have arrived in Palestine in c. 1250 B.C.E., the political framework of the culture was not established until c. 1000 B.C.E. when the Israelites successfully defended their territories against the Ammonites (from Jordan), the Philistines (from Palestine), and the Phoenicians (from Lebanon) and established the **Kingdom of Israel** under Saul (r. c. 1010-c. 1006 B.C.E.). Under Saul's successor, David (r. 1006-966 B.C.E.; with Bathsheba), the northern (Israel) and southern (Judah) regions of Israeli territory were united, the capital of the new state was established in Jerusalem, the Ammonites and Philistines were again defeated, and the Moabites and Edomites (both from Palestine) were also subdued as Israeli domination of Palestine was consolidated. The first Hebrew temple, the "Temple of Jehovah," was constructed (in Jerusalem) under David's successor, Solomon (r. 966-926 B.C.E.), but Aramaean (Syrian) and Edomite territories were lost and the Kingdom was again divided in the reign of Solomon. The culture was subsequently taken over by Assyria (under Sargon II) in 722 B.C.E., by Babylonia (under Nebuchadnezzar II) in 587 B.C.E., by Persia (under Cyrus the Great) in 539 B.C.E., and by Alexander the Great in 332 B.C.E. A brief period of partial independence was achieved with the revolt of the Maccabees (an Israeli sect) in 168 B.C.E. but Palestine was incorporated into the Roman Republic by Pompey in 63 B.C.E., came under the leadership of Herod the Great (r. 39-4 B.C.E.), who was appointed by the Romans in 39 B.C.E., was utterly subdued by the future Roman Emperor, Titus, in 70 C.E., and entered the Diaspora (the dispersion) after the unsuccessful revolt of Bar Kochba (d. 135 C.E.) against Roman rule in Palestine in 132-135 C.E.

The most telling and influential aspect of ancient Israeli, or Hebrew, culture was its unique religious, intellectual, and poetic genius. Human civilization is most deeply indebted to this culture:

- for its monotheistic and personalistic notion of divinity (of Yahweh, or Jehovah), which became the basis of **Judaism**, Christianity, and Islam;
- for the individualistic system of ethical and political secularism that is governed by this notion; and
- for the literature which so aptly expressed this notion; most notably, the Talmud, or oral traditions (compiled in c. 100-c. 500 C.E.), and the Scriptures, or written traditions, which, in turn, include the Torah, Pentateuch, or Mosaic Laws (the first five books of the Hebrew Bible [Genesis, Exodus, Leviticus, Numbers, and Deuteronomy, all written in c. 1000-c. 300 B.C.E.]) and the remaining historical (most importantly, Joshua, Judges, I Samuel, II Samuel, I Kings, and II Kings, all written before c. 300 B.C.E.), poetical (most importantly, Job, Psalms, Proverbs, and the Song of Solomon, all written in c. 300-c. 150 B.C.E.), and prophetical books (most importantly, Isaiah, Jeremiah, Lamentations, Ezekiel, Daniel, and Jonah, all written in c. 730-c. 600 B.C.E.) of the Hebrew Bible.

The education and sport of the ancient Hebrews were crafted principally by (and were expected to serve) the religious, intellectual, and poetic traditions of the culture.[83] Although only rarely occurring in formal schools, or synagogues (mainly for aspiring priests, bureaucrats, and scribes), and thus left largely to the informal auspices of the family, education in language, mathematics, and music was oriented to formal religious and ethical principles. Neither did the ancient Hebrews ever formalize their interest in sport in any terms other than military ones. Most widely practiced in this respect were archery, fencing, swimming, team ball games resembling handball, polo, and volleyball, weapons activities (shield, sling, and spear), and wrestling. The Hebrews nonetheless had a deep respect for sophisticated exercise habits, for high standards of personal and community hygiene, and for vigorous forms of physical activity including game-playing. Sporting metaphors appear in the Scriptures; perhaps most significantly, the wrestling contest between Jacob and Yahweh in Genesis 32: 24-32. The Mosaic Laws permit what they do not forbid and they do not forbid physical games. And the great heroes of the ancient Hebrews were of courageous and robust action:

- the patriarchs; most notably, Noah, Abraham, Jacob, Joseph, and Moses;
- the historical heroes; most notably, Joshua, Samson, Samuel, Saul, David, and Solomon; and
- the prophetical heroes; most notably, Daniel and Jonah.

Moreover, Alexander and Herod both successfully promoted sport among the Hebrews.

Persian Culture and Sport

Ancient Persian civilization was of Indo-European cultural and linguistic character and it developed in southwestern Asia (i.e., mainly in the region now occupied by the modern nation-state of Iran). The **Median Empire** (also of Indo-European cultural and linguistic character), which antedated the Persian in the region, had come to prominence in c. 835 B.C.E., fell to the Cimmerians and the Scythians (both from the Caucasus) in 647 B.C.E., reasserted itself in 625 B.C.E., conquered Assyria in 608 B.C.E., and was itself conquered, in turn, by Persia (under Cyrus the Great [d. 529 B.C.E.]) in 559 B.C.E. The **Persian Empire** took its formal beginnings from Cyrus' conquest of the Medes. It subsequently conquered Lydia (of Indo-European cultural and linguistic character; in western Turkey) in 546 B.C.E., Palestine in 539 B.C.E., Egypt in 525 B.C.E., India in 513 B.C.E., and Thrace and Macedonia (on the Balkan Peninsula) in 512 B.C.E. The military superiority of the Persians from the mid-sixth century to the mid-fourth century B.C.E. – a superiority based on mounted warriors armed with bows and arrows – allowed them to dominate extensive territories from Egypt and the Balkan Peninsula to the Aral Sea (in Kazakhstan) and from the Caucasus, Palestine, Syria, and Mesopotamia to India. The Persian Empire reached its widest influence under Darius I (r. 521-486 B.C.E.), began to decline under Xerxes I (r. 486-465 B.C.E.) with its failures against the Greek city-states, and was conquered by Alexander the Great in 331 B.C.E. Although largely finished as an imperial power with the conquest of Alexander, the culture nonetheless persisted under Seleucid (effectively, Greek) domination, 331-240 B.C.E., then under Parthian (effectively, Scythian) domination, 240 B.C.E.-226 C.E., to the effective re-establishment of the old, the Iranian-Persian, empire under the Sassanids, 226-636 C.E. The Islamic Arab conquest of 636 C.E. began the amalgamation of ancient Iranian-Persian and Islamic culture that effectively marked the end of ancient Persian culture as such. Principally in its Achaemenid form (the ruling dynasty from c. 550 to 330 B.C.E.), the Persian Empire developed:

- the institutions of a world government based on a new formula in which uniform justice pertained equally to ruler and ruled and in which disparate provinces were united under a strong central authority;
- an imposing and an ambitious military, a fervent militarism, and an exceedingly able warrior class;
- a unique form of monumental, ceremonial, and decorative relief sculpture and colossal, royal architectural complexes (most notably, the "Palace of Darius I" at Persepolis); and
- a vigorous, personalistic, and influential form of religious sentiment, **Zoroastrianism**, from Zoroaster, or Zarathustra (c. 660-c. 583 B.C.E.), whose teachings are collected mainly in the <u>Zend-Avesta</u>.[84]

Persian education and sport occurred almost entirely in military (and religious) contexts, took almost entirely military (and religious) forms, and served almost entirely military (and religious) aims.[85] Vigorous physical activities of a sport-like nature figured centrally in military preparation and in the present-oriented, thisworldly struggle for Zoroastrian enlightenment but was otherwise very little practiced. They were therefore of rather narrow scope and limited largely to those of elite station and to men. Not unlike the Babylonian and Assyrian cases, Persia had, by ancient standard, a fairly well-developed leisure resource and fashioned other qualities characteristically favorable to sport but it did nonetheless not practice sport at all widely, preferring instead to reinvest its resource and its taste for bodily vigor in military projects. Only martial forms of such activity very much prospered; most notably, archery, fencing, a game resembling field hockey , horse riding, polo, discus throwing, and javelin throwing.

Greek Culture and Sport

Ancient Greek civilization was of Indo-European cultural and linguistic character; it was the first of the distinctly European forms of cultural possibility; and it developed in the southern reaches of southeastern Europe (i.e., in the southern aspects of the Balkan Peninsula and in the adjoining islands of the Aegean Sea; mainly in the region now occupied by the modern nation-state of Greece). Its development was greatly influenced by two older, proto-Greek cultures (most notably, the Minoan and the Mycenaean cultures) and by a non-European culture (the Phoenician culture) of the region.

The proto-Greek period

The Minoan civilization was preceded in the developed Aegean world by the **Cycladic culture** which was also of likely Indo-European cultural and linguistic character and which first developed on the Cycladic Islands (in the central reaches of the Aegean Sea), c. 2400 B.C.E. Little is known of the Cycladic case except that it fashioned a stunning form of sculptural art (as, most notably, in the marble female fertility figures of sharply geometric and frontal proportion from as early as c. 2000 B.C.E.), that it had a taste for boxing (which it celebrated in a memorable, fresco wall painting, "Young Princes Boxing," c. 1500 B.C.E.), and that it passed into oblivion in c. 1100 B.C.E.

Minoan civilization was likely too of Indo-European cultural and linguistic character and it first developed on the island of Crete (in the southern reaches of the Aegean Sea) in c. 2200 B.C.E. The civilization was governed by a strong, central administration, excelled in maritime trade, constructed among the most remarkable ancient forms of royal palace complex (most notably, the "Palace of Minos" at Knossos, c. 1500 B.C.E.),and developed among the most accomplished ancient traditions of wall painting. It succumbed to the Mycenaean invasions from the Greek (Helladic) mainland in the late fifteenth century B.C.E. and passed as a distinctive entity in c. 1400 B.C.E. Whispers of the characteristically Greek religious, artistic, and sporting inclinations were apparent in Minoan culture. Minoan sport, not unlike Greek sport itself, was typically practiced in conjunction with religious festivals, largely as an expression of homage to divine figures (most significantly, to the mother goddess of fertility, the mother goddess of earth).[86] It was, moreover, less connected to military affairs than was the custom in the ancient world; it not untypically included both men and women; and it was commemorated in the art of the period (most notably, in the "Toreador Fresco," c.

1500 B.C.E.), which was itself of an unusually playful and animate character. Running, boxing, wrestling, bull leaping (which entailed vaulting the head and back of an onrushing bull, the Minotaur, the bull-headed monster of the Minoan labyrinth), gymnastics (acrobatics), and various forms of ball game were apparently the most widely practiced forms of sporting recreation.

Mycenaean civilization was likewise of Indo-European cultural and linguistic character; it first developed on the Helladic mainland (in the southeastern reaches of the Peloponnesus) in c. 1600 B.C.E. It was far more given to military affairs than was Minoan culture, a tendency which showed prominently in its political, religious, artistic, and sporting life. The Mycenaeans were governed by a strong, central authority of warrior kings who were renowned as charioteers, who lived in monumental fortresses (most notably, the thirteenth century B.C.E. citadels of Mycenae and Tiryns), and who were ceremonially buried in majestic, domed tombs (most notably, the "Treasury of Atreus" at Mycenae, thirteenth century B.C.E.). The germinal features of what would become the personalistic, anthropomorphic, polytheistic, and militant religion of the ancient Greeks themselves were owed to the Mycenaeans. The monumental sculptures of the Mycenaeans (most notably, the "Lions Gate" in the fortress walls at Mycenae, c. 1250 B.C.E.) likewise took a stylized martial, if fluid, form. And the sport of the Mycenaeans also tended to a martial emphasis; running, boxing, wrestling, chariot racing, and weapons activities were most prominent.[87] In the thirteenth century B.C.E., largely as a consequence of local disruptions, the Mycenaeans fell to decline and began extensive emigrations to Asia Minor (to the coastal regions of western Turkey, to Ionia). The Mycenaean state was brought to a conclusive end with the Trojan Wars in Asia Minor, c. 1180 B.C.E., and with the Greek conquest of Mycenaean fortifications, c. 1150 B.C.E.

Unlike the Cycladic, Minoan, and Mycenaean cultures, **Phoenicia** was of Hamito-Semitic cultural and linguistic character. It first developed in the eastern Mediterranean (in the region now occupied by the modern nation-state of Lebanon) in c. 1300 B.C.E. and it later came to great influence throughout the coastal regions of Egypt as well as those of north-central and northwestern Africa, the southern borders of the Iberian Peninsula, and the major islands of the Mediterranean Sea (including in proto-Greek and Greek societies of the area). With the collapse of the Mycenaean trade hegemony in c. 1200 B.C.E., Phoenicia became the dominant commercial power in the Mediterranean; it was governed by a strong, central authority, a king, who nonetheless administered to largely autonomous city-states; it established its eastern center at Tyre and developed the earliest form of alphabetic language, both in c. 1000 B.C.E.; it established its western center at Carthage in 814 B.C.E.; and it was conquered by Assyria (under Sennacherib) in 701 B.C.E., by Babylonia in 586 B.C.E., and by Alexander the Great in 332 B.C.E. Phoenicia had an authentic taste for religion and for sport, which, like its commercial prowess, had an enormous influence on Greek culture.[88] Ritual festivals and religious games were prominent in the practical and the mythological life of ancient Phoenicia. The principal god, the source of life, Baal, wrestled with El (his father) for power over the universe, with Yam (god of the sea) for rain, and with Mot (god of death) for fertility. Melkart, the great hero of Phoenicia, performed athletic feats worthy of Herakles. Exceptional athletes were considered the servants of the temple. Funerary games, in which gods were both portrayed and honored, were common in Tyre and elsewhere. The most commonly practiced forms of sport were boxing, equestrian activities, jumping, running, throwing, and wrestling.

The earliest migrations of the Greeks themselves into Greece itself and into Asia Minor (Ionia), sometimes referred to as the **Dorian migration**, occurred between 1200 and 1100 B.C.E. The Greeks displaced the indigenous population (which had fought as charioteers armed with weapons of bronze) by means of superior military tactics and weapons. They fought instead as mounted warriors armed with weapons of iron. Political and economic settlements were customarily formed about abandoned Mycenaean fortresses and established Ionian communities; these settlements became a loosely confederated group of city-states in the form of the Ionian League in c. 875 B.C.E. Greek culture unfolded from the migrations of the twelfth century B.C.E. in four major periods:

- the geometric period, c. 1200/1100-c. 750/700 B.C.E.: from the migrations to the beginning of extensive Greek colonization of the Mediterranean region and the beginning of the full development of Greek political life on the mainland (the beginning of the full development of the city-states);
- the archaic period, c. 750/700-c. 550/480 B.C.E.: from the beginning of the full development of the city-states to Persian domination;
- the classical period, c. 550/480-338 B.C.E.: from Persian domination to the Macedonian conquest; and
- the Hellenistic period, 338-146 B.C.E.: from the Macedonian to the Roman conquest.

The geometric period

The first of these periods, the geometric period, c. 1200/1100-c. 750/700 B.C.E., was marked by the development of a new class of political elite, the warrior nobles (or landed aristocracy), and the oligarchic form of government dominated by nobles. This class and this form came to displace kings and the monarchial form of government dominated by kings. Political franchise was broadened, at least modestly, by this tendency. The geometric period was too marked by the fashioning of an aboriginal mode of plastic artistry, a so-termed geometric mode (c. 1050/950-c. 700 B.C.E.), dominated by decorative stylizations, mainly on vase. This period was also significantly characterized by:

- the formal development of the uniquely Greek religion, its principal shrines, and its athletic proclivities; and
- the first appearance of European epic literature and its athletic proclivities, mainly from Homer and Hesiod.

In **Greek religion**, the natural dominated the supernatural; the natural and human worlds (i.e., the universe) were taken to create and to govern the divine; the divine was not taken to have created or to have governed the natural and human.[89] Greek religion entailed a worship of the beautiful and the otherwise compelling features of nature and humanity. It did not entail a humbling submission to otherworldly personalities or phenomena. The gods were conceived in ideal, human terms, as superpersons, different from ordinary persons only in respect to their quantitative superiority and in respect to their immortality (from a finite birth). Life was therefore measured by heroic, thisworldly, not by meditative, otherworldly, standards and religion functioned as an active influence on all aspects of individual and cultural experience, including the arts and sciences, education, and sport. This personalistic, anthropomorphic, polytheistic, and militant emphasis was very favorably disposed to activities with a strong individualistic sense of adversarial struggle such as sport. The mythic gods and heroes were themselves of imposingly athletic body and moment:

- the Titans deposed Uranus and Gaea and were of enormous proportion and strength; most notably, Kronus (Saturn), Prometheus, and Atlas;
- the Olympian gods deposed the Titans and were of cunning skill, strength, and speed; most notably, Zeus (Jupiter), the supreme god; Hera (Juno), wife and sister of Zeus and the goddess of marriage; Apollo, the god of truth, poetry, and gymnastics; Poseidon, the god of the sea: Athena (Minerva), the goddess of the civilized city and of reason; Hermes (Mercury), the messenger god; Aphrodite (Venus), the goddess of love and beauty; Artemis (Diana), the goddess of the hunt and of wildlife; and Ares (Mars), the god of war;
- the lesser gods of sky, earth, and the underworld; most notably, Demeter, the goddess of fertility and the harvest, who was characteristically associated with athletic festivals celebrating the harvest; Dionysus, the god of fertility and wine, who was of especially vital and raucous character; and Terpsichore, the muse of dance, who was extraordinarily graceful of movement; and
- the great heroic adventurers:
  - Theseus, who beat the Cretan monster of the labyrinth, the Minotaur, to death with his fists;
  - Herakles, whose stalwart adventures for glory included the twelve celebrated labors and the heroic freeing of Prometheus from the Caucasus and of Theseus from Hades;
  - Perseus, who slew the dreaded sea monster, the Medusa, by heroic and guileful means;
  - Jason, whose quest for the Golden Fleece entailed perilous adventures;
  - Atalanta, courageous huntress, who defeated Achilles' father, Peleus, in wrestling and who met all challenges (except Melanion's) in foot-races for her favor in marriage;
  - Phaeton, who drove his father's chariot across the sky setting the earth afire;
  - Hyacinthus, beautiful consort of Apollo, who was killed by a discus thrown by Apollo; and
  - the great heroes of the Homeric epics recounting the Trojan Wars, Achilles and Odysseus.

The principal shrines associated with Greek religion (associated mainly with the Olympian pantheon) were also established in this period. The most significant of these were at Olympia, Delphi, Corinth, and Nemea. Many of the most important chapters of ancient Greek sport, which were themselves of religious consequence, later developed about these sanctuaries.

The earliest fashioning of **European epic literature** and the earliest literary record of ancient Greek life is likewise owed to this time; this, in the form of Homer's epic masterpieces, the <u>Iliad</u> and the <u>Odyssey</u>, c. 900-c. 750 B.C.E., and in the form of Hesiod's more prosaic tomes, <u>Theogony</u> and <u>Erga</u> (Works and Days), c. 700 B.C.E. The <u>Iliad</u> and the <u>Odyssey</u> related the Greek adventures in the Trojan Wars (conflicts between

Mycenae and Troy [in Anatolia]), c. 1180 B.C.E., and they both reflected and formed the unified principles of intellectuality and physicality on which the rational traditions of the Greeks were based. Accounts of the harmonization of contemplative wisdom and physical vigor were first fashioned in these two works of towering genius and signal moment. The great hero of the Iliad, Achilles, embodied the Greek ideal of physicality, of bodily vigor and action. The great hero of the Odyssey, Odysseus, embodied the Greek ideal of intellectuality, of contemplative knowledge and wisdom. The principal aim of Greek culture, education, and sport would become the full development and the unification of these twin ideals; that is, the cultivation of an enduring harmony in respect to these ideals.[90]

Achilles, the Greeks most accomplished warrior, was betrayed by the leader of Greek forces, Agamemnon, and withdrew from battle. His friend, Patroclus, then took up Achilles' armor and fought bravely but was slain by Hector (son of Priam, king of Troy), the leading warrior of the Trojans. In the 23rd book of the Iliad, Achilles ordered funeral games (or athletic contests associated with funerary rituals) in honor of Patroclus. Games such as these were apparently a common feature of noble and military life in this time; such that, most any important occasion may have had athletic games associated with it. The first event on the program of Patroclus' funerary games was a chariot race, followed by boxing, then wrestling and foot-racing contests. Accounts of armed fighting, discus throwing, archery, and javelin throwing at these games are now widely thought bogus (or later interpretations of Homer's original account). The drawn wrestling match between colossal Ajax (a rival of both Achilles and Odysseus) and cunning Odysseus was perhaps the most memorable event of these games. Achilles resumed the battle after the games commemorating his fallen comrade had ended, turned back the Trojan route, killed Hector, and was himself killed by an arrow to the heel of his foot as he brought the Greeks to the walls of Troy. Achilles was felled by Paris, whose judgment preferring love to power and whose abduction of Helen (the wife of Menelaus, brother of Agamemnon) from Mycenae to Troy had started the entire conflict. Achilles magnificent arms were awarded to Odysseus (not to Ajax), who devised the ingenious strategy of filling a wooden horse with Greek soldiers, of having the horse taken into the besieged city by Trojans themselves, and of sacking the city once inside it. The destruction of the city complete, the Trojan affront had been avenged and Helen was returned to Menelaus.

The Odyssey portrayed Odysseus' long return journey to Greece following the war, a journey beset by great suffering and high adventure. There are several accounts of sporting contests in the Odyssey. After one of many shipwrecks, Odysseus succeeded in reaching the land of the Phaeacians where he was hospitably entertained by its king, Alcinous. Among the entertainments were athletic contests in running, jumping, wrestling, boxing, and discus throwing (won by Odysseus himself). On Odysseus return home, he disguised himself as a beggar and found his wife's (Penelope's) many wretched suitors amusing themselves in the court with discus throwing; he was himself challenged to a boxing match by one of them; and only he succeeded in stringing the bow of Odysseus (the condition for winning Penelope's favor in marriage) and eliminating the suitors.

Hesiod too wrote passingly of local athletic festivals. What is nonetheless found in Homer and Hesiod are largely informal and spontaneous forms of athletic expression. Such forms of expression were highly esteemed, largely for military, religious, and entertainment purposes, but they were not yet organized in strictly formal terms, their rules were not yet formally codified, nor was there yet a specialized preparation for them. They were, however, the precursors of the well-organized and formal athletic festivals and gymnastic institutions of the next several centuries.

The archaic period

The period that followed, the archaic period, c. 750/700-c. 550/480 B.C.E., was marked, at its beginning, by fairly extensive colonization and Hellenization of the Mediterranean region (owing largely to a shortage of the food supply); and, at its end, it was marked by the opening chapters of domination by Persia. It was further characterized by:

- the full development of the political life of the Greek mainland in the form of city-states;
- the political transformation from oligarchies to tyrannies and democracies;
- the earnest inceptions of the storied Greek traditions in plastic art, music, and philosophy; and
- the formal advent of Greek sport, including the celebrated local and national athletic festivals themselves.

The political life of the Greek mainland unfolded increasingly in the form of largely autonomous and largely self-sufficient **city-states** (poleis). These relatively small administrative entities were nonetheless united by a common language and religion; that is, by a common sense of Greek culture. They typically consisted in an upper city (acropolis), a place of refuge mainly for temples; a lower city, a place for public buildings, markets (agora), and residences; and surrounding agricultural and mining communities. In the end, there were approximately twenty-two major such entities; most notably, Attica (Athens), Laconia (Sparta), Boetia (Thebes), Argolis (Corinth, Nemea, and Argos), Elis (Olympia), Phocis (Delphi), Aetolia, Achaea, Arcadia, Messenia, Thessaly, Epirus, Euboea, Chalcidice, Thrace, and Miletus (in Ionia). Of these, Athens and Sparta became the most prominent. Athens developed out of a local monarchy in c. 700 B.C.E., became the most advanced and the most democratic of the Greek city-states, and became the dominant city-state with military victories over Sparta and Boetia in 506 B.C.E. Sparta was established in c. 900 B.C.E.; was governed principally by the autocratic tendencies of Lycurgus' (fl. ninth century B.C.E.) "Constitution of Sparta" from the ninth century B.C.E.; extended its influence over adjoining Messenia in the First and Second Messenian Wars (740-720 B.C.E. and 660-640 B.C.E. respectively); became the dominant military and political influence on the Peloponnesus, under the auspices of the Peloponnesian League, by 550 B.C.E.; developed a new military technique in which well-armed foot soldiers attacked and defended in phalanxes; sharply suppressed the very large class of peasants and slaves; and remained a powerful, but regressive, military state significantly untouched by democratic reforms elsewhere in the Greek world until its effective end in the fourth century B.C.E.

The passage from **oligarchic forms of political organization**, in which the landed aristocracy is the unconditional ruling class, to **tyrannies**, in which a prominent noble (or faction of nobles) allies with peasants and defends the poor, first occurred in c. 660 B.C.E. and was first formalized by the Draconian Code in 621 B.C.E. This transformation was caused primarily by peasant and middle-class resentment of nobles and by discontent of the urban unemployed and it marked a significant broadening of political franchise; most notably, in the Tyranny of Corinth, c. 650-570 B.C.E., and in the Athenian Tyranny of Pisistratus (c. 605-527 B.C.E.), 560-514 B.C.E. The gradual widening of franchise (to include skilled artisans and peasants as citizens and to include making magistrates responsible to the electorate) was taken still further by the evolution of **democracies** in the sixth century B.C.E.; most notably, by Solon (c. 639-c. 559 B.C.E.) in 594 B.C.E. (formalized by the "Athenian Constitution of Solon") and by Kleisthenes (fl. late sixth century B.C.E.) in 509 B.C.E. (formalized by the "Athenian Constitution of Kleisthenes"). With the development of democracies, all citizens came to both a direct and a representative participation in political affairs, came to own property, and also came to enjoy educational and sporting opportunity; the power of the aristocracy was curtailed; the equal rights of individuals were enhanced both by law and by judicial review; torture, usury, and enslavement for debt were abolished; and the currency was reformed. In even the most progressive of cases (in Athens), however, no more than roughly one-third of the city-state's inhabitants were citizens in the strict sense. The remaining approximately two-thirds continued to labor in servitude, performing all menial tasks and thus creating the remarkable (by ancient standard) leisure resource of the citizen class.

The **architecture and sculpture** of this period also assumed a markedly new and more studied form. Under the influence of near Middle Eastern tendencies, referred to as orientalizing tendencies (c. 700-c. 600 B.C.E.), Greek art departed from the geometric stylizations of the just-prior period and adopted a larger sense of variation and movement. Between c. 600 and c. 480 B.C.E., the first unmistakable glimpses of the Greek plastic genius showed themselves. The magnificent Doric (most associated with Sparta and Corinth) and Ionic (most associated with Athens) styles of temple architecture first developed in this time; most notably, the "Temple of Hera" at Paestum (c. mid-sixth century B.C.E.), the "Treasury of the Siphnians" at Delphi (c. 530 B.C.E.), and the "Temple of Aphaia" at Aegina (c. 500 B.C.E.). The free-standing male (kouroi) and female (korai) sculptural figures too first appeared in this time; these were frontal idealizations of athletic proportion with hints of tensile movement: most notably, the "Kouros of Sounion" (c. 600 B.C.E.), the "Calf Bearer" (c. 570 B.C.E.), the "Peplos Kore" (c. 530 B.C.E.), the "Anavyssos Kouros" (c. 525 B.C.E.), and the "Delicata Kore" (c. 525 B.C.E.). The tradition of architectural relief sculpture, its advanced sense of perspective, and its commandingly heroic orientation, all of which heralded the classical flowering which followed, likewise first appeared in this time; most notably, the "Archer" from the "Temple of Aphaia" at Aegina (c. 490 B.C.E.). And the stunning Greek tradition in vase painting, which was very significantly associated with athletic festivals and sporting subjects, achieved its highest mark in this time; most notably, in the work of Exekias (fl. last half of the sixth century B.C.E.), "Dionysus in a Ship" (c. 540 B.C.E.).

The earliest memorable achievements in Greek **lyric poetry** too occurred in the archaic period. Most significant in this respect were the development of formal patterns of poetic expression (most notably, iambic pentameter) and the development of passionate love lyrics (most notably, by Sappho [fl. early sixth century B.C.E.] and by Anacreon [563-478 B.C.E.]). Although Greek choral and instrumental music was monadic, monophonic, and otherwise fairly unentailed, Pythagoras (c. 570-c. 500 B.C.E.) nonetheless worked out the formal relation of tones also in this time. This relation is the fundamental basis of harmony and the fundamental basis of subsequent developments in Western music.

The origins of what became the most accomplished tradition in **Western philosophy**, the ancient Greek tradition, were likewise owed to the archaic period. The history of authentically philosophic discourse (discourse largely free of religious convention) and, in a sense, the history of ancient Greek science as well began with the reflective thought of the Milesian (from Miletus in Ionia) cosmologists and with the thought of Pythagoras in the sixth century B.C.E. The Milesians' realistic-tending thought had principally to do with the essential character and purpose of the objective, material, or cosmological realm and it attempted to explain this character and purpose by reference to natural (or scientific), not by reference to mythological (or religious) phenomena. The Milesians' commitment to direct observation and to the appeal of reason set them significantly apart from all prior tendency. They explained the whole of reality in terms of a single, concrete substance in which motion, or change, is inherent. The issues of substance and change were, for them and for most of the other leading pre-Socratic philosophers as well, the main issues of philosophic reflection. The most significant of the Milesians were Thales (c. 624-c. 550 B.C.E.), Anaximander (c. 611-c. 546 B.C.E.), and Anaximenes (c. 588-c. 524 B.C.E.).[91] Pythagoras, conversely, in idealistic-tending fashion, emphasized the formal relations among the various manifestations of fundamental substance. He characterized these relations in mathematical terms and thus equated the laws of mathematics and those of nature.

The **formalization of ancient Greek sport** grew out of the informal, largely military emphasis of the Homeric age and it began in earnest in the eighth century B.C.E. The fundamental nature and purpose of sport in what has become its modern form is owed, in its original formulation, to ancient Greek life. This development eventually formed the single most important chapter in the entire pre-industrial maturation of sport. Not only were the earliest sporting institutions of modern moment Greek but so too was the basic concept of modern sport itself. The terms 'athletics' and 'athlete' (άθλός, athlos, a contest; αθλόν, athlon, the prize of a contest; αθλείν, to contend for a prize; and αθλητης, athletes, those who contend for a prize), as well as the notions they signify, are Greek. These terms connote a sense of arduous effort, of trying struggle, a hard testing of oneself with others; effectively, a testing devoted to securing a widely sought and a difficult-to-obtain prize. Athletics (i.e., sport) had most to do with attempting to excel others in a vigorous, physical contest, with attempting to attain, by honorable means, the joy of victory in such a contest.

The **local athletic festivals** of ancient Greece grew up around the activities of the temples, markets, theaters, assemblies, and juries and they thus had close institutional bonds with such as religious, commercial, artistic, political, and juridical practices. Some even antedated the establishment of several of the national festivals. By 500 B.C.E., there were approximately 50 such festivals held at regular intervals in the Greek world; all city-states staged at least one; many city-states staged numerous such festivals; and the most prominent city-states conducted a local celebration in nearly every month of the year. In almost all cases, these festivals were eventually associated with military, agricultural, or religious gatherings. Although some were occasionally open to competitors from all city-states, most were reserved for the citizens of the host city-state. Their athletic programs typically consisted in large numbers of events (significantly more than in the national festivals), many of which were highly embellished (unlike the events of the national festivals), and the victors in these events were awarded very elaborate tangible prizes (such as, food, clothing, oil, amphorae, tripods, weapons, and women), also unlike the symbolic prizes formally awarded in national events. Unsurprisingly, the local festivals were a great deal more provincial, in both concrete and ideological terms, than the national festivals. Arguably, the most notable of the local festivals was the Panathenaea, established in Athens in c. 566 B.C.E., held in honor of Athena (and perhapsTheseus as well), and used as a means of promoting civic pride, the esteem of the city, and sport itself by no less than Solon and Pisistratus. There was both a lesser, annual Panathenaea, which may not have included sporting events, and a greater, quadrennial (in the third years of each Olympiad, or four-year cycle, marked, in the first year, by Olympic celebrations) Panathenaea, which went on for nine days, which included roughly the same sporting, musical, and dancing events as the national festivals, and which awarded valuable material prizes for both first-place and second-place performances. The site of the Panathenaean Games from the fourth century B.C.E., the Panathenaic Stadium, was the only stadium in the Greek world that made extensive provision for the seating of spectators (several dozen rows of marble seats to accommodate approximately 50,000 persons). This stadium was constructed by Lycurgus (396-325 B.C.E.), a student of Plato and Isocrates and the administrative superintendent of Athens in the mid-fourth century B.C.E., in the fourth century B.C.E.; it was rebuilt by Herodes Atticus (c. 104-c. 180 C.E.), a wealthy Athenian benefactor, orator, and teacher of Marcus Aurelius, in the image of the stadium at Delphi (which he also financed) in the second century C.E.; and it was restored/converted in the late nineteenth century into the modern stadium which hosted the 1870 version of Evangelis Zappas' "Pan-Hellenic" Games and the Games of the First Modern Olympiad in 1896.

The **national athletic festivals** of ancient Greece were too established in this period and they were also intimately connected to, and sharply influenced by, the other leading tendencies of the time. All of them evolved out of religious festivals (staged at religious shrines) and all of them retained an abiding relationship with religious ritual. All of them were significantly moved by the fractional political organization of city-states and the fervent nationalism/militarism which resulted. All of them were greatly affected by the athletic orientation of the leading artistic and intellectual movements of the time. All of them were conducted amid a truce order, were closely supervised by athletic officials, were often attended by as many as c. 45,000 spectators, and were conducted in the form of highly vigorous and highly competitive contests. All of them were held continuously from the time of their respective origins to the time of their common abolition in the late fourth and early fifth centuries C.E. All of them were likewise different than the local festivals in several important respects:

- athletes from all of the Greek city-states participated in them;
- only several athletic events of inelaborate proportion were included in them;
- only prizes of symbolic consequence were formally awarded in them, a practice that appreciated aristocratic prerogative and that depreciated the prerogatives of wage labor; wreaths of a sacred leaf were placed on the victors' heads in a solemn and impressive ceremony;
- prizes were formally awarded only to victors in them; and
- they more fully embraced the classical athletic ideal of Hellenism (which was most tellingly developed in the Greek Enlightenment of the fifth century B.C.E.) than did the local festivals.

There were four of these national, pan-Hellenic, or "crown" festivals: the Olympic Games, the Pythian Games, the Isthmian Games, and the Nemean Games.

The first and the greatest of these were the **Olympic Games**.[92] There are several mythological accounts of the Games' origin:

- The fifth celebrated labor of Herakles entailed his cleaning of the Augean stables by diverting the Alpheus River (which is adjacent to the site of the Olympic Games at Olympia) through them. Augeias, displeased with the result, took up arms against Herakles who successfully defended himself. The Games were instituted in celebration of Herakles' victory.
- Pelops, grandfather of Herakles, had sought the marriage favor of Hippodameia, daughter of Oinamaos. Oinamaos, however, required his daughter's suitors to stand the test of a chariot race against him. In this race, only the winner was spared his life. Thirteen unsuccessful aspirants passed before Pelops' dubious triumph. The Games were instituted in celebration of his victory and his marriage to Hippodameia. Herakles later re-established these Games.
- Tantalus dismembered his son, Pelops, threw Pelops' parts into a caldron of stew, and served the stew to his guests, the gods. A suspicious Zeus restored Pelops, however, and the Games were instituted in celebration.
- The Games were instituted to commemorate Zeus' deposition of Kronus.

Whatever the basis for the origin of the Games in these myths, the Games likely commemorated the heroic stature of Herakles (and his ancestors) in the form of victory, initiation, and/or harvest rites until the early sixth century B.C.E.; thereafter, they honored the god of gods, Zeus.

Although music, drama, recitation, dancing, and athletic contests of a sort were held at Olympia (on the western Peloponnesus at the confluence of the Alpheus and Cladeus Rivers) from at least c. 1300 B.C.E. (perhaps from as early as c. 1800 B.C.E.), the first Games for which there is documentary evidence were held in 776 B.C.E. They were staged every four years (in the first year of each Olympiad, or four-year cycle marking the intervals of Olympic celebration) continuously from that time to their abolition by the second Christian emperor of the Roman Empire, Theodosius I (Theodosius the Great) in 394 C.E. The only exceptions to this nearly 1200-year line of quadrennial celebration occurred in 364 B.C.E. (when the Arcadians occupied Olympia) and in 67 C.E. (when the Roman emperor, Nero, postponed and otherwise abused the ideal of the Games). In both instances, Olympic officials declared "anolympiads."

The Olympic site became the national sanctuary of the supreme god of the Olympian pantheon, Zeus, and the political, artistic, intellectual, and athletic forum of the entire Greek world. The Games themselves were held at the base of a beautiful hill (the hill of Kronus) amid groves of olive trees. The major features of the site were the Altis, which contained numerous altars (most significantly, the altar of Zeus at which a sacrificial fire burned perpetually), statues (most significantly, the Macedonian figures collected in the Philippeion), and temples (most significantly, the colossal temples of Hera and Zeus, the small temples of the various cities, the Treasuries, and the tomb of Pelops); the structures outside the Altis (most significantly, the gymnasium, exercise hall, baths, sculptors' workshop, banquet hall, and guest house); the stadium; and the hippodrome (now lost). The central athletic facility of the Olympic site was, of course, the stadium (στάδιον, stadeion). Ancient Greek stadiums differed in length owing to different standards of measurement and different topographical features at various sites. The athletic floor of the stadium at Olympia was 192.27 meters in length (at Delphi, 177.5 meters; at Nemea, 178 meters). There was also an additional approximately 15 meters of open space at each end of the stadium and the floor itself was approximately 30 meters in width. The stadium was enclosed on both sides by natural or constructed, earthen embankments. Stone basins for drinking water were put every approximately 30 meters along each side of the stadium floor and square pillars for measuring purposes were put at approximately 90-meter intervals along each side of the stadium floor. An arched, processional tunnel connected the Altis and the stadium floor; it was through this tunnel that athletes and officials entered the stadium. The platform for the awarding of prizes was located opposite the tunnel.

Throughout the first approximate half-century of the Games' practice (i.e., to the last quarter of the eighth century B.C.E.), participation was confined largely to inhabitants of the western Peloponnesus. The first champion, Coroebus, was from Elis itself. Thereafter, the Games came to include representatives from the other city-states of the Balkan Peninsula, Aegean basin, Asia Minor, Spain, Italy, and Africa. Sparta was the dominant sporting state at Olympia from 720 to 576 B.C.E.; Athens gained its first victory at Olympia in 696 B.C.E. The impulse to pan-Hellenism came to maturity in the sixth century B.C.E. when the spirit of Greek nationalism became more fully developed. Under the terms of this spirit, athletics was considered one among the trappings of human culture which distinguished Greeks from others, which distinguished Greeks from barbarians. Likewise under the terms of this spirit, only Greek citizens (all of whom were men) were permitted to participate as athletes. Solon's early sixth century B.C.E. constitutional reforms in Athens nonetheless defined Greek citizenry in broader respects than earlier/elsewhere; that is, in timocratic (by wealth as well as birth) as distinct from in aristocratic (strictly by birth) respects.

The Games were attended by anyone who wished to avail themselves of the opportunity, except married women. Because the athletes performed in the nude after 720 B.C.E. (in short pants earlier), married women were excluded because their presence was thought to constitute an undue challenge to the integrity of the family and because their presence was thought to diminish the resolve of athletes to inspire fear in their opponents. Although the attendance of unmarried women was not prohibited, few nonetheless chose to frequent the Games. Only Callipateira (mother of the grandson of the great Diagoras of Rhodes, arguably the most accomplished boxer in the entire history of ancient Greek sport), whose son, Eukles of Rhodes, won at boxing in 404 B.C.E., escaped the fate of married women who defied the custom prohibiting their attendance, to be thrown to their death from the Typaeum Rock, a cliff on the side of the Alpheus River opposite the stadium. Among women, only the priestess of Demeter was expected to attend the Games and had an established place of honor in them. Constructed seating was sparse and was reserved for the approximately 160 honored guests, deputations from the various city-states, and officials. The other 40,000-45,000 spectators customarily sat or stood on the earthen embankments. Neither were there any formal accommodations for the lodging of spectators; most relied on tents for such purposes. Attendance was without charge but it was also a chaotic experience without comfort.

Although Greek sport was born in the age of Homer of its associations with war (and other activities of the everyday), as either a preparation for war, a commemoration of war, or a diversion from war, it flowered under the playful terms of a qualified peace. The Olympic Games were always conducted amid a truce order (εχεχειρια, ekecheiria). Citizens of hostile, as well as friendly, city-states were to compete together in peaceful rivalry. Penalties for violating the truce were severe; in the most celebrated such instance, Sparta was expelled from the Games of the 90th Olympiad in 416 B.C.E. The truce was announced throughout the Greek world by the sacred truce bearers (spondophores) and it was enforced throughout the Greek world for several months prior to the Games and for one month following their conclusion. All travelers were thereby put under the protection of the gods and were assured safe passage to and from the Games. The truce did not pertain to military activities in any broader sense.

The Games were strictly supervised by official judges (hellinodikai) who were sworn to impartial and objective judgment. The judges supervised the competitions themselves as well as the final preparations of the athletes for the Games. As a condition of their participation, athletes were required to assemble for training at Olympia one month prior to the opening of the Games.

The only prize officially awarded victors in the Games was a crown of laurel, apple, palm, pine, or wild olive branches (στεφανιται, stefanitai) which was to symbolize the honor of victory. The official prize was not to do with material gain. From c. 700 B.C.E., however, many unofficial prizes were heaped on the victors of the Games by other-than-Olympic officials (even by state officials such as Solon), including prizes of great material value. The Greeks were "never" therefore amateurs in the strict modern sense although they did work out a distinction between professional athletes, who did sport on a full-time, vocational basis (and were thus well trained) and so-termed idiotai, who did sport on a part-time, avocational basis (and were thus little trained). Unlike the modern amateur-professional distinction, however, the Greek difference was not grounded in material compensation. Also unlike the early development of the modern amateur-professional distinction, professional Greek athletes came increasingly from all social classes.

The principal sporting events in the Olympic Games were foot-racing, jumping, discus throwing, javelin throwing, wrestling, boxing, pancrateion, pentathlon, chariot racing, and horse racing. Foot-racing, in turn, took four main forms: a sprint race, a middle-distance race, a long-distance race, and a race with armor. In all of these forms, athletes ran up and back the length of the stadium floor on a straight course as distinct from around an oval course (as in the modern instance). All races were run over distances that were multiples of one stadium length (192.27 meters in the Olympic case). Running in all races, except the long-distance event, started either:

- from stone blocks, or sills (4 feet/1.2 meters x 18 inches/50 centimeters), put flush with the running surface into which two grooved lines (γραμμη, gramme) had been carved approximately 7 inches/18 centimeters apart (for placement of each foot) and/or
- from behind vertical posts (νυσσαι, nussai), inserted into the sills, on which ropes or bars were hung.

In the latter case, all of the ropes or bars were apparently dropped simultaneously by a starting device (υσπλεχ, husplex) operated from a starter's pit. The posts may likewise have been used as guides for running from one end of the stadium to the other on a straight course. There is no evidence that lanes were roped (as in the early modern case) or that the track surface itself was marked for lanes (as in the later modern case). Fresh sand was nonetheless thrown over the course to enhance firm placement of the foot. In any case, races were started either by dropping the ropes/bars, by a herald's trumpet, or by a herald's voice command (απιτε, apite, go). Those who false started were variously struck with a rod and/or disqualified. Since all races finished at the same end of the stadium (the end nearest the processional tunnel and the Altis) and since not all races were defined as multiples of two stadium lengths, both ends contained starting sills; there were twenty sills at one end and twenty-one at the other, one for each runner in both cases. The runners started from a standing position with their feet put into the grooves of the stone sills and with their torsos forward leaning, their knees slightly flexed, and their arms apart. The style of running apparently resembled modern techniques.

The sprint race, the stade (σταδιον), was one stadium-length in distance (approximately 192 meters/210 yards). The middle-distance race, the diaulos (διαλος), was two stadium-lengths in distance (approximately 385 meters/420 yards); the runners turned left around the post in their "lane" at the conclusion of the first length and they finished at the post in their "lane" at the conclusion of their second length. The long-distance race, the dolichos (δολιχος), was run over various distances (7, 12, 20, and 24 stade; approximately 1346 meters/1472 yards, 2327 meters/1 mile 785 yards, 3845 meters/2 miles 685 yards, or 4654 meters/2 miles 1570 yards respectively; that is, from slightly less than one mile to slightly less than three miles). The athletes in the dolichos started together and did not run in "lanes" but en masse; they too ran repeatedly around center posts (καμπτηρες, kampteres), one at each end of the stadium floor. The race with armor, the hoplitodromos (οπλιτοδρομος) was run over the same distance (in the Olympic Games; it was run over longer distances elsewhere) and in the same way as the diaulos, except that athletes wore a battle helmet and carried a battle shield. In the stade and quite likely in the diaulos and the hoplitodromos as well, only the winners of preliminary heats (each including four runners) advanced to the final. In the dolichos, all entrants contested a final race only; there were no qualifying rounds. Dead heats resulted in re-runs; a winner had to be declared.

Since the Greeks hadn't the standardized measures or the technology to keep records of a fully modern type, there are few means of comparing ancient to modern performance. The Greek city-states nonetheless developed many celebrated athletes; most notable among runners were:

- Coroebus of Elis, the first Olympic champion, who won the stade in the Games of the First Olympiad in 776 B.C.E.;
- Chionis of Sparta, who won the stade and the diaulos in the Games of the 29th, 30th, and 31st Olympiads in 664, 660, and 656 B.C.E. respectively;
- Phanas of Pellene, the first triple victor at Olympia, who won the stade, the diaulos, and the hoplitodromos in the Games of the 67th Olympiad in 512 B.C.E.;

- Astylos of Kroton/Syracuse, among the greatest athletes of ancient Greece, who won the stade and the diaulos in the Games of the 73rd, 74th, and 75th Olympiads in 488, 484, and 480 B.C.E. respectively;
- Dandes of Argos, who won twenty-two pan-Hellenic running titles in four Olympiads of the early fifth century B.C.E. (including the stade in the Games of the 77th Olympiad in 472 B.C.E.);
- Ladas of Sparta, who died following his victory in the dolichos in the Games of the 85th Olympiad in 440 B.C.E.;
- Leonidas of Rhodes, among the greatest athletes of ancient Greece, who won the stade, the diaulos, and the hoplitodromos in the Games of the 154th, 155th, 156th, and 157th Olympiads in 164, 160, 156, and 152 B.C.E. respectively;
- Polites of Ceramus, who won the stade, the diaulos, and the dolichos in the Games of the 212th Olympiad in 69 C.E.; and
- Hermogenes of Xanthos, who won eight races (stade, diaulos, and hoplitodromos) in the Games of the 215th, 216th, and 217th Olympiads in 81, 85, and 89 C.E. respectively.

Although relay races (torch relays, or lampadedromoi) and ultra-long-distance races/runs (hemerodromoi) were an occasional feature of local festivals, they were never made a part of the pan-Hellenic celebrations. The most memorable achievements in these activities were attained by long-distance running military messengers:

- the unknown messenger (only Plutarch, in his Moralia, claimed that this was Eucles), who ran from Marathon to Athens (roughly 40 kilometers/25 miles) to announce the Greek victory over Persia in the Persian Wars, 490 B.C.E., then fell dead of the effort;
- Pheidippides, who (according to Lucian) ran from Athens to Sparta and return (approximately 480 kilometers/300 miles) in two days for reinforcements in the Persian Wars, 490 B.C.E.; and
- Philonides, who is said to have run approximately 218 kilometers/136 miles in one day in the fourth century B.C.E.

Although the Greeks foresaw most of the events now typically contested in modern track competitions, there is no evidence that they practiced any form of hurdling in any context.

Jumping events were a feature of the pan-Hellenic athletic festivals (including the Olympic Games) only insofar as one such event was among the five events of the pentathlon; these events did not hold an independent place on the program of the national festivals. The only form of jumping included in the Olympic Games (as an aspect of the pentathlon) was the running long jump with weights (αλμα, alma). This event entailed a rather slow and a relatively short approach run, a modest preparation for take-off in the context of the run, a one-foot take-off from a take-off threshold of stone or wood (βατηρ, bater, which was marked on each side by pillars or spears) in which the jumper thrust the arms, hands, and weights vigorously forward and upward, a flight position in which the arms and legs were extended, together, and parallel to one another, a preparation for landing in which the arms, hands, and weights were thrust downward and backward, and a landing with the feet together making a firm impression in the jumping pit (σκαμμα, skamma, which was comprised of turned over and leveled soil). The weights (halteres) were held in the hands and resembled dumbbells; they were constructed of metal or stone, were 12 centimeters/5 inches to 30 centimeters/12 inches in length, and weighed between 1 kilogram/2.2 pounds and 4.5 kilograms/10 pounds; and many were very artfully formed. The jump was marked by pegs (semeion) placed in the ground beside the jumping pit and they were later measured by rods (κανονες, kanones). Three to five attempts were evidently allowed to each contestant and the event was commonly performed to a flute accompaniment owing to its immense difficulty. Although widely thought fictional, greatly exaggerated, or wildly misinterpreted, the most extraordinary feats of jumping in the ancient world were allegedly achieved by Chionis of Sparta, who at the Games of the 29th Olympiad in 664 B.C.E. is said to have jumped 52 feet/16 meters, and by Phayllus of Kroton, who at the Pythian Games in Delphi in 482 B.C.E. is said to have exceeded the skamma by five feet (thus jumping 55 feet/17 meters) and to have fractured his leg on landing. It is plausibly the case that, owing to the articulate use of hand-weights, distances achieved by leading ancient Greek jumpers were comparable to those achieved by leading modern long jumpers (who do not use hand-weights). It is unlikely, however, that these distances approached those of leading modern triple jumpers. Among other forms of jumping event, standing long jumping with and without weights and perhaps running high jumping were practiced in some local festivals but not in the national celebrations. Standing high jumping, multiphasic horizontal jumping (such as triple jumping), and pole vaulting were evidently unknown to the Greeks.

Discus throwing (δισκος), like long jumping, did not have an independent place on the Olympic program; it was a part of this program only insofar as it was one among the five events of the pentathlon. 'Diskos' originally referred to any object to be thrown but came to signify a flat, circular implement resembling the modern discus. As such, it was eventually distinguished from the javelin (which was also among the events of the pentathlon) and the solos, or mass of stone or bronze usually thrown as in putting the shot or the stone (an event which was contested in local, but not in national, festivals). Like the modern implement, the ancient Greek discus was somewhat thicker at its center than at its edges. It was, however, typically much larger than its modern analog; it had no standard dimension or mass but was customarily from 15 centimeters/6 inches to 28 centimeters/11 inches in diameter and from 2.4 kilograms/3 pounds to 7 kilograms/15 pounds in weight. Too unlike the modern case, it was constructed of solid stone or brass, rubbed with sand to smooth its surface, and often crafted in a varied and artful way. It was thrown from a rectangular area (balbis) which was demarcated by lines on its front and on its sides, but not on its back. The space in the front of this area was also marked by stone slabs (balbides) which throwers were required to keep themselves behind. The discus was held flat in the hand, resting on the forearm, with the fingers on the outside, the thumb on the inside of the implement. Throwers were permitted to approach the balbides as they wished from whatever distance they wished so long as they remained within the designated area. The discus, however, was typically thrown from a twisting stand or from a two or three forward-stepping action. Customarily, the discus was held in both hands to the front of the body at head height, then swung back with steps backward and forward in the fashion of preliminary swings. The non-throwing-side leg was usually put backward, then brought forward to establish the throwing position just before the discus itself was brought forward for delivery and release fairly near to the throwing side of the torso; the reversal step followed. Throws were measured from the balbides to the place where the discus fell on the stadium floor. As in the case of long jumping, the three to five throws permitted were marked with pegs and measured with rods.

Javelin throwing (ακοντισις or ακων, akontisis or akon), like long jumping and discus throwing, was an Olympic event only insofar as it was among the five events of the pentathlon. Although thrown for accuracy in other precincts of ancient Greek sport, it was thrown only for distance in the pentathlon of the national festivals. The ancient Greek javelin, like the ancient Greek discus, was not of standardized dimension or mass; it nonetheless typically consisted in straight wooden (likely, elder) poles which were light in weight, nearly the height of a man in length, and roughly the circumference of a finger. Unlike the modern implement, its forward end was usually without a point; it was instead covered by a blunt bronze cap for purposes of safety and for purposes having to do with the mass and balance of the shaft. The implement was held in the throwing hand by means of a thong (αγκυλη, agkule), or amentum, which was a 30 centimeter/12 inch to 45 centimeter/18 inch long band of leather firmly bound around the approximate center (slightly forward of center) of the shaft in such a way as to leave an 8 centimeter/three inch to 10 centimeter/four inch loop on one or both ends and on one or both sides of the shaft and beneath it. The first or the first and the second fingers was/were inserted in this/these loop(s), all of which contributed significantly to the impressive distances achieved, both in terms of force application and in terms of flight stabilization. The javelin was thrown from a backward leaning and looking position; the amentum was fixed in the extended throwing arm and hand by gripping the shaft with that hand and by pressing the javelin shaft into that hand with the other hand; several short steps set the throwing position; and the implement was then delivered and released much as in the modern practice. It was thrown a similar number of times as the discus and from a similarly framed area as the discus; performances in it were also marked and measured in a way similar to the discus. Standard forms of modern throwing event other than the discus, solos (shot), and javelin -- that is, hammer and weight throwing -- were apparently unknown to the Greeks in any context.

Wrestling (παλη, pale) was one of three dual combative events included in the Olympic Games and in the other national festivals as well; the others were boxing and pancrateion. Unlike boxing and pancrateion, however, wrestling remained largely free of brutality throughout its practice in the Games, emphasizing the throwing of an opponent with skill, grace, and style. It was thereby the most widely respected of the three. There were two somewhat different styles of wrestling in ancient Greek sport, the upright (kulsis) and the ground styles. Only the upright style was contested in the national festivals; the ground style was practiced in other contexts. In the upright style, which somewhat resembled modern Graeco-Roman wrestling, the aim was to throw the opponent cleanly to the ground from a standing (an upright) position; the contest did not continue on the ground. In the ground style, which somewhat resembled modern freestyle wrestling and which was given to brutality, the contest began on the feet but continued on the mud-covered ground until one of the combatants acknowledged defeat. There were no classifications by bodyweight; the event was therefore the rather exclusive province of very large men. In the upright style, only clean throws to the back, hips, or shoulders of the opponent counted; throws to the appendages or to the front of the torso did not. A throw in which both athletes fell to the ground together did neither count. Three clean throws (τριασσειν, triassein) were required for victory. Leg holds (i.e., holds applied to or by the legs) were likely prohibited. The stance on the feet resembled the modern practice in which the wrestlers stand square to one another. Holds were engaged at the wrists, arms, trunk, neck, and head and, since there was much turning in ancient Greek wrestling, they were variously applied as well from both in front of and behind the opponent. The rectangular area in which wrestling contests were conducted (σκαμμα, skamma) was distinguished only by its turned over and leveled soil surface over which a thin layer of fresh sand was sprinkled. Pairings were drawn by lot from a helmet. Withdrawals and byes were frequent but disrespected; a victor without byes (anephedros) was more highly regarded than one with (ephedros). The most accomplished of the ancient wrestlers were:

- Hipposthenes of Sparta, who won five consecutive Olympic titles in the Games of the 39th to the 43rd Olympiads from 624 to 608 B.C.E.;
- Hetoimokles of Sparta, who won four consecutive Olympic titles in the Games of the 45th, 46th, 47th, and 48th Olympiads in 600, 596, 592, and 588 B.C.E. respectively;
- Milon of Kroton, among the greatest athletes of ancient Greece, who won five consecutive Olympic titles in the Games of the 62nd to the 66th Olympiads from 532 to 516 B.C.E., who won the Olympic boys wrestling title in the Games of the 60th Olympiad in 540 B.C.E., and who won 32 pan-Hellenic titles (six Olympic, seven Pythian, ten Isthmian, and nine Nemean) in the late sixth century B.C.E.; and
- Sostratos of Sikyon, who won three consecutive wrestling and pancrateion titles in the Games of the 104th, 105th, and 106th Olympiads in 364, 360, and 356 B.C.E.

Boxing (πυγμη or πυξ, pugme or pux) was also a major feature of the Olympic Games. Like wrestling, there were no classifications by bodyweight and so the event was dominated by quite large men. Also like wrestling, there was no standard ring, only an area marked off for the event. Neither were there rounds although pauses by mutual consent of the boxers were permitted. Matches were fought to the finish; that is, either until a boxer acknowledged defeat by holding up his hand or until a boxer was adjudged unfit to continue by an official of the contest. A boxer might be struck while on the ground and apparently only blows to the head were used (either by rule or by custom). The conventional technique was to hold the body upright, the head erect; one foot was put forward of the other; the knees were slightly flexed; and the hands were held well up. The lead arm was well extended, its hand was held open, and it was used both for guarding and for creating an opening for the other hand, which was held well back for striking (for crossing over the openings created by the clearing action of the lead arm). There was little inside or offensive fighting; the tempo was slow, the emphasis tactical and defensive. Hand pieces were worn throughout the sport's ancient Greek practice but, as boxing became progressively more brutal and less scientific, they became themselves progressively more dangerous. Early on, the hands were wrapped in simple ox hide thongs (himantes) which were dressed with animal fat to make them supple. These thongs were usually three to four meters/ten to twelve feet in length and they were wrapped several times about the fingers, then passed diagonally across the palms of the hands and about the wrists and forearms where they were secured. They both protected the hands as well as somewhat softened blows and they were used into the fourth century B.C.E. when they were replaced by more formidable coverings (sphairai). Sphairai were formed of thick bands of soft leather put over the hands and forearms and fastened to the hands by other, hard leather thongs, hard leather thongs which were wrapped about the fingers and which created sharp edges that tended to cut the opponent when struck. Later in the fourth century B.C.E., a still more perilous device, the hard thong, replaced the sphairai. The hard thong consisted in a strip of hard leather wrapped around a padded glove which covered the hand (but not the fingers) and forearm. Parts of the strip were bound further together by smaller straps and thongs, all of which left very sharp, cutting edges. And from the second century C.E. a still more hazardous device was used, the Roman caestus. In this, a large glove, held in place by leather thongs, was put over the entire hand and arm. Over the gloved hand, in turn, was put a hard, semi-cylindrical cast and inside the impenetrable cast was commonly put such as iron and lead weights as well as spiked protuberances. In this form, the boxing hand piece became a potentially lethal weapon. Arguably the most renowned of the ancient boxers were:

- Tisandros of Naxos, who won four consecutive Olympic titles in the Games of the 52nd, 53rd, 54th, and 55th Olympiads in 572, 568, 564, and 560 B.C.E. respectively;

- Diagoras of Rhodes, among the greatest athletes of ancient Greece, who won the Olympic title in the Games of the 79th Olympiad in 464 B.C.E. and who had a son and a grandson who also won Olympic boxing titles as well as two sons who won Olympic pancrateion titles; and
- Varasdates of Armenia, who won the Olympic title in the Games of the 291st Olympiad in 369 C.E. and who was the last known ancient Olympic champion.

The most brutal of the three dual combative events in the national Greek festivals was the pancrateion (πανκρατιον). Like the other two such events, there were no classifications by bodyweight in pancrateion; it was therefore also dominated by rather large men. Like ground-style wrestling, pancrateion was contested over mud-covered ground and without intervals to the finish, which was designated by one of the combatants admitting defeat. Almost any means, except gouging, biting, and perhaps strangling, were permitted in order to encourage an opponent's submission. Kicking, leaping onto, striking, and various types of submission hold were most commonly used. From the stand, most pancratiasts attempted to throw the opponent heavily to the ground in order to bring him disabling injury. If necessary, the attacks continued on the ground where the match was usually decided. The most celebrated pancratiasts were:

- Arrichion of Phigaleia, who won three consecutive Olympic titles in the Games of the 52nd, 53rd, and 54th Olympiads in 572, 568, and 564 B.C.E. respectively and who secured his final Olympic victory at the moment of his death;
- Theagenes of Thasos, who achieved more than 1400 sporting victories throughout Greece, who won the Olympic pancrateion title in the Games of the 76th Olympiad in 476 B.C.E., and who won the Olympic boxing title in the Games of the 75th Olympiad in 480 B.C.E.; he was one of only two to win both an Olympic pancrateion and an Olympic boxing title;
- Dorieus of Rhodes, who won three consecutive Olympic titles in the Games of the 87th, 88th, and 89th Olympiads in 432, 428, and 424 B.C.E. respectively;
- Polydamas of Thessaly, among the greatest athletes of ancient Greece, who won the Olympic title in the Games of the 93rd Olympiad in 408 B.C.E.;
- Kleitomachos of Thebes, who won the Olympic pancrateion title in the Games of the 141st Olympiad in 216 B.C.E. and who won the Olympic boxing title in the Games of the 142nd Olympiad in 212 B.C.E.; he was one of only two to win both an Olympic pancrateion and an Olympic boxing title; and
- Kapros of Elis, who won the Olympic pancrateion and wrestling titles in the Games of the 142nd Olympiad in 212 B.C.E.

The pentathlon (πενταθλον) began, not as a discrete event itself, but as a means of determining the best all-around athlete among those contesting all of the discrete events of a sporting festival. As a discrete event itself, it was comprised of five events in one. Three of these – the running long jump with weights, discus throw, and javelin throw – had a place on the program of the pan-Hellenic festivals, including the Olympic Games, only insofar as they constituted aspects of the pentathlon. The remaining two of these – the stade and (upright) wrestling – had both an independent place on these programs and constituted an aspect of the pentathlon. The method of scoring the pentathlon and the order of events in it are not known in detail and with assurance except that the performance of each competitor in each event was compared with the performance of every other competitor in each event in order to determine which competitor(s) had won most events relative to each other competitor; it is also known that wrestling was the final event. It is nonetheless thought that:

- any competitor who was defeated by any other competitor in three of the first four events – the stade, long jump, discus throw, and javelin throw – was eliminated; if a competitor defeated each of the other competitors in three (or, equivocally, all four) of these events, he was declared the victor of the pentathlon and wrestling was not contested; similarly, any competitor who defeated each of the other competitors in two of these events remained in the competition; typically two to four competitors remained in the competition after four events, each of them having defeated each of the others in two of these events; the remaining competitors then contested wrestling, the winner of which was declared the victor of the pentathlon (he thus became the sole triple victor, the triakter); or
- only victors in the first three events, those unique to the pentathlon – the discus throw, long jump, and javelin throw – advanced to the stade (which was staged only if no competitor had yet secured three victories over each of the other competitors); wrestling was then contested among the remaining two competitors only if no competitor had yet secured three victories over each of the other competitors.

The pentathlon appealed most to the ideal of Greek sport during its classical era and least to the highly specialized preferences of professional athletics that followed. The harmonious union and beauty of all physical qualities and skills were most characteristically embodied in the pentathlete. Arguably the most eminent of the ancient Greek pentathletes was the only three-time Olympic champion, Philombrotos of Sparta, who won consecutive Olympic titles in the Games of the 26th, 27th, and 28th Olympiads in 676, 672, and 668 B.C.E. respectively.

The equestrian events – chariot racing (αρμα, arma) and horse racing (κελης, keles) – were held in the hippodrome, a facility which was two to three times larger than the stadium (i.e., the length of the course was two to three times that of the stadium; it was thus two to three stade). These events were contested around two pillars, one at each end of the facility. They began with an elaborate procession consisting in not more than twelve officials (who worked in groups of three), the herald (ceryx), the trumpeter, and the competitors, horses, and chariots. The officials took their places as each of the competitors, horses, and chariots passed before them, the herald proclaimed the competitor's name and his city-state, then asked if any man had a charge against him. As these were typically the first sporting events of the Games, the Games were then declared open and the competitors were addressed by a distinguished person, usually a hellanodikai. Prior to each race, the herald announced the names of the competitors in it, lots were drawn for starting positions, competitors' names and starting positions were written on a sign board, and the competitors, horses, and chariots took their places at the start. These races started from an intricate, prow-shaped starting gate with stalls (σφησας, sphasis), in the center of which were a bronze eagle and dolphin. An official (likely by means of pulleys) made the eagle go up, the dolphin go down, and ropes drop away from the fronts of the stalls as a trumpet was sounded, all to designate the start of the race. The chariots were light, two-wheeled carts with space only for a standing charioteer and they were pulled by several horses abreast. The charioteer, who wore a long white chemise-like garment, was the only clothed athlete in the Games, carried a whip (which he used frequently), and held the reins in both hands. The fields were typically quite large (40-60 chariots), the races were very long (twelve laps, 24 lengths, c. 48-72 stade, c. 9000-c. 14,000 meters/c. 6-c. 9 miles), and accidents were common, most particularly at the perilous turns. The wealthy owner of the chariot that came first (who in very rare cases was a woman), not the charioteer, was declared the victor and received the prize for victory. Kyniska of Sparta was the first woman to win an Olympic title in this way; she owned the victorious four-horse chariot team in the Games of the 96th and 97th Olympiads in 396 and 392 B.C.E. respectively. Although several chariot races were briefly added to the Olympic program in the classical, Hellenistic, and Roman eras, the two most enduring such events were the four-horse race (tethrippon or quadriga) and the two-horse race (synoris or biga). Horse racing also took several forms but was most importantly done without saddle or stirrups, by one shoeless rider, over one lap of the hippodrome (two lengths, c. 4-c. 6 stade, c. 800-c. 1200 meters/ c. ½-c. ¾ mile).

The program of the ancient Olympic Games evolved progressively to include these events; the Games did not include all of them from their very beginning. The stade was the first Olympic event and it was the only such event through thirteen Olympiads. In the Games of the fourteenth Olympiad, 724 B.C.E., the diaulos was added; in the Games of the fifteenth Olympiad, 720 B.C.E., the dolichos. The others followed:
- pentathlon and wrestling in the Games of the eighteenth Olympiad, 708 B.C.E.;
- boxing in the Games of the 23rd Olympiad, 688 B.C.E.;
- four-horse chariot racing in the Games of the 25th Olympiad, 680 B.C.E.;
- pancrateion and horse racing in the Games of the 33rd Olympiad, 648 B.C.E.;
- hoplitodromos in the Games of the 65th Olympiad, 520 B.C.E.; and
- two-horse chariot racing in the Games of the 93rd Olympiad, 408 B.C.E.

Events for boys (beardless [ageneioi], 12-16 years of age, and others [paides], 16-20 years of age), as distinct from men (andres), were also eventually added for at least brief periods:
- foot-racing (over roughly 5/6th the distance of the men's stade) and wrestling in the Games of the 37th Olympiad, 632 B.C.E.;
- pentathlon in the Games of the 38th Olympiad, 628 B.C.E.;
- boxing in the Games of the 41st Olympiad, 616 B.C.E.; and
- pancrateion in the Games of the 145th Olympiad, 200 B.C.E.

This was likewise the case in respect to other equestrian events – most notably, the apene, or two-mule chariot race in the Games of the 69th Olympiad, 500 B.C.E. – and in respect to contests for heralds and trumpeters as well as contests in lyre-playing, religious dancing, scholarly recitation, and tragedic drama.

The Olympic Games were held alternately in the second or third full moon after the summer solstice, in the months of August or September. In its most memorable practice, in the classical era (beginning in the early fifth century B.C.E.), the Olympic festival was conducted over a five-day period. On the first day, no competitions were held; a solemn inspection of the competitors was staged instead. In this inspection, the competitors as well as their trainers, fathers, and brothers passed through a ceremony in which a pig was sacrificed and in which the competitors swore that they would use no unfair means to secure victory and that they had trained for at least ten months preceding the festival in a manner worthy of it. The judges then took final decisions concerning the eligibility of competitors and swore to make impartial judgments throughout the events of the Games themselves. The penalties for giving false information in these ceremonies or for cheating in the competitions themselves included expulsion from the Games, public floggings, and fines. What remained of the first day was taken up with training.

On the second day, the four-horse chariot race, the two-horse chariot race, the horse race, and the pentathlon were contested. The equestrian events were all staged in the hippodrome. The first four events of the pentathlon were held in the stadium; the fifth, wrestling, if contested, was staged in front of the altar of Zeus on the Altis. The evening was spent in revelry, eating, drinking, dancing, singing, and rejoicing. The third day was the most honored of the festival. In the morning, a formal sacrifice in which all official parties participated was offered at the altar of Zeus. A long procession was followed by the slaughter of one hundred oxen, the thighs of which were burned, the rest eaten. The afternoon was given to the competitions for boys, mainly in foot-racing, wrestling, and boxing. The evening was again spent in revelry. The principal athletic events of the Games were contested on the fourth day. In the morning, the stade, diaulos, and dolichos were held in the stadium. In the afternoon, wrestling, boxing, and pancrateion were conducted before the altar of Zeus on the Altis. The competitive day ended with the hoplitodromos in the stadium. And the evening was still again devoted to revelry. The fifth and final day of the Games was reserved for feasting and rejoicing. The victors made their vows at the altars of the gods. Other rites and sacrifices were performed. And the Games concluded with the entertainment of the victors at a feast in the banquet hall.

Although women were customarily excluded from all precincts of ancient Greek sport, except in Sparta and Cyrene (in northern Africa), there is some evidence to suggest that an approximately 150 meters/500 feet foot-race for three age-groups of maiden girls (children, adolescents, and young women) was staged at Olympia at approximate five-year intervals (but not in Olympic years). The Games in which these races occurred honored the main female figure in the Olympian pantheon, Hera, and they were thus known as the Heraean Games. The awards for victory in these Games were symbolic; viz., crowns of olive branch and leaf. The girls wore their hair loose and were clothed in a short, one-shoulder dress, or chiton. These Games were most likely inspired by Sparta, had a close association with the legend of Hippodameia, and signified the passage to civilized adulthood in ritual terms. Spartan women, unlike most other Greek women (including Athenian women), were highly active, took part in educational gymnastics, and (for eugenic reasons) performed nude before men in athletic activity. Other, less esteemed women's races were neither unknown in ancient Greece from the seventh and sixth centuries B.C.E.; most notably, the Gortyn in Crete, the Orthia in Sparta, and the Physkos in Olympia.

The other pan-Hellenic athletic festivals began approximately two centuries after the first documented edition of the Olympic Games; that is, in the sixth century B.C.E., when their political significance was acknowledged and when formal regulations were established for them. They passed from existence in the same time (the late fourth century C.E.) and under the same influences as the Olympic Games. Although they were somewhat less highly regarded than the Olympic Games, the four national celebrations together nonetheless formed a compelling cycle (περιοδος, periodos); a champion in all four (περιοδικεις, periodikeis) was greatly revered and exceedingly rare (only 46 men are known to have achieved this feat). Multiple victories in any one of these festivals were also very highly regarded; double (paradoxonikes) and triple (triastes) victors were likewise rare and celebrated.

The second-most-renowned of the national festivals, the **Pythian Games**, were established when the musical competitions at Delphi, then staged in eight-year cycles, were reordered in accord with the quadrennial schedule of the Olympic program in 586 and 582 B.C.E. These Games were held at Delphi in honor of Apollo (who defeated no less than Hermes in running and Ares in boxing) every four years thereafter in the third year of every Olympiad. The prize for victory was a wreath of bay branches and leaves. The festival at Corinth was similarly reorganized in 582 B.C.E. and became the **Isthmian Games**. They were conducted in honor of Poseidon every two years thereafter in the second and fourth years of every Olympiad. The prize for victory was a wreath of pine or dry parsley branches and leaves. And the Nemean festival was likewise reorganized and became the **Nemean Games** in 573 B.C.E. These Games were held variously at Nemea and Argos in honor of Nemean Zeus (a shepherd god) every two years thereafter in the first and third years of every Olympiad. The prize for victory was a wreath of fresh parsley branches and leaves.

The classical period

The period which followed, the classical period, c. 550/480-338 B.C.E., was among the most remarkable in the entire record of human civilization. It was marked, in its beginning, by Persian domination of Greece and, in its end, by the Macedonian conquest of Greece. It was most distinguished by:

- the successful wars of the Greeks against the Persian Empire, the Persian Wars;
- the fracture of Greek political "unity" and the routine and ruinous civil wars that resulted (most notably, the Peloponnesian, Corinthian, and Theban Wars);
- the long and unsuccessful struggle with Macedonia that concluded in the loss of Greek political independence, military influence, and commercial prowess;
- the apotheosis of Greek democratic experiments and their dissolution;
- the flowering of the Greek intellectual genius, the Greek Enlightenment, in philosophy, architecture, sculpture, drama, poetry, oratory, history, and music; and
- the flowering as well as the incipient decline of Greek athletics, Greek educational sport, and the athletic ideal of ancient Hellenism.

Although the Greeks did not begin to earnestly resist until 500 B.C.E., Persian domination of the Greek city-states in Ionia began as early as c. 546 B.C.E. Persian successes largely marked the conflict until 494 B.C.E. when the sweep of advantage began to shift. The decisive battles of the **Persian Wars** occurred at Marathon in 490 B.C.E. (victory of Miltiades of Athens over Darius I of Persia), at Thermopylae in 480 B.C.E. (effective victory of Leonidas of Sparta over Xerxes I of Persia), at Salamis in 480 B.C.E. (the battle strategy of the Athenian statesman, Themistocles [c. 525-c. 460 B.C.E.; r. 483-470 B.C.E.], himself an accomplished charioteer, prevailed over Xerxes I), and at Plataea in 479 B.C.E. (victory of Pausanias of Sparta over a depleted army abandoned by Xerxes I). Although Persia sacked Athens in 480 B.C.E. and again in 479 B.C.E. and although the Wars dragged on for another approximately thirty years until a second Greek victory at Salamis (and the Athenian statesman Cimon's [c. 502-449 B.C.E.] Peace of Callias) in 449 B.C.E. brought them to a full conclusion, the Persian expansion and significant Persian prerogative in Greece proper ended in 479/478 B.C.E. The Greek successes in these Wars were interpreted (by the Greeks) as the decisive victory of free city-states over Oriental despotism as well as the victory of trained athletes over effeminate barbarians. The national triumph found its largest expression in commerce and in sport, both of which prospered handsomely in this period.

The Greek Enlightenment followed as did the deepening alienation of Greek city-states from one another; most tellingly, the alienation of Athens and Sparta. The Delian League was established in 478 B.C.E. as a Greek alliance against the Persian danger. The League, however, was throughout an Athenian-dominated confederacy from which Sparta became increasingly estranged and from which Sparta was eventually expelled. A series of contending alliances among the Greek states developed as a result; conflicts between these alliances predictably escalated, in the end creating utterly fractural hostilities. The intensity of these hostilities, together with the invasions of the Persians, Macedons, and Romans, principal among others, kept Greek culture perpetually near to either the threat or the fact of military conflict. This sense of rivalry and its austere physical manifestations also importantly expressed itself in the sport of the period, mainly in the form of vehement sporting opposition.

By 431 B.C.E., the hostilities between Athens and Sparta had overwhelmed both. The **Peloponnesian War** was the calamitous result. The War began in the Athenian rule of Pericles (c. 495-429 B.C.E.; r. 461, 443-429 B.C.E.) and Aspasia, continued through the devastating plague in Athens that killed Pericles and one-third of the Athenian population, and went on through the rule of Cleon (d. 422 B.C.E.; r. 429-422 B.C.E.) and the treacherous persecution, defection, recall, and murder of Athenian statesman, Alcibiades (c. 450-404 B.C.E.), who was himself a great athlete and charioteer. It ended with the victory of the Spartans under Lysander at Aegospotami in 405 B.C.E. and with the siege and capitulation of Athens, the dissolution of the Delian League, and the establishment of the Spartan hegemony, all in 404 B.C.E.

Other, mostly civil wars and ongoing conflicts with Persia (concerning the Ionian states) and with Macedonia (concerning Greek political independence) continued through the next approximate two-thirds of a century:

- Sparta attempted to free the Ionian states of Persian influence in a series of mostly unsuccessful conflicts, 399-394 B.C.E.;
- Athens, Thebes, Corinth, and Argos opposed Sparta to little effect and unsteady conclusion in a series of conflicts referred to as the **Corinthian War**, 395-387 B.C.E.; and

- in a series of events, 379-362 B.C.E., referred to as the **Theban Wars**, Thebes (under Epaminondas [c. 418-362 B.C.E.]) defeated Sparta at Leuctra in 371 B.C.E., establishing the Theban hegemony, liberating much of the Peloponnesus from Spartan rule, and thus also initiating the decline of Sparta; in the last major event of this series, Thebes defeated an Athenian-Spartan alliance (under the Second Delian League which had been formed in 377 B.C.E.) at Mantinea in 362 B.C.E.

The **conflicts with Macedonia** began in 357 B.C.E. and continued to the Macedon defeat of the Greeks and the end of Greek political independence in 338 B.C.E. Philip II of Macedonia (382-336 B.C.E.; r. 359-336 B.C.E.) managed the unification of Macedonia in 358 B.C.E.; reorganized the military into an imposing and superior force of foot soldiers arranged in phalanges armed with maces, long lances, and small shields; and began a campaign of successful foreign conquest in 357 B.C.E. The approximately twenty warring years with the Greek states were most importantly marked by Philip's conquest of Chalcidice in 357-346 B.C.E.; by disintegration of the Second Delian League in 357-355 B.C.E.; by Philip's conquest of Thessaly in 352 B.C.E. and of Thrace in 343-342 B.C.E.; by the stirring debate in Athens between Isocrates (who urged Hellenic unity against Persia and who favored the unification of Greece and Macedonia) and Demosthenes (who favored continued opposition to Philip); by the formation of the Hellenic League against Philip in 340 B.C.E.; and by the decisive victory of Philip (and his son, Alexander III, or Alexander the Great) over the Greeks at Chaeronia in 338 B.C.E.

Among the principal casualties of these conflicts was the "perfection" of **Greek democracy** achieved by Pericles. Under Pericles, who was himself an accomplished wrestler, the citizen class of Athens expanded and political franchise was extended to all Attican citizens, an impressively large relative number of persons by ancient, if not by modern, standard. The triumphs of Pericles in this respect were, however, variously diminished by his successors and by the events which unfolded after his death. These triumphs were first seriously compromised by Cleon in the 420s B.C.E., then restored in 403 B.C.E. at the conclusion of the Peloponnesian War; they deteriorated thereafter under the military threat and the anti-democratic tendencies of Sparta. The classical Greek experiments in popular government eventually failed; such experiments nonetheless brought with them a respect for unfettered intellectual inquiry that is incompatible with despotism, itself a virtually characteristic feature of the ancient world's political economy. The democratic inclinations of the time, howsoever limited by modern perspective, likewise contributed favorably to the development of Greek sport, principally by heightening the sense of state and national patriotism (which expressed itself in sporting terms) and by broadening the scope of sporting participation.

The classical groundwork of the Greek Enlightenment and the **Greek Enlightenment** itself developed in the context of the commercial prowess, the economic prosperity, the internationalism, and the democratic reforms which followed the Persian Wars. Although this movement had scarce analog in the political life of ancient Greece (which, for prominent instance, excluded non-citizens, including all women) and was thus, even in its own time, more so an intellectual proposal than a matter of accomplished concrete fact, it nonetheless constituted among the most brilliant and most influential chapters in the entire record of human civilization. The Greeks were the first to conceive of humanity as the central issue of reflective discourse, as the principal subject and the principal object of truth. Reason, by the Greek view, was thought the impartial criterion of truth and humanity, in turn, the unique possessor, or guardian, of reason. The integral forms of human experience – science, sport, dance, art, religion, history, philosophy, and education – were, for the first time, explicitly endowed with purposeful reason and so with authentic humanity. They were, for the first time, explicitly interpreted as ends-in-and-for-themselves, as essential aspects of human life, as characteristically human and humanizing forms of expression. They had thus taken their first, tentative steps beyond the status of mere means. In only novel features of the medieval and modern Islamic Enlightenment (most especially, features of the Omayyad, Abbasid, Fatimid, Almoravid, Nasrid, Timurid, Mogul, and Ottoman developments), European (most especially, Italian, Burgundian, and German) Renaissance humanism, nineteenth-century (most especially, French, German, British/Irish, Russian, American, Scandinavian, Italian, and Spanish) romanticism/realism, and twentieth-century European (most especially, Scandinavian) democratic socialism and European (most especially, Germanic, French, Russian, and Finnish), American, and Mexican expressionism would this intrinsic possibility (and the tendency to political society that it entails) be very widely repeated.

In **political society**, as distinct from gentile and civil society, the humanities predominate; the fundamental and universal aspects of human experience (science, sport, dance, art, religion, history, philosophy, and education) take the form of distinctly and uniquely human consciousness. They thus take the shape of imaginative significations (or symbols) of life's self-conscious basis. They function primarily as "fully" developed ways of expressing (or revealing) humanity's fundamental nature and purpose, humanity's fundamentally (emotional and) rational character. They are, consequently, imitative (as in gentile society) only in germ and they are representative (as in civil society) only in negative sublimation. Effectively, political society is gentile society "fully" and explicitly elaborated; it is what results from the positivity (the implicit affirmation of human fulfillment) of gentile society after it (this positivity) has passed through and triumphed over the negative epoch (the epoch in which human fulfillment is not at primary issue) of civil society. Political society distinguishes the integral forms of human experience but it treats these forms as cooperative participants in an organic union of experience, as aspects of such a union which are necessarily connected to one another and to the whole of life. Each is thus not utterly separate from each of the others, as fragmented bits of knowledge unconnected to one another, but necessarily related to each of the others and as a necessary contributor to the fulfillment of human life as such. Each may be therefore authentically well understood, appreciated, and practiced if, and only if, it is understood, appreciated, and practiced both in-it-self and insofar as it relates to each of the others as well as to the whole. Each of the parts of life's whole thus stands in balanced, harmonious, and proportionate relation to each of the other parts and to the whole. By this view, human life is itself liberated from the discords of excess, deficiency, and division; it is itself conceived as an active search for its highest virtues, for its inherent virtues, for truth, justice, peace, beauty, and humility.[93] The "leisure" practices of political society are therefore self-consciously intrinsic to, and continuous with human experience in its broadest and deepest, in its fundamental disposition; they are explicitly and "fully" self-conscious.[94]

The governing principle of ancient Greek life throughout its most memorable and accomplished periods was most tellingly embodied in the Periclean anthropology and the Aristotelian ideal. This principle entailed cultivating the full development of, and the full relations among humanity's integral aspects, including sport. The unexcelled achievements of the Greeks in philosophy, architecture, sculpture, drama, poetry, oratory, history, and music -- which are owed mainly to the fifth and fourth centuries B.C.E. – are among the richest cultural accomplishments of any time or place.

In **philosophy**, the issues of substance and change continued (from the Milesians) to dominate thought in the first approximate half of the fifth century B.C.E. Heraclitus (c. 535-c. 475 B.C.E.), in materialistic-tending fashion, argued, against the Milesians, that change does not inhere in material substance but is itself the fundamental datum of reality, that nothing is permanent except the rational principle (the logos) by which change itself is ordered, and that reality is therefore constituted as a harmoniously arranged succession of transformations. The Eleatics (from Elea in Sicily), principally Parmenides (c. 515-c. 450 B.C.E.) and Zeno (c.490-c. 430 B.C.E.), in idealistic-tending manner, conversely, held that reality is fundamentally permanent, that it is fundamentally fixed, that nothing can be transformed, and that in order for there to be anything at all, there can be only one, indivisible, eternal being, only unchanging thought. The qualitative atomists, most notably Empedocles (c. 495-c. 435 B.C.E.) and Anaxagoras (c. 500-428 B.C.E.), attempted a conciliation of the extreme positions taken by Heraclitus and the Eleatics by arguing that a fully satisfactory account of the world must explain both its inclination to permanence and its inclination to change. According to this idealis-tic-tending view, the world is permanent in respect to its being comprised of numerous qualitative elements; it is changing insofar as the relations of these elements are in continuous flux.[95] The quantitative atomists, mainly Leucippus (fl. fifth century B.C.E.) and Democritus (c. 460-c. 370 B.C.E.), also construed the world as a mosaic of changeless, eternal particles, or atoms. Unlike the qualitative atomists, however, they surmised, in realistic-tending fashion, that atoms are without quality, that they are quantitatively defined, and that they move (i.e., change) by inherent, not by external, means.

The cosmological speculations of the Milesians, Pythagoras, Heraclitus, the Eleatics, and the qualitative and quantitative atomists invited both a deeply skeptical reply and an era of comprehensive systems. The skeptical reply came principally from the sophists and Socrates; the comprehensive systems, from Plato and Aristotle. The sophists, most notably Protagoras (c. 490-c. 421 B.C.E.), who was himself an accomplished wrestler, mounted a revolt against what they took as the unduly speculative views that had preceded them. They argued that the metaphysical ruminations of the past, which had gone on about universal truths, had not resolved and could not have resolved the matters at issue because the truth of such matters is inaccessible to human experience. If there is anything at all to such matters, the sophists held, it cannot be known by us. Instead of inquiries into the fundamental character of cosmological reality, the sophists made a critical study of what they held is accessible to human experience; namely, the capacity of human intelligence for subjective truth, or opinion. Humanity, accordingly, is the measure of all things in the sense that only the contingent perceptions of individual persons may be known and in the sense that only the virtues of an independent mind are worthily defended as the basis of freedom and happiness. Socrates (469-399 B.C.E.) also took a skeptical line in respect to the metaphysical flights of earlier Greek thought. He nonetheless attempted to reaffirm the rational and, thus, the shared foundations of human knowledge, morality, and the state which the sophists had devastated. By his view, philosophy is properly limited to practical, human matters, to an unfinishable search for human happiness and fulfillment (as the sophists had claimed), but it is also properly enlisted in the pursuit of universal solutions to moral and political dilemmas (a view that is contrary to the sophists' position).[96]

Plato and Aristotle took Socrates' challenge of the sophists still farther than had Socrates himself, developed far broader and less skeptical programs of philosophical reflection than had the sophists or Socrates, thought (unlike the sophists and Socrates) a resolution to the problem of metaphysical reality both obtainable and a necessary basis for dealing with more practical concerns, and constructed the first authentically comprehensive (and what have also proved to be among the most accomplished and durable) systems of philosophic discourse in the entire history of the subject. Plato (427-347 B.C.E.),[97] who fashioned an idealistic-tending system, argued that reality is fundamentally rational, that insofar as the basis of reality is knowable, it corresponds to that of knowledge. This is so for Plato because only rational knowledge, neither sense-perceptual consciousness nor subjective opinion, is capable of accounting for itself, only such knowledge is self-conscious and self-authenticating, and only such knowledge is about universal truths. Such truths are embodied in essential categories, or forms, of consciousness which are presupposed by our experience, exist prior to, and so independent of individual persons as the immortal vehicles of knowledge, and gather themselves into an enduring and systematic unity characterizing cosmic purpose, the Good, or the Absolute. The realms of form (or being) and matter (or non-being) are, by this view, therefore disparate. True knowledge, goodness, beauty, and justice are, accordingly, functions of the ideal realm and the measure by which they are experienced in other-than-perfect terms is a function of materiality's compromise of them. The body is itself regarded as a participant in the realm of matter and, thus, as a corporeal impediment to knowledge, an obstacle to be overcome in reason's search for itself.[98] Plato's philosophy of sport (physical education) is also sharply affected by his vehement dualism. His view of materiality and the body leads to the conclusion that the body (and its principal stewards, such as sport) is worthy of human attention only insofar as it sustains and enhances the cognitive faculties. For Plato, sport is a vital feature of human experience but its significance is limited to the instrumental contributions it makes to health, to civic and pedagogical projects, and to military preparation. Plato also cautions against an exceedingly competitive or spectatorial orientation to athletics by which one-sidedness, vainglory, or surfeit triumphs over virtuous action.

Aristotle (384-322 B.C.E.),[99] in naturalistic-tending fashion reminiscent of the Periclean anthropology, takes a notably more sympathetic view than Plato of the material realm, of the body, of movement, and of sport. This view more nearly embraces the central tenets of the Greek Enlightenment than did that of any other major philosophical personality of the ancient world, let alone of the classical period itself. Aristotle, arguably the most remarkable philosophic genius of any age, attempted to re-work the imposing system of Plato in what he regarded as more consistent and more plausible ways than had Plato himself. He argued that merely because there is something different than particular things (namely, the eternal forms that explain these things) is itself insufficient reason to suppose this something separate from such things. For Aristotle, unlike for Plato, forms are not apart from, but are inherent in particular things. This, together with Aristotle's high regard for the scientific study of concrete events, led him to a very much more sympathetic regard for nature (and all that nature entails) than Plato had managed. Accordingly, matter is not, by Aristotle's account, the inert, passive stuff of non-being (a mere imitation of the formal) as Plato had taught, but is itself dynamic being in which form (i.e., idea and purpose) invariably inheres. Although form is nonetheless the defining element of discrete entities, or substances, as for Plato, these entities are constituted as inseparable aggregations of form and matter according to Aristotle. Aristotle's keen taste for the temperate, middle ground runs through all aspects of his thought; most importantly, his ethics, politics, and philosophy of sport (physical education).[100] His ethical and political thought argues that the highest good is approached as a substance cultivates that which is essential to it; the highest good is approached from within as a substance nears fulfillment of its own basic character and purpose. In the case of humanity, the highest good is thus served as the rational faculties (themselves rooted in physical reality), the defining element, of the species are edified. The pursuit of virtue, the public interest, and so happiness is therefore characterized as an enrichment of our rational possibilities. This enrichment entails both the "perfection" of reason as such and the fashioning of a well-ordered soul, a soul in which a balanced and a proportionate relation of reason itself and its lower forms (feeling and desire) is achieved. A balanced, proportionate, and harmonious relation among the activities of the soul is, in turn, defined as a form of moderation, or golden mean, between the extremes of excess and deficiency with respect to any voluntary sentiment, action, or intent. Political life is also obliged to such a mean and is therefore obliged as well to pursue the good of each and so every person participating in it, for the good of all entails the good of each. Aristotle's philosophy of sport (physical education) too closely followed his basic orientation. This aspect of his thought is governed principally by his view of the body (as our material, or lower, aspect) and the mind (as our formal, or higher, aspect) and by his recognition that the development of lower order faculties provides a necessary foundation for the development of higher order ones. Aristotle thus advocated the practice of sport both as a preparation for, and as an accompaniment of predominantly intellectual forms of activity. He too thought of sport as making necessary contributions to a balanced, harmonious, and unified development of human beings, to the development of persons of high intellect and vigorous action, to the development of good citizens, and so to the development of a just social and political order.

The Greek genius likewise revealed itself superbly well in the plastic arts, mainly the **architecture and sculpture**, of the classical period. The sense of harmony, proportion, and organic grace, which constituted the governing themes of Periclean and Aristotelian philosophy, was likewise characteristic of classical art. The heroic dignity and intrinsic richness, the intensely dynamic, yet refined, sense of action and movement, the self-consciously expressive dignity, and the balanced unity of bodily and spiritual excellence, which marked the classical style, all conspired to make it one of the most memorable episodes in the entire record of artistic activity. The most significant work in the architecture and architectural sculpture of the fifth century B.C.E. was done in Olympia and in Athens. At Olympia, the "Temple of Zeus," 470-456 B.C.E., which is now largely lost, was designed by Libon of Elis (fl. fifth century B.C.E.) and included the colossal statute of "Zeus" by Phidias (500-431 B.C.E.), also lost, and the architectural sculpture, "Battle of the Lapiths and Centaurs." At Athens, the four major structures of the Acropolis, which are among the greatest triumphs of Western architecture, were all designed and constructed in the classical period. The "Parthenon," 447-438 B.C.E., was constructed under the patronage of Pericles, was designed by Iktinos (fl. fifth century B.C.E.) and Kallikrates (fl. fifth century B.C.E.), and included magnificent pediment sculptures ("Birth of Athens" on the east and "Contest Between Athena and Poseidon" on the west), likely supervised by Phidias, as well as Phidias' colossal "Athena Parthenos," which is now lost. The other major structures of the Athenian Acropolis were constructed somewhat later: the "Propylaia," or monumental gate, 437-432 B.C.E.; the "Temple of Athena Nike," c. 425 B.C.E.; and the "Erechtheion," also a temple, 421-405 B.C.E. The other major architectural masterpiece of the fifth century B.C.E. was Iktinos' "Temple of Apollo" at Bassai, c. 420 B.C.E., which included the first Corinthian column. Greek architecture of the fourth century B.C.E. was most distinguished by the "Mausoleum" at Halikarnossos, c. 353 B.C.E., and by the beautiful theaters of the period (most notably, the "Theater" at Epidauros, c. 350 B.C.E.).

The free-standing Greek sculpture of the fifth and fourth centuries B.C.E. is likewise unexcelled in organic magnificence and much of the best of it concerned sport. The Greeks were the only culture to have developed an entire style, or genre, of accomplished sculptural work devoted to the subject and to the basic spirit of sport. Greek sculptors found great inspiration in the beauty of accomplished athletes and of athletics. Contributing significantly to the intimate relation of Greek sport and Greek sculpture was the practice of commemorating life-size statues of victors in athletic festivals, either in the athletes' home city or in the national sanctuaries. In any case, the most striking artistic monuments to the high Greek respect for sport are found in the remarkable sculpture of these two centuries: the "Charioteer of Delphi," c. 470 B.C.E.; the "Diskobolus" (Discus Thrower), c. 450 B.C.E., of Myron (fl. second half of the fifth century B.C.E.); the "Doryphoros" (Spear Bearer), c. 440 B.C.E., and the "Diadumenus" (Victor Tying Head Ribbon), c. 430 B.C.E., of Polykleitos (fl. second half of the fifth century B.C.E.); the "Hermes with the Infant Dionysus," c. 330 B.C.E., of Praxiteles (fl. mid-fourth century B.C.E.); and the "Apoxyomenos" (Athlete with Scraper), c. 330 B.C.E., of Lysippos (fl. late fourth century B.C.E.). The other leading sculptural achievements of this period were the "Kritos Boy" (c. 480 B.C.E.), the "Zeus of Artemision" (c. 460 B.C.E.), Praxiteles' "Aphrodite of Knidos" (c. 350 B.C.E.), and "The Apollo Belvedere" (c. late fourth century B.C.E.).

Although next to nothing survives of ancient Greek painting as such, it is nonetheless known that the Greeks developed several methods of painting that had an enormous influence on all subsequent work in the medium. The most notable of these were tempera (egg yolk), encaustic (wax), and glazing. It is also known that the Greeks were the first to work out many of the mysteries of light depiction, emotional nuance, and perspective. Something of the wonder that has been lost is apparent in the arresting late fourth century B.C.E. mosaic copy of a painting, "Victory of Alexander over Darius III."

The literary arts, principally **drama and poetry**, also flourished greatly in the classical period. Like other forms of artistic expression, they too embraced the governing canons of thought in this period and they created among Western civilization's most stirring tragedic, comedic, and poetic tomes. The leading achievements in drama were the founding and fateful tragedies of Aeschylus (525-456 B.C.E.), "Prometheus Bound" (478 B.C.E.), "The Persians" (472 B.C.E.), "The Seven Against Thebes" (467 B.C.E.), and "Oresteia" (458 B.C.E.); the deeply ironic tragedies of Sophocles (496-406 B.C.E.), most notably "Antigone" (442 B.C.E.), "Oedipus Rex" (427 B.C.E.), and "Elektra" (410 B.C.E.); the iconoclastic tragedies of Euripides (480-406 B.C.E.), most notably "Alcestis" (438 B.C.E.), "Medea" (431 B.C.E.), "Hippolytos" (428 B.C.E.), "The Trojan Women" (415 B.C.E.), "Iphigenia in Taurus" (412 B.C.E.), and "Iphigenia in Aulis" (406 B.C.E.); and the incisively satirical comedies of Aristophanes (448-380 B.C.E.), most notably "The Clouds" (423 B.C.E.), "The Birds" (414 B.C.E.), "Lysistrata" (411 B.C.E.), and "The Frogs" (405 B.C.E.). Aeschylus, Sophocles, Euripides, and Aristophanes all commented variously and seriously on sport.

Like the leading sculptors of the classical age, the best of the lyric poets were also frequently employed to commemorate victories in the athletic festivals. This was done in the form of triumphal odes, or epinices, which were either sung or recited at victory celebrations. The most remarkable poet of this time, Pindar (518-446 B.C.E.), was often so employed and created among the most accomplished poetry of the age in this form. From 498 to 446 B.C.E., he wrote fourteen Olympian, twelve Pythian, eight Isthmian, and eleven Nemean odes in which he extolled the organic virtues of harmonious physical beauty expressing itself in beautiful deeds, expressing itself in high achievement, honorably, humbly, and modestly acknowledged without hint of arrogant pride. Excellence, by Pindar's characteristically classical view, could be attained only by the dignified and purposeful courage of risking defeat in the hard quest for victory. The other leading poets of the classical era were the (terse) epigrammatic lyricist, Simonides (556-468 B.C.E.), and the (emotional) dithyrambic lyricist, Bacchylides (505-450 B.C.E.), both of whom wrote memorable victory poems. The most celebrated orators of ancient culture were likewise of the classical age:

- Isocrates (436-338 B.C.E.), the greatest teacher of ancient Greek oratory and the author of "Panegyricus," who was an ardent opponent of competitive sport as it was increasingly practiced;
- Diogenes (c. 412-323 B.C.E.), who publicly condemned political corruption, who publicly advocated the virtues of the simple life from a bathing tub, and who also commented passingly on sport; and
- Demosthenes (384-322 B.C.E.), the greatest orator of ancient Greece and the author of "Philippics," who too commented variously on sport.

The origins of authentic **historical scholarship** were also owed to the classical Greek culture. Herodotus (484-425 B.C.E.) was the progenitor of such scholarship and the author of History of the Persian Wars, who was given to emphasizing the fateful, divine tendencies of history. Thucydides (460-396 B.C.E.), the author of History of the Peloponnesian War, was instead most impressed with the impartial, natural tendencies of history. And Xenophon (430-354 B.C.E.), the author of Anabasis (concerning Greek conflicts with and against the Persian Empire after the Peloponnesian War), was the master of forthright military narrative. Herodotus, Thucydides, and Xenophon all wrote passingly of Greek sport. And Thucydides was apparently associated with sport in some still more tangible ways.

Although there are few authentic remnants of ancient Greek **music**, it is nonetheless known that music played a large role in the artistic, the religious, and the sporting lives of the Greeks, functioning primarily as an accompaniment to religious and sporting, as well as to other types of artistic, event. It developed two main forms: the Apollinian (of rational proportion that typically accompanied poetic and epic recitations) and the Dionysian (of emotive proportion that typically accompanied dramatic performances). Instrumental music was otherwise customarily accompanied by dancing, by choral activities, or by both dancing and choral activities. Music was also an inseparable part of religious ceremony and occasionally (with dancing) accompanied athletic performances and ceremonies commemorating extraordinary athletic achievements.

It is in this broad context that the **athletic ideal of ancient Hellenism** and the ancient Greek sport of the classical period unfolded. This ideal and the sport it governed immortalized a harmonious reconciliation of the rival claims of mind and body aimed at most memorably in features of the thought of Homer, Pericles, and Aristotle. Although only partly realized -- for it excluded most social classes and most women and was routinely compromised in other terms as well -- this ideal nonetheless embraced that carved out for other fundamental aspects of Greek life, for religion, art, and education most notably. The result was that Greek religion, art, and education were very favorably disposed to sport and greatly enriched sport; sport likewise was very favorably disposed to religion, art, and education and greatly enriched religion, art, and education. Sport even became, in a sense, a religious, artistic, and educational agency, which is to say a distinctly human agency. Greek sport, which had its origins in military affairs, was most fully nurtured under the sublimated influence of religion, art, and education and it thus conformed to spiritual, aesthetic, intellectual, and moral, as well as to physical, standards.

The athletic ideal of ancient Hellenism aimed at a balanced, harmonious, and proportionate development of all integral aspects of human experience in sport. It entailed an affirmation of the unity and intrinsic merit of human life as against its fragmentation and its instrumental worth. The Greek view of life and sport was perhaps most aptly characterized by the notions of aidos (αιδος), arete (αρετη), and kalokagathia (καλοκαγαθια), all of which convey an organic sense of harmony among our various aspects and an organic sense of striving for elusive excellence. Aidos entails an absence of all arrogance and exaggeration; an expression of modest calm, dignified honor, and refined humility; and an authentic respect for oneself, for others, and for sport. It is the contrary of insolence, or hubris (υβρις), and self-ingratiated gain, stolen away as it is by secret and extrinsic franchise. Arete entails a sense of excellence with respect to good and virtuous conduct and with respect to relentless exertion. It is closely related to the concept of agon (αγων), or resolute assertion in the face of opposition, which is at the center of sport's competitive zeal; and it is too closely related to the concept of askesis (ασκησας), or rigorous self-discipline in the service of high purpose, which is at the center of sport's relation to exercise. And kalokagathia entails a sense of beauty and peace, both of which are circumscribed by the notion of unified development.

The athletic ideal of ancient Hellenism, unsurprisingly, like the **sport of political society**, assumed the humanistic and imaginative/expressive form of political society and was thus explicitly playful, competitive in a cooperative sense, and physical in an intrinsic sense. Classical Greek sport was playful in the sense that it functioned as an intrinsic type of human fulfillment, as an end-in-and-for-itself. In this circumstance, the rules of sport are self-legislated; they are respected as positive symbols of our distinctly human nature and they are therefore resolutely and cheerfully obeyed. Classical Greek sport was competitive in the sense that it attempted to achieve difficult-to-achieve standards of performance, the ultimate purpose of which is subjective (held within our experience) and having primarily to do with excellence and secondarily to do with winning/losing (the quest to gain victory/ evade defeat). The primary competitive end of sport, excellence, to which winning/losing is devoted, takes the shape of mutually inclusive edification, a shape that is shared by all participants, those who come first as well as those who do not. "Opponents" are consequently viewed as cooperative facilitators in a shared project, the mutual pursuit of excellence, of fulfillment; opponents constrain one another and thereby assist one another to this end. And classical Greek sport was physical in the sense that it respected skillful movement as its definitive medium, as an inherently compelling feature of human experience, as a fulfilling form of human experience.

Among the leading, novel manifestations of the classical period's view of sport as an essential aspect of human experience was the formal development of **educational sport**. Although education was, throughout the Greek record, available only to citizens and only to men (except in Sparta) and was provided in only informal terms until the classical period, it was nonetheless devoted to the central tenets of Greek life. That is to say, it was devoted to the progressive development of a broad, balanced, harmonious, and complete individual excellence, to a proportionate intellectual-rational and physical-bodily development (except in Sparta). This was nowhere more emphatically the case than in Athens. The Athenians fashioned these possibilities more fully than any other Greek peoples. This is so in broad cultural as well as in educational terms; it is likewise so in respect to physical education, or gymnastics. Physical education enjoyed what is quite likely its greatest acclaim in ancient Athens, where it flourished as a constituent aspect of national life.

The home was the informal, educational agency for all children to the age of seven years. This circumstance was dominated by many simple games and sports (such as, play with balls, rattles, hoops, jacks, swings, stilts, and carts). Although the formal education of male children of the citizen class was voluntary, it was nonetheless widely availed. It typically began at the age of seven years and continued for poor lads to the age of fourteen years, for wealthy youngsters to the age of eighteen years. Training for the military (in the Ephebic College) was then compulsory from the age of eighteen to the age of twenty years. The formal education of male youth was conducted in three types of institution: the didascaleum (or music school), the palaestra (παλαιστρα, or wrestling school), and the gymnasium (γυμνασιον).

The didascaleum was a private, elementary and secondary school supervised by the public governing council (the Areopagus), financed by wealthy benefactors (gymnasiarchs), and owned by the school's teachers (didaskaloi). It cared for intellectual education, giving instruction principally in mathematics, science, literature, and music. The palaestra was a private, elementary and secondary school supervised by the public governing council (the Areopagus), financed by wealthy benefactors (gymnasiarchs), and owned by the school's teachers (παιδοτριβης, paidotribes, the first formal cadre of physical education teachers). It cared for physical education, giving instruction principally in running, jumping, discus throwing, javelin throwing, wrestling, boxing, pancrateion, weapons activities, hoop bowling, light gymnastic activities, ball games, and dancing. Students were variously escorted by elderly slaves (paidagogus) and they attended the didascaleum and the palaestra concurrently until the age of fourteen to eighteen years. The palaestra was located inside the city and consisted in a series of rooms, each for a highly specialized purpose, arranged in a rectangular configuration surrounding an open, central, exercise court. The rooms were reserved for such as undressing (apodyterion), oiling (unctorion, where oil was put over the body for strength and invigoration both before and after bathing, then removed with a scraper, or strigil, in order to remove the residue), powdering (konisterion, where common earth, powder, or konis, was put over the body before exercise, as a vestige of ancient hunting rituals intended to obscure scent, and after exercise, as a means of cleansing and drying the skin), warm air bathing (tepidarion), hot air bathing (caldarion), cold water bathing (frigidarion), ball playing (sphaeristerion), and hitting bags or balls (korykeion). Most of the substantive activity occurred in the exercise court which was covered with a fine sand, which had a running track (dromos) about it that was distinguished from the court itself by a colonnade, and which had within it bowling strips (for hoop bowling) and pits for wrestling, boxing, and pancrateion.

Although there were numerous private gymnasia, the main gymnasium was publicly supervised, financed, and owned. It was effectively a secondary and higher school that also housed the Ephebic College (for military training). The gymnasia, found in virtually every Greek community, were mainly athletic facilities and religious sanctuaries which functioned as centers of civic sport and which served the daily athletic and intellectual needs of adult male citizens. They were strikingly similar to the palaestra in basic design except that they were located outside the city in tranquil and bucolic circumstance (near forests and streams). Among the most significant athletic features of the gymnasia were the running tracks, variously covered (xystos) and uncovered (paradromis), of varied length (from 170 to 195 meters/190 to 215 yards), and customarily dug up, rolled, and covered with a fine white sand. Also importantly included were baths, jumping pits, ranges for discus and javelin throwing, and open areas for such as combative activities, weapons activities, equestrian activities, and ball playing. The most widely practiced activities included all of those prominent in the national athletic festivals as well as swimming (breaststroke, sidestroke, and front crawl with and without lifebelts), diving, archery, fencing, gymnastics (acrobatics), weightlifting (with dumbbells and barbells, or pestles), rowing (with two to eight rowers in a vessel), sailing, hoop bowling, and elaborate forms of individual, dual, and team ball games, including games resembling football (pilla and follis), lacrosse (harpastum), tennis (trigon and shaeristike), rugby (episkyros), and field hockey (kereitelein). These activities were customarily practiced in the form of highly competitive and vigorous contests and they were too conducted under quasi-scientific conditions (such as, progressive methods of learning and training, curative medical techniques, special diet, massage, and attention to the physiological and psychological effects of exercise). Rigorous training was variously directed by teachers (paidotribes), by specialized athletic coaches (gymnastes), or by their assistants. The three most significant gymnasia, all very near Athens, were established in the sixth century B.C.E. and came to be associated with major religious symbols and philosophical figures: the Academea was associated with the cult of Prometheus and came under the influence of Plato in 388 B.C.E.; the Lyceum was associated with the cult of Apollo and came under the influence of Aristotle in 335 B.C.E.; and the Kynosarges was associated with the cult of Herakles and came under the influence of the Cynics (a philosophical school based on the pessimistic aspects of Socrates' moral thought which taught that the renunciation of pleasure is ethically primary) in the late fourth century B.C.E. Like the original notion and practice of athletics, the original notion and practice of gymnastics (from γυμναστικη, to exercise unclothed), or physical education, is also owed to the Greeks. There is little, moreover, in modern physical education that the Athenian Greeks failed to anticipate in some, fairly substantial way.

The circumstance in Sparta was quite different, however. There, a fervent and closed militarism excluded much of the cultural, intellectual, aesthetic, and democratic tendency that stood at the center of Athenian education and physical education. The education of male and female children was regarded as a state, a public, responsibility. The Spartan education was characteristically military in form: it was ascetic and it entailed severe discipline, rigorous training, and sparse diet, sleep, and clothing. It was one-sided, physical training ultimately devoted to military skills in the case of males and child bearing/rearing skills in the case of females. By the view of no less a figure than Lycurgus, such training was essential to the development of skillful, obedient, virtuous, and courageous warriors and to the development of fit mothers for such warriors. The educational system, the agoge (or "rearing"), effectively re-enacted the idealized cultural legacy of Lycurgus. Youth were taken into the system, conscripted to state service, at the age of seven years; the males to live permanently in barracks, the females to live at home. From seven to eighteen years of age, both males and females received an introductory education. At the age of eighteen years, females returned permanently to the home; males entered an advanced training to the age of twenty years, then began full military service to the age of thirty years; thereafter, males performed the duties of military administration (including the training of young men) to the age of fifty years. There were no professional teachers in the Athenian sense; effectively, all were teachers. The school itself was supervised by a man selected from among outstanding citizens, typically an accomplished military figure, the paidonomus. The paidonomus was assisted in his instructional responsibilities by the eldest and ablest of his students, the eiren, and he was assisted in his evaluative obligations by state inspectors, the ephors.

The schools and the local athletic festivals were the main precincts of ancient Spartan sport. The most notable of the local athletic festivals, which began as musical, oratorical, and dancing contests, were the Carnea (from c. 676 B.C.E.), the Gymnopaediae (from 668 B.C.E.), and the Hyacinthia (from the late fourth century B.C.E.). The most widely practiced forms of sporting activity in the schools and festivals were highly combative, of a team sort, had an initiatory significance, were connected to the cultic traditions of Herakles and Lycurgus, included sacred preliminary rituals (in some cases entailing animal sacrifice) that were followed by festive celebration, were distinguished by tribes and the ages of participants (boys, paides; youth, ageneioi; and men, andres), and were conducted amid spectators. The two most prominent such activities were platanistas and episkyros (or sphairomachia). In platanistas, two teams walked to an island by different bridges, then fought without civilizing restriction for its control. The principal aim was to push all opponents into the water by any means whatever. In episkyros, or ball tournament, two sides attempted to push one another, also largely without restriction, over a (goal) line. Yet other prominently practiced activities were dual in character, wrestling, boxing, pancrateion, and fencing most notably; still others were of an individual sort – running, jumping, discus throwing, javelin throwing, swimming, equestrian skills, ball playing, and dancing most significantly. Two forms of individual activity were especially novel and had an especially large cultural significance. In the endurance contest (ho tes karterias agon), boys were severely flogged, in some rare cases to their death. The principal aim was to hold out longer than anyone else. Those who passed the test were advanced to youth; those who did not were disgraced and banished. In the staphulodromos (or grape race), several runners pursued another. It was considered an omen of good fortune for the city if the fleeing runner were caught, an omen of misfortune if not. The schools and athletic festivals of the Spartans, unlike those of the Athenians, importantly included women and preferred team to individual activities but they also had far more to do with displaying useful military and domestic skills than with human development in the broad sense.

Like Greek culture generally constituted, the celebrated athleticism, the athletic festivals themselves, the system of educational sport, and the athletic ideal of ancient Hellenism reached their most refined mark in the period of the Persian Wars and in the Periclean decades immediately following the Persian Wars; that is, c. 510-c. 440 B.C.E. They then fell progressively away from the sense of enlightenment that had earlier governed them; they then fell into a discernible decline. The incipient **decline of Greek culture and Greek sport** was owed to several factors:

- the commercial successes that followed the Persian Wars and that brought great wealth to the Greek states also brought material excesses, excesses which eventually toppled the proportionate relations of intellectual and physical dimensions of experience, the proportionate relations of   rational knowledge and sense perception, and the proportionate relations of individual and common goods; the result of this tendency were increasingly one-sided emphases on intellectuality (and physicality), unexamined opinion, and individuality;
- the civil wars of the fifth and fourth centuries B.C.E., principally the Peloponnesian, Corinthian, and Theban Wars, had an increasingly divisive effect on political life; the result of this tendency was a ruinous political fractionalization , a heightened sense of militarism, and economic deterioration, all of which further chipped away at the balanced and harmonious sense of life, the sense of aidos, arete, and kalokagathia, so at the center of the enlightened Greek orientation; and
- the increasing dearth of educational leadership, which mistook license for freedom, developed neither intellect nor beauty of vigorous form and action; the result of this tendency was that unargued and uninformed expressions of preference came to dominate careful and reflective thought, students came to despise teachers, and teachers came to fear students (and to play the toady).

The affect of these broad developments on sport was enormous. Sport became increasingly specialized and so less fully visited by notions of balance, harmony, proportion, and unity. The pentathlon, for prominent instance, once the most deeply respected sporting event, became the least highly regarded. The connections between sport and other integral features of human experience waned; the view of sport as itself a form of human expression declined. Sport was cut increasingly off from other prominent forms of cultural illumination, functioning more so as an isolated diversion from life, as a mere amusement or exhibition for spectators, than as a distinctly human symbol. It thereby lost its intellectual, religious, and artistic significance, becoming in the end little more than an instrumental gambit. Sport suffered a diminished interest in participation and a heightened interest in spectatorial orientation. It likewise became progressively more commercial and less educational in basic inclination. It was, for salient example, increasingly taken over by professional athletic coaches of dubious credential (γυμναστης, gymnastes) who, unlike the paidotribes, were more concerned with performance in the strictest of senses than with the intrinsically human values of sport. The widespread proliferation of sporting competitions and the concomitant deterioration in their quality, which the commercial emphasis portends, further weakened the importance of the national festivals and the ideal underlying them. And the prodigious expansion in the quantity of prizes and their material worth also contributed significantly to the increasingly commercial practice of sport as well as to the tendency to make sport more fully restricted to the demands of wealth.

Many of the leading intellectual and political figures of the classical era recognized these tendencies for what they were and opposed them. Hippocrates held that athletics produces dangerously unstable conditions of the body. Socrates and Plato (himself an accomplished wrestler) lamented the disharmony of mind and body in sport and the excessive awards given to athletes. Aristotle (also an accomplished wrestler) objected to the immoderate nature of athletic training. Aristophanes and Isocrates were especially vocal opponents of competitive sport; both parodied its muscular excesses. Epaminondas disdained sport itself but tolerated it owing to its political utility. Euripides (too an accomplished wrestler) had an apparently high opinion of humanistic sport and variously used sporting metaphors in his celebrated dramas. He nonetheless issued an entirely venomous condemnation of what sport had become, characterizing athletes as overfed and unsophisticated louts and characterizing sport's one-sidedness, its tendency to advantage-taking, and its commercial corruption as the enemy of aidos, as morally inadequate, as among the worst evils of the day, as constituting no lasting good, as fraudulently honoring shallow victors over good and wise men, and as a pursuit of useless pleasures. Thus, within a century, the entire disposition of Greek sport had changed. Still at this, Olympia in particular influenced and was visited by virtually every major figure of the ancient Greek and Roman worlds. Even throughout the decline (which continued), the old ideal and practice were never wholly lost. Neither before nor since, with the possible exception of modern industrial society, has sport been such a full and integral part of the cultural mainstream as it was in classical Greek civilization.

The Hellenistic period

The final chapter of ancient Greek history as such, the Hellenistic period, 338-146 B.C.E., was marked, at its beginning, by the Macedonian conquest of Greece and, at its end, by the Roman conquest of Greece. It was most distinguished by:

- the triumphs of Philip II and Alexander III/Alexander the Great of Macedonia and the consequent Hellenization of the civilized world;
- the wars among Alexander's successors, the Wars of the Diadochi, and the resultant fragmentation of Alexander's empire, a development which ended with the Roman conquest;
- the flowering of ancient Greek mathematics and science (physics, astronomy, medicine, literature, and philosophy);
- continuing triumphs in the plastic arts which variously depended on, and departed from the proportionate tendencies of the classical period; and
- the ongoing decline of ancient Greek sporting institutions and their underlying ideals.

The **Macedonian conquests** of Philip and Alexander, which had begun in 357 B.C.E., brought Greece fully into the Macedon fold in 338 B.C.E. In the year following Philip's victory over the Greeks, in 337 B.C.E., he formed the Hellenic, or Corinthian, League under his own patronage. The League consisted in all Greek cities, all Greek city-states, except Sparta and it was created in order to oppose the common, the Persian, enemy. On Philip's assassination in 336 B.C.E., the crown, together with its program of foreign conquest, passed to Alexander (356-323 B.C.E.; r. 336-323 B.C.E.). In the first year of his reign, Alexander consolidated earlier successes in Thrace and Illyria and suppressed Greek revolts in Thebes, Athens, and on the Peloponnesus. In 335 B.C.E., he effectively destroyed Thebes and in the following year began the war against Persia. In 334 B.C.E. at the Battle of Granicus, he secured western Asia Minor from the Persians, then claimed Ionia and Phrygia. After several failures early in 333 B.C.E., Alexander achieved victory over Darius III of Persia at the Battle of Issus and the following year he completed the conquest of Syria at Tyre and at Damascus as well as the conquest of Egypt at Alexandria and at Memphis. In 331 B.C.E., Alexander again defeated Darius, in this instance at the Battle of Guagamela, and claimed Mesopotamia (including Babylon) and Persia (including Susa). In 330 B.C.E., he burned Persepolis itself, became the formal successor of the Achaemenids in Persia, conquered Afghanistan, and had his opponents in Macedonia murdered. In the period from 329 to 327 B.C.E., Alexander vanquished eastern Iran and Sogdiana (Uzbekistan), married Roxane, had the courageous historian, Calisthenes, executed, and murdered the great friend of his youth, Clitus. The campaigns in India (327-325 B.C.E.), the political fusion of Macedonia, Greece, and Persia (324 B.C.E.), and the death of Alexander in Babylon (323 B.C.E.), while preparing for campaigns against Carthage in the western Mediterranean, followed. Under Alexander's leadership, Greek became the universal language throughout his vast empire, Greek culture became the dominant intellectual canon throughout this empire, a common currency was established throughout this empire, and Greek cities (most notably, Alexandria) were established throughout this empire. The **Hellenization of the civilized world**, or much of it, which Alexander had effectively achieved, constituted the first authentic meeting of Western and Eastern civilization in both mercantile and cultural terms. Moreover, Alexander distributed the wealth of conquered territories throughout his empire in ways that fostered eminent works of science and art and in ways that also resulted in the establishment of the greatest libraries and museums of the ancient world: the Library and Museum of Alexandria (third century B.C.E.) and the Library of Pergamum (second century B.C.E.). The circumstance he left at his death, however, embodied wide extremes of enormous wealth and abysmal poverty that made for profoundly insecure and unstable political conditions.

The wars among Alexander's successors, the **Wars of the Diadochi**, gave apt expression to such an unsteady environment. They went on from Alexander's death in 323 B.C.E. to 280 B.C.E. and they included the murder of Alexander's mother, Olympia, in 316 B.C.E., the murder of his wife, Roxane, in 310 B.C.E., the still broader acceptance of Greek culture, and the struggle for fragmented power between Seleucis (who became governor of Babylon and Persia), Ptolemy (who became governor of Egypt), Antipater (who became governor of Macedonia and Greece), and Antigonus (who became governor of Anatolia). These wars resulted in the establishment of three great empires:

- that of the Antigonids in Macedonia, 279-168 B.C.E.; rule included the three Macedonian Wars against Rome (215-168 B.C.E.) and it ended with the Roman victory over the Macedonians at Pydna in 168 B.C.E.;
- that of the Seleucids in south-central Asia and the near Middle East (center at Antioch), 304-64 B.C.E.; rule included the Kingdoms of Bithynia (in north-central Anatolia), Pergamum (in northwestern Anatolia), and Bactria (in Pakistan, Afghanistan, and Tajikistan) as well as the Parthian Empire (in Iran and Turkmenistan) and it ended with the Roman victory of Pompey over the Seleucids in 64 B.C.E.; and
- that of the Ptolemies in Egypt (center at Alexandria), 304-30 B.C.E.; rule ended with the Roman victory over the Ptolemies at Alexandria in 30 B.C.E.

The Greeks themselves made several further attempts to regain their political independence after Alexander's death. The Lamian War (323-322 B.C.E.), which sparked the suicide of Demosthenes in 322 B.C.E., and the Chremonidean War (266-261 B.C.E.) nonetheless both failed. Confederations of Greek states (most notably, the Aetolian and Achaean Leagues) were formed in order to mount a more formidable challenge to Macedonian and Roman influence, but they too failed. Although a conditional autonomy was accorded Athens, Sparta, and Delphi, the **Roman conquest** of Greece was effectively completed at the Battle of Corinth in 146 B.C.E.

Greek **mathematics and science** came to its highest mark in the Hellenistic period. Euclid (fl. c. 300 B.C.E.) formulated the governing principles of plane geometry in his celebrated Elements. Archimedes of Syracuse (c. 287-212 B.C.E.) developed a primitive calculus, established the foundations of solid geometry, discovered the mechanical laws of the lever and the screw, and discerned the specific weight of material objects. Aristarchus of Samos (c. 310-c. 230B.C.E.) was the first to propose a heliocentric theory of the universe, a theory that entailed calculations concerning the revolution of the Earth about the Sun and calculations concerning the rotation of the Earth about its own axis. Eratosthenes of Cyrene (c. 275-c. 195 B.C.E.) determined the spherical shape and the dimensions of the Earth, devised a geological chronology of the Earth and a world map, and calculated the distance from the Earth to the Earth's moon and sun. And Hipparchus of Nicaea (c. 190-c. 120 B.C.E.) devised the first comprehensive catalog and chart of the stars and discovered the character of equinoxes and the periodicity of eclipses. In medicine, the seminal vision of Hippocrates (c. 460-c. 370 B.C.E.), who fashioned the traditions of objective observation and ethical practice a century to two centuries earlier, was carried forward by Herophilus (fl. third century B.C.E.), who discovered the character and relation of the brain and nerves, and by Erasistratus of Ceos (fl. third century B.C.E.), who conducted autopsies and discovered the character and relation of the heart, lungs, arteries, veins, and blood as well as the character and function of motor and sensory nerves.

Even the **literature and philosophy** of the Hellenistic period took on a more scientific cast than had classical Greek developments of the sort. Menander (342-292 B.C.E.) wrote comedic love plays with highly developed characters (and wrote passingly of sport as well) and Theocritus (fl. first half of the third century B.C.E.) wrote exacting, pastoral poetry. Callimachus (c. 310-c. 240 B.C.E.) fashioned a catalog that constituted a comprehensive history of literary pursuits. Many others systematically collected noteworthy literary manuscripts, made detailed commentaries on classical literary works, and wrote rigorous grammatical texts. Philosophy, in similar manner, fell away from the metaphysical emphasis given it by Plato and Aristotle. Hellenistic philosophy, principally in the form of Epicureanism, stoicism, and skepticism, thought the problems of metaphysics insufficiently practical and thus tended to naturalistic, realistic, and pragmatic renderings of ethical and political issues. Epicurus (341-270 B.C.E.) adopted a strict empiricism according to which knowledge is based primarily on clear sense impressions; general ideas are abstracted from such impressions. His ethics held that human happiness in the form of pleasure is the highest good and the principal issue of philosophy. Such pleasure, by his view, entails the elimination of pain (the acquisition of good health through proper exercise and diet) and the achievement of an informed tranquility (through the study of philosophy); it is construed in terms of the health of the body and the serenity of the soul, a sense of health and serenity which constitutes the self-interest of all persons and which it is the obligation of all political institutions to preserve. Zeno the Stoic (336-264 B.C.E.) shared Epicurus' empiricistic tendencies but took them in a notably different direction. Zeno and other leading stoics argued that humanity achieves happiness by purging itself of passionate sentiment (which effectively constitutes virtuous conduct), by gracefully arranging itself in accord with right reason, in accord with the will of the world, in accord with one's duty to justice. And Pyrrho (365-270 B.C.E.), principal among the skeptics, held that sensation is the sole form of human knowledge, that sensation reveals mere appearances, not the certitude required of true knowledge, that the ultimate character of reality is therefore inaccessible to human experience, and that human happiness and right action can thus reside only in a resignation to the impossibility of certitude and in a tranquility of the soul that accompanies such a resignation.

The **plastic art** of the Hellenistic period too turned in a more realistic and naturalistic direction as against its classical predecessors. Hellenistic art was done on a less proportionate, a more exaggerated scale than classical art and it also embodied a larger sense of emotional drama and frenetic action. It tended to overwhelm as well as edify. Its principal achievements were in city planning, temple architecture, and sculpture. The most accomplished instances of city planning occurred in western Asia Minor and took the form of geometrically rational designs which always included athletic stadia. The leading instances of temple architecture were the colossal "Temple of the Olympian Zeus" at Athens (174 B.C.E.-c. second century C.E.), the first major Corinthian temple, and the "Altar of Zeus" at Pergamum (181-159 B.C.E.), which included (in its friezes) the most accomplished architectural sculpture of the Hellenistic period. And the most significant achievements in sculpture were the "Demosthenes" (c. 280 B.C.E.), "Dying Gaul" (c. 230 B.C.E.), "Barberini Faun" (c. 220 B.C.E.), "Nike of Samothrace" (c. 190 B.C.E.), "Portrait of Alexander" (c. first half of the second century B.C.E.), Hagesandros' "Laocoon and His Two Sons" (c. second century B.C.E.), and Apollonius' "Seated Boxer" (c. second century B.C.E.).

Unsurprisingly, the **sport** of the Hellenistic period also turned in a more realistic, naturalistic, and scientific direction, which is to say in a less humanistic direction. With the rise of Macedonia, the Greek athletic festivals and precincts of educational sport persisted; they even prospered in a strictly practical way. The organic ideal underlying them a century before, however, continued to erode. Although Philip and Alexander (Alexander particularly) disdained sport as such, they nonetheless recognized its political utility and thus encouraged its practice as a means of maintaining the unity of the Greek world, an aim much to their own benefit and much to the benefit of Greek culture as well. Philip, who owned horses and chariots that won at Olympia (although he did not himself participate in Olympic contests), even established several festivals in Macedonia itself on the broad theme of the Olympic Games; most notably, the Olympic Games at Aegae and at Dion. Alexander, an accomplished, if indifferent, runner, also introduced athletic festivals to the conquered peoples of the East, used them as an entertainment for his soldiers, occasionally staged funerary games, and even promoted boating races in the Middle East. Although Greek sport remained deeply popular and widely practiced in the third and second centuries B.C.E., its classical ideals passed through an even more dramatic deterioration in Greece and its western colonies as the influence of Rome expanded in these periods and in these regions. Sport grew progressively more bizarre and more brutal, progressively less edifying, under the terms of this influence.

Etruscan and Roman Culture and Sport

The **Etruscan culture** was of Caucasoid ethnic character; it spoke a language evidently unrelated to others; it had been apparently transplanted from the Lydian territory in Asia Minor in c. 1100 B.C.E.; and it developed most notably in the central-western regions of the Italian peninsula (effectively, in the modern Italian province of Tuscany, from the Arno River in the north, near the medieval and modern city of Florence, to the Tiber River in the south, near the ancient, medieval, and modern city of Rome). It never formed a coherent political administration, developing instead as a confederation of largely autonomous city-states, first governed by monarchs, later by nobles (landed aristocracy). By c. 600 B.C.E., it had formed the League of Twelve Cities and expanded its influence somewhat farther north of the Arno and south of the Tiber. In 540 B.C.E., it allied with Carthage (the increasingly dominant power on the coastal regions of north-central and northwestern Africa, founded in 814 B.C.E.) and defeated Greece for maritime supremacy in the northwestern Mediterranean. Early in the fifth century B.C.E., however, the Tarquins (the ruling family of Etruria) were expelled from Rome (the expulsion of the Tarquins) and were defeated by Syracuse (a Greek city-state in Sicily) at the Battle of Cumae, 474 B.C.E. The Etruscan decline followed: the southern Etruscan center at Veii was conquered by the Romans in 396 B.C.E. and Celtic invasions[101] in the north, also in the fourth century B.C.E., put a conclusive end to the Etruscan cultural development.

Etruscan civilization was greatly influenced by early Greek culture and had itself a very large affect on Roman affairs, including Roman sport. It is most significantly remembered for:

- its distinctive religious cult, which was formally connected to both its artistic and its sporting practices;
- the stylized, elemental power of its architecture, sculpture, and painting; and
- its robust form of sporting activity, most particularly its blood sport.

The Etruscans buried their dead beneath earthen mounds in tombs often decorated with terracotta figures and wall paintings and in ceremonies often visited by sacrificial celebrations and combative forms of sporting performance. Etruscan temple architecture, which was of low and broad proportion, included arches, and was adorned with terracotta ornamentation, had its basis in Greek achievements but was of a more parochial orientation than the Greek; it too had a profound affect on comparable Roman developments. The finest Etruscan sculptures were painted, terracotta, funerary figures, figures which were remindful in their measured intensity of archaic Greek tendencies and which foreshadowed the realism of Roman inclinations. The most memorable of these was the "Apollo of Veii" (c. 515-c. 490 B.C.E.). Also noteworthy were realistic bronze sculptures drawn mainly on mythological themes; such as, the "She-Wolf" (c. 500-c. 480 B.C.E.). Etruscan painting was likewise most associated with the cult of the dead, mainly in the form of tomb wall paintings. Perhaps the most accomplished example of the rudimentary style characterizing these pieces is the "Hunting and Fishing Fresco" at Tarquinia (c. 510-c. 500 B.C.E.). **Etruscan sport**, like Etruscan art, was likewise systematically associated with religious, principally funerary, celebrations.[102] It was practiced from the earliest development of distinctly Etruscan culture (c. 1000 B.C.E.), included both men and women, tended to an exceedingly active orientation, and was given to brutal forms of blood sport (such as events resembling gladiatorial combats), forms that had a very large influence on Roman sport. Also widely practiced were boxing, wrestling, chariot racing, running, jumping, discus throwing, javelin throwing, acrobatics, and various forms of ball game.

The mythological **origins of ancient Roman culture**, not unlike those of ancient Greek culture, were grounded in the events of the Trojan War of the twelfth century B.C.E., most aptly recounted by Homer in the Greek case and by Vergil (70-19 B.C.E.) in the Roman. In Vergil's <u>Aeneid</u> (among the greatest epic poems in world literature), Aeneas, son of Venus and second in command to Hector on the Trojan side, escaped Troy when it was burned; long wandered through many heroic trials on land and sea (including an alliance with Dido, the beautiful founder and queen of Carthage); journeyed to Italy, where he defeated those who opposed his entering the region; married the daughter of a powerful local king; and founded the city of Rome. This is the city later re-established by the twin sons of Mars, Romulus and Remus, who were thrown to the Tiber River as youngsters by the usurper of their grandfather's throne, floated to shore, were suckled by a she-wolf and reared by a shepherd, avenged their grandfather's deposition, and founded the city of Rome in 753 B.C.E. on the site where they had been rescued from the Tiber. These accounts connected the origins of

Roman culture with the heroic traditions of Greece and Carthage and they also identified Rome as a perpetual enemy of Greece and Carthage. The more prosaic account of Roman origination claims that the city was likely formed as a conjunction of Latinus and Sabines (two cultures under Etruscan influence inhabiting the region near the Seven Hills of Rome and the Tiber River) in the eighth century B.C.E. Rome was thus one of many small and largely autonomous city-states then situated on the Italian peninsula. These states most importantly included Etruria, Greek colonies, Phoenician settlements, and Italic communities themselves.

Roman civilization, which was of Indo-European cultural and linguistic character, first developed in political terms as an absolute monarchy , a circumstance in which a king functioned as the culture's chief military, religious, and judicial authority. In the period, c. 750-c. 510 B.C.E., the practice of an inherited monarchy eventually and progressively gave way, first to a timocratic tendency in which propertied wealth became the ruling authority, then to representative bodies such as the Senate and popular assemblies which variously advised and commanded officials (consuls) of the government. A popular army was also organized in this period and the establishment of the Republic itself marked its close in c. 509 B.C.E. The approximate millennium that followed defined the central history of Roman civilization in terms of both its Republican and its Imperial epochs. The dominant tendencies of this period were variously political, military, economic, cultural, religious, artistic, and sporting in character; most notably:

- ongoing contestation within Roman society between the privileged order, the patricians, and the broader order of citizen, the plebeians;
- routine wars throughout the Republican epoch with other Italic states concerning domain over the Italian peninsula, with the Celts concerning the sovereignty of Italic states and Gallic communities, with Carthage concerning domain over the western Mediterranean region, and with the Hellenistic east concerning domain over the eastern Mediterranean region;
- the struggle for preservation of the Republic which "ended" with the establishment of the Empire in 27 B.C.E.;
- the near-to-perpetual disputes, throughout the Imperial epoch, concerning the throne and the expansion and maintenance of territory, disputes that brought economic, political, military, and cultural disintegration, the barbarian migrations, the fracture of the Empire (into western and eastern parts) in the fourth and fifth centuries C.E., and an end to the western Empire in 476 C.E.;
- the rise of Christianity, its philosophic groundwork, and its institutions throughout the Imperial epoch;
- a literary flowering in poetry, drama, history, and philosophy that developed principally in the last century of the Republic and the first century of the Empire;
- the development of increasingly utilitarian, realistic, and monumental styles in the plastic arts (from the second century B.C.E. to the fourth century C.E.); and
- the development of increasingly utilitarian, realistic, and brutal forms of sporting activity (from the sixth century B.C.E. to the fifth century C.E.).

Class struggles between **patricians and plebeians** deepened in the fifth century B.C.E. The plebeians increasingly took independent actions in order to secure a more just and palatable life. These actions threatened the patrician hegemony and resulted in much of the hoped-for reform. The Laws of the Twelve Tables, enacted in 450 B.C.E., raised the state above class allegiances, redressed legal inequities, and brought a partial reconciliation of the two groups. The Licino-Sextian Laws, enacted in 367-366 B.C.E., eased economic and political injustices previously suffered by the plebeians. These reforms established the Roman Republic as a state of laws and duties in which the highly disciplined paternalistic family formed the experiential and the institutional basis of social life. This basis was thus ancestral and domestic in formative character.

Rome incrementally gained domain over adjacent states on the Italian peninsula, in the end gaining domain over the entire peninsula. The most significant chapters in this development were the First Latin War (with Latins among other Italic peoples), 498-493 B.C.E.; the Ten Years War with Veii (Etruria), 406-396 B.C.E.; the Second Latin War (with Latins among other Italic peoples), 340-338 B.C.E.; the three **Samnite Wars** (with Samnites among other Italic peoples), 343-341 B.C.E., 326-304 B.C.E., and 298-290 B.C.E.; and the War with Tarentum (and other Greek colonies on the Italian peninsula), 282-272 B.C.E.

Celtic culture organized itself as military aristocracies and fashioned a rich sculptural style; it migrated from central Europe to what are now England, Ireland, France, Spain, and Italy in the late fifth and early fourth centuries B.C.E. The Celts had an important role in ending Etruscan influences in central Italy, sacked Rome in 387 B.C.E., and remained at sporadic war with Rome virtually throughout the Republican epoch. Rome was rebuilt in 380 B.C.E., entered a treaty with other Italic states against the Celts in 358-354 B.C.E., successfully defended its own sovereignty and that of other Italic sates in several waves of especially acute **conflict with the Celts** (285-282 B.C.E., 222 B.C.E., and 200-190 B.C.E.), and conquered Gaul (the Continental center of Celtic culture) in 51 B.C.E.

The disputes with Carthage began as trade disagreements. Rome conceded trade monopoly in the western Mediterranean to Carthage by way of three major treaties, accords enacted in 510 B.C.E., 348 B.C.E., and 306 B.C.E. Wide political differences in the third and second centuries B.C.E., however, led to the **Punic Wars** in which Rome asserted its dominance in the western Mediterranean region. In the First Punic War, 264-241 B.C.E., Rome secured Sicily and Sardinia from the Carthaginian general, Hamilcar Barca (fl. in the mid-third century B.C.E.). Between the First and Second Punic Wars, Carthage established its supremacy over southern Spain in 236 B.C.E. and Rome established its domain over the Illyrian coast (i.e., in the modern nation-state of Albania) in 228 B.C.E. and over Corsica in 227 B.C.E. In the Second Punic War, 218-201 B.C.E., Hannibal Barca (247-c. 182 B.C.E.), son of Hamilcar and among the most remarkable military figures in human history, achieved stunning early successes with brilliant victories in Italy at Trebia (217 B.C.E.) and Canae (216 B.C.E.) before suffering losses in Italy, Sicily, Spain, and Africa. Hannibal was defeated conclusively by Scipio Africanus Major (c. 234-c. 183 B.C.E.) in Africa at the Battle of Zama, 202 B.C.E., and committed suicide in c. 183 B.C.E. while being pursued by Rome. The Third Punic War, 149-146 B.C.E., ended with the Roman destruction of Carthage in 146 B.C.E.

The four **Macedonian Wars** and the War with Antiochus III defined the conflicts in the Hellenistic east. The First Macedonian War, 215-205 B.C.E., entailed Hannibal's alliance with Macedonia and the Roman defeat of Macedon advances into Illyria. The Second Macedonian War, 200-197 B.C.E., ended with the Macedon surrender of its hegemony in Greece. The War with Antiochus III of the Seleucid Empire, 192-188 B.C.E., ended with the defeat of Antiochus in Greece. The Third Macedonian War, 171-168 B.C.E., ended at the Battle of Pydna (in Macedonia) with the Roman suppression of Macedonia's attempt to regain control of Greece. And the Fourth Macedonian War, 149-146 B.C.E., ended with the Roman destruction of Corinth. Mainly by way of the Punic and Macedonian Wars, Rome became the commercial and political capital of the Mediterranean region and fell heir to Greek cultural pre-eminence in the ancient Western world.

The unsuccessful struggle for the preservation of the **Republic,** which unfolded over the next approximate century, was principally rooted in divisive civil conflicts between enfranchised elites and others as well as in related internecine struggles for political authority which vacillated between a semblance of representative government and dictatorship. The First Slave War, an insurrection of mainly Sicilian (agricultural) slaves, in which Pergamum became a Roman province and which went on from 136 to 132 B.C.E., failed. The attempted land and social reforms of the Gracchi, 133-121 B.C.E., reforms aimed at redressing the balance of power between large and small farmers, at the political empowerment of soldiers and middle-class commercialists, and at correcting private tax abuses in the provinces, likewise failed. The Jugurthine War, 111-105 B.C.E., brought parts of Numidia (in north-central Africa) under Roman rule and included the earliest international triumphs of the two most accomplished Roman generals of the first quarter of the first century B.C.E., Marius (155-86 B.C.E.) and Sulla (138-78 B.C.E.). Marius further distinguished himself by reforming the army into a professional agency and by defeating migrating Celtic peoples from Scandinavia in a series of conflicts that went on from 113 to 101 B.C.E. The War of the Allies, 91-89 B.C.E., was a civil dispute which resulted in the granting of citizenship to the allies. The First Mithridatic War, 88-84 B.C.E., began with an attack on Roman territories by Mithridates VI (c. 131-63 B.C.E.) of Pontus (in northeastern Anatolia); it included the replacement of Sulla by Marius as the Roman commander of the War, the conquest of Rome by Sulla, the death of Marius, and the defeat of Mithridates by Sulla. The Second Mithridatic War, 83-81 B.C.E., enforced the accords ending the First. Sulla returned to Rome in 83 B.C.E., destroyed his enemies (principally the devotees of Marius), and, in 82 B.C.E., established a brutal and cruel dictatorship (the Dictatorship of Sulla) which he voluntarily relinquished in 79 B.C.E. After Sulla's death in 78 B.C.E., Roman military and (increasingly) political leadership fell to Sulla's ally, Pompey (106-48 B.C.E.), who successfully defended Sulla's legacy in Spain, 77-71 B.C.E. In the Third Mithridatic War, 74-64 B.C.E., Pompey and Crassus (d. 53 B.C.E.) defeated the slave revolt of Spartacus (d. 71 B.C.E.), 73-71 B.C.E., established the Consulate of Pompey and Crassus which restored some of the civil and political rights abolished by Sulla, defeated Pontus, and reorganized the eastern provinces.

A broad and chaotic lawlessness and ongoing disputes among contending factions for political authority led to the private division of the government among Pompey, Crassus, and Julius Caesar (c. 102-44 B.C.E.), the First Triumvirate, 60-53 B.C.E. In this circumstance, Caesar reformed the calendar (the Julian Calendar) in 60 B.C.E. and conducted brilliant and successful military campaigns in Gaul (the Gallic Wars), 58-51

B.C.E., and Britain, 55-54 B.C.E. On Crassus' death in 53 B.C.E., the First Triumvirate was ended and Pompey was charged with defending the Republic against Caesar. In 50 B.C.E., Caesar was ordered by the Senate to dissolve his army unilaterally. He refused, crossed into Italy and conquered Rome in 49 B.C.E., defeated Pompey in Greece in 48 B.C.E., strengthened the hold of Cleopatra VII (69-30 B.C.E.) on Egypt in 48-47 B.C.E., was appointed dictator for ten years in 46 B.C.E., and enacted popular municipal, agrarian, and welfare reforms. In 45 B.C.E., Caesar defeated supporters of Pompey's legacy in Spain and was made dictator for life. A senatorial conspiracy led by Brutus (c. 85-42 B.C.E.) murdered him in 44 B.C.E.; the dictatorship was abolished and the Senate assumed power over the state. Caesar's principal heirs, his political ally, Marc Antony (c. 83-30 B.C.E.), and his adopted grandnephew, Octavian (later, Augustus; 63 B.C.E.-14 C.E.), first turned together against the conspirators, then they turned against one another in the form of the Mutinensian War, 44-43 B.C.E., won by Octavian. They then, with Lepidus (fl. in the last half of the first century B.C.E.), formed the Second Triumvirate, 43-33 B.C.E., which constituted a formal division of political authority and which was commissioned to reorder the government. After numerous further civil upheavals — which included a reign of murderous terror in 43 B.C.E. that took even the great philosopher, Cicero — the struggle for political superiority came down to a contest between Octavian and Antony, who had left Octavian's sister and married Cleopatra VII of Egypt in 36 B.C.E. In the civil war that followed, the Ptolemaic War, 32-30 B.C.E., Octavian's forces defeated those of Antony and Cleopatra at the Battle of Actium in 31 B.C.E., Alexandria was seized in 30 B.C.E., Antony and Cleopatra both committed suicide in 30 B.C.E., and Egypt became a Roman province also in 30 B.C.E., thus ending the Ptolemaic dynasties of ancient Egypt. In 27 B.C.E., the extraordinary powers of Octavian were reduced and his resignation occasioned a brief restoration of the Republic before the Senate bestowed on him very broad powers and the title of Augustus, thus marking the establishment of the Principate, the Empire.

The **Empire** was a compromise of sorts between monarchial and republican forms of government; effectively, authoritarian power was delegated based on a reverence for traditional values to the Emperor by the Senate and the citizens. The prerogatives of Augustus (r. 27 B.C.E.-14 C.E.) expanded over the approximately forty years that he stood atop the Roman state but so too did the rights of common citizens. Although the Senate retained power over the public treasury, Augustus commanded the army, the provinces, foreign policy, religious activities, and some internal functions. His reign was memorable: Rome renounced further expansion in 20 B.C.E., declared world peace (Pax Augusta) in 17 B.C.E., variously reorganized the Empire throughout, and widely supported public works and patronized the arts also throughout. Most of Augustus' successors were much less able, much less devoted to an even-handed administration of the Empire, and much more fully moved by the spoils of war and other selective misfortunes. Augustus was the first of the **Julio-Claudian Imperial Dynasty**; the four remaining emperors of this Dynasty succeeded him:

- Tiberius (42 B.C.E.-37 C.E.; r. 14-37 C.E.), adopted son of Augustus, had made several successful military campaigns in Germania before becoming Emperor (8-6 B.C.E. and 4-6 C.E.) and as Emperor strengthened the electoral role of the Senate, suppressed German dissent, established provinces in eastern Anatolia, and endured extended conspiratorial intrigues;
- Caligula (12-41 C.E.; r. 37-41 C.E.), grandnephew of Augustus, transformed the Principate into a divine monarchy, a ruthless and cruel autocracy, directed ostentatious military campaigns in Germania and Britain, and was murdered;
- Claudius (10 B.C.E.-54 C.E.; r. 41-54 C.E.), grandnephew of Augustus, renewed the orderly administrative traditions of Augustus, advanced the influence of women, directed successful military campaigns in Britain and the Balkans, and was murdered in a plot concerning imperial succession; and
- Nero (37-68 C.E.; r. 54-68 C.E.), stepson of Claudius, directed successful military campaigns in Britain and Asia Minor, then, with his last wife, Poppaea (d. 65 C.E.), began an arbitrary, autocratic, and brutal reign that entailed the murders of family and advisers (including the great philosopher, Seneca), the burning of Rome, the persecution of Christians, revolts in Gaul and Spain, the murder of his mother, his murder of Poppaea, and his suicide.

Disputes over imperial succession followed the death of Nero and resulted in the ascension of the **Flavian Imperial Dynasty**:

- Vespasian (9-79 C.E.; r. 69-79 C.E.) fashioned an ordered and frugal administration, commissioned architectural wonders, and suppressed revolts in Germania and Palestine (which entailed the conquest of Jerusalem in 70 C.E.);

- Titus (39-81 C.E.; r. 79-81 C.E.), son of Vespasian, conducted the conquest of Jerusalem before becoming Emperor, as Emperor fashioned a conciliatory and benevolent administration, and was Emperor on the eruption of Vesuvius which buried Pompeii and Herculaneum (and claimed the great scientist, Pliny the Elder) in 79 C.E.; and
- Domitian (51-96 C.E.; r. 81-96 C.E.), brother of Titus, completed the conquest of Britain in 84 C.E., directed military campaigns in Gaul, Germania, and Dacia (Romania), conducted limited persecutions of Christians, formed a despotic administration, and was murdered.

The five so-termed "adopted" or **"good" emperors** who succeeded Domitian came to the throne by adoption, effectively by way of perceived merit. They shaped a brilliant period of world government that entailed broad legal reforms in which all persons were equally entitled to basic human rights, in which all persons were regarded as possessing inalienable rights, in which government was interpreted as a contract between rulers and ruled, and in which the ultimate sovereignty of the state was thought to reside in the will of the people. A competent civil service was established, legal protections for the poor were enacted, cities became much more fully developed, peace initiatives were common, industry and commerce flourished, and the sense of oppression inherent in despotism declined. The "good" emperors were among the most eminent statesmen of the ancient world:

- Nerva (3-98 C.E.; r. 96-98 C.E.) conducted a beneficent and frugal administration;
- Trajan (53-117 C.E.; r. 98-117 C.E.), the first Emperor of provincial origin (Spain), conducted successful military campaigns in Dacia, Arabia, Parthia, Armenia, Mesopotamia, and Assyria, directed limited persecutions of Christians, and presided over the greatest extent of the Empire (from Britain in the north to northern Africa in the south, from the near Middle East in the east to the Atlantic Ocean in the west);
- Hadrian (76-138 C.E.; r. 117-138 C.E.) directed the construction of extensive fortifications in order to secure the frontiers of the Empire, directed the reconstruction of Jerusalem, and suppressed the revolt of the Jews under Bar Kochba (d. 135 C.E.) in Palestine, 132-135 C.E.;
- Antoninus Pius (86-161 C.E.; r. 138-161 C.E.) continued the construction of fortifications and the peace policies of his immediate predecessors; and
- Marcus Aurelius (121-180 C.E.; r. 161-180 C.E.), the distinguished stoic philosopher and fervent humanitarian, defeated insurrections in Britain, Parthia, and Germania (the First Marcomanni War, 167-175 C.E., and the Second Marcomanni War, 178-180 C.E.).

With Marcus Aurelius' successor, his dissolute son, Commodus (161-192 C.E.; r. 180-192 C.E.), dynastic inheritance was effectively restored and the discernible decline of the Empire began. Commodus reigned over a cruel, murderous, and extravagant administration, directed wars in Italy, Africa, and Britain, and was unsurprisingly murdered. The problem of imperial succession became again manifest on the death of Commodus. His eventual successor, Septimius Severus (146-211 C.E.; r. 193-211 C.E.), took the throne by force for himself and his family, the **Severi**. Under Severus, border disputes and provincial disturbances deepened, the military came to utterly dominate civilian affairs, legal and factual differences between the rich and the poor widened, political franchise contracted, the currency sharply inflated, taxation increased significantly, the balance of trade worsened, transportation languished, the farm economy failed as peasants fled the land, and imperial divinism reappeared. Severus was succeeded by his deranged son, Caracalla (188- 217 C.E.; r. 211-217 C.E.), whose savagery was legion, who did however extend citizenship to all free inhabitants of the provinces, and who was predictably murdered. Caracalla's cousin, Elagabalus (204-222 C.E.; r. 218-222 C.E.), continued the ineffective and debauched rule of his predecessor and was too murdered. Elagabalus' cousin, Severus Alexander (205-235 C.E.; r. 222-235 C.E.), was the last of the Severi as well as the most decent and able. In his reign, successful border attacks on the provinces by mounted peoples living on the frontiers of the Empire nonetheless began, indecisive military campaigns in Parthia and Germania were waged, and the Emperor himself was likewise murdered.

Over the next approximate half-century, domestic anarchy increased, border raids intensified, and political leadership weakened. The plague, which began in 250 C.E., greatly exacerbated civil unrest. Border skirmishes were virtually unrelenting; the most notable of these were Ostrogothic (Germanic) attacks in the north and Sassanian (Persian) raids in the east. The dominant political figures in this time are collectively referred to as the soldier, barracks, or **Illyrian emperors**. Most were proven, provincial generals, selected by the army, and murdered after brief reigns. The most significant of these were:

- Decius (r. 249-251 C.E.), who conducted the first general persecution of Christians;

- Valerian (r. 253-260 C.E.), whose reign was dominated by the general persecution of Christians and by border conflicts in the east, south, and west;
- Gallienus (r. 260-268 C.E.), who reformed the army and who issued a writ of toleration in respect to Christians; and
- Diocletian (245-313 C.E.; r. 284-305 C.E.), who temporarily eased the burden of imperial administration by decentralizing it, by dividing the Empire among contending rulers, who, in turn, strengthened the sense of the Empire as an absolute monarchy, the sense of Diocletian himself as a divine emperor, and the sense of citizens as mere subjects; he also conducted general persecutions of Christians and unsuccessfully attempted to correct severe currency inflation with tax reform, wage regulation, and price controls.

A period in which the throne was very uneasily shared followed, 305-312 C.E. A semblance of unity and stability was restored, however, with the victory of Constantine I, or Constantine the Great (c. 288-337 C.E.; r. 312-337 C.E.), against a rival for the throne, Maxentius (d. 312 C.E.), at the Milvian Bridge (near Rome) in 312 C.E. Constantine became ruler of the **Western Empire** on that occasion and he became ruler of the **Eastern Empire** as well (thus, the sole ruler of the entire Empire) on the occasion of his defeat of Licinius (250-325 C.E.) at Adrianople and Chrysopolis in 324 C.E. In 330 C.E., Byzantium was renamed Constantinople; it also became the capital of the Empire and, owing to Constantine's Christian sympathies, it too became the center of the new religion. Constantine ushered in a brief period of peace, significantly increased the size of the army (to c. 900,000), separated civil and military administration, and extended the absolutist and divinist nature of imperial rule installed by Diocletian.

In the approximately forty years after the death of Constantine:
- the problem of imperial succession again developed as the crown passed through several members of Constantine's dynasty and several others unrelated to Constantine;
- non-Christian religions gained currency;
- conflicts in the provinces and on the frontiers widened;
- some provinces were surrendered and established themselves as quasi-independent states; and
- the barbarian migrations in the north began with the Hunnic (the Huns were a prominent nomadic, mounted, Eurasian tribe) emigration from north-central Asia to Scythia (Ukraine) where the Huns defeated and displaced the Ostrogoths (a major Germanic tribe) to Pannonia (Austria and Hungary) in 375 C.E., with the Visigothic (the Visigoths were another major Germanic tribe) emigration (also under Hunnic pressure) from Pannonia to the Balkans in 376 C.E., and with the Visigothic defeat of the Romans at the Battle of Adrianople (in what is now European Turkey) in 378 C.E.

Theodosius I, or Theodosius the Great (c. 346-395 C.E.; r. 379-395 C.E.), became co-Emperor of the Eastern Empire in 379 C.E., Emperor of the Western Empire in 392 C.E., and sole Emperor in 394 C.E. Under his rule, pagan cults were prohibited, Christianity became the state religion in 391 C.E., and the pan-Hellenic athletic festivals (including the Olympic Games) were abolished in 394 C.E. On his death, the Empire was formally and permanently partitioned between his sons, Honorius (384-423; r. 395-423) and Arcadius (377-408; r. 395-408), into western and eastern parts respectively, thus conclusively ending the increasingly fragile unity of the Empire. The Eastern Empire had its center in Constantinople throughout and the Western Empire had its center in Rome until 404 C.E. and in Ravenna thereafter.

The most notable of the remaining Eastern Roman Emperors was Theodosius II (401-450 C.E.; r. 408-450 C.E.), grandson of Theodosius I, who deepened the influence of Christianity, who several times ordered the razing of Olympia from 408 to 426 C.E., who founded the University of Constantinople in 425 C.E., who established the Theodosian Code of folk law in 438 C.E., and who suffered the consequences of the Hunnic raids of Attila (d. 453 C.E.; r. 434-453 C.E.) in Scythia, Pannonia, Greece, Macedonia, Thrace, Germania, Byzantium, Persia, and Armenia. These raids ended with the carnage of Attila's defeat in Gaul in 451 C.E., with his conditional victories in Italy in 452 C.E., and with his death in 453 C.E. The circumstance in the Western Empire throughout the fifth century C.E. was still more desperate. The remaining Western Emperors (after Theodosius I) were weak and ineffective. The Visigoths sacked Rome in 410 C.E. and subsequently claimed bits of Italy, Gaul, and Spain. The Vandals (another major Germanic tribe) claimed bits of Gaul, Spain, and north Africa in the early-to-mid fifth century C.E. and subsequently sacked Rome in 455 C.E. And the Angles and Saxons (still other major Germanic tribes) successfully invaded Britain in the second half of the fifth century C.E. Governmental authority was further decentralized, senses of social community and duty were increasingly replaced by rapacious forms of self-absorbed individualism, trade and wealth declined, unemployment and poverty rose sharply, a barter economy prevailed, the cities depopulated, and peasants surrendered their land to large landowners for protection from brigands and tax officials. The increasing anarchy, corruption, and incompetence in the Roman government, together with the resolve of the mostly Germanic invaders, brought an effective end to the Western Roman Empire when Romulus Augustulus was deposed by the Gothic chieftain, Odoacer (c. 435-493 C.E.), at Ravenna in 476 C.E.

The second of the three major monotheistic and personalistic world religions, **Christianity**, was created at the virtual beginning of the Roman Imperial epoch and it matured as an ideology and as an institution throughout this epoch. The seminal vision of Christianity was, of course, owed to Jesus Christ (c. 4 B.C.E.-c. 30 C.E.). This vision alleges Christ as the son of a transcendent, infinite, and perfect God (Yahweh, or Jehovah) made mortal in order to save humanity from its inherently sinful nature and from death. Christianity grew out of Judaic tradition but is distinguished from that tradition principally by virtue of the literal significance of Christ as Savior, by the doctrines which issue from this significance, and by the sacraments expressing this significance. The distinctly Christian perception is most notably recorded in the New Testament, the distinctly Christian aspect of the Bible. The New Testament consists in:

- four biographical accounts of Christ – the Gospels of Matthew, Mark, Luke, and John – which were written in c. 70-c. 95 C.E. and which recount Christ's birth, childhood, adulthood, teachings, crucifixion, resurrection, and theological significance;
- a history of missionary activity, the Acts of the Apostles, which was written in c. 90 C.E. and which recounts the activities of the apostles and other disciples on behalf of the new religion immediately following Christ's death; most notably describes the Jewish/Gentile ministries and martyrdoms of St. Peter (d. 64 C.E.), the first bishop of Rome (effectively, the first Pope), and St. Paul (d. 64 C.E.), including Paul's conversion and his four great journeys throughout the eastern, northeastern, and north-central Mediterranean regions (45-49 C.E., 50-53 C.E., 53-57 C.E., and 57-59 C.E.);
- twenty-one letters, or epistles, written by disciples in the first century C.E.; the most significant of these were either of unknown source (Hebrews) or are attributed to St. Paul (Romans, I Corinthians, II Corinthians, Galatians, Ephesians, Philippians, Colossians, I Thessalonians, II Thessalonians, and Philemon), c. 56- c. 62 C.E.; they concerned the character and virtues of the new religion and were addressed to non-Jewish people (i.e., to Gentiles) throughout the northeastern and north-central Mediterranean; and
- a prophecy, the Apocalypse, or Revelation, which was written in c. 95 C.E. and which postulates the establishment of God's Kingdom in this world, the triumph of good over evil, and the Second Coming of Christ.

Christianity fashioned a rich corpus of philosophic disputation, disputation that constituted the most significant closing chapter of late ancient thought and the most significant inaugural chapter of early medieval discourse. This corpus of **early Judeo-Christian philosophy** was itself grounded mainly in ancient classical philosophy; it was grounded principally in the thought of Plato. The neo-Platonism of the first to the fifth centuries C.E. re-formed Platonic doctrine in Judaic and Christian terms, made philosophy a handmaiden of theology (that is, a rational elaboration of faith, an apologetic justification of faith to reason), and issued highly unfavorable, idealistic-tending interpretations of the body and its main expressions (often including sport). The most important exponents of this tendency were Philo (30 B.C.E.-50 C.E.), Tertullian (160-240 C.E.), Plotinus (204-269 C.E.), and St. Augustine (354-430 C.E.).

Philo led the endgame of Greek philosophy back to its origins in religion, albeit a very different form of religion. Alexandrian philosophy, which was centered in Alexandria and which was most incisively championed by Philo, united Greek and Jewish thought. The notion of God as a transcendent being (a being fundamentally apart from the world of human experience) and what follows from this, together with a taste for thisworldly denial, were common features of the Alexandrian teaching. Philo argued that the governing principle of reality is Jehovah, world-soul, or the Logos, the absolute, unitary, eternal, immutable, ineffable, and incorporeal creator. Jehovah is known by no means, only immediately by revelation, and is without imperfection. Evil owes its place in the world to material encumbrance. One is to live, therefore, in accord with the imperatives of the soul (the principle of good) and to deny the requirements of the material body (the principle of evil).This is to be done by means of an ascetic form of religious contemplation which entails an active turning away from the body.

Tertullian and the other leading Christian apologists of the period had a somewhat larger opinion of reason than Philo. He/they held that the source of truth is supernatural but it is nonetheless rationally comprehensible to divinely inspired minds. By this account, the order of the world is owed to the divine instantiation of reason in the incarnate Christ. Tertullian was nonetheless persuaded, like Philo, that the highest good consists in a resignation from the immanent domain of sense and in an aspiration to the transcendent domain of the supernatural, to the transcendent domain of God. Evil is accordingly construed as the human tendency to freely act otherwise. Plotinus defended as primary a form of knowledge that comes to one as a presence, as an intuitive apprehension of the system of ideas that constitutes reality as a whole; that is, a form of knowledge shared only by those who have experienced its immediate unity. The unity that composes reality in its most fundamental form, that frames the perfect source of all reality, God, the Good, the One, or the Supreme Consciousness, is construed as transcendent of all multiplicity and prior to it, as beyond all substance and rational thought, as ineffable. The world of multiplicity is explained in terms of emanations of God, from forms most resembling God, pure thought, to those least resembling God, matter. Matter, in turn, is construed as altogether passive and impotent, as the source and the principle of all privation and evil. Effectively, as for Plato, then, the world of multiple experience is determined by its correspondence to absolute exemplars and it is the basic aim of life to achieve a reunification with the highest aspect of reality. All entities thus live in search of a return to God. One comes to mystic experience, to ecstasy, by this view, only by a complete turning inward, only by a full turning away from the contaminating influence of the body.

Augustine[103] was the most accomplished and the most influential of the early Judeo-Christian philosophers. His thought marked the culmination of the apologetic tendency and it remained the dominant influence on Christian philosophy for several centuries. It stood majestically astride several worlds. Its metaphysical framework and its attack on skepticism harkened back a near-millennium to classical Greek tendency (most notably, to Plato) and looked forward a millennium to early modern tendencies (most notably, to Descartes). Its proclamation of faith foresaw the central tenets of medieval philosophy just ahead. By Augustine's view, the highest form of knowledge is of God and of self; the source of such knowledge is divine revelation. Reason provisionally judges the authenticity of revealed knowledge which revelation, in turn, affirms by faith. Although it is clearly faith that drives reason according to Augustine, only the Trinity (the three semblances of God: the Father, the Son, and the Holy Ghost) must be accepted on "indisputable" faith alone. All of this leads to the conclusion that one understands under the influence of reason in order to believe the revealed truth (credo ut intelligam). God, or Absolute Spirit, is, of course, the fount of such truth and is construed as the transcendent creator of all things, as omnipotent, as omniscient, as omnibenevolent, as free and self-sufficient, and as willing and doing at once without means. From nothing, God has created and God continuously sustains, in every moment and through every expanse, the most perfect, the best, of all possible worlds. Human selves, moreover, are conceived as rational and immutable souls inhabiting material and mortal bodies. The soul and the body are, thus, fundamentally different and distinct substances. The soul governs the body, effecting changes in it, without itself changing. Since, for Augustine, the presence of evil is necessary to that of good (and continuous with that of good), however, the body narrowly escapes the characterization given it by Philo, Tertullian, and Plotinus as the principle of evil itself. The moral ideal of humanity is nonetheless to achieve a union of the soul with God, to obtain an eternal blessedness in God, to gain the true life of pure form. This life is attained, according to Augustine, by dutiful exercise of the supreme virtue, love. The developmental record of this exercise, in turn, constitutes history and reveals the unfolding of the world in accord with the character and purpose of God through a perpetual conflict between the earthly kingdom (which is dominated by love of self and contempt of God) and the heavenly kingdom (which is dominated by love of God and contempt of self).[104] Despite his adult apprehensions about the earthly kingdom, however, Augustine apparently adored ball games in his youth.

The **institutional history of early Christianity** was mixed. The new religion, unlike others, quickly developed a telling sense of ideological unity, an established dogma, a sacred literature, and a communal framework of ecclesiastics, teachers, missionaries, administrators, and caretakers (principally in Rome, Constantinople, Antioch, Alexandria, and Jerusalem), much of which was incompatible with Roman citizenship, some of which explicitly challenged Roman prerogative. Christianity fell into frequent dispute with Roman authority, mainly, from the Christian perspective, over the issue of idolatry and, from the Roman perspective, over the issue of negligence of civic duty. Christianity opposed the notion of imperial divinism on ideological grounds; Roman authority, on practical and juridical grounds, took a dim view of the Christian separation of the worldly kingdom and the City of God and a dim view as well of Christians' related refusal to perform the duties of citizens and soldiers. The result was the selective Christian martyrdoms of the first century C.E., the limited persecutions of Christians by Nero (64 C.E.), Domitian (81-96 C.E.), and Trajan (98-117 C.E.), and the general persecutions of Christians by Decius (249-251 C.E.), Valerian (257-258 C.E.), and Diocletian (303-311 C.E.). There was nonetheless, from the mid-third century C.E., a progressive turning away from natural, civic, Roman gods, the effective architects of political and economic calamity, toward supernatural religion, toward Judeo-Christian spirituality. In this development, a world religion, which championed the uniquely individual soul, which was moved by the prospect of hope, love, and equality, and which was sympathetic to the poor and the oppressed, eventually replaced the Roman state, its interchangeable notion of citizens, and its mistreatment of individuals characteristic of such a notion. In 260 C.E., Gallienus issued an Edict of Toleration that temporarily suspended persecutions. On the Christian conversion of Constantine the Great in 313 C.E., the Edict of Milan granted complete religious freedom to the new dogma. In 325 C.E., the Council of Nicaea, convened by Constantine, dealt with the three major theological problems of Christianity – the finitude-infinitude of Christ (which entailed consideration of the immaculate conception and the resurrection), the Trinity, and the issue of evil (in a world created and sustained by a perfect Being) – and thus defused the heresies that had been developing around these problems from the second century C.E. And in 391 C.E., Theodosius the Great declared Christianity the state religion of the Roman Empire.

The **intellectual orientation of ancient Rome** – its worldly religious, educational, literary, and philosophic tendencies – was mostly borrowed from Etruscan and Greek culture. In practical affairs, such as city planning, engineering, trade, and military activities, it was most significantly affected by Etruria; in cultural affairs, such as religion, art, literature, and philosophy, it was most significantly affected by Greece. In all domains, however, Roman culture was foremost inclined to an emphasis on mechanistic utility and it was, thus, far more adept at organizing and applying theoretical knowledge than at propounding it. **Roman religion** adopted the basic outline of Greek polytheism but it interpreted that outline, not in anthropomorphic and heroic terms as had the Greeks themselves, but in animistic and cultic terms. Roman gods were usefully associated with such as the home, farm, and government; they were not universal, legendary figures in the full Greek sense. Roman culture clearly lacked the very broad, organic inclinations of classical Greek life but it excelled Greek culture in respect to gainful applications of intellectual achievement. **Roman education** also embodied a studious devotion to experiential utility as distinct from a classical Greek sense of organic fulfillment. It more so emphasized military, political, commercial, agricultural, domestic, and moral training than strictly intellectual attainment. From the establishment of the earliest formal schools shortly after the last of the Macedonian Wars (in the late second century B.C.E.) to the waning several centuries of the Empire, Roman education was highly disciplined, publicly financed and supervised, and available to both genders. In the final, the declining, several centuries of the Empire, however, the moral and physical aspects of education receded into the background, education was made increasingly available to fewer (to only the most privileged) persons, and it was increasingly sought as a conspicuous demonstration of social superiority.

Despite its fervent devotion to practical considerations, Roman culture could justifiably boast of some remarkable intellectual talents in poetry, drama, history, and philosophy. The literary flowering of the last century of the Republic and the first century of the Empire in particular was nonetheless wholly consistent with the predominantly realistic inclinations of ancient Roman life broadly characterized. The leading achievements in **Roman poetry and drama** were:

- the burlesque comedies of Plautus (c. 254-184 B.C.E.); most notably, "The Captives;"
- the urbane comedies of Terence (c. 194-159 B.C.E.); most notably, "Andria;"
- the epigrammatic, lyric poetry of Catullus (c. 87-c. 54 B.C.E.); most notably, "On the Death of Lesbia's Sparrow;"
- the exquisitely formed lyric poetry of Horace (85-8 B.C.E.); most notably, "Satires," "Odes," "Epodes," and "Epistles;"
- the pastoral poetry and epic literature of Rome's greatest writer, Vergil; most notably, "Eclogues" (37 B.C.E.), "Georgics" (30 B.C.E.), and Aeneid (19 B.C.E.);
- the love and mythological poetry of Ovid (43 B.C.E.-18 C.E.); most notably, "On the Art of Love" and "Metamorphoses;"
- the epigrammatic, satirical poetry of Martial (c. 40-c. 104 C.E.) and Juvenal (c. 58-c. 140 C.E.); and
- the robust, satirical prose dialogues of Lucian (c. 125-c. 180 C.E.).

Roman historical scholarship likewise flourished in the last two centuries B.C.E. and the first two centuries C.E. Cato the Elder (234-149 B.C.E.) wrote an insightful history of Italy and Rome (Origins). Polybius (c. 203-120 B.C.E.) wrote an extensive account of the rise of Rome (Universal History). Julius Caesar wrote brilliant commentaries concerning his campaigns in Gaul (Bellum gallicum) and in the civil war (Bellum civile). Livy (59 B.C.E.-17 C.E.) wrote a vivid and colossal history of Rome (Books from the Founding of Rome). Tacitus (c. 55-c. 117 C.E.) wrote severely critical interpretations of early imperial Rome (Germania, Histories, and Annals). Suetonius (c. 70-c. 146 C.E.) wrote revealing biographies (Lives of the Caesars). Plutarch (c. 46-120 C.E.) wrote comparative biographies of Greeks and Romans (The Parallel Lives). And Pliny the Younger (c.

62-c. 114 C.E.) wrote highly literate letters concerning Christian and Roman life of the late first and early second centuries C.E.

Roman philosophy, not unlike other forms of Roman scholarship, tended also to pragmatic orientations and was too greatly influenced by Greek achievements (most notably by Hellenistic thought). It was therefore governed mainly by an eclectic taste for Epicureanism and stoicism and it took the shape of skeptical, common-sense pronouncements about largely practical matters. Lucretius (c. 99-c. 55 B.C.E.) made the most notable Roman interpretation of Epicureanism in On the Nature of Things. The leading Roman stoics were the great dramatists and orators, Cicero (106-43 B.C.E.; most notably, On the State and On the Laws) and Seneca (3 B.C.E.-65 C.E.; most notably, Moral Essays and Moral Letters); the great rhetorician and teacher of oratory, Quintilian (c. 35-c. 95 C.E.; most notably, Education of the Orator); the great slave philosopher, Epictetus (c. 50-c. 138 C.E.; most notably, Discourses); and the great statesman, Marcus Aurelius (most notably, Meditations).

Roman science and music were likewise largely borrowed from the Greeks, took largely eclectic forms, and tended largely to practical inclination. Pliny the Elder (c. 23-79 C.E.) synthesized extant knowledge concerning natural phenomena in his encyclopedic Natural History. Galen (c. 130-c. 200 C.E.) synthesized extant medical knowledge and experimentally demonstrated the favorable influence of systematic exercise, diet, and massage on good health in his monumental On Good Health. And Ptolemy (fl. second century C.E.) synthesized extant knowledge concerning the physical universe and defended a geocentric notion (a static, earth-centered notion) of cosmology in his extensive Almagest. Although nothing remains of ancient Roman music, it was apparently little other than a fairly straightforward copy of the Greek.

Like other forms of Roman art, the architecture, sculpture, and painting of ancient Rome also tended to practical, utilitarian, mechanistic, and realistic, as distinct from mythological, heroic, organic, and universal, standards. These standards were less about aesthetic possibility as such than they were about representative recordings of fact; they were less about human inspiration and pathos of the Greek sort than they were about the world of utility. The Roman sense of plastic beauty eclectically combined foreign stylistic elements, mainly Greek and Etruscan elements, into its own stern and vital perception of coherent order. **Roman architecture** greatly improved the character and engineering use of concrete as well as mortar-and-brick construction and also greatly advanced arch-and-vault styles of design. These achievements freed the medium from its dominant earlier forms, post-and-lintel forms, greatly expanded design alternatives, and enabled the medium to effectively enclose monumental spaces. Although Republican architecture much resembled Greek and Etruscan design (as in the "Temple of Fortuna Virilis" at Rome, second century B.C.E., the "Basilica" at Pompeii, c. 120 B.C.E., and the "Maison Carée" at Nîmes, c. 1-10 C.E.), something of the colossal scale (in which columns are residual) characteristic of Imperial architecture can be seen in such as the "Sanctuary of Fortuna" at Praeneste (second century B.C.E.), the "Temple of the Sybl" at Tivoli (first century B.C.E.), and the "Pont du Gard" at Nîmes (late first century B.C.E.). The leading triumphs of characteristically Roman architecture were nonetheless achieved in the imperial reigns of Augustus ("Forum of Augustus" at Rome, late first century B.C.E.), Vespasian and Titus ("Colosseum" at Rome, 72-80 C.E.), Trajan ("Forum of Trajan" at Rome, 113 C.E.), Hadrian ("Pantheon" at Rome, 118-125 C.E., and "Hadrian's Villa" at Tivoli, 125-135 C.E.), Caracalla ("Baths of Caracalla" at Rome, 206-217 C.E.), Diocletian ("Palace of Diocletian" at Split, c. 293 C.E.), and Constantine the Great ("Basilica of Maxentius and Constantine" at Rome, 306-313 C.E.).

The realistic tendencies and developmental patterns of Roman architecture were also defining features of **Roman sculpture and painting**. Republican achievements tended to a symmetric and austere simplicity; most notably, in the bronze "L'Arringatore" (Portrait of Aulus Metellus), c. 90-c. 70 B.C.E., and in the marble "Head of Pompey," c. 55 B.C.E. Imperial achievements tended to a somewhat more elaborate and demonstrative simplicity. The leading triumphs of Imperial sculpture were variously Augustan (the historical relief sculpture of the marble "Ara Pacis" at Rome, 13-9 B.C.E., and the marble "Augustus of Primaporta," c. 15 B.C.E.), Flavian (the marble "Portrait of Vespasian," 75 C.E., and the historical relief sculpture of the marble "Arch of Titus" at Rome, 81 C.E.), Trajanic (the historical relief sculpture of the marble "Column of Trajan" at Rome, 113 C.E.), and Aurelian (the bronze "Equestrian Statue of Marcus Aurelius," 161-180 C.E., and the historical relief sculpture of the marble "Column of Marcus Aurelius" at Rome, 176 C.E.). In the third and fourth centuries C.E., a brutish and disordered emotionalism in the plastic arts came to accompany the broader chaos. The marble bust "Philip the Arab," c. 244-249 C.E., the historical relief sculpture of the marble "Arch of Constantine" at Rome, 312-315 C.E., and the colossal marble head "Constantine the Great," c. 315 C.E., were perhaps the most notable instances of this tendency. The inventive treatment of color and perspective in Roman wall painting, mainly landscape painting at Rome, Pompeii, and Herculaneum, from the first century

B.C.E. to the first century C.E. and in Roman mosaics at Sicily, north Africa, and Syria in the fourth century C.E. were also memorable.

Ancient **Roman sport**, like ancient Roman art, was greatly indebted to Greek (and Etruscan) practices.[105] The relationship of Roman and Greek culture in particular was nonetheless ambivalent. Roman society rarely tired of finding the contemptuous in Greek life even though it held a curious reverence for Greek achievements and owed much to them. There is, however, little of the Greek organicism in Roman sport. Unlike classical Greek culture, Roman society did never succeed in connecting its sporting activities to the comprehensive mainstream of authentic human experience (to such as religion and art for salient instance). Nor did Roman society consequently incorporate the Greek sense of balance, harmony, proportion, and beauty of bodily form and movement in its sporting exertions. There are several compelling reasons for this, not the least of which has to do with the mechanistic emphasis of Roman culture on the practical dimensions of life. According to this emphasis, sport (of the Greek variety) was considered unduly abstract; that is, insufficiently useful. Although much of the content of Roman sport was derived from Greek practices, Roman sport nonetheless embodied a studious devotion to utility and it therefore lacked the high Greek sense of cultural development. Other notable and related reasons for the stark differences in Greek and Roman sport most significantly include:

- the wide disparity between mechanistic, objective, and corporeal notions of reality, self, body, and movement held by Roman culture and organic, subjective, and lived such notions held by Greek culture;
- the relatively light influence of heroic religion on Roman culture and sport, the relatively heavy such influence on Greek culture and sport;
- the dissimilarities in Greek and Roman forms of government; the Romans did not develop a Greek sense of city-state "nationalism" nor the sort of sporting rivalry that accompanied this sense;
- the large influence of Etruscan forms of brutal, blood sport on Roman practices, the absence of such an influence on Greek practices;
- the large influence of Christianity on Roman practices, the absence of such an influence on Greek practices; and
- the customs of nudity in Greek sport that were much abhorred by the Romans.

Concisely said, Roman culture did never develop a Greek taste for sport. It did not conceive of sport as an essential form of human experience and it did never effectively make sport a part of the formal school curriculum.

Sport was expected to serve fairly narrow, somewhat pedestrian, albeit significant, ends in the Roman case. In the period of the Republic, Roman life was necessarily so occupied with the terms of agricultural and military survival that it developed little interest in sport as such and despised much about sport as useless. A simplicity of character defined sport in this period (from as early as the sixth century B.C.E.); sport was used primarily as a means to health and military purposes; strenuous exercise and recreation were well respected and far more highly prized than athletics (as for Terence, Cicero, Horace, and Ovid). Something of this simplicity is apparent in:

- Vergil's account of funeral games in Sicily honoring Aeneas' father, Anchises, in Book V of the Aeneid;
- Juvenal's deprecatory characterization of the vanity of human desire, as wishing for no more than "a sound mind in a sound body" (men sana in corpore sano), in his tenth satire; and
- Galen's view of athletics as pernicious but his spirited advocacy of progressive exercises for all body segments, at varying tempi, at various intervals, for various ages, and under various resistances in On Good Health.

In the period of the Empire, a contempt for exercise eventually developed and athletic practices became increasingly more elaborate, more commercial, more political, and more prominent; they were used primarily as a means to entertainment purposes. The Roman sport of this period more so took the form of extravagant spectacles, of amusing entertainments, of games (ludi) for spectators than the form of participatory contests for the human edification of athletes, athletic contests (agones, αγωνες) for participants in the Greek sense. Typically tending to great violence and to ostentation, the sport of Imperial Rome became progressively less redeeming, had increasingly less to do with humanizing possibilities, and had run its course by the early fifth century C.E. The uncivilized excesses into which Roman sport increasingly fell were many:

- it became a medium for conspicuously displaying the distinction between the leisured and literate class, the patricians, who comprised the majority of the spectatorial muse, and the unleisured class, the plebeians, captives, and slaves, who comprised the majority of the participatory corps; it thereby promoted the political, economic, and moral impoverishment of the lower classes and promoted as well an intemperate exploitation of the master-slave relation;

- it paid exorbitant honors to its champions, honors that far exceeded the contributions of accomplished athletes to social welfare; it likewise bestowed exorbitant resource and privilege on its athletic champions (rewards such as extraordinary money, meals, goods, and pensions as well as special exemption from taxation and from public service);
- it came to embody such debasements as extreme indolence among spectators, dissolute behavior among athletes and spectators, gambling, bribery, cheating, violent disputes, abuse of officials, spectators bellowing frenzied improprieties, fanatical approval of local athletes and malevolent abuse of their rivals, the development of a pretentious hierarchy of officials, and an exhibitionist increase in women's activities;
- it became a source of great material profit and thereby became more specialized and more spectatorial as well as more strenuous, regulated, consuming, and exclusive; the number of competitions and the value of prizes rose exponentially; the quality of competitive experience did not;
- it came to embody a highly artificial distinction between the life of an athlete and the life of other persons; and
- it became increasingly less devoted to the development of strength, beauty, health, or intellect.

These excesses predictably brought condemnation of sport, or at least condemnation of such practices in sport, from leading intellectuals. Many of the most prominent statesmen, physicians, poets, dramatists, orators, historians, and philosophers of ancient Rome wrote, in fragmentary terms, about sport: Plautus, Terence, Cicero, Horace, Vergil, Ovid, Tiberius, Seneca, Quintilian, Martial, Plutarch, Epictetus, Tacitus, Juvenal, Pliny the Younger, Suetonius, Hadrian, Marcus Aurelius, Lucian, Galen, Philo, and Tertullian. Some spoke well of it, others not. Martial, for significant instance, tended to an unconditional admiration for sport; Tertullian, conversely, to an unqualified disapproval of it. Most, however, were ambivalent of it, inclining to favor bodily fitness through regular, useful exercise but inclining also to oppose the spectacular and brutal entertainment sport of their day. Seneca, in his <u>Moral Letters</u>, gave perhaps the most characteristic and literate account of this type, condemning the corrupt spectacles, bemoaning the acclaim they received as "cultural projects," depreciating athletes, trainers, and spectators who make themselves the slaves of bodily appetites , and applauding the resolve and bodily vigor of athletes. The resolve and bodily vigor of athletes, it was nonetheless argued, may well be had by way of exercise and may well be thus gained without the attendant corruption, one-sidedness, or gluttony of the spectacles.

There were five major agencies of Roman sport. Two of these were mainly participatory in character (the military camps and baths) and three of these were mainly spectatorial in character (the athletic festivals, circuses, and gladiatorial combats). Military obligations formed the principal public responsibility of the Roman male citizen. The responsibilities of citizenship were imposed on Roman men between the ages of fourteen and seventeen years when they were conscripted to military service. They were expected to remain in such service until the approximate age of 47 years. It was in the **military camps**, such as the enormous Campus Martius near Rome, that Roman boys practiced martial exercises and games (which often included sporting exercises and games) under the tutelage of their soldier-fathers. This practice went on throughout much of the Republic and was customarily done in informal contexts but was also sometimes done in more formal ways. In the first century B.C.E., Augustus established formal associations, the Iuventus, for male youngsters in these camps. This initiative marked the only Roman attempt to make sport (or physical education) a formal part of education. The members of the Iuventus were typically drawn from the most distinguished patrician families of all regions of the Empire and they were trained for military and civil service. Although fairly well united in national service aims, these associations were nonetheless supported largely by wealthy, private patrons and they were otherwise rather independent as well. They, like the camps themselves, were, however, uniformly and heavily committed to vigorous physical activity. Pre-adolescent youngsters were principally devoted to the active and competitive games of childhood. Others were primarily devoted to various forms of archery, bowling, running, jumping, javelin throwing, swimming, boating, gymnastics (acrobatics), combative activities (boxing, wrestling, pancrateion/pancratium, fencing), equestrian activities (horse and chariot racing), contact, team ball games (trigon, a game resembling tetherball; sphaeromachiae, a game resembling lawn tennis; harpastum, a game resembling lacrosse, team handball, and hurling; a game resembling field hockey; a game resembling polo; and pilla and follis, games resembling football), paganica (a game resembling golf), and military maneuvers (forced marching with armor and miniature military games [ludus troiae]).

The **baths**, or thermae, also figured prominently in the physical recreative experience of ancient Roman life. Although the first of these public facilities was not constructed in Rome until 21 B.C.E., there were over 900 such facilities in Rome alone by the fourth century C.E. and virtually all Roman villages had made some provision for this type of recreation by the fall of the Western Empire. The largest and the most elaborate of these was the Baths of Caracalla, constructed in Rome between 206 and 217 C.E.; it was approximately 220 meters/240 yards x 114 meters/125 yards in full dimension; it could accommodate up to 3200 bathers in a session; and it was rivaled only by the Baths of Diocletian, which was constructed in Rome in the late third and early fourth centuries C.E. The baths either included separate rooms for women or scheduled special periods for their sole use. The larger of these facilities came to contain libraries, art galleries, and dining commons as well as exercise courts, swimming pools, and various rooms for undressing (apodyterium), oiling (unctorium), exercising with balls (spaeristerium), warm air bathing (tepidarium), hot air bathing (caldarium), and cold water bathing (frigidarium). In the late Empire, however, the baths, like the major spectatorial agencies of Roman sport, became increasingly elaborate, fell increasingly into unredeemable practice, and thus increasingly evoked church condemnation.

The spectatorial agencies practiced more strictly sporting activities than the participatory agencies; they were more fully given to a formalization of sporting activities than the participatory agencies; they were also, however, more fully inclined to violent excess than the participatory agencies; and, unlike the participatory agencies, they never became functional offices of physical recreation for the Roman people at large. The athletes who participated in the athletic festivals, circuses, and gladiatorial combats were acutely aware of their vulnerability and succeeded (by the first century B.C.E.) in organizing elaborate athletic guilds, Sacred Synods of the Xystos, which effectively functioned as trade unions, championing the political and economic welfare of athletes; the most notable of these, predictably, was the Synod of Rome.

The Romans both inherited the Greek athletic festivals, most importantly the pan-Hellenic celebrations, and established **athletic festivals** of their own. In neither case, however, did exactingly athletic events much appeal to the Romans. Both the festivals they inherited (and transformed) and those they created thus tended more so to artificial entertainments than to sporting contests of the Greek sort. And both were increasingly devoted to animal-dominated events – most especially to various forms of equestrian activity, horse racing and chariot racing in particular – as distinct from more strictly athletic forms of individual, dual combative, and combined event. The earliest of the distinctly Roman festivals (from the sixth century B.C.E. Republic), not unlike the earliest Greek festivals, were first practiced in conjunction with agricultural holidays and religious celebrations. Eventually (from c. 186 B.C.E.), however, the state established official games, wealthy "benefactors" established private games, and the festivals lost their original simplicity and religious significance. They became progressively more ornate and bizarre, progressively more political and fiscal in basic aim. As they grew more fully commercial, still greater numbers of them were established; by c. 100 C.E., more than 300 athletic festivals were conducted within the Roman Empire. The most notable of these were formed by Sulla (81 B.C.E.), Pompey (55 B.C.E.), Caesar (46 B.C.E.), Brutus (44 B.C.E.), Augustus (the Actian Games at Rome variously in the first century B.C.E. and the Augustalian/Sebastan Games at Naples in 2 C.E.), Caligula (variously in the first century C.E.), Nero (the Neronian Games at Rome in 60 C.E.), Domitian (the Capitoline Games at Rome in 86 C.E., for which the first permanent [Greek] athletic stadium in Rome, the Stadium of Domitian, was constructed, also in 86 C.E.), Antoninus Pius (the Eusebian Games at Puteoli in 138 C.E.), and Marcus Aurelius (the Olympic Games at Alexandria variously in the second century C.E.). Some of these festivals made fairly wide provision for women's events (most significantly, foot-races) although much of this was owing to the commercial benefits of exhibitionism. Many of them too, à la those of Philip II and Alexander the Great, were established for the principal purpose of appeasing foreign, particularly Greek, populations.

The temperament and programs of the Greek festivals that came under Roman influence were also sharply re-fashioned as against their original forms. Its affect on Greek populations aside, the Romans did not consider the distinction between Greek athletics and other forms of sport especially important. The national Greek sanctuaries and their festivals were qualitatively revised under Roman authority. This revision brought the organic tendencies of classical Greek sport to decline (by organic and classical Greek standard) and it replaced them with mechanistic orientations, typically with corrupt such orientations. The incipient origins of this decline antedated Roman influence; these origins were themselves Greek as has been said and they likely first showed themselves as early as the late fifth century B.C.E. The decline continued through the Macedonian hegemony and accelerated under Roman influence through the third, the second, and into the first centuries B.C.E., at least through the rule of Sulla (82-79 B.C.E.). The Olympic Games in particular were restored to something of their original character under the early government of Augustus (30-14 B.C.E.). Principally in order to regain the loyalty of the Empire's Greek colonies, to enhance a sense of Greek unity, and to provoke pride in the Greek city-states and in Hellenism, the esteem of Olympia and the practices of the old festivals were again encouraged. Although disrupted by such as Caligula and Nero, this restorative tendency continued, on balance, at least through the rule of Hadrian (117-138 C.E.). Then, with the invasion of the Goths in the third century C.E. and with the formal acceptance of Christianity in the fourth century C.E., the final descent began. The Gothic tendency to abhor anything cultivated, the Roman paganism (idol or emperor worship), the earlier Roman persecutions of Christians in "athletic" contests, the predominant Christian notion of the body as the principle of evil and as thus inviting ascetic restraint, and the moral degeneracy of the festivals (as well as the gymnasia) themselves were too much for the festivals to survive. They were all abolished by Theodosius the Great in 394 C.E., following the Olympic Games of 393 C.E. Although several festivals, particularly those dominated by chariot racing and other equestrian events, lingered emptily on in the Eastern Empire for a brief time – the Games at Antioch, which were held as late as 520 C.E., were perhaps the most notable of these – ancient sport had fallen into such disrepair by the end of the fourth century C.E. that it was effectively done by this time. Theodosius II several times ordered the razing of Olympia from 408 to 426 C.E., edicts largely executed by 450 C.E. What remained of the Olympic site after 450 C.E. was mostly destroyed by the earthquakes of 522 and 551 C.E. Olympia thereby remained covered over and forgotten until the archaeological excavations of the eighteenth century C.E.

The **circuses**, circenses, or ludi circenses, date in informal terms from the eighth century B.C.E. and in formal terms from 329 B.C.E. Like the late festivals, they were primarily devoted to animal-dominated activities. While the origins of the festivals were Greek and thus at least tenuously connected to the spirit of intrinsicality, however, the origins of the circuses were mainly Etruscan and thus firmly connected to the extrinsic traditions of blood sport and all that is entailed by such traditions (viz., violence, ostentation, extravagance, gambling, and corruption). The circuses were staged in cavernous and lavish amphitheaters, or hippodromes, effectively chariot and horse racing facilities. There were scores of these throughout the Roman ambit – in what are now Libya, Spain, France, Germany, Britain, the near Middle East, Greece, and Italy itself – but the most significant of these were in Antioch, Byzantium, Carthage, and Rome. Of these, in turn, the largest and most celebrated were the two major facilities, of five, in Rome; i.e., the Circus Maximus and the Circus Flaminius. The Circus Maximus was c. 140 meters/153 yards in overall width, c. 620 meters/678 yards in overall length; its floor was c. 79 meters/86 yards x c. 580 meters/634 yards; and it could accommodate 150,000 to 200,000 spectators in a single session. The Circus Maximus was a reconstruction of a facility first fashioned in the sixth century B.C.E. and not completed until the reign of Trajan in the early second century C.E. The Circus Flaminius was first constructed in 221 B.C.E. but was not brought to monumental dimension until the reign of Augustus (in the late first century B.C.E.). And the other most significant of the circuses, the fabled Circus of Constantinople, was designed in the reign of Septimus Severus (in the early third century C.E.) but was not completed until the reign of Constantine more than a century later (324-330 C.E.).

The most significant event of the circuses, by a wide margin, was chariot racing although horse racing, equestrian exhibitions in such as intricate movements of horses and desultores (foot-racing that included leaping to and from the backs of horses), as well as theatrical, dancing, and musical performances were also commonly included. The affairs of a racing day were announced in racing programs (tabella) and they customarily began with a solemn parade from outside the arena to within it. The parade consisted in the magistrate (who sponsored and financed the events by either public or private means) at its head followed by becoming youths, chariots/charioteers, commemorative statues, priests, consuls, actors, dancers, and musicians. Twelve to 24 races (although sometimes as many as 50) were typically staged, among men only, over the entire day (sometimes in one session, sometimes in two). Each race was customarily contested over an approximately 5 kilometers/3 miles distance (as many as 14 lengths, or 7 laps, of the hippodrome) among four (although sometimes among as many as twelve) chariots, one representing each of the four factions (White, Red, Green, and Blue). Each chariot was customarily drawn by either two or four (although sometimes by as many as ten) horses and directed by a single charioteer who was clothed in a (short) tunic and helmet and who held to the reins by passing them entirely about his body. The factions, which became the central organizing motif of the circuses, were of various types at various times and locations. Some were private, commercial syndicates that trained charioteers and provided the circuses with entertainers. Some organized themselves as political parties associated with residential areas, militias, and religious orientations. Still others were agencies representing socio-economic class distinctions; the Blues, for instance, were associated with the aristocracy and the Greens with non-aristocratic citizens. And yet others had strictly to do with sporting or theatrical enthusiasms and allegiances. Whatever their type, however, they invited fiercely passionate loyalties and embodied a sharply adversarial sense of rank partisanship. These loyalties and this sense often resulted in corruption, profligate expenditures for horses, trainers, physicians, attendants, and charioteers, gambling disputes, and full-scale riots (such as the extreme spectator violence in Rome in 509 C.E. and in Constantinople in 491, 498, 507, and 532 C.E.; this latter, the so-termed Nika Revolt, killed 30,000 persons). The original factions were the Whites and Reds; the Blues and Greens developed later; and the Whites eventually merged with the Greens, the Reds with the Blues. Spectators typically arranged themselves by faction and class but men and women commonly gathered together and often engaged in amorous intrigues.

In the chariot races themselves, pairings and starting positions were drawn by lot. At the start, attendants opened the gates, or traps (carceres), of the starting grid by drawing a cord attached to them and the race began. The starting gates were staggered along an arc; once the chariots cleared their gate, they were required to keep their "lane" until together passing a "break line." When that was successfully done, the presiding officer of the event, who functioned as the starter, threw a white cloth (mappa) to the track signaling the formal start of the race. The chariots raced around two large posts (meta), one at each end of the arena floor. These posts were customarily about 6 meters/20 feet in diameter; they were elaborately formed and decorated; and they were joined by a low wall (spina or euripus). The races were highly tactical affairs in which charioteers attempted to keep to the inside of the track, to obstruct opponents from achieving advantageous position, to gather information and advice from other horsemen of their faction who rode beside them, and to take strategic assistance from lesser chariots of their faction. In crashes, charioteers cut their reins with daggers in order to save themselves. Attendants gathered loose horses and ministered to fallen charioteers. Laps were counted by placing or tipping egg-shaped or dolphin-shaped objects in/into stipulated positions. The finish was marked by a white line put across the track opposite the turning post at the same end of the arena as the start. A herald waived the faction colors of the victorious chariot and announced the name of the victorious left-hand horse. Ties were re-run and the spectators could demand a recall or re-run by throwing their cloaks into the air. Victorious charioteers occasionally exchanged chariots with the vanquished for a rematch. Owing to the necessities of gambling, three places were recognized and received prizes. The winning charioteer saluted the presiding officer of the event and received a victory palm or crown from him. Leading charioteers were highly regarded and acclaimed and they received extravagant monetary and other material gifts, customarily from wealthy gambling enthusiasts, admiring women, and favorably affected political (including imperial) figures. Many charioteers were slaves who eventually purchased their freedom with prize money. Many were of notably higher station, however; Tiberius, for especially prominent instance, was an accomplished charioteer and Nero was also an avid and successful charioteer, albeit in largely contrived circumstances.

Like the baths and the athletic festivals, the circuses too became progressively less redeeming institutions in the late Empire and thus also fell into imperial and church disfavor. Chariot racing in particular (under the highly significant influence of its factions), but also some other equestrian events (such as horse racing and polo), nonetheless limped on, most notably in the Eastern Empire, in some cases even under imperial and church sanction, until the twelfth century C.E.

The **gladiatorial combats**, or exhibitions (munera), may date in informal terms from the sixth century B.C.E. and in formal terms they date from 264 B.C.E. They developed out of funerary rites for the male aristocracy into secular entertainments which in some cases included women combatants. Like the circuses, these entertainments were enormously popular well before the end of the Republic and they tended to become increasingly dominated by animal-related events throughout the Empire. Also like the circuses, the combats had their incipient origins in Etruscan blood sport and thus tended to the extrinsic orientation entailing violence, ostentation, extravagance, and corruption. Unlike the circuses, however, they were devoted mainly to dual and massed forms of combative activity. The earliest formal combats were staged in forums or on temporary grounds. The major combats of the Empire, however, were conducted in prodigious and luxurious amphitheaters that constituted among the leading architectural achievements of the day. Several hundred of these arenas were constructed throughout the Empire (even on the frontiers), principally as the sites of amusements intended to distract the Roman public for political purposes (games over bread), to expose the Roman public to electoral propaganda, to provide cathartic effect, to commemorate and to perpetuate Roman imperial domination in general and Roman political authorities in particular, to promote Roman myths of martial heroism and sacrifice, and to Romanize the provinces. The greatest of these was the Colosseum in Rome, begun under Vespasian in 72 C.E. and completed under Titus in 80 C.E. The amphitheaters in general, the Colosseum in particular, were impressively elaborate structures. They included subterranean chambers for gladiators and animals, a labyrinth of water pipes for flooding and draining the floor of the arena, and painstaking provisions for spectators (such as enormous awnings to shade them from direct sunlight and devices for spraying them with perfumed water). The Colosseum was c. 156 meters/171 yards in overall width, c. 188 meters/206 yards in overall length; its floor was c. 54 meters/59 yards x c. 86 meters/93 yards; and its area for spectators could accommodate 60,000 to 90,000 persons in a single session.

Some of the combats were conducted on a recurring schedule, others not. Some were done in a single day; others went on for as long as five days. Some included theatrical and musical displays as well as dual and massed forms of combative event; others did not. The affairs of a day at the combats began with a parade of dignitaries to their seated places, followed by a parade of gladiators, preparation of the gladiators for combat, and a trumpet call indicating the commencement of the combats themselves. An elaborate banquet for spectators often followed the completion of the sporting events. The combats were variously financed by public and by private means and variously sponsored by emperors, priests, and wealthy families. The sponsors of the combats also established and maintained organizations and facilities (effectively, schools) for the exceedingly rigorous training of gladiators (most notably, the Ludus Matutinus, Ludus Gallicus, Ludus Dacicus, and Ludus Magnus). Although gladiators were customarily of the underclass, captives, prisoners, and slaves (most memorably, Spartacus, who escaped from the gladiatorial school at Capua [near Naples] in 73 B.C.E., and fervent public advocates of Judaism and Christianity), and were thus "conscripted" to perform in the arena, there were some voluntary enrollments. Even some aristocratic women (most especially in the reigns of Nero and Domitian) and several emperors (most significantly, Caligula, Nero, and Commodus, who is said to have had 735 "successful" contests in the amphitheater) performed in the combats, albeit in the case of emperors under contrived circumstances. Although there were also some voluntary re-enlistments, gladiators customarily served for three years in the arenas, fighting two to three times per year, then served two years in the gladiatorial schools before winning their liberty. Spectators were admitted to the combats without charge and were segregated by class and gender.

The earliest, Republican combats were dual combative events accompanied by orchestral music, three to 60 pairs comprising a session, in which a gladiator opposed another in such as wrestling, boxing (with caestus), or armed battle (greaves, shields, and helmet). The victor received a palm in the arena and was later awarded money and precious objects. If the vanquished survived the contest, the sponsor of the event, often in consultation with spectators, decided if the beaten man was to be spared or put to death. If put to death, his throat was ceremonially cut, he was further struck and burned to assure his demise, and he was then carried away by attendants on a stretcher or dragged away by a horse. Sometimes both the victor and the vanquished survived by indecision. The tendency in the Republican combats was to spare; the tendency in the Imperial combats was otherwise. Some Imperial munera were altogether without mercy; gladiators were whipped to encourage aggression and only victory saved a combatant's life. In the Empire, many innovations on the theme of Republican dual events were fashioned. These innovations most importantly included the use of at least fifteen categories of weapon (different weapons always opposed one another), with and without coats of mail, with and without nets; designed mismatches between an armed and an unarmed (usually a criminal) gladiator; fighting from chariots with lances, tridents, and lassos, without shields; massed boxing contests; massed war battles among infantry and cavalry (horse and elephant) units; massed naval battles (naumachiae) among flotillas; and wild beast battles (venationes). Between 10,000 and 20,000 persons commonly contested massed events, typically to the death. The venationes took many unseemly forms, various beasts opposing one another and various beasts opposing humans. The most widely practiced of these entailed:

- tethered animals (usually bears or bulls) opposing one another;
- a mounted animal (usually an elephant) opposing a tethered animal (usually a bull);
- lions opposing tigers, bulls opposing boars, dogs opposing deer, lions opposing deer, bears opposing pythons, bears opposing seals, lions opposing crocodiles, and bulls opposing panthers;
- all order of other beast opposing one another (giraffes, rhinoceros, hippopotamuses, hyenas, leopards, ostriches, and eagles);
- armed humans opposing all order of beast;
- unarmed humans (usually criminals) opposing all order of beast;
- humans leaping from horse mount to the back of bulls and attempting to throw them;
- beasts making intricate movements at the direction of humans; and

- condemned people stripped of their clothing and either chained to a stationary post or given weapons for faint defense, then killed by beasts (usually lions, bears, tigers, bulls, or leopards).

Thousands of animals were typically used in a single session of the venationes. They were often taunted to enrage them to combat. Those that were not killed in the course of the events themselves were frequently killed following the events by persons armed with bows and arrows, swords, or lances. Approximately 9000 beasts were massacred, for prominent instance, in the inaugural celebration of the Colosseum.

The Theodosian edicts of the late fourth and early fifth centuries C.E., which were aimed principally at the athletic festivals, also had residual affects on the baths, the circuses, and the gladiatorial combats. The merciless brutality and the uncivilized savagery of the combats in particular eventually brought them imperial rebuke, church condemnation, and abolition. The gladiatorial schools were closed by order of the Western Emperor, Honorius, in 399 C.E.; the last munera were staged in 440 C.E.; and the last venatio was conducted in either 498 or 523 C.E. With their passing and the passing of the Western Empire, the history of ancient sport as well as the history of ancient culture broadly defined was done. So-termed medieval civilization (the culture of the Middle Ages) then came to replace the ancient equation.

Mayan, Aztecan, and Incan Culture and Sport

The major ancient cultural developments of the New World occurred significantly later than those of the Old. These developments were owed mainly to the Mayan, Aztecan, and Incan societies of central and South America. The **Mayan culture** was of Penutian cultural and linguistic character and it unfolded in the central regions of central America (i.e., in the modern nation-states of Guatemala [most notably, Tikal], British Honduras/Belize, and Honduras [most notably, Copan] as well as in the Yucatan peninsula of Mexico [most notably, Palenque, Uxmal, and Chichen Itza]). From c. 300 C.E., the Mayan peoples of these regions fashioned an exceptional culture out of tribal traditions that may have dated from as early as c. 1000 B.C.E. This culture was marked by a form of pictographic writing, advanced arithmetic calculation and astronomical observation, an animistic religion that included human sacrifice, an elaborate system of social classes (including slaves), a joint model of land ownership, a conquest form of tribal empire, an extensive network of bartered trade, a monumental (but proportionate) type of temple architecture, and a singular style of architectural sculpture. Mayan civilization came to its highest mark in the seventh, eighth, and ninth centuries C.E., then fell to gradual decline likely owing to agricultural failures, civil wars, and challenges from contiguous societies. The calamities of the fifteenth century C.E. ended its distinguished development an approximate century before the arrival of Spanish forces.

The **Aztecan culture** was of Aztecan-Tanoan cultural and linguistic character and it was centered in what is now south-central Mexico (most notably, Tenochtitlan, near modern Mexico City). From c. 1200 C.E., the Aztecan peoples of this region fashioned an exceptional culture out of tribal traditions that may have dated from as early as the ninth century C.E. This culture was marked by a form of pictographic writing, advanced arithmetic calculation and astronomical observation, an animistic religion that included human sacrifice, an inflexible system of social classes (including slaves), an accomplished program of collective agricultural production and bartered trade, a conquest form of tribal empire, and memorable achievements in engineering (most notably, road and bridge construction), metal technology, monumental architecture, sculpture, and music. Aztecan civilization flourished most strikingly in the fourteenth and fifteenth centuries C.E.; it was conquered by invading Spanish forces in the sixteenth century C.E.

The **Incan culture** was of Andean-Equatorial cultural and linguistic character and it matured in the central-western regions of South America (i.e., in the modern nation-states of Peru [most notably, Cuzco and Machu Picchu], Ecuador, Bolivia, Chile, and Argentina). From c. 1100 C.E., the Incan peoples of these regions fashioned an exceptional culture out of indeterminately older tribal traditions. This culture was marked by the absence of writing and private property, a conquest, theocratic, and welfare state (that included slaves), an animistic religion that included human sacrifice, a highly accomplished construction technology in respect to cities, roads, bridges, and irrigation projects, a collective program of agriculture, an efficient system of communication that made extensive use of runners and carriers, and a masterful style of small-scale sculpture and of architecture. Incan civilization reached its most distinguished stage in the fifteenth century C.E.; it was conquered by invading Spanish forces in the sixteenth century C.E.

The **sport of these cultures** (and of other prominent New World cultures such as the Olmecan, Teotihuacan, and Toltecan cultures) was dominated by team ball games.[106] Such games varied greatly

62

among these cultures and they varied also greatly across the manifold periods of each culture's development. They nonetheless customarily entailed highly vigorous competition between two teams of from two to as many as 1000 participants and they were sometimes contested on large and elaborate courts or fields. Some allowed the use of the arms-hands and/or legs-feet in order to advance the ball; some required that the ball be advanced by other than the arms-hands or legs-feet (that is, by the hips, buttocks, knees, chest, and/or shoulders). Still others advanced the ball by means of devices strapped to the arms-hands (basket-like devices); some used devices held in the hands (stick-like devices) in order to advance the ball. Some included only men, others only women, and yet others both. Some were strictly games of territorial acquisition; others defined "scoring" in terms of a special target or goal-like structure. Some involved governing officials and elaborate costumes (including protective equipment), some not, and some were attended by large gatherings of spectators, some not. Arguably the most widely known of these were the Olmecan game, ullamaliztli, the Mayan game, pok-ta-pok, and the Aztecan game, tlachtli.

The most elaborate and formal games were played in central America in the C.E., by which time they had clearly passed over the boundary from gentile society to the barbarism of civil society. These games were played between two teams usually of seven players to a side on oblong fields of impressive dimension (up to 150 meters/165 yards x 75 meters/80 yards), sometimes widened at the ends, sometimes with one end lower than the other, sometimes divided into halves or quarters, and usually with walls on all boundaries (very high walls on the sides, lower walls on the ends). A stone ring was customarily mounted in the vertical plane high on the middle of each of the side walls; these were the goals through which the ball was to pass in order to count as a score. The ball itself was of manifold dimension, mass, and composition but was typically of solid rubber and weighed less than three kilograms. The games served several significant religious and secular purposes. They were variously characterized as a violent and literal struggle between the cosmic forces of light and dark, life and death, plenty and scarcity, fertility and the barren, pleasing and displeasing futures and they were thought as well a rich source of recreation. The stakes in them were high; the victors often beheaded the vanquished or removed their beating hearts; the gods could be served only by the sacrifice of life itself. Gambling was also common and was likewise practiced over precious territory, even one's freedom and possession of one's children. These games were too widely commemorated in stone and terracotta sculpture and in vase and wall painting. They were played in a tamer form in western and northwestern Mexico into the early twentieth century.

Perhaps the most notable modern sporting derivative of the team ball games of the ancient Americas, however, is lacrosse, which was known to the North American Indians who played it most widely and who played it in its most organized form as 'baggataway'. Lacrosse evolved mainly out of the game-playing conventions of the Algonquian, Cherokee, and Iroquois peoples of the eastern woodlands of North America (i.e., in the eastern reaches of the modern nation-states of Canada and the United States of America). These precursors of lacrosse were customarily played between two very large (75-1000 members) and not always equal teams, on very large and frequently shifting fields of play, with the customary sticks for catching, throwing, and carrying the ball, according to rules in which scoring was assessed by advancing the ball beyond a specified boundary, amid extensive ceremony, and with the intent to damage opposing players sufficiently to discourage their continued participation in the contest.

MEDIEVAL CIVILIZATION AND SPORT

The Middle Ages are customarily taken to embody the approximate millennium from the conquest of the Western Roman Empire by Germanic tribes in 476 to the conquest of the Eastern Roman Empire by the Ottoman Turks in 1453.[107] They are sometimes further distinguished by their earlier and their later phases: the early Middle Ages, also in some contexts referred to as the Dark Ages, from the fifth to the tenth centuries and the late Middle Ages, aspects of which are also in some contexts referred to as the proto-Renaissance, from the tenth to the fifteenth centuries. The early Middle Ages, unsurprisingly, had its roots deep in antiquity; the late Middle Ages very significantly foreshadowed modern civilization.

Early Medieval Culture and Sport

With the dissolution of the Roman state in the west, the governing authority of Europe passed variously to northern and eastern tribal cultures; most notably, to Germanic, Slavic, and nomadic, mounted, Eurasian such cultures. The epoch of the Middle Ages is significantly defined by the assimilation of the remnants of the ancient Graeco-Roman and Celtic worlds into the Germanic, Slavic, and Eurasian cultures of medieval civilization. Early medieval culture is mainly characterized by:

- the chaotic intersection of these cultures with one another, with what remained of Celtic society in the west, and with what remained of the Roman Empire (mainly, the Byzantine Empire) in the east, each with its own novel educational, artistic, and sporting tendencies;[108]
- the development of a new political, economic, and social circumstance indicative of the decentralization of governing authority in Europe; that is, the development of the feudal and chivalric orders, together with accompanying educational, artistic, and sporting practices; and
- the philosophical and institutional maturation, as well as the sharply increasing influence, of the three major personalistic and monotheistic world religions, Judaism, Christianity, and Islam, each with its own novel educational, artistic, and sporting tendencies.

The **Germanic tribes** of the early Middle Ages (effectively, the fifth to the tenth centuries) were of Indo-European cultural and linguistic character. They lived as clans in small villages dominated by agricultural, animal husbandic, and related activity; they traded vigorously among themselves; and they arranged themselves in a tight social hierarchy from nobles (who were thought aligned with the gods) to freemen with full political rights, subject members of related tribes with limited political rights, and slaves (prisoners taken in war) without political rights. Like all barbarians, they were governed by oral, not by written, traditions. In the Germanic case, however, may be nonetheless found the germ of modern international law, the jury system of legal practice, the notion that leadership may accrue to any able man, and the view that nobles issue propositions which may be either accepted or rejected by freemen. Until Christianized by missionary initiatives, beginning in the fourth century (in which circumstance it achieved higher cultural levels and joined broader cultural movements), the Germanic religious orientation tended to a form of animism rooted in agricultural activity, principally in fertility cults practiced in festivals. These festivals most significantly honored such as Odin (the supreme god) and Thor (the god of farming) and they were conducted in sacred, natural groves governed by oracles. Until the Franks cultivated still broader and more exacting artistic styles, the other leading Germanic tribes (most especially, the Anglo-Saxons and the Vikings) developed rich, but circumscribed, visual traditions.

The Germanic migrations into Europe from the east began, in their earliest form, in the late third century B.C.E. These migrations were forced by population increases, land shortages, climatic shifts, advances of the mounted peoples, and a taste for warring adventure. The most notable of these were those of:

- the Goths, who had come to what is now Poland by c. 150 and to what is now Ukraine by c. 200 and who had divided into eastern (Ostrogoths) and western (Visigoths) factions, also by c. 200;
- the Ostrogoths, who had come to the region of the Black Sea by c. 200, to Pannonia (what is now Austria and Hungary) in 375, to the Balkans in 397, and to what is now Italy, where, mainly under Theodoric the Great (c. 454-526; r. 493-526), they defeated and murdered Odoacer at Ravenna and established the Ostrogothic Kingdom in 488; they then extended their influence to the south until defeated by the Byzantine Empire of Justinian in 552;
- the Visigoths, who remained in Ukraine until 376 when they migrated to Pannonia and the Balkans; who defeated the Romans at the Battle of Adrianople (in Thrace) in 378; who, mainly under Alaric I (c. 370-410; r. 394-410), pillaged in the Balkans from 395 to 401, in Italy from 401 to 410 (conquest of Rome, 410), in what is now Spain in 409, and in Gaul (what is now France) in 419; who established the Visigothic Kingdom in Gaul, 419-507, which prospered most under Euric (d. 484; r. 466-484) and Alaric II (d. 507; r. 484-507); and who established the Visigothic Kingdom in Spain, 507-7ll, which ended with the defeat of Roderic (d. 711; r. 710-711) by the Islamic Arabs under Tariq (fl. early eighth century) in 711;
- the Vandals, who had come to what is now Slovakia and Transylvania (Romania) by c. 400, to what are now Spain and Portugal in 409, and to northern Africa (what are now Morocco, Algeria, and Tunisia) in 429, where they established the Vandal Kingdom, 429-534, which seized Rome in 455, which was most memorably led by Genseric (c. 400-477; r. 428-477), and which was defeated by the Byzantine Empire of Justinian in 535;
- the Lombards, who had come to what is now northern Germany, to Scandinavia, and to Pannonia by c. 400 and who established the Kingdom of the Lombards throughout Italy (except for Byzantine hegemony over Ravenna, Rome, Naples, and Sicily), 568-774, until defeated by (and merged with) the Franks under Charlemagne in 774;
- the Burgundians, who had come to Poland and to what was until recently Czechoslovakia by c. 400, to Germany in 407, and to France and what is now Switzerland in 443, where they established the Kingdom of the Burgundians, 443-534, until defeated by the Franks under Clothar I in 534;
- the Suevi, who migrated from Germany and Poland to Spain and Portugal in 406 where they established the Kingdom of the Suevi, 406-575, until defeated by the Visigoths in 575;
- the Alamanni, who migrated from Germany to Austria and Switzerland in c. 475 until defeated by the Franks under Clovis I in 496;
- the Gepids, who migrated from Poland to Pannonia and Transylvania in c. 400 where they established the Gepid Kingdom until destroyed by the Lombards in 568;
- the Jutes, who migrated from what is now Denmark to what is now England in c. 450;
- the Angles, who also migrated from Denmark to England in c. 450;
- the Saxons, who migrated from what is now Netherlands to England in c. 450;
- the Vikings, who migrated from Scandinavia to England in c. 790; and
- the Franks, arguably the most advanced and influential of the Germanic tribes.

Of these, in turn, the Ostrogoths, Visigoths, Vandals, Lombards, Burgundians, Suevi, Alamanni, and Gepids were all taken over by either the Byzantine Empire, the Islamic Arabs, or the Franks, or they were taken over by one another, then by either the Byzantine Empire, the Islamic Arabs, or the Franks. Only the Jutes, Angles, Saxons, Vikings, and Franks developed independent political entities that survived the early Middle Ages.

The **Jutes**, **Angles**, and **Saxons** arrived in England from Denmark and Netherlands in the mid-fifth century, approximately one-half century after the Romans had abandoned the region in c. 400. They displaced the Celtic peoples left by the Romans (and in a sense they merged Celtic, Roman, and Germanic forms of cultural development), principally to what are now Scotland and Wales, events portrayed in the medieval Celt epics, <u>Sir Gawain and the Green Knight</u>, written in the fourteenth century, and <u>Le Morte d'Arthur</u>, written in the fifteenth century. The Christianization of England too occurred in this time; it is mainly owed to the missionary zeal of St. Augustine of Canterbury (d. 605; r. 601-605), the first Archbishop of Canterbury, dispatched in 597 by Pope Gregory I/Gregory the Great (c. 540-604; r. 590-604) to convert the Anglo-Saxons. The earliest, extant, English literature is also owed to the first several centuries of Anglo-Saxon rule in England, the anonymous Anglo-Saxon epic, <u>Beowulf</u>, likely written in the tenth century, portraying events two to three centuries earlier. The Jutes established themselves in Kent (in southeastern England); the Angles, in

Northumbria, Mercia, and East Anglia (in north-central and northeastern England); and the Saxons, in Essex, Sussex, and Wessex (in south-central England).

In the late eighth century, c. 790, the Viking, or Norman (Northmen), raids on Britain began. These raids came mainly from Danish (as distinct from Norwegian and Swedish) Vikings; they were caused principally by overpopulation in Scandinavia, by a growing dissatisfaction among prominent Scandinavian nobles in respect to royal prerogative over them, and by a taste for warring adventure; and they were made possible in technological terms by the development of the keeled long-boat (with reinforced bottom and mast), as distinct from the slower, less agile, and unreinforced ancient vessel. From the earliest Norman incursions in the late eighth century to the final Norman Conquest of England in the mid-eleventh century, the Anglo-Saxons opposed the invaders with mixed success. King Egbert of Wessex (c. 775-839; r. 802-839) attained dominion over the Anglo-Saxon states in 827 and briefly repelled the Viking raids. Systematic Viking conquests nonetheless began in 866 and England was governed by Danes from 870 to 926. King Alfred the Great of Wessex (849-899; r. 871-899) achieved victory over the Danes at Edington (near London) in 878 and seized London itself in 885 but he never succeeded in expelling the Danes altogether. Alfred is also justifiably well remembered for his having collected and ordered the laws of his realm; for his having promoted the education of youths and nobles at court; for his translations of the work of the leading historian of Anglo-Saxon life, St. Bede/the Venerable Bede (c. 673-735), mainly the Ecclesiastical History of the English Nation; and for his athletic temperament and skills as an accomplished archer. The Danish ambitions continued to be held in abeyance by Alfred's immediate successors: Edward the Elder (c. 870-924; r. 899-924), Ethelstan (d. 939; r. 924-939), and Edgar (943-975; r. 959-975). The Danes defeated Ethelred II/Ethelred the Unready (968-1016; r. 978-1013), however, and conquered all of England in 1013. Canute the Great of Denmark (c. 995-1035; r. 1016-1035) became King of England, Denmark, and Norway between 1016 and 1028. Edward the Confessor (c. 1004-1066; r. 1042-1066), son of Ethelred II, half-brother of Canute's son and successor, and last of the acknowledged Saxon kings of England, renewed the Saxon line and ascended the throne in 1042, came into conflict with the native Anglo-Saxon leader, Earl Godwin of Wessex (c. 990-1053), and was succeeded by Godwin's son, Harold (c. 1022-1066; r. 1066) in 1066. Harold, in a dispute over the throne, was, in turn, defeated and killed by Duke William of Normandy/William I/William the Conqueror (c. 1027-1087; r. 1066-1087), cousin of Edward the Confessor, at the Battle of Hastings (near Dover) in 1066. The final stage of the Norman Conquest and the first stage in the development of modern Britain had thus begun.

Although typically absorbed in cultural respects by the native populations they had subjugated, the Vikings dominated European trade from the eighth to the eleventh centuries and they had, of course, an especially profound affect on the political and cultural life of Scandinavia in this period as well as a very significant influence on early medieval political circumstances in Britain, in Ireland, in coastal western and northwestern Continental Europe, and in the north Atlantic. The **Danish Vikings** established a substantial kingdom, the Kingdom of Denmark (c. 935-1286), under King Gorm the Old (d. 945; r. c. 935-945) in c. 935; the Kingdom was Christianized under Sven Forked Beard (d. 1014; r. 985-1014); and, under Canute the Great, it subjugated England (in 1013-1016) and Norway (in 1028). The Danish Vikings most significantly raided Britain and plundered the coastal western and southwestern regions of Continental Europe (effectively what are now Netherlands, Belgium, France, Portugal, Spain, and Italy). These actions brought them into routine conflict with the Carolingian Empire in northwestern Europe, with the Islamic Arabs in Portugal, Spain, and Sicily, and with the Byzantine Empire in southern Italy. The Danish Vikings established "permanent" states, most notably in England (variously from the ninth century as has been said) and in Normandy (northwestern France in 911).

The **Norwegian Vikings** established the first substantial kingdom in Scandinavia, the Kingdom of Norway (c. 900-1280), under Harold I/Harold Fairhair (c. 850-c. 933; r. 872-c. 933) in c. 900; the Kingdom was Christianized under Olaf II/St. Olaf (c. 995-1030; r. 1016-1028); it was subjugated by Denmark in 1028; it expelled the Danes from 1035 to 1047; and it was defeated in an attempt to wrest England from Harold in 1066. The Norwegian Vikings most significantly raided what are now Scotland and Ireland and the territories of the north Atlantic (effectively, what are now Iceland [which they discovered in 860], Greenland [which they "discovered," under Eric the Red {fl. late tenth century}, in 984], and Vinland, or America [likely Newfoundland, which they "discovered," under Leif Ericsson {fl. early eleventh century}, son of Eric the Red, in c. 1002). These actions brought them into routine conflict the Celtic tribes of the North Sea. The Norwegian Vikings established a "permanent" state in Iceland where the earliest canons of Norse (and Germanic) mythology, the poetic Edda Elder (fashioned in c. 900, anonymously written in the thirteenth century, and included accounts of the origin and end of the world, of the leading Germanic gods [Odin and Thor], of the leading Germanic heroes and heroines [Siegfried and Brunhilde], and of the leading Germanic villains [the

Nibelungen]), were framed and where the earliest parliament, or assembly, in Europe, the Althing, was organized (in 930).

The **Swedish Vikings** established a substantial kingdom, the Kingdom of Sweden (995-1290), under Olaf Skutkonung (d. 1022; r. 995-1022), in 995 and also accepted Christianity under Skutkonung. They most significantly raided Britain and the coastal northern and northeastern regions of Continental Europe (effectively, what are now Poland, the Baltic states, Finland, and Russia). These actions brought them into routine conflict with the Slavic, Baltic, and Ural-Altaic (Finnic) tribes of the region. The Swedish Vikings established the earliest, unified Russian state under Rurik (d. 879; r. 865-879) in the north (about Novgorod) in 865. The descendants of Rurik ruled in Russia into the late sixteenth century. Oleg the Wise (d. 912; r. 879-912) united the northern tribes (about Novgorod) with the southern tribes (about Kiev) in 882 and made Kiev the capital of the Russian state. Igor (d. 945; r. 912-945) encouraged trade with the west and opened the state to Christian influence. Yaroslav the Wise (978-1054; r. 1019-1054) further unified the state and expanded it to the west, south, and east; he made the first compilation of Russian law; and he was also an important patron of architecture, painting, literature, and music. After 1054, the central state weakened and dissolved into principalities. In this form, it became vulnerable to attacks by the nomadic, mounted, Eurasian peoples, most particularly thirteenth-century Mongols.

The **Franks** had come to what are now Netherlands, France, and Belgium by the middle of the third century; they there established the Frankish Kingdom, variously under the Merovingians and the Carolingians. The Merovingian unification of the Kingdom was first achieved by Clovis I (466-511; r. 482-511) at the conclusion of Roman rule; it effectively conjoined Roman and Frankish culture. Clovis converted to Christianity in 498 and conquered adjoining tribes (most notably, the Alamanni in 496, the Burgundians in c. 500, and the Visigoths in France in 507). Clothar I (d. 561; r. 558-561) again subjugated the Burgundians (at the Battle of Autun) in 532-534 and the Kingdom fell episodically toward and from unification over the next approximate century and one-half. The state again approached full unification under Clothar II (d. 629; r. 613-629) and Dagobert I (c. 612-639; r. 629-639) but then lapsed to partition and was variously governed by the administrative stewards of the provincial sovereigns. Principal among these, Carolingian stewards were Pepin II (d. 714; r. 679-714), who again effected a measure of political unity, and his son, Charles Martel (c. 688-741; r. 714-741), father of Pepin III and grandfather of Charlemagne, who defeated the Spanish governor of the Moors, Abd ar-Rahman (d. 732; r. 721-732), at the Battles of Tours and Poitiers in 732, thus ending Islamic Arab expansion in Europe.

The last of the by-then-titular Merovingian monarchs was deposed in 743 and the first Carolingian in sole possession of the throne was installed in 751. The **Carolingian Empire** which followed, 751-814, constituted the most remarkable Germanic culture of the early Middle Ages. It showed the way out of the characteristically early medieval equation to the culture of the late Middle Ages and beyond. It was in this respect more so a transitional than a distinctly early medieval development. Pepin III/Pepin the Short (c. 714-768; r. 751-768), the first king of all Franks, won full papal endorsement by successfully wresting Ravenna and successfully protecting Rome from the Lombards in 754 and 756 and by returning them to the Papacy (as the Papal States) under Pope Stephen III (d. 757; r. 752-757). Pepin III was succeeded by his son, Charles I/Charles the Great/Charlemagne (c. 742-814; r. 768-814), arguably the most significant political and cultural figure of the early Middle Ages. Charlemagne expanded the Kingdom to the north and east in the Saxon Wars of the Low Countries (772-804), the wars against the Kingdom of the Lombards in Italy (773-774), the wars against the Islamic Arabs (the Moors) at the Spanish frontier in 778 (in which the Count of Roland, a commander and nephew of Charlemagne and the hero of the medieval epic, The Song of Roland [written in French in the eleventh or twelfth century], was killed), the wars against the Slavs (789-812), and the wars against the Avars, a nomadic, mounted, Eurasian tribe (791-796). In the end, Charlemagne reigned, by means of newly codified laws, highly efficient administration, and vigorous trade practices within Europe and between Europe and the Orient, over an enormous empire, an empire which included modern France, Germany, northern Italy, Austria, Switzerland, Netherlands, Belgium, Luxembourg, Slovenia, Serbia, Croatia, Hungary, Romania, Czech Republic, Slovakia, Ukraine, and Poland. He was crowned Emperor of the Western Roman Empire (a distinction that he had revived) by Pope Leo III (d. 816; r. 795-816) in 800; he thus became the secular protector of the Christian Church appointed by God (the Holy Ghost), effectively the temporal head of the Church and the ruling authority, the sacred monarch, of the predecessor state (the institutional basis) of the Holy Roman Empire of the mid-tenth century; he presided over the mass Christianization of western Continental Europe; and he was formally recognized as the Emperor of the West by the Eastern (Byzantine) Emperor in the Treaty of Aix-la-Chapelle (Aachen) in 812, an act which constituted the final separation of the Eastern and Western Roman Empires.

Charlemagne made Aix-la-Chapelle the political and cultural capital of the Carolingian Empire and the center of a vital intellectual and artistic revival, the **Carolingian Renaissance**. This revival was spawned by Charlemagne's summons of prominent scholars from England, Ireland, Spain, and Italy to his court, to the court at Aix-la-Chapelle. The most notable of these "scholars of the court," Alcuin of York (c. 730-804), directed the Palace School in Aix-la-Chapelle from 782 to 801 and the Cathedral School in Tours from 796 to 804. These schools became the model for other like institutions throughout the realm. They, and the courtly/monastic communities they embodied, developed into accomplished institutions of learning, fervent advocates of scientific inquiry, and effective conveyors of the literary traditions of classical and Christian antiquity. The principal vehicles of learning and culture in these schools were the liberal arts (artes liberales), studies worthy of free men, as distinct from the arts of the artisan (artes mechanicae). The liberal arts were themselves comprised of the trivium (grammar, rhetoric, and dialectics) and the quadrivium (arithmetic, geometry, astronomy, and music). Some informal types of physical recreation were nonetheless practiced by the students and the teachers of these schools; most notably, archery, running, swimming, throwing, wrestling, and ball games. Charlemagne himself is said to have been an excellent swimmer as well as an enthusiast of hawking and hunting.

The artistic images of the Carolingian Renaissance retained a hint of classical antiquity but, not entirely unlike the images of other early Christian and Byzantine cultures, they also tended predominantly to formalized and schematic patterns of religious (spiritual) abstraction in which the transcendental clearly dominated the natural and in which the beauty of natural phenomena as such, including the human body, was explicitly obscured. This tendency was most memorably embodied in mosaics and mural paintings now largely lost, in illuminated (illustrated) manuscripts, and in religious architecture; there was no free-standing sculpture in the Carolingian tradition. The most remarkable of the illuminated manuscripts were the Coronation Gospels (c. 795-810), Ebbo Gospels (816-841), Utrecht Psalter (c. 820-832), Lindau Gospels (c. 870), and Bible of Charles the Bald (grandson of Charlemagne; c. 875-877). Roman architecture was the model for Carolingian episcopal and monastery churches; most notably, the central-plan, "Palatine Chapel of Charlemagne," Aachen (792-805), designed by Odo Metz (fl. eighth century), and the basilica-plan, "Monastery of St. Gall, Switzerland" (c. 819).

On the death of Charlemagne in 814, the crown passed to his son, Louis I/Louis the Pious (778-840; r. 814-840), then to the sons of Louis as the Empire was formally partitioned in the Treaty of Verdun of 843. Further partitions led to the establishment of a western kingdom that effectively became the state of France, an eastern kingdom that effectively became the state of Germany, and a southern kingdom that effectively became the state of Italy; this, by the Treaty of Messen in 870 and the Treaty of Ribemont in 880. By 911, tribal duchies had become the dominant form of political organization, the Kingdom of Burgundy and the Kingdom of Normandy had achieved autonomy, and the Franks were unable to defend against intruding enemies (mainly, Hungarians and Normans). Although the Empire was nominally preserved into the late tenth century (in France), it was effectively done at least one-half century earlier as towns declined, rural (agricultural) economies became dominant, trade languished, barter increased, and the feudal system deepened.

The **Saxon emperors** (919-1024) were elevated to the throne by Franks and Saxons and effectively succeeded the Carolingians as the ruling agents of the German Empire in 919. Henry I (c. 876-936; r. 919-936), first of the Saxon emperors, variously gained and lost territories. Otto I/Otto the Great (912-973; r. 936-973), son of Henry, formally established the Holy Roman Empire in 962 under the same basic terms as Charlemagne had secured with the Papacy, brought Burgundy and Italy back into the German Empire, and secured the eastern frontiers of the Empire (mainly against the Poles, Bohemians, and Hungarians). Ongoing disputes with the Islamic Arabs, Bohemians, Byzantines, Danes, Italians, and Poles marked the reigns of the remaining Saxon emperors: Otto II (955-983; r. 973-983), Otto III (980-1002; r. 983-1002), and Henry II (973-1024; r. 1002-1024). The art of the Saxon epoch, Ottonian art, was renowned. It resembled Carolingian, (other) early Christian, and Byzantine tendencies in respect to its emphasis on spiritual abstraction and impersonal disembodiment. The Saxon state became the leading Germanic interpreter of painting, sculpture, and architecture in the tenth and eleventh centuries. Although virtually all Ottonian painting (in the form of church murals) has been destroyed, some illuminated manuscripts have survived; most notably, the Gospel Lectionary of Henry II (1002-1024), Bamberg Commentary (early eleventh century), Hitda Codex (early eleventh century), and Uta Codex (1002-1025). In sculpture, the "Crucifix of Archbishop Gero," Cathedral of Cologne (969-976) and the bronze doors (depicting scenes from the Old and New Testaments) of the Cathedral of Hildersheim (c. 1015) are most memorable. The Ottonian aesthetic developed its most novel perceptions in architecture, however; mainly in the construction of monastic buildings. The best of these – "St.

Michael's," Hildersheim (1001-1033) — were in the form of variously shaped (cubes, pyramids, octagons, cylinders) masonry block masses with uniquely arranged windows (that allowed light to pass easily into the interior) and with very assertive, multiplanar, exterior contours.

The German Empire again expanded to the south and the east under the **Frankish Salian emperors** (1024-1125), who were elected to succeed the Saxons in 1024. Conrad II (c. 990-1039; r. 1024-1039) strengthened the hold of the Empire over Burgundy and northern Italy. Henry III (1017-1056; r. 1039-1056) brought Hungary and Bohemia into the Empire. Henry IV (1050-1106; r. 1056-1105) waged largely successful disputes with the Saxons and with the Papacy. And Henry V (1081-1125; r. 1105-1125) achieved victories over Bohemia and Italy.

These Germanic developments were the dominant influence in western Europe throughout the early Middle Ages. In the east (i.e., in Asia Minor, the near Middle East, and southwestern Europe), however, what remained of the eastern Roman Empire, in the form of the **Byzantine Empire**, variously survived the entire millennium of the medieval epoch and preserved much of the ancient classical, the ancient Graeco-Roman, tradition that was under siege in the west, including the athletic festivals (briefly into the early sixth century) and the circuses (into the twelfth century). The chaotic upheavals of the fifth century, which undid the Western Roman Empire, were successfully resisted by the Byzantine state. The tribes of barbarians which threatened the east were largely driven into the west, the great cities of the east (principally, Alexandria as the center of agriculture, Antioch as the center of trade, and Constantinople as the intellectual and cultural center) were preserved, and a measure of stability was restored in the east. After codifying Roman law in Byzantium (529) and ending formal conflict with the neo-Persian Sassanid Empire in Iran (532), Justinian I/Justinian the Great (483-565; r. 527-565) and his wife, Theodora (508-548; r. 527-548), reclaimed, for a brief period, much of the western part of the Roman Empire from the Vandals in north Africa (535), from the Ostrogoths in Italy (552), and from the Visigoths in southern Spain (554). Justinian's reign, arguably the most significant in the entire 1000-year history of the Byzantine Empire, was marked by:

- ongoing heretical disputes with the Church having mainly to do with the variously divine and human character of Christ;
- ongoing disputes about the proper relation of the Church (and its leadership, the Pope) to the state (and its leadership, the Emperor);
- the Nika insurrection against Justinian of 532, a conflict involving the Green and Blue factions, respectively associated with non-aristocratic and aristocratic social classes and associated as well with the related, chariot racing events of the circuses;
- the great financial costs of the western campaigns, the insurrection, and an extravagant court, all of which brought increased taxation, social discord, and autocratic suppression; and
- the most extraordinary developments in early Byzantine (and early Christian) art.

The most accomplished architecture (and accompanying mosaics) of the early Middle Ages were owed to the "Age of Justinian:" the central-plan "San Vitale," Ravenna (c. 525-547), the basilica-plan "Sant' Appollinaire in Classe," Ravenna (c. 533-549), and the consummate creation of Anthemius of Tralles (fl. sixth century) and Isidorus of Miletus (fl. sixth century), the combination central-plan and basilica-plan, "Hagia Sophia" (Holy Wisdom), Constantinople (c. 532-537). Somewhat like earlier Roman-Christian and later Carolingian and Ottonian images, the most notable mosaics in these three magnificent churches — "Christ Enthroned Between Angels and Saints" (c. 525-547), "Emperor Justinian and Attendants" (c. 547), and "Empress Theodora and Attendants" (c. 547) in "San Vitale;" the half-dome, apse mosaic (c. 533-549) in "Sant'Appollinaire in Classe;" and the "Virgin and Christ Enthroned" (ninth century) in "Hagia Sophia" — tend to a form of spiritual abstraction in which there is little concern for real space, in which there is hardly a hint of movement or of robust body, in which figures are stylized and depicted ungrounded in strictly frontal plane, and in which a geometric sense of the natural is dominated by transcendental effect.

The history of the Byzantine Empire after Justinian was uneven. Italy was lost to the Lombards in 568. Maurice (c. 539-602; r. 582-602) re-established prerogative over Rome and Ravenna in the late sixth century. The Balkan peninsula was surrendered to Slavs in the first half of the seventh century. Islamic Arabs made significant gains against the Empire in Palestine, Syria, and north Africa throughout the second quarter of the seventh century. Avars, Slavs, and Persians made unsuccessful attacks on Constantinople throughout the seventh century. Byzantine power in Italy collapsed with the fall of Ravenna to the Lombards in 751, with the Papal-Carolingian alliance of the mid-750s, with the eastern recognition of Charlemagne as Western Emperor in 812, and with the provisional separation of the Eastern Orthodox Church (centered in Constantinople) and the Western Roman Church (centered in Rome) by Patriarch Photius of Constantinople (820-891) in 867. The period from 867 to 1025 (effectively, the period of the Macedonian Dynasty) constituted the pinnacle of Byzantine imperial power and the state's bureaucratization of political and economic affairs. In this time, Byzantine hegemony was restored in bits of Italy, in Crete and Cyprus, in Syria and Palestine, and in the Balkans despite Islamic Arab gains in Sicily and Greece; Bulgarian, Russian, and Islamic Arab attacks on the Empire were repulsed; and the Orthodox faith was disseminated successfully among the Slavs (most notably in Russia). The apex of these achievements was reached in the reigns of Constantine VII (905-959; r. 913-959) and Basil II (c. 958-1025; r. 976-1025). Thereafter, feudalization and so fragmentation of the Empire deepened, foreign advances on it increasingly succeeded, and a slow, but inexorable, decline of it ensued. The art of the Macedonian Renaissance (as well as that of the century and one-half prior to the Macedonian Renaissance) was greatly affected by the iconoclastic dispute of the eighth and ninth centuries. This dispute, in which mainly Jewish and Islamic influences were hostile to images as idolatrous and Christian agencies favored them as symbols of enlightenment, was settled against the iconoclasts by Pope Gregory III (d. 741; r. 731-741). The result were brilliant illustrated manuscripts of spiritualistic consequence (most notably, the Joshua Roll and the Paris Psalter, both of the tenth century) and domed monastic churches on the plan of the Greek cross (most notably, the "Katholikon" and "Theotokos" of the Monastery of Hosios Loukas, Phocis, Greece of the early eleventh century).

The other main tribal cultures that significantly affected the course of world history in early medieval Europe were the Slavic and the nomadic, mounted, Eurasian cultures. Like the Germanic tribes, the **Slavic tribes** were of Indo-European cultural and linguistic character; they lived as clans in small villages dominated by agricultural, animal husbandic, and related activity; they traded vigorously among themselves; they arranged themselves in a firm social hierarchy; they were governed by oral, not by written, traditions; and they tended to animism (and the fertility festivals and natural oracles typically associated with animism) in terms of religious sentiment until Christianized by missionary initiative, beginning in the sixth century. They too came into Europe from the east (likely from what is now western Russia by the sixth century) under pressure created by advances of the mounted peoples and they occupied territory east of the Elbe River (i.e., in eastern Europe) that had been earlier vacated by German migration. The most notable of these tribes were the Russians, Ukrainians, Belarussians, Poles, Moravians, Czechs (Bohemians), Slovaks, Serbs, Croats, Slovenes, Bosnians, and Macedonians. The Slavic migrations also had a telling affect on the development of other Indo-European cultures of the region; most significantly, the Baltic tribes (the Lithuanians in particular).

Of the Slavic tribes, only the Russians, Poles, Moravians, and Bohemians consolidated themselves into independent states in the early Middle Ages. This tendency to unification was greatly affected by the Christianization of these states from the sixth to the tenth centuries. Under Christian influence, all reached higher cultural levels and joined broader cultural movements than they had under prior, tribal circumstance. The Russian consolidation first occurred under the Rurik Dynasty of the Swedish Vikings in Novgorod in 865 and in Kiev in 882 as has been said; it was continued by the Ruriks until consumed by the Mongols (a nomadic, mounted, Eurasian tribe) in 1245; this latter despite the heroic efforts to the contrary of Aleksander Nevsky (1220-1263; r. 1236-1252), Prince of Novgorod. The Polish consolidation first occurred in 960 under Miezko I (d. 992; r. 960-992) of the Piast Dynasty; it variously came into successful and unsuccessful conflict with the German Empire to the west, with Moravia and Bohemia to the south, with the Kievan (Russian) Empire to the east, and with the Papacy; and it drifted between unification and disunification to the Mongol invasion of 1241. The Moravian consolidation (in the approximate region now occupied by Slovakia) first occurred in 830 under Moymir (d. 846; r. 830-846); it variously came into successful and unsuccessful conflict with the Carolingian Empire, Bohemia, and Poland; it was destroyed by the Magyars (a nomadic, mounted, Eurasian tribe) in 906; and it became closely tied to Bohemia in the eleventh century. And the Bohemian consolidation (in the approximate region now occupied by Czech Republic) first occurred in the ninth century under the Przemyslid Dynasty; it variously came into successful and unsuccessful conflict with Moravia and Poland; and it was incorporated into the German Empire in the tenth century. Wrestling contests, often brutal, sometimes fatal such contests became especially prominent features of Slavic life in the early Middle Ages. They functioned in this context as a means of settling social, economic, political, and military disputes in lieu of war as well as a means of commemorating significant events and persons.

The **nomadic, mounted, Eurasian tribes** came into Europe proper from the Eurasian steppes, the vast plains from eastern Europe (effectively, Poland) to eastern Asia (effectively, the Yellow Sea). These tribes were of Ural-Altaic cultural and linguistic character; they were bound by common interests in animals (mainly cattle and horses) and in protection from natural and human enemies, not by genetic resemblance; they arranged themselves in families, tribes, and hordes according to these interests; and they developed exceptional organizational skills which allowed them to dominate other cultures and to establish vast empires, all without racial prejudice. The tribes and hordes, in turn, were comprised principally of free warriors who held equal rights and who were led by a monarch (a prince). They embraced an animistic form of religious sentiment which successfully resisted attempts by Judaism, Christianity, Islam, and Buddhism to colonize it. The most notable of the Eurasian tribes were the Huns, Avars, Bulgars, Khazars, Magyars (or Hungarians), Patzinaks, Turks, Cumans, and Mongols (or Tartars). The Huns were forced out of China and Kazakhstan in the first and second centuries and they arrived in eastern and central Europe in the fourth century. They were most widely remembered for their largely successful raids in Scythia, Pannonia, Greece, Macedonia, Thrace, Byzantium, Persia, Armenia, Gaul, and Italy under their most accomplished leader, Attila (d. 453; r. 434-453). The Avars came out of the steppes to eastern and central Europe in the sixth century. The Bulgars came out of the steppes to eastern Europe (and adopted a European, a Slavic, language) in the seventh century. The Khazars came out of the steppes to eastern Europe in the seventh century. The Magyars came out of the steppes to Hungary in the ninth century. And the Patzinaks came out of the steppes to eastern Europe in the tenth century. The Turks, Cumans, and Mongols left the steppes and arrived in Europe in the late Middle Ages: the Turks in the eleventh century, the Cumans in the twelfth century, and the Mongols in the thirteenth century. After fairly wide successes against one another, the Romans, Germans, Slavs, and Byzantines, all except the Bulgars, Magyars, Turks, and Mongols were destroyed, either by one another or by the Romans, Germans, Slavs, or Byzantines. Moreover, only the Bulgars, Magyars, Turks, and Mongols, among the Eurasian tribes, established settled, independent states; the Bulgars and Magyars in Europe in the early Middle Ages, the Turks in the near Middle East in the late Middle Ages, and the Mongols in Asia also in the late Middle Ages. The provisional political unification of the Bulgars, in the form of the First Bulgarian Empire, first occurred in 681; the Empire reached its pinnacle in the early ninth century; and it was subjugated by the Byzantine Empire in 1018. The provisional unification of the Magyars, under Arpad (d. 907; r. 896-907) and the dynasty he founded (the Arpad Dynasty, 896-1301), first occurred in 896; it destroyed Moravia in 906; it became a Christian royal sovereignty under St. Stephen I (975-1038; r. 997-1038), and it collapsed under the weight of the Mongol invasion in 1241. Archery and animal activities (including brutal blood sports) were an especially prominent feature of Eurasian tribal life in the early Middle Ages.

It is mainly in the context of the Germanic, Slavic, and Eurasian developments, most emphatically the Germanic (in particular, the Frankish) developments, that the new (the early) medieval political, economic, and social order took shape. This order, **feudalism**, was mainly the result of the decentralization of governing authority and economic life occasioned by the dissolution of the Western Roman Empire and by the predominance of nothing more than barbarian perspectives to replace it. The Empire that the barbarians had overrun was in great disarray and about to come apart of its own devices and the political acuity of the barbarians themselves was insufficient to the task of governing the extensive and diverse territories they had seized. Cities were destroyed or abandoned, folk law came to replace common law, barter forms of exchange increasingly replaced moneyed forms of exchange, unemployment and poverty increased sharply, and the weak and impoverished fled to the sanctuaries of the powerful and wealthy. Public authority was dispersed to the prerogatives of many private persons who came to rule over a relatively large number of relatively small and significantly isolated castle communities, or manorial estates. The lords of these estates owned them and had virtually full jurisdiction over them and over those who served them (the vassals). The vassals were accorded personal security and some priorities over parcels of land (fiefs) in exchange for their labor, principally as (agricultural) peasants (serfs) or as gentry-soldiers (knights). The affect of feudalism on medieval civilization was profound. The European nobility were arranged into a fragmented hierarchy of upper and lower forms; the fiefs of the upper nobility became infant territorial states. The three major European monarchies of the late, early Middle Ages and the early, late Middle Ages were a direct consequence of the feudal equation: the tenth-century Ottonian monarchy in Germany, the tenth-century Capetian monarchy in France, and the eleventh-century Anglo-Norman monarchy in England. The power of monarchs was advanced by feudalism in France and England most importantly (owing to an exacting hierarchy of lords) and this power was diminished by feudalism in Germany most importantly (owing to an unexacting hierarchy of lords). The dislocations among manorial estates and the sense of self-sufficiency within manorial estates was so consuming, however, that activities depending on wider social communication and on leisure – activities such as trade, education, art, and sport – were, on balance, adversely affected by the feudal arrangement.

Ironically enough, it was within the context of the feudal equation and, in a sense, as a pre-condition of the feudal equation that a movement largely favorable to such as trade, education, art, and sport developed; namely, the **chivalric movement**. The emergence of independent knights and the cavalry techniques of medieval knights – the tangible bases of chivalry – were grounded principally in the Carolingian Empire of the

71

mid-eighth to the mid-ninth centuries. The well-mannered esteem for women, the taste for courageous adventure and supramundane glory, and the cult of fellowship that formed the intangible bases of chivalry were grounded in notions of loyalty to one another, honor to the lord, fidelity of the vassals to the fiefs, and service of the lord to the vassals. Although wrapped importantly in religious piety, the chivalric movement nonetheless contributed particularly much to the secularization of mid-to-late medieval culture and education and it also contributed particularly much to the promotion of mid-to-late medieval sport. It nonetheless had an inconsiderable, direct affect on the medieval working class, which enjoyed little leisure or educational opportunity, even though this class did practice some informal types of physical recreation such as running, swimming, wrestling, and ball games. Its principal influence was instead on the class of nobles who served the court as soldiers. The chivalric education was conducted in palace, or castle, schools and was primarily devoted to the customs of war, courtly gallantry, and religious morality. Both young women and young men attended these schools but each received a quite different education. Women were given instruction mainly in the graces of the court; men were trained primarily in military skills. Both began their formal education at the approximate age of seven years. The women served in the court under the supervision of noblewomen throughout their experience at school. The men also served in the court under the tutelage of noblewomen but only until the approximate age of fourteen years, during which period they were known as pages. From the age of fourteen years to that of twenty-one years, they served in the military field under the direction of accomplished soldiers (knights), during which period they were known as squires. And at the approximate age of twenty-one years, they were themselves advanced to knighthood.

Unlike the retiring manner of education in the cathedral and monastic schools, the chivalric education was dominated by vigorous physical activities. The most widely practiced of these activities were archery, fencing, riding, running, swimming, throwing, weightlifting, wrestling, various exercises with weapons (such as lances, swords, axes, and shields) in heavy armor, ball games, and several combative practices (or practices that trained knights for combative pursuits) unique to the chivalric experience:

- quintain, which entailed marksmanship with a lance from a mount against an inanimate target framed in the image of a man;
- tilting, which entailed marksmanship with a lance from a mount through a fixed ring;
- jousting, which entailed combat between two horsemen with lances riding toward one another;
- behourd, a mock battle in which a group attempted to defend a small fortress against the advances of another group; and
- mêlée, or grand tourney, which entailed a miniature war between two groups, each advancing on the other.

These several, uniquely chivalric activities were often contested in formal sporting fairs, or tournaments, and in arenas, or lists, constructed explicitly for them. The tournaments evolved mainly out of the martial games of Germanic societies. Direct participation of women in them was prohibited although women were encouraged to attend as spectators; some contests were even held in honor of prominent ladies of the court. These competitions began in earnest in the ninth century and they reached their greatest popularity in the eleventh to the fourteenth centuries. The early tournament was a brutal, war-like battle, the principal object of which was to capture opponents for ransom and for land. The rank brutality of these tournaments, which sometimes brought church condemnation, was not significantly diminished until the late Middle Ages when tournaments developed into more regulated spectacles, principally featuring jousting, tilting, and quintain forms of activity.

The signal achievements of early medieval literature (tracts of religious philosophy aside) were all grounded in the chivalric movement (or its rough equivalent) and in the feudal basis of the chivalric movement: the Anglo-Saxon epic, Beowulf; the Celtic epics, Le Morte d'Arthur and Sir Gawain and the Green Knight; the Norse epic, Edda Elder and its German sequel, Nibelungenlied; the French epic, The Song of Roland; the Spanish epic, Poem of the Cid; the Anglo-Norman and German epic, Tristan and Isolde; and the French and German epic, Parsifal. These achievements were, accordingly, all of heroic and romantic moment; they all included men and women of valorous athleticism and included significant episodes of vigorous, sport-like action as well; and they all emphasized the military utility of such action. The most notable instances of such action in these masterful, narrative poems included Beowulf's defeat of Grendel in "wrestling" and of Breca in "swimming;" Arthur's "wrestling" match with Gawain; the numerous references to "skiing," "wrestling" (including one involving no less than Thor), and ball games in the Nordic myths; Siegfried's "running" victory over Gunther and Hagen in Nibelungenlied; and the "fencing" exploits of Beowulf, Arthur, Galahad, Launcelot, Gawain, Siegfried, Roland, Rodrigo (El Cid), Tristan, and Parsifal.

The most pervasive intellectual influences on early medieval life were the three major personalistic and monotheistic world religions that came to philosophical and institutional maturation in the period. Judaism, Christianity, and Islam grew to immense authority in the early Middle Ages and gave this otherwise disordered time its only enduring sense of cultural, educational, and political cohesion. They likewise uniquely championed the revolutionary notion that all persons, the wealthy and the powerful as well as the impoverished and powerless, are equally worthy of knowledge, respect, and freedom, a notion which is, on balance, favorable to the wide sense of social intercourse and leisure that tends to go well for such as sport. They too, however, again turned civilization away from its natural and human ground in the direction of its divine possibilities, a tendency that, on balance, inclined medieval culture to be less favorably disposed to bodily matters in general and to sporting activity in particular than the ancient Greek and Roman cultures had been.

The **Judaic divinism** of this period was more so a continuation of the ancient traditions, traditions dating from Abraham (c. 2300 B.C.E.), than an utterly new development. Judaism was nonetheless first canonized in the fifth and sixth centuries. Although formally organized about the synagogue (the intellectual, educational, and political nucleus of the community), Jewish life had no national center from the sack of Jerusalem by Titus in 70 and the abortive revolt of Bar Kochba against Roman rule in Palestine in the second century. Jewish people were thereafter prohibited by the Romans from entering Jerusalem; they thus became a dispersed people; and they suffered subsequent degradations of a broad and sporting character in the reigns of Constantine, Theodosius II, and Justinian. In the Diaspora (the dispersion), they migrated most significantly to Babylon, Afghanistan, Persia, India, north Africa, the Caucasus, Spain, Italy, Germany, Lithuania, Poland, and the Balkans. Owing to perceived strategies of separation, to Jehovah's claims of exclusivity, to alleged practices of ritual murder, and to blasphemous treatments of elements of the Christian communion, the Jews were again greatly persecuted during the main age of the Crusades, 1096-1215, when they were prohibited from bearing arms and from holding political office. They were subsequently required to wear prescribed clothing; were made increasingly dependent in personal and fiscal terms on political offices; were expelled from England in 1290, from France in 1306, from Spain in1492, and from Portugal in 1496; suffered destruction of numerous communities in Germany in the fourteenth century; were greatly affected by the Black Death, the plague epidemic, of 1348-1350; and thereafter fled again to the east (mainly to Italy, the Balkans, north Africa, Palestine, Lithuania, and Poland). The dominant philosophical orientation of early medieval Judaic divinism, like the tangible traditions of the faith, was too more so continued (from Philo) than was it original with the period. Philo had held to a transcendent interpretation of Jehovah, to a mechanistic and dualistic sense of human purpose that devotes itself principally to obtaining divine favor, and to a form of asceticism that appreciates the intangible soul (as the principle of good in the world) and depreciates the tangible body (as the principle of evil in the world), views which all tend to an unfavorable attitude to sport. In accord with a traditional taste for robust bodily activity (as expressed in the stalwart character of the early Judaic prophets) and for personalistic views of the self, however, the Diaspora Jews in particular (more so than the Palestinian Jews who were held more fully under the Roman and Byzantine associations of sport with paganism and with debasement) continued to practice informal types of physical recreation.

The **Christian divinism** of the early Middle Ages was also significantly a continuation of late ancient traditions, traditions that had first developed in the era of the Roman Empire and that had ripened mainly in the neo-Platonic philosophy of St. Augustine. Like the Judaic circumstance, however, the Christian faith too came to a much firmer institutional ground in the early Middle Ages than it had in the ancient world. The two most conspicuous instances of this development concerned the rise of the Papacy and the formation of monastic orders. The (Roman) Papacy, which dated in its original form from St. Peter in 41, was formally established by Calixtus I (c. 160-222; r. 217-222) in 217. The Bishops of Rome, as distinct from those of Jerusalem, Antioch, Alexandria, and Constantinople most importantly, were thereafter installed as the primary governing authorities of the Christian Church. Theodosius I/Theodosius the Great, in the late fourth century, was the first Roman emperor to formally acknowledge this authority. The other, leading, early medieval Bishops of Rome were:

- Pope Leo I (c. 400-461; r. 440-461), the first authentic pope, the first pope widely accepted as the highest administrative, teaching, and judging authority in the Church;
- Pope Gregory I/Gregory the Great, the first monastic pope, who undertook the Christianization of Europe (which was largely successful with the Visigoths, Lombards, Suevi, Angles, and Saxons), who expanded the secular prerogatives of the Church (mainly with Germanic peoples), and who synthesized and revised the music of the Church[109] in the form of monophonic, impersonal,

unaffected, deeply spiritual, and profoundly beautiful choral accompaniments to the Latin liturgy (which became known as plainsong, or Gregorian chant);

- Pope Gregory III, who effectively settled the iconoclastic dispute in favor of the advocates of icons;
- Pope Stephen III, who founded the Papal States by means of an artful alliance with the Frankish state under Pepin III/Pepin the Short in 756; and
- Pope Leo III, who crowned Charlemagne, Emperor of the Western Roman Empire (the effective beginning of the Holy Roman Empire), in 800.

Monasticism first developed in the near Middle East, most especially in Egypt and Syria, in the early fourth century and it was dispersed to Europe in the late fourth century. Its basic aim was to preserve an austere form of Christianity by means of ascetic ideals, to achieve spiritual perfection through severe and methodic forms of self-denial and self-discipline such as poverty, chastity, obedience, piety, and manual labor. The monasteries served the poor, rendered hospitality to the unfortunate, engaged in missionary projects directed at spiritual reawakening, established schools, and functioned as centers of agriculture and broader forms of cultural life. They were the main organs of learning from the time of their inception to the eleventh century; they were the centers of manuscript translation (most notably, St. Jerome's translation of the Bible into Latin in 382) and manuscript reproduction (illuminated and unilluminated manuscripts) in this period; and they (together with the broader Church) alone sheltered, preserved, and transmitted the classical heritage of the West throughout the early Middle Ages. The earliest of these, predominantly rural institutions was organized in the near Middle East in the early fourth century; the first European monastery was established by St. Benedict of Nursia (480-543) in Italy in c. 529. The other leading exponents of the monastic movement were St. Martin of Tours (c. 316-397) in France, St. Basil (c. 329-378) in Byzantium, St. Ambrose (c. 333-397) in Italy, St. Jerome (c. 347-c. 420) in Byzantium, St. Patrick (c. 385-461) in Ireland, St. Gregory of Tours (c. 538-c. 594) in France, St. Augustine of Canterbury in England, St. Bede the Venerable in England, and St. Boniface (c. 675-754) in Germany. Monasticism was also ardently championed by no less than Pope Gregory the Great and Charlemagne. It nonetheless drifted toward deeper secular influences in the late, early Middle Ages and thereby invited numerous attempts to stabilize its fundamentally spiritual character, such as the reforms of the Cluniac movement in the tenth and eleventh centuries.

The monastic orders and the monastic schools (not unlike the cathedral schools) were established as the doctrinal complexities and civic implications of the new religion were being worked out and as Christ's expected return did not occur. These schools were attended by both prospective laity and prospective ecclesiastics of both genders from the ages of seven or eight years. The educational prescriptions of the monastic movement were predictably rooted in the universal human calling to the will of a Divine Being (God); these prescriptions were rooted in the quest for eternal salvation. They were therefore almost entirely taken up with catechetical objectives. The monastic schools were, consequently, devoted largely to the study of religion and to the study of what remained of ancient Graeco-Roman wisdom (in the form of the liberal arts) as it favorably related to religion. Although instruction in some limited forms of necessary craft and laboring activity was also customarily included in them, these schools were nonetheless dominated by a meditative and an ascetic form of unsparing discipline. These deeply reserved and austere tendencies have been customarily unfriendly to predominantly physical experiences of all types (except necessary labor), including physical recreation. St. Bede is nonetheless said to have enthusiastically played games of the field in his youth.

The typically low Christian regard for the body and movement of the early Middle Ages was also conspicuous in the philosophy and in the art of the period. The **Christian philosophy** of the early Middle Ages was dominated by the thought of St. Augustine but it lacked the speculative impulse of Augustine himself and was governed instead by uncritical appeals to religious authority, Augustine principal among them. Only the thought of Boethius (c. 475-525) and that of John Scotus Erigena (c. 810-c. 877) constituted notable exceptions to this tendency and even they inclined to apologetic forms of spiritual mechanism in which philosophy stands in the service of theology and in which the material (and bodily) dimension is trammeled beneath the immaterial (and spiritual). Boethius, who was executed by the Ostrogothic Kingdom of Theodoric in 525 on false charges of treason, gave a largely neo-Platonic (and Stoic) defense of religious/intellectual faith, most notably in his Consolation of Philosophy (c. 524). Erigena, who taught in the Carolingian court, gave a somewhat more characteristic, early medieval rendering, a rendering nonetheless also drawn mainly on idealistic-tending, neo-Platonic (and Augustinian) lines. This rendering effectively assimilated a Christian notion of reality into a universal system of thought. By Erigena's view, recorded most memorably in On the Divisions of Nature (c. 862-c. 866), God is conceived as the transcendent, omniscient, omnipotent, omnibenevolent, and ineffable creator and sustainer of the world. From God, all things flow, in God all things exist, and to God all things return. Reality is nothing other than God evidencing Itself to the world, nothing other than a reflection of the Divine Light. Erigena's division of nature distinguishes things that are not created but create (God), things that are both created and create (ideas), things that are created but do not create (concrete objects), and things that are neither created nor create (God in Its rest). Humanity, accordingly, is to lose itself in the Divine Darkness (to behold God and to dwell in God's life) by rising above sense and reason through mystic exaltation.

Early **Christian art** likewise conveyed a relatively low opinion of the body and its movement. Gregorian chant and the visual arts of early Roman Christendom, not unlike Carolingian, Ottonian, and early Byzantine expressions, portrayed a closed (a determined) and a static world, a world unendowed with substantial change. Human bodies were depicted in a schematic way (the bodies of different persons were of the same form) demonstrating their insignificance as individuating agents (or their singularly spiritual and transcendent significance). Individual persons came off as near-to-disembodied figures whose facial expressions likewise revealed an unaffected contentment, an atemporal serenity, and a passionless lack of tragic emotion. The largest and most innovative architecture of this period, the "St. Peter's," Rome (first half of the fourth century), which did not survive the Renaissance, was modeled on the Roman basilicas (meeting halls) and was without external decoration. The most accomplished mosaics of this time were done in "St. Peter's," in the "Mausoleum of Galla Placidia," Ravenna (most notably, "The Good Shepherd;" c. 425-426), and in the "Santa Maria Maggiore," Rome (most notably, "The Annunciation and Adoration of the Magi;" c. 432-440). The most memorable sculpture was done in marble sarcophagi; most notably, the "Sarcophagus of Junius Bassus," Rome (c. 359). The best painting was done in Egypt, so-termed Coptic art, in the form of murals in the fifth and sixth centuries. The most remarkable achievements of the period in the visual arts, however, were attained in illuminated manuscripts. Christian practice required books (paged volumes, or codices), as distinct from scrolls, for liturgy and disputation. Many of the most notable of these were crafted, copied, and illustrated in monasteries (some in convents by women). Likely the most noteworthy illuminated manuscripts of this period were the Saxon, <u>Lindisfarne Gospels</u>, England (698-721) and the Celtic, <u>Book of Kells</u>, Ireland (c. 760-820).

The dominant intellectual and cultural orientation of early medieval Christian divinism (not unlike that of early medieval Judaic divinism) -- in particular its views of humanity, the body, and movement -- was, on balance, unfavorable to such as sport. Its spiritualistic and dualistic notion of humanity, ephemeral concept of the body, and arrested sense of movement, together with its ascetic temperament which elevated the immortal principle of good (the soul) and disparaged the mortal principle of evil (the body), had the predictable effect of suppressing predominantly physical expressions, recreative such expressions prominent among them. Neither did the close associations of ancient sport with Roman activities augur well for it in the early Middle Ages. Religionists had been widely persecuted for centuries under Roman rule, including debasement in sporting events. And, the persistent associations of Roman sport with pagan religion -- attendance at some Roman sporting contests implied a demonstration of imperial divinism -- did neither bode well for **sport in Christian (and Judaic) communities** of the period.

There were nonetheless some features of the Christian faith that disposed it favorably to physical recreation, although these features were in the early Middle Ages covered over by those that opposed the practice. The personalistic tendencies of Christianity and the robust characteristics of its leading prophets are perhaps the most significant of these features. Christ was himself thought the perfect trinity, the perfect proportion of body, mind, and soul, and he did neither by his apparent example nor by his apparent teaching perceive anything inherently opprobrious in physical recreation. St. Paul was too of courageous and vigorous action, taught cautiously against false asceticism, held that matter is not inherently evil (Colossians 2:16-23), and argued in passages visited by sporting metaphors (particularly those of running contests) that the Christian sense of hope and love makes authentic participation in life's many and varied activities (presumably including sport) its own best reward (Romans 9:16; I Corinthians 9:24-27; Galatians 2:2, 5:7; Philippians 2:16, 3:12-14; and Hebrews 12:1). These are hardly ringing endorsements of bodily experience, let alone of sport, but they do include a tempered perspective of the body (and its expressions) as against unbridled condemnation of it. Paul apparently opposed the practice of (Roman) sport as it was known to him. He nonetheless had a high regard for Greek views of the agon and of askesis as they pertained to hoped-for achievements of the gospel. He had a high regard for resolute self-assertion in the face of rivalry and opposition, for rigorous self-discipline and self-denial in the service of high purpose, for the perfection of individuals through stern training, for engaging the hard quest to obtain the prize (to obtain victory), for the importance of participation vis-à-vis victory, and for the dignity of those who fail to obtain victory despite high effort, all notions that figure prominently in many aspects of sporting life. What little sport was practiced in Christian communities of the early Middle Ages, mainly in such as palace, cathedral, and monastic schools and in chivalric tournaments, was unsurprisingly most associated with the festivals of holy days, although some of these festivals restricted or prohibited sporting recreations as a means of protecting their primarily spiritual significance. Arguably the most important of these festivals were the Irish, Tailteann Games and Fair of Carman, and various other celebrations of little-known origin or character in England, Scotland, and France. The **Tailteann Games** were originally established as formal funerary rites for Queen Tailte by her son, Luguid, in 1829 B.C.E. They were allegedly contested on an annual schedule (with only occasional interruptions) mainly at Teltown (near Dublin) until 554 C.E. They were open to all persons except criminals and included commercial and cultural events as well as formal competitions in running, high jumping, long jumping, pole jumping, shot putting, hammer throwing, javelin throwing, archery, boxing, wrestling, equestrian activities, and games resembling handball and hurling. The Fair of Carman staged formal events in running, jumping, throwing, archery, boxing, wrestling, equestrian activities, and hurling. And the festivals in England, Scotland, and France primarily featured formal ball games resembling rugby, football, soccer, lacrosse, field hockey, and hurling, all typically practiced in ritualistic fashion.

Although the seminal developments of Judaism date from Abraham, the seminal developments of Christianity from Abraham's son, Isaac, and the ancestral developments of Islam from Abraham's son, Ishmael, and although Islam held onto the prophets of the Old Testament and onto the prophetic significance of Christ (but rejected the divine nature of Christ and thus also the Trinity), the **Islamic divinism** of the early Middle Ages was effectively unique to its time. Unlike comparable Judaic and Christian movements of the period, early medieval Islamic divinism was not in any strict sense a continuation of prior occurrences. Islam is the most recent of the three major personalistic and monotheistic world religions. The distinctly Islamic vision and its associations with Arabian life were owed to the teachings and the example of the religion's founding prophet, Mohammed (c. 570-632). The Arabian circumstance in which Islam first took shape and which greatly affected the incipient nature of the faith itself was of Hamito-Semitic cultural and linguistic character. The new religion was proclaimed by Mohammed after his calling in Mecca in 610; it entailed the declaration of Allah as the one, true, and indivisible God, the creator of the universe and the judge of humanity's impending fate (its reward or punishment); it dispensed (in its original form) with a priesthood, with sacraments, and with liturgy, holding that all have direct access to Allah by means of prayer; it embraced the notions of a last judgment and an eternal life in either heaven or hell; and it required several major obligations of its supplicants:

- confession of faith in Allah and His prophet, Mohammed ('Islam' itself signifies submission to the will of God);
- dutiful prayer five times daily;
- charitable gifts in the form of generous alms and taxes;
- abstention from alcoholic drink and some foods;
- fasting in the month of Ramadan (the period commemorating the earliest divine revelations to Mohammed); and
- an attempted pilgrimage, or haj, to Mecca.

The governing documents of Islam are the Koran (the sacred word of Allah as revealed to Mohammed and recorded in the form of 114 chapters, or suras), the Sunna (the traditions of habit, or hadith, and proclamations of the prophet), and the Ijma (the accord of the faithful).

After Mohammed's calling and years of mostly unsuccessful attempts to convert non-believers in Mecca (the city of his birth), he fled to Medina in 622 (the hegira, or flight, from which the Moslem era/calendar began) in order to escape murder threats against him. There, the spiritual transformation and the theocratic state embodying this transformation in Arabia, which he had ordained, were successfully established by 630, at which time he returned to Mecca and eliminated idol worship in the Kaaba (the ancient Arabian shrine). Mohammed died in Medina in 632 and was succeeded by four elected caliphs (or spiritual and temporal rulers), 632-661:

- Abu Bakr (573-634; r. 632-634), a father-in-law of Mohammed, who subjugated many not-yet-converted Arabian tribes and who began the great expansion of Islam outside of Arabia with armed advances (massed, mounted warriors with composite bows) to Syria, Mesopotamia, and Persia;
- Omar (d. 644; r. 634-644), another father-in-law of Mohammed, who transformed the national Arabian state left him by Abu Bakr into a world empire by conquests of Syria under the Byzantine Empire (Damascus, 635), Persia under the collapsing neo-Persian, Sassanid Empire (Ctesiphon, 636),

Palestine under the Byzantine Empire (Jerusalem, 638), and Egypt under the Byzantine Empire (Alexandria, 644) and who was murdered in 644;

- Othman (d. 656; r. 644-656), an Omayyad and a son-in-law of Mohammed, who continued the expansion of the empire into the coastal regions of north-central and northwestern Africa (from Libya to Morocco) and into the Caucasus, who first collected the written text of the <u>Koran</u> in 651, and who was murdered in 656 in an insurrection over the issue of succession, an issue which formed the basis of the distinction between Sunni Moslems (the orthodox Moslems who supported Othman) and the Shiite Moslems (the reform Moslems who supported Othman's rival and successor); and
- Ali (d. 661; r. 656-661), a Fatimid and another son-in-law of Mohammed, who was consumed by internal dissension which led to his murder in 661.

The **Omayyad Dynasty** (661-750) was established on Ali's death; succession was thereafter hereditary; the capital of the empire was moved from Medina to Damascus; the Shiites became the dominant Moslem sect in 680 at the Battle of Kerbela (in modern Iraq); the empire continued its expansion to the east with conquests of Turkmenistan (709), Pakistan/India (711), Uzbekistan (712), Afghanistan (712), and Kazakhstan (751); and it also continued its expansion to the west with conquests in 711 by Tariq of the Visigothic Kingdom (under Roderic) in southern and central Spain and in Gibraltar, an expansion that continued to the north until conclusively halted by the Frankish Kingdom under Charles Martel at Tours and Poitiers in 732.

The Omayyad Dynasty was defeated and replaced by the Abbasids at the Battle of Zab (in modern Iraq) in 750. The Omayyads nonetheless re-established an emirate/caliphate at Cordoba (in Spain) in 756, an entity that flourished most significantly under Abd ar-Rahman III (891-961; r. 912-961) and that endured until the incipient beginning of the Christian re-conquest of Spain and until major civil wars among the Arabs themselves brought it to dissolution in 1031. The Omayyads (in Spain) were succeeded in 1061 by the Almoravid Empire, which:

- extended Islamic influence into sub-Saharan west Africa in the eleventh century,[110] thereby upending the Ghana Empire (which had persisted from the sixth to the thirteenth centuries in regions now occupied by the modern nation-states of Senegal, Gambia, Mauritania, and Mali) and other centralized societies in regions now occupied by the modern nation-states of Sudan, Chad, Central African Republic, Cameroon, Nigeria, Niger, Dahomey/Benin, Togo, Ghana, Upper Volta/Burkina Faso, Mali, and Côte d'Ivoire/Ivory Coast; and
- extended Islamic influence into the coastal regions of eastern Africa also in the eleventh century, into regions now occupied by the modern nation-states of Eritrea, Djibouti, Somalia, Kenya, Tanzania, Comoros, Malagasy Republic/Madagascar, and Mozambique.

The Almoravid Empire gave way, in turn, to the Almohad Empire in 1147; the Almohad Empire was itself dissolved in 1250; and Spanish assaults brought an end to Islamic Arab (Moor) authority in Spain (except for Granada and Gibraltar in the extreme south) by 1248. The (Nasrid) Emirate of Granada (and Gibraltar), the last Arab state in Europe, passed through a period of cultural brilliance in the fourteenth century and was then conclusively taken from the Moors by the Spanish in 1492.

The **Abbasid Dynasty** (750-1258) moved the capital of the empire from Damascus to Baghdad, allowed Persians the dominant position (over Arabs) in the empire, and flourished most significantly under al-Mansur (d. 775; r. 754-775) and Harun al-Rashid (c. 765-809; r. 786-809). Although a major political, economic, and cultural power into the thirteenth century, the effective dissolution of the empire began in the eighth century with the fractional development of independent kingdoms; most notably, those in Spain, the Caliphate of the Fatimids in north Africa (910-1171), the Empire of the Ayyubids in the near Middle East (1171-1250), and the earliest of the Turkish dynasties (of central and western Asia) which came increasingly to leadership in the Islamic world (the Ghaznevids of Afghanistan/Pakistan, 962-1186, and the Seljuks of Turkmenistan, Persia, Mesopotamia, Syria, Palestine, Arabia, the Caucasus, and Asia Minor, 1030-1194). Despite modest gains in Sicily and Greece against the Byzantine Empire in the early ninth century, successes against the (western) Christian Crusades in the twelfth and thirteenth centuries, the deepening influence of Islam in west Africa in the thirteenth century, and the diffusion of Islam to Malaysia and Indonesia also in the thirteenth century, the Abbasid Dynasty was destroyed by invading Mongols in 1258. By the late thirteenth century, the dominant position in the Islamic world of the near Middle East and the Balkans had passed to the Ottoman Turks.

The Islamic Arabs assimilated very diverse cultures under the universal bonds of the Moslem faith, were tolerant of local civic customs that were not contrary to Moslem practice, and brought together the Oriental and the Hellenistic intellectual legacies in their splendid cultural centers (mainly, Mecca, Medina, Damascus, Baghdad, Cairo, Samarkand, Cordoba, and Granada), universities (mainly, Baghdad, Cairo, and Cordoba), and other schools. The earliest Islamic schools were established in the reigns of the four elected caliphs in the seventh century. They were similar in basic character and religious emphasis to the early Judaic and Christian schools; that is, mainly devoted to obtaining divine favor. Also like the early Judaic and Christian schools, analogous Islamic institutions were established as the doctrinal complexities and civic implications of the new religion became sufficiently well developed to require formal instruction.

While Europe was suffering the dislocations of the Dark Ages, the Islamic Arabs were passing through a flowering in science, technology, mathematics, the visual arts, literature, philosophy, and sport, a flowering that had an enormous affect on the course of world history, including the history of European culture (largely through Spain). In medicine, the Arabs contributed greatly to our understanding of disease and pharmaceutical treatments of disease; they also contributed greatly to the encyclopedic synthesis of medical learning (most notably, by way of Avicenna's widely celebrated and deeply influential, Canon of Medicine). In astronomy, the Arabs did much to refine ancient European knowledge concerning the motions of the sun, moon, and outer planets. In technology, the Arabs significantly improved ancient astronomical instruments, improvements which led to the development of telescopes and clocks, devices that have had a colossal affect on subsequent scientific discovery, transportation, and techniques of mass production. And in mathematics, Arab advances in numerals and trigonometric functions were especially noteworthy.

The **visual arts of the Islamic Arabs** -- in particular, the intricate and abstract character of its decorative designs -- were the result of a rich admixture of cultural influences; most notably, the iconoclastic orientation of medieval Islam itself and the formal inclinations of Byzantine and Sassanian (Persian) art. The most accomplished Islamic (abstract/calligraphic) design was done in the form of architectural (and manuscript) decoration, not in the form of painting or sculpture. The highly developed aesthetic taste of Islam, itself moved by a refined sense of mathematical proportion, was most apparent, however, in its thoroughly stunning architecture. The best architecture of medieval Islam (and its continuation/refinement in Timurid central Asia, Mogul India, and Ottoman Turkey in the fifteenth, sixteenth, and seventeenth centuries) is the only major instance of artistic achievement in world history that obtained an organic result by way of mediation between materialist and spiritualist orientations. The middle-ground tendencies of the organic ideal are elsewhere obtained by eschewing (or sublimating) materialist and spiritualist orientations, not by mediating them. This so because these (organic) tendencies conceive of the relation of the material and the spiritual realms in a characteristically different way than does either materialism or spiritualism itself; namely, in a monistic and intrinsic, as distinct from a dualistic/pluralistic and extrinsic, way. The mystery of the Islamic apotheosis is both deepened and relieved by the absence of contextual support; there are no other features of the Islamic case that achieve organic result. It is deepened by the isolation of the achievement; it is relieved because inherent, contextual support of a congruent sort is inconsistent with a fundamentally mechanistic contingency. The most memorable instances of medieval Islamic architecture are:

- the octagonal, central-plan, splendidly well decorated (in marble and glass mosaics) "Dome of the Rock," Jerusalem, late seventh century, on the alleged site of Abraham's abortive attempt to sacrifice Isaac and of Mohammed's ascent to heaven;
- the "Great Omayyad Mosque at Damascus," 705-711, which includes the first minarets and refined, geometrically intricate, decorative mosaics;
- the "Great Abbasid Mosque at Baghdad," 754-775, which was destroyed by the Mongols in the thirteenth century;
- the "Mosque of Ibn Tulun," Cairo, 877-879;
- the "Great Mosque at Cordoba," 786-987;
- the "Madrasah and Mausoleum of Sultan Hasan," Cairo, 1356-1363; and
- the "Alhambra," Granada, 1354-1391, which includes exquisitely delicate spaces, columns, arches, and (geometrical) mosaic decorations, all in monumental expanse but of distinctly human scale and proportion.

Although not quite up to its matchless genius in architecture, the **literary and philosophical achievements of medieval Islam** nonetheless rivaled, resembled, and influenced those of Europe in this time. Arguably the most memorable accomplishments in literature were the romantic prose tales of Sheherazade (in Arabic) in the anonymous, Thousand and One Nights, or Arabian Nights (likely tenth century); the graceful and skeptical poetic masterpiece (in Persian) of Omar Khayyam (fl. eleventh century), Rubaiyat; and the great epic poem (in Persian) of Firdausi (c. 940-1020), Book of Kings. The first significant philosophical interpretation of Islam was achieved by al-Kindi (fl. ninth century) and it tended, not unlike its Judaic and Christian analogs, to an idealistic-tending, neo-Platonic, mechanistic, and dualistic account. Its divinist inclinations argued that the world has been created out of nothing by Allah and was therefore of finite origin, that the world (but not Allah) will ultimately dissolve into the void from which it came, that divine revelation is superior to philosophical knowledge, that only revelation secures fundamental tenets of faith which are primary to knowledge, and that reason merely confirms what is (and can be) known only by means of faith. The other towering figure in early medieval Islamic philosophy was the great physician, Avicenna, or ibn-Sina (980-1037), who, unlike al-Kindi, argued from empirical fact to the necessary being of Allah but who, like al-Kindi, nonetheless came to idealistic-tending, neo-Platonic, mechanistic, and dualistic conclusions about the transcendent, omnipotent, omnibenevolent, and uncaused nature of Allah as well as about the immanent, caused nature of the world.

The predominant drift of early medieval Islamic philosophy was thus in the direction of an utter submission to divinity, a spiritual awakening, and in the concomitant direction of a bodily asceticism, a form of material depreciation. The **Islamic view of sport**, movement, the body, and humanity was not therefore fundamentally different than the Judaic and Christian views. Early medieval Islam nonetheless made a less strident distinction between the commands of the body and those of the soul than did early medieval Judaism and Christianity; it was given to a larger sense of change in the world than were early medieval Judaism and Christianity; and it allowed, too unlike early medieval Judaism and Christianity, that the good life on earth and in heaven include forms of (bodily) self-indulgence -- all qualities which are, on balance, favorable to predominantly physical expressions, including sport. The personalism of Islamic doctrine, its high regard for the general notion of exercise as the practice of disciplined order, its broad concern for bodily health, and the robust physical characteristics of its leading prophets also inclined it to a measured respect for bodily activity. Islam, of course, shared its leading prophets (and their vigorous ways) with Judaism and Christianity; and Mohammed was likewise of a vital physical nature. He made particularly much of the necessary unification of mind and body, is the subject of "wrestling" metaphors in the <u>Koran</u>, and is known to have favored acrobatic gymnastics, archery, fencing, horse riding, running, swimming, and wrestling for purposes of military training and relaxation. Although Islam did neither develop a leisure sub-culture nor make wide provision for sporting activity, was in principle opposed to games of chance and the practice of bodily exposure in public, and denied sporting opportunity to women, it nonetheless made especially much of the relation of sport and the waging of holy war and it therefore promoted sports of martial utility for men; most significantly, sports such as archery, fencing, polo (and other equestrian activities), gymnastics, weightlifting, and wrestling.

The early Middle Ages began to give way to a more modern development in the tenth and eleventh centuries. The events that formed late medieval culture continued to embrace the basic inclinations of early medievalism but in a more ordered way. In the late Middle Ages, Europe in particular began to put itself back together, began to centralize the governing authority that had been so widely dispersed in the just-prior epoch. Late medieval life also developed a more deeply secular tendency as against the early Middle Ages. This was a tendency that significantly tempered the influence of formal religion and advanced the prerogatives of temporal activity. Both the proclivity to centralization and that to secularization would come to have what was, on balance, a favorable affect on sport.

Late Medieval Culture and Sport

The political and military chaos of the early Middle Ages continued in the later epoch but in a somewhat more measured and less fragmentary manner. Late medieval culture (effectively, the tenth to the fifteenth centuries) was mainly characterized by:

- the development of the incipient, unifying groundwork of the leading modern nation-states of western and eastern Europe; the feudal order gradually yielded to the centralizing tendencies of royal law in Germany, France, England, Denmark, Norway, Sweden, Italy, Spain, Switzerland, Burgundy, Hungary, Bohemia, Lithuania, Poland, Russia, Bulgaria, Serbia, and Byzantine Turkey, each with its own novel educational, artistic, and sporting practices related most notably to military activities in general and to the Crusades in particular, all of which came to embody the apogee of the chivalric movement;

- a deepening attention to, and respect for secular affairs that manifested itself principally in a dramatic increase in trade and population, in the re-establishment of urban centers (towns, or cities) in which wealthy, middle-class artisans and merchants became the dominant influence and in which professional societies of artisans and merchants (guilds) were formed, and in the inception of universities, each with its own novel consequences for educational, artistic, and sporting activity;

- profound transformations in the Christian Church characterized most notably by a dilution of papal authority, the schism of Western (Roman) and Eastern (Orthodox) faiths, the Crusades, the germ of Protestant agitation, and a philosophical movement (scholasticism) that marked both the apotheosis of Christian thought and the basis of its diminishing influence, each with its own novel consequences for educational, artistic, and sporting activity;
- the development of the two crowning artistic styles of the Middle Ages in visual, musical, and literary terms, the Romanesque and the Gothic styles, each with its own novel consequences for educational, artistic, and sporting activity; and
- the continuing development, throughout the so-termed Middle Ages, of the two major Asian civilizations of the ancient world, India (which had also a telling affect on the incipient cultures of southeast and central Asia in this period) and China (which had also a telling affect on the incipient cultures of southeast Asia, Korea, and Japan in this period), each with its own novel educational, artistic, and sporting practices.

The late Middle Ages are significantly characterized by an increasing **centralization of government** in which strictly feudal law (and its sense of fragmentation and isolation) was gradually replaced by **royal law** (and its sense of unification and social intercourse). Glimpses of this tendency were apparent in the early Byzantine Empire, the early Islamic empire, and the Carolingian Empire, all of the early Middle Ages, but it came to distinctly medieval maturation in the major feudal monarchies of the late Middle Ages: the Ottonian Empire of the tenth century in Germany, the Capetian Empire of the tenth century in France, and the Anglo-Norman Empire of the eleventh century in England.

The **Ottonian Empire** was established in the eastern Frankish kingdom, in **Germany**, by the Saxon emperor, Otto I/Otto the Great, in 936 as has been said. The Saxons were succeeded by the Salian emperors in 1024 as has been also said. The period which followed that of the Salian emperors began in 1125 and was dominated by the **Hohenstaufen**, 1137-1254; most notably, by:

- Frederick I/Frederick Barbarossa (c. 1125-1190; r. 1152-1190), who continued (from his predecessor) the German colonization of the Slavic east in Poland, Bohemia, Moravia, Lithuania, Belarus, and Ukraine (a development that went on throughout the thirteenth century as well), who reconciled rival factions by judiciously awarding various regions to different families, by cooperation with the Papacy, and by means of an alliance with the Capetians in France (1187), and who played a major role in the Third Crusade;
- Henry VI (1165-1197; r. 1190-1197), who brought Sicily into the Empire; and
- Frederick II (1194-1250; r. 1212-1250), who surrendered some German territories to Denmark, who conducted ongoing campaigns in southern Italy, who participated very significantly in the Fifth Crusade, and who engaged in ruinous disputes with the Papacy which led to the decline of the Hohenstaufen and to the dissolution of the "hereditary" German monarchies of the Middle Ages.

It was in the context of Hohenstaufen rule that the leading epic literature of late medieval Germany was written, c. 1200-1210: Nibelungenlied, Tristan and Isolde, and Parsifal.

The **elective German monarchies** of the thirteenth, fourteenth, and fifteenth centuries followed. Intermittent feudal warfare demanded the renewal of imperial authority by several ecclesiastic and several secular electors. After an interim, the period proceeding the Hohenstaufen emperors was nonetheless also dominated by ruling families, the Hapsburgs and the Luxemburgs. The most notable of these were:

- Rudolf I of Hapsburg (1218-1291; r. 1273-1291), the first of the imperial Hapsburgs, who confirmed German possession of Austria;
- Albrecht I of Hapsburg (d. 1308; r. 1298-1308), who confiscated Bohemia and Moravia;
- Henry VII (c. 1275-1313; r. 1308-1313), the first of the imperial Luxemburgs;
- Charles IV of Luxemburg (1316-1378; r. 1346-1378), who expanded German influence to the north and who made Bohemia (Prague) the center of the Empire; and
- the Luxemburg sons of Charles IV, Wenceslaus (1361-1419; r. 1378-1419) and Sigismund (1368-1437; r. 1410-1437), who variously and, in the end, unsuccessfully attempted to establish a Greater Slavic Empire which included Bohemia and bits of Hungary, Poland, and Germany, who prosecuted the highly influential Hussite Wars (1419-1436) against a dissident Christian sect, and who presided over a weakening of the Bohemian and German crowns that resulted in the granting of Brandenburg (a northern German region) to the Hohenzollerns in 1415 and of Saxony (a central German region) to the Wettins in 1432.

With the extinction of the Luxemburgs in 1437, the German crown (including Austria, Switzerland, Bohemia, and Hungary) fell to the Hapsburgs; most notably, to Frederick III (1415-1493; r. 1440-1493), under whom a general lawlessness and harsh justice prevailed, native kings were raised to the throne in Hungary (Matthias Corvinus, c. 1443-1490; r. 1458-1490) and Bohemia (George Podiebrad, 1420-1471; r. 1458-1471), imperial losses to Poland and Burgundy were suffered (reversed in 1477), and Turkish and Hungarian attacks on Austria occurred.

France had begun its drift away from Germany in the partitions of the Carolingian Empire of the ninth century as has been said. The Franks nonetheless maintained a nominal hegemony in France until the late tenth century when the Saxon leader, Hugh Capet (d. 996; r. 987-996), acquired the throne (in 987). Although the **Capetian Empire** (987-1328) which followed was of German ethnicity, it came to adopt a predominantly Italic language, a language that had been most influenced by Latin. Capet's immediate successors in **France** served long reigns and strengthened the Capetian hold on the crown. Robert II/Robert the Pious (970-1031; r. 996-1031), son of Hugh Capet, acquired Burgundy; Henri I (c. 1008-1060; r. 1031-1060), son of Robert II, began the long French struggles with the Normans in France and in England; and Philip I (1052-1108; r. 1060-1108), son of Henri I, acquired Netherlands by marriage. Authentic French independence from Germany began in earnest, however, with the reign of Louis VI/Louis the Fat (1081-1137; r. 1108-1137), son of Philip I, who established a strong central administration and hospitable relations with the Papacy and with the new monastic orders. The remaining Capetian monarchs succeeded in developing an increasingly robust sense of French national consciousness and were largely taken up with the Crusades, with Papal disputes, with the formation of Parlement, and with offensive and defensive campaigns against the Holy Roman Empire (effectively, Germany), England, and Flanders (effectively, the region occupied by the modern nation-state of Belgium, together with bits of France and Netherlands): Louis VII/Louis the Young (c. 1120-1180; r. 1137-1180), Philip II/Philip Augustus (1165-1223; r. 1180-1223), Louis IX/Saint Louis (1214-1270; r. 1226-1270), Philip III/Philip the Bold (1254-1285; r. 1270-1285), Philip IV/Philip the Fair (1268-1314; r. 1285-1314), Louis X/Louis the Quarrelsome (1289-1316; r. 1314-1316), Philip V/Philip the Tall (1294-1322; r. 1317-1322), and Charles IV/Charles the Fair (1294-1328; r. 1322-1328), the last of the Capetians. It was in the context of eleventh-century, twelfth-century, and thirteenth-century Capetian rule that the leading epic literature of late medieval France was written, <u>The Song of Roland</u> (eleventh or twelfth century) and <u>Parsifal</u> (c. 1190).

The Capetian line went extinct in 1328 and was succeeded by the **House of Valois** (1328-1498). The defining event of the Valois dynasty was the **One Hundred Years War** with England (1337-1453), which began with England's (under Edward III) invasion of France (under the first Valois, Philip VI [1293-1350; r. 1328-1350]), which brought untold misery to the French people (famine, pestilence, oppression, anarchy), and which ended in French triumph and in the development of a secure and unified French national state and French national economy. The War had largely to do with rival territorial claims; that is, with England's claim to bits of France, the French crown, Flanders, fishing and other commercial rights in the English Channel, and Scotland. The French, conversely, intended to hold onto itself, Flanders, and commercial rights in the English Channel as well as to oppose England's attempted annexation of Scotland. Edward III invaded France in 1337 and achieved notable early successes at land and at sea, captured John II/John the Good (1319-1364; r. 1350-1364)[111] through his son, Edward the Black Prince, at the Battle of Poitiers in 1356, and negotiated a provisional end to the War that was largely favorable to England in 1359 (the Treaty of London) and that freed John II for ransom in 1360 (the Peace of Brétigny). The War was resumed by French King, Charles V/Charles the Wise (1338-1380; r. 1364-1380), and continued by his immediate successors, Charles VI/Charles the Mad (1368-1422; r. 1380-1422) and Charles VII/Charles the Victorious (1403-1461; r. 1422-1461). This phase of the War went fairly well for the French until Henry V of England defeated them at the Battle of Agincourt in 1415. Wide English gains then continued until Joan of Arc (the "Maid of Orléans;" c. 1412-1431), a divinely inspired peasant girl and the French national heroine, lifted the Siege of Orléans, variously engaged the English in armed combat elsewhere, and aroused Charles VII to action, all in 1429. She was captured in 1430 by the Burgundians (then English allies), condemned in a mock trial as a heretic (as one who falsely claimed direct communication with God), and burned at the stake in Rouen in 1431; her guilt was revoked in 1456. French victories nonetheless continued after Joan's death: the English alliance with Burgundy was broken in 1435, Paris was re-taken in 1436, and Normandy was re-acquired in 1450. The War ended with the French victory at Bordeaux in 1453. The remaining Valois, Louis XI (1423-1483; r. 1461-1483) and Charles VIII (1470-1498; r. 1483-1498), entangled themselves in largely inconsequential intrigues with England, Italy (Sicily in particular in 1494), and Austria. For the next approximate century, until the House of Bourbon came to power in 1589, France was governed by the Valois in association with other ruling families.

The **Anglo-Norman Empire** in **England** began with the dispossession of the Anglo-Saxons (under Harold) by Duke William of Normandy/William I/William the Conqueror at the Battle of Hastings in 1066. William had conquered the whole of England by 1071, ordered compilation of The Domesday Book (a survey, or census, of all properties in the realm and their annual yields; a record from which there was no relief) in 1085, and installed "The Salisbury Oath" (a pledge of loyalty to the king by subordinate vassals) in 1086. William thus gained virtually complete military, political, and economic dominion over England. He was succeeded by a son, William II (1056-1100; r. 1087-1100), who occupied Normandy in 1090 and who gained control of the Scottish crown in 1097. Henry I (1068-1135; r. 1100-1135), another son of William I, succeeded his brother and in 1106 defeated his other brother, Robert II (c. 1054-1134; r. 1087-1106; who had inherited the Duchy of Normandy from his father in 1087 and who had led Norman forces in the First Crusade), thus reuniting Normandy and England. Stephen of Blois (c. 1097-1154; r. 1135-1154), grandson of William I, succeeded Henry I but was subjected to a chaotic and a near-constant struggle to retain the throne, most notably against Matilda (1102-1167), daughter of Henry I. Stephen, the last of the Normans, was succeeded by Henry II (1133-1189; r. 1154-1189), son of Matilda (whose husband, Count Godfrey of Anjou [in western France] was nicknamed 'Plantagenet').

Henry II thus became the first of the **House of Anjou-Plantagenet**, 1154-1399. He reigned over England and much of France; fashioned the "Constitution of Clarendon" in 1164 (which was intended to limit the secular prerogatives of a quarrelsome Church); arranged the murder, in 1170, of the Constitution's principal opponent, his Chancellor of the Archbishop of Canterbury, Thomas à Becket (1118-1170); did penance for the misdeed in 1174; initiated the conquest of Ireland in 1171, of Wales in 1172, and of Scotland in 1173; established a permanent court at Westminster in 1178; and presided over the gradual development of English common law. Henry II was succeeded by his son, Richard I/Richard Lion-Heart (1157-1199; r. 1189-1199), who was a major and an especially courageous participant in the Christian Crusades of the late twelfth century and who suffered serious disputes with the Holy Roman Empire. Richard's brother, John (1167-1216; r. 1199-1216), succeeded him, lost territories in France to Philip II of France, suffered consequential disputes with the Papacy, and so aroused the barons by way of unwise fiscal policies and violations of feudal custom that he was obliged to grant the "Magna Carta" at Runnymede (near Windsor/London) in 1215. The "Magna Carta" stipulated the rights of barons against royal abuses, the limitations of royal authority, and the necessary respect for the law that all governing authority must avow. It was too in this approximate period (c. 1200) that the great Anglo-Norman epic, Tristan and Isolde, was written. Henry III (1207-1272; r. 1216-1272), son of John, followed his father and again aroused the barons, in this case by increasing ecclesiastic authority and taxation, by extravagant and futile campaigns in France, and by abortive attempts to obtain the German and Sicilian crowns. He prevailed in the Barons' War (1258-1267), directed by Simon de Montfort (c. 1208-1265), that resulted but the quarrel ultimately led, in the reign of his son and successor, Edward I (1239-1307; r. 1272-1307), to shared governance in the form of councils and parliaments. Edward I had prosecuted the Barons' War for his father, strengthened the crown through French acquisitions and legal reforms, annexed Wales in 1284 (after it had passed through its last period of independence under Llewelyn [d. 1282; r. 1263-1282]), claimed the throne of Scotland in 1296 after royal succession there had been broken (the Scottish crown was reclaimed by Robert I/Robert the Bruce [1274-1329; r. 1306-1329] in 1314), and staged the "Model Parliament" (which embodied a much broader participation in government as against prior practice) in 1295.

Edward I was succeeded by his son, Edward II (1284-1327; r. 1307-1327), who was weak, dissipated, and ineffective, who presided over great internal dissension and the loss of Scotland, and who was forced to abdicate, was imprisoned, and was murdered. His son, Edward III (1312-1377; r. 1327-1377), who succeeded him, put an end to the domestic turmoil and invaded France in 1337, thus setting off the One Hundred Years War with France. He and his son, Edward the Black Prince (1330-1376), took an active part in the War. Prince Edward won the Battle of Crécy in 1346 (in which guns, in the form of canons, were first successfully used) and the Battle of Poitiers in 1356 (in which John II was captured). King Edward negotiated a provisional end to the War in 1359 and the release of John for ransom in 1360. The War was resumed by the French, however, and, although inconclusive in Edward's reign, required concessions to Parliament by Edward in order to assure fiscal support for the War. The Black Death of 1348-1350 (a virulent epidemic of the bubonic plague) deepened the economic crisis occasioned by the War and it also brought social advancement to the lower classes. The decline in population effected by the plague resulted in a labor shortage, the demand for higher wages, and an enhanced station (including military obligations) for the habitually disadvantaged. The last generation of Edward's reign was dominated by economic crisis, class unrest, disputes concerning church reform (with John Wyclif and his disciples in particular), the adoption of English as the official language of the realm in 1362, the consequent development of distinctly English literature (most notably by Geoffrey Chaucer [c. 1340-1400]), and the impending publication of the first English translation of the <u>Bible</u> by John Wyclif (c. 1320-1384) in 1380. He was succeeded by the son of Prince Edward, Richard II (1367-1400; r. 1377-1399), the last of the Anjou-Plantagenets. Richard II was the victim of prolonged disputes over the throne (mainly with his uncles, with Chaucer's principal patron, John the Gaunt [1340-1399], son of Edward III, in particular), of military defeats in France, of official corruption, and of the failed Peasants' Revolt of Wat Tyler (d. 1381) over wage restrictions, poll taxes, and enforced serfdom in 1381. He was deposed and imprisoned in 1399 and likely murdered in 1400.

Henry IV (1367-1413; r. 1399-1413), son of John the Gaunt, established the royal **House of Lancaster** (1399-1461) by deposition of Richard II in 1399 and spent the sweep of his reign suppressing rebellions by the disciples of Richard, by other challengers to the throne, by protestant-tending ecclesiastics, by the Welsh under Owen Glendower (c. 1359-c. 1416), and by the Scots. He was succeeded by his son, Henry V (1387-1422; r. 1413-1422), who turned the One Hundred Years War with France again in the English favor with a brilliant victory at Agincourt in 1415 and with subsequent triumphs in Normandy, who further strengthened the English national character with armed victories over challengers to his throne and over Owen Glendower, and who endeavored to make English culture distinct from French culture. Henry V was succeeded by his son, Henry VI (1421-1471; r. 1422-1461), whose reign was marked by the triumphs of Joan of Arc, by her execution, by the conclusive victory of the French in the One Hundred Years War, and by domestic disorder and factionalism (most notably, the War of the Roses). The **War of the Roses** (1455-1485) was a dynastic dispute between the House of Lancaster (symbolized by a red rose), with Henry VI at its head, and the **House of York** (1461-1485; symbolized by a white rose), with Richard, Duke of York (d. 1460) first at its head. On Duke Richard's death in 1460, his son, Edward IV (1442-1483; r. 1461-1483), assumed the Yorkist claim and achieved the throne in 1461. Although Henry was briefly restored (in 1470-1471), he was then murdered, the crown was reclaimed by Edward, and it was subsequently passed to his son, Edward V (1470-1483; r. 1483), who was, like Henry, also murdered, likely by order of his uncle (a son of Duke Richard) and usurper, Richard III (1452-1485; r. 1483-1485), the last of the Yorkist kings. Richard was defeated and killed by the Welshman and Lancastrian claimant to the English crown, Henry Tudor, at the Battle of Bosworth Field (near Leicester) in 1485, ending the War of the Roses and the feudal equation in England. Henry married into the House of York (Elizabeth, daughter of Edward IV), thus uniting the warring factions and originating the royal House of Tudor (1485-1603) as Henry VII.

There developed a similar tendency toward national unification in the other leading states of late medieval Europe. **Denmark** began its rise to the status of a major, unified European power in the reigns of:
- Waldemar I/Waldemar the Great (1131-1182; r. 1157-1182);
- his son, Waldemar II/Waldemar the Conqueror (1170-1241; r. 1202-1241), who came to rule over a kingdom that included Denmark, southern Norway, southwestern Sweden, and the southern and eastern Baltic coast to what is now Estonia, before losing domain in Norway (to the Kingdom of Sweden-Norway, which it joined [with Iceland] in 1363/1397) and on the Baltic coast (to the Hanseatic League, a powerful German trade confederation that came to dominate the southern Baltic coast in the thirteenth and fourteenth centuries, and to the Teutonic Knights, a chivalric order that came to dominate the eastern Baltic coast in the thirteenth and fourteenth centuries);
- his grandson, Erik V Glipping (d. 1286; r. 1259-1286), who was compelled, in 1282, to accept the "Danish Magna Carta" installing the rule of law, limiting royal power, and extending political franchise; and
- Waldemar IV (c. 1320-1375; r. 1340-1375).

Norway established a unified, hereditary monarchy under Sverrir (d. 1202; r. 1184-1202) in the late twelfth century, conquered Greenland in 1261 and Iceland in 1262-1264 under Haakon IV (1204-1263; r. 1217-1263), and entered a union with Sweden under Magnus VII in 1319 and with Denmark under Haakon VI (d. 1380; r.1355-1380) in 1363, an arrangement that was formalized by the Union of Kalmar in 1397 and that endured in an unsteady form into the sixteenth century. **Sweden** began its modern drift toward national unification in the twelfth century under Eric IX (d. 1162; r. 1155-1162), conquered and Christianized southern Finland under regent, Jarl Birger (d. 1266; r. 1250-1266), in 1250-1266, extended protection to peasants from the nobility under Magnus Ladulas (d. 1290; r. 1275-1290), and entered a union with Norway under Magnus VII (1316-1373; r. 1319-1363) in 1319 and with Denmark under Haakon VI in 1363 (1397).

Late medieval **Italy** had a somewhat different experience; it did not tend to national unification so as the other major nations of Europe had. It became a part of the Holy Roman Empire, the German Empire, under Otto I in 962 as has been said. Its southern regions thereafter fell variously under Norman influence beginning in the eleventh century and under French and Spanish influence beginning in the thirteenth century. Beginning in the twelfth century, significantly as a result of the Christian Crusades, well-organized, adeptly administered, modern-tending, and largely autonomous commercial city-states -- principally, Venice, Genoa, Pisa, Florence, Milan, Siena, Naples, and Sicily -- became the dominant political entities of the peninsula. The Papal States, centered in Rome of course, remained prominent and survived the entire epoch of the late Middle Ages.

Late medieval **Spain** was primarily driven by the European attempt to reclaim the Iberian peninsula from the Islamic Arabs, by the "reconquista," which began in earnest in the eleventh century. The Arabs had occupied the southern reaches of the peninsula from the early eighth century as has been said. Small, independent, European, and Christian states -- most notably, Navarre, Barcelona/Catalonia, Asturia/Leon, Castile, Aragon, and Portugal -- had nonetheless and variously continued in northern Spain from the end of the eighth century to the opening of the eleventh. Beginning in the early eleventh century, these states began their assaults on the south. Aided by major civil wars among the Arabs themselves, which began in 1008:

- Castile, under Ferdinand I/Ferdinand the Great (c. 1000-1065; r. 1035-1065), obtained Leon in 1037 and Navarre in 1054 and reclaimed significant bits of central Spain from the Moors by the middle of the eleventh century;
- Rodrigo (c. 1040-1099), the hero of the romantic, medieval Spanish epic, <u>Poem of the Cid</u> (written in c. 1200), captured Toledo in 1085 and Valencia in 1094;
- Portugal gained autonomy in 1094 and, under its first king, Alfonso I (c. 1109-1185; r. 1139-1185), expanded its territory rapidly to the south at the expense of the Moors;
- Aragon, under Alfonso I/Alfonso the Warrior (d. 1134; r. 1104-1134), also significantly expanded its territory to the south, too at the expense of the Moors, and later (in 1137) it united with Catalonia;
- Ferdinand III/Ferdinand the Saint of Castile (1199-1252; r. 1217-1252) effectively completed the "reconquista" by claiming the remaining south of the peninsula (except the Emirate of Granada, but including Cordoba) by 1248;
- Alfonso X/Alfonso the Wise of Castile (1221-1284; r. 1252-1284) established a comprehensive system of common law and expanded the development of provincial parliaments, or cortes; and
- the Emirate of Granada, the last Arab state in Europe, was conclusively taken from the Moors in 1492 by the Spanish states of Castile and Aragon.

The remaining Spanish states, Castile (central and western Spain), under Isabella I of Castile (1451-1504; r. 1474-1504), and Aragon (eastern Spain), under Ferdinand II of Aragon (later Ferdinand V of Spain; 1452-1516; r. 1474-1516), were united by the marriage of Isabella and Ferdinand in 1469 and by the Peace of Alcacovas (which ended the Castilian War of Spanish Succession [1474-1479] against Portugal and France) in 1479. The unified Spanish state that resulted was responsible for the final Christian victory over the Moors in 1492; for the religious intolerance that brought the expulsion of the Moors and Jews and the establishment of the Spanish Inquisition, both in the late fifteenth century; and for what were among the earliest European journeys of world discovery and world conquest (most notably, those of Christopher Columbus), also in the late fifteenth century.

The **Swiss Confederation** (1291-1513) was first formed in the region of modern Switzerland from three small and largely autonomous territories, or cantons, in the late thirteenth century. These territories came together mainly for protection from the Hapsburgs in Austria. The Confederation expanded in the fourteenth to the sixteenth centuries in various disputes with Austria, Germany, Burgundy, and Italy and it became wholly independent, separating itself entirely from the German Empire, in 1499.

The **Kingdom of Burgundy** (1363-1477) was first formed as a complex of territories in the border regions of (eastern) France, (western) Switzerland, and (western) Germany by a branch of the House of Valois, the ruling family in France from the early fourteenth to the late fifteenth centuries. Philip the Bold (1342-1404; r. 1363-1404) was invested with the Duchy of Burgundy by his father, John II/John the Good, (Valois) King of France, in 1363. In 1384, Philip (and his successors) obtained Flanders; in 1433, Netherlands; and in 1443, Luxembourg. By means of entangling alliances with England, Castile, Aragon, and Austria against France and Switzerland, the grandson of Philip the Bold, Philip the Good (1396-1467; r. 1419-1467), and his son, Charles the Bold (1433-1477; r. 1467-1477), were variously defeated in armed conflict by (and lost most of the Kingdom by marriage to) the Austrian Hapsburgs at the Battle of Nancy (in France) in 1477. At its height, Burgundy was among the wealthiest states in Europe, passed through a late flowering of chivalric culture, and spawned a stirring chapter in European painting and music.

Late medieval **Hungary** was ruled by the Arpads until their extinction in 1301 as has been said. In 1307, it fell to the French House of Anjou (1307-1382) and entered a personal union with the Polish crown in 1347. In 1387, it came under the rule of the (German) House of Luxemburg, presided over by Sigismund (r. 1387-1437), who also became King of Germany in 1410, King of Bohemia in 1419, and Holy Roman Emperor in 1433. With the extinction of the Luxemburgs in 1437, Hungary fell to the (German) Hapsburgs. John Hunyadi (c. 1385-1456) contested Hapsburg claims in 1446 and defeated Turkish claims in 1456. His son, Matthias Corvinus, conquered hereditary Luxemburg territories from the Hapsburgs, was raised to the crown in 1458, and moved the capital to Vienna in 1485. The kingdom declined thereafter and was partially taken over by the Hapsburgs in 1526 and by the Ottoman Empire in 1541.

Late medieval **Bohemia** was incorporated into the German Empire in the tenth century as has been said. It became closely associated with Moravia in the eleventh century; it became a kingdom within the Empire in 1198; and it came to its greatest, independent power in the thirteenth century under Przemysl Ottokar II (d. 1278; r. 1253-1278), who obtained Austria in 1251, parts of Slovakia in 1260, and bits of Hungary in 1261. Ottokar fell in the Battle of Marchfeld (in Austria) in 1278 to Rudolf I of Hapsburg; Bohemia and Moravia again came firmly under the German hegemony (led by Luxemburg, Albrecht I) soon thereafter (in 1306). Bohemia was nonetheless at the center of the Holy Roman Empire under the Luxemburgs (who had unsuccessfully attempted to establish a Greater Slavic Empire centered in Prague), Charles IV, Wenceslaus, and Sigismund, from the mid-fourteenth to the mid-fifteenth centuries and it enthroned a native king, George Podiebrad, in 1458, even after the Hapsburg restoration of 1437. In 1471, its crown was joined to that of Poland and, from 1526, Bohemia was utterly dominated by the Hapsburgs.

Medieval **Lithuania** was formed by the consolidation of Baltic clans in c. 1250 for the main purpose of strengthening its defense against the Teutonic Knights (1226-1410), a chivalric order that was formed in Palestine in 1190 and that came to dominate the eastern Baltic coast in the thirteenth and fourteenth centuries. (Orthodox) Lithuania was united with (Catholic) Poland by marriage in 1386 and, in that form, it defeated the Teutonic Knights to the north and expanded its power to the east (into Belarus and Ukraine) in the early fifteenth century.

Early medieval **Poland** was undone by the Mongol invasion of it in 1241 as has been said. It nonetheless recovered a unified sense of itself under Vladislav I Lokietek (1260-1333; r. 1306-1333). In the early fourteenth century, under Casimir III/Casimir the Great (1310-1370; r. 1333-1370), it entered a personal union with the Hungarian crown (in 1347). And under Vladislav II Jagiello (c. 1350-1434; r. 1386-1434), the first of the Jagiellonians (1386-1572), it was united by marriage with Lithuania (in 1386) and, in that form, it defeated the Teutonic Knights in the early fifteenth century. In the reign of Casimir IV (1427-1492; r. 1447-1492), Prussia (a northern German region) came under Polish rule (in 1454), the Bohemian crown was joined to the Polish (in 1471), and the Polish-Lithuanian state extended from the Baltic to the Black Sea. Although Poland briefly defended Livonia (effectively, the region now occupied by the modern nation-state of Latvia) against the Russians and Swedes in the late sixteenth century and briefly occupied Moscow and laid claim to the Russian throne in the early seventeenth century, its expansion was at an effective end by the close of the fifteenth century as it was surrounded by powerful political enemies, by the Hapsburgs to the west, the Turks to the south, and the Grand Duchy of Moscow to the east.

Early medieval **Russia**, not unlike early medieval Poland, was vanquished by the Mongol invasion of it in 1245 as has been said. This resulted in the dissolution of the union of (Great) Russians, Belarussians, and Ukrainians and in a prolonged isolation from the west. (Great) Russians remained under Mongol sovereignty into the late fourteenth century; Belarussians and Ukrainians fell under Lithuanian and Polish sovereignty into the early fifteenth century. Under the first Russian prince, Ivan I (d. 1341: r. 1325-1341), Moscow became the center of the new Russian Empire and began an impressive expansion. The drift to unified independence started in earnest with the first Russian victory over the Mongols in 1380, the separation of the Greek and Russian Orthodox Churches in 1439, and the consolidation of the Grand Duchy of Moscow under Ivan III/Ivan the Great (1440-1505; r. 1462-1505), the first tsar (sole ruler) of all Russia, in 1480. Ivan significantly expanded the Grand Duchy to the north, mainly by confiscating the Republic of Novgorod, in 1478; he achieved a decisive disengagement from the Mongols in 1480; and he transformed his residence, the Kremlin (castle), into an architectural wonder. The most notable of Ivan's immediate successors was Ivan IV/Ivan the Terrible (1530-1584; r. 1533-1584), who renewed the Empire through absolute autocracy, awesome and arbitrary terror, and mass liquidations, all significantly occasioned by his severe mental illness; who reformed the law, central administration, bureaucracy, and army; who opened trade with the west (with England in particular); who presided over massive flights of peasants from the soil and the consequent decline of agriculture; who greatly expanded the Empire to the south against the Mongols (mainly by subjugating the

Khanates of Kazan and Astrakhan in 1552-1556); who unsuccessfully engaged Sweden and Poland in a dispute over Livonia in 1558-1582; who began the conquest of Siberia, a enormous expansion to the east, in 1581; and who ordered the construction of the "Cathedral of Saint Basil the Blessed" in Moscow in 1554. Ivan was effectively succeeded by Boris Godunov (c. 1551-1605; r. 1588/1598-1605), who came fully to the throne (by election of an assembly of the ruling class) with the death of the last of the Rurik Dynasty (Ivan's mentally deranged son, Feodor I [1557-1598; r. 1584/1588-1598]), the governing authority in Russia that had descended from the Swedish Vikings and that had in various senses ruled in Russia from 865. Godunov's reign was greatly troubled by famine, by peasant and military rebellions, by disputes over the throne, and by Polish occupation. Grave difficulties continued after Godunov's death and a new ruling dynasty closely related to the Ruriks (i.e., from a wife of Ivan IV), the Romanov Dynasty, was installed by election in 1613.

All major Balkan states of the late Middle Ages, except Greece, Albania, and Romania/Moldova, were of Slavic tradition; all (except Greece) threw off a reassertion of Byzantine sovereignty over them in the twelfth century; all (except Greece), like the other leading European states of the period, tended, at least briefly, toward a more unified national circumstance; then all (except Croatia and Slovenia) were defeated by the Ottoman Turks and became a part of the Ottoman Empire in the fourteenth, fifteenth, and sixteenth centuries. The First Bulgarian Empire was subjugated by the Byzantine Empire in 1018 as has been said. Ivan (fl. late twelfth century) overcame Byzantine domination of **Bulgaria** and established the Second Bulgarian Empire in 1186. The Empire expanded briefly before Mongol and again Byzantine advances of the thirteenth century substantially weakened it; it then disintegrated into feudal territories until absorbed by the Greater Serbian State in 1330; it became a province of the Ottoman Empire in 1396; and it remained an Ottoman possession until 1908. The **Greater Serbian State** (including Serbia, Bosnia, Herzegovina, Montenegro, Macedonia, Albania, and northern Greece) was formed by Stefan Nemanja (1151-1196; r. 1169-1196), who united tribal entities and overcame Byzantine domination in the late twelfth century. The Serbian Orthodox National Church was established in 1219 and functioned as a highly significant unifying influence. Serbia became the dominant power in the Balkans with its defeat of the Bulgarians in 1330; a generation later, it disintegrated into feudal principalities; it was then defeated by the Turks at the Battle of Kosovo in 1389; it was incorporated into the Ottoman Empire in 1459; and it remained an Ottoman possession until 1878. Greece was absorbed into the Ottoman Empire, from the Byzantine, in 1456 and it remained an Ottoman province until 1829. Late medieval Albania (of unique, Thraco-Illyrian, not Slavic, linguistic and cultural character) was formed by nomadic Wallachians and native Illyrians; it was under Serbian hegemony until the fourteenth century; led by Skanderbeg (c. 1404-1468), it made a heroic defense of itself against the Ottoman Turks in the mid-fifteenth century; it nonetheless fell to the Turks in 1478; and it remained an Ottoman province until 1912. Bosnia became a part of the Greater Serbian State in the mid-fourteenth century; it established an independent state under Stefan Tvrtko (1353-1391) in the late fourteenth century; it fell to the Ottoman Turks in 1463; and it remained an Ottoman province until 1878. Herzegovina also became a part of the Greater Serbian State in the mid-fourteenth century; it established an independent state in 1448; it fell to the Ottoman Turks in 1483; and it remained an Ottoman province until 1878. Latinic, not Slavic, Wallachia and Moldavia (in the approximate region now occupied by the modern nation-states of Romania, Moldova, and southwestern Ukraine) were formed in the eleventh century; they gained a sense of independence in 1365; they became provinces of the Ottoman Empire in 1394 and 1512 respectively; and they remained Ottoman dependencies until 1861. And Croatia was formed in the tenth century; it passed (with Slovenia) largely to the (Austrian) Hapsburgs in the fourteenth and fifteenth centuries; and it effectively remained an Austrian province until 1918.

In **Byzantine Turkey**, the Byzantine Empire began an inexorable decline after the period of the Macedonian Dynasty (867-1025) as has been said. Foreign advances on it were increasingly successful, its territories were increasingly diminished, and it fell into increasing fragmentation. The so-termed Middle Byzantine Empire (1025-1204), which followed the Macedonian Dynasty, was most notably marked by the Great Schism between the Eastern Orthodox (Greek) and Western (Roman) Churches in 1054; by wide Christian conversions of the Slavs (most significantly, of Russians); by an extension of the spiritualistic aesthetic of the Early Byzantine Empire, principally in painting and in architecture;[112] by attacks on it from Normans to the west, from Patzinaks, Cumans, Magyars, Bulgars, Serbs, and Croatians to the north and west, from Persians, Seljuk Turks, and Mongols to the east, and from Islamic Arabs to the south; and by conquests of Constantinople itself by Crusaders in 1203 and 1204. This latter, the Fourth Crusade's second conquest of Constantinople in 1204, established the Latin Empire (1204-1261), a political entity in which western European Christians took over most of the Byzantine Empire (then effectively reduced to Greece and to the Asian and European territories subtending Constantinople). The Latin Empire was partitioned among the western Europeans into the territories of and about Constantinople (under Flemish sovereignty) and those of Greece (under Italian sovereignty). Several Byzantine successor states also survived/developed on the borders of the Latin Empire and routinely challenged it; the most notable of these was the Nicaean Empire in western Asia Minor (Turkey). The Latin Empire was most tellingly characterized by the rise of Venice and Genoa as the leading commercial powers in the near Middle East and by the barbaric cruelties it heaped on the Greeks, including the pillage and ruin of many cultural and artistic treasures. The Empire was dissolved in 1261 by Michael VIII Paleologus (1234-1282; r. 1261-1282).

In the Late Byzantine Empire, under the Paleologi (1261-1453), Greek cultural independence was restored and Byzantium variously lost and gained territories (and prerogatives) against enemies that encircled it but it never recovered fully from the Latin incursion and neither did it ever succeed in reuniting the Eastern and Western Churches. Michael "regained" most of the Nicaean Empire and also reclaimed some territories in the Balkans. With the reign of his son and successor, Andronicus II (d. 1328; r. 1282-1328), however, civil wars and Mongol and Ottoman Turkish assaults from the east intensified. By the mid-fourteenth century, the Ottoman Turks[113] occupied the virtual whole of Asia Minor and the Byzantine Empire had been reduced to Constantinople and the European territories immediately surrounding it. The first Ottoman siege of Constantinople occurred in 1422; in 1453, the last of the Paleologi, Constantine XI (1394-1453; r. 1449-1453), was defeated and killed by the Islamic forces of the Ottoman Turkish Sultan, Mohammed II (1430-1481; r. 1451-1481). Constantinople itself thus fell (and became Istanbul); the Byzantine (Eastern Roman) Empire thus ended; the medieval epoch thus closed; the extensive Ottoman Empire and Turkey were thus born; and the modern era was thus inaugurated.

Although the dissolution of the Byzantine Empire is commonly taken as the concluding act of medieval civilization, the Empire and its demise nonetheless had an enormous affect on the earliest development of modern civilization. Byzantium had sheltered much of the ancient European heritage throughout the medieval millennium; Greek scholars fled, at the fall of Constantinople, with the terms of this heritage mainly to Italy; and this heritage provided the principal basis for the earliest development of modern European humanism. At the fall of Constantinople, the center of the Eastern Orthodox Church was transferred from Constantinople to Moscow. At the fall of Constantinople, Europe lost access to the Black Sea and was deprived of land routes to India and China; it thus began a search for a new sea route and stumbled over previously unknown (to the Europeans) bits of the Americas, Africa, Asia, and Oceania. And, the ongoing relationship of the Ottoman Empire, which was of predominantly Islamic orientation, and European states, which were of predominantly Christian orientation, would decide much of the most significant international, political, economic, and military activity of the next four to five centuries.

Arguably the most influential international events of the late Middle Ages were the **Crusades**, nine largely unsuccessful attempts of European Christianity which occurred between 1096 and 1291, which were ordered chiefly by papal authority, and which were aimed principally at recovering, by armed force, the Holy Land (Palestine) in general and Jerusalem (the Holy Sepulchre) in particular from the Moslems (and Jews), at reuniting the Latin (the Roman) and the Greek (the Eastern Orthodox) Churches, and at obtaining land, other forms of wealth, and trade advantages. The Crusades brought men from thousands of small and isolated castle communities together and brought European culture and learning into contact with Middle Eastern culture and learning. They brought previously isolated Christian communities into contact with one another and they brought Christian culture and learning into contact with Islamic (and Judaic) culture and learning. The Crusades were also instrumental in undoing the feudal system of political economy which marked the late Middle Ages, in establishing the intercultural conditions for the wide resumption of trade and commerce which marked the late Middle Ages, and in establishing the animate conditions necessary to educational, artistic, and sporting prosperity which marked the late Middle Ages.

The First Crusade, 1096-1099, was conducted by French, Flemish, and Norman (under Robert II) forces; it entailed the provisional conquest of Antioch (in Syria), Nicaea (near Constantinople), the (Seljuk) Sultanate of Iconium, and Jerusalem; and it resulted in the establishment of Crusader States in Palestine, Syria, and Asia Minor. The most notable of these States was the Kingdom of Jerusalem, 1099-1187, which was eventually weakened by disputes over imperial succession, conflicts with Byzantines, Seljuk Turks, and Islamic Arabs, and internal debility. The Kingdom was in the end defeated by the (Islamic, Kurdish) Sultan of the Empire of the Ayyubids, Saladin (c. 1137-1193; r. 1171-1193), in 1187. The Second Crusade, 1147-1149, was carried out by French (under Louis VII), German, and Italian forces, was instigated by successful Islamic attacks on the Crusader States, and ended in European defeat in Asia Minor and Damascus. The Third Crusade, 1189-1192, was conducted by German (under Frederick I), English (under Richard I), and French (under Philip II) forces, was immediately preceded by Saladin's re-conquest of Jerusalem in 1187, and entailed limited

European successes in Asia Minor and Palestine (including permission for Christian pilgrimages to Jerusalem). The Fourth Crusade, 1202-1204, was carried out by French, Flemish, and Italian forces and it most importantly included the conquest of Constantinople in 1203 and (after a brief loss of the city) a second victory over the Orthodox Byzantines for the city in 1204, all of which deepened the enmity between the established Christian Churches, the western, Latin and the Eastern, Greek Churches. The Latin Empire (1204-1261), in which western European Christians took over most of the Byzantine Empire, was the result; the Byzantine Empire was restored in these regions in 1261 as has been said. The so-termed "Children's Crusade" of 1212 followed; this abortive expedition was taken over by corrupt merchants who transported thousands of children from Marseille to Alexandria and sold them into slavery. The Fifth Crusade, 1217-1221, was aimed in a badly organized way at Egypt but failed. The Sixth Crusade, 1228-1229, was mainly conducted by the German Emperor, Frederick II, who obtained Jerusalem, Bethlehem, and Nazareth; the Moslems re-conquered these cities in 1244. The Seventh Crusade, 1248-1254, was carried out principally by French King, Louis IX, and, like the Sixth, unsuccessfully attempted to conquer Egypt. The Eighth Crusade, 1270, was also carried out by Louis IX of France; it entailed unsuccessful attempts to conquer north-central Africa. The final Crusade, the Ninth, 1291, was marked by the loss of the last of the Crusader States to the Moslems; sparse, terminal holdings in Egypt fell to the Mamelukes (originally warrior slaves of the Fatimids who secured independence and held ruling [Islamic] authority over most of Egypt from 1250 to 1517); and Crusader possessions in Palestine were abandoned.

The Crusades failed in the end because the Moslem and Byzantine resolve (as well as technological prowess) was great and because the national and commercial interests of the European states involved could not be evidently reconciled with the universal claims that had inspired them. The leading Mediterranean seaports of Italy and France in particular nonetheless flourished as a consequence of enhanced trade with the east; the money economy throughout the developed world quickened; a wealthy middle class of merchants and artisans developed; standards of living improved dramatically; and the cultural station of Europe rose by its association with superior Arab and Byzantine cultures.

The near-to-incessant military activity of the late Middle Ages, perhaps most notably that of the Crusades, was mainly conducted by chivalric institutions and the principles that governed them. Formal Orders of Knights -- most significantly, the Knights of St. John (formed in 1113), the Knights Templars (formed in 1120), and the Teutonic Knights (formed in 1190) -- combined the ascetic ideals of monastic life (mainly, poverty, chastity, piety, and obedience) with the principles of the medieval warrior (mainly, bravery, loyalty, continence, protection of the oppressed, and the waging of war against so-termed heretics). These ideals and principles, modeled on the examples of Alexander the Great and Charlemagne, were celebrated in the epic literature, the secular music, and the sport of chivalric court culture. Although court life fell typically well beneath the ideal standards claimed for it, these ideals and their practice nonetheless provided the inspiration for the lyric romances, the secular music, and the activities of the tournaments in the late Middle Ages.

The **lyric romances** were based principally in the heroic and vigorous customs of war and courtship in Germany, France, England, Scandinavia, and Spain. They most importantly included: Beowulf, Le Morte d'Arthur, Sir Gawain and the Green Knight, Edda Elder, Nibelungenlied, The Song of Roland, Poem of the Cid, Tristan and Isolde, and Parsifal. The **secular music** of the period differed significantly from the somber tendencies of early medieval liturgical song. Not unlike the literature of the late Middle Ages, the music was too of a more robust and vital character as against early medieval equivalents. It was originally of monophonic, later of polyphonic character and was often sung to instrumental accompaniment, sometimes with dramatic and dance texts as well; it was thus of a much more complex and active form than plainsong. It was developed in the eleventh to the fifteenth centuries, principally by troubadours and trouvères in France and by minnesinger and meistersinger in Germany, but also had an important presence in England, Italy, and Spain. These minstrels of love and war poems were themselves customarily of the lower nobility; they nonetheless typically performed for courtly audiences of the upper nobility. Arguably the most remarkable of these balladeers were William IX of Poitiers (1071-1127) and Adam de la Hale (c. 1230- c. 1288).

The **tournaments** of the late Middle Ages, like the literature and the music of the period, also functioned as telling secularizing agents. They were less strictly military and more strictly sporting events than their early medieval analogs had been. As royal law increasingly replaced feudal law and as capital concerns progressively blunted military objectives, the tournaments grew more artificial and more costly; they were increasingly corrupted by indulgence and expense; they were governed by increasingly detailed rules; they came to include non-military as well as military populations; they made larger accommodations for spectators (especially women); they were increasingly staged in formal enclosures; and they awarded increasingly more valuable prizes for success in them. They were nonetheless also, however, subject to aesthetic criteria; they were, for prominent instance, frequently visited by leading minstrels and by the sense of beauty conveyed by the singers of engaging song. They were as well rooted in moral principles/criteria characteristic of the chivalric movement (and courtly tradition) itself; criteria such as decent conduct, respect for opponents, and deference to rules. The first regulated tournaments in Germany were staged in 934, in France in 1066, and in England in 1194. The tournaments reached their greatest acclaim in the eleventh to the fourteenth centuries in Germany, France, England, Italy, Spain, and Flanders. It was in this period and in these places that the tournaments evolved from brutal war-like battles into more regulated (largely jousting, tilting, and quintain) spectacles as has been said. As regulated events, however, they relinquished much of the political and economic function (and status) they had earlier served (and held). This loss, together with church objections to the violence, drunkenness, ostentation, gluttony, and gambling associated with them and the diminished need for the skills they developed with the advent of gunpowder in Europe (and the consequent revolution in the techniques of warfare) in the fourteenth century, made them increasingly less useful, increasingly less necessary, and increasingly less popular after the fourteenth century. They nonetheless continued in some fashion (in the German case as national events staged at regular intervals) into the seventeenth century, largely in the revised form of elaborate archery contests among the bourgeoisie, known as schutzenfeste.

The royal and papal view of the tournaments was equivocal. Insofar as they contributed to the defense of the realm, they were favored. Insofar as they evoked public disorder and indecency, they were not. The English monarchs, William I, William II, Henry I, and Henry II, for salient instance, are known to have prohibited certain forms of tournament. Richard I, John, Edward I, and Edward II are known to have greatly favored the tournaments. Henry III variously forbade and licensed them. Richard II and Henry IV prohibited peasants from participating in them. The most accomplished of the medieval tournament professionals, William the Marshal (1146-1219), who made his greatest successes between 1173 and 1183, was nonetheless among the most celebrated personalities of his time. He captured 500 knights and their equipment in the able service of four kings (Henry II, Richard I, John, and Henry III) and was the frequent subject of popular poems and songs. The German and French perception of the tournaments, at least insofar as it was unaffected by papal views, was apparently less ambiguous and, on balance, approving. The papal opinion was itself ambivalent, however. Although the military-secular and ecclesiastical worlds were in a sense reconciled in the mid-eleventh century under Pope Leo IX (1002-1054; r. 1049-1054) and the tournaments were given tacit endorsement for purposes of supporting the Crusades from the late eleventh century forward, formal prohibitions against tournaments were nonetheless continued from the early Middle Ages. These prohibitions were accentuated by the Council of Clermont in 1130, the Council of Reims in 1131, the Second Lateran Council in 1139, the Synod of Reims in 1148, and the Third Lateran Council in 1179. Although such luminous philosophical leaders of the Church as Albertus Magnus and St. Thomas Aquinas accepted them in the thirteenth century, the papal injunction against them was not lifted until 1316 (by Pope John XXII [c. 1244-1334; r. 1316-1334]).

While the tournaments were arguably the most conspicuous and otherwise prominent form of late (as well as early) medieval sport, they were by no means the only significant form of sporting activity in the late Middle Ages. Sport was very much more widely practiced and more sympathetically regarded in the late medieval than in the early medieval epoch. It was also practiced in European contexts other than the courts and in circumstances other than those governed by chivalric principle; most notably, in inns, taverns, and holiday fairs/festivals, in schools (or at least in informal association with the new, emerging guilds and universities in particular), and in monasteries. And it was as well always practiced in the context of fairly sharp distinctions in socio-economic class. Although most of the sporting activities practiced in the schools and monasteries were the same (or very similar to) those practiced in inns, taverns, and holiday fairs/festivals, an account of late medieval sport in guilds, universities, and monasteries will be reserved for a forthcoming discussion about the broad character of these institutions.

Most of the **sport practiced in inns, taverns, and holiday fairs/festivals** (the fairs associated with holy days, Sundays, and secular celebrations) was done by peasants and other laborers and it had amusement as its principal aim; it functioned as a diversion from the onerous struggle for ordinary survival. It was customarily practiced in the outdoors, was typically fiercely physical, and was often visited by gambling and by violent, drunken, and disorderly behavior. There was also, in these recreations, little distinction between players and (sparse) spectators and little explicit attention given to gender distinctions (men and women variously participated together and apart from one another). There were neither uniforms nor officials included in them. Arguably the most prominent sporting practices of this type in this time were blood activities (most notably, fighting between and among bulls, bears, boars, cocks, and dogs), team ball games (most notably, precursors of campball/football/rugby, hurling, stickball/stoolball/cricket, field hockey, bandy, and shinty on ground and ice), dual combative activities (most notably, boxing, wrestling, and fencing), track and field athletic activities (most notably, running, jumping, casting the stone, and throwing the spear), aquatic activities (most notably, swimming and boating), winter activities (most notably, ice skating and precursors of curling), acrobatic gymnastics, archery, bowling, quoits, and precursors of golf.

Of these, in turn, most is known about the various forms of football, bat-and-ball games, acrobatic gymnastics, ice skating, and archery played in late medieval England and of the track and field athletic activities most widely practiced in late medieval Scotland. A form of football was played in England from at least 1175 among teams of persons from distinguishable villages, among teams that varied from several members to several hundred members, among both men and women together and apart, and on fields both small and very large (in some cases, the goals were several miles from one another). It was even, on occasion, played among aristocratic men to large audiences. Lower-class football was also the subject of numerous royal edicts prohibiting it. Henry II banned football in the late twelfth century because it caused disabling injury and because it distracted from the practice of archery. Edward II (1314) objected to football's displeasing affects on civil order and tranquility. And Edward III (1365), Richard II (1388), Henry V (1414), and Edward IV (1477) ruled variously against football, lawn bowling, tennis, and casting the stone in favor of archery. A similar Irish ban of a precursor of hurling was issued in 1367 and a similar Dutch ban of a precursor of golf was enacted in 1360. The most prominent bat-and-ball games of the time were the acknowledged precursors of cricket, stickball and stoolball, played in England from at least 1300. Acrobatic gymnastics were most widely practiced by the minstrels of late medieval England, France, and Italy. Ice skating was practiced by strapping long animal bones to the feet and was fairly widely done in England, Netherlands, and Scandinavia from at least the twelfth century. Archery was very widely practiced throughout late medieval Europe; most especially, after the colossal successes of English archers at the Battles of Poitiers (1356) and Agincourt (1415) in the One Hundred Years War and after the military enfranchisement of the lower classes following the Black Death of the mid-fourteenth century. Like football, archery was too the subject of numerous royal edicts; unlike football, however, it was promoted, not prohibited, by such edicts. The most memorable of these writs of advocacy were issued by English monarchs, Henry II, Henry III, Edward I (also proscribing fencing in 1281), Edward III (also proscribing field hockey in 1363), Richard II, Henry V, and Edward IV. William II is also said to have been himself particularly fond of archery. The sport was less widely practiced after the successful use of guns by Edward the Black Prince at the Battle of Crécy in 1346 and, more notably, by Henry Tudor in the defeat of Richard III at Bosworth Field in 1485.

The track and field athletic activity of late medieval England and Scotland was most influenced by the Irish, Tailteann Games, last contested in 554. The most significant, formal meetings of the age were the Scottish, **Highland Games**, or Gatherings, first staged in the late eleventh century under the direction of King Malcolm III (d. 1093; r. 1057-1093), who came to the throne by defeating (and killing) his predecessor, Macbeth (d. 1057; r. 1040-1057), and who was a leading advocate of Scottish independence (from England) in the late Middle Ages. The earliest editions of the Highland Games were devoted to the utilitarian task of selecting the fastest clansmen as postal runners; they awarded numerous and substantial prizes; and they were the precursors of what became the most important of the strictly athletic meetings, the Braemar Gathering. The Games continued until suspended briefly in the mid-eighteenth century.

The aristocracy (most conspicuously, English monarchs) was itself known to have participated in these activities, football and archery in particular, in this period. Edward I is thought to have been fond of wrestling and Edward II, of wrestling and swimming. But, tournament skills aside, the aristocracy was mainly devoted, in sporting terms, to animal sports (most notably, hunting, fishing, falconry/hawking, horse riding/racing, chariot racing, polo, and bull fighting), shooting, and precursors of billiards, croquet (pêle mêle), and handball/tennis. The lower classes also, on occasion, are known to have participated in hunting, fishing, falconry/hawking, horse riding/racing, and handball/tennis, but not always as a matter of course and not always lawfully. Among the sports of the aristocracy, most is known of hunting, fishing, falconry/hawking, horse riding/racing, chariot racing, polo, and handball/tennis. Hunting in England was a formal function of feudal privilege from 1066 and it was a leading recreation of William I, William II (who was killed in a hunting "accident"), Henry II, Thomas à Becket, John, Henry III, and Edward III. Fishing for sporting purposes was also widely done, particularly in late medieval England; and it owes its earliest book-length manuscript to this period, The Art of Fishing with an Angle by Juliana Berners in 1486, nearly two centuries before Izaak Walton's more celebrated treatise. Falconry/hawking was among the favorite recreations of William I, Henry II, Thomas à Becket, and Frederick II of Germany. Although the first public horse-race course, the Smithfield Track, was established in London in c. 1174, horse riding/racing, chariot racing, and polo were most widely practiced in Byzantium. The Roman circuses, which most importantly included horse and chariot racing, continued (from the ancient practice) into the twelfth century when the political and economic status of the factions associated with them changed significantly (the factions became publicly financed and sought imperial allegiances) and when excessive expense and church condemnation put an end to them. A game similar to polo was played most significantly by the Byzantine royal family between the tenth and twelfth centuries. The first known bullfight was staged at a coronation of Alfonso VII of Castile and Lyon (1104-1157; r. 1126-1157) in 1133. Billiards as such began to develop in fourteenth-century (and fifteenth-century) France and England out of attempts to craft an indoor version of lawn bowling; the game was first played on an enormous square floor or table with arches and stakes (cones) as targets for thrown, stone balls (pebbles), then for balls struck with a mace (a large wooden club). The most widely practiced form of non-animal sport among the late medieval aristocracy, however, was handball/tennis, variously played with implement and without (with the open hand). The game was most widely played in Ireland, England, and France, likely from as early as the eleventh, twelfth, and thirteenth centuries. Edward III constructed a court and advocated the playing of the sport before condemning it in deference to archery in 1365. Richard II, Henry IV, and Edward IV likewise prohibited its practice among the lower classes in 1388, 1410, and 1477 respectively. Although outlawed by Louis IX in the thirteenth century, several later French monarchs were greatly devoted to a form of the game known as "le jeu de paume;" most notably, Louis X and Charles V in the fourteenth century and others in the fifteenth to the eighteenth centuries.

Sport was also variously portrayed in leading illuminated and unilluminated manuscripts and in other artistic artifacts of the late Middle Ages. Included in the "Bayeux Tapestry" (1070-1082), depicting events of the Norman Conquest, are images of bull baiting, bear baiting, cock fighting, hunting, fishing, hawking, horse riding, football, stickball, throwing, and archery. In William Fitzstephen's "Description of the City of London," (c. 1175) are attributions of sport to the play impulse and documentary references to the gambling and violence associated with sport of the common folk. Chaucer's <u>Troilus and Criseyde</u> refers passingly to tennis and his <u>The Canterbury Tales</u>, to hunting and wrestling. One of the finest illuminated manuscripts of the period, the <u>Luttrell Psalter</u>, includes portrayals of fourteenth-century English hawking, horse riding, and archery. And Alfonso X of Castile arranged for the publication of a manuscript highly favorable to sporting games and their enjoyment, <u>Libro de Juegos</u>, in 1283.

The deepening sense of political centralization characteristic of late medieval life was importantly accompanied and abetted by the growing respect for secular affairs that likewise visited the age. This **secularization of cultural life** manifested itself in several important ways. For one, it manifested itself in an enormous increase in trade and population. The **resumption of trade** was significantly initiated and sustained by:

- the international and intercultural affects of the Crusades and other military adventures;
- advanced agricultural technology and productivity driven by such as the development of watermills and windmills for the processing of grain, of the replacement of oxen by horses as main draught animals, of improved systems of irrigation and methods of crop rotation, of improved ploughs, harrows, scythes, and flails, and of horse collars and shoes;
- advanced military technology and increased warfare having mainly to do with improved equipment for the martial use of the horse (stirrups and shoes);
- advanced manufacturing, communication, and transportation technology having principally to do with the development of the clock, furnace, and spinning wheel, with the first large-scale production of linen, paper, and books, and with the improvement of glass and ships;
- the establishment of advanced commercial and banking practices having mainly to do with credit, commissions, and innovative bookkeeping; and
- the establishment of corporate trade associations involving an assemblage of mercantile cities, formed in order to secure commercial advantage and prepared to defend itself by military means if necessary.[114]

The accelerated commerce of the period resulted in a dramatic quickening of the money economy, a dramatic increase in the standard of living (including dietary improvements), and a dramatic tendency toward urbanization.

The growing respect for secular affairs in the late Middle Ages manifested itself, for a second, in the **reestablishment of large urban centers** (towns, or cities). Agrarian populations migrated to an increasing number of progressively larger, more carefully planned, and more uniform cities, where increasingly numerous consumer goods and services were exchanged. With the economic recovery of Europe in the eleventh century, walled cities were either established (in advantageous geographical locations) or developed (around castle communities) by royal or by ecclesiastical authorities and became settlements of such authorities and other citizens (mainly, knights, artisans, merchants, and wage laborers) with a permanent market. These cities engendered the free right to own and to wander; they developed urban governmental frameworks; they gave administrative direction to the development of modern national/territorial states; they attempted to increase their liberties and to extend both their territories and their influence as centers of civilized life; and they signaled the decline of the feudal order. Somewhat as a basis for the cities and somewhat as a result of the cities, there developed in them a wealthy and powerful middle class of artisans and merchants. In some cases, this class became the dominant class and thus became the dominant governing influence. The rise of a large and powerful middle class was among the most significant occurrences in the widespread extension of the democratic spirit that also marked the late Middle Ages. It was this middle class, in turn, that created distinctive divisions of labor according to trade/craft and created as well professional societies (guilds) according to trade/craft. The **trade, craft, and merchant guilds** were private, mandatory associations operating under royal protection, designed to both plan, control, and guide the production of goods and services (in terms of quality, price, distribution, and profits) and to supervise the training, employment, and social welfare of artisans and merchants. They were first developed in the twelfth century and they became leading agencies of education and training in the late Middle Ages. Insofar as they were educational offices, they had various religious and social obligations but were primarily devoted to giving practical and vocational instruction in the rigors and standards of craft and commercial life. As such, the guild education was fairly narrow but it was too very importantly an education of a distinctly secular type and an education that both revered and improved the laboring activity which advanced medieval culture in economic (and, ultimately, in cultural) terms. The guilds were, however, established by the prosperous for the prosperous and did therefore not include peasants and unskilled wage laborers. Some of them nonetheless later evolved into town, or burgher, schools which served a broader constituency. Priests who gave adjunct instruction in linguistic and religious subjects aside, the teachers in the guilds were those who had passed successfully through the industrial ranks, from apprentice to journeyman to master craftsman.

The third major manifestation of the burgeoning respect for secular affairs that defined the late Middle Ages was the **inception of the European universities**.[115] In the eleventh and twelfth centuries, a revival of classical learning, based mainly on the recent re-discovery of Aristotle's thought, developed. This revival brought ancient classical and medieval religious philosophy together in a more modern way than previously; that is to say, in a way that called the revealed faith of religious devotion before the mantle of secular reason, in a way that required faith to account for itself in rational terms. The unique conjunction of ancient and medieval thought in the late Middle Ages framed the dominant intellectual movement of the period, scholasticism. The scholastic urge, in turn, spawned the formation of the late medieval universities. This formation was itself greatly abetted by the return to Europe of Byzantine scholars as the Byzantine Empire tumbled to decline and collapsed. The major cities of Byzantium, principally Constantinople, had preserved (together with the Church) the ancient Graeco-Roman heritage throughout the medieval millennium. The return of this heritage to its European ground contributed significantly to the renewed enthusiasm for classical learning then developing, most notably in Italy, France, England, Spain, Bohemia, Austria, and Germany.

Students at cathedral and monastic schools increasingly gathered, in a broader context, about eminent and sparse teachers, or masters, and paid fees to hear them. Corporations, or guilds, exclusively comprised of teachers and students, not others, formed around this practice and were granted judicial and administrative autonomy by imperial and ecclesiastical authority. These organizations were known as universities and they were principally about giving/taking demanding instruction in law, theology, philosophy, the arts, and medicine. They conducted their activities in existing rooms or buildings throughout the cities in which they were located. Masters read and commented on text in Latin; students, who owned no books of their own, listened intently and engaged masters in discussion. Students were granted baccalaureate degrees after four years of successful study, were themselves licensed to teach after approximately six years of such study, and won doctor's degrees after six to twelve years of such study. The southern European universities were mostly student formed and administered; the northern European universities were mostly teacher formed and administered. The first university in southern Europe, and the model for others in the region, was the University of Bologna, established in 1088. The first university in northern Europe, and the model for others in the region, was the University of Paris, established in 1150. Others soon followed, some by imperial or ecclesiastical command; most notably, Oxford (1167), Salerno (1173), Arezzo (1215), Padua (1222), Cambridge (1229), Toulouse (1229), Salamanca (1243), Seville (1254), Montpellier (1289), Rome (1303), Avignon (1303), Orléans (1309), Pisa (1343), Prague (1348), Krakow (1364), Vienna (1365), Heidelberg (1385), and Cologne/Koln (1388).

The resumption of trade, the town and guild movement, and the formation of universities all favored the basic pre-conditions of sport: a more secular emphasis which developed larger sympathies for the material, physical, and bodily aspects of life and a more fluid social fabric more widely open to change and to new possibilities for a wider compass of people. Still at this, owing mainly to vestiges of asceticism, neither the guilds nor the universities gave any formal attention to sport; in some cases, they even authorized sanctions against sporting (and related) activities. The townsmen, guildsmen, and university students of the age nonetheless enjoyed a rich informal experience of such activities. Humanity's universal and fundamental inclinations to sport again managed to get themselves expressed despite official efforts to suppress them. Most of this activity was done either spontaneously, in the course of ordinary community life, or done in inns, taverns, and holiday fairs/festivals. The **sporting recreations practiced in towns, guilds, and universities** principally entailed informal participation in most of the activities commonly practiced in inns, taverns, and holiday fairs/festivals. The most widely done forms of sport in this circumstance were: blood sports (most notably, fighting between and among bulls, bears, boars, cocks, and dogs), other forms of animal sport (most notably, tournament skills, hunting, fishing, falconry/hawking, horse riding/racing, chariot racing, and polo), team ball games (most notably, precursors of campball/football/rugby, hurling, stickball/stoolball/cricket, field hockey, bandy, and shinty on ground and ice), dual combative sports (most notably, boxing, wrestling, and fencing), track and field athletic activities (most notably, running, jumping, casting the stone, and throwing the spear), aquatic sports (most notably, swimming and boating), winter sports (most notably, ice skating and precursors of curling), acrobatic gymnastics, archery, bowling, quoits, shooting, and precursors of billiards, croquet (pêle mêle), golf, and handball/tennis. Like the chivalric tournaments as well as the sporting practices of the inns, taverns, and holiday fairs/festivals, however, the sporting recreations of the late medieval towns, guilds, and universities often included violence, drunkenness, and gambling and thereby often also invited church and political condemnation.

The secularizing tendencies of late medieval culture were likewise evident in the profound transformations through which the Christian Church passed in this time. Principal among these transformations were the dilution of papal authority, the schism of Western (Roman) and Eastern Orthodox faiths, the Crusades, the development of Protestant agitations, and the unfolding of scholasticism. Papal authority began to decline nominally in the tenth and eleventh centuries; the papal monarchy, the Papal States, in the thirteenth century. This authority was increasingly replaced by the prerogatives of secular monarchs who were more favorably disposed to the affairs of the material world, including the likes of sport. The **dilution of papal authority** began in earnest with the reform movements of the tenth and eleventh centuries, movements such as the Cluniac correction which, ironically enough, attempted to redress secular drifts of the Church. These movements installed priestly celibacy, limited the conduct of war, "eliminated" the corrupt purchase of ecclesiastic offices, denied rights of investiture (rights of assigning feudal estates and the authority accompanying them to lay persons; most notably, to secular monarchs), provided for the ecclesiastic election (as distinct from the imperial appointment) of the Pope, and established the Papacy as a centralized monarchy, and, thus, as a an absolute (a divine) monarchy. The investiture struggle was likely at the heart of these reforms and at the heart of the secular/anti-secular conflict. This struggle had principally to do with the influence of the Papacy and of secular monarchs over both secular and ecclesiastic affairs (over both temporal wealth and spiritual privilege), most memorably in Germany and England.[116] Despite the earnest efforts of Pope Leo IX to reconcile the secular and the ecclesiastical worlds, the issue of investiture was not formally "resolved" until the Concordat of Worms, concluded by Holy Roman Emperor and German King, Henry V, and Pope Calixtus II (d. 1124; r. 1119-1124) in 1122. In the Concordat, monarchs relinquished prerogatives over the internal affairs of the Church and gained larger secular powers; the Church relinquished influence over temporal matters and gained larger ecclesiastic powers. Not unlike the basic tendencies of scholasticism (in which matters of faith were ultimately distinguished from matters of reason), the Concordat effectively carved out different spheres for the secular and the ecclesiastical worlds. This was an arrangement that did not immediately or greatly diminish the influence of the Church but it was nonetheless an arrangement that would eventually diminish this influence as the relative dominance of the temporal realm over the spiritual deepened. Even at this, vestiges of the dispute between the secular and ecclesiastic realms have continued to our own time.

The eleventh and twelfth centuries were also occasioned by several other events that were, in their time, of equivocal affect on the Church but which, in the end, diminished its stature; to wit, the **Great Schism** and the Crusades. The provisional separation of the Western (Roman) and Eastern Orthodox Churches of 867 was effectively completed in 1054 by Pope Leo IX. This, the Great Schism, was caused by the conflicting universalistic claims of each and it entailed a rejection of papal jurisdiction over the Eastern faith as well as an Eastern modification of Western practices in respect to liturgy and celibacy. The Crusades effectively deepened the secular drift of the Church and also deepened the rift between Western and Eastern forms of it. The Crusades were a consequence of the intensified internal religiosity of the Church in the eleventh century and advances of the Seljuk Turks in the near Middle East, also in the eleventh century. Pope Gregory VII (c. 1020-1085; r. 1073-1085), at the head of an army of occidental knights, had planned to come to the aid of besieged, eastern Christians, to liberate Palestine (most notably, Jerusalem) from the Moslems (and Jews), and to reunite the Roman and the Eastern Orthodox Churches. Pope Urban II (c. 1042-1099; r. 1088-1099) persuaded the forces of chivalry to the wisdom of Gregory's plan at the Synod of Clermont in 1095 and the Crusades began in 1096. The Crusades predictably sharpened the enmity between Christians and Moslems (the Crusades were aimed mainly at the Moslems), between Christians and Jews (the sacks of Jerusalem in the First Crusade [1099], the late eleventh-century formation of the Crusader States in Palestine, and the formal persecution of Jews by Christians from 1096 to 1215 were the principal causes), and between Western and Eastern Christians (the sacks of Constantinople [1203 and 1204] in the Fourth Crusade, called by Pope Innocent III, and the subsequent establishment of the Latin Empire in the early thirteenth century were the principal causes).

The **Papacy** came to its pinnacle in the twelfth and thirteenth centuries. St. Bernard of Clairvaux (1091-1153) was the ideological architect of the deep, inelaborate, and intuitive piety that characterized the earliest phases of this time. Bernard emphasized the simple worship of God, the salvation of humanity, the necessity of love, humility, and faith, the virtue of doing good works, and the sacraments embodying this faith and these works (baptism, confirmation, marriage, extreme unction or last rites, admission to holy orders, penance or sorrow for sin, indulgence or dilution of penalty for sin, and communion). Pope Alexander III (d. 1181; r. 1159-1181) prevailed in 1174 over English King, Henry II, concerning undue royal influence in the internal affairs of the Church; he prevailed as well over Holy Roman Emperor and German King, Frederick I, concerning the leadership of Western Christianity. Pope Innocent III (c. 1160-1216; r. 1198-1216) centralized papal power, successfully asserted universal rule over much of Europe and the near Middle East, prohibited new orders (sects), and established the (episcopal) Inquisition (in 1215). Pope Gregory IX (c. 1143-1241; r. 1227-1241) established the (papal) Inquisition (formal tribunals against heretics which came to include punishment by death as well as by excommunication, torture, and imprisonment) in 1231 and asserted the independence of church law.

The political, fiscal, and administrative inefficiencies of the Papal monarchy and the corruption that it increasingly fell to, together with effective secular and ecclesiastic challenges to its authority, nonetheless brought it to discernible decline by the end of the thirteenth century. Pope Boniface VIII (1235-1303; r. 1294-1303) unsuccessfully demanded Church exemptions from taxation and from secular sovereignty, most notably from Philip IV of France. Philip, in turn, arranged the election of Pope Clement V (1264-1314; r. 1305-1314), first in a line of French popes, and compelled the transfer of the Papacy from Rome to Avignon (France) in 1309. The Avignon Papacy (1309-1378) was deeply corrupt and extravagant and the Church lost much of its authority throughout the period of its jurisdiction; heretical agitations for reform from outside the Church also accelerated throughout this period. Pope Gregory XI (1331-1378; r. 1370-1378) returned the exiled Papacy permanently to Rome (to the Vatican) in 1377 and the Schism of the West (1378-1417) began at his death the year following. This Schism refers to the sharp division in the Roman Catholic Church (and in related secular affairs as well) between the (western) Papacy of Avignon and the (eastern) Papacy of Rome. The Avignon line continued under Antipope Clement VII (d. 1394; r. 1378-1394) and held allegiance in France, Spain, Scotland, and southern Italy. The Roman line continued under Pope Urban VI (c. 1318-1389; r. 1378-1389) and held allegiance in England, Ireland, Scandinavia, Hungary, Poland, Lithuania, and northern and central Italy. The German Empire was variously divided between the two factions. The Schism was ended by the Council of Constance (1414-1418), which deposed the extant pope and antipope and which elected Pope Martin V (1368-1431; r. 1417-1431) as the sole, the Roman, authority over the entire Church. Although the Council and Martin attempted necessary reforms, these attempts failed, authority over secular matters further decreased, heresy and superstition further increased, and deep internal conflict persisted.

This conflict, which had national as well as ecclesiastic foundations, continued to disadvantage the Church. The institution's gradual turn from poverty to wealth, from spirituality to worldliness, from religion to banking and the failure of its many attempts to reform itself made it increasingly vulnerable to heretical agitations from what were mostly external sources. The **germ of Protestant agitations** began as proclamations of simple, personal, and deeply pious faith of the sort proposed by such as the Cluniac movement in the tenth and eleventh centuries and by St. Bernard of Clairvaux in the twelfth century; and they progressed to the sort of anti-papal appeals characteristic of the Reformations in the sixteenth century. They were all appalled by the increasing corruption and extravagance of the Church; they all proposed a retreat from the secular world and a renewed commitment to strictly spiritual concerns; and they all developed formal sects which were typically opposed by the established Church (mainly by means of military and judicial action against them). Ironically enough, they all contributed, in the end, to the advancing secularization of human civilization by effectively separating the spiritual domain (which was of diminishing significance) and the temporal domain (which was of rising significance), reserving the spiritual domain for the Church and allowing for the self-governance of secular affairs. These late medieval agitations developed in two main waves: the French sects of the twelfth and thirteenth centuries and the Lollard and Hussite movements of the fourteenth and fifteenth centuries.

The **French sects**, mainly the Albigensian and Waldensian sects, were fashioned in the twelfth century and they advocated an ascetic spirituality; a renunciation of property and other forms of wealth; a rejection of the formal church hierarchy, the death penalty, the adoration of saints, and the purchase of indulgences; and a preference for vernacular speech over Latin. The Church responded with the Inquisitions and with military action (most notably, the inconclusive and savage Albigensian Wars, 1209-1229).

The **Lollards and Hussites** were also moved by the doctrine of simple faith but, unlike the French sects, were opposed to formal religious institutions. The Lollards were led by Oxford professor, John Wyclif (c. 1320-1384), who achieved the first English translation of the Latin Bible in 1380. The Lollards believed in the supreme authority of the Scriptures, in a direct, unmediated relation of humanity and God, and in an austere and inelaborate life. They opposed the dogma and ritual of the established Church, denounced the Church hierarchy (including papal authority), defended the laity against the abuses of the Church, and held against celibacy and indulgences. The Hussites were led by the Bohemian reformer, Jan Hus (c. 1369-1415), who was greatly influenced by Wyclif and who held to the same approximate views as Wyclif. Hus' teachings were predictably condemned and suppressed, also like those of Wyclif, but, unlike Wyclif, Hus was executed (burned at the stake) for heresy (by the German King, Sigismund, in Prague, 1415). The inconclusive Hussite Wars (1419-1436), an uprising of Hussite forces against Sigismund (who claimed the Bohemian crown in 1419), followed.

Among the attempts to reform the Church from within that met with significant success, the establishment of the **mendicant orders** was the most telling. These orders, not unlike the French sects, the Lollards, and the Hussites, tended to a form of austere discipline also reminiscent of the chivalric movement and to an ascetic form of poverty and simplicity likewise remindful of early medieval monasticism. Unlike the French sects, the Lollards, and the Hussites, however, these orders were endorsed by the Church and constituted a type of monastic reform; they lived the life of Christ by engaging themselves fully in the secular world, effectively by rejecting permanent abbeys (including monasteries) and wandering, without homes, in the secular world as itinerant teachers and beggars; they were enormously popular; and they had the general effect of combating heresy and reviving the Church. The most notable of these orders, the Franciscan and the Dominican Orders, were established in the thirteenth century. The Franciscan Order was founded in 1209 by the Italian friar, St. Francis of Assisi (1182-1226), who also fashioned (or had fashioned about him) one of the literary masterpieces of the late Middle Ages, The Little Flowers. The Dominican Order was formed in 1216 by the Castilian friar, St Dominic of Caleruega (1170-1221). Both the Franciscan and the Dominican Orders would figure prominently in the scholastic debate that was forthcoming.

Likewise consistent with the increasing accommodation of temporal affairs within the Church were the modest **attentions given to sport by monastic life** in this time. Despite formal attempts to restrict its practice, sport, as a complement of demanding manual labor, was fairly commonly practiced by students in the monastic schools and by monks themselves, largely for religious and peaceful purposes, in late medieval monasteries from at least the twelfth century. The most notable forms of sporting activity in this circumstance were archery, bowling, and wrestling as well as precursors of football, cricket, and handball/tennis.

The dominant intellectual/philosophical movement of the late Middle Ages, **scholasticism**, also contributed significantly, if indirectly and unintentionally, to the secular tendencies of the period. Both the development and the dissolution of the scholastic movement were driven by the renewed enthusiasm for ancient classical, for ancient Graeco-Roman, scholarship (occasioned principally by the re-discovery of Aristotle's naturalistic-tending thought) that visited the late Middle Ages and that was too the originative basis of the late medieval universities. Scholasticism was mainly concerned with the character and relation of divine revelation, or faith (in which the will is dominant), and human reason (in which the intellect is dominant) as well as with the problem of universals (i.e., substantive classes of entities) in the form of the nominalist-realist debate. Scholasticism attempted to reconcile the rival claims of faith and reason in Judaism, Christianity, and Islam -- to explain the Judaic, Christian, and Islamic dicta of faith in rational terms. It therefore challenged the orthodox Judaic, Christian, and Islamic dogmas at least to the extent that it subjected these dogmas to a rational examination and attempted to make the dogmas intelligible, not only to divine disclosure, but also to human reason; it called the divine order to the bench of secular reason. The early result of these reasoned defenses of Judaism, Christianity, and Islam was to suppose that reason confirms revelation and is therefore continuous and consistent with revelation; the early result of scholasticism was to unite faith and reason. This conclusion was forwarded most significantly by the leading Judaic scholastic, Moses Maimonides (1135-1204), by the leading early and high Christian scholastics, St. Anselm of Canterbury (1033-1109), Peter Abelard (1079-1142), Albertus Magnus (c. 1193-1280), and St. Thomas Aquinas (1225-1274), and by the leading Islamic scholastic, Averroes, or ibn-Rushd (1126-1198).

The Spanish-Jewish philosopher, Maimonides, argued (most notably in his Guide for the Perplexed) that revelation secures all of the central tenets of Judaism (the notion of Jehovah as absolute existence, the I am who am, in particular) and is thus the primary source of knowledge. Rational discourse, by this view, ratifies revelation and is thus of derivative significance. Maimonides too held for spiritual (but not for bodily) immortality; he nonetheless favored bodily hygiene and moderate exercise, largely for purposes of health. Anselm, Italian philosopher and Archbishop of Canterbury, was exiled by Henry I in the investiture struggle and is best remembered for his celebrated Monologium and Proslogium in which he variously defends a characteristically scholastic view of the faith-reason relation, re-formulates Augustine's cosmological argument for the existence of God in ontological terms, and opposes, in "realistic-tending" fashion, the nominalist heresy of Roscelin (c. 1045-c. 1120). In respect to the faith-reason relation, Anselm embraced the view that one believes the revealed truth in order to understand reality under the influence of reason. Anselm developed his ontological argument for the existence of God in idealistic-tending manner; he argued from the notion of God's presumed perfection, from the notion that God is that than which none greater can be conceived, to the conclusion that God's existence is entailed by His perfection; God would otherwise lack the perfection of existence; He cannot be conceived, therefore, not to exist. The nominalism of Roscelin argued that universals are not themselves "real," but mere symbols signifying "real" entities. Anselm held to a "realistic-tending" alternative to nominalism, according to which universals have an existence qualitatively distinct from "real" entities but they nonetheless make appearances only in such entities. By Anselm's view, universals (most notably those of religious significance such as the Trinity) therefore exist in a far more substantial sense than they do by the nominalist argument.

The French philosopher, Peter Abelard, was a student of both Roscelin, the strictest of nominalists, and William of Champeaux (1070-1121), the strictest of realists. William argued that each and so every universal category is present in each and so every instance of that category. Abelard sought a conciliation of the two positions but failed himself, in the end, to give an altogether unequivocal interpretation, tending somewhat to the nominalist side of the debate. In both thought and practice, Abelard is arguably instead best revered as the most accomplished teacher of the Middle Ages; he stood to the medieval world in this respect rather as Socrates had stood to the ancient. His innovative, dialectical method of intellectual discourse, dicta pro et contra (which he recorded most memorably in his deeply influential, Sic et Non), became the standard in scholastic education and learned disputation. In it, both affirmative and negative arguments concerning major theological issues (about which there was typically widespread disagreement) were raised. The relative merits of these arguments were then left to the independent and informed judgment of students and teachers to decide. Peter Lombard (c. 1100-c. 1160), a student of Abelard, faithfully and importantly extended and applied Abelard's method.

The German philosopher and Dominican, Albertus Magnus, was the first Christian ecclesiastic to carefully set the system of Aristotle to scholastic themes; most notably in his widely celebrated, Summa Theologiae. It was his Italian student and Dominican colleague, St. Thomas Aquinas,[117] however, who worked this system out in fully articulate and comprehensive fashion and who achieved what arguably stands as the most astute philosophical account of the Christian faith yet achieved. In naturalistic-tending terms, both Albert and Aquinas attempted to demonstrate the rationality of the universe as a revelation of God. Aquinas' basic program argues that matter, or mere potentiality, constitutes the universal principle of changing individuation and that form, or actuality, constitutes the universal principle of enduring purpose. Nature is construed as the union of form and matter. God, by this view, is pure actuality, the cause of all spiritual and material entities. The world itself is constituted by bodies which are beneath humanity, human souls which are at the level of humanity, and intellectual substances which are above humanity. Humanity itself is construed as the autonomous unity (or substance) of a soul aspect and a bodily aspect, as a conjunction of intelligence and sensibility, as a composite being. The radical distinction, in Aquinas, between intelligence and sensibility requires the postulation of a linking principle, the agent intellect. It is by means of this principle that humanity raises sense impressions to intellectual knowledge. It is also by means of this dualistic-tending view of the mind-body relation that the incorporeal soul can live in an unembodied state and can achieve immortality by divine grace. Aquinas, moreover, sides with the realists (with such as Anselm, William, and Duns Scotus) against the nominalists (against such as Roscelin, Abelard, and Occam) in the ongoing medieval debate concerning the metaphysical status of universals. He claims in this respect that universals are the essences of entities and that they have no existence apart from their being in entities.

Aquinas' epistemology, too like Aristotle's, holds that all knowledge has its basis in the particularity of sense perception but that authentic knowledge consists in the universality of conceptual frameworks. Sensation is not what we know but that by which we know. For Aquinas, philosophy, in which the intellect is dominant, proceeds from facts (or known effects) to God (or unknown cause); theology, in which the will is dominant, conversely, proceeds from God to facts. A philosophic apprehension of God is therefore inferred from God's creation (i.e., from the facts of the created world). Such an apprehension is gained through an observation of God's effects in the created world (the five ways of Aquinas), effects that cannot be explained save by reference to God. Insofar as God's existence is not self-evident and insofar as it is outside the purview of direct demonstration, it may be known only by the appearances which are more known and more perfect to humanity, if less known and less perfect in themselves (that is, to God). This is the cosmological argument for the existence of God in its most fully developed form. There are nonetheless several cornerstones of the Christian dogma, according to Aquinas, most notably the Trinity and the doctrine of original sin, which are and can be known only by divine revelation (only by theological, not by philosophical, means), although they are in no sense nor measure contrary to reason.[118]

Aquinas' synthetic system, which effectively attempted to unite the domains of reason and revelation, the natural and the divine worlds, mediated the largely unfavorable views of the body (and its activity) characteristic of early medieval, neo-Platonic accounts and the highly favorable, humanist accounts of the body (and its activities) characteristic of the Renaissance. Its Aristotelian-tending sense of the middle ground and its typically scholastic reliance on the capacity of reason to demonstrate the certitude of virtually all matters was the distinctive mark of thirteenth-century European philosophy.

Significant developments in Arabian philosophy importantly paralleled Western achievements in the twelfth and thirteenth centuries. Like Christianity, Islam too fashioned a rational, a scholastic, defense of itself in this time. This tendency reached its apogee in the naturalistic-tending thought of the Spanish-Arabian philosopher and physician, Averroes, or ibn-Rushd, who was the leading Moslem commentator on Aristotle and on the compatibility of Aristotle's philosophy with the teachings of Mohammed. Like Aristotle, Averroes defended the validity of causal relations and the sciences which are grounded in such relations. He argued that science is the knowledge of causes by which even the existence of Allah is rendered probable. His system is principally devoted to securing demonstrative, scientific, or necessary knowledge of such causes, which he took as superior to the mere gathering of contingent explanations. The notions of corporeal and spiritual immortality, however, are accepted on divine authority alone. Averroes recorded his world vision most significantly in The Incoherence of the Incoherence, where he effectively prosecuted the central tenet of scholasticism, which is the claim that the domains of faith and reason are continuous and consistent with one another.

Confidence in reason as the worthy auxiliary of faith was, however, not universal, even in the thirteenth century, let alone in the fourteenth and fifteenth centuries. Opposition to scholasticism came most notably from a renewed enthusiasm for neo-Platonic and Augustinian thought (framed in mystical and aesthetic terms) by such as St. Bonaventura (1221-1274) and Marsilio Ficino (1433-1499); from an advocacy of empiricistic scientificism by such as Roger Bacon (1214-1294); from a form of pantheistic mysticism (which owed more to Plato than to Aristotle) by such as Meister Eckhart (1260-1327) and Nicholas of Cusa (1401-1464); and from the skeptical challenges of John Duns Scotus (c. 1266-1308) and William of Occam (c. 1280-1347). Of these, in turn, the mystical and the skeptical developments were the most telling. The German, Dominican philosopher, Eckhart, affirmed the primacy of faith over reason, depreciated the purely intellectual search for religious enlightenment, and sought a method for obtaining personal experience of God. In idealistic-tending fashion, recorded most notably in The Book of Divine Consolation, Eckhart characterizes God as the eternal, immutable, ineffable, spiritual substance in which all entities are united and which becomes manifest only in the Trinity. For him, all entities are in God and God is in all entities. The most fundamental obligation of humanity, consequently, is to gain an intuitive (a mystical) contemplation of, and unification with God, to gain a selfless conjunction of the one with the One. Nicholas too was German and also inclined to idealistic-tending thought as distinct from naturalistic-tending possibilities. Mainly in De Docta Ignorantia, he held that the infinite universe has no center; that the universe cannot be apprehended by rational means; that God is infinite, inaccessible to reason, and knowable only by mystic intuition; that religion can conceive of God only relatively because He incorporates all contradictions within Himself; and that each religion reflects a facet of Divine Truth and is thus worthy of tolerance by other faiths. His qualified pantheism, embodied in the claim that the world is distinct from, but nonetheless a mirror of God, challenged the utter transcendence of God. The broad asceticism advocated by the mystic program was also a central theme of the leading devotional literature of the late Middle Ages; most notably, The Imitation of Christ (1415) of the German monk, Thomas à Kempis (c. 1379-1471), and the anonymous, late fifteenth-century morality play, Everyman. In The Imitation of Christ, God is everything, humanity is nothing; God, as the chief good, collects and unites all else; and humanity is enjoined to devote itself to achieving a union with God. In Everyman, God is dismayed by humanity's neglect of spiritual concerns, demands a reckoning, and dispatches death with a summons for Everyman, who is saved only by the embrace of Good Deeds.

The **dissolution of scholasticism** is, however, most owed to the skeptical assertions of the main Franciscan opponents of Aquinas, Duns Scotus and Occam, both of whom challenged the limits of faith and reason outlined by the scholastic movement. The towering Scottish philosopher, Duns Scotus, argued, most notably in his major work, the Ordinatio, that human knowledge is flawed in several crucial respects. He imputes the imperfection of such knowledge to the Fall from grace and sets himself the task of defining its limits. With Aquinas, he held that, although there is no dispute between the truths of faith and those of reason, only faith can sustain the fundamental claims of Christianity. Duns Scotus, however, restricted the scope of reason much more fully than had Aquinas. This more skeptical tendency resulted in a bifurcation between the practical concerns of theology (which operate under the dicta of faith and in a divinely revealed fashion) and the theoretical concerns of philosophy (which operate under the dicta of reason and in a humanistically inspired way). This is the "doctrine of twofold truth" which Duns Scotus was convinced liberated both theology and philosophy. He nonetheless held to a "realistic-tending" notion of universals (not altogether unlike Anselm, William, and Aquinas) in which universals (acts of thought) correspond to concrete realities, in which universals exist prior to their instantiation in the world (i.e., in the "mind" of God), in which universals exist in the concrete objects of the world as their essence, and in which universals persist after the passing of concrete objects (i.e., as remembrances in the minds of human beings). This interpretation accounted for both the universality of thought necessary to Duns Scotus' metaphysics and the principle of individuation inherent in his view of matter. The highest universal, and so the most fundamental of metaphysical categories according to Duns Scotus, is being, for only it can be predicated of all things. God alone possesses, or is, pure being, pure form, pure actuality; God alone is unlimited, eternal, and independent; and God is thus the principal issue for being and for philosophical discourse. In naturalistic-tending fashion, not unlike Aquinas, Duns Scotus was too convinced that the only possible demonstration of God's existence is a demonstration which argues from God's effects in the world to His pure being. From these effects, he infers the possibility of God's existence and urges, from this possibility, that, if God did not exist, His existence would be impossible and that God, therefore, necessarily exists, that it is not possible that God not exist, that the very idea of God would be self-contradictory and so impossible if it were the case that God did not exist. It is likewise, for Duns Scotus, the existence of God which makes morality possible because the free will of God is taken as the fundamental source of all judgments in respect to right and wrong.

The skeptical inclinations of Duns Scotus prepared the way for an even more "radical" departure from the orthodoxy of Christian high scholasticism in the thought of Duns Scotus' talented student, the signal English philosopher, Occam. This departure is nominalistic in respect to the problem of universals; it is persuaded that there are no theological truths accessible to reason; and it is recorded most notably in Occam's major work, the Summa Logicae. According to Occam, the only source of true, demonstrable knowledge is experience. All knowledge which cannot be traced to a beginning in experience can be apprehended only by unprovable faith. The existence of God, for prominent example, cannot be demonstrated in any way, either by His effects in the world (à la Augustine, Aquinas, Averroes, and Duns Scotus) or by His inherent nature (à la Anselm); God's existence is wholly unintelligible to reason and, thus, can be known by faith alone. Occam held that only particular substances and their qualities demonstrably exist, that an appeal only to such substances and qualities is required in order to account for the whole of experienced reality. This propensity to metaphysical simplicity concludes in the view that all knowledge consists in organized bodies of proposition about particular things. Universals therefore exist only as objects of knowledge, or acts of intellect, abstracted from particular things. They are neither inherent in things nor are they held in the "mind" of God. This nominalistic concept of universals (which he effectively shared with Roscelin and Abelard) and the dualistic-tending presuppositions that underlie it nonetheless rest on the rational hypothesis that neither principles nor things are to be multiplied without necessity ("Occam's razor"). In the case of Occam's view of universals, this comes to the claim that there is insufficiently good reason for leaping to the realist conclusion which makes things of ideas and ideas of things.

Scholasticism had sought a rational explication of faith, an effective conjunction of faith and reason. The separation of theology and philosophy worked out in the thought of Duns Scotus and Occam brought the scholastic movement to an effective end. The result was the liberation of both theology and philosophy (from one another), the development of an intellectual/philosophical tradition increasingly independent of religious expectation (i.e., the loosening of the hold of orthodox religion on free, modern inquiry) and the prospect of a strictly secular, a modern, state. Both scholasticism and its passing accentuated the secularization of late medieval life. Scholasticism required divine revelation (and faith in it) to account for itself in terms of secular reason. Faith and its religious grounding had been previously (in the early Middle Ages) little challenged as the primary canon of knowledge and life. The dissolution of scholasticism evened the way for a yet more deeply secular orientation in the modern world. The scholastic movement itself as well as its passing were, moreover, largely devoted to limited intellectual and religious objectives. They likewise held to a measured form of bodily asceticism that was not entirely unreminiscent of early medieval monastic austerity. The retiring and contemplative temperament of these developments was therefore, unsurprisingly and on balance, unfavorable to bodily events, including sport.

The development of the two crowning artistic styles of the western European Middle Ages in visual, musical, and literary terms, the Romanesque and the Gothic styles, were likewise quick to reveal the great transformation that occurred in the late (as against the early) Middle Ages. This transformation functioned as a bridge linking the dualistic, extrinsic, ephemeral, and arrested tendencies of the early Middle Ages in which sport figured only passingly to the monistic, intrinsic, subjective, and lived tendencies of the Renaissance in which sport was more prominent. It is perhaps most conspicuous in respect to the enhanced sense of physicality and more vital interpretation of movement embodied in it.

The **Romanesque style** was the dominant orientation in the visual arts from the eleventh to the thirteenth centuries. It entailed a plastic tendency that was no longer Roman and not yet Gothic, a tendency that grew mainly out of early Christian and Byzantine influences, and a tendency that was developed principally in monumental religious architecture, in architectural sculpture, in mural painting, and in illuminated manuscripts and tapestries. The **Romanesque orientation in architecture** inclined to clear and precise lines, dignified and direct effect, ponderous and dense volume, and colossal scale. Its great churches were capacious (in order to accommodate large numbers of persons) and well-lit by the ample use of well-placed windows; they were framed in their interior aspect by high barrel-vaulted walls/ceilings and by radiating chapels; they were framed in their exterior aspect by inelaborate, slight load-bearing walls; and they were decorated in structure-related sculpture and mural paintings. The most remarkable of these were constructed in France, Italy, and England. The leading French instances of Romanesque religious architecture are the: "Abbey Church of St.-Étienne," Caen (1067-1120); "Sernin," St.-Toulouse (1080-1120); "Abbey Church of St.-Pierre," Cluny (c. 1085-1130), now largely destroyed; "Ste.-Madeleine," Vézelay (c. 1120-1132) with its portal sculpture, "Mission of the Apostles;" and "Cathedral of Autun" (c. 1130) with its high-relief portal sculpture, "Last Judgment." The leading Italian instances of such architecture are the: "Baptistery of San Giovanni," Florence (eleventh century); "Cathedral," (1063), "Baptistery" (1153), and "Campanile" (1174), Pisa; and "Sant'Ambrogio," Milan (late eleventh century-early twelfth century). The leading English instance of such architecture is the "Cathedral of Durham" (1093-1130). The unsurpassed genius of Romanesque sculpture was the Italian artist, Benedetto Antelami (c. 1150-c. 1230), whose delicate sense of line, melodic sense of composition, and full sense of body foresaw Renaissance sculpture. Antelami's masterpieces were architectural works: "Descent from the Cross," Cathedral of Parma (1178) and "King David," Cathedral of Fidenza (c. 1180-1190). The most significant mural painting of Romanesque moment is the fiercely energetic, "Christ Enthroned with the Archangel Michael Battling a Dragon," San Pietro al Monte, Civate, Italy (late eleventh century-early twelfth century). The most remarkable illuminated manuscript of Romanesque type is the Bible of Bury Saint Edwards, England (early twelfth century), which embodies a mastery of design and two-dimensional space and which is done in brilliant colors. And the most accomplished instance of Romanesque embroidery is the "Bayeux Tapestry," Cathedral of Bayeux, France (c. 1073-1083), depicting the Norman invasion of England by William the Conqueror in 1066 and including portrayals of sporting recreation practiced in that time.

Although the notion of Romanesque (as well as Gothic) style is customarily reserved for the visual arts, there was an analogous development in **music** that also warrants mention. In the eleventh century, Guido of Arezzo (c. 995-c. 1050), a French monk, crafted a form of notation that liberated music from an exclusive dependence on oral tradition. In the twelfth century, the earliest form of polyphony (the weaving together of several, independent melodies) was developed at the "Abbey of St.-Martial" in France -- the "St.-Martial Organum." The tendency to polyphony, together with the heightened sense of vital movement and temporal sensuality that it conveys (as against early medieval monophony), was further advanced by the leading

99

figures of the "Notre Dame Organum" in Paris in the twelfth and thirteenth centuries, Leonin (fl. last half of the twelfth century) and Perotin (c. 1183-c. 1238). At the beginning of the thirteenth century, virtually all music was sacred and grounded in the Gregorian chant; by its end, both sacred and secular compositions were common, albeit yet wrapped in a rather rigid theological framework, not unlike the philosophy and literature of the period. The passage from "ars antigua" (the old art) to "ars nova" (the new art) had nonetheless begun.

This passage was exemplified most notably in the development of the near-to-universal **Gothic style** of the thirteenth to the fifteenth centuries. This style was most conspicuous in **architecture** but was also apparent in sculpture, painting, music, and literature. It was owed in its original form to France; it then came to prominence most notably in England, Germany, Italy, and Spain. It was characterized by a continuing shift in aesthetic perception from a disembodied, one-sided spiritualism reminiscent of the early Middle Ages to the sense of proportion, balance, and harmony of spiritual and bodily dimensions that came to mark the earliest stages of modern civilization, the Renaissance. It was made possible by the various terms of increasing centralization and secularization that visited and defined the late Middle Ages as well as by technical innovations that were unique to this time. As national monarchs, no longer popes, came to direct vital political activity; as merchants and artisans, no longer ecclesiastics, came to direct pressing economic activity; and as universities, no longer monasteries, came to direct eminent learning; cities came to dominate rural communities. It was in these cities that a communal devotion to the construction of cathedrals developed and that the greatest achievement of thirteenth-century to fifteenth-century art and technology, the Gothic cathedral, was realized. Gothic cathedrals fully embodied the late medieval perception of the entire universe and were therefore given to a disciplined and geometric sense of order and hierarchy; they were technically governed by the fashioning of ribbed vaults, high-pointed arches, and flying buttresses, all of which concentrated load-bearing in columns and piers and all of which largely freed the walls of load-bearing function, giving them up instead to windows; they were richly, but tastefully, "decorated" in architectural sculpture and stained-glass windows; and they left the impression of a soaring, vertical, and graceful elegance. The very earliest of these were constructed in the twelfth century but most were done somewhat later. The most remarkable of the French Gothic cathedrals are the: "Abbey Church of St.-Denis," Paris (1140-1144), "Cathedral of Chartres" (1140-1150; rebuilt after fire, 1194-1220) with its solemn, serene, vital, and well-ordered portal figures of the west façade and the south transept and with its utterly brilliant windows of stained glass in the north transept; "Cathedral of Laon" (1160-1190); "Cathedral of Notre Dame," Paris (1163-1250); "Cathedral of Reims" (1210-1299) with its jamb statues of the west façade, "Annunciation" and "Visitation," and with its sculptural figures in the round of the west interior wall, "The Knight's Communion;" "Cathedral of Amiens" (1220-1230); and "Ste.-Chapelle," Paris (1243-1248) with its surpassing stained-glass windows. The most significant of the English Gothic cathedrals are the: "Salisbury Cathedral" (1220-1258), "Westminster Abbey," London (1245-1519), and "Gloucester Cathedral" (1332-1357). The greatest of the German Gothic cathedrals are the "Cathedral of Cologne/Koln" (1248-1322) with its metal relief sculpture, "Shrine of the Three Kings," and the "Cathedral of Strasbourg" (thirteenth and fourteenth centuries) with its portal sculpture of the south transept, "Death of the Virgin." The Italian Gothic achievements were especially extensive and especially noteworthy: "Siena Cathedral" (1280s), "Church of Santa Croce," Florence (c. 1294), "Cathedral of Florence/Duomo di Santa Maria del Fiore" (1296), "Palazzo Vecchio," Florence (1299-1310), "Palazzo Ducale," Venice (1340-1424), and "Cathedral of Milan" (1386-1813). And the most notable of the Spanish Gothic cathedrals is the "Cathedral of Gerona" (1312-1347, 1417-1604).

The great **sculpture and painting** of the thirteenth to the fifteenth centuries developed principally in the artistic guilds of the leading Italian city-states, Pisa, Florence, Venice, Siena, and Milan, and it constituted such a departure from the medieval and such a herald of the modern that it is perhaps better characterized as proto-Renaissance than Gothic. As against Romanesque tendencies, the Gothic was given to a more natural rendering of objects, humans, and light, to a more strictly three-dimensional perspective, to a more substantial, robust, and active sense of material existence, and to a more individualistic and expressive orientation. The leading sculptors of this period and this temperament nonetheless owed much to Antelami in particular; they were Nicola Pisano (c. 1220-c. 1284) and his son, Giovanni Pisano (c. 1250-c. 1314). Nicola's masterpiece is the relief images of the hexagonal marble pulpit for the "Baptistery of Pisa" (1259-1260); Giovanni's is the relief images of the octagonal marble pulpit for the "Sant'Andrea of Pistoria" (1298-1301). The leading painters of this period and this temperament were:

- the Florentine, Cenni di Pepi, or Cimabue (c. 1240-c. 1302), whose masterpiece is the tempera-on-panel, "Madonna Enthroned" (c. 1280);

- the Sienese, Duccio di Buoninsegna (c. 1260-c. 1320), whose masterpiece is the tempera-on-panel altarpiece for the "Siena Cathedral," "Maesta" (1308-1311);
- the Florentine, Giotto di Bondone (c. 1267-1337), whose masterpieces are the tempera-on-panel, "Madonna and Child Enthroned" (c. 1310) and the cycle of frescoes in the "Arena Chapel," Padua (near Venice), 1305-1306 (most notably, the "Raising of Lazarus," "Lamentation," and "Christ Entering Jerusalem");
- the Sienese brothers, Pietro Lorenzetti (c. 1280-c. 1348), whose masterpiece is the tempera-on-panel, "Birth of the Virgin" (1342), and Ambrogio Lorenzetti (c. 1285-c. 1348), whose masterpiece is the elaborate fresco, "Allegory of Good Government," in the "Palazzo Publico," Siena (1338-1339);
- the Sienese student of Duccio, Simone Martini (c. 1283-1344), whose masterpieces are the tempera-on-panels, "Annunciation" (1333) and "The Road to Calvary" (c. 1340); and
- Giovanni da Milano (fl. mid-fourteenth century), whose masterpiece is the tempera-on-panel, "Pieta" (1365).

The most notable illuminated manuscripts of this period and temperament are all French: <u>Bible Moralisée</u>, Reims (mid-thirteenth century), <u>Psalter of St.-Louis IX</u>, Paris (1253-1270), and <u>Belleville Breviary</u>, Paris (c. 1323-1326).

The music and literature of the Gothic era were too of a more robust and active character than those of the early Middle Ages. They were of a more secular and a more sensuous cast, albeit yet clothed in orthodox ecclesiastic garb. The "ars nova" of fourteenth-century **music** was of a more varied scale, was of broader range, and was more rhythmically diverse than the "ars antigua" had been. Its leading French exponent was Guillaume de Machaut (c. 1304-1377), who perfected multi-part, choral and instrumental balladic forms (of chivalric moment), secularized motet forms, and developed revolutionary polyphonic forms of the Mass (most notably in "Messe de Notre Dame") that importantly foresaw Renaissance music. Its leading Italian exponent was Francesco Landini (1325-1397), known mainly for the innovative melodies and harmonies of his ballads and madrigals. Fifteenth-century European music extended and elaborated on the central tendencies of the fourteenth century. Its leading figures were the English composer, John Dunstable (c. 1385-1453), known mainly for his novel sacred music; and the two major Burgundian composers of the period, Guillaume Dufay (c. 1400-1474) and Gilles Binchois (c. 1400-1460), known mainly for their inventive Masses, motets, and secular songs.

Late medieval **literature** was similarly disposed, giving larger attention to the material, empirical, and volitional aspects of human experience without seriously challenging any of the most cherished features of established theological canon. With Chaucer, the most remarkable literary figures of the late Middle Ages were the Italian (mainly the Florentine) poets:

- Dante Alighieri (1265-1321), whose masterpiece, <u>Divine Comedy</u> (written in Italian, 1314-1321), ranks with the greatest poems of any place or any time; it recounts the passage of the poet through Hell and Purgatory (guided by Vergil) and through Heaven (guided by his dead love, Beatrice);
- Francesco Petrarca, or Petrarch (1304-1374), who is best known for his love poems to Laura, the <u>Sonnets</u> (written in Italian, c. 1327-1374), and whose masterpiece, <u>Africa</u> (written in Latin, c. 1337-1341), is an epic of colossal eloquence; and
- Giovanni Boccaccio (1313-1375), whose masterpiece, <u>Decameron</u> (written in Italian, 1348-1353), is a surpassing collection of worldly stories set in the sobering context of the Black Death.

All were champions of a vernacular language (Italian), of ancient classical (Graeco-Roman) scholarship, and of the emerging humanism of the Renaissance. The magnificent English poet, Geoffrey Chaucer (c. 1340-1400), too championed a vernacular language (English), was also devoted to classical scholarship, and was likewise an important herald of modern humanism. His masterpieces are too among the greatest achievements of medieval literature: the extensive love poem, <u>Troilus and Criseyde</u> (1385), and the intensely vital series of poetic yarns, <u>The Canterbury Tales</u> (1387-1400).

While the defining elements of so-termed medieval culture (including medieval sport) were owed mainly to Europe, the Middle East, and north Africa, the two major Asian civilizations of the ancient world, India and China, also passed through a continuing, a memorable, and an influential development in this time. The earliest Islamic Arab incursions into **India**, into the Indian sub-continent (i.e., into the Indus River Valley in modern Pakistan and into what is now western India), from the west occurred in 711 as has been said. The Islamic transformation of India and the **Islamic influence** in India continued throughout the remaining centuries of the Middle Ages. The early Arab era was followed by the Ghaznevid (Turkish) incursions, into what are now southern Pakistan and northern India, from the north in 962 and the establishment of the first Turkish sultanate in the region under Mahmud the Great (c. 970-1030; r. 999-1030) in 999. The Ghaznevids, in turn, were defeated by Mohammed of Ghur (d. 1206; r. 1162-1206), from what is now southern Afghanistan, in 1186. Mohammed was murdered by his successor, Aibak (fl. late twelfth century-early thirteenth century), a slave, who established the Delhi Sultanate (1206-1526) in 1206. In the thirteenth and fourteenth centuries, the Sultanate successfully repulsed the Mongol advances of Genghis Khan and others from the north, broke the power of native Hindu princes, virtually destroyed Buddhism and sharply depreciated Hinduism in India, traded vigorously with the Arab world, and established a prosperous, albeit a despotic and a rigidly hierarchical, state. The Delhi Sultanate came to its widest influence, under Mohammed Ibn Tughluk (r. 1325-1351), with the conquest of some regions of southern India in c. 1330. The decline of the Sultanate began shortly thereafter (c. 1340), however, as Hindu resistance stiffened; most notably in the southern city/empire of Vijayanagar. The Mongol invasion of Timur in 1398-1399 annexed northern India, nearly destroyed Delhi itself, and limited sovereignty of the Sultanate to Delhi. By the fifteenth century, the regions now occupied by the modern nation-states of Bangladesh, Malaysia, and Indonesia (except Bali) had nonetheless migrated from predominantly Hindu to predominantly Moslem allegiance. The discovery of a sea route from Europe to India by Portugal in 1498 sharply accelerated European influence in the region at the end of the fifteenth century. And the amalgamation of Mongol and Islamic culture, in the form of the Mogul Empire (1526-1756), formally dissolved the Delhi Sultanate and brought the so-termed Middle Ages in India to an end by the early sixteenth century.

Although the Moslem influence in India throughout the medieval era was very considerable, Hinduism has remained the dominant native religion of the region from the ancient world to our own time. It was under **Hindu influence** that the great achievements of medieval Indian dance and of medieval Indian art and architecture occurred: the "Kandarya Mahadeva Temple," Khajuraho, and the ""Brihadesivara Temple," Thanjavur, both c. 1000, both of commanding proportion, and both adorned with intricately detailed and beautifully crafted relief sculptures of spiritualistic moment. Hinduism was dispersed from India throughout southeast and central Asia in the medieval period but became prominent only in Bangladesh (which became predominantly Moslem), in Nepal (which developed a form of temple architecture that rivaled, if not surpassed, analogous developments in India itself), in Cambodia (which became predominantly Buddhist and where the magnificent Khmer "Temples of Angkor Thom and Angkor Wat" were constructed in the twelfth century), in Malaysia (which became predominantly Moslem), and in Indonesia (which, Bali aside, became predominantly Moslem). Buddhism too had its origins in India as has been said but it had largely spent itself there by the thirteenth century. It was nonetheless dispersed in the ancient and medieval eras from India, either directly or by way of China, to Pakistan (which remained predominantly Moslem), China, Nepal (which became predominantly Hindu), Tibet, Afghanistan (which remained predominantly Moslem), Ceylon/Sri Lanka, Korea, Japan, Burma/Myanmar, Vietnam, Laos, Thailand, Cambodia, and Indonesia (which became predominantly Hindu, then predominantly Moslem). The stunning Buddhist sculpture, mainly spiritualistic images of the seated, reclining, or standing Buddha in stone or bronze (some of which are of monumental scale, some of which are not), of Pakistan, Nepal, China, Tibet, Afghanistan, Ceylon/Sri Lanka, Korea, Japan, Burma/Myanmar, Vietnam, Laos, Thailand, and Cambodia constituted a leading chapter in the annals of medieval art. The colossal Buddhist "Temple of Borobudur," Java, Indonesia (c. 800) is widely regarded among the greatest treasures of the pre-modern world.

The highly significant Islamic influence on the education and sport of medieval India was admixed with the native Hindu orientations to these activities. The Hindu emphasis, continuing from the ancient world, on otherworldly forms of spiritual experience, on deprecatory interpretations of the material/bodily aspect of life, and on preference for the future stage of time had a largely unflattering affect on sport. Sport was practiced only for marginal religious and for military purposes in medieval Hindu India and in the societies most influenced by Hindu India (most notably, that of Nepal). The characteristically Moslem orientation to bodily affairs in general and to sport in particular was somewhat different and, on balance, more favorable. The personalistic attributes of the religion, the sense of robust action that animated its leading figures, its typically high regard for bodily health and for disciplined effort, and its admiration for military defenses of itself, all inclined Islam to a measured respect for bodily activity and for sport.

The circumstance in **China** throughout the approximate millennium of the Middle Ages was also an uneven admixture of unifying and disunifying developments, native and foreign hegemonies. There were "eight" major, largely native dynastic periods from the passing of the Han (the last of the so-termed ancient dynasties) in 220 to the establishment of the foreign Yuan in 1260:

- Three Kingdoms (Wei, Wu, and Shu), 220-265, in which Confucianism was eclipsed by Taoism and Buddhism;

102

- Tsin, 265-420, which brought a temporary unification, then a separation of northern and southern China as Huns and Turks invaded the north;
- Six Dynasties, 222-589, which continued Chinese traditions in the south after the alien incursions of the north and in which (Mahayana) Buddhism was dispersed throughout China, c. 500-c. 550;
- Wei, 420-588, which effectively entailed the Chinese administration of Hunnic and Turkish kingdoms in the north;
- Sui, 581-618, which again achieved political unification under a central government, which instituted an accomplished governing bureaucracy, and which developed an intricate canal system;
- Tang, 618-907, in which China achieved the highest stage of its development (under Tai Tsung [d. 649; r. 627-649]), developed a highly efficient military, expelled or annihilated the Hunnic and Turkish invaders, moved its capital to Xian, further developed the governing bureaucracy of the nation, advanced to Korea and Formosa/Taiwan, and developed (under largely Buddhist influence) the finest Chinese poetry (most notably, the pastoral work of Li Po [c. 701-762]), painting (most notably, the delicate landscapes of Wang Wei [699-759], paintings which emphasize essential line as against renderings of perspective and light), and sculpture (most notably, magnificent, dispassionate, inanimate, and colossal Buddhist statues) of the ancient and medieval eras; foreign military successes on the western frontiers and internal persecutions of Buddhists brought it to eventual ruin;
- Five Dynasties, 907-960, which was characterized by political fragmentation, corruption, civil conflict, and warfare at the western borders; and
- Sung, 960-1279, in which political unification was again achieved then lost (c. 1127) as the north and the south were again separated (into the Southern Sung Dynasty in the south and the Chin Empire, a Manchurian contrivance, in the north), Confucianism again triumphed over Taoism and Buddhism, a technological flowering occurred (gunpowder, printing, and porcelain), a renewed enthusiasm for scholarship (not unlike the scholastic renewal in Europe) in the sciences, arts, and humanities developed, pagoda-style temple architecture was firmly established, and the modern Chinese language was created.

The foreign, Yuan Dynasty (1260-1368) of the **Mongols** replaced the Sung in 1260. The Turks and the Mongols were the most significant of the nomadic, mounted Eurasian tribes of the late Middle Ages and the only such groups to establish settled, independent states in this period. The first supreme ruler of a unified Mongol nation, the first Khan, was Temujin, or Genghis Khan (c. 1167-1227; r. 1196-1227), who eliminated all rivals for the distinction in 1196. The Khan was, from that time, selected from among the hereditary family of Temujin. Early in his reign, Temujin codified Mongol law, devoted the Mongol nation to world conquest by means of military excellence, and acknowledged a supreme god. In 1209, he completed the conquest of the Hsi-Hsia Kingdom in northwest China; in 1215, he completed the conquest of the Chin Empire in northeast China; and in 1225, he subjugated the Empire of Khorezm (an Islamic state) in Kazakhstan, Uzbekistan, Afghanistan, Turkmenistan, and Persia, thus extending the Mongol Empire from northern China/Mongolia to the Caspian Sea. At the death of Temujin in 1227, the Empire was partitioned among his four sons and Karakorum (in Mongolia) became its permanent capital. The Great Khan, Ugudei (fl. first half of the thirteenth century), son of Temujin, completed the subjugation of the Chin Empire (in northern China) by 1234 and of the Empire of Khorezm (in southern Persia) by 1241. Mongol campaigns in eastern Europe began in 1236, largely under Batu (fl. mid-thirteenth century), grandson of Temujin; these campaigns subdued Poland and Hungary in 1241 and Russia in 1245; they established the Golden Horde in Russia (largely out of the Khanates of Kazan and Astrakhan) in 1251. Hulagu (fl. mid-thirteenth century) destroyed Baghdad and the Abbasid Dynasty in 1258, then made triumphs in Syria, the Caucasus, and Byzantium (thus extending the Mongol Empire to the Black Sea), before being turned back by the Mamelukes (Egyptian warrior-rulers) in the region of the Black Sea in 1260. Kublai Khan (1214-1294; r. 1260-1294), grandson of Genghis Khan, attacked the Southern Sung Dynasty in (southern) China in 1258, established the Yuan Dynasty over the whole of China in 1260, made Beijing the political, cultural, and trade center of the Empire in 1264, completed the subjugation of southern China in 1279, gained control of Korea from 1274 to 1281, and was twice repulsed in attempts to vanquish Japan (in 1274 and 1281). The Yuan Dynasty was characterized by a technological flowering (canons, other guns, and experiments with flying machines, submarines, and telescopes), by dramatically heightened trade within Eurasia and with Europe (most notably exemplified in the adventurous expeditions of Venetian, Marco Polo [c.1254-c.1324], with the court of Kublai Khan, 1271-1295), by a form of religious tolerance for such as Christianity and Islam, and by failed attempts to expand Mongol influence to Korea, Japan, Tibet, Burma/Myanmar, Vietnam, and Indonesia.

The Mongols were in the end, however, unable to govern the vast territories they had overrun, were dominated in cultural terms by many of the superior cultures they had conquered (including the Chinese), were greatly opposed by the Chinese in particular, and lost dominance of their trade routes (the Asiatic caravan routes) to Arabian sea lanes. These trends, together with the famine of 1325 and consequent peasant insurrections, resulted in the contraction of the Mongol Empire in the fourteenth century, brought the expulsion of the Mongols from China in 1368, and effected the reestablishment of Chinese hegemony in China in the form of the first modern Chinese ruling authority, the Ming Dynasty (1368-1644). An attempt to renew the Mongol state in the late fourteenth century succeeded briefly, then collapsed. Timur, or Tamarlane (1336-1405; r. 1360-1405), a presumptive heir of Genghis Khan, conquered Kazakhstan, Uzbekistan, Turkmenistan, Afghanistan, Pakistan, Mesopotamia, Persia, and bits of northern India and Byzantium before his death in 1405; consistent with the high Eurasian regard for animal sport, Timur is known to have constructed an elaborate polo grounds in Samarkand in the late fourteenth century. Subsequent disputes over succession and unsuccessful wars against China resulted in the final deterioration of the Empire in the early fifteenth century. Even the extraordinary grandson of Timur, Ulug-Bek (1394-1449; r. 1447-1449) – who was an astronomical genius, who connected the medieval Arabic tradition in architecture with the Timurid ("Madrassah of Ulug-Bek," Registan Square, Samarkand, 1417-1420, and "Gur Emir," Samarkand, early fifteenth century), and who thereby foresaw the Mogul (architectural) Enlightenment by an approximate century – was unable to reverse the decline. Thereafter, the Mongol influence was limited mainly to Mongolia itself and to the Islamized descendants of Mongols in India, the Mogul Empire (1526-1756).

The contemplative, impersonalistic, ascetic, and past-oriented tendencies of ancient **Taoism and Buddhism**, together with the thisworldly inclinations of ancient **Confucianism** and the high ancient regard for military activity, intermittently continued to dominate Chinese culture in the so-termed medieval era. As in the ancient case, medieval Chinese culture was therefore ambivalent about sport and used it to secure rather narrow military, medical, or religious purposes, mainly in martial and court contexts. Most forms of sporting activity practiced in the ancient Chinese world predictably maintained a strong presence in the medieval and developed there as well in the direction of more modern characteristics. Perhaps the most important medieval forms of **Chinese sport** were the martial arts of the Shaolin-Temple tradition (386-534), various forms of boxing in particular, the most notable of which, ch'uan shu, took its current form as t'ai chi ch'uan in the period of the Yuan Dynasty. The ancient form of military sport, wu shu, was also formalized, as kung fu, in the period of the Yuan Dynasty (after the development of gunpowder, c. 1300), as was what became the traditional Chinese form of wrestling, jiaoli. The Yuan too especially widely played an ancient game resembling golf and established an ultra-long distance running contest in which imperial guards (and perhaps other soldiers) ran behind the Emperor's chariot for distances of up to 90 kilometers/56 miles, a practice by which postal runners were selected. Sport was a part of the education of the elite male until the period of the Sung Dynasty and was especially widely practiced in the periods of the Sui Dynasty, Tang Dynasty, Five Dynasties, and Yuan Dynasty. The period of broadest enlightenment in medieval China, the era of the Tang Dynasty, gave sport, like poetry, painting, and sculpture, a deeper and more favorable attention than any other. A game resembling association football/soccer and another resembling rugby football were especially widely played in this time, even by some emperors. Despite wide criticism by religious adepts of its violence and brutality, a game resembling polo was also widely contested, often to musical accompaniment, before numerous officials and thousands of spectators on enormous fields (of approximately 100 paces by 1000 paces), typically between two teams, among two to sixteen elaborately dressed players to a side (some of whom were women, some of whom were royal participants), in which a leather, wood, stone, or ceramic ball was struck by slender, elongated implements with crescent-shaped tips. The Emperor, Mu Zong (fl. early ninth century; r. 821-824), is said to have died of injuries suffered in a polo match. Acrobatic gymnastics, bull fighting, archery, diving, fencing, horse riding, hunting, ice skating, jumping, running, swimming, throwing, and weightlifting, as well as activities resembling badminton, field hockey, and golf were likewise deeply popular in the period of the Tang. The sport of the Tang was also unusually widely available to women, was exceptionally active, and was much accompanied by gambling practices. The rather exclusive intellectual and scholarly tendencies of the Sung Dynasty disinclined it to a fervent advocacy of sport, even though sport was not unknown, among men in particular, in this era, even though the earliest formal Chinese sporting societies (in archery and wrestling) were formed in this era, and even though the earliest codification of Chinese sporting rules (in golf and polo) were also achieved in this era.

Chinese culture (including Chinese sport) became widely influential among adjoining societies in the period of the so-termed Middle Ages. Southeast Asian, Korean, and Japanese circumstances were the most significantly affected. Most of the states of **southeast Asia** were first drawn (perhaps from as early as the third century B.C.E.) from gentile orientation and delivered to civil society by Indian (Hindu and Buddhist) influences; they were somewhat later greatly influenced by Chinese culture. Vietnam was the main exception; it came first under very large Chinese (Buddhist) influence, likely no later than the second century B.C.E. Thailand and Indonesia came under very large Chinese influence no later than the seventh century; Cambodia, Laos, and Malaysia, no later than the eighth century; and Burma/Myanmar, no later than the ninth century. Chinese culture even had a passing affect on Philippines, albeit notably later (i.e., from the sixteenth century). In many of these cultures, native forms of martial art, inspired by earlier Chinese examples (principally boxing examples), were developed:

- in Thailand, a form of muay Thai, or Thai boxing (which includes kicking);
- in Indonesia and Malaysia, a form of pentjak-silat (similar to jujutsu);
- in Burma/Myanmar, a form of bando (similar to jujutsu); and
- in Philippines, a form of arnis de mano (a type of hand and stick fighting).

A precursor of sepak takraw was also first played in Thailand, Malaysia, and Indonesia in the so-termed late Middle Ages.

The formative influence of China in Korea and Japan was still larger; there, the passage from gentile to civil society was first and mainly effected by Chinese culture. The earliest Chinese presence in **Korea** dates from c. 200 B.C.E. The earliest form of national unification, sparked by Chinese (largely Buddhist) inclinations, began to develop in c. 350 and was later formalized in the Silla (668-935) and Koryo (918-1392) Dynasties. The principal Korean form of martial art, taekwondo (similar to jujutsu), dates at least from the fourth century, perhaps from the first. The uniquely Korean form of wrestling, ssirum (which somewhat resembles sumo) also dates from at least the fourth century, perhaps from the first. Archery too was especially widely practiced in ancient and so-termed medieval Korea. The military elite of medieval Korea, the huarangdo, contributed particularly much to the formative development of Korean sport from the sixth to the tenth centuries. These great warriors made central contributions to the unification of Korea, were prototypes of body-soul harmony and morality, and were well-trained in martial sport (most notably, in equestrian, archery, fencing, and throwing activities).

The earliest Chinese presence in **Japan**, via Korea, dates from c. 100 B.C.E. Japan was governed, virtually throughout its early history, by an autocratic, central, military authority (a shogunate). Its so-termed medieval history, which followed an ancient period of quasi-Neolithic character and Korean domination, developed in five major periods:

- the Asuka, centered in Asuka (near Osaka), 552-645;
- the Nara, centered in Nara (near Osaka), 645-794;
- the Heian, centered in Kyoto, 794-1185;
- the Kamakura, centered in Kamakura (near Tokyo), 1185-1333; and
- the Ashikaga, centered in Kyoto, 1338-1573.

The dominant governing ideology of medieval Japan was framed by **Shintoism** (the native ancestral and animistic religion) and by (Mahayana) Buddhism (imported from China in the sixth century). In the eighth century, Shintoism and Buddhism were accommodated to one another; in the fourteenth century, a variation of the Buddhist teaching, **Zen Buddhism** (which emphasized meditative experience as against doctrinal concerns), was brought to Japan from China and came to great prominence. The distinctive and accomplished architecture, sculpture, painting, literature, drama, and sport of the Japanese have been most influenced by these religious sentiments and by the military imperatives of feudal warfare which were a characteristic feature of Japanese life. The earliest Buddhist temples of Japanese cast – most notably, the "Horyu-ji," Nara, c. 610 – were constructed in the Asuka period. The most memorable Buddhist temples of Japanese cast -- "Byodo-in," Uji (near Kyoto), eleventh century – were of rigid, but artful, simplicity and were owed to the Nara, Heian, and Kamakura periods. The most remarkable sculpture of medieval Japan -- principally, spiritualistic Buddhist figures in wood and bronze – were done in the Nara and Kamakura periods. The best painting – most notably, "Parinirvana of the Buddha" (1086) and "Winter Landscape" (fifteenth century) of Sesshu (1420-1506) – was of delicate and active outline and was achieved in the Heian, Kamakura, and Ashikaga periods. And the pre-eminent age of medieval Japanese literature and drama unfolded in the Heian period, the time in which the written Japanese language was formalized and the time in which one of the great romantic-heroic novels of world literature, the Tale of Genji, was written by noblewoman, Murasaki Shikibu (fl. late tenth century-early eleventh century), in the early eleventh century.

The earliest and most distinctive form of ancient and medieval **Japanese sport**, sumo, was first practiced, in its originative form, in the first century and was formally organized in ninth-century Heian society. Kemari (a cooperative game in which balls are kept from touching the playing surface) and games resembling polo and croquet were played from seventh-century Naran society; and horse racing, swimming, and weightlifting, from eleventh-century Naran society. The largest influences on Japanese sport, however, were the military orientations of the feudal armies of chivalric warriors, knights, or samurai and the religious orientation of Zen Buddhism. The samurai were governed by a strict moral code of honor and conduct (bushido) which was first organized in twelfth-century Kamakuran society, which was a very significant factor in the Japanese defeat of both attempted Mongol invasions of the thirteenth century (in 1274 and 1281), which was brought to a yet more exacting development in Ashikagan society, and which was characterized by robust forms of physical activity (including martial sport). Zen Buddhism was largely a product of fourteenth-century Kamakuran society and emphasized spiritual experience (which was taken to importantly included bodily dimensions). Japanese fencing and wrestling and the several major martial arts of the Japanese, including a re-formation of the earlier-practiced forms of sumo, were largely a function of these military and religious practices: jujutsu (which includes striking, kneeing, throwing, choking, kicking, and joint-locking and which is the main precursor of judo, karate, and aikido), kyudo (a traditional form of archery), and kenjutsu (a form of fencing that is the major precursor of kendo). As in some European cases, however, common people were customarily prohibited from participating in military-oriented forms of activity (including games).

The Middle Ages effectively ended in the fourteenth and fifteenth centuries and, not unlike their beginning, they ended none too well, most especially in Europe. In the political, economic, and social crises of the time, population and trade declined owing largely to widespread famine (agricultural failures made for a short food supply) and pestilence (the bubonic-plague epidemics killed approximately one-third of Europe's people); ruinous civil and international conflicts throughout the civilized, ecclesiastic and secular worlds variously invited social anarchy and oppression; and increasing exploitation of the poor further deepened already colossal disparities between the wealthy and others. Also amid the divisive chaos, however, was a continuing drift to political unification, a progressive extension of the democratic spirit, and an arising form of rational humanism, all of which established a firm ground for the maturing commerce, economic recovery, enhanced franchise, free inquiry, technological innovation, and common human values of the cultural flowering that followed. What emerged from the perilous environment of the late Middle Ages was the earliest period in the modern epoch of world history, the Renaissance.

EARLY MODERN CIVILIZATION

Modern civilization has both a pre-industrial, an early, and an industrial, a contemporary, phase.[119] Early modern civilization -- the fifteenth, sixteenth, seventeenth, and eighteenth centuries – drew the human condition out of its medieval occasion and delivered it to what became the contemporary life of the nineteenth and twentieth centuries. Early modern civilization itself is customarily distinguished by three main stages: the Renaissance of the fifteenth and sixteenth centuries, the seventeenth century (the so-termed "Age of [Scientific] Reason"), and the eighteenth century (the so-termed "Age of [the Modern European] Enlightenment"). The industrial era of the nineteenth and twentieth centuries – effectively, our own time – follows in turn.

The stage on which the earliest events of the modern era unfolded was, of course, late medieval. The centralizing tendencies of an advancing royalism, the maturing commerce and technology of the town and guild movement, the secularizing influences of the universities, the dilution of papal authority and increasing dissension within the Christian Church, the intercultural effects of the Crusades, the vigor of the chivalric movement, the spiritual prominence of Islam, Judaism, Hinduism, and Buddhism, the universality of Gothic art, and the intellectual triumphs of scholasticism's dissolution, all of the proto-Renaissance, conspired to evoke a new age. The most conspicuous and novel mark of this age was intellectual in character. Insofar as the political, economic, educational, and sporting events of early modern civilization were unique to this time, they were largely a function of the singular intellectual orientation that dominated it. There were, of course, many other respects in which these events continued in the unexceptional style of earlier periods. An account of the political and economic events which framed this period, many of which hadn't clear analogs in the dominant intellectual tendencies of the age, will be followed by an examination of the major intellectual, educational, and sporting developments of the time.

The political and economic tendencies of early modern civilization were by no means uniform. They nonetheless effected a gradual recovery from the social crises characteristic of the late Middle Ages, brought a new (a modern) sense of unsettled adversity to the human experience, and ultimately transformed civilization at its core. In political and economic terms, the approximately four centuries of world history at issue here are most tellingly marked by:

- the manifold ascent, decline, and reorganization of the Italian city-states, the Holy Roman Empire, the German Empire, Switzerland, Brandenburg-Prussia, Austria, the Austro-Hungarian Empire, Portugal, Spain, Netherlands, Poland, Sweden, Denmark, Russia, the Ottoman Empire, England, United States of America, France, China, Korea, Japan, and India in the context of the continuing drift to political unification (and its strident military implications) as well as the continuing drift to an extension of the democratic spirit (which "culminated" in the American and French Revolutions);
- the intellectual discord of the Protestant Reformation, the Catholic Counter-Reformation, and the religious wars that resulted;
- the rise of modern capitalism, the ongoing development of the commercial middle class that increasingly incited it, and the inventive creation of technological innovations that increasingly drove it (and that eventually brought it to the dawn of the industrial age); and
- the revolutionary voyages of European discovery, European colonialism in India (and elsewhere in Asia), the Americas, Africa, and Oceania, and the virtual world war (mainly concerning the European balance of power) that resulted.

Political Transformations

Italy, the **Italian city-states**, had been variously a part, in some instances a reluctant part, of the Carolingian and Holy Roman Empires since the eighth century as has been said. Its southern regions fell variously under Norman, French, and Spanish influences beginning in the eleventh century as has been also said. Increasingly, however, the Italian city-states -- principally, Venice, Genoa, Pisa, Florence, Milan, Siena, Naples, and Sicily — came themselves to great prominence as commercial and cultural centers (associated mainly with the Crusades). They likewise came increasingly to virtual independence from the Holy Roman Empire (and other states) beginning in earnest in the twelfth century. With the decline of the Hohenstaufen in the mid-thirteenth century, the hold of the Holy Roman Empire over Italy weakened further and a century later even nominal control over it effectively ended. In the fourteenth and fifteenth centuries, fractional struggles between the imperial, Ghibellines, and the papal, Guelphs, brought civil war among the social classes and among the city-states.

By the mid-fifteenth century, however, an uneasy balance of power obtained among the cities and between the cities and the Papal States. Also in the fifteenth century, the leading cities (Florence, Venice, and Milan as well as the Papal States) came under the dominant influence of staggeringly wealthy mercantile and banking families. Florence, Venice, and the Papal States were most affected by the **Medici**; Milan, by the Sforza. Although the quasi-democratic constitutions of the cities, which had been established roughly three centuries earlier, were outwardly upheld, the cities were nonetheless governed largely by the wealth and the political influence of these families, despite their having only rarely held formal public office. It is in these city-republics and in the context of the social unrest they embodied that one of the world's most remarkably creative periods, the Italian Renaissance, unfolded. The Medici and the Sforza were both ardent patrons of the arts and sciences that marked the characteristically humanistic perspectives of this period. Of these, the Florentine Medici were the most influential. Cosimo de' Medici/Cosimo the Elder (1389-1464; r. 1434-1464) was the first of the Medici to rule **Florence**; he was a major patron of Renaissance architecture, sculpture, and philosophy; he created the Medici Library; and he established the Platonic Academy (1440). His grandson, Lorenzo de' Medici/Lorenzo the Magnificent (1449-1492; r. 1469-1492), was arguably the most accomplished of the Medici to rule Florence; he was among the most influential figures of the Renaissance; he reigned over one of the era's most remarkable periods; and he too was a major patron of Renaissance art (mainly painting and sculpture).

Several of the Medici also became pope and exerted great influence over Florence (and other regions of Italy in particular and Europe in general) from Rome. The most notable of these were:
- Leo X (1475-1521; r. 1513-1521), son of Lorenzo the Magnificent, who was, like his father, a great patron of Renaissance art (mainly, architecture and painting) and whose renewal of indulgences and failed attempts at Church reform incited Luther to what became the Protestant Reformation; and
- Clement VII (c. 1475-1534; r. 1523-1534), last of the so-termed Renaissance popes, who presided over the sack of Rome by the Holy Roman Empire in 1527 and over the unsuccessful dispute with the English crown (under Henry VIII) in 1533.

The other most significant of the Renaissance popes were likewise ineffective administrators of the Church; under their leadership, the institution continued its moral and fiscal decline; they were nonetheless also highly notable advocates of humanistic study:
- Nicholas V (1398-1455; r. 1447-1455), the first of the so-termed Renaissance (or humanist) popes, established the Vatican Library;
- Pius II (1405-1464; r. 1458-1464) was himself a major humanist scholar;
- Sixtus VI (1414-1484; r. 1471-1484) was a major patron of architecture and established the Sistine Chapel;
- Innocent VIII (1432-1492; r. 1484-1492) was a major patron of music; and
- Julius II (1443-1513; r. 1503-1513) was a major patron of architecture, sculpture, and painting.

Although periodically deposed, exiled, and banished, the Medici continued to rule variously over a greatly diminished Florence (after the early sixteenth century) into the eighteenth century. Of the Sforza, Ludovico Sforza (c. 1451-1508; r. 1494-1499), an avid patron of the arts (architecture and painting most especially), was likely the most memorable.

The Italian city-states were, however, vulnerable to still larger, foreign political forces in southern Europe. These forces eventually swept them up (and they were too adversely affected by the Protestant Reformation). Naples, for prominent instance, was conquered by Spain in 1442; Sicily fell to Spain in 1479 and to France in

1494; and Milan was confiscated by France in 1515 and by Spain in 1559. The entire Italian "system" of city-states was in effective decline by the end of the fifteenth and the beginning of the sixteenth centuries. The competition for Italy, variously among France, Spain, Austria, England, Switzerland, Germany, the Papal States, and the Italian city-states themselves, was a major feature of early sixteenth-century European political life. The balance-of-power principle worked out over this competition has formed a central tenet of European and intercontinental political affairs to our own time. According to this principle, each of the major powers attempts to gather as much resource to itself as feasible through fluctuating and opposing coalitions and each of these coalitions threatens mutually destructive war against each of the others. The gambit entailed by this principle is thus to gather wealth by evading ruinous, but nonetheless perpetually threatened, war. In the Italian case, the principle was of equivocal effect as the peninsula fell under various foreign hegemonies – mainly the French and Spanish crowns – and it was fought over (largely by France and Austria) in the French Revolutionary Wars of the late eighteenth century before its successful struggle for political independence in the nineteenth century.

Throughout the fifteenth century, the **Holy Roman Empire** came to little other than Germany, Austria, Switzerland, Bohemia, and Hungary, all effectively governed by the German king who was anointed by a declining and a divided papal authority. By the mid-sixteenth century, German monarchs had dispensed with the pretext of papal approval and were crowned in Frankfurt. Even at this, the quarrels between the German crown and the Papacy continued without notable pause and without significant consequence. The hold of the Empire over Italy had been diminishing from the twelfth century as has been said. The disputes between the Ghibellines and the Guelphs of the fourteenth and fifteenth centuries in Italy and the rise of the Italian city-republics, also in this time, further curtailed the German influence in Italy and marked the twilight of medieval and early modern German imperial policy.

The **German Empire**, the German crown, itself had come into sole possession of the **Hapsburgs** in 1437 as has been said. After the long reign of Frederick III ended in 1493, his son, Maximilian I (1459-1519; r. 1493-1519), a renowned knight and patron of the humanities, became King, Emperor, and thus ruler of all hereditary Hapsburg lands. Less by imperial policy as such than by inheritance and marriage contracts (most importantly with Spain), Maximilian brought approximately one-half of the "civilized" world under his purview, incited the enmity of France (largely over his designs on Burgundy), and provoked domestic agitations for internal reform. The proposals for reform evoked by these agitations were considered in a series of imperial diets, or assemblies, which resulted in the full independence of **Switzerland** from the German Empire (by means of the Swabian War in 1499); the beginnings of an imperial constitution mainly concerning political authority, taxation, the raising of an army, and the keeping of public peace; and the reorganization of the German Empire in 1512 into Bohemia, Hungary (both of which came under full Hapsburg control in 1526; Hungary was captured by Ottoman Turkey in 1541), and ten imperial German districts, each under the direction of two princes (Burgundy [Flanders, Netherlands, Luxembourg], Lower Rhine-Westphalia, Lower Saxony [Holstein, Mecklenburg], Upper Saxony [Pomerania, Brandenburg], Rhineland, Franconia, Upper Rhine [Alsace, Lorraine, Savoy], Swabia [Baden, Wurttemberg], Bavaria, and Austria).

The first Holy Roman Emperor of the Spanish Hapsburgs, the King of Spain (as Charles I), and one of the most notable political figures of early modern history, Charles V (1500-1558; r. 1519-1556), succeeded his grandfather, Maximilian I, in 1519. Charles reigned over an enormous empire that included Spanish America and the virtual whole of continental western Europe (except the southern Balkans, the Papal States, Switzerland, France, and Scandinavia). He:

- was arguably the central political defender (the Papacy aside) of the Catholic Counter-Reformation;
- was effectively defeated by the German Protestant princes in his attempt to secure the unity of the Christian faith; this, by way of the Diet of Augsburg in 1530 and the Peace of Augsburg in 1555;
- urged Pope Paul III, in 1545, to convene the highly influential Council of Trent in order to settle the Catholic-Protestant dispute;
- established the Austrian Hapsburg line in 1521 by way of the Diet of Worms, which had condemned Luther;
- made Spain (Madrid in particular) the core of the Empire;
- was the patron of the first successful circumnavigation of the planet by Magellan in 1519-1521;
- prosecuted four somewhat successful wars against his principal continental rival (the Protestant German princes aside), Francis I of France:
  - the first, 1521-1526, entailed the capture of Francis;

- the second, 1526-1529, entailed the German sack of Rome in 1527 and the first siege of Vienna by the Ottoman Turks in 1529;
- the third, 1536-1538, entailed a Franco-Turkish alliance against Charles, coastal raids on Spain and Italy by the Turkish pirate , Khaireddin Barbarossa, and the Empire's seizure of Tunis from the Turks in 1535; and
- the fourth, 1542-1544, entailed the Turkish capture of Hungary from the Empire in 1541, another Franco-Turkish alliance against Charles, and an Empire-English alliance against France.
- presided over the inconclusive Schmalkaldic War of 1546-1547; and
- conducted unsuccessful territorial wars against France in 1552-1556.

Charles was succeeded as king by his son, Philip II, and as emperor by his brother, Ferdinand I (1503-1564; r. 1556-1564). As King of Hungary and Bohemia from 1526, Ferdinand brought both regions under full Hapsburg control. As Holy Roman Emperor, he attempted to keep the religious peace and continued the initiative for Catholic reform but, like his successors throughout the next approximate century, presided over a declining economy with diminishing imperial authority. Ferdinand was succeeded by his son, Maximilian II (1527-1576; r. 1564-1576), who promoted religious tolerance toward Protestants and ongoing Catholic reform and who reclaimed, by purchase, bits of Hungary from the Turks in 1568. Maximilian was succeeded, in turn, by his son, Rudolf II (1552-1612; r. 1576-1611), who pressed the Jesuit-inspired reforms of the Catholic Counter-Reformation and who was a leading patron of the natural sciences. Rudolf was deposed in 1611 and was succeeded by his brother, Matthias (1557-1619; r. 1612-1619), who attempted to restore Hapsburg imperial authority and to advance toleration toward Protestants. His policies nonetheless aroused Catholic enmity and enticed the Catholic-Protestant conflict into what became the Thirty Years War, 1618-1648. Ferdinand II (1578-1637; r. 1619-1637), grandson of Ferdinand I, had been the King of Bohemia (as Ferdinand III) from 1617 and was crowned Holy Roman Emperor in 1619. He was deposed as King of Bohemia in 1619 and replaced by the Protestant, Frederick the Winter King (1596-1632; r. 1619-1620), an event which effectively incited the Thirty Years War. Ferdinand defeated Frederick the following year but the War nonetheless continued through what remained of his reign and well into the reign of his son and successor, Ferdinand III (1608-1657; r. 1637-1657). Ferdinand III, also King of Hungary and Bohemia (1626/1627-1657), was forced to accept the unfavorable terms of the Peace of Westphalia, which ended the War, and Germany was left in virtual ruin. The Holy Roman Empire disintegrated into a confederation of states (which included the effective separation from it of Austria and Netherlands) and its long decline continued (although nominally preserved until 1806, it was of only honorific significance after 1648), as did that of the Hapsburgs themselves.

The devastations of the War were numerous: a sharp decline in population, extensive material damage, and widespread brutality, robbery, and dissipation. The German Empire, nonetheless made a fairly rapid recovery owing largely to the insight and enterprise of the Protestant princes, who centralized political administration, taxation, and military authority and who greatly expanded public educational and welfare services. Still at this, the Empire then consisted of approximately 300 sovereign parts. Out of this radically decentralized and otherwise troubled circumstance developed a permanent Imperial Diet (Reichstag) at Regensburg (near Munich) in 1663 (a body which was nonetheless of largely deliberative, not legislative, significance until the twentieth century) and several major territorial states, some of which were of an absolutist character and some of which were constitutional in nature. The most significant of these were:

- Bavaria (south-central Germany), centered in Munich and Regensburg and governed by the House of Wittelsbach;
- Saxony (north-central Germany), centered in Dresden and Leipzig, developed a personal union with Poland (1697-1763), and governed by the House of Wettin;
- Hanover (northwest Germany), centered in Hanover and Bremen, developed a personal union with Great Britain (1714-1837), and governed by the House of Brunswick-Luneburg; and
- Brandenburg-Prussia (northeast Germany), centered in Berlin and Potsdam and governed by the House of Hohenzollern.

The most notable of these, in turn, was **Brandenburg-Prussia**, which was ruled by the **Hohenzollerns** from 1415 to 1918. The central, early modern figures of this development were:

- Frederick William/Frederick William the Great Elector (1620-1688; r. 1640-1688), the principal architect of the Brandenburg-Prussian nation-state, who developed the political, mercantile, and military infrastructure of the state, who gained important successes in wars against Poland, France, and Sweden (1660-1678), who established a colonial presence in Africa, and who made Brandenburg-Prussia the leading German state next to Austria;

- Frederick I (1657-1713; r. 1688-1713), son of Frederick William the Great Elector, who established national academies of the arts and sciences in Berlin;
- Frederick William I (1688-1740; r. 1713-1740), who further developed the domestic edifice of the nation, who promoted a strong and absolutist central administration, military, and economy, and who significantly elevated the standards of public education; and
- Frederick II/Frederick the Great (1712-1786; r. 1740-1786), son of Frederick William I and among the most gifted military, political, and social leaders of early modern civilization.

Frederick the Great was:

- a major participant in the War of the Austrian Succession (1740-1748) in which he challenged Austrian claims to all Hapsburg lands by invading and successfully claiming Silesia (in what is now southern Poland) in 1740, by establishing alliances with France, Spain, and Bavaria against Austria, Great Britain, and Netherlands, and by therewith establishing Prussia as a major European state;
- the principal figure in the **War over Silesia** (1756-1763), the second and last (the European) phase of the Seven Years War, in which he again invaded Silesia, on this occasion as a pre-emptive action to combat joint French and Austrian designs against him, and by which Prussia significantly augmented its status as a leading European power;[120]
- a major participant in the First Partition of Poland in 1772, by which Prussia, Austria, and Russia gained significant Polish territory;
- the principal figure in the **War of the Bavarian Succession** (1778-1779) in which he effectively nullified Austrian claims over substantial parts of Bavaria (after the extinction of the Wittelsbach Dynasty in 1777) by entering alliances with Saxony and Russia and by invading Bohemia;
- mainly responsible for establishing the League of German Princes with Saxony and Hanover in 1785, by which Austria's alliance with Russia (in 1781) was effectively countered and by which Austria was no longer able to unilaterally assert itself against Prussia in the Empire;
- favorably disposed to the establishment of the Bank of Berlin in 1764; and
- among the eighteenth century's most enlightened despots, those who governed in partial accord with principles of humanitarian reason and created sovereign welfare states, modern bureaucracies, and uniform and equitable systems of law; Frederick advocated freedom of thought and religion for all subjects, established fixed state budgets, state control of the economy, state monopolies of staple foods, divisions of governmental powers, a bureaucracy of nobles, and a fiscal structure in which tax burdens were carried mainly by bourgeois artisans and commercialists, eliminated torture, royal intervention in legal proceedings, and the purchase of offices, and promoted road and canal construction, agriculture, animal husbandry, and forestry as well as literary, philosophical, and musical activities; he did himself engage successfully in literary and musical projects; although he transformed Prussia into a constitutional monarchy, he was nonetheless unable to free the serfs, who remained in hereditary dependence.

Frederick the Great was succeeded by his nephew, Frederick William II (1744-1797; r. 1786-1797), who entered an unsuccessful alliance with Austria/Holy Roman Empire in 1792 (to counter the influence of the French Revolution) and who participated very significantly in the Second (1793) and Third (1795) Partitions of Poland, by which the Polish state was effectively dissolved, a popular Polish insurrection was suppressed, and Prussia again took over sizable bits of Polish territory. Frederick William was also a leading patron of the musical arts.

Although the territorial states became the principal constituents of the German Empire in the seventeenth century, the Holy Roman Empire itself nonetheless limped on under the Hapsburgs after the Thirty Years War until 1806 as has been said. Its leadership fell in 1658 to Leopold I (1640-1705; r. 1658-1705), also King of Hungary and Bohemia (1655/1656-1705), son of Ferdinand III, who fared badly in several wars with France, who managed better results in conflicts with the Turks in Hungary, who went well in the early years of the War of the Spanish Succession (1701-1714) over Hapsburg claims to the Spanish crown, and who made Vienna the political, economic, and cultural center of the Empire. Leopold was succeeded by his son, Joseph I (1678-1711; r. 1705-1711), also King of Bohemia (1687-1711), who continued the War of the Spanish Succession and his father's successes in Hungary against the Turks. Joseph was succeeded by his brother, Charles VI (1685-1740; r. 1711-1740), also King of Hungary (1712-1740), in whose reign the War of the Spanish Succession was lost (1714), two major and largely successful wars with Turkey were undertaken (1716-1718 and 1735-1739), the largely indecisive War of the Polish Succession (1733-1735) was waged, and the so-termed "Pragmatic Sanction" settling all Hapsburg lands on his daughter, Maria Theresa, was issued. The "Pragmatic Sanction" was contested on Charles' death in the War of the Austrian Succession, however, most significantly by Frederick the Great of Brandenburg-Prussia and Charles Albert of Bavaria. Charles Albert became Holy Roman Emperor as Charles VII (1699-1745; r. 1742-1745) in 1742, was defeated by the Austrians in 1745, and was succeeded as Emperor by the husband of Maria Theresa, Francis I (1708-1765; r. 1745-1765) of Lorraine (in northeastern France). The Empire was effectively ruled by Maria Theresa (1717-1780; r. 1740-1780), Archduchess of Austria and Queen of Bohemia and Hungary, through Francis I and his successor, their son, Joseph II (1741-1790; r. 1765-1790), from 1745 to 1780. Joseph was, in turn, succeeded by his brother, Leopold II (1747-1792; r. 1790-1792), also King of Hungary and Bohemia (1765-1790), whose 1791 defense of Louis XVI of France (who was married to Leopold's sister, Marie Antoinette, daughter of Maria Theresa and Francis I) and 1792 alliance with Prussia (to counter the influence of the French Revolution) figured prominently in the French Revolutionary Wars. The Holy Roman Empire was dissolved by Napoleon I Bonaparte of France in 1806. Its last Emperor, Francis II (1768-1835; r. 1792-1806), son of Leopold, also King of Bohemia and Hungary (1792-1835) and (first) Emperor of Austria (1804-1835), was a major figure in the French Revolutionary Wars and the Napoleonic Wars as well as in the contemporary modern development of Austria.

The early modern development of **Austria** was marked most notably by its ascent to the status of an imperial district in the reorganization of the German Empire under Maximilian I in 1512, by Charles V's establishment of the Austrian Hapsburg line in 1521 (Austria had been a German Hapsburg possession from claims made for it by Rudolf I in 1282), and by its increasing independence from the Holy Roman Empire after 1648 (as per the Peace of Westphalia ending the Thirty Years War). Its late-seventeenth-century and eighteenth-century history was dominated by its disputes with Ottoman Turkey, by its associations with Hungary, and by its increasingly dominant place in the German and Holy Roman Empires. The wars with Turkey were mainly over mutual claims in the Balkans and in Hungary. The Turks had several times assaulted central Europe in the reign of Charles V; they had made a siege of Vienna in 1529 and captured Hungary in 1541 as has been said. Partial Turkish dominion over Hungary continued into the late seventeenth century. The First Turkish War (1663-1664) was caused by Turkish and Austrian intervention in Wallachia and Moldavia and it resulted in the further partition of Hungary. The **Second (Great) Turkish War** (1683-1699) entailed the second Turkish siege of Vienna (1683), the development of the Holy Alliance (Austria, Poland, Venice, and Russia) against Turkey (1684), the liberation of Hungary (1686-1697), full transfer of the Hungarian crown to the Hapsburgs (1687), the establishment of a dual Austro-Hungarian monarchy (1687) by the Imperial Diet of Pressburg/Bratislava, the eventual defeat of the Turks and the conclusive relief of central Europe from Turkish incursion (1699), and the rise of Austria as a major European power by means of the Peace of Karlowitz (near Belgrade) which ended the War in 1699. The Third Turkish War (1716-1718) was ended by the Peace of Passarowitz (also near Belgrade) in 1718 and marked the greatest extension of Hapsburg lands. And the Fourth Turkish War (1737-1739) was brought to conclusion by the Peace of Belgrade (1739), occasioned Austrian gains in the Balkans and Russian gains in the Crimea, and opened the era of Austro-Russian rivalry in southeastern Europe.

The **Austro-Hungarian Empire** was consolidated in the first several decades of the eighteenth century under a centralized and an absolutist administration; Holy Roman Emperor Leopold I made Vienna the political, economic, and cultural center of the German world in the last several decades of the seventeenth century; and the "Pragmatic Sanction" of Holy Roman Emperor Charles VI in 1713 brought Austria to the dominant position in the Holy Roman Empire, in the German sphere, and in the Hapsburg Dynasty by 1740-1745. Although Maria Theresa's claim to all Hapsburg lands was challenged in the **War of the Austrian Succession** (1740-1748), mainly by Frederick the Great of Prussia and by Charles Albert of Bavaria, she effectively prevailed in the Peace of Aix-la-Chapelle of 1748, became head of the Austrian (as well as the Bohemian and Hungarian) state(s) in 1740, governed jointly with her son, Joseph II, from 1765 to her death in 1780, and was the effective leader of the Holy Roman Empire through her husband, Francis I, and their son, Joseph II, from 1745 to 1780. The Peace of Aix-la-Chapelle did not altogether relieve international tensions between Austria and Prussia, however; Maria Theresa allied with France in the Silesian phase of the Seven Years War (1756-1763), mainly against Prussia, an act which confirmed, not resolved, the Prussian-Austrian struggle for German predominance. Maria Theresa was also a major participant in the First Russo-Turkish War (1768-1774) as an ally of Turkey and in the First Partition of Poland (1772) in which Austria, Prussia, and Russia gained Polish territory. And she was as well a significant participant in the War of the Bavarian

Succession (1778-1779) against Prussia in which her claims in Bavaria were largely nullified by Frederick the Great.

Maria Theresa and Joseph II were, with Frederick the Great of Prussia and Catherine the Great of Russia, among the eighteenth century's most enlightened despots. These towering figures governed in partial accord with principles of humanitarian reason and created sovereign welfare states, modern bureaucracies, and uniform and equitable systems of law. Maria Theresa followed the broad examples of her Prussian adversary, Frederick the Great, instituted agrarian and financial reforms, established training schools for the professions, and promoted the visual and musical arts. Joseph II was the Holy Roman Emperor from 1765 to his death in 1790, was the co-ruler (with his mother) of Austria from 1765 to 1780, and was the sole ruler of Austria, Bohemia, and Hungary from 1780 to 1790. He entered an important alliance with Russia in 1781 to counter Prussian influence, (with Russia) engaged the Turks in several largely successful conflicts in 1788-1789, and suffered the secession of the Belgian provinces from the Austrian Netherlands in 1790. He is nonetheless most widely remembered for his broad social reforms; most notably, his abolition of serfdom, the guilds, hereditary privilege, and capital punishment, his liberalization of legal codes and tax policies, his advocacy of public education, his establishment of public hospitals, orphanages, and institutions for the blind and the insane, his edict of religious toleration, and his promotion of the musical arts. The imperial record of Austria/Austria-Hungary as a wholly independent state (outside the contexts of the Holy Roman Empire) began in the early nineteenth century, in the first years of the contemporary modern era, as has been said.

The fates of Portugal and Spain were closely related in early modern civilization. Both figured prominently in the revolutionary voyages of world discovery and the colonial tendencies of the period. **Portugal** had gained an independent status from other Iberian states in 1094 and it participated significantly in the "reconquista" from the twelfth century as has been said. Its early modern history dated from the distinguished reign of John I/John the Great (c. 1357-1433; r. 1385-1433), the first of the Aviz Dynasty, who further secured Portuguese independence from the Spanish states and who was the father of Prince Henry the Navigator, a central figure in the Portuguese voyages and rising commercial prowess of the mid-to-late fifteenth century. Portugal became the leading commercial nation of Europe under Manuel I/Manuel the Great (1469-1521; r. 1495-1521), who promoted world exploration (most notably that of Vasco da Gama) and established Portuguese settlements in India, Asia, Africa, and Brazil. Most of Portugal's colonial holdings were lost to the Dutch and English after an overextension of resource and a break in royal succession brought weaknesses that were exploited by Spain. Portugal became a Spanish dependency in 1580 and remained under the Spanish yoke until 1640, when it was liberated by John IV (1604-1656; r. 1640-1656), the first of the Braganza Dynasty. Although politically independent from that time, it remained a commercially dependent nation, despite alliances with France and Great Britain, throughout the seventeenth and eighteenth centuries.

Spain, conversely, remained a leading European nation, if not the pre-eminent such nation, virtually throughout the early modern period. The several Spanish states unified in the late fifteenth century under Isabella I of Castile and Ferdinand II of Aragon (later Ferdinand V of Spain), who variously ruled the country until 1516, as has been said. The crown passed to the Hapsburg Dynasty through the husband of Isabella's and Ferdinand's daughter, the son of Holy Roman Emperor Maximilian I, in 1516. The grandson of Isabella, Ferdinand, and Maximilian became King of Spain in 1516 and Holy Roman Emperor as Charles V in 1519. Charles made Spain the center of European life and reigned over an enormous empire which included Spanish America and most of continental western Europe as has been said. He was a central figure in the Catholic Counter-Reformation, a highly significant patron of Spanish voyages of world discovery in the Americas and Asia (most particularly those of Magellan), established the Austrian Hapsburg line, and was a colossal presence in European political events until abdicating the Spanish throne to his son, Philip II (1527-1598; r. 1556-1598) in 1556. Philip (also King of Naples and Sicily, 1554-1598, and [as Philip I] King of Portugal, 1580-1598), like his father, was a fervent defender of Catholicism; he exerted unconditional authority over the national church, the national economy, and the colonies; and he virulently persecuted heretics, Jews, and Moslems by way of the Spanish Inquisition. Philip's reign was among the most eventful in the entire history of the country:

- Charles V's war against France was continued, 1556-1559, and realized modest Spanish gains;
- Philip married Mary I of England in 1554 (who died in 1558) but was greatly opposed in respect to his hegemonic military and commercial ambitions by Mary's Protestant/Anglican successor, Elizabeth I, whose forces (mainly under Sir Francis Drake) thoroughly defeated the Spanish attempt to conquer England by means of the Armada (a large naval fleet) in 1588;

- An insurrection in the Spanish Netherlands began in 1568 and succeeded in declaring independence from Spain for the northern provinces (what is effectively now Netherlands) in 1581; support of the rebellion by France and England deepened the enmity between those countries and Spain;
- Leading Catholic states, including Spain, broke the Turkish domination of the Mediterranean at the memorable Battle of Lepanto (Greece) in 1571;
- Philip conquered Portugal in 1580;
- The war of France, England, and Netherlands against Spain, 1595-1598, ended Spanish expansion in Europe and Spanish attempts to intervene in the internal affairs of France; and
- Depopulation, colonial overextension, burdensome taxation, and courtly extravagance significantly weakened the Spanish state by the end of Philip's life.

Philip II was succeeded by his son, Philip III (1578-1621; r. 1598-1621), also King of Naples, Sicily, and (as Philip II) Portugal (1598-1621), in whose reign peace treaties with England (1604) and Netherlands (1609) were negotiated; Spain entered the Thirty Years War; Spanish visual and literary arts flourished; and the national economy continued to decline. Philip III was, in turn, succeeded by his son, Philip IV (1605-1665; r. 1621-1665), also King of Naples and Sicily (1621-1665) and (as Philip III) King of Portugal (1621-1640), who was an ardent patron of the visual arts and in whose reign Portugal gained independence from Spain in 1640, the Thirty Years War ended badly for the Hapsburgs in 1648, Spain acknowledged the independence of Netherlands in 1648, still another prolonged war with France (1621-1659) closed in Spanish humiliation at the Peace of the Pyrenees (1659), and the decline of Spain as the most powerful nation in Europe continued. And Philip IV was succeeded, in further turn, by his son, Charles II (1661-1700; r. 1665-1700), also King of Naples and Sicily (1665-1700), the last of the Hapsburg Kings of Spain. Charles was mentally and physically infirmed and presided over the ongoing political, economic, and intellectual decline of the Spanish state. Succession to the Spanish throne after Charles' death endangered the European balance of political power, led to the formation of the Grand Alliance (Great Britain, Netherlands, Austria, Prussia, Hanover, Portugal, the Holy Roman Empire, and Savoy [northwestern Italy] against Bavaria [the Wittelsbachs] and France [the Bourbons]), and provoked a virtual world war, the War of the Spanish Succession (1701-1713/1714).

The **War of the Spanish Succession** overburdened the mercantile system and caused internal discord throughout Europe. It was largely finished with the Peace of Utrecht (Netherlands) in 1713, by which Spain and its colonies passed to the (French) Bourbon Dynasty, central and eastern European territories (including Naples but excepting Sicily) passed wholly to (Hapsburg) Austria, Sicily passed to Savoy, what remained of the Spanish Netherlands (principally Belgium) came under the control of Netherlands, and Gibraltar, much of eastern Canada, and the Latin American slave trade passed to Great Britain. Britain's balance-of-power policy had prevailed and an era of "cabinet politics" ensued over the next approximate one-half century, an era in which manifold forms of compromise (e.g., alliances, partitions, and territorial exchanges), as distinct from warring activity, were variously and mainly employed to resolve international conflict. Britain itself became arguably the most powerful nation in the world. Philip of Anjou (in west-central France), great-grandson of Philip IV of Spain and grandson of Louis XIV of France, was crowned the first Bourbon King of Spain, as Philip V (1683-1746; r. 1700-1746), in 1700. In Philip's reign, there were continuing disputes (particularly in Italy), notable patronage of the musical arts, and a modest recovery of the Spanish national economy. Bourbon rule of Spain continued throughout the eighteenth century; that is, to the Napoleonic intrusion of 1808. Philip V was succeeded, in turn, by his son, Ferdinand VI (c. 1712-1759; r. 1746-1759); by Ferdinand's brother, Charles III (1716-1788; r. 1759-1788); by Charles III's son, Charles IV (1748-1819; r. 1788-1808); and by Charles IV's son, Ferdinand VII (1784-1833; r. 1808, 1814-1833). Of the pre-industrial Bourbon Kings of Spain, Charles III was the most accomplished. He regained Naples and Sicily and ruled both from 1735 to 1759; he lost Florida to England in the Seven Years War (1763) but regained it in the American Revolutionary War (1783); and he presided over an impressively prosperous national economy. Charles IV entered the First War of the Coalition (1792-1797) against Great Britain in 1796 but was defeated by the English (1797) and also failed to check the populist influences of the French Revolution.

After an approximate century of quasi-autonomous development from (Valois) France, **Netherlands** (as a part of the Kingdom of Burgundy, together most notably with what are now Belgium and Luxembourg) came under Hapsburg rule in 1477 over a dispute concerning the Burgundian inheritance as has been said. In 1551, Holy Roman Emperor and King of Spain, Charles V, transferred it to the Spanish Hapsburg line. The "Low Countries," both the Latin (French), Catholic south, centered in Antwerp, and the German (Flemish), Protestant north, centered in Rotterdam, thereby became the Spanish Netherlands. When Philip II of Spain attempted to Hispanicize the region by brutally intensifying the Inquisition, by prohibiting political liberties, and by imposing pacification in it, an insurrection erupted. The **Dutch War of Independence** (1568-1648) that resulted was first directed by William I of Orange (1533-1584), under whom the northern provinces united in the Union of Utrecht in 1579 and under whom independence from Spain was declared in 1581. The United Provinces of the Netherlands, which developed as a consequence, continued its opposition to Spanish rule even after the assassination of William (in 1584) by order of Philip II. England and France came to the aid of the Provinces in 1585 and waged full-scale war against Spain in 1595-1598. The Dutch War of Independence had been effectively won by 1621 but was not formally acknowledged by Spain until the end of the Thirty Years War and the Peace of The Hague, both in 1648. The Dutch colonial empire was also established in the period of the struggle for political independence, principally by way of Dutch raids on Spanish and Portuguese military stations in Indonesia and Malaysia, by way of explorations in Oceania, and by way of slightly later settlements in south Africa. In the seventeenth century, Netherlands, with Amsterdam then at its center, became the world's leading commercial power, mainly by means of maritime trade, and it was also among the world's most ideologically tolerant and most culturally advanced nations, distinctions it relinquished to England and France in the eighteenth century. Its southern provinces (effectively, Belgium, or Flanders, and Luxembourg) nonetheless remained variously loyal to either Hapsburg Spain or Austria throughout the sixteenth and seventeenth centuries; that is, until they fell under manifold control of Netherlands and Austria after the War of the Spanish Succession in 1713/1714, were allied (as an effective part of Netherlands) with Great Britain and Austria against Prussia, Spain, France, and Bavaria in the War of the Austrian Succession (1740-1748), and were then (together with Netherlands itself) annexed by France in 1797.

The Polish crown had been united with the Hungarian in 1347, with the Lithuanian in 1386, and with the Bohemian in 1471 as has been said. Prussia came under Polish rule in 1454 as has been also said. By the end of the fifteenth century, **Poland** was the most powerful state in eastern Europe. It was, however, also surrounded by powerful enemies which incrementally took it over. By way of an alliance with Holy Roman Emperor Maximilian I for protection against Russia and by way of marriage, Sigismund I (1467-1548; r. 1506-1548), son of Casimir IV, passed Hungary and Bohemia fully to the Hapsburgs in 1526. The union with Lithuania was strengthened by Sigismund I's son and successor, Sigismund II (1520-1572; r. 1548-1572), the last of the Jagiellonians, in 1569. Sigismund II also acquired Courland and Livonia (effectively, the regions now occupied by modern Latvia), successfully opposed Protestantism, and presided over a humanistic flowering of Polish culture. The disorder that followed the death of Sigismund II was marked by several successful campaigns against Ivan the Terrible of Russia which brought Livonia and Estonia to Poland in 1582. This disorder continued under Sigismund III Vasa (1566-1632; r. 1587-1632), also King of Sweden (1592-1604), son of John III of Sweden and a nephew of Sigismund II, who briefly united the Polish and Swedish crowns (1592-1604), who promoted Catholicism, who temporarily occupied parts of Russia (1605-1612), who negotiated peace with Ottoman Turkey in 1621, and who conducted disastrous wars against Sweden (1600-1660) in which Poland lost both Livonia and Estonia in 1621 and Prussia in 1660.

Thereafter, Poland was bought and sold by virtually every major European power. It was an ally of Russia against Sweden in the Great Northern War (1700-1721). It attempted to settle rival claims to its throne in the **War of the Polish Succession** (1733-1735), which effectively put Russian and Austrian interests against French, Spanish, and Polish ones. Russian and Austrian efforts largely prevailed; Augustus III of Saxony (1696-1763; r. 1735-1763) became King of Poland in 1735 and territories in France and Italy were variously traded among the contestants. Foreign domination of Poland deepened yet further in the remaining decades of the eighteenth century under Stanislaus II Poniatowski (1732-1798; r. 1764-1795), the last King of Poland. He was chosen for the crown mainly by a 1764 alliance of Frederick the Great of Prussia and Catherine the Great of Russia and he presided over the dismemberment (ultimately the dissolution) of Poland by Prussia, Russia, and Austria. Russian and Prussian interference in the internal affairs of Poland led to the First Russo-Turkish War (1768-1774) and to the **First Partition of Poland** (1772) in which Prussia, Russia, and Austria (under Maria Theresa) gained Polish territory. The struggle among Prussia, Russia, and Austria over the political character of Poland as either an elective monarchy or a hereditary, constitutional monarchy -- effectively, a struggle concerning the prerogatives of the nobility -- nonetheless continued. This struggle brought the **Second Partition of Poland** (1793) in which Prussia, Russia, and Austria gained still more Polish territories. A popular insurrection in 1794, led by Polish national hero, Tadeusz Kosciuszko (1746-1817), was suppressed by Prussia and Russia and led to the **Third Partition of Poland** (1795) in which the Polish state was altogether dissolved. Lithuania (which had been part of Poland for roughly four centuries) fell under Russian dominion and Prussia, Russia, and Austria gained all remaining Polish territories. This final, early modern Partition brought Russia into contiguity with Prussia and Austria, brought a restive minority under

Prussian rule (the root source of modern Polish-German enmity), and brought large German migrations into eastern Europe.

The development of early modern Poland, Sweden, Denmark, Russia, and Turkey were quite closely related. **Sweden** had conquered southern Finland (which remained under Swedish sovereignty into the early nineteenth century) in the thirteenth century and entered a union with Norway, Iceland, and Denmark in the fourteenth century as has been said. Although Norway and Iceland remained under Danish sovereignty into the early nineteenth century, Danish domination of the union (and of Sweden) ended with the Swedish defeat of the Danes by Gustavus I (1496-1560; r. 1523-1560), first of the Vasas, in 1523. Gustavus is regarded as the founder of the modern Swedish state; he established a national Protestant church in Sweden; he freed Swedish commerce from the burdensome influence of the Hanseatic League; and he engaged Russia in the struggle for Livonia and Estonia in 1558. After a brief and unsuccessful reign by Gustavus' deranged son, Eric XIV (d. 1577; r. 1560-1568), the crown fell to Eric's brother, John III (1537-1592; r. 1568-1592), then to Sigismund III Vasa (r. 1592-1604) of Poland, son of John III and King of Poland (1587-1632), who briefly united the Polish and Swedish thrones (1592-1604), then to Charles IX (1550-1611; r. 1604-1611), still another son of Gustavus I. Charles deposed Sigismund and began the mostly successful wars against Poland of the early seventeenth century (1600-1660). He was, in turn, succeeded by his son, Sweden's most remarkable early modern political and military figure, Gustavus II Adolphus (1594-1632; r. 1611-1632). Gustavus Adolphus created the most efficient army in Europe mainly by making military service obligatory for peasants; he deprived Russia access to the Baltic Sea in 1617; he won Livonia and Estonia from Poland in 1621; and he was the principal figure in the Swedish phase of the Thirty Years War in which he invaded northern Germany to prevent German expansion, achieved astonishing victories, and died at the Battle of Lutzen (near Dresden) in 1632. His daughter, Christina (1626-1689; r. 1632-1654), succeeded him but she was far more interested in serious learning than in political life. In her reign, the country was governed principally by Sweden's greatest early modern statesman, Axel Oxenstierna (1583-1654). Sweden became the leading power in the Baltic region after the 1643-1645 war with Denmark and the favorable provisions of the Peace of Westphalia that ended the Thirty Years War in 1648.

On Christina's abdication in 1654, the throne fell to Charles X (1622-1660; r. 1654-1660), nephew of Gustavus Adolphus, who made the war against Poland (1654-1660) that won all of northern Sweden from Denmark and significantly enhanced Sweden's influence on the southern Baltic coast, thereby gaining him a reputation as the "Nordic Alexander." Under his son and successor, Charles XI (1655-1697; r. 1660-1697), Sweden unsuccessfully attacked Frederick William the Great Elector of Brandenburg-Prussia (1675-1678) and was unsuccessfully attacked by Denmark (1675-1679). Charles XI was succeeded, in turn, by his son, Charles XII (1682-1718; r. 1697-1718), the "last Viking," who was a brilliant general remembered mainly for his prosecution of the Great Northern War (1700-1721). The War was largely between Sweden and Russia for dominance in the Baltic region. Russia (under Peter the Great) made alliances with Poland, Denmark, and Saxony; Sweden was assisted by British and Dutch forces. The War went well for Charles in its early stages, which featured defeats of Denmark (1700), Russia (1700), Poland (1700), and Saxony (1704). Reversals soon followed, however; Peter founded St. Petersburg (on the Baltic) in 1703, achieved victories over Sweden in Russia, Livonia, and Estonia in 1704, thoroughly routed Charles at the Battle of Poltava (Ukraine) in 1709, occupied Finland in 1714, and invaded Sweden itself in 1719-1720. In the treaties ending the War, Sweden lost Livonia and Estonia to Russia and lost its German possessions to Hanover and Prussia; it was thereby replaced by Russia as the pre-eminent Baltic state. Throughout what remained of the eighteenth century, Sweden fell under heavy foreign influence (mainly that of France and Russia), was allied with Russia, France, and Austria (principal among others) against Prussia in the Seven Years War, and conducted an unproductive war with Russia.

The early modern history of **Denmark** was largely moved by its dominant position in the fourteenth-century alliance with Sweden, Norway, and Iceland as well as by its adversarial relationship with Sweden after the early sixteenth century. The union with Sweden ended in 1523 but that with Norway and Iceland continued into the early nineteenth century as has been said. Denmark's consequential disputes with Sweden were very nearly continuous from at least the early fifteenth century. The most telling of these disputes occurred in the seventeenth and eighteenth centuries, however, when Denmark was also marshaling a modest colonial ambition; to wit, the mostly unsuccessful wars of 1643-1645, 1654-1660, and 1675-1679 as well as the Great Northern War (1700-1721). Denmark's most notable political figures of the early modern period were Christian I (1426-1481; r. 1448-1481), the first of the Oldenburg Dynasty that ruled Denmark for approximately four centuries, and Christian IV (1577-1648; r. 1588-1648), who unsuccessfully prosecuted the

Danish phase (1625-1629) of the Thirty Years War in northern Germany. The eighteenth-century history of the country was unsteady and unexceptional.

The early modern history of **Russia**, conversely, was increasingly purposive and increasingly exceptional. The **Romanov Dynasty** (1613-1917) was installed by election in 1613 as has been said. The first of the Romanovs, Michael (1598-1645; r. 1613-1645), was unable to secure access to the Baltic Sea (1617) from Gustavus Adolphus. The second, Michael's son, Alexis (1629-1676; r. 1645-1676), greatly extended Russian influence to the east and to the west (most notably in Ukraine). Alexis was succeeded by his sons, in turn, Feodor III (1656-1682; r. 1676-1682), Ivan V (1666-1696; r. 1682-1690), and Peter I/Peter the Great (1672-1725; r. 1682-1725). The development of distinctly modern Russia began with the reign of Peter, who:

- attempted, with despotic brutality, to Europeanize (or Westernize) Russia;
- greatly improved the military, the economy, and industry;
- reorganized the government and transformed the bureaucracy into a meritocratic hierarchy;
- ruthlessly reformed agriculture by deepening the burdens of serfdom;
- strengthened the prerogatives of the tsar as head of the church and the government;
- promoted the construction of canals and ports and thus significantly improved transportation and trade;
- participated in the Holy Alliance (with Austria, Poland, and Venice) against Turkey in 1684;
- founded St. Petersburg in 1703 and began its earnest development as the new capital of the nation and as one of the great cities of the world in 1721;
- established advanced professional schools and the Academy of Sciences in St. Petersburg in 1725;
- commissioned Vitus Bering to make the first scientific exploration of Siberia;
- conducted a temporarily successful campaign against Turkey in Ukraine in 1696; and
- after suffering early defeat (1700) by Charles XII of Sweden in the **Great Northern War** (1700-1721), allied with Poland, Saxony, and Denmark, achieved great victories over Sweden (1704) in Russia, Livonia, and Estonia, thrashed Sweden at the Battle of Poltava (Ukraine) in 1709, occupied Finland in 1714, and invaded Sweden itself in 1719-1720.

In the Great Northern War, Russia gained Livonia and Estonia, won access to the Baltic Sea, and supplanted Sweden as the most powerful state in the Baltic region.

Peter was succeeded, in turn, by his wife, Catherine I (c. 1683-1727; r. 1725-1727); his grandson, Peter II (1715-1730; r. 1727-1730); his niece, Anna (1693-1740; r. 1730-1740); his great-grandnephew, Ivan VI (1740-1764; r. 1740-1741); his daughter, Elizabeth (1709-1762; r. 1741-1762); and his grandson, Peter III (1728-1762; r. 1762). In the approximate four decades following Peter the Great's death, the Russian court grew more extravagant, became more arbitrary, and was often dominated by foreign interests; the condition of the peasantry worsened; Russia intervened successfully (with Austria) in the War of the Polish Succession (1733-1735); Russia made successful war (with Austria) against Turkey (1735-1739) in the Crimea (southern Ukraine) thereby reaching the Black Sea; and Russia sided successfully (with Austria) against Prussia in the Seven Years War (1756-1763). Peter III made peace with Frederick the Great of Prussia, abolished the secret police, and extended religious freedoms before being forced to abdicate and being murdered by conspirators who included his wife and successor, Catherine II/Catherine the Great (1729-1796; r. 1762-1796).

Catherine was, with Frederick the Great of Prussia, Maria Theresa of Austria, and Joseph II of Austria, among the several most enlightened despots of the eighteenth century, figures who governed in partial accord with principles of humanitarian reason. She was a significant patron of humanistic literature, philosophy, and the arts and was herself an accomplished writer. She established the University of Moscow in 1755 and later unsuccessfully attempted to establish elementary and secondary schools. Her domestic political policies were nonetheless autocratic and regressive; she increased privileges of the nobility over the serfs, for prominent instance, an initiative that provoked a serious peasant uprising in 1773-1774. Her foreign policy was also despotic and it was too imperialistic. She increased Russian control of the Baltic provinces and Ukraine (formally annexing the Crimea in 1783) and began the colonization of Alaska (which was formalized in 1791). She variously allied with and against Prussia and Austria – with Prussia against Austria in the War of the Bavarian Succession (1778-1779) and with Austria to counter increasing Prussian influence in 1781 – for the purpose of preserving balance-of-power considerations. Russian and Prussian interference in the internal affairs of Poland and Russian occupation of Moldavia and Wallachia occasioned two major wars against Turkey in Catherine's reign. In the First Russo-Turkish War (1768-1774), Austria allied with Turkey to oppose the Russian occupation. Prussia mediated the dispute that resulted in Russian withdrawal from Moldavia and Wallachia, in Russian gains in the Crimea and on the Black Sea, and in the First Partition of Poland (1772), by which Russia, Prussia, and Austria obtained bits of Polish territory. In the Second Russo-Turkish War (1787-1792), Russia allied with Austria against Turkey and again achieved victory, becoming the dominant power in southeastern Europe. The Second and Third Partitions of Poland (1793 and 1795 respectively), in which Russia, Prussia, and Austria obtained all remaining Polish territory, followed; Lithuania came under Russian dominion; and Russia became a contiguous neighbor of both Prussia and Austria. Catherine was succeeded by her son, Paul I (1754-1801; r. 1796-1801), who, unlike his mother, tended to withdraw from Western influences and from policies of foreign expansion. Paul nonetheless participated in the Second War of the Coalition (1798-1801) against Napoleon and annexed Georgia (from the Ottoman Empire) in 1801.

The **Ottoman Empire** (the Ottoman Turks) had become the leading influence in the Islamic world by the late thirteenth century, the heir of the Byzantine Empire by the mid-fifteenth century, and the dominant political entity in the Middle East by the mid-sixteenth century as has been said. It was too the pre-eminent influence in southeastern Europe (in the Balkans) by the late fifteenth century; this was an arrangement that continued to the late nineteenth and early twentieth centuries. Its attempts to further expand its prerogatives in Europe and European attempts to prevent such an expansion were the distinguishing features of Ottoman Turkish history in the sixteenth, seventeenth, and eighteenth centuries. By deeply autocratic rule and the development of a surpassing army, the Empire reached its highest mark and its greatest extent in the early-to-mid-sixteenth-century reigns of Sultan Selim I (1467-1520; r. 1512-1520) and his son, Sultan Sulayman I/Sulayman the Magnificent (1494-1566; r. 1520-1566). In this period, Persia was defeated (1514); coastal bits of north-central Africa, Egypt, Syria, Palestine (all, 1516-1517), Mesopotamia (1534), and Arabia (1538) were added to the Empire; the first Turkish siege of Vienna occurred (1529); Tunis was lost to the Holy Roman Empire (1535); a Franco-Turkish alliance brought war (1536-1538) against Holy Roman Emperor Charles V; the Turkish pirate, Khaireddin Barbarossa (c. 1475-1546), made successful coastal raids on Italy and Spain (1533, 1544); Hungary was captured (1541); and another Franco-Turkish alliance again brought war (1542-1544) on Charles V. Under Sulayman I's son and successor, Sultan Selim II (c. 1524-1574; r. 1566-1574), the Holy Roman Emperor, Maximilian II, reclaimed parts of Hungary by purchase (1568) and Turkish domination of the Mediterranean was broken by the foremost Catholic states of Europe (most notably, by Spain under Philip II) at the Battle of Lepanto (Greece) in 1571.

The volatile political circumstance that followed was marked most notably by an organic flowering in architecture and by Persian and Polish defeats of Turkey in the early seventeenth century. This unsteady condition was stabilized somewhat in the reign of Sultan Mohammed IV (1641-1692; r. 1648-1687), mainly by his Grand Vizier, Mehmed Korprulu (1583-1661; r. 1656-1661). It was also in the reign of Mohammed IV that the principal seventeenth-century Turkish assaults on central Europe occurred. These conflicts were mainly with Austria (and the Holy Roman Empire under Leopold II) over mutual claims in Hungary and in the Balkans and they ended, on balance, badly for Turkey. The First Turkish War (1663-1664) was caused by Turkish and Austrian intervention in Wallachia and Moldavia and it resulted in the further partition of Hungary. The Second (Great) Turkish War (1683-1699) entailed the second Turkish siege of Vienna (1683), the formation of the Holy Alliance (Austria, Poland, Venice, and Russia) against Turkey (1684), the liberation of Hungary (1686-1697), the temporarily successful campaign of Peter the Great of Russia against Turkey in Ukraine (1696), the eventual defeat of the Turks, and the consequent and conclusive relief of central Europe from Turkish incursion (1699). The Turkish wars with Austria (and the Holy Roman Empire under Joseph I and Charles VI) continued in the early eighteenth century. The Third Turkish War (1716-1718) marked the greatest expansion of Hapsburg lands. And the Fourth Turkish War (1737-1739) entailed Austrian and Russian victories over Turkey in the Balkans and the Crimea and the beginning of Austro-Russian rivalry in the Balkans. The most telling Turkish conflicts of the eighteenth century were against Russia (under Catherine the Great) and they too went badly for Turkey. In the First Russo-Turkish War (1768-1774), Austria allied with Turkey to successfully oppose Russian occupation of Moldavia and Wallachia; Russia nonetheless achieved gains in the Crimea and on the Black Sea. The Turkish decline, both by internal corruption and dissension and by external insufficiencies, continued in the reign of Sultan Selim III (1761-1808; r. 1789-1807) who lost significant territories in the near Middle East and the Balkans and who also lost the Second Russo-Turkish War (1787-1792) against Russia and Austria.

The early modern era in **England** began with the conclusion of the War of the Roses (1455-1485) in which Henry Tudor defeated Richard III at the Battle of Bosworth Field in 1485, united the warring factions (the Houses of York and Lancaster) by marriage (thus establishing the **House of Tudor** [1485-1603]), and assumed the throne as Henry VII (1457-1509; r. 1485-1509). By way of his autocratic, but even-handed, style, Henry eventually restored a sense of civil order and prosperity, consolidated English rule in Ireland (1494), commissioned John Cabot's explorations of the Americas (1497-1498), and effected a peace treaty with Scotland (1499). He was succeeded by his son, Henry VIII (1491-1547; r. 1509-1547), who was among the most important political figures of early modern history. Henry entered six marriages; most were of significant historical consequence. He took his first wife, Katharine of Aragon (1485-1536), daughter of Ferdinand V and Isabella I of Spain and widow of Henry's brother, in 1509. She was the mother of Mary I but failed to produce a male heir. Henry fell out with the Papacy over his resolution to divorce Katharine and to marry Anne Boleyn (1505-1536) in 1533. He proclaimed the "Act of Supremacy" in 1535 by which he replaced the Pope as the head of the Church in England. This initiative brought a qualitative rupture with Rome, established the Church of England (the Anglican Church) as the successor of the Catholic Church in England, and signified the triumph of Protestantism in England. It was likewise this initiative that evoked his break with the celebrated author and statesman, Sir Thomas More, and that led to More's imprisonment and execution in 1535. Anne was the mother of Elizabeth I but, like Katharine, failed to produce a male heir. She was likely falsely accused of adultery and treason and was executed in 1536. Henry married Jane Seymour (c. 1509-1537) in 1536; she died giving birth to Edward VI in 1537. In 1540, he both married and divorced Anne of Cleves (1515-1557) and also married Catherine Howard (c. 1521-1542). Catherine, like Anne Boleyn, was accused of adultery and executed (in 1542). Henry's sixth and last marriage was to Catherine Parr (1512-1548) in 1543; she is said to have had a beneficent affect on him. His numerous and mostly failed marriages aside, Henry was otherwise occupied with the formal unification of Wales and England (1536), an unsuccessful war to unite Scotland and England (1542), a failed attempt to unite (Catholic) Ireland and (Anglican) England (1542), and an alliance with Holy Roman Emperor Charles V in two moderately successful wars (1522 and 1542-1544) against Francis I of France.

The remaining Tudor monarchs of England were: Edward VI (1537-1553; r. 1547-1553), son of Henry VIII and Jane Seymour; Mary I (1516-1558; r. 1553-1558), daughter of Henry VIII and Katharine of Aragon; and Elizabeth I (1533-1603; r. 1558-1603), daughter of Henry VIII and Anne Boleyn. Edward's reign included a more liberal interpretation of monarchial absolutism than that of his father, a deeper sympathy for the burdens of the peasantry than that of his father, a widening allegiance to Protestantism, and the disputed succession of the crown. In 1554, Mary married the man who, in 1556, became Philip II of Spain. Her reign was marked principally by a fervent renewal of Catholicism and a virulent prosecution of Protestants (which brought the appellation, "Bloody Mary"), by a continued, but unsuccessful, participation of England in Charles V's war against France, and by fiscal deterioration. Elizabeth stood astride the last approximate half of the sixteenth century as her father had stood astride the first approximate half of the century. Like her father, she too was among the most significant political figures of early modern civilization. Elizabeth inherited, from Mary, an unsettled religious, military, and economic circumstance. She nonetheless came to reign over one of the most accomplished and memorable periods in the whole of English, if not world, history. Her nationalist and Anglican/anti-Catholic orientation brought her into immediate conflict with Mary's husband, Philip II of Spain, whose 1559 marriage proposal she refused and whose hegemonic military and mercantile ambitions she opposed throughout the entire course of her reign. Elizabeth prosecuted numerous actions against Spain; most notably, the English defeat (by Sir Francis Drake) of the Spanish Armada's attempt to conquer England in 1588 and the assistance given (with France) to Netherlands against Spain in the Dutch War of Independence (1585, 1595-1598). She too variously and successfully supported the French Huguenots in their War of Religion (1562-1598) against Catholic domination. Her defeat of Spain and neutralization of France were central to the subsequent rise of England as the most powerful nation in the world. Elizabeth's nationalist and Anglican/anti-Catholic orientation also brought her into virtually immediate conflict with Mary Queen of Scots (1542-1587; r. 1561-1567), a Catholic, the mother of her own successor and Elizabeth's, James VI of Scotland (1566-1625; r. 1567-1625; later, James I of England), and the dominating wife (1558-1560) of Francis II of France. Mary, a person of uncommon intelligence, charisma, courage, and beauty, if equally uncommon wile, had attempted by numerous failed intrigues (which included strategic marriages and murders) to succeed Elizabeth by most any means; she was executed for her actions by reluctant order of Elizabeth in 1587. Elizabeth, who had an autocratic sense of rule but also an impressive ability to marshal popular support for her policies, too presided over the earnest beginnings of English colonialism and piracy in the Americas and Asia (carried out largely by Sir Francis Drake); over currency reforms, the stabilization of labor conditions, and the establishment of humane laws concerning the relief of poverty; over a significant improvement in agricultural, manufacturing, and commercial production; over the establishment of the London Stock Exchange in 1571; and over a literary flowering with few, if any, rivals in world intellectual history.

Elizabeth died without an heir in 1603; the English throne passed to the Scottish **House of Stuart** (1603-1714), then under James VI of Scotland, son of Mary Queen of Scots, who became James I of England (r.

1603-1625) in 1603. The reign of James was most notably marked by very sharp disputes with Parliament (which was suspended from 1611 to 1621), a herald of the English Civil War at mid-century, by a peace treaty with Philip III of Spain in 1604, by the authorized publication of the <u>King James Version of the Bible</u> in 1604 (published in 1611), by a varied advocacy of Anglicanism, by a condemnation of Catholicism and (Calvinist) Puritanism, by an enhanced commitment to colonial ambitions (particularly in the Americas), and by significant patronage of architecture and the literary arts. James was succeeded by his son, Charles I (1600-1649; r. 1625-1649), who continued his father's colonial expansion in the Americas and who further exacerbated his father's disputes with Parliament (ostensibly over issues of taxation), with Catholics, and with Puritans. Charles depreciated civil and religious liberties and dissolved Parliament from 1629 to 1640, suffered war with Scotland from 1638 over attempts to introduce Anglicanism to the country, massacred rebelling Irish Catholics in Ulster (northern Ireland) in 1641, and arrested Puritan leader, John Pym (c. 1583-1643), also in 1641. The result was the **English Civil War** (1642-1648) which put advocates of the Crown (Cavaliers, mainly nobles and Anglicans), who claimed the prerogative to rule by divine right, squarely against advocates of the Parliament (Roundheads), who claimed the prerogative to rule independently of the Crown. Scotland joined the Parliamentary Army (comprised mainly of Puritan elite aided by middle-class artisans and merchants) under Oliver Cromwell (1599-1658) in 1643; the Army had effectively vanquished the Cavaliers by 1647. Cromwell defeated the Scots, in turn, in 1648; Charles was arrested, also in 1648; he was executed and the monarchy was abolished in 1649.

Under the quasi-democratic Commonwealth (1649-1660) that followed, a form of parliamentary rule prevailed, albeit a form of such rule that entailed strict Puritan supervision of daily conduct. Scotland and Ireland were brought under Puritan heel, England gained success against Netherlands and Spain in the First English-Dutch Naval War (1652-1654), a conflict over trade disputes, and it was also victorious in a trade disagreement/war with Spain (1654-1659) that included the seizure of Jamaica (1655). After the death of Cromwell in 1658 and the abdication of his less-able son, Richard (1626-1712), in 1659, the monarchy was restored. The Stuart Restoration of 1660 under Charles II (1630-1685; r. 1660-1685), who had been educated at the court of Louis XIV of France where he spent the period of the Commonwealth (after having unsuccessfully attempted to defeat Cromwell by attacking him from Scotland), brought enhanced parliamentary prerogatives (which included the development of political parties [most notably, the Protestant, Whigs, and the Catholic, Tories] and the protection of individual persons from arbitrary arrest) and enhanced colonial ambitions as well, most particularly in the Americas, Africa, and India. Charles nonetheless attempted to imitate French absolutism; his concessions to representative government were begrudging. He inverted the religious order of the Commonwealth by restoring the Anglican state church and persecuting Puritans. His reign was also marked by:
- the Second English-Dutch Naval War (1665-1667) in which Dutch Guiana/Suriname was exchanged for what became New York City;
- the virtual destruction of London by plague (1665) and fire (1666); and
- the Third English-Dutch Naval War (1672-1674) which was unpopular and indecisive.

Charles was succeeded by his brother, James II (1633-1701; r. 1685-1688), who attempted an exceedingly unpopular Catholic restoration and who deepened mutual hostilities between the Crown and the Parliament. With the birth of James' son (the would-be James III) in 1688, the threat of permanent Catholic rule in England incited anti-Catholic political authorities to summon William III of Orange (Netherlands; 1650-1702; r. 1689-1702) to the throne for the purpose of defending Protestantism and a free parliament. William had earlier distinguished himself in the Third Dutch War against Louis XIV of France (1672-1678). He was the grandson of William I of Orange (the great hero of the Dutch War of Independence) and Charles I of England and he was the husband (from 1677) of James II's daughter, Mary (1662-1694), with whom, as Mary II (r. 1689-1694), he ruled jointly until her death in 1694. "The Glorious Revolution," led by William, was a largely bloodless coup d'état in which James II was permitted to escape to France; James, who had marshaled the support of Irish Catholics, was conclusively defeated by William in Ireland in 1690. The "Revolution" brought acceptance of the "Declaration of Rights" (1689) which enacted a sharp reduction of royal power, a significant augmentation of parliamentary prerogative, a more impartial system of taxation, an increased provision for religious toleration, and an extension of speech freedoms. In a series of continental wars with Louis XIV of France, the War of the Grand Alliance (1688-1697), the English (Protestant) notion of constitutional monarchy came to replace French (Catholic) absolutism as the prevailing view of domestic government and the English (Protestant) axiom of balance-of-power came to replace the French (Catholic) maxim of hegemony as the governing principle of international affairs. Owing principally to the force of its cultural achievement, its mercantile pre-eminence, and its naval superiority, England was becoming the leading nation in the world by the end of William's reign.

William was succeeded in 1702 by the last of the Stuarts, Anne (1665-1714; r. 1702-1714), daughter of James II. Unlike her father, like her sister (Mary II) and William III himself, Anne was a devout Protestant in a predominantly Protestant, not a predominantly Catholic, nation. The transition to parliamentary government continued in her reign and the formal union of Scotland and England-Wales, as Great Britain, likewise occurred in her time on the throne. The principal event of the period in which she ruled, however, was the War of the Spanish Succession (1701-1713/1714) through which Britain's stature in the world grew yet more imposing. Gibraltar, much of eastern Canada, and the Latin American slave trade accrued to her in the Peace of Utrecht that ended the War. Britain's balance-of-power policy and its inclination to "cabinet politics" had again prevailed.

The "Act of Settlement" (1701) regulated royal succession after Anne. It stipulated that if Anne died without an heir (which, it turned out, she did), the throne would pass to the (German) Hanovers and their Protestant descendants (which, it turned out, it did). The great-grandson of James I (whose granddaughter, Sophie, had married into the House of Brunswick-Luneburg/House of Hanover), George I (1660-1727; r. 1714-1727), an important patron of the musical arts, thus became King of Great Britain in 1714. The **House of Hanover** ruled Britain for the next approximately two centuries (1714-1901). George I was succeeded by his son, George II (1683-1760; r. 1727-1760), also an important patron of the musical arts, who presided over great prosperity due largely to successful, mercantilist colonial policies in the Americas, Africa, and India and who formulated and advanced the modern party system of the nation in which the parliamentary majority provides the ministry of the government (headed by the Prime Minister). Robert Walpole (1676-1745; r. 1721-1742) was the first formally acknowledged Prime Minister under this arrangement. In the War of the Austrian Succession (1740-1748), Britain was allied with Austria and Netherlands against Prussia, Spain, France, and Bavaria. In the Seven Years War (1756-1763), Britain successfully engaged France in colonial disputes in North America, the Caribbean, and Africa (moved mainly by Prime Minister William Pitt the Elder [1707-1778; r. 1757-1761], among the leading architects of British colonial policy) and successfully allied with Prussia against Austria and France in the Silesian (the European) phase of the War. George II was succeeded by his grandson, George III (1738-1820; r. 1760-1820), in whose long and eventful, early modern reign:

- the Seven Years War came to an end (1763) in North America; Britain obtained Florida from Spain and Canada, the western United States (east of the Mississippi River), and Senegal from France;
- Britain consolidated its political and fiscal domination of India through the British East India Company, which was itself transformed into a British administrative agency in 1773:
- a wide expansion of international trade occurred and the incipient development of modern industrialism unfolded;
- transportation improved and trade, manufacturing, and agriculture prospered; there nonetheless developed a short food supply due to sharp increases in population;
- the American Revolutionary War (1775-1783) gained political independence from Britain for the thirteen American colonies (which became the United States of America) in 1783; Florida was also lost to Spain in 1783;
- colonial claims in Oceania (most notably in Australia, 1788) were greatly expanded;
- Canada was re-organized into French-speaking (Quebec) and English-speaking (elsewhere) regions in 1791;
- Britain entered the First War of the Coalition (1792-1797) against France owing to conflict over colonial interests with the French, the growing French threat to the European balance of political power, and opposition to the principles and practices of the French Revolution; leadership of the government throughout the period following the American Revolutionary War (in which war debts greatly burdened the state) and the period of the war against France (in which early results were mixed but in which Britain ultimately prevailed) fell to William Pitt the Younger (1759-1806; r. 1783-1801, 1804-1806), son of William Pitt the Elder and among Great Britain's most celebrated Prime Ministers; and
- a flowering of arts and letters occurred, mainly in painting, music, literature, and philosophy.

The earliest European explorations of North America (what are now Canada and the United States of America), eleventh-century Viking voyages aside, were done by the English and the Spanish in the late fifteenth and early sixteenth centuries. Spain made its first permanent settlement in North America in the sixteenth century; England, France, and Netherlands made their first such settlements in the seventeenth century. From the virtual beginning of the European presence in North America, conflicts over territory for farming, hunting, fishing, trapping, mining, trading, residing, and dictating prerogatives developed among the colonizing powers, among the indigenous peoples, and between the colonizing powers and the indigenous peoples. These conflicts, sometimes collectively referred to as the so-termed Indian Wars, were virtually perpetual. In the end, they resulted in the wide displacement, in some cases the extermination, in almost all cases the disadvantage, of indigenous cultures. By the mid-eighteenth century, the North American continent, not unlike the European, was poised for a virtual world war. The French and Indian War began in 1754 and became the North American phase of the **Seven Years War** (1756-1763). It was mainly a dispute between France and Great Britain (with native American peoples caught amid) over colliding colonial interests in the Americas. The Treaty of Paris that ended the War in 1763 effectively finished French control of what are now Canada and the (western) United States (east of the Mississippi River) in favor of the British, finished Spanish control of Florida in favor of the British, eliminated the French threat to British settlers, and opened the drift to independence from Great Britain for the American colonies (which had fought on the victorious British side in the War).

This drift toward the political independence of what became the **United States of America** was accelerated by the imperial policies of George III toward the colonies. Control of settlements west of the Appalachian Mountains (effectively, at the western border of the colonies), trade, and taxes were the main issues of contention. The Stamp Act (1765-1766) imposed taxes on documents, newspapers, and books; the Townsend Acts (1766) decreed import duties. The colonists, centered in Boston, replied in 1770 with a boycott of British goods. Colonial demands for representation in Parliament were rejected; all special taxes (except the duty on tea) were nonetheless eliminated. In 1773, colonists threw the cargoes of three ships into Boston Harbor (the Boston Tea Party); the government closed the Harbor and declared martial law. Britain executed the so-termed Intolerable Acts limiting the geographical and political freedoms of the colonists. Separatist movements, independence movements, developed under the exhortations of Samuel Adams (1722-1803), Thomas Jefferson (1743-1826), and Thomas Paine (1737-1809). Delegates of the thirteen colonies convened in Philadelphia in 1774 (the First Constitutional Congress) and suspended trade with Great Britain. The **American Revolutionary War**, or the American War of Independence (1775-1783), began on April 19, 1775 at Lexington and Concord, Massachusetts. The Second Continental Congress convened at Philadelphia in 1775; it made George Washington (1732-1799), a Virginia farmer and British antagonist who had nonetheless fought in the French and Indian War on the British side, commander-in-chief of the Continental Army; and, on July 4, 1776, it ratified Thomas Jefferson's "Declaration of Independence."

The early results of the War were mixed; major colonial victories were achieved in Boston (1775), Ticonderoga, New York (1775), Trenton, New Jersey (1776), Princeton, New Jersey (1776), and Saratoga, New York (1777); major British victories were achieved in New York City (1776), Philadelphia (1776), and Quebec (1776). France and Spain entered the War on the American side against Britain in 1779; prominent European aristocrats volunteered their services to the colonists and played a highly significant role in the colonists' ultimate success. The most important of these were the French general, Marquis de Lafayette (1757-1834), who later had a largely unsuccessful role in the French Revolution and in the July Revolution of 1830; the Polish national hero, Tadeusz Kosciuszko, who later led an unsuccessful popular insurrection in Poland against Prussia and Russia; and the Prussian general, Baron von Steuben (1730-1794), who had an especially large part in training the Continental Army. After fairly wide British successes in the Carolinas and Georgia in 1780, the British resource wavered significantly and the conclusive colonial triumph over Britain was achieved at the Battle of Yorktown (Virginia) in 1781. The Peace of Paris, which formally ended the War, was concluded in 1783, largely by Benjamin Franklin (1706-1790), an accomplished writer and scientist, who had earlier played a major role in crafting the "Declaration of Independence" (1776) and who would later play a major role in formulating the "Constitution of the United States of America" (1787). The Peace established the political independence of the thirteen American coastal colonies (Delaware, Pennsylvania, New Jersey, Georgia, Connecticut, Massachusetts, Maryland, South Carolina, New Hampshire, Virginia, New York, North Carolina, and Rhode Island) and most of the remaining territory east of the Mississippi River; it returned Senegambia (what are now Senegal and Gambia) to France (from Great Britain); and it returned Florida (west to New Orleans) to Spain (from Great Britain).

The thirteen American colonies of Great Britain were the first colonial possessions to win political independence from European domination and, as the Unites States of America, the first nation in the world to tangibly organize itself in accord with the principles of Enlightenment democracy. These principles were allegedly based on natural law and secular reason; they were to eradicate the tyrannies of the absolutist, monarchial systems of government and to replace the feudal state with democratic, class society; and they were to assure popular sovereignty, the legal and social emancipation of the individual person, personal liberty, and popular equality. They achieved some of this for many people but also continued to enslave many others. The American (and French) Revolutions were mainly middle-class and upper-class insurrections (bourgeois revolutions); they were not peasant-class, working-class, and lower-class movements although they had a great affect, in some respects a salutary affect, on peasants, workers, and lower-class persons; and, of course, they yet rested very significantly on the formal institutions of slavery themselves.

The immediate aftermath of the War was trying on virtually all sides. Britain's international pre-eminence and its transatlantic empire were severely damaged. France suffered heavy war debts. And the very loose confederation of American states itself very nearly collapsed; it lost loyalist population to Canada, encountered continuing border conflicts with native American people, experienced serious inflationary tendencies, and endured continuing constitutional problems. A federal constitution, the "Articles of Confederation" (1781), and state constitutions were developed on the model of Jefferson's "Virginia Bill of Rights" (1776). These documents assured popular sovereignty by means of democratic rights, the elective principle for all offices of state, the separation of executive, legislative, and judicial powers, and the independence of church and state. The weak central government of the "Articles" made it (the central government) ineffective, however. A Federal Constitutional Convention was staged in Philadelphia in 1787 to address the constitutional crisis. In it, Benjamin Franklin and James Madison (1751-1836) mediated the debate between advocates of a very strong central government (the Federalists; most notably, George Washington, John Adams [1735-1826], and Alexander Hamilton [1755-1804]) and those who emphasized the prerogatives of the individual states (the Republicans, later the Democrats; most notably, Thomas Jefferson). The constitution of the first modern democracy, the "Constitution of the Unites States of America," was issued by the Convention in 1787 and became the governing document of the new nation in 1789. It secured the liberties assured by the "Articles of Confederation" and established a federal republic in which the chief responsibilities of the national government concerned the conduct of foreign policy and the chief responsibilities of the state governments concerned the conduct of domestic policy; in which the executive, legislative, and judicial functions of government were separated; and in which a system of checks and balances decided the relation of federal and state authorities as well as the relation of executive, legislative, and judicial functions of the federal government. George Washington (r. 1789-1797) was elected the first President of the Unites States of America, the first head-of-state, in 1789; Vermont (1791), Kentucky (1792), and Tennessee (1796) joined the union of states in his presidency. Alexander Hamilton, who had served brilliantly under Washington in the American Revolutionary War, became his Secretary of the Treasury, also in 1789, and, in that capacity, became also the principal architect of the new nation's fiscal policy, a policy that stabilized the economy in respect to debt, in respect to a system of excise taxes and tariffs, and in respect to banking; that presided over the establishment of the New York Stock Exchange in 1790 and the Bank of the United States of America in 1791; that invested the power of American capitalism in the prerogatives of the wealthy elite; that developed a national program of commerce and industry; and that urged an isolationist form of foreign policy.

The early modern history of **France** was dominated by the sixteenth-century Valois (in association with other ruling families), the House of Bourbon (which ruled France from 1589 to 1792), and the French Revolution and the French Revolutionary Wars (which, in various forms, occupied the last approximate decade of the eighteenth century). The last of the direct Valois line, Charles VIII, died in 1498 as has been said. He was succeeded by his cousin, Louis XII (1462-1515; r. 1498-1515), who was a major patron of music and who unsuccessfully continued Charles' wars in Italy. Louis was followed, in turn, by his cousin, Francis I (1494-1547; r. 1515-1547), whose reign was (with that of Charles VII) arguably the most eventful of the Valois. He:

- successfully resumed Louis' wars in Italy (most notably in Milan, 1515);
- was a serious candidate for Holy Roman Emperor in 1519 but was defeated by Charles V of Spain, who became his principal continental rival;
- suffered four largely unsuccessful wars against Charles V:
  - 1521-1526, entailed opposition of Henry VIII of England and the capture of Francis;
  - 1526-1529, brought mainly inconclusive results;
  - 1536-1538, entailed a Franco-Turkish alliance against Charles; and
  - 1542-1544, entailed opposition of Henry VIII of England and another Franco-Turkish alliance against Charles.
- fervently persecuted the (Protestant) Huguenots; and

- was a significant patron of painting and literature.

Francis was succeeded by his son, Henri II (1519-1559; r. 1547-1559), who resumed his father's wars against Charles V in 1552-1556 but with somewhat broader success, who continued these conflicts less successfully with Charles' Spanish successor, Philip II, in 1556-1559, who, also like his father, widely persecuted the Huguenots, and who died accidentally in a tournament. Henri was succeeded, in turn, by three sons, the last of the Valois: Francis II (1544-1560; r.1559-1560), Charles IX (1550-1574; r. 1560-1574), and Henri III (1551-1589; r. 1574-1589). Francis II married Mary Queen of Scots in 1558 and was dominated by her family; he too continued his father's virulent persecution of the Huguenots. Charles IX likewise continued his immediate predecessor's oppression of the Huguenots and presided over the beginning of the Huguenot Wars (1562-1598) in which Protestantism briefly triumphed. And Henri III was also deeply, in the end fatally (he was assassinated), engaged in the Huguenot intrigues. He too, with England, came to the aid of Netherlands in the Dutch War of Independence against Spain in 1585.

The **House of Bourbon** (which was connected in distant terms to the Capetians) began its rule of France in 1589. The first of the Bourbon monarchs of France, Henri IV (1553-1610; r. 1589-1610), was a Protestant and a central figure in the Huguenot Wars which ended under the influence of Henri's conciliatory populism in 1598 with the Edict of Nantes. The Edict granted Huguenots liberty of conscience, freedom of worship, and political equality. In Henri's reign, a French, Dutch, and English alliance made successful war against Philip II of Spain in 1595-1598. This conflict effectively ended Spanish expansion in Europe and Spanish attempts to intervene in the internal affairs of France as has been said. Also in his reign, the crown and the unitary sense of a national state were strengthened, agriculture and trade were improved, and the first French colony was established in Canada (1603). Henri was assassinated in 1610 and was succeeded by his son, Louis XIII (1601-1643; r. 1610-1643), a major patron of painting, in whose reign the French Academy (Académie Française) for the promotion of arts and sciences was established (1615) and whose government was dominated by his chief minister, Cardinal Armand Richelieu (1585-1642; r. 1624-1642). Richelieu promoted philosophy, resumed hostilities with the Huguenots, further centralized and absolutized royal authority, further depreciated parliamentary prerogative (the Estates-General was not convened from 1614 to 1789), allied successfully with Sweden/Denmark and the Protestant princes of Germany against the Holy Roman Empire (the Hapsburgs) in the Thirty Years War (1618-1648), and was largely responsible for directing the final phase, the Franco-Swedish phase (1635-1648), of the Thirty Years War which ended with the Peace of Westphalia (1648), the restoration/enhancement of the nation's natural frontiers (the Pyrenees Mountains and the Rhine River), and the rise of France to pre-eminence among world nations.

Louis XIII was succeeded by his son, Louis XIV/Louis the Sun King (1638-1715; r. 1643-1715), the longest reigning monarch in the history of the country and among the most memorable figures of early modern world history. The early reign of Louis XIV was dominated by his chief minister, Cardinal Jules Mazarin (1602-1661; r. 1643-1661), who favorably negotiated the Peace of Westphalia, successfully ended the prolonged war (1621-1659) with Philip IV of Spain in the Peace of the Pyrenees (1659), and continued Richelieu's absolutist and repressive domestic policies (which evoked notable public discord). By his own direction, Louis:

- greatly refined and expanded the mercantilist character of the national economy by developing state craft enterprises made productive, in large measure, by definitive division-of-labor practices, by developing trade associations, by developing an extensive system of roads and canals for the transport of goods, by invoking protective tariffs, by raising internal taxes, by fixing agricultural prices, and by prohibiting emigration, all of which emphatically accentuated the hierarchical nature of French class society, significantly augmented the prosperity of the upper and middle classes, and substantially deepened the burdens and the misery of the lower classes;
- greatly improved techniques of warfare and strengthened the French military which carried out repressive police actions within France, expansionist ambitions elsewhere in Europe, and aggressive colonial policy virtually throughout the world; the principal manifestations of these tendencies were:
  - the creation or refinement of prisons such as the Bastille (in Paris) for the arbitrary and secret detention of state enemies;
  - the numerous alliances and wars against Netherlands, Spain, the Germanies, and the Holy Roman Empire which most notably included losses to Frederick William the Great Elector of Brandenburg-Prussia in his actions against France, Poland, and Sweden (1660-1678), territorial successes against the Holy Roman Empire under Leopold I in the late seventeenth century, the largely indecisive Third Dutch War (1672-1678) against William III of Orange (which, like the first two such wars, also involved English opposition to Netherlands and which aimed at

diminishing Dutch commercial successes), the somewhat indecisive War of the Grand Alliance (1688-1697) mainly against the Holy Roman Empire, the Germanies, Spain, and William III of Orange (Netherlands)/William III of England (which was caused by Louis' designs on German territory and which resulted [by the Peace of Rijswijk {near Amsterdam}, 1697] in the triumph of English [Protestant] notions of constitutional monarchy and balance-of-power over French [Catholic] notions of absolute monarchy and hegemonic domination), and the War of the Spanish Succession (1701-1713/1714) in which France lost colonial territories in eastern Canada to Great Britain but in a sense gained the Spanish crown (which passed to the [French] Bourbon grandson of Louis XIV, Philip V, in 1700) as has been said; and

- colonial acquisitions, most significantly in the Americas and in Africa.
- greatly persecuted French Protestants (the Huguenots in particular), revoked the Edict of Nantes (in 1685) by which the Huguenots had been granted tolerance, and protected the Catholic state church; and
- greatly promoted accomplished architecture (such as the "Palace of Versailles"), painting, music, dance, and literature in the context of a brilliant court life.

Louis XIV was succeeded by his great-grandson, Louis XV (1710-1774; r. 1715-1774), whose extravagant court, costly foreign adventures, and unexceptional leadership brought near-bankruptcy to the government and prepared the way for the French Revolution. The troubled economy was stabilized briefly under the chief minister of his early reign, Cardinal André Fleury (1653-1743; r. 1726-1743), but deteriorated markedly thereafter. The decadence of the absolutist equation likewise deepened. The standard of living and prerogative of the aristocracy (the upper class; those of inherited or purchased wealth) and the bourgeoisie (the middle class; wealthy manufacturers, bankers, merchants, physicians, lawyers, and priests) were greatly favored by the mercantilist system. The peasantry (propertyless agricultural workers comprising at least one-half of the population) and the manufacturing working class were greatly disadvantaged by this system. The upper class was largely exempt from taxation; the increasingly onerous tax burden fell largely on the peasantry; price inflation further reduced real income. As the disparities between wealth and poverty, power and powerlessness, privilege and restriction grew, the quasi-democratic tendencies of the Enlightenment elevated opposition to the government. The aristocracy exhorted limitations on absolute monarchy but retention of their own prerogative; the bourgeoisie urged social equality and political representation for themselves; the peasants and workers had had quite enough of doing virtually everything and getting virtually nothing. Approximately fifteen years after the death of Louis XV, the open insurrection, the French Revolution, invited by him (among others) erupted.

The most significant of the profligate foreign intrigues of Louis XV's reign were the War of the Polish Succession (1733-1735), the War of the Austrian Succession (1740-1748), and the Seven Years War (1756-1763). French involvement in the War of the Polish Succession was occasioned by Louis' marriage to a Polish princess and it effectively ended with Russian and Austrian interests prevailing over French, Spanish, and Polish ones. In the War of the Austrian Succession, France was successfully allied with Frederick the Great of Prussia, with Spain, and with Bavaria against Austria, Great Britain, and Netherlands. The earliest phase of the Seven Years War began in North America as the French and Indian War in 1754 and it became a global conflict between France and Great Britain, largely over colliding colonial assertions. This phase of the War ended with French losses to Britain of what are now Canada, the (western) United States of America (east of the Mississippi River), Senegal, and parts of India. The other, the second phase of the War went on in Europe and principally entailed a French, Austrian, Swedish, and Russian alliance against Prussia and Great Britain. This, the so-termed War over Silesia, ended with a re-statement of Prussian eminence and further dilution of French influence on the continent. Although Louis XV reigned over an especially unfortunate period of early modern French political and economic history, he did nonetheless also preside over an especially memorable era in French painting, music, and literature as well as over the establishment of the first public bank (1715).

The misfortunes of absolute monarchism deepened yet further in the reign of Louis XV's grandson and successor, Louis XVI (1754-1793; r. 1774-1792). Several factors contributed to Louis XVI's ruin, not the least of which were his own retiring and indolent nature, the deteriorating circumstance he inherited, the large public debts incurred by his alliance with the American colonies against Great Britain in the American Revolutionary War, the quasi-democratic appellations of the American Revolution itself, failed proposals for domestic political reform (having mainly to do with taxation), peasant starvation, the intransigence of privilege, and economic crises caused by British commercial successes, diminished agricultural production, and public bankruptcy (1788). The economic crises in particular encouraged Louis to re-convene (from 1614) the Estates-General in 1789 and to face the prospect of a limited monarchy; the deluge that had been threatened for decades, if not centuries, was upon him. The **French Revolution** effectively began on June 17, 1789, when the Estates-General, meeting in Versailles (near Paris), commenced work on a new constitution and was taken over by its lowest ranking members (who declared themselves the National Assembly). Suspicious troop movements ordered by Louis aroused apprehensions that the Assembly may be forcibly dissolved; the Bastille (a political prison in Paris which was taken as a symbol of despotic repression) was stormed on July 14, 1789; public administration and the absolutist equation it defended collapsed; the army was dissolved; Marquis de Lafayette, who had earlier distinguished himself in the American Revolutionary War, formed a militia of citizens (the National Guard); peasant rebellions exploded throughout the country; and large numbers of aristocrats fled the country. Later in 1789, the peasants were freed and the "Declaration of the Rights of Man" (August 26, 1789), proclaiming the universal brotherhood of humanity, personal liberty, and judicial equality, was adopted. Famine and the fear of counter-revolution incited the masses of Paris to further acts of violence. In order to relieve fiscal difficulties, Bishop Charles Maurice de Talleyrand (1754-1838) proposed the confiscation of church property with compensation, a measure which produced onerous inflation and greatly heightened church-state conflict, conflict that was made still worse by the dissolution of religious orders and monasteries and by the opposition of ecclesiastics to the new constitution. Closed and efficient political parties were established in Paris, then throughout the country. The most notable of these figured prominently in the remaining course of the Revolution: the moderate (by the standards of the day) Feuillants (including Lafayette) were qualified loyalists; the Girondists were mainly propertied bourgeoisie; the radical (by the standards of the day) Cordeliers were led by Jean Paul Marat (1743-1793); and the ultra-radical (by the standards of the day) Jacobins were led by Maximilien Marie Isidore Robespierre (1758-1794).

Louis XVI attempted to flee the chaos in 1791 but was apprehended, returned to Paris, deprived of all political powers, imprisoned in 1792, and executed in 1793. The new "Constitution" was proclaimed in 1791; it established a constitutional monarchy with a weak executive, a popular assembly/parliament elected indirectly on the basis of limited suffrage (by active, propertied citizens only), elected officials, judges, and jurors, open courts, and assurances of basic human rights (including such for Jewish people) and of private property. The monarchy was abolished and the first stage (the National Convention, 1792-1795) of the **First Republic** (1792-1804), under a new constitution, was established in 1792. A massacre, the "September Massacre," of impassioned royalists in 1792 brought a second significant wave of aristocratic emigration, which, together with ongoing famine, inflation, and social discord, further threatened the revolution. The domestic result of all of this was the "Reign of Terror" (1793-1794) in which the Cordeliers and the Jacobins, under Marat and Robespierre respectively, established public education and welfare for the poor but also established a virtual dictatorship, a dictatorship in which judicial terror and mass liquidation (that swept up even Marie Antoinette) effectively abolished human rights. Sufficient opposition was raised to put an end to the "Reign" in 1794; Marat was murdered in 1793 and Robespierre was executed in 1794. A royalist campaign of terror predictably followed. In 1795, a new constitution brought in a new government, the Directory (1795-1799), and also brought in a larger recognition of the prerogatives of the propertied bourgeoisie; the "Terror" had dissuaded from universal suffrage. The Directory was, however, run through with corruption, fiscal chaos, militant excess, and a resurgence of royalist sentiment; it was replaced in 1799 by the Consulate (1799-1804) in a coup d'état that assured the victory of the bourgeoisie and that was effectively led by the Corsican-born military and political colossus, Napoleon Bonaparte/Napoleon I (1769-1821; r. 1802-1815).

The French Revolution precipitated a series of general European wars, the **French Revolutionary Wars** (1792-1802), that had mainly to do with the opposition of foreign monarchs, aristocrats, and clergy to the republican tendencies of the Revolution; most particularly, to do with such tendencies as they may have affected the enhanced prerogatives of the lower classes. The Holy Roman Empire under Leopold II (son of Archduchess Maria Theresa of Austria and Holy Roman Emperor Francis I; brother of Holy Roman Emperor Joseph II and Marie Antoinette [1755-1793], wife of Louis XVI and an especially important patron of the musical arts) defended Louis XVI in 1791 and aroused fears among the revolutionaries of a Hapsburg invasion. An Austrian-Prussian alliance in 1792 raised further apprehensions among the revolutionaries and elicited a French declaration of war on Austria (and so also Prussia) in 1792, the ongoing gambit of the so-termed **First War of the Coalition** (1792-1797). Great Britain, Spain, Portugal, and Netherlands entered the War against France in 1793. Napoleon Bonaparte became commander-in-chief of the French Revolutionary Army in 1796 and conducted a brilliant campaign in northern Italy in 1796-1797 to "end" the War by the Treaty of Campo Formio (near Venice) in 1797. Prussia and Spain were altogether defeated; Netherlands (Batavian

Republic), Belgium, Luxembourg, Milan (Cisalpine Republic), Savoy (Kingdom of Sardinia), and Genoa (Ligurian Republic) effectively went to France; Venice went to Austria; and Great Britain occupied Dutch territories in South Africa (1795) and Ceylon/Sri Lanka (1796). In the course of the War, Italian artistic treasures had been confiscated (i.e., taken to the Louvre in Paris by Napoleon), the French army had been thoroughly reformed into arguably the finest military organization in the world, and the techniques of warfare had been qualitatively revised. The notion of unlimited/total war, in which both military and civilian populations are significantly included and in which universal conscription of citizens for military duty and labor services pertain, was born of the First War of the Coalition. So too were the contemporary military practices of large, offensive, flexible, and varied massing of soldiers for battle, dispersed and mobile systems of logistic supply, and meritocratic bases of military rank.

The war with Great Britain nonetheless continued from 1798 to 1802 in what became the **Second War of the Coalition**. It entailed:

- Napoleon's at-first successful campaign against the British in Egypt (which included scholarly investigations of the region, the occupation of Malta, and the capture of Cairo from the Mamelukes in 1798) and his ultimate defeat by Admiral Horatio Nelson (1758-1805) at the Battle of Aboukir (near Alexandria) in 1798, an event that halted Napoleon's advancement in the region, that effectively won predominant control of the Mediterranean for the British by 1799, and that allowed the British to annex Malta in 1800;
- a second failed coalition (1798-1801) of Great Britain, Russia, Austria, Turkey, Portugal, and Naples against France;
- the transformation of Switzerland into the Helvetian Republic in 1798, of the Papal States into the Roman Republic in 1798, and of Naples into the Parthenopian Republic in 1799;
- Napoleon's dissolution of the incompetent Directory in 1799, his advancement to head of the new government (the Consulate, 1799-1804, a military dictatorship in democratic clothing), and his:
  - broad transformations of the (centralized) administration and the tax system;
  - establishment of a national system of primary, secondary, and higher education;
  - stabilization of public finances and control of inflation;
  - creation of the Bank of France (1800);
  - negotiation, with Pope Pius VII (1740-1823; r. 1800-1823), of the Concordat (1801), which reestablished the Roman Catholic Church in France but brought it largely under state control;
  - codification of the laws of the revolution (the Code Napoleon, 1804), personal liberty, legal equality, private property, and civil marriage and divorce; and
  - intolerance of dissent and taste for censorship, secret police repression, and military conscription.
- the French acquisition of Louisiana from Spain in 1800; and
- Napoleon's defeat of Austria at the Battle of Marengo (near Milan) in 1800, an event that occasioned the Treaty of Lunéville (near Strasbourg) with Austria in 1801 and the Treaty of Amiens (near Paris) with Great Britain in 1802; these treaties effectively ended the War.

The conflicts that would frame the early course of contemporary modern civilization, the Napoleonic Wars (1803-1815), followed almost immediately.

The history of so-termed early modern **China** was marked by the reign of a native dynastic succession, the Ming (1368-1644), and the reign of a foreign dynastic succession, the Manchu, or Qing (1644-1911). Administrative inadequacies, trade failures, famine, and peasant insurrections conspired to expel the Mongols, the foreign, Yuan Dynasty, from China in 1368 as has been said. The principal figure in this transformation and the first emperor of the **Ming Dynasty** was the Buddhist monk, Chu Yuan-chang (d. 1398; r. 1368-1398), who moved the capital from Peking/Beijing to Nanking and who established a strong central government (with accompanying bureaucracy, judicial authority, and police apparatus), an imperial academy, and public schools. In the fifteenth and sixteenth centuries, Confucianism was reinstated, the capital returned to Peking/Beijing (1421), the "Great Wall" was extended, new trade routes were developed in Asia and Africa, European trading stations were first established (by the Portuguese) in Canton/Guangzhou (1516) and Macau (1557), European (Catholic) missionaries gained influence from 1581, political/cultural expansion deepened in southeast Asia, significant medical advancements (including acupuncture) were achieved, and architecture (most notably, the imperial palace, "Forbidden City," in Peking/Beijing and the "Royal Ming Tombs" near Peking/Beijing) and ornamental porcelain flourished. There were as well, however, in the period of the Ming the customary sieges by Mongols, Japanese, and Manchus and the customary calamities of flood, famine, and pestilence.

At the beginning of the seventeenth century, Nurhachi (1583-1628) united the Tungu tribes of Manchuria (northeastern China) to form the nation of the Manchu. Approximately a decade later (in 1637), the Manchu subjugated Korea. The accomplished military organization of the Manchu and an internal military rebellion against the Ming brought down the last Ming emperor, Tsung-tseng (d. 1644; r. 1628-1644), in 1644 and opened the era of the last dynastic ruling authority of China, the **Manchu (or Qing) Dynasty**. In the reign of the Manchu's most significant emperor, K'ang Hsi (1655-1722; r. 1662-1722), Formosa/Taiwan (1683), Mongolia (1696), and (slightly later) Tibet (1724) were straightforwardly or effectively conquered. The nation achieved its approximate current boundaries with the addition of Sinkiang (now northwestern China) in 1757. The enormous Manchu empire that resulted was governed by a dogmatic Confucianism, an uncompromising central sense of authority, an inflexible form of social hierarchy which greatly and unfavorably affected the lower classes in particular, and an oppressive police apparatus. Until the late eighteenth century, however, population increased, European trade was expanded, and painting and literature flourished. In the last several decades of the eighteenth century, prohibitions of Christian missionaries were enacted, literary censorship was increased, and distrust of foreign trade interests intensified. In the nineteenth century, these interests (most notably, those of Great Britain, France, Germany, Russia, United States of America, and Japan) virtually took the country over. The most notable nineteenth-century conflicts with imperialist powers all went badly for the Chinese: the Opium War (1839-1842), by which Hong Kong was ceded to Britain; the Taiping Rebellion (1850-1864), mainly over excessive foreign influence in China; the First Sino-Japanese War (1894-1895), by which Korea and Formosa/Taiwan were lost to Japan; and the Boxer Rebellion (1898-1900), by which foreign influence over internal Chinese affairs was further increased. The Russo-Japanese War was fought in 1904-1905 over rival Russian and Japanese claims in Manchuria and Korea and resulted in Japanese control of those regions. The lot of these humiliations and wide domestic dissatisfaction with the archaic Manchu incited an insurrection which overthrew the Qing Dynasty in 1911; a new republic was established the following year.

The very large influence of Chinese culture in southeast Asia and in central-east Asia dated from the late ancient and early medieval eras as has been said. This influence continued in early modern civilization, most notably in Korea and Japan. The Koryo Dynasty of **Korea**, framed mainly by Chinese Buddhism, was briefly taken over by the Yuan (Mongol) government of China, 1274-1281, and was, in 1392, replaced by the Yi Dynasty (1392-1910) as has been also mostly said. The Yi Dynasty was governed by Confucian doctrine, established its capital at Hanyang (what is now Seoul), was subjugated by Japan from 1592 to 1598, was subjugated by the Manchu from 1637 to (in various senses) 1894, was subject (like China itself) to much unwelcome attention by foreign missionaries and commercialists throughout the nineteenth century most especially, and was tangibly occupied by the Japanese from the First Sino-Japanese War (1894-1895) and the Russo-Japanese War (1904-1905). Korea was formally annexed by Japan in 1910.

Early modern **Japan** was mainly distinguished by the self-destruction of the Ashikaga Shogunate (1338-1573), by a brief period without a shogunate, the Momoyama (1573-1603), and by the last shogunate, the Tokugawa Shogunate (1603-1867). The Ashikaga Shogunate, centered in Kyoto, descended into ruinous civil wars as early as the late fourteenth century, was visited by European armaments and Catholic missionaries from the mid-sixteenth century, and was conclusively undone by the great warrior, Oda Nobunaga (1534-1582; r. 1573-1582) in 1573. The Momoyama, centered in Osaka, was dominated by Nobunaga and his effective successor, the brilliant statesman, Hideyoshi Toyotomi (1535-1598; r. 1582-1598). Toyotomi established a trenchant central administration and directed the subjugation of Korea from 1592 to 1598. His successor, in turn, was defeated by Ieyasu Tokugawa (1542-1616; r. 1603-1616) at the Battle of Sekigahara (near Kyoto) in 1600 and established the **Tokugawa Shogunate** in 1603. The Tokugawa was centered in Edo (what is now Tokyo); it took the form of a rigid and hierarchical police state which greatly depreciated the peasantry; it reigned over an extended period of domestic repose; it persecuted and excluded all foreign influences (commercialists and missionaries principally); and it presided over a rich artistic development in architecture, painting, and drama. Its isolationist tendencies, not unlike those of the Manchu, so aroused imperial market concerns, however, that it was forced open to foreign trade by the Unites States of America in 1854. The shogunate itself was abolished in 1867 by the Emperor Meiji (1852-1912); the emperor was restored to the head of government (the Meiji Restoration) in 1868; and a period of Westernization and industrialization followed.

The amalgamation of Mongol and Islamic culture in what are now Afghanistan, northern Pakistan, and north-central **India** (in Delhi and the broad regions subtending Delhi) brought the Delhi Sultanate to dissolution and established the **Mogul Empire** (1526-1756) in 1526 as has been said. The final Islamic advance into India was led by the last Timurid, Babar (1483-1530; r. 1525-1530), a descendant of Genghis Khan, a man of great learning, an accomplished writer, the conqueror of the Sultanate of Delhi at the Battle of Panipat (near Delhi) in 1526, and the founder of the Mogul Empire. Babar was succeeded by his son, Humayun (1508-1556; r. 1530-1540), who was deposed by an Afghan usurper but who made a second conquest of Delhi with his son and successor, Akbar (1542-1605; r. 1556-1605) in 1555. Akbar was arguably the most remarkable of the Mogul emperors; he extended the Empire, made peace with the Hindus and other religionists by issue of the "Edict of Toleration" (1583), reorganized the administrative, judicial, and educational systems, established libraries and universities, and greatly promoted creative activities such as the visual and literary arts and the study of history. Akbar was succeeded by his dissolute and wasteful son, Jahangir (d. 1627; r. 1605-1627), in whose reign significant European colonial intrusions (English intrusions most notably) began (1612-1613). And Jahangir was, in turn, followed to the throne by his son, Shah Jahan (c. 1592-1666; r. 1628-1658), who expanded the Empire to the south and who presided over the cultural fusion of Hindu, Islamic, Mongol, and Persian[121] traditions that produced one of the most exceptional chapters in the entire history of the visual arts (most significantly in architecture, à la the "Taj Mahal"). Shah Jahan was deposed and imprisoned by his son, Aurangzeb (1618-1707; r. 1658-1707), who was the last significant governing authority of the Empire, who again expanded the Empire (n this case to its greatest extent), and who so persecuted Hindus that they responded with challenging insurrections. Hindu sects had been proliferating in India throughout the period of the Mogul Empire. Arguably the most notable of these were the Sikhs who were originally formed around the vision of the extraordinary mystic teacher, Nenak (c. 1469-c. 1539). In any case, as mistreatment of Hindus (such as destruction of their temples, special taxes on them, and overt attacks of them) deepened, particularly under Aurangzeb, they became increasingly ardent and increasingly militant enemies of the (Moslem) Empire. The internal dissolution of the Empire effectively began with the Hindu persecutions of the late seventeenth century and with the increasingly successful Hindu raids on the Empire that these persecutions incited. The most influential of these raids came from the Sikhs of northern India and from the Marathi Empire of central India. These forays had largely vanquished the Empire by the mid-eighteenth century, although serious Hindu-Moslem conflicts on the Indian sub-continent have variously continued to our own time. The external dissolution of the Empire was owed mainly to the English and French dispute over colonial prerogatives in the country. This dispute, and the Mogul Empire, largely ended with the English victory at the Battle of Plassey (near Calcutta) in 1757, an event that marked the beginning of a nearly two-century British domination of India.

The Reformations

The very considerable political discord of early modern civilization had its ideological equivalent in the Protestant Reformation, the Catholic Counter-Reformation, and the religious wars that these colossal events provoked. The Protestant and Catholic movements of this period constituted one of the most extensive and influential cultural transformations of early modern history and they had themselves highly significant political consequences. These movements came full blown in the sixteenth century but they had their germinal roots in the monastic reforms of the tenth and eleventh centuries, the ascetic spirituality of the Albigensian and Waldensian sects of the twelfth century, the nominalist heresies of Roscelin in the twelfth century and of Occam in the fourteenth century, the prescriptions of simple faith attributed to such as St. Francis and St. Dominic in the thirteenth century, Duns Scotus' "doctrine of twofold truth" in the fourteenth century, the mystic teachings of Eckhart in the fourteenth century and of Nicholas in the fifteenth century, the anti-papal agitations of Wyclif and Hus in the fourteenth and fifteenth centuries respectively, and the aesthetic religion of Ficino in the fifteenth century. They were also importantly encouraged by the secular orientations of modern mercantilism and humanism.

The conceptual groundwork of the Protestant Reformation proclaimed biblical supremacy and clerical (including papal) fallibility, the doctrine of simple faith (an unmediated, personal relation of individual persons with God that is alone necessary to salvation), and the necessity of ecclesiastic purification through charitable works and institutional reform. The Catholic Counter-Reformation held steadfastly to the supremacy of the Church (and the Papacy) in all matters, even secular matters, and to the formal hierarchy of salvation; but it did also attempt an internal revitalization of the Church that resulted in a more austere and purposeful, a less extravagant and corrupt, institution. The principal consequences of the Protestant-Catholic disputes of early modern civilization were the increasing separation of church and state (secular) functions, the further reduction of church prerogative over economic and political affairs, and the further enhancement of secular prerogative over economic and political affairs.

The **Protestant Reformation** had its center in northern Europe, principally in Germany, where a relatively weak central political authority had prevented the establishment of a national church (unlike in France, England, and Spain for prominent instance). By the early sixteenth century, very considerable dissatisfaction with the established Church had developed in Germany (and elsewhere) for several important reasons:

- heavy papal taxation which raised concerns about foreign domination;
- the turn of the Church away from spiritual values to extravagant forms of clerical life and to an accompanying indifference to the poor and otherwise disadvantaged;
- the impersonal and extrinsic orientation of the Church which weakened its moral commitment to social enhancement and to authentically charitable works; and
- the deterioration of ecclesiastic means of salvation into legal forms of exchange; that is, the purchase of indulgences, or relief from punishment for sin.

By the early sixteenth century, ritual ceremonies of the Church had also become more numerous and more elaborate; the cult of relics, veneration of saints, and imposition of pilgrimages and penitential journeys (often associated with profit-taking and indulgences) had increased; and the persecution of witches and non-Christians had been well formalized.

In short, the internal perversion of the Church and the external opportunity of the increasingly independent German princes to do something tangible about it had reached incendiary proportions by the early sixteenth century. The principal figure, the instigating figure, of the Protestant Reformation was the German priest, Martin Luther (1483-1546), who, in 1517, posted 95 theses at the Castle Church in Wittenberg calling mainly for a disputation concerning abuses in the traffic of indulgences (such as that renewed by Pope Leo X for the reconstruction of the "Basilica of Saint Peter's," Vatican City, Rome in 1514). After several failed attempts at reconciliation, Luther widened his proposals for reform, was issued a papal condemnation by Leo X in 1520, which he burned publicly, also in 1520, and was excommunicated by the Diet of Worms (near Cologne) in 1521. He was widely supported by many leading German humanists and by the (Protestant) German princes, who dissolved convents and monasteries, confiscated ecclesiastic property, and rejected priestly celibacy. Luther's revision of the Catholic Mass (the German Mass, 1526) and of the Catholic sacraments (1529), as well as his three memorable essays of 1520 ("An Appeal to the Christian Nobility of the German Nation," "The Babylonian Captivity of the Church," and "Of the Liberty of a Christian") contain the entire basis of Protestant reform and worship. His German translation of the Bible, which was completed in 1534, contributed especially much to the secular accent of Protestantism.

Despite the ban on Luther, great enthusiasm for him and his proposals developed very quickly. Within several decades, deep allegiances for Protestantism had evolved in northern Germany, Netherlands, Bohemia (including Moravia), northern Poland, Denmark (including Iceland and Norway), Sweden (including Finland), the Baltic states (except Lithuania), Switzerland, England, Scotland, northern Ireland, Austria, Hungary, western Ukraine, and the northern Balkans. All fell mainly under Luther's influence except Switzerland, Netherlands, and Scotland (which were primarily Calvinist) and England and northern Ireland (which were primarily Anglican).

The other major figures of the movement – Zwingli, Calvin, Henry VIII, and Knox – came soon to the fore. Ulrich Zwingli (1484-1531), a Swiss priest who worked mainly in Zurich, became, like Luther, deeply critical of the Church, made public protests against its abuses (in 1522), and issued a program of reform for it (in 1523). His celebrated Commentary on True and False Religion of 1525 summarizes the full sweep of his religious views. John Calvin/Jean Cauvin (1509-1564), a French Protestant theologian who worked mainly in Geneva (1536-1538, 1541-1564), fashioned an especially severe brand of the new doctrine which included unconditional obedience to God, a notion of predestination by which most are irretrievably condemned, an austere sense of morality, severe punishment (including death) for offenses against the faith, and the germ of social Darwinism (the capitalist ethic which claims that worldly success and wealth are an indication of divine election). Calvin's The Institutes of the Christian Religion (1536) is arguably the most systematic and comprehensive account of Protestantism and thus among the canons of Reformationist thought. Henry VIII, second Tudor king of England, was an unwitting, but important, contributor to the new faith. He fell out with Pope Clement VII over his proposal to divorce Katharine of Aragon and to marry Anne Boleyn in 1533; he instituted the "Act of Supremacy" in 1535 by which he replaced the Pope as the head of the Church in England; he thereby broke with Rome and established the Church of England (the Anglican Church); and he dissolved the Catholic monasteries and sold Catholic Church property. Although Anglicanism more so resembled Catholicism than Protestantism in doctrinal terms, its schism with the Papacy nonetheless significantly affected the political course of the Reformations. So too did the failed attempts to restore Catholicism as the state religion in England by Mary I, Mary Queen of Scots, and James II. Anglican disputes with Calvinists/Puritans were likewise significantly responsible for the English Civil War of the mid-seventeenth century. And John Knox (c. 1514-1572), a Scottish priest, was mainly responsible for the establishment of Calvinist-inspired Presbyterianism in Scotland after 1567.

The **Catholic Counter-Reformation**, or Catholic Reformation, was an attempt to renew and to stabilize the Church by means of overt resistance to Protestantism and by means of internal reforms. Some of these reforms had begun prior to Luther's act of rebellion and some were replies to Protestant agitations and tendencies to unorthodox religious fanaticism. While Protestantism was primarily a northern European phenomenon, Catholicism continued its domination of southern Europe; mainly, Italy, Spain, and France as well as Portugal, the southern Balkans (which were variously under the influences of Catholicism, Orthodox Christianity, and Turkish Islam), southern Germany, southern Poland, Lithuania, and southern Ireland. Eastern Europe continued its allegiance to Orthodox Christianity. In Italy, the so-termed reform Papacy was the motive force of the Catholic Counter-Reformation. The leading figures of this movement were:

- Pope Paul III (1468-1549; r. 1534-1549), the first of the papal reformers, who was an important patron of the arts (painting in particular), who promoted charitable and missionary orders, who reintroduced the papal Inquisition in 1542, and who convened the Council of Trent (near Milan; 1545-1563) in 1545; the Council, in which the Protestants refused to participate, unsuccessfully attempted to secure the unity of the faith and the Church against Protestant challenge, it affirmed some established Catholic views (mainly concerning the sacraments, the education and conduct of the clergy, and the doctrine of original sin) and revised others (mainly those concerning the purchase of spiritual and temporal benefits), it established the index of prohibited books, and it shaped the entire development of modern Catholicism;
- Pope Julius III (1487-1555; r. 1550-1555) re-convened the temporarily suspended Council of Trent in 1551, attempted, with Mary I of England, to reunite England and Rome, and significantly patronized the musical arts;
- Pope Paul IV (1476-1559; r. 1555-1559) attempted to correct the moral laxity of the clergy, to alleviate the burdens of the poor, and to even the dispensation of justice; and
- Pope Pius V (1504-1572; 1566-1572) vigorously executed the commands of the Council of Trent against corruption, widely persecuted heretics, revised the catechism and the Mass, and excommunicated Elizabeth I of England over her Anglican sympathies and their affect on Catholic property.

In Spain, a vibrant national consciousness rooted in established religious conviction, in the uncompromising invocation of the (Spanish) Inquisition, and in voluntary internal reforms of the Church prevented the advance of Protestantism. Charles V, the first Spanish Hapsburg Emperor of the Holy Roman Empire, staunchly and effectively defended Catholicism in southern Europe but failed to preserve the unity of the faith elsewhere on the continent. By principal way of the Diet of Augsburg in 1530 (which irrevocably sealed the Catholic-Protestant rift), the Schmalkaldic League of Protestant imperial estates, formed in 1531, the inconclusive Schmalkaldic War of 1546-1547, the compromises of the Peace of Augsburg in 1555 (which confirmed the various regional patterns of Catholic and Protestant domination, which granted predominantly Protestant states the right to religious self-determination, and which thus opened the modern era of the secularized state embodying religious toleration), and the failures of the Council of Trent (which concluded in 1563), the Protestant German princes in particular largely succeeded in defending the new faith in northern Europe. The obedience of the Spanish state to the Papacy in this time, Spain's national sense of charity (if not tolerance), and its commitment to reform were perhaps most significantly embodied in the Society of Jesus (the Jesuits), an order of the Church formally established in 1540 by the Basque priest and author of the mystical-ascetic treatise, Spiritual Exercises (1548), St. Ignatius of Loyola (1491-1556). The Jesuits were major defenders of the Counter-Reformation and were mainly devoted to highly disciplined teaching and missionary projects in Europe, the Americas, India, China, and Japan, projects that aimed principally at the reform of heretics and the conversion of heathens.

And in France, Protestants were widely persecuted throughout the first approximate half of the sixteenth century; most efficiently by Francis I and Henri II. After the Protestant conversion of the highly influential Bourbon family in 1559, however, the most striking of the French Protestants, the Calvinist-inspired

Huguenots, developed a formal political party. In the eight **Huguenot Wars**, or Wars of Religion (1562-1598), which followed, the Huguenots were supported by England and Protestantism gained the upper hand. Huguenots were granted formal toleration of conscience, freedom of worship, and political equality by the Edict of Nantes (1598), which ended the Wars. Persecutions were nonetheless revived under the centralizing tendencies of the Bourbons in the seventeenth century and the Edict was itself revoked by Louis XIV in 1685. France thus remained largely Catholic. Even England had its brief, if unsuccessful, flirtation with Catholic revival; most notably, in the mid-sixteenth century reign of Mary I and in the late seventeenth-century reign of James II.

The wars of religious persecution inspired by the Protestant-Catholic disputes of the sixteenth and seventeenth centuries were numerous and brutal. Although most of the military conflict of the sixteenth and seventeenth centuries was significantly marked by the Reformations, the most important of the largely religious wars were the Great Peasant War (1524-1525), the Thirty Years War (1618-1648), and the previously mentioned Schmalkaldic War and Huguenot Wars. The **Great Peasant War** was aroused by the Protestant challenge to established authority and by mounting peasant dissatisfaction with the servile vestiges of feudalism. Driven by famine, poverty, and overt injustice, peasant unrest had been on the rise in Germany from at least the late fifteenth century. Emboldened by Protestant successes, the uprising began in Germany and came also to include Austria. From the beginning, it lacked coherent aims and effective leadership and, after initial successes, deteriorated into murderous pillage, elicited the opposition of Luther, and was defeated by the princes. The peasants suffered grievously as a result, becoming even more servile (into the nineteenth century); they were deprived of political rights and were little other than the private property of landlords. The War greatly strengthened the territorial state and the Reformations thereafter became as much a political as a religious movement.

The **Thirty Years War** began as a religious conflict between increasingly strident and dogmatic assertions of Catholic and Protestant belief; it ended as a colossal European political struggle, as a general European war. Its immediate cause was embodied in the dispute between the Spanish and the German (Bohemian) Hapsburgs and it came ultimately to a struggle between the German Protestant princes (and allied foreign powers; most significantly, Denmark, Sweden, and France) and the unity and power of the (Hapsburg) Holy Roman Empire (and allied Catholic German princes). The War unfolded in four main phases:

- the Bohemian phase (1618-1623), which began in Prague and in which Protestant Bohemian nobles deposed the Catholic (Spanish Hapsburg) King of Bohemia (Ferdinand III, later Emperor Ferdinand II) in 1619 and installed a Protestant (German) monarch (Frederick the Winter King); Ferdinand defeated Frederick in 1620 and subjugated Bohemia but the War continued;
- the Danish phase (1625-1629), in which Charles IV of Denmark invaded northern Germany in order to prevent Hapsburg expansion into the region; ended with the defeat of Denmark and the loss of its provinces in northern Germany;
- the Swedish phase(1630-1635), in which Gustavus II Adolphus of Sweden invaded northern Germany, too fearing German expansion in the region; ended in Swedish victory and a provisional peace which partially reconciled Catholic and Protestant factions; and
- the Franco-Swedish phase (1635-1648), in which Cardinal Richelieu of France pressed the offensive against Hapsburg power, expanded the War beyond German territory into the Low Countries, Italy, Scandinavia, and Spain, and, in the end, prevailed.

The War ended with the Peace of Westphalia (near Cologne), by which France became the leading state in Europe, Sweden and Netherlands rose also to great political power, Germany was left in virtual ruin, the Holy Roman Empire continued its long decline, and the Hapsburgs began their long descent from hegemonic prerogative.

The Protestant-Catholic schism continued to exert an enormous influence on early modern civilization even after the Thirty Years War; it has continued, for that matter, to exert an enormous influence over the whole of modern life's political, economic, and intellectual fabric to our own time. In the late seventeenth century, ongoing religious conflict between Anglican, Catholic, and Calvinist-Puritan communities in western Europe was significantly responsible for such notable events as the English Civil War and "The Glorious Revolution;" formation of the Religious Society of Friends, the Quakers, by Englishman, George Fox (1624-1691), in 1668; the wide civil contention evoked by continuing strife between Catholic and Huguenot factions in France; and significant emigration, mainly to North America, by those attempting to escape the contentious environment of western Europe. Although these tendencies persisted into the eighteenth century, the Enlightenment values of that period brought a somewhat larger sense of religious toleration to it. The only very notable new development of the Reformationist movement in the eighteenth century was the emergence of Methodism, which entailed a strict interpretation of personal salvation through faith in Christ alone, which opposed slavery and advocated compassionate care of the poor, which grew out of Anglicanism, and which was owed, in its original formulation of 1729, to Englishman, John Wesley (1703-1791).

Economic Developments and Technological Innovations

The progressive transformation of the European political economy of the early modern period from a predominantly barter system to a predominantly money system began with the Crusades in Italy, then came to France, Germany, and Netherlands, then moved throughout the continent. The animating force of early modern capitalism was the opportunity, principally among middle-class artisans and merchants, to strive for calculated profit, an opportunity driven more by talent and temperament than by inherited station and resource. The commercial and banking practices of the late Middle Ages were further advanced in early modern civilization. The influence of commerce itself and of commercialists themselves over political and cultural affairs rose dramatically in this time. Stock exchanges were established for the purpose of organizing investment-trading markets; the most notable early modern exchanges were the London Stock Exchange (1571) and the New York Stock Exchange (1790). Private trading companies were increasingly established by leading merchants in order to produce and to distribute goods over increasingly more extensive, international routes, in order to gain monopoly over particular commodities, and in order to administer the colonial policies of the state. The most notable of these were the British East India Company (1600), the Dutch East India Company (1602), the Dutch West India Company (1621), and the French East India Company (1664) of the seventeenth and eighteenth centuries. Enormous banks were established by those of great wealth in order to finance very large commercial, political, and cultural projects; the most notable of these were the banks of the Medici of Florence in the fifteenth century, the banks of the Fuggers of Augsburg in the sixteenth century, the Bank of Amsterdam in 1609, the Bank of England in 1694, the first public bank (in France) in 1715, the Bank of Berlin in 1764, and the Bank of the United States of America in 1791. Increased urban demands for food brought about specialty farming and dairying practices and also brought about new forms of landowning that tended to prefer renting or leasing land for agricultural production to the feudal custom of utter serfdom. The emphasis on production-for-profit, export-for-profit, and state support of the money economy and its owners – that is, for mercantilism – also, however, fashioned periodic patterns of overproduction, price inflation and currency devaluation, widening disparities between rich and poor, and deepening tendencies to social insecurity and instability.

The commercial (as well as colonial and scientific) adventures of the Renaissance were greatly aided by major technological innovations of the fifteenth and sixteenth centuries; most notably, the development of an improved compass, navigational instruments, the printing press, and the pocket watch. The commercial (as well as colonial and scientific) adventures of the seventeenth century were likewise importantly assisted by major technological innovations of that time; most notably, the development of the adding machine (1642), pendulum clock (1657), air pump (1663), and calculating machine (1673). And the commercial (as well as colonial and scientific) adventures of the eighteenth century were too significantly driven by major technological innovations of that period, innovations that prepared the seminal groundwork for the Industrial Revolution, innovations such as the development of the weaving shuttle (1733), cast iron (1735), the breach-loading rifle (1751), the lightening conductor (1752), the coke-fed blast furnace and the sheet-iron mill (1754), the spinning jenny (1767), the steam engine (1769), the steam car (1769), the diver's helmet (1778), the hot-air balloon (1783), the mechanical power loom (1785), the spinning mill (1790), the cotton gin (1793), the hydraulic press (1795), lithography (1796), and cement (1799). Although industrialism did not become a pervasive world phenomenon until the nineteenth century, the incipient origins of the Industrial Revolution are owed to the mass production of textiles and steel by steam-driven machines in mid-eighteenth-century England.

Voyages of World Discovery and Colonialism

It was the technological innovations of early modern civilization, as well as the inquiring spirit of its humanist inclinations, its mercantile proclivities, and its missionary (religious) zeal, that significantly impelled the revolutionary European voyages of world discovery, European colonialism, and the virtual world wars associated with the balance of European colonial power in the fifteenth to the eighteenth centuries. It was too these innovations and this spirit that significantly brought European culture and the cultures of the other continents authentically together and that thus opened the epoch of "universal" human history. In the period of the Renaissance, Portugal, Spain, England, and Italy were the foremost nations of world discovery. The Portuguese Prince, Henry the Navigator (1394-1460), son of John I of Portugal and grandson of John the Gaunt of England, established the first navigational school in 1434 and planned the first circumnavigation of Africa in order to establish direct trade connections with the gold and slave markets of east Africa, in order to limit Islamic influence in Africa and the Middle East, in order to conquer Palestine (the Holy Land), in order to circumvent high Ottoman customs tolls in the Middle East, and in order to establish direct trade routes to India, Malaysia, Dutch East Indies/Indonesia, and China. Although Islamic traders had reached the coastal regions of eastern Africa (including Malagasy Republic/Madagascar) and the regions of sub-Saharan central and western Africa (in some cases) several centuries earlier as has been said, **Portuguese expeditions** were the first to reach Atlantic islands west of west Africa in the mid-to-late fifteenth and early sixteenth centuries: the Azores, discovered in 1431; the Cape Verdes, discovered in 1445; the Canaries, reached in 1496; and Saint Helena, discovered in 1502. They were also the first Europeans to explore what are currently French West Africa/Mauritania (1444), French West Africa/Senegal (1444), Gambia (1444), Guinea-Bissau (1446), French West Africa/Guinea (1446), Gold Coast/Ghana (1456), Sierra Leone (1460), Sao Tome e Principe (discovered, 1471), Nigeria (1471), French Equatorial Africa/Cameroon (1472), Spanish Guinea/Rio Muni/Equatorial Guinea (1472), French Equatorial Africa/Gabon (1482), French Equatorial Africa/French Congo/Middle Congo/ Republic of the Congo/People's Republic of the Congo/Republic of the Congo (1482), Belgian Congo/Democratic Republic of the Congo/Zaire/Democratic Republic of the Congo (1482), Angola (1482), German Southwest Africa/Southwest Africa/Namibia (1487), South Africa (1487), Mozambique (1498), German East Africa/Tanganyika/Tanzania (1498), Kenya (1498), Malagasy Republic/Madagascar (1500), and the Seychelles (discovered, 1502). They were too the first to pass around the Cape of Good Hope, the southernmost reaches of Africa (1487), and the first to circumnavigate the continent. This latter was first achieved in 1497 by Vasco da Gama (c. 1469-1524), who also discovered a sea route from Europe to India (1497-1499) and was the first to establish the Portuguese colonial empire in Africa and in India (in the early sixteenth century). The other most notable European adventurers/explorers of the fifteenth and sixteenth centuries were:

- Christopher Columbus (1451-1506), a Genoese in the service of Spain, who, in his search for a westward sea route to India, became the first to sail over the vast, open expanse of one of the world's great oceans (as distinct from coastal seafaring), the first European in the Americas since Leif Ericsson, and the first European to explore the Caribbean and central America; he came upon the West Indies (what are currently Bahamas, Turks and Caicos Islands, Cuba, Haiti, and Dominican Republic) after a 61-days journey in 1492 and upon other Caribbean islands (what are currently Dominica [1493], Guadeloupe [1493], Montserrat [1493], Saint Kitts-Nevis [1493], Antigua and Barbuda [1493], Saint Martin/Sint Maarten [1493], Anguilla [1493], the Virgin Islands [United States of America and British; 1493]), Puerto Rico [1493], Jamaica [1494], Saint Vincent and the Grenadines [1498], Grenada [1498], Trinidad and Tobago [1498], Saint Lucia [1502], Martinique [1502], and the Cayman Islands [discovered, 1503]) as well as the coastal mainlands of what are currently French Guiana (1498), Dutch Guiana/Suriname (1498), British Guiana/Guyana (1498), Venezuela (1498), Colombia (1498), Honduras (1502), Nicaragua (1502), Costa Rica (1502), and Panama (1502) in three additional journeys to 1504;
- Giovanni Caboto/John Cabot (c. 1461-1498), a Venetian in the service of England, who was the first European since Leif Ericsson to explore North America (1497) and the first European to explore what is currently the United States of America (1498);
- Amerigo Vespucci (1452-1512), a Florentine in the service of Spain and Portugal, who developed a more exacting method of calculating longitude and who was the first European to explore South America (mainly the northern coast of what is currently Brazil [1499)] and the Netherlands Antilles [1499]);

- Pedro Alvares Cabral (c. 1460-c. 1526) of Portugal, who was the first European to explore the east coast of South America (what is currently Brazil [1500]);
- Vasco Nunez de Balboa (c. 1475-1519) of Spain, who was the first European to reach the Pacific Ocean (by crossing the Isthmus of Panama in 1513);
- Ferdinand Magellan (c. 1480-1521), a Portuguese in the service of Spain, who was the first to circumnavigate the planet (1519-1521), who was killed in the Philippines by native peoples (a ship under his original command nonetheless returned to Lisbon in 1522), who was the first to effectively pass around Cape Horn, the southernmost reaches of South America (1520), who was the first to reach Asia by sailing west from Europe, who was the first European to explore what are currently Guam and the Mariana Islands (1521) as well as the Philippine Islands (1521), and who was the first to render wholly tangible proof of the Earth's spherical shape and to confirm the continental status of the Americas;
- Hernan Cortes (1485-1547) of Spain, who in 1519-1521 conquered the Aztec Empire under Montezuma II (c. 1480-1520; r. 1502-1520) in what is currently central and southern Mexico and who was the first European to explore what are currently the Yucatan (of Mexico), Guatemala, and British Honduras/Belize (where he defeated some Mayan communities) in 1523-1524;
- Francisco Pizarro (c. 1476-1541) of Spain, who in 1531-1534 conquered the Incan Empire under Atahualpa (d. 1533; r. 1526-1533) in what is currently Peru and who was the first European to explore what are currently Ecuador (1524) and Peru (1524);
- Diego de Almagro (1475-1538) of Spain, who accompanied Pizarro in his "discovery" of Ecuador and Peru in 1524, who also accompanied Pizarro in his conquest of the Incan Empire in 1531-1534, and who was the first European to explore what are currently Bolivia (1535) and Chile (1535);
- Juan Ponce de Leon (c. 1460-1521) of Spain, who was the first European to explore what is currently Florida (1513);
- Hernando de Soto (c. 1500-1542) of Spain, who was the first European to explore what is currently the southeastern United Sates of America (1539-1542), Florida excepted;
- Francisco Vasquez de Coronado (c. 1510-1554) of Spain, who was the first European to explore what are currently northern Mexico and the southwestern, south-central, and central United States of America; and
- Sir Francis Drake (c. 1540-1596) of England, who achieved the second circumnavigation of the planet (1577-1580), who was the first European to visit what are currently the western United States of America and British Columbia, and who inaugurated the era of the English/British colonial empire.

Other Spanish explorers, **Spanish expeditions**, were the first Europeans to reach what are currently the other leading nations of the Americas: Mexico (1502), Bermuda (discovered, 1503), Argentina (1515), Uruguay (1516), Barbados (1518), and Paraguay (1537). Although Spanish (and Portuguese) hegemony over the Americas was not immediate, the Spanish colonial empire was formally established in 1494 by the Treaty of Tordesillas (in northwestern Spain). This Treaty was proclaimed by the corrupt Spanish pope of the Borgia family, Alexander VI (c. 1431-1503; r. 1492-1503), and it effectively carved up the non-European world between Spain and Portugal. Slave importations to the Americas from Africa began as early as 1510 and the hold of the Spanish (and Portuguese) over the Americas was largely assured by the mid-sixteenth century. The Dutch colonial empire was first established in what are now Dutch East Indies/Indonesia and Malaysia in 1585. The French colonial empire was first established in what is now Canada in 1603. The other most significant European "discoveries" of the sixteenth century were: Dutch East Indies/Indonesia in 1511, (East) Timor in 1515, New Guinea/Papua New Guinea in 1528, the Marshall Islands in 1528, the Caroline Islands/Federated States of Micronesia in 1543, Palau in 1543, Réunion (discovered) in 1545, the Solomon Islands in 1568, the Falkland Islands/Malvinas Islands (discovered) in 1592, and Mauritius (discovered) in 1598. The Europeanization of world culture had begun in earnest, as had racial admixture, wide intercultural knowledge, and world trade. Mercantile domination shifted to the Atlantic Ocean from the Mediterranean, North, and Baltic Seas; such as Lisbon, Seville, London, Rotterdam, Amsterdam, Brussels, Bruges, and Antwerp replaced the likes of Venice, Genoa, Florence, Augsburg, and Lubeck as the trade and banking capitals of the world. The center of international political and economic power was transferred from central to western Europe.

The **principal European explorations of the seventeenth and eighteenth centuries** were those associated with the search for a northern passage from the Atlantic to the Pacific Oceans and those of the central and southern Pacific, all of which were driven mainly by commercial and political ambition as well as by the spirit of scientific discovery. In the former category were explorations of Siberia, Alaska, and the Aleutian Islands (mainly by the Russians), explorations of the Arctic (mainly by the Dutch), and explorations of northeastern and north-central Canada (mainly by the English/British). In the latter category were the mainly Dutch expeditions of the seventeenth century and the mainly British expeditions of the eighteenth.

Ivan the Terrible of Russia provided a prominent family of merchants, the Stroganovs, with Siberia in 1558, obliging it to colonize the region (which principally became Asiatic Russia) from Mongols, Turks, Chinese, and wasteland. The family achieved this end by commissioning Cossacks (escaped Russian and Ukrainian serfs) to the task. Western Siberia was reached in 1581-1584, central Siberia in 1604-1610, eastern Siberia in 1632-1650, the Sea of Okhotsk in 1645, the Bering Strait (which joins the Asian and the North American continents, the Pacific and the Arctic Oceans) in 1648 (by Simon Dezhnev [fl. in the mid-seventeenth century]), and the Kamchatka Peninsula in 1679. In the eighteenth century, Vitus Bering (1680-1741), a Dane in the service of Russia, made the first scientific exploration of Siberia (1728) and was the first European to reach what are currently Alaska (together with bits of the Yukon Territory; 1741) and the Aleutian Islands (1741), both of which became part of the Russian colonial empire in 1791. William Barents (c. 1560-1597) of Netherlands discovered what are now the Barents Sea (in northwestern Russia) and the Arctic Ocean in 1594 and Spitzbergen in 1596. Henry Hudson (c. 1570-1611) of England was the first European to reach what is now Hudson Bay (in north-central Canada) in 1610. And William Baffin (c. 1584-1622) of England was the first European to reach what is now Baffin Bay (in northeastern Canada) in 1616.

The principal Dutch explorer of the seventeenth century, Abel Tasman (c. 1602-1659), discovered Mauritius in 1642, was the first European to visit what are now Tasmania (1642), New Zealand (1642), Tonga (1643), and Fiji (1643), and was the first person to circumnavigate what is now Australia (1642). The other most important European "discoveries" of the seventeenth century in the Pacific were: Australia in 1601, French Polynesia/Tahiti in 1605, and the New Hebrides Islands/Vanuatu in 1606. The principal British explorer of the eighteenth century, James Cook (1728-1779), was the first European to visit what are now the Cook Islands (1773), New Caledonia (1774), and the Hawaiian Islands (where he was killed by native peoples; 1778), discovered the Antarctic Ocean and (by implication) Antarctica in 1774, and contributed greatly to knowledge concerning pre-literate cultures, the continents, and the oceans. The other most important European "discoveries" of the eighteenth century in the Pacific were: Easter Island in 1721, Samoa in 1722, the Ellice Islands/Tuvalu in 1764, the Gilbert Islands/Kiribati in 1765, Pitcairn Island in 1767, and Nauru in 1798.

Competition among the **colonial empires** of the early modern period (mainly, Spain, Portugal, France, England/Great Britain, Netherlands, Denmark, and Russia) for the resources (principally slave-labor, tobacco, and exotic and rare metals, stones, and foods) and the souls of the pre-literate cultures they had encountered on their monumental journeys was predictably intense. The main sites of conflict among these empires were **Asia** (most significantly India), the Americas, Africa, and Oceania. In India, the dissolution of the Mogul Empire and Hindu-Moslem conflicts evened the way for the establishment of new European trading centers. The Portuguese made the first permanent European settlement in India in 1510 and came to control several trading posts in the western and eastern coastal regions. The Dutch, largely by means of the Dutch East India Company (1602-1798), pushed the Portuguese out of Ceylon/Sri Lanka in 1609. The English, largely by means of the British East India Company (1600-1858), held increasing sway over Calcutta, Madras, and Bombay beginning in 1612-1613. And the French, largely by means of the French East India Company (1664-1769), controlled most of the eastern coastal region from the mid-seventeenth century. Conflicts between the French and British in particular escalated dramatically in the mid-eighteenth century, ending in the British victory at the Battle of Plassey (near Calcutta) in 1757, an event that marked the definitive beginning of British domination in India. Elsewhere in early modern Asia, the Portuguese established governing authority in Macao in 1557, in Formosa/Taiwan in 1590, and in East Timor in 1701; the Spanish became the dominant influence in the Philippine Islands beginning in 1565; the Dutch gained a large influence in the Dutch East Indies/Indonesia and Malaysia beginning in 1585; and the British had gained a firm place in Dutch East Indies/Indonesia by 1600. Colonial ambitions and disputes in Asia heightened yet further in the nineteenth and twentieth centuries.

In the **Americas**, Spain was the dominant influence from at least 1535; it established eventual hegemony over the virtual whole of central America (except what became British Honduras/Belize), over the virtual whole of South America (except what are currently the Guianas, Brazil, and the Falkland Islands/Malvinas Islands), over what is currently Florida and the entire western United Sates of America, and over what are now Cuba, Dominican Republic, and Puerto Rico. Portugal was the dominant influence in what is currently Brazil from at least 1537. France installed the first governor of what is currently Canada, Samuel de

Champlain (1567-1635), claiming what are now New Foundland and Nova Scotia, in 1603 and claiming what is now Quebec in 1608. What is currently French Guiana came under French sovereignty in 1604, Dominica in 1611, Guadeloupe and Martinique in 1635, Saint Martin in 1648, Grenada in 1650, Haiti in 1655, and the central United States of America (Louisiana) in 1682. England/Great Britain made its first "permanent" settlement in North America (Jamestown, Virginia) in 1607; it claimed Bermuda in 1609, Massachusetts (effectively including New Hampshire) in 1620, Maryland in 1632, Rhode Island and North Carolina in 1635, Connecticut in 1638, Maine in 1647, New York, New Jersey, and Delaware in 1667, South Carolina and the Northwest Territory (Canada; including parts of Ontario, Manitoba, Saskatchewan, and Alberta) in 1670, Pennsylvania in 1683, New Foundland and Nova Scotia in 1713, Georgia in 1733, and Vermont in 1741. In central America and the Caribbean, England/Great Britain laid claim to Saint Lucia in 1605, Saint Kitts-Nevis in 1623, Barbados in 1624, Bahamas in 1629, Antigua and Barbuda in 1632, Montserrat in 1632, British Honduras/Belize in 1638, Anguilla in 1650, Jamaica in 1655, the British Virgin Islands in 1666, the Cayman Islands in 1670, the Turks and Caicos Islands in 1670, Dominica in 1763, Saint Vincent and the Grenadines in 1763, Grenada in 1783, and Trinidad and Tobago in 1797. Netherlands, significantly by means of the Dutch West Indies Company (1621-1791), claimed what are now New York City in 1616, the Netherlands Antilles in 1634, Dutch Guiana/Suriname, British Guiana/Guyana, and French Guiana in 1636, and Sint Maarten in 1648. Denmark claimed what are now the Danish West Indies/United States of America Virgin Islands in 1666 and Greenland in 1721. And Russia's colonial claims in Alaska, the Aleutian Islands, and parts of the Yukon Territory were all formalized in 1791.

The circumstance in **Africa** was somewhat less formal. The leading colonial powers – mainly Portugal, France, England/Great Britain, and Netherlands – variously established trading stations on the continent's western, southern, and eastern coastal regions throughout the early modern era. Except for wide French claims in Malagasy Republic/Madagascar from 1643, Réunion from 1654, Senegal from 1659, Mauritius from 1715, and Seychelles from 1768, the Dutch incursions in South Africa from 1652, the British claims over Gambia from 1661 and over Seychelles from 1794, and ongoing Islamic influence in northern Africa and in the coastal regions of eastern Africa, the Portuguese domination of Africa continued into the nineteenth century when formal patterns of broader annexation by the colonial states and intensified disputes among them accelerated. Portuguese rule continued to independence (in the twentieth century), however, in Angola, the Cape Verde Islands, Guinea-Bissau, Mozambique, and Sao Tome e Principe. The central and southern interior of Africa remained largely unexplored by European adventurers until the nineteenth century.

In **Oceania**, the most intensely adversarial conflicts among colonial cultures were likewise reserved for the nineteenth and twentieth centuries. From European "discovery," most of the Melanesian, Micronesian, and Polynesian cultures of the central and south Pacific remained either largely undeveloped (by European standard) or under the heavy influence of (original) colonizing descendants into the nineteenth and twentieth centuries. The only very notable exceptions were:

- the Caroline Islands/Federated States of Micronesia, likely "discovered" by the Portuguese, came under predominantly Spanish influence in 1686;
- French Polynesia/Tahiti, likely "discovered" by the Spanish, came under predominantly British influence in 1767; and
- Australia, likely "discovered" by the Portuguese, came under predominantly British influence in 1770.

Many of these territories in Asia, the Americas, Africa, and Oceania were predictably fought over by the colonial factions; some were fiercely contested and possession of some was several times exchanged. Some of these conflicts were so wide-ranging and pervasive, engaged all of the world's leading political entities as well as others, and were waged not merely across national boundaries but across continents that they came to **virtual world wars**. Arguably the most significant conflicts of this type were between the French and the British; most notably, the Seven Years War (1756-1763). The Seven Years War entailed very wide international tensions and the inclination to resolve them in military terms. The global conflict between French and British colonial interests began in germinal terms in North America in the form of the French and Indian War. Border conflicts between the French and the British (in what are now Canada and the United States of America) were common by the mid-eighteenth century and they erupted into open warfare in 1754. Early French successes brought a change of government in Britain; William Pitt the Elder, among the leading architects of British colonial policy, became Prime Minister and engineered succeeding British triumphs. The British seizure of Quebec (1759), Guadeloupe (1759), Montreal (1760), Martinique (1762), Cuba (from Spain after Spain entered the War in 1762), and French bases in India (1757), Senegal (1760), and Nigeria (1760) brought the War to conclusion. By way of the Treaty of Paris in 1763, Great Britain obtained what is now

Canada, the (western) United States of America (east of the Mississippi River), Dominica, and Senegal from France and Florida from Spain; Guadeloupe and Martinique were returned to France; and Cuba was returned to Spain. The other, the second stage of the War, the War over Silesia (1756-1763), went on in Europe and principally involved an Austrian, French, Swedish, and Russian alliance against Prussia and Great Britain as has been said.

The spirit of political, ideological, economic, and technological innovation and the soul of world discovery were themselves very significantly influenced by the unique intellectual orientation of early modern civilization; this is, by the rise of humanism, its devotion to free inquiry, and its tendency to effect common human values. In intellectual terms, early modern civilization was most notably marked by:

- the humanist metamorphosis of the visual, musical, and literary arts and of philosophy; and
- utterly transforming discoveries in mathematics and in the natural and social sciences.

Humanism in the Arts and in Philosophy

The seminal stage of early modern civilization, the (European) Renaissance, was the third of five main episodes in world intellectual history that have been predominantly governed by the organic thesis and all that is entailed by this thesis; namely, political society, a monistic view of the mind-body relation, a subjective concept of body, a lived notion of movement, and an intrinsic respect for humanity and its principal expressions (science, sport, dance, art, religion, history, philosophy, and education). In only the ancient Greek (most especially, the Athenian) Enlightenment, novel aspects of the medieval and modern Islamic Enlightenment (most especially, aspects of the Omayyad, Abbasid, Fatimid, Almoravid, Nasrid, Timurid, Mogul, and Ottoman developments), nineteenth-century (most especially, French, German, British/Irish, Russian, American, Scandinavian, Italian, and Spanish) romanticism/realism, and twentieth-century European (most especially, Scandinavian) democratic socialism and European (most especially, Germanic, French, Russian, and Finnish), American, and Mexican expressionism would these remarkable possibilities be very widely repeated. The Renaissance case was mainly driven by the doctrine of rational humanism, according to which humanity is the primary agency of the created order; humanity is endowed (at least potentially) with all that is knowable, beautiful, and just of the universe; humanity is constituted as a balanced, harmonious, and proportionate unity of physical and intellectual qualities continuous with nature and divinity; and humanity is perfectible in the context of an unrestricted study of the humanities (and the common human values such a study portends). Rational humanism elevated the thisworldly, distinctly human condition, as against the otherworldly, divinist depreciation of this condition characteristic of medieval culture; it attempted to renew, to reawaken, the robust, active, tangible, and individualistic orientation of ancient classical scholarship. The germinal maturation of this more progressive, liberating, tolerant, expansive, and creative spirit was owed principally to the Italian proto-Renaissance of the late Middle Ages, which was itself greatly moved by a deep respect for ancient classicism. In the end, Renaissance culture came largely to a modern synthesis of ancient Graeco-Roman individualism and the collective morality of medieval Judaism, Christianity, and Islam. This culture achieved its first clearly modern form in the universities and other schools of the small, wealthy, and insecure Italian city-republics (most notably, Florence and Venice) and in the small, wealthy, and insecure Duchy of Burgundy (most notably, the regions of Flanders and Netherlands).

The visual arts

The new, the modern, spirit of the Renaissance first showed itself in the early fifteenth century and it was most conspicuous in the visual arts of the period. The familiar distinctions among the early, high, and late stages of the Renaissance pertain strictly only to the visual arts of Europe. The early Renaissance is commonly taken to begin in c. 1410 and to end in c. 1495; the high Renaissance, to begin in c. 1495 and to end in c. 1520; and the late Renaissance, to begin in c. 1520 and to end in c. 1600. The **Renaissance standard of beauty** in the arts was defined in terms of a sonorous balance, harmony, and proportion of parts to one another and to a whole of universal human appeal; effectively, the standard that unites form and content, the standard by which nothing may be added to nor taken from (nothing may be altered in) a composition to its benefit. The great artistic achievements of the Renaissance aptly reveal the robust and vigorous sense of body, the vibrant and vital quality of movement, the deep attention to natural detail, and the heroic perspective of humanity and nature that characterized the era in its broadest respects. There is about these achievements a virile grandeur, a powerful definition of personality, and an abundance of emotional content and passionate tension that demonstrate well their likeness to classical Greek tendencies and that set them decisively apart from the retiring inclinations of the Middle Ages. Multiple centers of action tend to replace solitary centers; luminous, varied, and vibrant colors tend to replace solemn and uniform ones; ongoing senses of unposed movement occurring in multiple planes tend to replace a posed and uniplanar inclination; the relative importance of natural backgrounds is enhanced and tends to replace a disproportionate emphasis on foreground; a dramatic turning variously toward and away from a central point or line tends to replace a formalistic attention to geometric order; and varying impressions at different angles, distances, and under different conditions of light tend to replace fairly even such impressions. In the Renaissance, nude figures, recognizable portraiture and landscape, free-standing human and animal figures, rounded senses of space and perspective, and rigorous forms of self-consciousness reappear after a hiatus of an approximate millennium to two millennia.

In Florence most especially, classical humanism had never been entirely stilled; remnants of the classical Roman architecture as well as the Latin language lingered there throughout the Middle Ages; Byzantine scholars (who had held onto much of the ancient European heritage throughout the Middle Ages) widely sought refuge there as the circumstance for European culture in Constantinople worsened; and there was sufficient wealth, leisure, freedom, and respect for learning there to support humanist studies. On the substantive ground prepared mainly by the Pisanos, Cimabue, Duccio, and Giotto and on the fiscal ground established mainly by the patronage of the ruling family of Florence (and, in a sense, Venice as well), the Medici, the early Renaissance took its first breath. The first phase of this development, the **Florentine phase of the early Italian Renaissance**, began with the surpassing genius of the Florentine masters: Filippo Brunelleschi (1377-1446) in architecture, Donatello/Donato di Niccolo-Bardi (c. 1386-1466) in sculpture, and Masaccio/Tommaso di Ser Giovanni (1401-c. 1428) in painting. Brunelleschi, who was significantly patronized by Cosimo the Elder, created the Renaissance style in architecture, a style which embodies a reasoned, inelaborate, massive, and (mathematically) proportional relation of rectangular and circular elements in white and colored marbles. His masterpieces are the colossal dome which completed the Gothic "Cathedral of Florence/Duomo di Santa Maria del Fiore," 1417-1446; the "Ospedale degli Innocenti," Florence, 1419; the "Church of San Lorenzo," Florence, 1421-1469; the "Church of San Spirito," Florence, 1434-1435; and the "Pazzi Chapel, Church of Santa Croce," Florence, c. 1440-1461. The other great architects of the early Italian Renaissance were the Florentines:

- Michelozzo di Bartolommeo (1396-1472), whose masterpiece is the "Palazzo Medici-Riccardi," Florence, 1444; and
- Leonbattista Alberti (1404-1472), who wrote brilliantly on architecture, sculpture, and painting and who is best remembered for his masterpieces, "Palazzo Rucellai," Florence, 1446-1451, and "Sant' Andrea," Mantua, 1470.

The most remarkable sculptor of this period was Donatello, who was also significantly patronized by Cosimo the Elder and whose masterpieces are numerous; most notably, the marble "Saint Mark," Orsanmichele, Florence, 1411-1413; the marble "Saint George," Orsanmichele, Florence, 1415-1416; the marble "Habbakuk/Lo Zuccone (Big Squash)," Campanile, Cathedral of Florence, 1423-1425; the bronze relief baptismal font "Feast of Herod," Cathedral of Siena, c. 1425; the bronze "David," c. 1440; the bronze "Equestrian Monument of Gattamelata," Padua, 1443-1453; and the wood "Mary Magdalene," 1454-1455. The other great sculptors of the early Italian Renaissance were (mostly) Florentines:

- Lorenzo Ghiberti (c. 1381-1455), who was too significantly patronized by Cosimo the Elder and whose masterpieces are the two sets of bronze doors for the Baptistery of San Giovanni, Florence, most particularly the second, "Gates of Paradise," 1425-1450, which is comprised of ten remarkable scenes in relief (most notably, "Story of Abraham" and "Story of Jacob and Esau");
- Nanni di Banco (c. 1385-1421), whose masterpiece is the marble "Four Crowned Martyrs," Orsanmichele, Florence, c. 1413;
- the Sienese, Jacopo della Quercia (c. 1374-1438), whose masterpieces are the bronze reliefs on the main doors of the Church of San Petronio, Bologna, 1425-1438 (most notably, "Creation of Adam" and "Expulsion from Eden");
- Antonio del Pollaiuolo (c. 1431-1498), whose masterpiece is the bronze "Hercules and Antaeus," c. 1475; and

- Andrea del Verrocchio (1435-1488), teacher of Perugino and Leonardo, whose masterpieces are the bronze "Doubting of Thomas," Orsanmichele, Florence, 1465-1483, and the bronze "Equestrian Monument of Bartolommeo Colleoni," Venice, 1481-1496.

The leading painter of the early Italian Renaissance, Masaccio, is among the singular talents in the entire record of human civilization. Although the fourteenth-century path from Giotto to Masaccio was well prepared by such as the Lorenzettis, Martini, and Milano, and by a somewhat older Florentine contemporary of Masaccio in the early fifteenth century (i.e., Gentile da Fabriano [c. 1380-1427], whose masterpiece is the tempera-on-panel altarpiece, "Adoration of the Magi," 1421-1423), the towering genius of Masaccio revolutionized painting and opened its authentically modern era. Masaccio's brilliant sense of exuberant color, light, space, and perspective, together with the enormous dignity and strength of his classically formed figures, make a deserving monument of him and of his stunning work. His masterpieces are the frescoes "Tribute Money" and "Expulsion from Eden" in the Brancacci Chapel, Church of Santa Maria del Carmine, Florence, c. 1425; the tempera-on-panel "Enthroned Madonna and Child," 1426; and the fresco "Trinity," Church of Santa Maria Novella, Florence, c. 1428. The Florentine masters (some of whom were borrowed) who followed Masaccio fleshed out the remaining detail of the early Italian Renaissance and likewise rank among the greatest painters in the history of the medium:

- Fra Angelico/Guido di Pietro (c. 1400-1455), whose masterpieces are the tempera-on-panel "Descent from the Cross," c. 1434, and the fresco "Annunciation," Monastery of San Marco, Florence, 1438-1445;
- Fra Filippo Lippi (c. 1406-1469), teacher of Botticelli, whose masterpieces are the tempera-on-panel "Annunciation," c. 1434, and the tempera-on-panel "Madonna and Child," c. 1452;
- Paolo Uccello (1397-1475), whose masterpiece is the tempera-on-panel "Battle of San Romano," c. 1445;
- Domenico Veneziano (c. 1410-1461), whose masterpiece is the tempera-on-panel "Saint Lucy Altarpiece," c. 1445;
- Piero della Francesca (c. 1420-1492), whose masterpieces are the fresco "Legend of the True Cross," Church of San Francisco, Arezzo, c. 1453-1454, the oil-on-panel "Portrait of Federigo da Montefeltro," c. 1474, and the oil-on-panel "Portrait of Battista Sforza," c. 1475;
- Antonio del Pollaiuolo, also an exceedingly talented sculptor, whose masterpiece in painting is the tempera-on-panel "Martyrdom of Saint Sebastian," 1475;
- Sandro Botticelli (1445-1510), who was significantly patronized by Lorenzo the Magnificent and whose masterpieces are the tempera-on-panel "Primavera," c. 1482, and the tempera-on-canvas "Birth of Venus," c. 1482; and
- Pietro Perugino (c. 1445-1523), teacher of Raphael, whose masterpiece is the fresco "Giving of the Keys to Saint Peter," Sistine Chapel, Vatican City, 1481.

The **Venetian phase of the early Italian Renaissance** developed in the last half of the fifteenth century; it combined penetrating Florentine senses of perspective and form with rich Venetian senses of color and texture; and it was dominated by two great masters: Andrea Mantegna (1431-1506) and Giovanni Bellini (c. 1430-1516). Mantegna's masterpieces are the fresco "Saint James Led to His Execution," Church of the Eremitani, Padua, 1454-1457, the tempera-on-canvas "Dead Christ," c. 1466, and the fresco "Arrival of Cardinal Francesco Gonzaga," Palazzo Ducale, Mantua, 1474. Bellini's masterpieces are the oil-on-panel "Saint Francis in Ecstasy," c. 1485, the oil-on-panel "Transfiguration of Christ," late 1480s, and the oil-on-panel "Madonna and Child Enthroned," 1505.

The major artistic achievements of the early Renaissance in northern Europe were owed entirely to the Duchy of Burgundy (most tellingly, to the regions of Flanders and Netherlands) and they were largely confined to the media of painting and music. The great cities of Flanders and Netherlands, Brussels and Bruges in particular, were worthy artistic rivals of Florence and Venice throughout the fifteenth century. New oils and glazes were used to great effect in the **Burgundian phase of the early Renaissance**, creating a depth and resonance of color and light unobtainable in tempera and influencing virtually all subsequent work of the sort. The incipient development of this tradition can be seen in the illuminated manuscript, "Très Riches Heures du Duc de Berry," c. 1413-1416 of the Limbourg brothers (Paul, Herman, and Jean), all of whom flourished in the early fifteenth century. In the "Labors of the Months" most revealingly, the brothers aptly capture the new spirit, including a reference to hunting and to ball games. The ranking geniuses of the Burgundian movement followed:

- Robert Campin (likely the Master of Flémalle; c. 1378-1444), teacher of van der Weyden, whose masterpieces are the oil-on-panel "Nativity," c. 1425, and the oil-on-panel "Mérode Altarpiece," c. 1425-1426;
- Jan van Eyck (c. 1385-1441), among the greatest painters of any age, who was in the direct employ of Philip the Good and whose masterpieces are the oil-on-panel "Ghent Altarpiece," 1429-1432, the oil-on-panel "Man in a Red Turban," 1433, the oil-on-panel "Arnolfini Wedding," 1434, and the oil-on-panel "Madonna of Chancellor Rolin," c. 1433-1434;
- Rogier van der Weyden (c. 1399-1464), whose masterpieces are the oil-on-panel "Descent from the Cross," c. 1435, and the oil-on-panel "Last Judgment," c. 1444-1451; and
- Hieronymous Bosch (c. 1450-1516), whose masterpieces are the oil-on-panel "Crowning with Thorns," c. 1500, and the oil-on-panel "Garden of Delights," c. 1505-1510.

The heroic sense of the active and the universal inherent in the early Renaissance was further magnified in the high and late Renaissance. The **high Renaissance in central Italy** was based largely in Florence, Rome, and Milan and it was dominated by four of the most richly talented and accomplished visual artists in world history: Leonardo, Bramante, Raphael, and Michelangelo. Leonardo da Vinci (1452-1519), who was significantly patronized by Ludovico Sforza and by Francis I of France, was the archetype of the age, a person of very broad interests and knowledge (a brilliant architect, painter, sculptor, musician, physicist, botanist, anatomist, geologist, geographer, engineer, and inventor), a person struck by the mysteries of nature, and a person of skeptical bent who accepted only the insights of direct, experiential observation and thus accepted no unexamined or dogmatic authority, not even that of the Church nor that of ancient classicism. It was too with Leonardo that the evolution of the artist from a guild craftsman to an academically trained and deeply respected professional began. Although Leonardo constructed no buildings, his architectural designs were nonetheless memorable; they were based on geometry and nature and thus tended to central-plan structures. His high reputation as a visual artist is secured mainly, however, by his drawings (most notably, the "Battle of Anghiari," 1503-1506, which was the basis of a since-destroyed mural) and his paintings. Instead of bringing light to objects (the customary tendency), Leonardo's paintings seemed to bring forms out of darkness. The most remarkable of these are: the oil-on-panel "Madonna of the Rocks," 1483; the fresco "Last Supper," Church of Santa Maria delle Grazie, Milan, 1495-1498; the oil-on-panel "Madonna and Saint Anne," c.1501-1503; and the oil-on-panel "Mona Lisa," 1503-1506.

Donato Bramante (1444-1514), who had worked with Leonardo in Milan and was much influenced by him and who was significantly patronized by Ludovico Sforza and Pope Leo X, received the commission for the re-building of the "Basilica of St. Peter's," Vatican City from Pope Julius II in 1506. His revolutionary central plan (1506-1514) for the Renaissance structure that was to replace the Constantinian building razed by Julius owed as much to the hemispheric shapes of the "Pantheon" as to the ribbed forms of the Gothic style and it established the basic groundwork of high Renaissance architecture. The inclination to central-plan classicism is repeated in his other masterpiece, the marble "Tempietto" in the Church of San Pietro in Montorio, Vatican City, c. 1511.

Raphael/Raffaello Sanzio (1483-1520), who was significantly patronized by Pope Leo X and Pope Julius II, employed uniquely spiral shapes to convey subtle movement and achieved an unsurpassed sense of compositional harmony. His masterpieces are the oil-on-panel "Marriage of the Virgin," 1504; the oil-on-panel "Madonna of the Meadows," 1505; the frescoes of the Stanze Chambers, Vatican City, "Disputation over the Sacrament" (1509), "School of Athens" (1510-1511), and "Expulsion of Heliodorus" (1512); the oil-on-canvas "Sistina Madonna," 1513; the fresco "Galatea," Villa Farnesina, Rome, c. 1513; the oil-on-panel "Transfiguration of Christ," 1517; and the oil-on-panel "Pope Leo X with Cardinal Giulio de' Medici and Luigi de' Rossi," c. 1517.

Although neither a skeptic nor a universal man in the sense of Leonardo, Michelangelo Buonarroti (1475-1564) developed a heroic style unmatched in his, perhaps in any, time. Michelangelo, who was significantly patronized by Lorenzo the Magnificent, brought the spirituality of Christianity and the bodily beauty of classical antiquity together in a more convincing and compelling way than any other visual artist. His early sculptural masterpieces were all in marble: "Pieta" (c. 1498-1500), "David" (1501-1504), "Dying Slave" (c. 1512), "Rebellious Slave" (c. 1512), "Moses" (c. 1515), and "Cross-Legged Slave" (1527-1528). His early masterpieces in painting were the ceiling frescoes of the Sistine Chapel, Vatican City, 1508-1512, commissioned by Pope Julius II. Michelangelo's later work, that after c. 1520, departs somewhat from his earlier triumphs; it is of more tormented and gymnastic figures (the Florentine Republic and the Papal States were themselves in great turmoil in this time), of less graceful, more turbulent poses, and of busier and more ornamental composition. This herald of the Baroque (which comes to dominance in the seventeenth and the early eighteenth centuries) is known as "mannerism" and it is almost entirely a central Italian phenomenon (Florence, Siena, Parma, and Rome) of the final three-quarters of the sixteenth century. Michelangelo is the most accomplished exponent of **mannerism** and the final approximately forty-five years of his life were moved primarily by it. The masterpieces of this period most notably include: the marble "Tomb of Giuliano de' Medici" (1519-1534; Giuliano, 1479-1516, was a son of Lorenzo the Magnificent) and the marble "Tomb of Lorenzo de' Medici" (1519-1534; Lorenzo, 1492-1519, was a grandson of Lorenzo the Magnificent), both in the Medici Chapel, Church of San Lorenzo, Florence; the end-wall frescoes ("Last Judgment") of the Sistine Chapel, Vatican City, 1536-1541, commissioned by Pope Paul III; the "Campidoglio (Capitol)," Rome, 1538-1564; the continuation of the central-plan "Basilica of Saint Peter's," Vatican City, 1538-1564; the marble "Deposition," 1550-1555; and the marble "Rondanini Pieta," c. 1554-1564. The other leading mannerists were:

- Correggio/Antonio Allegri (1494-1534), whose masterpieces are the oil-on-panel "Holy Night" (1522), the fresco "Assumption of the Virgin," Cathedral of Parma (1526-1530), and the oil-on-canvas "Jupiter and Io" (early 1530s);
- Parmigianino/Francesco Mazzola (1503-1540), whose masterpiece is the oil-on-panel "Madonna with the Long Neck" (1534-1540);
- Benvenuto Cellini (1500-1571), whose masterpiece is the bronze "Perseus and Medusa" (1545-1554);
- Bronzino/Agnolo Tori (1503-1572), whose masterpiece is the oil-on-panel "Exposure of Luxury" (c. 1546);
- Giorgio Vasari (1511-1574), whose architectural masterpiece is the "Palazzo degli Uffizi," Florence, 1560-1580;
- Giacomo della Porta (1541-1604), whose architectural masterpiece is the central-plan "Church of Il Gesu," Rome (1575-1584); and
- Giovanni Bologna (1529-1608), whose masterpiece is the marble "Rape of the Sabine Woman" (1583).

The **Venetian high and late Renaissance** was largely untouched by mannerism; throughout the sixteenth century, it effectively continued and elaborated on the strictly Renaissance equation first brought to it by Mantegna and Bellini. Italian artistic preeminence passed from Florence to Venice in the sixteenth century owing largely to the more favorable political and economic circumstance in Venice at this time. The uniquely Venetian sense of color and light was made possible mainly by the development of new glazes and by the adoption of flexible resins which encouraged painting in oil on canvas (as distinct from on panels). The great masters of the Venetian high and late Renaissance rank with the great masters of any age:

- Giorgione da Castelfranco (c. 1475-1510), whose masterpieces are the oil-on-panel "Enthroned Madonna with Saint Liberalis and Saint Francis" (c. 1505) and the oil-on-canvas "The Tempest" (c. 1505-1510);
- Titian/Tiziano Vecellio (c. 1490-1576), student of Bellini and Giorgione, who employed a uniquely triangular sense of composition and whose masterpieces are all done in oil on canvas except the oil-on-panel "Assumption of the Virgin" (1516-1518): "Sacred and Profane Love" (c. 1515), "Madonna of the House of Pesaro" (1519-1526), "Bacchanal of the Andrians" (c. 1520), "Man with the Glove" (c. 1520), "Venus of Urbino" (1538), "Portrait of Pope Paul III and His Grandsons" (1546), "Rape of Europa" (c. 1559-1562), and "Crowning with Thorns" (c. 1570);
- Palladio/Andrea di Pietro (1508-1580), whose architectural masterpieces are the "Villa Rotonda," Vicenza (1550) and the "Church of San Giorgio Maggiore," Venice (1566);
- Tintoretto/Jacopo Robusti (1518-1594), who employed a uniquely diagonal sense of composition and whose masterpieces are all done in oil on canvas: "Saint Mark Freeing a Christian Slave" (1548), "Crucifixion" (1565), "Christ Before Pilate" (1566-1567), and "Last Supper" (1592-1594); and
- Veronese/Paolo Caliari (1528-1588), whose masterpiece is the oil-on-canvas "Feast in the House of Levi" (1573).

Italian and Burgundian Renaissance art had a profound influence on aesthetic developments elsewhere in Europe, particularly in the period of the high and late Renaissance, most significantly in Germany, Netherlands, and Spain. The senses of line, proportion, perspective, composition, and heroic humanism characteristic of **sixteenth-century German, Flemish, and Spanish painting** rivaled those of early, high, and late Renaissance Italian painting as well as those of early Renaissance Burgundian painting. The leading figure in the German development was Albrecht Durer (1471-1528), an ardent disciple of Luther, whose masterpieces are the woodcut "Four Horsemen of the Apocalypse" (c. 1497-1498), the oil-on-panel

"Self-Portrait" (1498), the engraving ""Adam and Eve" (1504), the oil-on-panel "Adoration of the Trinity" (1508-1511), the engraving "Knight, Death, and the Devil" (1513), the engraving "Saint Jerome" (1514), the engraving "Melancolia I" (1514), and the oil-on-panel "Four Apostles" (c. 1526). The other foremost German figures of the period were:

- Matthias Grunewald (c. 1475-1528), whose masterpieces are the oils-on-panel "Crucifixion," "Annunciation," "Resurrection," and "Virgin and Child with Angels" of the "Isenheim Altarpiece" (c. 1512-1515);
- Lukas Cranach the Elder (1472-1553), a fervent devotee of Luther, whose masterpieces are the oils-on-panel "The Judgment of Paris" (1530) and "Apollo and Diana" (n. date); and
- Hans Holbein the Younger (c. 1497-1543), who was in the direct employ of Henry VIII of England and whose masterpieces are the oils-on-panel "Erasmus of Rotterdam" (c. 1523), "Madonna of Burgomaster" (1526), "French Ambassadors" (1533), and "Portrait of Henry VIII" (1539-1540).

The Flemish painter, Peter Bruegel the Elder (c. 1525-1569), and the Greek-born Spanish painter, El Greco/Domenikos Theotokopoulos (1541-1614), were the most accomplished and significant non-Italian, late-sixteenth-century harbingers of the emerging Baroque; Bruegel for his emphasis on the mundane affairs of the lower classes (including many peasant games) and El Greco for his mannerist tendencies. Bruegel's masterpieces are the oils-on-panel "Children's Games" (1560), "Landscape with the Fall of Icarus" (c. 1554-1555), "Triumph of Death" (c. 1561-1562), "Harvesters" (1565), "Hunters in the Snow" (1565), and "Peasant Wedding" (c. 1565). El Greco's masterpieces are the oils-on-canvas "The Burial of Count Orgaz" (1586), "Resurrection" (c. 1597-1604), "Grand Inquisitor Don Fernando Nino de Guevara" (c. 1600), "Toledo" (c. 1600-1610), and "Fra Felix Hortensio Paravicino" (c. 1605).

The seventeenth century marked a new turn in the progressive secularization and the progressive humanization of Western culture. This turn was most affected by the triumph of absolutism over the Renaissance "republics" and by the earnest inception of modern science. The seventeenth century, the so-termed "Age of (Scientific) Reason," held onto the humanistic tendencies of the Renaissance but it developed those tendencies in a new direction, in a scientific, or realistic, direction. In the arts, this direction predictably manifested itself in a new style, the **Baroque style**, which was nonetheless yet moved by ancient classical and medieval Christian theses, but which was also governed by a more precise sense of line, color, and perspective (a scientific standard of clarity), by a more intensely emotional and sensuous form of expression, by a more dramatic sense of worldly energy, by a more frenetic and varied sense of movement, by a still more expansive sense of scale, and by a more elaborate sense of decoration than had characterized Renaissance humanism. In the Baroque, humanity is conceived as a sense-perceptual agent, as a participant in the natural world of sensory phenomena, as a reflective body. This is a notion wholly consistent with the mechanistic, dualistic/pluralistic, empiricistic, objective, corporeal, and extrinsic inclinations of seventeenth-century intellectual life; that is, with the inclinations of seventeenth-century science. The result is a materialistic-tending departure from the rich sense of balance, harmony, and proportion that had been at the organic, monistic, subjective, lived, and intrinsic axis of Renaissance art.

In the visual arts, the Baroque extended, at its outside, from c. 1590 to c. 1725 and it was centered in Catholic Italy, Flanders (Belgium), France, and Spain and in Protestant Netherlands and England. The **Italian Baroque** developed most significantly in Rome and had as its principal exponents:

- Annibale Carracci (1560-1609) of Bologna, whose masterpieces are the ceiling and side-wall frescoes of the "Palazzo Farnese," Rome (1597-1600);
- Caravaggio/Michelangelo Merisi (1573-1610), who is said to have killed a man in a tennis match and whose masterpieces are the oils-on-canvas "Calling of Saint Matthew" (c. 1599-1600) and "Conversion of Saint Paul" (c. 1601);
- Gianlorenzo Bernini (1598-1680) of Naples, who was arguably among the greatest sculptors in all of world history, who was widely patronized by Pope Urban VIII (1568-1644; r. 1623-1644), Pope Innocent X (1574-1655; r. 1644-1655), Pope Alexander VII (1599-1667; r. 1655-1667), Pope Clement IX (1600-1669; r. 1667-1669), and Louis XIV of France, and whose masterpieces are the marble "Apollo and Daphne" (1622-1624), the marble "David" (1623), the bronze "Baldachin" (altar canopy), Basilica of Saint Peter's, Vatican City (1624-1633), the marble "The Ecstasy of Saint Theresa," Church of Santa Maria della Vittoria, Rome (1645-1652), the marble "Fountain of the Four Rivers," Piazza Navona, Rome (1648-1651), the marble and bronze "Cathedra Petri (Chair of Peter)," Basilica of Saint Peter's, Vatican City (1657-1666), and the "Colonnade of Saint Peter's," Vatican City (1656);

- Francesco Borromini (1599-1667), whose masterful central-plan churches are done in the characteristically Baroque form of sculptural plasticity: "Church of San Carlo alle Quattro Fontane," Rome (1638-1641), "Church of Sant'Ivo della Sapienza," Rome (1642-1660), and "Church of Sant'Agnese," Piazza Navona, Rome (1652-1666); and
- Baldassare Longhena (1598-1682) of Venice, whose masterpiece is the central-plan "Church of Santa Maria della Salute," Venice (1631-1687).

The **Flemish Baroque** developed mainly in Antwerp and was dominated by a learned genius of towering stature, Peter Paul Rubens (1577-1640). Rubens' acknowledged masterpieces are the oils-on-panel: "Raising of the Cross" (1609-1610), "Marie de' Medici Landing in Marseilles" (1622-1623), and "Landscape with the Chateau of Steen" (1636); and the oils-on-canvas: "Fall of the Damned" (1614-1618), "Rape of the Daughters of Leucippus" (1616-1617), "Henry IV Receiving the Portrait of Marie de' Medici" (1621-1625), and "Garden of Love" (c. 1638). The other major figure of the Flemish Baroque was Rubens' able student, Anthony van Dyck (1599-1641), whose masterpiece is the oil-on-canvas "Portrait of Charles I in Hunting Dress" (1635).

The **French Baroque** flowed from Rome and was dominated by another intellectual colossus, Nicolas Poussin (c. 1593-1665), who was patronized significantly by Louis XIII, who worked in Rome after 1624, and whose neo-classical tendencies importantly linked the Renaissance to the Enlightenment. Poussin's masterpieces are the oils-on-canvas: "Inspiration of the Poet" (c. 1628-1629), "Cephalus and Aurora" (c. 1630), "Rape of the Sabines" (c. 1636), "Landscape with the Burial of Phocion" (1648), and "Holy Family on the Steps" (1648). The other most significant contributors to the French Baroque were the painter, Claude Lorrain/Claude Gelée (1600-1682), who also worked in Rome, and the architect, Jules Hardouin-Mansart (1646-1708), whose principal work was done in or near to Rome. Lorrain's most memorable achievement is the oil-on-canvas "Embarkation of Saint Ursula" (1641); Mansart's are the "Palace of Versailles" (1669-1710) for Louis XIV and the central-plan "Church of the Invalides," Paris (1676-1706).

The **Spanish Baroque** was centered in Madrid and was owed most significantly to still another person of surpassing brilliance, Diego Rodriguez de Silva y Velazquez (1599-1660). Velazquez was significantly patronized by Philip IV and he is yet among the most widely acclaimed masters of composition. His most admired masterpieces are the oils-on-canvas: "The Water Carrier of Seville" (c. 1619), "Triumph of Bacchus" (c. 1628), "Garden of the Villa Medici, Rome" (c. 1649-1651), and "The Maids of Honor" (1656).

The Protestant Baroque, mainly in Dutch painting and English architecture, was likewise remarkable. The **Dutch Baroque** was centered in Amsterdam; it was significantly and uniquely devoted, in thematic terms, to mundane forms of leisured enjoyment; its greatest achievements were virtually all done in oil on canvas; and its leading figures worked typically without patrons and were thus tellingly subject to market conditions established primarily by prosperous commercial families. The most notable of its exponents were:
- Frans Hals (c. 1581-1666), whose masterpieces are the "Banquet of the Officers of the Saint George Guard Company" (1616), "The Laughing Cavalier" (1624), "The Jolly Toper" (1627), "Malle Babbe" (c. 1630-1633), and "Regentess of the Old Men's Almshouse" (c. 1664);
- Rembrandt van Rijn (1606-1669), the unexcelled master of light, considered by many the finest painter in the entire history of art, whose most memorable masterpieces are "Tobit and Anna with the Kid" (oil-on-panel; 1626), "Anatomy Lesson of Dr. Tulp" (1632), "The Blinding of Samson" (1636), "Angel Leaving Tobit and Tobias" (1637), "The Night Watch" (1642), "Supper at Emmaus" (1648), "Christ Preaching" (etching; c. 1652), "The Three Crosses" (etching; 1653), "The Polish Rider" (c. 1655), "Jacob Blessing the Sons of Joseph" (1656), "Self-Portrait" (c. 1667), and "Return of the Prodigal Son" (c. 1669);
- Jan Steen (c. 1625-1679), whose masterpieces are "The Eve of Saint Nicholas" (c. 1660-1665) and "The World Upside Down" (c. 1663);
- Jacob van Ruisdael (c. 1628-1682), whose masterpiece is the "View of Haarlem" (c. 1670); and
- Jan Vermeer (1632-1675), among the leading masters of color in the history of painting, whose masterpieces are "Kitchen Maid" (c. 1658), "View of Delft" (c. 1662), "The Letter" (1666), and "Allegory of the Art of Painting" (c. 1670-1675).

English Baroque architecture had its nucleus in London and owed especially much to Italian Renaissance architecture and to the 1666 fire of London, which destroyed most of the city's central district. The movement's two principal figures were Inigo Jones (1573-1652) and Christopher Wren (1632-1723). Jones was significantly patronized by James I; his masterpiece is the "Banqueting House," London (1619-1622). Wren's masterpiece is "Saint Paul's Cathedral," London (1675-1710).

The eighteenth century continued the progressive secularization and the progressive humanization of modern Western culture that had begun in earnest in the Renaissance and that had deepened in the seventeenth century. This tendency was most driven by the period's burgeoning democratism, by its advancing sense of political and intellectual individualism/independence, by its continuing commitment to the natural sciences, and by its quite original interest in the social sciences. The eighteenth century, the so-termed "Age of (the Modern European) Enlightenment," again turned the humanistic inclinations of the Renaissance and the seventeenth century in a somewhat new direction, in a naturalistic direction. In the arts, this direction manifested itself in terms of a more cosmopolitan, a more international, and a more tolerant orientation than had prevailed in the seventeenth century as well as in terms of a neo-classical form of naturalism. Naturalism itself was governed by a persisting respect for the rational and universal tendencies of ancient classicism, by the preeminence of the natural, uncontrived, discoverable order of the world, by a celebration of the regular patterns of the natural realm, and by a perception of humanity as a social participant in nature. In the visual arts, these inclinations expressed themselves in a more measured sense of color, composition, and sensual intensity than had been the case in the Baroque. These inclinations expressed themselves in a way that was wholly consistent with the political and scientific perspectives of the period and thus in a way that was yet fundamentally mechanistic, materialistic, dualistic/pluralistic, empiricistic, objective, corporeal, and extrinsic, not in a way that was fundamentally organic, monistic, subjective, lived, and intrinsic.

The neo-classical **naturalism** of eighteenth-century (visual) art tended to take either a largely naturalist form or a largely neo-classical form, both of which continued to be heavily influenced by Baroque tendencies. The painting of the period inclined to the naturalist emphasis (with the notable vestigial exception of Poussin and the notable strict exception of David); the architecture and sculpture of the period inclined to the neo-classical emphasis. The most distinguished eighteenth-century painting was French, Italian, English, and American. The leading French painters of this period were:

- Antoine Watteau (1684-1721), whose masterpieces are the oils-on-canvas "A Pilgrimage to Cythera" (1717) and "Signboard of Gersaint" (c. 1721);
- Jean-Baptiste-Siméon Chardin (1699-1779), whose masterpieces are the oils-on-canvas "Kitchen Still Life" (c. 1730-1735), "Back from the Market" (1739), and "House of Cards" (1741) and the oil-on-panel "Copper Cistern" (c. 1733); and
- Jean-Honoré Fragonard (1732-1806), a student of Chardin, whose masterpiece is the oil-on-canvas "The Bathers" (c. 1765).

The foremost Italian painter of this period was the Venetian, Giovanni Battista Tiepolo (1696-1770), whose masterpieces are the frescoes "The Banquet of Anthony and Cleopatra," Palazzo Labia, Venice (c. 1750) and "The Investiture of Bishop Harold," Residenz, Wurzburg (1750-1753). The leading English painters of this period were:

- William Hogarth (1697-1764), whose masterpiece is the oil-on-canvas "Marriage à la Mode: Signing the Contract" (1743-1745);
- Joshua Reynolds (1723-1792), whose masterpieces are the oils-on-canvas "Lady Sarah Bunbury Sacrificing to the Graces" (1765) and "Mrs. Siddons as the Tragic Muse" (1784); and
- Thomas Gainsborough (1727-1788), whose masterpieces are the oils-on-canvas "Robert Andrews and His Wife" (c. 1748-1750), "Mary Countess Howe" (c. 1765), "The Blue Boy" (1770), "Mrs. Siddons" (1785), "Mountain Landscape with Peasants Crossing Bridge" (c. 1785), and "Market Cart" (1787).

And the leading American painters of this period were:

- Benjamin West (1738-1820), whose masterpiece is the oil-on-canvas "Death of General Wolfe" (c. 1770);
- John Singleton Copley (1738-1815), whose masterpieces are the oils-on-canvas "Watson and the Shark" (1778) and "Paul Revere" (1783); and
- Gilbert Stuart (1755-1828), whose masterpiece is the oil-on-canvas "George Washington" (c. 1796).

The most distinguished **eighteenth-century architecture and sculpture** was German, English, French, and American. Enlightenment architecture, not unlike elements of Baroque architecture, was very heavily influenced by Italian Renaissance paradigms. The foremost German figures of this period were Balthasar Neumann (1687-1753), whose masterpiece is the "Residenz," Wurzburg (1719-1750), and Karl Langhans (1733-1808), whose masterpiece is the "Brandenburg Gate," Berlin (1789-1794). The leading English figure of this period was Richard Boyle/Earl of Burlington (1695-1753), whose masterpiece is "Chiswick House," London (1725-1729). The most significant French architect of the eighteenth century was Germain Soufflot

(1713-1780), whose masterpiece is the "Panthéon (Church of Sainte-Geneviève)," Paris (1757-1790). The most accomplished sculptor of this period was the Frenchman, Jean Antoine Houdin (1741-1828), whose masterpieces are the marbles "Voltaire" (1778) and "George Washington" (1788-1792). And the leading American figure of this period was the exceptional political theorist and statesman, Thomas Jefferson (1743-1826), whose architectural masterpieces are "Monticello," Charlottesville (1796-1800) and "The Lawn, University of Virginia," Charlottesville (1817-1825).

The **neo-classicism** of the late eighteenth and early nineteenth centuries in painting tended to a rational (not an emotive) sense of classical proportion (and virtue) and was the main plastic connection between Enlightenment tendencies and nineteenth-century romanticism. This movement was dominated by two brilliant French artists, one of whom, Jacques-Louis David (1748-1825), worked predominantly in the late eighteenth century, and the other of whom, Jean-Auguste-Dominique Ingres (1780-1867), a student of David, worked predominantly in the early nineteenth century. David, a Jacobin, was the great master of the French Revolution and the French Revolutionary Wars. His most remarkable works are the oils-on-canvas "Oath of the Horati" (1784-1785), "The Death of Socrates" (1787), "Death of Marat" (1793), and "Coronation of Napoleon and Josephine" (1805-1807).

Although there were two particularly rich artistic movements in early modern Asia and India – the Ming in China and the Mogul in India – the visual arts of this time and these places came more so to an elaboration on so-termed medieval themes than to an utterly fresh development. There was no Asian correlate of the European Renaissance, mainly because the humanistic, secular, and individualistic groundwork of early modern Europe hadn't an Asian or Indian analog. The traditional spiritualism of Asia and India prevailed instead. Even **Ming art** (1368-1644) was largely a synthesis of earlier possibilities. It nonetheless created an especially elegant form of porcelain wares and fashioned the majestic and monumental spaces of the new (seventeenth-century) imperial palace, the "Forbidden City," Peking/Beijing and the "Royal Ming Tombs," near Peking/Beijing. Manchu, or Qing, art (1644-1911) effectively continued the inclinations of the Ming. Ink scrolls emphasizing natural themes and a keen sense of essential line nonetheless became the dominant form of artistic expression in the Qing. So too in Korea, Japan, and southeast Asia, the tendency was to an embellishment of established conventions. Only the Japanese, "Himeji Castle," near Osaka (1581) of the Momoyama and the ink-on-paper painting of Uragami Gyokudo (1745-1820), such as "Forbidden to the Vulgar" (c. 1800) of the Tokugawa, impress as notable early modern exceptions.

The great anomaly to these claims of Asian and Indian constancy was, of course, **Mogul art** (1526-1756). There was much very fine painting in the Mogul Empire, largely in illuminated manuscripts and on cloth, largely in the late sixteenth and early seventeenth centuries, and largely under Persian auspices, but its most remarkable achievements were made in architecture. The organic magnificence of Mogul architecture in particular rivals that of even ancient Greek and early modern European triumphs in the medium as has been said. The admixture of Hindu, Islamic, Mogul, and Persian influences that signify the Mogul style produce an utterly breathtaking effect. Its most stunning examples are the "Mausoleum of Humayun," Delhi (1556-1605), the "Taj Mahal," Agra (1630-1648), and the "Badshahi Mosque," Lahore (c. 1676). Of these, in turn, the "Taj" is by any fair organic standard among the most beautiful buildings, among the most beautiful objects, in the world. It was constructed as a tomb (a mausoleum) for the Mogul ruler, Shah Jahan, and his favorite wife, Mumtaz Mahal (d. 1629). Its red sandstone and marble exterior of four cylindrical minarets, a large and graceful pointed dome flanked by four smaller such domes, and numerous pointed arches conspire to an intricate harmony of elegant detail, to an unmatched sense of unified whole. The compelling parts draw one's attention inextricably to the whole; the whole illumines the proportion of the parts and the refined relation of the parts to one another. Elsewhere in the early modern Islamic world, a sense of the organic was also achieved in the architecture of (Ottoman) Turkey; most notably, in the "Sultanahmet Cami (Mosque of Sultan Ahmet I [1589-1617; r. 1603-1617])," Istanbul (1609-1617).

The musical arts

The musical arts of early modern (European) civilization passed through similar transformations as the visual arts of the period, albeit slightly later. **Renaissance music**, like Renaissance painting, sculpture, and architecture, was governed by an organic, a humanistic, sense of balance, harmony, and proportion. It thereby became still more robust, active, diverse, and secular in character and emphasis as against the tendencies of the fourteenth and fifteenth centuries. Its personal vigor and spirited energy, its heroic sense of sonorous universality and of human life, as well as its abundance of emotional content and passionate tension set it clearly apart from all prior developments in the medium. The maturation of purely instrumental music (augmented by the invention of new and more diverse instruments), the adaptation of vocal music to instruments, the evolution of the modern chorus, and the formal development of balletic dance were principal among the technical achievements of the Renaissance that greatly affected the enhanced sense of vitality characteristic of its music. The leading composers of the Renaissance were of the Netherlands (Holland, Flanders, Luxembourg, and bits of northern France) and Italy. The most notable of the **Netherlander tradition**, who were the effective heirs of Burgundian genius in the visual arts, were:

- Johannes Ockeghem (c. 1430-1495), known mainly for his Masses (such as the "Missa Prolationum"), motets, and chansons;
- Jacob Obrecht (1452-1505), known mainly for his Masses, motets (such as "Parce Domine"), chansons, and instrumental compositions; and
- Josquin des Prez (c. 1440-1521), the acknowledged master of Renaissance music and one of the most significant figures in the entire history of the medium; variously patronized by the Sforza, Pope Innocent VIII, and Louis XII of France; wrote approximately twenty Masses (such as "Hercules dux Ferrariae" and "Faysans Regres"), 100 motets (such as "Ave Maria" and "Tu Pauperum Refugium"), and 70 chansons (such as "Faulte d'Argent" and L'Homme Armé"); and was the first to develop distinctly modern forms of harmonic structure and counterpoint.

The last of the towering Netherlanders (save Orlando di Lasso), Adrian Willaert (1490-1562), spent the final approximately four decades of his life in Venice and there assisted in the establishment of a national musical tradition, the **Italian tradition**, that supplanted his own as the dominant European tradition by the end of the sixteenth century. Willaert is known principally for his motets (such as "Victimae Paschali Laudes") and for his indirect, but nonetheless telling, influence on the first of the major Italian composers of the Renaissance, Giovanni Gabrieli (c. 1557-1612). Gabrieli is mainly known for his motets (such as "In Ecclesiis" and "Sonata Pian' e Forte"), for his development of the concerto form in which themes variously oppose one another, and for his inventive use of dynamic markings concerning volume and temperament. The Italian madrigal (vocal chamber music in which each of several parts is performed by one singer) and new forms of secular song – most notably, frottole in Italy, chansons in France, and lieder in Germany – were the dominant forms of composition in the last half of the sixteenth century. The two most remarkable composers of this period were the Netherlander, Orlando di Lasso (1532-1594), and the Italian, Giovanni Pierluigi da Palestrina (c. 1525-1594). Lasso, who worked mainly in Germany (Munich) but who also had a very large influence in France and Italy, was the most accomplished interpreter of the new songs in madrigal form (such as "Ich Armer Mann" and "Bon Jour, Mon Coeur"). He was too among the most prolific composers in the entire history of the musical arts, creating more than 2000 works, the most memorable of which are his dynamic and emotional, secular motets. Palestrina, conversely, who worked mainly in or very near to Rome, was the principal composer of religious music in this period. He wrote 102 Masses (such as "Pope Marcellus Mass," "Veni Sponsa Christi," "Missa Brevis," and "Improperia"), 450 motets (such as "Stabat Mater"), and 56 spiritual madrigals; his mostly somber and impersonal music was widely patronized by Pope Julius III; and he was the most notable musical interpreter of the Catholic Counter-Reformation. Although the Protestant Reformation had an important, if equivocal, affect on music, particularly on Lutheran church music in Germany, it did not produce a figure of Palestrina's stature until the seventeenth century.

Although it persisted somewhat longer than similar tendencies in the visual arts (i.e., to c. 1750), **Baroque music**, not unlike Baroque tendencies in the visual arts, inclined to a scientific sense of precision but also to a more emotionally expressive and a more flamboyantly decorative temperament than Renaissance music. The engaging tension between order and variation in the Baroque made for a novel sense of dramatic contrast that distinguished the music of this era from all prior developments in the medium. The highly inventive spirit of the seventeenth century produced a formalization of major-minor tonality and gave rise to numerous new forms of composition; most notably, the cantata, capriccio, chaconne, concerto grosso, fantasia, fugue, oratorio, overture, passacaglia, prelude, serenade, sonata, suite, theme and variation, toccata, and opera. Of these, the opera, which entails a unique conjunction of music, literature, drama, poetry, and sometimes dance, has been likely the most influential. Although the precedents of modern opera had been long-standing – ancient Greek drama, the medieval troubadour tradition, early modern Chinese music, and six-teenth-century madrigal cycles – the original formulation of modern European opera as such was owed to seventeenth-century Florence, Rome, and Venice. Its first great master, Claudio Monteverdi (1567-1643), who was the principal musical bridge from the Renaissance to the Baroque, wrote the first noteworthy operatic score of strictly modern moment, "Orfeo," in 1607. His exceptional madrigals (such as "The Combat of Tancred and Clorinda," 1624) and his other operatic masterpieces followed: "Ulysses' Homecoming" (1641) and "Poppea" (1642).

The other leading composers of the Baroque were mainly Italian, French, English, and German. The most notable figures of the **Italian Baroque** (with Monteverdi) also worked in Florence, Rome, or Venice; they were:

- Girolamo Frescobaldi (1583-1643), mainly known for his organ works (such as "Musical Flowers," 1635);
- Arcangelo Corelli (1653-1713), mainly known for his several dozen violin sonatas (1681-1700) and for his dozen concerti grossi (1682-1700);
- Giuseppe Torelli (1658-1709), the Bolognese, who was principally responsible for the ongoing refinement of the concerto form, most importantly in his final dozen violin concerti (1709);
- Alessandro Scarlatti (1660-1725), the Neapolitan, mainly known for his approximately 600 cantatas (such as "Cease, O Cease") and his approximately 100 operas (most notably, "Mitridate," 1707; "Tigrane," 1715; and "Griselda," 1721);
- Antonio Vivaldi (c. 1678-1741), who perfected the Italian Baroque concerto and concerto grosso, who wrote 447 concerti, most for violin (1712-1740), and who composed one of the great masterpieces of the concerto grosso form ("The Four Seasons," 1725);
- Domenico Scarlatti (1685-1757), son of Alessandro, who was significantly patronized by Philip V and Ferdinand VI of Spain and who is chiefly known for his more than 550 masterful harpsichord sonatas (most notably, those from 1738) and for his creation of modern keyboard technique; and
- Giovanni Battista Pergolesi (1710-1736), the Neapolitan, mainly known for his religious music (such as "Stabat Mater") and a comic opera ("The Maid as Mistress," 1733).

The **French Baroque** in the musical arts was centered in Paris; its most notable exponents were Jean-Baptiste Lully (1632-1687), François Couperin (1668-1733), and Jean-Philippe Rameau (1683-1764). Lully, who was Italian-born and who was significantly patronized by Louis XIV, fashioned the modern overture and wrote several memorable ballets and operas (most notably, "Alceste," 1674, and "Amadis," 1684). Couperin is mainly known for his church organ compositions and for his chamber music (most notably, his trio sonatas, such as "Les Nations Sonades et Suites de Simphonies en Trio," 1726). And Rameau, significantly patronized by Louis XV, was the leading musical theorist of the Baroque (<u>Treatise on Harmony Reduced to Its Natural Principle</u>, 1722) and the leading composer of French Baroque ballet and opera (most notably, "Hippolyte et Aricie," 1733; "Les Indes Galantes," 1735; "Castor et Pollux," 1737; "Dardanus," 1739; and "Zoroastre," 1749). The most significant figure in the **English Baroque** was Henry Purcell (c. 1659-1695), who worked in a wide variety of musical forms, mainly in London, who was the acknowledged master of English Baroque opera (most notably, "Dido and Aeneas," 1689; "King Arthur," 1691; and "The Fairy Queen," 1692), and who foresaw the development of the oratorio ("Ode to Saint Cecilia's Day," 1692).

The **German Baroque**, effectively Lutheran-inspired music, did not come to its full development until the approximate century following the Thirty Years War (i.e., c. 1650-c. 1750). It was too a more geographically diffuse movement than the Italian, French, or English forms of the musical Baroque. Its first major proponent was Heinrich Schutz (1585-1672), who worked mainly in Dresden and who is chiefly remembered for his oratorios (most notably, "The Seven Last Words," c. 1645, and "Christmas Oratorio," 1664). The other most widely acclaimed composers of the German Baroque prior to the appearance of its giant figures, Bach and Handel, were Dietrich Buxtehude (c. 1637-1707), who was Swedish-born and who worked principally in Lubeck, and Georg Philipp Telemann (1681-1767), who worked principally in Leipzig and Hamburg. Both are largely remembered for their Lutheran church music: Buxtehude for his monumental organ compositions in toccata and fugue forms and Telemann for his more than 3000 compositions (including 40 operas) in an imposingly wide range of forms.

The two crowning figures of the German Baroque in the musical arts, the two colossal geniuses of the Baroque more broadly defined, and two of the very most significant figures in the entire history of music, Johann Sebastian Bach (1685-1750) and Georg Friedrich Handel (1685-1759), brought seventeenth-century and early-eighteenth-century music to its highest mark and made the final preparations for the classical age that followed. Bach, who worked mainly in Weimar (near Leipzig) and Leipzig and who once collaborated in a musical project with no less than Frederick the Great of Prussia, wrote a staggering volume (well better than 1000 published compositions) of magnificent music in virtually all of the major forms of his time, except opera; he likewise wrote for chorus, orchestra, and most major instruments (most significantly, violin, cello, flute, organ, and clavichord/harpsichord). He is said to have perfected the Baroque cantata, chaconne, piano concerto, violin concerto, concerto grosso, fantasia, fugue, motet, overture, passacaglia, prelude, sonata, suite, theme and variations, and toccata. His instrumental masterpieces are numerous; arguably the most notable of these are the six concerti grossi of 1721 ("The Brandenburg Concerti"), the two systematic sets of twelve preludes and twelve fugues for clavichord/harpsichord of 1722 and 1744 respectively ("The Well-Tempered Clavier"), the set of theme and variations for clavichord/harpsichord of 1742 ("The Goldberg Variations"), and the instrumental fugues of 1749-1750 ("The Art of the Fugue"). His vocal masterpieces, monumental oratorio-like compositions for chorus and orchestra, are likewise copious: "Saint John Passion" (1724), "Saint Matthew Passion" (1729), "Magnificat" (1734), and "Mass in B Minor" (1733-1749). Bach's inventive abundance, measured sense of harmony, melody, and rhythm, clarity of form and proportion, intensity of demonstration, and technical superiority rank him among the foremost civilizers of early modern culture.

Still at this, Handel excelled him in operatic composition and was very nearly his equal in another sense or two as well. Handel's grandiose style and emphasis on melody and harmony may too have had a still larger affect on the music of the classical age than the contrapuntal and apportioned fashion of Bach. The early work of Handel was done in Hamburg, Rome, Florence, Venice, and Hanover; all of his mature work, however, was done in London, where he was widely patronized by George I and George II. Although he left a prodigious corpus of orchestral works — most notably, cantatas, organ concerti, oboe concerti, harpsichord suites, twelve stupendous concerti grossi (1739), "Water Music" (c. 1717), and "Fireworks Suite" (1749) -- Handel is principally known as the leading Baroque composer of operas and oratorios. The best of his 46 operas are: "Ottone" (1723), "Giulio Cesare" (1724), "Tamerlane" (1724), "Rodelinda" (1725), "Admeto" (1727), "Orlando" (1733), "Alcina" (1735), "Atalanta" (1736), and "Serse" (1738). The most remarkable of his 32 oratorios are: "Acis and Galatea" (c. 1720), "Esther" (1732), "Alexander's Feast" (1736), "Saul" (1739), "Messiah" (1742), "Judas Maccabeus" (1747), and "Jeptha" (1751).

Classical music (the classical era of modern music), which developed and flowered in the last approximate half of the eighteenth century, was the rough equivalent of neo-classical naturalism in the visual arts. Its cosmopolitan sense of uncontrived order and its agreeably moving, yet noble, effect set it securely between the first half of the eighteenth century and the romanticism of the nineteenth century. In the age of classicism, music became the dominant form of art, the German-Austrian axis became the dominant influence in music, and Vienna (mainly under Maria Theresa and Joseph II) became the center of the musical world. The string quartet and the symphony were the most significant compositional inventions of the period. The three major early champions of classical music were Carl Philipp Emanuel Bach (1714-1788), Christoph Willibald Gluck (1714-1787), and Luigi Boccherini (1743-1805). Bach was among the twenty children of Johann Sebastian Bach; he worked mainly in Berlin (where he was in the service of Frederick the Great of Prussia) and in Hamburg; and he was the likely founder of the innovative melodic and harmonic characteristics of the classical style which were most importantly embodied in his imaginative sonatas and symphonies (the earliest of which dates from 1742). Gluck was Bohemian-born, worked principally in Vienna (under the patronage of Maria Theresa and Joseph II) and Paris (under the patronage of Marie Antoinette), and wrote the foremost operas of early classicism (most notably, "Orfeo ed Euridice," 1762; "Alceste," 1767; "Iphigénie en Aulide," 1774; and "Iphigénie en Tauride," 1779). And the Italian, Boccherini, wrote the definitive chamber music of early classicism (125 string quintets and 91 string quartets) as well as four memorable cello concerti and twenty symphonies.

Musical classicism came to its culmination in the work of three colossal figures: Franz Joseph Haydn (1732-1809), Wolfgang Amadeus Mozart (1756-1791), and Ludwig van Beethoven (1770-1827). Haydn, an Austrian, worked mainly in the service of the Hungarian princes Esterhazy at Eisenstadt (near Vienna) from 1761 to 1790, in London from 1791 to 1795, and in Vienna itself in his last years. He was among the greatest composers in the history of music and also among the most prolific. Haydn wrote 23 operas, 6 Masses, 52 piano sonatas, and countless other, mostly instrumental compositions (including two cello concerti [number 1, 1783, in particular] and a trumpet concerto [1796] of surpassing beauty) in most major forms of the period. He is, however, best known for his:

- four oratorios (most notably, "The Creation," 1798, and "The Seasons," 1801), which were greatly influenced by Handel;
- 83 string quartets (most notably, opus numbers 17 [1771], 20 [1772], 33 [1781], 42 [1785], 50 [1784-1787], 54 [1789], 55 [1789], 64 [1790], 76 [1797], and 77 [1799]), a form of composition in which he was considered the undisputed classical master; and

149

- 104 symphonies, the first 92 of which were written between 1759 and 1788 (including the Paris symphonies, numbers 82 to 87 [1785-1786]) and the last twelve of which were written between 1791 and 1795.

The most memorable of his symphonies were numbers 44 ("Trauer"), 45 ("Farewell"), 47, and 56, all written between 1771 and 1774, as well as numbers 92 ("Oxford"), 94 ("Surprise"), 100 ("Military"), 101 ("Clock"), 103 ("Drum Roll"), and 104 ("London"), all of which were significantly influenced by Mozart. Haydn brought the measured assurances of the classical equation, inherited from such as C.P.E. Bach, Gluck, and Boccherini, to maturity, most tellingly in the form of the string quartet and the symphony.

Haydn's friend and notably younger colleague, Mozart, also Austrian, worked principally in Salzburg and Vienna, was greatly influenced by Haydn, had himself a large affect on Haydn's mature work, excelled even Haydn in virtually all genre of musical composition except the string quartet, and was seriously patronized by no less than Holy Roman Emperor Joseph II and Frederick William II of Prussia. Mozart was a genius of the first rank, a precocious talent of peerless brilliance whose music is characterized by an unexcelled grace, clarity, and sense of technical perfection, by a consummate synthesis of form and content, by an impeccable conjunction of German gravity and Italian radiance. In a very brief life, he wrote more than 600 published works, an astonishing number of which are widely included among the masterworks of Western music. Of these, the very most notable are his "Requiem" (1791) and the best of his:

- piano sonatas, violin sonatas, piano trios, sonatas for piano and violin, string quartets, string quintets, flute concerti, horn concerti, serenades, divertimentos, fantasies, and Masses;
- five violin concerti; most notably, numbers 3, 4, and 5, all 1775;
- 27 piano concerti; most notably, numbers 20 (1785), 21 (1785), 25 (1786), and 27 (1791);
- 41 symphonies; most notably, numbers 31 ("Paris," 1775), 35 ("Haffner," 1782), 36 ("Linz," 1783), 38 ("Prague," 1786), 39 (1788), 40 (1788), and 41 ("Jupiter," 1788); and
- several operas; most notably, "Idomeneo" (1781), "The Abduction from the Seraglio" (1782), "The Marriage of Figaro" (1786), "Don Giovanni" (1787), "Cosi Fan Tutte" (1790), "La Clemenza di Tito" (1791), and "The Magic Flute" (1791).

Beethoven stood astride the closing stages of eighteenth-century classicism/neo-classicism and the opening stages of nineteenth-century romanticism in the musical arts somewhat as David and Ingres had straddled the distinction in the visual arts. Also like David, he was greatly affected by the humanitarian tendencies of the French Revolution. Beethoven, German-born, worked mainly in Vienna and was briefly a student of Haydn there. Beethoven published less music than either Haydn or Mozart but wrote what he did many times over and with a meticulous care that approached both obsession and perfection. His early music, that to c. 1802, owed more to the classical tradition he inherited than to the original (romantic) tendencies he later and so brilliantly initiated. Throughout, Beethoven nonetheless brought a tumultuous, a romantic, sense of self-expression to the rational form, proportion, and unity of classicism. Of his masterworks, only the first several (six) of his sixteen string quartets, the first several (ten) of his 30 piano sonatas (most notably, the "Pathétique," 1799, and the "Moonlight," 1802), the first three of his five piano concerti (1796, 1795, and 1800 respectively), and the first two of his nine symphonies (1799 and 1802 respectively) are of this formative period.

The development of **balletic dance** was closely affiliated with European musical tendencies and its germinal stages were owed to early modern Europe. The Italian, Domenico da Piacenza (fl. in the mid-fifteenth-century), wrote the first manuals (c. 1440-1450) in which dance was characterized as a preservable art form. The sixteenth-century French court of Catherine de Medici (1519-1589; queen of Henri II and mother of Francis II, Charles IX, and Henri III) staged the first formal ballet in 1581. Louis XIV of France established the Royal Academy of Music and Dancing in Paris in 1661, significantly patronized the dance, and danced well and enthusiastically himself. It was, however, with the eighteenth-century formalization of European court dancing (which had been variously maturing from at least the fourteenth century) in France, Russia, Denmark, and Italy that contemporary modern traditions in balletic dance began to take recognizable shape. The Russian Imperial School of Ballet (St. Petersburg) was established in 1738, the Royal Danish Ballet (Copenhagen) was formed in 1748, and the two early modern giants of the medium, Jean-Georges Noverre (1727-1810) and Gaetan Vestris (1729-1808), also worked in the period of the Enlightenment. Noverre, the French, an associate of Vestris and Auguste Bournonville, first fashioned the modern sense of drama, action, and narrative in balletic dance, significantly refined dance technique itself, wrote approximately 150 ballet scores in the new style, and authored the definitive eighteenth-century text on the subject of the dance (Letters on the Dance, 1760). Vestris, the Italian-French, an associate of Noverre and Bournonville, was the dancing master to Louis XVI of France and the leading choreographer (with Noverre) of the late eighteenth century.

The literary arts

The course of early modern literature roughly corresponded to that of early modern architecture, sculpture, painting, and music. In the Renaissance, the literary arts were consequently moved by the organic, robust, and heroic form of humanism that was the characteristic intellectual mark of the period. The four-teenth-century heralds of modern literary humanism – mainly, Dante, Petrarch, Boccaccio, and Chaucer -- had established the groundwork on which distinguished Renaissance traditions developed in France, Netherlands, Italy, Portugal, Spain, and England. The leading figures of **French Renaissance literature** were:

- François Villon (c. 1431-c. 1464), a vagabond poet of irreverent, rebellious, and ribald, but nonetheless penitent, cast whose masterpieces are Little Testament (1456) and Testament (1461-1463);
- François Rabelais (c. 1490-1553), a Benedictine monk, physician, and person of very broad learning, significantly patronized by Francis I, and widely acknowledged as among the age's most persuasive advocates of mirthful joy and among the great comedic geniuses of modern literature, who is mainly known for his deeply satirical and thoroughly disrespectful prose masterpiece, Gargantua and Pantagruel (1532-1562);
- Pierre de Ronsard (c. 1524-1585), known mainly for his love sonnets (most notably, Sonnets pour Hélène, 1578); and
- Michel de Montaigne (1533-1592), the master of the early modern essay, serendipitous in style, tolerant and liberal of view, who is mainly known for his three books of Essays (c. 1571-1580, c. 1580, and c. 1588) in which he discusses a broad diversity of subjects having principally to do with the inconstant, but nonetheless edifying, character of nature and humanity.

The principal figure in **Dutch Renaissance literature** (the principal Dutch contributor to the literary development of early modern humanism) was Desiderius Erasmus (c. 1466-1536), a Catholic priest of vast learning, keen style, and engaging humor, of tolerant, pious, and moderate inclination, and an intimate friend of Sir Thomas More. Erasmus satirically reproved the chief institutions, persons, customs, and beliefs of his time; most notably in The Praise of Folly (1509) and The Education of a Christian Prince (1515). In these remarkable books, Erasmus declares folly necessary to human happiness, proposes the purification of corrupt religion through rigorous and impartial scholarship and through authentic action, and argues that individual persons find their principal capacity for fulfillment in the context of their species, not elsewhere.

The main figure in **Italian Renaissance literature** was Baldassare Castiglione (1478-1529). Castiglione was among the most accomplished knights of his age, was a confidant of many leading European men and women of his time (including Ludovico Sforza, Henry VII of England, Louis XII of France, Pope Leo X, and Pope Clement VII), and was the author of one of the most influential manuscripts of the Renaissance, Il Cortegiano/The Book of the Courtier (1528). In the Book, Castiglione fashions the character of the ideal man and woman of the court, the refined ideal of aristocratic etiquette and social grace, the universal ideal of intellectual and physical development.

The foremost figure in **Portuguese Renaissance literature** and the foremost figure in the entire record of Portuguese letters was Luis de Camoes (c. 1524-1580), whose varied and troubled, but adventurous, life and whose elegance of style conspired to create one of the great epic poems of modern civilization, The Lusiads (1572). The poem is an homage to the heroic voyages of discovery and conquest (most particularly those of Vasco da Gama) which marked the Portuguese national character in the late fifteenth and early sixteenth centuries.

The leading figure in **Spanish Renaissance literature** was Miguel de Cervantes (1547-1616) who, like Camoes, lived a turbulent and perilous life. He was partially disabled at the Battle of Lepanto, was enslaved by pirates, and was several times jailed for financial irregularities. In his masterpiece, Don Quixote de la Mancha (1605, 1615), which was the first modern novel and among the greatest of the genre, Cervantes frames the protagonist, Don Quixote, as a vividly imaginative and idealistic knight-adventurer who irrepressibly upbraids a mad world, who heroically undoes injustice and defends the oppressed, who enlists the assistance of a good-natured peasant squire, Sancho Panza (the paradigm of unrefined resignation in the face of horror and evil), and who invents a love-interest in the charming peasant girl, Dulcinea (the paradigm of unrefined beauty). All ends in predictable defeat for the Don who is unable to survive the unprincipled world in which he has lived.

The **Elizabethan literary Renaissance** of the late sixteenth and early seventeenth centuries formed among the most brilliant chapters in English literary history, perhaps among the most memorable chapters in the entire history of the literary arts. Its principal exponents were:

- Edmund Spenser (c. 1552-1599), who is mainly acclaimed for his classically inspired poetry of heroic moment and musical style; most notably, the pastoral allegory, "The Shepheardes Calendar" (1579), the love sonnets, "Amoretti" (1595), the wedding poems, "Epithalamion" (1595) and "Prothalamion" (1596), and the epic masterpiece, "The Faerie Queene" (1589-1596), a chivalric romance venerating high adventure, moral virtue, and gentle discipline;
- Christopher Marlowe (1564-1593), whose fame rests principally: on his long love poem, "Hero and Leander" (1598), in which Leander swims the Hellespont (part of the strait separating European and Asian Turkey), eventually drowning with his love, Hero; and on his utterly exceptional tragedic dramas in which men of commanding personality are gradually destroyed by their own blood-soaked passions and ambitions (most notably, Tamburlaine the Great, c. 1587; Doctor Faustus, c. 1588; The Jew of Malta, 1589; and Edward II, c. 1592);
- William Shakespeare (1564-1616), arguably the greatest of English writers, part-owner of the fabled Globe Theater (London) from 1599, patronized in a sense by James I, author of the tragic love poems, "Venus and Adonis" (1593) and "The Rape of Lucrece" (1594), and author of the more than 150 celebrated Sonnets (1590s), which largely concern the redeeming graces of love and art as against the unsettling transformations of life; most widely acclaimed, however, for his more than thirty historical, tragedic, and comedic plays of masterful attribute which tend to raise, but leave nonetheless unresolved, the boundless complexities of human life, mainly in respect to the relation of good and evil, order and chaos; the most notable of Shakespeare's peerless dramas are: Henry VI (c. 1590), Richard III (c. 1592), The Taming of the Shrew (c. 1593), Romeo and Juliet (c. 1594), Richard II (c. 1595), A Midsummer Night's Dream (c. 1595), The Merchant of Venice (c. 1596), Much Ado About Nothing (c. 1598), Henry V (c. 1598), Julius Caesar (c. 1599), As You Like It (c. 1599), Twelfth Night (c. 1599), Hamlet (c. 1600), Troilus and Cressida (c. 1601), Measure for Measure (c. 1604), Othello (c. 1604), King Lear (c. 1605), Macbeth (c. 1605), Antony and Cleopatra (c. 1606), and The Tempest (c. 1611);
- John Donne (1572-1631), an Anglican priest and metaphysical poet, who attempted to overcome the disillusions of human experience by reconciling the rival claims of passion and reason, of religion and science; most notably, in his romantic poetry, Songs and Sonnets (1601-1617), and in his religious poetry, Devotions (1624); and
- Ben Jonson (1572-1637), widely patronized by James I, who is mainly known for his moralistic and bitingly satirical poetry (most notably, Epigrams and The Forrest, both 1616) and for his comedic drama (most notably, Every Man in His Humour, 1598; Volpone, 1606; The Alchemist, 1610; and Bartholomew Fair, 1614).

Although holding onto the fundamentally humanistic sentiments of the Renaissance, seventeenth-century European literature, not unlike analogous tendencies in the visual and musical arts, inclined to a more scientific sense of precision and a more realistic sense of psychological experience than Renaissance literature had. The most remarkable literary achievements of the seventeenth century occurred in English poetry and in French drama. The towering figure of **seventeenth-century English poetry** was John Milton (1608-1674), an official in Cromwell's government and an ardent defender of Puritanism. Milton wrote among the finest sonnets in the English language, (23) Sonnets (done throughout his adult life); arguably the finest pastoral poetry in the English language, "Lycidas" (1638); the most stirring defense of intellectual and press freedoms in any language, Areopagitica (1644); and, after suffering blindness, the greatest epic poem in the English language, Paradise Lost (1667), as well as its sequel, Paradise Regained (1671), and a brilliant poetic tragedy, Samson Agonistes (1671). Also worthily mentioned in respect to the English literary circumstance of this time is the Diary (1660-1669) of Samuel Pepys (1632-1703) which is among the most compelling personal narratives in the English language.

The leading figures in **seventeenth-century French drama** were Pierre Corneille (1606-1684), Jean Baptiste Poquelin Molière (1622-1673), and Jean Racine (1639-1699). Corneille and Racine, not unlike Poussin in the visual arts, were highly significant harbingers of eighteenth-century neo-classicism and they were also the most accomplished tragic dramatists in the long and distinguished tradition of French literature. Molière was the French master of comedic drama. Corneille beatified the subordination of passion to duty and the willful striving for perfection; most notably in his acknowledged masterpiece, Le Cid (1637).

Molière, who was significantly patronized by Louis XIV, wrote many incisive satires, most of which derided a flaw of character or a form of excess by lampooning a person who embodied such flaws or who practiced such forms. His most memorable work took aim at religious hypocrisy, Tartuffe (1664); obsessive honesty, The Misanthrope (1666); parsimony, The Miser (1668); and medical quackery, The Imaginary Invalid (1673). And Racine, who was also significantly patronized by Louis XIV, penetratingly explored the character of violent treachery; most notably, in Andromaque (1667), Brittanicus (1669), Bérénice (1670), and Phèdre (1677).

Eighteenth-century European literature was unsurprisingly oriented to the cosmopolitan, reformist, naturalistic, individualistic, and democratic inclinations of the Enlightenment. It tended to a clean, precise, and uncontrived, but nonetheless flexible, sense of reasoned (classical) order and it was dominated by English, German, and French writers. The most memorable giants of the **English literary Enlightenment** were:

- John Dryden (1631-1700), best remembered for his artful poetry (most notably, "Annus Mirabilis," 1667, and "Alexander's Feast," 1697), original criticism (most notably, Essay on Dramatic Poesy, 1668), penetrating drama (most notably, All for Love, 1677), and poetic satire (most notably, "Absalom and Architophel," 1681-1682);
- Daniel Defoe (c. 1659-1731), who wrote the first authentic English novels (most notably, The Life and Strange Surprising Adventures of Robinson Crusoe, 1719; Moll Flanders, 1722; and A Journal of the Plague Year, 1722);
- Jonathan Swift (1667-1745), a master of social satire, mainly known for his merciless attacks on human folly, ignorance, and predacity (most notably, The Battle of the Books, 1704; Gulliver's Travels, 1726; and Modest Proposal, 1729);
- Joseph Addison (1672-1719), among the leading essayists in the history of English literature, nonetheless mainly known for his epic poem commemorating a prominent English military victory, "The Campaign" (1704);
- Richard Steele (1672-1729), also among the leading essayists in the history of English literature, nonetheless too best known for a comedic play that swipes satirically at the instrumental family, The Conscious Lovers (1722);
- Alexander Pope (1688-1744), whose poetic masterpieces concern literary criticism ("Essay on Criticism," 1711, and "The Dunciad," 1728-1743), satirical distaste for the fashionable life ("The Rape of the Lock," 1714), melancholic forms of love ("Eloise to Abelard," 1717), and humanity's relation to itself, the universe, society, and happiness ("Essay on Man," 1734);
- Henry Fielding (1707-1754), mainly known for his magnificent social novels in which innocent poor people are routinely victimized by sociopathic persons of influence and by uncaring institutions, but in which, after much travail, the simple virtues of goodness and charity triumph (most notably, Joseph Andrews, 1742; Jonathan Wild, 1743; Tom Jones, 1749; and Amelia, 1751);
- Samuel Johnson (1709-1784), the most influential and talented literary savant and critic of his time whose conversational acumen may have outdone even his very considerable scholarly talents; mainly known for his definitive Dictionary of the English Language (1755), Shakespeare (1765), and The Lives of the English Poets (1779-1781), as well as for his philosophical romance concerning the vain search for human happiness, The History of Rasselas, Prince of Abyssinia (1759);
- James Boswell (1740-1795), whose masterpiece, The Life of Samuel Johnson (1791), ranks with the most vivid and accomplished biographies in the whole of modern literature; and
- three dramatists who wrote among the most memorable social satires of comedic moment in the entire record of English literature:
  - John Gay (1685-1732), the English writer and close associate of Alexander Pope, mainly remembered for his "The Beggar's Opera" (1727) and "Polly" (1729);
  - Oliver Goldsmith (1728-1774), the Irish-English writer and close associate of Samuel Johnson, mainly remembered for his "The Good-natur'd Man" (1768) and "She Stoops to Conquer" (1773); and
  - Richard Brinsley Sheridan (1751-1816), the Irish-English writer, politician, and orator extraordinaire, mainly remembered for his "The Rivals" (1775) and "The School for Scandal" (1777).

The **German literary Enlightenment** was dominated by Gotthold Ephraim Lessing (1729-1781), Johann Wolfgang von Goethe (1749-1832), and Johann Friedrich Schiller (1759-1805). Lessing's best works are his dramas of toleration and conciliation: Minna von Barnhelm (1767), in romantic terms, and Nathan the Wise

(1779), in religious contexts. Goethe was among the most remarkable literary talents of any place or time. Not unlike David and Ingres in the visual arts and Beethoven in the musical arts, Goethe straddled the basic inclinations of the eighteenth and nineteenth centuries. He nonetheless belonged mainly to the classical/neo-classical characteristics of the Enlightenment. He is principally remembered for the love novel, The Sorrows of Werther (1774); the tragedic dramas, Iphigenie auf Tauris (1787), Egmont (1788), and Faust (1808-1831); the novel of education, The Apprenticeship of Wilhelm Meister (1796); the epic poem, "Hermann und Dorothea" (1797); and his engaging autobiography, Poetry and Truth (1811-1833). The classical heroism of Goethe had an enormous influence on Schiller, who wrote at least three great historical plays (Wallenstein, 1799; Mary Stuart, 1800; and William Tell [the famed Swiss archer], 1804) and many stunning poetic ballads (such as "Ode to Joy," 1785).

The basic spirit of political revolution characteristic of late-eighteenth-century European life was nowhere more vividly expressed than in the comedic dramas of the principal figure of the **French literary Enlightenment**, Pierre Augustin Caron de Beaumarchais (1732-1799). Chiefly in The Barber of Seville (1775) and The Marriage of Figaro (1784), Beaumarchais trenchantly satirizes the corrupting privilege and low character of the aristocracy and acclaims lower-class virtues and sinews.

The several most significant **literary achievements outside of Europe** in the early modern period occurred in India, Japan, China, and the United States of America. In India, the most notable triumph was the stunning sixteenth-century autobiography of Babar, the founder of the Mogul Empire, Memoirs. In Japan, the most important achievements were the seventeenth-century development of kabuki (the leading form of Oriental opera) and the eighteenth-century novels of Chikamatsu Monzaemon (1653-1725), most memorably the tragedic account of the common person's struggles in respect to love and duty, Love Suicides at Amijima. In China, the most remarkable achievement was the eighteenth-century tragic love intrigue of novelist, Tso Hsueh-chin (1719-1764), Hung Lou Meng, arguably the most momentous (and the most intricate) of polished Chinese novels. And in the United States of America, the most memorable feats were the eighteenth-century, common-sense, worldly, and optimistic musings of Benjamin Franklin (most notably, Poor Richard's Almanack, 1733-1758, and Autobiography, 1757).

Philosophy

The philosophical discourse of early modern civilization, not unlike the visual, musical, and literary arts of the time, made a telling response to the philosophical disputations of the Middle Ages. The liberation of philosophy from theology predictably deepened throughout the period; most notably, in terms of a renewed interest in free and independent inquiry, an increasing emphasis on secular and distinctly human affairs, an advancing attention to the significance of science and individuality, and a regained confidence in the virtues of reason. The period's debt to classical antiquity (as well as to medieval religiosity) in all of these respects cannot be easily overstated. Plato and Aristotle (as well as Augustine and Aquinas) in particular continued to exert enormous influence throughout the entire development of early modern thought.

Renaissance philosophy nonetheless yet had one foot in the medieval world and the other in the modern. There was therefore no strict and explicit philosophical equivalent of the organic richness that so characterized Renaissance painting, sculpture, architecture, and music (as well as, to a lesser extent, Renaissance literature). The accomplished philosophical thought of the fifteenth and sixteenth centuries was grounded both in the dissolution of (medieval) scholasticism, largely by way of the skeptical assertions of Duns Scotus and Occam as has been said, and in the rise of the new (the modern) humanism of the pro-to-Renaissance. The two leading figures of **fifteenth-century philosophy** were the idealistic-tending German philosopher-cleric, Nicholas of Cusa, and the idealistic-tending Florentine philosopher-cleric, Marsilio Ficino; both aptly conjoined the orientations of late medieval and early modern thought. Nicholas, for all of his orthodoxy and his advocacy of pantheistic mysticism (that tended to depreciate the roll of reason in theological and human affairs), nonetheless qualified the utter transcendence of God and held that the universe is infinite and without a center. Ficino, who was patronized significantly by Cosimo de' Medici, who translated and commented on all of Plato's dialogues and on the thought of all major neo-Platonists, who was himself a devoted neo-Platonist, and who wrote his main philosophic work, Theologica Platonica de Immortalitate Animarum, in 1469-1474, embraced the hierarchy of orthodox cosmology, the immortality of the soul, and the scholastic relation of philosophy and theology. He nonetheless framed his view of religion in active, human, and aesthetic terms and he conceived of God as an expression of beauty.

The two most significant figures of **early sixteenth-century phliosophy** were principally concerned with social and political thought. Niccolo Machiavelli (1469-1527), a Florentine statesman and political philosopher, demonstrated the unflattering social conclusion to which the depraved character/behavior of human beings (and the amoral character/behavior of their institutions) tends. In The Prince (1513) and in the Discourses (1513), writing from the perspective of the brutal Italian civil wars of the fifteenth and sixteenth centuries and writing as well from the wholly practical perspective (from the wholly practical necessity) of acquiring, maintaining, and extending political power (neither on the basis of universal moral principles nor on the basis of the abstract rights of humanity), Machiavelli fashioned a republican form of centralized, secular government in which political authority is exercised according to expedient (not ideal) standards. Such a government was to gain the respect of its subjects by considering their interests, by assuring the internal and external security of the state, and by pledging the benefits of trade. This was also, by Machiavelli's view, the best way to achieve Italy's unification and its liberation. The political vision of Machiavelli likewise contains the germinal basis of what would become the modern nation-state and it too demonstrates the vast divide between the political imperatives of the Renaissance and the humanist ideals of its intellectual life. Sir Thomas More (1478-1535), the English statesman, author, and friend of Erasmus, was of a significantly different mind than Machiavelli. In Utopia (1516) most notably, he developed the notion of an ideal state based on reason and he asserted that the misfortunes of states are grounded in war, the idle rich, and private property. Although once in the service of Henry VIII, More was imprisoned and executed (beheaded) by order of Henry for refusing to assent to the "Act of Supremacy," a declaration by which the King replaced the Pope as the head of the Church in England.

The two most significant figures of **late sixteenth-century philosophy**, conversely, were principally concerned with matters of still broader cosmological, ontological, and theological dimension. Both were Italian-Dominican scholars and both were horribly persecuted; they were also, astonishingly enough, of quite different philosophical orientation. Giordano Bruno (1548-1600) defended a notion of relative truth according to which the world is a function of the many perspectives from which it is apprehended. His opposition to the doctrine of absolute truth, his idealistic-tending claim that God is the rationally unobtainable unity of all things (but is nonetheless immanent and active), and his view of the universe as infinite, as without a center, and as comprised of irreducible elements in uninterrupted motion, all conspired to bring charges of heresy down on him. He was arrested in 1591, tried before the papal Inquisition, and burned at the stake in 1600. On the basis of his philosophical masterpiece, On the Infinite Universe and Worlds (1584), his defense of Copernicus, and his martyrdom, Bruno is widely regarded as among the poetic harbingers of modern science, art, and philosophy and among the great early modern advocates of free inquiry. Tommaso Campanella (1568-1639) developed a naturalistic-tending system (most notably in Philosophia Sensibus Demonstrata, 1591, and Civitas Solis, 1623) which variously held that nature is a revelation of God, that human knowledge is based fundamentally on sensation, and that the ideal form of social and political organization is grounded in shared, in communal, knowledge. Campanella was imprisoned in Spain and Italy from 1599 to 1629 on charges of heresy and conspiracy before escaping to France where he was honored by Cardinal Richelieu and Louis XIII.

Seventeenth-century philosophy took on the characteristic disputations of early modern science even more emphatically than Renaissance philosophy had. The genius of early modern science and its philosophical groundwork discredited some of the most cherished ancient and medieval beliefs, propelled modern thought significantly beyond the strict authority of the ancient and medieval past, and generally demanded that deductive principles (previously taken to govern the world) consult the evidence of scientific experimentation. The central debate of seventeenth-century philosophy, a debate that continued throughout the eighteenth century as well, concerned the origin and the basic character of knowledge. The Renaissance philosophers who dealt seriously and instructively with this issue – mainly, Nicholas, Ficino, Bruno, and Campanella – gave largely theological explanations of it. In the seventeenth century, two main lines of contending argument concerning this issue emerged, the empiricist and the rationalist lines. Both held that nothing can be known independently of experience but they differed widely over the origin of knowledge and its model (its basic character). By the empiricist view, all knowledge originates in sense-perceptions (visual, auditory, olfactory, gustatory, and tactile perceptions) and takes the form of sensation; empiricism argues inductively, from particular instances to universal law. According to the rationalist view, all knowledge originates in concepts and takes the form of reason; rationalism argues deductively from universal law to particular instances. The foremost empiricists were British, gave realistic-tending and thus dualistic/pluralistic-tending accounts of the world, were the intellectual descendants of ancient atomism and medieval nominalism, and had, not unlike Machiavelli, More, and Campanella, an especially fervent interest in social and political philosophy. The foremost rationalists were Continental Europeans (mainly French, German, and Dutch), gave idealistic-tending and thus dualistic-tending accounts of the world, were the intellectual descendants of Plato, Aristotle, and the medieval "realists," and had, not unlike Nicholas, Ficino, and Bruno, an especially fervent interest in metaphysical issues.

The first major advocate of modern **empiricism** and the first modern scientific philosopher (the first to give searching philosophical expression to the new scientific age) was the extraordinary English statesman (mainly under James I) and thinker, Francis Bacon (1561-1626). The principal task of Bacon's philosophy — worked out most notably in Essays (1597-1625), The Advancement of Learning (1605), Novum Organum (1620), and New Atlantis (1624) — was to develop a formal system of inductive logic free of religious dogmatism and extrapolated from the operations of experimental observation, a system that was to replace Aristotle's deductive logic as the ideal of knowledge, morality, and society. This new method, new instrument, or new organ was to achieve a reconstruction of the whole of human knowledge, morality, and society in accord with the experimental inclinations of scientific inquiry. It was to explain the world (except the divine revelations of heavenly mystery known only by faith) as a mosaic of material causes and effects. Bacon characterized philosophy itself in scientific terms and considered it the highest form of knowledge, for it serves, by force of reason, to combine all experimental insights, to demonstrate the broadest human significance of such insights, and to establish the utopian political and educational framework by which such insights may contribute to the common good.

The second major figure in the development of early modern empiricism, the English philosopher, Thomas Hobbes (1588-1679), emphasized (like Bacon) the empirical source of knowledge, the notion of the world as a mosaic of material causes and effects, the practical utility of science and philosophy, and the radical distinction between the reason and experience of science and philosophy and the faith relation of theology and religion. Unlike Bacon, however, Hobbes also accounted for the highly significant role of deduction (as well as induction) in scientific demonstration. In Human Nature (1640) most notably, Hobbes argued that the mind is constituted as a mosaic of material appearances, a mosaic of appearances of material causes and effects, an epiphenomenon of the body. Hobbes' most significant and enduring contribution to the history of early modern philosophy, however, is his inventive social and political thought. In this aspect of his philosophy, developed most notably in Elements of Law (1640) and Leviathan (1651), Hobbes argued that it is right and reasonable for human beings to do whatever they must to preserve themselves, to do whatever they must to evade violent death. In a state of nature, a state deprived of socio-political custom and law, human beings are led, by their inherently depraved character and by the natural scarcity of commodities requisite to survival, to a perpetual conflict of each against each of the others. A state of nature always tends to a state of war for the means of self-preservation are of necessity perpetually contested. In such a state, there is no peace, security, right, wrong, justice, or property and one's preservation is not so much assured as it is the object of endless assault; each person must attempt to possess all power in order to assure its not being used against her/him, thereby nullifying the preservation most desired. Accordingly, there is the greatest need for an agent (in Hobbes' view, a sovereign) to rescue human society from self-annihilation. The natural "right" to do harm to others must be relinquished in order to obtain security and all that may be entailed by security; one must be content with only so much liberty as one is prepared to allow others. Human beings, consequently, must voluntarily agree to enter a social contract, agree to be bound by duty to a commonwealth and its sovereign, even though it is contrary to their fundamentally individualistic and adversarial character to do so. They must do this in order to save themselves from themselves, in order to save themselves from the perpetual state of war to which they naturally incline. This contract (this commonwealth) must be formed in such a way as to compel all persons equally to honor their avowed obligations to it. For Hobbes, this entails a commonwealth in which absolute power is invested in one person or in an assembly of persons by those constrained to such power (not by divine authority). This person or assembly is Hobbes' "Leviathan," the agent in which the supreme power of the sovereign is invested and in which the wills of all become one. The sovereign, in turn, represents the subjects who have granted it authority and it holds authority only so long as it assures peace, security, right conduct, justice, and property.

Although hardly of empiricist bent (nor of British heritage either for that matter), an important seventeenth-century corollary to the "natural law" and "social contract" theories of Hobbes (among others) was proffered by the Dutch jurist and statesman, Hugo Grotius (1583-1645). Grotius, the so-termed father of international law, argued, most notably in Concerning the Law of War and Peace (1625), that nations are based on free contracts made by humans to provide for their security, that the natural law prescribes rules of conduct for nations as well as for individuals, that nations are therefore obliged to assure international order and peace, that nations are morally justified in making war only for defensive purposes, and that nations which make (even justifiable) war are morally obliged to conduct it in "humane" ways.

The third, last, and most influential major British advocate of seventeenth-century empiricism was John Locke (1632-1704), a man of very wide learning and very high genius. Both of Locke's main philosophic concerns (education aside), the origin and nature of knowledge (developed most notably in Essay Concerning Human Understanding, 1689) and the character of ideal government (developed most notably in Two Treatises on Government, 1690), entailed critical replies to Hobbes. His examination of human knowledge was inspired by the alleged conflict in Hobbes' variously rationalistic (Hobbes considered reason the proper model for knowledge) and empiricistic (Hobbes considered sense-perception the source of knowledge) leanings on the subject as well as on Descartes' rationalism. Locke argued that the scope of human knowledge is both more problematically determined and more limited than the rationalists had claimed. He also held, against the rationalists, that the natural sciences provide a more suitable model for knowledge than does mathematics. According to this view, the (natural) sciences and philosophy need to be liberated from the alienation of mathematics by demonstrating the correspondence of ideas to observable data. In Locke's program is found one of the earliest and one of the most telling challenges to rationalism.

From the self-evident claim that we are conscious of having ideas produced by things that are distinct from ideas and the self-evident notion that these ideas correspond to the things producing them, Locke argues that these things and these ideas are occupants of qualitatively independent worlds. He then sets out to demonstrate how such ideas come into the mind. The two possibilities, according to Locke, are that ideas come into the mind either by experience or they are innate. They cannot be innate, however, because we are all unable to discern any ideas (let alone any common ideas) that we bring into the world with us and the concept of unconscious ideas is barren for it fails to show what is native to the mind and what is not. All knowledge, therefore, must come from experience; all knowledge, by Locke's view, is empirical. The mind, accordingly, is an empty closet, an unmarked tablet ("tabula rasa"), on which sensory experience impresses itself. The mind, therefore, thinks only in the sense in which it abstracts, compares, remembers, generalizes, combines, and repeats ideas; it does neither bring these ideas into the world with it (these ideas are not its ideas) nor does it subsequently generate them. There are, on this account, no ideas which haven't an empirical source, even those of substance, motion, causality, space, time, and existence. Bodies cause us to have the ideas that we do but our consciousness is only of sensations and what the mind variously does with them. Locke nonetheless held to the self-evident (the rationalistic) existence of God, self, minds, and bodies and to the interactionist view of the relation of minds and bodies which does no better than stipulating this relation as an indemonstrable truth. Even at this, he argued, in a skeptical way characteristic of modern scientific inquiry, that all knowledge is probable, that it is not certain in the mathematical sense claimed by seventeenth-century rationalism.

As there are no innate metaphysical or epistemic truths for Locke, neither are there any such moral or socio-political verities. Such verities are also empirically acquired; in their case, they are rooted in inherently individual pleasure and pain. That which is likely to produce self-interested pleasure is thought good; that which is likely to effect self-interested pain is thought evil. Social and political life is also grounded in the principle of self-interested pleasure according to Locke. Unlike Hobbes, Locke argued that, although bound by natural law, human beings are otherwise free, good, and equal in a state of nature; every person naturally seeks the preservation of self and others in peace, tolerance, and goodwill. What compels humanity to enter a socio-political order (a social contract) is not, therefore, the impulse to preserve itself against the natural inclination of others to the contrary, as Hobbes had supposed, but rather a sense of convenience, disposition, and security against those aberrant others unattuned to natural law. The formal end of government, by Locke's view, is to assure the common good by extending the natural state of individualism, by preserving the personal safety, liberty, and property of the governed, and by securing the social and political order itself. The sovereign, or executive, who is explicitly responsible for achieving the formal end of government, is installed by the people to protect their natural liberties. Because, however, the sovereign may, and often does, act contrary to this trust, strong provisions must be enacted for her/his deposition. The otherwise excessive powers of the sovereign must also be limited by independent legislative agencies. Locke, unlike Hobbes, thought absolute monarchy inconsistent with civil liberty.

Locke's influence on modern thought and modern life has been enormous. His systematic and comprehensive theory of knowledge picked up on and extended the earlier forms of empiricist inclination in Bacon and Hobbes; it launched the most compelling phase of modern British empiricism soon to be taken over by Berkeley and Hume in the eighteenth century and later taken over by Bentham and Mill in the nineteenth century; it was to have a significant hand in inciting Kant also in the eighteenth century; and it inspired much of the empirical psychology of the eighteenth and nineteenth centuries. His ethical and socio-political philosophy had a profound affect on those who framed the ideological basis of the American and

French Revolutions (Rousseau most notably) in the eighteenth century. At bottom, Locke was among the most conspicuous and the most discerning heralds of the modern European Enlightenment.

Rationalism was cast of a quite different mold as has been said. Its earliest of three major early modern exponents was the French-Catholic mathematician (founder of analytic geometry) and philosopher, René Descartes (1596-1650), who was patronized by no less than Queen Christina of Sweden and who wrote what are among the formative texts of early modern philosophy (most notably, Discourse on Method, 1637; Meditations on First Philosophy, 1641; and Principles of Philosophy, 1644). Descartes asserted mathematics the model of all knowledge and hoped to attain mathematical certainty even in characteristically philosophic matters. The ardent skepticism of his thought both distinguished it from the scholastic and Renaissance traditions and established it as a basis of early modern science. Descartes argued that knowledge must be grounded in and constructed on an indubitable foundation, a foundation that cannot be plausibly doubted, a foundation that is an altogether certain, self-contained, and formal system of thought. This is Descartes' celebrated "methodological skepticism" which is somewhat reminiscent of Augustine's strategic orientation. By the principle of systematic doubt, which accepts as true only that which there is no occasion nor reason to doubt (namely, self-evident propositions and what follows inexorably from such propositions), Descartes first called the testimony of the senses (which have on occasion deceived us) into serious question; then the existence of others, the existence of the external world, and even the truths of mathematics were challenged. This strategy was pursued until he came on a notion that by its nature could not be plausibly doubted. Much as for Augustine, this notion is entailed by the character of doubt itself. Descartes argued that doubting itself necessarily entails thinking, which, in turn, entails being. The act of doubting thus gives rise to the "cogito ergo sum" (I think, therefore I am). It is from the certitude of the "cogito" that Descartes draws other so-termed clear and distinct ideas; most notably, the existence of an external world (to which our ideas correspond and by which they are awakened), the existence of human beings as extended (material, bodily) and unextended (immaterial, minded) substance, the veracity of well-considered sense-perceptions, and the existence of a benevolent God (by which humanity achieves a valid knowledge of the world).

Descartes' radically dualistic concept of reality and humanity resembled Plato's and Augustine's. It held that humanity is comprised of both intellectual substance, mind ("res cogitans"), and material substance, body ("res extensans"). By this view, the body, which is extended and unthinking, is merely some thing that humanity possesses; the mind, conversely, which is unextended and thinking, is what humanity essentially is, what makes humanity peculiarly human. The primary status of the mind in human nature and human activity then predictably forms the basis of Descartes' moral imperative, the search for the mind's freedom from material influences. The extreme amplitude of his mind-body dualism, however, left him with an untenable linking principle, the infamous "pineal gland hypothesis," by which the mind and the body mysteriously interact in the pineal gland. This amplitude likewise left him with the daunting task of reconciling the determined and passive order of nature (the fair domain of science, effectively thought primary by Bacon, Hobbes, and Locke) and the free and active order of divinity (the fair domain of theology, effectively thought primary by Nicholas, Ficino, Bruno, and Campanella). The reconciliation of nature, humanity, and divinity offered by Descartes is hauntingly remindful of Duns Scotus' "doctrine of twofold truth." In it, science and theology operate in qualitatively distinct domains; each influences the other, if at all, only by spurious means; and humanity (the fair domain of philosophy), which has one foot in the determined order of nature and the other in the free order of divinity, is caught between, at once both free and determined as well as neither free nor determined. In short, the philosophic reconciliation of science and religion, nature and divinity, reason and faith, what is unchangeable (and so determined and enduring) and what is open to choice (and so free and ephemeral), so earnestly sought by Descartes, ends in fragmentary estrangement.

In the end, Descartes was convinced that he had achieved the promised reconstruction of human knowledge. Although few features of his system disturbed anything in the established world view of orthodox Christianity, the system nonetheless, according to Descartes' himself, elevated the terms of this view to knowledge. He thought that he had discovered, by rational means, the a priori ideas (the necessary presuppositions of experience and their consequences) held innately in the mind which explain the whole of things. Not everyone, not even everyone of rationalistic persuasion, agreed. It was the radically dualistic aspects of Descartes' philosophy – aspects that precluded the development of a plausible linking principle between the material bodies of science and the immaterial minds of theology – that variously inspired and provoked the richest responses over the following several centuries. So influential was his thought that much of what remained of early modern philosophy was devoted to commentaries on (and critical replies to) it. The learned voices opposing his dualism in particular were numerous and telling. Arnold Geulincx (1624-1669), the Flemish metaphysician, argued that Descartes' mind-body relation is better formulated either as a continuous, divine intervention or as a pre-established harmony. Blaise Pascal (1623-1662), the French mathematician, scientist, inventor, religious philosopher, and author of the celebrated reflections on universal moral and religious problems, Pensées (1670), defended Descartes' dualism but thought ultimate knowledge unobtainable. He likewise, in accord with Bruno, postulated the scientifically erudite notion of an infinite universe. And Nicolas Malebranche (1638-1715), the French theologian and philosopher, held that, although we are aware (by revelation), of a world of material things, we cannot know it as a world of extended things (it is a world of unknown constitution to us); we can know only ideas of bodies, not bodies themselves, only a world of ideas, an intelligible world in ideal space.

Among the most instructive and accomplished rationalistic critiques of Cartesianism was given by the renowned German-Protestant mathematician (co-founder of the differential and integral calculus), logician (founder of symbolic logic), statesman (most notably in the service of the House of Hanover), inventor, and philosophic essayist, Gottfried Wilhelm Leibniz (1646-1716). In his most exceptional philosophical work (Discourse on Metaphysics, 1686; New Essays on Human Understanding, 1704; Theodicy, 1710; and Monadology, 1714), Leibniz attempted to discover the true organon, or ideal language, of reason for the sciences and to reconcile modern science, modern philosophy, and Christian theology through this language. He regarded Descartes' methodological skepticism as incapable of yielding any knowledge whatever, arguing instead that a definitive system of thought necessarily rests on plausible assumptions, or first principles. Leibniz constructed his system on the principle of contradiction (which considers false all that may be contradicted), the principle of sufficient reason (which postulates that all which has come into existence has been caused and is thus explainable by rational precept), the "cogito" (effectively the existence of thought and selves), the existence of the external world, and the existence of God. For Leibniz, the universe is a harmonious whole governed by necessary and synoptic principles of a logical and mathematical sort. The world is so constituted that it can be explained by the application of these innate principles to our experience. This experience does not create these principles; it furnishes instead the occasion in which they are demonstrated. Leibniz's confidence in reason as the ultimate instrument of knowledge – as the means of discovering all that our finite perspectives allow – is virtually unqualified.

Leibniz was further convinced that, since bodies gain and lose motion, and since the continuity of nature is always preserved, there must be a ground of motion, something more fundamental than motion itself, which explains its (motion's) varying presence. Leibniz termed this something, "force," the inherent and unrelenting tendency of bodies to move. According to this view, all substances are expressions of "force;" "force," in turn, is comprised of units (variously termed, essential forms, formal atoms, or "monads"), which are themselves constituted as the union of souls (or active, unitary, and psychic substances) and matter (or passive, differentiated, and corporeal substances). An infinite number of "monads" formally make up the world and, though no one of them is extended (i.e., tangible), groups of them are extended (as in the case of a point's relation to a line). They are eternal (neither created nor, except by miracle, perishable) and so also immaterial, or unextended (i.e., intangible). Leibniz thus fashioned a dynamic and energetic, as distinct from a geometric and static, world view; he accounts for the enduring status of substance as well as for transformations of it (as well as for the motion in/of it). Although every "monad" is a self-contained microcosm of the entire universe, each also represents the universe in a unique way. "Monads" are alike in their broad character, different in respect to their tangible detail. And they arrange themselves in a hierarchy according to clarity. The lowest monads are dominated by obscurity and confusion; the highest, the "monad" of "monads," the perfect "monad," or God, is construed as purely clarified activity. Humanity is distinguished by its possession of a dominant "monad," which is capable of a priori (of necessary) knowledge. The animals share sense-perceptual, empirical, or a posteriori knowledge with humanity and with plants; and inorganic bodies are comprised of largely comatose "monads." Sense-perceptual impressions are distinguished from conceptual understandings in respect to their being made up of more obscure psychic "monads" than understandings; the continuity of sensation and understanding is thereby assured. Leibniz explains knowledge, morality, and history by claiming that every "monad," except God of course, evolves by inner necessity to a realization of itself. "Monads" are consequently free in the sense in which they are not externally determined; in Leibniz's terms, they have no windows. Each thereby contains within itself the terms of its own truth, goodness, past, present, and future and each inherently tends to a fulfillment of its own basic character thus defined.

Like Descartes (and the empiricists as well for that matter), Leibniz too was given to dualism. He conceived of the mind and body as independently existing substances, of the mind as the dominant entity in the relation, and of the body as the material expression of the mind. Leibniz's resolution of the implacable dualistic problem of the mind-body relation differed significantly from Descartes' interactionism, however. It more nearly resembled Geulincx's parallelism instead. Leibniz argued that these two substances (the mind and the body) appear to influence one another (to interact) but they do not. They act in a harmony pre-established by God and in accord with the principle of universal perfection inherent in God. Likewise following from this principle (and what it presupposes in respect to the fundamental character of God and the relation between God and the created world) is the view that our world attains the greatest perfection possible, that this is the best of all possible worlds, a view widely criticized by the politically astute philosophers of the eighteenth century who had every intention of improving the very imperfect national and international political orders of the time. The other leading "pre-Kantian," German philosophers, all of the eighteenth century, were deeply beholding to Leibniz. Christian Wolff (1679-1754) is mainly remembered for his attempted systematization of Leibniz's thought and for his attempted reconciliation of rationalism and empiricism. The other such philosophers were the most significant influences on the formative development of modern aesthetic theory: the philosopher, Alexander Gottlieb Baumgarten (1714-1762), and the dramatist, Gotthold Ephraim Lessing.

The remaining of the three leading Continental European rationalists of the seventeenth century was the brilliant and courageous Dutch-Jewish philosopher and professional lens grinder, Baruch (Benedict) de Spinoza (1632-1677). Mainly in his most remarkable manuscripts (Tractatus Theologico-Politicus, 1670; Ethics, 1677; Tractatus de Intellectus Emendatione, 1677; and An Essay on the Improvement of the Understanding, 1677), Spinoza, not unlike Descartes and Leibniz, attempted to unveil the true nature of the understanding through rational discourse (through clear and distinct thought), to obtain a universal knowledge of the world by appeal to reason. Unlike either Descartes or Leibniz, however, Spinoza's profound love of truth and his ascetic disposition led him to stake his happiness, his basis for living, on the successful completion of a mathematically precise, internally coherent system. For Spinoza, we can come to knowledge and to happiness only if we can come to an understanding of what is absolutely certain, only if we can come to an understanding of what is logically necessary. Based on the necessary consequences of a logical principle, which is fundamental and given, Spinoza spins out an elaborate and an ingenious determinism. As in Descartes and Leibniz, the rational system is taken to reflect the character of reality; experience provides the primitive data of this system. Spinoza argued that we possess an idea based on logically necessary precepts (the principle of non-contradiction most significantly) which, although otherwise indefensible, is nonetheless itself necessarily true. This idea is "substance," the conception and sustained existence of which requires nothing other than itself; it is the cause of and for itself, or "causa sui;" it is God (or Nature). From the notion of "substance," by Spinoza's account, all "else" (all equally certain ideas) is deduced, all "else" is derived, for there can be no "substance" outside of God; whatever is, is in God. God thereby entails existence and is infinite, independent, indivisible, free, and the immanent, active principle (the underlying structure) of the world. Thought and extension, thus, cannot be considered qualitatively distinct substances (utterly different sorts of things), as Descartes, Leibniz, Bacon, Hobbes, and Locke had taught; they must be two (among an infinite number of other) attributes, or aspects, of God. While independent in themselves, they are nonetheless processes of the same thing expressed in two different ways. Spinoza's philosophy is therefore pantheistic, organic (in a qualified sense), monistic, and humanistic (in a qualified sense); it is a remnant of Renaissance humanism and a herald of nineteenth-century romanticism.

The world is not, for Spinoza, the aggregate of finite things but God viewed through the attribute of extension. Individual minds and bodies are temporal modes of substance which correspond to one another; the order and connection of ideas are the same as the order and connection of objects. The idea of an object and the object are one in God, although we perceive the two as different attributes. A transformation of thought therefore entails a transformation of extension; the mind apprehends all bodily states and bodily occurrences inexorably entail corresponding minded events. The human body is conceived as the most complex of extant extensions and the human mind is construed as the idea of body. The mind and body are qualitatively inseparable. The mind is passive insofar as it is affected by bodies, but it is active insofar as it operates in accord with logical precept. Under the terms of this view, humanity is considered a temporal mode of substance possessing the attributes of thought and extension; humanity is knowledge of its body. Knowledge of self is thereby made dependent on, it is constituted by, the variety of ways in which the body may be influenced and this variety, in turn, is a function of the body's capacity for being influenced, a function of the body's complexity. Humanity is distinguished from other modes of substance by the greater complexity of its body and so by the quantitative superiority of its intelligence.

As for Leibniz, Spinoza held that our knowledge is defective only insofar as we claim contingent possibilities for it. By his view, all exists necessarily in this, the best and only possible world. Spinoza's ethical and socio-political thought is grounded in his epistemic and metaphysical allegiances. The highest good, accordingly, entails the rational necessity of knowing and loving God (or Nature). For only through such a knowledge and affection does/can one come to the necessary understandings which qualify as authentic knowledge and authentic happiness. Human beings governed fully by reason (fully by their own basic nature) are, therefore, inherently virtuous and (socially) trustworthy. Contra Hobbes in particular, such beings allow everything to function through their natural inclination to preserve and fulfill themselves, through their natural inclination to goodness; they desire nothing for themselves that they are not also prepared to desire for all persons.

Eighteenth-century philosophy, the accomplished philosophy of the modern European Enlightenment, took three main forms: 1) French, British, and American social and political philosophy (most notably, the thought of Rousseau), which emphasized the cosmopolitan, secular, reformist, individualistic, and democratic inclinations of the period and which was couched in naturalistic world views; 2) the continuing development of British empiricism (most notably, in the thought of Berkeley and Hume), which extended the seventeenth-century form of the doctrine in metaphysical and in scientific directions; and 3) the apotheosis of the age in the thought of Kant, which, at bottom, achieved the long-sought reconciliation of empiricism and rationalism, the contending doctrines that had dominated early modern philosophy. Although the earliest of the French Enlightenment figures, Pierre Bayle (1647-1706), was not primarily a social and political philosopher, his skeptical orientation, advocacy of religious toleration, and uncompromising belief in the virtues of free thought (all developed most significantly in the Historical and Critical Dictionary, 1695-1697) prepared the way for the great personalities of **French social and political philosophy** who followed:

- Charles-Louis de Montesquieu (1689-1755), whose Persian Letters (1721) gave a sharp critique of French absolutism, whose Spirit of the Laws (1748) argued that personal liberty is possible only in a moderate state such as a constitutional democracy in which each branch of government (the monarchial executive, the elected legislative, and the appointed judicial) is separated from each of the others and enacts checks and balances on each of the others, and whose vision of government, greatly affected by Locke, had a profound influence on the American and French Revolutions;
- François Marie Arouet de Voltaire (1694-1778), who was several-times imprisoned and banished for his outspoken criticism of established institutions (monarchial despotism in particular), who was patronized by Frederick the Great of Prussia, who argued fervently for the separation of church and state and for the establishment of a free, secular state, and who satirically assaulted the Church, the canons of intolerant faith that governed the Church, and the conservative optimism (which opposed significant change) advocated by the Church, all in his most celebrated works, The Age of Louis XIV (1751), Candide (1758), and Philosophical Dictionary (1764);
- Denis Diderot (1713-1784), who was devoted mainly to Bacon's view of science, who was patronized by Catherine the Great of Russia, who did pioneering work in art criticism, and who was the principal editor of the Encyclopédie (1751-1777), an enormously influential manuscript that included "all" extant knowledge (principally concerning the sciences and practical arts) interpreted in an "enlightened" spirit; and
- Jean-Jacques Rousseau (1712-1778).

The tendency to independent and free inquiry, that had increasingly marked Renaissance and seventeenth-century culture, spilled significantly into eighteenth-century thought and life where it also acquired a burgeoning sense of optimism. This sense embodied itself in the view that human consciousness (mainly reason) is capable of rendering human life intelligible and capable of resolving even the most intractable of human problems. Unsurprisingly, the sciences, the arts, and philosophy were increasingly marshaled to a consideration of social, political, and educational issues. These characteristically Enlightenment inclinations were nowhere more fully and persuasively developed than in the thought of the French reformers, most notably Rousseau. Rousseau, an associate of Diderot and Hume, held to a naturalistic-tending form of humanism -- recorded most skillfully in Discourse on the Origin of Inequality (1755), Émile (1762), Social Contract (1762), and Confessions (1781) -- reminiscent of analogous tendencies in the sciences and in the visual, musical, and literary arts. According to this view, humanity is considered an organic participant in the natural order, humanity is thereby a function of natural law, and humanity is thus construed as possessing the inherent rights of nature, the rights of equality, fraternity, liberty, simplicity, and temperance. The basic thesis of Rousseau's philosophy entailed the notion that nature and humanity (and humanity in a state of nature) are fundamentally good and the right basis of just society. Contrary to such as Hobbes, more nearly in accord with Locke, Rousseau argued that nature tends toward democracy, tends toward the free expression of will, the liberation of persons. (Existing) social and political institutions, conversely, by his view, tend toward autocracy, tend toward the imposition of alien demands (dishonesty and hypocrisy for prominent instance), tend toward the oppression of persons. Largely by way of property and commerce, social and political institutions have made human beings unequal and subjugated; such institutions have distorted and corrupted the natural inclinations of the species. Nature, then, constitutes the ideal condition, the condition invested with all of the good and proper qualities that the existing social and political condition lacks. Rousseau held that a form of government is nonetheless necessary because there are some aberrant persons in the state of nature who demand power and freedom at the expense of others and because the innocence of nature is not restorable. For him, political institutions must be reformed and upbuilt in the image of nature; the privileged aristocracy and hereditary monarchs must be deposed, by revolutionary means if necessary. In enlightened, or natural, politicality, sovereignty rests with the people (and their representatives), conventions and laws are freely and unanimously agreed to by all, the imperatives of political life are fashioned so as to promote equality and social justice for all, and liberty exists only in the context of such equality and justice. By this view, politicality is defined as a general will (not the mere aggregate of self-interested wills), or social contract, which has as its formal end the realization of the common good. Rousseau's social and political philosophy attempted to demonstrate that freedom entails obedience to self-legislated law and that such freedom naturally conforms to the public interest. Socio-politicality is thereby construed as a manifestation of that which is naturally and universally felt, thought, willed, and good. The other major feature of Rousseau's thought, his educational philosophy, follows straightforwardly from his social and political philosophy.

Rousseau's influence was staggering, arguably greater than that of any other eighteenth-century intellectual figure. His articulate emphasis on natural volition, emotions, and feeling and on the force of the will as the prime mover of reason had a very significant affect on the development of nineteenth-century Continental European romanticism. His articulate account of political freedom, justice, and liberty had a very telling affect on the American and French Revolutions. And his articulate philosophy of natural education had a profound, a formative, affect on the educational thought and practice of the next two centuries.

The other leading social and political philosophers of the eighteenth century were also greatly influenced by Rousseau, as well as by Montesquieu, Voltaire, and Diderot. The most notable of these others were the foremost contributors to the **British and American social and political philosophy** of the period. Edmund Burke (1729-1797), the British statesman and political commentator, is most widely remembered for his advocacy of political parties (in Thoughts on the Cause of the Present Discontents, 1770), his proposed conciliation with the American colonists, and his conservative opposition to the French Revolution (in his masterpiece, Reflections on the Revolution in France, 1790). Thomas Paine, the Anglo-American political theorist, wrote the most virulent condemnation of British monarchism and the most inspiring defense of American independence (in the pamphlet "Common Sense," 1776) and also wrote the most influential reply to Burke's unflattering portrayal of the French Revolution (in The Rights of Man, 1791-1792) in which he affirms the virtues of rule by majority vote, the natural right to freedom and happiness of all human beings, and the obligation of the state to assure the freedom and happiness of all people. And Thomas Jefferson, the third President of the United States of America, accomplished architect, and resolute advocate of the arts and sciences, was mainly responsible for the founding documents of the American republic: the "Declaration of Independence" (1776), among the first modern formulations of human rights (including the right to oppose established political institutions); the "Virginia Bill of Rights" (1776); and the "Constitution of the United States of America" (1787), the governing document of the first modern democracy.

The **continuing development of British empiricism** also exerted great influence over eighteenth-century philosophy. The empiricist gauntlet passed in this time to the idealistic-tending metaphysico-epistemic vision of Berkeley and to the very much more widely influential, pragmatic-tending, skeptical, and scientific rendering of Hume. George Berkeley (1685-1753), the Anglo-Irish philosopher, Anglican bishop, and associate of Addison, Steele, Pope, and Swift, gave a deeply penetrating analysis of the origin and nature of human knowledge that did not come to the typically materialistic and dualistic/pluralistic conclusions of the other leading empiricists, but rather to a spiritualistic account of the doctrine. Most notably in A Treatise Concerning the Principles of Human Knowledge (1710) and Three Dialogues between Hylas and Philonous (1713), Berkeley attempted to dispel the then-fashionable skepticism (apparent in Locke among prominent others) over knowledge and religion and to put an end to non-empirical speculations about the nature and purpose of the world. With Locke and against the rationalists, Berkeley argued that it is meaningless and self-contradictory to hold that there is anything but what the senses provide. There are, therefore, no innate ideas; all ideas are abstracted from experience. With the rationalists and against Locke, however, Berkeley was convinced that we can know all that there is to know of reality. It is simply that there are no non-empirical facts to know of it; the limits of human experience are defined by sense experience; all "else" is unknown to us. Berkeley thus also broke with Locke's view that we can know bodies as material things persisting apart from our experience of them. He regards this view as unduly speculative and as contrary to Locke's own, fundamentally empiricistic principles. Since our knowledge, moreover, is limited to what our senses provide, it is limited to ideas, which cannot be like material objects but only like other ideas. Reality is thereby constituted by ideas and only by ideas. According to Berkeley, these ideas are by their nature active and indivisible; they are thereby also indissoluble and so immortal. This argument for the immortality of ideas is also taken to establish the immortality of the soul and to demonstrate that a passive material world (should it exist, which we cannot know) could not influence the world of ideas. The alleged passivity of an "extended world," consequently, cannot be the cause of our perceptions as Locke had claimed. All so-termed material things are, therefore, nothing other than the ideas we perceive "of them." "Their" existence consists in "their" being conceived by the mind; this is Berkeley's infamous notion, "to be is to be perceived" ("esse est percipi"). Things exist only as complexes of ideas; there are no unthinking substances. Berkeley is, in the end, persuaded that the belief in an independent world of matter challenges the universality (and so the existence) of God and constitutes a tumble to skepticism and materialism.

Among those "things" of which we have a "direct" perceptual experience, according to Berkeley, are the conscious operations of "the mind." From this experience is deduced the existence of mind itself as that in which ideas (or conscious operations) exist and that by which ideas are perceived. The mind is consequently thought distinct from its ideas; it is thought the substratum in which ideas appear and persist. Berkeley asserts this basically rationalistic conclusion even though our consciousness of mind as such is inferred from our consciousness of its operations, or ideas, and from the implicitly invoked principle that ideas inhere in a substance. Our direct experience is nonetheless only of ideas; it s not of mind itself. Although our ideas, moreover, are private (we directly perceive only our own ideas), the existence of other minds is implied by the existence of our own. Berkeley's acceptance of this implication saves him from the extreme fall to solipsism (the view that the individual self alone exists). Berkeley also admits to the existence of selves, bodies, and God on rationalistic-tending grounds which are an apparent violation of his own, empiricistic allegiances. The self is thought a further ground of mind or that which possesses mind. The body is construed as a discrete mosaic of ideas that we know to exist from our perceptions of it and that must exist else we be pure idea (a distinction befitting only God). Although our minds, then, make us what we are, they are nonetheless inseparably connected to a corporeal notion, or body. This formulation of the mind-body relation is reminiscent of Spinoza's; the relation occurs between sets of ideas, not between ideas and something other than ideas. And in respect to the existence of God, Berkeley held that the existence of an eternal, omniscient, omnipotent, active, indivisible, immaterial, and transcendent Being is presupposed by our perceptions; God is thus the cause of perception and the perceiver of all "things."

Eighteenth-century British empiricism was taken to its sophisticated end (itself a bridge to nineteenth-century British utilitarianism) in the thought of the Scottish philosopher and historian, David Hume (1711-1776). Most notably in <u>A Treatise of Human Nature</u> (1739), <u>An Enquiry concerning the Human Understanding</u> (1748), <u>An Enquiry concerning the Principles of Morals</u> (1751), and <u>Dialogues concerning Natural Religion</u> (1779), Hume accepted Berkeley's "esse est percipi" and attempted to work out its implications with a care, rigor, and consistency that had eluded Berkeley himself. In this elaboration, Hume hoped to demonstrate the untenability of rationalism and to show philosophy's tangible need for the experimental method. He was convinced that the rationalists' reconstruction of knowledge was unduly speculative, remote, abstruse, contrary to the uncertain nature of things, and unachievable. He claimed that the negative function of philosophy is to expose the metaphysical excursions of rationalism for the masquerades that they are. And for the positive side of the subject, Hume reserved an exploration of the nature of the mind and human knowledge. For Hume, philosophy is exclusively devoted, in its positive aspect, to a descriptive account of our minded faculties and experience. Although Hume was little impressed with the practical or existential significance of such an account, thereby differing greatly from such as Spinoza, he did consider philosophic truth valuable in itself and preferable to illusion, if more limited and less useful in the course of mundane affairs than illusion. He was highly skeptical, in particular about the successful operation of philosophic insight in the mundane world (where the forces of passion seem more prominent) and about the capacity of reason to effectively apprehend such as ultimates, substances, causality, souls, and the external (the material) world.

The first principle of Hume's empiricism is that human knowledge is exhausted by our sense-perceptual experiences. Humanity, consequently, cannot have knowledge of "entities" outside such experiences. While we are able to speak of, and to have beliefs about such "entities," we cannot have knowledge of them. One cannot, therefore, either establish that something exists independently of our sense-perceptual experience or that nothing so exists, let alone determine the presumably spiritual or material constitution of this something/nothing. Hume thereby rejected both realism/naturalism/materialism and idealism/spiritualism, considering both untenable. Among the customary issues of philosophic discourse that Hume thought meaningless (i.e., residing outside the nexus of sense-perceptual experience) are substance, souls, and material objects. He nonetheless distinguishes the realities of mental and physical events but withholds ascribing substance to them. Mind is thereby construed as nothing other than the collection of our perceptions and the body as nothing other than the collection of perceptions commonly (but wrongly) conceived as existing intimately with, but nonetheless apart from ourselves. Although we do customarily think of our bodies as existing independently of our perceptions (and they may well), we cannot know if this is so or not so, because we can rightly claim to know only what we perceive. We cannot likewise claim to have knowledge of self (as that collection of perceptions which we are) or to have knowledge of the means or manner by which minds, minds and bodies, or bodies "interact."

Despite Hume's strict interpretation of empiricist teaching, he nonetheless claims that there is no truth so certain as the existence of God. In what impresses as an openly rationalistic appeal, Hume argues for the existence of God from the principle of sufficient reason. According to Hume's handling of this principle, God exists as the absolutely perfect first cause and continued sustainer of the universe and the foundation of all truth, happiness, morality, beauty, and socio-political decency. Although God's existence is indubitable, according to Hume, Its basic character cannot be known; any claim to such knowledge commits the calamity of ascribing inferior, human qualities to a superior, non-human Being. The "truths" of religion, moreover, not unlike those of ethics and politics, are "truths" of passion; they are practical, active, and free "truths" of the will, as distinct from conceptual truths. In religion, one seeks a happiness left unfulfilled by nature, a happiness which obeys the natural law of causality and seeks a fulfillment of one's instinct for a coherent world. Morality too rests on an instinct, not on a rational necessity, according to Hume. The basic sentiment which leads us to live a morally just life is an altruistic sympathy for the happiness of humanity, for enlightened self-interest in Hume's terms. His utilitarian ethic claims that goodness is that which pleases oneself and is in concert with the interests of humanity in general. A social and political order is required in order to save humanity from the chaotic and self-destructive tendencies of its unenlightened inclinations. As one's base self-interest is educated (or enlightened) by knowledge, it gives way quite by its nature to governmental convention, to enforced rules of social cooperation and resource distribution. This convention effectively puts necessary restraints on self-interest and reconciles it to the common good. Hume's aesthetics is too grounded in the passions, in the passion for beauty, in the passion for that which arouses to pleasure.

Early modern philosophy came to its highest mark and to its effective conclusion in the monumental genius of the German philosopher, Immanuel Kant (1724-1804). Kant's idealistic-tending, neo-classical system – developed most notably in what are among the masterworks of Enlightenment philosophy, Critique of Pure Reason (1781), Prolegomena to Every Future Metaphysics (1783), Foundations of the Metaphysics of Morals (1785), Critique of Practical Reason (1788), and Critique of Judgment (1790) – largely resolved the empiricist-rationalist debate which had so dominated the just-prior two centuries; Kant's masterful system largely achieved the long-sought **reconciliation of empiricism and rationalism**. Kant attempted to demonstrate the functions necessarily served by both reason and sense-perceptual experience in human knowledge. With the success of this demonstration also came Kant's triumph over the then-somewhat-fashionable skepticism with respect to the capacity of either and both reason and sense-perception and with respect to the free prerogatives of the will in moral and religious contexts. Kant was at first most influenced by Leibniz, later by Locke and Hume, and in the end broke independently away to a line of insight that summed one age, inaugurated another, and yet ranks with the most memorable achievements of philosophic discourse. As had been the case for most of the major figures of the early modern period, the problem of knowledge remained the central issue of philosophy for Kant. With both the rationalists and empiricists, Kant held that sense-perceptual experience provides the raw data, the primitive content, of knowledge. With the rationalists, against the empiricists, however, he argued that the mind frames the content of the senses in necessary accord with its own nature, in necessary accord with its own form; the character of empirical reality thus corresponds to the formal character of the mind. With the empiricists, against the rationalists, he claimed that rationalism imposes a dogmatic, a stipulative, form on content and that human knowledge of the sort thought possible by rationalism is unachievable. And, against both the rationalists and empiricists, Kant was convinced that neither mathematics nor the sciences provide an ideal model for human knowledge. This is Kant's arbitration of rationalism and empiricism, his so-termed "second Copernican revolution," which turns the empirical argument on its head (while nonetheless acknowledging the partial merits of the argument) and which accounts for the relationship of form and content in far more plausible ways than rationalism.

In Kant's judgment, the traditional objects of philosophic inquiry, nature, humanity, divinity, knowledge, and value, are unknowable as universal and necessary truths. All that can be known are "possible objects of experience," or appearances. The character of the reality that lies beneath these appearances (as their cause) can neither be known, for we have no direct experience of this reality as such. The concrete fact of appearances nonetheless establishes the existence of such a reality for Kant. This reality is made up of what Kant calls "material things-in-themselves," or "transcendental objects," "objects" which themselves transcend our direct experience, but which such experience nonetheless presupposes. These "objects" provide our perceptions, our direct experience, with a cause and they establish as well the limits of human knowledge. We know that they are but we cannot know what they are. By Kant's view, then, philosophy cannot aspire to an authentic knowledge of the ultimate nature of things, the "noumenon" (the discrete world corresponding to the form of our minds as the cause of that form), which rationalists supposed that it could, but only to a knowledge of what experience provides, the "phenomenon" (the world of appearances), which is nonetheless more than the empiricists typically allowed. Our knowledge cannot penetrate beyond the limits of experience; the world is nothing other than the sum of all "possible objects of experience." Kant's "transcendental method of argument," which is neither mathematical nor scientific, but humanistic, in character, therefore moves from the indubitable character of all "possible objects of experience" to what must be universally and necessarily presupposed by these "objects" in order to make experience possible at all. It moves from the empirical facts to the necessary conditions of their possibility.

The epistemic thrust of Kant's philosophy is to show that all ideas cannot be mere copies of sense-perceptions, but are in some meaningful way reflections of the mind as well. This is done by pure reason, by reason with all of the data of experience removed. And it is done in order to demonstrate the terms in which the mind (the understanding, the "transcendental ego") structures our experience, mainly in respect to the categories of time, space, quantity, quality, relation, and modality. According to Kant, knowledge itself presupposes the existence of mind, the competence of reason to examine itself, and the cooperation of sensation and thought. Although outside the limits of "possible objects of experience" and thus unknowable by means of "pure reason," Kant nonetheless allowed that knowledge of other significant entities may be gained by other means, by means of "practical reason." He argued that so-termed "Ideas" (most notably, the existence of God, human freedom, the immortality of the soul, and the purposeful nature of the world) do not constitute knowledge in the strictest of pure senses but are nonetheless of telling practical significance and are natural to reason in terms of their organizing and guiding it, assuring its unity, and being methodologically useful to it. Among the most important laws of practical reason, and the law which forms the basis of Kant's celebrated ethics, entails the duty to conduct ourselves so as to deserve happiness. Inherent in the voluntary acts that form this duty is the freedom of the good will and the constraint to choose what is highest and best in us by its exercise. Kant's conciliation of determinism and free will intuits humanity as a unified consciousness at once a participant in the world of sense by which it is determined and in the world of reason by which it is free. Humanity is consequently free insofar as it acts in accord with the self-legislated laws of reason and it is moral insofar as it submits to the universal and necessary moral law of reason, the "categorical imperative." This law unconditionally, or categorically, commands humanity to conduct itself always so that the governing principle of action becomes universal law and to intend this action out of a respect for one's duty to the self-legislated law (out of a respect for one's duty to happiness). The "imperative" commands a treatment of every person always as an end-in-and-for-itself, never as a means to an end without itself. A social and political order of persons commanded by the "imperative" results in a kingdom of ends, a community of rational spirits characterized by the coalescence of individual and common goods. This, the moral, dimension, in turn, introduces humanity to a world transcending the phenomenal, a world that implies (although not altogether plausibly) the existence of God, the immortality of the soul, and the purposeful nature of the world (which itself entails a universal and non-utilitarian form of aesthetic judgment). Kant's philosophy of education too issues mainly from his moral perspective.

The high place accorded Kant in the history of philosophy is as secure as that of any other figure. Much of the philosophy since him has taken the form of either a response to his thought or an extension of his thought. An especially great deal of nineteenth-century philosophy was heavily occupied with the "completion" of the Kantian program from its critical foundations. Kant's "second Copernican revolution," his dualistic tendencies and the unsympathetic interpretation of nature that accompanied them, and his acceptance of entities which neither conform to the categories of the mind nor of which we have direct experience, entities such as "material things-in-themselves" and "Ideas," brought him wide criticism. Among the most important, early replies to Kant came from the German Enlightenment philosopher of (evolutionary) history, Johann Gottfried Herder (1744-1803), the German Enlightenment poet, Johann Friedrich Schiller, and the German Enlightenment philosopher, Friedrich Heinrich Jacobi (1743-1819). Herder and Schiller both rejected Kant's dualism, discounted his unsympathetic treatment of nature, and argued for the balanced (the aesthetic) education of humanity. Jacobi was convinced that the critical foundations of Kant's philosophy and the sharp order of skepticism entailed by these foundations could not yield an authentic knowledge of either "material things-in-themselves" or "Ideas." The towering German figures of the early nineteenth century who took the critical philosophy of Kant as their point of departure, Fichte, Schelling, Schleiermacher, and Hegel, followed. Kant, as well as Rousseau, Goethe, Beethoven and David, had prepared the ground for a return to organicism (in the form of romanticism) in the early nineteenth century.

Discoveries in Mathematics and the Sciences

The extraordinary intellectual vitality of early modern culture had an especially profound affect on the development of one of the most storied and brilliant chapters in human history, that of modern mathematics and science. This development continued to respect the ancient classical and medieval canons, at least insofar as these canons were taken to contain the rudimentary ideals of human existence, but it challenged (and to a significant extent overturned) these canons as matters of scientific erudition. It was principally through a theretofore unique commitment to the empirical sciences (the natural sciences), and to the methods of careful observation, controlled experimentation, and mathematical calculation which underlie these sciences, that many of the most cherished scientific truths of ancient and medieval scholarship were discredited and revised. Conventional views concerning perfection, change, certainty, the unique character of the Earth and of humanity, and the broader character of the physical universe were in clear retreat in this time. The new science demonstrated that ancient and medieval scholarship did not hold the sum of all knowledge, that each age is not in every significant respect governed by prior ages, that every age has its own truths to discover, and that truth is not therefore utterly fixed, but evolving. This movement was greatly buoyed by the empiricistic doctrines of Francis Bacon and of later British philosophic adepts; it was significantly influenced by the mathematical inclinations of the Continental European rationalists; it was governed mainly by the skeptical and mechanistic presuppositions characteristic of experimental activities; and it was most devoted to mathematics, the physical sciences (physics, chemistry, geology, and astronomy), the biological sciences, and the social sciences. Although it had been on its formative way since the early university studies of the thirteenth and fourteenth centuries (which importantly included the scientific exhortations of Roger Bacon) and was in significant measure made possible by technological innovations worked out in the late Middle Ages and the early Renaissance, it owed its earnest origins to the sixteenth century and (yet more emphatically) to the seventeenth century (itself, the so-termed "Age of [Scientific] Reason").

The most notable technological innovations, or **technical inventions**, of the early modern period that significantly influenced the mathematical and scientific achievements of the age had most to do with the invention of the printing press, with improvements in the glass industry, and with advancements in steam and electrical energy. The printing press (with moveable, metallic type) was fashioned by the German craftsman, Johann Gutenberg (c. 1397-1468), at Mainz in c. 1445; it had a profound affect on communication among intellectuals as well as others; and it thereby very notably accelerated the rate of change/progress in intellectual (as well as other) pursuits. Many of the most significant achievements of early modern science were also greatly affected by inventive developments in glass technology, developments that made possible the fashioning of novel scientific instruments. The microscope was invented by the Dutch opticians, Hans and Zacharias Janssen (both fl. in the late sixteenth century), in c. 1590. The telescope was created by the celebrated German astronomer, Johannes Kepler (1571-1630), in c. 1605. The mercury barometer was developed by the Italian physicist and associate of Galileo, Evangelista Torricelli (1608-1647), in 1643. The reflecting telescope was conceived by the English genius, Isaac Newton (1642-1727), in 1669. The mercury thermometer was devised by the German physicist, Gabriel Daniel Fahrenheit (1686-1736), in 1720. And the principal advancements in steam and electrical energy of the early modern period were made respectively by James Watt (1736-1819), the Scottish engineer, who developed the steam engine in 1769, and by Alessandro Volta (1745-1827), the Italian physicist and inventor, who created many important electrical devices, including a cell that converts chemical to electrical energy (1800).

The most striking achievements of this period in **mathematics** were those of John Napier (1550-1617), the Scottish mathematician, who "discovered" logarithms in 1614; René Descartes, the French mathematician and philosopher, who fashioned the analytic geometry in 1637; Blaise Pascal, the French mathematician, scientist, inventor, and philosopher, who invented the adding machine in 1642 and who founded the modern theory of probability in the 1650s; Isaac Newton, the English mathematician, physicist, and inventor, who co-founded (with, but independently of, Leibniz) the differential and integral calculus in c. 1665; and Gottfried Wilhelm Leibniz, the German mathematician, statesman, inventor, and philosopher, who co-founded (with, but independently of, Newton) the differential and integral calculus in 1672 and who invented the calculating machine in 1673. Differential and integral calculus in particular had an utterly colossal affect on all subsequent thought in mathematics and the sciences; it provided precise values for quantities that are incessantly changing. The **physical sciences** of early modern culture were likewise dominated by crowning genius. The leading contributors to the stunning achievements in these subjects were:

- Nicholas Copernicus (1473-1543), the Polish astronomer and student of Nicholas of Cusa, who affirmed the spherical shape of the Earth (from the Hellenistic judgment of Eratosthenes of Cyrene in the third century B.C.E.), who demonstrated (mainly in his revolutionary masterpiece, <u>On the Revolutions of the Heavenly Bodies</u>, 1543) that the Earth rotates on its own axis, that the Sun is at the center of the universe, and that the planets (including the Earth) revolve in circular paths about the Sun; this heliocentric (sun-centered) notion of the universe confirmed and refined the Hellenistic claims of Aristarchus of Samos from nearly two millennia earlier and it upended the geocentric (earth-centered) view of Ptolemy (from the second century C.E.) and of medieval science;

- Philippus Aureolus Paracelsus (1493-1541), the Swiss alchemist and physician, whose pioneering work concerning the interaction of chemical elements and substances established the seminal basis of modern chemistry;

- Georg Agricola (1494-1555), the German scholar, whose formative work in metallurgy and mineralogy established the seminal basis of modern geology;

- Tycho Brahe (1546-1601), the Danish astronomer, who was the teacher of Johannes Kepler, who was patronized by Holy Roman Emperor Rudolf II, who erected the first astronomical observatory, who was the first to observe a supernova, who compiled the first modern star catalog (after the Hellenistic work of Hipparchus of Nicaea in the second century B.C.E.), and whose precise observations of lunar and planetary movements provided much of the raw data for subsequent studies in cosmology;

- Galileo Galilei (1564-1642), the colossal Italian physicist, astronomer, and apostle of modern scientific experimentation, whose work went still further than Copernicus' had gone in correcting prevailing conceptions of the universe and the natural laws that govern it; Galileo discovered the four largest satellites of Jupiter and the stellar composition of the Milky Way; he showed that all material bodies fall at the same rate, not at rates proportional to their mass as Aristotle had argued, that the path of projectiles is a parabola, that the natural state of material bodies is motion, not rest as Ptolemy had taught, that such bodies move by inherent inertia, they are not pushed from without as Aristotle had held, that celestial bodies, like terrestrial ones, are not changeless and so perfect in this sense as Ptolemy had supposed, but in a continuous state of change, and that celestial bodies, like terrestrial ones, are neither perfectly spherical nor homogenous (they are instead slightly flattened at the poles and have numerous "imperfections," such as spots, craters, and mountains) nor do they move in perfectly circular paths, all as Ptolemy had taught; his defense of the Copernican system, as against the Ptolemaic, in one of the great masterpieces of scientific literature, <u>Dialogue Concerning Two Chief Systems of the World</u> (1632), brought him before the papal Inquisition of Urban VIII in 1633 where he was forced under threat of torture and imprisonment to recant his views and was condemned to seclusion;

- Johannes Kepler, the German astronomer, mathematician, and student of Brahe, who was patronized by Holy Roman Emperor Rudolf II and who discovered the elliptical paths (as distinct from the circular paths postulated by Ptolemy and Copernicus) of the planets as well as the mathematical properties of planetary motion, all most notably in a work of masterful insight, <u>Astronomia Nova</u> (1609);

- Blaise Pascal, the French mathematician, scientist, inventor, and philosopher, who discovered vacuums in 1646;

- Robert Boyle (1627-1691), the Anglo-Irish chemist and physicist, who was the first to give an exacting definition of a chemical element, a chemical reaction, and chemical analysis, thereby distinguishing the mysteries of alchemy from the mechanistic truths of chemistry; he also discovered the relation of pressure, volume, and temperature in gases in 1662;

- Christiaan Huygens (1629-1695), the Dutch physicist, who discovered several major properties of light and who developed the wave theory of light in 1690;
- Isaac Newton, the English mathematician, physicist, and inventor, who is widely regarded as among the most incisive geniuses in the history of the human species, who refined the collective judgments of the age and organized them into a coherent, mechanistic system (most notably in what is among the great books of Western science, <u>The Mathematical Principles of Natural Philosophy</u>, 1687), who in 1666 discovered the law of universal gravitation which signifies the attractive relation of material (celestial and terrestrial) bodies in respect to their masses and the distances between them, who constructed the first reflecting telescope in 1669, and who formulated the corpuscular (or particle) theory of light in 1704; Newton is also well remembered for his discovery that white light is composed of all spectral colors and for his celebrated laws of motion (inertia, acceleration, and reaction);
- Olaus Roemer (1644-1710), the Danish astronomer, who discovered the velocity of light in 1675;
- Charles Du Fay (1698-1739), the French physicist, who discovered the positive and negative charges of electricity in c. 1737;
- James Hutton (1726-1797), the Scottish geologist, who proposed (mainly in <u>The Theory of the Earth</u>, 1795) that the Earth did not develop abruptly in brief periods of catastrophic transformation by novel occurrence as commonly supposed but very gradually over very long periods of time by ongoing types of geological event (the doctrine of uniformitarianism);
- Henry Cavendish (1731-1810), the English physicist and chemist, who discovered hydrogen in 1766;
- Joseph Priestley (1733-1804), the English scientist, who discovered oxygen in 1774;
- William Herschel (1738-1822), the German-English astronomer, who was patronized by no less than George III of England and who discovered the vast character of the local galaxy (the Milky Way), the character of nebulae (immense bodies of interstellar gas and dust) as the possible origin of new worlds, and in 1781, Uranus, the seventh planet from the Sun (Mercury, Venus, Earth, Mars, Jupiter, and Saturn were known to the ancient world; this was the first planetary discovery since);
- Antoine Laurent Lavoisier (1743-1794), the French chemist and physicist, who formulated a classification of substances that distinguished chemical elements and chemical compounds and that established the basis of modern chemical nomenclature, who was the first to use quantitative methods in the study of chemical reactions, who demonstrated the central role of oxygen in combustion, and who was executed in the "Reign of Terror" over his concern for the improvement of social and economic conditions in France; and
- Alessandro Volta, the Italian physicist and inventor, who did much of the pioneering work in modern electrical theory.

Early modern advancements in the **biological sciences** were likewise highly significant. The most memorable and influential achievements in these subjects were made by:

- Philippus Aureolus Paracelsus, the Swiss alchemist and physician, who dramatically reformed medicine (largely at Galen's expense) by explaining the physical and chemical forces of life on their own terms and who transformed modern notions of disease by scientifically demonstrating the causes of specific diseases and by scientifically advocating specific chemical remedies for such diseases;
- Andreas Vesalius (1514-1564), the Flemish anatomist, who revolutionized the science of human anatomy (largely also at Galen's expense) in his renowned manuscript, <u>On the Fabric of the Human Body</u> (1543); unlike Galen, who had relied mainly on animal dissections, Vesalius based his work on human dissections; he narrowly escaped a death sentence on charges of heresy by the Spanish Inquisition and served as a court physician to Holy Roman Emperor Charles V and his son, Philip II, King of Spain;
- William Harvey (1578-1657), the English physician, who first correctly demonstrated the nature of the cardiovascular system (largely too at Galen's expense) in his celebrated manuscript, <u>On the Movement of the Heart and Blood in Animals</u> (1628);
- Antony van Leeuwenhoek (1632-1723), the Dutch biologist, who discovered and first fully described micro-organisms (mainly bacteria and protozoa) and microscopic features of human anatomy (mainly capillaries, red corpuscles, sperm, and nerve, muscle, and epidermal tissue);
- Carolus Linnaeus (1707-1778), the Swedish botanist, who originated the modern scientific nomenclature and taxonomy (system of classification) of plants and animals; most notably, in <u>Systema Naturae</u> (1735) and <u>Genera Plantarum</u> (1737); and

- Luigi Galvani (1737-1798), the Italian physician, who discovered that animal tissues manifest electrical properties.

The scientific life of Renaissance and seventeenth-century Europe concentrated mainly on the natural sciences and on the principal means of treating the data of the natural sciences, mathematics. Eighteenth-century European culture continued to be deeply devoted to the natural sciences and to mathematics but it also developed a quite original interest in the natural laws governing social scientific phenomena; it developed a quite original interest in the **social sciences**. In the period of the modern European Enlightenment, the age of individualism, of enhanced franchise and civil rights, of constitutional democracy, and of political revolution, these laws (which were taken to obey rational expectations) were applied to psychological, cultural, political, economic, historical, and educational events in the hope of putting an end to the barbarities and the absurdities of the old, patently exploitative order. Of particularly large influence were the empirical psychologies of French philosophers, Étienne Bonnot de Condillac (1715-1780) and Claude-Adrien Helvetius (1715-1771). Condillac's Traité des Sensation (1754) and Helvetius' De L'Espirit (1758) explained human behavior in strictly environmental terms, in sole terms of sense-perceptual responses to environmental stimuli. Arguably the most significant eighteenth-century social scientists, however, were the French "physiocrats" and the classical British economists, the first modern political economists, who systematically demonstrated the character and consequences of competitive, laissez-faire (unregulated) markets. Of the "physiocrats," their founder, François Quesnay (1694-1774), a physician to Louis XV, was the most prominent. Chiefly in The Economical Table (1758), Quesnay argued that land is the root source of all wealth and that only absolutely unrestrained trade in abundant agricultural products assures prosperity. Adam Smith (1723-1790), the Scottish economist and leading early modern apostle of capitalism, gave the most sanguine account. Mainly in a volume that qualifies on any fair standard as a masterpiece of social scientific thought, An Inquiry into the Nature and Causes of the Wealth of Nations (1776), Smith advocated the largely unregulated operation of supply and demand, postulated the surplus value of labor as the true source of wealth (a century before Marx), recognized the importance of labor division to productivity and prosperity, and argued that the unfettered conduct of self-interest naturally (if instrumentally) evokes the public welfare and social progress. On Smith's view, the function of the state is not strictly economic; it is not regulatory, but political; it is to protect from foreign enemies and to keep domestic tranquility. (Thomas) Robert Malthus (1766-1834) and David Ricardo (1772-1823), both English economists, came to notably less buoyant conclusions about the virtues of the new capital order. Malthus, principally in his widely influential masterpiece, An Essay on the Principle of Population (1798), foresaw the colliding relation between population and the resource necessary to sustain it. By Malthus' view, only war, famine, and disease, themselves great misfortunes, can mitigate the poverty and misery of inevitable overpopulation. And Ricardo, in his widely acclaimed masterpiece, The Principles of Political Economy and Taxation (1817), demonstrated the terms in which the value of any good is a function of the labor required to produce it and the terms in which wages in an unregulated marketplace tend always to subsistence levels.

The earliest systematic, archaeological excavations of significant ancient sites were likewise unique and highly significant features of eighteenth-century social science. Such excavations began at Herculaneum in 1738, at Pompeii in 1755, and at Olympia in 1766. The historical scholarship of the Enlightenment must too be counted among the major scientific achievements of the time. English historian, Edward Gibbon (1737-1794), mainly in the foremost historical manuscript of the century (The History of the Decline and Fall of the Roman Empire, 1776-1788), embraced the anticlerical and democratic tendencies of eighteenth-century French liberalism and argued that human progress (in the form of the Roman Empire) declined with the advent of Christianity.

Educational and Sporting Developments

The dominant intellectual tendencies of early modern civilization, humanist tendencies, had an especially large affect on the educational developments of the age. In the period of the Renaissance, the broad urge to rational humanism, to the organic thesis and its distinctly human orientation, and to free inquiry produced an educational ideal reminiscent of the Athenian. This ideal reaffirmed the balanced, harmonious, and unified development of humanity's intellectual and physical aspects, the fashioning of a fertile intellect and a robust sense of the physical. Humanism held that the subjective body contains the spiritual and conceptual faculties and thereby acts as the individual person's window on the world. The body, consequently, was thought continuous with consciousness and as itself capable of expressing great beauty. By this view, the body signifies neither an ephemeral nor an objective impediment to fulfillment, but a form of subjective, uniquely human fulfillment itself. Insofar as sport[122] was practiced in educational contexts (in the form of physical education), and it was far more widely practiced in such contexts in the Renaissance than it had been in medieval circumstance, it too was greatly influenced by the humanist inclination. Insofar as it was practiced in non-school contexts, it was much less deeply affected -- in some cases, it was almost entirely unaffected -- by the humanist inclination.

The Renaissance curriculum was framed by the progressive, liberating, and creative needs of the individual person and of the social order. It was somewhat less formal and less austere than its medieval antecedents but it was nonetheless appropriately demanding. It gave significant attention to both the searching content of education and its inventive methods of instruction. It customarily included a study of mathematics, Greek and Latin languages, vernacular languages, Greek and Roman literature, natural science, history, philosophy, the visual, musical, and dancing arts, and physical education. As is typical of circumstances with an authentic respect for education, teachers were carefully selected and were themselves well educated. The earliest Renaissance form of institutional education was conducted in privately established and maintained schools for the sons of wealthy merchants, bankers, and aristocrats. Some provision was customarily also made for young women and for the talented sons of poor scholars and peasants. These institutions were known as town, or burgher, schools; some were the descendants of guild schools and some did also evolve into public, town schools. Extant universities likewise fell increasingly under the governing spell of the recent movement and new universities were too established as embodiments of it.

Renaissance education and physical education in southern Europe was most significantly affected by individualistic interpretations of the humanist doctrine and by the Catholic Counter-Reformation. The foremost architects of educational (and physical educational) humanism in the southern European Renaissance effectively worked out the educational implications of the broad thought of proto-Renaissance litterateurs such as Petrarch and they fervently endorsed education and physical education as media of individual expression (as well as pleasure and health). The most notable of these were the Italian reformers:

- Petrus Paulus Vergerius 1349-1420), who wrote the first and the most widely read humanist discourse on education and physical education, On Good Morals and Liberal Studies;
- Vittorino da Feltre (1378-1446) and Guarino da Verone (1370-1461), both accomplished teachers, who established the pioneer humanist schools at Mantua ("La Giocosa/The Pleasant House") and Ferrara respectively, schools that importantly included physical education;
- Aneas Sylvius Piccolomini (1405-1464), who became Pope Pius II and who wrote an exceedingly influential manuscript, De Liberorum Educatione, in which physical education was explicitly and enthusiastically advocated for both biological and psychological purposes;
- Leonbattista Alberti, the great architect, who also wrote widely on the subjects of education and physical education; most significantly in On the Care of the Family;
- Baldassare Castiglione, who wrote the most influential humanist manuscript of the sixteenth century, Il Cortegiano/The Book of the Courtier, in which he fashions the ideal man and woman in organic terms, in terms of a balanced, harmonious, and unified development of our intellectual and physical qualities; and
- Hieronymus Mercurialis (1530-1606), an accomplished physician, who importantly discussed the value of exercise to the maintenance of good health in De Arte Gymnastica.

Moreover, many of the leading political and intellectual figures of this period were themselves tangibly and seriously devoted to educational projects. Marsilio Ficino and Cosimo de' Medici/Cosimo the Elder were instrumental in establishing the Platonic Academy in Florence in the mid-fifteenth century; Pope Nicholas V established the Vatican Library, also in the mid-fifteenth century; and Tommaso Campanella wrote tellingly of a universal philosophy of education (which included an advocacy of vigorous forms of sporting activity) in the early seventeenth century. In Mogul India, Akbar reorganized the educational system, established libraries, and formed universities. In Ming China, public schools and an Imperial Academy were established.

Renaissance education and physical education in northern Europe was most significantly affected by social interpretations of the humanist doctrine and by the Protestant Reformation. The foremost architects of educational and physical educational humanism in the northern European Renaissance effectively worked out the educational implications of the broad thought of northern European Renaissance humanists such as Erasmus and they fervently endorsed education and physical education as media of social human expression (as well as pleasure and health). The most notable of these were the English scholars, teachers, and reformers who wrote the defining texts of the movement: Thomas Elyot (1490-1546), the author of The Boke Named the Governour and The Castle of Health, and Roger Ascham (1515-1568), the author of The Scholemaster and Toxiphilus/Of Archery. The northern form of educational humanism was, however, more heavily influenced by religious concerns than the southern form and it thereby also gave somewhat less attention to affairs of the body, including physical education. Moreover, the attention it did accord physical education was more so associated with the courts (political agencies) and the guilds (commercial agencies) than with the schools (educational agencies). The transformative affects of the new printing technology also had larger consequences in the north than in the south. The invention of the modern printing press in the mid-fifteenth century made for very much more readily available and very much less expensive books, for a vast increase in lay learning, in communication, in rates of change and progress, and in formal censorship, as well as for a diminished attention to oral traditions.

Predictably, physical education prospered under the humanist influence. Not unlike the Athenian form of the subject, **Renaissance physical education** tended to high vigor, was customarily practiced in a quasi-scientific way, served expressive as well as biological, psycho-social, and military purposes, and emphasized individual (as against dual and team) activities. The most widely practiced physical activities (in Renaissance education) were archery, gymnastic exercises, swimming, track and field athletic exertions (most notably, walking, running, jumping, vaulting, and weight throwing), weightlifting, games resembling lawn bowling, golf, and tennis, dual combative endeavors (most notably, boxing, fencing, and wrestling), tournament skills (most notably, weapons exercises, equestrian games, tilting, and jousting), and team ball games resembling field hockey, football, hurling, and soccer.

The other major influence on Renaissance education and physical education was the Reformations. The ideological leaders of the Protestant Reformation, together mainly with the victorious Protestant German princes, were especially zealous in their attempts to expand welfare services in broad respects and to reform Christian education in particular. They established schools for the purpose of framing **education in Protestant terms**:

- elementary (or parish) schools, which gave instruction in largely vocational subjects by massed means to most poor children;
- secondary (or Latin grammar) schools, which provided wealthy youth (and some others of intellectual promise) a liberal education by tutorial means; and
- universities (most notably, the German institutions, University of Koenigsberg, 1544, and University of Jena, 1558), which provided an advanced education for accomplished scholars.

By this arrangement, the elementary and secondary schools did not furnish a progression of educational levels from simple to more complex subjects. They were instead schools devoted to giving instruction in different subjects by different means to students of different social classes. The earliest forms of Protestant education did therefore already exhibit an affection for the sort of class differentiation with which it is yet widely identified, an affection consonant with its economic (and political) allegiances. The Protestant Reformation opposed the scholastic mechanization of faith, favoring instead a simple faith in the Scriptures and a direct teaching of them to all persons. It therefore too favored education in the languages of most people, in vernacular (as distinct from classical) languages. All of the major Protestant reformers wrote and acted energetically in these several respects concerning education. Luther's main views concerning education are recorded in "Letter to the Mayors and Aldermen of All the Cities of Germany in Behalf of Christian Schools" and "Sermon on the Duty of Sending Children to School;" Zwingli's are found in Brief Treatise on the Christian Education of Youth; Calvin's are included in his magnum opus, The Institutes of the Christian Religion; and Knox's are inscribed in Book of Discipline for the Scottish Church. Others, however, tangibly instituted the educational prescriptions of the great reformers. The most notable of these were Johannes Bugenhagen (1485-1558), who was the principal author of ordinances governing the organization of Protestant education, and Philip Melanchton (1497-1560), who established among the earliest secondary schools (a gymnasium) devoted to the new reforms. The Reformationist aims of education, outlined in these manuscripts and these acts, were harmonized with the increasingly influential practices of mercantile capitalism. Christian education (in its Protestant form) was thus integrated with the secular life of the community in a far larger sense than it had been in the medieval era. This integration was nonetheless devoted to the ends of religious piety (i.e., personal salvation) and vocational austerity (i.e., commercial profit); that is, education was to serve a form of otherworldly ambition and worldly asceticism governed by stern discipline, hard work, efficiency of action, and thrift. Ironically enough, the Protestant Reformation nonetheless further diminished (or significantly prepared the way for a further reduction of) the influence of formal religion over secular affairs (over the state, the economy, and education most notably). It likewise had a liberating affect on the religious and secular life of the laity; it made education a public obligation; and it insisted on a sparse orientation and a rigid discipline in both religious and secular matters for all classes.

The leading figures of the Catholic Counter-Reformation, Loyola most notably (in his <u>Spiritual Exercises</u>), were too much devoted to educational matters and they were even also moved to educational reform, albeit a type of reform which re-framed **education in Catholic terms**. Their reforms were nonetheless more modest than the Protestant revisions. The Catholic schools remained under the firm control of the Church and continued to teach the orthodox dogma; they did as well, however, develop quite unique opportunities for young women and were less given to prosecuting inegalitarian differences in social class than the Protestant movement.

Reformationist physical education and sport was governed principally by an equivocal interpretation of the bodily dimension. Both the Protestant and Catholic Reformations developed a more favorable view of secular affairs in general and bodily activities in particular than the medieval circumstance. Neither, however, fashioned a respect for such affairs and activities that rivaled the organic, monistic, subjective, lived, and intrinsic sympathies of Renaissance humanism. By the Reformationist view, there may be a heroic quality about vigorous bodily activities (if they serve the purposes of spiritual enlightenment and its practical consequences as well as the purposes of military preparation), but this quality is more limited and reserved than in the Renaissance case. The Reformationist view of vigorous bodily activities was neither wholly dispassionate in the medieval sense nor was it fervently exuberant in the Renaissance sense. Humanity, thus, need not altogether renounce its physical aspect in order to win personal salvation; the expression of this aspect is nonetheless not without fetters. Laboring activity and relief from laboring activity (that effectively abets labor itself and the mercantile ambitions and religious fulfillment served by labor itself), in the form of physical recreation for prominent instance, were amply endorsed. Physical exercise was widely advocated by virtue of its favorable effects on good health (i.e., it keeps the body free of infirmity) and on forthright behavior (i.e., it keeps individuals from delinquent behavior by occupying them with something other than such behavior). These strictly instrumental regards for physical education, together with the inherent dualism of Reformationist Christianity, nonetheless evoked an ambivalent view of the subject and kept the movement from an authentic, a positive, respect for it. There were also in Reformationist Christianity deep reservations about the potentially frivolous and sensually pleasurable/indulgent qualities of sport. Unsurprisingly, then, the Protestant and Catholic Reformations are not well known for their broad commitment to physical education and sport; they did not typically include it in their schools; and they restrained and condemned much that it entailed. It was more so tolerated than actively embraced; it was interpreted as an activity at least slightly more worthy than ennui, infirmity, and delinquency. Still at this, Luther and Zwingli favored bowling, gymnastic exercise, fencing, and wrestling; even Calvin, who greatly disdained idleness and inclined to a tempered, ascetic, and serious view of spontaneous appetites and bodily pleasures, defended and practiced bowling and quoits; and Loyola emphasized the importance of physical exercise. There were as well several other synoptic features of the Reformations (the Protestant Reformation most notably) that positioned them well for the very large and supportive influence they came to have over the development of modern sport (in the nineteenth and twentieth centuries particularly):

- its emphasis on the productive uses of leisure;
- its resolute striving for competitive worldly and spiritual success;
- its characterization of self-worth in conspicuous achievement; and
- its orientation to individualistic self-reliance.

Renaissance sport outside the schools was fairly extensive but it was much less conspicuously influenced by either humanist or Reformationist tendency than the physical education of the time. Most of this activity occurred in military training days, fairs, festivals, inns, and taverns, effectively in the centers of municipal affairs and entertainment. Much of it occurred over the objections of the churches and schools and was therefore informal. The game-playing spirit of the species nonetheless often prevailed, even in defiance of formal proscriptions of physical recreation. The most widely practiced forms of such sport were archery (from mount and foot), rowing, ice skating, skiing, shooting, swimming, tobogganing, track and field athletic exertions (most notably, running of various sorts including pedestrianism, jumping of various horizontal and vertical sorts including vaulting, and weight throwing of various sorts including casting the stone and throwing the javelin), and weightlifting; games resembling billiards, bowling, croquet (pêle mêle), curling, golf, (court) handball, and tennis; dual combative activities (most notably, boxing, fencing, and wrestling); tournament skills (most notably, equestrian games, weapons contests, tilting, and jousting); team ball games resembling cricket, field hockey, football, ice hockey, hurling, and soccer; and blood sports such as bear and bull baiting, bullfighting, cock fighting, dueling, fishing, and hunting.

Of these, the continuing (but declining) practice of tournament skills (particularly jousting) and somewhat new interpretations of football, tennis, and golf were arguably the most prominent, received the greatest formal attention, and had the most lasting consequences. The **chivalric tournaments** of the Renaissance were less violent and more allegorical spectacles than their medieval equivalents had been. In them, grace of movement counted equally with physical strength. As the military significance of the tournaments declined, owing to technical improvements in martial archery and in the weaponry of gunpowder and owing as well to the enhanced importance of courtly good manners, aesthetic considerations significantly augmented competitive ones. High danger nonetheless remained; Henri II of France, for salient instance, died at the joust in 1559, ending the practice in France; and Henry VIII of England very nearly died of injuries suffered at the joust. Likely the most memorable of the Renaissance tournaments was that between Henry VIII of England and Francis I of France in 1520, an event that may have included an impromptu wrestling (or angry brawling) match between the two sovereigns or their immediate representatives. Although the first formally written rules of jousting were framed in 1465 (in Italy) and in 1466 (in England), the tournaments were nonetheless in decline by the fifteenth century throughout Europe, even in England, France, and the Germanies where they had been most prominent. The last tournament in France was staged in 1559; the last tournament in England was conducted in 1621; the tournaments continued into the seventeenth century in the Germanies as well, but largely in the form of archery contests. Several other sports were greatly influenced by the tournaments in this time and began to take their distinctly modern form as a result of that influence. Fencing of the one-hand/arm (as distinct from two-hand/arm) type, for prominent example, began to take such a form in its growth out of Italian, German, English, and French tournaments in the fourteenth, fifteenth, and sixteenth centuries. A formal fencing school was established at the University of Bologna in 1413; formal fencing guilds had developed in Germany by 1480, in England by 1540, and in France by 1570; fencing contests were routinely staged in association with the entrepreneurial interests of the sixteenth-century English theater; and major texts concerning modern fencing were first published in the sixteenth century (most notably, Opera Nova by Achille Marozzo of Italy in 1536 and Traicté by Henri de Sainct Didier of France in 1573). Modern equestrian activities grew out of Italian and Austrian tournaments in the fifteenth, sixteenth, and seventeenth centuries. Horse racing, which owed most to the palio (the often-violent Italian race of armored knights on mount), and dressage were arguably the most significant instances of the equestrian case in this time.

Likely the most renowned sporting contests of the Renaissance were the elaborate and spectacular **football tournaments** played in England, Ireland, France (la soule), the German states (fussball), Netherlands, Belgium, Italy (calcio), and Spain (la pelota), perhaps from as early as the thirteenth century. These were combative, team contests played on the feet (as distinct from the mount); they entailed variously advancing a "ball" on a goal defended by the opposing team; they were "civilized" versions of still older contests from the ancient and medieval worlds; and they were the precursors of all major forms of modern football. Their most notable immediate precedents were the late medieval peasant football games in England and the neighborhood brawls (fist-fights and stone-throwing contests) on bridges in Venice which date from the fourteenth century. English football was among the most notable forms of the sport; it varied so greatly that it sometimes included up to 1000 players to a side, was sometimes played on "fields" of several miles in dimension, sometimes included the kicking, throwing, catching, and carrying of balls, sometimes included only one, two, or three of these, and was sometimes staged under civilizing regulations and sometimes not. The most remarkable of the football tournaments, however, were of calcio, played between aristocratic teams (other social classes were customarily excluded) of 27 members each, to large audiences, on fields twice as long as wide. Although variously played, conducted in ritualistic fashion, and regulated, little in respect to contact among the players was prohibited. The ball games of the Mayan, Aztecan, and Incan cultures in the New World also continued in the period of the European Middle Ages and Renaissance (and into the twentieth century for that matter) as has been said. Hernan Cortes even transported Mesoamerican Indian players to Spain for a demonstration of their skills at the court of Holy Roman Emperor and Spanish King Charles V in 1528.

Modern tennis grew out of similar ancient and medieval games and was first played in the Renaissance (in fifteenth-century Netherlands, France, and England) as "le jeu de paume" (court, royal, or real tennis), a game conducted on elaborate (indoor and outdoor) four-walled courts in which the ball was originally struck with the hands (handball), then with bat-like implements, then, beginning in the sixteenth century, with stringed rackets. It was reserved in this time largely for the upper classes; Netherlands forbade its practice by others in 1401 and 1413; Tudor monarchs in particular (most notably, Henry VIII in 1541 and Mary I in 1555) issued formal prohibitions against its practice by others (servants and laborers mainly); and it was ardently endorsed and played by many of the leading political figures of the age. Tennis was patronized and played by French King Louis XI in the fifteenth century; by Henry V and Henry VII of England in the fifteenth century; by Philip I of Spain as well as James IV and James V of Scotland in the sixteenth century; by most major French kings of the sixteenth century, Louis XII, Francis I, Henri II, and Charles IX; and by Henry VIII of England also in the sixteenth century, including a celebrated match with Holy Roman Emperor and Spanish King Charles V in 1522. The first formal rules of court tennis were written in France in 1592. More, Rabelais, Cellini, and Montaigne all variously referred to the game, several included it in their views of the ideal education of youth; Cellini played it avidly; Erasmus emphasized the expression of honor as its principal feature; and Shakespeare had a metaphorical word of it in <u>Henry V</u>. Moreover, the main precursor of jai alai, a game similar to handball/tennis, first appeared in sixteenth-century Basque Spain and was variously referred to by no less than Cervantes.

Modern golf, like modern football and tennis, owed much to similar games of the ancient and medieval worlds. Its distinctly modern development, however, began in fourteenth-century Netherlands, Belgium, France, and (most significantly) Scotland. Several Scottish monarchs of the fifteenth and sixteenth centuries (most importantly, James II in 1457 and James IV in 1491) prohibited golf (and football) in favor of archery for those of other-than-royal (for those of unprivileged) station. James IV and James V of Scotland were nonetheless themselves avidly devoted to the game; James IV was also himself favorably disposed to archery and lawn bowling. The alleged and fabled "birthplace" of modern golf, the course at St. Andrews (near Edinburgh, Scotland) was established in 1552.

Of the **other major sports** of the Renaissance that were other than a mere continuation of earlier practices, cricket, curling, field hockey, hurling, pedestrianism, rowing, and skiing were the most conspicuous. Cricket began its modern development in mid-sixteenth-century England out of similar bat-and-ball games that had been taken to England from France and Flanders in the late fifteenth century. Modern curling, in its seminal form, is owed to early sixteenth-century Scotland; modern field hockey, to early sixteenth-century Ireland; and modern hurling, to fifteenth-century Ireland (where it was widely played by men of the royal family). Pedestrianism developed out of the practice of aristocrats putting their footmen (those who attended carriages on foot) up against one another in long-distance foot-races for wagers. These contests customarily entailed walking and/or running prodigious distances, typically from one place to another, often under highly bizarre circumstances. They first came to notable prominence in late sixteenth-century England. Modern rowing dates from mid-sixteenth-century competitive activities of professional watermen on the Thames River (in and near London). And the formative development of modern skiing is owed mainly to early six-teenth-century Sweden.

The most notable multi-sport festival of the medieval world that survived the Middle Ages likewise survived the Renaissance. The **principal multi-sport festival of the Renaissance** was the Celtic, Highland Games of Scotland, which dates from the eleventh century C.E. and which has variously continued to the present. Celtic (most especially, Irish and Scottish) culture, together mainly with Germanic culture (and various derivatives of Germanic culture; i.e., English, French, Italian, Spanish, Dutch, Flemish, Swedish, and Austrian culture), were the dominant social influences on the sport of the European Renaissance.

As has been implied, the **relation of Renaissance sport and class society** was intimate. Much of Renaissance sport was framed and governed by the character of class society; much of Renaissance sport tended both to express and to exacerbate differences in social class. The propertied, aristocratic class preferred sports requiring great wealth and leisure, such as chivalric tournament events, ice skating, tennis, golf, horse racing, yachting/sailing, and hunting, but did also engage in activities more characteristic of the middle and lower classes. The middle class of merchants, bankers, and artisans tended to prefer more useful and less exclusive activities, such as rowing, archery, and fencing, but did to an extent also emulate the activities of the aristocracy and borrow some lower-class amusements. Laborers and peasants inclined to still less exclusive activities, such as track and field athletic events, swimming, bowling, boxing, wrestling, cricket, field hockey, football, ice hockey, hurling, and soccer. Among the most strident ways in which class differences were manifested in the sport of this time included attempts by the aristocracy to regulate the sporting recreations of other social classes. There were several notable ideological, religious, economic, and political reasons for this tendency:

- the aristocracy claimed intrinsic participation in sport (the incipient origins of modern amateurism), ascribed lesser aims (extrinsic aims) to the sporting activities of others, and installed their own standards as those against which all others were to be unfavorably judged (the standards against which others were often adjudged indulgent and unsavory);

- the sporting recreations of the lower classes occurred mainly and unavoidably on the Sabbath and thus violated the Christian day of worship and rest;
- the sporting recreations of the lower classes distracted (in time, effort, and public order) from the central concerns of their work (that is, from producing advantages for the upper classes);
- the sporting recreations of the lower classes were often violent and sometimes brought disabling injury, further and adversely affecting their work and the advantages of the upper classes based on their work;
- the sporting recreations of the lower classes were more publicly visible than those of other classes and could thereby be more easily regulated than those of other classes;
- the upper classes had the prerogative and the resource to regulate others; others hadn't sufficient prerogative or resource to effectively resist; and
- sport's sense of freedom from established authority portended its revolutionary potential, its potential for political dissent.

The attempts of the aristocracy to regulate the sporting recreations of other classes were nonetheless only partly successful; the lower classes continued to vigorously practice sport in largely informal contexts such as fairs/festivals, inns, and taverns. In this highly discriminatory circumstance, women were among the most systematically disenfranchised. Although widely and deeply admired in the Renaissance, women were largely excluded from participation in sport. This tendency pertained most emphatically to aristocratic women whose standard of courtly manners did not include such participation. It was nonetheless the case that some Renaissance women of the lower class did participate, in running and rowing contests most particularly, throughout central, western, and southern Europe.

As has been also claimed, many of the leading cultural personalities of the fifteenth and sixteenth centuries were connected to sport in some noteworthy way. Of the **foremost political and intellectual figures of the Renaissance concerned with sport**, the English royal families of the period (the Houses of Lancaster, York, and Tudor) had an especially large penchant for the activity:

- Henry IV and Henry V regularly renewed bans on popular sports (in 1401, 1409, 1410, and 1414) but were nonetheless well disposed to aristocratic sport; Henry V was himself a tennis enthusiast as has been said;
- Henry VI lifted the ban on lawn bowling in 1455, imposed bans on football and golf in favor of archery in 1471 and 1491, presided over the first known use of the term, 'sport,' itself in c. 1440, and otherwise reigned over a period favorably inclined to popular sports and the disorder, gambling, and drunkenness associated with them;
- Edward IV promoted chivalric tournaments and forbade idle sports in order to protect archery in 1474 and 1477;
- Richard III also promoted chivalric tournaments;
- in addition to his already-cited taste for tennis, Henry VII was likewise fond of chivalric tournaments, archery, and wrestling;
- in addition to his already-cited taste for chivalric tournaments and tennis, Henry VIII widely patronized horse racing, presided over the establishment of the first permanent horse-race course (at Chester in 1540), and successfully practiced long jumping, high jumping, pole vaulting, shot putting, hammer throwing, wrestling, lawn bowling, hunting, and cock fighting, all allegedly in the service of fitness, not pleasure; in 1511 and 1526, he forbade idle games for archery; in 1540, he revoked the ban on fencing; and in 1541, he restricted the practice of lawn bowling to those owning valuable land;
- Edward VI had a guarded view of sport; and
- Katharine of Aragon had an apparent enthusiasm for golf; Anne Boleyn was evidently affected by archery; Mary I, by golf and bear baiting; Elizabeth I, who popularized chivalric tournaments as entertainments, by archery, tennis, and hunting; and Mary Queen of Scots, a Stuart, by golf and croquet.

Despite the rising specter of Puritanism, the English proclivity for sport was significantly advanced in the reign of Elizabeth (i.e., in the last approximate half of the sixteenth century). Tudor sympathies for the activity, a prosperous commercial circumstance, the beginnings of English colonialism, as well as both a taste and a sense of tolerance for revelry and the "vulgarities" of the body all conspired to this end.

The Medici, moreover, were enthusiastic supporters of chivalric tournaments in Italy. Louis XI of France was an avid player of billiards as well as tennis. The illuminated manuscript, "Très Riches Heures du Duc de Berry" of the Limbourg brothers, depicted early fifteenth-century French hunting and ball games. The Flemish

175

<u>Book of Hours</u> (1530), an illustrated calendar, included peasant and aristocratic forms of sport, golf most particularly. Leonardo da Vinci was a person of uncommon strength and was exceedingly adept at mountaineering, running, swimming, vaulting, and wrestling. Peter Bruegel the Elder depicted sporting games in several of his most celebrated paintings; most notably, "Children's Games" (1560). Pope Pius V prohibited bullfighting, by papal writ, in 1567. Edmund Spenser characterized sport as a noble and heroic pursuit. In addition to his already-cited reference to tennis in <u>Henry V</u>, Shakespeare variously accounted "Olympian Games" in <u>Henry VI</u> and <u>Troilus and Cressida</u>, lawn bowling in <u>Richard II</u>, wrestling in <u>As You Like It</u>, fencing (dueling) in <u>Twelfth Night</u>, football in <u>The Comedy of Errors</u> and <u>King Lear</u>, and billiards in <u>Antony and Cleopatra</u>. Ben Jonson spoke passingly in verse of sport. And several sixteenth-century French kings were avidly devoted to sport, most especially to tennis, as has been said.

The **dispersion of European Renaissance education and sport** to other regions of the world (mainly to the Americas and to Australasia) was first realized by the sixteenth-century voyages of world discovery. Even in other regions, however, these activities retained their European patterns of class (and gender) specificity, patterns which aggravated both the relations among Europeans and those between Europeans and indigenous peoples. The game-playing recreations of native peoples, which were customarily associated with animistic religious rituals having principally to do with "survival" activities (such as, soldiering, farming, hunting, fertility, and territorial acquisition), too had a significant influence on the development of sport outside Europe. Most early modern European immigrants to the Americas and to Australasia were Spanish, English, French, Italian, Portuguese, or Dutch. In the sixteenth century, the social-class sports of the Spanish were the most influential. Of these, the most notable were the festivals established by the conquistadores in central America. These festivals were mainly about displaying equestrian and other skills of combat. They were also often accompanied by Mesoamerican Indian sporting exhibitions. Likely the most important formal sporting consequence of these festivals was the development of bullfighting; the first public bullfight was staged in Mexico City in 1535. The Spanish too established universities in Lima (1551), Mexico City (1553), and Bogota (1592) where the humanist orientation prospered. In the seventeenth and eighteenth centuries, as well as the nineteenth and twentieth for that matter, the English traditions of outdoor sport became the singularly most compelling cultural influence on the development of modern sport in Europe and elsewhere. Contemporary world sport, the sport of our own time, is most the result of the English national sporting heritage, a heritage which had been developing in formal terms from at least the twelfth century.

Like the broad tendencies of European Renaissance culture, those of the seventeenth and eighteenth centuries also had a profound influence on the European education and sport of the period. In the empiricist-rationalist debate concerning the origin and nature of knowledge that pervaded the seventeenth century (and the eighteenth as well for that matter), empiricism gained the dominant ground in respect to education and physical education. **Seventeenth-century European education and physical education** were governed mainly by the empiricist doctrine, a doctrine which taught that the content of all knowledge is acquired through the bodily senses and takes the form of sense-perceptual impressions, impressions of a visual, auditory, olfactory, gustatory, and tactile sort. The mind, by this view, contributes nothing substantial to knowledge; it comes to nothing other than an empty receptacle endowed with the faculties of receiving, organizing, and recollecting the impressions brought to it by the senses. Empiricism gave a respectful interpretation of the body as the vehicle of the senses. A fit body was thought necessary to all forms of learning, for all forms of learning (i.e., all forms of knowledge) are grounded in bodily sense discrimination. Empiricism thereby widely advocated and widely promoted the practice of physical education. The subject occupied a prominent place in the broad and demanding empiricist curriculum, together with classical (Greek and Latin) and vernacular languages, logic, mathematics, the natural sciences (mainly physics), history, philosophy, and the arts. The realist-empiricist notion of the mind-body relation is not merely empiricistic, however, it is also dualistic/pluralistic, or of the view that the mind and body are qualitatively distinct substances which variously interact; it too holds to an objective concept of body and a corporeal view of movement.[123] Although on first inspection favorable to bodily events in general and to physical education in particular, empiricistic dualism/pluralism tends to interpret physical education as little other than an exercise modality, a means of enhancing bodily faculties. It acknowledges other worthy purposes (social, military, religious, and recreational purposes mainly) but so emphasizes health-oriented objectives that it fails to promote a fully humanistic, an intrinsic, respect for the activity; it tends to cut physical education off from its higher than biological, principally its humanistic, possibilities. The most prominently practiced forms of physical education in this period were: archery, gymnastic exercises, swimming, track and field athletic exertions (most notably, walking, running, jumping, and weight throwing), weightlifting, games resembling bowling, golf, and tennis, dual combative activities (most notably, boxing, fencing, and wrestling), tournament skills (most notably, equestrian games), and team ball games resembling field hockey, football, hurling, and soccer.

The realistic, or scientific, humanism of the seventeenth century, and its Baroque corollary, required a more scientifically oriented curriculum than had been earlier in fashion. This was so both in respect to curricular content and in respect to curricular method. The educational content of natural/empirical science and scientific/empirical methods were the governing factors of seventeenth-century European education and physical education. The seventeenth-century curriculum continued to include the study of logic, mathematics, vernacular languages, the natural sciences, history, philosophy, the arts, and physical education as has been said. It too continued (from the Renaissance) to embrace classical literary scholarship but it interpreted the significance of this scholarship in more instrumental ways than the Renaissance had. This scholarship was thought mainly important because it contained prescriptions for usefully improving the quality of human existence, for usefully improving the quality of practical life. Seventeenth-century educational method was also grounded in the procedural tendencies of the natural sciences; it was effectively grounded in inductive orientation and it was too devoted to expelling the groundless conclusions of the deductive tradition. Seventeenth-century education and physical education was, thus, not driven in every problematic case by either the ancient classics or the revealed texts of medieval religion. The inductive approach argues from particular instances to general cases, from example to principle, from what is known to what is unknown. It thereby makes extensive use of sensory techniques such as direct experience, observation, experimentation, creative problem-solving, and illustrated examples; it likewise recognizes developmental and individual learning differences, fashions sophisticated teaching-learning progressions, and acknowledges a role for entertainment in education. It too greatly favors the careful training and selection of teachers and it prefers a public, universal, and massed education to a private, exclusive, and tutorial one.

In this time and largely under the terms of the empirical equation, physical education was enthusiastically endorsed by some of the period's most remarkable literary and philosophic talents. Juan Luis Vives (1492-1540), a Spanish scholar, wrote the earliest realist tracts on subjects pertinent to education and physical education in the sixteenth century, On a Plan of Studies for Youth, On the Instruction of a Christian Woman, Concerning the Teaching of the Arts, and Concerning the Mind. François Rabelais, the exceptional sixteenth-century French ecclesiastic and educational satirist and critic, characterized the proper education of youth in his masterpiece, Gargantua and Pantagruel. Gargantua's lessons very importantly included the rigorous practice of physical education. Richard Mulcaster (c. 1531-1611), the English headmaster of the "Merchant Taylors' School" and the "St. Paul's School," both in London, greatly favored the education (and vigorous physical education) of all persons (including women), construed physical education (mainly in the form of hunting, horse riding, walking, running, leaping, swimming, shooting, fencing, wrestling, handball, tennis, and football) as a form of human expression, pleasure, and enjoyment as well as a means of enhancing and maintaining health, and was the first to practice the realist education and physical education in concrete, school circumstance. Mulcaster also wrote two penetrating and influential volumes, Positions and Elementaire, on the subject. Michel de Montaigne, the celebrated sixteenth-century French essayist, wrote two extraordinary essays concerning the realist education and physical education, "On the Education of Children" and "On Pedantry." In both, physical education was greatly favored as a worthy and necessary accompaniment of intellectual learning. Francis Bacon, the first of the legendary British empiricists and the first modern scientific philosopher, included favorable treatments of the realist education and physical education (having mainly to do with health) in several of his philosophical masterworks, The Advancement of Learning, Novum Organum, and New Atlantis. John Amos Comenius (1593-1670), the renowned Moravian bishop and scholar and the most skillful educational interpreter of Bacon, wrote several accomplished and influential manuscripts concerning educational reform in which he championed the realist view of education and physical education, Great Didactic, School of Infancy, and Orbis Pictus/The World in Pictures. John Milton, the illustrious English poet, referred metaphorically to "Olympian Games" in Paradise Lost and wrote an important realist account of education and physical education, Tractate on Education, in which physical expressions (particularly fencing and wrestling) put to good purpose (i.e., effecting good consequences; most notably, health) were highly praised. And John Locke, the quintessential British empiricist, authored an especially memorable interpretation of the realist education and physical education, Some Thoughts Concerning Education, in which he outlined the formal purpose of education for both men and women as progressing, by inductive means, to happiness through pleasurable experience. This experience entails perfecting the sense-perceptual faculties (as the bodily source of all knowledge) by means of physical education (mainly fencing, swimming, and exercise) and perfecting the faculties of the mind (as the ultimate form of all knowledge) by means of intellectual education. The result of such experience, if all has gone well, is a person of high intellectual prowess, vigorous action, practical good sense, and exemplary moral and socio-political character.

Several leading political authorities and institutions were likewise significantly devoted to the new scientific education. The French Academy (of arts and sciences) was established in 1615 in the reign of Louis XIII; the Royal (scientific) Society of London was established in 1662 in the reign of Charles II. And Frederick William the Great Elector of Brandenburg-Prussia meaningfully elevated German standards of public education in the mid-to-late seventeenth century.

Eighteenth-century European education and physical education was also profoundly affected by the broad tendencies of the age, by the naturalistic humanism (and its neo-classical corollary) of the Modern European Enlightenment. Many of the leading political and intellectual figures and institutions of the eighteenth century were themselves tangibly and seriously devoted to educational projects; some of these figures were themselves accomplished teachers/professors. Frederick I of Brandenburg-Prussia established a (national) Academy of Sciences in Berlin in 1707. The Imperial Academy of Qing China published an encyclopedia in 1716 that greatly influenced Chinese and European scholarship and education. Secret international societies, such as the freemasons, were increasingly created to promote the ideals (including the educational ideals) of the Enlightenment; the first of these, the Grand Lodge of London, was established in the reign of George I in 1717. Christian Wolff, the methodical German philosopher, amplified the educational implications of Leibniz' thought in the early-to-mid eighteenth century. Peter the Great of Russia established and promoted advanced professional schools and the Academy of Sciences (St. Petersburg, 1725). Catherine the Great of Russia unsuccessfully attempted to establish public elementary and secondary schools and successfully founded the University of Moscow in 1755. Maria Theresa of Austria created training schools for the professions in Vienna in the mid-to-late eighteenth century. Joseph II of Austria was a fervent advocate of public education in the late eighteenth century. Benjamin Franklin advocated practical and public forms of education in his "Proposals Relating to the Education of Youth" of 1743 and played a major role in the establishment of the University of Pennsylvania in 1751. Thomas Jefferson, as Governor of Virginia, enacted the "Virginia Public Education Bill" in 1779. The "doctrine of sensationalism" (the view that sensation is not only the source of all knowledge but the sole form of knowledge as well), inspired mainly by the seventeenth-century philosophy of John Locke and developed explicitly and principally by the French philosophers, Étienne Bonnot de Condillac and Claude-Adrien Helvetius, created the basis of modern empirical psychology, a subject that has had an altogether profound influence on modern education. Gotthold Ephraim Lessing, the celebrated German dramatist, wrote tellingly of Enlightenment education in <u>The Education of the Human Race</u> (1780). Johann Wolfgang von Goethe, the German literary colossus, wrote among the great novels of education in modern literature, <u>The Apprenticeship of Wilhelm Meister</u>, in 1796. The other towering figure of German Enlightenment literature, Johann Friedrich Schiller, and the leading German Enlightenment philosopher of history, Johann Gottfried Herder, persuasively advocated a balanced, an aesthetic, education of humanistic dimension (which foresaw nineteenth-century romantic prescriptions) in the late eighteenth century; perhaps most notable in this respect was Schiller's "Letters on the Aesthetic Education of Mankind" (1794-1795). And Immanuel Kant, the apotheosis of German Enlightenment philosophy, in <u>On Education</u> (1803), which was written significantly under the influence of Rousseau, outlined the principal obligations of education: to cultivate and to advance humanity's unique and inherent (natural) inclination to acquire theoretical knowledge, to act morally (in accord with the "categorical imperative"), to apprehend God, and to form an aesthetic awareness. Education, by this view, is to develop an organism of alert mind, sturdy body, and moral, aesthetic, and socio-political sensitivity. Physical education was thought an important medium through which these various aims were to be taught and learned.

The singularly most important educational interpreter of naturalistic humanism, the defining personality of eighteenth-century European education and physical education, however, was the French social and political philosopher, Jean-Jacques Rousseau. Rousseau's philosophy of education, recorded most notably in <u>Émile</u>, advocated a development of the individual personality toward the inherent virtues of nature, a natural development in which the individual is made free from bogus and contaminating forms of social and political expectation and free for discovering her/his natural character and purpose. Education was thought to make life intelligible, to give all persons an understanding of what democratic citizenship in an ideal (a natural) state entails, and to make for the harmonious development of one's intellectual and physical aspects. Rousseau's naturalistic interpretation of education, his liberal and universal interpretation of education, awarded major emphasis to physical education, principally as a means of protecting and enhancing health, physique, and psychomotor skill, of developing rich sense experiences, of fashioning moral and social character, and of embodying recreational pleasure. In his educational prescriptions, he reserved a very prominent place for the vigorous, spontaneous, and natural movements of physical education. Rousseau traced the education of a male child, Émile, through five successive stages of development from birth to marriage. Complete freedom to exercise dominates the animal stage (birth to five years); a variety of games and sports, the savage stage (five to twelve years); physical exercise and intellectual activity of immediate interest and use (linguistic and mathematical activity mainly), the pastoral stage (twelve to fifteen years); physical exercise and the formal study of social, religious, and moral problems, the social stage (fifteen to twenty years); and the physical and intellectual challenges of marriage and life, the adult stage (thereafter).

Physical education figured very prominently in the educational and recreative prescriptions of eighteenth-century European life. The philosophical basis of these prescriptions remained fundamentally realistic, however. Naturalistic humanism continued to hold to an objective concept of body, a corporeal view of movement, a dualistic/pluralistic notion of the mind-body relation, and an empiricistic interpretation of knowledge, all ostensibly conducive to the wide pursuit of vigorous physical expressions, but all ultimately casting such expressions in extrinsic profile. As a function of the quite original eighteenth-century interest in the social sciences, naturalistic programs of physical education nonetheless added authentically social experience to the realist emphasis on largely biological purposes and thereby more nearly approached humanistic and intrinsic possibilities than realist such programs had. The most widely practiced forms of physical education in this period were: archery, gymnastic exercise, ice skating, rowing, swimming, track and field athletic exertions (most notably, walking, running, standing and running horizontal and vertical jumping, vaulting, and weight throwing), weightlifting, games resembling badminton, bowling, golf, and tennis, dual combative activities (most notably, boxing, fencing, and wrestling), equestrian activities, and team ball games resembling cricket, field hockey, football, hurling, lacrosse, and soccer.

Rousseau was arguably among the several most profound and influential thinkers and writers of the eighteenth century. He was, by both inclination and practical necessity, however, a wandering bohemian who never attempted to set either his political or his educational thought to concrete practice. The first to venture a tangible practice of Rousseau's educational philosophy were German schoolmasters and teachers. The earliest of these was Johann Bernhard Basedow (1723-1790), who founded the first school in which naturalistic humanism was the governing tenet, the universal Philanthropinum (1774-1793) at Dessau, and who wrote two important books on the subject of naturalistic education, A Book of Methods and Elementary Book. It was at the Philanthropinum that naturalistic physical education took its first tentative steps. The physical education classes there were greatly emphasized and they were first entrusted to Johann Friedrich Simon (fl. in the late eighteenth century), who is thereby known as the first teacher of modern, naturalistic physical education. In subsequent decades, several new schools, fashioned on the example of the Philanthropinum, were established. The most notable of these was the Schnepfenthal Educational Institute, created by Christian G. Salzmann (1744-1811) at Schnepfenthal in 1785. After the brief tenure of Christian Carl André (fl. in the late eighteenth century), the physical education instruction at the Schnepfenthal was taken over by the man who was to become the most prominent physical educator of the eighteenth century, the so-termed "grandfather of modern (naturalistic) physical education," Johann Friedrich GutsMuths (1759-1839). GutsMuths taught geography and physical education at the Schnepfenthal for nearly fifty years (1786-1835). It was during his tenure there that he wrote his two most memorable books, Gymnastics for the Young (1793) and Games (1796), and that he formulated the detailed ground of the new system. GutsMuths' program of physical education was predictably of broad scope, democratically inclined, and highly scientific. It was divided into three parts: gymnastic exercises properly so-called (in which bodily exercises were classified according to kind [running, leaping, vaulting, throwing, lifting, climbing] and according to educational function [observation, alacrity, imagination, memory]), manual labors, and social games. And it was based on the vigorous movements to which human beings incline when they are left to do as they will in an uncontrived, a natural, environment; that is, large-muscle, integrative activities such as running, leaping, vaulting, throwing, lifting, balancing, and climbing. This makes for a substantially different type of gymnastic system than its main alternative, the militaristic system, which was first sketched in the nineteenth century.

Not unlike Renaissance sport, **seventeenth-century and eighteenth-century sport outside the schools**, sport in the wider than strictly educational sense, was remarkably extensive and it was also less explicitly affected by the ideological tendencies of the period (by realistic and naturalistic humanism) than was physical education. It also continued, however, to be greatly influenced by broad patterns of cultural development, many of which were ongoing from the Renaissance. It continued, for one, to develop in the contentious context of class society; the aristocracy continued to prefer exclusive sporting activities and to regulate the recreations of the lower classes; the middle class continued to emulate the recreations of the upper classes and to borrow some lower-class amusements; and the lower classes continued to practice inclusive sporting activities, largely in informal terms. It continued, for another, to be significantly affected by colonialism, by patterns of immigration related to colonialism, and by the recreative practices of native peoples. The singular most significant cultural influences on the development of sport in the seventeenth and eighteenth centuries (as well as the nineteenth and twentieth centuries for that matter) in Europe and elsewhere were the English traditions as has been said. With the earnest advent of English colonialism in particular (and associated immigration patterns) in the late sixteenth century, the practice of English sport (like that of other English conventions) was variously transported about the world; most importantly, to what would become the sovereign nations of Ireland, Australia, Canada, New Zealand, South Africa, India, the British West Indies, and the United States of America. The new settlers in these regions brought with them the social-class sports of seventeenth-century and eighteenth-century Europe. The **sporting recreations of native peoples** also continued to influence sporting life in these regions, most emphatically in the Americas and Australasia. In the Americas, the game-playing conventions of the Eskimos, the North American Indians (such as, the Algonquian and the Siouan), the Mesoamerican Indians (such as, the Aztecan and the Mayan), and the South American Indians (such as, the Incan) were most significant. Kayaking and lacrosse are likely the most notable sporting derivatives of these conventions. In Australasia, the game-playing conventions of the Polynesians were most significant. Canoeing and surfing are likely the most notable sporting derivatives of these conventions. The sport of this period was too importantly affected by the **sporting recreations of indentured peoples**; most notably, by the sporting recreations of African slaves in the Americas. Most of these recreations, which were surprisingly extensive, grew out of animistic religious ceremonies (of the broad type practiced by native peoples), the sparse leisure allowed by quasi-seasonal duties, and the need for the sort of catharsis, self-respect, and group cohesion that slavery lacks and that sport can impart. Capoeira, a highly acrobatic form of martial art fashioned by Brazilian slaves in the sixteenth and seventeenth centuries, is likely the most notable sporting derivative of these recreations.

The most significant sporting developments novel to the seventeenth and eighteenth centuries unfolded in Europe, North America, and Asia. In Europe, **English/British sport** was by far the most extensive and the most influential. As in the medieval and Renaissance instances, the relation of sport and formal religion consequentially determined the course of English/British sport (as well as other forms of European sport, American sport, and Asian sport) in this period. Church objections to sport softened somewhat in the seventeenth and eighteenth centuries; they would soften still further in the nineteenth and twentieth centuries. Anglicanism's generally favorable treatment of sport and the high taste for sport in the English royal family (the Tudor monarchs of the sixteenth century most notably) continued, on balance, in the seventeenth and eighteenth centuries. The Stuarts, the dominant political entity in England throughout the seventeenth century, were too, on balance, very fond of sport and attempted to standardize sporting regulations and to fix the schedules (the times and places) of sporting events. Sport flourished throughout the reign of the Stuarts despite the ongoing objections of Puritanism to vigorous expressions of the physical body and despite (or perhaps because of) sport's brutally violent practice, its telling associations with gambling, and its domination by commercial interests. James I (r. 1603-1625), the first Stuart, greatly favored popular sports and, in 1618, authorized publication of the <u>Book of Sports</u>/<u>King's Declaration on Sports</u>, a volume that enthusiastically endorsed sporting activity as highly constructive, as promoting fitness for war, and as discouraging folly, idleness, and discontent. He also authorized (in 1612) practice of the Cotswold, or "Olympick," Games by Captain Robert Dover (1582-1652) at Dover's Hill (near Stratford); these Games had been established in 1604 and they were variously carried on until 1857 (revived in 1951). They included a wide variety of activities – most notably, wrestling, leaping, pitching the bar, throwing the hammer, and tossing the pike – practiced for purposes of merriment and national defense. Although James forbade tennis to laborers and servants (in 1618) and tended to protect the sanctity of the Sabbath from sport, he lifted earlier royal bans on archery and football, established a horse-racing course at Newmarket (near Cambridge) in 1622, and was himself devoted to croquet, golf, horse racing, hunting, and lawn bowling.

Charles I (r. 1625-1649) re-issued the <u>Book of Sports</u> in 1633, again over Puritan protests, but enacted a formal ban on Sunday sports in 1644; he was himself taken with tennis, golf, lawn bowling, horse racing, and hunting; and he established the Newmarket Gold Cup in horse racing in 1634. The Puritan-inspired Commonwealth that followed (1649-1660) was, on balance, deeply unfriendly to sport. The rigid, uncompromising, and austere fundamentalism of the Puritan movement encouraged a view of sport as a form of sensual indulgence, as a type of indecent revelry, as a profligate opponent of industrious employment, and as embodying a lack of admirable restraint. Puritanism likewise opposed the barbarous and cruel practices of many sports (particularly football, horse racing, and blood sports such as bull baiting, hawking, and hunting), the dissolute practices of inns and taverns where sports were often conducted, and the practice of Sunday sports. The result was formal bans (which were routinely defied) on football and animal sports in 1654; the Cotswold Games had been suspended in 1642; and Sunday sports had been too prohibited in 1644 as has been said. Vigorous forms of physical expression were tolerated by the Puritan leadership only for purposes of useful toil, of exercise when demanding physical labor were unavailable, of promoting a sense of the body's connections to spirituality, and of encouraging a resourceful ethic. Oliver Cromwell himself was nonetheless apparently fond of sport within the rough parameters of Puritan restraint. He had played football and cricket in his youth and later developed a taste for lawn bowling and horse racing; he did neither greatly disturb the recreations of the rich despite his enthusiasm for restricting popular sporting amusements. With the Stuart Restoration of 1660, Anglicanism regained its ideological preeminence, the Puritan influence declined sharply, and popular sports again flourished. The bans on football and animal sports were lifted in 1659 and the Cotswold Games were resumed in 1660. The sport of the late Stuart years was nonetheless more fully committed to combining enjoyment with good taste, with gaining pleasure without abandoning reason and style, than the sport of the early Stuart years had been. Charles II (r. 1660-1685) was himself committed to a broad range of sporting activities: swimming, ice skating, croquet, tennis, lawn bowling, archery, fencing, wrestling, yachting/sailing, football, horse racing (in which he rode his own horse in races, established the Newmarket Racecourse in 1665, and formed the first King's Plate race at Newmarket in 1666), and hunting. James II (r. 1685-1688) played tennis, golf, and lawn bowling; Mary II (r. 1689-1694), golf and billiards; William III (r. 1689-1702) had a guarded view of sport; and Anne (r. 1702-1714), the last of the Stuarts, had a great affection for hunting and horse racing (she standardized breeding regulations, originated the notion of stakes races, established the practice of races for cash prizes, and opened the Royal Ascot Racecourse [near London] in 1711).

The enormous popular appeal of English/British sport, so prominent in the Tudor and Stuart eras, was effectively continued in the Hanoverian (1714-1901). Sport of both the formal, professional sort (most particularly, boxing, cricket, and horse racing) and the informal, non-professional sort (in such as schools, inns, and taverns) flourished throughout the eighteenth century. Church influence over sport again declined; the commercial utilization of leisure activities expanded; the comprehensive regulation of sport significantly increased, principally in order to optimize popular rivalries and the profits that could be turned from such rivalries; brutal, unsavory, and corrupt practices, typically associated with attempts to protect the investments of gamblers, crept prominently back into sport; characteristically democratic notions of individual achievement in sport, equal opportunity to participate in sport, and class integration in sport were advanced as were characteristically capitalistic notions of private property rights pertinent to sport and the sense of exclusivity such rights entail; and national sporting tendencies were promoted. The eighteenth-century British crown after Anne, however, was governed by a sense of reasoned moderation that more so tolerated sport as a means of social control than actively endorsed the activity. George I (r. 1714-1727) was nonetheless interested in boxing, horse racing, and hunting; George II (r. 1727-1760), in boxing, cricket, horse racing, and yachting/sailing; and George III (r. 1760-1820), in yachting/sailing and horse racing. By the late eighteenth century (c. 1780), moreover, a new moral voice, mainly from religionists, had made its way through Great Britain. This voice of piety and virtue objected to the brutality, violence, and corruption in many popular sports (most notably, boxing and blood sports; cock fighting, for prominent instance, was outlawed provisionally in Great Britain in 1795); it successfully attempted to make established sports less offensive to changing tastes, to provide wholesome public recreation, to reduce the sense of spectacle in sport, and to increase the sense of fair play and equal opportunity for success in sport; it encouraged local sports (such as bandy in Wales and hurling and shinty in Ireland); and it allowed some sports to be practiced in some schools (formal inter-class football was played at Trinity College, Dublin as early as 1780 and inter-class rowing was contested at Eton College [public school] and Oxford University as early as 1793 for especially prominent instance). This voice also became prominent among commercialists/industrialists whose concern for public order and the discipline of labor increasingly overwhelmed all other considerations.

Although the **institutionalization of national and international sport**, out of local sports (governed mainly by oral reminiscences), was a largely nineteenth-century and twentieth-century phenomenon, the (written) formalization of some modern sporting codes, rules, and institutions in national and international terms was nonetheless owed to the eighteenth century. The earliest of the strictly athletic endeavors to thrive under the terms of this formalization was **boxing**. Curiously enough, the early popularity of boxing in England/Great Britain was significantly due to a growing antipathy for blood sports such as cock fighting, bear and bull baiting, gouging, and dueling, which had been main forms of sporting amusement to at least the early eighteenth century. Astonishingly by late twentieth-century standards, boxing had a taming affect on early modern English/British sport. The codification of boxing rules and the sport's first great champions "civilized" the sport and brought it respectability by the middle of the eighteenth century. Broughton's Rules, which governed formal boxing matches, then contested with ungloved hands ("bare knuckles"), from 1743 to 1838:

- prohibited gouging and striking a felled opponent with hands or feet but yet allowed upper-body "wrestling;"
- characterized segments (or rounds) of a match by falls (when a fighter is put to the turf) after which the fallen fighter was given one-half minute to stand at a square in the center of the ring and continue the match or be declared beaten; and
- defined the conclusion of a match by the inability of a fighter to continue.

James Figg (1695-1740) became the first generally acknowledged male boxing champion of England before the advent of Broughton's Rules when the sport included wrestling practices and was little other than continuous fighting. He reigned from 1719 to 1734; had between 277 and 300 fights, losing but once; was also an accomplished wrestler and fencer; operated an influential school for boxers, Figg's Academy for Boxing, in London from 1719; was patronized by no less than Jonathan Swift, Alexander Pope, and William Hogarth; and was portrayed in several of Hogarth's most accomplished paintings. Elisabeth Stokes (fl. in the early eighteenth century) became the first generally acknowledged female boxing champion of England in 1720. John "Jack" Broughton (1704-1789), a pupil of Figg's Academy, was the author of Broughton's Rules, invented the boxing glove (then used only for sparring), and reigned as the stylish, resolute, and upstanding champion of England from at least 1740 (perhaps 1734) to 1750. He was arguably the most important figure in the early (i.e., eighteenth-century) development of modern boxing. He was beaten by the disreputable Jack Slack (fl. in the mid-eighteenth century; r. 1750-1760) in 1750, after which the sport fell into nearly forty years of corruption and neglect. In this period, only the reign of the first Irishman to hold the English title, Peter Corcoran (fl. in the late eighteenth century; r. 1771-1776), a punching master, and the reign of Tom Johnson (1750-1797; r. 1783-1791), a technical master of the ring, a fighter of great strength, and a man of wide popularity, were at all noteworthy. The honorable and technically masterful Jewish fighter, Daniel Mendoza (1763-1836), effectively rescued the sport in the early 1790s. Mendoza, a man of exceedingly modest height and weight, held the English title from 1791 to 1795, revolutionized boxing technique, and greatly popularized the sport in both England and Ireland. He was defeated for the title in 1795 by "Gentleman" John Jackson (b. 1776) who retired as champion in 1800 without having fought again.

The **other major European sports** of the seventeenth and eighteenth centuries were: archery, billiards, bowling, cricket, croquet, curling, fencing, football, golf, (acrobatic) gymnastics, (court) handball, field hockey, ice hockey, horse racing, hunting, hurling, pedestrianism, rowing, shooting, ice skating, skiing, soccer, swimming, tennis, track and field athletics, weightlifting, wrestling, and yachting/sailing. Some of these were more widely practiced in this period than in any prior period; some were themselves devoted to producing commercial profit, had substantial prizes associated with them, were deeply involved with gambling activities, and had a wide spectatorial following; and many encouraged women's participation, sometimes with men, usually not (most particularly, archery, cricket, football, horse racing, hunting, pedestrianism, rowing, shooting, swimming, and yachting/sailing). Several even developed still more modern forms and passed through significant formal developments in this time. In archery, the Royal Scorton (near York, England) Arrow (the oldest continuing archery tournament in the world) was established in 1673, the Royal Company of Archers was formed in Scotland in 1676, the Society Royal Toxophilite (which included women) was established in England in 1781, and the Royal British Bowmen (which also admitted women) was formed in England in 1787. In billiards, from as early as the seventeenth century in France, England, Spain, and the Germanies, the practice of striking stone balls with a mace through and at arches and stakes was replaced by the practice of striking wooden and brass balls (i.e., cue and object balls) at one another and at pockets, all with slender, tapered sticks (or cues); the tables in this time were themselves wooden, were of varying dimension, and had at first two pockets (one at each end of the table), then four (one at each of the four corners of the table), and, when they were made rectangular, six (one at each corner and one at the middle of each of the two sides of the table). In bowling, the first written rules of pin bowling were crafted in England in 1670; the first formal lawn bowling club, the Kilmarnock Bowling Club, was formed in Scotland in 1743; and the first written rules of lawn bowling were framed in Scotland in 1771. In cricket as such, the first recorded match (with wickets) was staged in England in 1700; the first formal rules were developed in England in 1727; these rules were codified by the London Cricket Club in 1744 and significantly refined in 1774 (to establish what are yet the approximate specifications of the balls and bats) and 1788 (to allow overarm, albeit straight-arm, bowling); the first county match was played in 1728 between Kent and Sussex; legal restrictions prohibiting cricket in England were lifted in 1748; the sport was passed from England to Scotland in the

1740s, to Continental Europe in the 1760s, and to Wales in the 1780s; the first major clubs, the London Cricket Club and the Hambledon Cricket Club, were established in England in 1744 and 1756 respectively; (aristocratic) women's cricket was first organized in England in 1777 (although smock races for women had been common at cricket matches from the seventeenth century); and arguably the most important institution in the entire history of the sport, the Marylebone Cricket Club (the effective national governing body of cricket in England), was established in 1787. Modern croquet evolved out of a medieval and Renaissance game, pêle mêle, in seventeenth-century France; coincident with the elimination of arches and stakes in billiards was an attempt to maintain these features on a large playing surface; the incipient development of croquet as an outdoor sport was the result. Modern curling first developed in sixteenth-century Scotland out of older attempts to translate lawn bowling to ice; the first formal club in the sport, the Dudingston Curling Club of Edinburgh, was established in 1795. In fencing, the saber was fashioned in Italy in 1686 and protective masks were created in eighteenth-century France. The earliest discernible precursors of Gaelic-rules football as such, which entailed both the kicking and the catching of balls, were played in Ireland in 1670. The first formal golf club, the Royal and Ancient Golf Club of St. Andrews, and the first formal rules of the game (including the standard round of eighteen holes) were established in Scotland in 1754 on the site of the approximately two-centuries-old golf course.

In horse racing, the Jockey Club of England, which thereafter significantly governed the sport, was established in 1750; the St. Leger, typically for 3-year olds over I mile 6 furlongs 132 yards (c. 3000 meters) at Town Moor (near Manchester and York), the oldest stakes race in the world, was first run in 1776 (and later became the third-leg in the British triple-crown series); the Oaks, typically for 3-year old fillies over 1½ miles (c. 2400 meters) at Epsom (near London) was first run in 1779; and the English, or Epsom, Derby, typically for 3-year olds over 1½ miles at Epsom, was first run in 1780 (and later became the second-leg of the British triple-crown series). Rowing regattas among gondoliers in Venice began in the early seventeenth century (although rowing regattas of some type had been apparently conducted in Venice from perhaps as early as the thirteenth century); English rowing on the Thames River continued from the Renaissance, most notably in the form of Doggett's Coat and Badge, a ferrymen's boat race between London and Chelsea Bridges (c. 4½ miles/c. 7000 meters), which began in 1716 and which was once won by the fabled boxing champion, Jack Broughton. Modern ice skating began as informal speed skating contests (some of which included women) on metal (iron, as distinct from bone or wood) skate blades (first fashioned in the late sixteenth century) in seventeenth-century Netherlands; it established its first formal organization, the Skating Club of Edinburgh, in 1742; and it conducted its first formal competition, a 15-mile (c. 25,000 meters) race on the Fen River in England, in 1763. The development of modern skiing continued from the Renaissance in seventeenth-century and eighteenth-century Sweden and Norway; cross-country skiing of a sort was also practiced in eighteenth-century Canada. A snow-ice carnival (which included skiing) was held in Canada from as early as 1759; the first modern, organized cross-country skiing competitions (some of which resembled modern biathlon contests) were staged in the Norwegian military among border guards on the Norway-Sweden frontier in 1767. Tennis likewise continued its formal modern development from the Renaissance as "le jeu de paume" (court, royal, or real tennis), most notably in France and England. All three seventeenth-century French kings, Henri IV, Louis XIII, and Louis XIV, ardently played the sport; Charles I, Charles II, and James II of England were also devoted to it; a trade union of tennis players was developed in seventeenth-century France; and the equipment used in the sport was greatly improved (a net dividing the court replaced the earlier chord and stuffed leather balls replaced the earlier cloth implements, all in the eighteenth century). The semblance of world championships in court tennis was held on a challenge basis in men's singles, first in 1740 in France and again twice before the end of the eighteenth century (in 1765 and 1785). And the formative development of modern yachting/sailing was owed to seventeenth-century Netherlands, Venice, Ireland, and England; the earliest clubs, the Water Club of Cork Harbor, Ireland (1720) and the Cumberland Fleet of England (1775), were established in this time; and the first regatta was staged in England also in this time (1775). Ice boating, a form of yachting/sailing, was first done in eighteenth-century Netherlands and skate sailing, also a form of yachting/sailing, was first practiced in eighteenth-century Scandinavia (mainly Denmark and Sweden).

The most significant developments in European animal sports of the seventeenth and eighteenth centuries (other than horse racing and other than largely English restrictions on blood sports) was the widespread practice of blood sports (mainly cock fighting, dog fighting, badger baiting, bear baiting, bull baiting, and coursing [the chasing of hares by dogs]) throughout this period and the ongoing, the distinctly modern amplification of bullfighting in eighteenth-century Spain. The eighteenth century was also witness to the earliest development of aerial nature sport in the form of hot-air ballooning. The first balloon flights, the unmanned efforts of the Montgolfier brothers, Joseph Michel (1740-1810) and Jacques Étienne (1745-1799), in Lyons, France in 1783, were scientific projects of a characteristically Enlightenment sort. The first manned flight was achieved in a Montgolfier balloon by Pilatre de Rozier (fl. in the late eighteenth century) and François Laurent (fl. in the late eighteenth century) in Paris, also in 1783. And the earliest major mountain climbing triumph was too owed to the eighteenth century; Montblanc (4807 meters/15,819 feet) in the French Alps was first scaled in 1786.

Both of the **principal multi-sport festivals of early modern civilization** survived the period and continued into the era of contemporary modern civilization (the nineteenth century). The Highland Games of Scotland, which began in the eleventh century, were suspended in the mid-eighteenth century (1747) over a dispute with England concerning the attempted Anglicization of Scottish society, but were revived in 1781. And the Cotswold Games of Dover's Hill, England, which began in 1604, were variously carried on until 1857 as has been said.

Most of the **sporting experience of the colonial period in North America** (from colonization by European powers in the seventeenth century to political independence from European powers in the eighteenth century) was the consequence of English developments a generation or less before. The American colonists, like the English themselves, were divided most importantly into Anglican and Puritan communities, communities that differed widely over the subject of sporting activity. The English colonists who first migrated to America in 1607 and formed the Virginia Company were primarily upper-middle-class Anglicans who were largely motivated by mercantile aims. The influence of this group was dominant among the gentry of New York, of the middle colonies (most notably, Maryland and Virginia), of the southern colonies (most notably, the Carolinas), and of the frontier (most notably, Kentucky, Ohio, Indiana, Illinois, and Michigan). In these regions, sport was much encouraged, particularly sports of the English aristocracy, mainly as expressions of social, national, and economic status but also as means of pleasurable recreation.

The English colonists who first migrated to America in 1620 and formed the Massachusetts Company were primarily lower-middle-class Puritans who were largely motivated by religious aims. The influence of this group was dominant in the colonies of New England (most notably, Massachusetts), in the colonies to which dissidents from New England fled (most notably, Connecticut and Rhode Island), and in Pennsylvania (which was most notably governed by the "Holy Experiment," the Quaker experiment, of William Penn [1644-1718]). Although serious restrictions were enforced in these regions on peasant and working-class sport for military purposes (sport distracted from duty), for political purposes (sport distracted from public order), and for economic purposes (sport enhanced the prospect of disabling injury and the subversive notion of self-sufficiency), the most telling restrictions were religious. Religious restrictions on sport were based primarily on the typically violent, disorderly, and unsavory behavior associated with sporting events, on the detestation of gambling, idleness, self-indulgence, and frivolous amusement, and on sporting profanations of the Sabbath. As in England, Puritan-inspired laws prohibiting Sunday recreations were well known in America. Mainly in order to impede gambling and to preserve virtue, sobriety, and a strict Sabbath, formal legal restraints on Sunday sport were enacted in New England in 1624, 1632, 1643, 1644, 1648, and 1653 and exacting Quaker laws against Sunday sport were enforced in Pennsylvania, most strictly from acts of 1682 and 1740. The most devout of the puritanical tendencies in colonial American religion and culture, the Great Awakenings, went on intermittently from the late seventeenth century to the late nineteenth century and were led most significantly in the seventeenth and eighteenth centuries by Cotton Mather (1663-1728) and Jonathan Edwards (1703-1758). This movement tended to tireless and severe condemnations of sport. The Great Awakenings nonetheless failed in the end, both in general terms and in respect to sporting activity. Their sharply limited and limiting view of life was unable to successfully defend itself against the deepening sense of secular wealth, leisure, diversity, and tolerance that moved through American culture in these periods. Religious prohibitions of sport were too routinely defied (recreations were often covertly pursued despite authoritative prohibitions of them); these prohibitions were themselves progressively loosened; the antipathy of (most influential forms of) religious sentiment for sport was progressively softened; and American religion increasingly accommodated sport. Under the terms of the Colonial Enlightenment, American religion came, in the end, to embrace many forms of sport as contributing, by catharsis, to the efficiency of work, as a means of good health, and as a form of salutary recreation.

Wherever colonial sport appeared, however, it was largely a function of local perceptions of economic utility, religious observance, and personal-community rights. The imperatives of everyday life were nonetheless so overwhelming and leisure resource so sparse that sport did not become an integral feature of American life in the colonial period. Its practice was mainly limited to spontaneous and informal game-playing by colonists and British soldiers at such as fairs, festivals, inns, taverns, and schools (colleges, grammar schools, secondary schools, and academies). Arguably the most notable such development first occurred in leading colleges of the eighteenth century, for this development heralded what became one of the most significant chapters in the history of American sport, the formal maturation of intercollegiate athletics in the nineteenth century. On the broad models of Oxford University and Cambridge University and at institutions now known as Harvard University (Cambridge, Massachusetts; established in 1636), William and Mary College (Williamsburg, Virginia; established in 1693), Yale University (New Haven, Connecticut; established in 1701), Princeton University (Princeton, New Jersey; established in 1746), University of Pennsylvania (Philadelphia; established in 1751), Columbia University (New York City; established in 1754), Brown University (Providence, Rhode Island; established in 1764), Rutgers University (New Brunswick, New Jersey; established in 1766), and Dartmouth College (Hanover, New Hampshire; established in 1769), informal game-playing among students was fairly common. This was the case even though the administrative leadership of early American schools was typically opposed to sporting activity. In addition to the conventional political, economic, and religious objections, school authorities also opposed the unruly and unsavory behavior that typically accompanied such activity.

The most widely practiced sports in early modern North America were of English/British pedigree as has been said. The most notable of these were billiards, blood sports (cock fighting and fox hunting in particular), lawn bowling, boxing, cricket (and other precursors of baseball such as rounders, one old cat, and stoolball), fencing, football/soccer, golf, field hockey, horse racing, swimming, tennis, track and field athletic exertions, wrestling, and yachting/sailing. Of these, the most significant by a wide margin was horse racing; horse racing was the earliest form of organized sport in North America. It was first developed in the mid-seventeenth century in the southeastern region of the United States of America; most importantly, in Maryland, Virginia, and South Carolina. It then became popular throughout the colonies, mainly among the wealthy, leisured, and landed aristocracy of the agrarian field. The first American club devoted to horse racing, the Maryland Jockey Club (1745), was owed to this time. Billiards, blood sports, pin bowling, fencing, football/soccer, tennis,, track and field athletic exertions, and wrestling were also first practiced in North America in the seventeenth century; boxing, cricket, golf, field hockey, swimming, and yachting/sailing, in the eighteenth century. Moreover, the first American international sporting contest, a cricket match between Londoners and the victorious colonists, was staged in 1751; the first American sporting club, The Colony, was established in Philadelphia in 1732; and the earliest American sporting books were published in the eighteenth century: Edward Blackwell's A Compleat System of Fencing (1734), Hugh Gaines' A Little Pretty Book (mainly about cricket; 1762), and Benjamin Franklin's The Art of Swimming Rendered Easy (mid-eighteenth century). Lacrosse, as a derivative of Native American Indian games, was likewise and importantly played in the eighteenth century; a massacre of American soldiers by Native American (Sac and Ojibway or Sac and Chippewa) Indians in Michigan/Ontario in 1763, for prominent instance, occurred on the pretext of a lacrosse match between the two.

From the early years of the French and Indian War through the period of the American Revolutionary War itself, 1758-1781, the dominant events of colonial life in North America were not readily conducive to sport. Ascetic middle-class values unfavorable to sport gained sway, a certain resentment toward aristocratic pleasures including sport emerged, and a war-time austerity unfriendly to sport increasingly prevailed. A proclamation of the First Continental Congress in 1774 argued for suspended interest in recreational extravagance and dissipation; all resource was to be marshaled for the impending effort against Great Britain. Much of the resource that was poured into this effort was taken from the racing stables of the landed aristocracy. The Revolution, therefore, on balance, significantly impeded the practice of sport, most notably among the aristocratic classes. Even the period immediately following the War was not well disposed to sporting enthusiasms because the economic depression caused mainly by the inflationary consequences of the War, which crested in 1786, limited "inessential" activities, particularly for the middle and lower classes. As the trauma of the War and its economic devastations receded, however, and as the new federal government and its economic policies became well established, a renewed interest in sport among all social classes crept back into American life in the 1790s.

Sport in early modern Asia, in China and Japan most significantly, continued an ambivalent earlier development. In China, the contemplative nature of Taoism and Buddhism pulled in one direction vis-à-vis sport and the thisworldly features of Confucianism, military life, and medical concerns pulled in the other. The intellectual orientation of the Ming Dynasty (1368-1644) encouraged the practice of archery, golf, and the martial arts (particularly, kung fu) but discouraged the practice of ch'uan shu (a form of boxing) and polo. The military orientation of the Qing Dynasty (1644-1911) periodically suppressed the martial arts (particularly, ch'uan shu), largely owing to their revolutionary potential, but encouraged the playing of folk sports such as

185

football and polo. Otherwise, the sports of medieval China were fairly widely practiced in the periods of the Ming and Qing. Near the end of the Qing Dynasty (in the late nineteenth century), Western sporting practices gained increasing prominence (largely through the YMCAs and YWCAs) despite formal Chinese opposition to them. Religious, political, and military considerations were also the leading influences on early modern Japanese sport. The martial arts continued as the preeminent forms of Japanese sport in this period. Although the practice of sumo waned from the twelfth to the nineteenth centuries, this practice was significantly revived in the nineteenth century. Judo developed out of jujutsu and kendo out of kenjutsu, also in the nineteenth century. Kyudo had an ongoing prominence from the medieval through the early modern period. The abolition of the warrior cult, samurai, by the Meiji Restoration of 1868 encouraged the transformation of largely martial orientations in the martial arts to increasingly artistic/sporting orientations in these activities. Despite the distaste of the Tokugawa Shogunate (1603-1867) for Western culture, Western sports were introduced to Japan in the seventeenth century. They did not, however, come to great popularity until after the Meiji Restoration in the late nineteenth century. The other forms of sport widely practiced in medieval Japan continued a notable presence throughout the early modern period. Of these, swimming was likely the most significant; Japan was the first large political entity to formally organize swimming contests on a national basis, that in the first year of the Tokugawa Shogunate (1603). Elsewhere in so-termed early modern Asia, the most notable sporting developments were the ongoing practice of martial arts in Korea and in southeast Asia, the formalization of sepak takraw (out of practices that may date from the eleventh century) in sixteenth-century Thailand, the introduction of cricket by the British to India in 1721 and to Pakistan in 1784, and the establishment by the British of the Calcutta Cricket Club in 1792.

As in the case of all prior periods, many of the leading cultural personalities of this time were connected to sport in some noteworthy way. Of the **foremost political and intellectual figures of the seventeenth and eighteenth centuries concerned with sport**, few were more influential than the English/British and French monarchs of the period. Most English kings of this time were significantly concerned with sport as has been said. Most of the French kings of this time were likewise devoted to sport (tennis in particular) as has been also said. Louis XIII played billiards as well as tennis; Louis XIV was too an accomplished tennis player and acrobatic gymnast, did dressage, and played billiards and croquet; and Louis XVI was especially fond of hunting. Thomas Hobbes, John Locke, David Hume, and Jean-Jacques Rousseau in particular authored influential philosophic systems postulating the primacy of the body; Hobbes also played tennis avidly until 75-years of age and Rousseau was allegedly too a tennis enthusiast. Samuel Pepys widely chronicled seventeenth-century English sport. John Dryden was fond of playing football. Jonathan Swift, Alexander Pope, and William Hogarth were moved by boxing as has been said; Hogarth featured sport in several of his best paintings. Samuel Johnson was an especially accomplished swimmer. Catherine the Great of Russia issued a decree regulating boxing in 1726. Antonio Vivaldi wrote an opera, "L'Olimpiade," based on ancient Olympic mythology in 1734. Joseph Addison, Richard Steele, and François Marie Arouet de Voltaire were critical of sporting violence, although Addison enthusiastically played football. Denis Diderot included accounts of eighteenth-century French aristocratic sports (most notably, billiards, lawn bowling, croquet, and tennis) in his celebrated Encyclopédie. Benjamin Franklin, George Washington, and Thomas Jefferson recognized the educational, recreative, and health benefits of vigorous forms of game-playing. Franklin also advocated that physical education be included in the formal school curriculum, argued that a "rugged animalism" significantly governs human achievement (a notion that greatly influenced GutsMuths), wrote instructively about swimming as has been said, and was himself a highly accomplished swimmer. Washington was himself a remarkable wrestler and long jumper, enjoyed billiards, and was too an avid fox hunter. Jefferson was apparently taken with billiards. Johann Wolfgang von Goethe had a broad interest in sport. Marie Antoinette was a keen ice skater. Wolfgang Amadeus Mozart was exceedingly adept at billiards. And Benjamin West was an accomplished ice skater.

CONTEMPORARY MODERN CIVILIZATION

The most recent epoch of world history, contemporary modern civilization, the nineteenth and twentieth centuries, effectively our own time, is characterized by several broad developments. In political, economic, and social terms, it is characterized by:

- a deepening sense of nationalism and militarism which entailed:
    - alliances and wars of unprecedented dimension and brutality;
    - the continuing drift to national unification and independence of all world nations; and
    - the expansion, then the twilight of classical colonialism-imperialism and the advent of neo-colonialism-imperialism.
- the ongoing democratization of modern life which entailed:
    - the progressive triumph of liberal democratism, socialism, and communism over conservative monarchism, despotism, and fascism;
    - the progressive political, economic, and social enfranchisement of women and minorities; and
    - the advent of universal educational franchise (of free, compulsory, public education for all) and the incipient eradication of illiteracy.
- the capital industrialization and the urbanization of the developed world which entailed:
    - a technological revolution of previously unknown scale, invention, and effect;
    - a continuing agenda of terrestrial and celestial world discovery;
    - dramatic revisions in emigration/immigration patterns and in the development of remaining frontiers; and
    - an utter transformation of the tangible and intangible conditions of everyday life.

In intellectual terms, it is characterized by:

- the progressive triumph of immanence over transcendence, of the sciences, philosophy, and relativism over orthodox religion, theology, and absolutism;
- a brilliant era of discovery in the natural and social sciences;
- the conclusion of "modern" philosophy, history, and literature and the development of "post-modern," effectively skeptical, alternatives; and
- the conclusion of "modern" traditions in the visual, musical, and movement arts and the development of "post-modern," effectively abstract, alternatives.

And in sporting terms, it is characterized by a qualitative revision and a quantitative expansion of the activity in broad accord with the dominant political, economic, social, and intellectual tendencies of the period.

Political, Economic, and Social Developments

The period to the First World War

Although nationalistic and militaristic inclinations had a long and a firmly established history well before the nineteenth century, the scale on which nationalistic and militaristic contests were waged in the nineteenth and twentieth centuries has been without precedent. The ferocity and broad scope of these contests were grounded in a burgeoning necessity and appetite for national unification and independence and in an analogous bent for international expansion, effectively for the exploitation of foreign people, their territories, and their natural resource. Much of this necessity, this appetite, and this bent was driven by the new political, economic, and military imperatives of capital industrialism and it was made possible by the remarkable technological invention of the period. In this circumstance, patriotic loyalties based mainly on common national (ethnic, linguistic, historical, and/or ideological) traditions and characteristics were greatly emphasized and intensified; especially much was made of the differences among various national traditions and the terms in which certain of these traditions could be "plausibly" thought superior to others. The signal national and international violence of the past two centuries began with the Napoleonic Wars of the early nineteenth century.

The French Revolutionary Wars (1792-1802), in the form of the First and Second Wars of the Coalition, effectively continued in the early nineteenth century as the Third, Fourth, and Fifth Wars of the Coalition – collectively, the **Napoleonic Wars** (1803-1815). Between the end of the Second War of the Coalition and the beginning of the Third, Haiti liberated itself from France in 1804, Napoleon Bonaparte declared himself Emperor of France (thus ending the Consulate and establishing the **First Empire**) in 1804 and King of Italy in 1805, and the Third Coalition (Great Britain, Russia, Austria, Sweden, and Naples) was formed against Napoleon in 1804. The **Third War of the Coalition** (1805) was most significantly marked by:

- Napoleon's defeat of Austria at the Battle of Ulm (near Stuttgart) and his entry into Vienna;
- Admiral Nelson's defeat of French and Spanish forces at the Battle of Trafalgar (near Gibraltar), which established British naval superiority and which ended both Nelson's life and Napoleon's ambitions to conquer England;
- Napoleon's brilliant victory over Austria and Russia at the Battle of Austerlitz (in western Moravia);
- Prussia's acquisition of Hanover in exchange for a treaty agreement with France aimed against Great Britain; this was the opening gambit in Napoleon's largely unsuccessful Continental System intended to isolate British from Continental trade; and
- the Peace of Pressburg/Bratislava which brought the War to conclusion and by which Austria ceded Venice to France.

In 1806, Napoleon broke the (1805) treaty with Prussia by offering Hanover to England and Prussia initiated the **Fourth War of the Coalition** (1806-07) but was quickly isolated and, with Saxony, collapsed after the decisive French victory at the Battle of Jena (near Leipzig) in 1806. Napoleon then captured Berlin (1806) and attacked Russian troops advancing on Berlin. His stunning victory over the Russians at the Battle of Friedland (near Koenigsberg/Kaliningrad) in 1807 brought the Peace of Tilsit (likewise near Koenigsberg/Kaliningrad), also in 1807. The Peace brought Russia into the Continental System against Great Britain, created the Duchy of Warsaw (under French domination), and made Napoleon the effective master of Continental Europe. In the broad context of the Fourth War of the Coalition, the French also:

- occupied Naples in 1806 and declared Napoleon's brother, Joseph Bonaparte (1768-1844; r. 1806-08), king;
- reframed the Batavian Republic/Netherlands as the Kingdom of Holland in 1806 and declared Napoleon's brother, Louis Bonaparte (1778-1846; r. 1806-10), king; and
- reorganized the German Empire by dissolving the Holy Roman Empire (then under Francis II as has been said) in 1806 and by establishing, also in 1806, a new German state, the Confederation of the Rhine, governed by western German princes (excluding eastern German states, Prussia and Austria), but allied with and subordinate to France.

Soon after the Peace of Tilsit, France occupied nearby states that had refused to participate in the Continental System; it conquered Portugal in 1807, the Roman Republic/Papal States in 1808, and Spain in 1808. In Spain, Joseph Bonaparte replaced the Bourbon kings, Charles IV (1748-1819; r. 1788-1808) and Ferdinand VII (1784-1833; r. 1808, 1814-33), in 1808 (-13), and a lengthy insurrection against the French with British support (the Peninsula War) began. Alarmed by French aggression, Austria declared the **Fifth War of the Coalition** in 1809 but was in the end decisively defeated by Napoleon at the Battle of Wagram (near Vienna), also in 1809. The Peace of Schoenbrunn (near Vienna), likewise in 1809, brought Austria and Prussia into the Continental System. The Fourth and Fifth Wars of the Coalition also sparked significant democratic reforms in the Prussian monarchy of Frederick William III (1770-1840; r. 1797-1840), son and successor of Frederick William II. Although these reforms were significantly truncated by Prussian participation in the Holy Alliance of 1815, they nonetheless constituted especially fertile possibilities for future development. The most telling of these were: the abolition of serfdom, assurances of personal liberty, freedom to own property, freedom of occupational choice, legal equality, emancipation of the Jews, independent judicial review, and humanistic reform of the educational system. Prussian educational reform was carried out mainly by Karl Wilhelm von Humboldt (1767-1835), who promoted academic freedom and the unity of teaching, learning, and research, who established public gymnasia (secondary schools) and elementary schools emphasizing instruction in the liberal arts, and who founded the fabled University of Berlin (at which many of the greatest scholars of the nineteenth century taught, including Fichte, Schleierrmacher, and Hegel) in 1810.

Napoleon further strengthened his hold on Austria by divorcing (in 1809) his Martinique-born wife, Josephine Beauharnais (1763-1814), whom he had married in 1796, and by marrying (in 1810) the daughter of Francis I (as Francis II, the Holy Roman Emperor until 1806; he had become the first Emperor of Austria, as Francis I, in 1804 [-35]), Archduchess Marie Louise (1791-1847). The greatest extent of the Napoleonic Empire was achieved in 1810-12 by which time France largely, if variously, controlled the whole of Europe except Great Britain, Russia, the Ottoman Empire, Portugal, and Sweden; that is, approximately one-third of the Continent's population. Napoleon's bourgeois hegemony over Europe had many modernizing consequences: the extension of liberal political, legal, and educational ideas and institutions, the development of centralized governing bureaucracies, a further increase in nationalistic sentiment, economic instability and corruption, and a diminished respect for and status of feudalism.

Nationalistic opposition to the Napoleonic system was nonetheless growing, most notably in Portugal, Spain, Russia, and Germany. British general and statesman, Arthur Wellesley/Duke of Wellington (1769-1852) effectively liberated Portugal in 1808 and Spain in 1813; Ferdinand VII was restored to the Spanish throne in 1814; John VI was restored to the Portuguese throne in 1816. Russia had benefited significantly from its participation in the Continental System; it obtained Finland from Sweden in 1809 and obtained Bessarabia (part of what are now Moldova and Ukraine) in a conflict with Turkey (Russo-Turkish War), 1806-12. Napoleon's tenuous alliance with Russia was nonetheless broken in 1810 when Tsar Aleksander I (1777-1825; r. 1801-25), son and successor of Paul I, rejected the Continental System and turned to British trade for urgently needed industrial goods. In an attempt to reassert the Continental System, Napoleon allied with Prussia and Austria and invaded Russia in 1812 with the largest army to its time. Russia, conversely, allied with Sweden, which sought restoration of a union with Norway (then joined to French ally, Denmark) in order to compensate for the loss of Finland (ironically enough, to Russia). Napoleon reached Moscow but was then routed in a disastrous retreat caused mainly by supply difficulties and harsh winter climate. Emboldened by the French defeat, Prussia, Austria, and Spain, as well as Great Britain, entered what became the **Wars of Liberation** (1813-15) on the Russian side in 1813. Russia obtained Poland, Prussia (to include Saxony) was restored to independence, and the allied powers "conclusively" defeated Napoleon at the Battle of Nations, Leipzig, all in 1813. In 1814, the Napoleonic system collapsed; the allies (mainly Wellington and Aleksander I) captured Paris; Napoleon abdicated and was exiled to the north-central Mediterranean island of Elba; the Bourbon crown was restored, largely by the efforts of Bishop Charles Maurice de Talleyrand, in Louis XVIII (1755-1824; r. 1814-24), brother of Louis XVI and uncle of Louis XVII (1785-95; r. 1793-95 in titular terms only); a liberal constitution was granted by Louis XVIII; the Confederation of the Rhine was dissolved; Germany, Holland, Upper Italy, and Naples were liberated; and Denmark (under Frederick VI [1768-1839; r. 1808-39]) lost Norway to Sweden. In 1815, Napoleon escaped from Elba, entered Paris, promised radical democratic reforms, deposed Louis XVIII, made several military successes before falling to final defeat by the Prussians and British (directed mainly by Wellington) at the Battle of Waterloo (near Brussels), and was deported to the isolated, British-controlled island of Saint Helena (in the South Atlantic Ocean) where he died in 1821.

The allies again entered Paris in 1815 and again reinstated Louis XVIII to the throne, also in 1815. The peace accords that followed – the **Congress of Vienna** (1814-15) – attempted to restore the political circumstance of 1792, to re-establish the legitimacy of monarchial rule, to reject the liberal agenda of revolutionary political reform, and to assure, as a basis for enduring peace, a balance-of-power among the strongest nations of Europe, mainly Great Britain, Russia, Austria, Prussia, and France. The principal architects of the accords were the French representative, Talleyrand, the British, Viscount Robert Stewart Castlereagh (1769-1822), and the Austrian, Prince Klemens von Metternich (1773-1859). Great Britain was the main beneficiary, regaining its union with Hanover, reasserting its colonial prerogatives over the southern region of South Africa/Cape Colony (from 1795), Ceylon/Sri Lanka (from 1796), Malta (from 1800), and Mauritius (from the French, 1810), gaining colonial prerogative over the western region of Dutch Guiana/Suriname (as British Guiana/Guyana) in 1815, and becoming the most powerful nation in the world. In the final two decades of George III's long reign (1800-20), Britain also prohibited the slave trade (but not yet slavery itself) in 1807; suffered the first anti-industrial riots (by the Luddites, who attributed high unemployment and low wages to the textile machines which they attempted to destroy) in 1811-16; passed through the first organized pacifist movement (which entailed the rejection of force as a means of resolving international disputes) in contemporary modern civilization (England's Peace Society, formed in 1816); and asserted hegemony over Ireland (by the Act of Union joining Ireland to Britain in 1801), Sierra Leone (for liberated slaves, 1808), Nepal (by means of a conflict with the dominant cultural group in the region since 1768, the Gurkhas; the Gurkha War, 1814-16), and Singapore (1819). Austria relinquished claims to Hapsburg Netherlands (Belgium) in exchange for gains in Upper Italy (mainly Venice, Lombardy, and Tuscany) and Dalmatia (the Adriatic coast of modern Slovenia and Croatia). Sardinia, Piedmont, Savoy, and Monaco (which had been a virtual French possession from 1641 and a virtual Spanish possession from 1542 to 1641) — Sardinia and northwest Italy — were united as the Kingdom of Sardinia. The Papal States were liberated and Naples joined Sicily as the (Bourbon) Kingdom of the Two Sicilies. Holland, Belgium, and Luxembourg were liberated and united as the Kingdom of the Netherlands under (Bourbon) King William I (1772-1843; r. 1815-40). Switzerland regained independence and was guaranteed eternal neutrality. Denmark obtained Greenland from Norway in 1815. Although France reconfirmed its colonial prerogative over the eastern region of Dutch Guiana/Suriname (as French Guiana) in 1815 and had Senegal returned to it by Great Britain, also in 1815, French borders themselves were effectively reduced to their pre-revolutionary locations. And Germany (the Germanies) became a loose confederation of approximately forty entities with a legislative assembly at Frankfurt, the German Confederation (1815-66). Although only parts of Austria and Prussia held membership in the Confederation, they were the dominant forces in it. The Confederation of the Rhine and the German Confederation — which effectively replaced the Holy Roman Empire (the First German Empire/Reich) — established the foundations of modern German nationalism and the foundations of the modern unified and independent German state. Although the modern unified German state was not achieved until the late nineteenth century, the nationalist sentiments that provoked this achievement were most articulately and fervently argued by the leading German intellectuals of the early nineteenth century, including the great poets, Johann Wolfgang von Goethe and Friedrich Holderlin, and the great philosophers, Johann Gottlieb Fichte, Friedrich Daniel Ernst Schleiermacher, and Friedrich Wilhelm Joseph Schelling.

In order to assure international cooperation in protecting the Vienna accords (that is, in order to assure international cooperation in protecting the established dynasties) and to prevent a resurgence of French imperialism, the leading European states established an alliance system that further certified the balance of prerogative among them. The most significant element of this supranational system was the **Holy Alliance** of 1815. Tsar Aleksander I of Orthodox Russia, King Frederick William III of Protestant Prussia, and Emperor Francis I of Catholic Austria, largely under the direction of Austrian Prince Metternich, attempted to enforce the reactionary policies of pre-revolutionary Europe by means of the Alliance. The repressive Bourbon restorations of Louis XVIII in France and Ferdinand VII in Spain and the Braganza restoration of John VI (1769-1826; r. 1816-26) in Portugal later joined the Alliance and contributed measurably to its conservative agenda. The increasingly repressive government of Tsar Aleksander I of Russia was replaced by the equally despotic regime of his brother, Nicholas I (1796-1855; r. 1825-55), on Aleksander's death in 1825. At least until mid-century, the Alliance (or its vestiges) successfully defended the divine right of monarchial authority (with modest, constitutional restraints on arbitrary rule), "successfully" made domestic government by Christian principle (the unification of throne and altar), and successfully kept international peace among the major powers through solidarity in foreign affairs. The Alliance's conservative opposition to revolutionary movements, even to liberal reforms, was nonetheless at sharp odds with Enlightenment (and romantic) inclinations to individual liberty, social equality, and national sovereignty. The result was the fervent opposition of Great Britain, the leading defender of European liberalism, to the Alliance and three ardent waves of domestic insurrection in the Continental Europe of the 1820s, of 1830-33, and of 1848-49.

The British commitment to Enlightenment liberalism entailed an allegiance to secular reason, to individual freedoms (of conscience, thought, and press), to legal equality, to popular elections of legislative representatives, to separation of governmental powers, and to unrestricted economic activity. It was most aptly defended in the utilitarianism of Jeremy Bentham and John Stuart Mill. Because, however, utilitarianism conceives of freedom, not as a natural (or inherent) right but as a useful one, it leaves uncorrected the enormous inequalities of unregulated markets; it thus leaves unremedied the privations of the lower classes; and it therefore comes to a de facto defense of plutocracy.

The **liberal revolutions of the 1820s** occurred mainly in southern Europe, principally in the Italies, Spain, Portugal, and Greece. Except for the **Greek War of Independence**, 1821-29, they were largely unsuccessful. The Greek struggle against the Ottoman Empire was supported by Great Britain, Russia, and France; it was opposed by Austria; and it thus divided and somewhat undid the Holy Alliance. The memorable Greek victories at the Battle of Missolonghi (on the southwestern Greek mainland), 1826, and the Battle of Navarino (on the southwestern Peloponnesus), 1827, brought Greek independence by the Peace of Adrianople (in what is now European Turkey) in 1829. Otto I of Bavaria (1815-67; r. 1832-62) was chosen king, however, and, despite modest gains in civil rights (including such for Jewish people), an unpopular foreign autocracy effectively replaced another. Otto, who was forced to abdicate, was succeeded by a son of the Danish king (Christian IX), George I (1845-1913; r. 1863-1913 [assassinated]), and George I, in turn, by his son, Constantine I (1868-1923; r. 1913-17, 1920-22), both of whom were importantly involved in the staging of the first modern Olympic Games in 1896. Russia also annexed Armenia and Azerbaijan (both from Persia/Iran in 1828), likewise in the broad context of 1820s European turmoil. Even Great Britain was unable to escape the unrest of the 1820s. After the Napoleonic Wars, Britain, under George IV (1762-1830; r. 1820-30), son of George III, suffered a severe economic depression, caused mainly by overproduction and declining prices. The rising unemployment that resulted severely affected workers, who responded with public demonstrations against the government. Freedom of the press and assembly were curtailed but the criminal code was reformed in 1822, trade unions were legally recognized in1824, and religious equality was declared in 1828-29. The United Arab Emirates came under British control in 1820; northern Burma/Myanmar (which had been politically unified in 1758) was brought under British dominance by means of the First Burmese War in 1824-26; and Malaysia/Straights Settlement came under British sway in 1826.

The Spanish and Portuguese colonial empires in the Americas were also under heavy siege throughout the approximate decade prior to 1820 and throughout the 1820s as well. The liberal, independence movements against the Spanish and Portuguese were inspired, in ideological terms, primarily by the American and French Revolutions and their Enlightenment groundwork. These movements were aimed mainly at ending colonial exploitation and the repressive policies of the Spanish throne. Their incipient phase was led, from 1810 to 1812, by the Venezuelan military officer, Francisco de Miranda (c. 1754-1816). The foremost figures (also military authorities) in the **liberation of South America** from Spanish rule, however, were Venezuelan Simon Bolivar (1783-1830), Venezuelan Antonio Jose de Sucre (1793-1830), Argentinean Jose de San Martin (1778-1850), and Chilean Bernardo O'Higgins (1778-1842). After several large failures, Bolivar liberated Venezuela and Colombia (including Panama) in 1817-20 and (with Sucre) liberated Ecuador in 1819. Gran Colombia (effectively, what are now Colombia, Venezuela, Ecuador, and Panama) was proclaimed in 1819 and it was broken up into the United States of New Granada (Colombia and Panama; after 1861, Colombia only), Venezuela, and Ecuador in 1830. Sucre participated (with Bolivar) in the liberation of Ecuador and achieved a masterful victory over the Spanish at the Battle of Ayacucho (in Peru) in 1824, an event that conclusively secured the liberation of the continent. San Martin liberated the United States of the Rio de la Plata (Argentina) in 1816, Chile (with O'Higgins) in 1818, and Peru (with Bolivar) in 1821. The southern regions of Peru established independence, as Bolivia, in 1825. Paraguay was declared independent by a military junta in 1811. Brazil, under Emperor Pedro I (1798-1834; r. 1822-31), heir to the Portuguese crown (which he relinquished), achieved independence from Portugal without struggle in 1822 and it enjoyed one of the most benign governments on the continent under Pedro I's son and successor, Emperor Pedro II (1825-91; r. 1831-89), who made Brazil the last nation in the world to formally abolish slavery in 1888. Uruguay was confederated to Argentina and followed the general course of Argentinean independence until it was annexed by Brazil in 1817; allied with Argentina, it achieved independence at the conclusion of a war against Brazil (1825-28) in 1828. Although the rule of the Spanish and Portuguese crowns in the Americas (except in Cuba and Puerto Rico) ended with the liberation movements of the 1810s and 1820s, the new governments were often as severe as those they replaced. European dictators of reactionary orientation had been replaced by local despots of reactionary orientation. Bolivar's vision of a united South America was a major casualty of local despotism and reaction, including his own.

Liberation movements in central America and the Caribbean were likewise carried out in the first several decades of the nineteenth century. In central America, Mexico (most of what are now the western United States of America and the whole of central America except Panama) won independence from Spain under Colonel Augustin de Iturbide (1783-1824) in 1821. Iturbide declared himself Emperor in 1822, was deposed and exiled in 1823 by General Antonio Lopez de Santa Anna (1794-1876), and was executed in 1824. Santa Anna ruled by dictatorial means throughout most of the period between 1824 and 1855. The Central American Federation (effectively the regions now occupied by Guatemala, Honduras, El Salvador, Nicaragua, and Costa Rica) separated from Mexico in 1823. The Federation was dissolved in 1839 and the constituent states became autonomous nations: Costa Rica, Honduras, and Nicaragua in 1838, El Salvador and Guatemala in 1839. In the Caribbean, Toussaint L'Ouverture (c. 1774-1803), a former Haitian slave, took over the entire island of Hispaniola and abolished slavery de facto in both the French west and the Spanish east, all in 1801. In 1804, Jean-Jacques Dessalines (c. 1758-1806; r. 1804-06), also a former slave, who became an accomplished general, won independence for the island from France, made Haiti the second independent nation in the Americas (to the United States of America), made Haiti the first nation in the world to formally abolish slavery, and suffered severe French reparations in exchange for recognition. Dessalines ruled as an utter despot until assassinated in 1806. The eastern part of the island separated from the western in 1808 and was returned to Spanish rule. The Spanish east was occupied by Haiti from 1822 to 1844; it became an independent nation, as the Dominican Republic, in 1844. Only Cuba and Puerto Rico then remained as Spanish (or Portuguese) colonial possessions in the Americas; some English, French, Dutch, Russian, and Danish possessions nonetheless remained.

The **United States of America of the early nineteenth century** was too greatly affected by the Napoleonic Wars and by the quest for national unification and enduring independence. John Adams (r. 1797-1801), the second president of the country and a very significant contributor to its formation, presided over the establishment of Washington, District of Columbia as the nation's capital in 1800 and struggled with the dissatisfactions of the southern states in respect to the Alien and Sedition Acts of 1798. In response to the threat of war with France, these Acts proscribed criticism of the government and allowed for the expulsion of dangerous aliens. Adams' successor, Thomas Jefferson (r. 1801-09), who had had a still larger influence on the creation of the country, opposed the Alien and Sedition Acts and the slave insurrections in Haiti and presided over an enormous westward expansion of the country. The United States of America purchased Louisiana (a region west of the Mississippi River extending from New Orleans on the Gulf of Mexico north and northwest very nearly to the current border with Canada and including most of what is now the central territory of the country) from the French – the Louisiana Purchase – in 1803, doubling the land area of the country. Jefferson also organized the expedition of Meriwether Lewis (1774-1809) and William Clark (1770-1838), 1803-06, which explored Louisiana and the regions west of Louisiana to the Pacific Ocean. The expansion of the United States entailed by the Purchase encouraged established American and European immigrants to settle in the deep interior and it also included the persecution of native peoples inhabiting the deep interior. Jefferson too founded the University of Virginia (1803-19) and supervised the admission of Ohio to the union of states (1803).

The expansionist tendencies of the United States continued in the term of its fourth president, James Madison (r. 1809-17), who (like Adams and Jefferson) had been also instrumental in the establishment of the nation and who had also (like Jefferson) opposed the Alien and Sedition Acts. The principal event of Madison's presidency was the **War of 1812** (1812-15), also inappropriately known as the Second War of American Independence. Its main causes were American designs on British territory in Canada and British trade disputes with the United States relating to its struggles against France in the Napoleonic Wars. The most significant episodes of the War were:

- the prelude disputes with American Indians (who were British allies) under Tecumseh (c. 1768-1813) which effectively ended with the victory of General William Henry Harrison (1773-1841; later the ninth president of the nation) at the Battle of Tippecanoe (in Indiana) in 1811;
- the American naval victory on Lake Erie in 1813;
- the British capture of Washington, D.C. in 1814;
- the American victory at the Battle of Fort McHenry (Baltimore) in 1814; and
- the victory of General Andrew Jackson (1767-1845; later the seventh president of the nation) at the Battle of New Orleans in 1815.

The War ended indecisively with borders largely restored to pre-war locations but with British influence in North America further diminished. In Madison's terms, Louisiana (1812) and Indiana (1816) joined the union of states.

European influence in the Americas was also the principal issue in the administrations of James Monroe (1758-1831; r. 1817-25), fifth president of the United States of America. The Monroe Doctrine of 1823 proscribed European intervention (most notably that of the Holy Alliance) in the Americas; it declared the Western Hemisphere closed to further European colonialism. It likewise tacitly declared the Hemisphere the rightful domain of the United States, a self-proclaimed prerogative that the government has routinely invoked since. The Doctrine thus formalized the opening of American colonialism/neo-colonialism/imperialism in the Hemisphere. Also in Monroe's presidency, Florida was purchased from Spain (1819); Mississippi (1817), Illinois (1818), and Alabama (1819) joined the union of states; the Missouri Compromise (1820-21) marked the first major political crisis of many concerning the status and expansion of slavery (Maine entered the union in 1820 as a free state and Missouri in 1821 as a slave state); Liberia was established in 1822 for the settlement of freed American slaves; and an economic crisis swept the nation in 1819. The presidency of John Quincy Adams (1767-1848; r. 1825-29), son of John Adams, which followed was largely ineffective.

The second major wave of European revolutionary activity since the conclusion of the Napoleonic Wars – the **revolutions of 1830-33** -- began in France and spread throughout the continent (mainly to Belgium, the

Italies, Saxony, Hanover, and Poland). Louis XVIII was succeeded by his brother, Charles X (1757-1836; r. 1824-30), in 1824. Charles deepened the ultraroyalist, repressive, and reactionary policies of the French crown. The liberal reply (which importantly included Lafayette) began in Paris with the July Revolution of 1830. This Revolution brought a constitutional revision that broadened suffrage, loosened press censorship, and increased the prerogatives of the propertied bourgeoisie (the de facto middle class) but left the bondage of the working class largely unchanged. The new constitutional monarchy, under Louis Philippe (1773-1850; r. 1830-48), a Bourbon descendant of a son of Louis XIII, of a brother of Louis XIV, presided over the colonization of Algeria (from the Ottoman Empire in 1830), of the Comoros (in 1841), and of French Polynesia/Tahiti (from the British and the local Pomare Dynasty [1743-1880], which nonetheless survived, in 1843) and over the capital industrialization of France. It nonetheless became itself increasingly given to the police-state methods of Metternich. Catholic Belgium gained independence from the largely Protestant Kingdom of the Netherlands in 1830; Prince Leopold I (1790-1865; r. 1831-65) of the central Germanies, who married a daughter of Louis Philippe in 1832, became the nation's first king in 1831 and granted a new constitution instituting a parliamentary system, civil rights (including such for Jewish people), and a measure of popular sovereignty. Catholic Luxembourg was partitioned by Belgium and Netherlands in 1839. The drift to Italian national unification likewise began in earnest in this period. The leading early figure of this drift was the poet, Giuseppe Mazzini (1805-72), who organized the agency of liberation (Young Italy), proposed a democratic and cooperative league of nations, beginning in 1831-32, organized popular insurrections against the monarchy (including the Revolution of 1848-49 and the Garibaldi expeditions), advocated a liberal Italian republic, and defended the working classes, all of which brought him imprisonment, then banishment. In Saxony and Hanover, liberal agitations provoked constitutional transformations and an accelerated movement for national German unification (Young Germany), led by the poet, Heinrich Heine (1797-1856). And in Poland, Tsar Nicholas I of Russia violated the Polish constitution sparking an 1830 insurrection in Warsaw which briefly ousted the Russians and established a national government. Russian rule was reestablished the following year (1831) with severe reprisals, however, and large numbers of Poles (including the celebrated composer, Frédéric Chopin) emigrated to the west, mainly to Paris.

Even the most powerful and the most liberal nations in the world, Great Britain and the United States of America, were affected by the revolutions of the 1830s. In Great Britain, under William IV (1765-1837; r. 1830-37), brother of George IV, electoral franchise was greatly enhanced (to the middle class) in 1832; child and female labor was limited by the First Factory Act of 1833; slavery was formally abolished in 1833; a general concern for the welfare of animals, for the poor (including their education), and for public opinion rose; the Malvinas Islands/Falkland Islands were formally colonized in 1833; and Saint Helena was formally colonized in 1834. The presidency of Andrew Jackson (r. 1829-37) in the United States of America witnessed a dramatic increase in abolitionist sentiment (sentiment opposing slavery), the elimination of all restrictions on male, white suffrage, a vigorous debate about states' rights vis-à-vis the federal government and federal patronage, and an ascending sense of unity among (southern and western) farmers and workers against (northern and eastern) capital. Jackson's tenure was also importantly marked by the 1835-36 American insurrection in Texas against Mexico (which most notably included the Mexican victory of General Santa Anna over Davy Crockett [1786-1836] at the Battle of the Alamo [San Antonio] in 1836 and the American declaration of Texas independence, also in 1836). Arkansas (1836) and Michigan (1837) joined the union of states in Jackson's second term.

The struggle for the rights and prosperity of all people and so the search for domestic stability were elusive, however. Although some gains had been made in these respects by the revolutions of the 1820s and those of 1830-33, the misfortunes of the lower classes (workers and peasants) were left largely unimproved and the ambitions of many nations for national unification and independence remained largely unrealized. The late 1830s and the whole of the 1840s were especially turbulent economic times. The burgeoning capital industrialism and urbanization of the period created an enormous transformation in the conditions of ordinary life, created a new and a large middle and lower class of urban industrial workers, and also created periodic financial crises of colossal scale. In **late 1830s and 1840s Great Britain**, (Queen) Victoria (1819-1901; r. 1837-1901), granddaughter of George III, came to the throne in 1837, effectively breaking the union with Hanover.[124] In her early reign, Britain unsuccessfully attempted to colonize Afghanistan (which had been politically unified in 1747 under the Durani Dynasty; by way of the First Afghan War, 1838-42); successfully colonized Aden/Yemen (southwest Arabia, 1839), Hong Kong (by way of the Opium War against China, 1839-42), the central-eastern coastal region of South Africa (Natal, 1843),[125] Brunei (1849), and southern Burma/Myanmar (by way of the Second Burmese War, 1852); greatly expanded British holdings in northwest India (mainly in Kashmir and the Punjab) and the wide British hold over India (1846-58); was a major participant in the Crimean War (1853-56); and ushered in a loyal and a respectful regard for constitutional government, for reforming the election laws (to approve universal male suffrage), and for advancing public education. Many social ills nonetheless remained: poverty, squalor, child abuse, commercial and judicial iniquity, imprisonment for debt, and abuse of workers prominent among them. The magnificent English writers, Thomas Carlyle (1795-1881) and Charles Dickens (1812-70), penned especially insightful and especially critical accounts of these miseries. The social reformer, Robert Owen (1771-1858), importantly attempted to develop self-sufficient agricultural-industrial communities governed by cooperative, as distinct from adversarial, relationships (such as New Harmony in 1810s Indiana, United States of America). Owen argued that human beings are inherently good, that human society is perfectible, and that working hours ought to be reduced, wages increased, and housing improved. His social experiments achieved modest, temporary successes in Scotland but failed in America, demonstrating that political and economic power must accompany purposive intentions in order to reform liberal governments. Savings and loan associations were first established in 1854 to finance such efforts. The international anti-slavery campaign and the pursuit of workers' rights were arguably the most conspicuous social movements of this period. The most prominent event in the anti-slavery campaign was the World Anti-Slavery Convention in London in 1840. The most striking events in the pursuit of workers' rights were the creation of the first political workers' movements, the Chartists (1838) and the National Association for the Protection of Labour (1845), and the first attempt of a general strike in 1842. The Great Irish Potato Famine (1845-49) killed nearly one million people (of starvation and disease), forced emigration of another approximate million (mainly to North America), and significantly deepened the social crisis, a crisis which was not relieved by the unrestricted, the free-trade policy of the British government under Prime Minister Robert Peel (1788-1850; r. 1834-35, 1841-46).

In **late 1830s and 1840s United States of America**, the presidency of the nation's eighth chief executive, Martin Van Buren (1782-1862; r. 1837-41), was dominated by a severe economic depression, the Panic of 1837, likely caused by the intentional contraction of credit for land purchase in Jackson's second term. Van Buren's immediate successors, William Henry Harrison (r. 1841), John Tyler (1790-1862; r. 1841-45), and James Knox Polk (1795-1849; r. 1845-49), presided over economic recovery, a further expansion of the country, and the continuing maturation of the frontier. In 1845, the United States annexed Texas and admitted it to the union of states. In the **Mexican War** of 1846-48 which resulted, the United States, led by General Zachary Taylor (1785-1850; later the twelfth president of the country), baited Mexico, led mainly by General Santa Anna, into attacks on its alleged territory, then routed it, reaching Mexico City in 1847. By the Treaty of Guadalupe-Hidalgo (near Mexico City), which ended the War in 1848, Mexico lost approximately two-fifths of its territory (all territory north of the Rio Grande River, most of what is now the southwestern United States, Texas, New Mexico, Arizona, Colorado, Utah, Nevada, and California). In 1846, the Oregon Treaty with Great Britain fixed the border with Canada and the approximate current (lower continental) boundaries of the country were established. The United States had thus become a transcontinental nation, significantly by way of the colonial/neo-colonial policy of Manifest Destiny and significantly at the expense of native peoples, other colonial powers (mainly Spain, France, and Great Britain), and Mexico. The central and western regions newly acquired by the Louisiana Purchase, the Mexican War, and the Oregon Treaty were also increasingly populated in the 1840s by means of overland trails. Established Americans and large groups of European (mainly English, Irish, and German) immigrants scrupulously and unscrupulously developed the "limitless" possibilities of the frontier in this period, largely in terms of agricultural cultivation and the mining of precious minerals (most notably expressed in the California Gold Rush of 1848-49). In addition to Texas, Florida (1845), Iowa (1846), and Wisconsin (1848) also formally joined the union of states in the 1840s and Liberia became an independent nation in 1847. American imperialism, the country's abuse of native peoples, and its commitment to slavery in particular did not go entirely unchallenged, however, even from within. The legendary American writer, Henry David Thoreau (1819-62), among the most notable of many thoughtful critics, earnestly and persistently reproved such practices.

In **late 1830s and 1840s Continental Europe**, the re-establishment of reactionary agendas (after the revolutions of 1830-33) accompanied wide economic strife. The Romanov autocracy of Tsar Nicholas I in Russia (which sparked a vibrant romantic reply in literature and music), for prominent instance, deepened. In Hapsburg Austria, Francis I was succeeded by his son, Ferdinand I (1793-1875; r. 1835-48), who continued the reactionary policies of Metternich. In Bourbon Spain, Ferdinand VII was succeeded by his daughter, Isabella II (1830-1904; r. 1833-68), whose disputed and despotic reign sparked numerous conservative-liberal conflicts. Even the government of Frederick William IV of Prussia (1795-1861; r. 1840-61), son and successor of Frederick William III, which came nearer to satisfying liberal aspirations than any other Continental regime of the period, grew increasingly unforgiving and increasingly opposed to reformist options.

In France, the economic crisis of 1846-47, caused mainly by systematic overproduction and crop failures, radicalized industrial workers and elements of the middle class. The **seminal development of contemporary modern socialism** is owed mainly to early nineteenth-century French culture. First detected in the sixteenth-century and seventeenth-century utopias of Sir Thomas More and Tommaso Campanella and first tangibly practiced in the early nineteenth-century cooperative communities of Robert Owen, the new movement argued for equal rights and equal opportunity for all people (including the so-termed subordinate classes), for a social order based on inherently human senses of justice (not on the power of whoever may seize or maintain it), for universal suffrage, for a just distribution of property, for the elimination of privilege in education, and for reconciliation of all people in a confederacy of world peace. The revised order was to be achieved by progressive social reform, overt class struggle, or outright revolution. The principal early architects of this view were the French social and political philosophers:

- Count Claude Henri de Saint-Simon (1760-1825), who held, most notably in The New Christianity (1825), that economic progress is the driving force of human history, that capital (which is the principal manifestation of economic value and the principal basis of property, power, and happiness) ought to be transferred to the state for scientific and fair distribution to all people for the purpose of effecting social harmony among all people, and that the governing principle of social life should encourage each person to contribute according to capacity and to receive according to contribution;
- Charles Fourier (1772-1837), who held that social harmony is a function of liberating labor from coercion, exploitation, and misery in voluntary cooperatives (such as Brook Farm in 1840s Massachusetts, United States of America); and
- Pierre Joseph Proudhon (1809-65), who held, most notably in What is Property? (1840) and The Philosophy of Property (1846), that social harmony is grounded in a just existence for all people and that such an existence entails the communal and peaceful abolition of all forms of coercion (including laws and the state).

The incisive French novelists, Victor Hugo (1802-85) and Émile Zola (1840-1902), also wrote especially insightful and especially critical accounts of existing social conditions. The other major mid-century exponents of contemporary socialism were the celebrated Russian and German revolutionaries:

- Mikhail Bakunin (1814-76), who argued, most notably in God and the State (1882), that human beings are inherently good and are thus worthy of a form of freedom unbridled by the state or the church (the doctrine of anarchism); existing governments and the church, Bakunin taught, are impediments to virtue and freedom and are to be justifiably and violently overthrown;
- Karl Marx (1818-83); and
- Friedrich Engels (1820-95).

In any case, the economic turmoil of late 1840s France evoked an intensification of reactionary policies, a renewed persecution of revolutionaries, and increased restrictions on the collective activities of workers; but it also evoked the first tangibly effective expressions of contemporary modern socialism and the February Revolution of 1848.

The **Revolutions of 1848-49** began in Paris and came to directly involve all major European states except Great Britain and Russia. They were moved primarily by the same type of liberal aims and the same type of ambition for national unification and independence that had stirred the revolutions of the 1820s and of 1830-33. As in the case of the earlier insurrections, these aims and ambitions were largely disappointed; they were met with still another wave of reaction; and they greatly disturbed faith in the power of liberal ideas over established, concrete reality; but they were neither without their measured successes. They toppled, for instance, the Bourbon throne of Louis Philippe in France and installed the **Second Republic** under President Louis Napoleon Bonaparte (1808-73; r. 1848-52), son of King Louis Bonaparte of the Kingdom of Holland (brother of Napoleon I). The triumph was nonetheless hollow, more so nominal than substantial; Louis Napoleon governed as an anti-liberal autocrat, suppressing legislative prerogatives and workers' reforms and colonizing French West Africa/Guinea (in 1849) and French West Africa/Dahomey/Benin (in 1851). Similarly, in Hapsburg Austria, the dismissal of Metternich by Ferdinand I and the forced abdication of Ferdinand himself, both in 1848, brought Ferdinand's nephew, Franz Joseph I (1830-1916; r. 1848-1916), to the throne. Although Franz Joseph proclaimed a new and more liberal constitution, the nation functioned as an absolute monarchy; it thwarted several liberal insurrections in regions under its direct influence; most notably, those in Italy (largely directed by the celebrated revolutionary, Giuseppe Garibaldi [1807-82]) and Hungary (largely directed by the celebrated revolutionary, Lajos Kossuth [1802-94]), both in 1849; and it reasserted its leadership in the German Confederation in 1850. Luxembourg broke from its Dutch and Belgian partition and became an autonomous state under Dutch suzerainty in 1848. Netherlands itself, under King William II (1792-1849; r. 1840-49), son and successor of William I, ordained moderately enhanced civil rights (including such for Jewish people). Struggles for the unification and independence (mainly from Austria) of the Italian states and for the unification and independence (also mainly from Austria) of the Germanies continued with some liberal reforms at the constitutional level, but without achievement of their fundamental goals. In the end, the forces of reaction had again prevailed in the Revolutions of 1848-49 but a new world was nonetheless on its larger way than it had previously been; the discernible retreat of the European monarchs and the European aristocracy had begun.

The political economy of the early nineteenth century, of the first approximate half of the nineteenth century, differed substantially from the economic circumstance of all prior periods, including the eighteenth-century circumstance that it replaced. The **beginnings of modern capital industrialism** are owed to mid-eighteenth-century English textile and steel production as has been said. Industrialism did not, however, become pronounced until the period following the Napoleonic Wars and the War of 1812, after which the United States of America, France, Germany, Sweden, Belgium, Holland/Netherlands, and Switzerland joined Great Britain as the leading industrial states in the world. Capital industrialism entailed the mass production of material goods by means of machines driven by generated power, set up in urban factories (as distinct from domestic or rural circumstance), and financed by private investment capital. It was motivated by a striving for personal profit beyond the satisfaction of individual needs; it was made possible by the ingenious technologic inventions of the eighteenth and nineteenth centuries; and it was accompanied by the virtual absence of restrictions on it (from such as Adam Smith's laissez-faire account of economic activity) as well as by the frenzied sense of change and the ardent individualism (and self-confident initiative) characteristic of constitutional democracies. The social consequences of capital industrialism were profound and enduring:

- it installed materialism as the dominant ethos of contemporary modern civilization and pragmatism as the dominant view of materialism's utilitarian application;
- it mechanized laboring activity;
- it Europeanized the world;
- it gradually urbanized what to that time had been a predominantly agrarian and rural economy;
- it very significantly increased population, the middle class, national incomes, material standards of living, easy credit, consumer goods, consumerism, trade, and financial insecurity;
- it utterly transformed the tangible and the intangible conditions of everyday life, making these conditions at once less onerous in material terms and, in some respects, more threatening in psycho-emotional terms;
- it steadily expanded the ranks and the influence of urban middle-class and lower-class factory workers (the so-termed proletariat);
- it widened already very large socio-economic class differences and heightened the already very large sense of opposition among such classes;
- it established new and broader (effectively, world) markets for material goods and services;
- it sharply affected emigration patterns, most importantly from Europe to North America, South America, Australia, and New Zealand and it also sharply affected the development of the frontiers in these "new" regions;
- it substantially diminished the influence of small-scale commerce, small-scale agriculture, craft activity, and the peasantry on economic affairs;
- it greatly exacerbated the exploitation of nature in the form of its overuse and pollution;
- it turned over the economic and political life of the planet to entrepreneurs (owners of large accumulations of private capital), to high finance, and to the tentacles of monopoly capitalism, large banks, stock-issuing corporations, cartels, syndicates, and trusts; and
- it significantly revised the character of human exploitation and the form of labor's very considerable disadvantages in respect to capital.

The incipient development of the Industrial Revolution was accompanied by a qualitative transformation in agricultural production, a transformation which entailed the dispossession of small farmers, the re-distribution of open fields, the fashioning of modern mass-farming techniques, as well as an increase in yields and in healthful food. The first major phase of the Revolution itself, which unfolded mainly in the early nineteenth century, was most influenced by revolutionary advances in mining, textile manufacturing, agricultural manufacturing, and metallurgical manufacturing, advances that were driven principally by coal and iron (as distinct from wood) technologies. Transportation and communication were especially much affected in this phase; canals, harbors, and highways, for prominent instance, were widely constructed in developed countries, the first mass-produced newspaper (The Times, London, 1814) was created, and the first railroad (Liverpool-Manchester, England, 1830) was established. The steamship (1807), cylinder printing press (1812), steam locomotive (1814), weaving mill (1815), vulcanization of rubber (1830), and harvesting machine (1831) were all developed in this phase. The second major phase of the Industrial Revolution, which unfolded mainly in the late nineteenth century, was most influenced by a continuing refinement of manufacturing techniques and by a sharp increase in monopolistic business practices. It was driven primarily by oil and electrical technologies and it had an especially large affect on medicine, transportation, communication, construction, and armaments; the first national postal service (Great Britain, 1840), the first world industrial/technological exposition/fair (Great Exhibition of the Works of Industry of All Nations, London, 1851), and the first central, electric power-plant (New York City, 1882) were established in this time. The electric motor (1834), revolver (1835), photography (1839), wire telegraph (1844), sewing machine (1846), submarine (1850), telephone (1861-76), stop-watch (1862), dynamite (1867), reinforced concrete (1867), typewriter (1867), electric generator (1867), internal-combustion (gasoline) engine (1867-84), barbed wire (1873), cable car (1873), phonograph (1877), electric locomotive (1879), incandescent light-bulb (1879), machine gun (1883), linotype (1884), automobile (1885), seamless pipes (1885), electric streetcar (1887), pneumatic tire (1888), diesel engine (1893), cinematography (1895), wireless telegraph (1895), subway (1897), dirigible (1900), motorized airplane (1903), cast concrete (1907), synthetic rubber (1909), propeller-turbine engine (1910), tank (1911), and tube transmitter (1913) were all developed in this phase.

The leading inventive geniuses of contemporary modern civilization were among those responsible for many of these remarkable **technological innovations**: Gottlieb Daimler (1834-1900), German engineer, the automobile; Thomas Alva Edison (1847-1931), American inventor, the phonograph, incandescent light-bulb, cinematography, and cast concrete; Charles Goodyear (1800-60), American inventor, the vulcanization of rubber; Guglielmo Marconi (1874-1937), Italian physicist, the wireless telegraph; Cyrus Hall McCormick (1809-64), American inventor, the harvesting machine; Samuel F.B. Morse (1791-1872), American inventor, the wire telegraph; William Siemens (1823-83), German-English engineer, the electric generator and locomotive; and the Wright brothers, Wilbur (1867-1912) and Orville (1871-1948), American inventors, the motorized airplane. The spirit of inquiry central to the work of such inventive genius also affected ongoing patterns of celestial and terrestrial world discovery. Neptune, the eighth planet from the Sun, was discovered in 1846. American-Canadian navigator, Captain Joshua Slocum (1844-1909), became the first person to sail alone around the world in 1898. The Antarctic was first tangibly discovered and circumnavigated in 1820-21 and was first tangibly reached in1895. Aided by new modes of land, sea, and air transport, the Arctic (beginning in 1893), the Antarctic (beginning in 1901), and Greenland (beginning in 1906) were first widely explored in this period. American explorer, Robert Edwin Peary (1856-1920), was the first to reach the North Pole in 1909. Norwegian explorer, Roald Amundsen (1872-1928), and British explorer, Robert Falcon Scott (1868-1912), were the first to reach the South Pole in 1911 and 1912 respectively.

The **origins of the modern labor movement** were also owed to the early industrial age. This movement was first devoted to organizing workers according to craft and to obtaining improved wages and working conditions for workers by means of negotiation, collective agreement, and strike. In this time, most every gain of middle-class and upper-class capitalists deepened the misery of lower-class workers. The so-termed liberal middle class was largely indifferent to this suffering and had a vested interest in preventing reform. Even the liberal concessions of the American and British governments and of Continental European governments responding to the revolutions of the 1820s, of 1830-33, and of 1848-49 did little to relieve the plight of the lower classes; these concessions were aimed principally at the middle and upper divisions of the social order. The crime, disease, and vice of the industrial cities, the want of effective public administration in them, the wretched housing available to workers, and the outright exploitation of workers (overwork, low wages, frequent and disabling injuries, insecurity, lack of insurance, and abusive treatment of women and children) incited the proletariat itself to self-defensive action. Such action achieved some hoped-for results even in the first half of the nineteenth century as has been said; most notably, the anti-industrial riots of the machine-breakers (the Luddites) in Great Britain, 1811-16; the anti-government demonstrations in 1820s Britain that won legal recognition of trade unions in 1824; the limitations on child and female labor included in the First Factory Act in Great Britain in 1833; the creation of the first political workers' movements, the Chartists and the National Association for the Protection of Labour, both in Great Britain, in 1838 and 1845 respectively; and the first attempted general strike, also in Great Britain, in 1842. Likewise significant in this time were the attempted development of cooperative communities by Robert Owen and the social criticism of Thomas Carlyle, Charles Dickens, Victor Hugo, Émile Zola, and Henry David Thoreau as has been too said.

Moreover, France granted workers the right to collective organization in 1864, Prussia in 1869, and laws prohibiting such organization gradually disappeared throughout Europe; cooperative societies, similar to Owen's, were fashioned in France and Prussia in the first half of the nineteenth century (most notably, the League of the Just [Germany] which became the Communist League in 1844); and some forms of organized religion, Protestantism in particular, also called for relief of workers' misery and of poverty (most notably, the Young Men's Christian Association [YMCA], 1844, and the Salvation Army [of William Booth, 1829-1912], 1865-78). Arguably the most significant development in this movement, however, was the seminal cultivation of contemporary modern socialism in the thought of Saint-Simon, Fourier, Proudhon, and Bakunin, the flowering of this cultivation in the thought of Karl Marx and Friedrich Engels, and the establishment of formal socialist (and other labor) institutions in the late nineteenth and early twentieth centuries.

The scientific socialism of Marx demonstrated the structural laws governing the development of capital and of capitalism. It held that all history is that of class struggles over economic ground, class struggles between those who own and control the means of economic production (mainly, land, natural resource, labor, and money), the aristocracy and the bourgeoisie, and those who do not, the workers (proletariat), between the exploiters and the exploited, the ruling and the oppressed classes, masters and slaves. The exploitation of workers brings owners surplus value (i.e., profit); as large accumulations of invested capital, this value:

- drives technological-industrial growth;
- increases the reserve of workers (because unsteady markets routinely produce unemployment, because large accumulations of capital, to which the process tends, require proportionately less labor than lesser accumulations, and because jobs themselves became more mechanized and less skilled which made workers more easily replaceable, more readily interchangeable), increases competition among workers, increases the pressure on wages, and increases the misery of workers;
- eventually decreases competition among capitalists (owing to the inherent laws of capital by which large concentrations consume lesser concentrations) and thus creates monopolistic and autocratic control of the markets; and
- systematically effects periodic crises of overproduction which are caused by the incessant necessity of raising the rate of profits (as the only viable alternative to withering capital according to the laws of capital themselves).

By Marx's view, these internal contradictions will drive capitalism into the socialist revolution; power will be seized by the proletariat from the bourgeoisie (the expropriators shall be expropriated); the means of production will be socialized (owned in common and equitably distributed); class differences will be eliminated; and the coercive state will give way to economic cooperation, guaranteed justice, authentic freedom, and self-fulfilled humanity. The collective ideology of Marx may have taken insufficient account of individual prerogative; Marx's economic determinism may have taken insufficient account of such non-economic factors as intellectual-religious and political (particularly, nationalistic) phenomena; and Marx may have misread the consequences of capitalist appeasement of workers. The thought of Marx nonetheless established the formal groundwork by which socialism became a major force in the world and the formal groundwork by which the liberal state of the nineteenth century (dominated utterly by the upper and middle classes) gave way to the welfare state of the twentieth century (that took significant account of the concerns and rights of all people, including the lower classes).

Marx also participated importantly in sparking a substantial crusade among workers themselves. In 1843, he left his native Germanies (variously, Trier, Bonn, Berlin, Jena, and Cologne) bitterly opposed to the Prussian autocracy of Frederick William IV most especially. In Paris, he met Engels and began a momentous literary partnership and a lasting friendship (in which Engels contributed indispensable financial assistance to Marx, his family, and his work). In 1845, Marx was expelled from France, went to Brussels, then back to Paris and Cologne, where, after the Revolution of 1848-49, he was arrested, tried for sedition, acquitted, and expelled. He lived the rest of his life (from 1849) in London. His partnership with Engels produced the Communist Manifesto in 1848 and the International Workingmen's Association/the First International (London), the first organization expressing the common interests of labor in all nations, in 1864. Engels made Marx's thought more accessible to popular consumption than Marx himself, mainly through the explicit development of dialectical materialism (the official philosophy of modern communism, effectively a re-statement of economic determinism and its historical development) in Anti-Duhring (1878) and The Origin of the Family, Private Property and the State (1884). Engels also completed the last two volumes of Marx's stupendous, three-volume, Das Kapital (1867-94), left unfinished at Marx's death in 1883.

Leading episodes in the institutional development of the contemporary socialist and labor movements in the late nineteenth and early twentieth centuries gradually turned what had been a clandestine, revolutionary inclination into an open political campaign, gradually as well fashioned organizations on a national and international scale with autonomous fiscal status and prerogative, and gradually too won deeper rights and more advantageous circumstances for workers by overtly disrupting or threatening to disrupt the productive process. The most significant of these episodes were the establishment of:

- the General Association of German Workers (the first German political party of socialist bent) by Ferdinand LaSalle (1825-64) in 1863;
- the First International in London in 1864 and its dissolution from dissension (between the socialists of Marxist persuasion and the anarchists of Bakunin) in 1876;
- the National Grange of the Patrons of Husbandry (a cooperative society that argued for public regulation of private utilities) in the United States of America in 1867;
- the Trades Union Congress (a national organization governing local syndicates) in Great Britain in 1868;
- the Knights of Labor (the first major labor organization in the United States) in 1869;
- the Fabian Society (which advocated progressive state socialism and which included no less than the great Irish playwright and critic, George Bernard Shaw) in Great Britain in 1884;
- the American Federation of Labor (the most powerful national labor organization in the United States) by Samuel Gompers (1850-1924) in 1886;
- the Second International in Paris in 1889 (-1914);
- the Social Democratic Party of Austria in 1889;
- the Social Democratic Party in Germany in 1890;
- the Italian Socialist Party in 1892;
- the Polish Socialist Party in 1892;
- the General Confederation of Work in France in 1895;
- the Social Democratic Workers' Party in Russia in 1898, largely under the influence of Georgi Valentinovich Plekhanov (1857-1918) and Vladimir Ilyich Ulyanov/Lenin (1870-1924);
- the Industrial Workers of the World (the "Wobblies") in the United States in 1905;
- the Labour Party in Great Britain in 1906, mainly by Ramsay MacDonald (1866-1937), first Labour Prime Minister (1924) and again Prime Minister in 1929-35; and
- the International Federation of Trade Unions in Australia in 1913.

Of these, the Russian development has had arguably the largest affect on the course of world history. In London in 1903, the Social Democratic Workers' Party split into the Menshevik faction (largely under the doctrinal influence of Plekhanov, who opposed political terror and who argued, most notably in Anarchism and Socialism [1894] and Fundamental Problems of Marxism [1908], that the socialist revolution in Russia could occur only after the further development of capitalism) and the Bolshevik faction (largely under the leadership of Lenin, who was opposed to any collaboration with capitalism and who favored assertive revolution at the earliest feasible moment). In 1912, the Bolsheviks formed an independent party which became the leader of world communism in 1917 and the linchpin of the Third International (created in 1919).

The Congress of Vienna and the Holy Alliance canonized the legitimacy of established monarchism and discouraged liberal reform, a circumstance which kindled the enormous domestic turmoil of the period from the close of the Napoleonic Wars to the Revolutions of 1848-49 as has been said. The Congress and the Alliance also established a balance-of-power among the leading states of Europe, an arrangement that discouraged international military conflict among European nations until shortly past mid-century. The resumption and the intensification of international warring activity in Europe were mainly driven by two closely related factors:

- the escalating competition inherent in capital industrialism among developed nations for the world's natural resource (principally in the form of raw materials for industrial and military production), for the world's human resource (principally in the form of labor for industrial and military production), and for the world's markets (principally in the form of capital and trade); and
- the ongoing struggle for national unification and independence, for national self-sufficiency, and for power among nations.

The first major international European war in nearly forty years, the **Crimean War** (1853-56), between Russia and the Ottoman Empire (Turkey), began in the Balkans in 1853. It was principally caused by disputes over military access of the two countries to the Black Sea and the Danube River and by a largely pretextual dispute over Eastern Orthodox prerogatives at holy sites in Palestine. Russia, under Nicholas I, invaded the Ottoman-controlled states of Moldavia and Wallachia in 1853. In order to protect their own commercial interests in the Middle East and to check Russian expansion (which threatened the balance of European power), Great Britain, France, Austria, Prussia, and Sardinia entered the War on the Turkish side in 1854-55. The two most celebrated features of the conflict were:

- the wrenching siege of Sebastopol (in the Crimea, southern Ukraine; 1854-55), which included the first instance of modern trench warfare and its accompanying brutalities (about which Leo Tolstoy wrote a stirring anti-war account) and which also included the fabled and ill-fated incident of the Charge of the Light Brigade at nearby Balaklava (about which Alfred Tennyson wrote a memorably heroic account); and
- the pioneering and inestimably great contributions of the courageous English nurse, Florence Nightingale (1820-1910), who established the foundations of modern scientific nursing during the War.

Sebastopol fell to the allies in 1855; Austria occupied Moldavia and Wallachia also in 1855; and the new (Romanov) tsar, Aleksander II (1818-81; r. 1855-81 [assassinated]), son and successor of Nicholas I, negotiated the Peace of Paris that ended the War in 1856. The Peace made the Black Sea and the Danube River neutral military territory; attempted to restore the balance of European power by diminishing Russian, Austrian, and Prussian influence and by enhancing British, French, Turkish, and Sardinian influence; and established the foundations for the unification and independence of Moldavia (in the northeast) and Wallachia (in the southwest) as the autonomous state of Romania in 1861. Romania crowned its first sovereign, King Carol I (1839-1914; r. 1866/1881-1914), a (Hohenzollern) German, who reigned over the early independence and the early industrialization of the nation, in 1866/1881.

From mid-century to the First World War (1914-18), Great Britain was the foremost nation in the world, the most powerful and prosperous nation in the world, and the leading colonial power as well. **Great Britain from the mid-nineteenth century to the First World War** continued to be dominated by the long reign of Victoria (which had begun in 1837). This reign extended its largely auspicious genesis (by nineteenth-century standards in respect to monarchial rule) until c. 1886: standards of living improved, male suffrage was significantly expanded (mainly to include the working class), government bureaucracy was modernized, class conflicts diminished on balance, liberal reform of poor laws, prisons, public health, factory regulations, and education accelerated, industrialization expanded, leading political parties were transformed from aristocratic to mass democratic (middle-class) organizations, and fiscal policy was reformed. Much of this was achieved by the leading British parliamentary statesmen and Prime Ministers of the last half of the nineteenth century: Henry John Temple/Lord Palmerston (1784-1865; r. 1855-58, 1859-65), Benjamin Disraeli (1804-81; r. 1868, 1874-80), and William Ewart Gladstone (1809-98; r. 1868-74, 1880-86, 1892-94). After c. 1886, however, more conservative persuasions gained sway, reform slowed, the economy faltered, and social unrest (mainly in the form of labor activism) rose.

Throughout the reign of Victoria, however, the qualified British enthusiasm for political reform (advocated most notably by Victoria, Gladstone, Carlyle, and Dickens) was accompanied by an even larger ardor for **British colonial expansion** (advocated most notably by Victoria, Palmerston, Disraeli, and Carlyle, if not by Gladstone and Dickens). Some of this zeal for colonial ambition was moved by a sense of perceived obligation to promote progress and civilization (of the industrial and British types of course) elsewhere in the world; much of it was governed by significantly less noble, political, economic, and religious aims; and none of it granted to others the prerogatives of self-determination reserved for British subjects themselves. In the last approximate forty years of Victoria's rule (which ended in 1901), the Victorian taste for colonial expansion continued: Bahrain was brought under British dominance in 1861; Bhutan, in 1865; Basutoland/Lesotho, in 1868; Gold Coast/Ghana, in 1874; Fiji, in 1874; the Suez Canal (constructed for Egypt by France, 1859-69; purchased by Britain), in 1875; Baluchistan (effectively, Pakistan), in 1876-87; Cyprus (by way of the Russo-Turkish War of 1877-78), in 1878; Afghanistan (by way of the Second Afghan War, 1878-80), in 1880; Egypt (although yet under Ottoman suzerainty) and Sabah (northeast Borneo), in 1882; the southern region of Papua New Guinea, in 1884; Nigeria, in 1885; New Hebrides Islands/Vanuatu (with France) and the Maldive Islands, in 1887; the Cook Islands, Sarawak (northwest Borneo), and Brunei, in 1888; Sikkim (northeast India) and Zanzibar, in 1890; Oman (southeast Arabia), in 1891; the Gilbert Islands/Kiribati and the Ellice Islands/Tuvalu, in 1892; the southern Solomon Islands, in 1893; Kuwait, in 1897; and Tonga (from the local Tupou Dynasty [1845-   ], which nonetheless survived) and the northern Solomon Islands (from

Germany), in 1900. Great Britain also participated in the successful foreign intervention that defeated the Boxer Uprising in China, 1898-1900.

In southern and eastern Africa, late nineteenth-century and early twentieth-century British colonialism was most affected by the explorations of the Scottish adventurer, David Livingstone (1818-73), and by the activities of the English financier, Cecil John Rhodes (1853-1902), and his British South Africa Company. Livingstone most importantly explored the regions now occupied by the sovereign states of Botswana, Zimbabwe, and Zambia. Rhodes gained a monopoly over the gold and diamond fields of southern Africa in the 1870s, amassed enormous power and wealth as a consequence, and used much of his influence to promote British expansion in the region. In 1884, British (northern) Somaliland/Somalia came under British dominance; in 1885, Bechuanaland/Botswana; in 1886, Kenya; in 1888-91, Southern Rhodesia/Rhodesia/Zimbabwe and Northern Rhodesia/Zambia; in 1889, Nyasaland/Malawi; in 1894, Swaziland; in 1895, Uganda; and in 1899 (with Egypt), Sudan (although yet nominally under Ottoman suzerainty). As Prime Minister of the Cape Colony, 1890-96, Rhodes exercised nearly dictatorial prerogatives over southern Africa and effectively initiated the **Boer War**, or South African War (1899-1902), between Great Britain (the ruling authorities of the Cape Colony and Natal) and the Dutch, the Afrikaner, people of South Africa (the ruling authorities of the Orange Free State and the Transvaal). The British had annexed the Transvaal in 1877 but were defeated by a Boer (Dutch) uprising in 1881. The British again made threatening gestures toward the Transvaal in 1895-99; the government of the Transvaal had impeded British commercial (mainly mining) activities in the province. After several initial Boer successes under General Jan Christiaan Smuts (1870-1950), the British, mainly under General Horatio Herbert Kitchener (1850-1916), prevailed and the Boer states lost their independence by the Treaty of Vereeniging (near Johannesburg) which ended the War in 1902.

There also developed, however, effective **opposition to British colonial adventures** in the waning decades of the Victorian Age; most notably, in India, Ireland, Canada, and Australia. In a way typical of classical colonial practice, Great Britain had developed the modern industrial, agricultural, administrative, and educational infrastructure of India but it had also seriously damaged the traditional Indian form of self-identity and added significantly to the staggering overpopulation, unemployment, famine, and pestilence of the sub-continent. A resistance movement, the Indian National Movement, was formed largely by Europeanized elites who attempted to reconcile the ancient Hindu and the modern Western learning, to promote Indian dignity, and to win at least a measure of political self-determination. The Hindu mystic, Ramakrishna (1836-86), and the Indian National Congress (1885), which eventually won some modest governing prerogatives from the British, made perhaps the largest contributions to this movement in the late nineteenth century. Similarly, Irish opposition to its union with Great Britain (in 1801) went on throughout the nineteenth century, from the agitations of the Irish politician, Daniel O'Connell (1775-1847), in the first half of the century, to the alienations of the Great Irish Potato Famine at mid-century (in the 1840s), to the several attempts by Gladstone to secure effective independence ("home rule") for Ireland in the 1880s and 1890s. Although the reform efforts all failed in their principal objective, they nonetheless established a groundwork for Irish independence that eventually (in large) won the day in the early twentieth century.

The contemporary political formation of **Canada** as an autonomous state within the British Empire/Commonwealth was also owed principally to the late nineteenth century. The country had, by this time, developed an adequate infrastructure to form a viable modern industrial, agricultural, and trading state; it was thus a favorable candidate to be cut loose from British control and from British fiscal support; its fears of the expansionist and bellicose tendencies of the United States of America impelled it to unification; and its distaste for British interference in its domestic affairs moved it to a larger measure of political autonomy. Canada won its effective independence (that is, its self-governing status as a dominion within the British Empire/Commonwealth) from Great Britain in 1867. Ontario, Quebec, New Brunswick, and Nova Scotia were the original provinces; Northwest Territories (1869), Manitoba (1870), British Columbia (1871), Prince Edward Island (1873), Yukon Territory (1898), Alberta (1905), Saskatchewan (1905), Newfoundland (1949), and Nunavut (1999) have since joined the confederation. **Australia**, for like reasons, achieved a similar status within the British Empire/Commonwealth (as a self-governing state, a dominion) and thus effective independence from Great Britain in 1901. The new nation was formed by uniting the previously disparate colonies of New South Wales (1786), Tasmania (1825), Western Australia (1829), South Australia (1834), Victoria (1851), and Queensland (1859). Northern Territory came into the confederation in 1911. Australia assumed British possession of southern Papua New Guinea in 1905.

Victoria died in 1901; she was succeeded by her son and Albert's, Edward VII (1841-1910; r. 1901-10); Edward, in turn, was succeeded by his son, George V (1865-1936; r. 1910-36). The reigns of Edward and

George marked the authentic beginnings of the **House of Windsor** (1901-); they were also distinguished by a continuation of the reformist and colonial agendas of Victoria. The principal reformist achievements of early twentieth-century British political life were the enactment of old-age pensions in 1908 and sick and unemployment insurance in 1911, both under the leadership of Prime Minister Herbert Henry Asquith (1852-1928; r. 1908-16); the uncompromising and courageous feminist demonstrations of Emmeline Goulden Pankhurst (1858-1928), who campaigned tirelessly for the emancipation of women and for female suffrage and who founded the Women's Social and Political Union in 1903; and the labor strikes that disrupted the economy and the domestic order of the period. The colonial aims of this (and later) time(s) had increasingly more to do with balance-of-power and with trade considerations vis-à-vis other colonial states than to do with the objectives of classical, predatory colonialism. These aims nonetheless continued to arouse the resistance of occupied peoples. In India, a failed British partition of Bengal (northeast India) into a predominantly Hindu state (centered in Calcutta) and a predominantly Moslem state (what has since become the sovereign nation of Bangladesh) in 1905 strengthened nationalist claims, mainly under frequently imprisoned activist, Bal Gangadhar Tilak (1856-1920). A boycott of British textiles and guerrilla bombings undid the partition. By the Pact of Lucknow (near Delhi), Hindus and Moslems called jointly for independence from Britain in 1916. In Persia/Iran, the New Persian Empire of the Safavid Dynasty was undone in 1736 as has been said. Over the next approximate century and three-quarters, largely under the Kajar Dynasty (of Turkish origin) established in 1779 (-1921), the nation at first descended still further into butchery and anarchy before establishing relations with leading European states (manly Great Britain and Russia) and attempting to enact some liberal, European-style reforms. In order to protect commercial interests (including oil interests) from the political uncertainty of the region, however, and over Persian objections, Great Britain and Russia variously occupied and divided the country into respective spheres of influence beginning in 1907. In Ireland, the resistance to British rule stiffened yet further; the militant Catholic resistance formed the Sinn Fein (1905) which soon became the dominant nationalist organization in the country. **New Zealand**, which had been originally a part of the Australian colony of New South Wales, became a discrete colony in 1841, became the first nation in the world to grant voting franchise to women in 1893, gained control of the Cook Islands in 1901, and attained autonomous status (self-governing status) in the British Empire/Commonwealth (as a dominion à la Canada and Australia before it), effectively independence from Great Britain, in 1907. (The Union of) **South Africa** came to the same end, to political unification and independence (as a self-governing dominion) within the British Empire/Commonwealth, in 1910.

France from the mid-nineteenth century to the First World War likewise continued to be among the leading states of Europe. From its successful participation in the Crimean War to its unsuccessful participation in the Franco-Prussian War (1870-71), it was likely the most powerful nation on the European Continent. The presidency of Louis Napoleon Bonaparte (r. 1848-52) consolidated conservative sentiment and suppressed efforts at liberal reform as has been said. These sentiments and efforts brought in a new constitution in 1852; this constitution granted Louis Napoleon dictatorial powers; the Second Republic was thereby replaced by the **Second Empire** and Louis Napoleon became King Napoleon III (r. 1852-70) also in 1852. The early reign of the new sovereign was marked by highly authoritarian policy; a more liberal temperament characterized the last several years of his rule (owing largely to public discontent over foreign policy failures). Throughout his tenure, however, the industrialization and the commercialization of the country was greatly accelerated; enormous urban construction projects were completed (the rebuilding of cities, the creation of railways, and the formation of public libraries in particular); the arts flourished; and important international expositions were staged (most notably, the Paris World Exhibitions of 1855 and 1867). The historical record of the Second Empire is also inscribed by several major international developments:

- the construction of the Suez Canal in Egypt (connecting the Mediterranean and Red Seas and greatly reducing the sea-traveling distance between Europe and Asia) by the French engineer, Ferdinand de Lesseps (1805-94), in 1859-69;
- the French military protection of the Papal States (1849-70) which strained relations with the other Italies;
- the French support of the Italies in the Franco-Sardinian War against Austria in 1859;
- the French possession of Monaco (from Sardinia) in 1861 and the effective independence (self-governing status) of Monaco (under the ongoing Grimaldi Dynasty) also in 1861;
- the failed colonial intervention in Mexico; despite opposition by the American government as well as by the Mexican government (under President Benito Juarez), the French installed (Austrian Hapsburg) Archduke Maximilian (1832-67), brother of Franz Joseph I and husband to the daughter of

Leopold I of Belgium, as Emperor of Mexico in 1864; French troops withdrew in 1866-67 and Maximilian was executed in 1867;

- the continuing amplification of French colonialism in Asia, Africa, the Middle East, and the south Pacific; France became the dominant political and economic influence in New Caledonia in 1853, in French Indonesia/Vietnam in 1858-84, in Syria (including Lebanon; although yet under Ottoman suzerainty) in 1860, and in French Indonesia/Cambodia in 1863; and
- the Franco-Prussian War of 1870-71 which ended in a resounding Prussian victory and in a unified German state; Prussia secured the neutrality of Great Britain, Austria, and Italy as well as the support of the other German states and supplanted France as the leading power on the European Continent; by the Peace of Frankfurt, which concluded the War in 1871, France lost Alsace-Lorraine (then in northeastern France) to Germany.

Monarchial rule in France (the Bourbon Dynasty in general and the Second Empire of Napoleon III in particular) ended with the crushing French defeat in the Franco-Prussian War, Napoleon was himself captured at the decisive Battle of Sedan (near Reims); he was deposed and exiled; and, after several months of ruinous civil war, a new government with a new constitution, the **Third Republic** (1870-1940), was formed, all in 1870-71. The new constitution established universal male suffrage and freedom of assembly and the press. The life of the Third Republic from its formation to the First World War was dominated by a state bureaucracy but by unstable governments; by continuing disputes between conservative and liberal political agendas and personalities, between workers and employers, between civil and military authorities, and between church and state; by rising anti-German sentiment; by a vast expansion of public, secular education (largely under the direction of Jules Ferry [1832-93; assassinated], who twice served brief terms as Prime Minister, 1880-81 and 1883-85); and by thoroughly brilliant developments in technology, science, the arts, and sport. This was also importantly the period in which:

- the Panama Canal was begun (in 1881) by Ferdinand de Lesseps (who had earlier supervised construction of the Suez Canal); construction in Panama was nonetheless discontinued in 1892-93 due to financial scandal;
- the Paris World Fair of 1889 (for which the Eiffel Tower was constructed) was successfully staged;
- the Dual Entente was formed with Russia in 1890 and the Entente Cordial was arranged with Great Britain in 1904; these became the Triple Entente in 1907;
- the nineteenth century's most celebrated case of explicit government duplicity and official racism, the Dreyfus Affair, unfolded; in 1894, Alfred Dreyfus (1859-1935), a Jewish military officer, was falsely accused and convicted, by contrived means, of espionage for reasons having largely to do with reactionary militarism against Germany and with anti-Semitism; Dreyfus served five years in prison, was vigorously and courageously defended by no less than Émile Zola (himself convicted of libel for these efforts) and Georges Clemenceau (later the prime minister of the country), and was fully exonerated in 1906; and
- the ongoing development of **French colonialism** in Asia, Africa, the Middle East, and the south Pacific; France became the dominant political and economic influence in Tunisia (from the Ottoman Empire) in 1881, French West Africa/Gabon in 1886, New Hebrides Islands/Vanuatu (with Great Britain) in 1887, French Somaliland/Djibouti in 1888, French Equatorial Africa/French Congo/Middle Congo/ Republic of the Congo/Peoples' Republic of the Congo/Republic of the Congo in 1889, French West Africa/Niger in 1891, French Indochina/Laos in 1893, French West Africa/Côte d'Ivoire/Ivory Coast in 1893, French Equatorial Africa/Central African Republic in 1894, French West Africa/Upper Volta/ Burkina Faso in 1896, French West Africa/Mali in 1898, French West Africa/Mauritania in 1903, Morocco (with Spain) in 1912, and French Equatorial Africa/Chad in 1913; it also participated in the successful foreign intervention that defeated the Boxer Uprising in China in 1898-1900.

The nineteenth-century German and Italian struggles for national unification and independence were significantly related. Both had begun in earnest in the 1830s and both were greatly affected by French and by Austrian initiatives. The German case was vigorously opposed by the French and Austrians; the Italian case was ardently supported by the French and opposed by the Austrians. Prussia was the foremost state in **Germany from the mid-nineteenth century to the First World War**. William I (1797-1888; r. 1861-88), brother and successor of Frederick William IV, came to the Prussian throne in 1861 and appointed Otto von Bismarck (1815-98; r. 1862-90) prime minister in 1862. Virtually throughout his tenure, Bismarck was the dominant political figure in Prussian-German political life. Of deeply conservative and militaristic bent, he unconstitutionally dissolved the parliament in 1862 and began a series of wars aimed at expelling Austria from the German Confederation and at uniting the remaining German states under Prussian leadership. In the German-Danish War of 1864, Prussia and Austria attacked and annexed the then-Danish provinces of Schleswig-Holstein (southern Denmark/north-central Germany). In 1866, Prussia defeated Austria in the Austro-Prussian War, took sole possession of Schleswig-Holstein, and formed the North German Confederation, which included all northern German states except Hanover and Saxony, which excluded Austria, and which became the dominant political voice in German affairs. Austria and Liechtenstein (which had been a part of the German Confederation from 1815 and a part of the Holy Roman Empire from 1719) thus became independent states (states independent of formal German affiliation) in 1866. In 1870, Bismarck provoked the **Franco-Prussian War**, largely over the prospect of a Hohenzollern (the royal family of Brandenburg-Prussia from 1415 to 1918) succession to the new elective monarchy in Spain, a prospect to which the French government of Napoleon III greatly objected. The emphatic Prussian victory and the 1871 treaty manifesting it (the Peace of Frankfurt) brought Alsace-Lorraine into the German fold and united the southern German states (mainly Bavaria and Wurttemberg) with the northern.

The new German state, the **Second German Empire**/Reich (1871-1918), came under Prussian hegemony (that is, domination by the House of Hohenzollern centered in Berlin); William I was proclaimed emperor and Bismarck chancellor (virtual dictator), both in 1871. In domestic terms, the new constitution provided a largely perfunctory parliament (Reichstag), which was unable to effectively oppose the autocratic and repressive policies of Bismarck despite liberal, socialist, and religious opposition to them. In order to defuse some of this opposition, Bismarck nonetheless allowed the passage of child labor laws, working-hour legislation, and aged, illness, and unemployment insurance programs, all in the period from 1883 to 1887. Despite the economic crisis of 1873, Bismarck also presided over a colossal expansion in economic activity and prosperity; industrial production, commercial prowess, and banking proficiency all significantly increased. In terms of foreign policy, Bismarck intended no further European expansion; he developed instead an extensive system of alliances designed to defend the new state and to preserve the conservative social order of the Continent. The most notable of these alliances were the League of the Three Emperors (Germany, Russia, and Austria-Hungary) in 1872 and the Triple Alliance (Germany, Italy, and Austria-Hungary; later joined by Romania and Serbia) in 1882. Although intending no further European expansion, Bismarck nonetheless established the **German colonial empire** in Africa and the central-south Pacific. Germany became the dominant political and economic influence in Cameroon, German Southwest Africa/Southwest Africa/Namibia, and northern Papua New Guinea in 1884, German East Africa/Tanganyika/Tanzania, the northern Solomon Islands, and the Marshall Islands in 1885, Togoland/Togo in 1886, and Nauru in 1888.

High liberal hopes were invested in William I's progressive son and successor, Frederick III (1831-88; r. 1888), who was also Queen Victoria's son-in-law and a renowned and heroic military commander in both the Austro-Prussian War and the Franco-Prussian War, but his reign was very brief and uneventful. The last emperor of the Second German Empire and the last of the Hohenzollern rulers was Frederick III's son and successor, William II (1859-1941; r. 1888-1918). William had few of his father's very considerable talents and little of his father's congenial character. He neither had any good use for Bismarck whom he dismissed in 1890. His reign was most significantly marked by:

- a vain overestimation of German military and commercial power which brought deteriorating relations with Great Britain, France, Russia, and the United States of America;
- a continuing increase of corporate power, industrial production, and military armaments; Germany became the most industrialized and the most heavily armed nation in Continental Europe in this time;
- ongoing political dissension among the numerous factions of conservative and liberal advocates, most of which favored reactionary tendencies;
- further development of the German colonial empire in Africa, the central-south Pacific, and Asia; Germany became the dominant political and economic influence in Burundi and Rwanda in 1890, purchased Palau, the Northern Mariana Islands, and the Caroline Islands/Federated States of Micronesia from Spain in 1899, and partitioned the Samoan Islands (with the United States of America), acquiring the western islands, also in 1899; it too participated in the successful foreign intervention that defeated the Boxer Uprising in China in 1898-1900 and importantly contested French and Spanish claims in Morocco in 1912; and
- two significant disputes with France over colliding interests in Morocco and over support for Austrian policy in the Balkans in the early twentieth century, both of which contributed notably to causing the First World War.

The other major sector of German culture in the late nineteenth and early twentieth centuries, Austria-Hungary, was a diverse multi-national state which then included (or soon came to include) Austria and Hungary themselves, as well as Bohemia, Moravia, Silesia, Galicia, Transylvania, Croatia, Slovenia, Bosnia-Herzegovina, and northern Serbia. That is, in addition to Austria, Hungary, Croatia, Slovenia, Bosnia-Herzegovina, and northern Serbia, it also included good bits of what are now the Czech Republic, Slovakia, Poland, Romania, and Ukraine. Austria-Hungary, under Hapsburg Emperor Franz Joseph I, was excluded from the North German Confederation and the new, the unified, Germany as has been said. After successful participation in the Crimean War, it lost Lombardy to Sardinia in the Franco-Sardinian War against Austria of 1859; it lost Venice to Italy and Schleswig-Holstein to Prussia in the Austro-Prussian War of 1866; it acceded to continuing Hungarian demands for effective domestic independence in the form of the Dual Monarchy, the **Austro-Hungarian Empire** (1867-1918), in 1867 (Franz Joseph also became King of Hungary in 1867; r. 1867-1916); and it increasingly granted autonomous prerogatives to the non-German (mainly, the Slavic) regions of the Empire, principally to Czech, Polish, Serbian, and Croatian regions as well as to Romanian territories. The political decline of Austria, of the Austro-Hungarian Empire, was further augmented by continuing conservative-liberal disruptions and by the relatively modest pace with which the country was industrialized. Its status and power were nonetheless buoyed by its alliances with Germany; most importantly, by the League of the Three Emperors (1872) and the Triple Alliance (1882). These alliances as well as their connections to the Balkan policy of the Austro-Hungarian Empire and to the assassination of the heir apparent to Franz Joseph I, his nephew, Austrian Archduke Franz Ferdinand (1863-1914), and of his wife, Sophie, by a Serbian nationalist in Sarajevo, Bosnia in 1914, were significantly implicated in the causes of the First World War.

Italy from the mid-nineteenth century to the First World War was largely dominated by its struggle for political unification and independence. The political unification and independence of the Italies (the **Risorgimento**, or revival), like those of the Germanies, had begun in the 1830s and were especially closely related to Austrian and to French policies of the mid-nineteenth century as has been said. The Kingdom of Sardinia (Sardinia itself and northwest Italy; that is, Sardinia, Piedmont, Savoy, and Monaco), under the **House of Savoy** (r. Sardinia, 1720-1861; r. Italy, 1861-1946), centered in Piedmont, came to leadership of the Risorgimento in 1848. In the context of the Revolutions of 1848-49, King Charles Albert (1798-1849; r. 1831-49) twice attempted unsuccessfully to expel the Austrians, then abdicated. His son and successor, Victor Emmanuel II (1820-78; r. Sardinia, 1849-61; r. Italy, 1861-78), and the Sardinian Prime Minister, Count Camillo Benso di Cavour (1810-61; r. 1852-59, 1860-61), then developed a modern liberal state, participated successfully in the Crimean War, and cultivated a program to unify Italy under Sardinian (i.e., Piedmontese) leadership. Sardinia prevailed, with French assistance, against Austrian aggression in the Franco-Sardinian War of 1859 and also prevailed in the broader conflict with Austria, the Austrian-Piedmont War of 1859-61. In the former encounter, Sardinia acquired Lombardy (north-central Italy). In the latter, Tuscany, Modena, Parma, and Romagna – effectively, the remainder of northern Italy except Venice and Umbria – voluntarily joined the Italian union. Also in 1860, the brilliant campaign of Giuseppe Garibaldi captured the (Bourbon) Kingdom of the Two Sicilies (the effective whole of southern Italy) and Umbria (central-eastern Italy) was annexed to the union. The united Kingdom of Italy was proclaimed in 1861 with King Emmanuel II as its first sovereign. Except for the South Tyrol, Venice, and Istria (all in the northeast), which remained with Austria, the Papal States (in central-western Italy), which remained under papal authority and French protection, and Savoy and Monaco (in the northwest), which were ceded to France, the entire peninsula (and its Italian extensions) achieved political unification and independence from Austria in the north and from the Sicilian Bourbons (who were of Spanish lineage) in the south. Venice came to Italy in 1866 by way of the Austro-Prussian War and the Papal States came to it in 1870 by way of the Franco-Prussian War. Pope Pius IX (1792-1878; r. 1846-78), the longest reigning pope in the entire history of the institution, and his successors nonetheless retained sovereignty over Vatican City; Rome became the capital city of Italy in 1871.

The period in contemporary modern Italian history from independence to the First World War, largely under Victor Emmanuel II's son and successor, Humbert I (1844-1900; r. 1878-1900), who was assassinated by an anarchist, and under Humbert I's son and successor, Victor Emmanuel III (1869-1947; r. 1900-46), was an era of highly significant transformation. Population, agricultural production, industrialization, nationalism, militarism, worker agitations and reforms, political franchise, and public education all rose sharply in this time. In foreign policy, Italy became a major European political and military factor on its joining the Triple Alliance (with Germany and Austria-Hungary) in 1882 and it practiced an expansionist colonial strategy throughout the period. Italy became the dominant political and economic influence in Italian (eastern) Somaliland/Somalia in

1889, in Eritrea in 1890, and in Libya (from the Ottoman Empire) in 1911. Its attempted annexation of northwest Abyssinia/Ethiopia in 1889 was defeated by the Abyssinians in 1894-96.

The **other major states of western Europe from the mid-nineteenth century to the First World War** passed through developments of the same basic type as those experienced by Great Britain, France, Germany, Austria-Hungary, and Italy. In **Spain**, nationalists, liberals, and socialists opposed monarchists and Catholics in the struggle for political influence; political and economic stability declined as a consequence. The Bourbon monarchy teetered and the throne itself was contested; Isabella II was succeeded by brief and unsteady experiments with an elective (or constitutional) monarchy (1869-73) and with a republic (the First Republic, 1973-74). The Bourbon crown was restored in Isabella II's son, Alfonso XII (1857-85; r. 1874-85), and continued in Alfonso II's son and successor, Alfonso XIII (1886-1941; r. 1886-1931). Liberal-conservative disputes and challenges to what remained of the Spanish colonial empire continued. A new constitution (1876) and some progressive reforms briefly stabilized the country before several waves of insurrection in Cuba (1868-78 and 1895-98) brought about the Spanish-American War in 1898 and the expiration of the Spanish colonial empire in the Americas (that is, in the only two remaining Spanish colonies in the Americas, Cuba and Puerto Rico, both of which passed to American hegemony). Spain's remaining possessions in the central and south Pacific were either also claimed by the War in 1898 – Guam and the Philippines (both of which too passed to American hegemony) – or were sold to Germany in 1899: Palau, the Northern Mariana Islands, and the Caroline Islands/Federated States of Micronesia. By 1899, then, only several small African possessions remained in the once-extensive Spanish colonial empire: the Canary Islands, bits of Morocco (most notably, Spanish Sahara/Western Sahara, which had been claimed in 1884), and Spanish Guinea/Rio Muni/Equatorial Guinea.

Similarly, in **Portugal**, conservative-liberal altercations, significant advances in the industrial, commercial, and educational life of the nation, and transformations in its colonial empire marked the period from the death of John VI in 1826 to the First World War. John VI's son, Brazilian Emperor, Pedro I, who was heir to the Portuguese throne, relinquished it to his daughter, Maria II (1819-53; r. 1834-53), and remained in Brazil. Maria's reign (not unlike Isabella II's tenure in Spain) was both disputed and troubled. Political turmoil continued throughout the remaining Braganza sovereigns to the last, Manuel II (1889-1932; r. 1908-10), the last king of Portugal, who was deposed by a republican revolution in 1910. Brazil achieved independence from Portugal without struggle in 1822 as has been said. Portugal otherwise largely formalized its prerogatives over other long-held territories in Africa and Asia: Angola, the Azore Islands, the Cape Verde Islands, Guinea-Bissau, Mozambique, Sao Tome e Principe, East Timor, and Macao.

Switzerland became a more centralized federal state in the nineteenth century, passed through several stages of conservative-liberal dissension and constitutional revision, and achieved significant enhancements of its industrial, commercial, and educational life. A nineteenth-century Swiss citizen, Jean Henri Dunant (1828-1910), was likewise responsible for establishing the inviolability of hospital services and an organization to care for war wounded, the International Red Cross, in Geneva in 1864, a distinction for which he became the co-recipient of the first Nobel Peace Prize in 1901. The Universal Postal Union, uniting the postal services of sovereign nations, was also established in Switzerland (Berne) in this period (1874).

The **Low Countries** too passed through drifts to national identity, liberal-conservative struggles, democratic constitutional revisions, impressive industrial, commercial, and educational gains, and colonial upheavals from the middle of the nineteenth century to the First World War. Luxembourg broke from its Dutch and Belgian partition and became an autonomous state under Dutch suzerainty in 1848 as has been said; it achieved full independence as a duchy, under the ongoing Nassau Dynasty, in 1890. Belgium was governed in this period by Leopold II (1835-1909; r. 1865-1909), son and successor of Leopold I, and by his nephew and successor, Albert I (1875-1934; r. 1909-34). It acquired the Congo Free State/Belgian Congo/Democratic Republic of the Congo/Zaire/Democratic Republic of the Congo with the assistance of British explorer and journalist, Henry Morton Stanley (1841-1904), in 1884-85; it administered the territory in an utterly rapacious way, abusing (slave) labor and amassing enormous private wealth. Netherlands was governed in this period by the son and successor of William II, William III (1817-90; r. 1849-90), and by his daughter and successor, Wilhelmina (1880-1962; r. 1890-1948). Its colonial record in this time was somewhat more benign than Belgium's but was nonetheless troubled; the ongoing treatment of native peoples by Dutch descendants and by the Dutch government itself in South Africa, the Dutch East Indies/Indonesia, and Dutch Guiana/Suriname was not without injurious incident.

From the middle of the nineteenth century to the First World War, the **Scandinavian states** likewise experienced a sharp rise in nationalistic (and regional Scandinavian) sentiment, agitations for national unification and independence, democratic social, constitutional, and educational reform, industrial and agricultural production, and commercial prowess. In Denmark, the period was most importantly marked by the reign of Frederick VII (1808-63; r. 1848-63), the last of the Oldenburg Dynasty, by that of his successor, Christian IX (1818-1906; r. 1863-1906), by that of his son and successor, Frederick VIII (1843-1912; r. 1906-12), who was also the brother of George I of Greece, and by that of his son and successor, Christian X (1870-1947; r. 1912-47). Schleswig-Holstein was lost to Prussia and Austria in the German-Danish War of 1864 and Iceland remained in personal union with Denmark but became otherwise a largely autonomous state in 1874-1918. In Sweden, the period is most importantly marked by the establishment of the Nobel Prizes in peace, chemistry, physics, physiology or medicine, and literature in 1901 and by the reigns of Charles XIV (1763-1844; r. 1818-44), a French revolutionary general and the adopted son of his childless predecessor who had effectively governed the country from 1810, of Oscar II (1829-1907; r. 1872-1907), a grandson of Charles XIV and an accomplished linguist, historian, and poet, and of Gustavus V (1858-1950; r. 1907-50), son and successor of Oscar II. Charles forced Denmark to cede Norway to Sweden in 1814 as has been said; he was also largely responsible for arranging the post-revolutionary government of Sweden. Oscar, conversely, negotiated dissolution of the union with Norway in 1905; Norway thereby became an independent constitutional monarchy under Haakon VII (1872-1957; r. 1905-57), ironically enough a member of the Danish royal family (i.e., a son of Frederick VIII). Finland had been obtained by Russia from Sweden in 1809 (as has been said) and it remained a subject of the Russian throne throughout the nineteenth century. A resolute independence movement nonetheless developed in the late nineteenth and early twentieth centuries, most notably under the influence of the national epic, Kalevala, compiled by Finnish philologist, Elias Lonnrot (1802-84), and under the influence of the Young Finns crusade. Finland became the first European state to grant female suffrage in 1906.

The political, economic, and social developments that shaped western European life from the approximate middle of the nineteenth century to the First World War were roughly those that also shaped life elsewhere in the world in this time; that is, in the Americas, Africa, the central and south Pacific, Asia, eastern Europe, and the Middle East. By mid-century, the United States of America was becoming a major political and economic force in international affairs; **late nineteenth-century United States of America** was among the leading national societies in the world. The country was unusually large and wealthy; it had a still largely undeveloped frontier; it was of widely varied climate; it attracted European immigrants (which greatly added to its population and to its store of inexpensive labor); and it hadn't an established cultural commitment to special castes or churches other than commercialists and commerce. James Polk was succeeded as president by the leading American military figure in the Mexican War, Zachary Taylor (r. 1849-50), and Taylor, in turn, by Millard Fillmore (1800-74; r. 1850-53), Franklin Pierce (1804-69; r. 1853-57), and James Buchanan (1791-1868; r. 1857-61). The two most significant issues in American political affairs of the 1850s were the ongoing expansion of territory (and influence) and slavery (including the sectional and economic implications of slavery). In respect to the expansionist issue, the United States:

- aggressively opened previously closed Japanese ports and trading inclinations to foreign influences, largely through the efforts of Commodore Matthew Calbraith Perry (1794-1858) in 1853-54; and
- negotiated the purchase of extreme southern Arizona and New Mexico (the Gadsden Purchase) from Mexico in 1853.

California (1850), Minnesota (1858), Oregon (1859), and Kansas (1861) joined the formal union of states in the presidential terms of Fillmore and Buchanan. In respect to the issue of slavery, the Compromise of 1850 left the question of slavery to the popular sovereignty of the disparate states. The Kansas-Nebraska Act (1854) repealed the Missouri Compromise (1820-21), threatened the introduction of slavery in the western states/territories, and led to the establishment of the (new) Republican Party (which opposed such an introduction), to the dissolution of the Whig Party (which tended to favor the Compromise of 1850), and to subsequent Democratic-Republican divisions in American political life. And the Dred Scott Case of 1856-57 held that slaves are property who cannot be freed by escaping from slave to non-slave states and that the government has no legitimate power to limit slavery in the disparate states/territories. The abolitionist cause was greatly advanced by private attempts to assist the escape of fugitive slaves (such as those of the principal heroine of the Underground Railroad, Harriet Tubman [c. 1820-1913], herself an escaped slave), by the publication of articulate anti-slavery literature (such as that of Uncle Tom's Cabin by Harriet Beecher Stowe [1811-96] in 1852), and by armed acts of public defiance (such as the retaliatory insurrection of John Brown [1800-59] at Harpers Ferry, Virginia-West Virginia in 1859). The American Civil War was well on its way at least a decade before it formally began. Moreover, the transatlantic telegraph cable was completed in this time (1858), the cause of public education was also greatly advanced in the decade prior to the Civil War, and the country passed through a severe economic depression, the Panic of 1857 (1857-60), as the 1850s came to an end.

The **American Civil War** (1861-65) was the war of American national unification. It put the northern states (the Union states), effectively industrial, protective-tariff states, against the southern states (the Confederate states), effectively agricultural states devoted to unrestricted trade. The political economy of the south (its world monopoly of cotton in particular) and the aristocratic form of plantation life characteristic of southern culture (with its heavy reliance on the institution of slavery) were greatly threatened by the capital industrialism of the north. South Carolina seceded from the union in 1860; ten other states followed, forming the Confederate States of America, under President Jefferson Davis (1808-89; r. 1861-65), in 1861. The Confederacy had its capital in Richmond, Virginia and was led by Davis and his two ablest military commanders, General Robert Edward Lee (1807-70) and General Thomas Jonathan "Stonewall" Jackson (1824-63). The Union had its capital in Washington, D.C. and was led by its newly elected president, the sixteenth president of the country, Abraham Lincoln (1809-65; r. 1861-65), and his two ablest military commanders, General William Tecumseh Sherman (1820-91) and General Ulysses Simpson Grant (1822-85; later the eighteenth president of the nation). When Union troops were garrisoned at Fort Sumter (Charleston), South Carolina in 1861, the Confederate army attacked and the War was on. The Confederate victory at Sumter was followed by other major southern successes early in the conflict, all in Virginia under the direction of Lee and/or Jackson: the First Battle of Bull Run (Manassas) in 1861, the Second Battle of Bull Run in 1862, the Battle of Fredericksburg in 1862, and the Battle of Chancellorsville (at which Jackson was killed) in 1863. In 1862, however, the War began to turn in the Union's favor; attempting to invade the north, Lee and Jackson were defeated at the Battle of Antietam (Maryland). In 1863, again attempting an invasion of northern territory, Lee was defeated at the horrific Battle of Gettysburg (Pennsylvania). The vast numerical and technological superiority of the north then overwhelmed its opposition in the western and southern campaigns of Grant and Sherman; most notably, in Grant's victories at the Battles of Vicksburg (Mississippi) in 1863, Petersburg (Virginia) in 1864, and Richmond in 1865 and in Sherman's victory at the Battle of Atlanta in 1864. Lee surrendered to Grant at Appomattox (near Richmond) in 1865, effectively ending the War in the Union's favor.

Lincoln's presidency was utterly dominated by the War. Slavery was effectively abolished by the Emancipation Proclamation of 1863 and the union of states was preserved under northern, industrial leadership. Shortly before the conclusion of the War, Lincoln had been elected to a second term; within a week after Appomattox, he was assassinated. His "Gettysburg Address" (1863) and "Second Inaugural Address" (1865) are widely considered among the foremost achievements of American oratorical literature. His first term was also notable for the Homestead Act (1862), which awarded land to western pioneers (trappers, farmers, merchants, speculators, and craftsmen), which contributed notably to the development of the frontier, and which further displaced native peoples; for the inception of the transcontinental railroad (1862); and for the admission of West Virginia (1863) to the formal union of states.

The American Civil War left the south in virtual ruin, killed more Americans than any other conflict in the nation's history, made the United States of America a major industrial and economic power, and established the basis on which the next chapter of American history, **Reconstruction**, unfolded. The period of Reconstruction (1865-77) was circumscribed by the presidencies of Lincoln's two successors, Andrew Johnson (1808-75; r. 1865-69) and Ulysses Simpson Grant (r. 1869-77). It entailed the renovation of the Union, principally in terms of providing a federal military occupation of the south, in terms of re-admitting seceded states to the union of states, and in terms of accommodating (or contriving ways to evade accommodating) the new status of former slaves. Although African-Americans won formal rights of citizenship in 1868 and the formal right to vote in 1870, severe limitations were nonetheless placed on the de facto exercise of their civil rights. Terrorist organizations (such as the Ku Klux Klan, established in 1866) intimidated black persons by threatening, whipping, and lynching them; literacy tests and poll taxes disenfranchised them; acutely differential occupational, educational, and investment opportunities greatly disadvantaged them; and sharply segregated and inferior housing and living conditions severely limited their life chances. Johnson's presidency was also importantly marked by an impeachment of him on specious grounds (which narrowly failed to convict) in 1868, by completion of the transcontinental railroad in 1869, by the purchase of Alaska from Russia in 1867, and by the admission of Nebraska to the formal union of states in 1867. Grant's presidency was mainly distinguished by pervasive corruption, by punitive measures against southern farmers in particular, by a severe economic depression in 1873-78, and by the admission of Colorado to the formal union of states in 1876. His Personal Memoirs (1885-86) nonetheless rank among the most extraordinary military narratives in the history of the genre.

The colossal industrial (and agricultural) expansion of the country after the Civil War was advanced still further in the presidential terms of Grant's immediate successors: Rutherford Birchard Hayes (1822-93; r. 1877-81), James Abram Garfield (1831-81; r. 1881 [assassinated]), Chester Alan Arthur (c. 1830-86; r. 1881-85), (Stephen) Grover Cleveland (1837-1908; r. 1885-89, 1893-97), Benjamin Harrison (1833-1901; r. 1889-93), grandson of William Henry Harrison (the nation's ninth president), and William McKinley (1843-1901; r. 1897-1901 [assassinated]). Despite the severe economic depression of 1893-94, there was enormous economic growth in the approximate quarter-century from the end of Grant's presidency to the end of McKinley's. Much of this had to do with technological innovation and much of it also had to do with the domination of the government by corporate interests, with private initiative and risk-taking, and with overt and covert criminal license. Hard currency policies linked to the gold standard and protective tariffs were the dominant government policies of the period. The insatiable and the largely unrestrained pursuit of profits characteristic of the time produced immense concentrations of wealth for the few, substantial prosperity for many others, and utter destitution for alarmingly large numbers of still others. American business combined its resources to fix prices, control markets, and dilute to eliminate the expense of competition. The monopolies which resulted – most notably, the New York Central Railroad of Cornelius Vanderbilt (1794-1877), the Standard Oil Company of John Davison Rockefeller (1839-1937), the Carnegie Steel Company of Andrew Carnegie (1835-1919), and the banking, insurance, mining, manufacturing, and shipping interests of John Pierpont Morgan (1837-1913) – threatened both equality (by discriminating against the poor) and liberty (by investing vast power in the wealthy). These monopolies also sparked:

- wide labor unrest; most significantly, the Haymarket Square riot in Chicago in 1886 and organization of the American Federation of Labor, also in 1886;
- reform of government regulation in respect to commerce; most significantly, the Interstate Commerce Act of 1887 and the Sherman Antitrust Law of 1890; and
- the most remarkable epoch in American philanthropy, led by preeminent industrial magnates whose charitable gifts and endowments included universities, libraries, museums, research institutes, artistic foundations, and welfare organizations.

The last approximate quarter of nineteenth-century American life also included Hayes' withdrawal of federal troops from southern states (which formally ended Reconstruction) in 1877; staging of the first Pan-American Conference (which established the Pan-American Union and which was aimed mainly at protecting and advancing substantial American commercial investments in central and South America and at securing American political and economic domination of the region) in Harrison's presidency (1889-90); formal admission to the union of states of North Dakota (1889), South Dakota (1889), Montana (1889), Washington (1889), Idaho (1890), Wyoming (1890), and Utah (1896); and McKinley's prosecution of the Spanish-American War (1898), the Boxer Uprising in China (1898-1900), and the annexation of Hawaii (1898) and (American) Samoa (1900). The **Spanish-American War** effectively began with the insurrection for Cuban independence from Spain in 1895-98 (brought about largely under the leadership of revolutionary poet, Jose Marti [1853-95]) and was most influenced by American commercial losses in the Cuban guerrilla actions, by imperial American ambitions in the region (mainly in respect to the Panama Canal), by the suspicious sinking of an American battleship in Havana, and by a rebellion in the Philippines against Spanish rule inspired by accomplished physician and author, Jose Rizal (1861-96 [executed]). In the brief conflict which followed, the United States decisively defeated Spanish colonial forces virtually wherever it engaged them, claimed Cuba (which enjoyed only ostensible independence), Puerto Rico, Guam, and the Philippines (over armed local objection, 1899-1901) from Spain by the Treaty of Paris (which ended the War), and established itself as a leading international political and military power. The United States too participated in the successful foreign intervention that defeated the Boxer Uprising in China in 1898-1900. The Hawaiian Islands had been politically consolidated under a local monarchy founded by Kamehameha I (c. 1738-1819; r. c. 1790-1819) in c. 1790. The monarchy continued to Queen Liliuokalani (1838-1917; r. 1891-93) who was dethroned by constitutional exponents (mainly American sugar tycoons). The United States, which had increasingly dominated the political and economic life of the Islands since the 1820s, largely through Christian missionaries and agricultural commercialists, annexed the region in 1898. The Samoan Islands were partitioned between Germany and the United States in 1899 as has been said; Germany acquired the western islands and the United States annexed the eastern islands, which thus became American Samoa.

The three American presidential administrations which followed McKinley's, effectively the society of **early twentieth-century United States of America**, were of a more moderate temperament in respect to business affairs. The administrations of Theodore Roosevelt (1858-1919; r. 1901-09), William Howard Taft (1857-1930;

r. 1909-13), and (Thomas) Woodrow Wilson (1856-1924; r. 1913-21) all attempted to bring corporate prerogative within the ambit of social responsibility without injuring this prerogative's sense of invention, its productivity, or its contributions to prosperity. Roosevelt, who had earlier served with distinction in the Spanish-American War, formulated a vigorous program of government regulation concerning industrial and agricultural commerce, a program aimed mainly at restraining the monopolies and conserving the environment. He also presided over the economic depression of 1907, supervised the admission of Oklahoma to the formal union of states in 1907, and prosecuted an imperialistic foreign policy, principally in central America and the Caribbean. The construction of the Panama Canal had been abandoned by France in 1892-93 as has been said; the project was left to the United Sates in 1901. The United States provoked a revolution in 1903 by which Panama seceded from Colombia and became an independent state under heavy American "supervision." The Canal itself was constructed by the American military between 1904 and 1914. The United States, which had earlier occupied Cuba (1898-1902) following the Spanish-American War, made an armed intervention in a civil rebellion there and again occupied the island from 1906 to 1909. Roosevelt's successful mediation of the treaty ending the Russo-Japanese War in 1904-05 won him the 1906 Nobel Peace Prize.

Taft continued the progressive domestic and the imperialistic foreign tendencies of Roosevelt, if somewhat less emphatically than had Roosevelt himself. The most notable instances of these tendencies were the anti-trust legislation enacted in Taft's term and the armed intervention in a civil war in Nicaragua in 1912 (which became a military occupation lasting until 1933). New Mexico and Arizona joined the formal union of states also during Taft's tenure; i.e., in 1912. Wilson's inclinations were more progressive still; his administration restricted protective tariffs, executed progressive taxation measures, and further reduced the power of the trusts by regulating banking and trading practices and by enacting anti-trust legislation (the Clayton Antitrust Act, 1914). Conflicts in Haiti, the Dominican Republic, Mexico, the Danish West Indies/Virgin Islands, and Europe, however, truncated his domestic agenda.

The approximate events which shaped western European and North American political, economic, and social circumstances in this period were likewise the principal influences on such circumstances **elsewhere in the world from the early nineteenth century to the First World War**. The period from independence, effectively the 1820s, to the First World War in **Latin America** (central and South America) was a time of enormous instability, inequality, and injustice. Spanish and Portuguese autocracy was replaced by unsteady local regimes that were increasingly dominated by American capital interests and their politico-military enforcers. Despite the introduction of modern constitutions, incompatible class, race, and ideological (liberal-conservative, secular-clerical) differences carved routine civil conflict; the well-known competition among nations for natural and human resource produced routine international strife. The industrial (most notably, in tin and copper mining) and agricultural (most notably, in coffee, fruits, grains, rubber, and cattle) productivity of the region nonetheless increased dramatically in this time, as did population (in part the result of heavy European emigration), transportation and communication services, commercial prowess, and educational promotion. Arguably the most significant political events of the period in South America were:

- the forced Argentine cession of the Malvinas Islands/Falkland Islands to Great Britain in 1833;
- the War of the Triple Alliance in 1865-70 between Paraguay and the victorious allies, Argentina, Brazil, and Uruguay;
- the War of the Pacific, or Nitrate War, in 1879-84 between victorious Chile and beaten Bolivia and Peru;
- the bloodless overthrow of the Brazilian monarchy and the establishment of a republic in 1889;
- the annexation of Easter Island by Chile in 1888;
- the acquisition by Argentina of Patagonia (now southern Argentina) in 1902; and
- the secession of Panama from Colombia in 1903.

The most significant political events of this time in central America were:

- the dissolution of the Central American Federation and the consequent autonomy of Guatemala, Honduras, El Salvador, Nicaragua, and Costa Rica in 1838-39;
- the Mexican dictatorship of General Santa Anna, the American insurrection in Texas in 1836, the American annexation of Texas in 1845, the Mexican War of 1846-48 (by which Mexico lost nearly one-half of its territory to the United States of America), and the Gadsden Purchase of 1853 (by which the United States purchased other bits of Mexico);
- the overthrow of the Santa Anna regime in Mexico in 1855 and its replacement by the reformist government of Benito Juarez (1806-72; r. 1857-65, 1867-72) in 1857; Juarez brought immense

clerical possessions into the public domain, abolished clerical and military privilege, and expelled the French intervention under Austrian Archduke Maximilian in 1867;

- the despotic Mexican government of Porfirio Diaz (1830-1915; r. 1876-1911), which was mainly influenced by foreign investments, which enriched few and impoverished many, and which provoked the revolution of 1910 led by democratic reformer, Francisco Indalecio Madero (1873-1913; r. 1911-13 [murdered]), Mexican nationalist, Francisco "Pancho" Villa (c. 1877-1923), and Indian-rights advocate, Emiliano Zapata (c. 1879-1919 [murdered]);
- the violent and corrupt Mexican autocracy of Victoriano Huerta (1854-1916; r. 1913-14), which overthrew the Madero presidency and which was itself forced from power by popular revolt;
- the independence of Panama from Colombia in 1903 and the subsequent construction of the Panama Canal by the United States of America in 1904-14;
- the American military intervention in a civil war in Nicaragua in 1912-33; and
- the failed 1916 American military invasion of Mexico in pursuit of Pancho Villa, who had raided border communities in the United States.

The defining events of nineteenth-century and early twentieth-century **Caribbean** life were the ongoing colonial presence of Great Britain, France, Netherlands, and Denmark in the region, the diminishing significance of the region as a center for the slave trade (with the abolition of the trade and of slavery itself in Europe and North America throughout the nineteenth century), and the Spanish-American War of 1898. The Cuban insurrections of 1868-78 and 1895-98, among other influences, led to the Spanish-American War (as has been said), to the appearance (but not the fact) of Cuban independence, to American military occupations of Cuba (1898-1902 and 1906-09), and to the American annexation of Puerto Rico. Before entering the First World War in 1917, the United States of America also began a nearly twenty-year (1915-34) military occupation of Haiti (ostensibly to regulate political insurrections), began a somewhat shorter (1916-24) military occupation of the Dominican Republic (ostensibly also to regulate political insurrections), and purchased the Danish West Indies/(southwestern) Virgin Islands (which thus became the United States Virgin Islands) from Denmark (in 1917).

The historical record of nineteenth-century and early twentieth-century **Africa** was dominated largely by European colonial actions on the continent, by the collision of such actions with native cultures, by conflicts among native cultures themselves, and by the continuing Arab-Islamic presence (mainly in the form of Ottoman influence) in north Africa (Morocco, Algeria, Tunisia, Libya, Egypt, and Sudan) and bits of east Africa (Tanzania, Zanzibar, and Madagascar). The African cultures of this period were mostly decentralized tribal societies or they were feudal despotisms, many of which exploited the tribes and conspired for benefit with European commercialists in the slave trade (most notably, in sub-Saharan west and central Africa). Although centralized African states (like the Fulani of inland western Africa and the Sultanate of Morocco) were not unknown, the European powers – Great Britain, France, Germany, Portugal, Spain, Netherlands, Belgium, and Italy – and the Ottoman Empire were the dominant political and economic influences in African affairs of the time. The declining slave trade was gradually replaced by colonial interest (mainly) in mineral discovery. Only two African states "escaped" colonial domination and remained, at least formally, independent, Liberia and Abyssinia/Ethiopia. Liberia, which is a qualified case, had been established in 1822 as a settlement for freed and returned American slaves and became an independent republic in 1847 as has been said.; it has since suffered periodic episodes of foreign interference, economic and political instability, official corruption, extreme poverty, civil unrest, tribal conflict, and civilian-military dispute. After several centuries of ruinous civil wars and interpositions by Egypt and Great Britain, the Coptic (a form of Christianity with an unorthodox view of the Trinity) peoples of Abyssinia/Ethiopia were unified under Emperor Menelik II (1844-1913; r. 1889-1913) in the late nineteenth century. The Italian attempt to annex the country in 1889 was defeated by the Abyssinians in 1894-96 as has been said.

Similarly, in the central and south Pacific and in Asia, the nineteenth century and the early twentieth century were dominated by colonial activity and its engagement with native cultures. No major island or island group in the **central and south Pacific** was untouched by such English, French, Spanish, German, American, Australian, or Japanese activity (as has been largely said). In **Asia**, only China (although large parts of it were occupied and other parts annexed by foreign states), Japan, and Siam/Thailand evaded full colonial domination, either by Great Britain, France, Germany, Spain, Netherlands, Portugal, Russia, or the United States of America, or by China or Japan themselves, in this period. Although Siam/Thailand had been threatened with colonization by both Great Britain and France and although it lost its claims to Cambodia and Laos (to France) in the nineteenth century, the country retained its independence as an absolute or constitutional monarchy throughout this and subsequent periods. The nation was transformed into a modern state, most significantly by (Chakri) King Chulalongkorn I/Rama V (1853-1910; r. 1868-1910) in the late nineteenth century.

As foreign trade interests increasingly took over **China** in the early nineteenth century, the government of the Manchu, or Qing, Dynasty (1644-1911) attempted to restrict such interests as has been said. When China prohibited the importation of British opium and destroyed large shipments of it, Great Britain declared war in an effort to end the restrictions. In the **Opium War** of 1839-42, Britain prevailed; by the Treaty of Nanking, which ended the War in 1842, Hong Kong was ceded to Britain and several ports were opened to British trade. A second conflict in 1856-58, the Lorcha War, opened yet other ports to France, Russia, and the United States of America. The Taiping Rebellion of 1850-64 was caused mainly by the Qing inability to deal effectively with western powers and by the Qing exploitation of the masses for the purpose of enriching the ruling elite. It was suppressed with the assistance of western armies (most notably, the British) and resulted in the further enhancement of foreign (particularly Russian and British) influence over the governmental, commercial, and educational life of the country. As the French hold over Indochina and the British hold over Burma deepened in the late nineteenth century, Chinese prerogatives in these regions also further declined. The First Sino-Japanese War of 1894-95 likewise went badly for China; the War was fought over Japanese intrusions in Korea (which was, at that time, Chinese territory) and resulted in the Japanese occupation of Korea (provisional Korean independence), the Japanese occupation of Formosa/Taiwan (which was also, at that time, Chinese territory), and the further proliferation of foreign (particularly, Japanese, German, and British) influence over internal Chinese affairs. A final nineteenth-century attempt to resist the foreign menace, the **Boxer Uprising** of 1898-1900, too failed dismally. A massacre of European Christians by anti-foreign revolutionaries (the Boxers) brought a punitive colonial expedition of British, French, German, Russian, American, and Japanese troops which brutally suppressed the insurrection, which came just short of formally partitioning the country (settling instead for an open-door, or common-market, trade policy among the occupying powers), which nonetheless tangibly occupied parts of the country, and which opened China to the importation of inexpensive western industrial goods that destroyed native crafts and trades, sharply diminished urban standards of living, and significantly increased popular sentiment against foreign influence. The Russo-Japanese War of 1904-05 was fought over rival Russian and Japanese claims in Manchuria (which, until 1900 when invaded by Russia, had been Chinese territory) and Korea (which, until 1894-95 when occupied by Japan, also had been Chinese territory). Japan unexpectedly prevailed, displaced Russia and China as the leading indigenous power in Asia, and became a significant influence in world affairs.

Finally, in 1905, Dr. Sun Yat-sen (1866-1925; r. 1911-12), a physician from Canton/Guangzhou, organized the Revolutionary Alliance that plotted to overthrow the Qing Dynasty and to establish a democratic republic with an autonomous national life and a guaranteed income for all persons. The Revolution of the Young Chinese forced the abdication of the Qing in 1911; (Outer) Mongolia and Tibet declared their independence from China in 1911 and 1912 respectively; the Alliance became the Kuomintang (the National People's Party) in 1912 and organized a republican government which soon fell under dictatorial leadership. The Party was outlawed in 1913 but continued a secret revolutionary program of domestic liberal reform and national liberation (from foreign domination) into and past the First World War and into and past the civil wars that followed.

Early nineteenth-century **Japan**, not unlike early nineteenth-century China, too opposed and excluded foreign influences. The Tokugawa Shogunate (1607-1867) was a rigidly stratified, feudal and police state that attempted to isolate the country from alien cultural, commercial, and religious persuasion as has been said. In 1853-54, however, largely by efforts of American Commodore Matthew Perry, repeated American and Russian attempts to open Japanese ports and trading inclinations for foreign commerce succeeded. The Shogunate soon collapsed under the weight of foreign influence, its own fiscal decline, and its systematic mistreatment of the lower classes. The last shogun (feudal military dictator) abdicated and the shogunate (feudal military dictatorship) itself was abolished in 1867. Emperor Meiji/Mutsuhito (1852-1912; r. 1867-1912) was installed as the head of government (the **Meiji Restoration**) in 1868; the ancient/medieval feudal order (which included the samurai class and its code of honor, the bushido, and which also included the ancestral worship characteristic of Shintoism) was gradually replaced by a centralized administration, a constitutional monarchy, and a reformed fiscal, judicial, and military bureaucracy. The development of modern Japan, in significantly Western terms, followed. This development was characterized by a sharp rise in industrial and economic expansion, in communication infrastructure, in press freedoms, in public health services, and in public education. Accompanying the new Japanese taste for Western tendencies was an imperial/colonial ambition. The **First Sino-Japanese War** of 1894-95 was fought over Japanese encroachments in (Chinese)

Korea and, by the 1895 Peace of Shimonoseki (near Hiroshima), resulted in Japanese occupation of Korea (provisional Korean independence) and of (Chinese) Formosa/Taiwan as has been said. Japanese influence in China was further advanced by Japan's successful participation in the international suppression of the Boxer Uprising in 1898-1900 and by its victory in the **Russo-Japanese War** of 1904-05. In this latter conflict, Japan defeated Russian claims in Korea (from 1897) and Manchuria (from 1900) and, by the 1905 Peace of Portsmouth (in New Hampshire, United States of America) mediated by American President Theodore Roosevelt, became the dominant political and economic influence in those regions, the dominant indigenous power in Asia, and a major participant on the world geo-political stage. The heightened sense of Japanese nationalism engendered by these several conflicts and the imperatives of capital industrialism by which the developed world "necessarily" lived brought Japan to the outright annexation of Korea in 1910 and to its participation in the First World War. Emperor Meiji died in 1912 and was succeeded by the liberal-tending administration of his son, Emperor Taisho/Yoshihito (1879-1926; r. 1912-26).

In eastern Europe and the Middle East, the politico-economic circumstance from the middle of the nineteenth century to the First World War was still more dangerously volatile than elsewhere. It was here that the decisive events leading to the First World War occurred. The unstable Russian, Ottoman, and Balkan environments, together with their connections to western European alliances, were most at issue. In **eastern Europe**, the long-standing tendencies to Russian expansionism continued in this period. The repressive regimes of Aleksander I and Nicholas I and their equivocal records in the Napoleonic Wars, the Holy Alliance, and the occupations of Finland and Poland were replaced by the regime of Aleksander II in 1855 as has been said. The Crimean War (1853-56), mainly against archrival Turkey (Ottoman Empire), was significantly occasioned by the Russian invasion of Moldavia and Wallachia in 1853 as has been also said. Although the War ended badly for **Russia** (in 1856) and diminished its European stature, the next approximate half-century was moved by notable Russian expansion in the Caucasus, Siberia, and central Asia. Under the last three Romanov tsars, Aleksander II (r. 1855-81 [assassinated]), Aleksander III (1845-94; r. 1881-94), son and successor of Aleksander II, and Nicholas II (1868-1918 [assassinated]; r. 1894-1917), son and successor of Aleksander III, Russia:

- strengthened its hold over the Caucasus (mainly over Georgia [which had been acquired in 1801], Armenia [which had been acquired in 1828], and Azerbaijan [which had been also acquired in 1828]);
- advanced its trading prerogatives in Japan and China from the 1850s;
- annexed Kazakhstan (1853-76), Kirgyzstan (1855-76), Uzbekistan (1864-76), Turkmenistan (1864-84), and Tajikistan (1868);
- extended its holdings in Siberia (most notably, the cession by China of the Amur [1858] and Coastal Provinces [1860], regions to the immediate north and east of Manchuria, a cession which very importantly included the warm-water seaport of Vladivostok);
- brutally suppressed (with Prussia) a Polish insurrection in 1863;
- sold Alaska to the United States of America in 1867;
- entered a significant alliance with Austria-Hungary and Germany, the League of the Three Emperors, in 1872;
- prosecuted yet another, in the end largely unsuccessful, war against Turkey (the Russo-Turkish War of 1877-78) that ended with the Congress of Berlin (1878), by which Russian expansion in the Balkans and the Middle East was checked (largely by British and Austrian intervention), Turkey was nonetheless diminished (largely by the independence of Serbia and Montenegro, by a larger sense of autonomy for Bulgaria, and by the loss of Bosnia and Herzegovina to Austria-Hungary), the League of the Three Emperors (1872-81) was dissolved, and the political circumstance in the Balkans was further destabilized;
- entered a significant alliance with France, the Dual Entente, in 1890 (became the Triple Entente when Great Britain joined in 1907);
- successfully participated in the international suppression of the Boxer Uprising in China in 1898-1900;
- was defeated by Japan in the Russo-Japanese War of 1904-05 over Russian claims in Korea (from 1897) and Manchuria (from 1900); and
- (with Great Britain) partitioned Persia/Iran in 1907.

The capital industrialization and the liberal reforms that had been evolving most emphatically in western Europe, North America, and Australasia throughout this period also influenced Russian political, economic, and cultural affairs. Serfdom as such was abolished in 1861; other improvements followed: academic freedom from political influence, loosening of press censorship, emancipating transformations of the judicial system and penal code, and marginal provisions for regional self-government. The burdens of the peasants nonetheless continued to increase in other terms, in terms having principally to do with taxation, and social unease therefore also continued to rise. Political uprisings, driven mainly by impoverishment and the revolutionary ferment that unrelieved impoverishment (and its accompanying injustices) invites, were near to perpetual after the Crimean War and especially intense from at least the 1870s. A mystic faith in the simple virtues of the peasantry and sympathy for the fate of poor persons, in such as the work of the unexcelled Russian novelist, Count Lev Nikolayevich Tolstoi/Leo Tolstoy (1828-1910), contributed significantly to justifying the burgeoning unrest of the time. Capital industrialization began in earnest in the 1880s (late by western European standards) with construction of the Trans-Caspian Railway (1883-86) and the Trans-Siberian Railway (1891-1904); it was accompanied by a dramatic increase in population and taxation, by a sharp rise in production for export (and the sort of elite profit and foreign control entailed by such production), by an alarming increase in public and private (mostly peasant) debt, and by a decline in the purchasing power of the poor. The formation of the Russian proletariat and its guerilla insurrections aimed at toppling tsardom (the divine right of inherited autocracy) and eradicating social injustice brought intensified repression of the reform agenda and its liberal advocates, the press, the universities, the judiciary, the ethnic and religious minorities, and the peasants. The reigns of Aleksander III and Nicholas II in particular were run through with reactionary government policy and with worker-peasant revolts. The contemporary socialist and labor movements which had been developing throughout Europe in the middle-to-late nineteenth century came to their most consequential results in the Russian circumstance of the period as has been said. Largely under the doctrinal influence of Mikhail Bakunin, Karl Marx, and Friedrich Engels (as well as their French predecessors, Saint-Simon, Fourier, and Proudhon) and mainly under the tangible leadership of Georgi Valentinovich Plekhanov and Vladimir Ilyich Ulyanov/Lenin, the revolutionary activities of late nineteenth-century and early twentieth-century Russian culture unfolded to monumental consequence. Plekhanov and Lenin established the earliest social democratic organizations in Russia and led their main factions, the Mensheviks (the minority under Plekhanov) and the Bolsheviks (the majority under Lenin). The Bolshevik view of Lenin, which opposed any collaboration with the established capital order and which favored assertive revolution, eventually prevailed. Among the most significant revolutionary figures of modern history, Lenin elaborated on the dialectical materialism of Marx and Engels, principally in terms of the basic character of imperialism (as rooted in the economic monopolies of the few and in the tendencies of these monopolies to divide the world into spheres of colonial influence, established and maintained by armed force if necessary) and in terms of practical action (to the end of achieving a proletarian revolution and a classless society in Russia, then elsewhere). He asserted these views most notably in <u>What Is to Be Done?</u> (1902), <u>One Step Forward, Two Steps Back</u> (1904), <u>Materialism and Empirio-Criticism</u> (1909), <u>Imperialism, the Highest Stage of Capitalism</u> (1916), and <u>State and Revolution</u> (1918). Lenin was imprisoned for revolutionary activity from 1895 to 1897, exiled to Siberia from 1897 to 1900, and lived variously in western Europe (principally in London, Munich, and Geneva) from 1900 to 1917 (except for a brief period of political agitation associated with the First Russian Revolution from 1905 to 1907), before returning to Russia where he led both the Second Russian Revolution and the subsequent government.

The **First Russian Revolution** for the liberation of the middle, working, and peasant classes was caused by the government's corrupt and disastrous handling of the Russo-Japanese War of 1904-05 and by its having fired on a peaceful protest of liberal demonstrators in St. Petersburg in 1905. The worker strikes, military mutinies, and political revolts (most notably in Finland, Poland, Ukraine, and the Baltic states) that followed persuaded the government to adopt a constitution (which included basic civil liberties), to establish a parliament (the Duma), and to enact agrarian reforms. These actions also brought severe counter-revolutionary measures, however, by which the constitution was ignored, the parliament was dissolved, the monarchy was preserved, the plight of the lower classes was substantially unimproved, and opponents of the government were severely persecuted. The utter devastations of the First World War and the increasingly conspicuous incompetence and vacuity of the established government led directly to the dissolution of the Romanov throne and to the Second Russian Revolution, both in 1917.

In the **Middle East**, the **Ottoman Empire** (Turkey) continued its decline throughout the nineteenth century and the early years of the twentieth. Although this decline was not precipitous and the influence of the Empire in the Middle East, north Africa, the Caucasus, and the Balkans remained highly significant, the Empire was nonetheless incrementally weakened by:

- its own supranational nature and national liberation movements against it in the Balkans (mainly in Greece, Romania, Bulgaria, Serbia, Montenegro, Bosnia, Herzegovina, and Albania) and in Arabia (mainly by indigenous, Islamic fundamentalists, the Wahabites); these movements brought independence to Greece (by the Greek War of Independence) in 1829, to Romania (by extended consequence of the Crimean War) in 1861, to Montenegro and Serbia (by the Russo-Turkish War of 1877-78) in 1878, to Bulgaria (by extended consequence of the Russo-Turkish War of 1877-78) in 1908, and to Albania (by the First Balkan War) in 1912; Bosnia and Herzegovina were brought under Austro-Hungarian suzerainty (by the Russo-Turkish War of 1877-78) in 1878; and the Wahabites (founded in the eighteenth century) of Ibn Saud (1881-1953; r. 1912-53) secured control of the northern interior regions of the Arabian peninsula by 1912;

- ongoing European colonial incursions mainly in the Caucasus and in north Africa; Russia had annexed Georgia in 1801; Great Britain had become the dominant political and economic influence in the United Arab Emirates in 1820, in Aden/southern Yemen in 1839, in Bahrain in 1861, in Egypt in 1882, in Oman in 1891, in Kuwait in 1897, and in Sudan in 1899; France had come to dominate Algeria in 1830 and Tunisia in 1881; France also had a very large influence in Syria (including Lebanon) from 1860; and Italy gained sway over Libya (by the Tripolitan War) in 1911;
- civil disturbances in Egypt led by Muhammad Ali (1769-1849: r. 1803-49), who took power on the defeat of Napoleon I in 1801 (and his withdrawal in 1803), who conclusively deposed and destroyed the Mamelukes (the warrior caste who were the dominant native political influence in Egypt from at least the thirteenth century) in 1811, who ably defended the Ottoman hegemony in Arabia, Sudan, and Greece, but who took an increasingly independent course by which he obtained Syria in 1831-33;
- the seminal development of contemporary modern Zionism and agitations for the establishment of a Jewish national state in Palestine; this movement was first directed by Theodore Herzl (1860-1904), who was convinced that European anti-Semitism (based increasingly on racial, as distinct from religious, grounds and on the politico-economic tentacles of race) required the establishment of an independent nation in which Jewish people were to possess full civil rights and governing prerogatives (in which Jewish people were not merely a tolerated or a discriminated-against faction of the population), who recorded the characteristic terms of the movement in The Jewish State (1896), and who organized the first World Zionist Congress in Basel in 1897; and
- domestic insufficiencies having mainly to do with obsolete state organization, corrupt administrative practices, and a divisive social order; the attempted reforms of Sultans Selim III (r. 1789-1807), Mahmud II (1784-1839; r. 1808-39), and Medjid (1823-61; r. 1839-61) all largely failed.

Even the measured successes of the Crimean War had a significantly unfavorable affect on the Empire for they opened it to increasing domination by western capital, to increasing debt to foreign interests, and eventually to public bankruptcy (1875). Its first constitution (1876) was routinely set aside by Abdul Hamid II (1842-1918; r. 1876-1909) who also presided over the misfortunes of the Russo-Turkish War of 1877-78 and the insurrection of Christians in Armenia (which was met with an attempt to exterminate them from c. 1894). From c. 1860, a liberal resistance movement, the Young Turk Movement, which opposed the autocracy and the heavy influence of foreigners over Turkish affairs, developed. This movement's most prominent early leaders were Enver Pasha (1881-1922), who led the Revolution of 1908 by which he became the effective head-of-government, and Mustafa Kemal/Ataturk (1881-1938). Pasha's affections for German militarism led the Empire to its final calamities, the First and Second Balkan Wars (1912-13), the Armenian massacre (1915), and the First World War (1914-18).

Colliding Russian (Slavic, Orthodox), Turkish (Altaic, Islamic), and Austrian (Germanic, Catholic) interests in the **Balkans** had been most apparent in the Greek War of Independence (1821-29), the Crimean War (1853-56), and the Russo-Turkish War of 1877-78. It was principally by means of these conflicts that several of the major national groups of the Balkans had won political independence (or its rough equivalent) by 1908 as has been said. Croatia, Slovenia, Bosnia, and Herzegovina then remained under Austro-Hungarian supervision. Albania was then soon-to-be-independent and Macedonia was then claimed by other Balkan states. In that year (1908), Austria fully annexed Bosnia and Herzegovina; King Ferdinand I (1861-1948; r. 1908-18), who was of (central) German descent, declared Bulgarian independence from Ottoman Turkey; and Enver Pasha (and the Young Turk Movement) attempted to transform the Ottoman Empire into a constitutional state. Alarmed by the Austrian expansion and in preparation for an anticipated partition of European Turkey, Serbia, Bulgaria, Greece, and Montenegro declared war on Turkey, the **First Balkan War**, in 1912. By the Peace of London (1913), which formally ended the conflict, very nearly all of European Turkey and all Aegean islands were lost to the Balkan states and Albania won its independence (declared in 1912), largely through the efforts of Essad Pasha (c. 1865-1920; r. 1914-20). The **Second Balkan War** (1913) was fought largely over contending claims of the Balkan states in respect to Macedonia. By the Peace of

Bucharest (1913), which formally ended the conflict, Serbia, Montenegro, Greece, Romania, and Turkey all won bits of the region from Bulgaria.

The contending factions in the Balkan Wars were all connected, by means of formal (and informal) alliances, with the major industrial powers of western and eastern Europe, Great Britain, France, Germany, Russia, Austria-Hungary, and Italy. All had significant interests in the Balkans and many of these interests were incompatible. The major industrial powers of Europe were also variously connected to one another, too by means of formal (and Informal) alliances, in ways that made the perpetual unrest in the Balkans the main flashpoint of the First World War and in ways that made the Balkan Wars the main prelude to this catastrophic discord. The most important of these alliances were formalized in the late nineteenth and the early twentieth centuries and divided Europe into two contending power entities: Germany, Austria-Hungary, and Italy, for one, and Great Britain, France, and Russia, for the other. The Triple Alliance was formed in 1882 and allied Germany, Austria-Hungary, and Italy (the so-termed Axis Powers). The Dual Entente allying France and Russia was formed in 1890 and was expanded under the terms of an agreement between France and Great Britain (the Entente Cordial, 1904) to form the Triple Entente (the so-termed Allied Forces) in 1907.

The period of the two World Wars and between

The struggles associated with an upended balance of European power (mainly under the influence of Italian and German national unification), the struggles associated with colliding colonial ambitions (mainly in the Balkans and in Morocco), and the struggles between autocratic and democratic forms of government (mainly in respect to the rights and prerogatives of the disparate social classes) were all long-standing by the early twentieth century. All nonetheless intensified still further and became yet more unsteady in this period. The unsettled balance of European power inclined the major alliances to offensive (as distinct from defensive) actions and encouraged Germany in particular to overestimate its authority over other nations; the competition for foreign possessions destabilized an already tenuous international environment; and the antagonisms among the main divisions in the socio-economic order made for an especially volatile political and economic milieu, most particularly in the multi-national states (Austria-Hungary, the Ottoman Empire, and Russia). The result was a still sharper rise in nationalistic sentiment and militaristic orientation, unaccompanied by a comparable sense of cautious restraint. When Austrian Archduke Franz Ferdinand and his wife, Sophie, were assassinated by Serbian nationalist, Gavrilo Princip (c. 1893-1918), in Sarajevo, Bosnia on June 28, 1914, the Great War, the War-to-end-all-wars, arguably among the most epoch-turning events in human history, the **First World War**, effectively began. The First World War was waged on an unprecedented scale, on a scale that involved not only all military personnel and some non-military persons (as had several major hostilities since the First War of the Coalition against Napoleon I, 1792-97), but on a scale involving virtually everyone. It was also waged with an unprecedented ferocity and the technological means (most notably, in respect to the modern machine-gun and poison gas) to make this ferocity destructive beyond foreseeable possibility. For the first time in human history, it was palpably clear that human ingenuity is adequate to the task of eradicating the species and that human predacity may well be up to the task of allowing, even perhaps encouraging, self-extinction. The flaws in the dominant world form of political economy, a form that requires individual persons and national groups of such persons to devour one another as a condition of their own survival, were also made abundantly conspicuous. The transformation in human perceptions of itself and of the world in which it lives was qualitative.

One month after the assassinations in Sarajevo, Austria-Hungary declared war on Serbia and virtually all major world nations mobilized. In large, the **Axis Powers** of the Triple Alliance (Germany and Austria-Hungary but not Italy) and their colonies, as well as Turkey and Bulgaria, went to war against the **Allied Powers** of the Triple Entente (Russia, France, and Great Britain/Ireland) and their colonies, as well as Serbia, Romania, Greece, Italy, Portugal, Belgium, Luxembourg, Japan, Australia, New Zealand, South Africa, Canada, and eventually the United States of America (and its colonies), China, Tibet, Mongolia, Siam/Thailand, all the nations of central America (except Mexico), Cuba, Haiti, Dominican Republic, Peru, Uruguay, Ecuador, Bolivia, and Liberia. Among European nations, only Spain (and its colonies), Netherlands (and its colonies), the Scandinavian states (Sweden, Norway, Denmark, and Iceland), Switzerland, and the Vatican (under Pope Benedict XV [1854-1922; r. 1914-22]) remained neutral. Outside of Europe, only the just-mentioned Spanish and Dutch colonies, Afghanistan, Persia/Iran, Abyssinia/Ethiopia, Mexico, Venezuela, Colombia, Chile, Argentina, and Paraguay did not participate actively in the conflict.

Although vastly outnumbered, the industrial and military efficiencies, as well as the resolve, of the Axis Powers allowed them to prevail in the early aspects of the conflict, most particularly in the east. German

General Paul von Hindenburg (1847-1934), who later (1925-34) served as his country's president, directed German successes, mainly against Russian forces in Prussia, Poland, Hungary, the Baltic states, and the Balkans from 1914 to 1917. In the west, the early going was less decisive; the French halted German advances at the First Battle of the Marne (near Reims) in 1914 and what had been a mobile conflict became dominated by the brutalities of trench warfare and by a tendency to stalemate. British naval superiority was first established at the Battle of the Falkland Islands, also in 1914. In 1915, poison gas was first used at the Battle of Ypres (Belgium), the Allies' Gallipoli campaign (at the Dardanelles Strait near Constantinople/Istanbul) against Turkey failed, and the Turks very nearly completed their several-decades-long campaign to exterminate recalcitrant, separatist Christian Armenians with the appalling massacre of approximately one million persons. In 1916, the indecisive and savage Battles of Verdun (near Reims), Battle of Jutland (Denmark), and Battle of the Somme (near Calais) were waged; the Americans unsuccessfully attempted to broker a peace agreement after the German-submarine sinking of the British ocean-liner, Lusitania (1915); David Lloyd George (1863-1945; r. 1916-22) became the inspirational and reformist Prime Minister of Great Britain (owing to public dissatisfaction over Prime Minister Asquith's conduct of the War); and Austro-Hungarian Emperor Franz Joseph I died and was succeeded by his grandnephew, the last Emperor of Austria and (as Charles IV) King of Hungary, Charles I (1887-1922; r. 1916-18). In 1917, the stalemate was broken:

- Owing to military failures, severe civilian suffering, and government ineptitude, the **Second Russian Revolution** began in March in the form of food riots, worker strikes, and military desertions in St. Petersburg/Petrograd. These incipient tumults were followed by the abdication of Tsar Nicholas II, the return of Lenin from Switzerland, the return of Joseph Vissarionovich Dzhugashvili/Stalin (1879-1953) from Siberia, the return of Lev Davidovich Bronstein/Leon Trotsky (1879-1940 [murdered]) from the United States of America, and the establishment of a Soviet Republic. The new Republic entailed nationalization of the banks and landed estates; worker domination of the factories; formation of a provisional government, eventually under Prime Minister Aleksander Fyodorovich Kerensky (1881-1970; r. 1917); failure of the provisional government to re-distribute land, to stage elections, and to end the War; and the culmination of the armed insurrection in the form of the November/Bolshevik Revolution by which Lenin became the effective head-of-state, land was re-distributed, elections of a sort were held, the World War was declared at an end, and a period (1917-20) of fierce civil wars began.
- Owing to self-interested financial concerns and the resumption of unrestricted German submarine warfare, the United States of America entered the War on the Allied side.
- Owing to public dissatisfaction with the conduct of the War, a change of government was fashioned in France under the animated leadership of Prime Minister Georges Clemenceau (1841-1929; r. 1906-09, 1917-20).

The American entry into the War was likely the deciding factor. The successful campaigns of the American Expeditionary Force, under General John Joseph Pershing (1860-1948), beginning at the Battle of Château-Thierry (near Reims) in 1917 and the successful 1918 campaigns of the Allies (mainly British, French, and American armies), under French Marshal Ferdinand Foch (1851-1929), beginning at the Second Battle of the Marne (near Reims), together with domestic upheavals (effectively socialist/communist revolutions in Russia and Germany), brought the War to a conclusive end on November 11, 1918. Its costs had been staggering: 10-11 million died, roughly twice that number had been wounded, and c. $350 billion had been consumed.

The terms of cessation were based on the peace proposal ("Proclamation of the Fourteen Points") of American President Woodrow Wilson (r. 1913-21). The "Proclamation" stipulated that all covenants were to be open (not secret) and to be openly (not secretly) decided, that the seas were to be free and neutral territory, that international trade barriers were to be eliminated, that armaments were to be limited, that colonial claims were to be adjusted, that the Axis Powers were to withdraw from Russia, that Belgium was to be restored (from German occupation during the War), that Alsace-Lorraine was to be returned to France, that the borders of Italy were to be adjusted in accord with the principle of nationality, that the national groups of the Austro-Hungarian Empire were to develop autonomous states, that the Axis Powers were to withdraw from Romania, Serbia, and Montenegro, that Turkey was to be independent, to open the Dardanelles and Bosporus Straits to foreign vessels, and to grant autonomy to the non-Turkish peoples of the Ottoman Empire, that Poland was to establish an independent state, and that a League of Nations was to be established. The terms of the peace were negotiated by several conferences and took the form of several treaties; most importantly, the Treaty of Brest-Litovsk (1918), which largely ended the War in the east, and the

Treaty of Versailles (1919), which largely ended the War in the west and the War altogether. In the Treaty of Brest-Litovsk (near Warsaw), Russia surrendered Estonia, Livonia/Courland (effectively, Latvia), Lithuania, and Poland to the Axis Powers and recognized the independence of Ukraine, Belarus, Armenia, Azerbaijan, Georgia, and Finland. The **Treaty of Versailles** (near Paris), which was mainly fashioned by American President Wilson, British Prime Minister Lloyd George, French Prime Minister Clemenceau, and Italian Prime Minister Vittorio Emanuele Orlando (1860-1952; r. 1917-19), nullified some of the provisions of the Treaty of Brest-Litovsk and was driven principally by Wilson's "Proclamation of the Fourteen Points." The most telling consequences of the various treaties (and other events) ending the War were the adjustments of numerous national borders (customarily in favor of Allied nations); the dissolution of the German monarchy, disarmament of the German military, surrender of German war criminals (including William II), payment of German war reparations, and surrender of German colonies; the dissolution of the Austro-Hungarian Empire and the Ottoman Empire as well as the monarchial systems that governed them; the establishment of several independent nations (mainly out of national groups included in the Austro-Hungarian Empire, the Ottoman Empire, and the Russian Empire); and the establishment of Allied mandates over several national groups previously included in the Ottoman Empire.

Germany, Austria, and Hungary were significantly diminished in territory and in prerogative; all became independent republics in 1918-19. Turkey was also significantly diminished in territory and prerogative; under Mustafa Kemal/Ataturk (r. 1923-38), it rebelled against the allied occupation of Istanbul and other parts of western Turkey in 1918-21, abolished the sultanate (then under Muhammad VI [1861-1926; r. 1918-22]) in 1922, became a republic (centered in Ankara) in 1923, formally disestablished Islam as the state religion in 1924, incrementally transformed the educational system of the country, and gradually Westernized. Bulgaria was likewise significantly diminished in territory and prerogative but continued its monarchial system of government (under the son and successor of Ferdinand I, Boris III [1894-1943; r. 1918-43]). Czechoslovakia became an independent republic (from the Austro-Hungarian Empire), under the accomplished philosopher, the leader of its independence movement, and its first president, Thomas Garrigue Masaryk (1850-1937; r. 1918-35), in 1918. The Kingdom of Serbs, Croats, and Slovenes (effectively, Serbia, which included Macedonia and Montenegro [both of which had been independent before the War], as well as Croatia, Slovenia, Bosnia, and Herzegovina, all of which had been part of the Austro-Hungarian Empire) became an independent nation in 1918, continued for a time as a constitutional monarchy under the Karadjordjevic Dynasty (from 1842), King Alexander I (1888-1934; r. 1918-34 [assassinated]), and became Yugoslavia in 1929. Poland, which had been thrice partitioned among Prussia, Austria, and Russia in the late eighteenth century as has been said, had not been an autonomous state for over a century; it became an independent republic in 1918 under Prime Minister Josef Pilsudski (1867-1935; r. 1918-22, 1926-35). Romania acquired Bessarabia (parts of modern Moldova and Ukraine) also in 1918 and continued its Hohenzollern monarchy under King Ferdinand (1865-1927; r. 1914-27), nephew and successor of Carol I, under Carol II (1893-1953; r. 1930-40), son of Ferdinand, and under Michael I (1921- ; r. 1927-30, 1940-47), son of Carol II. Ukraine (1918), Belarus (1918), Armenia (1918), Azerbaijan (1918), Georgia (1918), Lithuania (1918), Estonia (1920), and Latvia (1920) all won independence from Russia shortly after the War. Finland declared its independence from Russia before the end of the War (1917) and shortly thereafter (1918) fell into a civil war between the victorious, nationalist White Guard (supported by Germany and led by General Karl Gustav Emil Baron von Mannerheim [1867-1951; r. 1918-19, 1944-46]) and the vanquished, Bolshevik Red Guard (supported by Russia); a republic was established in 1919.

Great Britain further strengthened its formal hold over Cyprus in 1914 (from 1878) and over Egypt also in 1914 (from 1882); the League of Nations granted it mandates in 1920-22 over Mesopotamia/Iraq, Palestine (which included Transjordan/Jordan until 1923), and Arabia (the Kingdom of Arabia had been declared in 1916; Great Britain also became the dominant political and economic influence in Qatar in 1916), all of which had been part of the Ottoman Empire. France was granted a League of Nations mandate in 1920 over Syria (which included Lebanon until 1926); it had nonetheless controlled Syria from 1860 (despite Syria having been a formal part of the Ottoman Empire). And all German colonies were lost; Allied states either annexed them during the War or they were granted League of Nations mandates over them after the War. Nauru and northern Papua New Guinea went to Australia in 1914 and 1920 respectively. Burundi and Rwanda went to Belgium in 1919. German East Africa/Tanganyika/Tanzania went to Great Britain in 1918. Cameroon and Togoland/Togo went to Great Britain and France in 1918. The Caroline Islands/Federated States of Micronesia, Marshall Islands, Northern Mariana Islands, and Palau went to Japan in 1914. Western Samoa went to New Zealand in 1914. And German Southwest Africa/Southwest Africa/Namibia went to South Africa in 1918.

The second term of American President Woodrow Wilson was significantly affected by the enactment of prohibition (laws prohibiting the manufacture, distribution, and consumption of alcoholic beverages) in 1919-20, by the establishment of women's suffrage (the right of women to vote) in 1920, and by the economic depression of 1920-21. Wilson's second term was nonetheless largely dominated by the War, by the repressive measures taken to eliminate dissent during the War, and by the consequences of the War, tangible and hoped-for. Wilson's "Proclamation of the Fourteen Points" and his influence over the Versailles Peace Conference and the consequent Treaty of Versailles were the leading factors in determining the immediate post-War, international political environment and won for him the 1919 Nobel Peace Prize. Among Wilson's most cherished proposals, the **League of Nations**, was formally established in 1919 and began its work in Geneva, Switzerland in 1920; it had Great Britain, France, Russia, Italy, Japan, and Germany as its principal members; it participated significantly in executing the terms of the peace accords; it enforced its policies by the collective exercise of arbitration, economic sanction, and military force; and it created a permanent international court and a permanent international chamber of labor as affiliated institutions. The United States of America itself, however, never joined; the League was also weakened by numerous defections; it was unable to deal effectively with several major international military crises involving powerful nations; and it failed in its disarmament aims. It largely collapsed under the weight of uncompromising advantage-taking among leading nations in the late 1930s and dissolved itself in 1946. There was nonetheless in the period immediately following the War an especially large interest in actively encouraging international peace and in actively discouraging military conflict. Some of this interest was continuing; many national and international peace societies had been fashioned in the nineteenth century (perhaps most notably the International League for Permanent Peace, 1867) and several international peace conferences had also been staged before the First World War. The Nobel Peace Prize (as well as Nobel Prizes in physics, chemistry, medicine, and literature) had been established in 1901 by the estate of Swedish chemist, inventor (of dynamite), and pacifist, Alfred Bernhard Nobel (1833-96), to encourage the promotion of international peace (and scholarship). The labor and socialist movements were typically very favorably inclined to the notion of international peace. In 1928, an international agreement, the Briand-Kellogg Pact, banned war as a means to settle disputes between/among nations. Although all of these efforts failed to prevent even another world war, they nonetheless made important contributions to the ongoing struggle against international militarism.

The **period between the two World Wars**, 1918-39, was characterized by:

- economic recovery from the War, driven significantly by a prodigious expansion of commercial activity, the development of new technologies, and the inventive spirit of discovery;
- the accelerated domination of large corporate business enterprises and their eventual collapse;
- the continuing retreat of aristocratic monarchism and the further rise of constitutional democracy, communism, and fascism;
- an attempted restoration of the international balance-of-power through disputations over unbalanced peace treaties and through realignment of international alliances;
- the continuing tendency to national independence by colonized societies and the transformation of imperial styles by colonizing societies; and
- the qualitative enhancement of political, economic, and educational opportunities for women.

The **transition to a peace economy** after the First World War was slowed by several factors inherent in the war economy itself: the curtailment of foreign investments and international trade; an increased tendency to protect national economies by means of import tariffs; an increased tendency to national economic self-sufficiency in order to assure adequate supply; expansion of the armament industry; restrictions on the production of consumer goods; the rationing of basic and consumer goods; the decline of gold reserves; the instabilities of currency inflation and collapse caused by paper financing of the War; the instabilities and value disruptions of property destruction and confiscation; and the depressive effects of war debts and reparations. The United States of America benefited most from the political and economic transformations of the War; it also recovered more rapidly than any other nation from the devastations of the War. Its productive capacity increased dramatically; it was transformed from a debtor to a creditor nation; it increased its gold reserves; it brought women more fully into the wage-earning economy; and it (not a European state) became the foremost military and economic power in the world by the conclusion of the War. The somewhat progressive presidency of Woodrow Wilson gave way, in the 1920s, to an era (not entirely unlike the final quarter of the nineteenth century) in which so-termed "big business" utterly dominated the political and economic landscape. The presidential terms of Warren Gamaliel Harding (1865-1923; r. 1921-23), Calvin Coolidge

(1872-1933; r. 1923-29), and Herbert Clark Hoover (1874-1964; r. 1929-33) turned against the reformist policies of Wilson; fashioned a reactionary reply to the communist threat (the so-termed "red scare") which was marked by strikes, violence, suspensions of civil rights, and executions; pursued a policy of foreign isolation that included high protective tariffs, immigration restrictions, the recall of European war debts (selectively postponed and excused), and racial intolerance; and presided over:

- fraudulent government-business relationships and a declining role of government in the regulation of business practices; Liberia, for prominent instance, was virtually taken over in 1925-31 (with the tacit approval of the American government) by the Firestone Rubber Plantation Company, which enslaved vast numbers of native people, obliged forced labor contracts on others, systematically and perpetually indebted the nation to it, and very nearly bankrupted the country;
- the enforcement of prohibition and the corruption and crime associated with prohibition (1919-33);
- neglect of the agricultural sector which resulted in overproduction, oversupply, soil erosion, declining farm prices, and extreme debt and poverty among farmers;
- the establishment of a price system based on the mass consumption (not on the inherent value) of goods;
- the rapid rise of stock prices and stock markets; and
- an enormous expansion in industrial technology and production (mainly by large corporations such as automobile, chemical, and machine manufacturers) and in industrial prosperity (including gains of the industrial working class).

Much of the commercial prosperity which marked the first approximate decade after the War (and also greatly affected the 1930s and 1940s) was the result of **imaginative technologies and discoveries**, many of which were themselves the consequence of collective efforts and corporate projects. The most significant technological inventions of the inter-War period were the development of new bio-medical procedures and substances; of synthetic fibers (1925), (vastly improved) synthetic rubber (1936), and synthetic insecticides (1939); and of transformative advances in transportation (the helicopter in 1922, the rocket in 1926, and the jet engine in 1929-30) and communication (the radio in 1915, audio motion pictures in 1919, the wireless telephone in 1927, television in 1923-32, and microwave transmission in 1935). The most important of the new bio-medical procedures and substances were:

- the widespread diagnostic use of x-rays (discovered in 1895);
- the discovery of blood groups and blood typing, mainly by Austrian-American physiologist and 1930 Nobel laureate in medicine, Karl Landsteiner (1868-1943), from 1909 to 1940;
- the isolation and use of insulin in the treatment of diabetes by Canadian physiologist, Charles Herbert Best (1899-1978), Canadian physician and 1923 Nobel co-laureate in medicine, Frederick Grant Banting (1891-1941), and Scottish physiologist and 1923 Nobel co-laureate in medicine, John James Rickard MacLeod (1876-1935), in 1921;
- the development of antibiotics for the treatment of bacterial infections (such as plague, syphilis, tetanus, and typhoid fever) in humans; most notably, the discovery of penicillin by Scottish bacteriologist and 1945 Nobel co-laureate in medicine, Alexander Fleming (1881-1955), in 1928, of sulfonamides by German pathologist and 1939 Nobel laureate in medicine, Gerhard Domagk (1895-1964), in 1932, and of streptomycin in 1944;
- the development of yellow fever immunization in 1930 and the subsequent development of highly effective vaccines for diphtheria, hepatitis, measles, and typhoid fever; and
- the development of synthetic vitamins in 1934.

The principal celestial discovery of the period was of the ninth (and farthest) planet from the Sun, Pluto, in 1930. The principal terrestrial discoveries of the time were largely elaborations on earlier achievements in the Arctic (including Greenland) and Antarctic. American explorer, Richard Evelyn Byrd (1888-1957), was the first to fly over the North Pole in 1926 and the first to fly over the South Pole in 1929. The Arctic was divided into American, Canadian, Danish, Norwegian, and Russian spheres of interest; the Antarctic, into American, Argentine, Australian, Chilean, French, Norwegian, and New Zealand spheres of influence. The most notable other major adventuring achievements of this time were: the first solo. non-stop transatlantic flight (1927) by American aviator, Charles Augustus Lindbergh (1902-74); the first solo, non-stop transatlantic flight (1932) by a woman of American aviatrix, Amelia Earhart (1897-1937), who died in an attempt to fly around the world in 1937; and the first around-the-world flight of any kind (1929) by the German dirigible, Graf Zeppelin.

An overextension of credit markets, a largely unrestrained speculation in stock prices, and overproduction were the main causes of the collapse (the wholesale selling of stocks) of the New York Stock Market on

October 24, 1929. Industrial production, prices, and trade declined sharply, unemployment rose sharply, large numbers of businesses fell into bankruptcy, banks failed, liquid capital contracted, sparse government attempts to reverse these tendencies failed, and one of the great calamities of human history, the **Great Depression** of the 1930s, followed. The consequences of the American turmoil soon adversely affected all other industrial economies throughout the world. The industrial prosperity of the 1920s had ended very badly; the American government in particular was convinced that wide government intervention would not repair the devastation and that the inherent laws of capital industrialism would themselves operate in the direction of recovery if left to their own devices. They did not so operate and governments eventually intervened by creating public works, by engaging in public partnerships with business enterprises (such as subsidizing the purchase of raw materials), by socializing business enterprises, by invoking production, price, and wage controls, and/or by eliminating the gold standard. The theoretical basis of these policies was advanced by the most influential economist of the twentieth century, the Englishman, John Maynard Keynes (1883-1946). Principally in his widely celebrated, The General Theory of Employment, Interest and Money (1936), Keynes departed from the classical notions of laissez-faire economics and advocated active government intervention in private markets. This intervention was aimed at stimulating business activities, at reducing unemployment, at increasing national income, and at increasing the purchasing power of all people, even if necessary by deficit-spending of the government.

The American case was again the fulcrum of the other cases, of the other national economies. In the **United States of America**, the presidency of Franklin Delano Roosevelt (1882-1945; r, 1933-45), which began at the height of the crisis in 1933, was left to deal with the ruin. Roosevelt, who was a cousin of Theodore Roosevelt (the nation's 26th president), declared a national emergency and quickly introduced extensive fiscal and social reforms aimed at reviving the economy through an immense expenditure of public funds. These reforms were collectively referred to as the New Deal and they entailed a reorganization of agriculture and industrial production, of banking and investment activities, and of currency policy, all under government supervision/regulation. They also entailed public works projects (mainly construction projects such as public buildings, public bridges, and public power and water management facilities), public regulation of the relation between employers and employees (National Labor Relations Act, 1935, which established the right of workers to strike and to bargain collectively), and public insurance for unemployment, retirement, and disability (Social Security Act, 1935). Although very late to such reforms – Great Britain, France, and Germany, for prominent instance, had enacted similar worker and social provisions in the nineteenth century as has been said – the United States, when threatened with the expiration of its capital edifice, eventually came to them. Roosevelt, together with his brilliant, reformist wife, Eleanor Roosevelt (1884-1962), a niece of Theodore Roosevelt, argued both for the freedoms of commission (of speech and worship) and for the freedoms of omission (from want and fear), the doctrine of the four freedoms. The reforms of the Roosevelt administration were also greatly aided by the repeal of prohibition in 1933 and by the eradication of the corruption and crime associated with the phenomenon.

Roosevelt's foreign policy was also enormously influential and marked a significant departure from that of his presidential predecessors (with the feasible and qualified exception of Wilson). It aimed at international cooperation, neither overt exploitation nor implicit isolation. He resumed diplomatic relations with the Soviet Union in 1933, ended the American military occupations of Nicaragua in 1933 and of Haiti in 1934, instituted the "good neighbor policy" in Latin America in 1934, and prohibited the sale of armaments to belligerent states (Neutrality Act) in 1935. As the Second World War loomed in Europe and Asia and as the infeasibility of neutrality became increasingly evident, however, the United States began rearmament (1938), reenacted military conscription (1940), and instituted the Lend-Lease Act (1941) by which war materials were supplied to any country vital to American interests.

Post-war European economies were more adversely affected by the War than was the American economy. They also recovered less rapidly owing to the tangibly greater destruction of life, property, and emotional stability they suffered, to burdensome war reparations, and to the dislocations of new political imperatives (new countries and new political systems in transformed countries). The European (and other industrial) economies were too very deeply affected by the American strife of 1929; they were overextended and overdependent and were thus devastated by the contraction of American capital and by the American recall of European debt (even though some of this was selectively postponed). The leading nations of Europe responded to the crisis in the same approximate ways as the United States; that is, by immense expenditures of public funds.

The War had as well significantly diminished the status of Europe in the world (most especially in respect to the United States of America) and it significantly revised European political realities themselves. The aristocratic monarchies of (Romanov) Russia, (Hapsburg) Austria-Hungary, (Hohenzollern) Germany, and (Ottoman) Turkey had been dissolved. The **struggle between constitutional democracy and totalitarianism** nonetheless continued in somewhat revised forms. The practice of constitutional democracy gained ground in the first approximately half-dozen years after the War but then gave way, on balance, to a new form of totalitarianism, to one-party military dictatorships, in which powerful, often minority, factions imposed their will by force (or by threat of force) on the entire life of a society. Crises in the new democracies -- inexperience with the notion of political equality for all persons, power struggles among domestic political factions, disputes over the inequities of the peace treaties in respect to national borders, disarmament, reparations, and trials, the intensification of nationalism and its propaganda machinery (i.e., its tendency to control the patterns of public information, to manipulate elections, to suppress the opposition, and to disrespect individual rights), and economic depression -- brought a renewed trust in the necessities and the virtues of armed force, either by the few against the many or by majority populations against minorities. Between 1922 and 1936, the triumph of nationalist sovereignty over collective sentiment, the failure to achieve general disarmament, and the vain efforts of the League of Nations variously delivered single-party governments to Hungary, Italy, Bulgaria, Spain, Turkey, Albania, Poland, Portugal, Lithuania, Yugoslavia, Romania, Germany, Austria, Estonia, Latvia, and Greece. Of these, the ultranationalist, virulently anti-communist, fascist regimes of Benito Mussolini in Italy (1922), Adolf Hitler in Germany (1933), and Francisco Franco in Spain (1936) were the most influential. By 1938, then, the only remaining constitutional democracies in Europe were Great Britain, Ireland, France, Netherlands, Belgium, Luxembourg, Switzerland, Sweden, Norway, Denmark/Iceland, Finland, and Czechoslovakia. Russia/Soviet Union became a one-party communist state in 1920. The same approximate forces that pushed European nations in extreme nationalist directions likewise encouraged Japan and China to similar ends. The fascist government of Emperor Hirohito in Japan (1926) and the independent Chinese government of Chiang Kai-shek (1926) had the largest affect on world affairs between the two World Wars among non-European nations (except, of course, the government of the United States of America). The expansionist inclinations of Germany, Italy, and Japan, when put with their belligerent, fascist form of nationalism, were significantly implicated in the causes of the Second World War.

The Second Russian Revolution and the Treaty of Brest-Litovsk had effectively ended Russian participation in the First World War in 1917-18 as has been said. These events also launched a period (1917-20) of fierce civil wars that:

- closed with the formation of the first modern communist state, the first modern state to advocate the abolition of private property and the development of a classless society;
- put the Bolshevik (the "Red") faction against the several Menshevik (the "White") factions;
- established a provisional Bolshevik government and constitution under Lenin in 1918;
- included a sporadic, armed intervention by western European and American forces in support of the "Whites" (1918-19);
- included the assassination by Bolsheviks of the last tsar of Russia, the last of the Romanov rulers of Russia, Nicholas II, and his family in 1918;
- entailed the establishment of the Third International in Moscow in 1919 (-43), by which the strictly disciplined and centrally controlled Communist Party of Russia/Soviet Union became an organization of professional revolutionaries, the governing organ of the country, the leading organ of world communism, the leading organ of attempts at world communist revolution, and the leading organ of attempts to secure the international solidarity of trade unions; and
- included the Russo-Polish War (1920) over border disputes between the two states.

The Bolsheviks prevailed in these conflicts significantly because they developed an efficient military organization (the Red Army), because the Mensheviks lacked cohesion and a clear alternative to the reactionary views that were a central cause of the conflicts, and because the Allied effort against the Bolsheviks was uneven and ineffective. The very early development of the new country (1920-22) was nonetheless exceedingly troubled; western powers continued attempts to destabilize it, Lenin's nationalized economy effectively collapsed, and strikes/mutinies threatened public order. A partial return to state capitalism, which included foreign investment and international trade agreements, international recognition of the new government, and the prohibition of all opposition groups (thus transforming the country into a one-party state), eventually steadied the way, however. The Union of Soviet Socialist Republics (U.S.S.R.), the **Soviet Union**, was formally established in 1922 and revised its constitution (mainly in terms of defining the powers of the central government and those of the member republics) in 1923. Armenia, Azerbaijan, Belarus, and Kazakhstan joined Russia in the new Union (or what was soon to become the new Union) in 1920;

Georgia, in 1921; Ukraine, in 1922; Kirgyzstan, Turkmenistan, and Uzbekistan, in 1924; Tajikistan, in 1929; and Latvia, Lithuania, and Estonia, in 1940.

Lenin died in 1924 and the fateful struggle for succession was won by Joseph Stalin (r. 1924-53) over Leon Trotsky. Stalin's main contributions to Marxist-Leninist ideology were his views that socialism may be successfully developed in one country (it does not require a wider acceptance, howsoever desirable a wider acceptance may be) and his view that socialist revolution may be initiated by party leadership, by the state (it is not necessarily initiated from below by the peasant and working classes). The dictatorship of Stalin was especially brutal; his univocal domination of the government was achieved by eliminating all opposition through repression, terror, imprisonment, banishment, and/or execution. The most celebrated such cases were those of Trotsky (who was removed from office, then expelled from the Party, banished, and murdered) and the Great Purges (which reached their height between 1934 and 1942 and which entailed the mass arrest and execution of millions). Stalin also presided over the development of universal education, the rigorous and largely successful collectivization of Soviet agriculture, and the transformation of the Soviet Union into a modern industrial state. He instituted five-year economic plans to this end in 1928-29 and revised the constitution to secure unchallengeable control (through the Party) over all aspects of domestic and foreign affairs in 1936. Not only did the state not wither away in Stalin's nationalistic autocracy (as Marx had supposed it would in democratic socialism) and not only were the workers not liberated (as Marx had also taught), the communist state was omnipotent and workers were uniformly exploited, were otherwise mistreated, and had virtually every feature of their lives (including their political, educational, and aesthetic perceptions) ruled by the Party. In foreign policy, Stalin formed alliances with other eastern European states as a buffer against western Europe (mainly against Germany) and also attempted to negotiate alliances with Great Britain and France (too aimed principally at protection from German expansion).

China also developed in ultra-nationalist directions and passed through a period of intense civil wars in the period between the two World Wars. Disappointed that its successful participation in the First World War did not bring a substantial reduction in western and Japanese influence over its internal affairs and impressed with the achievements of the Second Russian Revolution against foreign interference and wealthy elites, the Kuomintang (National People's Party, formed in 1912), under Sun Yat-sen and Chiang Kai-shek (1887-1975; r. 1928-49) and governed by the "Three People's Principles" of nationalism (unity of the people), democracy (rights of the people), and socialism (livelihood of the people), and the Communist Party of China (formed in 1921), eventually under Mao Tse-tung and governed by Marxist-Leninist principles, cooperated to oust (in 1926) the warlords who had been prosecuting civil wars among themselves and between themselves and the Kuomintang since 1916. In 1927, however, Chiang Kai-shek turned against his communist allies and thus began another wave of civil wars (1927-36, 1945-49) that did not end until 1949. In the first phase of these wars, Chiang suppressed peasant rebellions and attempted to liquidate the communists by execution (most notably, the Shanghai massacres of 1927) and forced relocation (most notably, the Long March from southeastern China to the north-central interior of 1934-35). The communists organized the Red Army in 1928, established military bases in the southeast of the country, and redistributed land to peasants in the areas they controlled. In 1928, Chiang completed the effective unification of China as a one-party military dictatorship and solidified the national government that had been established in Nanking in 1927. Although Chiang made no land reform and generally sided with banks and wealthy merchants against the poor, the Kuomintang (largely under him) ruled China without disabling equivocation from 1927 to 1936. When the Second Sino-Japanese War, effectively the Second World War in China, began in 1937, the nationalists and communists formed an uneasy armistice between themselves and an uneasy alliance against the Japanese invaders.

Inter-war developments in Germany, Italy, Spain, and Japan were also exceedingly turbulent; they were likewise driven by acute nationalism; and they too had a colossal affect on the subsequent course of world history. Germany struggled throughout this period to redress the great disadvantages it suffered in the treaties ending the First World War, the disadvantages it suffered principally in respect to territorial contraction, war reparations, disarmament demands, and foreign military occupation. It had agreed to the terms of these treaties only under threat of renewed Allied invasion and it made several attempts to revise the Treaty of Versailles throughout the inter-war period. The collapse of the Second Reich (1871-1918) under William II at the conclusion of the War resulted in a long struggle for political power among leftist, rightist, and centrist factions. The centrists prevailed in the formation of a new constitution at Weimar (near Leipzig) in 1919. The so-termed Weimar Republic (1919-33), a parliamentary democracy, that followed was, however, routinely and seriously challenged by leftist and rightist opponents of it, most particularly in the period from 1919 to 1923 and again from 1930 to 1933. The government drifted significantly to the right under the leadership of General/President Paul von Hindenburg (r. 1925-34) and under the influence of the domestic turmoil, the threats of foreign invasion, and the deteriorating economic circumstance of the mid-to-late 1920s and the early 1930s. It was also in this time and context that the fascist movement gained a firm ground in German political life. This movement became the rightist alternative to monarchism; it thus opposed both parliamentary democracy and communism. Fascism developed as a distinctive political ideology after 1918 and it entailed a virulent nationalism that is defined in radical terms and that prosecutes or excludes non-native races (which are perceived as threats to the native race). Although it authenticates a rigidly hierarchical system of social classes, greatly favors large financial interests, and assures social order to such interests, it nonetheless also assures social justice to workers of native race and sharply regulates all economic and political activity in the interests of the national community. It prosecutes its domestic agenda by terrorist, secretive, paramilitary methods, by mass propaganda, and by collusion with professional lawyers, physicians, teachers, and bureaucrats; its foreign policy tends to expansionist and aggressive military action. Leadership of German fascism fell early on to Adolf Hitler (1889-1945; r. 1933-45 [suicide]), who had been born in Austria, who had moved from Vienna to Munich in 1913, and who had been injured by poison gas and gunfire in the First World War. Hitler had become the charismatic and authoritarian chairman of the fascist party in Germany, the National Socialist German Workers' Party (formed in 1919) in 1921, fashioned an insurrection in 1923 (for which he was imprisoned from 1923 to 1924), wrote the defining text of the movement, <u>Mein Kampf</u>, in 1923-27, and led the transformation of the country to a one-party military dictatorship, the **Third Reich** (1933-45), in 1933.

The deteriorating and chaotic economic circumstance of the country (declining wages, prices, and spending and rising taxes and unemployment), the increasingly anti-parliamentary attitudes of the country, the unsuspecting attitude of the established government in respect to Hitler's ultimate intentions, and Hitler's own very considerable political erudition conspired to bring him virtually unchecked power by 1933. Germany was approaching civil war when Hitler became head-of-state (Der Fuhrer), invoked emergency powers of the constitution, suspended basic constitutional rights, established a central police apparatus and an extensive system of concentration (prison, forced-labor, and extermination) camps (Dachau [near Munich] was the first, 1933), folded legislative, judicial, and military power into the prerogatives of the party executive, effectively abolished the federal system by centralizing all authority in Berlin, dismissed "undesirables" (principally Jews, Slavic minorities, communists, dissidents, homosexuals, and the disabled) from the government and the professions, imprisoned or liquidated political enemies, and outlawed opposition political parties and trade unions, all in 1933-34. The practice of denying selected populations (mainly Jews and Slavic minorities) legal equality began with the Nuremburg Laws in 1935; the practice of organized pogroms, of extralegal arrests and summary executions, and of isolating ethnic minorities (mainly Jews) in impoverished ghettos began in 1938. Hitler attempted to achieve economic self-sufficiency and to reverse the economic decline by instituting land reform for peasants and state supports for agriculture, extensive public works projects (such as construction of the federal highway system), a national workers' service, and general military conscription; all organizations and individuals (including educational and cultural agencies) were brought under public control by 1936. These measures were, on balance, impressively successful; unemployment declined precipitously, the middle class recovered, and productivity soared. The cost to many ethnic non-Germans and to those who would not or could not cooperate in state production and propaganda, however, was staggering.

The foreign policy of the Third Reich was aimed primarily at escaping the bondage of the Treaty of Versailles, at obtaining additional "living space" for the German people, at uniting the German ethnic lands, and at preserving international peace through bilateral agreements (not by collective security). Germany explicitly violated the Treaty of Versailles by its program of rearmament in 1935 and by its unchallenged military occupation of the demilitarized zone (a part of the Rhineland near the German borders with Netherlands, Belgium, Luxembourg, and France) in 1936. The most significant of the bilateral agreements were with the Vatican, Poland, Great Britain, France, Austria, Japan, Italy, Spain, and the Soviet Union and they were, from the German perspective, mainly to assure non-aggression against (in some cases, cooperation with) Germany as a basis for its own expansionist intentions. The assistance it provided to the fascists in the Spanish Civil War (1936-39), the agreement with Austria, and the Munich Pact were likely the most fateful of these. Germany proclaimed its reunification (the Anschluss) with Austria and occupied the country over League of Nations objections in 1938. Between Germany, Italy, Great Britain, and France, the agreements of Munich, also in 1938, ceded German ethnic territories in Czechoslovakia (the Sudetenland) to Germany, enacted Anglo-German and Franco-German accords of non-aggression, settled remaining Franco-German border disputes, and gave assurances that Germany would make no further territorial demands.

The German invasions of Czechoslovakia and Poland in 1939 straightforwardly violated these (and other) agreements; they were also the opening, formal gambits of the Second World War in Europe.

Although **Italy** had received the long-disputed Tirol and Istria (in the northeast) from Austria as a condition of the peace accords, it too (like Germany) had been disappointed with the Treaty of Versailles (mainly in respect to costly, ongoing military obligations and in respect to ethnic Italian regions on the northern Adriatic coast having been ceded to the Kingdom of the Serbs, Croats, and Slovenes). After brief quasi-democratic flirtations, it too (like Germany) turned to fascism for restoration of its national identity and stature, for a revival of the disciplined and totalitarian traditions of ancient Rome. Among the most influential early leaders of the fascist movement in Italy was the accomplished soldier and poet, Gabriele D'Annunzio (1863-1938). The Partito Nazionale Fascista was formed in 1921, largely by Benito Mussolini (1883-1945; r. 1922-45 [executed]), who (like Hitler) served and was wounded in the First World War, who (also like Hitler) became a virulent nationalist and a fervent advocate of one-party military dictatorship as a result, and who (too like Hitler) came to oppose monarchism, liberalism, and populism in almost any form by almost any means. Mussolini's 1922 "March on Rome" persuaded King Victor Emmanuel III (r. 1900-46) to turn the government largely over to him. By 1926, virtually all parliamentary restrictions on (and political opposition to) Mussolini had been eliminated, a party militia had been established to enforce domestic compliance, and the full support of the monarchical, corporate, military, and religious sectors of Italian society had been secured. Although Mussolini (Il Duce) embraced the standard fascist agenda, he did not prosecute this agenda with the unrestrained form of domestic terrorism that became characteristic of the German case; political opponents (mainly socialists and communists), but not typically others, were nonetheless harshly treated. Not unlike German fascism, let alone the foremost liberal and conservative states of Europe, North America, and Asia, however, Mussolini continued to pursue the imperialist ambitions of his Italian predecessors. To this end, he framed a mutual-assistance agreement with Germany and Japan in 1936, sided with the fascists in the Spanish Civil War (1936-39), and strove for Italian hegemony in the Mediterranean and in parts of east Africa. In 1935, Italy again invaded Abyssinia/Ethiopia (the Italo-Ethiopian War), then under Emperor Haile Selassie/Negus Tafari Mekonnen (1891-1975; r. 1930-36, 1941-74), grandnephew of Emperor Menelik II; it annexed the country over League of Nations objections in 1936 (-41). In 1939 (-44), it occupied Albania, then under President/King Ahmedi Zogu/King Zog (1895-1961; r. 1925-39).

Spain, unlike Germany and Italy, had been neutral in the First World War as has been said. Its economy thus suffered less than the economies of Germany and Italy in this time. Tensions between the conservative upper class and radicalized workers nonetheless increased and Spanish governments in the inter-war period vacillated between liberal-progressive democracies and military dictatorships. The Bourbon monarchy, under Alfonso XIII (r. 1886-1931), was replaced in 1931 by the Second Republic. Catalonia (in the northeast) and the Basque provinces (in the north-central region) were granted autonomy in 1931 and 1936 respectively. When a coalition of liberals (republicans, socialists, and communists), supported by such as the remarkable Spanish philosopher, Jose Ortega y Gasset (1883-1955), was elected to lead the government in 1936, counterrevolutionaries (monarchists, fascists, and Catholics), principally under General Francisco Franco (1892-1975; r. 1939-75), initiated the **Spanish Civil War** (1936-39). The nationalists of Franco were assisted by Germany and Italy; the republicans (or loyalists) were aided by the Soviet Union and brigades of international volunteers. Franco (Il Caudillo) and his Fascist Falange Party (formed in 1933) prevailed in 1939 (thus putting an end to the Second Republic), established a corporate state of standard fascist type, dealt ruthlessly with the political opposition, and remained largely neutral in the Second World War.

Under Emperor Taisho (r. 1912-26), **Japan** became a major commercial and military power. Its successful participation in the First World War had brought it enhanced international stature and possession of German colonies in the central Pacific (the Caroline Islands/Federated States of Micronesia, Marshall Islands, Northern Mariana Islands, and Palau). As economic and political stability declined (owing largely to trade deficits and the devastating Tokyo earthquake of 1923) and as relations with the Soviet Union and the United States of America grew less stable (owing largely to territorial and immigration disputes), however, conservative-liberal conflicts intensified. When the progressive-tending Taisho died in 1926, he was succeeded by his son, Emperor Hirohito/Showa (1901-89; r. 1926-89), and the drift to a regressive one-party state began in earnest. This drift entailed a deepening sense of strident nationalism based significantly on a renewal of Shinto traditions (and their divinist view of ancestors in general and of the Emperor in particular), economic depression, wide corruption, political assassinations, a sharp rise in population, and attempts to establish large spheres of economic domination. This latter was driven principally by the basic nature of the world economy (which requires raw materials, foreign markets, and trade surpluses), by high foreign tariffs and import restrictions on Japanese goods, and by the country's own fascist sense of militaristic superiority.

225

Japan's attempted domination of Asia (which began in 1927) resulted; in 1931, over League of Nations objection, it again invaded Manchuria, separating the province from China in 1932, establishing a Japanese state (Manchukuo) in the region (northeastern China) also in 1932, fighting over Shanghai in 1932 as well, joining Germany and Italy in an anti-communist, pro-fascist pact in 1936, and preparing the way for the **Second Sino-Japanese War** (1937-45), the opening salvo of the Second World War in Asia.

The leading constitutional democracies of western Europe – Great Britain and France – passed through much less profound and turbulent transformations in the inter-war period than the Soviet Union, China, Germany, Italy, Spain, or Japan. The liberal-conservative debates that had been a central feature of political life throughout the nineteenth and twentieth centuries nonetheless continued in these (not unlike most) countries. In **Great Britain**, the government was variously led by liberal/labor Prime Ministers David Lloyd George (r. 1916-22) and (James) Ramsay MacDonald (r. 1924, 1929-35) and by conservative Prime Ministers Stanley Baldwin (1867-1947; r. 1923-24, 1924-29, 1935-37) and (Arthur) Neville Chamberlain (1869-1940; r. 1937-40). All dealt with labor unrest, unemployment, economic recovery (from the War and the Depression), as well as conflicts with the Soviet Union, France, Germany, and Italy in particular. Lloyd George presided over the extension of suffrage to women (1918) and was an important moderating influence on the Treaty of Versailles (1919). MacDonald formally recognized the Soviet Union amid ideological disputes concerning loyalty issues and the relative merits of capitalism and communism. Baldwin negotiated a settlement with France over Middle Eastern oil (in 1926) that resulted in the eventual independence of Iraq from Great Britain in 1930-32. And Baldwin and Chamberlain both attempted to evade war with Germany and Italy by way of negotiated appeasements; most notably, by way of Chamberlain's Munich Pact of 1938. The British crown became an increasingly titular/ceremonial distinction in this period, which was reigned over by George V (r. 1910-36) and two of his four sons, Edward VIII (1894-1972; r. 1936 [abdicated]) and George VI (1895-1952; r. 1936-52).

The **British Empire/British Commonwealth of Nations** passed through two major revisions in the inter-war period: the independence of Ireland from Great Britain and the alteration of commonwealth status itself for Ireland, Canada, Australia, New Zealand, and South Africa. The approximate century-long struggle for Irish independence reached its "final" stage with the Easter Rebellion of 1916, the assumption of nationalist leadership by Sinn Fein (which suffered numerous executions by the British for its role in the Rebellion), the proclamation of Irish independence by Sinn Fein in 1918, the nationalist guerilla war against the British (1919-21), and the 1920 partition of **Ireland** into the predominantly Catholic south (Irish Free State/Eire/Republic of Ireland) and the predominantly Protestant northeast (Ulster, or Northern Ireland). Northern Ireland remained a part of the United Kingdom and the Irish Free State/Ireland gained dominion status in the British Empire/Commonwealth in 1922. The Irish Republican Army, which became the military component of Sinn Fein in 1916, nonetheless continued its opposition to British rule in Northern Ireland and continued its advocacy of Irish national unification. The other dominions of the British Empire/Commonwealth, Canada, Australia, New Zealand, and South Africa, all of which had sided with Great Britain in the First World War, also passed through the customary liberal-conservative debates and the customary periods of economic prosperity and depression characteristic of the inter-war period. They became as well more fully autonomous states within the Empire/Commonwealth by means of the Statute of Westminster (1931), according to which they were united only by their common allegiance to the British crown and by loose agreements to political and economic cooperation among them. These dominions (except Canada) themselves gained control of foreign territories in Africa and the Pacific either shortly before, during, or immediately following the First World War as has been said. The British colonial empire otherwise consisted in subordinate crown colonies in Africa, Asia, the Pacific, central America, South America, and the Caribbean. These colonies were administered in the customary colonial way: native political participation was limited to marginal roles; native peoples were assimilated to European orientations by active means and by suppression of native traditions; the political, economic, and educational infrastructure of colonial societies was further developed; and the lives of settlers in particular were improved. Great Britain also took possession of several former German colonies in 1918 as has been too said: German East Africa/Tanganyika/Tanzania, Cameroon (with France), and Togoland/Togo (with France). Great Britain, together with its dominions and colonies, had draped itself over approximately one-fourth of the world's population by the end of the First World War.

Ireland was not the only British possession clamoring for and achieving independence in this time. European notions of the nation-state and its self-determining nature also strengthened movements for national independence in Asia and the Middle East. Afghanistan, under Emir Amanullah (1892-1960; r. 1919-29), achieved independence in 1921 by way of the Third Afghan War/Afghan War of Independence of 1919. In Persia/Iran, Reza Shah Pahlevi (1878-1944; r. 1925-41) overthrew the Kajar Dynasty (1779-1921) in 1921;

ended the British-Russian partition of the country and achieved independence by installation of the Pahlevi Dynasty (of Cossack, Ukrainian-Russian, origin) in 1921-25; made significant progress toward modernizing the society in Western terms; first negotiated major international oil agreements in 1933; and reconciled Iran's predominantly Shiite form of Islam with the predominantly Sunni form of other Middle Eastern nations in 1937. Nepal was granted independence (as a monarchy) in 1923. In the Middle East, Egypt, under King Ahmed Fuad I (1868-1936; r. 1922-36), a descendant of Muhammad Ali, won quasi-autonomous status in 1922 and, under Fuad's son, King Farouk I (1920-65; r. 1936-52), won virtually full independence in 1936. Britain's League of Nations mandate over Mesopotamia/Iraq ended with Iraqi independence in 1930-32; Emir Faisal I (1885-1933; r. 1921-33) became the new nation's first head-of-state. Faisal had earlier participated, with the British adventurer, Colonel Thomas Edward Lawrence/T.E. Lawrence/Lawrence of Arabia (1888-1935), in the Arab revolt against Ottoman Turkey in Arabia that resulted in the declaration of the Kingdom of Arabia, under his father, Sherif Hussein Ibn Ali (1856-1931; r. 1916-24), in 1916; he had earlier been briefly declared the King of Syria (1918-20) before expulsion by the French mandate; he had come to the Iraqi throne by British assent in 1921; he had established a constitutional monarchy in Iraq in 1925; and he presided over Iraq's first large international oil agreements in 1925-34. Saudi Arabia was united and declared its independence under the Wahabite leader who had earlier gained control of the northern interior regions (1912) and the northern coastal regions (1926) of the Arabian peninsula, King Abdul Aziz Ibn Saud (c. 1881-1953; r. 1912-53), in 1932. Ibn Saud presided over his nation's first large international oil agreements in 1936-38.

The other sector of the British Middle Eastern mandate, Palestine, did not gain independence in the inter-war period but was nonetheless importantly partitioned into Palestine and Transjordan/Jordan in 1923 and was importantly the site of virtually continuous Jewish-Arab conflict throughout this time. Although the Balfour Declaration of 1917 had promised British support for a national homeland for Jewish people in Palestine, the mandate continued until shortly after the Second World War. Likewise in India, the struggle for independence continued without full success but nonetheless resulted in a larger measure of self-determination. The Amritsar massacre of 1919 in which British troops shot into an unarmed assembly of Indian nationalists both further inflamed the Indian passion for autonomy and the British commitment to reform. Leadership of the Indian National Congress fell to Mohandas Karamchand Gandhi (1869-1948 [murdered]), the "Mahatma" (the noble-hearted), after the death of Tilak in 1920. Gandhi had earlier defended the rights of Indian people in South Africa and, like Tilak, was frequently imprisoned for his nationalist views in respect to India. He lived a life of physical abstinence and spiritual purification; advocated the loving, spiritual union of humanity in a moral system consistent with the teachings of Hinduism, Islam, and Christianity; opposed the traditional and highly discriminatory caste system of India; and promoted a program of passive, non-violent resistance to British rule in India (largely by withholding cooperation with the British and by actively boycotting the cotton and salt monopolies of the British). His courageous pacifism and hunger strikes, together with his resolute and persuasive rhetoric, were most responsible for the achievement of a revised constitution (that increased Indian self-government) in 1937 and the achievement of Indian independence itself shortly after the Second World War.

France had suffered far greater war damage than Great Britain and also struggled through a more difficult recovery, less stable governments, and more telling economic crises in the inter-war period. A reduction of population owing to war casualties and to emigration, the high cost of war debts, of repairing war damage, and of policing treaty provisions, declining currency values, heavy tax burdens, the impoverishment of the middle and lower classes, unrest in the colonies, ongoing liberal-conservative disputes, and the classic consequences of economic depression (including staggering unemployment) were most the cause. Although France came into partial possession (with Great Britain) of two German colonies, Cameroon and Togoland/Togo, in 1918 as has been said and continued its colonial empire elsewhere in sub-Saharan Africa, in the Caribbean, in South America, in Asia, and in the south Pacific, its colonies in the Middle East (Syria and Lebanon) and in north Africa (Morocco, Algeria, and Tunisia), where Islamic-Arab nationalism and a rejection of European civilization were on the rise, were moving emphatically and turbulently toward autonomy. France itself was moving emphatically and turbulently toward another confrontation with Germany in the form of the Second World War.

Elsewhere in Europe, the most significant, as-yet-unmentioned developments of the inter-war period were:
- the continuation of modernization and social-reform agendas in the Papacy; Pope Pius XI (1857-1939; r. 1922-39) renewed and extended the efforts of Pope Leo XIII (1810-1903; r. 1878-1903) to reconcile Catholic ideology and contemporary industrial democracy as well as to oppose the abuses of capitalism, communism, and fascism; and

- the development of uniquely cooperative societies in Scandinavia (most notably, in Sweden, Norway, Denmark, and Iceland).

The Scandinavian development was among the most telling, if untypical, of the inter-war period. The tendency to pan-Scandinavianism increased significantly in this time and relatively stable, centrist governments and welfare states genuinely opposed to militaristic nationalism and favorably disposed to trade and military neutrality became increasingly prevalent. The first tangible glimpses of the **modern socialist democracies**, states in which equal rights, equal opportunities, equal franchise, and the basic needs of all persons are assured, are owed to the leading Scandinavian nations of the inter-war period. Theses nations were the first in world history to embody (in incipient, socio-political terms) the characteristic tenets of the organic thesis and all that is entailed by the organic thesis (i.e., an intrinsic-monistic-expressive interpretation of reality in general, humanity and sport in particular; a preference for political, as against gentile or civil, society). Democratic socialism found its intellectual analog in twentieth-century European (most especially, Germanic, French, Russian, and Finnish), American, and Mexican forms of expressionism. Likewise in this period, Iceland came largely independent of Denmark in 1918 as has been said.

Elsewhere in the world, the most significant, as-yet-unmentioned developments of the inter-war period occurred in Mongolia, Indonesia, and Latin America. Outer Mongolia/Mongolia broke "fully" free of Chinese and Menshevik domination and became an "independent" Soviet satellite in 1921. Its monarchy was replaced by a communist government in 1924. In the Dutch East Indies/Indonesia, the nationalist movement, principally under President Achmed Sukarno (1901-70; r. 1945-66), won limited autonomy from Netherlands in 1918 on its way to full independence after the Second World War.

The dependency of small, poor nations on large, wealthy ones, the tendency to national identity, and conservative-liberal debates about the relative merits of alternative political systems and about the wisdom of reform measures also played themselves out to especially uneven and to especially turbulent effect in **Latin America**. The pace of economic, political, and social change in central America, South America, and the Caribbean overwhelmed local capacities. Industrialization, urbanization, population, political instability, and exploitation of working-class people and the environment increased exponentially. Land reform languished; methods of industrial and agricultural production were inadequate to the prevailing standards of (international) political economy; widespread illiteracy prevented the development of sufficiently skilled labor; dependence on foreign trade and capital investment was routinely disappointed; and the price of raw materials indigenous to the region fell precipitously. The result was severe popular dissatisfaction and routine domestic insurrection, systematic intervention of the military in domestic political affairs, the installation of governments that gave the appearance of democratic, of parliamentary, orientation but behaved like smothering dictatorships, international border disputes (most notably, the Chaco War of 1932-35 between Bolivia and Paraguay), and systematic military intervention by the United States of America. The most significant of the American military occupations of this period occurred in Nicaragua (1912-33), Haiti (1915-34), Mexico (1916), and the Dominican Republic (1916-24) as has been said. Less direct, but nonetheless profound, political and economic interference (with some military involvement) by the American government in the internal affairs of Latin American nations also continued; most importantly in Cuba, Panama, and Honduras. Most all of this ended with American President Roosevelt's proclamation of the "good neighbor policy" in 1934 but it resumed after the Second World War. Curiously enough, all of the nations so affected (except Mexico and Panama) had already, with American "assistance," installed among the most repressive and corrupt governments on the continent before or shortly after the American withdrawal and these nations unsurprisingly continued (after the withdrawal) to act in rather strict accord with American expectations for them. Of these, in turn, the most notable and notorious were the regimes of Rafael Leonidas Trujillo (1891-1961; r. 1930-61 [assassinated]) in the Dominican Republic, Fulgencio Batista (1901-73; r. 1933-44, 1952-59) in Cuba, and Anastasio Somoza (1896-1956; r. 1937-56 [assassinated]) in Nicaragua. The Nicaraguan and Cuban repressions sparked two of the most stirring popular revolutions in Latin American, if not world, history: the unsuccessful insurrection led by Augusto Cesar Sandino (1895-1934) in 1930s Nicaragua and the successful insurrection led by Fidel Castro (1926- ; r. 1959-) in 1950s Cuba. The major exception to the regressive tendency in Latin American political life during the inter-war period was Mexico, which inclined to a more progressive orientation than either before the First World War or following the Second. After popular revolt forced the dictatorship of Victoriano Huerta from power in 1914, the leadership of Venustiano Carranza (1859-1920; r. 1914-20 [murdered]), Alvaro Obregon (1880-1928; r. 1920-24 [assassinated]), Plutarco Elias Calles (1877-1945; r. 1924-28), and Lazaro Cardenas (1895-1970; r. 1934-40) strengthened the national commitment to constitutional government, instituted agrarian, labor, and educational reforms favoring peasants and workers, enhanced the rights of native peoples, and limited the prerogatives of clerics and foreign investors.

228

By the late 1930s, then, the ongoing competition among nations for the world's scarce, raw material and labor resource, the economic turmoil of the period, the collision of fascist and democratic political systems, the contentions of capitalistic and communistic economic orientations, and the instabilities in the international balance-of-power conspired to kindle another world war. These instabilities provoked a realignment of international alliances, all struck, of course, out of self-interested aims against common enemies, not out of a wider commitment to world peace. This realignment was extensive and it effectively determined the sides on which the combatants of the **Second World War** participated. As in the case of the First World War, the Second put the leading Axis Powers (then, Germany, Japan, and Italy) and their colonies as well as other supporters (mainly, Albania, Austria, Bulgaria, Czechoslovakia, Finland, Hungary, and Romania) against the leading Allied Powers (Great Britain, France, Russia, China, and the United States of America) and their colonies as well as other supporters (virtually all other nations of the world including most independent nations of central and South America, Australia, Belgium, Canada, Denmark, Greece, Iceland, Luxembourg, Netherlands, New Zealand, Norway, Turkey, and Yugoslavia). Among major world nations, only Ireland, Portugal, Spain, Sweden, Switzerland, and the Vatican (under Pope Pius XII [1876-1958; r. 1939-58]) remained neutral throughout the most extensive and devastating conflict in human history.

The opening gambit of the Second World War in Asia, the Second Sino-Japanese War (1937-45), was an intensified continuation of the Japanese invasion of (Chinese) Manchuria which began in 1931 as has been said. It was also an intensified continuation of Japan's designs on the entire Asian continent which were first tangibly formulated in 1927 as has been also said. The War began with an exchange of gunfire between Japanese and Chinese soldiers near Peking/Beijing in 1937 and went very much Japan's way until 1945. The major cities in the country, Peking/Beijing, Shanghai, Nanking, and Canton/Guangzhou, soon fell to the Japanese. The United States of America cancelled its main trade agreements with Japan, thus restricting the import of raw materials for war production, but the Japanese expansion continued nonetheless. In 1941, Japan installed General Hideki Tojo (1884-1948 [executed]; r. 1941-44) as prime minister, negotiated a non-aggression pact with the Soviet Union, and occupied French Indo-China (Vietnam, Cambodia, Laos), Hong Kong, and Guam. Tojo became the leading exponent of Emperor Hirohito's authoritarian government and imperialist ambitions and he directed the remaining course of Japan's participation in the Second World War, including the aerial attack on Pearl Harbor (Honolulu, Hawaii) on December 7, 1941, an attack that brought the United States into the War in all three main theaters, the Pacific, Europe, and north Africa. Japan had been in effective possession of Taiwan and Korea since the First Sino-Japanese War (1894-95) and of the Caroline Islands/Federated States of Micronesia, Marshall Islands, Northern Mariana Islands, and Palau since the First World War (1914-18) as has been said. In 1942, it occupied most of the remaining territories in southeast Asia and the central-southwest Pacific: the Philippines (Battle of Corregidor), Dutch East Indies/Indonesia, Brunei, Singapore, Malaysia, Thailand, Burma/Myanmar, Papua New Guinea, Solomon Islands, Aleutian Islands, and Gilbert Islands/Kiribati.

The War in Europe effectively began with Germany's military occupation of the Rhineland's demilitarized zone in 1936, Germany's Anschluss with Austria in 1938, Germany's Sudetan cession of 1938, and the German invasions of Czechoslovakia and Poland in 1939 as has been said. In 1939, Italy occupied Albania and, after the successful German invasion of Czechoslovakia, Germany incorporated Bohemia and Moravia (i.e., western and central Czechoslovakia), negotiated a secret non-aggression pact with the Soviet Union, and successfully invaded, occupied, and enslaved western Poland, the act which convinced the Allies that Germany's true aims were not limited to the pan-German agenda, the act which convinced the Allies of the futility of appeasement, and the act which brought Great Britain and France into the War. The Soviet Union responded by occupying eastern Poland in 1939 and by occupying Bessarabia (northeastern Romania), Karelia (southeastern Finland), Lithuania, Latvia, and Estonia in 1940. As in the case of the three partitions of the country (which effectively obliterated it from the late eighteenth century to the end of the First World War), independent Poland was again eradicated. In 1940, the German expansion accelerated; Denmark, Norway, Netherlands, Belgium, Luxembourg, and northern France were occupied; German troops reached the English Channel where they resoundingly defeated French and English forces at the Battle of Dunkerque (northwest France); France was partitioned into the occupied north and the unoccupied south; and Italy invaded Egypt, Greece, and southern France. The established French government, the Third Republic, centered in Paris, was extinguished; the new government in the unoccupied south, centered in Vichy (thus, the Vichy government), was formed in 1940, came under the direction of Marshal Henri Philippe Pétain (1856-1951; r. 1940-44), and somewhat unavoidably, albeit selectively, acceded to German demands and oriented itself to fascist conduct. The British government of (conservative) Neville Chamberlain also fell in 1940; it was replaced by the conservative leadership of Prime Minister Winston Leonard Spencer Churchill (1874-1965; r.

1940-45, 1951-55), whose stirring oratory and prose (for which he was awarded the 1953 Nobel Prize in Literature) and whose unyielding defiance of fascist and communist aggression were significant factors in the eventual victory of the Allies. In 1941, Germany occupied Greece and Yugoslavia (creating an independent Croatian state under fascist rule) but the German reach began to exceed its grasp, particularly in respect to British and Russian opposition. The German air offensive against Britain (most notably, against London, the Battle of Britain) of 1940-41 failed; the British navy sank the German super-battleship, Bismarck; the United States of America ended its neutrality in respect to the conflict and variously began to supply war materials to the Allies (mainly Great Britain and China) by way of the Lend-Lease Act; Britain (together with the Soviet Union) occupied Syria, Lebanon, and Iran; Allied forces defeated the Italian annexation of Italian Somaliland/Somalia (which had begun in 1889), of Eritrea (which had begun in 1890), and of Abyssinia/Ethiopia (which had begun in 1936); and Germany itself took one of the most ill-advised and ill-fated decisions of the War, the invasion of the Soviet Union.

The Second World War, unlike the First, was decided less by strategic position than by powerful, destructive, and efficient movement. The military use of airplanes was the principal reason. In the early years of the War (1937/1939-42), the Axis Powers exercised their prowess in the air (as well as on the ground and the sea) with such skill, resolve, and tactical acumen that they dominated the conflict. The pattern of the First World War (early on dominated by the Axis Powers but ultimately decided in the Allies' favor) began to repeat itself in the Second, however, in 1942. Also as in the case of the First World War, it was the American entry into the War – the extraordinary American resource, leadership, productive capacity, incentive, and research aptitude – that made the principal difference. The aerial attack on Pearl Harbor, which the Japanese considered a pre-emptive measure against American opposition to Japan's Chinese ambitions and against American trade embargoes (principally of oil and vital metals) and threatened naval quarantines/blockades of Japanese ports, convinced the United States that its own interests were seriously at issue and brought the country into all three theaters of the War, the Pacific, Europe, and north Africa, as has been said. The turn of fortune was nonetheless not so abrupt as it had been in the First World War. Axis success continued into 1943 but not without notable qualification. German submarine triumphs in the Atlantic continued for significant instance but they were slowed notably by Allied use of radar, naval destroyers, and extensive air support. In 1942-43:

- the United States and Great Britain began a prolonged and successful bombing campaign of German war industries and urban population centers;
- Allied counteroffensives in north Africa, mainly under British General Bernard Law Montgomery (1887-1976) and American General Dwight David Eisenhower (1890-1969; later, the 34th president of the nation), resulted in wide victories over Italian and German forces, mainly under German General Erwin Rommel (1891-1944 [suicide]);
- Montgomery's victory over Rommel at the Battle of El Alamein (near Alexandria) in 1942 and subsequent Allied successes brought the war in north Africa to an end in 1943;
- the Allied invasion of Italy following the final triumph in north Africa (1943) brought an end to Italian colonial prerogatives in Libya, the temporary demise of Mussolini, the dissolution of the Partito Nazionale Fascista, a German counteroffensive that occupied Rome, and the Italian declaration of war on Germany;
- early German successes in eastern Poland, the Baltic states, Belarus, Ukraine, and Russia (German forces had captured Kiev, Minsk, Vilnius, Riga, and Tallinn and they had reached Moscow in 1941; they captured Sebastopol and Stalingrad/Volgograd in 1942) faltered; a Russian counteroffensive recaptured Stalingrad/Volgograd in 1943;
- active resistance movements in Germany and in the occupied countries (mainly among social democrats, trade unionists, intellectuals, and religionists, but also among some military officers, politicians, and diplomats), which had been first organized in 1941, began to have a telling affect despite brutal German reprisals against them; these movements were aimed variously at eliminating Hitler and his dictatorship, at restoring constitutional government in Germany, and at expelling Germany from the occupied countries; and
- Japanese advances in China were increasingly repelled and Allied counteroffensives in the Pacific, principally under American General Douglas MacArthur (1880-1964) and American Admiral Chester William Nimitz (1885-1966), were increasingly successful; Papua New Guinea (Battle of the Coral Sea), Aleutian Islands, Gilbert Islands/Kiribati (Battle of Tarawa), and Solomon Islands (Battle of

Guadalcanal) were recaptured in 1943 and American air attacks on Japanese industrial centers also began in 1943.

The final year to two years of the War, 1944 and 1945, brought accelerated Allied successes and, in the end, decisive Allied victory. In 1944:

- the Soviet Union penetrated the Balkans, the resistance movements in Yugoslavia (under Marshal Josip Broz Tito [1892-1980]; later, prime minister/president of the country) and Albania (under General Enver Hoxha [1908-85]; later, the leading political figure in the country) succeeded in expelling German and Italian forces respectively, Germany withdrew from Greece and Hungary, and Romania, Bulgaria, and Hungary (under heavy Soviet pressure and malevolent German treatment) declared war on Germany;
- the especially brutal German occupations of Ukraine, Belarus, the Baltic states, Czechoslovakia, and Poland, which included the execution of local political leadership, forced resettlement and military conscription, and severe exploitation of workers, aroused fierce Soviet opposition, opposition which succeeded in reclaiming these territories;
- the Allied invasion of northern France and Belgium under General Eisenhower and the Allied invasion of southern France, together with significant assistance from the French resistance under General Charles De Gaulle (1890-1970; later president and prime minister of the country), reached the western German, Swiss, and Italian borders, thus liberating France, Belgium, and Luxembourg from the German occupation; the last major German offensive of the War (Battle of the Bulge), into Belgium, failed;
- an unsuccessful assassination attempt against Hitler brought vengeful murders, including the forced suicide of General Rommel; and
- the Allied counteroffensives in the Pacific, under General MacArthur and Admiral Nimitz, reclaimed the Marshall Islands, the Northern Mariana Islands, and Guam; the final assault on the Philippines (Battle of Leyte Gulf) also began.

By the beginning of 1945, the Allies were approaching victory. Mainly American and British forces were entering Germany itself from the west. Mainly Soviet forces were entering western Poland and Germany itself from the east. And mainly American, British, and Chinese (an uneasy alliance of nationalist and communist) forces were advancing on Japan itself from the south and the west. The fascist aggression had overextended itself and was at the edge of collapse.

In the final several months of the Second World War in Europe, Hitler ordered suicidal defense measures in an attempt to avert the defeat that was coming. By the end of April, the climax of the Allied air war against German cities had been achieved with the terror/firestorm raids on Dresden (between Berlin and Prague), then flush with refugees (many of whom were among the c. 35,000-c. 135,000 civilians killed by incendiary bombs and aerial machine-gun fire); the Soviet conquest of western Poland (including Warsaw), Slovakia (including Pressburg/Bratislava), eastern Austria (including Vienna), and eastern Germany were virtually complete; the American and British conquest of western Germany was virtually complete; German resistance in northern Italy had capitulated (and Mussolini, attempting an escape to Switzerland, had been executed by Italian partisans); Hitler had committed suicide; and the National Socialist German Workers' Party had been dissolved. The remaining centers of German culture, Berlin and Prague, fell in early May and Germany surrendered unconditionally to General Eisenhower at Reims, France on May 7.

The war in Asia nonetheless continued. The Allied reconquests of the Philippines and of Burma/Myanmar were completed; American forces landed in Japan itself (in Iwo Jima and Okinawa; south of the main islands) and prepared for a land invasion of the main islands; conventional air attacks by American forces on Japanese cities (including Tokyo) intensified; and on August 6 at 0815 hours, allegedly in order to forestall a land invasion and the Allied casualties entailed by a land invasion, the United States dropped an atomic bomb, code-named "Little Boy" (a uranium bomb with an explosive force of c. 12.5 kilotons of TNT), on Hiroshima (southwestern Honshu), killing c. 140,000 (mostly civilian Japanese) persons by the end of the year and destroying c. 90% of the city instantaneously. The Soviet Union then declared war on Japan and invaded Manchuria and Korea. On August 9 at 1102 hours, the United States dropped a second atomic bomb, code-named "Fat Man" (a plutonium bomb with an explosive force of c. 20 kilotons of TNT), on Nagasaki (western Kyushu), killing c. 70,000 (mostly civilian Japanese) persons by the end of the year and destroying c. one-third of the city instantaneously. Japan surrendered without condition on August 14 ending the most destructive war in world history. Approximately five times the number of persons who had been killed in the First World War lost their lives in the Second (i.e., 55 million); approximately 35 million had been wounded; approximately three million were never found and were presumed vaporized; and the fiscal costs were incalculable. The greatest losses were suffered by the Soviets, Chinese, Poles, and Germans.

The German and Japanese conduct of the War had been especially brutal, even by the low standards prevailing in such matters. Both treated the people of countries they had occupied with utter contempt, enslaving, imprisoning, and executing vast numbers of such people with little compassionate restraint and with virtual impunity. The human and natural resources of these countries were shamelessly exploited, arousing spirited resistance movements which were themselves very harshly suppressed. The domestic circumstance in Germany (and in German-occupied territories) was also visited by one of the most systematic and devastating programs of genocidal madness in the entire record of human misconduct, itself a long and unflattering record. This program was ordered by Hitler and variously carried out by his closest associates: Heinrich Himmler (1900-45 [suicide]), Paul Joseph Goebbels (1897-1945 [suicide]), who had directed the largely unsuccessful propaganda campaign associated with the 1936 Olympic Games, and Hermann Wilhelm Goering (1893-1946 [suicide]). Mainly Jewish people, Slavic minorities, communists, dissidents, homosexuals, and the disabled variously had their property destroyed or confiscated, were excluded from national life, were isolated in impoverished ghettos, were imprisoned as enemies of the state, were consigned to slave labor and often worked to death, or were liquidated as "undesirables." This program, the so-termed Holocaust, was aimed principally at Jewish people, whose business practices were blamed for Germany's humiliation in the First World War. In the end (beginning in 1941), it attempted an ethnic extermination of the Jews mainly in concentration-extermination camps in Poland; most notably, Auschwitz (near Krakow). At least eleven million people perished in these camps; at least six million of these were Jewish people, virtually the entire European Jewish community. Only those who had successfully emigrated and a very few others had survived.

Except for the involuntary internment by the American government of Japanese-American citizens in concentration camps from 1942 to 1945, the major Allied atrocities of the War were more antiseptic and more random. The firebombings of Dresden and the nuclear detonations over Hiroshima and Nagasaki were aimed principally at non-military, non-industrial targets (i.e., they were tests of incendiary and nuclear devices on defenseless human populations and their property) and at dissuading the Soviet Union from a larger presence in post-war Europe and Asia than Soviet allies would tolerate. They were acts for which there were likely more benign and effective alternatives, alternatives that did not target civilians unengaged in war production and alternatives that would likely have equally well hastened the end of the War. There may have been, however, less viable choice over the development of incendiary and nuclear weapons by the Allies than over the uses to which they were put, mainly because the Germans were known to be also attempting their development and presumed use. The American effort that fashioned the first atomic weapons, the Manhattan Project, was directed by American physicist, J. Robert Oppenheimer (1904-67), from 1942 to 1945. This Project was itself based on the development of the first nuclear reactor by Italian-American physicist and 1938 Nobel laureate, Enrico Fermi (1901-54), at the University of Chicago in 1942. It exploded the first atomic weapon, a plutonium bomb, near Alamogordo, New Mexico on July 16, 1945 and it assembled the devices dropped on Hiroshima and Nagasaki the following month.

The extraordinary government expenditures of the war years at last ended the Great Depression and the War itself framed the political, economic, and social environment of the period that has unfolded since. By the Atlantic Charter of 1941, Roosevelt and Churchill formulated the terms by which international peace could be achieved: disavowal of national ambitions for territorial gain, universal rights of national self-determination, universal access to essential raw materials by international trade, and the renunciation of raw force. By the Washington Pact of 1942, Allied Powers agreed to seek only a mutually agreeable armistice (not disparate armistices) with the Axis Powers. The Atlantic Charter, the Washington Pact, and subsequent **war-time conferences**, together with the longer-standing groundwork of the League of Nations, established the basis on which the United Nations was later established. By the Casablanca Conference of 1943, Roosevelt and Churchill formulated war plans concerning the bombing of Germany, the invasions of Italy and France, and the use of atomic weapons. By the First Cairo Conference of 1943, Roosevelt, Churchill, and Chiang Kai-shek planned military operations against Japan and agreed to the independence of Korea and other territories occupied by Japan. By the Tehran Conference of 1943, Roosevelt, Churchill, and Stalin formulated war strategy in Europe, agreed to a revised status for Poland, and formulated plans for post-war cooperation in the form of the United Nations. And by the Yalta (in the Crimea) Conference of 1945, Roosevelt, Churchill, and Stalin settled on spheres of Anglo-American and Soviet influence in post-war Europe (mainly in Germany, Poland, and the Balkans) and came to further agreements about the organization of the United Nations. The various **war-end treaties** themselves (most notably, the Potsdam [near Berlin] Agreement in

1945, the Paris Peace Treaties in 1947, and the Peace of San Francisco in 1951), treaties which formalized the concluding accommodations of the War, ordered German and Japanese war reparations, the demilitarization and reorganization of Germany and Japan, the withdrawal of Japan from Formosa/Taiwan, Korea, all other occupied territories, and its Pacific colonies (the Caroline Islands/Federated States of Micronesia, Marshall Islands, Northern Mariana Islands, and Palau), the American and Russian partition of Korea, the restoration of Austria, Czechoslovakia, and Poland as independent republics, the forfeiture of all remaining Italian colonies (Libya, Eritrea, and Italian Somaliland/Somalia), the reduction of Hungarian territory (mainly in Transylvania), the re-conjunction of Croatia with Yugoslavia, and the forfeiture of Bessarabia/Moldova (by Romania) and Karelia (by Finland) to the Soviet Union. The unsettled character of several central and south Pacific nations (and their strategic significance) brought them under American trusteeship in 1944-47: Solomon Islands (became independent in 1978), Palau, Caroline Islands/Federated States of Micronesia (became self-governing in 1979), Marshall Islands (became self-governing in 1983), and Northern Mariana Islands. Guam reverted to its pre-war status as a United States territory and American Samoa remained a United States territory. In the Caribbean, Puerto Rico and the United States Virgin Islands also remained United States territories.

The period since the Second World War

Recovery from the War, from the unprecedented devastations of the War, was astonishingly swift, particularly in the leading industrial nations on the Allied side. The damages of the War were fairly soon overcome by the technological progress of the war years themselves and of the immediate post-war period. The period since the Second World War has been marked by yet another prodigious expansion of **technological innovation and imaginative discovery**. This most recent stage in the maturation of industrialism has managed yet another vast increase in production, consumption, prosperity for many, quality-of-life expectations for all, population,[126] life expectancy, international trade, corporate domination, consumer goods, consumerism, leisure resource, specialization, and rates of profound and uncertain change. It has also, however, deepened the environmental crisis in respect to overuse and pollution; it has advanced crime and politico-commercial corruption; it has heightened the sense of insecurity and alienation associated with profound and uncertain change; it has created significant dislocations related to natural shifts in the business cycle, related to periodic expansion and contraction of markets, rates of economic growth, production, and consumption (such as, the recessions of the late 1940s, mid-1950s, late 1950s, early and late 1960s, early 1970s, mid-1970s, late 1970s, early and late 1980s, and early 1990s); and it has pointed paradoxically at either the "final perfection" of civilization or its obliteration. This stage has been mainly driven by the development of plastics, transistors, computers, and nuclear power. It has had its chief affects on bio-medical practice, communication, transportation, armaments, and space exploration.

Astonishing advancements in **bio-medical practice** have been an especially incisive and an especially salutary influence on the period since the Second World War. Although cholera and malaria (from which some relief had been achieved in the nineteenth century) continued to haunt various, mostly developing, regions of the world where climate and sparse health provisions conspired to promote the conditions of their development, most serious infectious diseases that had not been earlier beaten were conquered in this time. The most notable of these are influenza, which can now be at least temporarily controlled by immunization, and poliomyelitis, which has been nearly eradicated through the use of vaccines developed by Jonas Edward Salk (1914-95) in c. 1955 and by Albert Bruce Sabin (1906-93) in c. 1959. Diseases caused mainly by injudicious nutritional and life-style practices (such as cardiovascular deterioration) and by environmental pollution (such as cancer) have nonetheless continued to prosper as such practices and such pollution have prospered. Also owed to this period are the development of:

- innovative pharmaceutical substances; most notably, oral contraceptives, sophisticated antibiotics (mainly those treating infections resistant to such as penicillin and streptomycin), and psycho-therapeutical modalities (mainly, tranquilizers and anti-depressants);
- innovative diagnostic technologies; most notably, ultrasound, cat scan, and magnetic resonance imaging;
- mechanical methods of procreation; most notably, artificial insemination and in vitro fertilization (the first "test-tube" baby, Louise Joy Brown, was born in Great Britain in 1978);
- pharmaceutical and mechanical methods for the postponement of death/the extraordinary prolongation of life (mainly, intravenous feedings, respirators, and artificial kidney machines), often

"meaningless" life, and thus the concurrent development of the euthanasia movement (Netherlands was the first nation to de-criminalize euthanasia in 1993);

- striking achievements in bio-medical engineering; most notably, organ transplantation techniques and artificial organs-tissues; the first major, successful organ transplantation in humans was of the kidney and it was done by Dr. Joseph E. Murray (1919-) of the United States in 1954 (Murray won the 1990 Nobel Prize in Medicine for this and related work); the first successful heart transplantation was done by Dr. Christiaan Neething Barnard (1923-) of South Africa in 1967; and the first permanent artificial implantation of a major organ in humans was done in 1982 of a heart principally developed by Dr. Robert Koffler Jarvik (1946-) of the United States;
- singular achievements in nutritional science;
- the human genome project of 1990-2000, by which the entire genetic code of the human species – c. 100,000 genes and c. 3 billion DNA units – has been deciphered and by which the function of disease in respect to this code has been widely studied; and
- the advent of the AIDS epidemic (and quasi-successful attempts to curtail it) in 1981.

The period since the Second World War has been also one of exceptional achievement in **communication and transportation**, achievement that has been grounded mainly in electronic technology. Arguably the most significant of these achievements have been the development of:

- the digital computer (artificial intelligence) in 1946;
- the transistor in 1948;
- lasers in 1960;
- integrated circuits/semiconductors in 1961;
- the compact disc in 1983;
- personal computers in the 1980s;
- the worldwide web (the internet) and its fiberoptic groundwork in the 1990s;
- the first supersonic flight by American aviator, Charles Elwood "Chuck" Yeager (1923-), in 1947; and
- the commercial aviation industry in the 1940s, 1950s, and 1960s.

Alarming advancements in **armaments**, most particularly biological, chemical, and nuclear armaments, have also characterized this most recent period of our development. Weapons and weapons systems have become progressively more sophisticated and steadily more capable of extinguishing all life on the planet many times over. The American nuclear program and armament industry have been the most ardent and successful contributors to this tendency. The United States was the first to develop biological and chemical weapons in 1943. It was also the first to develop nuclear weapons, an achievement which was based on the nuclear reactor fashioned by Enrico Fermi and which formally began in 1942 with the Manhattan Project directed by J. Robert Oppenheimer as has been said. It detonated the first nuclear weapons in 1945 as has been also said. In 1946, it established the Atomic Energy Commission (to direct and regulate American nuclear technology); in 1952, it detonated the first hydrogen/thermonuclear bomb (on Eniwetok, Marshall Islands); in 1954, it created the first atomic submarine (Nautilus); and in 1957, it crafted the first intercontinental ballistic missiles with nuclear warheads, missiles capable of reaching any location on the planet. Other leading nations soon followed suit. The Soviet Union first exploded a fission (atomic) bomb in 1949 and a fusion (hydrogen) bomb in 1953; it was the first to establish an atomic power station in 1954; and it developed intercontinental ballistic missiles in the same year as the United States (1957). Great Britain detonated an atomic bomb in 1952; France, in 1960; China, in 1964; and India, in 1974. It is suspected that Pakistan, Israel, and South Africa have since developed atomic weapons. The catastrophically ruinous powers of these weapons, the incapacity to defend against them, and the prospect of their being used in offensive scenarios incited all sides to form international regulatory agencies and to consider international armament/disarmament treaties, both of which effectively defined the terms of nuclear deterrence, the terms of cooperative co-existence, the terms by which unwinnable wars were to be avoided, the terms of mutually assured destruction, the terms of the balance-of-terror. Likely the most notable of these agencies were the United Nations Atomic Energy Commission (1946) and the International Atomic Energy Agency (1956). Likely the most notable of these agreements, mainly between the United States and the Soviet Union, were the Nuclear Test Ban Treaty of 1963 (which prohibited the testing of nuclear devices in the atmosphere, in outer space, and under water), the Nuclear Non-Proliferation Treaty of 1968 (which limited the production and deployment of nuclear weapons), the Strategic Arms Limitation Talks I Treaty of 1972 (which limited the deployment of antiballistic missiles and offensive nuclear weapons), and the Strategic Arms Reduction Talks II Treaty of 1993 (which further limited the deployment of antiballistic missiles and offensive nuclear weapons).

Space exploration was often closely affiliated with military (particularly, reconnaissance and weapons) projects, but was also moved by more strictly scientific aims, aims concerning such as astronomical, biological, communication, geographical, materials, medical, navigation, resource mapping, and weather research/technological development. It was made possible by the manufacture of rockets capable of penetrating space (capable of escaping Earth's atmosphere) and capable as well of deploying earth satellites. The rocket and satellite technologies first came successfully together in 1957 when the Soviet Union deployed the first artificial earth satellite, Sputnik 1. The United States responded in 1958 with the formation of the National Aeronautics and Space Administration (NASA), the organization which directs the American space program and which has made among the most stunning achievements (and among the most colossal failures as well) of the space age. The Soviet Union nonetheless continued for a time with pioneering accomplishments. In 1959, it sent the first human-made object, Lunik 1, to the Sun (circumnavigation), sent the first human-made object, Lunik 2, to the moon (hard landing), and took the first photographs of the far-side of the moon (Lunik 3). In 1960, it sent the first inhabited (dogs) space capsule into earth orbit; on April 12, 1961, it achieved the first manned space flight (put the first human being in space) when Major Yuri Alekseyevich Gagarin (1934-68) orbited the planet once aboard Vostok 1; in 1963, it sent the first woman, Valentina Vladimirovna Tereshkova (1937-), into space aboard Vostok 6; in 1965, Soviet cosmonaut, Aleksei Arkhipovich Leonov (1934-), performed the first extravehicular activity in space aboard Voskhod 2; in 1966, it achieved the first soft landing on the moon (Luna 9) and achieved the first lunar orbit (Luna 10); in 1967, it made the first entry into the atmosphere of Venus (Venera 4); in 1968, it made the first circumlunar flight which returned to Earth (Zond 5); in 1970, it returned the first automatically obtained lunar-soil sample to Earth (Luna 16), engineered the first automatic lunar-surface vehicle (Luna 17), and became the first to reach the Venusian surface (Venera 7); in 1971, it created the first earth-orbit space station (Salyut 1); and in 1973, it became the first to enter the Martian atmosphere (Mars 6).

The United States was, however, not far behind and, by the late 1960s, began to excel the Soviets in the "race for space." In 1958, it became the second nation to place an artificial satellite in earth orbit; in 1960, it placed the first communications satellite in earth orbit; in 1961, it became the second nation to achieve manned space flight; in 1962, it became the second nation to achieve orbital space flight; and in 1973, it became the second nation to create an earth-orbit space station. It was, however, in manned, lunar space flight and in deep-space probes that the Americans eventually pulled ahead. The United States achieved the first:

- observational flyby of Venus, by Mariner 2, in 1962;
- observational flyby of Mars, by Mariner 4, in 1964;
- manned docking of space vehicles, by Gemini 8, in 1966;
- manned circumlunar flight, by Apollo 8, in 1968;
- manned lunar landing, by Apollo 11, in 1969; American astronaut, Neil Alden Armstrong (1930-), became the first human being to visit a celestial body, the first to walk on the moon, an epic accomplishment, on April 21, 1969;
- probe to orbit another planet (Mars), Mariner 9, in 1971;
- observational flyby of Mercury, by Mariner 10, in 1973;
- observational flyby of Jupiter, by Pioneer 10, in 1973; later (1983), the first human-made object to leave the solar system;
- space laboratory, Space Lab, in 1973;
- landing on Mars, by Viking 1, in 1976 (also entailed the first tangible search for Martian life);
- observational flyby of Saturn, by Pioneer 11, in 1979;
- re-usable space vehicle, Space Shuttle (Columbia), in 1981;
- observational flyby of Uranus in 1986 and Neptune in 1989, both by Voyager 2; and
- deployment (with European cooperation) of a space observatory, Hubble Space Telescope, in 1990.

There have been many other memorable successes in space exploration and discovery since these seminal achievements -- other satellites, space stations, and deep-space probes (aimed mainly at planets, the natural satellites of planets, asteroids, comets, and the Sun). There have even been five successful, manned lunar landings (all American efforts) since the first, but none since 1972 (Apollo 17). And there have been successful satellite deployments by prominent technological societies other than the United States and the Soviet Union; most significantly, Germany, Japan, Great Britain, France, China, and India. There have been some tragic accidents as well, however; most notably, the deaths of three American and one Soviet astronauts/cosmonaut in 1967, the near-fatal and abandoned American moon expedition in 1970 (Apollo 13), the deaths of three Soviet cosmonauts aboard Soyuz 11 in 1971, and the fatal explosion of the American Space Shuttle, Challenger, in 1986.

These stunning technological achievements and their commercial employments, together with ongoing refinements of technologies first developed before the Second World War, were the principal bases of significant gains in prosperity after the War. They were also, however, the principal bases of an accelerated pattern of environmental degradation in this time. This pattern most notably included alarmingly frequent oil spills, chemical contamination of land, air, and water, depletion of the atmosphere's ozone layer (discovered in 1979), and nuclear accidents (most notably, the Three-Mile Island, U.S.A. accident of 1979 and the Chernobyl, Ukraine accident of 1986). This pattern also sparked a movement to protect, restore, and conserve the environment and the largely defenseless creatures that inhabit it. The **environmental and animal-rights movements**, which included the defense of endangered species, of the post-war period are perhaps most conspicuously expressed by the proclamation of Earth Day in 1970.

The **global political and economic circumstance since the Second World War**, which was closely related to technological-commercial developments, has been dominated by the rivalry between the United States and the Soviet Union, by the systems of American and Soviet alliances with other countries, by the development of a movement among unaligned (mostly, developing) nations opposed to either American or Soviet domination of them, and by formation of transnational/international political and trade organizations attempting ostensibly to make one world out of many. The United States of America emerged from the Second World War as an even more imposing and an even more dominant power than it had from the First World War. The era of European world domination had clearly passed; the United States became indisputably the most influential of all nations. Its capitalistic orientation was nonetheless fervently opposed by the communist inclinations of the second most powerful nation in the world, its World War II ally, the Soviet Union. As classical colonialism/imperialism waned still further (vis-à-vis earlier modern periods) and almost all national groups won political independence in strictly formal terms, a new colonial/imperial order was established. In this order, wealthy industrial nations continued their domination of poor foreign cultures, less by overt force (the classical case) than by control of the new, native leadership in such cultures. This control (of local elites) was achieved mainly by the manipulation of capital investment and of trade practices as well as by fiscal and political corruption (including electoral fraud). Only if such manipulation and corruption failed to win the desired objectives were covert, then overt military options typically invoked. The terms of independence were therefore European and American, not local; these terms masqueraded as democratic but were more typically organized by and for the few; and these terms customarily continued the sense of dependence (on foreign capital and markets) and subservience (to foreign capital and markets), as well as the sense of repression, characteristic of classical colonialism, if somewhat differently wrapped. The newly independent nations, particularly the developing nations, were customarily left and maintained in desperate straits: with burgeoning, mostly uneducated, populations, massive migrations to deteriorating cities, insufficient technological resources, declining economies, staggering unemployment, currency failures, unstable and insecure political groundworks, feudalistic social hierarchies, contending class, ethnic, religious, cultural, and military-civilian factions, and the sort of violence, crime, discrimination, poverty, famine, pestilence, squalor, standardized misery, and political radicalization characteristically associated with such chaotic and exploitative disorder. The basic character of that form of political economy which has governed the world for the past approximate two centuries, capital industrialism, requires such an arrangement. The bellicose nature of the major powers did neither resist this arrangement. The United States and the Soviet Union thus set about to create their own imperial spheres of influence (which were already well along by 1945 as has been said), allying with other developed societies and taking over as many of the yet others (i.e., the developing societies) as they were plausibly able to take over. The result was the **Cold War** in which the two superpowers (and their minions) stared one another down, by nuclear and conventional means (that is, by threat of mutually assured destruction), throughout the world for over forty years.

In the **United States of America**, the war in Europe was within one month of its end when President Roosevelt died in office. He was succeeded by Harry S. Truman (1884-1972; r. 1945-53), who conditionally attempted to continue Roosevelt's (New Deal) domestic policies and who presided over the closing days of the war in Europe, the ominous, but war-ending, decision to use nuclear weapons against Japan, the 1945 establishment of the major transnational/international political and trade organizations of the post-war era (the United Nations, World Bank, and International Monetary Fund), the independence of the Philippines from the United States (granted in order to discourage communism in Asia) in 1946,[127] the establishment of American military bases elsewhere in the world, the opening gambits of the Cold War, and most of the Korean War (1950-53). Truman's commitment to the New Deal of his predecessor was truncated somewhat by the occurrence of two events which he opposed: the passage of the Taft-Hartley Act in 1947 (which limited the influence of trade unions) and communist (espionage) show trials inspired mainly by Senator Joseph Raymond McCarthy (1908-57) in the late 1940s and early 1950s. The opening stages of the Cold War, the American bombings of Dresden, Hiroshima, and Nagasaki, and the Soviet invasions of Manchuria and Korea were followed in 1947 by formal declarations of American and Soviet designs on the post-war world. The Truman Doctrine stipulated containment of communist expansion and extension of American interests; the Molotov (from the Soviet Foreign Minister) Plan stipulated containment of capitalist expansion and extension of Soviet interests. The five principal expressions of the Truman Doctrine were the demilitarization and reorganization of German political life, the demilitarization and reorganization of Japanese political life (including stabilization of the Japanese economy), the negotiation of three major international alliances, the Marshall Plan, and the Korean War.

The American occupation government in Japan (1945-50), under General MacArthur, demilitarized Japanese society, exacted war reparations, conducted trials of Japanese war criminals, effected significant land reform that blunted the old feudal order, and transformed the political realities of the country. A new, western-style constitution was installed; this constitution established a parliamentary democracy which ascribed only ceremonial significance to the imperial throne (yet under Hirohito as has been said). This government also reorganized the Japanese economy in western, capitalist terms and thereby established the foundations of what would become one of the leading economies in the world by the end of the century. After Japan adopted political and economic reforms that made it more nearly like the United States, that made it a viable trading partner for the United States, that eliminated it as a military threat to the United States, and that made it of strategic military significance to the United States, it became a staunch ally of the United States and had its sovereignty returned to it by the United States in 1952.

The Truman administration also negotiated three major international alliances, all aimed at collective defense measures, political cooperation, and economic agreement against communism: the Organization of American States (OAC; among nations of the Americas) in 1948, the North Atlantic Treaty Organization (NATO; among nations of the Atlantic community, the United States, Canada, and most major nations of western Europe) in 1949, and the ANZUS Pact (among Australia, New Zealand, and the United States) in 1951. The Marshall Plan of 1947-51 was proposed and mainly directed by the American Secretary of State, General George Catlett Marshall (1880-1959), a distinction for which he was awarded the 1953 Nobel Peace Prize. The Plan was principally devoted to the economic recovery (from the War) of western Europe, whose markets were to become the foremost post-war trading partners of American business corporations.

The **Korean War** was too a fixture of Cold War political imperatives. Korea had been promised independence by the Allies but was nonetheless divided into zones of American and Soviet occupation at the conclusion of the Second World War as has been said. In 1948, the agricultural south, the American zone, was organized as the Republic of Korea/South Korea and was governed by an American-puppet regime (that had been elected by specious means), under the autocratic capitalist leadership of Syngman Rhee (1875-1965; r. 1948-60). Also in 1948, the industrial north, the Soviet zone, was organized (without elections) as the Democratic People's Republic of Korea/North Korea, under the autocratic communist leadership of Kim Il Sung (1912-94; r. 1948-94). When Allied promises of free elections, unification, and independence were continuously disappointed, North Korea invaded South Korea in 1950. The United Nations authorized member states (mainly the United States) to aid the south, whose forces were early on commanded by American General MacArthur. The north was assisted by the People's Republic of China and the Soviet Union. The early months of the War were won by the north; United Nations forces were pushed back to Pusan and the region surrounding Pusan (in the extreme southeast). The next several months were won by the south which advanced to the Chinese border at the Yalu River (in the extreme north). When General MacArthur insisted on the invasion of the People's Republic of China itself, he was dismissed by President Truman, who feared another world war if Chinese sovereignty were breached. After the Chinese army entered the War late in 1950, the conflict stagnated at roughly the pre-war border (between the capital of the north, Pyongyang, and that of the south, Seoul). The War ended in an effective stalemate by the Armistice of Panmunjom (near Seoul) in 1953; the border of the two Koreas was restored to its approximate location at the beginning of the War. The Korean War claimed c. 415,000 South Korean military lives, c. 200,000 North Korean and Chinese military lives, c. 62,000 American military lives, and c. 3 million North Korean and South Korean civilian lives. North Korea has since the War remained under heavily autocratic communist leadership and has since also been allied with China and the Soviet Union. South Korea has remained in the capitalist ambit, allied principally with the United States; it has since the War passed through a succession of military and civilian governments, virtually all of them deeply autocratic; and it has too experienced a measure of prosperity unknown in the north.

The presidential administrations of the United States' leading military figure in the Second World War, Dwight Eisenhower (r. 1953-61), followed. They were characterized by a largely prosperous economy, by the beginnings of an effective civil/minority-rights movement, and by an exceedingly aggressive foreign policy directed primarily against communist nations (and movements) or against any action opposed to major American corporate interests. The economic expansion of the immediate post-war period continued under Eisenhower. Racial segregation in public education was declared unconstitutional (Brown v. Board of Education) in 1954; the successful 1955-56 non-violent boycott of public buses in Montgomery, Alabama, led by the civil rights bellwether, stirring orator, and 1964 Nobel Peace laureate, Reverend Martin Luther King, Jr. (1929-68 [murdered]), began the effort to desegregate public transportation and had a large affect on the integration of other institutions and on the civil-rights achievements of the 1960s broadly defined; federal troops enforced school desegregation orders in the south in 1957; and the Civil Rights Bill, mainly concerning the voting rights of minorities, was enacted in 1957. Alaska and Hawaii also joined the formal union of states (as the most recent additions) in Eisenhower's second term (1959). In foreign policy, the armistice ending the Korean War was formalized in 1953 and Eisenhower's conservative inclinations and virulent anti-communism brought:

- routine disputes with the People's Republic of China (mainly over Korea, Vietnam, and Formosa/Taiwan);
- deteriorating relations with the Soviet Union (mainly over "territorial" disputes in central Europe, over Cuba, and over American espionage flights in Soviet airspace);
- routine hostility for the Arab cause against Israel and routine hostility as well for other third-world liberation movements;
- the 1953 execution of Ethel (1916-53) and Julius (1918-53) Rosenberg on espionage charges that were at best dubious;
- a 1953 covert operation (mainly with Great Britain) which overthrew an elected government in Iran under Premier Muhammad Mussadegh (1880-1967; r. 1951-53), who had nationalized the British oil industry in the country and who had forced the pro-western shah, Muhammad Reza Shah Pahlevi (1919-80; r. 1941-79), himself installed by invading Russian and British troops in 1941, into temporary exile;
- the 1954 formation of the anti-communist defense alliance, the Southeast Asia Treaty Organization (SEATO), among the United States and southeast Asian nations opposed to communism;
- a military invasion of Guatemala in 1954 which overthrew an elected government under Jacopo Arbenz Guzman (1913-71; r. 1951-54), who had nationalized some American corporate (agricultural) assets; the country since has passed through a troubled series of regimes, most of them military juntas, strongly supported by the United States, and with abysmal civil-rights records;
- the opening rounds of the American effort in French Indo-China/Vietnam in 1955; after the Vietnamese defeat of the French in the First Indo-China War/French Indo-China War/Franco-Vietnam War (1946-54) in 1954 and the formal partition of Vietnam into a northern and a southern region in 1954-55, the United States installed a corrupt minority (Catholic, western-educated, anti-Buddhist, anti-communist) dictatorship in the south under President Ngo Dinh Diem (1901-63; r. 1955-63 [assassinated]) in 1955; when Diem refused to hold the elections agreed to by the peace accords which ended the First Indo-China War, communist insurgents in the south, the Vietcong, began the Second Indo-China War/Vietnam War/American War (1957-75) in 1957;
- a military invasion of Lebanon in 1958 which subdued a pan-Arab rebellion against pro-western policies; and
- the end of the corrupt, regressive, American-dominated government in **Cuba** under Fulgencio Batista (r. 1933-44, 1952-59) in 1959; a long and courageous guerilla insurgency (1953-59) led by the Cuban revolutionary, Fidel Castro (r. 1959-), and the Argentine revolutionary (later executed in Bolivia), Ernesto "Che" Guevara (1928-67 [executed]), toppled Batista, collectivized agriculture, nationalized industry, universalized education and health care, diminished the prerogatives of foreign capital, and advanced the welfare of peasants and workers; when Cuban overtures for economic and political relationships with the United States were rebuffed, Cuba turned to the Soviet sphere for such relationships and the unsuccessful American effort to destroy the new government in Cuba (that has been going on since) began.

238

The Eisenhower presidency was followed by the terms of John Fitzgerald "Jack" Kennedy (1917-63; r. 1961-63 [assassinated]) and Lyndon Baines Johnson (1908-73; r. 1963-69), both of whom took a notably more liberal course in domestic affairs than Eisenhower but pursued a similarly bellicose, Cold War path in foreign policy. Kennedy's term was brief but tumultuous. His domestic agenda, the so-termed New Frontier, included progressive tax reform favoring the poor, federal aid to education, medical care for the aged, an extension of civil rights for minorities and women, and a dramatic expansion of the space program. His foreign policy most importantly included the establishment of the Peace Corps (by which trained volunteers assisted developing nations in infrastructure formation) in 1961, the Alliance for Progress (by which special economic and technological assistance was extended to Latin American nations in order to discourage communist agitations) in 1961, and the Nuclear Test Ban Treaty of 1963. It also included, however, sharp increases in nuclear and conventional armaments, foreign military aid, and foreign military interventions:

- The Soviet-American interface in Germany continued;
- Ongoing American attempts to depose the increasingly corrupt, repressive, and unmanageable, if efficient, regime of Rafael Trujillo (r. 1930-61) in the Dominican Republic succeeded with his assassination in 1961; the economic stability and orientation of the country has since improved, on balance;
- Primarily in order to protect rubber and banking interests, the American military presence in South Vietnam increased qualitatively from 1961 to 1963; the regime of Diem became increasingly corrupt, repressive, and unmanageable; he was assassinated in 1963 (with American duplicity) and was succeeded by several equally dictatorial and corrupt, but more manageable, military regimes, mainly under Marshall Nguyen Cao Ky (1930- ; 1965-67) and General Nguyen Van Thieu (1923- ; r. 1967-75); Soviet and Chinese assistance to the North Vietnamese effort also increased substantially;
- Ongoing American attempts to depose the Castro government in Cuba failed; a ruinous trade embargo, numerous assassination schemes against Castro himself, and the Bay of Pigs invasion of 1961 (an internationally embarrassing fiasco that was quickly and decisively defeated) were the most notable of these attempts; and
- The Cuban Missile Crisis of 1962 ended peacefully; the American government successfully demanded the removal of missile sites that had been constructed in Cuba by the Soviet Union after the Bay of Pigs invasion in exchange for comparable American concessions in Turkey.

The presidency of Lyndon Johnson was similar in basic character. Johnson's domestic agenda, the so-termed Great Society program, included major civil-rights initiatives (the Civil Rights Act of 1964 and the Voting Rights Act of 1965), publicly funded medical programs for the poor and aged, and federal aid to education, housing, community development, and transportation (the heart of the War on Poverty). His foreign policy was marked by (another) military intervention in the Dominican Republic (1965), by negotiation of the Nuclear Non-Proliferation Treaty with the Soviet Union in 1968, and by another sharp escalation of the Vietnam War. A contrived attack on American naval vessels in the Gulf of Tonkin (near Hanoi/Haiphong) in 1964 provided the pretext for the very large commitment of ground troops to the War, for the bombing of North Vietnam, Da Nang, and Hue, for incendiary bombing throughout Vietnam, and for the commission of war atrocities (such as the 1968 massacre of unarmed civilians at My Lai). Increasing communist successes (most notably, the Tet offensive of 1968 in Saigon/Ho Chi Minh City and Hue), increasing American casualties and expenditures, and an American public increasingly skeptical of its government's credibility brought widespread social turmoil to the country (most notably, anti-war and anti-government riots in the cities and universities and political assassinations of prominent civil-rights and anti-war activists, Malcolm X [1925-65], the militant black separatist leader, in 1965, Reverend Martin Luther King, Jr. in 1968, and Senator Robert Francis Kennedy [1925-68], the former president's brother, in 1968).

President Johnson did not stand for re-election and had many of his social and economic welfare programs and his commitment to governmental enforcement of racial equality reversed by his immediate successors, Richard Milhous Nixon (1913-94; r. 1969-74) and Gerald Rudolph Ford (1913- ; r. 1974-77). Nixon achieved rapprochement with the People's Republic of China (which included "ping-pong diplomacy") in 1972; negotiated the Strategic Arms Limitations Talks I Treaty with the Soviet Union also in 1972; de-stabilized the elected, democratic socialist government of President Salvador Allende Gossens (1908-73; r. 1970-73 [assassinated]) in Chile in 1973 (a project that was moved by Allende's nationalization of industry and landed property, a project that resulted in the assassination of Allende, and a project that produced the installment of one of the most repressive military governments in the Americas, an elitist, pro-American government under General Augusto Pinochet [1915- ; r. 1973-90]); and at first attempted to decisively win the

Vietnam War, then attempted to end it. He ordered the illegal invasions of Cambodia (1970) and Laos (1971) and the saturation bombing of North Vietnam, suffered allegations of American duplicity throughout the War (most notably, in respect to the arranged disposal of Diem, the treachery of Tonkin Gulf, and the commission of numerous, concealed war atrocities), and (after a massive North Vietnamese offensive in 1972) negotiated a cease-fire agreement in Paris in 1973 by which all American troops were withdrawn from the country. The War itself ended in 1975 with the final victory of North over South Vietnam, the fall of Saigon/Ho Chi Minh City, and the communist reunification of the nation. More bomb tonnage had been dropped on Vietnam (and adjoining territory) by the United States than had been dropped by all combatants throughout the Second World War; c. 2.2 million Vietnamese had been killed (of which 1.5 million were civilians); and c. 58,000 American military had died. The most powerful nation in the world had been beaten by the vastly superior resolve of an impoverished and beleaguered people.

The political circumstances in Laos and Cambodia nonetheless remained unsettled. The protracted civil war in Laos between communist insurgents (the Pathet Lao), aided by the Vietminh, and the established monarchy began in the final years of the First Indo-China War (c. 1949-52), intensified in the early years of the Second Indo-China War (c.1962-64), and ended in the final years of the Second Indo-China War (1973-75) with the victory of the Pathet Lao. In Cambodia, which was (like Laos) increasingly implicated in the Vietnam War, the established monarchy, under King/Prime Minister Norodom Sihanouk (1922- ; r. 1941-55, 1960-70, 1975-76, 1991-), was deposed by a military coup led by General Lon Nol (1913-85; r. 1970-75) in 1970. Nol's government was, in turn, felled in 1975 by a combination of the efforts of exiled Sihanouk supporters and of the communist insurgency of the Khmer Rouge under Prime Minister Pol Pot (c. 1928-98; r. 1976-79). The Pot regime was among the most ruthless and unsuccessful governing agencies of world history. It attempted to transform the country into an agrarian collective and to that end made a peasant of virtually everyone, compelling millions into rural relocation and forced labor. It brutally imprisoned, tortured, and/or summarily executed anyone who so much as hinted at opposing it, effectively destroyed an already failing economy, produced endemic famine, and variously killed c. 3 million persons (the "killing fields"). Its border disputes with Vietnam in 1977-78 provoked a Vietnamese invasion in 1978-79 that ended its barbarous reign in 1979. Cambodia has since been governed by a pro-Vietnamese administration opposed to Pot and later by an uneasy coalition of communist, non-communist, and aristocratic (monarchical) interests. The other major nation in the immediate region, Thailand, was never formally colonized as has been said. After the Japanese occupation ended in 1945, the country came under the leadership of Chakri King Bhumipol Adulyadej/Rama IX (1927- ; r. 1946-), refined its constitutional monarchy, leaned to western orientations, was an American ally in the Vietnam War, passed through routine disputes with neighboring states, and vacillated between unsteady military and civilian governments.

Nixon's domestic record was neither enviable; his presidency was troubled by economic difficulties, by the youth rebellion, by a 1973 Native American Indian insurrection in South Dakota, and by widespread corruption. The Watergate scandal (1972-74), which entailed highly illegal political espionage, influence-peddling, and obstruction of justice, eventually did him in. He was impeached and resigned in 1974. Although several of his associates were put to prison, Nixon himself was pardoned by his successor, Gerald Ford, and he was never prosecuted for his leading role in one of the most insidious, known episodes of official misconduct in the history of the American republic. President Ford effectively continued Nixon's foreign policy initiatives and also, like Nixon, dealt unsuccessfully with inflationary and recessionary tendencies in the world economy.

The economic strife of the Nixon and Ford presidencies continued unresolved in the term of Ford's successor, James Earl "Jimmy" Carter (1924- ; r. 1977-81). President Carter's foreign policy was also of mixed effect:

- The (Panama) Canal Zone was returned by the United States to Panama (under General Omar Torrijos Herrera [1929-81; r. 1968-81]) in 1978-79; it came into full Panamanian control in 1999;
- A treaty between Israel and Egypt concerning territorial issues and Palestinian autonomy, the Camp David Accords, was negotiated under American supervision in 1979;
- In 1979, the American-supported, modernizing, but repressive, government of Muhammad Reza Shah Pahlevi (r. 1941-79) of Iran was deposed by a (Shiite) Islamic revolution under Ayatollah Rudollah Khomeni (1900-89; r. 1979-89); the new regime was anti-western and repressive; it presided over considerable social turmoil, a hostage crisis at the American embassy in Tehran (1979-81), and a ruinous war with (Sunni) Iraq over largely territorial issues (1980-88); and

- The American-inspired boycott of the 1980 Olympic Games in Moscow in protest of the Soviet invasion of Afghanistan in 1979 further heightened Cold War anxieties.

After President Carter left office, he became a widely respected advocate for the dispossessed and for world peace.

His immediate successors, Ronald Wilson Reagan (1911- ; r. 1981-89) and George Herbert Walker Bush (1924- ; r. 1989-93), were of a significantly different cast. Neither was impressed with the role of public institutions in social affairs and both were devoted to destroying the Soviet Union and any other nation that dared to oppose American corporate prerogatives. Enormous public debts were accumulated throughout the 1980s and recessionary tendencies also continued to haunt the decade (as well as the early 1990s). Anti-union practices of the government and pro-business fiscal policy further denuded working-class prerogatives. The privatization and globalization of the world economy began in earnest in the Reagan-Bush tenure; national restrictions on world trade were increasingly eliminated; the prerogatives of private, transnational corporations were increasingly appreciated; and the welfare of workers and the environment were increasingly discounted – all in broad accord with the free-trade views of American economist and 1976 Nobel laureate, Milton Friedman (1912-), and with the theoretical groundwork of such views provided by the likes of game theory, which explained human behavior as a mosaic of maximizing one's own prerogatives and minimizing the prerogatives of others in a non-cooperative environment (first developed by Hungarian-American mathematician, John von Neumann [1903-57]). Crime, incarceration, state-execution, and poverty rates increased as did zealous enforcement of drug-prohibition laws and the contraction of civil rights associated with such enforcement. The terms of Reagan and Bush were also characterized by near-routine foreign military interventions; most notably:

- the invasion of Cuban-aligned (1979-83) Grenada in 1983 which effectively killed the head-of-government, Prime Minister Maurice Rupert Bishop (1944-83; r. 1979-83) of Aruba and Grenada, and returned the island to American-dominated interests;
- the bombing of Libya in 1986 in retaliation for a terrorist attack on American interests later attributed to Syria;
- covert operations in Guatemala, Honduras, El Salvador, Nicaragua, and Haiti aimed at defeating revolutionary movements that were themselves devoted to toppling long-standing, oppressive, corrupt, foreign-dominated, elite (often military) oligarchies; of these movements, only the socialist insurrections in Nicaragua in 1979 and in Haiti in 1990 succeeded, if only briefly; the Nicaraguan insurrection was led principally by the revolutionary poet, Daniel Ortega Saavedra (1945- ; r. 1980-90), who had been imprisoned from 1967 to 1974 by the government he ousted, the government of Anastasio Somoza Debayle (1925-80 [assassinated]; r. 1967-72, 1974-79), son of Anastasio Somoza; it was defeated in 1989-90 by an American financed and directed counterrevolutionary effort that included the Iran-Contra scandal of 1986, a scandal which linked the Iranian hostage crisis and the illegal provision of arms to the counterrevolutionaries;
- the Haitian insurrection of 1990 which was led principally by Father Jean-Bertrand Aristide (1953- ; r. 1990-91, 1994-95) and which attempted to put an end to the grinding poverty of Haiti and to the plundering thievery of previous, recent governments; most tellingly, the governments of François "Papa Doc" Duvalier (1907-71; r. 1957-71) and his son, Jean-Claude "Baby Doc" Duvalier (1951- ; r. 1971-86); it was defeated in 1991 by a military coup likely connected to North American interests;
- the invasion of Panama in 1989-90 on highly specious and deeply suspicious grounds;
- the **Persian Gulf War** of 1991 in which the United States invaded Kuwait and Iraq in order to reverse Iraqi encroachment against Kuwait in 1990, in order to protect oil interests in the region, in order to test military alliances and new weapons systems in tangible combat circumstances, in order to punish the Iraqi leadership, under President Saddam Hussein (1937- ; r. 1979-), for its indiscretions in Kuwait and for its nationalistic, anti-American belligerence, and in order to discourage others from such belligerence; curiously, the Americans had supported and armed Iraq in its war against Iran (1980-88); the Persian Gulf War was very decisively won by the United States in fairly short order and it included the American destruction of an Iranian passenger jetliner and staggering civilian casualties; devastating American air strikes and economic sanctions against Iraq continued throughout what remained of the twentieth century; Moslem replies to American Middle Eastern policy in the Reagan-Bush years included the bombing of the American embassy and of military facilities in Lebanon in 1983 and 1984, of an American passenger jetliner in Scotland in 1988, and of the World Trade Center in New York City in 1993;

- the invasion of Somalia in 1992, ostensibly in order to resolve ongoing civil wars, in order to reestablish a central government, and in order to relieve the consequences of famine; and
- intervention in the Bosnian conflict in 1991.

The American campaign against eastern European communism in general and the Soviet Union in particular also came to significant success in the era of Reagan and Bush (1989-91).

The record of the most recent American chief executive, William Jefferson "Bill" Clinton (1946- ; r. 1993-), among the most brilliant and charming of American presidents, was profoundly ambivalent. It was characterized by several (mostly failed) attempts at progressive domestic reform (most importantly concerning universal medical care and social welfare), by broad (but not universal) economic prosperity, by a decline in crime rates but a substantial rise in incarceration rates, by several personal scandals (the implications of one of which brought impeachment in 1998 and acquittal in 1999), by several (mostly failed) attempts to achieve a Palestinian-Israeli peace agreement (most notably, the 1993 accords), by assistance with peace negotiations in Northern Ireland, by the 1993 Strategic Arms Reduction Talks II Treaty with Russia, and by a foreign policy little distinguished from that of his pugnacious predecessors. Drug-enforcement intervention, most significantly in Mexico, Colombia, Ecuador, Peru, and Bolivia, again thrust the country directly into military (and political) intrigues in Latin America. The bombing of Iraq (and economic sanctions against it) continued. The military-political conflict in Somalia continued and was abandoned unresolved in 1994 as the civil wars there went on. Military intervention in Haiti in 1994 reinstated the democratic socialist government of Father Aristide (r. 1990-91, 1994-95) for the ultimate purpose of restoring business-friendly order to the country under the leadership of someone other than Aristide. The Bosnian conflict was stabilized in 1995-96. Trade relations with Vietnam and the People's Republic of China were restored in 1995 and 2000 respectively. Sudan and Afghanistan were bombed in 1998 as retaliation for attacks on American embassies in Kenya and Tanzania. And Yugoslavia (including Belgrade) was bombed in 1999 in connection with the Kosovo crisis. Moslem replies to the Middle Eastern policy of the Clinton administrations included: the World Trade Center (New York City) bombing in 1993, bombings of American military installations in Saudi Arabia in 1995 and 1996, the American embassy bombings in Kenya and Tanzania in 1998, and the bombing of an American naval vessel in Aden/Yemen in 2000. Domestic terror in the Clinton era included the deadly government attack on a religious compound in Texas in 1993 and the also-deadly retaliatory bombing of a federal building in Oklahoma in 1995. The Clinton years too importantly included a further acceleration of the globalization process in respect to the world economy; many of the foremost trappings of this American-dominated process were established in these years: the North American Free Trade Agreement (NAFTA; 1994), the World Trade Organization (WTO; 1995), and the General Agreement on Tariffs and Trade (GATT; 1995).

The principal western European allies of the United States in the Second World War, Great Britain and France, likewise participated significantly in the Cold War and its economic and cultural consequences. In **Great Britain**, the conservative war government of Winston Churchill (r. 1940-45, 1951-55) was replaced by the progressive leadership of Clement Richard Attlee (1883-1967; r. 1945-51) in 1945. Attlee dealt with the economic strife of the immediate post-war years (mainly, heavy indebtedness, loss of capital, and currency devaluation) by nationalizing major industries and the national bank, by expanding social welfare programs, and by enacting austerity measures. The government of the country thereafter, not altogether unlike that of the United States, vacillated between conservative and liberal/progressive tendencies. This is roughly how many nations in the post-war period negotiated the territory between a necessary preservation of past and present realities (the conservative tendency) and attempts to improve the future prospects for more/most, if not all, people (the liberal tendency). Winston Churchill (r. 1940-45, 1951-55), Anthony Eden (1895-1977; r. 1955-57), (Maurice) Harold Macmillan (1894-1986; r. 1957-63), Alec Douglas-Home (1903-95; r. 1963-64), Edward Richard George Heath (1916- ; r. 1970-74), Margaret Thatcher (1925- ; r. 1979-90), and John Major (1943- ; r. 1990-97) led the conservative governments to the end of the century. (James) Harold Wilson (1916-95; r. 1964-70, 1974-76), James Callaghan (1912- ; r. 1976-79), and Anthony Charles Lynton "Tony" Blair (1953- ; r. 1997-) led the liberal governments to the end of the century. The British (Windsor) sovereign at the end of the century was Elizabeth II (1926- ; r. 1952-), who succeeded her father, George VI, to the throne in 1952. Great Britain became a nuclear nation in 1952 but has suffered economic strife since the Second World War and is no longer the most powerful nation in Europe, let alone the world.

With the pervasive wave of agitations for independence among national groups that had not earlier broken free of their colonial bonds and with the advent as well of neo-colonialism (in which foreign nations are controlled by indirect capital and trade manipulation), Great Britain also lost most of what remained of its once-vast colonial empire. In Mediterranean Europe, Malta achieved independence from Great Britain in 1964; Gibraltar remained in the British ambit. The dominions of the Commonwealth itself, Australia, Canada, Ireland, New Zealand, and South Africa, took increasingly independent courses, passed through customary conservative and liberal shifts of government, and inclined broadly, not unlike Britain itself, in the direction of social democratic welfare states. In **Northern Ireland**, however, a near civil war between the Catholic minority (represented by the Irish Republican Army) and the Protestant majority (represented by the Ulster Defense Association and Britain itself) evoked British military occupation in 1969 and direct British rule of the country in 1972-73. The peace accords of 1994 and 1998 diminished somewhat the sense of sectarian conflict that marks the society. In **South Africa**, the nationalist Afrikaners came to power in 1948, formally enacted strict laws of racial segregation and disenfranchisement (and their attendant discriminations), the laws of apartheid, pursued policies of extreme racial and political repression (such as the Sharpeville [near Johannesburg] massacre of 1960), and, in the 1970s and 1980s, established politically independent but horribly impoverished (and thus economically dependent) black homelands (mainly, Bophuthatswana, Transkei, Ciskei, and Venda). The Soweto (near Johannesburg) insurrection (and massacre) of 1976 and other acts of civil disobedience and non-cooperation, including boycotts and strikes (all directed most notably by the African National Congress, which had been established in 1912), together with international banking and trade sanctions, ended the nationalists' grip on the government and delivered governing authority to the majority in 1994. The brilliant and charismatic leader of the resistance movement in the country and the 1993 Nobel Peace co-laureate, Nelson Rolihlahla Mandela (1918- ;r. 1994-99), who had been imprisoned for 27 years (1962-90) by the nationalists, became the first majority head-of-state (president) and eliminated apartheid in 1994. Social unrest has nonetheless continued in the country, substantial economic improvements have been elusive, and South Africa suffers one of the most devastating AIDS epidemics in the world. An autonomy-inspired guerilla war against South African occupation of German Southwest Africa/Southwest Africa/Namibia (which had been going on in earnest from the 1970s), continuing demands from the United Nations to withdraw from the country, and the approaching end of the Afrikaner government in South Africa itself brought independence to Namibia in 1990.

Remaining British mandates over the nations of the **Middle East** also ended in the period since the Second World War. Political independence came to Transjordan/Jordan (under the Hashemite Dynasty of King Abdullah ibn Hussein [1882-1951; r. 1946-51 {assassinated}], brother of Faisal I of Syria and Iraq) in 1946, Kuwait (under the al-Sabah Dynasty) in 1961, Aden/Yemen in 1967, Bahrain in 1971, Oman in 1971, Qatar in 1971, and United Arab Emirates in 1971; all, except Aden/Yemen, as monarchies. Three of the Middle Eastern cases, however, were especially problematic: Cyprus, Egypt, and Palestine/Israel. Cyprus became independent in 1960 but was thereafter greatly troubled by disputes between its majority Greek and minority Turkish populations. It was originally governed by its first president, (Greek Eastern Orthodox) Archbishop Makarios III (1913-77; r. 1960-77), whose attempted conciliation of the Greek and Turkish communities failed. The civil war that resulted (1963-64) brought United Nations intervention in 1965, a Turkish invasion in 1974, and the formal partition of the country into a Turkish northern sector and a Greek southern sector also in 1974. The British mandate in Egypt had ended in 1936, as has been said, but British control of the Suez Canal Zone continued until Egyptian agitations encouraged British evacuation in 1954. The corrupt Egyptian monarchy under King Farouk I (r. 1936-52) was deposed in 1952 by a military coup d'état led by pan-Arab nationalist, Colonel Gamal Abdal Nasser (1918-70; r. 1954-70). Nasser became the first prime minister (1954) and president (1956) of the country, instituted land reform and ambitious economic development programs, aligned with both the Soviet Union and the United States, and nationalized the Suez Canal (1956). The nationalization of the Canal precipitated a brief British, French, and Israeli invasion (1956) that was quickly defused (in significant part by the diplomacy of the United Nations, the United States, and the Soviet Union) but that nonetheless disrupted the 1956 Olympic Games in Melbourne. Nasser played a pivotal role in the Arab-Israeli Wars of his generation. He was succeeded by 1978 Nobel Peace laureate, President Anwar al-Sadat (1918-81; r. 1970-81 [assassinated]), who also figured prominently in the Arab-Israeli conflicts of the time and in conciliatory, western-assisted efforts to end them.

Among the most intractable vestiges of British colonialism has concerned **Palestine/Israel**. The Balfour Declaration of 1917 had promised British support for a national Jewish homeland in Palestine as has been said. The British mandate over Palestine nonetheless continued until after the Second World War as has been also said. As Jewish immigration to the region increased after 1933, Arab resistance to Zionism in general and to a Jewish state in particular intensified and civil war resulted (1936-39). British attempts to satisfy both parties effectively failed and the issue was turned over to the United Nations Commission on Palestine in 1947. The Commission recommended partition, a proposal accepted by the Jewish community

243

but rejected by the Arab. When the British abandoned the mandate in 1948, the First Arab-Israeli War erupted (and an approximate half-century of virtually perpetual and formalized Arab-Israeli conflict began), the state of Israel was proclaimed under the leadership of David Ben-Gurion (1886-1973; r. 1948-53, 1955-63), and the new state was attacked by Egypt, Syria, Transjordan/Jordan, Lebanon, and Iraq. The 1948-49 war ended in Israeli victory and a United Nations sponsored armistice in 1949. The armistice effectively doubled the territory of the new country, partitioned Jerusalem, displaced and dispossessed c. 750,000 Palestinians, and awarded the West Bank of the Jordan River to Transjordan/Jordan and the Gaza Strip to Egypt. An enormous emigration of Jewish people from throughout the world to Israel followed and the country was developed through the establishment of a technological infrastructure, through large irrigation and forestation projects that reclaimed much of the desert, and through the formation of cooperative villages. In 1956, Israel (together with Great Britain and France) attacked Egypt (the Second Arab-Israeli War) in response to the Egyptian nationalization of the Suez Canal as has been said. The crisis was again mediated by the United Nations (among others), which occupied the Gaza Strip and the Sinai Peninsula. In 1967, the Third Arab-Israeli War, the Six-Day War, was fought over continuing military provocations among Israel, Egypt, Transjordan/Jordan, and Syria and resulted in another resounding Israeli success and Israeli occupation of the Sinai Peninsula (from Egypt), the Gaza Strip (from Egypt), the West Bank of the Jordan River (from Jordan), and the Golan Heights (from Syria). The Fourth Arab-Israeli War, the Yom Kippur War, of 1973-74 produced especially wide losses on both the Israeli and the Arab (Egypt, Syria, Iraq) sides but resulted in no territorial gains on either side. And the Fifth Arab-Israeli War of 1978-82 entailed Palestinian guerilla attacks from Lebanon on Israel, a measured Israeli invasion of Lebanon which established an occupied zone in southern Lebanon (adjacent to the Israeli border), and a massive Israeli invasion of Lebanon (to Beirut) that forced Palestinian guerillas from the country.

Most of the major Arab nations of the Middle East were significantly transformed by the establishment of Israel, by the perpetual conflict with Israel, by the inherent instabilities in the region that were greatly aggravated by contending western oil interests and contending Cold War ambitions, and by the imperatives of Arab life themselves in the decade-to-two-decade period immediately following the Second World War. These nations formed two alliance systems that assisted in maintaining non-aggression against one another and in encouraging political and military cooperation (at least in respect to their common opposition to Israel): the Arab League of 1945 and the Central Treaty Organization of 1955, both of which included most Moslem nations from Iran in the east to Morocco in the west. These nations also became independent of direct colonial rule either between the World Wars or since the Second World War. Egypt passed from a pro-western monarchy to an other-than-strictly-aligned, authoritarian, and ultra-nationalist parliamentary republic in 1952. Iraq too passed from a pro-western monarchy (under Faisal II [1935-58; r. 1939-58 {assassinated}], grandson of Faisal I) to an other-than-strictly-aligned and an authoritarian parliamentary republic in 1958; claimed Kuwait in 1961; encountered a near-continuous Kurdish (secessionist) insurrection from 1962; came under the control of the ultra-nationalist Baath Party (mainly directed by President Saddam Hussein [r. 1979-]) in 1963; endured a ruinous territorial war against Iran in 1980-88; and was the primary target of American invasion in the Persian Gulf War of 1991. Syria, conversely, had been customarily aligned with the Soviet Union but it also tended to an increasingly anti-western and authoritarian parliamentary republic (in 1961); came under the control of the ultra-nationalist Baath Party (mainly directed by President Hafez al-Assad [1928-2000; r. 1965-2000]) in 1963; and unsuccessfully supported Palestinian guerillas in Lebanon from 1976 to 1982. Libya, under Colonel Muammar al-Qadaffi (1942- ; r. 1969-), also passed from a pro-western monarchy (under Idris I [1890-1983; r. 1951-69]) to an increasingly anti-western, ultra-nationalist, and authoritarian parliamentary republic (in 1969) and has been the frequent target of American military, political, and economic attacks (most notably, the American bombing of Libya in 1986). Jordan continued its Hashemite monarchy under the grandson of Abdullah ibn Hussein, King Hussein I (1935-99; r. 1953-99); fought and won a brief civil war against Palestinian guerillas in Jordan in 1970-71 but in 1974 renounced its lingering claims to the West Bank in favor of a Palestinian state being established there; and has since attempted a moderate, non-aligned, but pro-Palestinian course in the region. Saudi Arabia continued the fundamentalist, Wahabite monarchy of Ibn Saud (r. 1912-53); the nation has been governed autocratically by sons of Ibn Saud since his death in 1953, has become one of the leading oil producers and among the wealthiest states in the world, has developed an industrial sector, has steered an increasingly moderate course in the international political affairs of the region, and has amassed one of the region's least commendable civil-rights records. Lebanon attempted a still more emphatically neutral path but was shaken by a Moslem rebellion against pro-western policies of the minority Christian government in 1958; endured an American military invasion to subdue the rebellion also in 1958; suffered grievously in a 1975-76 civil war between the conservative Christian and the revolutionary Moslem factions that dominated the political life of the country; was nearly destroyed by Syrian and Israeli attempts to decide the civil war in 1976-82, attempts that included the 1982 massacre of unarmed Palestinian civilians in the concentration camps of Sabra and Shatila (near Beirut); and has since attempted to rebuild itself, attempted a more moderate official course, but nonetheless suffered ongoing sectarian violence. The refugee Palestinians, principally under the Palestinian Liberation Organization (PLO), founded in 1964 and led, since 1969, by Chairman Yasir Arafat (1929- :r. 1969-), have been significantly dispossessed by Israel (and its western supporters, mainly the United States) and variously dispersed. They have also conducted a long and arduous campaign against the occupation/confiscation of their (entire) country; most notably in the form of the intifada, the overt insurrections of 1987-94 and 2000. This campaign has evoked ongoing Israeli reprisals, including assassinations, the bombing of civilian sectors, and the destruction of essential property.

There have been several serious attempts to resolve the disputes between Israel and the predominantly Moslem populations of the Middle East. These disputes center on, but are not limited to, the issue of an independent homeland for the Palestinian people and the status of Israeli settlements in so-termed occupied territories (mainly the West Bank and the Gaza Strip). The first major agreement was the Camp David Accords of 1979 between Israel (under Prime Minister Menachem Begin [1913-92; r. 1977-83]) and Egypt (under President Anwar al-Sadat [r. 1970-81]). The Accords were brokered by American President Carter; their promise won the 1978 Noble Peace Prize for Begin and Sadat; they provided for the return of the Sinai Peninsula to Egypt (formally achieved in 1982) and for the negotiation of Palestinian autonomy (unachieved); and they were widely condemned throughout the Moslem world (as providing ground for the Israeli invasion of Lebanon in 1978-82). Subsequent attempts – most notably, the Israeli-Palestinian accords of 1993, negotiated by Israeli Prime Minister and 1994 Nobel Peace co-laureate, Yitzhak Rabin (1922-95; r. 1974-77, 1992-95 [assassinated]), Palestinian Liberation Organization Chairman and 1994 Nobel Peace co-laureate, Yasir Arafat (r. 1969-), and American President Clinton – likewise failed to win a lasting peace in the region.

The twilight and conclusion of classical British colonialism in Asia, Oceania, Africa, and the Americas followed a similar pattern as it had in the Middle East. In **Asia**, the resolute movement for the independence of **India** was long-standing by the end of the Second World War as has been said. Non-violent agitations, inspired and directed mainly by Mahatma Gandhi and Jawaharlal Nehru (1889-1964; later, the [first] prime minister of India), won full Indian independence in 1947. Over the objections of Gandhi (who was murdered in 1948 owing to his tolerance for Moslems), the nation was partitioned in 1947 into two independent states, predominantly Moslem, Pakistan (distinguished by a western sector, West Pakistan, on the western reaches of the Indian sub-continent, and an eastern sector, East Bengal/East Pakistan, on the eastern reaches of the Indian sub-continent), and predominantly Hindu, India. Pakistan came under the leadership of Governor-General Muhammad Ali Jinnah (1876-1948; r. 1947-48), the principal architect of Pakistani independence. India came under the leadership of Prime Minister Nehru (r. 1947-64). Approximately one million persons died in the sectarian violence associated with partition; the India-Pakistan Wars of 1947-48, 1965-66, and 1971 were fought mainly over territorial disputes between the two countries (most notably, disputes over the status of Kashmir [in the north]), disputes that continued throughout what remained of the twentieth century. In 1971, East Pakistan declared its independence, as Bangladesh, from West Pakistan and (with Indian assistance) won the civil war that resulted; another approximately one million persons perished in this conflict. Pakistan, Bangladesh, and India have attempted to pursue a neutral (unaligned) course in international affairs; they have attempted industrial development with mixed results; India and Pakistan have developed nuclear weapons; and India and Bangladesh in particular have struggled with what are among the most intractable cases of poverty, famine, and squalor in the world, staggeringly deep cases which neither country has approached correcting. Pakistan and Bangladesh have been principally administered by an unstable series of authoritarian, military governments. India has been principally administered by a series of variously benign and authoritarian governments, led and dominated by wealthy elites; the world's largest "democracy" is among the least egalitarian societies in the world. Likely the most significant of these governments, after Nehru's largely benign tenure, was that of his daughter, Prime Minister Indira Gandhi (1917-84; r. 1966-67, 1980-84 [assassinated]), and that of her son, Prime Minister Rajiv Gandhi (1944-91 [assassinated]; r. 1984-89). Indira Gandhi was convicted of electoral fraud; suspended civil liberties; presided over monumental population growth, environmental degradation, poverty, labor strife, religious discord, and class violence; and was assassinated (because of her perceived attacks on Sikhism). Rajiv Gandhi succeeded his mother, governed to no very great effect, and was also assassinated (because of his opposition to the Tamil secession movement in Sri Lanka).

Elsewhere in Asia and in **Oceania**, independence from Great Britain was achieved by:
- Bhutan (as a monarchy) in 1947 (achieved independence from India in 1949);
- Burma/Myanmar in 1948;
- Ceylon/Sri Lanka in 1948 (has since encountered a secessionist movement by the Tamil minority);
- Malaysia in 1957 (came to include Sabah and Sarawak in northern Borneo in 1963);
- Singapore in 1959;
- Maldive Islands in 1965;
- Fiji in 1970;
- Tonga (as a monarchy) in 1970;
- Ellice Islands/Tuvalu in 1978;
- Gilbert Islands/Kiribati in 1979;
- New Hebrides Islands/Vanuatu (also from France) in 1980; and
- Brunei (as a monarchy) in 1984.

Great Britain returned Hong Kong to China/People's Republic of China in 1997. And four nations in the Pacific that had been administered since the early twentieth century by British Commonwealth dominions also won independence in the period since the Second World War: Western Samoa from New Zealand in 1962, Cook Islands (self-governing) from New Zealand in 1965, Nauru from Australia in 1968, and Papua New Guinea from Australia in 1975. Pitcairn Island has remained in the British ambit.

The retreat of British colonialism in Africa and the Americas was similarly dramatic. In **Africa**, anti-colonialism and African nationalism were the dominant themes of the Organization of African Unity (formed in 1963), which was instrumental in the success of independence movements throughout the continent. Since the Second World War, independence from Britain was achieved by:
- Eritrea in 1952; the British continued to administer Eritrea after the expulsion of the Italians from it and from Ethiopia in 1941; in 1952, Eritrea was effectively annexed by Ethiopia and in 1962 an open insurrection against Ethiopian feudalism (under American-supported, pan-African advocate, Emperor Haile Selassie [r. 1930-36, 1941-74]), began; Selassie was himself deposed in 1974, significantly over a 1964 conflict with Somalia, the Eritrean question, and the severe famine of the early 1970s; a military dictatorship (under Colonel Mengistu Haile Miriam [1937- ; r. 1974-91]), supported by the Soviet Union, was then installed; the economy was nationalized; political opposition was brutally suppressed; social chaos became endemic; a territorial war with Somalia again erupted in 1977-79; devastating famines reappeared (throughout the 1980s and early 1990s); economic collapse came in the early 1990s; and the Ethiopian war against Eritrean secession continued until it was lost (and full Eritrean independence was achieved) in 1993; more moderate governments have ruled Ethiopia since;
- Sudan in 1956; recurring famines and ruinous civil wars between the Moslem north and the animistic-Christian south (1955-72 and 1983-), which have claimed several million lives, followed; the instabilities and brutalities in Sudan, significantly under Colonel/President/Prime Minister Muhammad Gaafur al-Nimeiri (1930- ; r. 1969-85), have been among the most unsettling in post-colonial Africa;
- Gold Coast/Ghana (which had come to include British Togoland) in 1957; under Prime Minister/President Kwame Nkrumah (1909-72; r. 1957-66), Ghana was the first Black African state to gain political independence; the recent military administration of President Jerry Rawlings (1947- ; r. 1981-) has been among the most influential nationalist governments devoted to social welfare programs and to economic self-sufficiency on the continent;
- Nigeria in 1960; the country has been since greatly troubled by tribal and regional rivalries (most notably, the Biafran War of 1967-70, in which the unsuccessful secessionist movement of the southwest region produced several million deaths and lingering misery); it has been governed by a series of unstable and abusive civilian and military administrations; and it has become one of the most openly corrupt societies in the world;
- British Somaliland/Italian Somaliland/Somalia in 1960; the British continued to administer Somalia after the expulsion of the Italians in 1941; since independence, the country has variously danced between Soviet and American allegiances, conducted several unsuccessful territorial wars against Ethiopia (most notably, 1964 and 1977-79), descended into chaotic and devastating civil wars, and suffered an American military invasion in 1993;
- Cameroon in 1961;

- Sierra Leone in 1961; since independence, the country has been greatly troubled by political and economic instability and by civil unrest;
- German East Africa/Tanganyika/Tanzania in 1961; Tanzania merged with Zanzibar (which had become independent in 1963) in 1964; it came under the leadership of one of the most laudable figures in modern African political life, Julius Kambarage Nyerere (1922-99; r. 1961-85), who was a leading advocate of independence, who served as the nation's first prime minister and first president, who supported liberation and anti-fascist movements throughout east and south Africa, who unsuccessfully attempted to achieve economic self-sufficiency for Tanzania, and who resolutely aimed at achieving educational opportunity, equality, and justice for all persons;
- Uganda in 1962; under (Apollo) Milton Obote (1925- ; r. 1962-71, 1980-85), the nation's first prime minister and president, Uganda fell to autocracy; Obote was forced from power by one of the continent's least commendable figures, General Idi Amin (1925- ; r. 1971-79), an accomplished boxer, who deepened the established tendency to dictatorship and who presided over chaotic brutality, official terrorism, civil disorder, tribal warfare, and ethnic discrimination; Amin was himself forced from power (by the Tanzanian military) and Obote was restored to office in 1979-80; the circumstance since has been also disordered and unstable, made worse by the 1981-85 civil war (characterized by deep ethnic and factional conflict) and by one of the most devastating AIDS epidemics in the world;
- Kenya in 1963; the armed Mau Mau insurrection (1952-56) and other agitations brought independence under leading pan-African advocate, President Jomo Kenyatta (c. 1893-1978; r. 1964-78), who had been earlier implicated in the uprisings for independence and imprisoned (1953-59) for this involvement; Kenyatta's reign was run through with tribal conflict; it was followed by that of Daniel arap Moi (1924- ; r. 1978-), who presided over one of the most corrupt governments on the continent;
- Nyasaland/Malawi in 1964; under President Hastings Kamuzu Banda (c. 1902-97; r. 1966-97), Malawi became an autocratic, one-party state;
- Northern Rhodesia/Zambia in 1964; Zambia came under the autocratic and corrupt leadership of its foremost nationalist agitator for independence and its first president, Kenneth Kaunda (1924- ; r. 1964-91);
- Gambia in 1965;
- Southern Rhodesia/Rhodesia/Zimbabwe in 1965/1980; a white-supremacist, minority government, under Prime Minister Ian Douglas Smith (1919- ; r. 1964-79), proclaimed independence in 1965 over British and native black objections; a guerilla war ensued, led mainly by Robert Gabriel Mugabe (1924- ; r. 1980-), who had been imprisoned by the Smith regime from 1964 to 1974, who eventually won independence for the majority black government, as Zimbabwe, in 1980, and who became the new nation's first prime minister;
- Bechuanaland/Botswana in 1966; originally under its exceptional first president, Seretse Khama (1921-80; r. 1966-80), Botswana has become among the most moderate, stable, egalitarian, and peaceful nations on the continent;
- Basutoland/Lesotho (as a monarchy) in 1966;
- Mauritius in 1968;
- Swaziland (as a monarchy) in 1968; and
- Seychelles in 1976.

Saint Helena has remained in the British ambit.

In the **Americas**, independence from Great Britain was achieved by: Montserrat (self-governing) in 1960; Jamaica in 1962; Trinidad and Tobago in 1962; Barbados in 1966; British Guiana/Guyana in 1966; Saint Kitts-Nevis in 1967; Bermuda in 1968; Bahamas in 1973; Grenada in 1973; Dominica in 1978; Saint Lucia in 1979; Saint Vincent and the Grenadines in 1979; Antigua and Barbuda in 1981; and British Honduras/Belize in 1981. Anguilla, British Virgin Islands, Cayman Islands (which had been a dependency of Jamaica until 1962), and Turks and Caicos Islands (which had been also a dependency of Jamaica until 1962) have remained in the British ambit. British hegemony in the Falkland Islands/Malvinas Islands, which had been long-contested by Argentina, likewise continued; the Argentine occupation of the Islands in 1982 was defeated by the British later in the year.

In **France**, General Charles De Gaulle (r. 1945-46, 1958-69) became the principal political leader in the immediate post-war period. De Gaulle had been the leading figure in the French resistance during the War, was President of the provisional government in 1945-46, was Prime Minister at the end of the Fourth Republic (1946-58) in 1958, and became the first President of the Fifth Republic (1958-) in 1958 (-69). He presided variously over the persecution of German collaborators in the Vichy government, the nationalization of major industries, the decline in production and increase in public debt just past the War, the constitutional shifts from the provisional government to the Fourth and Fifth Republics, the development of the French nuclear deterrent in 1960, the political independence of many colonial possessions, the devastating war of Algerian independence, and severe worker-student demonstrations against his conservative policies in 1968. The Fourth Republic fell owing to severe economic instability, labor unrest, and the perceived failure of colonial policy (the First Indo-China War had ended badly for the French in 1954, the Algerian insurrection had begun in 1954, and the abortive invasion of Egypt, with Great Britain and Israel, over the nationalization of the Suez Canal occurred in 1956). Until the election of France's first democratic socialist president, François Maurice Mitterrand (1916-96; r. 1981-95), in 1981, the Fifth Republic was dominated by De Gaulle's sense of independence from American and British domination and by his elitism. Mitterrand was mainly devoted to the nationalization of banks and other industries and to the administrative decentralization of the government.

The **French colonial empire**, like the British, effectively ended after the Second World War. Except for the Algerian and Indo-Chinese cases, the demise of the empire was mostly negotiated without disabling military action. The Middle Eastern mandates over Syria and Lebanon ended in independence for both nations in 1944 and 1945 respectively. In the south Pacific, New Hebrides Islands/Vanuatu gained independence from France (and Great Britain) in 1980. In Africa, independence from France was achieved by:

- Morocco (also from Spain), as a monarchy, in 1956; under King Muhammad V (1910-61; r. 1957-61), the leading advocate of political independence, and his son, King Hassan II (1929-99; r. 1961-99), the country has tended to pro-western sympathies, has inclined to repressive rule, and has engaged in continuing border disputes with Spain, Algeria, and Mauritania over Spanish Sahara/Western Sahara;
- Tunisia in 1956; under President Habib Bourguiba (1903-2000; r. 1957-87), the leading advocate of political independence, the country became a moderate, if authoritarian, pro-western, Moslem republic;
- French West Africa/Guinea in 1958; under President Sékou Touré (1922-84; r. 1958-84), the country became an unaligned, one-party, socialist state;
- French West Africa/Dahomey/Benin in 1960;
- French West Africa/Upper Volta/Burkina Faso in 1960;
- French Equatorial Africa/Cameroon in 1960;
- French Equatorial Africa/Central African Republic in 1960; the country eventually fell under the brutal military dictatorship of Colonel Jean Bedel Bokassa (1921-96; r. 1966-79), who looted the place and massacred substantial numbers of its people;
- French Equatorial Africa/Chad in 1960; the country has been among the least stable on the continent and has been dominated by conflicts between the Moslem north and the African south;
- French Equatorial Africa/French Congo/Middle Congo/Republic of the Congo/People's Republic of the Congo/Republic of the Congo; the country has been governed mainly by socialist military administrations; most notably, that of Colonel Denis Sassou-Nguesso (c. 1943- ; r. 1979-92, 1997-);
- French Equatorial Africa/Gabon in 1960;
- French West Africa/Ivory Coast/Côte d'Ivoire in 1960; under President Felix Houphouet-Boigny (1905-93; r. 1960-93), the leading advocate of political independence, the country became a one-party state and has pursued a characteristically independent course in African affairs;
- Malagasy Republic/Madagascar in 1960;
- French West Africa/Mali in 1960; the country has been routinely troubled by severe droughts and by the economic and social turmoil caused by such droughts;
- French West Africa/Mauritania in 1960; the country has been greatly affected by Moslem-African conflict, by severe droughts, and by its contestation, with Spain, Morocco, and Algeria, of Spanish Sahara/Western Sahara (which it abandoned in 1979);
- French West Africa/Niger in 1960; the country has been routinely troubled by severe droughts and by the economic and social turmoil caused by such droughts;
- French West Africa/Senegal in 1960; under President Léopold Sédar Senghor (1906- ; r. 1960-81), the leading advocate of political and cultural independence and a renowned poet, the country suffered severe drought, economic instability, and civil unrest;

- French West Africa/Togoland/Togo in 1960; the country eventually fell under the leadership of Colonel Étienne Gnassingbe Eyadema (1937- ; r. 1967-), who has become arguably the most influential statesman in west Africa;
- Algeria in 1962; the struggle for **Algerian independence** (1954-62) was long and violent; on independence, it became a one-party, socialist state under the leading advocate of political and cultural independence, Prime Minister Ahmed Ben Bella (c. 1919- ; r. 1962-65), who was deposed in 1965 and imprisoned from 1965 to 1980; since independence, the country has suffered routine sectarian conflict and civil unrest, has pursued an unaligned, nationalist tendency, and has supported the political independence of Spanish Sahara/Western Sahara against Spanish, Moroccan, and Mauritanian claims over the region;
- Comoros in 1975; and
- French Somaliland/Djibouti in 1977.

The struggle for **Indo-Chinese independence** was the most intractable of the French colonial cases. Vietnam and Cambodia declared themselves independent after the Japanese occupation of southeast Asia ended in 1945. Following brief occupations of North Vietnam (centered in Hanoi) by China and of South Vietnam (centered in Saigon/Ho Chi Minh City) by Great Britain (1945-46), however, the French attempted to reassert control over the country, to again install Emperor Bao Dai (1913-97; r. 1926-45, 1949-55) as the head-of-state, and to deny political leadership to the leading advocate of national liberation, the head of the principal movement for national liberation (the Vietminh, established in 1941), and the Communist Party Chair/President, Ho Chi Minh (1890-1969; r. 1954-69). Bao Dai had collaborated with the French and the Japanese throughout their tenures in the country; Ho was opposed to foreign domination and was also the presumed and the favored heir to political authority in Vietnam. The conflict resulted in the First Indo-China War/French Indo-China War/Franco-Vietnam War (1946-54), which ended in the independence of Cambodia and Laos in 1953 and in French defeat at the Battle of Dien Bien Phu (near the northwest border with Laos) in 1954. The treaty that formalized the conclusion of hostilities, the Geneva Treaty, ended the French colonial regime in Indo-China, established the sovereign (independent) state of Vietnam, partitioned Vietnam into a communist northern sector (North Vietnam under Ho) and a so-termed nationalist southern sector (South Vietnam), and ordered free elections in South Vietnam to decide its final status (i.e., its presumed reunification with North Vietnam). When the American puppet-regime of South Vietnamese President Ngo Dinh Diem (r.1955-63) refused to hold the elections (which the communists were very likely to have won) and declared South Vietnam independent of North Vietnam, the war to liberate Vietnam from the United States, the Second Indo-China War/Vietnam War/American War (1957-75), began as has been said. The remaining French colonial possessions – French Guiana, French Polynesia/Tahiti, Guadeloupe, Martinique, New Caledonia, Réunion, and Saint Martin – have continued in the French ambit.

Elsewhere in western Europe (as in Great Britain and France), there developed a drift to economic, political, and military integration-solidarity. This tendency was set off most significantly by the American-directed Marshall Plan (European Recovery Program) of 1947-51 and it was advanced most notably by the establishment of the North Atlantic Treaty Organization (NATO), which included the United States and Canada, in 1949 and by the establishment of the European-inspired European Economic Community/European Union in 1957. The inclination to solidarity was most effective in respect to economic issues; that is, in respect to customs/tariffs, trade, energy, currency, and prices.

In southern Europe, Spain, Andorra, Portugal, Italy, Vatican, Switzerland, Liechtenstein, Austria, Greece, and Turkey all passed through noteworthy transformations. The independent principality of Monaco under the Grimaldi Dynasty (from 1297) and the independent republic of San Marino (from 1243) under a democratic system of parliamentary rule continued largely unchanged. **Spain** was significantly isolated from other western European nations throughout what remained of the regime of General Francisco Franco (r. 1939-75) after the War. The last of the major European (and Asian) fascist states effectively died with Franco in 1975. The (Spanish) Bourbon monarchy was restored (from 1931) in 1975 under the grandson of King Alfonso XIII, Juan Carlos I (1938- ; r. 1975-). King Juan Carlos I and (socialist) Prime Minister Marquez Felipe Gonzalez (1942- ; r. 1982-96) were most responsible for directing the country from the dictatorship of Franco to a constitutional monarchy and a parliamentary democracy; they were likewise most responsible for dealing with protracted Basque (in the north-central region) and Catalan (in the northeast region) separatist agitations. The Spanish colonial empire, not unlike the British and French, was also further diminished in the period since the Second World War. Morocco gained independence (too from France) in 1956, Spanish Guinea/Rio Muni/Equatorial Guinea gained independence in 1968, and claims over Spanish Sahara/Western Sahara[128] were relinquished in 1976; only the Canary Islands have remained in the Spanish ambit. The independent principality of Andorra (effectively from 1289), once governed by Spanish (and French) nobles, became a constitutional democracy in 1993.

Portugal has been among the least stable nations of western Europe since the Second World War. The struggles between conservative rightism and progressive leftism impressed themselves with special acuity on Portugal. Like Great Britain, France, and Spain, it too relinquished nearly all that remained of its colonial empire in this period. Independence from Portugal was achieved by mostly violent means; it nonetheless came to Guinea-Bissau in 1973, Angola in 1975, Cape Verde Islands in 1975, Mozambique in 1975, and Sao Tome e Principe in 1975. (Portuguese) East Timor was annexed by Indonesia in 1975-76 and became independent in 1999. Portugal returned Macao to China/People's Republic of China in 1999. Only the Azore Islands have remained in the Portuguese ambit. The former Portuguese colonies were left in especially desperate straits at independence; political instability (often entailing rapacious civil conflicts such as the Cold War contests between Soviet-supported and American-supported factions in Angola and Mozambique) and economic desolation were rife.

Italy has also passed through great political inconstancy in the period since the Second World War. The last (Savoy) king of Italy, Humbert II (1904-83; r. 1946), son of Victor Emmanuel III, was deposed at the establishment of a republic, mainly under Prime Minister Alcide de Gasperi (1881-1954; r. 1945-53), in 1946; Humbert II was succeeded by numerous governments of variously liberal, conservative, and centrist types as well as by numerous political assassinations and shifts of economic fortune and misfortune. As has been said, the Italian annexation of Abyssinia/Ethiopia, Eritrea, and Italian Somaliland/Somalia ended in 1941; the Italian occupation of Albania, in 1944; and Italian colonial prerogatives over Libya, in 1943. Libya became independent in 1951. After the death of the wartime pope, Pius XII (r. 1939-58), in 1958, the papacy developed a notably larger concern for church reform, world peace, and social welfare (the eradication of hunger, poverty, and injustice). Under John XXIII (1881-1963; r. 1958-63), Paul VI (1897-1978; r. 1963-78), John Paul I (1912-78; r. 1978), and John Paul II (1920- ; r. 1978-), the Vatican also turned to a more ecumenical attitude concerning world religious ideologies and institutions.

Elsewhere in southern Europe, Switzerland maintained its constitutional democracy and its strict neutrality during and after the War; it has become the banking, industrial, charitable, and scientific center of the continent. The independent principality of Liechtenstein has become very closely allied to Switzerland and has continued to flourish as a constitutional monarchy. Austria was liberated from Germany by the Allies in 1945; it nationalized major industries shortly thereafter; it was occupied by the Allies from 1945 to 1955, when it became a sovereign republic; and it has since become among the most stable and prosperous nations of Europe, mainly under (socialist) Chancellor Bruno Kreisky (1911-90; r. 1970-83). In Greece, conversely, the political turmoil of the inter-war period continued after the Second World War. After the civil war of 1946-49, between Soviet-supported communist and (victorious) American-supported royalist factions, the country vacillated among civilian, military, and monarchical governments, all conservative and all pro-western. The monarchy, under King Constantine II (1940- ; r. 1964-73), great-grandson of George I and Olympic yacht champion, was abolished in 1973. The Turkish occupation of northern Cyprus in 1974 resulted in the formal partition of the nation as has been said. And the reform administration of Greece's first socialist government, under Prime Minister Andreas Papandreou (1919-96; r. 1981-89, 1993-96), finally brought an evening stability to the country. Turkey has also passed through enormous political turmoil and economic instability since the Second World War. Its conflicts with Greece (mainly over Cyprus) and its unenviable record dealing with minority Armenian and Kurdish populations continued; it too was variously administered by conservative military and civilian governments; and it likewise inclined to pro-western, anti-Soviet allegiances.

In north-central Europe, the **Low Countries**, Netherlands and Belgium mainly, recovered quickly from the War despite enormous destruction, restored their constitutional monarchies/democracies, tended to major industrialization efforts and to domestic social-welfare reform (principally aid to the poor), inclined to integration with the larger European community, and lost their remaining colonial possessions. Queen Wilhelmina (r. 1890-48) resumed the Dutch throne, was succeeded by her daughter, Queen Juliana (1909- ; r. 1948-80), and Juliana, in turn, by her daughter, Queen Beatrix (1938- ; r. 1980-), all without disabling incident. The son and successor of King Albert I, King Leopold III (1901-83; r. 1934-51), who had surrendered Belgium to the Germans at the beginning of the War and was accused of collaborating with them, conversely, reclaimed the Belgian throne under extreme duress; he was exiled to Switzerland (1945-50) and abdicated in favor of his son, King Baudouin (1930-93; r. 1951-93), in 1951; Baudouin was succeeded, in turn, by his brother, King Albert II (1934- ; r. 1993-), in 1993. Netherlands has become among the most prosperous, best educated, and most peaceful nations in the world. Belgium has suffered numerous ethnic disruptions between the Flemish north and the French south. The independent duchy of Luxembourg has continued to flourish under the Nassau Dynasty. The colonial empires of both Netherlands and Belgium ended in the period since the Second World War. The Dutch East Indies/Indonesia declared its independence from Netherlands in 1945; it formally achieved its long-sought independence in 1949 after a several-year war with the Dutch (1946-49). Largely under dictatorial, communist-tending President Achmed Sukarno (r. 1945-66) and his successor, dictatorial, right-tending General/President Suharto (1921- ; r. 1966-98), post-independence Indonesia passed through enormous turmoil: routine inefficiency, corruption, repression, and social chaos; the 1965 massacre of communist insurgents; the 1975-76 annexation (from Portugal) and torture of East Timor; and the 1999 independence of East Timor from Indonesia. Dutch Guiana/Suriname won independence from Netherlands in 1975; Sint Maarten and the (southern) Netherlands Antilles (Aruba, Bonaire, and Curacao) became self-governing in 1954 but have remained otherwise in the Dutch ambit; Aruba separated from the other islands of the Netherlands Antilles in 1986. The struggle for independence among Belgian colonies left a still more problematic and a still less edifying result. The most severe of these struggles occurred in the Belgian Congo/Democratic Republic of the Congo/Zaire/Democratic Republic of the Congo which gained independence in 1960 after the 1959 Leopoldville/Kinshasa insurrection and a long nationalist campaign led mainly by (future) President Joseph Kasavubu (c. 1917-69; r. 1960-65) and by (future) Prime Minister, Patrice Emergy Lumumba (1925-61; r. 1960-61 [murdered]). The ethnic and provincial chaos that followed, known as the Congo Crisis (1960-65), entailed the secession of the country's principal mining region, Katanga/Shaba Province (in the southeast) in 1960, a consequent civil war (1960-63) in which Belgian forces supported the secessionist side for largely economic reasons, an agreement brokered by the United Nations which ended the secessionist movement and the civil war in 1963, and the coup d'état that brought Colonel/President Joseph Désiré Mobutu/Mobutu Sese Seko (1930-97; r. 1965-97) to head-of-state in 1965. Mobutu's regime became among the most openly corrupt in the world; it systematically looted the treasury of the country, failed to develop Zaire's infrastructure despite favorable resources and opportunities, and failed as well to limit the execrable human-rights violations of its own military. The other remaining Belgian colonies, Burundi and Rwanda, both achieved independence in 1962 and both also, not unlike Zaire, descended into ethnic butchery (mainly the slaughter of Hutu by the dominant Tutsi minority in Burundi in 1972, 1988, and 1993 and the slaughter of Tutsi by the dominant Hutu majority in Rwanda in 1994, conflicts which claimed at least one million lives).

In **Scandinavian northern Europe**, recovery from the War was astonishingly rapid; vital market economies were quickly resumed; the tendency to pan-Scandinavianism deepened; the development of socialist democracy and the egalitarian, social-welfare, and progressive orientations entailed by socialist democracy continued; and broad organic inclinations made the nations of Scandinavia among the most decent, most edifyingly purposeful, best educated, and most prosperous in the world. Unsurprisingly, the Swedish, Norwegian, and Danish crowns became largely ceremonial distinctions in the larger context of constitutional democracy. The Swedish throne was occupied in this time by Gustavus V (r. 1907-50), son of Oscar II, by Gustavus VI (1882-1973; r. 1950-73), son of Gustavus V and himself an accomplished scientific scholar, and by Charles XVI Gustavus (1946- ; r. 1973-), grandson of Gustavus VI. The leading political figure in post-war Swedish (and Scandinavian) life, however, was (socialist) Prime Minister Olof Palme (1927-86; r. 1969-76, 1982-86 [assassinated]), who supported national liberation (anti-colonial) movements throughout the world, condemned superpower interventions in the Third World, and promoted disarmament programs in all heavily armed nations. The Norwegian throne was occupied in this time by Haakon VII (r. 1905-57), son of Frederick VIII of Denmark, by Olaf V (1903-91; r. 1957-91), son of Haakon VII, and by Harald V (1937- ; r. 1991-), son of Olaf V and an Olympic yachtsman. And the Danish throne was occupied in this time by Christian X (r. 1912-47), son of Frederick VIII, by Frederick IX (1899-1972; r. 1947-72), son of Christian X, and by Margaret II (1940- ; r. 1972-), daughter of Frederick IX. Finland variously repelled both German and Soviet attempts to dominate it during and after the War; it was led mainly by (centrist) Prime Minister/President Urho Kaleva Kekkonen (1900-86; r. 1950-81). Iceland declared and achieved full independence from Denmark in 1944. And Greenland became self-governing in 1979 but remained otherwise in the Danish ambit.

The nation in which the Soviet-American, Cold War rivalry was most profoundly and most troublingly expressed was **Germany**, itself of course at the epicenter of the storm in both World Wars. The German question remained unresolved in the immediate post-war environment. The Potsdam Agreement of 1945 (struck by the leading Allies in the War itself, the United States [Truman], the Soviet Union [Stalin], and Great Britain [Churchill and Attlee]) formalized earlier provisions of the Yalta Conference (1945). It attempted most importantly to flesh out the basic principles of post-war German development: elimination of German

251

nationalism, militarism, and fascism; Allied control of industry for the main purpose of increasing production (significantly by means of forced labor) and planning an economy favorable to the Allies; payment of war reparations; conduct of tribunals for Axis war criminals (Nuremberg Trials, 1945-46); formation of new political parties; enactment of land reform (including confiscation of property without compensation), constitutional revision, and currency reform; and the partition of the country into zones of Allied occupation (governing authority was to be exercised by the United States, the Soviet Union, Great Britain, and France). Execution of the Agreement was uneven, however, and the mutual antagonisms and suspicions between the United States and the Soviet Union brought routine breaches of it. The Soviets, alarmed by western currency reform and eager to evict western powers from the eastern sector of Germany, ordered a blockade of West Berlin in 1948-49, an act thwarted by a massive Allied airlift. A western German government, the Federal Republic of Germany/West Germany (centered in Bonn, near Cologne), the Second Republic, was established in 1948-49 under President/Chancellor Konrad Adenauer (1876-1967; r. 1948-63). Under Adenauer's right-tending administration, West Germany began its economic reintegration with western Europe (mainly by developing trade unions, full employment, state agricultural and industrial subsidies, and welfare reform) and began as well its spectacular economic rebirth; well before the end of the century, it was among the best educated, most productive, and most prosperous nations in the world. Also under Adenauer's leadership, West Germany made steady progress toward national sovereignty; foreign occupation (1945-52) was gradually withdrawn and full independence was achieved in 1955. The Soviet-occupied sector of the country too formed a new government, the German Democratic Republic/East Germany (centered in East Berlin), in 1949. Mainly under Communist Party Chairman/President Walter Ulbricht (1893-1973; r. 1950-73) and Communist Party leader, Erich Honecker (1912-94; r. 1971-89), East Germany adopted a Soviet-style government and economy (a communist government and a planned economy) but it never approached the productivity or the prosperity of West Germany. The administration of Ulbricht dealt brutally with a workers' insurrection in 1953, an act which encouraged wide East German emigration to western Europe and greatly disappointed reunification efforts (which had been a major objective of Adenauer, who was openly hostile to the partition of the country). The Berlin Wall was erected by the Ulbricht government in 1961 in order to curtail desertions and to impede a western attack. Honecker, who had been imprisoned by the fascists from 1935 to 1945, presided over the political repressions and the industrial gains of the 1970s and 1980s. The Berlin Wall and the East German government were effectively dismantled at the end of the Honecker regime in 1989. The West German economy leapt further forward under Chancellors Ludwig Erhard (1897-1977; r. 1963-66), Kurt Georg Kiesinger (1904-88; r. 1966-69), Willy Brandt/Herbert Ernst Karl Frahn (1913-93; r. 1969-74), Helmut Schmidt (1918- ; r. 1974-82), and Helmut Kohl (1930- ; r. 1982-98). The conservative governments of Erhard and Kiesinger established diplomatic relations with Israel in 1965-66. The social democratic governments of the great Brandt, an ardent anti-fascist and the 1971 Nobel Peace laureate, and of Schmidt in particular, while favoring the reunification of the country, nonetheless softened relations notably with East Germany and the Soviet Union. It was in the right-tending administration of Kohl, however, that the Soviet Union came undone, that the Berlin Wall was dismantled (1989), and that the German state was reunified in accord with West German political, economic, and cultural orientations (1990). Kohl's government was succeeded by the liberal administration of Chancellor Gerhard Schroeder (1944- ; r. 1998-) in 1998.

The **Soviet Union**, the principal adversary of the United States in the geo-political life of the Cold War (most notably, in Germany and Korea, but in some telling sense virtually throughout the world), had contributed centrally to the Allied victory in the Second World War, principally by way of military advances into central Europe (Poland, Germany, Austria, and the Balkans) and by way of its invasion of Manchuria and Korea. It nonetheless recovered less rapidly from the War than western European states. The planned, demand-side form of economic organization increasingly prominent throughout eastern Europe, the wide devastation suffered by the Soviet Union in the War (approximately two-fifths of all casualties were Soviet), and the antipathy of western nations were most responsible. The immediate post-war years continued to be dominated by the utterly authoritarian personality and administration of Joseph Stalin (r. 1924-53); by the continuing collectivization of agriculture, development of heavy industry (including armaments), and implementation of construction projects; by the ongoing reign of terror, use of forced labor, and economic exploitation of domestic and foreign workers; by the establishment of Soviet military bases in foreign territories; by the 1948 Yugoslavian defection; by the unsuccessful Soviet blockade of West Berlin in 1948-49; by the development of nuclear weapons in 1949; and by Soviet support of North Korea in the Korean War (1950-53). Formalization of the Soviet systems of alliance and the Soviet satellite system is also owed to this period. The principal economic alliance of eastern European nations (the approximate equivalent of the European Economic Community [EEC] in western Europe), the Council for Mutual Economic Assistance

(COMECON), was established in 1949. The principal political and military alliance of eastern European nations (the approximate equivalent of the North Atlantic Treaty Organization in western Europe), the Warsaw Pact, was established in 1955. The Soviet sphere of dominant European influence (the satellite system) had been effectively endorsed by Roosevelt, Churchill, and Stalin at the Tehran Conference of 1943 and the Yalta Conference of 1945. This sphere originally included all of the nations that bordered the Soviet Union to the west (except Finland and Norway) – that is, Poland, Czechoslovakia, Hungary, and Romania – as well as East Germany, Bulgaria, Yugoslavia, and Albania. The expansion of Soviet power in eastern Europe entailed the military occupation and militarization of the region, nationalization of industry, collectivization of agriculture, broad economic planning, opposition to organized religion, and suppression of political competition, all on the Soviet model. The satellite system led eventually, however, to a fracture of Communist Party unity, first in Yugoslavia, then elsewhere; it led also eventually to the isolation of the Soviet Union in foreign affairs; and it contributed eventually to a structural crisis in Soviet economic life.

Stalin died in 1953 and the monolithic dogmatism and brutality that had characterized his regime began to die with him. The country became slightly more diverse in political terms, gave some attention to consumer goods, improved peasant life on the collective farms, moderated the severity and the arbitrary nature of penal justice, improved standards of living, and widened its commitment to educational development. The leadership of the country passed mainly to the new leader of the Communist Party/Premier Nikita Sergeyevich Khrushchev (1894-1971; r. 1953/1958-64), Foreign Minister Vyacheslav Mikhailovich Molotov (1890-1986; r. 1939-49, 1953-56), Premier Georgi Maksimilianovich Malenkov (1902-88; r. 1953-55), and Premier Nikolai Aleksandrovich Bulganin (1895-1975; r. 1955-58). Of these, Molotov and Khrushchev had the greatest influence. Molotov had contributed significantly to the establishment of the United Nations and, in 1947, formulated the Soviet equivalent of the Truman Doctrine, the Molotov Plan, which stipulated the terms in which capitalist expansion was to be contained and Soviet interests were to be extended. Khrushchev effectively presided over the 1956 uprisings in Poland and Hungary; the enormous early successes of Soviet space technology, space exploration, and armament production; the 1960 conflict with the United States concerning American espionage flights in Soviet airspace; the 1961 construction of the Berlin Wall by the East German government (with Soviet approval); the 1961-68 Albanian defection; the 1962 Cuban Missile Crisis; the 1963 Nuclear Test Ban Treaty with the United States; and the 1959-64 ideological rift with the People's Republic of China. The Soviets had favored nuclear-testing treaties and peaceful coexistence with western nations, surmising that economic competition would eventually undo the capitalist juggernaut; the Chinese were opposed to such treaties and favored armed struggle with western interests. Owing mainly to the Cuban and Chinese conflicts, Khrushchev was removed from office in 1964. The Soviet leadership since has continued to struggle with the vestiges of Stalinism, with periodic tumbles in agricultural and industrial production, with further breaches in the unity of world communism, and with hostilities with western societies.

At Khrushchev's political demise, Leonid Ilyich Brezhnev (1906-82; r. 1964-82) became the new leader of the Communist Party and Aleksei Nikolayevich Kosygin (1904-80; r. 1964-80) became Premier. Together, they dealt with ongoing conflicts with the People's Republic of China, supported the Arab cause against Israel and also other liberation movements in the Third World, opposed the American intervention in Vietnam, negotiated the 1968 Nuclear Non-Proliferation Treaty and the 1972 Strategic Arms Limitations Talks I Treaty with the United States, opposed the 1968 Czechoslovakian insurrection, invaded Afghanistan in 1979, and imposed martial law in Poland in 1981-83. The decade of the 1980s was among the most turbulent and transformative in Soviet history. Brezhnev was succeeded by Communist Party Chairmen Yuri Vladimirovich Andropov (1914-84; r. 1982-84) and Konstantin Ustinovich Chernenko (1911-85; r. 1984-85). Andropov presided over the 1983 destruction of a Korean passenger jetliner that had strayed into Soviet airspace; Chernenko, over the 1984 Soviet boycott of the Olympic Games in Los Angeles. The war in Afghanistan and the virulent anti-communism of American President Reagan brought détente with western nations to its lowest level since the 1950s. The Soviet economy, greatly taxed by the deepening failures in Afghanistan and unable to keep pace with western (mainly American) production of armaments (as well as western, mainly American, threats to use them), was severely strained and about to fail when Mikhail Sergeyevich Gorbachev (1931- ; r. 1985-91), the 1990 Nobel Peace laureate, became Communist Party Chairman and Premier in 1985. Gorbachev attempted to re-structure the Soviet economy (perestroika) in order to increase production of consumer goods and to improve the quality of all goods; he attempted also to open more fully the Soviet political system (glasnost) in order to better account for the prerogatives of the individual person. This attempt to liberalize the country and to restore its status as a leading world power failed; the result was a measure of rapprochement with the People's Republic of China in 1989, an end to the disastrous war in Afghanistan in 1989, the effective demise of the Soviet satellite system in 1989 (i.e., the dismantling of the Berlin Wall and of the hold of the Soviet Union over eastern European states), and the disassembly of the Soviet Union itself in 1990-91.

The **Afghan-Soviet War** (1979-89) was presaged by the overthrow of the Afghan monarchy (the Durani Dynasty, 1747-1973) in 1973. The government that resulted was itself undone by a Soviet-backed coup in 1978 and this, in turn, by a nationalist coup in 1979. The Soviet Union invaded the country in 1979 and installed another communist government. Despite colossal technological advantages which brought wide devastation to Afghanistan, the guerilla forces of the Mujaheddin (a coalition of Afghan and foreign Moslem insurgents aided mainly by the United States of America, the People's Republic of China, and Saudi Arabia) prevailed in a rapacious conflict that claimed c. one million Afghan and c. 15,000 Soviet lives over ten years. As in the case of the Vietnam War, an utterly impoverished and thoroughly beleaguered, but enormously resolute, people had sent one of the two most imposing military juggernauts on the planet packing. The War nonetheless left Afghanistan with staggering political, economic, and ecological problems, problems, which when put with the long-standing tribal, ethnic, and religious divisions of the country, brought ongoing civil conflict after the War with the Soviets and a deeply fundamentalist Moslem government, under the Taliban (selective remnants of the Mujaheddin), to power in 1996.

The fifteen **Soviet republics** – Armenia, Azerbaijan, Belarus, Estonia, Georgia, Kazakhstan, Kirgyzstan, Latvia, Lithuania, Moldova, Russia, Tajikistan, Turkmenistan, Ukraine, and Uzbekistan – became independent states in 1990-91. Some engaged in armed struggle with the Soviet Union for their sovereignty (e.g., Lithuania), others not (e.g., Ukraine); some remained closely aligned with Russia (e.g., Belarus), others not (e.g., Estonia); most attempted, with very mixed results, to develop pluralistic (multi-party) political systems, market economies, and western-style cultures. Russia itself, the largest and most influential of the republics, came under the leadership of President Boris Nikolayevich Yeltsin (1931- ; r. 1991-99) and Prime Minister/President Vladimir V. Putin (1952- ; r. 1999-); negotiated the Strategic Arms Reduction Talks II Treaty with the United States in 1993; framed a new constitution in 1993; prosecuted a convulsive civil war against a separatist movement in Chechnya (1994-96, 2000-); and flirted with economic ruin. In particular, Putin, an accomplished wrestler, attempted to eradicate corruption and to institute further market and democratic reforms, all to very mixed effect.

The **Soviet satellite system in eastern Europe** too collapsed in 1989 as has been said; this, owing largely to the same political and economic transformations that felled the Soviet Union itself. Yugoslavia and Albania had nonetheless successfully withdrawn from the Soviet sphere notably earlier. In 1948, under Marshal/Prime Minister/President Josip Broz Tito (r. 1945-80), the leading figure in the resistance movement against German occupation during the Second World War, Yugoslavia abolished its Karadjordjevic monarchy, then under King Peter II (1923-70; r. 1934-41/45), son of Alexander I, broke with the Soviet Union, pursued a more moderate economic course than Moscow but the same approximate political orientation in domestic terms, and chose an unaligned alternative in foreign affairs. Agitations for political autonomy among Yugoslavia's six republics – Croatia, Slovenia, Macedonia, Bosnia-Herzegovina, Serbia, and Montenegro – intensified in the late 1960s and again following Tito's death in 1980. When the cohesion of eastern European communism came largely undone in 1989, these essentially ethnic agitations eventually brought national independence to Croatia, Slovenia, and Macedonia in 1991. The Croatian and Slovenian insurrections were overtly opposed by the Yugoslav (Serbian) government, under (nationalist-communist) Serbian-Yugoslav President Slobodan Milosevic (1941- ; r. 1989-2000), and resulted in violent, if relatively brief, armed struggles. The Serbian population in Croatia and the Albanian population in Macedonia nonetheless continued to express acute discontent with their treatment as minority peoples. Bosnia-Herzegovina declared its independence from Yugoslavia in 1992 and, like Croatia and Slovenia, was opposed by the Yugoslav (Serbian) government. The brutal civil war that followed (1992-96) pitted the Bosnian Serbs against the Croat and Moslem populations of the nation, left the nation in virtual ruin, and ended in 1996 in a compromise government which included all three factions and independence from Yugoslavia. The Serbian province of Kosovo, which is populated by a large Albanian majority, also agitated for a more autonomous status within the Yugoslav republic; uprisings throughout the 1980s and 1990s intensified still further in 1998-99 and brought military intervention by the United Nations (mainly the United States). Only Serbian-dominated Serbia (which includes Kosovo) and Montenegro thus remained in the once-much-larger Yugoslav confederation. Not unlike the former Soviet republics, the former Yugoslav states (including the new Yugoslavia itself) attempted, with very mixed results, to develop pluralistic (multi-party) political systems, market economies, and western-style cultures. Albania, under General/Premier/Communist Party Chairman Enver Hoxha (r. 1944/1946-85), the leading figure in the resistance movement against Italian occupation during the Second World War, transformed the nation from a quasi-feudal state to an industrial economy, sharply reduced illiteracy, and broke with the Soviet Union in

254

1961-68, largely over its opposition to the liberalization of Soviet political and economic life after the death of Stalin. It then aligned primarily with the People's Republic of China until taking an altogether independent, nationalist course (which included a continuation of its inflexibly repressive domestic agenda) in 1978. After the death of Hoxha in 1985, the country became gradually more open and moderate; it made the transition to representative government in 1992.

The other Soviet satellites likewise became independent states and attempted to develop pluralistic (multi-party) political systems, market economies, and western-style cultures in 1989 or shortly thereafter. East Germany collapsed in 1989 and was reunited with West Germany on West German standards in 1990 as has been said. Poland, like Hungary and Czechoslovakia, had unsuccessfully attempted to break somewhat free of the Soviet Union significantly earlier. In 1956, widespread riots against Soviet control brought Communist Party Chairman Wladyslaw Gomulka (1905-82; r. 1956-70) to power. Gomulka liberalized the economy in a measure but eventually reverted to the rigid political policies of his immediate predecessors. Continued worker alienation and protest evoked the development of an independent labor union, Solidarity (under the leadership of tradesman, 1983 Nobel Peace laureate, and [future] President Lech Walesa [c. 1943- ; r. 1990-95]), in 1980. A period of severe government repression (which included the 1981-83 declaration of martial law approved by the Soviets) and deteriorating economic conditions followed. Poland became independent in 1989. Hungary too, like Poland, attempted to moderate the Soviet hold over it in 1956. Mainly under Premier Imre Nagy (1896-1958 [executed]; r. 1953-55, 1956), the **Hungarian Revolution** was waged and in the end suppressed (by the Soviet military). Nagy's Soviet-approved successor, Communist Party Chairman/Premier Janos Kadar (1912-89; r. 1956-88), not unlike Gomulka in Poland, was nonetheless successful in moderating the political, economic, and cultural life of the country. Hungary became independent in 1989. Czechoslovakia came under the communist presidency of Klement Gottwald (1896-1953; r. 1948-53) in 1948 and followed the customary eastern European path of Sovietization. Like Poland and Hungary, it too developed a taste for a more moderate course. In 1968, Aleksander Dubcek (1921-92; r. 1968-69) assumed leadership of the Communist Party in the country and instituted liberal political and economic reforms. The Soviets disapproved of the reforms, invaded the country in 1968, installed a new government (under Communist Party Chairman Gustav Husak [1913-91; r. 1969-89]) in 1969, and reversed many of Dubcek's moderating policies. Czechoslovakia became independent in 1989, mainly under the leadership of its renowned playwright-poet-humanitarian, President Vaclav Havel (1936- ; r. 1989-92, 1993-). The country divided into the sovereign states of the Czech Republic (the western region) and Slovakia (the eastern region) in 1993.

The Romanian monarchy, then under (Hohenzollern) King Michael I (r. 1927-30, 1940-47), son of King Carol II, was abolished in 1947 and the government was taken over by Communist Party Chairman/Premier Gheorghe Gheorghiu-Dej (1901-65; r. 1947-65) and subsequently by Communist Party Chairman/President Nicolae Ceaucescu (1918-89; r. 1965-89 [executed]), both of whom pursued a foreign political course somewhat independent of Moscow, a course that included reconciliation with western nations and with the People's Republic of China. Ceaucescu also, however, prosecuted ruinous domestic economic policies, installed one of the most repressive and despised systems of public terror in eastern Europe, and was executed without ceremony in 1989. Romania became independent in 1989-90 but continued to be ruled by the old regime until 1996. Similarly, the Bulgarian monarchy, then under King Simeon II (1937- ; r. 1943-46), son of Boris III, was abolished in 1946 and the government was taken over by Communist Party Chairman/Premier Georgi Dimitrov (1882-1949; r. 1946-49) and subsequently by Communist Party Chairman/Premier/President Todor Zhivkov (1911-98; r. 1954-89), both of whom pursued political and economic policies in strict accord with Soviet expectations. Bulgaria became independent in 1989-90 but continued to be ruled by the old regime until 1991.

Most nations of the world were not formally or were not exclusively aligned with either the Soviet Union or the United States, preferring instead an unaligned status opposed to either Soviet or American domination of them. These nations, the **unaligned nations**, were mostly the recent victims of colonial predacity (some few the beneficiaries of colonial prudence); they were developing not developed, poor not wealthy, industrializing not industrialized societies; and they were therefore by necessity much influenced by the behavior of the wealthier states and deeply vulnerable to the prerogatives of the wealthier states. Among the principal ways that these nations have danced as successfully, if warily, as they have among the wealthier states have been by means of political and economic solidarity, by means of playing both sides of Cold War diplomacy equally, or by means of playing with neither side, all perilous, if unavoidable, alternatives to overt subjugation.

The post-Second World War records of all nations (except Liberia, the states of Latin America, and China), aligned and unaligned — the major powers, their formal allies, their colonies/dominions/satellites, their former colonies/dominions/satellites, and uncolonized developing societies -- have now been considered. Although formally independent (mainly from the United States) since 1847, Liberia became a classic west African case of post-colonial corruption, instability, civil unrest, and wrenching poverty; most notably, in the regime of Charles McArthur Ghankay Taylor (1948- ; r. 1997-). In **Latin America**, the states of central America (except Belize, a non-Latin case) and of South America (except Guyana, Suriname, French Guiana, and Falkland Islands/Malvinas Islands, all non-Latin cases except French Guiana) have all been independent of their main colonizers for well more than a century and one-half as has been said. The great instabilities of the region — the economic turmoil; the military-civilian, conservative-liberal, and clerical-secular conflicts; the colossal inequality, injustice, corruption, and poverty; and the wide human-rights abuses — effectively continued, in some instances deepened. The United States contributed especially much to these miseries in Mexico, Guatemala, Honduras, El Salvador, Nicaragua, Panama, Ecuador, Colombia, Peru, Bolivia, and Chile (as well as in the Caribbean states, Cuba, Haiti, Dominican Republic, and Grenada) as has been said. Even nations that did not suffer direct American intervention — Venezuela, Brazil, Uruguay, and Argentina — experienced great instability and the misfortunes that are both the cause of violent change as well as often too the result of it. Mexico, Chile, and Paraguay eventually achieved stable governments but largely by totalitarian means, means that did not relieve the suffering of the poor. Mexico had been a conservative one-party state since 1926; retreated since the Second World War from the progressive tendencies of the inter-war period; passed through numerous deeply corrupt administrations (such as that of President Gustavo Diaz Ordaz [1911-79; r. 1964-70], who presided over the 1968 Olympic demonstrations that killed several hundred students in Mexico City); inspired an insurrection of native Indian peoples (the Zapatistas) in Chiapas (in 1994-); and began to develop a functional multi-party system of political culture (in 1993-). Chile, under Pinochet, was a very stable country after the murder of Allende but it was also among the most repressive in the hemisphere as has been said; it became a stable, representative democracy in 1990. Likewise, Paraguay, mainly under General/President Alfredo Stroessner (1912- ; r. 1954-89), achieved constancy at the expense of liberty. Following turbulent developments just after the Second World War, Costa Rica (beginning in the 1950s), Uruguay (beginning in the 1980s), and Argentina (beginning in the 1980s) developed uncommonly orderly and uncommonly democratic governments by the standards of the region. After 1950 (after the junta of 1948-49 had passed), Costa Rica became a committed, representative democracy, de-emphasized military institutions, devoted itself principally to ecological, health, and educational issues, and ardently supported international peace initiatives. Its exceptional president, Oscar Arias Sanchez (1941- ; r. 1986-90), won the 1987 Nobel Peace Prize and has continued to work effectively for world peace since leaving office. Uruguay suffered significant social, economic, and political turmoil following the Second World War; was eventually stabilized, but deeply repressed, by a regressive military regime (1973-85); and, since 1985, has become a tolerant and progressive representative democracy. Argentina came under the ambivalent leadership of Colonel/President Juan Domingo Peron (1895-1974; r. 1944/46-55, 1973-74) in 1944/46. Among the most enigmatic political figures of the post-war era, Peron attempted to achieve national self-sufficiency by dictatorial, but nonetheless revolutionary means; his welfare state greatly increased public support for education, health, and labor and it eventually opposed the regressive influence of the Church in public affairs. Economic woes destabilized his administration, however, and he was succeeded by a mostly troubled series of highly repressive and unstable military governments which largely ended in 1983 after the ruinous 1982 war against Great Britain over possession of the Falkland Islands/Malvinas Islands. The Argentinean governments since 1983 have attempted to develop the standard trappings of representative democracy and have attempted as well to redress the very considerable crimes of the military governments from 1974 to 1983.

China was in an extremely impoverished and demoralized condition at the end of the Second Sino-Japanese War/the Second World War. The uneasy alliance that had been arranged during the War between the National People's Party (the Kuomintang), of Chiang Kai-shek (r. 1928-49), and the Communist Party of China, under Party Chairman Mao Tse-tung (1893-1976; r. 1949-76) and (future) Premier Chou En-lai (1898-1976; r. 1949-76), expired with the War and with the expulsion of the Japanese. The civil wars between the nationalists and the communists that had begun in the inter-war period (1927-36) were then resumed (1945-49). Despite assistance from the United States, the corrupt and dictatorial, one-party, rightist regime of Chiang Kai-shek was defeated and the (dictatorial, one-party, leftist) People's Republic of China (centered in Peking/Beijing) was established in 1949. The Kuomintang fled to Formosa/Taiwan (which, like the mainland, had been reclaimed from Japan in 1945) and established the Nationalist Republic of China, also in 1949. The new government of the mainland transformed the country in accord with established communist prescriptions: a new constitution was enacted; the economy was nationalized; a vigorous program of industrialization was initiated; enormous communes were developed and agriculture collectivized in them; currency and land reform were instituted; and a pervasive re-education of the people was organized. But all did not go well: economic progress was painfully slow; famine and pestilence were common; counterrevolutionary unrest and plunder were ample; and foreign military obligations were costly. In matters of foreign weight, the People's Republic of China occupied Tibet in 1949-51 and has dealt with several uprisings there since; it fought on the North Korean side in the Korean War and supported North Vietnam in the Vietnam War; it initiated offensive measures against Formosa/Taiwan (which brought it into open dispute with the United States) in 1957-58; and it broke with the Soviet Union in 1959-64, largely over its opposition to what it interpreted as undue Soviet appeasement of western nations. It became a nuclear nation in 1964 and achieved rapprochement with the United Nations in 1971 and with the United States (which included "ping-pong diplomacy") in 1971-72. The domestic history of the country has been also uneven. At times of economic misfortune in particular, the People's Republic of China has tended to exceedingly inflexible, to highly regimented, and to decidedly doctrinaire orientations. The most notable such instance was the "Great Proletarian Cultural Revolution" (1966-76), which was most severe in its first several years (1966-69) but which continued in some form until 1976; it thus occupied the final decade of Mao's rule-life and Chou's. The "Cultural Revolution" was aimed at eradicating reactionary opposition to the Party, opposition that was rooted mainly in the bourgeois, foreign tastes and influences of the elite class. Its extreme repression and fiscal myopia brought the nation to the edge of ruin. After the deaths of Mao and Chou in 1976, the People's Republic of China, mainly under Communist Party leader and Vice-Premier Deng Xiaoping (1904-97; r. 1977-97), pursued notably more liberal trade policies, rapid economic modernization with market elements, and a more moderate domestic course in political affairs. The purges and reform that followed the end of the "Cultural Revolution" were, however, insufficient to discourage a burgeoning movement for a more democratic form of political culture. The Tienanmen Square (Beijing) insurrection of 1989 was the most notable demonstration of public dissatisfaction with the government; although the insurrection brought some loosening of political shackles, the country was yet characterized by deep political dissension and great economic disparity. Crime rates in the People's Republic of China also remain high and incarceration and execution rates are the highest in the world. A measure of rapprochement with the Soviet Union was achieved in 1989.

The period since the Second World War was too characterized by the development of major **transnational/international political and trade organizations**, organizations that have effectively attempted to make one world of the many just chronicled. Although these organizations typically framed their activities in accord with the interests of the foremost political and economic powers in the world (interests which are often not in concert with the interests of others), they have in some cases also provided a forum for the less fortunate. By far the most significant, if not the most influential, of these international organizations is the **United Nations**, the effective sequel to the failed League of Nations (dissolved in 1946). The establishment and bureaucratic infrastructure of the United Nations had been proposed at the Tehran Conference of 1943, the Dumbarton Oaks Conference of 1944, and the Yalta Conference of 1945. The Charter of the United Nations (i.e., its founding and governing document) was formulated principally by the United States, the Soviet Union, Great Britain, and China; it was enacted in San Francisco in June 1945 and became effective on October 24, 1945; it originally included fifty nations; by the end of the century, it included all but a handful of world states. The purpose of the organization was to promote world peace and security by non-violent means, national self-determination (de-colonization) throughout the world, equal human rights for all people, and improvement of living standards (mainly in respect to justice, discrimination, crime, pollution, health, hunger, disease, poverty, and education). The United Nations has been especially effective defusing conflict among developing nations but has also contributed significantly to managing disputes between major Cold War adversaries. It has played exceedingly noteworthy peacekeeping roles in the countless wars of national liberation/oppression of the last two generations; most notably, the India-Pakistan Wars, the Arab-Israeli Wars, the Congo Crisis, and the partition of Cyprus. The organization has also participated variously and importantly, as a moderating agent, in the Chinese civil wars; the Chinese occupation of Tibet; the partition of Germany; the Korean, Vietnam, and Persian Gulf Wars; conflicts in Afghanistan, Bosnia, Burundi, Cambodia, Cuba, El Salvador, Guinea, India, Indonesia, Iran, Iraq, Kosovo, Mozambique, Namibia, Pakistan, Rhodesia, Rwanda, Somalia, South Africa, and East Timor; and the American trusteeship of central and south Pacific nations. It has too had a major, salutary affect on humanitarian relief associated with the imposing problems of refugees, problems caused principally by war, other forms of ideological, ethnic, and religious conflict, the twilight of classical colonialism, and extraordinary emigration patterns. For these manifold achievements, the United Nations has been four times awarded the Nobel Peace Prize (1954, 1965, 1981, and 1988). The permanent headquarters of the United Nations was established in New York City in 1946. Its leadership, in the form of the Secretary-General, has fallen to a succession of very able men:

- Trygve Halvdan Lie (1896-1968; r. 1946-53) of Norway;
- Dag Hammarskjold (1905-61; r. 1953-61) of Sweden, who won the 1961 Nobel Peace Prize;
- U Thant (1909-74; r. 1961-72) of Burma/Myanmar;
- Kurt Waldheim (1918- ; r. 1972-81) of Austria; later, President of Austria (1986-92);
- Javier Perez de Cuellar (1920- ; r. 1982-91) of Peru; later, Prime Minister of Peru (2000-);
- Boutros Boutros-Ghali (1922- ; r. 1992-96) of Egypt; and
- Kofi Annan (1938- ; r. 1997-) of Ghana.

The most significant of the other major international agencies of humanitarian bent have been the International Red Cross (established in 1863), which is broadly devoted to the relief of human misery and which has thrice won the Nobel Peace Prize (1917, 1944, and 1963); Amnesty International (established in 1961), which has campaigned dauntlessly against human-rights abuses throughout the world and which won the 1977 Nobel Peace Prize; and Greenpeace (established in 1971), which has been among the most intrepid defenders of environmental integrity (i.e., the protection of natural resources and plant and animal life) throughout the world. The most significant of the international trade (and banking) organizations/agreements – the World Bank (1945), International Monetary Fund (IMF; 1945), North American Free Trade Agreement (NAFTA; 1994), World Trade Organization (WTO; 1995), and General Agreement on Tariffs and Trade (GATT; 1995) – have tended to operate on a lesser, on a not entirely edifying, level, promoting privatization schemes, the prerogatives of wealthy, First-World corporations over public entities (including the internal affairs of Third-World states), and the globalization of commercial incentives. Their imposing resource, high esteem among wealthy and influential elites (who profit handsomely from them), deeply coercive tactics, and regressive agendas (i.e., disregard for the welfare of workers and of the environment) made them more powerful than most nations and gave them enormous power over most nations. Numerous acts of civil disobedience throughout the world have opposed the activities of these organizations but none has succeeded in substantially transforming them.

Intellectual Developments

The sweep of human intellectual experience, throughout its ancient, medieval, and early modern development, had tended, on balance, in the direction of a purposive certainty; that is, in the direction of an optimistic affirmation of the permanently constant and absolute character of nature and humanity, of the unique and superior character of human life as against other forms of life, and of the ultimate perfectibility of nature and humanity. Contemporary modern civilization, conversely, has gradually chipped away at the dominant ancient, medieval, and early modern world views in these several, pivotal respects. Largely under the influence of an ardent skepticism, itself driven mainly by the brilliance of modern science, by industrialism, and by calamitous human conflict, the optimistic affirmations of earlier periods were progressively replaced by a sense of impermanence, a sense of purposeless uncertainty, and a sense of pessimistic resignation. This prodigious transformation constitutes a radically substantive shift in which the most fundamental notions of reality in general and of humanity in particular have been qualitatively revised. This cultural and intellectual metamorphosis was grounded primarily in:
- convincing scientific demonstrations revealing the fundamentally variable (inconstant) and the fundamentally relative character of nature and humanity;
- convincing scientific demonstrations revealing the dependent and continuous relation of human life with other forms of life; and
- a measure of brutality so colossal, so staggering, and so appalling as to call into compelling question any serious claims of human perfectibility.

This thoroughly profound transformation has, moreover, evoked the progressive triumph of immanence over transcendence, of science over orthodox religion, and of critical philosophy over speculative theology.

At first, the scientific conquests of the nineteenth century, together with the material gains of the period, encouraged a sense of optimistic progress in the capacity of science and technology to ultimately resolve the perplexities and to solve the problems of human existence. As the rate of substantive, seemingly uncontrollable, and unedifying change reached unprecedented magnitudes in the twentieth century particularly, as the sciences increasingly revealed a world that threatened, not enhanced, human happiness, and as the epoch-turning events of the First World War unfolded (events in which human genius was devoted to human extinction), however, a sense of disillusioned futility, resigned alienation, and pessimistic uncertainty became the dominant tendency. Although this transformation did not take on the broad and pervasive cultural significance that is now widely recognized in it until after the devastating dislocations and disaffections of the First World War, it predictably had its beginnings in a much earlier time. The germinal tendencies of this upheaval are recognizable in the skeptical orientations of Confucius, Heraclitus, the sophists, and Hellenistic and Roman science, philosophy, and literature. They are too apparent in the early European university studies of the thirteenth and fourteenth centuries and in Renaissance literature and philosophy, all of which called pure faith to the reckoning of cautious reason. These tendencies have their earnest origins, however, in the extraordinary mathematical and scientific discoveries of the sixteenth, seventeenth, and eighteenth centuries and in the philosophical and artistic corollaries of these discoveries. They are carried to their most recent "conclusions" by the ingenious disclosures of nineteenth-century and twentieth-century science and its philosophical and artistic corollaries.

Ironically enough, the age of skeptical uncertainty – contemporary modern civilization – began with a triumphant acclamation, a triumphant reinterpretation of the dominant ancient, medieval, and early modern tendency. Inclinations to nineteenth-century romanticism/realism were developing in the neo-classicism of the eighteenth century as has been said. Romanticism/realism itself (in its French and German forms most notably, but also in significant British/Irish, Russian, American, Scandinavian, Italian, and Spanish forms) was the fourth of five main episodes in human history to embrace at all seriously the organic thesis and that which is entailed by the organic thesis; i.e., political society, a monistic view of the mind-body relation, a subjective concept of the body, a lived notion of movement, and an intrinsic respect for humanity and its principal expressions (science, sport, dance, art, religion, history, philosophy, and education). Only the ancient Greek (most especially, the Athenian) Enlightenment, novel aspects of the medieval and modern Islamic Enlightenment (most especially, aspects of the Omayyad, Abbasid, Fatimid, Almoravid, Nasrid, Timurid, Mogul, and Ottoman developments), European (most especially, Italian, Burgundian, and German) Renaissance humanism, and twentieth-century European (most especially, Scandinavian) democratic socialism and European (most especially, Germanic, French, Russian, and Finnish), American, and Mexican expressionism have also claimed an abiding allegiance to the organic vision. The dualistic/pluralistic and extrinsic tendencies that romanticism/realism opposed and that are arguably among the principal impediments to a full and authentic humanity (as well as a full and authentic experience of sport) run through the virtual whole of our intellectual development. Such ancient tendencies before the Greeks were partially overcome by the most enlightened of the Greeks. These tendencies were again exacerbated by the Romans and to a yet greater extent by medieval divinism and scholasticism. Modern life has, on balance, come to a development in the direction of "restoring" and "completing" humanity's lost sense of harmony, the lost sense of harmony between its physical and its intellectual aspects. Modern progress in the direction of putting the basic mistake of dualism/pluralism (and instrumentality) right turned first toward "re-establishing" the ancient Greek sense of proportion in the form of Renaissance humanism. It then turned toward a more distinctly modern interpretation of the unity of human experience culminating in nineteenth-century romanticism/realism.

Romanticism/realism was the dominant intellectual orientation through the first approximate two-thirds of the nineteenth century. Positivism/impressionism/post-impressionism came to the fore in the last approximate one-third of the nineteenth century and began the dominant turn away from organic, monistic, and intrinsic orientations toward materialistic, dualistic/pluralistic, and extrinsic orientations. This turn constituted the earliest movement away from the modern intellectual equation (as it had developed through the modern European Enlightenment and its romantic-realist apotheosis) in the direction of post-modernism. The enormous transformation that this turn portended was hastened by the burgeoning industrialism and militarism of the period and by the dominant intellectual tendencies of the twentieth century itself: the relativism of the natural and social sciences, the skepticism of philosophy, history, and literature, and the abstractionism of the visual, musical, and movement arts. These tendencies were nonetheless importantly interrupted by two developments which capture/re-capture the central tenets of organicism:

- European (most notably, Scandinavian; i.e., Swedish, Norwegian, Danish, and Icelandic) democratic socialism, which was the first tangible and enduring political manifestation of the organic view, which embodied the characteristic tenets of political (as distinct from gentile or civil) society, which was explicitly devoted to equal rights, equal opportunities, and equal franchise for all persons, which was committed to assuring satisfaction of the basic needs of all persons, and which won sporadic acclaim elsewhere in western Europe, as well as a semblance of approbation in Australia, Canada, and New

Zealand (all of the latter of which nonetheless have had a troubling history of mistreating native populations); and

- European (most especially, Germanic, French, Russian, and Finnish), American, and Mexican abstract expressionism, which has been the most recent intellectual movement of organic moment.

The natural and social sciences

Among the most richly creative periods in human intellectual history, the nineteenth and twentieth centuries are in no domain more distinguished than in scientific erudition. The stupendous scientific discoveries of this most recent period were greatly abetted by the development of ingenious methodological technologies; most notably, the development of exceedingly powerful and discriminating telescopes, microscopes, spectroscopes, computers, and particle accelerators. Grounded in an analytic study of the material world, the natural sciences of the period penetrated the mysteries of this world more deeply than any prior development. The principal achievements in mathematics and the physical sciences concerned number and probability theory, the laws of electricity (including electromagnetism), radioactivity, atomic structure, the laws of the sub-atomic universe (quantum theory), the laws of the macrocosmic universe (fractal geometry and relativity theory), and the geological character and development of the Earth. Arguably the most accomplished and influential figure in **nineteenth-century mathematics** was the German genius, Carl Friedrich Gauss (1777-1855), whose greatest work, <u>Disquisitiones Arithmeticae</u> (1801), ranks with the most remarkable manuscripts in the entire history of mathematics and whose insights concerning number theory, probability theory, and non-Euclidean geometry significantly prepared the way for quantum and relativity theory in the twentieth century.

On grounds established by eighteenth-century studies concerning electricity by such as Charles Du Fay, Luigi Galvani, and Alessandro Volta, the **laws of electricity and electromagnetism** were further elaborated in the nineteenth century; most notably, by:

- Danish physicist, Hans Christian Oersted (1777-1851), who demonstrated a relation between electricity and magnetism and thus discovered the phenomenon of electromagnetism in 1819;
- French physicist, André Marie Ampère (1775-1836), who discovered the mathematical relation of electrical current and magnetism in 1822;
- German physicist, Georg Simon Ohm (1787-1854), who discovered the mathematical relation of electrical force (voltage) and resistance (ohms) to electrical current (amperes) in 1827;
- English scientist, Michael Faraday (1791-1867), who discovered the phenomenon of electromagnetic induction (in 1831), a phenomenon which explained the production of electrical force by alterations in the magnetic field surrounding electrical conductors; this was the basis for the technological development of primitive generators capable of mass producing electrical from mechanical energy and the technological basis as well of many other forms of electrical machinery for industry; Faraday also came to a refined mathematical understanding of electrolysis (in 1833), a phenomenon which explained the decomposition of some chemical compounds into their elemental constituents under the influence of electromagnetism; this was the basis of technological innovation in industrial electrochemistry;
- Scottish physicist, James Clark Maxwell (1831-79), who postulated electromagnetic radiation (waves of invisible electrical and magnetic energy that behave like visible light) in 1864 and who, in <u>A Treatise on Electricity and Magnetism</u> (1873), greatly refined mathematical understanding of electromagnetic fields and showed the mathematical relation of such fields to the character and speed of visible light;
- German physicist, Heinrich Rudolf Hertz (1857-94), who, in 1887, confirmed Maxwell's electromagnetic theory of light (the view of light as electromagnetic radiation) and who demonstrated that electricity can be transmitted by a type of electromagnetic wave (in this case, by long-length, low-frequency radio waves) which move at the speed of visible light and, like visible light itself, can be reflected, refracted, and polarized; this was the basis for the technological development of wireless telegraphy, radio, and television; it was too the basis for the development of other technologies grounded in other forms of electromagnetic radiation (microwave, infrared, ultraviolet, x-ray, and gamma ray); and
- German physicist, Wilhelm Conrad Roentgen (1845-1923), who discovered the short-length, high-frequency form of penetrating, electromagnetic radiation, x-rays (in 1895), a technology that has had an enormously favorable affect on medical practice and an achievement that won him the first Nobel Prize in Physics in 1901.

The discovery of electromagnetic radiation and its main forms and properties was closely followed by the discovery of **radioactivity** (in which the atoms of some elements naturally disintegrate by emitting particles from their nuclei) and by the discovery of the structural (and functional) properties of atoms themselves (by the discovery of **atomic structure**). French physicist, Antoine Becquerel (1852-1908), was the first to critically observe natural radiation (in uranium) in 1896. He shared the 1903 Nobel Prize in Physics for this distinction with Marie Sklodowska Curie (1867-1934), a Polish-French physicist and chemist, and her husband, Pierre Curie (1859-1906), likewise a French physicist. The Curies discovered radium and polonium in 1898 and observed their inherent and continuously changing energy, their radioactive properties; Marie Curie also won the 1911 Nobel Prize in Chemistry for this work. A still more detailed account of radioactivity, which included discovery of its two principal forms (alpha-particle and beta-particle radioactivity) as well as the terms in which atoms are transformed by radioactivity, was formulated by the New Zealand-Canadian-English physicist, Ernest Rutherford (1871-1937) in 1905, an achievement that won him the 1908 Nobel Prize in Chemistry. In 1911, Rutherford began to surmise the fundamental structure of the atom (the basic unit of all matter), the differentiated structure of the atom — a small, dense, and positively charged nucleus surrounded by yet smaller, exceedingly light, and negatively charged orbital electrons. The three basic elementary particles (constituents of atoms), electrons and the two main particles comprising the nucleus, protons and neutrons, were discovered between 1897 and 1932. English physicist and 1906 Nobel laureate in physics, Joseph John Thomson (1856-1940), discovered the electron in 1897; Rutherford, who was, among his numerous colossal distinctions, the first to split atomic nuclei by artificial means, discovered the proton in 1919; and English physicist and 1935 Nobel laureate in physics, James Chadwick (1891-1974), discovered the neutron in 1932. Dozens of other elementary particles have been discovered since; most notably, antiparticles/antimatter (particles that correspond to ordinary electrons, protons, and neutrons but carry the opposite electrical charge), quarks (among the most elemental types of particle), and strings (the very most basic form of matter). All elementary particles are now nonetheless thought to take one or several of four major forms, to participate in one or several of the four fundamental forces of nature: gravitational, electromagnetic, strong nuclear, and weak nuclear forces.

The great mysteries of atomic structure (and function) had been very loosely foreseen by the qualitative and quantitative atomists (most notably, Democritus) in the fifth and fourth centuries B.C.E. as has been said. The atomic theory of matter was first tellingly revived in the modern world by the English mathematician and scientist, John Dalton (1766-1844), in 1808. This theory was carried further forward by the distinguished chemists of the early-to-mid nineteenth century, the heirs of Philippus Paracelsus, Robert Boyle, and Antoine Lavoisier; most notably:

- Swedish chemist, Jons Jakob Berzelius (1779-1848), who developed the modern system of chemical symbols and formulas and who devised an accurate table of atomic weights for known elements in 1818;
- German chemist, Justus Liebig (1803-73), who made an exacting analysis of known elements in 1831, who demonstrated the relation of inorganic and organic compounds, who greatly advanced the science of organic chemistry, and who had an enormous influence on the practice of agriculture and medicine; and
- Russian chemist, Dmitri Ivanovich Mendeleyev (1834-1907), who, in 1869, formulated the periodic table of elements, which classified known elements according to structure (and function) and thus revealed the chemically determined order of the natural (and human) worlds.

It was, however, the study of electromagnetic radiation and radioactivity in the late nineteenth and early twentieth centuries that brought experimental confirmation of atomic structure itself. And it was the development of quantum theory in the early twentieth century that achieved a fully exacting account of the atomic/sub-atomic universe.

Quantum theory was first conjured by German physicist and 1918 Nobel laureate in physics, Max Planck (1858-1947), and later elaborated most significantly by Danish physicist and 1922 Nobel laureate in physics, Niels Henrik David Bohr (1885-1962), and by German physicist and 1932 Nobel laureate in physics, Werner Heisenberg (1901-76), who had been a student of Bohr. Planck, beginning in 1900, Bohr, beginning in 1913, and Heisenberg, beginning in 1927, ushered in the relativist revolution in science by observing, contrary to the view of classical physics, that atoms do not emit and absorb energy continuously but only sporadically in discrete packets (or quanta), that sub-atomic matter is characterized by constantly changing relational shifts among particles and quanta, and thus that sub-atomic matter is significantly unpredictable. The original vision of quantum theory is owed to Planck; Bohr expanded the theory to explain atomic structure (and function), which included the postulated existence of numerous elementary particles (many of which have been experimentally confirmed since); and Heisenberg fashioned the celebrated "uncertainty principle," according to which the more accurately the position of a particle is measured, the less accurately its velocity can be measured and vice versa. By Heisenberg's account, the laws of physics are thus about relative, probable, approximate, not about absolute certainties/uncertainties and the observer is a factor in the observed.

Coextensive with the development of quantum theory (which accounted for the atomic/sub-atomic universe) was the formulation of **relativity theory** (which accounted for the macrocosmic universe, the large-scale structure and function of the universe). Relativity theory was importantly foreseen by the extraordinary Dutch physicist and 1902 Nobel laureate in physics, Hendrik Antoon Lorentz (1853-1928); its principal exponent, however, was the brilliant German-American physicist and 1921 Nobel laureate in physics, Albert Einstein (1879-1955). Einstein's "special theory of relativity" (1905) compromised no less fundamental principles of classical physics than Newton's celestial mechanics. In it, Einstein argued that:

- the speed of light is constant for all observers irrespective of the motion of observers or the source of light (it is the universal, limiting feature of the material world in the sense that it is everywhere the same and in the sense that nothing exceeds it);
- phenomena which occur at or near the speed of light (macrocosmic phenomena) differ substantially from those that do not (middle-range phenomena described by classical physics);
- energy is a function of mass and velocity ($E = mc^2$);
- objects appear to contract (in the direction of motion) and time to slow as velocity increases (in particular, as the speed of light is approached);
- the appearance of events to those moving very rapidly differs from that of those observing such movement and not moving very rapidly; and
- even time and space, but not the speed of light, are therefore relative, not unchanging, not absolute (i.e., even time and space are an inconstant function of something that is unchanging; namely, the speed of light).

Einstein's "general theory of relativity" (1915) expanded the earlier claims, arguing that:

- space and time are not independent entities but a four-dimensional continuum (the three dimensions of space and the lone dimension of time), space-time;
- space-time is not flat, but curved, warped, or bent, by the material bodies and energies in it;
- gravitational force is a function of this curvature;
- the path of material bodies in space-time is determined by this curvature; and
- this curvature deflects even light (which is to say that everything occurs in it).

The character of the macro-atomic universe proposed by Einstein has been since largely confirmed and significantly elaborated by astronomical observation and experimentation. The principal achievements in **astronomy** since publication of the "general theory of relativity" were attained by:

- Harlow Shapley (1885-1972), an American astronomer, who, on the basis of Herschel's work concerning the character of the local galaxy (the Milky Way), in 1918, made the pioneering discoveries concerning the size of the galaxy and the position of our solar system in it;
- Edwin Powell Hubble (1889-1953), an American astronomer, who, in 1924-29, was the first to discover galaxies other than the Milky Way, to discover that these galaxies are distributed almost uniformly in all directions (that the known universe has no center and no boundary), to discover that the universe is not static but expanding (and expanding uniformly at accelerating rates), and to discover the approximate finite age of the universe; these were the bases on which the Big Bang theory of the universe's finite origin was developed; this theory holds that the known universe was created in a colossal explosion approximately 14-18 billion years ago, an explosion that began the continuing expansion of all that is; the Hubble Telescope, which was deployed in 1990, honored the illustrious Hubble and has contributed profoundly to our knowledge of the physical universe; and
- Arno Allan Penzias (1933-), German-American physicist-astronomer, and Robert Woodrow Wilson (1936-), American physicist-astronomer, co-recipients of the 1978 Nobel Prize in Physics, who, in 1965, discovered the most convincing corroborating evidence for the Big Bang theory, the electromagnetic remnants of the Big Bang, the background radio radiation that comes to the Earth equally from all directions.

A planet outside the local solar system, an extra-solar planet, was first discovered (by spectrographic means) in 1995. It is presumably this type of body (with life-sustaining possibilities) that human beings and other life forms, as well as the creations of human cultural achievement, will need to occupy if they are to survive the prospective death of the local solar system.

The most perplexing problem of the physical sciences in the last half of the twentieth century concerned the relation of quantum theory (which explains the sub-atomic universe) and relativity theory (which explains the macro-atomic universe). Concisely said, these two main theoretical constructs by which we understand the material world, the two brilliantly conceived constructs which have very significantly transformed the world views of classical physics and astronomy developed mainly by Nicolas Copernicus, Tycho Brahe, Galileo Galilei, Johannes Kepler, and Isaac Newton, are in substantial disagreement. Quantum theory argues that reality is governed by unpredictable chance; relativity theory holds that reality is ultimately predictable. Einstein was himself centrally devoted in his final years to the search for a theory that unified these two constructs, to the search for a **unified field theory**. This search, which eluded even the great Einstein, has resulted in the development of super-symmetry, or super-string theory, according to which the four fundamental forces (gravitational, electromagnetic, strong nuclear, and weak nuclear forces) were all symmetrically united in the circumstance of the universe's origin; these forces and the elementary particles they embodied were variously dispersed in the first moments of the universe and these particles (under the influence of these forces) variously combined to form the subsequent asymmetries (the somethings instead of nothings) of the created world.

Similarly, **twentieth-century mathematics** has been principally devoted to attempts to explain the quantitative and qualitative properties of natural phenomena at all levels of generality-specificity (at the small-scale, middle-range, and large-scale levels), to explain the similarities-dissimilarities of natural phenomena at these levels and the continuities-discontinuities of natural phenomena among these levels. Set theory, monster functions, dynamical systems theory, and chaos theory have all aimed in this broad direction. The highest mark of this development, however, has been the fractal geometry of Polish-French-American mathematician, Benoit B. Mandelbrot (1924-), developed most notably in <u>Fractals: Form, Chance, and Dimension</u> (1975) and <u>The Fractal Geometry of Nature</u> (1982). According to Mandelbrot Sets, which have been generated with the significant aid of computer graphics, the order in apparently erratic shapes and processes is infinitely expandable-contractible; it is infinitely complex (indeterminate/unpredictable); but it is nonetheless governed by simple laws (determinate/predictable). There is, by this view, sufficient variation in the phenomena which these laws govern that it is not possible to predict future events utterly. The result is a sense of simple order in the middle-range of local experience which nonetheless occurs in the context of universal chaos in the small-scale and the large-scale universes.

The astounding achievements of nineteenth-century and twentieth-century mathematics and science concerning electromagnetic radiation, radioactivity, atomic structure, quantum theory, relativity theory, and unified field theory have also predictably had a formative affect on the production of **nuclear energy** for terrestrial (and celestial) use. On the basis of these achievements, French scientists, Irène Joliot-Curie (1897-1956), daughter of Marie and Pierre Curie, and her husband, Frédéric Joliot-Curie (1900-58), were the first (in 1934) to produce radioactive substances by artificial means, an accomplishment that won them the 1935 Nobel Prize in Chemistry. German scientist and 1944 Nobel laureate in chemistry, Otto Hahn (1879-1968), was the first (in 1938) to achieve nuclear fission (by splitting the uranium atom) and to discover the possibility of nuclear chain reactions. Italian-American physicist and 1938 Nobel laureate in physics, Enrico Fermi, was the first (in 1942) to create self-sustaining chain reactions (in uranium) as has been said. The (American) Manhattan Project, under the direction of American physicist, J. Robert Oppenheimer, then became the first (in 1945) to produce nuclear weapons as has been also said. The fashioning of still more destructive nuclear armaments and of nuclear energy programs for industrial, domestic, and space-exploration uses followed in turn.

Geology likewise passed through a profound transformation in the period of contemporary modern civilization: from the catastrophism that had been the main view of the Earth's character and development through the eighteenth century, to the uniformitarianism of the nineteenth century, to the notion of continental drift/plate-tectonics of the twentieth century. On the basis of James Hutton's uniformitarian claims, Charles Lyell (1797-1875), an English geologist, asserted that the Earth has developed very gradually over eons by means of ongoing geological events that are yet observable; the Earth has not, by this view, developed very abruptly over short periods by means of catastrophic geological occurrences novel to earlier periods. Principally in his celebrated, <u>Principles of Geology</u> (1830-33), Lyell prepared the geological way for the biological evolutionism of Charles Darwin and Alfred Wallace. The uniform alterations to which Lyell referred came to be still better understood in the twentieth century. German geologist-meteorologist, Alfred Lothar Wegener (1880-1930), was the first (in 1922) to convincingly propose the notion of continental drift, itself the basis for the subsequent recognition (at mid-century) of plate-tectonics. Mainly in his <u>The Origin of Continents and Oceans</u> (1915), Wegener argued that the Earth's continents were joined until c. 200 million years ago when they separated and very gradually migrated, largely by means of thermal convection cells in the planet's mantle (the layer immediately beneath the crust [its outermost layer]), to their current, very different positions. Plate-tectonic theory holds that the Earth's crust is divided into contiguous, moving plates (very large, discrete land masses) which carry the continents and which explain such as continental drift, volcanic activity, sea-floor spreading, mountain-formation, and earthquakes.

The revolutionary transformations in the biological sciences of contemporary modern civilization were as telling as those in the physical sciences of the period. These transformations had principally to do with the biological development of the species (mainly in respect to the character of genetic transmission and the influence of environmental factors on evolution), with pioneering etiological studies and the medical treatment of disease, and with biological influences on behavior. The most significant contributions to genetic study, to the new science of **genetics**, were achieved by:

- Gregor Johann Mendel (1822-84), Austrian botanist, who discovered the fundamental laws of heredity in 1866; according to these laws, traits are inherited by the combination of biological units (genes) from each parent; this discovery revealed the central dependence of life (including human life) on genetic transmission, on inherited qualities over which we have little-to-no prerogative, as distinct from achieved qualities over which we have notably larger choice;
- Theodor Boveri (1862-1915), German zoologist, who discovered discrete chromosomes as the carriers of hereditary traits in 1887-90;
- Thomas Hunt Morgan (1866-1945), American zoologist and 1933 Nobel laureate in medicine, who, in 1910-19, discovered the relation of chromosomes and genes (genes are transmitted through the actions of chromosomes), inaugurated the science of gene-mapping (identifying the position of discrete genes [on chromosomes] and their function), accounted for hereditary contributions to evolution, and incited the deeper study of eugenics (methods to improve inherited characteristics);
- James Dewey Watson (1928-), American zoologist, and Francis Harry Compton Crick (1916-), English zoologist, co-recipients of the 1962 Nobel Prize in Medicine, who, in 1953, discovered the double-helix physical and chemical character of deoxyribonucleic acid (DNA), the principal constituent of genes (known from 1944) and the substance that determines the identity of living organisms; this discovery explained the detailed nature of heredity, including the role of mutation (influenced largely by radiation and chemical factors) in evolutionary development; it also initiated revolutionary advances in molecular biology such as genetic engineering (the manipulation of genetic material); and
- Harold Clayton Urey (1893-1981), American chemist-geophysicist and 1934 Nobel laureate in chemistry (for other work), and Stanley Miller (1930-), American chemist-biologist, who, in 1953, demonstrated (in the celebrated "Miller-Urey Electric-Discharge Experiment") that the inorganic compounds which dominated the Earth's early atmosphere (mainly, ammonia, carbon dioxide, methane, and water) may be transformed, under conditions of electrical stimulation, into organic molecules (mainly, amino acids, the basic chemical stuff of life); this discovery explained the fundamental mechanism by which life may have evolved from inanimate matter.

Environmental accounts of biological evolution (themselves closely related to prior claims, particularly uniformitarian claims, concerning geological evolution) antedated the earliest convincing work about genetic transmission and were also significantly corroborated by this work. French naturalist, Jean Baptiste Pierre Antoine Lamarck (1744-1829), mainly in his <u>Invertebrates</u> (1801) and <u>Zoological Philosophy</u> (1809-30), was the first modern scientist to suggest a cogent theory of biological evolution. Lamarck asserted that all forms of life originated and developed as an ongoing process of gradual modification to shifting environmental factors over very long geological periods. By this view, new traits are acquired in the process of modification and these traits are variously transmitted to subsequent generations, thus producing organisms that are progressively better fitted to surviving extant (and changing) environments. The towering genius of biological evolutionism, English naturalist, Charles Robert Darwin (1809-82), owed much to Lamarck's natural, as distinct from miraculous, explanation of the origin and development of living organisms. Darwin's world voyage aboard the H.M.S. Beagle from 1831 to 1836 provided him with the experience and the empirical data on which his celebrated theory was based. Much influenced too by Robert Malthus and Charles Lyell, Darwin formulated the unifying principles of organic existence. These principles characterize evolution as a gradual process of descent within and across species (they thus establish the mutability of species), a process driven by the struggle for survival and the terms in which natural selection decides this struggle. The struggle for survival is itself moved by the tendency of species to produce populations which greatly exceed the capacity of their environment to sustain them and by the shifting nature of biological (and geological) environments themselves. Those creatures best adapted to the changing conditions of their environment survive and reproduce at a rate notably above that of creatures less fit to such adaptation; that is, they are naturally selected by their superior fitness to survive. Darwin's evolutionism, recorded most notably in <u>On the Origin of the Species by Means of Natural Selection, or the Preservation of Favored Races in the Struggle for Life</u> (1859) and <u>The Descent of Man, and Selection in Relation to Sex</u> (1871), utterly transformed the life sciences, philosophy, and theology; it showed the continuity of human life with other forms of life and thereby significantly diluted the qualitative distinction between human life and these other forms. The basic sweep of Darwin's insights was coextensively devised but less convincingly defended by English naturalist, Alfred Russel Wallace (1823-1913), who had, like Darwin, traveled and studied extensively in South America and the Pacific and who, in <u>The Geographical Distribution of Animals</u> (1876), importantly added geographical perspectives to the broader claims of evolutionism. The Darwinian vision was explicitly extended into the social and humanistic arenas, in the form of social Darwinism, by other prominent thinkers of the age; most notably, by Herbert Spencer.

The modern **study of disease**, its causes and treatments, which had begun in earnest with Philippus Paracelsus and Antony van Leeuwenhoek, continued in still more revealing and useful ways in the nineteenth century. The foundations of modern scientific immunology are owed to English physician, Edward Jenner (1749-1823), who discovered a preventive vaccine for smallpox in 1796-98. German pathologist, distinguished social scientist, and progressive political reformer, Rudolf Virchow (1821-1902), pioneered the science of cellular pathology (1858) and the practice of public health/sanitation (beginning in 1859 in Berlin). French chemist and microbiologist, Louis Pasteur (1822-95), made the first conclusive, scientific demonstration that micro-organisms (germs) are the cause of infectious disease and thus also conclusively demonstrated the dependence and vulnerability of human life on/to other biological organisms, even organisms of microscopic proportion. Pasteur's early work on fermentation constituted the formative contribution to the science of bacteriology. He also importantly developed a process of sterilizing food and drink, pasteurization (1864), produced a vaccine for rabies (1885), and became the founding director of the foremost research organization in the world devoted to the prevention of infectious disease, the Pasteur Institute in Paris (1888). On the basis of Pasteur's bacteriological discoveries, English surgeon, Joseph Lister (1827-1912), developed antiseptic treatments for wounds, formulated the basis of modern antiseptic surgery, and dramatically decreased the incidence of post-operative fatalities from infection (1867). Also on the basis of Pasteur's formative demonstrations, German bacteriologist, Robert Koch (1843-1910), refined the techniques of bacteriological study; he, most notably in this respect, developed a unique method of staining and identifying bacteria as well as novel methods of cultivating bacteria for study. Koch too discovered the bacterial cause of many infectious diseases; most significantly, anthrax (1876), tuberculosis (1882), and cholera (1884). His studies of malaria and plague also contributed tellingly to the eventual conquest of these diseases. It was on the groundwork of these discoveries that vaccines/immunizations and inoculations were developed for the prevention, diagnosis, and treatment of what were among the most lethal diseases of the time. Few persons in human history have relieved more suffering than Koch; he won the 1905 Nobel Prize in Medicine for his 1890 discovery of a test for tuberculosis. Arguably the most significant achievement of nineteenth-century medicine unrelated to etiology as such was the discovery and use of general anesthesia (ether) by American scientist, Charles Thomas Jackson (1805-90), and American dental surgeon, William Thomas Green Morton (1819-68), in 1841-46. The enormous corporate expansion of bio-medical technology, characteristic of the twentieth century, followed as has been said.

The seminal development of experimental methods and of experimentally ascertained insights in the social sciences, in psychology and sociology most notably, are also owed to the nineteenth century. Although much influenced by the French empirical speculations of the eighteenth century (by such as the empirical psychologies of Étienne de Condillac and Claude-Adrien Helvetius) and by the German empirical speculations of the early nineteenth century (by such as the empirical psychologies of Johann Friedrich Herbart and Gustav Theodor Fechner), **experimental psychology** as such (psychology as a rigorous scientific subject) began in the late nineteenth century. The earliest scientific studies concerning biological influences on consciousness/behavior, the connections of biology and psychology, were made in this time. The German physiologist, psychologist, and philosopher, Wilhelm Max Wundt (1832-1920), fashioned the first experimental methods and principles of physiological psychology in his most important text, <u>Principles of Physiological Psychology</u>, in 1874 and established the first laboratory of experimental psychology (the

Institute for Experimental Psychology) in Leipzig in 1879. Wundt's work also inspired the early development of psychological systems; most significantly, structuralism (discerning the elements of mind/consciousness), functionalism (discerning the operations of mind/consciousness), and experientialism (discerning the character of concrete human experience).

The electrical-neurological connections of the inanimate and biological realms first recognized by Luigi Galvani were extended to psychological phenomena by the eminent Russian physiologist-psychologist and 1904 Nobel laureate in medicine, Ivan Petrovich Pavlov (1849-1936). In animal experiments concerning digestive function, Pavlov discovered the conditioned reflex, the neurophysiology of reflexive responses to environmental stimuli, in 1889. Pavlov's major work, <u>Conditioned Reflexes</u> (1926), contained the basic principles of animal and human psychology according to its reflexive properties. These principles were widely accepted as the official psychological doctrine of the Soviet Union and they had a profound influence on the subsequent development of twentieth-century psychology, most particularly on the development of behaviorism. American psychologist, John Broadus "J.B." Watson (1878-1958), was the principal architect of behaviorism. In his most celebrated manuscripts, <u>Behavior: An Introduction to Comparative Psychology</u> (1914) and <u>Psychology from the Standpoint of a Behaviorist</u> (1919), and on the basis of animal and human experiment, Watson argued that psychological phenomena are rooted in observable response to environmental stimuli; they are rooted in behavior, not in consciousness. This stridently mechanistic assertion and its possibilities for tightly controlled experiment as well as for programmed learning greatly influenced the subsequent course of contemporary modern psychology and contemporary modern education; most notably, by way of <u>Walden Two</u> (1961), the foremost manuscript of American psychologist, Burrhus Frederic "B.F." Skinner (1904-90). Arguably the most accomplished work concerning the relative contributions of heredity and learning, of genetic transmission and environmental influence, to individual and collective patterns of behavior was done by Swiss psychologist, Jean Piaget (1896-1980), who had been a student of the remarkable Carl Jung, and by Austrian zoologist and 1973 Nobel co-laureate in medicine, Konrad Zacharias Lorenz (1903-89). Piaget, mainly in <u>Judgment and Reasoning in the Child</u> (1924) and <u>Genetic Epistemology</u> (1970), demonstrated the universal, genetically determined stages of human development, the characteristic nature of each of these stages, the differing senses of knowledge in each of these stages, and thus the intellectual terms in which children differ from adults. Lorenz, mainly in <u>On Aggression</u> (1966), demonstrated that much of what constitutes individual and collective patterns of behavior is learned very quickly very early in life and very rarely changes much, that animal and human language and behavior are continuous (not qualitatively distinct), and that aggressive (adversarial) impulses in animals and humans are significantly (although not entirely) innate. Behaviorism's utterly analytic character provoked several major synthetic replies; most importantly, psychoanalysis and Gestalt.

Psychoanalysis was grounded mainly in the phenomenon of human motivation and it was developed principally by the Austrian physician-psychiatrist, Sigmund Freud (1856-1939). Freud, principally in <u>Interpretations of Dreams</u> (1899) and <u>Introductory Lectures in Psychoanalysis</u> (1916), argued that human behavior is driven primarily by unlearned impulses, or instincts, primarily by the sex-instinct (the instinct to act) and the death-instinct (the instinct to withhold action). These instincts operate, in their originative state, at the unconscious, or sub-conscious, level of awareness; they are not subject to (conscious) recall at will; they are manifestly developed largely in the coercive environment of childhood; but they are nonetheless the basis of all experience. Humanity is thus decided principally by non-rational, "accidental" factors; it is tellingly influenced by factors which are unchosen, imposed, and unknown. According to Freud, if the sex-instinct and the death-instinct are unbalanced (either by heredity or by childhood experience), human beings develop emotional/psychological dysfunctions; they do not express their instincts but repress them. They do this in order to relieve the anxieties that result from the disproportion and to make their experience more tolerable. But the internal conflict caused by repression deepens, not relieves, the dysfunction; only a bringing of dysfunctional, sub-conscious repressions to consciousness by means of psychotherapy (an expression and an analysis of "unmediated" experience in the form of free-association and dreams) relieves the dysfunction (brings catharsis). Freud also developed an elaborate, tripartite theory of human personality that figured heavily in his psychoanalytic vision and which (like psychoanalysis itself) has had an enormous influence on the contemporary modern social sciences in general and on contemporary modern education in particular. According to this theory, the most basic level of personality (the id) is constituted as the reservoir of unconscious instincts which are devoted to their own immediate gratification; the level of conscious experience (the ego) is constituted as personal identity; and the level of moral conscience (the superego) is constituted as transpersonal, or social, awareness (awareness of environment and of other persons).

Freud's emotive mechanism was both broadened (to account for a larger influence of cultural factors in human experience) and muted (to account for a larger influence of free agency in human experience) by subsequent developments in psychoanalysis. Arguably the most significant contributor to these tendencies was the Swiss psychiatrist, Carl Gustav Jung (1875-1961), whose Psychology of the Unconscious (1912) added collective unconsciousness to Freud's strictly personal characterization, emphasized the role of creative agency (as distinct from the role of Freud's sexual repression) in the life of the unconscious, and asserted that the principal aim of our experience is to harmonize the unconscious and conscious dimensions of personality. The collective consciousness, according to Jung, is constituted as patterns of emotion, thought, and action that manifest themselves as archetypes shared by members of discrete cultures, in some cases shared by all human beings. These archetypes customarily take the form of dreams or fantasies and they frame the basic themes of mythology and religion. Jung's Psychological Types (1921) importantly acknowledged wide variations in personality and distinguished extroverted types of personality (which orient themselves to the external world) from introverted types of personality (which orient themselves to the inner world). A still more synthetic perspective was sought by **Gestalt theory** in the early twentieth century. The seminal vision of Gestalt was owed largely to German psychologist, Max Wertheimer (1880-1943), who argued that human perception is best explained as organized wholes, phenomena greatly affected by human values; it is not best explained as aggregates of distinct parts unaffected by such values.

The critical study of society, in the form of scientific sociology, was likewise taken in new directions in the nineteenth and twentieth centuries. On the eighteenth-century legacy of the French physiocrats (most notably, François Quesnay) and the classical British economists (most notably, Adam Smith, Robert Malthus, and David Ricardo), the earliest contemporary modern social scientists fashioned:

- stirring literary critiques of mass, industrial culture (most notably, from Thomas Carlyle, Charles Dickens, Victor Hugo, Émile Zola, and Henry David Thoreau in the nineteenth century and from many yet-to-be-discussed twentieth-century figures);
- brilliant philosophical critiques of mass, industrial culture (most notably, from Robert Owen, Claude Henri de Saint-Simon, Charles Fourier, Pierre Proudhon, Mikhail Bakunin, Karl Marx, Friedrich Engels, and Vladimir Ilyich Lenin in respect to the rise of contemporary socialism and from Arthur Schopenhauer, Soren Kierkegaard, Friedrich Nietzsche, Martin Heidegger, Karl Jaspers, and Jean-Paul Sartre in respect to other [largely existential] perspectives); and
- ongoing erudition in social and political philosophy (most notably, from Georg Wilhelm Friedrich Hegel, Auguste Comte, Jeremy Bentham, John Stuart Mill, Karl Marx, Herbert Spencer, John Rawls, and Italian and German neo-Marxism).

The development of modern, **experimental sociology**, however, is owed principally to French sociologist, Émile Durkheim (1858-1917), and German sociologist, Max Weber (1864-1920). Durkheim's The Rules of Sociological Method (1895) in particular demonstrated the terms in which the methods of natural science, empirical and statistical methods, apply to the experimental study of society. According to Durkheim, morality and religion have their source in the collective, social mind, not in individual personality; social cohesion/order/success is a function of the common, cultural values inherent in morality and religion; and social (and individual) disintegration results from the loss of such values. Weber, most memorably in The Protestant Ethic and the Spirit of Capitalism (1904-05), explained the development of various types of society ("ideal types," or generalized social models drawn from a comparative study of tangible societies) mainly in terms of their ideological and religious character and leadership, as distinct from such as their technological and economic condition (the view of Marx et al.). The subsequent development of twentieth-century sociology has been principally dominated by:

- the social behaviorism of American psychologist, sociologist, and philosopher, George Herbert Mead (1863-1931), which argued that the individual is developed (in consciousness and behavior) in a purposeful interaction with social environment, in a dynamic relational process of symbolic communication, and which was most importantly recorded in Mind, Self and Society from the Standpoint of a Social Behaviorist (1934);
- the structuralism-functionalism of American sociologist, Talcott Parsons (1902-79), which searched for a unified nexus that accounts for the characteristics of all societies and which was most importantly recorded in The Social System (1951); and
- the moderate economics of American economist, Louis O. Kelso (1913-91), which proposed a conciliation of communistic and capitalistic economic orientations in the form of worker ownership of private corporations, a form of ownership that assures quality production, broadly shared affluence,

and social justice, and which was most importantly recorded in The Capitalist Manifesto (with Mortimer J. Adler; 1958).

The development of cultural and physical anthropology and of archaeology as scientific subjects too forms an important chapter in the maturation of contemporary modern social science. **Cultural anthropology** has been most significantly devoted to a study of linguistics (the structure of language, the relations of languages, and the cultural role of language in human behavior), a study of the origin and character of human culture, and comparative studies of human cultures. The principal architects of cultural anthropology were Swiss linguist, Ferdinand de Saussure (1857-1913), German-American ethnologist-anthropologist, Franz Boas (1858-1942), American anthropologist, Ruth Fulton Benedict (1887-1948), American anthropologist, Margaret Mead (1901-78), and Belgian-French anthropologist, Claude Lévi-Strauss (1908-). Saussure turned the fertile linguistic ruminations of the late eighteenth and early nineteenth centuries in rigorously scientific directions; his studies of the structure of language examined the relation of language to what is signified by it as well as the enduring and changing characteristics of language; his most notable published work was Course in General Linguistics (1916). Boas pioneered the use of experimental techniques and statistical methods in ethnographical-anthropological investigations; he examined the character of American aboriginal (mainly Eskimo and North American Indian) language and culture by such techniques and methods; his most significant published works were The Mind of Primitive Man (1911) and Anthropology and Modern Life (1928). Benedict, a student of Boas, studied North American Indian and contemporary European and Asian cultures; she emphasized the role of culture in personality development and the terms in which cultures integrate themselves around discernible values; her most notable published work was Patterns of Culture (1934). Mead, a student of both Boas and Benedict, studied the cultures of Oceania, mainly in respect to child-rearing, gender, and personality; she compared the tendencies of the Pacific Islanders in these respects to those of developed Western cultures in ways that were not entirely favorable to so-termed developed society; and she demonstrated the immense role of cultural environment in human development and behavior; her most important published work was Coming of Age in Samoa (1928). And Lévi-Strauss characterized human behavior as a formal system of communication ordered by cultural phenomena; he compared such systems among cultures in order to reveal the structural similarities of all cultures, of all mythologies; his most significant published works were Structural Anthropology (1958) and The Savage Mind (1962). Language (not unlike mathematics) also became a central philosophical datum in the twentieth century; an account of it in this respect has been reserved for the discussion concerning twentieth-century philosophical scholarship. The still more expansive anthropological and historical visions -- mainly those of Lewis Henry Morgan, Oswald Spengler, and Arnold Toynbee -- are both descriptively compelling and philosophically engaging. They are as much studied philosophies of history as they are memorable anthropological proclamations and will be later discussed as prominent contributions to the philosophical and historical scholarship of contemporary modern civilization.

Physical anthropology has been most notably devoted to a study of human evolution (human origins, human variations, and human ecology). Arguably the most notable seminal contributors to this subject were Kenyan-English anthropologist, Louis Seymour Bazett Leakey (1903-72), and his wife, English anthropologist, Mary Douglas Leakey (1913-96). Beginning in 1931, the Leakeys discovered (tool and fossil) evidence in east Africa (mainly in Tanzania and Kenya) which established the African origins of human beings, the approximate stages in the evolution of human beings, and the approximate chronology of these stages. This evidence was also squared with earlier fossil discoveries (from as early as the late nineteenth century); it too surmised the originally/fundamentally cooperative nature of humans; and it was most notably published in Stone Age Africa: An Outline of Prehistory in Africa (1936) and Adam's Ancestors: The Evolution of Man and His Culture (1953). Extensive, subsequent investigations of this (fossil-gathering and fossil-comparing) sort and of genetic phenomena pertinent to the evolution of living organisms have brought us progressively nearer to understanding and appreciating the full scope of our development as such organisms.

Although modern **archaeology** had begun in earnest with eighteenth-century excavations of Herculaneum, Pompeii, and Olympia as has been said, its rigorously scientific basis was developed in the nineteenth century by German archaeologist, Heinrich Schliemann (1822-90), and English archaeologist, Arthur John Evans (1851-1941). Both worked principally in the Aegean; Schliemann is known primarily for his pioneering excavations of ancient Troy (beginning in 1870) and Mycenae (beginning in 1876); Evans, for his pioneering excavations of ancient Crete (beginning in 1893). Extensive, subsequent investigations, principally twentieth-century investigations, have contributed profoundly to our knowledge of ancient, medieval, and modern culture, to our knowledge of gentile, civil, and political society.

Philosophy, history, and literature

Enlightenment philosophy came to its highest mark, as has been said, in the neo-classical idealism, rationalism, and optimism of Immanuel Kant, the socio-political naturalism, vitalism, and meliorism of Jean-Jacques Rousseau, and the scientific empiricism, skepticism, and pessimism of David Hume. The dominant tendencies of nineteenth-century and twentieth-century philosophy were evoked, at bottom, by the thought of these three crowning figures. From Kant issued:

- idealistic-tending German romanticism that attempted to "complete" the critical philosophy of Kant in the early nineteenth century;
- German neo-Kantianism that attempted to reconcile the Kantian view of knowledge and the character of contemporary modern science in the late nineteenth and early twentieth centuries;
- English and American idealism that attempted to reformulate the Kantian and romantic programs in the late nineteenth and early twentieth centuries; and
- French and Italian idealism that attempted to reformulate the Kantian and romantic programs in the late nineteenth and early twentieth centuries.

From Rousseau issued the mostly nineteenth-century French, German, and Russian social and political philosophy of naturalistic bent that formed the reflective basis of contemporary socialism, a movement highly critical of the new industrial and technological order and a movement which held that the ultimate fate of the world is grounded, not in inherent qualities but, in the free actions of human beings. And from Hume issued the main programs which opposed the Kantian, romantic, and socialist legacies; these programs tended to deeply skeptical, materialistic, empiricistic, relativistic, and scientific orientation; and they were manifoldly indifferent to, supportive of, or resigned to the new industrial and technological order. These programs were influential throughout the nineteenth and twentieth centuries and they were of strictly realistic/positivistic inclination: positivism as such, utilitarianism, evolutionism, (German) phenomenology, English and American realism as such, pragmatism, and the sundry forms of analytic philosophy. The remaining major current in contemporary modern philosophy cut variously into and across the other major currents and was largely unique to the nineteenth and twentieth centuries. Existentialism and its main derivatives, intuitionism, philosophical anthropology, and (French) phenomenology, opposed both idealistic-tending and realistic-tending accounts of the world (favored by those systems which issued from Kant and Hume respectively), were customarily opposed to collective ideologies (favored by those systems which issued from Rousseau), and were most favorably inclined to direct, distinctly human experience and individualistic prerogative. Its customary vitalism, skepticism, pessimism, and distaste for capital industrialism nonetheless connected it to several other contemporary modern tendencies in philosophy. Commentary on comparable developments in literature (including historical literature) is made in the context of the following discussions about the major philosophical tendencies of the past two centuries.

Few movements in the entire history of philosophy have been as fully consumed with the spirit of searching thought or with the passion for ultimate truth as **post-Kantian German (romantic) philosophy**. It was a movement of great exuberance and encyclopedic scope that began with the work of Johann Gottlieb Fichte (1762-1814), unfolded through the efforts of Friedrich Wilhelm Joseph Schelling (1775-1854) and Friedrich Daniel Ernst Schleiermacher (1768-1834), and concluded in the genius of Georg Wilhelm Friedrich Hegel (1770-1831). It began its development in idealistic-tending directions; in the end, it embraced romantic, organic, and monistic possibilities; it aimed at achieving rigorously systematic and sweepingly comprehensive perspectives; it thought itself working out the completion of Kant's critical philosophy; and it constituted the effective conclusion of the modern philosophical equation. Fichte, Schelling, Schleiermacher, and Hegel took the free world of mind (or spirit) to which Kant's moral law points as the departing basis of their philosophy. By their view, reality is intelligible only as self-determining rational (or spiritual) activity, only as a historical evolution of reason (or spirit) toward itself, toward its knowing itself as such. In their systems, emphasis therefore rests on what was called the science of knowledge, wissenschaftslehre.

Fichte, not unlike Spinoza, had intended to show the terms in which philosophic reflection transforms/reforms human knowledge of human life. Principally in Critique of All Revelation (1792), The Science of Knowledge (1794), The Science of Ethics as Based on the Science of Knowledge (1798), The Vocation of Man (1800), and Addresses to the German Nation (1807-08), Fichte argued that authentic knowledge is possible only by faith in an act of freedom, only in a self-determining expression of will, ego, intelligence, reason. Against Kant, then, Fichte held that this expression cannot be caused by something external to reason (Kant's material thing-in-itself), for we have no experience of such a something, for one, and because, for another, only that which is freely created by intelligence can be known by it (this, according to the principle of sufficient reason). Otherwise, the notions of freedom and knowledge themselves are arbitrary, stipulative, and contradictory. Fichte therefore attributed not only the form of knowledge to intelligence, to the Absolute Ego, to Kant's transcendental ego (as had Kant), but the content of knowledge as well (contra Kant). Our experience (the phenomenal world), consequently, is nothing other than the concrete manifestation of Absolute Ego. Fichte's philosophy thereby ends in a radical, one-sided form of idealism according to which there is Absolute Ego and nothing but Absolute Ego, the entity that is both the sole cause of its own content (thus, an immaterial thing-in-itself) and the formal ordering principles of that content in one, the infinite ground of being and knowledge. The science of knowledge completes itself by becoming freely conscious of itself; it completes itself in the free thought of philosophy. It is the freedom of rational self-determination characteristic of philosophy that both makes knowledge possible according to Fichte and invests humanity with a moral dimension. This dimension draws humanity above the amoral, causal succession of natural events and eternally constrains humanity to ethical standards, to universal purpose (to God). For Fichte, consequently, morality itself implies immortality of the soul and the existence of God. By this view, humanity is morally obliged to perpetually strive for, to perpetually serve, universal purpose. Such purpose embodies both the good of individuals and the common good; it too directs concrete historical evolution. This evolution and the purpose underlying it are likewise the governing principles of education, a process properly devoted to giving directions for intellectual, moral, and social development consistent with universal aims. Fichte, who taught most importantly at the University of Jena (near Leipzig) and the University of Berlin and who was an acquaintance of Kant, Goethe, Schiller, and Hoelderlin, was also a fervent and influential advocate of German culture and German nationalism, most significantly in the period of the Napoleonic Wars.

Schelling carried the critique of Kant still further and in that broke too with Fichte, claiming that it is no more legitimate to argue that the transcendental ego of Kant (the Absolute Ego of Fichte) and concrete human experience (the phenomenal world) are causally related (as had Fichte) than to conceive of the phenomenal world as causally related to a material thing-in-itself (as had Kant). Principally in Ideas toward a Philosophy of Nature (1797), System of Transcendental Idealism (1800), and Of Human Freedom (1809), Schelling construed the phenomenal world as the concrete realization of a principle (the Absolute, the fundamental interpretive principle of reality) which is by itself mere potentiality. The Absolute cannot consequently be said to exist prior to, and independently of the phenomenal order (as Kant had supposed in respect to the material thing-in-itself and as Fichte had supposed in respect to the Absolute Ego), but as a potentiality actualized in that order; It has no "real" existence apart from its phenomenal "manifestations." Likewise against Kant, Schelling inclined to a view of nature as something other than barren interpretations by which we are morally constrained. He thought of it instead as itself possessed of purpose, life, and reason. For Schelling, nature is neither opposed to, nor is it utterly discrete from reason; it is an epoch in the organic evolution of the Absolute. This process of evolutionary development occurs dialectically in the form of opposing events (theses and antitheses) reconciling themselves in progressively higher syntheses. According to Schelling's organic form of idealistic-tending thought, the formal end of this development is reason coming to know itself in-and-for-itself, reason coming to self-consciousness, to freedom. Moreover, the highest stage of this end, the stage which completes it, is artistic expression. Schelling, who taught most importantly (like Fichte) at the University of Jena and the University of Berlin, who was most beholding to Spinoza, Kant, and Fichte, and who was an acquaintance of Goethe, Schiller, Fichte, Hegel, and Hoelderlin, was the quintessential romantic philosopher, devoted to dissolving the conflict of nature and consciousness, to unifying the finite and the infinite, to giving the volitional and rational features of human experience their harmonized due.

Fichte's fervent moralism and Schelling's ardent aestheticism were matched in early nineteenth-century German philosophy by the zealous (Protestant) religiosity of Schleiermacher. Principally in On Religion: Speeches to Its Cultural Despisers (1799), Outline of a Critique of Previous Ethical Theory (1803), and The Christian Faith (1822), Schleiermacher, who (like both Fichte and Schelling) taught at the University of Berlin, developed a sweepingly comprehensive and systematic program that was arguably the most incisive philosophy of (Protestant) religion in the nineteenth century. This essentially theological program, which had been most influenced by Plato, Augustine, Kant, and the other German idealists, sided with Schelling, against both Kant and Fichte, in its sympathetic regard for nature, to which it imputed reason, will, and moral substance. With Kant, and against Fichte and Schelling, however, Schleiermacher held to the existence of material things-in-themselves, although his position in this regard was not strictly Kantian. He argued that reality is not known merely as phenomena (Kant's position), but in terms of a yet more fundamental realm, a transcendent ground, absolute principle, or God. The absolute principle cannot be known by reason, but only immediately by religious feeling, or divining intuition; this principle is construed by Schleiermacher as the identity of thought and being, a spaceless and timeless unity of spatio-temporal plurality. Accordingly, humanity is morally constrained to move in the direction of this infinite unity, to live the moments of its life as though extended into eternity. Although he thought the notion of personal immortality implausible, Schleiermacher nonetheless envisioned the working out of synoptic world purpose and the working out of individual moral obligation coming together in one's free movement toward God, coming together in a vertical eternity.

Fichte, Schelling, and Schleiermacher had made significant progress beyond Kant. But it was Hegel who completed the resolution of Kant's critical philosophy, who thus fully connected eighteenth-century and nineteenth-century thought, who brought the organic inclinations of romanticism to their highest philosophical mark, and who carried the traditions of modern philosophy to their effective conclusion. Hegel ranks among the crowning geniuses of human history; his main works rank among the masterpieces of philosophical literature: Phenomenology of Spirit (1807), Science of Logic (1816), Encyclopedia of the Philosophical Sciences in Outline (1817), The Philosophy of Right (1821), Lectures on the History of Philosophy (1836), Lectures on the Philosophy of History (1837), and Lectures on Aesthetics (1838). Like Fichte and Schelling, Hegel, an acquaintance of Schelling and Hoelderlin, taught principally at the University of Jena and the University of Berlin. Like Spinoza and Fichte most notably, he based his life and happiness on the successful completion of his philosophy. The substantive foundations of Hegel's imposing and encyclopedic system were owed principally to Aristotle, Spinoza, Kant, Fichte, and Schelling. Much in the spirit of harmonization characteristic of Aristotle's and Spinoza's thought, which he greatly admired, Hegel protested the fragmentation of humanity evident in modern philosophy, most importantly for him in the philosophy of Kant. Although Hegel found much in Kant to his liking – the second Copernican revolution, the transcendental method, and the insistence on human freedom in particular – he sided with Fichte and Schelling in rejecting Kant's material thing-in-itself as unduly speculative, as violating Kant's own premises, and as throwing humanity into a regrettable dualism. Hegel's monistic result improves on Kant insofar as it achieves a more refined harmony among reality's manifold aspects than had Kant, insofar as it corrects Kant's ambiguous view of causality, nature, and freedom, and insofar as it shows, unlike Kant, the creative flow of human knowledge and experience throughout its history.

Hegel's epistemic orientation is nonetheless similar to Kant's. This orientation claims that, although all knowledge commences with (or has its source in) experience, experience itself simply provides an occasion for thought and does not therefore constitute true knowledge. Accordingly, knowledge depends on a mutual refinement of the rational and empirical features that make it up. This leads Hegel to the conclusion that an understanding of all empirical parts of the rational whole is necessary to an understanding of the whole itself and that an understanding of the whole itself is necessary to an understanding of all empirical parts. Thus, with Kant and Schelling most significantly, Hegel overcame both the limitations of strict rationalism (according to which reality is construed as conforming to a stipulative model) and the limitations of strict empiricism (according to which the mind is construed as conforming to the ad hoc impressions of an unreflective world).

The spirit of harmonization, which ran especially deep in nineteenth-century post-Kantian German (romantic) idealism, ran nowhere deeper than in the thought of Hegel. Hegel sought, as a grounding tenet of his organic vision, the harmonization of such classical polarities as universality and particularity, reason and nature, thought and being, mind and body. In this, Hegel held to the unity of reason and so to the view that a single Spirit permeates all individuated forms. Accordingly, what exists is consciousness in its various forms. All existence reveals itself, and is constituted as, conscious event; reality discloses itself as a mosaic of rational laws which explains such event. This system of rational laws, spiritual laws, or laws of consciousness, is called Idea and it is constituted as determinate substance and active, self-actualizing principle. The Idea is manifest in the phenomenal world (in our experience) as Spirit. With Schelling, Hegel argued that it is no more plausible to regard the transcendental ego (of Kant), the Absolute Ego (of Fichte), the Absolute (of Schelling), the God (of Schleiermacher), or the Idea (of Hegel himself) as existing prior to, and as causally related to the phenomenal world (as had Kant, Fichte, and Schleiermacher) than to regard a material thing-in-itself as causally related to the phenomenal world (as had Kant). The relationship of Idea and the phenomenal world was instead conceived in terms of potentiality concretely actualizing itself as phenomena. The phenomenal world is therefore considered the product of neither Kant's transcendental ego, Fichte's Absolute Ego, Schelling's Absolute, Schleiermacher's God, Hegel's own Idea, nor Kant's material thing-in-itself, else it violate the principles of the critical philosophy, for one, and be gratuitous, for another. The phenomenal world is thus regarded as the first stage in the developmental actualization of Idea. And the system of reason itself, the Idea, exists only as it is embodied in phenomena, only as it is revealed in human experience. According to Hegel, then, the concrete manifestations of Idea inherently work their way toward an idealization, a perfection, a progressively more authentic embodiment. This development unfolds in stages which together signify a hierarchy (a "circular" progression) from primitive forms of consciousness in which all things appear differentiated to absolute forms of consciousness in which all things are apprehended as a unity. Each of these stages depends necessarily on the prior one (s) and each develops toward pure rationality, toward a rational consciousness of its universal participation, in the end to rational self-consciousness itself. All stages are both a product (a discrete result of prior stages) and, except for the "final" stage, a prophecy (a preparation for higher stages). The Idea acquiring bare inanimate existence is the physical world; the physical world acquiring animate existence is life; life acquiring subjective, individual, or personal consciousness is Subjective Spirit; Subjective Spirit acquiring interpersonal, or social, existence is Objective Spirit; and Objective Spirit acquiring self-knowledge, acquiring consciousness of itself as such and thus existing in-and-for-itself, is Absolute Spirit, or God.

Absolute Spirit is, therefore, the full embodiment of the system of reason, the perfection of a world which exists prior to its perfection but which is nonetheless moving inexorably, if not uniformly, through its development in the direction of its own perfection (in the direction of its defining characteristics). Hegel thus accounts for the world as both an inherently (not an arbitrarily) purposeful order and as a changing/free order. Absolute Spirit itself, moreover, takes several integral forms according to Hegel; namely, art, religion, and philosophy, each of which invites and embodies a progressively higher expression of self-consciousness. The arts concern the self-consciousness of beauty; in them, spiritual truth is revealed in sensuous forms. The three basic forms of art, symbolic, classical, and romantic, represent the three orders of unity between the spiritual and the sensuous as these orders have revealed themselves throughout the historical development of the arts. Religion, in turn, makes a tacit and a veiled expression of self-consciousness, a semiotic expression that reigns above the sensuous but falls short of the fully self-conscious. And philosophy, in further turn, obtains an explicit and a complete apprehension of self-consciousness. Only in philosophy, by Hegel's view, is the Idea, the fundamental principle of reality, fully revealed. Philosophy shows the reason in all things and thereby shows the development and the unity of reason itself. Philosophy is at once the self-apprehension and the self-actualization of Idea and Spirit. The network of rational laws, the Logic (which is actual, and the actual, it), constitutes philosophy, constitutes Thought thinking itself as such. For Hegel, consequently, philosophy is the highest manifestation of Idea, the highest expression of Spirit, and the noblest form of human activity.

Hegel's brilliant philosophy of history was perhaps the most serious and authentic effort of the sort to that time, or at least since Augustine. Hegel envisioned history as the development of the world toward Absolute Spirit, as consciousness of the developmental self-actualization of knowledge. Humanity's freedom (its achievement of rational self-consciousness, of itself) and the significance of its existence ultimately reside in its being a manifestation of absolute knowledge. The philosophy of history apprehends the developmental patterns of this knowledge and, ultimately, the unity of its subjective, objective, and absolute stages; it perceives the logical self-unfolding of thought. According to Hegel, history develops by a dialectic process in which all events are connected in mutual dependence and in which all events, or theses (i.e., broad dominant tendencies), give rise to separated opposites (to the inherently conflicting, or negative, aspects of those events), which, in turn, give way to a conciliation, a resolution, of such opposition in a higher unity (a synthesis). These patterns recur cyclically to the perfection of the world in Absolute Spirit. The most compelling empirical "confirmation" of Hegel's broad view of history was effectively achieved by American anthropologist, Lewis Henry Morgan (1818-81), whose studies of North American Indians were of pioneering significance in the development of modern anthropology and whose stunning philosophy of history, Ancient Society: On Researches in the Lines of Human Progress from Savagery through Barbarism to Civilization (1877), classified world cultures by progressive stages, from savagery (which begins with hunter-gatherer societies) to barbarism (which begins with agricultural societies) to civilization (which begins with written language). Morgan's notions of gentile, civil, and political society, later fleshed out by Friedrich Engels in The Origin of the Family, Private Property and the State (1884), signify the passage from pre-literate, implicitly intrinsic culture (gentile society) to instrumental, implicitly and explicitly extrinsic culture (civil society) to self-actualizing, explicitly intrinsic culture (political society). Hegel's metaphysics and philosophy of history, together with Morgan's and Engels' scientific and philosophical ruminations on human history, frame the formative basis of the current text as has been said. This is the case despite the very considerable disagreements between Hegel and Morgan and Engels in respect to the virtues of contemporary political institutions. Hegel had a generally favorable view of the established state; Morgan and Engels, a generally unfavorable view. The current text shares the latter, not the former, view and is convinced that Hegel's social and political philosophy – particularly its endorsement of constitutional monarchies of the Prussian type – is inconsistent with his broader vision, a vision that did not have the example of socialist democracies before it.

For Hegel, the final stages in the development of human knowledge and freedom develop only in the context of a moral life which is itself possible only within the state, only within a political circumstance, only within a constitutional monarchy. The fundamental obligation of the state, by his view, is to establish and maintain laws and social institutions that optimize humanity's progress toward self-knowledge and freedom. The state, therefore, is conceived as a rational, self-actualized system of laws and institutions concerning property, contract, and punishment, a system which promotes such progress, progress that informs our conduct with impartial reason and establishes, preserves, and extends the common good by critical refinement of subjective (i.e., personal) interests. Hegel's philosophy of education follows straightforwardly from his broader program. It predictably argues that education ought to be devoted to promoting the rational self-actualization (the subjective, objective, and absolute fulfillment) of all persons. The influence of Hegel's thought on what remained of distinguished nineteenth-century philosophy – most notably on the work of Marx, Herbart, Schopenhauer, Kierkegaard, and Nietzsche – was staggering.

The travail of the human condition and its (subjective) longing for fulfillment also dominated the romantic movement in contemporary modern literature. **Romantic literature**, however, more so than romantic philosophy, championed the emotive (the vitalistic) as against the intellectual and thus aligned itself more resolutely with the volitional emphasis of Rousseau's naturalism than with the completion of Kant's neo-classical orientation. Although philosophical romanticism very importantly accounted for and very importantly esteemed the passions, it was less dominated by them than was literary romanticism (and romanticism in the visual, musical, and movement arts for that matter). The compelling (i.e., the organic) nature of both philosophical and literary romanticism, as well as of their underlying ideologies (eighteenth-century neo-classicism and eighteenth-century naturalism respectively), is nonetheless grounded in at least a tacit (if in some cases begrudging) acknowledgement by both of the necessary contributions of reason and emotion (even, the continuity and balance of reason and emotion) to human experience. The moderating and synthesizing influence of Hegel's organic metaphysics and philosophy of history portends the necessity of this conclusion.

Literary romanticism, not unlike its philosophical corollary, was too rooted in deep historical perspectives (including perspectives of pre-literate and other pre-modern cultures), in deep socio-political sympathies (including egalitarian and nationalistic sentiments, mainly evoked by the French Revolution), and in deep respect for individual and collective heroism. The leading figures of this movement were British, French, German, Russian, Italian, and American. The most notable exponents of **British literary romanticism** were among the greatest poets and novelists of any age:

- William Blake (1757-1827), the English mystic poet and artist, author of two highly memorable collections of poems, Songs of Innocence (1789) and Songs of Experience (1794), the latter of which included his acknowledged masterpiece, "The Tyger;"
- Robert Burns (1759-96), the Scottish poet of rural life, author of "Auld Lang Syne" (1788), "Tam o'Shanter" (1790), "A Red, Red Rose" (1794), and "A Man's a Man for A' That" (1795);
- William Wordsworth (1770-1850), the English poet of nature, author of Lyrical Ballads (with Coleridge; 1798; most importantly included "Lines Written a Few Miles Above Tintern Abbey"), "The Prelude" (1805), "Ode on Intimations of Immortality from Recollections of Early Childhood" (1807), and "The Excursion" (1814);
- (Sir) Walter Scott (1771-1832), the Scottish historical poet and novelist, author of "The Lay of the Last Minstrel" (1805), "Marmion" (1808), "The Lady of the Lake" (1810), Guy Mannering (1815), The Heart of Midlothian (1818), Rob Roy (1818), The Bride of Lammermoor (1819), Ivanhoe (1820), Kenilworth (1821), Quentin Durward (1823), and The Talisman (1825);
- Samuel Taylor Coleridge (1772-1834), the English poet (of exotic and supernatural themes) and literary critic, author of Lyrical Ballads (with Wordsworth; 1798; most importantly included "The Rime of the Ancient Mariner," "Christabel," and "Kubla Khan");
- Jane Austen (1775-1817), the English novelist of ironic propriety, author of Sense and Sensibility (1811), Pride and Prejudice (1813), Emma (1816), and Northanger Abbey (1818);
- George Gordon Noel (Lord) Byron (1788-1824), the notoriously unsettled English poet (of love and melancholy), satirist, and political revolutionary (who died in the Greek War of Independence campaigning on the Greek side), author of "Childe Harold's Pilgrimage" (1812-18), "The Prisoner of Chillon" (1816), "Manfred" (1817), and "Don Juan" (1818-24);

273

- Percy Bysshe Shelley (1792-1822), the English lyrical poet who had an especially deep respect for the grandeur of human reason and the prospects for freedom from tyranny, author of "Alastor; or, The Spirit of Solitude" (1815), "Hymn to Intellectual Beauty" (1816), "The Cenci" (1819), "The Indian Serenade" (1819), "Ode to the West Wind" (1819), "Prometheus Unbound" (1820), "To a Skylark" (1820), and "Adonais" (1821); and
- John Keats (1795-1821), the English poet of rich, sensuous, and dignified melody, author of "Endymion" (1818), "Hyperion" (1818-19), "Isabella" (1818), "The Eve of St. Agnes" (1819), "Lamia" (1819), "Ode on a Grecian Urn" (1819), "Ode to a Nightingale" (1819), and "Ode on Melancholy" (1820).

The leading champions of **French literary romanticism** were:

- François René de Chateaubriand (1768-1848), author of tragic, passionate, and melancholic love novels; most notably, Atala (1801);
- Stendhal/Marie Henri Beyle (1783-1842), author of tragic, passionate, and melancholic love novels; most notably, The Red and the Black (1831) and The Charterhouse of Parma (1839);
- Alexandre Dumas (1802-70), author of historical adventures; most notably, The Three Musketeers (1844) and The Count of Monte Cristo (1845);
- Victor Marie Hugo, fervent opponent of Napoleon III and author of stirring historical novels that included remarkably compassionate renderings of human suffering, particularly among the victims of unjust and corrupt society; most notably, Nôtre Dame de Paris (1831) and Les Misérables (1832); and
- Charles Pierre Baudelaire (1821-67), author of despairing and deeply expressive poetry; most notably, "Les Fleurs du Mal" (1857).

German literary romanticism owed much to the neo-classicism and the romantic leanings of Johann Wolfgang von Goethe as has been said. Its central proponents, however, were the lyric poets, Johann Christian Friedrich Holderlin (1770-1843) and Heinrich Heine. Holderlin, a close acquaintance of Schiller, Fichte, Schelling, and Hegel, was, like Goethe, much influenced by Enlightenment classicism and by nineteenth-century romanticism. His high regard for classical Greek literature and his unexcelled command of modern German idiom together fashioned a uniquely classico-romantic style. He is principally remembered for his prose elegy, the novel, Hyperion (1797-99), and for the most remarkable of his many anguished poems, "Bread and Wine" (1797-1801). Heine was a leading figure in the movement for German national unification and liberal reform (Young Germany) as has been said; he was accordingly much affected by both the burgeoning realism of the time and by the passing prominence of romanticism. He is primarily remembered for his despairing early poems, "The Grenadiers" (1819) and Book of Songs (1827), and for his satirical late poems, New Poems (1844) and "Atta Troll" (1847).

Literary romanticism eventually came to Russia as well but not until after the Napoleonic Wars. The principal exponents of **Russian literary romanticism** were Aleksander Sergeyevich Pushkin (1799-1837), Nikolai Vasilyevich Gogol (1809-52), and Mikhail Yurevich Lermontov (1814-41). Pushkin, poet and novelist, wrote melodic, narrative verse-dramas of great moment; most notably, "Ruslan and Ludmila" (1820), "Boris Godunov" (1825), and "Eugene Onegin" (1825-33). Glinka, Moussorgsky, and Tchaikovsky respectively wrote memorable operatic scores based on these works. Pushkin's most accomplished novel, the historical manuscript, The Captain's Daughter (1832), was, like his poems, a text of uniquely Russian intrigue; it juxtaposed cruel indecency and conscientious kindness, arrogance, humility, grief, and joy. Gogol was the leading novelist of Russian romanticism whose later works embraced the new, emerging realism. He is primarily remembered for his epic novel of seventeenth-century Cossack life, Taras Bulba (1834), and for his ironic and satirical portrayals of nineteenth-century Russian society, The Inspector General (1836), The Cloak (1842), and Dead Souls (1846). And Lermontov, who (like Pushkin) died from wounds suffered in a duel and who (also like Pushkin) excelled in both poetry and prose, is primarily remembered for his adventurous novel, A Hero of Our Times (1840), which disdains the imbecility of both the aristocratic and the common herd.

Like most of the major Russian figures, the foremost interpreter of **Italian literary romanticism**, Alessandro Manzoni (1785-1873), also wrote memorable poetry and extraordinary prose. Manzoni's poem, "Fifth of May" (1821), and his great novel, The Betrothed (1825-26), were signal contributions to early nineteenth-century world literature. Verdi's magnificent "Requiem" commemorated the death of Manzoni.

Literary romanticism came tellingly to the United States at roughly the same time as it came to prominence in Russia. **American literary romanticism** produced among the most exceptional achievements in the entire history of American poetry and prose. The movement's leading personalities were:

- Washington Irving (1783-1859), of graceful and elegant prose style, author of The Sketch Book (1819-20), which included the two most celebrated of his short stories, "The Legend of Sleepy Hollow" and "Rip Van Winkle;"
- James Fenimore Cooper (1789-1851), the first major American novelist, who wrote mainly adventurous accounts of the American Revolution and purposeful descriptions of life on the American frontier (which included deeply sympathetic treatments of Native American peoples); author of The Spy (1821) and the five novels of the Leatherstocking Tales (1823-41), The Pioneers (1823), The Last of the Mohicans (1826), The Prairie (1827), The Pathfinder (1840), and The Deerslayer (1841);
- William Cullen Bryant (1794-1878), the first major American poet, of nobly simple style, author of "To a Waterfowl" (1815) and "Thanatopsis" (1817);
- Ralph Waldo Emerson (1803-82), mystical essayist and poet, close acquaintance of Thoreau, known principally for his essays, "The American Scholar" (1837) and "Self-Reliance" (one of many memorable texts of the Essays [1841]);
- Nathaniel Hawthorne (1804-64), early American master of the short story and the deeply symbolic novel, mainly remembered for his collection of short stories, Twice-Told Tales (1837), and for his penetrating novels of human conflict, The Scarlet Letter (1850) and The House of the Seven Gables (1851);
- Henry Wadsworth Longfellow (1807-82), who wrote verse of unique and compelling rhythms, primarily known for his masterful narrative poetry, "The Village Blacksmith" (1842), "Evangeline" (1847), "The Song of Hiawatha" (1855), "The Courtship of Miles Standish" (1858), and "Paul Revere's Ride" (1861);
- Edgar Allan Poe (1809-49), who wrote stunning short stories and poems of musical quality; the most memorable of his mostly macabre short stories were "The Fall of the House of Usher" (1839), "The Murders of the Rue Morgue" (1841), "The Pit and the Pendulum" (1842), "The Tell-Tale Heart" (1843), and "The Cask of Amontillado" (1846); the most memorable of his many gripping and remorseful poems were "The Raven" (1844), "Annabel Lee" (1849), and "The Bells" (1849); and
- Walt Whitman (1819-92), who was greatly affected by his service in the American Civil War and who wrote poems emphasizing the freedom, dignity, and fraternity of human beings and their continuity with nature; author of arguably the greatest poem in the history of American literature, "The Leaves of Grass" (1855-91), which most significantly included "Song of Myself" (1855), "Drum-Taps" (1865), and "Sequel to Drum-Taps" (1865-66).

Philosophical (and literary) romanticism was not the end of the Kantian legacy as has been said. German neo-Kantianism, English and American idealism, and French and Italian idealism also continued to reformulate the Kantian (and romantic) programs into the late nineteenth and early twentieth centuries. **Neo-Kantianism** represented a renewed interest in Kant among late nineteenth-century and early twentieth-century German thinkers. It was provoked by materialistic critiques of Kant (as well as post-Kantian German idealism/romanticism) and by the development of contemporary modern science since Kant. It attempted to reconcile Kantian method and recent developments in science to the end of opposing the irrational character of the new materialism and to the end of establishing philosophy itself as a form of scientific inquiry. Its principal advocates were: Gustav Theodor Fechner (1801-87), Rudolf Hermann Lotze (1817-91), Wilhelm Max Wundt, Rudolf Christoph Eucken (1846-1926), the 1908 Nobel laureate in literature, and Wilhelm Windelband (1848-1915).

Late nineteenth-century and early twentieth-century **English idealism** turned decisively away from the empirical legacy of British philosophy. It even regarded nineteenth-century British empiricism as a regressive interlude in the development of European thought. It much preferred Kant, Fichte, Schelling, and Hegel to Locke, Hume, Bentham, and Mill. This movement effectively came to an independent reformulation of early nineteenth-century German idealism. Easily the most prominent figure in the movement was Thomas Hill Green (1836-82). Green's radical form of idealistic-tending thought, which most nearly resembled Fichte's among those to whom he was most indebted, held that an all-uniting Universal Self-consciousness, a noumenal or spiritual world, is presupposed by, and makes possible the phenomenal world (and our knowledge of it). The determinate order of nature is not therefore the source of consciousness, as the empiricists had argued, but itself a product of consciousness. Green conceived of humanity, of the human self, as a free, eternal, and unifying consciousness (a consciousness not formally unlike universal mind) which organizes impressions or sensations in such a way that they are made intelligible and that they qualify as knowledge. According to this view, humanity is a moral agent in virtue of its capacity to conceive of an idealized state of itself and to willfully aspire to that state. Humanity is so endowed, for Green, because it is a replica, albeit an imperfect replica (owing to its participation in nature), of Universal Self-consciousness, a participant in the consciousness of God (as well as in the natural order). The idealized state of humanity, in turn, the good, is a perfection to be attained or fulfilled, something absolutely intrinsic, independent, supreme, and desirable. Humanity's moral and socio-political duty entails an active pursuit of the good, a pursuit implying a form of universal equality and respect among all persons, a pursuit which implies Kant's categorical imperative. In this, all persons must be treated as ends-in-and-for-themselves; no self-interest can be therefore realized apart from, let alone contrary to the common good. The perfection of others is consequently entailed by the notion of ourselves as perfectible and morality is itself thought a function of rational community. There can be, moreover, no notion of political obligation except in the context of this ideal, an ideal by which the rights of all are mutually recognized and honored in a fraternal world order. Although humanity obtains only an incomplete glimpse of this ideal and never fully obtains it, we nonetheless move fragmentally in the direction of its fulfillment. The most significant of Green's works were Prolegomena to Ethics (1883) and Lectures on the Principles of Political Obligation (1895).

Like Green, English idealist, Francis Herbert Bradley (1846-1924), too argued that humanity has an inherent, but an incomplete perception of the Absolute and that this perception is contrary to an apprehension of the world as fragmented appearances. Also like Green, Bradley was convinced that this spiritual Absolute, or unifying principle of reality, is necessarily presupposed by our knowledge and by our disparate experience. This is tantamount to claiming, somewhat as had Schelling (to whom Bradley was most beholding), that a knowledge of particular things entails a knowledge of them as harmonious participants in one fundamental reality, a knowledge of them in the unity of all experience. Bradley's ethics and politics also predictably resemble Green's. Accordingly, humanity is a moral agent in virtue of its possessing an intent to realize itself as an infinite whole, as a self-conscious participant in the Absolute. The ultimate ends of reality, morality, and socio-politicality are thereby coextensive for Bradley. Bradley's most significant works were Ethical Studies (1876), Principles of Logic (1883), and Appearance and Reality (1893). The most emphatic Hegelian tendencies in the English idealism of this period were formed in the thought of Bernard Bosanquet (1848-1923), who argued that human fulfillment resides in the "completion" of the system of knowledge, morality, and beauty, resides in humanity coming to one with Absolute Unity. Also contributing significantly to this movement were the pluralistic and personalistic idealism of John Ellis McTaggart (1866-1925) and the subjectivistic and idealistic aesthetics of Robin George Collingwood (1889-1943).

Neo-Hegelianism also had a noteworthy affect on late nineteenth-century and early twentieth-century American philosophy. The leading figure in the **American idealism** of this period was Josiah Royce (1855-1916), who construed the whole of reality as consisting in ideas. For Royce, the fundamental interpretive principle of reality is an orderly, rational, omniscient, and knowable Logos which includes all finite selves and all finite forms of consciousness (and is, as such, personalistic) but which is also more than any or all of the finite selves and the finite forms of consciousness comprising it. It is more than any or all such selves and forms in virtue of its completing, unifying, and making self-conscious these selves and forms. The moral dimension of human existence entails a faith in, and a loyalty to this universal omniscience, this highest good. Royce's most significant works were The Religious Aspect of Philosophy (1885) and The World and the Individual (1901-02).

The development of idealistic tendencies in late nineteenth-century and early twentieth-century French philosophy was more the result of critical replies to the positivism of Auguste Comte than the result of an independent reconsideration of post-Kantian German idealism. The major contributions to the **French idealism** of this period were:

- the pluralistic and personalistic system of Charles Bernard Renouvier (1815-1903), which denied the existence of a noumenal world and confined knowledge to the relativity of phenomenal relations;
- the vitalistic and evolutionistic reconciliation of idealism and naturalism (realism) of Alfred Fouillée (1838-1912), which interpreted reality as a singular, active, psychic force, as idée-force; and
- the program of Émile Boutroux (1845-1922), which construed reality as unfolding in the form of a hierarchy of existential levels from highly determinate (and devoid of freedom), to progressively more indeterminate and free, to altogether indeterminate and ultimately free (to God).

The idealistic movement in twentieth-century Italian philosophy was governed mainly by critical replies to what it considered the unduly static world views of the recent British Hegelians (principally Bosanquet). Unsurprisingly, the **Italian idealism** of this period thereby emphasized the historical (as distinct from the logical and metaphysical) aspects of Hegel's thought. It consequently interpreted reality as the evolution of active and creative thought, as the progressive evolution of human achievement. The most prominent exponent of this view was Benedetto Croce (1866-1952). Embracing the central tenet of idealism, that reality is spiritually constituted and that spirit is manifest in thought and experience, Croce construed the manifestation of spirit in tangible, human, and present (as distinct from ethereal, transcendent, and past or future) terms. His organic (and humanistic) form of idealistic-tending philosophy took as primary the character and purpose of the concrete human experiences of thinking (humanity's theoretical aspect) and willing (humanity's practical aspect). He further bisected the theoretical aspect into its intuitive (or aesthetic) and its conceptual (or rational) stems. The intuitive stem is that by which the content of human experience is obtained. It entails both perception and the expression of perception in imaginative media; it entails both the basal impressions from which all experience and thought springs and the transformation of those impressions in artistic images. The conceptual stem formally organizes the material which intuition brings to it. Willing, in turn, impels us to action, impels us to act in accord with the theoretical insights which ground the will itself. Education, it follows according to Croce, is nothing other than a dutiful cultivation of the theoretical and practical aspects of reality. Croce's most significant works were <u>Aesthetic as Science of Expression and General Linguistic</u> (1902), <u>Logic as Science of Pure Concept</u> (1905), <u>What Is Living and What Is Dead in the Philosophy of Hegel?</u> (1915), <u>History -- Its Theory and Practice</u> (1917), and <u>La Poesia</u> (1936).

Although a close associate of Croce (until the formal advent of fascism in Italy to which Croce was fervently opposed) and sharply influenced by Croce, the other major advocate of idealism in early twentieth-century Italian philosophy, Giovanni Gentile (1875-1944 [assassinated]), nonetheless argued that Croce's unity of experience and his view of this unity's multiple expressions (in various activities) are incompatible. Gentile consequently opted for a position which, in his judgment, better accounted for the ideal unity of subject and object in self-conscious experience. This position, which signifies the fulfillment of self-consciousness, entails the synthesis of all disparate manifestations; most notably, the synthesis of art, religion, history, and education. Gentile was ardently devoted to educational reform and briefly held a formal government post to that end; he was assassinated as a consequence of his fascist sympathies. His most significant works were <u>Summary of Education as Philosophical Science</u> (1913-14), <u>The General Theory of the Spirit as Pure Act</u> (1916), and <u>System of Logic as Theory of Knowing</u> (1917).

What remained of distinguished contemporary modern philosophy (and literature) was occupied principally with critical replies to the doctrines of contemporary modern idealism. These replies took three main forms: the socio-political materialism that issued, at bottom, from Rousseau's thought; the scientific materialism that issued, at bottom, from Hume's; and the existential anti-materialism that was largely unique to the nineteenth and twentieth centuries. All of these forms tended to a more skeptical (and pessimistic) attitude than idealism had typified and all tended as well to emphasize concrete experience more fully than idealism had.

The new, mass industrial-technological order of the nineteenth century made many significant contributions to human progress as has been said. It too, however, brought many intractable and entirely unedifying problems to the human and the ecological conditions as has been also said. **Socio-political materialism** offered the most strident, discerning, and influential critique of capital industrialism (and idealistic/romantic philosophy as well). The leading figures of this movement were the social and political thinkers who established the basis of contemporary socialism and who were the most incisive advocates of a transformed social and political order: Robert Owen, Claude Henri de Saint-Simon, Charles Fourier, Pierre Proudhon, Mikhail Bakunin, Karl Marx, Friedrich Engels, and Vladimir Ilyich Lenin. Of these, only Marx achieved high renown for philosophical work concerning subjects other than strictly social and political ones and this work, this fundamentally materialistic thought, was itself greatly influenced by that of German philosopher, Ludwig Andreas Feuerbach (1804-72). Feuerbach rejected the idealistic-tending content of Hegel's philosophy while nonetheless holding on to its method (i.e., its dialectical historicism). He was convinced that Hegel's thought was a disguised form of illusionistic/supernatural religion, a form of religion that depreciated humanity and nature, which he interpreted, in turn, as the proper subjects of philosophic reflection. Feuerbach, mainly in <u>The Essence of Christianity</u> (1841), flayed Christianity and its Judaic roots (as well as Hegelianism) as an inhumane and egoistic religion that obscures and distracts from, not illumines and fulfills, human experience and its natural-material ground.[129] Feuerbach was at the vanguard of the liberal movement in nineteenth-century intellectual and political affairs, a movement that brought radical criticism down on existing conditions. He thus presided over the first major cracks in contemporary modern religious and political orthodoxy, cracks that Marx (principal among others) entered and significantly widened.

Few intellectual talents have so profoundly affected the course of human history as the German thinker, Karl Marx. Marx himself characterized his philosophical anthropologic-tending thought as a naturalistic/materialialistic mediation of the equally untenable excesses of idealism and realism. He rejected the idealistic view of reality as essentially spiritual owing to its undue abstractness and he dismissed the realistic conception of reality as exclusively concrete in virtue of its apparent mindlessness. Marx argued instead that humanity can be understood only in terms of what it has actually made of itself through its own practical activity, through its own economic and social conditions, through its own labor. According to this view, consciousness is a faculty of natural humanity and is therefore derivative of nature; it is not, as Hegel had insisted, the constitutive principle of reality, nature, and humanity. For Marx, then, unlike for Hegel, Schelling, and Fichte, there are natural entities which exist independently of consciousness. Marx does not make abundantly clear, however, how this can be known, how it affects any compelling account of the limits of human knowledge, how it figures in explaining the balanced relation of humanity's various aspects, or how it influences the place of purpose and freedom in the world. Despite Marx's ostensibly sharp disagreement with Hegel, he owed a great deal to Hegel, the dialectic tendencies of his program and his philosophical sense of history most especially. A feasible argument can even be made for the claim:

- that Hegel's very unique form of idealism, his romantic organicism effectively, is the most plausible, modern basis on which Marx's social and political philosophy may be grounded, that Hegel's organicism is presupposed by Marx's social and political philosophy; and
- that Hegel's conservative political conclusions are not entailed by his broader vision (as expressed in his metaphysics and philosophy of history) so much as Marx's social and political conclusions are entailed by this vision.

By such an argument, Hegel provides the most plausible metaphysical basis for Marx and Marx establishes the most plausible socio-political formulation for Hegel. The two together, accordingly, bring the modern intellectual equation (the equation which had largely prevailed since Descartes) to a tentative conclusion, a conclusion that is first earnestly and enduringly manifest in the socialist democracies of the twentieth century.

Marx was convinced, somewhat as Locke and Rousseau before him, that, in a state of nature, humanity is free and inclined to use its natural milieu to actively further its own self-determination. Humanity is nonetheless characteristically moved to social participation, principally because its self-determination cannot be realized autonomously. In any case, such participation is itself considered an expression of humanity's naturalistic constitution. Likewise bound up in this constitution, for Marx, is the distinctly human obligation to treat other persons in an other-than-exploitative fashion as well as the distinctly human inclination to refine productive activity (which alone characterizes and fulfills humanity) beyond the animal impulse to biological subsistence. According to this account, productive activity must be undertaken as an intrinsically creative act, an act that sets one in the direction of self-determination. By Marx's view, however, prevailing political and economic circumstance, autocratic and capitalistic circumstance, was inadequate to the task of human liberation. This circumstance, acting as it has out of feudal and civil, not out of natural allegiances, actively curtails the development of authentic humanity. This is so because the means available for such development have been controlled by the few at the expense of the many; the many have been consequently alienated from the means of their own self-determination, from the means of their own self-expressive labor, and so from themselves; and a rapacious sense of self-interest has been everywhere apparent. This extreme form of self-interest, in turn, has set everyone against everyone else and required all to regard all others as little other than means to the gratification of their own self-interest. Such an excessive egoism, Marx argued, cannot be overcome by a natural progression of thought beyond it, as Hegel had claimed, but only by a revolutionary transformation of the autocratic and capitalistic, the private, institutions which are at its foundation, only by a revolutionary form of class struggle. Only a transformation of this sort can emancipate the masses from the hold of capitalist exploitation and propel socio-political life out of its feudal and civil bondage and into the liberating possibilities of communism. The role of philosophy in this transformation is not merely to make interpretive descriptions of it, but to actively show the way to revolutionary transformation itself and give this way passionate and persuasive defense. Marx's principal work of broad philosophical moment was the Economic and Philosophic Manuscripts (1844). The most important of his socio-political tracts were the Communist Manifesto (with Engels; 1848) and Das Kapital (completed by Engels; 1867-94) as has been said.

The accomplished disciples of Marx have been numerous. The most notable of these have variously repeated, extended, refined, and corrected aspects of Marx's thought: German revolutionary philosopher, Friedrich Engels; Russian revolutionary statesmen, Georgi Valentinovich Plekhanov (1857-1918) and Vladimir Ilyich Lenin (1870-1924); and twentieth-century Italian, German, and German-American neo-Marxists, Antonio Gramsci (1891-1937), Max Horkheimer (1895-1973), Herbert Marcuse (1898-1979), Theodor Ludwig Wiesengrund Adorno (1903-69), and Jurgen Habermas (1929-), who had been a student of Horkheimer and Adorno. **Neo-Marxism**, in particular, variously acknowledged both the materialistic and the idealistic elements of Marx's philosophy, developed a "critical theory" aimed at transforming and emancipating human consciousness and culture, and muted Marx's economic determinism by also privileging cultural and intellectual phenomena. Gramsci's <u>Prison Notebooks</u> (1926-37), Horkheimer's and Adorno's <u>Dialectic of Enlightenment</u> (1947), Marcuse's <u>One-Dimensional Man</u> (1964), and Habermas' <u>The Theory of Communicative Action</u> (1984, 1987) were the defining texts of the Italian and German neo-Marxist movement.

Literary realism, **realist literature**, effectively paralleled the materialist development in philosophy. It tended to interpret life more so as it is than as it ought to be (the romantic inclination). Its characteristically sharp critiques of contemporary mass culture, not unlike those of philosophical materialism, nonetheless framed recommended directions of reform in terms that are not inconsistent with romantic senses of purpose (i.e., with romantic senses of what ought to be). Its compelling (i.e., organic) nature thus depends on its (at least) tacit debt to the formal aspects of romanticism and on its continuity with the formal aspects of romanticism; as, perhaps, the compelling (i.e., organic) nature of romanticism had depended on the anticipation of realism's contextual erudition. The leading contributors to the historical scholarship of literary realism were the French writer, Alexis Charles Henri Clérel de Tocqueville (1805-59), and the Swiss historian, Jacob Christoph Burckhardt (1818-97). Tocqueville, mainly in <u>Democracy in America</u> (1835), gave a measured assessment of contemporary democracy, acknowledging its virtues, predicting that it would likely prevail over aristocratic alternatives, but warning of its egalitarian dangers (that is, the tyrannical power and shallow judgment of the majority). Burckhardt, mainly known for his definitive work in Renaissance history, <u>Civilization of the Renaissance in Italy</u> (1860), adjudged the egalitarian tendencies of contemporary democracy even more harshly, as a new barbarism of civilization, and gave a generally pessimistic interpretation of the largely tragic aspects of world history. The foremost realist poets, essayists, and novelists also emphasized the numerous depravities of human society; they nonetheless too customarily acknowledged the redeeming features of human life and thus also the measured hope for an improved future. Arguably the most stirring exponents of the realist genre in these respects (or at least of its tendency to social criticism, to skewer social predacity in particular) were Thomas Carlyle, Charles Dickens, Victor Hugo, Émile Zola, and Henry David Thoreau as has been said. There were as well, however, many other highly momentous contributors to this remarkable movement. The most notable of the literary realists were British/Irish, French, American, Russian, Scandinavian, and German figures. The leading exponents of **British/Irish literary realism** were:

- Thomas Carlyle, the Scottish-English scholar and social critic, whose disdain for the narrow, pretentious, and material perspectives of aristocratic-bourgeois society knew few limits; author of <u>Sartor Resartus</u> (1833-34), <u>French Revolution</u> (1837), <u>On Heroes, Hero-Worship, and the Heroic in History</u> (1841), and <u>Past and Present</u> (1843);

- Elizabeth Barrett Browning (1806-61), the English lyric poet and the wife of Robert Browning, who wrote mainly of romantic love and social injustice; author of "Sonnets from the Portuguese" (1850) and "Aurora Leigh" (1857);

- Robert Browning (1812-89), the English poet and the husband of Elizabeth Barrett Browning, who mainly wrote dramatic monologues portraying human virtues and vices and the search for creative freedom and integrity; author of "My Last Duchess" (1842), "Pied Piper of Hamelin" (1842), "The Bishop Orders His Tomb at St. Praxed's Church" (1845), "Andrea del Sarto" (1855), "Fra Lippo Lippi" (1855), "The Last Ride Together" (1855), "Rabbi Ben Ezra" (1864), and "The Ring and the Book" (1868-69);

- Alfred (Lord) Tennyson (1809-92), the English poet (laureate under Queen Victoria), whose work primarily emphasized the heroic quest for love, knowledge, and justice and the often-tragic consequences of this quest; author of "The Lotus-Eaters" (1832), "The Lady of Shalott" (1842), "Locksley Hall" (1842), "Ulysses" (1842), "Idylls of the King" (1842-45), "The Princess" (1847), "In Memoriam" (1850), "The Charge of the Light Brigade" (1854), "Maud" (1855), "Enoch Arden" (1864), and "Crossing the Bar" (1889);

- William Makepeace Thackeray (1811-63), the English novelist, whose sharp satirical wit was directed mainly at human frailties (particularly in respect to romantic love) and at shallow and wasteful social conventions; author of <u>Vanity Fair</u> (1847-48), <u>The History of Pendennis</u> (1848-50), <u>Henry Esmond</u> (1852), <u>The Newcomes</u> (1855), and <u>The Virginians</u> (1857-59);

- Charles Dickens, the English novelist, among the greatest writers of fiction in any language or age, who thundered against abuses of wealth and power, against social injustices, and against mean-spir-ited decadence, who created among the richest collection of variously loathsome and benevolent characters in the history of literature, and who also crafted among the most miraculous and becoming transformations of personal character in the history of literature; author of <u>Posthumous Papers of the Pickwick Club</u> (1837), <u>Oliver Twist</u> (1838), <u>The Life and Adventures of Nicholas Nickleby</u> (1839), <u>The Old Curiosity Shop</u> (1841), <u>Barnaby Rudge</u> (1841), <u>A Christmas Carol</u> (1843), <u>The Life and Adventures of Martin Chuzzlewit</u> (1844), <u>Dombey and Son</u> (1848), <u>The Personal History of David Copperfield</u> (1850), <u>Bleak House</u> (1853), <u>Hard Times</u> (1854), <u>Little Dorrit</u> (1857), <u>A Tale of Two Cities</u> (1859), <u>Great Expectations</u> (1861), <u>Our Mutual Friend</u> (1865), and <u>The Mystery of Edwin Drood</u> (1870);

- Anthony Trollope (1815-82), the English novelist, who framed the lives of ordinary people in extraordinary, sometimes satirical, terms; author of <u>The Warden</u> (1855), <u>Barchester Towers</u> (1857), and <u>The Last Chronicle of Barset</u> (1867);
- Charlotte Bronte (1816-55), the English novelist and the sister of Emily Bronte, who fashioned poor, but spirited and independent female characters and transported them through grave misfortune to love, happiness, and success; author of <u>Jane Eyre</u> (1847) and <u>Shirley</u> (1849);
- Emily Jane Bronte (1818-48), the English novelist and the sister of Charlotte Bronte, who wrote of the tragic intersections of love, social station, and vengeance; author of <u>Wuthering Heights</u> (1847);
- George Eliot/Mary Ann Evans Cross (1819-80), the English novelist, who wrote brilliantly of the intricacies of anguished moral choice and their consequences, some happy, some not; author of <u>Adam Bede</u> (1859), <u>The Mill on the Floss</u> (1860), <u>Silas Marner</u> (1861), and <u>Middlemarch</u> (1871-72);
- Matthew Arnold (1822-88), the English poet, essayist, and critic and the son of Thomas Arnold (the English schoolmaster who had a significant, if indirect, influence on the development of the modern international Olympic movement), principally known for the austere moralism, universal range, and deep respect for enlightened culture in his literary and social criticism; author of <u>Essays in Criticism</u> (1865, 1888) and <u>Culture and Anarchy</u> (1869);
- Algernon Charles Swinburne (1837-1909), the English lyric poet and critic, of sensuous and musical style, who trenchantly condemned conservative social conventions (Victorian and Christian conventions mainly) and who greatly admired political liberation movements; author of <u>Poems and Ballads</u> (1866), <u>Songs Before Sunrise</u> (1871), and <u>Poems and Ballads</u> (1878);
- Thomas Hardy (1840-1928), the English novelist and poet, of somber moment, who wrote primarily of the cruelty of nature, the artifice of society, and the ruinous influence of both on the high aspirations of people in humble circumstance; author of <u>Far from the Madding Crowd</u> (1874), <u>The Return of the Native</u> (1878), <u>The Mayor of Casterbridge</u> (1886), <u>Tess of the d'Urbervilles</u> (1891), <u>Jude the Obscure</u> (1895), and "The Dynasts" (1904, 1906, 1908);
- Henry James (1843-1916), the American-English novelist and the brother of pragmatic philosopher, William James, who wrote masterful, subtle, and complex accounts of human character (most particularly in romantic intrigues); author of <u>Daisy Miller</u> (1878), <u>The Portrait of a Lady</u> (1881), <u>The Bostonians</u> (1886), <u>The Turn of the Screw</u> (1898), <u>The Wings of the Dove</u> (1902), <u>The Ambassadors</u> (1903), and <u>The Golden Bowl</u> (1904);
- Robert Louis Stevenson (1850-94), the Scottish novelist and poet, who wrote of high adventures in an unusually clear and rhythmical style; author of <u>Treasure Island</u> (1883), <u>A Child's Garden of Verses</u> (1885), <u>Kidnapped</u> (1886), <u>The Strange Case of Dr. Jekyll and Mr. Hyde</u> (1886), and <u>The Master of Ballantrae</u> (1889);
- George Bernard Shaw (1856-1950), the Irish dramatist and critic and 1925 Nobel laureate in literature, who wrote deeply satirical and critical accounts of conventional morality concerning class, war, poverty, religion, love, marriage, and commerce; author of "Candida" (1893), "Mrs. Warren's Profession" (1893), "Arms and the Man" (1894), "The Devil's Disciple" (1897), "Caesar and Cleopatra" (1898), "Man and Superman" (1903), "Major Barbara" (1905), "Androcles and the Lion" (1912), "Pygmalion" (1912), and "Saint Joan" (1923); and
- Rudyard Kipling (1865-1936), the English poet and novelist, 1908 Nobel laureate in literature, and close associate of Cecil Rhodes and Theodore Roosevelt, who wrote in highly energetic rhythms of deeply robust adventures and who customarily defended the conservative imperialism of the Victorian era; author of <u>Departmental Ditties</u> (1886; most importantly included "The Betrothed"), <u>Plain Tales from the Hills</u> (1888), <u>Wee Willie Winkie and Other Child Stories</u> (1888), <u>The Light that Failed</u> (1890), <u>Barracks-Room Ballads and Other Verses</u> (1892; most importantly included "Dauny Deever," "Gunga Din," and "Mandalay"), <u>The Jungle Books</u> (1894-95), <u>Captains Courageous</u> (1897), "Recessional" (1897), <u>Kim</u> (1901), and <u>Rewards and Fairies</u> (1910; most importantly included "If -- ").

The foremost interpreters of **French literary realism** were:

- Honoré de Balzac (1799-1850), the masterful novelist, who fashioned among the most memorable characters and among the most detailed accounts of everyday life in the history of literature; his principal work, The Human Comedy (1829-50), was a vast collection of novels and short stories; most notably, The Curé of Tours (1832), Eugénie Grandet (1833), Père Goriot (1834), César Birotteau (1837), Cousin Bette (1847), and Cousin Pons (1847);
- Victor Marie Hugo, the romantic-realist novelist;
- Gustave Flaubert (1821-80), the novelist of painstakingly exacting style, who wrote of the futility of mediocre existence; author of Madame Bovary (1857), Salammbô (1862), The Sentimental Education (1869), The Temptation of Saint Anthony (1874), and Three Tales (1877);
- Émile Edward Charles Antoine Zola, the stupendous novelist and incisive social critic, who wrote powerful and unflattering portrayals of French working-class life in the Second Empire, who was persecuted for his opposition to the government's execrable treatment of Alfred Dreyfus, and who fashioned evolutionistic accounts of the Rougon-Macquart family (1871-93) in particular, accounts which included both hereditary and environmental factors; author of The Dram Shop (1877), Nana (1880), Germinal (1885), and The Downfall (1892); and
- Henri René Albert Guy de Maupassant (1850-93), the author of pessimistic short stories and novels; most notably, Pierre et Jean (1888).

The leading figures of **American literary realism** were:

- John Greenleaf Whittier (1807-92), the poet of rural life, of the common person, and of abolitionist causes; author of "Moll Pitcher" (1832), "Songs of Labor" (1850), "The Barefoot Boy" (1856), "Barbara Frietchie" (1864), "Snow-Bound" (1866), and "Maud Muller" (1867);
- Henry David Thoreau, the essayist and close acquaintance of Emerson and Alcott, who championed the simplicities of nature over the inanities of industrialism, who emphasized the importance of individual self-reliance in life, and who opposed as unjust American imperialist treatments of native, indentured, and Mexican peoples; author of "Civil Disobedience" (1849), A Week on the Concord and Merrimack Rivers (1849), and Walden (1854);
- Herman Melville (1819-91), the philosophical novelist whose sea-tales were largely disguised allegories of the human struggle for virtue against contending, material tendencies; author of Typee (1846), Omoo (1847), Moby Dick (1851), Pierre (1852), The Piazza Tales (1856; most importantly included "Bartleby the Scrivener"), and Billy Budd, Foretopman (1891);
- Walt Whitman, the romantic-realist poet;
- Emily Dickinson (1830-86), the reclusive poet who wrote unusually concise and bold verse, mainly of love and death; almost all of her major work was published posthumously in waves, beginning in 1890 (Poems by Emily Dickinson); author of "Because I Could Not Stop for Death," "I Died for Beauty," and "Parting;"
- Louisa May Alcott (1832-88), the novelist and close acquaintance of Thoreau, who was, like Whitman, greatly affected by her service in the American Civil War and who wrote principally of the charms of child-dominated family life; author of Little Women (1868) and Little Men (1871);
- Mark Twain/Samuel Langhorne Clemens (1835-1910), the essayist and novelist who also wrote engaging short stories, best known for his anti-racist and anti-imperialist sentiments and for his satirical, ironic, and humorous accounts of life, often framed in vernacular language; author of "The Celebrated Jumping Frog of Calaveras County" (1865), The Innocents Abroad (1869), The Adventures of Tom Sawyer (1876), The Prince and the Pauper (1882), Life on the Mississippi (1883), The Adventures of Huckleberry Finn (1884), A Connecticut Yankee in King Arthur's Court (1889), and The Tragedy of Pudd'nhead Wilson (1894); and
- Stephen Crane (1871-1900), the novelist and writer of short stories, who wrote mainly of the struggle for redemption from poverty and danger; author of Maggie: A Girl of the Streets (1893), The Red Badge of Courage (1895), and "The Open Boat" (1898).

The most notable champions of **Russian literary realism** were:

- Ivan Sergeyevich Turgenev (1818-83), the novelist, dramatist, and writer of short stories, who stridently denounced the privileged antics of the aristocracy, defended the oppressed (mainly, the serfs), and gave stirring accounts of the heroic search for authenticity and happiness; author of Sportsman's Sketches (1847-51; most importantly included "Biryuk," "The District Doctor," and "Khor and Kalinich"), "A Month in the Country" (1850), Rudin (1855), A Nest of Gentlefolk (1858), On the

Eve (1860), <u>Fathers and Sons</u> (1861), <u>Smoke</u> (1867), <u>Torrents of Spring</u> (1871), and <u>Virgin Soil</u> (1876);

- Feodor Mikhailovich Dostoyevsky (1821-81), the novelist, among the towering figures of world literature, who fashioned the inherent paradox and madness of human life, the spiritual crisis of humanity, a species caught between malice and benevolence, driven to emotional turbulence and despair by its nature and by its tangible miseries, and lifted to redemption only by religious faith; imprisoned for his youthful liberalism, he was transformed by religious orthodoxy and its special brand of madness; author of <u>Poor Folk</u> (1846), <u>The House of the Dead</u> (1862), <u>Notes from Underground</u> (1864), <u>Crime and Punishment</u> (1866), <u>The Idiot</u> (1868), <u>The Eternal Husband</u> (1870), <u>The Possessed</u> (1871-72), <u>A Raw Youth</u> (1875), and <u>The Brothers Karamazov</u> (1880);
- Lev Nikolayevich "Leo" (Count) Tolstoy, the novelist, among the greatest writers in the entire history of world literature, who fashioned an account of social life that routinely corrupts the ideals of natural humanity and overwhelms human decency and happiness; not unlike Dostoyevsky, he was transformed by a religious conversion in which he attempted to break through the inherent injustices of class difference and to embrace a sense of basic Christian simplicity, love, and peace; author of <u>Sebastopol</u> (1855-56), <u>War and Peace</u> (1863-69), <u>Anna Karenina</u> (1875-77), <u>A Confession</u> (1879), <u>The Death of Ivan Ilyich</u> (1886), and <u>Resurrection</u> (1899);
- Anton Pavlovich Chekhov (1860-1904), the dramatist and writer of short stories, also an accomplished physician who worked mainly in the relief of famine and disease among the poor; characterized the decline of aristocratic life in both comic and tragic terms, in terms principally of the irrational and hopeless despair of a spent society and of persons in such a society whose values no longer sustain them; author of "The Steppe" (1888), "The Sea Gull" (1896), "Uncle Vanya" (1899), "The Three Sisters" (1900), and "The Cherry Orchard" (1904); and
- Maxim Gorky/Aleksei Maximovich Pyeshkov (1868-1936), the writer of plays, short stories, and novels depicting the vigor, nobility, and joyless poverty of peasants and workers and the savagery, dishonesty, and profligacy of the bourgeoisie and aristocracy; himself a poor and greatly disadvantaged youth, he became a revolutionary socialist, sided with the anti-tsarist forces in both the 1905 and 1917 revolutions, and was the literary architect of social realism; author of <u>Foma Gordeyev</u> (1899), "Twenty-Six Men and a Girl" (1899), "The Night's Lodging" (1902), <u>Mother</u> (1906), <u>My Childhood</u> (1913), <u>In the World</u> (1916), <u>My Universities</u> (1923), and <u>The Life of Klim Samgin</u> (1927-36).

The leading advocates of **Scandinavian literary realism** were also among the giants of the broader movement. Their work, of tragic tendency, inclined to psychological drama of deeply introspective color, opposed the restrictive and unjust conventions of contemporary society, and included elements that looked clearly forward to the impressionistic, existentialistic, and expressionistic orientations of the late nineteenth century and of the twentieth century. Henrik Ibsen (1828-1906), the Norwegian dramatist, was among the most influential figures in contemporary modern theater; he was the author of "Brand" (1866), "Peer Gynt" (1867), "A Doll's House" (1879), "Ghosts" (1881), "An Enemy of the People" (1882), "The Wild Duck" (1884), "Hedda Gabler" (1890), and "The Master Builder" (1892). (Johan) August Strindberg (1849-1912), the Swedish dramatist, was likewise an innovative genius; he was the author of "The Father" (1846), "Miss Julie" (1888), and "A Dream Play" (1902). The most significant contributor to **German literary realism** was the dramatist and 1912 Nobel laureate in literature, Gerhart Hauptmann (1862-1946). Hauptmann emphasized the great suffering of disadvantaged workers, the fateful terms in which human decency is corrupted by social problems, and the necessity of liberal reform. His most memorable works were "The Sunken Bell" (1886), "Before Dawn" (1889), "The Weavers" (1892), "Hannele" (1893), "Drayman Henschel" (1898), and "Rose Berndt" (1903).

Although the notion of post-modernism as such was first explicitly employed in architecture surprisingly enough, and in the 1960s (not the 1860s) no less, the seminal stages of the notion are here taken to have occurred in the gradual turn away from the organic, monistic, and intrinsic orientations of romanticism/realism (the apotheosis of modernism) toward the materialistic, dualistic/pluralistic, and extrinsic orientations of **scientific materialism**, of positivism/impressionism/post-impressionism, in the late nineteenth century. This turn was moved primarily by the scientific-technological discoveries, skeptical temperaments, and relativistic tendencies of the time and it was first systematically expressed in philosophical terms by the (scientific) **positivism** of the French thinker and close acquaintance of Saint-Simon, Auguste Comte (1798-1857). Comte's realistic-tending philosophy owed its fundamental roots to Hume; it was recorded most notably in <u>Course of Positive Philosophy</u> (1830-42), <u>The System of Positive Polity</u> (1851-54), and <u>The Catechism of</u>

<u>Positive Religion</u> (1852); and it sought an empirical knowledge of the natural laws of social and political life, a rigorously scientific knowledge of socio-political phenomena. Comte argued that human knowledge has developed through three successive stages, from earliest to most recent, from least well developed to most fully developed: the theological (emphasis on the supernatural), metaphysical (emphasis on ideas), and positive stages. According to Comte, theology and metaphysics both attempt the unachievable, both attempt the futile task of explaining the world in absolute terms. The positive stage, conversely, explains the true nature of things in relativistic terms by direct experience and by the laws of experimental science. Comte's observations concerning the historical evolution of knowledge led him to a systematic classification of the sciences (to a hierarchy of human knowledge) according to the order in which they have appeared in the positive stage. This hierarchy progresses from the simplest and most specific science, mathematics, to the most complex and general form of knowledge, sociology (which is taken to include philosophy, most notably ethics). Although each level of the hierarchy presupposes each prior level, Comte nonetheless evaded the fall to reductionism and the most extreme forms of realism by arguing that no level in the hierarchy is reducible to any of the others. He also held to a view of the social and political order in which the egoistic interests of the individual are cultivated in accord with the nobility of reason and in the form of humanity's social impulse, or feeling, of love. For Comte, the central ethical command and the central principle of his religion of humanity is to live for others and thus to live in harmony and comfort with others. It is not altogether clear, however, that such a principle is derivable from direct experience of the empirical sort that Comte thought primary. He nonetheless advocated achieving this principle in a progressive revision of existing social and political institutions and by institutional means, by evolutionary means, as distinct from in a radical destruction and reconstruction of such institutions by means of civil disobedience, by revolutionary means. Also unlike the leading French philosophers of the Enlightenment and too despite his sympathies for all human beings, Comte opposed popular representation in government on the grounds that it makes the informed dependent on, and victim of, the uninformed. This, of course, supposes that the uninformed stand in the majority, a phenomenon that authentic, public education is designed to redress.

The new scientificism had had a significant influence, albeit a less systematic influence, on nineteenth-century philosophy even before Comte. This influence was nonetheless more so an empiricistic reaction to earlier developments – as in the thought of German philosopher, Johann Friedrich Herbart (1776-1841) – or an empiricistic extension of earlier tendencies – as in the utilitarianism of British thought. Although he had been a student of Fichte at the University of Jena, Herbart stood largely against the characteristically idealistic orientations of the post-Kantian German development. He regarded this development as an aberration of the Kantian principles which it had variously proposed to follow, refine, and complete. In its place, Herbart proposed, principally in <u>Main Points of Metaphysics</u> (1806), <u>General Practical Philosophy</u> (1808), and <u>General Metaphysics</u> (1828-29), a realistic-tending orientation, a form of **German empiricism**, that more so resembled modern British than modern German philosophy. With Kant, he argued that thought has its basis in experience, that experience reveals only phenomena, and that the fact of phenomena presupposes the independent existence of material things-in-themselves (as the cause of such phenomena). Against Kant and the idealistic interpreters of Kant, however, Herbart denies the mind itself any formative capability. He is therefore left with a strictly pluralistic metaphysics and a strictly empiricistic epistemology in which the mind unconsciously and passively receives sensations (or ideas) from the material world; these sensations then raise themselves (and the relationships among themselves) to consciousness by inherent (not by the mind's imposed) means. Herbart's ethics and his social and political philosophy, moreover, argue for the formal union of will and reason in order to achieve a harmonious social and political order. His epistemology, ethics, and politics, in turn, formed the basis of his celebrated philosophy of education, which owed especially much to Kant and Johann Heinrich Pestalozzi. Mainly in <u>General Theory of Education</u> (1806), Herbart insisted that the educational process must begin by disturbing the mass of unconscious ideas, by exhorting them to consciousness, and it must proceed from this disturbance to an active participation in new and unique experiences, an increasing assimilation of what these experiences reveal to general ideas, and an application of these ideas to practical concerns. It is the first obligation of education, by this view, to create and maintain the interest by which unconscious ideas are disturbed, by which ideas tend to associate, and by which new experiences are sought. This obligation is best achieved through an established curriculum of essential subjects and it is ultimately devoted to the cultivation of virtuous conduct.

The empiricistic legacies of modern British philosophy – primarily through Locke, Berkeley, and Hume – were continued in the late eighteenth century and the early-to-mid nineteenth century by the utilitarianism of Jeremy Bentham (1748-1832) and John Stuart Mill (1806-73). These legacies were continued in the late nineteenth century by the evolutionism of Herbert Spencer (1820-1903). Bentham, principally in <u>Introduction</u>

to the Principles of Morals and Legislation (1789) and Deontology or Science of Morality (1834), gave the first major interpretation of the modern ethical doctrine, **utilitarianism**. Bentham's realistic-tending thought was mainly devoted to establishing a principle of moral conduct for the individual and a scientific basis for the legislative improvement of the social and political order. His self-evident "principle of utility" approves of all actions which produce happiness in the form of pleasure and disapproves of all actions which produce unhappiness in the form of pain. Accordingly, the system of jurisprudence and legislation that governs the socio-political fabric of life must have as its primary obligation the formation of humanity's actions so as to produce pleasing consequences; that is, the greatest possible quantity of happiness. Bentham's philosophy of education, his "chrestomathia," was likewise based on the principle of utility and on a hedonistic calculus that, at once, determines the quantities of pleasure and happiness and, thus, too the relative merits of alternative courses of action.

The formative affect of Bentham's thought (as well as the philosophy of Saint-Simon and Comte and the poetry of Wordsworth and Coleridge) on that of Mill was immense as was the influence of Mill's liberal teaching on the pattern of nineteenth-century reform in government (most particularly in respect to women's rights, labor unions, and proportional representation). Mainly, if variously, in System of Logic (1843), Principles of Political Economy (1848), On Liberty (1859), and Utilitarianism (1861), Mill argued that a fully satisfactory examination of social and political life (including social and political reform) depends on a sound, probable knowledge of it and that such knowledge, in turn, depends on the use of sound methods of inquiry. He therefore concerned himself, as a first priority, with fundamental logical and psychological issues; that is, with establishing a valid and reliable system of inductive logic. Assuming the uniformity of nature and the doctrine of the association of ideas, Mill attempted to demonstrate that all knowledge, all inference and proof (except self-evident truths), consists in inductions, in inferences from known to unknown particulars. Deduction, accordingly, ends at the beginning of argument for it merely repeats what is known by induction; there are no a priori truths. Mill nonetheless held, with Kant, that only phenomena, not noumenal entities, not noumenal things-in-themselves, are known and that noumenal things-in-themselves must be thought to exist in order to explain the cause of our sensations. Mill's realistic-tending and empiricistic allegiances kept him a notable distance from Kant on most other significant issues, however. He conceives of mind as nothing other than a series of feelings and of the self as a permanent possibility of feelings which has its character formed through the liberal exercise of its own free will (that is, through the science of education). He is too persuaded, against Kant, that even the most basic laws of logic and mathematics are explainable by exclusive reference to experience. Mill's hoped-for reform of the social and political sciences and of social and political institutions is grounded in the fundamental judgments of logical experience. The terms of this reform are governed by a correspondence between social and political life and by a humanitarian type of Benthamesque ethic which claims that the measure of goodness (or happiness) is pleasure and that the sine qua non of morality is bound up in the utilitarian principle, the greatest good of the greatest number. Mill's hedonism differs from Bentham's, however, in that pleasures are taken to differ not only in quantitative, but also in qualitative respects. This allows Mill to hold that intellectual pleasures reign over sensuous ones and are readily recognized as superior to sensuous ones by all those well informed with respect to the character of both. The utilitarianism of Mill is also distinguished from that of Bentham in virtue of its interpretation of happiness as exceeding pure self-interest, as a disinterested social sentiment as well, a desire for the unity and welfare of all persons.

The naturalistic-tending philosophy of Spencer carried the doctrine of **evolutionism** into broader-than-biological spheres, principally into psychological, sociological, educational, and philosophical spheres. Mainly in a vast multi-volume work, Synthetic Philosophy (1860-93), which most importantly included First Principles (1862) and Principles of Ethics (1879-93), Spencer fashioned a highly favorable account of capital industrialism and a thoroughly optimistic assessment of human progress entailed by laissez-faire capitalism. In this account, Spencer missed most of the misery caused by the new industrial and the new capital order, rejected socialist prescriptions for correcting this misery, and championed the hierarchical arrogance of social Darwinism (the view that social wealth and power, not unlike biological survival, accrue to superior, and thus deserving, people; misery, conversely, accrues to inferior, and thus deserving, people), while being nonetheless wary of the nationalistic, militaristic, and imperialistic implications of social Darwinism. Spencer's philosophy was primarily devoted to correcting the fragmentation and the inconsistency of so-termed common sense (mostly realistic-tending) forms of thought. In this, he sought a fully informed knowledge of reality, a universal knowledge, a synthetic philosophy. His program was given to discovering the highest truths, the self-evident truths, from which the principles of the special sciences could be deduced. For Spencer, these principles are, however, not only deducible from such truths, they are also empirically accessible and thus possess the faculty of introducing themselves into the unified system. His alleged resolution of the rationalist-empiricist dispute suggests that, while knowledge is based on a priori forms of the mind (conceptual categories such as relation, difference, and likeness) which have evolved as consequences of the species experience, it is nonetheless also owed to an empirical source. This source, in turn, has progressively and variously upbuilt itself in the form of the a priori categories and thus made such categories visible. Accordingly, all knowledge is of finite and limited things and is thereby also relative. Spencer nonetheless embraces the existence of an Absolute Being as the objective correlate of humanity's subjective feeling of activity, power, and force and as underlying (and explaining) the activity of all nature and all experience. By Spencer's view, the indestructible persistence of this subjective feeling is independently expressed in mind (or subjectivity) and also in matter (or objectivity). The basic terms of Spencer's evolutionism, the fundamental basis of the species' development, is thereby grounded in an unknowable, albeit continuous, dualistic-tending adaptation of internal (or psychological) to external (or physical) events.

The crown of Spencer's synthetic philosophy is his ethics. Like Bentham and Mill before him, Spencer held that happiness in the form of pleasure constitutes the first principle of morality. More nearly like Mill than Bentham, however, he was convinced that the end of the evolutionary process, the ideal of this process, is a permanently peaceful social and political order in which every constituent achieves their self-interest and assists in achieving the self-interest of others. In this order, the notion of justice requires that all persons be free to do as they will except interfere with the freedom of others to do likewise. This thesis, which aims at reconciling what Spencer considered the extremes of egoism and altruism, regards the welfare of social and political life as a means of promoting the welfare of its individual agents. It is a thesis which therefore tends to prefer the least feasible interference of the state with the exercise of individual freedom. Surprisingly, however, and unlike either Bentham or Mill, Spencer's ethics is taken to have a (qualified) rational (as distinct from empirical) origin; it is deduced from the basic principles of the special sciences. Spencer's naturalistic inclinations are likewise conspicuous in his philosophy of education, which owed especially much to Pestalozzi. Largely in Essays on Education (1861), Spencer opposed the classical/neo-classical tradition and advocated instead a fiercely individualistic education, an education that is science-dominated and ultimately devoted to a preparation for complete intellectual, moral, and physical experience.

The new scientificism continued to exert an enormous influence, perhaps the dominant influence, on distinguished twentieth-century thought; most notably in the form of German phenomenology, English and American realism, pragmatism, and the sundry forms of analytic philosophy. Twentieth-century phenomenology developed in two main and quite different forms. The earliest was German and was scientific in basic orientation; the more recent was French and humanistic/existentialistic in basic orientation. The foundations of **German phenomenology** were rooted in the realistic-tending (and so also the dualistic-tending) aspects of Plato's metaphysics and epistemology, of Descartes' notion of the self, and of Kant's view of the phenomenal world, as well as in the realist-nominalist debate of the Middle Ages concerning the problem of universals. In customarily realistic-tending fashion, German phenomenology held to the qualitatively independent existence of objects (of knowledge) and knowing minds. The earliest notable advocate of this tendency was Franz Brentano (1838-1917), who established an empirical philosophy of mind that examined the (active) nature of mental processes by which the mind apprehends objects, mainly in Psychology from an Empirical Standpoint (1874, 1911, 1925). Brentano distinguished this philosophy, and its scientific order of skepticism, from what he considered the unduly speculative flights, the "psychologism," of nineteenth-century British empiricism, which focused on the unknowable genesis of thought. Brentano's analysis centers on an examination of the mind's central characteristic, of the characteristic that defines it, and on an examination of the products of this characteristic. For Brentano, this characteristic is the mind's referential capacity, its capacity to refer to something outside itself, to an intentional object. The framework of this claim was carried further by Brentano's talented Austrian student, Alexius Meinong (1853-1921). Most importantly in On Assumptions (1902), Meinong constructed a theory of intentional objects from a conception of such objects as anything that can be thought or intended. In this theory, the various kinds of intentional objects, together with the characteristic properties of each, are distinguished. Principal among these kinds are particular (e.g., tables), ideal (e.g., numbers), and imagined (e.g., golden mountains, square circles) objects.

This form of phenomenology reached its highest development in the thought of Edmund Husserl (1859-1938), who, like Meinong, had been a student of Brentano and who, like both Brentano and Meinong, concerned himself with both the method and the content of phenomenological analysis. Principally in Logical Investigations (1900-01), Ideas – General Introduction to Pure Phenomenology (1913), Formal and Transcendental Logic (1929), Cartesian Meditations (1932), and The Crisis of European Philosophy and the Transcendental Phenomenology (1936), Husserl grounded his sense of life purpose and his happiness on a rigorously scientific study of consciousness, a study of the foundations of human knowledge, of the laws of human experience. For him, pure phenomenology is the description of subjective processes, or phenomena, the description of what is found in, or what is presented to experience. Phenomenology thereby differs from psychology in virtue of its limiting itself to descriptions of what is displayed in experience, as distinct from giving an explanation of such displays in causal or genetic terms. According to Husserl, phenomenology takes no more and presupposes no more than what it finds in experience; psychological inquiries that pretend to do more than this (that pretend to speak of the character of the objective world itself and of the relation of the objective world and the mind, for prominent instance) fall over into speculative excess. The objects of phenomenological description are consequently intentional objects and Husserl's interest in them is in their pure, their ideal essences, in what they formally are when the particular facts encumbering them are eliminated, or bracketed away. For Husserl, only knowledge of such essences qualifies as authentic.

Although English and American realism were bedeviled throughout their development by the predictable consequences of realism's inherently dualistic character (i.e., its resort to gymnastic explanations of the relation between/among independent aspects of reality), they nonetheless exerted enormous influence on twentieth-century philosophical disputation. Their scientific orientation, wholly consistent with the dominant intellectual tendency of the period, was itself most influenced by the perceived excesses of contemporary idealism, by Hume's epistemology, and by twentieth-century advances in logic (and mathematics). The leading exponents of **English realism** were English philosopher, George Edward "G.E." Moore (1873-1958), Welsh-English philosopher-mathematician, Bertrand Arthur William Russell (1872-1970), and Australian-English philosopher, Samuel Alexander (1859-1938). Mainly in Principia Ethica (1903), Ethics (1912), and Philosophical Studies (1922), Moore, acting out of a notion earlier developed by Meinong and opposing Berkeley in particular, expanded the distinction between the act of knowing and that (object) which is known. According to Moore's original position on this issue, the object of knowledge exists independently of the act of consciousness by which it is known; the object exists irrespective of its perception. His mature position on this issue, however, significantly modified the terms of independence objects enjoy in relation to sense perceptions of them. Moore takes this move in order to show a relationship of some sort between humanity's impressions of physical objects, or "sense data," and physical objects themselves. He comes in the end to adopt the view that, while sense data may persist unsensed, physical objects do so in only a naive and hypothetical fashion. In order to explain humanity's knowledge of physical objects, by Moore's mature view, such objects must be construed as permanent possibilities of perception.

Russell, who won the 1950 Nobel Prize in Literature, had a wider audience than any other twentieth-century philosopher. His general pacifism and heretical opinions concerning liberal social and political reform (including educational reform, espoused mainly in Education and the Social Order [1932]) brought him sharp condemnation from conservative British and American governments in particular and brought him respectful acclaim from progressive devotees. His courageous social activism twice brought him imprisonment. His pioneering work in symbolic logic, moreover – mainly in The Principles of Mathematics (1903) and Principia Mathematica (with his professor, Alfred North Whitehead; 1910-13) – demonstrated that the laws of mathematics are all deduced from the basic axioms of logic. His principal contribution to contemporary realism, however, was grounded in the thought of Meinong and Moore, was recorded mainly in An Inquiry Into Meaning and Truth (1940) and Logic and Knowledge (1956), and held to the strict realist position that physical objects persist in-themselves irrespective of perception or awareness of them. He argued that this strict view is the most tenable explanation for sense perception even though the independent existence of physical objects cannot be proved. With Moore, Russell claimed that sense data are distinct from humanity's conscious sensation; but, against Moore, that they do not exist unsensed and that they are private, or immediately known only by individual subjects. Humanity's a priori knowledge is explained by the independent existence (that is, the extramental and extraphysical existence) of qualitative and relational universals; these universals stand in a direct relation with mind and with objects but they are nonetheless distinct from both minds and objects. The precise character of the relations among universals, sense data, physical objects, and minds, however, is nowhere unambiguously clear in Russell's thought.

Alexander was arguably the most systematic thinker of this tendency and he likewise came nearer to embracing the naturalistic metaphysics of Whitehead than any other major advocate of this tendency. Principally in Space, Time, and Deity (1920), Alexander identified the fundamental interpretive principle of reality as Space-Time, which he conceived as a natural, infinite, continuous, and irreducible union of spatial expanses and temporal moments. The primordial properties of this union are identity, diversity, existence, relation, substance, causality, quantity, intensity, and motion. For Alexander, however, unlike for Kant, these properties are not contributions of the mind to experience, but empirically rooted concepts. They do not prescribe laws to nature; they are themselves features of nature. The mind is itself construed, by Alexander, as a naturally evolved event. According to this account, the universal space-time matrix is the basic groundwork within which all qualitative levels of reality develop or emerge; most notably, the highest of such levels, life, mind, value, and Deity. Alexander's epistemology develops within the broad context of his metaphysical system. In it, he distinguishes two forms of knowledge, both provoked by sense perception: "enjoyment," or the mind's direct awareness of itself, and "contemplation," or the mind's indirect awareness of entities other than itself.

Although the thought of English philosophers, Moore, Russell, and Alexander, formed the central precincts of twentieth-century realism, an American form of the doctrine also contributed significantly to it. The foremost advocate of **American realism** was the Spanish-American philosopher, George Santayana (1863-1952). American realism was principally devoted to an exacting analysis of the origin and nature of human knowledge. It first took the form of epistemological monism, according to which objects of knowledge are directly apprehended by conscious agents; but it later developed along more critical lines which held to a form of epistemological dualism, according to which material objects are thought to exist independently both of mind and of the sense data by which they are known. Santayana was the leading exponent of critical realism in American philosophy. His thought more so resembles the naturalistic inclinations of Alexander's (and Whitehead's) than the more strictly realistic teachings of Moore and Russell. Principally in The Life of Reason (1905-06), Scepticism and Animal Faith (1923), and Realms of Being (1927-40), Santayana argued that all things have their source in the determinations of nature, even rational interpretations of humanity's scientific, social, religious, artistic, and philosophical activities. Such creative activities, which distinguish and dignify humanity, are thus construed as expressions of nature. In his epistemology, Santayana takes as self-evident the independent existence of physical objects and intelligent consciousness. Knowledge is construed as a system of universals, or "essences," which persist independently of physical objects (but are nonetheless representations of these objects) and independently of intelligent minds (but are nonetheless apprehended by these minds). Of the three main "realms of being" (matter, essences, and minds), matter is primary, for the form and content of its own character, as well as the content of essences and of minds, issue from it.

Arguably the most celebrated feature of Santayana's thought was his aesthetics, expressed most notably in The Sense of Beauty (1896). For him, humanity's sense of beauty is its highest inclination because it is the sense that evokes the greatest pleasure. According to this view, beauty is not a quality of objects, nor is it an intellectual, moral, or practical phenomenon; it is instead a function of one's unmediated, one's emotional response to things; it is a function of vital, free, spontaneous, and intrinsically valued response to things. Although referring only to an ephemeral moment and pertaining only to conditions peculiar to that moment, aesthetic judgments nonetheless establish an absolute ideal by Santayana's account. That is to say, although everyone responds in their own way, although everyone thereby establishes their own aesthetic standard, and although there cannot consequently be a common standard of taste with respect to aesthetic content, the form of aesthetic response is nonetheless universal and all persons make aesthetic responses and judgments as though making them for all persons. The universal form of aesthetic response, according to Santayana, and the form that makes such response aesthetic, is defined by a unique type of aesthetic pleasure. The objective features of an art product may arouse such pleasure but they do not constitute this pleasure because such features do not raise peculiarly aesthetic responses in all persons. The differentia of aesthetic pleasure, for Santayana, is the illusion of objectifying pleasure. Although its intrinsicality, disinterestedness, and universality are prominent among its features, it is this illusion that characterizes it. Accordingly, beauty is intrinsic, disinterested, universal pleasure which is thought to be inherent in the qualities of objective things, but which is instead a subjective response to such qualities. Science, religion, art, and sport are among the activities that Santayana counts as especially capable of significant aesthetic development. Such activities, he argues, qualify as ends-in-and-for-themselves, as fundamental forms of human expression, as vital features of an authentic education, and as conspicuous opponents of instrumentality.

The **process philosophy** of English philosopher-mathematician, Alfred North Whitehead (1861-1947), is closely related to the development of English and American realism, most particularly to the thought of Alexander and Santayana. Whitehead's early work concerning symbolic logic – mainly in On Mathematical Concepts of the Material World (1906) and Principia Mathematica (with his student, Bertrand Russell; 1910-13) – ranks among the most important of the century. His later work was principally devoted to an account of the universe as an organic process of becoming, to a systematic metaphysico-epistemic account of the world from a scientific perspective; it was expressed mainly in An Enquiry Concerning the Principles of Natural Knowledge (1919), Science and the Modern World (1925), Process and Reality (1929), and Adventures of Ideas (1933). Whitehead's naturalistic-tending form of humanism construed Nature as an organic system of spatio-temporal events, occasions, objects, and universals (or eternal objects that appear in concrete objects, occasions, and events), as an organic system constituting the whole of reality. God, by this view, is interdependent with the world and developing from it; God is the ground of reason, or the principle that determines which universals are to appear in concrete objects, occasions, and events. Experience thus flows from objectivity to subjectivity, not (as for Kant) from subjectivity to objectivity. With Alexander, Whitehead thus thought himself to have inverted Kant's second Copernican revolution. Whitehead's epistemology is consequently empirical. In it, he considers "prehension" the fundamental form of knowledge; prehension is unconscious in the sense of its being pre-cognitive; it takes rudimentary and implicit account of particular objects, occasions, and events; and it contains the characteristic pattern of knowledge that recurs at all levels of abstraction (i.e., at the prehensive, perceptual, and conceptual levels). Perception explicitly attends to the terms of prehensive experience and cognition brings prehensive and perceptual experience to self-conscious unity; cognition thus also shows the relations among the lower levels of abstraction. Whitehead rejects the sense datum theories of perception and knowledge, advocated most prominently by Moore and Russell, as excessively speculative and abstract, as fallaciously treating abstractions of concrete experience as though they were themselves concrete; this is Whitehead's celebrated "fallacy of misplaced concreteness." For Whitehead, the doctrine of prehension avoids such an error by bringing the fundamental nature and origin of knowledge into direct and present experience. His philosophy of education – developed primarily in <u>The Aims of Education and Other Essays</u> (1929) – flows predictably and consistently out of these broader tendencies and is widely considered a landmark contribution to twentieth-century thought on the subject. It is effectively a protest against dead, inert, useless, and insignificant ideas. Whitehead conceived of education as the use of knowledge, as the concrete and intelligent experience that defines self-development. Accordingly, the process of active experience is given more emphasis than the product and the relations of ideas are more fully accentuated than their discrete character.

Pragmatism was among the most significant movements in twentieth-century philosophy. Its highly skeptical character and its scientific orientation fashioned one of the most pervasive intellectual influences on the period. This movement, which was primarily American in origin, development, and culmination, likely constitutes the principal contribution of American thought to the entire history of philosophic discourse. Although its major figures were twentieth-century Americans, it nonetheless had its germinal roots deep in ancient, early modern, and nineteenth-century skepticism; it also owed especially much to nineteenth-century and twentieth-century European advances in the empirical sciences and in positivistic and analytic philosophy. Its founder and one of its most profound interpreters was the brilliant American philosopher, Charles Sanders Peirce (1839-1914). Peirce's work was done altogether in the form of essays which were collected and published after his death as <u>The Collected Papers of Charles Sanders Peirce</u> (1931-35, 1958); the most notable of these was "How to Make Our Ideas Clear" (1878). Peirce claimed that logic is the basis of all philosophic study; he emphasized the analytic function of philosophy in clarifying the meaning of concepts and propositions; and he developed the notion that such meaning is obtained only from an analysis of the practical consequences of concepts and propositions. His metaphysics is phenomenologic-tending; it describes phenomenal experience as it is given immediately to consciousness. His epistemology is governed by similar inclinations; it is largely taken up with a theory of signs, or "semiotic," a theory about that which refers to an object but which is nonetheless qualitatively independent of that object. In this, Peirce defends a correspondence notion of truth according to which a proposition, in the form of a sign, is true in virtue of its corresponding to its referent object, false in virtue of its not. Peirce's "doctrine of fallibilism" nonetheless persuades that no synthetic proposition (no proposition about the so-termed world) can ever be verified absolutely, by correspondence or otherwise. Peirce likely ranks among the titans in the history of philosophy, figures who have spawned intellectual revolutions or who have at least put the mark of philosophy on such revolutions. He provided pragmatism with its formative principles, principles that were later more systematically and more elaborately worked out by two other remarkable American philosophers, William James (1842-1910) and John Dewey (1859-1952).

James, brother of novelist Henry James and close acquaintance of Peirce, Dewey, Bergson, Santayana, Renouvier, Royce, and Bradley, was also a pioneering contributor to the seminal development of pragmatism and too significantly influenced the early development of scientific psychology. Mainly in <u>Principles of Psychology</u> (1890), <u>The Will to Believe and Other Essays in Popular Philosophy</u> (1897), <u>The Varieties of Religious Experience</u> (1902), and <u>Pragmatism: A New Name for Some Old Ways of Thinking</u> (1907), James conceived of philosophy as an analytic process of clarifying ideas and thereby making them useful in getting from various parts of our experience to various other parts. The test of knowledge, by this view, is the expediency (the utility) of its practical consequences in life, its problem-solving capacity. According to James, reality is best conceived as pure experience, as passionate, instinctive vision from which consciousness emerges; consciousness merely explains such experience in a posterior fashion. This experience, in turn, reveals the world as multiple, diverse, and comprised of novel and opposed events. Only such pluralistic experience, according to James, can account for the most significant features of life, practical moral and religious features. In moral respects, James argued that the world is neither inherently good nor inherently evil, but inclined in the direction of its constituents' active striving either for its success or for its failure; his ethics is therefore melioristic. In religious respects, James argued for a transcendent but compassionate God because only such a notion satisfies humanity's emotional disposition. In his epistemology, James construed the mind as the unity in/of the stream of conscious process and he employed a method of investigating conscious activity which turns the mind, and so consciousness, to an examination of consciousness itself. He also developed a unique interpretation of the doctrine of free will which conceives of the will as the capacity of mind to focus on a freely chosen, well-defined idea, exclusive of other ideas, a capacity that entails action governed by choice. The psychological orientation of James' thought also greatly affected his philosophy of education. Acting out of his characteristically relativistic inclinations, James advocated an experience-oriented, a practical, and an individual-centered education in which learning occurs fundamentally through instinct and in which the goods of society and of individuals are mutually enhanced.

Dewey, a student of Peirce and a close acquaintance of James and the celebrated sociologist, George Herbert Mead, immersed himself in social reform (most notably educational reform) as well as philosophical problems, transformed the University of Chicago and Columbia University (New York City) in both social and philosophical terms, and became the most influential American philosopher of the twentieth century. Mainly in Democracy and Education (1916), Reconstruction in Philosophy (1920), Experience and Nature (1925), Philosophy and Civilization (1931), Art as Experience (1934), and Logic: The Theory of Inquiry (1938), Dewey, not unlike James, argued that the world is constituted by indeterminacy and evolutionary change; it is a mosaic of particular, relative events unknowable in the absolute terms of traditional philosophy. For Dewey, these events are knowable only in virtue of their being consequential, or useful, in the consciously experienced lives of human beings; that is, in practical human experience. He thereby takes concrete human experience as the groundwork of his philosophy and he considers philosophy itself as the basic method of analysis used to obtain a fundamental understanding of such experience. This method is to empirically verify the useful, the instrumental, consequences (the imminent and hypothesized consequences) of practical experience. Dewey was convinced that this interpretation of the world had achieved the conciliation of rationalism and empiricism so daringly, but unsuccessfully, attempted by Kant. According to Dewey, then, experience itself is not alien to nature, but the means of discovering nature; it is the confrontation of the unified self (the knowing and willing moral, social, aesthetic, and religious self) with its environment. The culmination of human experience and happiness, by this view, is found in an aesthetic refinement and intensification of ordinary experience. Such a refinement and intensification entail a bringing order and harmony to otherwise disordered experience; the aesthetic (which pervades all integral features of life authentically lived) resolves the fragmented and suspended aspects of experience and thereby enhances the experience of living. Likely Dewey's most prominent philosophical descendants were American philosophers, Clarence Irving Lewis (1883-1964) and Richard McKay Rorty (1931-). Lewis is most remembered for his "conceptual pragmatism," according to which experience is best explained in terms of human needs embodied in a priori (conceptual) categories. Rorty is mainly known for his "neopragmatism," according to which truth can be meaningfully explained and human freedom authentically defended only in terms of intersubjective, socially circumscribed solidarity.

Dewey's philosophy of education was greatly influenced by the thought of Johann Heinrich Pestalozzi and Friedrich Froebel and it is arguably itself the most exacting as well as the most influential, reflective treatment of the subject in contemporary modern civilization. His meliorism, like James', holds that only by active social and educational involvement can the human ideal of living in harmonious community with others be realized. Also like James' educational philosophy, Dewey's is relativistic, experience-oriented, practical, and individual-centered. It advocated the development of an integrated personality (a unified moral, social, aesthetic, and religious individual) through self-ordered experience and a natural method of inquiry. By Dewey's view, education is the experimental study of humanity and its world. Education must therefore not only be brought into contact with the circumstance of everyday learning, it must be itself an experience in everyday, in democratic learning. It must acculturate by giving instruction in the skills and knowledges of intelligent doing and effective social living. Dewey reserved a high place in educational experience for physical education, considering it an excellent medium for learning such skills and knowledges as well as a fertile source of aesthetic pleasure.

So-termed **analytic philosophy** has been perhaps still more fully influenced by the genius of contemporary science than any other recent philosophical development. It has been especially much affected by the scientific inclinations of contemporary realism, by the deeply skeptical orientation of pragmatism, and by recent achievements in mathematics and symbolic logic. The analytic traditions have customarily held that there is no sufficiently good reason to suppose scientific concepts and theories literally accurate representations of the objective world despite their indispensably useful contributions to humanity's understanding of its practical life and to humanity's living out the terms of this life. Such concepts and theories are useful fashions but we cannot know with assurance if they do or they do not give valid accounts of phenomena. The depth of analytic skepticism thus leads it to reject traditional metaphysics as unduly speculative and meaningless. The major, mostly twentieth-century traditions of analytic philosophy have taken many forms; most notably, conventionalism, fictionalism, logical positivism, and manifold treatments of moral, aesthetic, and socio-political life. The earliest of these traditions were the conventionalist doctrines of Austrian mathematician-physicist-philosopher, Ernst Mach (1838-1916), French-German-Swiss philosopher, Richard Heinrich Ludwig Avenarius (1843-96), and French mathematician-philosopher, Jules-Henri Poincaré (1854-1912). Conventionalism argued that the knowable world consists solely in pure experiences, sensations, or perceptions and that our knowledge is therefore nothing other than a description of such experiences. Scientific concepts and theories are consequently regarded as handy characterizations, or conventions, which are apparently consistent with the unknowable facts but which cannot be verified by such facts. The skepticism of German philosopher, Hans Vaihinger (1852-1933), runs yet deeper. In his fictionalism, Vaihinger held that scientific concepts and theories constitute useful practical insights but that these insights are nonetheless contradictory of reality. By this view, such concepts and theories are useful fictions, the "doctrine of the 'as if'."

Logical positivism was most affected by Hume, by conventionalism, and by the symbolic logic of Russell, Whitehead, and German mathematician-philosopher, Gottlob Frege (1848-1925). It emphasized the criteria of verifying knowledge, the direct (in common practice) and the indirect (in symbolic principle) verifiability of experiential knowledge. It claimed that philosophy can achieve no other plausible end than a clarification of the meaning of all cognitively significant statements, which it took as entailing a clarification of the structure and function of ordinary and scientific knowledge. German-Austrian physicist-philosopher, Moritz Schlick (1882-1936), who had been a student of the celebrated physicist, Max Planck, and his Vienna Circle, which came to include German-American mathematician-philosopher, Rudolf Carnap (1891-1970), who had been a student of Frege, stood at the early center of this movement. The work of the Vienna Circle was most importantly enlarged by Austrian-English philosopher, Karl Raimund Popper (1902-94), by American philosopher, Willard Van Orman Quine (1908-2000), who had been a student of Carnap, by British philosopher, Alfred Jules Ayer (1910-89), and by Austrian-English philosopher, Ludwig Josef Johann Wittgenstein (1889-1951). Wittgenstein, a student of Russell, was the foremost exponent of linguistic analysis. He was convinced that most philosophical statements, particularly those of a traditional metaphysical sort, entail subtle misuses of language that raise rather than relieve ambiguity, imprecision, and perplexity and that such statements are not so much false as nonsensical, meaningless, and undecipherable. He taught that the proper function of philosophy is nothing other than making our propositions clear. In his early analysis of logically structured language, in his widely acclaimed <u>Tractatus Logico-philosophicus</u> (1921), Wittgenstein allowed for the existence of phenomena that are outside knowledge but are nonetheless acknowledged by language (e.g., non-verifiable things and nonsensical things) but argued mainly that language, thought, and reality are formally and closely related, that language and thought function as a literal photograph of the real world, and that an understanding of the world rests on an understanding of the relation among linguistic terms/thoughts and between these terms/thoughts and their real-world referents. In his later treatment of ordinary language, in his <u>Philosophical Investigations</u> (1953), Wittgenstein postulated that language and thought do not merely reproduce the real world but also respond significantly and creatively to it.

The analytic traditions since Wittgenstein have taken many additional forms, most driven by logical empiricism, by logical analysis of scientific language and knowledge. Arguably the most notable contributors to this development have been:

- Gilbert Ryle (1900-76), the English philosopher, best remembered for his philosophy of mind;
- Nelson Goodman (1906-98), the American philosopher, best remembered for his aesthetic philosophy;
- Jean-François Lyotard (1924-98), the French philosopher, best remembered for his social and political philosophy;

- Noam Chomsky (1928-   ), the American philosopher, best remembered for his philosophy of language, for his libertarian socialism, and for his courageous social activism; and
- John Rogers Searle (1932-), the American philosopher, best remembered for his philosophy of mind. Some few nonetheless turned away from the skeptical limitations of the analytic tendency. Perhaps the most influential of these were American philosophers, John Rawls (1921-   ) and Alasdair C. MacIntyre (1929-   ). Rawls' social and political philosophy – recorded most notably in A Theory of Justice (1971) – argued that social justice ought to be based on fairness, not utility, and that liberal democratic states ought to devote themselves to assuring such justice. MacIntyre's ethical philosophy – recorded most notably in After Virtue: A Study in Moral Theory (1981) – argued for a neo-Aristotelian transformation of moral principle by which inherently human properties (internal goods) and their institutional expressions govern other considerations (external goods) and their institutional expressions.

Twentieth-century literature, like twentieth-century philosophy, was greatly influenced by the scientific and analytic emphasis of intellectual life in this time. It responded to this emphasis more so in existential than in scientific and analytic ways, however; it more so took the form of humanistic protest than of homage. The most notable exception to this claim occurred in historical literature. The foremost **analytic literature** of the twentieth century was written by the leading historical scholars of the period, the German historian, Oswald Spengler (1880-1936), and the English historian, Arnold Joseph Toynbee (1889-1975). Spengler, mainly in The Decline of the West (1918-22), and Toynbee, mainly in A Study of History (1934-61), developed synoptic philosophies of history which attempted to discern the laws (indeterminate for Spengler, determinate for Toynbee) that characterize the origin, development, and demise of civilizations; claimed that all cultures rise, mature, and decline in cyclic, curvilinear, or repetitive patterns; and gave deeply pessimistic interpretations of the deterioration of modern (Western) civilization.

The remaining major current of contemporary modern philosophy, **existentialism** (and its derivatives), shares the vitalistic, skeptical, pessimistic, and critical orientation of other prominent post-modern movements but it takes this orientation in a novel direction. As its central aim, it makes a unique interpretation of distinctly human experience, of subjective human experience. The most significant nineteenth-century advocates of existentialism were the German philosopher, Arthur Schopenhauer (1788-1860), the Danish philosopher, Soren Aabye Kierkegaard (1813-55), and the German philosopher, Friedrich Wilhelm Nietzsche (1844-1900).

Schopenhauer, mainly in The World as Will and Idea (1818-19) and Parerga und Paralipomena (1851), established himself as an ardent opponent of post-Kantian German idealism, particularly Hegel, against whom he railed tirelessly when both taught at the University of Berlin. As with many of the major figures who followed in the shadow of Kant, Schopenhauer accepted the master's second Copernican revolution but rejected his paradoxical allegiance to the material thing-in-itself. According to Schopenhauer, reality is construed as Idea and Will. It is Idea insofar as all knowledge of it comes in the form of perceptions, perceptions which are themselves nothing other than ideas in the mind that reveal the world as a mosaic of ideas apprehended by subjects. It is Will insofar as humanity is conceived as more than a mere knowing subject; humanity is also an active, doing, striving, craving, and yearning being who has a consciousness of this other dimension of itself that cannot be explained fully in rational terms. Schopenhauer was especially ardent in opposing Hegel's virtually complete appeal to reason and held, against Hegel, that the fundamental interpretive principle of reality is Will, not Idea; the fundamental interpretive principle of reality is this blind, irrational force. By this view, then, Will is primary; all else (such as body, mind, and nature) is derivative of Will, in the form of being an outward manifestation of it. Schopenhauer infers, by analogy, the existence of other wills, minds, and bodies from the existence of his own. Since, however, Will is itself perceived as Idea by the mind and since Idea as such is not apprehended in a fully explicit sense by Will, it is not altogether clear in what terms Will justifiably establishes primacy over Idea.

According to Schopenhauer's view, the most fundamental expression of Will is that of preserving one's existence, the will to live, the will to be. In the higher animals and in humanity, this primitive force may be touched and, in a measure, influenced by intelligence because it sometimes manifests itself in the world of ideas. In lower forms of existence, life proceeds by this compulsion alone; such forms are characteristically and utterly devoid of intelligence. It is the universal presence of willing in all forms of life, as distinct from the selective presence of intelligence in such forms, which persuades Schopenhauer that Will is more fundamental than Idea. Presupposed by this view, however, is a certain discontinuity between willing and thinking that is never fully resolved and, of course, the properties of inanimate existence (which are shared with animate entities) are yet more widely present in the world than willing. In any case, the source and substance of Schopenhauer's infamous pessimism are rooted in the notion of Will's primacy over Idea and in the contention that the ceaseless will to live (as the most fundamental expression of Will itself, as the universal necessity of consuming others in order to sustain oneself) is the cause of all selfishness, sorrow, struggle, and evil in the world. Human life as such is therefore construed as predominantly evil, base, selfish, painful, miserable, meaningless, and, thus, unworthy of preservation. With neither a god nor immortality to sustain life, according to Schopenhauer, one is left with nothing much other than the bottomless void, the despair of human experience itself. The perpetuation of life, to which life is fundamentally devoted, is therefore equivalent to the perpetuation of pointless suffering and is less preferable than eternal oblivion.

Humanity can hope to free itself from the wicked will only by actively suppressing its inherent selfishness and by acting out of a pure sympathy for others. This liberation may occur in several ways according to Schopenhauer. Philosophy enlightens with respect to the character and limits of human understanding and action and, through this achievement, shows the way to obviating sensual engagements and other yearnings of will; it thus shows the way to obviating suffering itself. The arts suppress the will to live by viewing the world as it is in-itself, as it is independently of will, independently of a desire for its (the world's) use and manipulation. Concisely said, the arts obtain a will-less experience by viewing the world as pure idea. The palliative consequences of philosophy and the arts are nonetheless inferior to a more direct, a stoic-tending denial of pleasure and acceptance of pain in which life is properly abhorred and the impulse to be is annihilated. Even such an ascetic resignation gives only temporary relief from the incessant craving of will, however, and it thus also fails in the end to render life palatable. For life is, at bottom, suffering and enduring happiness is unrealizable. Accordingly, Schopenhauer's escape from an advocacy of self-destruction is at best narrow. He argues that an act of such rational appeal as suicide is at odds with the fundamentally irrational character of reality and so an untenable denial of reality; although why this should count for much in an essentially meaningless world is not at all clear. Schopenhauer's influence on subsequent thought, on Nietzsche and Freud in particular, was nonetheless great and it was the central concern of Kierkegaard's thought to rescue humanity from the sort of despair that Schopenhauer so embraced.

Like Schopenhauer, however, Kierkegaard made the character of human existence the centerpiece of his philosophy, was openly contemptuous of Hegel, and thought himself passing significantly beyond Hegel. Although most of what Kierkegaard knew of Hegel came from misleading secondary sources or from Schelling's equally misleading interpretations, Kierkegaard nonetheless believed himself exploding the Hegelian demon no less in culture and religion than in philosophy. Principally in Either/Or: A Fragment of Life (1843), Fear and Trembling (1843), The Concept of Dread (1844), Philosophical Fragments (1844), Concluding Unscientific Postscript (1846), and The Sickness Unto Death (1849), Kierkegaard sought a thoroughgoing reform of human life by recalling the individual to herself/himself, by working out a renaissance of human freedom, self-determination, and personal dignity, by formulating a basic transformation in individual human existence. In characteristically existentialistic fashion, he hoped to raise individuals from their public and complacent condition to an active, personal, and authentic reflection on life and happiness; in the end, he hoped to raise individuals to what he considered the highest mode of existence, to a Christian allegiance. As for Schleiermacher, then, religion (neither philosophy as for Fichte and Hegel nor the arts as for Schelling and Schopenhauer) forms the capstone of human existence. Philosophy "merely" shows the way to the formal end of life, to the religious end of life; it does not itself constitute this end. The central issue of Kierkegaard's philosophy is the distinctive character of human existence, the distinctive character of uniquely human subjectivity. For him, humanity is the only authentically existential being, the only being endowed with freedom and a consciousness of freedom's ominous responsibilities. In emphatic opposition to Hegel, Kierkegaard's program proclaims that the essential character of humanity resides, not in its impersonal and general features by which every person is like every other, but in its uniquely personal and novel features by which every person is distinct from every other.

According to Kierkegaard, truth and happiness are grounded in subjective, in individual existence and they are best obtained by self-governed, experiential confrontations. The highest of these confrontations, the confrontation that signifies the culmination of unique human subjectivity, of personal identity, is the confrontation with the transcendent God of Christianity (not with the Hegelian God of reason realizing itself as such in humanity). To be truly human, in Kierkegaard's view, is to orient one's life toward God, to freely choose the "God-relation," to freely choose a personal faith in, and a personal allegiance to God. The achievement of unique individuality, truth, and happiness is, therefore, a function of one's free and personal relation to God. This achievement, in turn, is a constitutive expression of the logical impossibility of the Trinity, infinite God becoming finite humanity, which Kierkegaard calls the greatest of paradoxes, or the "absolute paradox." The supreme test of faith requires belief in the most absurd of "possibilities," for it is this test which raises the greatest and the most individualizing passion. According to Kierkegaard, then, Christian faith is the supreme existential allegiance because in its "conciliation" of humanity's finite immanence and God's infinite transcendence is found the most uniquely personal and revealing of experiences, experiences without which life falls over into a Schopenhauerian meaninglessness. This seems to commit Kierkegaard to the dubious position of arguing, in at least partially rational terms, that truth is a function of paradoxical absurdity; it is a function of what makes least rational sense to us because that raises the most deeply individualizing passions in us. By organic standard, this comes to gaining individuality, truth, and happiness by actively relinquishing them, the paradox to end all paradoxes.

For Kierkegaard, the dialectic of human existence occurs in three basic modes: the aesthetic, the ethical, and the religious. Humanity enters the lowest of these, the aesthetic, from an altogether public milieu in which its conformity to convention, domination by others, and lack of individual autonomy and responsibility are central. In the aesthetic mode, humanity leaps from the utterly public to a conformity with its own sensuality, to a life dominated by the pleasures of sensual desire, a life which ends in merely ephemeral accomplishment, doubt, emptiness, and despair. The barrenness of the aesthetic leads to the ethical mode of existence in which life is experienced through the relative categories of right and wrong. The sense of capricious pleasure characteristic of the aesthetic is exceeded by the personal, passionate, and "intrinsic" choices required of the ethical; the ethical therefore engenders a more enduring sense of happiness, peace, and tranquility than the aesthetic. It is yet grounded in finitude, however, and it is thus unworthy of ultimate devotion; like the aesthetic, it too ends in the despair and devastation associated with falling short of eternal truth. Its principal significance resides in its presaging the faith-relation of the highest mode of existence, the religious. In the religious mode, one rejects (by explicit means of either/or choice) all thisworldly, self-interested inclinations in pursuit of a unity with God. For Kierkegaard, only this paradoxical leap of faith, unsupported as it is by anything thisworldly, only this quest for unity with an infinite and eternal, albeit personal, being, delivers the complete individuality, truth, and happiness which are the formal ends of life authentically lived. Kierkegaard further argues that the several modes of human existence are not mutually exclusive, nor are they suspended or abolished by ascent to a higher mode; each (save the highest) supports the advance to a higher mode in the form of making such an advance possible and each persists in the higher mode (s) as vestigial tendencies. In a sense, Kierkegaard inverted the metaphysical hierarchy of Hegel; he argued that the subjective (of a sort) reigns over the absolute (of a sort). Kierkegaard nonetheless sharply condemned the institutional framework of this subjectivity (that is, established religion) as self-satisfied, conformist, and insufficiently devoted to the faith-relation.

Among the towering geniuses of contemporary modern philosophy and literature, Nietzsche, like Schopenhauer, resolved to come to grips with the implications for human existence of a godless world. He took the basic insights of Schopenhauer and, unlike Schopenhauer himself, developed them in affirmative and optimistic directions. His penetrating account of modern thought and modern life – developed principally in The Birth of Tragedy (1872), Human, All-too-human (1878), The Gay Science (1882), Thus Spoke Zarathustra (1883), The Will to Power (1884-88), Beyond Good and Evil (1886), Toward a Genealogy of Morals (1887), The Twilight of the Idols (1888), The Antichrist (1888), and Ecce Homo (1888) – concluded neither in Schopenhauer's pessimistic resignation nor in Kierkegaard's Christian sense of happiness. It ends instead in a rejection of Christianity (as well as all otherworldly philosophies, nationalism, militarism, imperialism, racialism, democracy, socialism, materialism, and idealism) and an affirmation of this life.[130] Nietzsche's philosophy (like most philosophy of the late nineteenth century) was profoundly affected by Darwin's leveling of the qualitative distinction between humanity and other forms of animal life. This leveling undermined many of Western civilization's most cherished and enduring assumptions, assumptions which had provided the main foundations of human existence. With nothing compelling to put in the place of these assumptions and foundations, Nietzsche foresaw an intellectual and cultural crisis in which the fall to nihilism, to groundlessness, was all but inevitable. Both Schopenhauer and Kierkegaard had been convinced that human life can be meaningfully sustained only in relation to a transcendent God. Schopenhauer rejected such a belief and thereby fell into the pessimistic torment which is the characteristic mark of his philosophy. Kierkegaard embraced belief in such a God and thereby found the meaning he had sought. Nietzsche adopted both Schopenhauer's atheism and Kierkegaard's affirmation of life by denouncing the notion, popular with both Schopenhauer and Kierkegaard, that only belief in a transcendent being saves humanity from oblivion. Nietzsche argued instead that one denies the will to live by embracing the view that life is meaningful only as it is created and sustained by God. The great crime of Christianity, according to Nietzsche, lies in its demand for such a denial and in its consequent deprivation of this life. Nietzsche was convinced that human life is endowed with authentic meaning and significance – it is redeemable and capable of happiness – only to the extent that it is considered meaningful and significant on its own terms. He therefore held that life can be saved from utter despair and ardently affirmed only by a distinctly human standard of value; life is to be optimistically embraced despite its godlessness and its suffering.

Nietzsche followed Schopenhauer in the view that the world is constituted as will and idea. Nietzsche's most elegant expression of this view is found in his brilliant account of ancient Greek tragedy, which he interpreted as a fusion of the Dionysian (the reflection of the sensuous will, most importantly in the form of music) and the Apollinian (the reflection of the conceptual idea, most importantly in the form of sculpture) impulses of humanity. Against Schopenhauer's Buddhist-like negation of the will, however, Nietzsche argued, in characteristically Greek terms, for a celebration of the joy and power inherent in human life. Also against Schopenhauer, Nietzsche held that human life is more fundamentally rooted in the will to power than in the will to be, for the latter is often risked for want of the former; and the former, which expresses itself most notably in creative activity, produces the greatest happiness. For Nietzsche, the creative expression of the will to power affirms life and provides the courage and strength to oppose weakness, suffering, and evil and to promote happiness and goodness. Evil is itself construed, in this view, as that which diminishes the will to power; goodness is that which enhances it. Even truth and beauty are worthily pursued only insofar as they augment the will to power; only activities that purposefully contribute to the quantitative and qualitative development of creativity, of the will to power, are authentically valued. Nietzsche conceived of art as a world of idealized illusions which heightens creativity, as a world that provides a palliative for life in the form of importing a renewed enthusiasm for it. When the will to power is sublimated in the largest sense and measure and is thereby developed away from the common tendency to express it as a primitive brutality, persons of great creative and intellectual prowess ("overmen" or "supermen") are the result. These are not ordinary persons in Nietzsche's view, not persons of the "herd," not persons who are "human-all-too-human," not persons who are more characteristically animal than human, but persons who embody the realization of humanity's highest possibilities. Higher persons are distinguished from lower both in terms of their quantum (or strength) of power and in terms of their qualitative (or moral) superiority. According to this account, the only defensible standard of human value is the overman, the realization of human life's highest form, the highest cultivation of the will to power. All other than overman is significant only insofar as it contributes to humanity's highest possibilities signified by overman. The herd, or "underman," is therefore something to be overcome, a bridge between animality and overman. For Nietzsche, even the higher persons -- as approximated by such as Homer, Socrates, Plato, Alexander the Great, Caesar, Dante, Leonardo, Spinoza, Frederick the Great, Kant, Napoleon, and Goethe – are nonetheless themselves largely insignificant as individuals. They are primarily significant as contributors to the fulfillment of what is highest in the human species. Nietzsche's fundamental concern is consequently somewhat afield of Kierkegaard's; it is more so to do with humanity as species, with "lebensphilosophie," than with unique human (individual) subjectivity, with "existenzphilosophie." It is therefore more fully connected with a tributary of existentialism, philosophical anthropology, than with the core of existentialism itself.

Although the meaning and significance of life are confined to thisworldly events for Nietzsche, they are not located in the social circumstance of everyday life, in a "comfortable security." This meaning and this significance are instead realized in a fellowship of uncommon persons; not a commiserative fellowship, but a competitive circumstance in which persons mutually respect and assist one another to the end of achieving creative lives. Such uncommon individuals and circumstances have been deliberately suppressed by an impersonal public and institutional environment, however. In its democratic inclinations, this environment has preferred the standardized, common, tranquil, complacent, and mediocre person, who is unable to bear the whole truth of life, to the genuinely extraordinary person, who is. Much of Nietzsche's attack on Christianity, no less than his attack on democracy, concerns the distressing repletion with which both promote the ordinary and the weak as against the extraordinary and the strong. This tendency, Nietzsche argues, is fundamentally evil because it diminishes the will to power and dignifies a "slave morality." For him, Christianity is the highest corruption because it encourages humanity to believe in a myth which, once exploded, undermines life altogether, leaving only despair in its place. According to Nietzsche, Christianity renounces life; it renounces the will to power and the will's thisworldly (including its physical) expressions; and it does this against the only terms (the thisworldly terms) which make life meaningful. Everyday social and political experience, most particularly democratic such experience, too promotes a destructive and decadent weakness. Such experience is, by Nietzsche's view, the means by which the herd consolidates its mediocrity and preserves the conventional standards and myths that make life palatable for it. Such experience effectively suppresses the unusual on the grounds that customary, albeit illusory, modes of existence are threatened by the extraordinary. Higher persons conform to such modes only insofar as such conformity is necessary to enhance their will to power. Higher persons fashion their lives around carefully self-chosen values which support and enhance their creativity; they do not fashion their lives around the inherited values of the herd. Although all higher persons cultivate the common virtues of a noble human soul (such as courage, solitude, sympathy, and wisdom), they nonetheless transfigure these virtues in relation to their own will to power. For higher persons, this is likewise a transfiguration which coincides with (which constitutes) the creative expression of humanity's highest possibilities. If such persons allow the herd its illusions. however, they come to be pitied instead of destroyed; though hardly understood or respected, they are at least thereby preserved and the free pursuit of their creativity, which is the formal end of their lives, survives. The numerical superiority of the herd, by Nietzsche's view, requires a "submission" of this sort to the slave morality. It is nonetheless a higher morality that is sought by this "submission."

As the broad end of striving is human creativity, so too is this the formal end of education for Nietzsche. He characterizes the educational process as inherently arduous (for life proceeds only at the expense of other life) and largely solitary (for the herd contaminates), as requiring an order of discipline and devotion far exceeding the capricious tendencies of everyday life, and as successively entailing an unbiased understanding of one's cultural heritage, a critical assessment of that heritage, and a release of one's own creative faculties in view of that heritage. In this process, one is to cultivate one's talents to the level of higher persons, then, if feasible, surpass that level in one's own terms. Based on an extraordinarily sympathetic concern for the body (as significantly more than an instrument of the mind, as inseparable from the mind, and as an essential mode of the reality of a person), Nietzsche too advocated active, intense, and courageous participation in daring and arduous forms of physical activity. He was convinced that such forms constitute a prominent medium in which the will to power may be fulfilled. The highly original thought of Nietzsche is among the most significant achievements of nineteenth-century intellectual life; it is also among the most telling intellectual influences on the twentieth century (most particularly on the continuing development of existentialism and philosophical anthropology but too on psychoanalytic psychology and accomplished literature; his thought was also falsely implicated in the formation of fascist ideology).

The leading existential philosophers of the twentieth century were the German thinkers, Martin Heidegger (1889-1976) and Karl Jaspers (1883-1969), and the French thinkers, Jean-Paul Sartre (1905-80) and Gabriel Marcel (1889-1973). Heidegger, mainly in <u>Being and Time</u> (1927) and <u>Introduction to Metaphysics</u> (1953), was principally devoted to explaining the nature and significance of distinctly human existence (of uniquely human subjectivity); he was principally devoted to showing what constitutes such existence and what the meaning of being human comes to; he was principally devoted to revealing the existential, as distinct from the objective, traits of human existence. In his "existential analytic," Heidegger, who had been a student of Husserl, established the "doctrine of ontological difference," according to which "Being" is the determinate ground of "beings," the determinate basis of all thought and experience. The distinctly human mode of existence is then taken as at once swept up in Being and as constituting the guardian of Being. The human condition is thus determined by its "residence in" Being and Being is itself fulfilled only in the form of human existence. For only in the human condition, only in being, is there the sort of Being that can apprehend and experience itself and the world as such. Only in this sort of Being, or "Dasein" (the highest form of human experience and action for Heidegger), does Being (and so reality) become aware of itself as itself. Being is therefore a form of consciousness embodied in the world as finite and temporal; it is not a transcendent form as for Kierkegaard. It is, in turn, by Heidegger's view, humanity's self-conscious awareness of itself as finite and temporal that makes its existence unique. The highest form of human experience and action, Dasein, is variously dominated, moreover, by "essential thinking" (the form of explicit thought proper to philosophy) and by "poetic thinking" (the form of metaphorical expression proper to the arts). A subordination of essential and/or poetic thinking to social and practical "imperatives" is therefore considered an inversion of life authentically lived and thus a perversion of thought and experience itself. Such a subordination is formally equivalent to frustrating the experience of Being.

Heidegger's basic program, not unlike Nietzsche's, emphasized the anxiety and the guilt inherent in human life, a form of life caught between the dead world of religious faith and the unborn world of authentic existence. By his view, only an abiding attention to the fundamental terms of one's authentic existence can "relieve" such anxiety and guilt and can "deliver" humanity to a genuine state of being, to a distinctly personal state of being, to "existenz." Authentic existence is itself construed as a freely chosen living in accord with one's fundamental, one's existential nature; it is a living in recognition of one's highest possibilities as well as one's death. The call to authenticity is a call to recognize, and to live in concert with, the true and fundamental character of reality, to thereby evade self-deception, and to freely make oneself into what one most basically is. The prospect of falling into inauthenticity, into "das man," is nonetheless great. In inauthentic modes of existence, dominated as they are by "everydayness" and impersonality, one fails to recognize the full nature and purpose of the distinctly human mode of existence; one acts primarily out of a conformity to environment (which is at odds with human fulfillment), thereby alienating oneself from one's own potential for authenticity. In a state of inauthenticity, one is lost to publicness, other-directed, and so living in accord with one's natural ("being-in-the-world") and social ("being-with-others") tendencies as though interchangeable with other persons. In such a state, one lives out one's "ontic" possibilities as a functional and impersonal part of other-than-distinctly human modes of existence. Only anxiety, guilt, and death arouse from the inauthenticity of the everyday and allow one to live out one's "ontological" possibilities as a free, self-directed, and individual personality. Heidegger characterizes anxiety as a peculiarly human discomfort arising from the realization that, relative to the human condition, the world is hostile and meaningless; humanity is thrown into the world as a concrete and discontinuous fact. Guilt is taken as a peculiarly human discomfort which results from humanity's choosing to fulfill certain of its alternatives and consequently, but regretfully, being unable to fulfill others. One's personal confrontation with death, by Heidegger's view, is the most radically individualizing and humanizing possibility of Dasein. It is only through the urgency entailed by death, accordingly, that humanity is at all capable of authenticity. An authentic orientation to these features of distinctly human life requires a resolute confrontation of them, a seeing them for what they are, a recognition that they are not publicly manageable, impersonal events, but events faced in the solitude which brings self-knowledge.

Jaspers, who had been a student of the renowned sociologist, Max Weber, began in much the same place as Heidegger. Mainly in Man in the Modern Age (1932) and Philosophie (1932), Jaspers argued that the tragic conflicts of our age are due largely to an excessive dedication to the ends of merely empirical being and to the tendency of such a dedication to disregard the fundamental issue of human existence. As for Heidegger (and Nietzsche), the nineteenth and twentieth centuries come to an age with neither spiritual purpose nor personal autonomy according to Jaspers; it is an age "between," an age of basic purposeless-ness. Jaspers argued that only philosophy leads humanity out of the despair left by such an age. Jaspers' highly salutary regard for philosophy is most apparent in his deeply sympathetic and charitable account of the history of the subject, of the history of philosophizing. In this account, Jaspers characterized the history of philosophical thought as a common search for the personal meaning of reality in general and of human existence in particular; the history of philosophy is thus construed as a community of authentic spirits in shared quest of fundamental, existential truth. By this view, humanity realizes itself only in such a community, only in relation to the "other-than-oneself," and so only by the sort of communication inherent in such community and in such relation. The truth of human existence, which is the principal issue of philosophizing, is intelligible for Jaspers, moreover, only as a free subjectivity; it is not intelligible as a knowable object. Although reason arouses distinctly human subjectivity ("Existenz") and the two mutually cultivate one another, reason and Existenz are nonetheless the poles of "Being." Existenz is infinite in the sense of its being wholly unto itself, in the sense of its being unconditioned by finite things, and thus in the sense of its being neither rationally nor objectively determinate. The limits of Existenz, "boundary situations," are therefore inherent to it. The most significant of these situations, death and guilt, are accepted freely and lovingly as the characteristic marks of Being. Existenz is therefore a synoptic consciousness of the uniqueness of the individual self; It is the human impulse to self-determination, to independence, to "Transcendence." Jaspers' philosophy of sport issues from his wider vision. In it, he argues that, although sport is customarily a trapping of purposelessness, it is nonetheless capable of contributing to the vitality of unique human subjectivity, of participating in the revolt against the self-destructive tyranny of the objective and the everyday, of functioning as a form of uniquely human expression, and of affirming and enhancing (as distinct from merely sustaining) distinctly human experience.

Sartre was a highly notable literary talent and a major progenitor of existential psychology as well as the leading French advocate of existential philosophy. He participated in the French resistance during the Second World War, was a German prisoner-of-war, won the 1964 Nobel Prize in Literature (which he declined), was a student of Edmund Husserl, and was a close associate of Maurice Merleau-Ponty, Albert Camus, and Simone de Beauvoir. Like Jaspers, Sartre was greatly influenced by Heidegger; unlike Jaspers, he was also significantly moved by a form of Marxism. Principally in Being and Nothingness (1943) and Critique of Dialectical Reason (1960), Sartre claimed a radical distinction between the mode of existence which is unaware of itself (the non-human mode, the "in-itself," the "en-soi") and that which is aware of itself (the distinctly human mode, the "for-itself," the "pour-soi"). The en-soi is determined by the causal order of the world, is exhausted by its empirical qualities, and is therefore incapable of free choice. The pour-soi, conversely, is determined by free choice, by what humanity makes of itself, by humanity's transcendence of the causal order. As such, the pour-soi lacks the permanence of the en-soi which it nonetheless vainly seeks. Sartre characterizes the human circumstance itself as a passionate but futile quest for the synthesis of en-soi and pour-soi, for the unattainable absolute. The irresolvable, inescapable, and gnawing result signifies humanity's condemnation to freedom, alienation, isolation, and despair. According to Sartre's atheistic view, then, humanity and the world are ontological opposites: "Being" is identified with the positive (the unchanging) character of the world and "Nothingness" with the negative (the impermanent, the unfulfillable) character of human existence. Only Nothingness is free to choose as it will; only human actions, which entail the freedom of the pour-soi, are therefore significantly meaningful. For it is only by the free choice of self-determination, according to Sartre, that one escapes being a merely causal event, an inauthentic project. Humanity's awareness of this freedom, together with the grave personal responsibility that accompanies it, leads us to the dread, anguish, and solitude which mark the basic character of the pour-soi. That is, human beings choosing for themselves, as though choosing for all humanity, entails the dread, anguish, and solitude of the pour-soi. Although in this sense characteristically free, by Sartre's view, humanity is nonetheless not free in every respect. Humanity is not altogether free; it is conditioned and limited by the inherited terms of its circumstance, by the terms of the circumstance into which it has been thrown (in which it finds itself), by its "facticity;" humanity is not free, for prominent instance, not to be. Because it is in no meaningful respect freely chosen, the facticity of human existence, whatever its terms, holds no intrinsic value for Sartre. While the circumstance in which human life persists is in many ways determined (human life is confined to the sense-perceptive world), its value is not among those ways; human life is characteristically distinct from material objects in this respect. It is this judgment that gives rise to Sartre's celebrated doctrine, "existence precedes essence." That is, the free choice which is the distinctive feature of human existence is more fundamental than the determinate circumstance in which it occurs; effectively, value is a function of human choice, not an inherent aspect of the determined and hostile order awaiting discovery.

Sartre's ethics follows close suit. In this aspect of his thought, he rejected the existence of a transcendental ego in which humanity is made the consequence of its essential (its conceptual) nature and reasserted his view that the ground of humanity resides instead in its non-conceptual, its spontaneous freedom of consciousness. Humanity is uniquely what it determines itself to be through its actions and it is thereby the sole source of moral value. According to Sartre, it is humanity's excessive absorption in the inauthentic demands of the "everyday" which distracts it from the rigors of dread, anguish, and solitude and which thus obscures its vision of freedom and the responsibility for genuine truth. This flight to the everyday, to a living with the collective determinations of the natural and social orders instead of with oneself, is tantamount to being what one is not and to not being what one is. Sartre calls this flight into which human beings all too commonly tumble, a state of "bad faith," or self-deception. It is ultimately our authentic response to death (the most radically individualizing event of our lives), however, that brings us to a fully resolute confrontation with human existence and with ourselves. It is facing the solitude and absurdity of death which, in the end, reveals ourselves to ourselves, makes us entirely and authentically human, and preserves our dignity through a circumstance that seems actively opposed to such a preservation.

Sartre's notions of body, play, and sport have also been among the most influential such notions in the twentieth century. The body, by his view, is the pour-soi engaged in the world. This engagement takes three main forms: what the body is immediately for a given subject (as a subjective center of self-reference with respect to the world), what the body is as an object for others (as an object which figures in the experience of others), and what the body is as an awareness of its being observed by others (as a self-alienating perception of oneself as though another, as a perception of oneself as others perceive us, as en-soi). Sartre construed play as a fundamental expression of our subjectivity and thus a resolute turning away from objective characterizations of ourselves. Sport, in turn, as a prominent form of play, was interpreted as a meaningful act of self-appropriation, a meaningful attempt to appropriate the permanence of the en-soi.

Unlike Heidegger, Jaspers, and Sartre, who had espoused secular brands of existentialism, Marcel fashioned a religious form of the doctrine. Like Heidegger, Jaspers, and Sartre, however, Marcel too resolutely opposed the intolerable contemporary preference for the impersonal, functional, and technical as against the personal, aesthetic, and affective. Mainly in Metaphysical Journal (1927), Being and Having (1935), and The Mystery of Being (1951), Marcel argued that such classical polarities as mind-body, subject-object, and thought-being are basically inaccessible to the objective inquiries of empirical science. This is so because such polarities have their basis in subjective experience which is the fair province of philosophy alone. Even at this, philosophy can do no better than reveal them as the mysteries that they are. Because the human self, which is the existential center of reality, is more than the sum of its empirical qualities, it cannot be scientifically verified, but only borne reflective witness to. The mysterious, the self-evident source and foundation of experience, as distinct from the consequences of experience, is thus repulsed by objective analysis. One's relations with what one has consequently differ, and they differ in qualitative respects, from one's relations with what one is and others are. In the special case of one's body, however, there is a compelling conjunction of having and being, for the body is evidently both a part of the world of objective things (and thus scientifically apprehensible) and a constituent of one's fundamentally subjective character as well (and thus only philosophically apprehensible). The concrete and immediate participation of one's body in the objective world nonetheless provides a window to that world, a window through which the mind grasps the existential integrity of "being." Marcel likewise held that humanity's response to being, and so humanity itself, is fundamentally free even though this response and humanity itself are influenced in significant ways and measures by one's inherited and conditioned character as well as by God. The supreme ontological mystery, for Marcel, is the union of the self with the transcendent "Being," with God. This union issues from the renunciation of one's self-sufficiency and the affirmation of God's transcendence. It is through and only through this renunciation and this affirmation that humanity makes itself authentic (makes itself what it is); humanity's authentic participation in being is a function of such a renunciation and such an affirmation, for Marcel, as well as a function of sympathetic respect for nature and community.

The other major contributors to twentieth-century existential philosophy were Spanish philosopher, Miguel de Unamuno y Jugo (1864-1936); Austrian-Jewish philosopher, Martin Buber (1878-1965), author of I and Thou (1923); Spanish philosopher, Jose Ortega y Gasset; German-American philosopher, Paul Johannes Tillich (1886-1965), author of The Courage To Be (1952); American philosopher, Reinhold Niebuhr (1892-1971), author of Moral Man and Immoral Society (1932); French philosopher, Simone de Beauvoir (1908-86), author of The Second Sex (1949-50) and a close associate of Sartre and Merleau-Ponty; French philosopher, novelist, and 1957 Nobel laureate in literature, Albert Camus (1913-60), a close associate of Sartre; and French philosopher, Michel Foucault (1926-84). The remaining, major currents in twentieth-century philosophy were effectively derived from the central tenets of existentialism; namely, intuitionism, philosophical anthropology, and French phenomenology.

Among the most influential humanistic replies to realism and to idealism was made by the **intuitionism** of French philosopher and 1927 Nobel laureate in literature, Henri Bergson (1859-1941). Bergson – mainly in Time and Free Will: An Essay on the Immediate Data of Consciousness (1889), Matter and Memory (1896), Introduction to Metaphysics (1903), Creative Evolution (1907), The Two Sources of Morality and Religion (1932), and The Creative Mind (1934) – proposed a strict, dualistic-tending cleavage between the proper objects of scientific, logical, and mathematical study, which are indirectly apprehended by rational intellect, and those befitting philosophic reflection, which are directly apprehended by intuitive consciousness. According to Bergson, science apprehends only matter, only the inert, static, predictable, and determined, only that which is without memory and creativity, only that which is incapable of penetrating to the essential character and purpose of reality. Philosophy, conversely, apprehends the basis of life, the center of all things, the individualizing life-force, the "élan vital;" it reveals the world as free, willing, conscious, living, evolving, moving, remembering, and creative force. The religious, moral, and socio-political imperative of this view is to cultivate the pure vitality that forms the fundamental interpretive principle of reality. Predictably, Bergson's notions of intuition, change, and creativity also formed the basis of his philosophy of education.

The seminal principles of **philosophical anthropology** were owed principally to Marx, Nietzsche, and Bergson. In its twentieth-century, not unlike its nineteenth-century, form, philosophical anthropology took the human species, the personal, social, and cultural character of distinctly human experience, as its basis and its end. The most notable twentieth-century advocate of this view was the German philosopher, Max Scheler (1874-1928), a student of Rudolf Eucken and a close associate of Franz Brentano. Scheler, mainly in Contributions to the Phenomenology and Theory of Sympathy and of Love and Hate (1913) and The Place of Man in the Universe (1928), made an ethical and religious interpretation of Edmund Husserl's thought which led him to a view of humanity as a concrete unity of acts. Humanity, according to Scheler, is a form of intentional existence whose "being" (whose authentic character and purpose) is disclosed to it by love (by a sympathetic immersion in the world). The other major contributors to the development and maturation of philosophical anthropology in the twentieth century were German philosopher, Ernst Cassirer (1874-1945); German philosopher, Helmut Plessner (1892-1985), a student of Husserl; and American philosopher, Susanne K. Langer (1895-1985).

French phenomenology, unlike its German analog, took a humanistic (as distinct from a scientific) course closely associated with existentialism. It was most memorably championed by Maurice Merleau-Ponty (1908-61), a close acquaintance of Sartre (who also contributed significantly to the phenomenological literature) and Beauvoir. In his celebrated reflections on perception, recorded mainly in Phenomenology of Perception (1945), Merleau-Ponty emphasized the active and free nature of distinctly human experience and he thus sharply opposed scientific (i.e., passive and determined) characterizations of it. He argued that such characterizations cannot explain bodily experience in particular. This experience cannot be explained by a view of the body as a participant in the causal order, as an object among other objects. It can be explained instead only as the embodiment of mind or consciousness, only as a subject actively and meaningfully existing in the world, only as a lived experience.

The accomplished literature of the twentieth century was very significantly affected by the scientific emphasis of the period as has been said. It was especially much affected by the relativistic and experimentalistic inclinations of the sciences. It thus rooted its perspective in individual, social, cultural, and historical tendencies of the period (as distinct from universal tendencies) and it routinely rejected traditional themes and styles for utterly novel possibilities. It nonetheless turned these possibilities in largely existential directions as has been also said. The dominant themes of this literature, this **existentialist literature**, concerned the character and purpose of the human condition amid the horrors of an exceedingly troubled century; that is to say, amid the absurdity, alienation, anguish, barrenness, brutality, corruption, decadence, dehumanization, despair, dissipation, fear, futility, grief, illusions, immorality, inanity, injustice, irony, violence, and vulgarity of the time. Some of this literature explicitly and (most often) satirically condemned, protested, and rebelled against these tendencies; some of it embraced the prospect of escaping these tendencies; some little of it even affirmed the expressive potential of human life despite these tendencies; and the rest of it settled into inevitable disillusionment. Most of the leading figures of twentieth-century literature have been American and western European people but a blossoming corpus of stunning work has been also done by enormously talented writers elsewhere in Europe and the Americas as well as in Africa, Asia, and Oceania. The foremost literary personalities of this period were:

- Oscar Fingal O'Flahertie Wills Wilde (1854-1900), the Irish writer of complex and symbolic plays, novels, and poems, who was imprisoned for two years on charges of sexual immorality; author of the novel, The Picture of Dorian Gray (1891), the play, "The Importance of Being Earnest" (1895), and the poems, "The Ballad of Reading Gaol" (1898) and "De Profundis" (1905);
- Joseph Conrad/Josef Teodor Konrad Walecz Korzeniowski (1857-1924), the Polish-English novelist, who wrote adventurous accounts of individuals suffering the alienation and moral decay of mass, industrial society; author of The Nigger of the Narcissus (1897), Lord Jim (1900), Heart of Darkness (1902), Typhoon (1903), Nostromo (1904), and Victory (1915);
- Alfred Edward "A.E." Housman (1859-1936), the English poet, who wrote mainly of the ephemeral joys of youth and their pitiless extinction; author of A Shropshire Lad (1896; most importantly included "To an Athlete Dying Young" and "When I Was One-and-twenty") and Last Poems (1922);
- Edith Newbold Jones Wharton (1862-1937), the American-French novelist, who wrote superbly crafted accounts of the despairing ironies and vulgarities of bourgeois society; author of The House of Mirth (1905), Ethan Frome (1911), and The Age of Innocence (1920);
- Gabriele D'Annunzio, the Italian writer of plays, novels, and poems, who also participated significantly (in both literary and military-political terms) in the First World War and in the rise of Italian fascism; author of the poem, "Canto Nuovo" (1882); the novels, The Child of Pleasure (1889), The Triumph of Death (1894), and The Flame of Life (1897); and the plays, "La Gioconda" (1898) and "Francesca da Rimini" (1901);
- William Butler Yeats (1865-1939), the Irish poet and dramatist and 1923 Nobel laureate in literature, who wrote intensely nationalistic pieces and brilliantly soulful passages, mainly of human melancholy; author of the poems, "The Wanderings of Oisin" (1889), The Rose (1893; most importantly included "The Lake Isle of Innisfree" and "When You Are Old"), The Wind Among the Reeds (1899; most importantly included "The Secret Rose"), Responsibilities (1914), "The Second Coming" (1921), The Tower (1928; most importantly included "Among School Children" and "Sailing to Byzantium"), and Collected Poems (1933); also author of the plays, "The Land of Heart's Desire" (1904) and "Deirdre" (1907);
- Luigi Pirandello (1867-1936), the Italian dramatist and 1934 Nobel laureate in literature, who wrote highly innovative and grimly humorous plays concerning the coming triumph of instinctive humanity over the false and decaying conventions and prejudices of the bourgeoisie; author of "Six Characters in Search of an Author" (1921) and "Enrico IV" (1922);
- André Gide (1869-1951), the French novelist and 1947 Nobel laureate in literature, who wrote mainly of human vices and their contributions to moral collapse and social disintegration; author of The Immoralist (1902) and The Counterfeiters (1926);

- Theodore Dreiser (1871-1945), the American novelist, who brilliantly portrayed modern humanity as the victim of shallow and ungovernable social values and social forces; author of <u>Sister Carrie</u> (1900), <u>Jennie Gerhardt</u> (1911), <u>The Financier</u> (1912), <u>The Titan</u> (1914), <u>The Genius</u> (1915), <u>An American Tragedy</u> (1925), <u>The Bulwark</u> (1946), and <u>The Stoic</u> (1947);
- Marcel Proust (1871-1922), the French novelist, who chronicled the decline of French aristocratic society and who championed the cause of the creative artist against aristocratic values (which he characterized as vulgar, malicious, trivial, false, and without redeeming sympathy for individual persons) in brilliant metaphor and rich psychological insight; author of the monumental, six-part <u>Remembrance of Things Past</u> (1913-27; most importantly included <u>Swann's Way</u>);
- Gertrude Stein (1874-1946), the American-French writer of short stories and novels, whose unusual style, freely associating the sounds and rhythms of words, emphasized the medium of literary language even above its content; author of <u>Three Lives</u> (1909) and <u>The Autobiography of Alice B. Toklas</u> (1933);
- Robert Frost (1875-1963), the American poet, who wrote principally of simple, isolated life and the search for self-understanding; author of <u>A Boy's Will</u> (1913), <u>North of Boston</u> (1914), "The Road Not Taken" (1916), <u>New Hampshire</u> (1923), "A Lone Striker" (1936), <u>A Witness Tree</u> (1942), "A Masque of Reason" (1945), <u>Steeple Bush</u> (1947), and <u>In the Clearing</u> (1962);
- Thomas Mann (1875-1955), the German-American novelist and 1929 Nobel laureate in literature, who denounced German fascism and who brilliantly portrayed the decline of German bourgeois society, the travail of the human journey in contemporary modern life, and the neurotic life of the creative artist in twentieth-century culture; author of <u>Buddenbrooks</u> (1900), <u>Death in Venice</u> (1911), <u>The Magic Mountain</u> (1924; a massive educational novel), <u>Joseph and His Brothers</u> (1925-43; a colossal four-part novel), and <u>Doctor Faustus</u> (1947);
- Rainer Maria Rilke (1875-1926), the inestimable Czech-German lyric poet and close associate of the celebrated sculptor, Auguste Rodin, whose introspective search for enduring merit in a constantly shifting world, whose high praise of human existence even in the face of its contemporary desolation, and whose ardent dedication to his art more nearly approached the organic tendencies of twentieth-century abstract expressionism than any other literary figure of the time (despite his deeply religious nature); author of <u>The Book of Pictures</u> (1902), <u>The Book of Hours</u> (1906), <u>New Poems</u> (1907), <u>Duinese Elegies</u> (1911-12), and <u>Sonnets to Orpheus</u> (1922);
- Wallace Stevens (1879-1955), the American poet, who wrote philosophical verse that aimed at creating order out of chaos; author of <u>Harmonium</u> (1923), <u>The Man with the Blue Guitar</u> (1937), <u>Transport to Summer</u> (1947), and <u>Collected Poems</u> (1954);
- Jean Giraudoux (1882-1944), the French dramatist, who mainly wrote bitter satires of the idealistic aspirations and the realistic betrayals of the human predicament; author of "The Enchanted" (1933), "The Tiger at the Gates" (1935), "Electra" (1937), "Ondine" (1939), "The Apollo of Bellac" (1942), and "The Madwoman of Chaillot" (1945);
- James Joyce (1882-1941), the masterful Irish novelist and among the most innovative experimental writers of the century, who fashioned the stream-of-consciousness novel with its complex shifts of conscious and sub-conscious perception and who proffered a celebration of individual life despite social narrowness, ignorance, and malice; author of <u>The Dubliners</u> (1914; a collection of short stories), <u>Ulysses</u> (1914-22; a monumental masterpiece), <u>Portrait of the Artist as a Young Man</u> (1916), and <u>Finnegan's Wake</u> (1939);
- Franz Kafka (1883-1924), the Czech-German novelist, who wrote principally of the modern human burdens of anxiety, guilt, and isolation and the futile quest of modern human beings for personal salvation; author of <u>Metamorphosis</u> (1916), <u>The Penal Colony</u> (1919), <u>The Trial</u> (1925), <u>The Castle</u> (1926), and <u>Amerika</u> (1928);
- David Herbert "D.H." Lawrence (1885-1930), the English novelist, who condemned mass, industrial society as dehumanizing and who canonized the redeeming possibilities of nature in general and love in particular; author of <u>Sons and Lovers</u> (1913), <u>The Rainbow</u> (1915), <u>Women in Love</u> (1921), <u>The Plumed Serpent</u> (1926), and <u>Lady Chatterley's Lover</u> (1928);
- Sinclair Lewis (1885-1951), the American novelist and 1930 Nobel laureate in literature, who brilliantly satirized the hypocritical and smug dullness, the egocentric disregard for community, and the contempt for progressive reform, authentic education, and accomplished learning that characterizes

middle-class American life; author of <u>Main Street</u> (1920), <u>Babbitt</u> (1922), <u>Arrowsmith</u> (1925), <u>Elmer Gantry</u> (1927), and <u>Dodsworth</u> (1929);

- Ezra Loomis Pound (1885-1972), the American-European poet, who espoused fascism (for which he was prosecuted by the American government on charges of treason and was eventually committed to a mental hospital for twelve years), who was nonetheless a highly influential literary figure, and who developed a uniquely twentieth-century style that featured obscure allusions, free, conversational associations, and measured dissonance; author of "Sextus Propertius" (1918), "Hugh Selwyn Mauberley" (1920), and "Cantos" (1925-60);

- Thomas Stearns "T.S." Eliot (1888-1965), the American-English poet, dramatist, and critic, 1948 Nobel laureate in literature, and among the most accomplished and influential figures in twentieth-century literature, who wrote mainly about the sterile, sordid, and anguished character of modern life; author of the poems, <u>Prufrock and Other Observations</u> (1917), <u>Poems</u> (1920), "The Waste Land" (1922), "Ash Wednesday" (1930), <u>Four Quartets</u> (1935-43), and <u>Collected Poems</u> (1936); author of the verse-dramas, "Murder in the Cathedral" (1935), "The Family Reunion" (1939), and "The Cocktail Party" (1950); and author of the critical essay, "The Metaphysical Poets" (1921);

- Eugene Gladstone O'Neill (1888-1953), the American dramatist and 1936 Nobel laureate in literature, who wrote uniquely experimental plays, principally of social disintegration and strident personal unhappiness in acquisitive, materialist culture; author of "Beyond the Horizon" (1920), "The Emperor Jones" (1920), "Anna Christie" (1921), "The Hairy Ape" (1922), "Desire under the Elms" (1924), "The Great God Brown" (1926), "Strange Interlude" (1928), "Mourning Becomes Electra" (1931), "Ah, Wilderness" (1933), "The Iceman Cometh" (1946), "A Moon for the Misbegotten" (1947), and "Long Day's Journey into Night" (1956);

- Boris Leonidovich Pasternak (1890-1960), the Soviet poet and novelist and 1958 Nobel laureate in literature (which he was compelled by the Soviet government to refuse), whose intellectual integrity remained uncorrupted by the repressive Soviet state and whose passionate accounts of the tragic upheavals in twentieth-century Russian life won wide acclaim; author of the poems, <u>The Twin in the Clouds</u> (1914), <u>Over the Barriers</u> (1916), and <u>My Sister, Life</u> (1922), and the novel, <u>Doctor Zhivago</u> (1955);

- Pearl Sydenstricken Buck (1892-1973), the American novelist and 1938 Nobel laureate in literature, who wrote principally of the troubled transformations in pre-revolutionary Chinese life, transformations from the old feudal order to the new industrial circumstance; author of <u>The Good Earth</u> (1931);

- Edward Estlin "e.e." Cummings (1894-1962), the American poet, who was interned in France during World War One and who wrote highly innovative, experimental poems; author of <u>Tulips and Chimneys</u> (1923), <u>Is 5</u> (1926), and <u>95 Poems</u> (1958);

- Aldous Leonard Huxley (1894-1963), the English novelist, who wrote trenchantly satirical accounts, mainly concerning the decadence, repression, artificiality, and deterioration, of materialist, technological society; author of <u>Antic Hay</u> (1923), <u>Point Counter Point</u> (1928), and <u>Brave New World</u> (1932);

- Francis Scott Key "F. Scott" Fitzgerald (1896-1940), the American novelist, who wrote mainly about the degenerate nature of American materialism and class society; author of <u>This Side of Paradise</u> (1920), <u>The Beautiful and the Damned</u> (1922), <u>The Great Gatsby</u> (1925), <u>Tender is the Night</u> (1941), and <u>The Last Tycoon</u> (1941);

- William Faulkner (1897-1962), the American novelist and 1949 Nobel laureate in literature, who wrote principally about the torment of American decadence; author of <u>The Sound and the Fury</u> (1929), <u>As I Lay Dying</u> (1930), <u>Sanctuary</u> (1931), <u>Light in August</u> (1932), <u>The Hamlet</u> (1940), <u>A Fable</u> (1954), and <u>The Reivers</u> (1962);

- Thornton Niven Wilder (1897-1975), the American dramatist and novelist, who wrote mainly about the plain beauties, agonies, and ironies of ordinary life; author of the novel, <u>The Bridge of San Luis Rey</u> (1927), and the experimental plays, "Our Town" (1938) and "The Skin of Our Teeth" (1942);

- Bertolt Brecht (1898-1956), the German-American dramatist, whose deeply political epics (he was an ardent Marxist and anti-fascist), experimental techniques, and expressionistic tendencies had an especially profound affect on twentieth-century literature; author of "Man is Man" (1926), "Three Penny Opera" (1928), "Mother Courage and Her Children" (1941), "Private Life of the Master Race" (1941), "The Good Woman of Setzuan" (1943), "Galileo" (1947), and "Caucasian Chalk Circle" (1955);

- Ernest Miller Hemingway (1899-1961), the American writer of novels and short stories and 1954 Nobel laureate in literature, who was a soldier in the First World War and a correspondent in the Spanish Civil War, who developed a uniquely forthright and concise style, and who wrote principally about human freedom, courage, and love as well as about the ostensibly purposeless drift of life; author of The Sun Also Rises (1926), A Farewell to Arms (1926), "The Snows of Kilimanjaro" (1936), For Whom the Bell Tolls (1940), The Old Man and the Sea (1952), and the celebrated exposition concerning bullfighting, Death in the Afternoon (1932);
- Thomas Clayton Wolfe (1900-38), the American novelist, who portrayed life as a bitter and restless pilgrimage; author of Look Homeward Angel (1929), Of Time and the River (1935), The Web and the Rock (1939), and You Can't Go Home Again (1940);
- John Steinbeck (1902-68), the American writer of novels and short stories and 1962 Nobel laureate in literature, who gave enormously compelling and compassionate accounts of the deprived and dispossessed victims of political and economic oppression; author of Tortilla Flat (1935), Of Mice and Men (1937), The Long Valley (1938; a collection of short stories, including "The Red Pony"), Grapes of Wrath (1939), Cannery Row (1945), East of Eden (1952), and The Winter of Our Discontent (1961);
- George Orwell/Eric Arthur Blair (1903-50), the English novelist, who wrote most memorably about the terrifying and dehumanizing consequences of totalitarianism; author of Animal Farm (1946) and Nineteen Eighty-four (1949);
- Pablo Neruda/Neftali Ricardo Reyes Basualto (1904-73), the Chilean poet, 1971 Nobel laureate in literature, and diplomat in the government of Salvador Allende, who was profoundly affected by the Spanish Civil War, who raged against the exploitation of native peoples, against oppression in all forms, against fascism, and against imperialism, and who advocated revolutionary socialism as an antidote to the grief and despair of domination; author of Twenty Love Poems and One Song of Despair (1924), Residence on Earth (1933), Canto General (1950), and A New Decade (1958-67);
- John-Paul Sartre, the French writer of plays, short stories, and novels, the leading figure in French existential philosophy, and the 1964 Nobel laureate in literature (a distinction that he declined), who wrote riveting accounts of the ironic terrors of life in a meaningless universe; author of the short story, "The Wall" (1939); the plays, "The Flies" (1943), "No Exit" (1944), and "The Respectful Prostitute" (1947); and the novels, Nausea (1938) and The Age of Reason (1945);
- Samuel Beckett (1906-89), the Irish-French dramatist and novelist and 1969 Nobel laureate in literature, who portrayed the inescapable absurdities and anguish of apparently normal experience; author of the novels, Murphy (1938) and Molloy (1951), and the plays, "Waiting for Godot" (1952) and "Endgame" (1957);
- Wystan Hugh "W.H." Auden (1907-73), the English-American poet, who wrote experimental and satirical verse about the bleak edges of modern life; author of The Double Man (1941), Collected Poems (1945), The Age of Anxiety (1947), Nones (1951), and About the House (1965);
- Eugène Ionesco (1912-94), the Romanian-French dramatist, who wrote principally about the absurdity of bourgeois values, the futility of human endeavor in a purposeless world, and the oppressions of communism; author of "The Bald Soprano" (1950), "The Lesson" (1951), "The Chairs" (1952), and "Rhinoceros" (1959);
- Albert Camus (1913-60), the French novelist, existential philosopher, and 1957 Nobel laureate in literature, who asserted the absurdity of the human condition and advocated courageous rebellion against the meaninglessness of life as the principal way of redeeming it; author of The Myth of Sisyphus (1942), The Stranger (1942), The Plague (1947), The Rebel (1951), and The Fall (1956);
- Thomas Lanier "Tennessee" Williams (1914-83), the American dramatist, who depicted the passionate, futile, and unfulfilling tensions of life; author of "The Glass Menagerie" (1945), "A Streetcar Named Desire" (1947), "Summer and Smoke" (1948), "Cat on a Hot Tin Roof" (1955), "Sweet Bird of Youth" (1959), "The Night of the Iguana" (1961), and "Small Craft Warnings" (1972);
- Arthur Miller (1915-), the American dramatist, who wrote deeply moral plays about barren values and their political bases and implications; author of "All My Sons" (1947), "Death of a Salesman" (1949), "The Crucible" (1953), "A View from the Bridge" (1955), "After the Fall" (1964), "The Price" (1968), and "The Creation of the World and Other Business" (1972);
- Aleksander Isayevich Solzhenitsyn (1918-), the Soviet-American novelist and 1970 Nobel laureate in literature, who wrote deeply critical and heart-rending accounts of Soviet oppression, who was deported in 1974 for his criticism of the Soviet system, who returned to Russia in 1994 after the fall of

the Soviet Union, and who was also deeply critical of western democratic societies, preferring instead a state governed by benevolent Christian authority; author of <u>One Day in the Life of Ivan Denisovich</u> (1962), <u>The First Circle</u> (1968), <u>Cancer Ward</u> (1968), <u>August 1914</u> (1971), <u>The Gulag Archipelago</u> (1973-75), <u>The Oak and the Calf</u> (1975), and <u>Lenin in Zurich</u> (1975);

- Jack Kerouac (1922-69), the American novelist, who wrote mainly about the rejection of traditional values and the frenzied pursuit of new and deeply intense experiences; author of <u>On the Road</u> (1957);
- Kurt Vonnegut, Jr. (1922-   ), the American novelist, who was a German prisoner-of-war in the Second World War (in which circumstance he survived the Allied firebombing of Dresden) and who, with dark humor, protested the horrors of the twentieth century; author of <u>Player Piano</u> (1951), <u>Slaughterhouse Five</u> (1969), and <u>Deadeye Dick</u> (1982);
- Edward Albee (1928-   ), the American dramatist, who wrote engagingly satirical accounts of modern life's stark edges; author of "The Zoo Story" (1959), "Who's Afraid of Virginia Woolf?" (1962), "Tiny Alice" (1965), "A Delicate Balance" (1967), "Seascape" (1975), and "Three Tall Women" (1994); and
- Athol Harold Lannigan Fugard (1932-   ), the South African (Afrikaner) dramatist, who wrote enormously powerful and sharply disapproving critiques of apartheid, who asserted the common humanity of all people, and who opposed the oppression of some by others (which he characterized as a form of collective suffering); author of "The Blood Knot" (1961), "People are Living There" (1968), "Boesman and Lena" (1969), "Sizwe Bansi is Dead" (1972), "A Lesson from Aloes" (1981), "Master Harold . . . and the Boys" (1981), and "The Road to Mecca" (1985).

The **cinema** developed as an increasingly significant corollary of accomplished literature, eventually as an art form itself, throughout the twentieth century. Like literature as such, it was too principally governed by the scientific and technological orientation of the time and the best of it turned to largely existentialist themes. The technology of film was first effectively conjured by American inventor, Thomas Edison, in 1893-95 as has been said. This technology was greatly refined by French brothers, Louis Jean Lumière (1864-1948) and Auguste Lumière (1862-1954) in 1895. In its seminal form, cinema functioned mainly as novelty ("Le Voyage Dans La Lune," 1902, for prominent instance) and as crude documentary ("The Great Train Robbery," 1903, for prominent instance). Although it has been most widely employed since as commercially viable entertainment, its development as a serious art form, in both technical and aesthetic terms, followed. The leading artistic directors of the silent era (to 1927, perhaps slightly beyond in some cases) were:

- David Wark "D.W." Griffith (1875-1948), the American, best known for "Birth of a Nation" (1915) and "Intolerance" (1916);
- Charles Spencer "Charlie" Chaplin (1889-1977), the English-American-Swiss, best known for "The Kid" (1921) and "City Lights" (1931);
- Friedrich Wilhelm "F.W." Murnau (1889-1931), the German, best known for "Nosferatu, A Symphony of Horrors" (1922) and "Sunrise" (1927); and
- Sergei Mikhailovich Eisenstein (1898-1948), the Russian, best known for "Potemkin" (1925).

The foremost artistic directors of the first several decades of the sound era (from c. 1927 into the 1960s) were:

- Fritz Lang (1890-1976), the German-American, best known for "M" (1931);
- Jean Cocteau (1889-1963), the French, who also worked with wide success in literature, drama, opera, and ballet, best known for the films, "The Blood of the Poet" (1932) and "Beauty and the Beast" (1945);
- Alfred Hitchcock (1899-1980), the English-American, best known for "The Man Who Knew Too Much" (1934), "The Lady Vanishes" (1938), "Suspicion" (1941), "Rear Window" (1954), "Vertigo" (1957), and "Psycho" (1960);
- Leni Riefenstahl/Helena Berthe Amalie (1902-   ), the German, best known for "Triumph of the Will" (1935) and "Olympia" (1938);
- Jean Renoir (1894-1979), the French, son of the great painter, Pierre Auguste Renoir, best known for "The Grand Illusion" (1936) and "The Rules of the Game" (1939);
- John Ford (1895-1973), the American, best known for "The Grapes of Wrath" (1940) and "How Green Was My Valley" (1941);
- Orson Welles (1915-85), the American, best known for "Citizen Kane" (1941);
- Vittorio De Sica (1901-74), the Italian, best known for "The Bicycle Thief" (1949) and "Umberto D" (1952);

- Akira Kurosawa (1910-98), the Japanese, best known for "Rashomon" (1950) and "Ikiru" (1951);
- Elia Kazan/Elias Kazanjoglou (1909-), the Greek-Turkish-American, best known for "A Streetcar Named Desire" (1951) and "On the Waterfront" (1954);
- Federico Fellini (1920-93), the Italian, best known for "La Strada" (1954), "The Nights of Cabiria" (1957), "La Dolce Vita" (1960), and "8 ½" (1963);
- Satyajit Ray (1921-92), the Indian, best known for "The Song of the Road" (1955), "The Unvanquished" (1957), and "The World of Apu" (1958);
- Ingmar Bergman (1918-), the Swede, best known for "The Seventh Seal" (1956), "Wild Strawberries" (1957), "The Silence" (1963), "Cries and Whispers" (1972), "Autumn Sonata" (1978), and "Fanny and Alexander" (1982);
- Jean-Luc Godard (1930-), the French, best known for "Breathless" (1959);
- François Truffant (1932-84), the French, best known for "The 400 Blows" (1959) and "Fahrenheit 451" (1966); and
- Michelangelo Antonioni (1912-), the Italian, best known for "The Adventure" (1960) and "Blow-Up" (1966).

In the1960s and since, the leading films have given especially explicit portrayals of the aversions of modern life and the sense of social protest such aversions evoke; most notably:
- the American films, "To Kill a Mockingbird" (1962), "Who's Afraid of Virginia Woolf?" (1966), "The Swimmer" (1968), "Last Summer" (1969), "A Clockwork Orange" (1970), "They Shoot Horses, Don't They" (1970), "One Flew Over the Cuckoo's Nest" (1975), "The Deer Hunter" (1978), "Apocalypse Now" (1979), "Reds" (1981), "Kiss of the Spiderwoman" (1985), "Brazil" (1986), "Do the Right Thing" (1988), "The Unbearable Lightness of Being" (1988), and "Roger and Me" (1989);
- the Greek film, "Z" (1969);
- the Australian films, "Breaker Morant" (1979) and "Year of Living Dangerously" (1983);
- the German films, "The Marriage of Maria Braun" (1979) and "Das Boot" (1982);
- the Polish film, "Moonlighting" (1982);
- the English-American films, "The Killing Fields" (1984) and "City of Joy" (1992);
- the Italian film, "Cinema Paradiso" (1990); and
- the Hungarian film, "The Taste of Sunshine" (2000).

The visual arts

The visual arts of contemporary modern civilization developed in the same basic, richly creative pattern as the philosophy and literature of the period. Humanistic inclinations to romanticism/realism were tacitly apparent in the neo-classical naturalism of the late eighteenth century. These inclinations were made explicit in romanticism/realism itself, a movement which occupied the first approximate two-thirds of the nineteenth century. Romanticism/realism was replaced by the scientific-positivistic orientations of impressionism/post-impressionism, orientations that dominated the last approximate one-third of the nineteenth century. And these orientations, in turn, were replaced in the twentieth century by various forms of abstractionism. This development began with the largely organic-intrinsic sympathies of romanticism/realism and it "ended" with the largely mechanistic-instrumental allegiances of abstractionism.

The foremost visual artists of **neo-classical naturalism** in the late eighteenth and early nineteenth centuries were:
- the English naturalist painter, Thomas Gainsborough, and the French naturalist painter, Jean-Honoré Fragonard; and
- the French neo-classical painters, Jacques-Louis David and Jean-Auguste-Dominique Ingres.

The naturalists, broadly connected to the philosophy of Rousseau and its literary correlates, made a celebration of the natural realm primary and portrayed humanity as a participant in nature. The neo-classicists, broadly connected to the philosophy of Kant and its literary correlates, eschewed sentiment for reason and adopted a classical sense of virtue. David worked predominantly in the eighteenth century as has been said; Ingres worked predominantly in the nineteenth. David and Ingres in particular straddled the fundamental inclinations of the two centuries, not unlike Hegel in philosophy, Goethe in literature, and Beethoven in music. Ingres was an extraordinary fashioner of color and form, achieved a remarkably sensual treatment of active reserve, and painted numerous masterpieces; most notably, the oils-on-canvas "Valpinçon Bather" (1808),

"Odalisque" (1814), "Apotheosis of Homer" (1827), "Louis Bertin" (1832), "Comtesse d'Haussonville" (1845), and "The Turkish Bath" (1862).

Artistic **romanticism**, broadly connected to post-Kantian German philosophical romanticism and its literary correlates, held on (in a formal sense) to the rational classicism of the late eighteenth and early nineteenth centuries but imbued this classicism with intensely emotional content. Although this content was very passionately, exuberantly, and dramatically expressed, it was nonetheless firmly influenced by (not bereft of) rational principle. This principle was of uniquely organic moment, moved by a balanced, harmonious, and unified sense of both our intellectual and our physical possibilities, dominated by an authentically human longing for freedom and fulfillment, and customarily affiliated with heroic revolutionary movements of liberal social reform, national unification, and political independence. The principal architects of romanticism in the visual arts were Spanish and French figures (who had been most influenced by neo-classicism) and English masters (who had been most influenced by naturalism). The earliest of these, the major figure of **Spanish romanticism**, was the colossal painter, Francisco Jose Goya y Lucientes (1746-1828). Goya was the court painter of Charles III and Charles IV but was nonetheless contemptuous of monarchical authority and abuses of monarchical power. His most remarkable work was vividly colorful, intensely human, bitingly satirical, deeply remorseful in respect to human suffering, thoroughly run through with social protest, and insightfully foresaw twentieth-century Germanic expressionism. His masterpieces are the oils-on-canvas "Family of Charles IV" (1800), "Maja Desnudo" (1800), "The Third of May, 1808, at Madrid" (1814), and "Saturn Devouring One of His Sons" (1820-22).

The leading French contributors to this movement, the main figures of **French romanticism**, were also geniuses of the first rank, the painters, Jean-Louis André Théodore Géricault (1791-1824) and Ferdinand Victor Eugène Delacroix (1798-1863), and the architect, Charles Garnier (1825-98). Géricault was himself a person of deeply romantic temperament and heroic proportion who fervently espoused the interests of the poor, the infirmed, the disabled, and the dispossessed, who was dedicated to the life of emotional turmoil, and who disdained his own safety (he was, for prominent instance, killed when thrown from a horse). His greatest work ranks with the masterpieces of any age: the oils-on-canvas "Officer of the Imperial Guard" (1812), "Raft of the Medusa" (1818-19), "Madwoman" (1822-23), and "Madman" (1821-24). Delacroix, who had been a student of Géricault, who was also a close associate of many other artistic giants of the time (including the great composer, Frédéric Chopin), who became an ardent champion of the Greek cause in the Greek War of Independence, and who worked out of an exceptionally cosmopolitan perspective, too painted among the most notable pictures of the romantic age: the oils-on-canvas "Bark of Dante" (1822), "Massacre at Chios" (1822-24), "Death of Sardanapalus" (1827), "Greece Expiring on the Ruins of Missolonghi" (1827), "Women of Algiers" (1834), "Frédéric Chopin" (1838), and "Odalisque" (1850). Romanticism was most celebrated, among the visual arts, in painting, neither in sculpture nor in architecture. Only Garnier's "Opéra," Paris (1861-75) comes to much of an exception and it is a qualified one at that; it is as much an extension of earlier inclinations (neo-Baroque inclinations in particular) as a distinctly romantic achievement.

The principal figures of **English romanticism** were also painters and they were as well of monumental significance. John Constable (1776-1837) painted mainly passionate landscapes which featured a mystic sense of light that foresaw impressionism. His most accomplished pictures are the oils-on-canvas "Hampstead Heath" (1821), "The Hay Wain" (1821), and "Stoke-by-Nayland" (1836). Joseph Mallord William Turner (1775-1851) is principally remembered for his inventive landscapes which depicted the elemental forces of nature and which foresaw abstract expressionism. His most accomplished works are the oils-on-canvas "The Slave Ship" (1840) and "Rain, Steam, and Speed" (1844). In English architecture, only the "Houses of Parliament," London (1836-60) of Charles Barry (1795-1860) and A. Welby Pugin (1812-52) are worthily mentioned in this context and their eclectic, Gothic, and neo-classical tendencies make them (not unlike Garnier's "Opéra") more so extensions of earlier inclinations than distinctly romantic achievements.

The development of **realism** in the visual arts effectively paralleled its development in philosophy and literature. The relationship of realism to romanticism in the visual arts also resembled this relationship in philosophy and literature. That is, realism deepened romanticism's perception of the harsh imperatives of life; it thereby connected the new social order (the capital-industrial order) and its wide injustices (particularly for the peasant and working classes) to the ideal aspirations of romanticism; it thereby too fleshed out the contextual erudition of romanticism's organic groundwork, an erudition consonant with this groundwork. Realism thus emphasized the character of visual and social reality more explicitly than romanticism had; its sense of color, action, and emotion more nearly resembled what is than what ought to be; and it thereby prepared the way for the approaching revolution of impressionism in the visual (and musical) arts. The basic sentiments of realism nonetheless belonged far more compellingly to the (humanistic) romanticism of the

305

early nineteenth century than to the (scientific) impressionism of the late nineteenth century. Faint glimpses of realism were apparent from as early as the 1820s but the movement did not develop in earnest until the 1840s. Its leading figures were French painters, one of whom was most conspicuously related to the (natural) romanticism of Constable and Turner and the others of whom were most conspicuously related to the (neo-classical) romanticism of Géricault and Delacroix. The earliest major champion of **French realism** was Jean-Baptiste Camille Corot (1796-1875), who, not altogether unlike Constable and Turner, painted scenes from ordinary life without salient political content. Corot made quiet landscapes which featured the serene harmony of nature and humanity; most notably, the oils-on-canvas "Island of San Bartolomeo" (1825), "Chartres Cathedral" (1830), and "Ville d'Avray" (1870). The others – Honoré Daumier (1808-79), Jean-François Millet (1814-75), and Gustave Courbet (1819-77) – owed especially much to Géricault and Delacroix. Although they too, like Corot, painted scenes from everyday life, their work, unlike that of Corot, had a simple human grandeur about it and was awash in salient political content. Daumier, who approached blindness at the end of his life, who was imprisoned for his merciless ridicule of contemporary bourgeois society (including King Louis Philippe), who foresaw the style and political content of Germanic expressionism in particular, and who was also a great sculptor, painted among the most powerful and expressive human figures in the entire history of the genre, satirized (mainly by way of masterful caricature) ruling authority virtually without restraint, and ardently sought reform of a society that he considered thoroughly and hypocritically corrupt. His masterpieces are unforgettable portrayals of human dignity and pathos in the face of elite predacity; most notably, the lithograph "Rue Transnonain, April 15, 1834" (1834) and the oils-on-canvas "Uprising" (1860), "Third-Class Carriage" (1862), and "Don Quixote Attacking the Windmills" (c. 1866). Millet, himself a peasant, too painted figures of powerful simplicity, but figures who accepted their humble fate more gracefully than Daumier's. His masterpieces, like Daumier's, are also profoundly moving: the oils-on-canvas "The Sower" (1850), "The Gleaners" (1857), "Summer, the Buckwheat Harvest" (1868-74), and "Winter" (1868-74). Courbet, like Daumier, was a zealous advocate of working-class rights and liberal social reform (sentiments for which he too was imprisoned); he was likewise a close associate of French socialist, Pierre Proudhon. Courbet's political acuity, vigorous style, and compositional genius are the characteristic marks of his stunning masterpieces: the oils-on-canvas "The Stone Breakers" (1849), "A Burial at Ornans" (1849-50), and "The Studio: A Real Allegory Concerning Seven Years of My Artistic Life" (1854-55).

French realism also significantly influenced late nineteenth-century English and American painting; most memorably, the **American realism** of Winslow Homer (1836-1910) and Thomas Eakins (1844-1916). Homer is best remembered for his masterful treatment of color in the oils-on-canvas "The Croquet Game" (1866) and "The Morning Bell" (c. 1866). Eakins is best remembered for his masterful treatment of perspective in the oil-on-canvas "The Gross Clinic" (1875). The cause of realism in both Europe and America was too greatly enhanced by the development of **photography**, a medium at which several leading realist painters excelled (most notably, Courbet and Eakins). The French chemist, Joseph Nicéphore Niépce (1765-1833), developed the basic technology of photography in the 1820s, making the first surviving photograph in 1826. He then enlisted the assistance of the French scenic artist, Louis Jacques Mandé Daguerre (1789-1851), who perfected the process in the 1830s. Photography quickly became a threat to painting (owing to its discriminating sense of representation), an aid to painting (in the form of its providing a representational guide to painters), a stimulus to painting (in the form of its providing a challenge to furnish non-representational interpretation), and an artistic medium itself. The first great artistic master of the new medium was the French caricaturist, Gaspard-Félix Tournachon/Nadar (1820-1910), who photographed many leading personalities of late nineteenth-century French society. The first to explore fully the possibilities of the new medium in respect to movement was the British-American photographer, Eadweard Muybridge (1830-1904), who made extensive photographic studies of animal and human locomotion. The first to use searchingly artistic photography for social aims was the celebrated Danish-American journalist and social-recreational reformer, Jacob August Riis (1849-1914), whose "Home of an Italian Ragpicker" (1888) ranks with the most accomplished photographs of the nineteenth century.

Realism had a less distinctive affect on architecture and sculpture than on painting. In architecture, the wide use of cast iron as a structural and ornamental material, beginning in the 1840s and 1850s, created new possibilities for enclosing and artfully designing very large, very well-lit spaces. Likely the most outstanding instance of this tendency was the "Crystal Palace," London (1850-51; constructed for the first world industrial/technological exposition/fair, the Great Exhibition of the Works of Industry of all Nations, but since destroyed by fire) of English architect, Joseph Paxton (1801-65). The work of the greatest sculptor of the nineteenth century, the French genius, (François) Auguste Rodin (1840-1917), importantly embodied aspects of all of the major artistic movements of the period: the sense of natural beauty, classical proportion, and intensely expressive emotion of romanticism; the harsh, concrete imperatives of realism; the spontaneity of impressionism; and the representational irregularities of abstractionism. His masterpieces are among the most remarkable and stirring sculptural achievements of any age: "The Man with the Broken Nose" (bronze, 1864), "The Age of Bronze" (bronze, 1876), "Gates of Hell" (bronze, 1880-1917; most importantly included "The Thinker"), "The Burghers of Calais" (bronze, 1884-86), "The Kiss" (marble, 1886), and "Balzac" (bronze, 1893-97).

The momentous advent of **impressionism** marked the beginning of what became a larger break with prior tendency than any other movement in the entire history of the visual arts. Impressionism embodied the first conspicuous stage in the revolutionary transformation from the organic, monistic, and intrinsic orientation of romanticism/realism (the terminal stage of modernism) to the materialistic, dualistic/pluralistic, and extrinsic orientation that characterizes all subsequent movements (the sweep of post-modernism) except the main forms of twentieth-century expressionism. Impressionism began in the 1860s and 1870s, was most associated with the positivism-scientificism of the mid-nineteenth century, was notably more reserved than the romantic and realist movements it replaced, and was profoundly influenced by photography (in the sense that it attempted to provide the interpretive content missed by photography). Its scientific perspective had most to do with light, color, and motion; this perspective had most to do with our perceptions of light (our perceptions of its shifts in particular) and of color (as an ephemeral moment in the affect of light on us). Impressionism, at bottom, was concerned with perceptual appearances, neither with the underlying character of the material world (which is the apparent source of these appearances) nor with the underlying character of the conscious world (which is the apparent tablet on which these appearances are recorded). It took the skeptical (or at least the agnostic) attitude of modern science in these several respects and, thus, more so acknowledged the searching issues of human existence (truth, freedom, virtue, beauty, justice, love, happiness, fulfillment) than proposed a searching solution to them. It was rather the value-neutral center of impressionism that brought an end to the impassioned humanism of romanticism/realism and that set into motion the clinical dispassion of the twentieth century. Impressionism thus constituted more so the inaugural stage of post-modern abstractionism than the terminal stage of the modern traditions.

The impressionist movement was overwhelmingly French; it was dominated by French geniuses and it was inspired by the unique cast of varying light in disparate regions of France (most particularly in and near Paris). The great masters of **French impressionism**, most of whom knew one another well (they often studied, worked, and exhibited together), were:

- Édouard Manet (1832-83), who developed the germ of the movement with his sense of spontaneous perception (which included the emotional disposition of figures) and who thus evoked the passage from realism; his masterpieces are the oils-on-canvas "Luncheon on the Grass" (1863), "Olympia" (1863), "The Fife Player" (1866), "Execution of the Emperor Maximilian of Mexico" (1867), and "A Bar at the Folies-Bergère" (1881-82);

- Claude Monet (1840-1926), the central figure of the movement, who was principally a landscape painter, who was most devoted to capturing the spontaneous moment of experience in light, and whose work became increasingly abstract; his masterpieces are the oils-on-canvas "Women in the Garden" (1866), "The River" (1868), "Impressionism – Sunrise at Le Havre" (1872), "Gare Saint-Lazare" (1877), "Rouen Cathedral in Full Sunlight" (1892-93), and "Water Lilies" (c. 1920);

- Hilaire Germain Edgar Degas (1834-1917), who was more interested in moving figures than in landscape, who distinguished himself in sculpture and photography as well as in painting, who was especially fascinated with horse racing and with the dance, and who suffered near blindness in his late years; his masterpieces are the oils-on-canvas "The Rehearsal" (1874), "Glass of Absinthe" (1876), and "Two Laundresses" (1884) and the pastels "Prima Ballerina" (c. 1876) and "Woman Bathing in a Shallow Tub" (1885);

- Pierre Auguste Renoir (1841-1919), who had been a student of Monet and who was concerned both with the emotional temperament (the deeply sensuous temperament) of figures and with landscape; his masterpieces are the oils-on-canvas "Les Grands Boulevards" (1875), "Le Moulin de la Galette" (1876), and "Luncheon of the Boating Party at Bougival" (1881);

- Berthe Morisot (1841-95), who was a grandniece of Fragonard and a sister-in-law (as well as an especially close associate) of Manet and who painted in a strictly impressionist style; her masterpiece is the oil-on-canvas "In the Dining Room" (1886); and

- Camille Pissarro (1830-1903), who was born of Portuguese-French parents in St. Thomas, West Indies, who had been a student of Corot, who was a close associate of Cassatt, Cézanne, and

Gauguin, and who painted in a strictly impressionist style; his masterpiece is the oil-on-canvas "Boulevard des Italiens, Paris – Morning Sunlight" (1897).

Impressionism also had a major influence on American art and on American artists. The foremost contributors to **American impressionism** all lived for significant periods in France and were very heavily affected by the great French masters of the movement. The most accomplished of these were painters who made memorable contributions to the broad development of impressionism:

- James Abbott McNeill Whistler (1834-1903), whose commanding technique and rendering of color won especially wide acclaim; his masterpieces are the oils-on-canvas "Arrangement in Gray and Black, No. 1: The Artist's Mother" (1871) and "Portrait of Thomas Carlyle: Arrangement in Gray and Black, No. 2" (1872) and the oil-on-panel "Nocturne in Black and Gold: Falling Rocket" (c. 1874);
- Mary Cassatt (1845-1926), whose style was impressively personal and vigorous, who had an enormous influence over the popularity and the collections of impressionist art in the United States, and who suffered blindness in her late years; her masterpiece is the oil-on-canvas "The Bath" (1891); and
- John Singer Sargent (1856-1925), especially well remembered for his masterful sense of texture; his masterpiece is the oil-on-canvas "Portrait of Lady Agnew" (c. 1892-93).

Rodin's affinities for impressionism aside, the only entirely noteworthy sculptors of impressionist leaning were the French-Irish-American artist, Augustus Saint-Gaudens (1848-1907), and the American sculptors, Daniel Chester French (1850-1931) and (John) Gutzon Borglum (1867-1941). All emphasized the optical immediacy characteristic of impressionism in the fashioning of heroic public monuments. Saint-Gaudens' masterpiece is the bronze (with stone pedestal) "Monument to Admiral Farragut," New York City (1881); French's are the bronze "Minute Man," Concord, Massachusetts (1875) and the marble "Abraham Lincoln," Lincoln Memorial, Washington, D.C. (1922); and Borglum's are the monumental heads of American Presidents George Washington, Thomas Jefferson, Abraham Lincoln, and Theodore Roosevelt, "Mount Rushmore National Monument," on a mountain face near Rapid City, South Dakota (1927-41). Not unlike romanticism and realism, impressionism also inspired little distinctive architecture. The innovative architecture of the late nineteenth century, except that of Antoni Gaudi, was driven mainly by technological advancements in structural steel and in steel-reinforced concrete. These advancements made possible the construction of very large, multi-story, steel-frame, emphatically rectangular buildings in which the walls were little more than curtains, often nearly replaced by glass windows. Most of these buildings accentuated functional efficiency and were industrial and commercial structures such as factories, office buildings, warehouses, department stores, apartment houses, and railway stations. The acknowledged masters of this style were American architects, Henry Hobson Richardson (1838-86), known principally for his "Marshall Field Wholesale Store," Chicago (1885-87), and Louis Henry Sullivan (1856-1924), known principally for his "Wainwright Building," St. Louis (1890-91).

With impressionism, the immediacy of perceptual experience replaced the object itself as the central datum of art; what followed in the history of art further deepened this tendency and increasingly made aesthetic judgment a function of personal (and private) feeling (i.e., a relative matter). This is the "essence" of the post-modern revolution in art, philosophy, literature, and culture. Impressionism had concerned itself with perceptual appearances, neither with the underlying material source of these appearances nor with the consequences of them for conscious reflection. Beginning in the 1880s, a movement spinning off of impressionism and eventually replacing it – that is, **post-impressionism** – developed to examine the formal properties of appearance. This movement came in two main forms: one emphasized the material form of reality and owed most to impressionism's sense of color and to neo-classicism's sense of construction; the other emphasized the emotive-spiritual form of reality and owed most to impressionism's sense of color and to romanticism's sense of passion. Both tended to liberate themselves from a strict adherence to realistic (or literal) observation. As in the case of impressionism itself, both too were dominated by imposing French figures and by the novel beauties of Paris (and southern France).

The foremost advocates of the first of these forms, the **material form of post-impressionism**, were French painters, Paul Cézanne (1839-1904) and Georges Pierre Seurat (1859-91), both of whom sought accounts, in a sense scientific accounts, of the enduring permanence of the material world, the material source of our sense-perceptual impressions. Unlike the impressionists, then, Cézanne and Seurat gave interpretations of our visual experience that were sharp abstractions of that experience. Both embodied a sense of quiet constancy devoid of movement and both attempted an analysis of material form through color and light. Cézanne was a close associate of Manet, Renoir, Pissarro, and the celebrated author, Émile Zola; he painted among the most influential and masterful pictures of the nineteenth and twentieth centuries: the oils-on-canvas "Self-Portrait" (1879), "Mont Sainte-Victoire" (1885-87), "Card Players" (c. 1890-92), "Woman with the Coffeepot" (c. 1895), "Still Life with Apples and Oranges" (1895-1900), and "The Bathers" (1898-1904). Seurat painted in small jots of pure color which were mixed in our perception of them to form discernible images (pointillism); his very considerable masterpieces were also among the most influential and accomplished pictures of the nineteenth and twentieth centuries: the oils-on-canvas "The Bathers at Asnières" (1883-84) and "Sunday Afternoon on the Island of La Grande Jatte" (1884-86).

The leading exponents of the second of these two forms, the **emotive-spiritual form of post-impressionism**, were the magnificent painters, Vincent Van Gogh (1853-90 [suicide]), Paul Gauguin (1848-1903), and Henri de Toulouse-Lautrec (1864-1901), all of whom gave intensely personal, impassioned, and (largely) discontented accounts of human experience. Unlike the impressionists, then, Van Gogh, Gauguin, and Toulouse-Lautrec fashioned accounts, humanistic accounts, which were significant abstractions of our experience. Unlike Cézanne and Seurat, these abstractions embodied a sense of turbulent sentiment and attempted an essential statement concerning the emotive-spiritual consequences of our sense-perceptual impressions, consequences expressed in intense color, imaginative line, and rich texture. Van Gogh, the Dutch-French painter and the colossus of this form of post-impressionism, suffered epilepsy, depression, emotional instability, a debilitating sense of betrayal and failure, and a disastrous friendship with Gauguin. Near the end of his brief and troubled life, he cut off one of his ears, was sent to an asylum, and finally shot himself to death. His masterpieces are nonetheless unexcelled: the oils-on-canvas "The Potato Eaters" (1885), "The Night Café" (1888), "A View of La Crau" (1888), "Self-Portrait" (1889), "The Starry Night" (1889), and "Wheat Field and Cypress Trees" (1889). Gauguin, the French eccentric, broke emphatically with his middle-class business life, wandered the French-speaking world (most notably, France itself, Martinique, and Tahiti) in search of himself, and died in poverty and despair in the south Pacific. He was partly (native) Peruvian and brought a non-European aesthetic, a gentile, archaic aesthetic (mainly, an Oceanic aesthetic), to European art, adopting a style reminiscent of primitive abstractions. His masterpieces are among the finest and most influential paintings of the late nineteenth century: the oils-on-canvas "Vision After the Sermon: Jacob Wrestling with the Angel" (1888) and "The Day of the God" (1894). Toulouse-Lautrec, also French, too lived only briefly and likewise very unhappily. He suffered a crippling accident in his youth from which he never fully recovered, lived throughout as a disabled dwarf, was alienated from his wealthy family's fashionable existence, and took sanctuary in Parisian cafés and related establishments of the night. His major works were of the café and entertainment worlds; most notably, the oil-on-canvas "At the Moulin Rouge" (1892).

The two stems of post-impressionism, the material and the emotive-spiritual stems, provided the groundwork on which all subsequent developments in the arts unfolded. Twentieth-century art was dominated by the abstractions (from immediate experience) signaled by the two main forms of post-impressionism. From the material stem issued movements that concerned:
- the physical and social structure, the composition, of material reality; and
- the physical and social function, the operations, of material reality.

From the emotive-spiritual stem issued movements that concerned:
- the psychological character of conscious (ordinary sense-perceptual, emotional, and rational) experience; and
- the psychological character of sub-conscious (fantastic) experience.

Some developments/movements embodied a rather strict concern for one of these tendencies, others cut across the characteristics distinguishing them. All, however, included the most fundamental of abstractionist allegiances, the commitment to exploring the basic elements of visual perception themselves (space-time, light, color, shape, texture, scale, proportion, and composition), which comes to exploring the basic character of the work of visual art as such. In this sense, and others, the artistic creativity of the twentieth century is among the most remarkably innovative in the entire history of the medium.

The **basic elements of post-modernism** are most conspicuous in the abstractionist movements of the twentieth century; they became especially conspicuous after the First World War and have become still more pronounced since the Second World War. The most notable of these elements are the tendency to:
- deny a universal standard of truth and beauty and thus emphasize ambiguity, contradiction, and the relative "basis" of life and art, which has effectively diminished the sense of coherence but enhanced the sense of variety, novelty, and license in artistic creativity;

- emphasize sensory-based, bodily, and active standards as against rational, reflective, and passive standards, which has effectively brought a sense of mechanistic one-sidedness to artistic creativity and a close association of artistic creativity with physical culture (with dance, sport, war, and sex most notably);
- collapse the distinction between art and other activities, which has effectively made the aesthetic qualities of the everyday more special and what-once-counted-as-art less special;
- collapse the distinction between high and popular culture, which has effectively made all cultural phenomena popular and many not terribly high;
- turn against established traditions in respect to continuity, subject, and medium, which has effectively:
    - denied a coherent historical narrative to artistic creativity;
    - widened and diversified the subjects acceptably addressed by artistic creativity; and
    - widened and diversified the materials acceptably used in artistic creativity, to include such as cut paper, textiles, cardboard, linoleum, wood, sand, leather, glass, rope, rubber, plastic, metal, newspaper, food, plants, nails, photographs, cinematographs, computer graphics, machines, even one's own flesh, necrotic flesh, blood, and excrement.
- diminish the sense of tangibly recognizable form, which has effectively enhanced the significance of non-representational objectives in artistic creativity and enhanced as well the inclination to more so "construct" visual reality than to reflect it; and
- commodify art as a form of market entertainment, a tendency that is well served by the other marks of post-modernism and a tendency which has effectively reified art, enthroned a commercial, industrial, and technological aesthetic, and further diminished the significance of artistic traditions and of art history.

As such, the drift of twentieth-century art, the drift of the various forms of **abstractionism** that distinguish twentieth-century art, is in the direction of mechanistic, not in the direction of organic inclinations. Only the several major forms of twentieth-century expressionism – Germanic, French, Russian, Finnish, American, and Mexican expressionism – have oriented themselves to organic persuasion. These forms, the intellectual correlates of democratic socialism, have achieved a balanced attention to formal outline and contextual content, a harmonious relation of our material and our spiritual aspects, and an explicit embodiment of the abstractions implicit in the art and culture of gentile society. Expressionism thus best unified the two stems of post-impressionism, stood best against the most tendentiously dehumanizing features of post-modernism, and best synthesized the historical development of human (artistic) experience from its gentile origins through its civil journeys to the intrinsic fulfillment of political society.

We shall first consider the three major movements (together with their corollaries) of contemporary modern art (excluding expressionism) in the first approximate half of the twentieth century (i.e., from the passing of post-impressionism in the last decade of the nineteenth century to the Second World War) -- fauvism, cubism, and futurism – then look at expressionism (which began in the 1890s and continued well past the Second World War), and conclude with an examination of the blizzard of innovative developments since the Second World War. **Fauvism** (of wild beasts), not unlike impressionism and post-impressionism, was an essentially French movement centered in Paris. It was first suggested by the remarkable French painter, Henri Matisse (1869-1954), in c. 1897 but not fully developed, also by Matisse, much before 1905. It was most influenced by impressionism, the scientificism of Cézanne and Seurat, Van Gogh's acute sense of color and texture, the primitivism of Gauguin, and recent Japanese painting. Its appreciation of sensual freedom, intensely emotional effects, and sense of rebellion against the prevailing conditions of life made it an especially fertile target for political, financial, and critical condemnation. It nonetheless quickly succeeded in installing the avant-garde as conventional expectation, a characteristic mark of twentieth-century intellectual life. Fauvism made masses of bold color, uniquely juxtaposed, the fundamental structural principle of painting. It held (with Cézanne and the impressionists) that painting must be representational of nature in some respect, (with the impressionists against Cézanne) that painted images must be dynamic, (with Cézanne against the impressionists) that painted images must be enduring, and (against both Cézanne and the impressionists) that painted images must be of solid (not of indistinctly mixed) color. The principal exponents of fauvism were Matisse himself and three other richly talented French painters, Georges Roualt (1871-1958), Maurice de Vlaminck (1876-1958), and André Derain (1880-1954). Matisse painted with a uniquely rich sense of color and contour; his masterpieces are the oils-on-canvas "Green Stripe (Madame Matisse)" (1905), "Joie de Vivre" (1905-06), "Harmony in Red" (1908-09), "Red Studio" (1911), and "Decorative Figure Against an Ornamental Background" (1925) and the gouache-on-cut-pasted-paper "Zulma" (1950). Roualt painted mainly sorrowful figures with a fiercely turbulent style; his masterpieces are the oil-on-paper "Head of Christ" (1905), the oil-on-cardboard "Prostitute at Her Mirror" (1906), and the oil-on-canvas "The Old King" (1916-37). Vlaminck and Derain, who were close associates, too painted deeply and boldly colored pictures; Vlaminck's masterpieces are the oils-on-canvas "Paysage" (1908-14) and "Village in the Snow" (c. 1927); Derain's is the oil-on-canvas "Westminster Bridge" (1907). Pablo Picasso and Georges Braque also made brief but significant forays into the fauvist movement; both, however, were principally devoted to other aspects of contemporary modern art.

Cubism, like fauvism, post-impressionism, and impressionism, was likewise a largely French movement centered in Paris. Its original development occurred between 1907 and 1909 and it was owed primarily to the colossal Spanish-French artist, Pablo Ruiz y Picasso (1881-1973). It was devoted to an analytic exploration of pure form, or structure, neither to function nor to psychological experience. In cubism, structure replaced the color-emphasis of fauvism as the dominant feature of plastic art; an imaginative coordination of the subject's constituent planes became the governing principle of plastic media; and the commitment to visual reality, to representational images, was further eroded (as against fauvism). Unsurprisingly, cubism was most influenced by Cézanne and by pre-literate African sculpture. Cubism was importantly foreseen by the geometric representations of French sculptor, Aristide Maillol (1861-1944), whose masterpiece is "Mediterranean (Crouching Woman)" (bronze, 1901), and by the pre-1907 geometric representations of Picasso himself. Picasso's so-termed blue period (1901-04) made especially strong associations with the miseries of the disadvantaged and the disabled; it included several acknowledged masterpieces; most particularly, the oils-on-canvas "Absinthe Drinker" (1902) and "The Old Guitarist" (1903). His rose period (1904-06) made especially strong associations with nostalgic figures; it included the masterpiece, the oil-on-canvas "Saltimbanques" (1905). Cubism as such began with Picasso's monumental and revolutionary oil-on-canvas "Les Demoiselles d'Avignon" (1907), among the most powerful, influential, and accomplished works of twentieth-century art. It was further developed in the oils-on-canvas "Seated Woman" (1909), "The Accordionist" (1911), "Three Musicians" (1921), and "Three Dancers" (1925), in the collage with rope and caning "Still Life with Chair Caning" (1911-12), and in the collage and charcoal-on-canvas "The Bottle of Suze" (1913). In his classical period, which began in 1917 and continued variously throughout the remainder of his life, Picasso returned to more strictly representational tendencies, some of which were associated with surrealism, but most of which continued to be driven mainly by cubist perspectives. Arguably the most notable of the latter were the oils-on-canvas "Three Women at the Spring" (1917) and "Mother and Child" (1921-22).

The other major cubist painters were French: Georges Braque (1882-1963), Fernand Léger (1881-1955), and Robert-Victor-Félix Delaunay (1885-1941). Braque's earliest cubist work is virtually indistinguishable from Picasso's earliest cubist work (the work following "Les Demoiselles d'Avignon") and, also like Picasso, Braque too increasingly included bits of found-objects in his compositions and increasingly emphasized the textural plane of painting. The most notable of his masterworks are the oil-on-canvas "The Portuguese" (1911) and the collage "The Courrier" (1913). Léger was principally concerned with the function of the industrial world and created flattering, geometric, and complex abstractions of a mechanized utopia; most notably, in his masterworks, the oils-on-canvas "Disks" (1918) and "The City" (1919). And Delaunay also primarily did imaginative and brilliantly colored abstractions of the industrial world; most memorably, the tempera-on-canvas "Homage to Blériot" (1914). Cubism too had a significant presence in sculpture (from Maillol); most notably, in the work of:

- the French, Raymond Duchamp-Villon (1876-1918), an elder brother of Marcel Duchamp killed in the First World War, who principally did mechanized images, such as "The Great Horse" (bronze, 1914);
- the Ukrainian-American, Alexander Archipenko (1887-1964), who made especially much of empty space as a central element in sculptural figures, as in "Walking Woman" (bronze, 1912); and
- the Lithuanian-French-American, Jacques Lipchitz (1891-1973), who made alarmingly stark and arresting images, such as "Figure" (bronze, 1926-30).

A form of cubism, neo-cubism, orphism, or de stijl (the style), took the cubist emphasis on the structure of nature and society still further, to a consideration of structure itself. The leading exponent of this tendency was the highly imaginative and influential Dutch-French painter, Piet Mondrian (1872-1944), who reduced cubist planes to an abstract, geometric, largely rectilinear pattern of primary colors (red, yellow, and blue), all colors (white), no color (black), and the admixture of all colors (gray); most memorably, in the oils-on-canvas "Composition in Line and Color" (1913), "Composition" (1925), and "Composition with Red, Blue, and Yellow" (1930).

Cubism and de stijl had a thoroughly profound affect on the development of twentieth-century architecture, mainly in respect to the design and construction of uniquely large buildings ("skyscrapers") in the American architecture of the first several decades of the century and in respect to the so-termed "International Style" in western European architecture after the First World War. The earliest of the accomplished "skyscrapers" had been significantly inspired by the work of Louis Sullivan, were steel-frame rectangular solids of sixty stories and more in New York City and Chicago, and were in their time the tallest buildings in the world. The most notable of these were the "Woolworth Building," New York City (1911-13) of American architect, Cass Gilbert (1859-1934), and the "Chrysler Building," New York City (1928-30) of American architect, William Van Alen (1882-1954). Still larger buildings followed, some of which entailed increasingly inventive intersections of rectangular (and other) shapes and some of which made especially inventive use of glass. The best buildings of American architect, Philip Courtelyou Johnson (1906-), such as the "Seagram Building," New York City (done with Mies Van Der Rohe, 1956-58), are perhaps the most memorable of these. The "International Style" was first fashioned by German-American architect, Walter Gropius (1883-1969), who had begun to cultivate its basis shortly before the First World War, perhaps from as early as 1910, and who brought the notion to fruition shortly following the First World War. In 1918, he became Director of the Weimar School of Art and the next year transformed the School into the fabled Bauhaus. The Bauhaus became the center of the International Style and an international axis for all forms of design (mainly, architecture, furniture, and textiles) based on structure. The International Style itself was governed by a functional attention to the industrial design of mass-produced goods; it aimed to unite the disparate spheres of art and craft. It tended to make austere, geometric buildings (mainly, residences, schools, commercial and government offices, factories, theaters, transport terminals, churches, and sport stadiums) of largely uniform appearance from steel, concrete, and glass (not from natural materials); these buildings, moreover, emphasized flat, unornamented, usually white surfaces that gave a rigidly rectangular impression. The Style came to especially great prominence in Germany, Netherlands, France, and United States. Its principal advocates were:

- Gropius himself, mainly known for his (new) "Bauhaus," Dessau (1925-26);
- Gerrit Thomas Rietveld (1888-1964), the Dutch architect and designer, mainly known for his "Shroeder House," Utrecht (1924) and for his chairs;
- Le Corbusier/Charles-Édouard Jeanneret (1887-1965), the Swiss-French architect, mainly known for the very wide influence of his inventive genius, for his mechanism (his notion of buildings as machines), and for the weightless effect he produced by constructing buildings (at least partly) on posts; his early masterpiece is the "Villa Savoye," Poissy, France (1928-30); his later work (after the Second World War) departed from the International Style; and
- Ludwig Mies Van Der Rohe (1886-1969), the German-American architect, mainly known for his exacting reduction of plastic elements to their essential levels and for his formative contributions to the refinement of the glass skyscraper; the most notable of his buildings are the "Lake Shore Drive Apartments," Chicago (1950-52) and the "Seagram Building," New York City (done with Philip Johnson, 1956-58).

The Bauhaus itself was moved from Weimar to Dessau in 1926; Gropius resigned as Director in 1928; Mies Van Der Rohe became Director in 1930; the institution was moved again, to Berlin, in1932; and it was closed by the fascist German government in 1933.

   Futurism and its two main sequels, dada and surrealism, were very sharply influenced by cubism and they did themselves, in turn, significantly affect the ongoing development of cubism. Futurism also owed especially much to Gauguin, in particular the view that painting is most fundamentally a representation for emotion. Its seminal vision is nonetheless owed to the Italian poet, novelist, and critic, Filippo Tommaso Marinetti (1876-1944), whose proclamations of 1908-10 (most significantly, Manifesto of Futuristic Painters, 1910) argued for an iconoclastic break with traditional values, for an emphasis on dynamic function as the dominant feature of experience and art, for the glorification of industrial achievement and warfare, and for a fascist form of government. The movement was centered in Turin, Paris, London, and Berlin although its principal exponents were Italian painters and sculptors:

- Carlo Carra (1881-1966) superimposed simultaneous elements in order to create an impression of frenetic movement; most notably, in the oil-on-canvas "Funeral of the Anarchist Galli" (1910-11);
- Umberto Boccioni (1882-1916), who was killed in the First World War, portrayed the breathtaking turbulence of movement and change; most notably, in the oils-on-canvas "The City Rises" (1910-11) and "Dynamism of a Cyclist" (1913) and in the bronze sculpture of a running man, "Unique Forms of Continuity in Space" (1913);

- Joseph Stella (1877-1946), the Italian-American, painted interpenetrating forms suggesting great movement; most notably, the oil-on-bedsheet "Brooklyn Bridge" (1917-18); and
- Marcel Duchamp (1887-1968), the colossal French artist and a younger brother of Raymond Duchamp-Villon, painted one of the masterpieces of futurism, the cinematic, oil-on-canvas "Nude Descending a Staircase, No. 2" (1912), and also contributed very tellingly to dada and surrealism.

The emotive spontaneity of futurism and its iconoclastic view of traditional values deepened in the first of its two major sequels, **dada**. Futurism's embrace of industrial and military activity did not. Originally centered in Zurich, beginning in 1915, and later most importantly dispersed to New York City, Berlin, Cologne, and Paris, dada protested the entire fabric of European society. Reviled by the slaughter, ignorance, and corruption of the First World War and contemptuous of the established political, moral, and aesthetic values that caused and prosecuted the War, dada aimed to destroy these values by emancipating our emotional framework from the rational twaddle of the established order and by liberating the human, political, and artistic imagination from the bondage of this twaddle. Dada (hobbyhorse) attempted to irreverently demonstrate the meaninglessness of the established order by adopting a form of anti-art, a form of nihilistic absurdity which embraced the random, unpredictable, contradictory, and nonsensical. It did this in three main ways:
- through disconnected and disconcerting dream images;
- through complex, non-functional machinery; and
- through found-objects, or ready-mades.

Although many leading surrealists (the work for which they are most renowned) had participated memorably in dada, the three most distinctive and accomplished advocates of dada as such were:
- Jean (Hans) Arp (1887-1966), the German-French sculptor and painter, who experimented with accidental art and vaguely biomorphic shapes; most notably, in the oil-on-cardboard with cutouts "Mountain Table Anchors Navel" (1925);
- Marcel Duchamp, the French artist, who was arguably the central figure in the plastic aspect of the movement, who also made significant contributions to futurism and surrealism, who constructed haunting, enigmatic, and irregular images (most significantly, the oil, lead foil, and quick-silver-on-plate-glass "The Bride Stripped Bare by Her Bachelors, Even," 1915-23, and the oil-and-graphite-on-canvas with battle brush, safety pins, and nut and bolt "Tu m'," 1918), who crafted intricate and purposeless machines, and who was the acknowledged master of found-objects, or ready-mades (ordinary objects such as urinals, snow shovels, and bicycle wheels displayed in a way that accentuates their aesthetic qualities and thus objects that limit creation to the act of choice alone); and
- Max Ernst (1891-1976), the German painter, who also made significant contributions to surrealism and who produced alarmingly stark and ferocious images; most notably, the collage "I Piping Man" (1920) and the oil-on-canvas "The Elephant of the Celebes" (1921).

The second of futurism's two main sequels, **surrealism**, had both a phase that antedated dada and significantly influenced it, a phase that unfolded coextensively with cubism – namely, fantastic art – and a phase that effectively replaced dada in the 1920s, surrealism in the strict sense. Not unlike futurism and dada themselves, both fantastic art and surrealism proper were driven principally by psychic emotivism. Both were also convinced that imaginative fantasy is more basic to human experience in general and to art in particular than the external world. And both therefore emphasized the illogical tendencies of the sub-conscious and crafted mainly dream-like and child-like images. **Fantastic art** owed most to the primitive abstractions of Gauguin and it was importantly foreseen by the French painter, Henri Julien Rousseau (1844-1910), who is mainly known for his highly inventive, primitivistic, fanciful, and mysterious landscapes; most notably, the oils-on-canvas "The Sleeping Gypsy" (1897) and "The Dream" (1910). The seminal contributions to fantastic art itself, however, were made by:
- Marc Chagall (1887-1985), the Russian-French-American painter and sculptor, who created sets and costumes for the ballets of fabled composer, Igor Stravinsky, who did several magnificent stained-glass windows and monumental murals, and who fashioned pictures of uniquely personal and child-like fantasy; most notably, the oils-on-canvas "I and the Village" (1911) and "Self-Portrait with Seven Fingers" (1912);
- Giorgio de Chirico (1888-1978), the Greek-Italian-French painter, who continued to develop his style in the period of surrealism itself and who made powerfully barren and melancholic landscapes; most memorably, the oils-on-canvas "The Nostalgia of the Infinite" (c. 1913-14) and "Mystery and Melancholy of the Street" (1914); and

313

- Paul Klee (1879-1940), the Swiss-German painter, who was briefly associated with German expressionism, who served on the faculty of the Bauhaus, who continued to develop his style in the period of surrealism itself, who conceived of visual art in terms of ordered shapes that are images of ideas, and who fashioned an utterly unique style dominated by child-like innocence; most notably, in the ink-on-paper "Heads" (1913), the mixed-media-on-gauze "Dance, Monster, to My Soft Song!" (1922), the watercolor, pen, and ink-on-paper "Twittering Machine" (1922), the oil-on-canvas "Ad Parnassum" (1932), and the oil-and-gouache-on-burlap "Death and Fire" (1940).

Marcel Duchamp's oil-on-canvas "The Bride" (1912) also importantly tended to fantastic perspectives as well as having foreshadowed dada.

Surrealism as such developed out of the basic character of fantastic art and out of the self-destructive excesses of dada. It was most explicitly inspired by the charismatic personality and the literary declarations of French writer, André Breton (1896-1966), beginning in 1919 and coming to full effect after 1924 (when Breton issued his first Manifesto of Surrealism). Surrealism, like fantastic art and dada, was primarily governed by our awareness of the sub-conscious, by the immediacy of Freud's free association of unmediated dream images, by the psychoanalytic symbolism of the id. It rejected the self-conscious perspectives of reason and convention in order to embrace poetic spontaneity. It was too, like dada, deeply moved by the devastations of the First World War and fervently devoted to an agenda of political (as well as intellectual) transformation. Unlike the fascist allegiances of futurism and the nihilistic anarchism of dada, however, surrealism was devoted to an international, socialist revolution. The styles of its leading figures varied widely but tended to stark, precisely outlined images, mostly biomorphic, but not always representational shapes, and unsettling psychological effects. The most significant exponents of artistic surrealism as such were:
- Joan Miro (1893-1983), the Catalan painter, who fashioned compositions of delicate and fluid lines, brilliant colors, and freely associated forms; most notably, in the oils-on-canvas "Harlequin's Carnival" (1924-25), "Composition" (1933), and "Painting, 1933" (1933);
- Salvador Dali (1904-89), the Spanish-American painter, who portrayed uniquely personal fantasies and obsessions, often nightmares; most notably, in the oils-on-canvas "The Persistence of Memory" (1931) and "Soft Construction with Boiled Beans: Premonition of Civil War" (1936);
- René Magritte (1898-1967), the Belgian painter, who mockingly depicted the absurd and the ironic in everyday life; most notably, in the oil-on-canvas "Delusions of Grandeur" (1961);
- Alberto Giacometti (1901-66), the Swiss-French sculptor and painter, who crafted gaunt, elongated human figures; most notably, in "Walking Man II" (bronze, 1948); and
- Matta/Roberto Sebastian Antonio Matta Echaurren (1912-), the Chilean-American painter, who did the most abstract and the most expressionistic work of the surrealists; most notably, in the oils-on-canvas "Listen to Living" (1941) and "To Give Painless Light" (1955).

The European painters, Pablo Picasso and Max Ernst, also made important contributions to the surrealist movement, mainly in the form of enormously powerful portrayals of social protest and social resistance. Picasso's celebrated oil-on-canvas "Guernica" (1937) conveys the terror of the (fascist) German bombing of a Basque city in the Spanish Civil War. Ernst's wrenching oil-on-canvas "Europe After the Rain" (1940-42) depicts the desolation of civilized life in the Second World War. And two major American painters, who developed rather unique styles, inclined primarily to surrealism: Georgia O'Keefe (1887-1986), wife of Alfred Stieglitz, made stark images of clear and strong color (such as the oil-on-canvas "Blue and Green Magic," 1919) and Edward Hopper (1882-1967) made menacingly lonesome images portraying the banality of American life (such as the oil-on-canvas "Automat," 1927).

Expressionism developed in the same approximate period as fauvism, cubism, and futurism and was greatly influenced by them. It effectively:
- raised the manifold tendencies of fauvism, cubism, and futurism (themselves implicit in impressionism and post-impressionism) to authentically human status;
- achieved a proportionate attention to the contextual and the formal, the material and the spiritual, aspects of our experience;
- embodied the possibilities of humanity's organic fulfillment in a way reminiscent of the other four main episodes in our world-historical development to compellingly embrace the organic thesis and all that is entailed by this thesis: the ancient Greek (most especially, the Athenian) Enlightenment, novel aspects of the medieval and modern Islamic Enlightenment (most especially, aspects of the Omayyad, Abbasid, Fatimid, Almoravid, Nasrid, Timurid, Mogul, and Ottoman developments), European (most especially, Italian, Burgundian, and German) Renaissance humanism, and

nineteenth-century (most especially, French, German, British/Irish, Russian, American, Scandinavian, Italian, and Spanish) romanticism/realism; and

- supplied the intellectual equivalent of European (most especially, Scandinavian) democratic socialism.

Twentieth-century expressionism unfolded in two main forms:

- a representational, or figurative, form that tended to emphasize the psycho-emotive features of human experience, that transformed tangible objects, and that was most influenced by post-impressionism and futurism; and
- a non-representational, or abstract, form that began with an ostensible emphasis on the structuro-functional features of human experience but that ended with an emphasis on distinctly human experience itself, that emancipated visual symbols from a strict attachment to tangible objects and delivered them to an inner necessity as well, and that was most influenced by fauvism and cubism.

The seminal development of the **representational form of expressionism** was owed to the 1890s; this form went variously on until well past the Second World War; and it was dominated by Germanic, Mexican, French, and Finnish artists. The basic tenor of the movement was foreseen by Belgian-English painter, James Ensor (1860-1949), who made visual elements subservient to emotional factors in his existential condemnations of contemporary human existence. As early as the mid-1880s, in the reign of post-impressionism, Ensor crafted pictures of vivid color, inventive shapes, and unsettling intensity; most notably, the oils-on-canvas "The Entry of Christ into Brussels in 1889" (1886) and "Intrigue" (1890). The principal harbinger of the earliest explicit phase of the movement, **Germanic expressionism**, however, was the magnificent Norwegian painter, Edvard Munch (1863-1944). Munch, a close associate of the celebrated Norwegian dramatist, Henrik Ibsen, painted deeply moving and profoundly agitated images dominated by existential senses of isolation, fear, and anxiety; most notably, the oils-on-canvas "The Scream" (1893), "Death in the Sick Chamber" (1893-94), "Anxiety" (1894), and "The Dance of Life" (1899-1900). The formal origins of Germanic expressionism as such were subsequently developed by an insurgent group of young artists in Dresden, Die Brucke (The Bridge), beginning in 1905. The basic vision of Die Brucke was provided by Ernst Ludwig Kirchner (1880-1938 [suicide]), who was soon joined by Karl Schmidt-Rottluff (1884-1976) and Emil Nolde (1867-1956). All were German, except Nolde (who was Danish), all were exceptional painters and woodcut artists, and all developed very powerful styles of sobering temperament, bold statement, existential melancholy, and social protest, variously reminiscent of Rouault, Munch, and Daumier. Kirchner is perhaps best remembered for his oils-on-canvas "The Street" (1907) and "Five Women in the Street" (1913); Schmidt-Rottluff, for his oil-on-canvas "Woman with Bracelets" (1912) and his woodcut "Way to Emmaus" (1918); and Nolde, for his oils-on-canvas "Last Supper" (1909), "Doubting Thomas" (1912), and "Landscape" (1931) and his woodcut "Prophet" (1912).

Although Die Brucke dissolved in 1913, its great influence continued; most significantly among Germanic and Mexican artists. Of the Germanic figures, the Austrian-German painter, Oskar Kokoschka (1886-1980), the German artists, Max Beckmann (1864-1950) and Otto Dix (1891-1969), and the German-American artist, George Grosz (1893-1959), who had also significantly participated in dada, were arguably the most memorable. Kokoschka, although no less alienated from human society than Beckmann, Dix, and Grosz, veiled his displeasure in solitary, psychological tensions that condemned less stridently than the others. His masterpieces are the oils-on-canvas "Self-Portrait" (1913), "The Bride of the Wind" (1914), and "Woman in Blue" (1919). Beckmann, Dix, and Grosz were thoroughly estranged from (and hostile to) bourgeois society and the official cruelties it had heaped on innocent people, most particularly in the First and Second World Wars; all painted bitingly satirical pictures that indicted the material and existential mutilations of the Wars and installed spiritual disillusionment as the only apt response to such mutilations. Beckmann's masterpieces are the oils-on-canvas "The Night" (1918-19), "The Dream" (1921), and "Blindman's Bluff" (1945). Dix's etching and aquatint "Lens Bombed" (1924) and Grosz's oil-on-cardboard "Metropolis" (1917) and oil-on-canvas "Germany, a Winter's Tale" (1918) are especially poignant examples of the ferocious caricatures at which both excelled. The talented Italian-French painter, Amedeo Modigliani (1884-1920), also tended in the broad direction of representational expressionism. His uniquely elongated and languidly fateful figures portrayed spiritual deprivation; most notably, in the oils-on-canvas "Portrait of Max Jacob" (1916) and "Jeane Hebuterne with White Collar" (1919).

The representational form of expressionism also developed a major presence in the Americas. The increasing influence of French and German artistic ideas in the Americas and the rather typical American inclination to eclecticism encouraged the maturation of a unique form of representational expressionism in the

United States, a form that tended to admix prominent European styles with distinctly North American perceptions. Arguably the most notable of those devoted to this tendency were art collector, exhibitor, photographer, and husband of Georgia O'Keefe, Alfred Stieglitz (1864-1946), and painter, John Marin (1870-1953). Stieglitz's magnificent photograph "The Steerage" (1907) and Marin's imaginative watercolors "Lower Manhattan" (1922) and "Boat off Deer Isle" (1926) are especially accomplished examples of the American sense of representational expressionism, futurism, cubism, and fauvism. Still more significant, however, are the leading figures, the colossal painters, of **Mexican expressionism**, Diego Rivera (1886-1957), Jose Clemente Orozco (1883-1949), and Rufino Tamayo (1899-1991). All were very significantly influenced by European artistic ideas, by pre-Colombian aesthetic perspectives, by Mexican life, history, and social problems, by humanitarian sympathies with the working-class struggles against industrialists, and by the revolutionary governments of Mexico between the two World Wars. Rivera and Orozco were also inclined to Marxist interpretations of the world's very considerable troubles and gave entailed, colorful, and impassioned accounts of these interpretations and troubles (some of which foresaw the paler development of social realism in eastern Europe) in monumental mural (fresco) paintings; most notably, Rivera's "Night of the Rich," Ministry of Education, Mexico City (1928) and Orozco's "Mankind's Struggle," New School for Social Research, New York City (1930). Tamayo tended to less overtly political statements but to a nonetheless comparably symbolic style; most notably, in the oils-on-canvas "Women of Tehuantepec" (1939) and "The Singer" (1950).

Representational expressionism also had a significant affect on twentieth-century sculpture and architecture. The organic forms of Norwegian sculptor, Gustav Vigeland (1869-1943), Romanian-French sculptor, Constantin Brancusi (1876-1957), English sculptor, Henry Moore (1898-1986), and American sculptor, Alexander Calder (1898-1976) all aimed at the essential and the proportionately elegant line characteristic of representational expressionism. The masterworks of these towering figures were among the finest plastic achievements of the century: Vigeland's "Young Man and Woman" (marble, 1906), "Mother and Child" (marble, 1909), and magnificent "Skulpturpark," Oslo (1924-59); Brancusi's "The Sleeping Muse" (plaster, 1909-26), "Mademoiselle Pogany" (marble, 1912), and "Bird in Space" (bronze, 1928); Moore's "Two Forms" (stone, 1936) and "Recumbent Figure" (stone, 1938); and Calder's abstract immobile sculptures (stabiles) and biomorphic kinetic sculptures (mobiles, which brought the temporal dimension more conspicuously to sculpture in the fashion of wire and metal forms hinged together as delicate and balanced moving compositions; such as "Lobster Trap and Fish Tail," 1939). In architecture, expressionism fashioned among the greatest talents in the entire history of the medium: the Catalan genius, Antoni Gaudi i Cornet (1852-1926), the American genius, Frank Lloyd Wright (1867-1959), and the Finnish-American and Finnish geniuses, Eliel Gottlieb Saarinen (1873-1950), his son, Eero Saarinen (1910-61), and the brothers, Timo Suomalainen (1928-) and Tuomo Suomalainen (1931-88). Gaudi was the master of irregular, exuberant, and enormously imaginative shapes, mainly curvilinear shapes, effectively sculptural shapes, and architectural designs. His masterpieces are the "Temple Expiatori de la Sagrada Familia," Barcelona (1883-1926) and the "Casa Mila," Barcelona (1905-07). Wright was the master of environmental design in which architecture and the natural spaces it inhabits are intimately and harmoniously related, in which strong common interior spaces are greatly influenced by exterior space, in which inventively projected planes establish a balanced relation between horizontal and vertical lines, and in which significant consideration is given to the experience of those occupying the spaces framed by architectural design. His masterpieces are the "Robie House," Chicago (1909) and the "Kaufmann House (Falling Water)," Bear Run, Pennsylvania (1936). And the great Finns were masters of inventive shape, elegant proportion, and environmental reference. Eliel Saarinen's most memorable work is the "Central Railway Station," Helsinki (1910-14); Eero Saarinen's, is the "Dulles Airport Terminal," Chantilly, Virginia (1961-62); and the Suomalainen's, is the stunning church "Temppeliaukio," Helsinki (1966-70). The magnificent Finnish sense of shape, line, proportion, and function also created an unexcelled tradition in design, led mainly and most brilliantly by architect, Hugo Alvar Henrik Aalto (1898-1976).

The seminal development of the non-representational form of twentieth-century expressionism, **abstract expressionism**, was owed to the period immediately preceding the First World War. Like the representational form, it too went on until well past the Second World War. Unlike the representational form, it was dominated by Russian and American artists. Its earliest marks were made by a brilliant group of artists, Der Blaue Reiter (The Blue Horseman), formed in Munich in 1911-12. Its leading figure was the principal exponent of **Russian abstract expressionism** and among the giants of contemporary art, the Russian-German painter, Wassily Kandinsky (1866-1944). Kandinsky was soon joined by no less than Paul Klee, mainly known for his pioneering contributions to fantastic art as has been said. Kandinsky was most affected by the cubist emphasis on form and the fauvist emphasis on color. Out of these dual influences, he developed a view of painting as a musical communication of the vital energy within us, a communication conducted by means of non-figurative symbols, a universal (transpersonal) view of art devoted to a form of spiritual experience free of human tragedy. His masterpieces are the extensive series of improvisations and compositions variously done between 1909 and 1921 – such as, the oils-on-canvas, "Improvisation 30" (1913), "Sketch I for 'Composition VII'" (1913), and "Composition 238: Bright Circle" (1921) – and the more geometric triumphs thereafter – such as, the oil-on-canvas "Yellow Accompaniment" (1924). In addition to his pioneering efforts with Der Blaue Reiter (which effectively disbanded in 1914), Kandinsky also served on the Bauhaus faculty and was importantly associated with two closely related Russian movements, suprematism and constructivism. Both suprematism and constructivism were dominated by wholly abstract, geometric shapes, by minimalist, structuro-functional shapes; both were centered in Moscow; and both unfolded mainly in the chaos and deprivation of the revolutionary years. Suprematism was the creation of Russian painter, Kasimir Malevich (1878-1935), whose masterpieces are the oils-on-canvas "Suprematist Composition" (1915) and "White on White" (c. 1918). Constructivism was the creation of the brothers, Russian-French sculptor, Anton (Antoine) Pevsner (1886-1962), and Russian-German-American sculptor, Naum Gabo (1890-1977). Among Pevsner's foremost work is his "Portrait of Marcel Duchamp" (celluloid-on-copper, 1926); among Gabo's, is his "Space Construction C" (plastic, c. 1922).

Kandinsky was arguably the first entirely abstract artist and had a thoroughly staggering influence on the subsequent course of contemporary art; most notably, on the subsequent course of abstract expressionism. The horrifying devastations of the two World Wars in Europe brought many prominent European artists to the United States, which became the artistic capital of the world after the Second World War. New York City in particular replaced Paris as the most important international center for the arts in the decades immediately following the War. Among the most creative and otherwise extraordinary movements in the entire history of artistic endeavor, the most significant American contribution to the entire history of the visual arts, and the dénouement of the organic triumphs of expressionism, **American abstract expressionism** was developed in the approximately fifteen years just past the War. American abstract expressionism exalted individual freedom, the intensely emotional and reflective character of our inner life in symbolic terms, and the act of artistic creativity/fulfillment itself. It thus opposed totalitarianism and those disinclined to liberating enunciation; it was itself, conversely, condemned by regressive materialism and its official defenders throughout the world (including in the United States itself). Its major figures, most of whom knew one another well, rank among the most remarkable artistic talents of any age:

- Arshile Gorky (1904-48 [suicide]), the Armenian-American painter of unexcelled genius, created deeply inventive, organic forms of sensuous color; most notably, in the oils-on-canvas "Garden in Sochi" (1941), "How My Mother's Embroidered Apron Unfolds in My Life" (1944), "The Liver in the Cock's Comb" (1944), "Water of the Flowery Mill" (1944), "Waterfall" (1944), and "Dark Green Painting" (1948);

- Jackson Pollack (1912-56), the American painter, developed the "drip" method of painting in 1946, an innovation that liberated painting from the brush, and created images of complex, rhythmic pattern; most notably, in the oils-on-canvas "One" (1950), "Number Five" (1951), and "Blue Poles" (1953);

- Willem de Kooning (1904-), the Dutch-American painter, created images of great energy and varied color; most notably, in the oil-on-canvas "Woman II" (1952) and the oil-and-enamel-on-canvas "The Time of the Fire" (1956);

- Hans Hofmann (1880-1966), the German-American painter, created exuberant images of sharply contrasting color; most notably, in the oils-on-canvas "Exuberance" (1955) and "The Gate" (1960);

- Franz Kline (1910-62), the American painter, created dynamic, intersecting, black-and-white images; most notably, in the oils-on-canvas "Accent Grave" (1955) and "Mahoning" (1956);

- Mark Rothko (1903-70 [suicide]), the Russian-American painter, created ominous and carefully ordered rectangular shapes of varying scale and color; most notably, in the oils-on-canvas "White and Greens in Blue" (1957) and "Two Openings in Black over Wine" (1958);

- Louise Nevelson (1900-88), the Russian-American sculptor, created complex and mysterious assemblages of wood, metal, and found-objects, customarily arranged in rectangular, box-like containers; such as, "An American Tribute to the British People" (wood painted gold, 1960-65); and

- David Smith (1906-65), the American sculptor, created bold and powerful, mostly welded steel constructions; such as, the stainless steel "Cubi XVII" (1963), "Cubi XVIII" (1964), and "Cubi XIX" (1964).

Although created largely by European expatriates in the United States as well as by American artists themselves, the universal scope of abstract expressionism also brought it a wide presence in Europe; most notably, in the tachism of French painter, Georges Mathieu (1922-), who created exceedingly fine, script-like shapes of sharp and engaging color; such as, the oils-on-canvas "Painting" (1952) and "Festival in Norwich" (1957). The movement was the dominant artistic influence on the intellectual life of accomplished world culture into the 1960s. Although it persisted variously since that time, it was overwhelmed in this and later periods by largely unflattering reactions to its impassioned nature, by ongoing forms of international conflict and treachery that called everything established into serious disrepute, and by an unrestrained promotion of commercial ambition (and its marketing, which is to say its propagandistic, corollaries) that required something new and different every several seconds. The result was a bewildering, but imaginative variety of views and styles that turned away from the organic texture of abstract expressionism in the direction of mechanistic dispassion and novelty. This dispassion and novelty, unsurprisingly, often had as much to do with attracting profitable attention as with strictly aesthetic concerns.

The iconoclasm and sense of social protest that moved predominantly through the post-Second World War era since the effective passing of abstract expressionism was most conspicuously expressed in the **pop-art movement**. This largely American movement emphasized the banal aspects of technological society by reinterpreting popular imagery, called attention to the aesthetic properties of everyday objects (not unlike dada), developed an anti-aesthetic aesthetic (also reminiscent of dada), and was dominated by:

- Robert Rauschenberg (1925-), the American painter and sculptor, who accentuated the nature of the material itself and included found-objects (bottles, clocks, quilts, photographs, tires, and stuffed goats for prominent example) in the construction of his intensely uninhibited collages; such as, the mixed media "Bed" (1955) and the oil-on-canvas with silkscreen "Trapeze" (1964);
- Jasper Johns (1930-), the American painter, who painted common objects in an artistic context; such as, the encaustic-and-collage-on-canvas "Flag above White with Collage" (1955) and the encaustic-and-newspaper-on-canvas with plaster casts "Target with Four Faces" (1955);
- Roy Lichtenstein (1923-97), the American painter, who fashioned audacious, comic-strip-like, commercial graphics; such as, the magna-on-canvas "Whaam" (1963);
- Claes Oldenburg (1929-), the Swedish-American sculptor, who made enlarged parodies of consumer goods that conveyed a sense of mechanized triviality and soulless dissatisfaction; such as, the vinyl, kapok, cloth, and plexiglass "Soft Typewriter" (1963); and
- Andy Warhol (1930-87), the American artist, who is mainly known for his long, avant-garde films (such as those of a man sleeping, a building, and his friends' casual activities) and for his highly repetitive, silkscreen images of such as commercial products (soup cans and boxes of cleaning compound for prominent example), macabre objects and events (electric chairs, automobile crashes, and race riots for salient example), common objects (flowers and two-dollar bills for instance), and celebrities (most notably, Marilyn Monroe, Elvis Presley, Jackie Kennedy, and Mao Tse-tung).

The **other major tendencies of the visual arts in the period since the Second World War** were: color-field art, conceptual and performance art, optical and kinetic art, minimal and process art, and earth and site art. Color-field art dealt with the emotionless language of visual art itself (mainly pure color and scale); in it, fields of hard-edged color were crafted to exacting scale and inventively juxtaposed. Its principal exponents were American painters, Barnett Newman (1905-70) and Frank Stella (1936-). Newman's oil-on-canvas "Who's Afraid of Red, Yellow and Blue III" (1966-67) and Stella's aluminum-paint-on-canvas "Avicenna" (1960) are among the finest examples of this genre. Conceptual and performance art aimed typically to offend orthodox sensibilities and was politically and morally subversive; it was often done in multi-media contexts (to include music, drama, dance, as well as plastic expanse) and also emphasized written text; and it was governed mainly by the novel idea of the work as distinct from its skillful execution. Its most memorable advocates were the Italian artist, Lucio Fontana (1899-1968), known mainly for his slashed canvases (such as, "Spatial Concept," 1960), and the French artist, Yves Klein (1928-62), who was among the most daringly experimental figures of the century. Klein did such as exhibit empty galleries, expose painted canvases to rain and fire (the painted-and-burned-asbestos "Fire Painting," 1961-62, for instance), and encouraged nude women covered in paint to move over paper and canvas surfaces (the paint-on-paper "Large Anthropology – Homage to Tennessee Williams," 1960, for example). Optical and kinetic art was devoted to a dispassionate, largely non-representational evocation of visual illusions in respect to mass, position, and motion. Minimal art created hard, simple, and permanent shapes (of metal or plastic for instance) divested of all human meaning; process art fashioned soft, complex, and impermanent shapes (of sand or steam for instance) divested of all human meaning. And earth and site art excavated and/or decorated large natural environments (such as plains, valleys, mountains, and islands).

There were nonetheless two major tendencies that gave a new and compelling twist to earlier developments: the admixed, surrealistic-expressionistic inclinations of French painter, Jean Dubuffet (1901-85), and the admixed, realistic-expressionistic inclinations of American sculptors, George Segal (1924-2000) and Edward Kienholz (1927-94). Dubuffet, in a fashion most reminiscent of Klee, expressed a profound and a mocking pessimism in images characteristic of primitive peoples, children, and the insane (such as, the oil-on-canvas "La Marée l'Hourloupe," 1963). Segal and Kienholz, in a fashion most reminiscent of Daumier, expressed deep disaffections concerning the grim and shabby character of contemporary industrial life; Segal, in white-plaster molds of living persons (such as, "The Bus Riders," 1964); and Kienholz, in exceedingly artful, satirical, and damning installations (such as, "Back Seat Dodge '38," 1964; "The Beanery," 1965; "The State Hospital," 1966; and "The Portable War Memorial," 1968).

The innovative erudition in the visual arts of the period since the Second World War, which was most evident in painting and sculpture, also conspicuously showed itself in photography and architecture. Arguably the most notable photographers of this period were the Americans, Ansel Adams (1902-84), who mainly did superbly detailed landscapes (such as, "Bridal Veil Fall, Yosemite," c. 1927), Diane Arbus (1923-71), who mainly did profoundly disadvantaged and troubled human figures (such as, "Child with Toy Hand Grenade, New York," 1962), and Robert Mapplethorpe (1946-89), who mainly did erotic figures (such as, "Leatherman II," 1970). Finnish expressionism aside, the most strikingly visionary designs of post-Second World War architecture were owed to the great Swiss-French architect, Le Corbusier, to American architect, Richard Buckminster Fuller (1895-1983), and to the Italian-American architect, Paolo Soleri (1919-). After the War, Le Corbusier departed from the International Style he had earlier embraced and created abstract, sculptural shapes; most notably, the apartment house "Unité d'Habitation," Marseilles (1947-52) and the chapel "Notre-Dame-du-Haut," Ronchamp, France (1950-54). Fuller created pre-fabricated, centrally planned, urban residential buildings which emphasized material, energy, climate, and cost efficiency; most notably, the geodesic dome "Biosphere," Montreal (1967). And Soleri created mushroom-shaped and dome-shaped, self-contained communities; most notably, "Arcosanti," Cordes Junction, Arizona (1970-).

The musical and movement arts

The musical and movement arts of the nineteenth and twentieth centuries passed through the same approximate stages as the philosophy, literature, and visual arts of this time and for roughly the same reasons. The classicism/neo-classicism of the late eighteenth century (mainly that of Haydn, Mozart, and the early Beethoven) gave way in the early nineteenth century to the new romanticism. The new movement, however, had an even larger influence on music, opera, and dance (itself driven principally by developments in music) than it had on the visual arts and it also persisted as the dominant tendency much longer in the musical and movement arts than it had in painting, sculpture, and architecture. In the late nineteenth century, moreover, (musical) romanticism was greatly affected by two major developments:

- the increasing attentions given to themes peculiar to various national-ethnic (folk) traditions, themes which were broadly aimed at the realist objectives of tangible social reform and national unification-independence; and
- transformations in the basic harmonic structure of music itself (heralded by Richard Wagner as early as the 1840s) and even more dramatic shifts in the basic tonality of music itself (first fashioned by Claude Debussy in the 1890s).

Although notably influenced and tellingly modified by these developments, romanticism (or neo-romanticism) remained the governing force of the musical and movement arts well into the twentieth century. As in the visual arts, it was nonetheless impressionism (in this case, that of Debussy in the 1890s), and its affiliations with scientific perspectives, that marked both the beginning of romanticism's end and the seminal stages of (musical) post-modernism. Impressionism itself developed quickly in the last decade of the nineteenth century and was followed in the first decade of the twentieth by the earliest whispers of atonality and dissonance (mainly from Arnold Schoenberg and Igor Stravinsky) that characterized post-modern (abstract) music in the strictest of senses. This form of music then became the dominant form after the loathsome terror of the First World War and its experimental cast deepened yet further in the period following the Second (mainly under the influence of John Cage).

Unsurprisingly, the romantic movement in the musical and movement arts closely resembled the romantic movement in philosophy, literature, and the visual arts. **Romanticism** added intensely emotional content to the rational classicism of the Enlightenment, was devoted to a balanced, harmonious, and unified sense of both our intellectual and our physical possibilities, was dominated by an authentically human longing for, and an authentically heroic pursuit of distinctly human freedom and fulfillment, and was thus committed to an organic, an intrinsic, view of life that inclined to the richness of political society. Its volcanic exuberance, elemental power, abrupt contrasts of temperament, and impassioned energy, its perception of the ideal in human and natural affairs, its compelling sense of struggle for meaningful and robust expression, its triumphant faculty of resolution, and its universal scope set it clearly apart from the classical movement it replaced and from the impressionist and abstract movements that would supplant it. By organic standard, it constitutes the most striking chapter in the entire history of music.

This chapter was centered in Vienna and Paris and it began, as has been said, with Ludwig van Beethoven, who straddled the eighteenth and nineteenth centuries in music as Goethe had in literature, as David and Ingres had in the visual arts, and as Hegel had in philosophy. Beethoven's contributions to the transformation from classical/neo-classical to romantic music were pioneering; they opened a substantially new world. His early compositions (to c. 1802) belonged to the former idiom; his later music, to the latter. From c. 1802, when he noticeably began to lose his sense of hearing, a tumultuous, a romantic, quality of self-expression was added to the rational form, unity, and proportion of his classical stage. In the last approximate decade of his life, which was haunted by total deafness, Beethoven tended to a still more deeply romantic orientation. Most of the magnificent music for which he is so deservingly well remembered was thus written in the new idiom after 1802; the best of the unsurpassed compositions of this period are:

- the last twenty of his 30 piano sonatas; most memorably, "Appassionata" (1804) and "Waldstein" (1804);
- his lone opera, "Fidelio" (1805);
- the most significant of his eleven overtures: the three "Leonore Overtures" (1805, 1806, 1806), the "Coriolan Overture" (1807), and the "Egmont Overture" (1810);
- his wonderful triple concerto (for violin, cello, and piano, 1805) and violin concerto (1806);
- the last ten of his sixteen string quartets; most significantly, the three "Rasumovsky Quartets" (1806) and the last five quartets, the "Grosse Fugue" (1826);
- the last two of his five piano concertos: numbers 4 (1806) and 5 (1809);
- the best of his two Masses, "Missa Solemnis" (1822);
- his variations for piano, "Diabelli Variations" (1823); and
- the last seven of his nine colossal symphonies: numbers 3 ("Eroica," 1803), 4 (1806), 5 (1807), 6 ("Pastoral," 1808), 7 (1812), 8 (1812), and 9 ("Choral," 1824).

Most of the other leading figures in the formative development and in the maturation of romantic music were Germanic (either Austrian or German), French, or Italian, many of whom were acquainted with one another (and importantly influenced one another) and many of whom were also the routine recipients of significant royal (and other institutional and private) patronage. Of these, the foremost figures of **Germanic romanticism** were arguably the most prominent:

- Carl Maria Friedrich Ernst von Weber (1786-1826), the German, was the virtual originator of distinctly German romantic opera; he wrote ten operas (most notably, "Peter Schmoll" [1803], "Abu Hassan" [1810], "Der Freischutz" [1821], "Euryanthe" [1823], and "Oberon" [1826], each of which begins with a stunning overture), many fine works for piano (most notably, the "Concertstuck for Piano and Orchestra" [1821]), and several memorable works for orchestra (most notably, "Invitation to the Dance" [1819]);
- Franz Peter Schubert (1797-1828), the Austrian, created a stupendous volume of remarkable work in many forms, piano sonatas, string quartets, songs, Masses, operas, and symphonies; mainly known for his more than 600 masterful songs (most notably, the cycles "Die Shoene Mullerin" [1823] and "Die Winterreise" [1827]), his extensive corpus of chamber music (most notably, the "Quintet in A Major" ["The Trout," 1819] and the "Quartet in D Minor" ["Death and the Maiden," 1824]), and the dramatic color of his nine symphonies (most notably, numbers 5 [1816], 6 [1817-18], 8 ["Unfinished," 1822], and 9 ["Great," 1828]);
- Jacob Ludwig Felix Mendelssohn-Bartholdy (1809-47), the German, also created a stupendous volume of remarkable work in many forms, piano sonatas, violin sonatas, string quartets, songs, concertos, overtures, Masses, operas, oratorios, and symphonies; principally remembered for his elegantly sensitive "String Octet" (1825), "Overture to Midsummer Night's Dream" (1826), "Songs Without Words" (for piano, 1830), "Hebrides Overture" (1832), "Violin Concerto in E Minor" (1844),

two colossal oratorios ("St. Paul" [1836] and "Elijah" [1846-47]), and wonderfully lyrical (last three) symphonies (numbers 3 ["Scottish," 1842], 4 ["Italian," 1833], and 5 ["Reformation," 1844]);

- Robert Alexander Schumann (1810-56), the German, had a very turbulent emotional life, was the quintessential romantic, and wrote brilliant piano music (most notably, "Papillons" [1831], "Carnaval" [1835], "Kinderszenen" [1838], and the stunning "Piano Concerto in A Minor" [1845]), the lovely "Overture to Manfred" (1849), the memorable "Concerto for Cello and Orchestra in A Minor" (1850), and four towering symphonies (numbers 1 ["Spring," 1841], 2 [1846], 3 ["Rhenish," 1850], and 4 [1853]);

- Franz Liszt (1811-86), the Hungarian-Austrian-German-French-Italian, was arguably the greatest pianist of the nineteenth century and among the most remarkable composers of the period as well; best remembered for his original development of the symphonic poem (in the broad symphonic style but with formal liberties and programmatic references), of which he wrote thirteen (most notably, "Les Preludes," 1854), transformation of the sonata form in "Piano Sonata in B Minor" (1853), numerous piano transcriptions of compositions originally written for other instruments by other composers, numerous piano études, "Totentantz" (for piano and orchestra, 1849), two symphonies ("Faust Symphony," [1854] and "Dante Symphony" [1856]), two piano concertos (numbers 1 [1855] and 2 [1856]), "Mephisto Waltz" (for piano, 1860), "Hungarian Coronation Mass" (1867), and twenty "Hungarian Rhapsodies" (most notably, numbers 1 and 2, both 1851);

- Richard Wagner (1813-83), the German, was among the greatest composers in the entire history of music (if not among the most congenial members of his profession), participated in the Revolution of 1848-49 on the insurgents' side to near-disastrous effect, and (whose thought) has been implicated in the development of German fascist ideology; he wrote two youthful works of such merit – "Symphony in C Major" (1832) and "Faust Overture" (1840-55) – that his future as a master of orchestral music may have rivaled the stature he achieved as the colossus of contemporary German opera; he is nonetheless mainly remembered for his revolutionary transformation of opera into a form of music-drama (a continuous flow of brilliant melody that united all arts in the universal themes of German mythology), for the new tone colors and expressive harmonies of his music which foresaw later impressionist and abstract possibilities, and for his prodigious corpus of unexcelled operatic scores (for which he also wrote the librettos); the most notable of these scores, several of which include powerful and masterful orchestral overtures, are: "Rienzi" (with overture, 1838-40), "The Flying Dutchman" (with overture, 1841), "Tannhauser" (with overture, 1843-44), "Lohengrin" (1846-48), "Tristan und Isolde" (1857-59), "Meistersinger von Nurnberg" (with overture, 1862-67), "Der Ring des Nibelungen" (arguably the most remarkable work in the entire history of opera and among the most remarkable works of art in any genre of any age, 1853-74; included "Das Rheingold" [1853-54], "Die Walkure" [1854-56], "Siegfried" [1856-69], and "Gotterdammerung" [1874]), and "Parsifal" (1877-82);

- Anton Bruckner (1824-96), the Austrian, wrote monumental compositions of complex, extended melody à la Wagner but with a more solemn sense of pious weight and grandeur than any other major nineteenth-century composer; most notably, "Mass in D Minor" (1864), "Mass in E Minor" (1866), "Mass in F Minor" (1867-71), "Te Deum" (1881-84), and nine symphonies (most significantly, numbers 7 [1881-83], 8 [1892], and 9 [1894-96]);

- Johann Strauss the Younger (1825-99), the Austrian, was a son of Johann Strauss the Elder (1804-49), who too wrote several hundred engaging (mainly) marches and waltzes (most notably, "Radetzky March," 1848); the younger Strauss wrote over 500 (mainly) celebrated and spirited waltzes (most significantly, "The Blue Danube Waltz" [1866], "Tales from the Vienna Woods" [1868], and "Emperor Waltz" [1888]) and numerous operettas (most significantly, "Die Fledermaus" [1873]);

- Johannes Brahms (1833-97), the German, was among the great masters of musical composition, wrote copiously in virtually all forms of musical life except opera, and fashioned a sonorous and resonant style of neo-romantic brilliance strongly touched by classicism; he is mainly remembered for his numerous songs and (Hungarian) dances, two outstanding piano concertos (numbers 1 [1857] and 2 [1881]), three stunning variations ("Variations and Fugue on a Theme of Handel" [1861], "Variations on a Theme of Paganini" [1863], and "Variations on a Theme of Haydn" [1873]), "German Requiem" (1868), four colossal symphonies (numbers 1 [1876], 2 [1877], 3 [1883], and 4 [1885]), magnificent violin concerto ("Violin Concerto in D Major," 1878), "Academic Festival Overture" (1880), "Tragic Overture" (1881), and engaging "Double Concerto in A Minor" (for violin and cello, 1887); and

- Max Christian Friedrich Bruch (1838-1920), the German, is mainly remembered for his three melodic violin concertos (most notably, number 1, 1866-68).

Brilliant French composers also made signal contributions to the formative development and ongoing maturation of musical romanticism. The most notable exponents of **French romanticism** were:

- Giacomo Meyerbeer/Jacob Meyer Beer (1791-1864), the German-Italian-French, mainly known for his spectacular French operas, "Robert le Diable" (1831), "Les Huguenots" (1836), and "L'Africaine" (1864);
- Louis-Hector Berlioz (1803-69), the French, acknowledged early French romantic master of orchestration and of programmatic music; principally remembered for his three radiantly powerful symphonic scores ("Symphonie Fantastique" [1830], "Harold en Italie" [1834], and "Roméo et Juliette" [1839]), "Requiem" (1837), "Roman Carnival Overture" (1844), "Te Deum" (1855), and three trenchantly dramatic operas ("Benvenuto Cellini" [1838], "Damnation of Faust" [1846], and "Les Troyens" [1856-58]);
- Frédéric François Chopin (1810-49), the Polish-French, who established the piano as a commanding solo instrument and who wrote the most coherent nineteenth-century music for the instrument; most notably, his numerous, graceful and elegant compositions for solo piano (études, preludes, nocturnes, ballads, waltzes, sonatas, and [Polish] nationalist polonaises and mazurkas) and his two piano concertos (numbers 1 [1833] and 2 [1836]);
- Charles François Gounod (1818-93), the French, principally known for his "St. Cecilia Mass" (1855) and his numerous operatic compositions (most notably, the magnificently melodic "Faust" [1859] and "Roméo et Juliette" [1867]);
- Jacques Levy Offenbach (1819-80), the German-French, mainly remembered for his numerous comic operettas (most significantly, "Orpheus in the Underworld" [1858], "La Belle Hélène" [1864], and "Tales of Hoffmann" [1880]);
- César Auguste Jean Guillaume Hubert Franck (1822-90), the Belgian-French, principally known for his extensive chamber, choral, and organ literature and for his two main orchestral works, "Symphonic Variations" (for piano and orchestra, 1885) and "Symphony in D Minor" (1886-88);
- Charles Camille Saint-Saens (1835-1921), the French, perhaps the most remarkable instance of romanticism's characteristically encyclopedic interests and talents, a literary and critical genius with a studied concern for, and facility in all forms of art, the sciences, and performance as well as theoretical matters concerning music; wrote a prodigious volume of brilliantly crafted and orchestrated works in virtually all forms of musical composition; most notably, five piano concertos (in particular, numbers 2 [1868], 4 [1875], and 5 ["Egyptian," 1895]), two cello concertos (in particular, number 1, 1872), four symphonic poems (in particular, "Danse Macabre," 1874), numerous operas (in particular, "Samson et Dalila," 1877), and three symphonies (in particular, number 3 ["Organ," 1886]);
- Clément Philibert Léon "Léo" Delibes (1836-91), a student of Adolphe Adam, who is principally known for melodic and vividly orchestrated ballets (most notably, "Coppélia" [1870] and "Sylvia" [1876]) and operas (most notably, "Lakmé," 1883); and
- Alexander César Léopold Georges Bizet (1838-75), the French, who is mainly remembered for his operas (most notably, "The Pearlfishers" [1863] and "Carmen" [1875]), his "Symphony in C Major" (1868), and his orchestral suite, "L'Arlésienne" (1872).

Italian contributions to musical romanticism were also very telling. The most exceptional contributions to composition for the violin and to opera (save Wagner) were made by the leading figures of nineteenth-century **Italian romanticism**:

- Niccolo Paganini (1782-1840), arguably the most accomplished violinist of the nineteenth century, also wrote among the most inventive and otherwise remarkable music for the instrument in this period; most notably, his 24 caprices for solo violin and his five violin concertos (in particular, number 1, c. 1817);
- Gioacchino Antonio Rossini (1792-1868), whose "Stabat Mater" (1841) was a major contribution to nineteenth-century church music, mainly remembered for his 34 masterfully theatrical and melodic operas (most of which begin with stirring orchestral overtures); most notably, "The Silken Ladder" (1812), "Tancredi" (1813), "The Italian Woman in Algiers" (1813), "The Barber of Seville" (1816), "Otello" (1816), "La Cenerentola" (1817), "The Thieving Magpie" (1817), "Semiramide" (1823), and "Guillaume Tell" (1829);

- Gaetono Donizetti (1797-1848) composed in a wide variety of musical forms but is principally known for his 64 melodic and theatrical operas; most notably, "L'Elisir d'Amore" (1832), "Lucrezia Borgia" (1833), "Lucia di Lammermoor" (1835), "La Fille du Régiment" (1840), "Linda di Chamonix" (1842), and "Don Pasquale" (1843);

- Vincenzo Bellini (1801-35) wrote ten searchingly lyrical, harmonically refined, and intensely expressive operas; most notably, "La Sonnambula" (1831), "Norma" (1831), and "I Puritani e i Cavalieri" (1835); and

- Fortunino Giuseppe Francesco Verdi (1813-1901), the crowning genius of Italian opera, wrote a thoroughly magnificent "Requiem" (in honor of the great Italian writer, Alessandro Manzoni; 1874), perhaps the most accomplished composition of its type in the entire history of music, and also wrote 26 operas of commanding moment, most of them consummate masterpieces, tangible human dramas of superbly melodic invention, deeply emotive effect, unique orchestral color, incisive clarity of phrase, and (often) revolutionary national account (concerning Italian national unification and independence); most notably, "Nabucco" (1842), "Ernani" (1843), "I Lombardi" (1843), "Macbeth" (1847), "Luisa Miller" (1849), "Rigoletto" (1851), "Il Trovatore" (1853), "La Traviata" (1853), "I Vespri Siciliani" (1855), "Simone Boccanegra" (1857), "Un Ballo in Maschera" (1859), "La Forza del Destino" (1862), "Don Carlo" (1867), "Aida" (in commemoration of the Suez Canal; 1871), "Otello" (1887), and "Falstaff" (1893).

Romanticism continued to exert governing influence over accomplished music well into the twentieth century as has been said. Beginning in the late nineteenth century, however, it was increasingly affected by ambitions to liberal social reform and national-ethnic unification-independence. This new, realistic-tending perception of the tangible imperatives of life (which had been also conspicuous in the work of Liszt, Wagner, Chopin, and Verdi), effectively this musical **realism**, more fully connected the new social order (the order of capital industrialism and its nationalist tentacles) to romanticism's ideal aspirations and significantly prepared the way for the still-more-pragmatic inclinations of impressionism. Distinctive national traditions in music, based typically in unique national-ethnic customs, developed most prominently in Russia, Bohemia, Romania, Norway, Spain, and Finland. The Russian case was the earliest and arguably the broadest of these. The principal early champions of **Russian realism**, most of whom were well acquainted with one another (and importantly influenced one another), were:

- Mikhail Ivanovich Glinka (1804-57), mainly known for his operas, "A Life for the Tsar" (1836) and "Russlan and Ludmilla" (1842);

- Mili Alekseyevich Balakirev (1837-1910), principally remembered for his piano fantasia, "Islamey" (1867), and symphonic poem, "Russia" (1887);

- Aleksander Porfirevich Borodin (1833-87), a professional chemist, primarily known for his two symphonies (in particular, number 2, 1876), symphonic poem, "In the Steppes of Central Asia" (1880), "String Quartet in D Major" (1887), and unfinished opera, "Prince Igor" (1887);

- Modest Petrovich Moussorgsky (1839-81), a civil-service clerk, mainly remembered for his symphonic poem, "Night on Bald Mountain" (1866), piano suite, "Pictures at an Exhibition" (1874), song cycles, "Without Sun" (1874) and "Songs and Dances of Death" (1875), and monumental opera, "Boris Godunov" (1874); and

- Nikolai Andreyevich Rimsky-Korsakov (1844-1908), principally remembered for his "Capriccio Espagnol" (1887), "Russian Easter Overture" (1888), symphonic suite, "Scheherazade" (1888), and fifteen operas (most notably, "Sadko" [1897] and "Le Coq d'Or" [1908]).

The other great figures of Russian music of the romantic/realist/nationalist type were less affected by distinctly national idioms and more significantly influenced by the mainstream of western European composition. The most notable of these were:

- Peter Ilyich Tchaikovsky (1840-93), likely the most accomplished master of musical composition in the entire history of Russian music (although Igor Stravinsky, Sergei Prokofiev, and Dmitri Shostakovich may also lay some justifiable claim to this distinction), whose intensely emotional, richly melodic, and brilliantly orchestrated scores are among the most memorable of any kind or age; most significantly, his seven symphonic poems (in particular, "Romeo and Juliet" [1869] and "Francesca da Rimini" [1876]), three piano concertos (in particular, number 1, 1875), three colossal ballets ("Swan Lake" [1876], "The Sleeping Beauty" [1889], and "The Nutcracker" [1892]), six symphonies (in particular, numbers 4 [1877], 5 [1888], and 6 ["Pathétique," 1893]), "Marche Slave" (1876), "Violin Concerto in D

Major" (1878), eleven operas (in particular, "Eugene Onegin" [1879] and "The Queen of Spades" [1890]), "Serenade for String Orchestra in C Major" (1880), and "1812 Overture" (1880);

- Aleksander Konstantinovich Glazunov (1865-1936), a student of Rimsky-Korsakov, mainly remembered for his ballets, "Raymonda" (1898) and "The Seasons" (1900), eight symphonies, and "Violin Concerto in A Minor" (1904);
- Sergei Vasilyevich Rachmaninov (1873-1943), the Russian-American, principally known for his stirring music for the piano; most notably, his "Prelude in C Sharp Minor" (for solo piano, 1892), four piano concertos (in particular, numbers 2 [1901], 3 [1909], and 4 [1926]), and "Rhapsody on a Theme by Paganini" (for piano and orchestra, 1934); and
- Aleksander Nikolayevich Scriabin (1872-1915), also mainly remembered for his (enigmatic) piano music, which was especially much influenced by the harmonic and tonal shifts inaugurated by Wagner and Debussy; most notably, his piano concerto, nine piano sonatas, three symphonies, and two other orchestral works, "Poem of Ecstasy" (1907) and "Prometheus: The Poem of Fire" (1910).

The romantic/realist/nationalist movement in Bohemia and Romania was more emphatically connected to the central course of European music than it was in Russia. The two crowning figures of nineteenth-century Czech music, the foremost exponents of **Bohemian realism**, Bedrich Smetana (1824-84) and Antonin Dvorak (1841-1904), nonetheless wrote compositions of distinctly Bohemian flavor as well as compositions of bright melodic line, most of which were programmatic in basic aim. Smetana's most notable creations are his opera, "The Bartered Bride" (1866), two string quartets, "From My Life" (1876, 1882), and six-part symphonic poem, "Ma Vlast (My Fatherland)," which includes "The Moldau" (1879). Dvorak's creative corpus is even more impressive; it most significantly includes his "String Quartet in F Minor" (1873), "Serenade for String Orchestra in E Major" (1875), first eight "Slavonic Dances" (for orchestra, 1878), "Violin Concerto in A Minor" (1879-81), "Stabat Mater" (1883), nine symphonies (in particular, numbers 8 [1889] and 9 ["From the New World," 1893]), and "Concerto for Cello and Orchestra in B Minor" (1894-95). Similarly, the leading figure in **Romanian realism**, Georges Enescu (1881-1955), a student of Gabriel Fauré, fashioned music of distinctly Romanian flavor, too with very bright melodic lines; most notably, "Romanian Rhapsodies, Numbers 1 and 2" (c. 1907).

Norwegian composer, Edvard Hagerup Grieg (1843-1907), the leading figure in **Norwegian realism**, also played a major role in the development of the romantic/realist/nationalist movement. He was too (like Smetana and Dvorak) more intimately linked to other western European tendencies than were most of the foremost Russian composers of the period. Grieg is most known for the deeply poetic melodies of his "The Holberg Suite" (for orchestra, 1864), "Piano Concerto in A Minor" (1868), cantata, "Olav Trygvason" (1873), and two "Peer Gynt Suites" (incidental music for Henrik Ibsen's fabled play; 1875). Spanish composers, Isaac Albeniz (1860-1909) and Manuel de Falla (1876-1946), the most prominent exponents of **Spanish realism**, likewise fashioned a peculiarly Spanish idiom out of western Europe's romantic perspective. Albeniz is principally remembered for his piano suite, "Iberia" (1909) and de Falla, for his opera, "La Vida Breve" (1905), symphonic suite for piano and orchestra, "Nights in the Garden of Spain" (1916), ballet, "The Three-Cornered Hat" (1917), and "Concerto for Harpsichord and Orchestra" (1926).

Among the most remarkable composers of this broad orientation was the main interpreter of **Finnish realism**, Johan Julius Christian "Jean" Sibelius (1865-1957). If the tendencies of (figurative and abstract) expressionism can be plausibly ascribed to music, which they are typically not (except in a very different capacity concerning the music of such as Arnold Schoenberg and Alban Berg), they may be most believably ascribed to the organic music of the great Finn. Sibelius, a first-rate genius, embodied the sense of robust reflection characteristic of nineteenth-century romanticism, crafted these characteristics in the pathos of distinctly Finnish inclinations (which, among many other sentiments, were opposed to Russian domination of the country), and also responded to the post-modern orientations of the twentieth century. His compositions gather the main currents of contemporary modern music into their most memorable synthesis/unity. His most celebrated works are the "Karelia Overture" (1893), the symphonic poems, "The Swan of Tuonela" (1893), "Finlandia" (1899), "Valse Triste" (1903), and "Tapiola" (1925), the "Violin Concerto in D Minor" (1903), and the seven symphonies (numbers 1 [1899], 2 [1901], 3 [1907], 4 [1911], 5 [1915-19], 6 [1923], and 7 [1924]).

The other major composers who straddled the major styles of the nineteenth and twentieth centuries (and who were strict adherents of neither impressionism nor abstractionism) continued to be greatly affected by the romantic equation. They were also greatly affected by impressionism and abstractionism (as well as the harbingers of impressionism and abstractionism) but did not become devotees of the new movements in the strong sense. Their compass had more fully to do with the inherent features of musical composition, less to do with national-ethnic themes, than that of the so-termed romantic/realist/nationalist proponents. Among the most accomplished and influential of these composers were several French, British, Italian, Germanic, and American figures. The most notable of the French were:

- Alexis Emmanuel Chabrier (1841-94), primarily known for his "Espana: Rhapsody for Orchestra" (1887);
- Jules Emile Frédéric Massenet (1842-1912), mainly remembered for his twenty operas; in particular, "Manon" (1884), "Werther" (1892), and "Thais" (1894);
- Gabriel Urbain Fauré (1845-1924), a student of Saint-Saens, principally known for his numerous songs, two cello sonatas (in particular, number 1, 1884), "Requiem" (1887), and opera, "Pénélope" (1907-12);
- Paul Marie Théodore Vincent d'Indy (1851-1931), a student of Franck, primarily remembered for his "Symphony on a French Mountain Air" (for piano and orchestra, 1886) and "Istar Variations" (for orchestra, 1896); and
- Paul Dukas (1865-1935), mainly known for his symphonic poem, "The Sorcerer's Apprentice" (1897).

The most notable of the British were:

- William Schwenck Gilbert (1836-1911), the librettist, and Arthur Seymour Sullivan (1842-1900), the composer, who together crafted brilliantly satirical operettas; most notably, "H.M.S. Pinafore" (1878), "The Pirates of Penzance" (1879), "Patience" (1881), "Iolanthe" (1882), "Princess Ida" (1884), "The Mikado" (1885), "Ruddigore" (1887), "The Yeomen of the Guard" (1888), and "The Gondoliers" (1889);
- Edward William Elgar (1857-1934), primarily known for his "Enigma Variations" (for orchestra, 1899), oratorio, "The Dream of Gerontius" (1900), numerous "Pomp and Circumstance Marches" (1901-30), and "Concerto for Cello and Orchestra in E Minor" (1919);
- Ralph Vaughan Williams (1872-1958), a close associate of Gustav Holst, mainly remembered for his "Norfolk Rhapsodies" (for orchestra, 1907), "Fantasia on a Theme by Thomas Tallis" (for string orchestra, 1909), song cycles (such as, "Five Mystical Songs," 1911), and nine symphonies (most notably, numbers 2 ["A London Symphony," 1914], 3 ["Pastoral," 1921], 5 [1943], and 6 [1947]); and
- Gustavus Theodore "Gustav" Holst (1874-1934), a close associate of Ralph Vaughan Williams, principally known for his "St. Paul's Suite" (for string orchestra, 1913), orchestral suite, "The Planets" (1916), and "The Hymn of Jesus" (for chorus and orchestra, 1917).

The most notable of the Italians were all great operatic composers:

- Ruggiero Leoncavallo (1858-1919) is known primarily for his "I Pagliacci" (1892);
- Giacomo Puccini (1858-1924), among the high masters of Italian opera, wrote articulately orchestrated scores and beautifully lyrical melodies (sung most memorably by the great Italian tenor, Enrico Caruso, 1873-1921); he is remembered mainly for his numerous masterworks; most notably, "Manon Lescaut" (1893), "La Bohème" (1896), "La Tosca" (1900), "Madame Butterfly" (1904), "The Girl of the Golden West" (1910), "Gianni Schicchi" (1918), and "Turandot" (1924);
- Pietro Mascagni (1863-1945) is known principally for his "Cavalleria Rusticana" (1890); and
- Umberto Giordano (1867-1948) is remembered primarily for his "Andrea Chenier" (1896).

The most notable of the Germanic figures all spun variously off of the revolutionary achievements of Wagner (and other Germanic composers heavily influenced by Wagner):

- Engelbert Humperdinck (1854-1921), the German, is known primarily for his opera, "Hansel and Gretel" (1893);
- Hugo Wolf (1860-1903), the Austrian, was among the great masters of the song; he brought music and poetry into a new and more intimate relation and is remembered mainly for his nearly 300 virtually unexcelled songs (most notably, the "Goethe Lieder," 1890);
- Gustav Mahler (1860-1911), the Austrian, significantly expanded the form and complex texture of the modern symphony; he wrote ten large and memorable symphonies (numbers 1 ["Titan," 1888], 2 ["Resurrection," 1894], 3 [1893-96], 4 [1899-1900], 5 [1901-02], 6 ["Tragic," 1903-04], 7 [1904-05], 8 ["Symphony of a Thousand," 1906], 9 [1908-09], and 10 [unfinished; 1903-04, 1910-11]), four of which are for voice and orchestra (numbers 2, 3, 4, and 8), and wrote four large and memorable song cycles for voice and orchestra that closely resembled symphonies (most notably, "Songs of a Wayfarer" [1883-84], "Kindertotenlieder" [1901-04], and "Song of the Earth" [1908]);
- Richard Strauss (1864-1949), the German, is known mainly for his approximately 150 artful songs, two engaging horn concertos (numbers 1 [1882-83] and 2 [1942]), richly orchestrated orchestral poems (most notably, "Death and Transfiguration" [1889], "Don Juan" [1889], "Till Eulenspiegel's

Merry Pranks" [1895], "Thus Spake Zarathustra" [1895], "Don Quixote" [1897], "Ein Heldenleben" [1898], and "Alpine Symphony" [1915]), and complex and dramatic operas (most notably, "Salomé" [1905], "Elektra" [1909], "Der Rosenkavalier" [1911], "Ariadne auf Naxos" [1912], and "Arabella" [1933]); and

- Franz Lehar (1870-1948), the Hungarian-Austrian, is remembered primarily for his several operettas; most significantly, "The Merry Widow" (1903).

And the most notable of the Americans were:

- John Philip Sousa (1854-1932), who is principally known for his approximately 100 marches; most notably, "Semper Fidelis" (1888), "The Washington Post March" (1889), "El Capitan" (1896), "The Stars and Stripes Forever" (1897), and "Hands Across the Sea" (1899); and
- Edward Alexander MacDowell (1861-1908), who was plausibly the most significant American composer prior to the First World War (with the arguable exception of Charles Ives) and who is mainly remembered for his four piano sonatas, two piano concertos (numbers 1 [1885] and 2 [1890]), two piano suites ("Woodland Sketches" [1896] and "Sea Pieces" [1898]), and "Indian Suite" (for orchestra, 1896).

The romantic/neo-romantic movement in music and its realist-nationalist corollary also embodied:

- the establishment of contemporary modern customs associated with individual virtuosi (first developed around such as Franz Liszt and Niccolo Paganini);
- the establishment of what are yet among the world's leading musical organizations (in particular, great symphonic orchestras [on the order of Leipzig Gewandhaus, 1743] and opera houses [on the order of Paris Opera]); most notably, the new (from the old, 1778) La Scala (Milan, 1812), New York Philharmonic (1839), Vienna Philharmonic (1839), new (from the old, 1669) Paris Opera (1875), Festspielhaus (Bayreuth, Germany, 1876), Boston Symphony (1881), Berlin Philharmonic (1882), Amsterdam Concertgebouw (1883), Metropolitan Opera (New York City, 1883), Philadelphia Orchestra (1900), and London Symphony (1904); and
- the development of contemporary modern ballet.

The dance had been maturing as an art form throughout the eighteenth century, largely under the influence of the French choreographer, Jean-Georges Noverre, and the Italian-French choreographer, Gaetan Vestris, as has been said. It was, however, in the nineteenth-century romantic context that modern ballet notation and technique, the leading modern ballet companies and theaters, virtuoso modern ballet dancers, and the modern ballet literature blossomed. The French and Italian styles continued (from the eighteenth century) to dominate most of the nineteenth century; Russian styles, however, came to preeminence in the late nineteenth and twentieth centuries. The Bolshoi Ballet (Moscow, 1856) and Kirov (Maryinsky) Ballet (St. Petersburg, 1889) were established in this time. Ballet Russes was created (in Paris) mainly by Russian impresario, Sergei Pavlovich Diaghilev (1872-1929), in 1909. The greatest female and male dancers of the period performed for Ballet Russes -- Anna Matveyevna Pavlova (1881-1931) and Vaslav Nijinsky (1890-1950), both Russians -- and contributed very significantly to the artistic maturation of the dance; most notably, to the artistic maturation of **romantic ballet**. The earliest romantic ballet, "La Sylphide," was written in 1832. Among the greatest composers of the age – Frédéric Chopin, Léo Delibes, and Peter Ilyich Tchaikovsky – wrote stunning compositions for the ballet; most notably, Chopin's "Les Sylphides" (music adapted from that of Chopin, 1909), Delibes' "Coppélia" (1870) and "Sylvia" (1876), and Tchaikovsky's "Swan Lake" (1876), "The Sleeping Beauty" (1889), and "The Nutcracker" (1892). Other very able composers – the French, Adolphe Charles Adam (1803-56), and the Austrian-Russian, Ludwig "Léon" Minkus (1826-1917), for prominent instance – wrote mainly for the ballet. Adam's "Giselle" (1841) and "Le Corsaire" (1856) and Minkus' "Don Quixote" (1869) and "La Bayadère" (1877) rank among the finest ballet scores in the entire history of the medium. The leading chorographers of the romantic idiom were likewise among the most remarkable of any age:

- Auguste Bournonville (1805-79), the Dane, who had been an associate of Noverre and a student of Vestris in Paris, had a major role in the development of modern ballet technique and wrote revived choreography for "La Sylphide" (1836);
- Jules Perrot (1810-92), the French, who had been a student of Vestris in Paris and an associate of Petipa, wrote the original choreographic score for "Giselle;"
- Marius Petipa (1822-1910), the French-Russian, who had been an associate of Perrot and Ivanov, greatly refined modern ballet technique, wrote the original choreographic scores for "Le Corsaire,"

"Don Quixote," "Swan Lake" (with Ivanov), "La Bayadère," "The Sleeping Beauty," and "Raymonda" (music by Glazunov, 1898), and wrote a revived choreographic score for "Coppélia" (1884); and

- Lev Ivanov (1824-1901), the Russian, who had been an associate of Petipa, fashioned a deeply intimate relation between music and the dance and wrote the original choreographic scores for "Swan Lake" (with Petipa) and "The Nutcracker."

The turn away from the organic and intrinsic tendencies of romanticism toward the mechanistic and extrinsic orientation of post-modernism began resolutely in the musical and movement arts, as it had in the visual arts, with the advent of **impressionism**. Although the impressionist inclination came to music several decades after it had first visited the visual arts, its musical form resembled its visual in several notable respects. Musical, like visual, impressionism embodied the formative origins of a sharp break with traditional perspectives, embodied a more skeptical, relative, analytic, and reserved attitude than romanticism, an attitude that eventually opened into still more positivistic and pragmatic perspectives, and embodied the beginnings of a governing concern for the basic character of (visual perception and) organized sound itself. The seminal development of impressionism was heralded by Wagner's harmonic transformations from as early as the 1840s but the dramatic shifts in basic tonality characteristic of impressionism as such were first owed to the revolutionary French composer, Claude-Achille Debussy (1862-1918). Debussy was most influenced by Wagner's sense of harmonic color (but emphatically rejected Wagner's notion of philosophical program) and by contemporary tendencies in French literature, painting, and music (the music of César Franck, Camille Saint-Saens, and Emmanuel Chabrier in particular). Beginning in the 1890s, he fashioned a new form of programmatic music intended to evoke a mood (an impression, neither a narrative nor a view), a mood created by a unique use of the whole-tone scale, irregular rhythms, and artful dissonance. Debussy's most remarkable and innovative compositions were his numerous piano preludes and études, other works for piano (most notably, "Suite Bergamasque" [including "Claire de Lune," 1893] and "Estampes" [1903]), "String Quartet in G Minor" (1893), epoch-turning works for orchestra (most notably, "Prélude à l'après-midi d'un Faun" [1894], "Trois Nocturnes" ["Nuages," "Fêtes," and "Sirènes," 1899], "La Mer" [1905], and "Images" [1912]), and opera, "Pelléas et Mélisande" (1902). The other principal contributors to musical impressionism were the German-English composer, Frederick Delius (1862-1934), the French, Maurice Ravel (1875-1937), the Italian, Ottorino Respighi (1879-1936), and the Swiss-American, Ernst Bloch (1880-1959). Delius is mainly remembered for the free structure and rich harmonies of his orchestral works (most notably, "Brigg Fair" [1907], "On Hearing the First Cuckoo in Spring" [1912], and "North Country Sketches" [1914]) and opera, "A Village Romeo and Juliet" (1907). Ravel, a student of Fauré and a master of intricate orchestration, wrote highly original pieces for the piano (most notably, "Pavane for a Dead Princess" [1899], "Jeux d'Eau" [1901], "Miroirs" [1905], "Gaspard de la Nuit" [1908], "Valses Nobles et Sentimentales" [1911], "Le Tombeau de Couperin" [1917], and "Piano Concerto for the Left Hand" [1931]) and for orchestra (most notably, "Rhapsodie Espagnole" [1907], "La Valse" [1920], "Bolero" [1928], and the ballet score, "Daphnis et Chloé" [1909-11]). Respighi is primarily known for his three stunning symphonic poems, "The Fountains of Rome" (1917), "The Pines of Rome" (1924), and "Roman Festivals" (1929). And Bloch is best remembered for his "Schelomo: Hebrew Rhapsody for Cello and Orchestra" (1916) and symphonic poem, "Israel Symphony" (for voice and orchestra, 1916).

The impulse to post-modernism became still more evident, the break with the nineteenth century still more conspicuous, in the **abstractionism** that supplanted the impressionist development. The skeptical, relative, and analytic character of impressionism deepened yet further in the ingenious innovations that succeeded impressionism in the musical and movement arts of the twentieth century. The technical and existential sense of being without a foundation or center, and thus without an ascertainable purpose, basis for fulfillment, or unified consensus, became still more prominent, certitude became still more obscure, unobtainable, open to spontaneous chance, and grounded in the everyday. The abstractionist path from impressionism took five main forms, all of which turned even more fully away from the romantic equation. The first was predominantly French and was led by Alfred Erik Leslie Satie (1866-1925); this form rejected impressionism but nonetheless resembled it. The second was predominantly Germanic and was led by Arnold Schoenberg (1874-1951); this form departed significantly from all prior musical tendencies. The third was dominated by Igor Fedorovich Stravinsky (1882-1971) and sought a development from romanticism and impressionism other than that offered by Schoenberg. The fourth attracted various national identities and was led by Bela Bartok (1881-1945); this form systematically worked national idioms into the new tonalities of the twentieth century. And the fifth attracted a diverse following but was mainly an American movement led by John Cage (1912-); this form was deeply experimental and attempted to discern the basic character of organized sound itself.

The French composer, Erik Satie, was an acquaintance of Sergei Diaghilev, Pablo Picasso, and Jean Cocteau; he was too both an acquaintance and an avowed opponent of Debussy, often satirizing him; and he was also an ardent iconoclast in the broad style of surrealism. His compositions nonetheless made fairly wide use of unresolved chords in ways hauntingly reminiscent of impressionism. Satie's work likewise tended to a positivistic economy of texture, a severe, everyday sense of harmony and melody, and a spare emotional effect. He is mainly remembered for his piano compositions (most notably, "Gymnopédies" [1888], "Sport et Divertissements" [1914], and "Nocturnes" [1919]) and symphonic drama for voice and orchestra, "Socrate" (1918). Satie's influence was wide, particularly among French composers of the next generation; most memorably, Arthur Honegger (1892-1955), Darius Milhaud (1892-1974), and Francis Poulenc (1899-1963). Honegger, the Swiss-French, fashioned sharply dissonant, violently energetic harmonies of programmatic bent; most notably, his symphony, "Horace Victorious" (1921), oratorio, "King David" (1921), symphonic movement, "Pacific 231" (1923), "Concertino for Piano and Orchestra" (1925), and operas, "Judith" (1926) and "Antigone" (1927). Milhaud is known principally for his inventive sense of tonality and complex dissonances; most significantly, in the eighteen string quartets, ballet, "La Création du Monde" (1923), "Suite Provençale" (for orchestra, 1937), and operas, "Les Euménides" (1924), "Le Pauvre Matelot" (1926), and "Christophe Colomb" (1928). And Poulenc wrote music that left the appearance of uncontrived spontaneity; most notably, his extensive chamber works, ballet, "Les Biches" (1924), "Mass in G" (1937), and opera, "Dialogues of the Carmelites" (1956).

The revolution crafted by the Austrian-American composer, Arnold Schoenberg, beginning in the first decade of the twentieth century, entailed a dramatic departure from the history of musical composition to that time. This revolutionary development was, in this among other respects, the approximate equivalent of the abstract movements then dominating the visual arts. Schoenberg's first two string quartets (1905 and 1908) and his first "Chamber Symphony" (1906) in particular expanded even Wagner's and Mahler's sense of harmonic invention. His slightly later works (those from 1908 to 1917) – mainly, the song cycle with piano accompaniment, "Book of the Hanging Gardens" (1908), "Five Orchestral Pieces" (1909), "Expectation" (for solo voice and orchestra, 1909), and song cycle for solo voice and chamber ensemble, "Pierrot Lunaire" (1912) – abandoned standard tonal, harmonic, and melodic formulas (they were atonal in this sense), employed extreme ranges and wide leaps of tonal and harmonic shift, deepened rhythmic complexity, fragmented melodic line, made wide use of unresolved chords, and adopted a smaller and a very sparse texture. It was in this context that so-termed expressionism in twentieth-century music developed, as an account not of humanity's organic possibilities but of humanity's existential condition, desperate and rebellious. By 1923, Schoenberg had perfected his twelve-tone system of serial composition in which tones are related only to one another and by which the internal architecture of music is exposed (à la cubism in the visual arts and German phenomenology in philosophy). The most notable works of this most recent period are his five piano pieces op. 23 (1923), "Suite for Piano Op. 25" (1924), "Third Quartet" (1926), "Variations for Orchestra" (1928), unfinished opera, "Moses and Aaron" (1931-32), "Violin Concerto" (1936), and "Fourth Quartet" (1937).

Schoenberg's influence was enormous, as extensive as any twentieth-century composer. It was especially noteworthy in the work of his two most celebrated students, both Austrian, Alban Berg (1885-1935) and Anton von Webern (1883-1945). Berg followed Schoenberg's twelve-tone, atonal standard but made a deeper emotional rendering of it than had Schoenberg himself. His principal compositions were the two deeply expressive, existential operas, "Wozzeck" (1917-21) and "Lulu" (unfinished; 1928-35), "A Lyric Suite" (for string quartet, 1926), and the "Concerto for Violin and Orchestra" (1935). Webern also followed Schoenberg's twelve-tone, atonal standard but developed this standard in a more inelaborate and sparing manner and with more complex rhythmic patterns than any other composer. His most remarkable compositions are the "Five Pieces for Orchestra Op. 10" (1913), "Symphony Op. 21" (1928), "Concerto for Nine Instruments Op. 24" (1934), "Piano Variations Op. 27" (1936), and "String Quartet Op. 28" (1938).

Arguably the most prominent musical figure of the twentieth century, the Russian-French-American composer, Igor Stravinsky, crafted music (not unlike Pablo Picasso in the visual arts) that cut across virtually all major tendencies of the time and raised those tendencies to a higher level. His earliest, strikingly original work – the three monumental ballets commissioned by Sergei Diaghilev, "The Firebird" (1910), "Petrouchka" (1911), and "Le Sacre du Printemps" (1913) – respectively embodied highly articulate treatments of national Russian folk idioms (inspired by Stravinsky's celebrated teacher, Nikolai Rimsky-Korsakov), the realist (everyday) orientation, and the primitivist tendency. "Le Sacre du Printemps" in particular was a masterpiece of post-modern music; it embodied the elemental, percussive power of pre-literate, gentile existence (à la features of post-impressionism, fauvism, cubism, surrealism, and expressionism in the visual arts) and it incorporated the remarkably inventive, irregular rhythms and harsh dissonances that became characteristic of Stravinsky's singular music. After c. 1913 (and until c. 1951), Stravinsky attempted to develop a new style, a style that went clearly beyond romanticism and impressionism but that was also an alternative to Schoenberg. This style continued the use of irregular rhythms and harsh dissonances inherent in the early ballets; it also employed novel and austere harmonies, a wide use of silence, and unusual combinations of musical instruments. The most notable compositions of this period are the ballets, "The Wedding" (1917-23), "The Soldier's Tale" (1918), "Pulcinella" (1919), and "Apollon Musagète" (1928); "Octet for Wind Instruments" (1923); "Concerto for Piano and Wind Instruments" (1924); "Suite in A for Piano" (1925); opera-oratorio, "Oedipus Rex" (1927); "Symphony of Psalms" (for chorus and orchestra, 1930); "Violin Concerto" (1931); "Dumbarton Oaks Concerto" (for chamber orchestra, 1938); "Symphony in C" (1940); and "Symphony in Three Movements" (1945). Somewhat ironically, Stravinsky's music after 1951 somewhat resembled that of Schoenberg and Webern; most notably, the opera, "The Rake's Progress" (1951), the ballet, "Agon" (1954-57), and "Canticum Sacrum" (for tenor, baritone, chorus, and orchestra, 1956). A more systematic and less harshly dissonant sense of tonality was achieved by the renowned German-Swiss composer, Paul Hindemith (1895-1973), whose most memorable compositions were the six string quartets, the song cycle for soprano and piano on poems by Rainer Maria Rilke, "The Life of Mary" (1923), the opera, "Mathis der Maler" (1934), and "Game of Tonalities" (for piano, 1942).

The romantic/realist/nationalist movement in nineteenth-century music extended into the twentieth century as has been said. A new orientation in respect to national musical idioms nonetheless developed in the twentieth century. This orientation was significantly more systematic and scientific than its largely nineteenth century predecessor, for one; it operated on a more fundamental level than its nineteenth-century form, for a second; and it worked national idioms into the new tonalities of the twentieth century, creating largely new styles, for a third. The leading progenitor of this orientation was the Czech composer, Leos Janacek (1854-1928), mainly known for his operas ("Jenufa" [1902], "Kata Kabanova" [1921], "The Vixen" [1924], and "The Makropulas Case" [1926]), his symphonic rhapsody ("Taras Bulba," 1918), and his "Glagolithic Mass" (1926). The colossus of this orientation, however, was the momentous Hungarian composer, Bela Bartok, who achieved the most inventive articulation of folk and post-modern elements. Bartok's synthetic genius made especially large use of tonal ambiguity, dissonance, and percussive primitivism in the broad context of mostly Hungarian (and Romanian) folk themes. His most notable compositions are the six stunning string quartets (numbers 1 [1908], 2 [1917], 3 [1927], 4 [1928], 5 [1934], and 6 [1939]), opera ("Duke Bluebeard's Castle," 1911), ballet ("The Miraculous Mandarin," 1918-19), two violin sonatas (numbers 1 [1922] and 2 [1923]), "Mikrokosmos" (153 piano pieces, 1926-37), three piano concertos (numbers 1 [1926], 2 [1931], and 3 [1945]), "Piano Sonata" (1926), "Cantata Profana" (1930), "Music for Strings, Percussion, and Celesta" (1936), "Sonata for Two Pianos and Percussion" (1937), "Violin Concerto" (1938), and "Concerto for Orchestra" (1943). The basic themes of this orientation were variously repeated and extended by many other exceptional twentieth-century composers; most significantly by:

- Charles Edward Ives (1874-1954), the American insurance executive, who independently anticipated many of the most radical tendencies of twentieth-century music, mainly in respect to dissonance, polytonality, polyrhythm, and daring experiment; most memorably, in his five symphonies (numbers 1 [1898], 2 [1902], 3 ["The Camp Meeting," 1904], 4 [1909-16], and "Holidays Symphony" ["Washington's Birthday," "Decoration Day," "The Fourth of July," and "Thanksgiving," 1909-13]), "The Unanswered Question" (for small orchestra, 1906), two piano sonatas (most notably, number 2 ["Concord," 1911-15]), and "Three Places in New England" (for orchestra, 1912);

- Zoltan Kodaly (1882-1967), the Hungarian, who is mainly known for his "Psalmus Hungaricus" (for solo tenor, chorus, and orchestra, 1923), opera ("Hary Janos," 1926), and "Missa Brevis in Tempore Belli" (1945);

- Heitor Villa-Lobos (1887-1959), the Brazilian, who is principally remembered for his nine "Bachianas Brasileiras" (variously for solo instruments, instrumental ensemble, chorus, and orchestra, 1932-44);

- Sergei Sergeyevich Prokofiev (1891-1953), the Russian-Soviet student of Rimsky-Korsakov, who wrote an impressive volume of masterful music; most notably, the five piano concertos (most memorably, numbers 1 [1911] and 3 [1921]), seven symphonies (most memorably, numbers 1 ["The Classical," 1916-17], 5 [1944], 6 [1945-47], and 7 [1951-52]), "Scythian Suite" (for orchestra, 1916), two operas ("Love for Three Oranges" [1921] and "War and Peace" [1941]), two violin concertos (most memorably, number 2, 1935), orchestral suite ("Lieutenant Kije," 1934), ballet ("Romeo and Juliet,"

1935-36), "Peter and the Wolf" (for narrator and orchestra, 1936), and cantata ("Alexander Nevsky," for solo soprano, chorus, and orchestra, 1938);

- Carl Orff (1895-1982), the German master of neo-primitive rhythm, who is best known for his secular oratorio, "Carmina Burana" (1936), and operas, "The Moon" (1939), "The Wise Woman" (1943), and "Antigonae" (1949);
- George Gershwin (1898-1937), the American, who is best remembered for his "Rhapsody in Blue" (for piano and orchestra, 1923), "Piano Concerto in F" (1925), symphonic poem, "American in Paris" (1928), numerous musical comedies (most notably, "Of Thee I Sing," 1931), and opera, "Porgy and Bess" (1935);
- Edward Kennedy "Duke" Ellington (1899-1974), the African-American master of jazz, who raised the African-American spiritualist dialect and the improvisatory tradition of African-American folk (mainly work) music, earlier canonized by Stephen Collins Foster (1826-64) and Scott Joplin (1868-1917), to its highest and most complex mark with such compositions as "Creole Rhapsody" (1932), "Black, Brown, and Beige" (1943), "Liberian Suite" (1947), "Harlem" (1951), and "Night Creatures" (1955);
- Aaron Copland (1900-90), the American, who is mainly known for his "Piano Concerto" (1927), "El Salon Mexico" (for orchestra, 1936), ballets ("Billy the Kid" [1938], "Rodeo" [1942], and "Appalachian Spring" [1944]), "Third Symphony" (1946), and song cycle, "Twelve Poems of Emily Dickinson" (1950);
- Dmitri Shostakovich (1906-75), the Russian-Soviet, who wrote what are among the century's most expressive symphonies, fifteen in sum (most notably, numbers 1 [1925], 5 [1937], 7 ["Leningrad," 1941], 10 [1953], and 11 ["The Year 1905," 1957), as well as two memorable operas ("The Nose" [1930] and "Lady Macbeth of the Mtsensk District" [1934]), a celebrated ballet ("The Golden Age," 1930), and two widely acclaimed scores mainly for piano ("Piano Concerto" [1933] and "Piano Quintet" [1940]); and
- Benjamin Britten (1913-76), the English, who is remembered principally for his choral and orchestral scores (most notably, "A Ceremony of Carols" [1942], "A Young Person's Guide to the Orchestra" [1945], and "War Requiem" [1962]) and his most accomplished operas ("Peter Grimes" [1945], "The Turn of the Screw" [1954], and "Death in Venice" [1973]).

As in the case of the visual arts, the most recent tendency in serious music has been innovatively eclectic and also deeply experimental. Much of it challenged the notion of music itself as intentionally organized sound and thus examined the basic character of the medium in unprecedented ways. This tendency was primarily, but not exclusively, an American phenomenon. Arguably the leading composers of creatively eclectic bent (in respect to old and new senses of tonality, harmony, melody, and rhythm) were the American composers, Leonard Bernstein (1918-90) and Carlisle Floyd (1926-   ). Bernstein, together with the remarkable Italian personality, Arturo Toscanini (1867-1957), may have been the greatest conductor of the century. He also wrote wonderful music; most notably, three symphonies (numbers 1 ["Jeremiah," 1942], 2 ["The Age of Anxiety," 1949], and 3 ["Kaddish," 1963]), several musical dramas (in particular, "On the Town" [1944], "Candide" [1956], and "West Side Story" [1957]), and two especially noteworthy choral works ("Chichester Psalms" [1965] and "Mass" [1971]). Floyd wrote among the finest operas since the Second World War; most significantly, "Susannah" (1955) and "Of Mice and Men" (1970). The Armenian-American composer, Alan Hovhaness/Alan Vaness Chakmajian (1911-2000), experimented to impressive effect with unique sonorities and with animal (and other natural) sounds; most notably, in his nearly 70 symphonies (in particular, number 2 ["Mysterious Mountain," 1955]), symphonic poem, "Ukiyo-Floating World" (1965), and "God Created Great Whales" (for orchestra and recorded humpback whale sounds, 1970). The German composer, Karlheinz Stockhausen (1928-   ), a student of Milhaud, and the American composer, Philip Glass (1937-   ), successfully explored the possibilities of electronic sound; Stockhausen's "Kontakte" (1959) and Glass' "Music in 12 Parts" (1971-74) and operas, "Einstein on the Beach" (1976) "Satyagraha" (1980), and "The Marriages between Zones 3, 4, and 5" (1997) are among the most outstanding examples of this tendency. Among Stockhausen's other notable innovations is his "Gruppen" (1959) in which three orchestras play at the same time, variously by chance, across one another. Quite likely the most iconoclastic and challenging work of broad experimental significance, however, was done by the American genius, John Cage, a student of Schoenberg and a close associate of the celebrated pop-artist, Robert Rauschenberg, and the celebrated choreographer, Merce Cunningham. Cage challenged the limits of what counts as music more deeply than any other figure. He investigated, for prominent instance, the prospects of making music with randomly selected sound, with free improvisation, with non-standard instruments and instruments modified from the standard, with everyday noise, and with utter silence. Arguably his most noteworthy creations are "Bacchanale" (for altered piano, 1938), "Sonatas and Interludes" (for altered piano, 1946-48), "Music for Changes" (sounds selected from pre-existing charts, 1951), "433" (four minutes and 33 seconds of silence filled, if at all, by random environmental sounds, 1952), "Imaginary Landscape No. 4" (for twelve radios randomly tuned, 1953), and "Telephones and Birds" (for orchestra, 1977).

The wide transformations in the musical arts marked by impressionism and by the several other forms of post-modernism that followed impressionism also had a profound affect on the movement arts. The drift from romantic-organic perspectives in dance, as in philosophy, literature, the visual arts, and the musical arts, brought a more skeptical, relative, and analytic orientation to the medium, an orientation without an unambiguous foundation or center, an orientation more open to chance-like spontaneity. The earliest post-modern choreographers of great significance, the earliest major devotees of **abstract dance**, fashioned dance scores for Stravinsky's three crowning (early) ballets; these are scores that included both established and avant-garde elements. Michel Fokine (1880-1942), the Russian-American who had effectively co-founded Ballet Russes with Sergei Diaghilev and who had composed choreographic scores for the great Russian dancers, Anna Pavlova and Vaslav Nijinsky, wrote the original choreographic scores for "The Firebird" (1910) and "Petrouchka" (1916). Nijinsky himself wrote the original choreographic score for "Le Sacre du Printemps" (1913). Fokine, who is considered the founder of twentieth-century ballet, also fashioned the original choreographic scores for "Les Sylphides" (music by Chopin, 1909), "Prince Igor" (music by Borodin, 1909), "Scheherazade" (music by Rimsky-Korsakov, 1910), "Daphnis et Chloé" (music by Ravel, 1912), and "Le Coq d'Or" (music by Rimsky-Korsakov, 1914). Nijinsky too wrote the original choreographic score for "Afternoon of a Faun" (music by Debussy, 1912).

Twentieth-century dance then turned in even more emphatic post-modern directions, particularly after the First World War. Dance notation became still more precise and accurate, largely under the influence of cinematography and the written system of Slovakian choreographer, Rudolf von Laban (1879-1958), whose Principles of Dance and Movement Notation (1956) in particular greatly advanced the scientific groundwork of the dance. American and German dancers-choreographers significantly widened the scope of avant-garde dance and its expressive techniques, thereby departing still further from traditional nineteenth-century standards. The most noteworthy of these were the Americans, Ruth St. Denis/Ruth Dennis (1877-1968) and Isadora Duncan (1878-1927), and the German, Mary Wigman (1886-1973), a student of Laban and of the Swiss educator, Émile Jacques-Dalcroze. This tendency was advanced and more exactingly formalized by American choreographers, Martha Graham (1895-1991), Agnes George De Mille (1906-93), and Merce Cunningham (1919-). Graham, who was a close associate of St. Denis, created especially stark and angular works; most significantly, "Appalachian Spring" (music by Copland, 1944) and "Archaic Hours" (1969). De Mille is mainly remembered for her choreographic scores to "Rodeo" (music by Copland, 1942) and "Fall River Legend" (1948). And Cunningham, who was a student of Graham and a close associate of John Cage and pop-artists, Andy Warhol, Jasper Johns, and Robert Rauschenberg, is principally known for his highly innovative scores, "Suite by Chance" (1952) and "Symphonie pour un Homme Seul" (1952).

The century's great master of abstract dance, of the avant-garde tendency in dance, however, was the Russian-American genius, George Balanchine/Georgi Melitonovich Balanchivadze (1904-83), an associate of Milhaud. Although he had been early on associated with the Kirov Ballet and Ballet Russes, then with the American Ballet Theatre (founded in 1937, New York City), his most memorable work was done with the New York City Ballet which he helped create in 1946. Balanchine crafted patterns of pure dance, patterns free of nineteenth-century textual restrictions and symmetrical imperatives. Arguably the most revolutionary of his approximately 200 choreographic scores are the memorable collaborations with Igor Stravinsky, "Apollo" (1928), "Orpheus" (1948), and "Agon" (1957). The most significant of the others are "Prodigal Son" (1929), "Serenade" (music by Tchaikovsky, 1934), "Seven Deadly Sins" (1958), "Kammermusik No. 2" (1978), and "Robert Schumann's Davidsbundlertanze" (1980). The other most notable dance figures of the Second World War era and since were the British choreographers, Frederick Ashton (1906-88) and Anthony Tudor (1909-87), the American choreographers, Alvin Ailey, Jr. (1931-89) and Twyla Tharp (1941-), and the German choreographer, Pina Bausch (1940-). Ashton wrote precise, lyrical scores of both traditional and abstract form; most significantly, "Symphonic Variations" (1946), "Cinderella" (music by Prokofiev, 1948), "Sylvia" (music by Delibes, 1952), "Ondine" (1958), and "A Month in the Country" (1976). Tudor wrote deeply psychological dramas of abstract form; most significantly, "Lilac Garden" (1938), "Romeo and Juliet" (music by Delius, 1942), and "Tiller in the Fields" (1979). Ailey wrote dramatic, abstract scores on African motifs; most significantly, "Creation of the World" (1954), "Revelations" (1960), and "At the Edge of the Precipice" (1983). Tharp wrote innovatively abstract and eclectic pieces, often without musical accompaniment; most significantly, "Deuce Coupe" (1973), "Push Comes to Shove" (1975), and "When We Were Very Young" (1980). And Bausch, a student of Tudor, emphasized the expressive movements of everyday life (not unlike St. Denis, Duncan, and Wigman); most significantly, in "Café Muller" (1978) and "Carnations" (1982).

Sporting Developments

The panoply of sport history up to the nineteenth and twentieth centuries effectively constituted the pre-history, the anthropological history, of sport in its contemporary, its modern institutional form. While it is mostly earlier forms of sporting activity that were formalized in this period, this formalization nonetheless made something quite new of sport. The novel development of contemporary modern sport is principally a function of the unique nature of the past approximately two centuries. In broad political, economic, and social terms, this most recent epoch of world history has been characterized by a deepening sense of nationalism and militarism, the ongoing democratization of modern life, and the capital industrialization and urbanization of the developed world. In intellectual terms, the nineteenth century was moved early on by romanticism and realism and near its end by positivism, impressionism, and post-impressionism. Twentieth-century intellectual life was governed, in turn, by the relativism of the natural and social sciences, the skepticism of philosophy, history, and literature, and the abstractionism of the visual, musical, and movement arts. The affect of these general tendencies on sport was profound.

The political, economic, and social imperatives of contemporary modern civilization had an especially large influence on the development of sport. The **affect of capital industrialism on sport** was particularly great. It was the rise of capital industrialism, and all that is variously entailed by this phenomenon, which utterly transformed human life in general and sport in particular. It was capital industrialism that produced the technology, the wealth, and the leisure that have made modern institutional sport possible. It was capital industrialism that softened, then broke, and eventually reversed the antipathy of formal religion and the power elite for sport. And it was capital industrialism that reordered the demographic, political, and intellectual realities of modern life in ways that have allowed sport to become what it has. Although industrialism's earliest views of sport were not entirely favorable – concerns for labor discipline and social order tended to overwhelm sentiment for physical recreation – the industrial spectacle had effectively embraced sport by the mid-nineteenth century. The new economy and its tentacles:

- deepened the material and mechanistic groundwork of sport, made sport an even larger feature of popular culture, and encouraged mass participation in sport;
- altered the character of work and its schedule in ways that augured for the development of corporate-sponsored, industrial sport; this, in order to promote social harmony, health, and the esteem of the power elite as well as in order to counter the sense of meaningless (self-estranging) work, the sense of alienation from the impersonal conditions of work (and their products), and the sense of powerlessness over the conditions of work;
- so increased population, leisure, and disposable income among the middle class (significantly too under the influence of labor reforms) that participation in sport also greatly increased;
- so increased per capita incomes that private patronage of sport in terms of prizes, facilities, equipment, and administrative support likewise increased;
- transformed our sense of interdependent divisions of labor and our sense of time (its measurement and management) in ways that have made sport a more precisely ordered and regulated activity and in ways that have diminished (but clearly not eliminated) violence and other unsavory behavior in sport;
- altered the family in ways that augured for the development of youth sport and of sport for the aged; and
- replaced a challenge-system of sporting organization with a schedule-system.

The **affect of the technological revolution on sport** was likewise significant. This nineteenth-century and twentieth-century revolution, itself a corollary of capital industrialism, contributed a great deal to the development of modern sporting activity. Advances in manufacture, communication, and transportation were particularly noteworthy in this respect. Inventions such as the steamship (raced regularly on major rivers), the stop-watch, the roller skate, rubber balls and tires, cinematography, the lawnmower, the bicycle, the automobile, the motorboat, and the motorcycle had an even more direct influence on sport. Also highly significant were technical improvements in the construction of sporting facilities (such as, gymnasia, stadiums, arenas, country clubs, pitches, courts, running tracks [and associated venues], swimming and diving pools, ice rinks, sledding tracks, and ski jumping hills), in the manufacture of sporting goods themselves (such as, angling rods and reels, saddles, shooting implements, billiard tables and balls, bowling alleys and balls, cricket, baseball, and softball bats, balls, and fielding gloves, running and other sporting shoes, protective and other sporting apparel, throwing implements, hurdles, diving boards, archery bows and arrows, inflated and uninflated balls, racquets, curling stones, croquet mallets and balls, boxing gloves, gymnastics apparatus, vessels and stroking implements for water sports, lifting weights, golf clubs and balls, fencing implements, ice skates, skis, sleds, hockey sticks, and lacrosse sticks), and in the mass production of sporting books (mainly concerning technique and rules), magazines and newspapers (mainly concerning recent events), and art prints (mainly of memorable events and experiences). Commercial firms were established to construct, manufacture, distribute, and sell these facilities, equipment, and documents. The earliest major firm of this type was A.G. Spalding and Brothers (United States, 1876). The earliest major, contemporary books concerning sporting technique and rules were the Spalding Sports and Athletic Guides (United States, 1877) and the Badminton Library of Sports and Pastimes (England, 1882). The earliest major, sporting magazines and newspapers were The Sporting Magazine (Great Britain, 1792), Bell's Life in London (Great Britain, 1821), American Turf Register and Sporting Magazine (1829), Festivals, Games, and Amusements (United States, 1831), The Spirit of the Times (United States, 1831), Bell's Life in Sydney (Australia, 1845), Sporting Life (Great Britain, 1859), Sporting Chronicle (Great Britain, 1871), Athletic News (Great Britain, 1875), National Police Gazette (United States, 1877), The Sporting News (United States, 1886), and the regular sport pages of The World (Great Britain, 1787), Bell's Weekly Messenger (Great Britain, 1796), New York Herald (late 1860s), New York World (1883), New York Sun (1880s), and New York Journal (1895). And the earliest art prints to feature sporting images were those of Currier and Ives (United States, 1857).

The **commercial tendencies of contemporary modern sport** were greatly affected by these developments and by the fervent consumerism that grew increasingly around them and around professional forms of sport themselves. Although commercial treatments of sport were not uncommon in pre-industrial civilization as has been said, the entrepreneurial organization of sport for capital gain was taken to unprecedented levels in the industrial age. Very large and very powerful institutions embodying professional sporting aims were successfully established throughout the world in the nineteenth and twentieth centuries. These institutions:

- fashioned sport a form of mechanistic work, a form of instrumental labor, thereby collapsing the distinction between joyless work and fulfilling leisure in the direction of work and thereby also crafting leisure as a form of production for profitable consumption, as a form of popular entertainment;
- sanctified the business model for sport (an emphasis on gate receipts, assets, compensation, tax privileges, public propaganda, and political influence), thereby promoting rampant consumerism (indiscriminate purchasing) in sport and transforming sport into a disposable product for sale in a global market;
- installed "the achievement principle" (the notion of limitless progress, quantifiable specialization, and adversarial triumph) as the formal end of sport in order to maximize the profit of the few;
- made the imperatives of corporate capitalism (the imperatives of the upper class and of the middle-class allies of the upper class) the dominant ideology of contemporary sport;
- embellished the significance of pervasive, commercially useful novelty and diminished the sense of cultural tradition in sport;
- enlarged the distinction between athletes and spectators and diminished the proportion of athletes to spectators;
- greatly increased the opportunities for the talented poor and otherwise disenfranchised to make a decent living in sport; and
- greatly increased the resource devoted to the enhancement of sporting skill among talented athletes.

Capital industrialism was also responsible for the urbanization of the developed world in the nineteenth and twentieth centuries. The industrial cities of rapidly expanding economies grew by enormous measures in this time. This growth was the result of a remarkable industrial expansion, of what industrial factories require (namely, vast numbers and great specialization [sharp divisions of labor]), of related patterns of immigration to urban centers, and of a moderate alienation from the isolation of agrarian experience. Urban life came to embody concentrations of population and quanta of working-class leisure and income unprecedented in the entire history of the world. The **affect of urbanization on sport** was great; the conditions of urbanization were highly favorable to organized forms of sporting activity; these conditions were far more favorable to such activity than were comparable features of agrarian-rural life. They established the demographic, economic, and social basis for the development of contemporary modern sport. The popularity and importance of sport grew to such an extent that it even competed successfully against other significant activities for scarce resources of land and capital. Sport also contributed notably to urban catharsis, to relieving the extraordinary malignancies of urban experience; that is, the corrupt, exploitative, alienating, barren, mean-spirited, overcrowded, squalid, and sedentary character of urban experience. It too participated very significantly in the search for both assimilation and folk identity among immigrants who came mainly to inhabit the cities.

As colonialist-imperialist ambitions expanded and as political and economic conditions worsened in Europe in the approximate middle of the nineteenth century, especially large numbers of Europeans emigrated, most importantly to North America, South America, Australia, and New Zealand. The **affect of immigration patterns on sport** was highly significant. Sport was prominent among the trappings of European culture dispersed throughout the "new worlds;" most notably, by means of commercial, educational, and military activity. The English, by far the most influential in these respects, were most instrumental in dispersing and popularizing archery, badminton, cricket, croquet, field hockey, horse racing, rowing, rugby, soccer, squash, swimming, table tennis, tennis, water polo, and yachting/sailing. The Irish were most instrumental in dispersing and popularizing boxing, (court) handball, and wrestling; the Germans, (pin) bowling, gymnastics, and weightlifting; the French and Italians, cycling and fencing; the Scandinavians, winter sports; the Scottish, (lawn) bowling, curling, golf, and track and field; the Spanish, animal sports and jai alai; and the Dutch, ice skating. Sport itself was significantly transformed within the European colonial and emigrant ambit in this period. In the United States, Canada, Australia, and New Zealand most emphatically, sport was less governed (but certainly not altogether unaffected) by class society than in Great Britain itself. Canada passed rugby on to the United States, developed its own form of football, refined curling, and codified canoeing, ice hockey, and lacrosse. The United States developed its own form of football, fashioned baseball (largely out of cricket), invented basketball, softball, and volleyball, and passed many sports (most tellingly, baseball) on to central America (most notably, Mexico), the Caribbean (most notably, Cuba), Oceania (most notably, Guam), and east Asia (most notably, Japan, Korea, and the Philippines). Ireland developed its own unique form of football and invented/codified hurling. Australia crafted its own brand of football. And India formalized badminton and polo, passed them back to Britain and beyond, and perfected field hockey. Among the immigrants in the Americas and in Australasia particularly, sport acted as a vehicle for introducing them to, as well as incorporating them in, the foreign culture (by participation in foreign sports on foreign terms) and as a vehicle for preserving their own individual, community, ethnic, and national identities (by participation in their own sports on their own terms). In this circumstance, sport functioned as a form of cultural assimilation into the new world, as a form of cultural cohesion in respect to the old world, and as a form of cultural confrontation between the old and the new worlds.

Outside the cities, in agrarian-rural circumstance and on the frontiers (particularly, the American, Canadian, Australian, and Argentinean frontiers), sport too prospered but in a different way. **Rural and frontier sport** was less formal, less organized, more irregular, more diverse, and (like pre-industrial sport) more closely connected to the uncontrived activities of everyday life (particularly work activities) and their rituals. The unbridled senses of robust, strenuous, and violent physicality, of competitive strife, of spontaneous practicality, of experiential and participatory immediacy, and of individual initiative characteristic of rural and frontier life were all wholly consistent with the (mechanistic) ethos of contemporary sport. The resource of this life – population, leisure, and disposable income principally – was not early on sufficient to develop formal sporting institutions of the urban type, but as this resource matured the sport of rural and frontier experience came more fully to resemble that of the cities. When the frontiers closed, sport often functioned as a substitute for its otherwise lost qualities.

The expansion of capital industrialism also promoted the advancement of partisan nationalism; the **affect of nationalism on sport** was colossal. Nationalism was centered in the patriotic fervor associated with traditional places and customs and it was expressed most tangibly in the quest for unification of these places and customs as well as the quest for political independence of these places and customs from alternative traditions. It tended to emphasize the likenesses within national groups and the differences among these groups; it tended also to assert the superiority of certain groups over others. It thus inclined likewise to colonialist-imperialist forms of expansion which entailed the exploitation of foreign people, their territories, and their natural resources. This sense of superiority and expansion, as well as its devastating military manifestations, together with an escalating competition among the developed nations for the world's scarce natural and human resource required by capital industrialism itself, created a deeply adversarial (a deeply mechanistic) circumstance, a circumstance that contributed significantly to the development of contemporary modern sport in several notable respects:

- The thirst for national unification and political independence had a large influence on the establishment of national and international forms of sport, forms that emphasized the national character of various sports and attempted to affirm the superiority of national sporting traditions over other such traditions in international contests; sport became a form of national identity and a vehicle for enhancing international status;

- European sport was dispersed throughout the world in the sixteenth, seventeenth, eighteenth, nineteenth, and twentieth centuries where it was imposed in the standard colonialist-imperialist manner on established populations, a process that included the establishment by colonial authorities of sporting clubs for established populations (albeit clubs controlled by colonial authority and devoted to socializing established populations in the practices and values of the colonial authority); anti-colonialist-imperialist sentiment, mainly among established populations in the Americas and Australasia (many of whom were originally Europeans themselves), nonetheless opposed this imposition; sport thus carried the colonialist-imperialist equation, assisted in prosecuting this equation, and was implicated in resistance to this equation;

- The martial emphasis of sport under the direction of nationalism, militarism, and capital industrialism encouraged its larger use in military and paramilitary institutions themselves, in which context it functioned as a counter to combat desertion, prostitution, and alcoholism and as a fertile source of entertainment, adversarial spirit, obedience to command, group cohesion, and physical proficiency, effectively as a diversion from the oppression and repression of military life and as a preparation for war; in this circumstance (among others), sport became as much a permanent rehearsal for war as a civilized substitute for it; and

- Sport itself increasingly took on the conventional values of nationalism, militarism, and capital industrialism: the severe, martial strife of competition, the primacy of materiality as life's basis, the hierarchical character of social Darwinism, the conspicuous display of distinction, and the achievement principle; it thus became a more fully accepted and a more fully integrated part of orthodox cultural life, of mechanistic cultural life.

The **affect of militarism on sport** was likewise immense. The phenomenon of industrial war itself further augmented the development of contemporary sport. The pre-industrial wars of the eighteenth and early nineteenth centuries, wars of the agrarian field effectively, tended to impede the development of sport, both in their immediate course and in their immediate aftermath. They all drew off capital from non-military pursuits in general, most especially leisure activities, and they all drew off sporting resource from the racing stables of the landed gentry in particular. They all had a depressive affect on property, produced economic recessions-depressions from which recovery was typically quite slow, and tended to a sense of austerity, division, and isolation, none of which proved favorable to the development of sport. The wars of capital industrialism, the major wars of the last half of the nineteenth century and of the twentieth century, conversely, all tended to favor the conditions on which contemporary sport developed. Unlike earlier modern conflicts that had tended to deplete the means of production, these conflicts greatly expanded industrial capacity, surplus capital, and post-war markets. They consequently widened the economic basis for the social expansion of sport. Although capital-intensive forms of sport (mainly professional and aristocratic-bourgeois forms of sport) declined in the immediate course of these wars (and in periods of economic depression as well), labor-intensive, mass forms of sport (mainly school, club, industrial, municipal, and military sport as well as sport in inns, taverns, fairs, festivals, streets, sandlots, parks, and playgrounds) greatly expanded in these periods (and also in periods of economic depression). In the special case of military sport, which was practiced on an unprecedented modern scale in the last half of the nineteenth century and in the twentieth century, the gospel of sport was dispersed to the remotest parts of developed countries by returning soldiers at war's end. The capital expansion created by these wars likewise made post-war environments (particularly in the victorious nations but also in the vanquished) all the more receptive to sporting recreations because these environments were all the more fully endowed with leisure, with disposable, surplus capital, and with the desire to relax in the shadow of war rigors. Virtually all forms of sport, capital-intensive and labor-intensive, expanded by dramatic measure in the periods immediately following the major wars of the past approximate century and one-half.

The **affect of democratization on sport** was too very considerable. Liberal reform in institutional government and the development of constitutional democracies had a largely salutary affect on the advancement of contemporary sport. This reform and these democracies were, on balance, friendly to the fashioning of formal, impartial, and egalitarian codes of sport rules and to the sense of progress, individual achievement, and group identity-cohesion inherent in sport. Sport was widely thought, at least according to official pronouncements on the subject, a great equalizer, a liberating force in the world, an apt preparation for and an apt expression of democratism. Although religious and political opposition to sport continued in the nineteenth and twentieth centuries from earlier periods, largely on grounds concerning Sabbatarianism (profanation of the Sabbath), moralism (objection to the brawling, drinking, and gambling often associated with sport), and utility (the ostensible uselessness of play and popular amusements), the social benefit of sport in the liberal state (later, in the communist and fascist states as well) gradually blunted, then reversed opposition to popular sport by formal religion and also by the power elite. Sport was increasingly viewed as an effective means of dissipating sexual energies in socially edifying ways, of combating crime and juvenile delinquency, of reducing interpersonal violence, of discouraging the consumption of intoxicating drink, and of gaining and maintaining good health (particularly of workers, on whose labor much gain is based). Opportunities for sporting participation and success among all classes, both genders, racial and aged minorities, and the handicapped expanded very significantly under the terms of these tendencies. This expansion was nonetheless aimed at affirming, not at transforming, the themes of domination and subordination that characterize the relation of the capital upper class and the laboring lower classes in the industrial age. Aristocratic-bourgeois sport was practiced for leadership socialization; working-class sport was encouraged by the upper classes in order to instruct the working classes of their subservient status, in order to make conspicuous the authority of the upper classes over the lower, in order to promote a sense of obedient and prideful community among workers, in order to maintain a productive and satisfied work corps, and in order to divert, fragment, pacify, and defuse the potentially revolutionary political energies, the resistance to hegemonic structures, of the lower classes. Insofar as feasible, working-class sport (in schools, clubs, industrial organizations, municipal agencies, the military, inns, taverns, fairs, and festivals as well as in professional contexts) was therefore formalized and brought under the explicit supervision of the upper classes. Informal sporting recreations of the working classes (those of the streets, sandlots, parks, and playgrounds mainly) were often disruptive of public order, often damaged property, and were often politically unmanageable. They were thus too brought increasingly under the control of the dominant class by the dominant class and they were unsurprisingly infused with the values of the dominant class.

The progressive **enfranchisement of women in sport** has been a long and an uneven struggle and it has been too a class-specific phenomenon. In the nineteenth century, working-class women were largely excluded from sport on the grounds that it had an unfavorable affect on character, modesty, health, femininity, and emotional stability and on the grounds that women are less proficient in sport than men. Curiously, these concerns were not so strictly turned on upper-class and middle-class women who participated more widely and more freely in sport than those beneath them in the social hierarchy and who participated more widely and more freely in sport than their analogs in early modern civilization. In the twentieth century principally, persuasive medical evidence countered the health-related objections to women's sport by demonstrating the favorable effects of sporting participation on the fitness of women. Although women were yet expected to conform to traditional domestic and subordinate roles and were yet expected to avoid interfering with the traditional and dominant status of men, sport was, in the twentieth century, notably more widely and freely practiced by women of all social classes and it became, among women, progressively more active/athletic, more independent, and more resolute. Male and female sport nonetheless continued to develop quite different, often sexist, temperaments until the late twentieth century when sport for both genders took on largely male traits. The male model turned outward, was sharply confrontational, adversarial, assertive, and aggressive, was governed by hard discipline, sacrifice, and conflict, and was considered an antidote to effeminacy. The female model turned inward, was essentially cooperative, loyal, obedient, and pleasurable, and was considered a preferred alternative to masculinity. The male model tended to mechanistic orientations; the female, to organic. There was nonetheless, for largely commercial and social reasons, a progressive attempt to make male sport more suitable to the presence of women and to make female sport more appealing to men.

The **expansion of sporting franchise for racial and aged minorities and for the handicapped** has been also a long and an uneven struggle and it has been too a class-specific phenomenon. Although not yet fully won at the end of the twentieth century, this struggle has been waged to great effect (most notably in the second half of the twentieth century) by the minorities and the handicapped themselves and it was also eventually encouraged by the power elite as an incentive to profit, as a way to bring dominant, upper-class values to such persons, and as a means of directing the sporting passions of such persons. Even **sport among indentured peoples**, some of it in the context of formal clubs, expanded significantly in the nineteenth century where it continued to serve the enslaved as an antidote to bondage, as catharsis from burdensome oppression, as a means to self-respect, and as a basis for group cohesion. Its most conspicuous, institutional forms nonetheless stood primarily in the service of upper-class interests. In the most notable of these forms, black workers in the Americas and convicts in Australia labored variously as cock trainers, jockeys, and prizefighters.

Although the previously disenfranchised made very significant gains in their standard of living, the quality of their lives, and their opportunities for educational and sporting participation in the nineteenth and twentieth centuries, they did so largely because they fought very hard for such gains against great odds, because such gains were eventually too in the best interests of the dominant classes, and because such gains did not upend the basically unequal character of capital industrialism. Democratic egalitarianism was thus as much a myth as an accomplished fact in contemporary modern civilization. In respect to sport, the appearance (but not the fact) of equal opportunity before impartial law as well as the appearance (but not the fact) of social integration buoyed the legitimacy of a political, economic, and social order that was at telling odds with these appearances. This fundamental illusion and its attendant benefits were further augmented by the advent of:

- universal educational franchise and its colossal influence on school (as well as other forms of) sport;
- the cult of sporting celebrity-heroism; and
- the amateur-professional distinction in sport.

It was largely under the sway of capital industrialism, nationalism-militarism, and democratism that free, compulsory, and **universal public education** became an accomplished fact in the developed and the developing nations of the nineteenth and twentieth centuries. The new political, economic, and social order demanded a citizenry well indoctrinated in the conventional ideology of the state and a literate citizenry at least passingly competent in the basic skills of contemporary life. The cultivation, by education, of intellectual proficiency, of patriotic fervor, and of national ideals based on a common language, literature, and history, as well as on friendly religious, vocational, and sporting customs, greatly served the industrial and nationalistic ends of the time. Although the effective message in the private education of the privileged concerned leadership dominance and the effective message in the public education of others concerned subordinate obedience, the development of public education for virtually all persons significantly expanded sporting opportunities for the lower classes, women, minorities, and the handicapped. These were, of course, not equal opportunities nor was their character open to entirely free development, but they were nonetheless opportunities that the upper classes could not in every respect regulate. The establishment of universal public education predictably had a profound affect on the development of physical education and sport in the schools and on the development of other forms of sport related to the schools, such as club, industrial, municipal, and professional sport. Physical education and sport, like other prominent school subjects and activities, were taken to make a notable contribution to the industrial and nationalistic objectives of contemporary modern civilization, principally in terms of biological fitness and psycho-social character.

The **cult of sporting celebrity-heroism** was also connected to orthodox behavior in the context of class-society; it was in some respects the epitome of orthodox behavior in class-society. The notion of sporting heroism was constructed mainly around athletes who courageously and independently overcame great adversity by means of enormous resolve, effort, and self-discipline to achieve high distinction, who played skillfully, earnestly, and fairly over unusually long periods, who were loyal, modest, and forgiving in basic character, and who were given to self-denial and devoted everything of themselves to a wider community of established values. Sporting heroes were customarily effective models of upper-class dominance or lower-class obedience although they in some cases also signified the transformative consequences of social mobility and too embodied qualities worthily admired by organic standard (but in a more just context of course).

The **amateur-professional distinction in contemporary sport** was still more obviously run through with the inequalities and the injustices of class-society despite its attempt to leave a quite different impression. The incipient development of modern amateurism was owed to the aristocratic sport of Renaissance Europe as has been said. The institutional development of the notion occurred in mid-nineteenth century, in Victorian, England, however. The governing principle of contemporary modern amateurism was to distinguish those of substantial means who could treat sport as an avocational expression (the so-termed "gentlemen" amateurs) from those of lesser means who either had to, needed to, or inclined to accept payment for their sporting participation (the so-termed "pugs," or professionals). Amateurism, by this account, prohibited extrinsic employments of sport; that is, commercial, political, racial, national, and sectarian forms of exploitation, discrimination, or propaganda. It put an emphasis instead on sport's intrinsic possibilities, on its internal goods, on its social, educational, aesthetic, and moral possibilities, on its prospects for correcting (or preventing) social malignancy and for promoting conventionally defined forms of decency (fair play, mutual respect, modesty, loyalty, and sacrifice), and on its apolitical character. Professionalism, conversely, was dominated by extrinsic orders of "respect" for sport (by respect for sport's external goods), mainly commercial such orders and goods, which put an emphasis on advantage-taking, humiliation, and resentment. The concept of intrinsic orientations to sport, of virtuous orientations to sport, was thus reserved for those who had fashioned it (the aristocratic-bourgeois classes), was explicitly denied to others by those who had fashioned it (and who had the power to deny it to others), and was ascribed the higher sentiment by those who had fashioned it. Those who had fashioned it were those who had most resolutely and successfully achieved private gain in non-sporting sectors; such gain was nonetheless condemned by them as it pertained to sport. This does in a sense privilege sport as a form of activity that prospers most in a non-exploitative context, but this was, of course, not a universally shared context. In an authentically democratic and an authentically human circumstance (i.e., in democratic socialism), the inherently intrinsic richness of amateur sport, the organic richness of amateur sport, is the universal standard, the standard for all persons, and it does not exclude pecuniary considerations. As an antagonist among many others in the rapacious class struggle, however, amateurism made human fulfillment, decency, and excellence, shared truth, freedom, and beauty, in sport the sole province of the power elite. As such, the amateur-professional distinction, which has been such a prominent feature of sport over the past approximate century and one-half, has come to still another attempt to consolidate the prerogatives of a social class (the capital class) at the expense of prerogatives open to other such classes (the laboring classes). Amateurism was thus implicated in establishing and maintaining the hegemony of the dominant class, in securing the acceptance of established orthodoxy and authority, and in preserving unequal class relations. The dynamics of these distinctions have nonetheless changed very substantially since their original formulation:

- many in the lower classes have come to distinguish themselves very notably in so-termed amateur sport;
- some in the upper classes have come to distinguish themselves very notably in so-termed professional sport;
- the amateur code was always problematically enforced at best in all forms of politico-economic circumstance (capitalist, communist, and fascist); and
- the amateur code's basic provisions had been reduced to little more than nominal significance by the late twentieth century as virtually all forms of sport (even street, sandlot, park, and playground sport) became predominantly afflicted with the instrumental orientations of professionalism.

Still another conspicuous mark of sport's increasingly prominent place in contemporary modern civilization was its stature among leading political, economic, and social personalities of the time. Many such personalities of the nineteenth century had a great interest in sport; some participated themselves earnestly and successfully in it. Virtually all major twentieth-century leaders had either an authentic concern for sport or at least acknowledged its great significance; many patronized it and/or participated in it themselves, some at impressively high levels. Arguably the **foremost political, economic, and social figures of the nineteenth and twentieth centuries concerned with sport** were British monarchs and American presidents:

- George IV was taken with archery, boxing, and horse racing and had a well developed inclination to gamble on sporting events;
- William IV was fond of golf and yachting/sailing;
- Victoria was a horse racing enthusiast;
- Edward VII had a taste for croquet, horse racing, hunting, tennis, and yachting/sailing;
- George V had a great enthusiasm for physical fitness as well as for cricket, golf, horse racing, hunting, rugby, shooting, soccer, and tennis;
- Edward VIII played squash competently well;
- Elizabeth II is a horse racing enthusiast;
- John Adams liked ice skating, shooting, swimming, wrestling, and yachting/sailing;
- Thomas Jefferson favored moderate exercise for fitness and for the enhancement of individual and social character;
- John Quincy Adams recognized the educational, recreational, and health benefits of vigorous forms of physical game-playing and was especially fond of billiards, horse racing, and swimming;
- Andrew Jackson had a great taste for robust and courageous physical activity in general and for cock fighting and horse racing in particular;

- Abraham Lincoln was accomplished at handball, horseshoes, weightlifting, and wrestling;
- Theodore Roosevelt had an enormous enthusiasm for boxing, football, hunting, rowing, tennis, and wrestling;
- William Howard Taft, Warren Harding, and Calvin Coolidge were fond of golf;
- Woodrow Wilson had an especially high opinion of baseball, football, and golf;
- Harry Truman avidly played horseshoes;
- Dwight Eisenhower, Richard Nixon, and Gerald Ford played intercollegiate football and later recreational golf;
- John Kennedy and Bill Clinton were deeply avid sportsmen;
- Ronald Reagan played intercollegiate football, did sport broadcasts on radio, and made sport films; and
- George Bush played intercollegiate baseball.

Many prominent persons in the British and American governments, other than heads-of-state, were also variously accomplished athletes and avid sporting enthusiasts; most notably:

- British prime ministers, Henry Temple Palmerston, a swimmer; David Lloyd George, a golfer; Ramsay MacDonald, a golfer; Winston Churchill, a polo player; and John Major, a cricket and soccer devotee;
- British army general, Arthur Wellesley Wellington, a tennis player; and
- American Supreme Court justices, John Marshall (1755-1835; the longest reigning chief justice, 1801-35), an excellent player of quoits, and Byron Raymond "Whizzer" White (1917-), among the most outstanding intercollegiate and professional football players of the immediate pre-Second World War era.

Numerous lower-ranking members of the British royal family, the civil British government, and the American government were also fervently devoted to sport; some even achieved Olympic participation and professional sporting success. Several leading Continental European monarchs were likewise deeply committed to the activity; most significantly: Napoleon I of France, a tennis player; Franz Joseph I of Austria-Hungary, a billiards player; Napoleon III of France, an ice skater; Alfonso XIII of Spain, a tennis player; William II of Germany, a tennis player; Nicholas II of Russia, a tennis player; Gustavus V of Sweden, a tennis player; Pope John Paul II, a soccer player; Olaf V of Norway, a ski jumper; Harald V of Norway, an Olympic yachtsman; Constantine II of Greece, the 1960 Olympic dragon-class yachting champion (several years before his ascent to the throne); and Pope Pius XI and Pope Pius XII both affirmed the high value of modern sport. Numerous other lower-ranking members of Continental European royal families and civil governments also won sporting distinction, including Olympic participation and professional sporting success. Moreover, Dominican president, Rafael Trujillo, and Nicaraguan president, Anastasio Somoza, were both avid baseball enthusiasts; Argentinean president, Juan Peron, was an especially ardent advocate of sport, largely for political purposes; Canadian prime minister, Pierre Elliott Trudeau (1919-2000), was a fine lacrosse player as a young man; Ugandan president, Idi Amin, was an accomplished boxer; and Russian prime minister and president, Vladimir Putin, was a skilled wrestler in his youth. And several of the foremost revolutionary figures of the nineteenth and twentieth centuries were too taken with sport or with selective features of it: Jose Marti favored vigorous forms of physical activity (particularly baseball), mainly owing to their health benefits, but opposed professional sport and American influence over the sporting life of Cuba; Vladimir Lenin favored physical exercise, valued physical fitness, admired and practiced many sports (particularly, cycling, ice skating, shooting, and walking), and interpreted sport as a social phenomenon intimately connected to the political and intellectual environment in which it is practiced; Ho Chi Minh was an avid devotee of exercise; Mao Tse-tung was an outstanding swimmer; and Fidel Castro was an exemplary baseball player.

The unique intellectual tendencies, like the dominant political, economic, and social realities, of contemporary modern civilization have also had a profound influence on the development of sport. The **affect of romanticism and realism on sport** was especially sweeping. The romantic and realist movements of the nineteenth century held to an organic, monistic, and intrinsic view of life that was very favorably disposed to a balanced, proportionate, harmonious, and unified sense of material and spiritual fulfillment. These movements were too very favorably inclined to a subjective characterization of the body and a lived sense of movement, to an abiding respect for vigorous bodily expressions as integral aspects of authentic humanity, and to sport as an expression of distinctly human nature, freedom, and beauty. Human life (including its sporting expressions), by such views, is accordingly lived as a heroic, reflective, and impassioned search for itself. Romanticism and realism thus admired a type of sport that embodied organic ideals; both nonetheless condemned mechanistic forms of sport, material, brutalizing, and deeply adversarial forms of sport. The intrinsic sweep of amateurism's governing principle as well as its sense of fair play and virtuous character appealed to them; amateurism's negative and instrumental use of sport to forestall savagery and other social ills, the explicit inclination of amateurism to disconnect sport from the social reality in which it lives, the implicit institutional connections of sport to orthodox, conservative political agendas endorsed by amateurism, and the inegalitarian features of amateurism's social reality did not. Romanticism and realism endorsed universal educational franchise and provision of universal opportunity for sporting participation; they too endorsed the liberating aspects of nationalism and national and international sport. They conversely opposed instrumental scientific and commercial tendencies in sport, elitist forms of sport, and the divisive aspects of national and international sport. The intimate connections preferred by romanticism and realism between sport and other forms of human expression opened sport to the possibilities of religious awareness and aesthetic self-revelation. These connections contributed significantly to the acceptance of sport by formal religion and by scientific and humanistic subjects. Many of the leading figures of the romantic and realist movements referred to sport in their work and/or participated earnestly themselves in sport. Among leading philosophical and literary figures of the romantic and realist orientations:

- Johann Gottlieb Fichte enthusiastically recommended physical exercise for health-related and moral purposes;
- Friedrich Daniel Ernst Schleiermacher had a very keen interest in physical education;
- William Wordsworth was much interested in sport;
- Sir Walter Scott played soccer in his youth;
- Lord Byron was a competent boxer, was also fond of cricket and horse riding, and was a highly accomplished long-distance swimmer;
- Percy Bysshe Shelley was fond of sailing and died in a sailing accident;
- Ralph Waldo Emerson, Nathaniel Hawthorne, Henry David Thoreau, and Louisa May Alcott thought of sport as keenly self-revealing and deeply educative, as a means of instilling individual self-reliance and spiritual greatness, and as a way of promoting the ideal harmonization of body, mind, and spirit; Emerson, Hawthorne, and Thoreau also did long river journeys on ice skates; and Alcott wrote fondly of physical activity in general and of croquet in particular (in Little Women);
- William Makepeace Thackeray had a broad interest in sport;
- Charles Dickens was a boxing and cricket enthusiast and wrote of racquets (in Posthumous Papers of the Pickwick Club);
- Anthony Trollope was a fanatical fox hunter and commented extensively on all popular forms of English sport;
- Karl Marx abhorred physical exercise but advocated physical education for health-related and military purposes;
- Mark Twain had great affection for baseball;
- Josiah Royce recommended gymnastic (in particular, Swedish) exercise;
- George Bernard Shaw was exceedingly fond of boxing; and
- Rudyard Kipling argued that Britain's taste for sport was at the root of its poor showing in the Boer War.

Among leading romantic and realist figures in the visual and musical arts:

- Francisco Goya was devoted to bullfighting;
- Théodore Géricault was an avid boxing enthusiast;
- Felix Mendelssohn played billiards very well;
- Stephen Foster composed engaging folk songs concerning sport (such as "Camptown Races," 1850);
- Winslow Homer portrayed the appeal of sport in painting (as in "Skating in Central Park" [1858] and "The Croquet Game" [1866]);
- Georges Bizet composed a musical score based on the games of children, "Jeux d'Enfants" (1872); and
- Thomas Eakins, who was himself exceedingly adept at cycling, ice skating, jumping, horse riding, rowing, running, sailing, and swimming, did magnificent photographs of vigorous locomotive activities and painted engaging canvases featuring sport (such as, "Max Schmitt in a Single Scull" [1871], "Taking the Count" [boxing, 1898], and "Between Rounds" [boxing, 1899]).

The mid-to-late-nineteenth-century turn away from the organic, monistic, and intrinsic orientations of romanticism and realism toward mechanistic, dualistic/pluralistic, and extrinsic orientations – the seminal turn from modernism to post-modernism – occurred principally under the influence of capital industrialism and its scientific, technological, and intellectual corollaries. This turn took a largely materialistic form; adopted an objective characterization of body and a corporeal sense of movement; was governed in intellectual terms by various forms of positivism (mainly, empiricism, utilitarianism, and evolutionism), by impressionism, and by post-impressionism; and was very favorably inclined to sport, albeit sport of a mechanistic type. The new emphasis on change, on tangible, secular, material activity (including bodily activity), on mechanized practice, on direct, energetic experience, on the (biological and social) Darwinist notion of progress, and on a robust, an athletic, standard of physical beauty and personal character all conspired to deepen popular acclaim for sport. This form of sport was, however, more so grounded in a one-sided cult of the body than in the sense of mind-body harmony reminiscent of romanticism and realism, in the sense of mind-body harmony by which physicality is itself endowed with the distinctly human call of reason, freedom, and beauty. The **affect of positivism, impressionism, and post-impressionism on sport** was immense and many of the leading figures of these movements importantly included sport in their most meaningful experiences:

- Herbert Spencer incorporated physical education in his vision of the new scientific education;
- Eadweard Muybridge did pioneering photographic studies of animal and human (including sporting) locomotion;
- Édouard Manet painted sporting scenes (such as, "The Races at Longchamps" [horse racing, 1872] and "Boating" [c. 1874]);
- Claude Monet painted sporting scenes (such as "Regatta at Argenteuil," 1872);
- Edgar Degas portrayed horse racing in painting (such as, "Carriage at the Races" (1871-72] and "The Races" [c. 1873]);
- Pierre Auguste Renoir portrayed rowing and sailing in painting (such as, "Regatta at Argenteuil" [c. 1874], "Oarsmen at Chatou" [1879], and "The Luncheon of the Boating Party at Bougival" [1881]);
- Mary Cassatt painted sporting scenes (such as "The Boating Party," 1893-94);
- Paul Gauguin painted an allegorical portrayal of wrestling in "Vision After the Sermon: Jacob Wrestling with the Angel" (1888); and
- Henri de Toulouse-Lautrec was a cycling enthusiast and depicted acrobatic circus scenes in painting (such as "In the Circus Fernando: The Ringmaster," 1888).

The preeminent intellectual tendencies of the twentieth century – relativism in the natural and social sciences, skepticism (principally in the form of German phenomenology, English and American realism, pragmatism, and the various types of analytic philosophy) in philosophy, history, and literature, and abstractionism (principally in the form of fauvism, cubism, futurism, pop art, and atonal-dissonant music) in the visual, musical, and movement arts – continued to be very significantly driven by post-modern scientificism. They too continued to be formally disposed to mechanistic notions of reality, to relative standards of value, to the material world of the body, to vigorous movement, and to sport. The **affect of relativism, skepticism, and abstractionism on sport** was great and many of the foremost personalities of these movements were connected to sport in some significant way:

- William James implied a reference to sport as the moral equivalent of war;
- Henri Rousseau painted sporting subjects such as "The Football Players" (1908);
- John Dewey reserved a high place for physical education in educational experience, considering it an excellent medium for learning the skills and knowledges of intelligent doing and effective social living, for acculturation in the experience of everyday, democratic life, for dynamic and healthful self-renewal, for character formation through tangible, pragmatic, and experimental action, and for cultivation of aesthetic pleasure;
- George Santayana fashioned sport an inherently intrinsic form of human expression, a vital feature of authentic education, a conspicuous opponent of instrumental orientations, and as capable of a unique and significant aesthetic development;
- Erik Satie wrote three piano compositions inspired in part by sporting images on an ancient Greek vase, "Gymnopédies" (1888), and twenty miniature sketches for piano inspired by sporting diversions, "Sports et Divertissements" (1914);
- Maurice de Vlaminck was an accomplished competitive cyclist in his youth;
- Pablo Picasso was an adept acrobatic gymnast;
- James Joyce commented on the horrors of school sports;
- Robert Delaunay painted sporting subjects such as "Runner" (1924);

- Arthur Honegger composed a memorable symphonic movement, "Rugby" (1928); and
- Aaron Copland (with Agnes De Mille) wrote the ballet score, "Rodeo" (1942).

Only existentialism and its main derivatives (philosophical anthropology, intuitionism, and French phenomenology) in philosophy and literature and (representational and abstract) expressionism in the visual arts have stood tellingly against the strictly analytic emphasis of the sciences in this time. Both existentialism and expressionism embodied the possibilities of humanity's organic fulfillment; existentialism in an inchoate and incomplete way, expressionism in an explicit and fully developed fashion. Both too acknowledged bodily activity as a central datum in the harmonies of edifyingly creative experience; both valued organically framed forms of sport as especially fertile engagements of such experience; and both denounced the mechanistic excesses of contemporary sport. Existentialism most valued robust activities that serve distinctly human, subjective (vitalistic, or willed) experience and what is characteristic of such experience (that is, free choice and responsibility, together with the sense of utterly personal, individuating experience that free choice and responsibility entail). Expressionism also greatly valued arduous activities that serve uniquely human purposes; in its case, however, these purposes are governed by a more complete and balanced sense of willed and reasoned perspective, of bodily and spiritual proportion. The **affect of existentialism and expressionism on sport** was large and many of the leading personalities of these movements were connected to sport in some significant way:

- Arthur Schopenhauer enthusiastically recommended physical exercise for health-related and palliative reasons;
- Friedrich Nietzsche fashioned an extraordinarily sympathetic regard for the body (as notably more than an instrument of the mind, as inseparable from the mind, and as an essential mode of the reality of a person) and advocated an active, intense, courageous, and self-determining participation in daring and strenuous physical activities as a prominent way of fulfilling the will to power;
- A.E. Housman crafted the moving poem, "To an Athlete Dying Young" (1896);
- Ernst Kirchner painted sporting subjects such as "Hockey Players" (1937);
- Karl Jaspers argued that sport is customarily a trapping of purposelessness but that it is nonetheless capable of contributing to the vitality of unique human subjectivity, of participating in the revolt against the self-destructive tyranny of the objective and the everyday, of functioning as a form of uniquely human expression, and of affirming and enhancing (as distinct from merely sustaining) distinctly human experience;
- Jose Ortega y Gasset identified playful activity (including sport) as that self-determining, self-re-newing, spontaneous, and exuberant mood which constitutes authentic doing and intrinsic living, which demonstrates the achievement of freedom from the instrumentalities of everyday experience, and which frames a characteristically human endeavor;
- Max Beckmann painted sporting subjects such as "The Trapeze" (1923) and "The Skaters" (1932);
- Ernest Hemingway had a fervent interest in boxing and wrote the celebrated exposition concerning bullfighting, <u>Death in the Afternoon</u> (1932);
- George Grosz painted sporting subjects such as "Sportsman" (1922);
- Bertolt Brecht was an avid boxing enthusiast;
- Jean-Paul Sartre construed play as a fundamental expression of our free, personal, and authentic subjectivity (and thus a resolute turning away from objective characterizations of ourselves) and he construed sport as a prominent form of play and a meaningful act of self-appropriation; and
- Albert Camus had a wide affection for sport as an expression of existential freedom, a confrontation with life's absurdity, and an antidote to alienation.

Of course many accomplished and prominent intellectual figures other than the very most exceptional included sport variously and significantly in their authentic experience. Arguably the most notable of these were:

- Horace Mann (1796-1859), the American statesman, educator, and abolitionist lawyer, who argued for the improvement of schools, of the conditions of teaching, and of the standards of educational achievement, for the establishment of free public schools for all persons, for the elimination of religious domination of the schools, for the co-education of men and women, for the establishment of public normal schools, and for the high place of physical education in the standard school curriculum;

- Frederic Remington (1861-1909), the American artist, who painted several noteworthy pictures featuring sport (such as, "Steeplechase at Cedarhurst" [1885] and "Yale-Princeton Football Game, Thanksgiving Day, 1890" [c. 1891]);
- Burt L. Standish/William George "Gilbert" Patten (1866-1945), the American author, who wrote heroic and popular, youth sport stories, "The Frank Merriwell Series" (1896-1916) in Tip Top Weekly;
- Robert Tait "R. Tait" McKenzie (1867-1938), the Canadian-American physician and educator, who had a major role in the early development of North American physical education, who was himself an avid and successful sportsman (principally in fencing, football, gymnastics, ice skating, skiing, sledding, and track and field), and who was arguably the finest sculptor of athletic subjects in the twentieth century (as in "Sprinter" [1902], "Competitor" [running, 1906], "Joy of Effort" [hurdling, 1912], "The Pole Vaulter" [1923], "Pennsylvania Relays" [1925], "Shot Putter" [1928], "The Shield of Athletes" [1932], and "Passing the Baton" [1934]);
- John Griffith "Jack" London, the American author, who wrote tellingly of boxing in the novel, The Game (1905);
- George Wesley Bellows (1882-1925), the American painter, who was himself an accomplished interscholastic and intercollegiate baseball, basketball, and football player and who made especially memorable portrayals of boxing (such as, "Both Members of the Club" [1908], "Stag at Sharkey's" [1909], and "Firpo Knocking Dempsey Out of the Ring" [1924]);
- Ringold Wilmer "Ring" Lardner (1885-1933), the American journalist, who crafted masterful stories, mainly about baseball (such as You Know Me, Al, 1916);
- Archibald Vivian "A.V." Hill (1886-1977), the English physiologist and 1922 Nobel co-laureate in medicine, who did the pioneering work in muscle and exercise physiology;
- Henri de Montherlant (1896-1972), the French novelist, athlete, and bullfighter, who wrote articulate, if harsh, accounts of sport (such as, The Dream [1922] and Les Olympiques [1924]); and
- Joseph "Joe" Brown (1909-85), the American artist and student of McKenzie, who was himself an accomplished boxer, football player, and intercollegiate boxing coach and who fashioned extraordinary sculptural images featuring sport (such as, "Punter" [football, 1947], "Hook-Slide" [baseball, 1949], and "The Supplicant" [boxing, 1951]).

Near-to-countless films concerning sport (or including sport in significant respect) have been also produced in the twentieth century. Among the earliest major such efforts were the American films, "Casey at the Bat" (baseball, 1899), "Knute Rockne – All-American" (football, 1940), "Pride of the Yankees" (about baseball legend, Lou Gehrig; 1942), and "Gentleman Jim" (about world heavyweight boxing champion, Jim Corbett; 1942). Among the most commendable of these efforts have concerned the Olympic Games (such as, the 1938 German film of the 1936 Games, "Olympia," and the 1981 British film of the 1924 Games, "Chariots of Fire"), boxing (such as, the American films, "Requiem for a Heavyweight" [1956], "Somebody Up There Likes Me" [about Rocky Graziano; 1956], and "Raging Bull" [about Jake La Motta; 1980]), and baseball (such as "Bang the Drum Slowly," 1973). Sport has too significantly influenced (and has been significantly influenced by) twentieth-century architecture; most notably, in respect to the inventive design of sporting facilities (such as, gymnasia, stadiums, arenas, and country clubs). And, of course, the popular arts of the twentieth century were awash in sporting references.

The evolution of sporting activity in the nineteenth and twentieth centuries developed on two main, and sometimes closely related, fronts: for one, programs of physical education that were found largely, but not entirely, in the schools and, for a second, athletic programs that were found largely, but not entirely, in non-school circumstance. The seminal systems of contemporary physical education developed mostly as regimens of calisthenic exercise known as gymnastics and they were owed primarily to Continental Europe. The seminal development of contemporary modern athletic institutions, conversely, was owed primarily to Great Britain and to the main colonies/dominions or former colonies/dominions of Great Britain; most notably, Ireland, Australia, Canada, New Zealand, South Africa, India, British West Indies, and United States of America.

Contemporary modern physical education and closely related activities

Free, compulsory and universal public education was increasingly organized in the developed nations of the nineteenth century and in the developing nations of the twentieth as has been said. Educational franchise was gradually extended to all social classes and had the utilitarian consequence of indoctrinating virtually everyone in standardized national ideologies, cultivating wide patriotic zeal, and serving the industrial aims of the age. Physical education (or gymnastics) was taken enthusiastically into the schools of the nineteenth and twentieth centuries (in some cases as a required subject) where it predictably functioned as one of many useful means to nationalistic and industrial success. The earliest and most characteristic systems of gymnastics were fashioned in the Germanies, Sweden, and Denmark. Other important systems were also developed in France, England, Switzerland, United States, Bohemia, and Russia. The German, Swedish, and Danish developments each grew out of humiliating military failures and the intense nationalist and reformist sentiments that these failures evoked.

The earliest, most characteristic, and otherwise most significant of these movements occurred in the Germanies. The leading German states of the early nineteenth century (most notably, Prussia) were among the most severely affected casualties of the Napoleonic Wars. The German struggles against France, together with Germany's impulse to liberal reform and political unification, encouraged a fervent nationalism that greatly influenced education and physical education. The foremost advocate of reform in government, education, and gymnastics, the principal figure in **German gymnastics**, was Friedrich Ludwig Jahn (1778-1852), who became known as the "father of modern (naturalistic) physical education." Jahn argued tirelessly and courageously for German national unity, for freedom of the German masses, for the use of education as a social and political instrument, and for the inclusion of physical education as an essential aspect of education. His broad political vision, which had been greatly influenced by the thought of the celebrated German philosopher, Johann Gottlieb Fichte, was most importantly recorded in German Nationality (1810). His views concerning educational and gymnastic issues were most importantly expressed in Die Deutsche Turnkunst (German Gymnastics, 1816), among the most notable nineteenth-century manuscripts concerning physical education. Jahn's earliest tangible work concerning gymnastic activity made an informal use of physical education in a private boarding school for boys in Berlin (Prussia), at which he formally taught mathematics, language, and history. This work went on from 1808 to 1811 without special success. Beginning in 1810-11, Jahn began the work in non-school circumstance for which he is so justifiably well remembered. This work entailed the development and administration of gymnastic activity (turnkunst), practiced in distinctive playground facilities (turnplatze), under the auspices of formal gymnastic societies (turnvereine), sometimes in the context of formal gymnastic exhibitions (turnfeste). This, the so-termed Turner's, movement had become a nationally acclaimed institution by 1814, principally because it promoted physical proficiency of a martial type and thereby served well the German (in particular, the Prussian) effort against Napoleon I; Jahn himself participated successfully in the 1813 military campaign against Napoleon. Reactionary rule again prevailed, however, following the defeat of Napoleon, the enactment of the Congress of Vienna accords, and the establishment of the German Confederation. The populist agitations of the Turner's movement brought it into such disfavor with the governing authorities – mainly with Frederick William III of Prussia and Austrian Prince Klement von Metternich – that it was effectively outlawed in 1818-19; Jahn was tried (but acquitted) of murder charges associated with the assassination of a political opponent; he was nonetheless put under strict government surveillance from 1819 to 1825; and he never again worked actively in the movement. Frederick William IV of Prussia lifted the ban in 1840-42; the Revolutions of 1848-49 further rehabilitated the movement; but it was not until it renounced its political ambitions and established the Deutsche Turnerschaft (a union of German and Austrian gymnastic societies) in 1868 that it regained its stature as an authentically national society. The Turner's movement nonetheless established an especially significant presence in North America by 1825, in Italy by 1833, in England by 1849, in Netherlands by 1849, in central and South America by 1853-59, and (despite Jahn's anti-Semitic inclinations) in the dispersed Jewish communities of Europe and the Middle East (the first Jewish sports organization, the Israelitischer Turnverein, a gymnastics club, was established in Constantinople in 1895) by 1895.

Jahn's system of gymnastics itself had been greatly influenced by the naturalistic program of Johann Friedrich GutsMuths and was thus of broad scope, democratically inclined, scientifically grounded, and oriented to the fundamental activities and movements that human beings incline to when they are left to do as they will in an uncontrived, a natural, environment (i.e., large-muscle integrative activities and movements). It was rigorous (in intrapersonal terms), individual (not massed), egalitarian (in the senses that innovation was permitted, persons of virtually all ages and social classes were included, and a common uniform was worn in order to eliminate an awareness of social-class differences), and conducted under firm but friendly persuasion (for instructional and safety reasons). The turnplatz itself – most notably, the first, the Hasenheide in Berlin, 1810 – consisted in an enclosed rectangular area that was filled with roughly made pieces of apparatus constructed in the image of natural objects such as several that would become standard features of gymnastic sport (parallel bars, high bar, rings, vaulting horse, pommel horse, balance beams, and climbing ropes), several that would become standard features of track and field sport (high jumping standards, pole vaulting standards, long jumping pits, and a walking-running track), as well as areas for acrobatic gymnastics, gymnastic exercises, hoop and rope jumping, throwing balls, clubs, and weights, weightlifting, wrestling, fencing, and various forms of folk game-playing and dancing. The naturalistic system of gymnastics that Jahn fashioned differed qualitatively from its main nineteenth-century alternative, so-termed militaristic systems of gymnastic activity.

Jahn's system had been first established in the leading northern German state, Prussia, in the second decade of the nineteenth century and was devoted mainly to non-school contexts. It was not until the 1840s in the southern German state of Hesse that a system of gymnastics suitable for German school use was developed. Adolph Spiess (1810-58), who had been greatly influenced by GutsMuths, Jahn, and Per Henrik Ling, who was himself an accomplished and devoted gymnast and fencer, and who had earlier (1833-44) worked with Friedrich Froebel as a teacher of gymnastics and the arts in Burgdorf, Switzerland (near Berne), first succeeded in securing the German adoption of physical education as an integral school subject in Darmstadt (near Frankfurt) in 1848. His active leadership, pedagogical expertise, reformist inclinations, and major published work on the subject, System of Gymnastics (1840-46), were major influences on German physical education throughout the nineteenth century. Spiess held that education must concern itself with the harmonious development of the whole individual (a customary romantic claim) and that physical education must be therefore accorded the same status as other school subjects. His militaristic system of gymnastics nonetheless differed characteristically from the naturalistic programs of GutsMuths and Jahn in most notable respects. It tended to a rigid discipline and order, to strict and autocratic supervision, and to strenuous interpersonal forms of competition. It entailed a progressive series of compulsory activities for each age and gender performed in massed circumstance. These activities, taken principally from Ling (who had been himself somewhat influenced by Franz Nachtegall), most importantly included simple hanging, supported, and marching exercises, rhythmically arranged and sometimes performed to musical accompaniment. Like the activities constituting other notable militaristic systems of the period, these too were grounded in scientific tabulations of the various attainable positions and movements of all body segments displaced by all of the body's major muscle groups about all of the body's major movable joints. It was designed to effect a systematic exercise of the entire body; it was not designed to develop natural movement patterns in a natural environment.

In the great controversy between naturalistic-tending systems (based essentially on GutsMuths' and Jahn's work) and militaristic-tending systems (based essentially on Nachtegall's, Ling's, and Spiess' work), a controversy that occupied the nineteenth century particularly but also spilled significantly over into the twentieth, the naturalists accused the militarists of being unnatural because they (the militarists) prescribed activities that are not naturally inclined to. The militarists, conversely, who also had a stake in being natural (effectively, acting in accord with our defining tendencies), accused the naturalists of being unnatural because they (the naturalists) used contrived apparatus, apparatus that dictated movement conformity, albeit apparatus formed in the image of natural objects. The militarists likewise accused the naturalists of being unscientific because they (the naturalists) did not carefully study the consequences of their activity nor did this activity produce a systematic and comprehensive exercise of the entire body. On balance, the naturalistic systems of the nineteenth century tended to give way in the twentieth century to programs of physical education dominated by sport-like forms of game-playing; these programs were typically more popular among men than women. The militaristic systems of the nineteenth century, conversely, tended to give way in the twentieth century to programs of physical education dominated by dance-like forms of activity; these programs were typically more popular among women than men.

The other major figures in contemporary modern German physical education were:

- Hans Ferdinand Massman (1797-1874), an assistant of Jahn, who unsuccessfully attempted to incorporate Jahn's system of gymnastics into the schools (1842-48) and who also unsuccessfully attempted to organize a professional preparation center for gymnastics teachers in Berlin (1848-49); and

- Hugo von Rothstein (1810-65), a Prussian military officer, who introduced Ling's Swedish system of gymnastics variously to the German military and the German schools (1847-62) and who organized and directed the first successful and permanent professional preparation center for military and school gymnastics teachers in the Germanies, the Royal Central Gymnastic Institute, Berlin, 1851 (courses for women were added in 1866).

The formal systems of gymnastics that had dominated the first one-half to three-quarters of nineteenth-century German physical education grew progressively more rigid and less engaging, however. Beginning in c.

1879, vigorous forms of sport-like game-playing began to work their way into the schools and into the broader precincts of German physical recreation, often over the objections of formal gymnastic traditions. Arguably the most prominent and effective advocate of this tendency was the Prussian statesman, Emil Theodor Gustav von Schenkendorff (1837-1915), who championed the playground movement throughout the Germanies. This movement favored English-style forms of sport (mainly team games and track and field activities) over the gymnastics systems of Jahn and Spiess, sponsored playdays (spielfeste) for the wide community practice of such forms, and established a national governing body to promote itself, the Central Committee for the Advancement of Folk and Child Play in Germany, in 1891. German physical education did nonetheless not broaden very significantly beyond the scope of gymnastic exercise until after the First World War, in the period of the Weimar Republic (1918-33). Carl Diem (1882-1962) was likely most responsible for the development of mass national sport in Germany in the inter-war era. Diem successfully agitated for the replacement of formal gymnastics programs in the schools by sport-like forms of game-playing; was instrumental in the formation of what has become the leading institution of sport studies in Germany (supplanting the preeminence of the Royal Central Gymnastic Institute) and among the most remarkable institutions of its type in the world, Die Deutsche Hochschule fur Leibesubungen (Berlin, 1920-34: moved to Cologne and became Die Deutsche Sporthochschule in 1947); and was a major figure in the organization and conduct of the 1936 (winter and summer) Olympic Games in Germany. The physical recreative life of modern Germany since the passing of the Weimar Republic continued to emphasize sports and games over formal gymnastics programs, a pattern that is also evident in the other leading world nations of the twentieth century.

Sweden, like the Germanies, also suffered a decline in its political, economic, and military fortunes in the early nineteenth century. In the Swedish case, this decline had begun in the early eighteenth century with Russian victories over it in the Great Northern War. Although it regained its union with Norway in 1814, Sweden was otherwise disadvantaged by its varied opposition to France throughout the Napoleonic Wars and it lost Finland to Russia in 1809. Sweden's tumble from European prominence, like Germany's, evoked an intensely nationalistic and reformist fervor. Among the most prominent advocates of Swedish educational and cultural revival was Per Henrik Ling (1776-1839), the so-termed "father of modern (militaristic) gymnastics," the leading figure in **Swedish gymnastics**, and among the most prominent figures in the entire history of physical education. Ling's ardent respect for gymnastics dated from his five-year tenure in Copenhagen (1799-1804), where he observed the establishment of the Military Gymnastic Institute, became an adept fencer, acquired a refined taste for Norse literature, and fell under the influence of the German romantic-idealist philosopher, Friedrich Wilhelm Joseph Schelling. On his return to Sweden in 1804, he became a lecturer in Norse mythology, poetry, and history and the fencing master at the University of Lund (in southern Sweden, near Malmo) where he had studied as a young man. Throughout his eight-year appointment in Lund, Ling developed the basic principles and methods of his celebrated gymnastics. In 1813, he proposed the establishment of a professional preparation center for gymnastics teachers in Stockholm, the approximate Swedish equivalent of the Military Gymnastic Institute in Copenhagen. Mainly on the grounds of its military utility, the proposal was approved by Charles XIV, also in 1813, and the Royal Central Institute of Gymnastics was opened, with Ling as its Director (1814-39), in 1814. It was at the Institute that Ling fashioned his enormous reputation as the author of the best Norse literature of his time (most notably, Asarne [Northern Gods], 1816) and the creator of modern militaristic gymnastics. Like the other leading romantic reformers in nineteenth-century education and physical education, Ling was of very wide learning and connected gymnastics to the broader scope of human affairs; in his case, to patriotic literature and the revival of Swedish cultural and political preeminence. Ling hoped to bring new resolve to the demoralized Swedish society and to inspire Swedish youth to develop the physical prowess and courage of the ancestral Norsemen.

Ling's system of gymnastics itself was recorded most memorably in Manual of Gymnastics (1836) and General Principles of Gymnastics (1839-40). It was intended to effect a balanced development of body, to function as an integral feature of a harmonious life, to secure a unity among the various aspects of human experience, and to satisfy our demands for beauty. Unlike naturalistic programs of gymnastic activity (such as Jahn's), which Ling considered unscientific in formulation, execution, and result, Swedish militaristic gymnastics was based on known anatomical and physiological laws, effectively on tabulations of the various positions and movements of all body segments displaced by all of the body's major muscle groups about all of the body's major movable joints. It consisted in a scientifically based, precisely ordered, and progressive arrangement of fundamental calisthenic exercises, peculiar to various ages and both genders, dominated by movements from held to held position and done in massed circumstance on command. The prescribed regimen of activities was known as "tables of movement" (later, as "gymnastic day's order"); it was comprised of introductory exercises (marching), arch-flexions (backward flexions of the trunk), heaving-movements

346

(lifting oneself by means of the arms on a bar, rope, or ladder), balance-movements (easy leg movements), shoulder-blade-movements (stretching of upper arms in respect to shoulders), abdominal exercises (raising of legs against fixed abdomen), lateral trunk-movements (lateral bending and twisting of the thorax), slow-leg movements (stretching of legs in running positions), jumping and vaulting, and respiratory exercises (arm movements in rhythm with deep respiration). Most of this was done without apparatus and was in that sense free exercise (a practice that has become a prominent feature of modern gymnastic sport). Some of it, however, was done on apparatus uniquely fashioned by Ling (most notably, Swedish boxes, stall bars, and balance beams [which also became a prominent feature of modern gymnastic sport]). The system was developed in the form of four major parts: pedagogical gymnastics (intended to create a well-balanced organism, a unity of body and will), military gymnastics (intended to raise physical proficiency in the military, to cultivate a unity of body and weapon in relation to the actions of an antagonist), medical gymnastics (intended to relieve physical disabilities, to restore the lost unity of health), and aesthetic gymnastics (intended to give bodily expression to inner emotions and thoughts, to fashion a unity of bodily and mental being).

Ling's many Swedish disciples greatly extended his work and the influence of his system. The most immediate and significant of these were:

- Lars Gabriel Branting (1799-1881), a student of Ling, who succeeded him as Director of the Institute (1839-62) and who made especially significant contributions to medical gymnastics;
- Hjalmar Frederick Ling (1820-86), son of Per Henrik, who worked at the Institute (1842-82), who made especially significant contributions to pedagogical gymnastics, who was instrumental in introducing physical education to Swedish schools, and who came to incorporate sport-like forms of game-playing in physical education programs; and
- Gustafva Lindskog (1790-1851), who became the first woman instructor at the Institute in 1848 (-51) even though formal courses for women were not introduced there until 1864.

Although Ling's legacy was profound, twentieth-century Swedish physical education, not unlike that in other developed nations of the period, expanded beyond the somewhat inflexible restrictions of gymnastic regimens to an emphasis on sports and other forms of game-playing. An international gymnastics celebration of near-Olympic proportion, the Lingiad, was nonetheless first staged (together with an international congress concerning physical training) in Stockholm on the centenary of Ling's death, 1939: the second such celebration was conducted in 1949.

The circumstance in early-to-mid nineteenth century Denmark was formally similar to that in early-to-mid nineteenth century Germany and Sweden. Political, economic, and military humiliations produced fervent nationalist and reformist sentiment in the country. Denmark was drawn begrudgingly into a regrettable alliance with France and England in the context of the Napoleonic Wars; it thereby lost Norway to Sweden in 1814. Although it obtained Greenland from Norway in 1815, Denmark fell to further political, economic, and military decline in the German-Danish War of 1864, by which Schleswig-Holstein was lost to Prussia and Austria. The project of restoring Danish national pride from this humbling turmoil fell in significant measure to the nation's foremost director of gymnastics, Denmark's leading champion of nationalistic gymnastics, and the most notable figure in nineteenth-century **Danish gymnastics**, Franz Nachtegall (1777-1847). Unlike Jahn and Ling, Nachtegall did not formulate an original system of gymnastics, adopting instead GutsMuths' naturalistic program. He nonetheless organized and directed the first modern institutions for the professional preparation of gymnastics teachers, mainly teachers of military and school gymnastics:

- his own private outdoor gymnasium in Copenhagen (1799-1804), which so inspired Ling and at which the future king of the country, Frederick VI, studied; and
- the Military Gymnastic Institute at the University of Copenhagen, established by Frederick VI in 1804.

Nachtegall was appointed Professor of Gymnastics at the University of Copenhagen (the first professorial appointment in the subject anywhere in the world) and the first Director of the Military Gymnastic Institute, both in 1804 (-42). It was principally through the Institute and under Nachtegall's leadership that Denmark became the first nation in the world to introduce physical education as an integral school subject (1801-04), the first nation in the world to organize training courses for teachers of gymnastics (1804; came to include women in 1838), and the first nation in the world to authorize, write, and distribute national manuals for physical education teachers (Manual of Gymnastics for the Village and Town Schools of Denmark, 1828, and Manual of Gymnastics and Regulations for the Secondary Schools of Denmark, 1834). In the customarily expansive style of romanticism, Nachtegall taught Latin, geography, and history as well as gymnastics and was himself especially proficient at vaulting and fencing. In the customarily nationalistic perspective of

347

nineteenth-century education, he was also convinced that broad bodily fitness is the most compelling source of national vitality and solidarity.

Although Ling's Swedish system became prominent in Denmark after 1884, it was not until the work of Niels Bukh (1880-1950) in the early twentieth century that Danish physical education broadened significantly beyond the vision of Nachtegall. As the Director of the Ollerup Gymnastic High School (mainly for young adults) from 1914 to his death in 1950 and as the author of Primary Gymnastics (1922), Bukh fashioned a dance-like system which was variously called primary, fundamental, or primitive gymnastics and which was not altogether dissimilar to Ling's in basic movement pattern and regimentation. This system differed from Ling's principally in respect to its larger emphasis on flexibility, its diminished emphasis on exercises devoted to the musculature of breathing, and its attention to the absence of held positions. Bukh crafted a progressive series of exercises that first aimed at correcting the imbalances associated with industrial life (i.e., at restoring natural harmonies), then attempted to develop the flexibility, strength, and agility commonly associated with accomplished performance in sport. He conceived of gymnastics as a noble and rational cultivation of our bodily faculties that is to be practiced throughout life. His system entailed a graceful flow, a continuity of movement, sequences of movement performed through impressively large ranges without a break. These movements resembled athletic patterns but they were performed largely without apparatus; they most significantly included marching, individual exercises, dual exercises, tumbling activities, and vaulting. Bukh greatly popularized gymnastics by way of numerous mass demonstrations that he performed throughout the world, including at five Olympic celebrations, beginning with the 1912 Games in Stockholm.

The intense nationalistic emphasis in nineteenth-century French education and physical education originated with Napoleon I, who did himself direct the establishment of a national system of public education (1799-1804). The systems of early nineteenth-century French gymnastics were largely borrowed, however. Colonel Francisco Amoros (c. 1770-1848), a Spanish refugee and military figure, established the seminal foundations of French military (and, to a lesser extent, school) gymnastics. His earliest work was done at a private gymnasium in Paris in 1817. When the military utility of this work was acknowledged in 1819, he was commissioned to organize and to direct the new Gymnase Normal Militaire et Civil, a professional preparation center for gymnastics teachers, which opened in Paris in 1820 (-34). After the Gymnase closed in 1834, Amoros continued giving instruction at his own private gymnasium in Paris to the end of his life (1834-48). His Manual d'Éducation Physique, Gymnastique et Morale (1830), which reflected the great influence of the fabled Swiss educator, Johann Heinrich Pestalozzi, established the partial basis of French military (and school) gymnastics, both of which made wide use of free exercise and exercise on apparatus. Phokion Heinrich Clias (1782-1854), an American-Swiss educator, who was himself proficient at gymnastics and swimming, also made pioneering contributions to the development of French school (and, to a lesser extent, military) gymnastics. Clias earliest work in both school and military gymnastics was done in Switzerland (1814-22), France (1817, 1819), and England (1822-25); his most mature work in both school and military gymnastics was done in France (1841-48). His An Elementary Course of Gymnastic Exercise (1825), which showed the deep influence of GutsMuths and Jahn, established the partial basis of French school (and military) gymnastics. After the Revolutions of 1848-49, Napoleon III established the Institut National de Gymnastique at Vincennes (near Paris) in 1852. Following the Franco-Prussian War (1870-71), a national and a nationalist organization of French gymnastic associations, Union des Sociétés Françaises de Gymnastique, was established in 1873 and staged annual festivals thereafter. And in 1888, a national organization devoted to physical education, Ligue Nationale d'Éducation Physique, was formed.

The two other major figures in nineteenth-century French physical education were French nationals. François Delsarte (1811-71), a teacher of vocal and dramatic activity and a popular public lecturer, devised a system of exercise designed to develop the vigor, rhythm, and poise of ideal dramatic poses and graceful gestures. This system was comprised of aesthetic movements intended to express identifiable emotions and ideas, to accompany theatrical oratory, to emphasize beauty and nobility of flowing gesture, and to make most of flexibility and relaxation. These movements were fundamentally dance-like; the system of movements constituted among the earliest explicit associations of gymnastics and dance; and the program of movements became especially prominent among women. The singularly most important figure in the French movement, however, was Pierre Frédi, Baron de Coubertin/Baron Pierre de Coubertin (1863-1937), who was mainly responsible for the establishment of the modern international Olympic movement. Coubertin, himself an avid, if unaccomplished, sportsman, also figured very significantly in the development of late nineteenth-century French physical education and sporting activity. His notion of pedagogical sport, which was drawn principally from ancient Greek and modern British models, constituted the most significant modern association of gymnastics and sport. It represented the main contribution to the increasing tendency of nineteenth-century and twentieth-century physical education to emphasize sporting activities as over and against regimens of calisthenic exercise. The most notable political motivation for Coubertin's work, the foremost source of his ardent nationalism and his fervent patriotism, was the humiliating defeats suffered by France in the Franco-Prussian War. Coubertin's reforms were intended to redress the French decline signified by the failures against Prussia.

The circumstance in England was quite different than in the Germanies, Sweden, Denmark, or France. The intensity of nationalistic sentiment most responsible for the growth of gymnastic systems in Continental Europe took a less strident form in England. England had been securely unified for centuries before the other leading European nations, for one; it did not fear foreign invasion so as the contiguous peoples of Continental Europe did, for another; and it had developed a more liberal political and cultural climate than was common in the Continental powers, for a third. Nationalistic systems of gymnastic exercise of the sort that had prospered on the Continent were therefore much less prominent in England. The English clearly preferred outdoor sporting games and track and field activities to gymnastic exercises. Sporting activity had been a prominent, if a largely informal, part of English life from the twelfth century at least, as has been said, but it was not much formalized and standardized until the schools took an interest in it in the early-to-mid nineteenth century, at which time a very large concern for organized competitive sport of a uniquely English-British sort developed.

The English-British were nonetheless not entirely insulated from the nationalistic consequences of the Napoleonic Wars, of course, and they were also a central participant in the Crimean War as well as in other international political intrigues of the nineteenth century. To the extent that they were not so insulated, they adopted some form of gymnastic system. Ling's militaristic Swedish system was brought to England in 1838 (where it gained especially large favor among women). The nationalistic German systems of GutsMuths and Jahn came to England with special affect after the Revolutions of 1848-49 (where they gained some currency particularly among men). Phokion Clias had also done some influential work in both school and military gymnastics in England from 1822 to 1825 as has been said. Among **British gymnastics** regimens themselves, only the eclectic program of the Scottish educator, Archibald Maclaren (c. 1820-84), made much of a mark. Maclaren opened a private fencing school in Oxford (c. 1850) and a private gymnasium for fencing and gymnastics also in Oxford (1858). Beginning in 1861-62, largely under the influence of the Crimean War, the military commissioned him to develop a health-dominated program of physical training for teachers of military gymnastics, the first such professional preparation program in the United Kingdom. Maclaren laid out his program of military gymnastics most notably in <u>A Military System of Gymnastic Exercises for the Use of Instructors</u> (1862). He also insisted that his system of progressive exercises on apparatus, together with recreational games, were entirely suitable for school use and that exercise constitutes an essential aspect of education. His program of school gymnastics was recorded most notably in <u>A System of Physical Education, Theoretical and Practical</u> (1869). A national organization devoted to physical education, Physical Education Association, was established in Great Britain in 1899. From at least the approximate middle of the nineteenth century, however, the physical recreative life of Great Britain was dominated instead by organized, competitive athletic contests.

The Swiss circumstance too differed substantially from the other main Continental European circumstances. Like the British, the Swiss did neither develop nationalistic gymnastic systems; its multi-lingual and somewhat decentralized political character, its policy of war neutrality, and its remote topography kept it from the sort of nationalistic attitude common elsewhere in Europe. **Swiss gymnastics** is instead best known for its ingenious contributions to innovative pedagogical uses of physical activity. The colossus of this disparate development was Johann Heinrich Pestalozzi (1746-1827), among the most articulate and influential educators of the nineteenth century. Pestalozzi, an acquaintance of Johann Wolfgang von Goethe and Johann Gottlieb Fichte, was most influenced by the pedagogical visions of Jean-Jacques Rousseau (his social advocacy of which brought him brief imprisonment) and Immanuel Kant and, in turn, had himself an especially large affect on Francisco Amoros, Johann Friedrich Herbart, Friedrich Froebel, and John Dewey. Mainly in <u>Leonard and Gertrude</u> (1781) and <u>How Gertrude Teaches Her Children</u> (1800) and mainly at the schools he directed for children (even poor children) and teachers at Burgdorf (near Berne; 1800-04) and Yverdon (near Lausanne; 1804-25), Pestalozzi worked out the theoretical and practical implications of Rousseau's and Kant's philosophies of education in experimental terms and thereby laid the foundations of modern scientific pedagogy. He made especially much of the transformative significance of education and conceived of education as an empirical method encouraging natural, individual development through concrete, active experiences. He was most fundamentally committed to a process of learning by direct and self-expressive involvement in subjects, in the beginning reduced to their primitive simples and raised progressively to more complex levels. This process was to have been elaborated through a rich variety of

349

sense experience and intellectual challenge. It was to have been ultimately devoted to a harmonious development of the thinking, feeling, willing, and social aspects of human experience. This experience, according to Pestalozzi, entailed a close relation between intellectual and physical education. Pestalozzi thus greatly favored physical education, mainly for its salutary affects on health, social character, and proportionate development. He even created a system of bodily movements arranged progressively according to difficulty and consequence, a system which also included fencing, hiking, skating, and swimming.

Pestalozzi had many immediate disciples, including Phillip Emenuel von Fellenberg (1771-1844), who appropriated the master's broad vision concerning education to create the vocational education movement in 1804 at a school in Hofwyl (near Berne). This movement wedded manual labor and exacting study for children of all classes and it prominently featured physical education (fencing, gymnastics, horse riding, and swimming). The most notable of Pestalozzi's immediate disciples, however, was the German-Swiss, Friedrich Wilhelm August Froebel (1782-1852). Froebel had studied at the University of Jena and at the University of Berlin and was thus greatly influenced by German romanticism (by Fichte, Schelling, and Hegel in particular); he was a student and colleague of Pestalozzi at Yverdon (1808-10); he became an acquaintance of Jahn in Berlin; and he participated in the Napoleonic Wars on the German side in 1813-14. He is most significantly remembered, however, for the pioneering work he did in Keilhau, Germany (near Leipzig; 1817-29), in Burgdorf (as a colleague of Spiess; variously in the 1830s), and in Blankenburg (near Keilhau; 1837-44). In the context of his teaching duties at the schools in Keilhau and Burgdorf and in his memorable book, <u>The Education of Man</u> (1826), Froebel developed the play theory of education, according to which education is best experienced through concrete, spontaneous, self-expressive, and socially grounded action. Froebel conceived of play as a natural expression of life, as a defining factor in the expression of life's unity through self-activity, and as an essential aspect of education. In the context of his teaching duties at the school in Blankenburg and in his manuscript, <u>Mother Play</u> (1844), Froebel established the seminal basis of the kindergarten movement in contemporary education. He held to the view that early childhood constitutes an utterly formative period in the development of human life and to the view that play constitutes the fundamental groundwork of this period. Both the play and kindergarten movements, themselves closely related of course, greatly favored physical education; both considered it an indispensable feature of the liberal curriculum, an awakening and a strengthening of body, intelligence, and moral compass.

The other major Swiss figure in the development of contemporary modern physical education was the Austrian-Swiss, Émile Jacques-Dalcroze (1865-1950), an accomplished teacher of music in Geneva, who formulated a system of rhythmic gymnastics, called eurythmics (movement in rhythm), intended to improve the facility of musical expression. Jacques-Dalcroze, who had studied music with no less than the remarkable Austrian composer, Anton Bruckner, and the remarkable French composer, Léo Delibes, created an effective language of rhythmic emotions for all segments of the body and their relations; every feature of the music corresponded to a specified movement. Although mainly devoted to rhythmic movements as they pertain to music, to rhythmic movements in the service of musical beauty, harmony, and creativity, the system was also eventually applied more broadly. Beginning in 1906, Jacques-Dalcroze organized training courses for teachers of eurythmics in Geneva. These courses had a very wide affect; Rudolf Bode (1881-1970), the German author of noteworthy, dance-like, expressionistic, and rhythmic gymnastic programs, and Mary Wigman, the fabled German expressive dancer-choreographer, were both students. The system also greatly influenced the pioneering Slovakian choreographer, Rudolf von Laban, and the brilliant Russian dancer-choreographer, Vaslav Nijinsky. It was among the most significant, explicit associations of art and gymnastic activity in contemporary modern civilization.

The development of contemporary modern physical education in the United States of America, the development of **American gymnastics**, was principally affected by Continental European and by local influences. Among the European influences, the German, Swedish, and Danish programs were the largest. Of these, in turn, the German system made the earliest and the most profound impact. Physical education became a regular part of the instructional program for the first time in the United States in a school that fell under the German authority, the Round Hill School in Northampton, Massachusetts. The Round Hill School was established in 1823 by Harvard University scholars, Joseph Green Cogswell (1786-1871) and George Bancroft (1800-91); it was closed in 1834. A private, college preparatory school, the Round Hill was broadly patterned after Fellenberg's Hofwyl institution; it gave individualized instruction in classical subjects, manual labors, and physical education (mainly, gymnastics, archery, boxing, dancing, ice skating, jumping, horse riding, running, swimming, vaulting, walking, wrestling, and team ball games); and it hired its first teacher of physical education, Charles Beck (1798-1866), in 1825. Beck, a German political refugee and an acquaintance of Jahn, assisted his friend, Charles Follen (1796-1840), also a German political refugee and an acquaintance of Jahn, in establishing the first college gymnasium in the United States at Harvard University (Cambridge, Massachusetts) in 1826, taught naturalistic gymnastics and Latin at Round Hill from 1825 to 1830, eventually took an academic post at Harvard, and also actively supported the abolition of slavery. It was principally Beck and Follen who introduced German naturalistic gymnastics, the gymnastics of Jahn, to the United States. The American enthusiasm for German gymnastics grew steadily from this modest beginning. The Turner's movement in the United States was further strengthened by the numerous German immigrants who came to the country in the wake of the Revolutions of 1848-49 and who brought their gymnastic enthusiasms with them. The first Turner's club, United Turnverein of North America, was established in Cincinnati in 1848; the first turnfest was held in Philadelphia in 1851; the governing body of the Turner's movement in North America, the North American Gymnastics Union, was formed in 1865; the movement's professional preparation center, the Normal School of the North American Gymnastics Union, was established in New York City in 1866; and it began publishing among the most notable nineteenth-century and twentieth-century periodicals concerning physical education, Mind and Body, in 1894 (-1935). Not unlike its European analogs, however, the movement fell into frequent public disfavor over its populist political agenda, most particularly in the periods of the American Civil War and the two World Wars. Its agitations for acceptance of physical education in the schools (which first succeeded in Cincinnati in 1855), for abolitionist causes, and for the political unification of the disparate states, together with its tendencies to German chauvinism, were the main causes of its disputes with established authority.

The Swedish system came to prominence in the United States somewhat later than the German. It was not until the 1880s that Ling's system caught hold and began to challenge the influence of the German teaching. From this time, a long-ranging debate between the two systems ensued. This debate effectively mirrored the European argument concerning the relative merits of naturalistic (largely German) and militaristic (largely Swedish) systems of gymnastics. In it, the Germans accused the Swedes of an excessive formalism; the Swedes accused the Germans of a disregard for scientific foundations. The Swedish system, like Delsarte's dance-like program of physical culture, nonetheless far surpassed the German, particularly in respect to its practice among women. The singularly most significant figure in the transplantation of Swedish gymnastics to the United States was Baron Nils Posse (1862-95). Posse variously taught the Swedish system in the Boston public schools from 1887 to 1889; was the Director and teacher of professional preparation courses concerning Swedish gymnastics at the Boston Normal School of Gymnastics (the center of Swedish gymnastics in the United States, fashioned on the model of the Royal Central Institute of Gymnastics in Stockholm where Posse had studied; 1889-1909) from 1889 to 1890; published The Swedish System of Educational Gymnastics in 1890, his seminal work concerning kinesiology, The Special Kinesiology of Educational Gymnastics, also in 1890, and the journal, Posse Gymnastic Journal, beginning in 1892 (-1915); and established his own very influential school of Swedish gymnastics, the Posse School of Gymnastics, in Boston in 1890 (-1942). The other major contributors to Swedish gymnastics in the United States were both connected to Posse and to one another. Edward Mussey Hartwell (1850-1922), a physician, had been a student of Edward Hitchcock at Amherst College (Massachusetts), taught Swedish gymnastics at Johns Hopkins University (Baltimore) from 1882, became Director of Physical Training for the Boston public schools (the first such public school title) in 1890 (-98), and is also remembered as the first major historian of modern physical education. Hartvig Nissen (1856-1924), a Norwegian-Swedish diplomat, taught Swedish gymnastics in the Washington, D.C. schools from 1883 and at Johns Hopkins University from 1887, was centrally involved in the Boston public schools from 1891 to 1900, variously taught Swedish gymnastics at Harvard University, and became Director of the Posse School of Gymnastics in 1915.

The Danish fundamental gymnastics of Niels Bukh did not make its way to the United Sates until the 1920s. Largely under the influence of Helen McKinstrey (1878-1949) in New York City, the Danish system effectively displaced the German and Swedish systems among formal regimens of calisthenic exercise, most emphatically among women. Throughout the twentieth century, however, the prominence of foreign systems of gymnastics in the United States declined steadily and the influence of local programs increased steadily. Local programs of physical education had been developing in germinal terms since the early nineteenth century in any case. The most notable contributors to the development of distinctly American programs were:

- Catharine Esther Beecher (1800-78), a sister of the celebrated abolitionist author, Harriet Beecher Stowe, of the influential clergyman, Henry Ward Beecher, as well as of several other prominent suffragettes and abolitionists, who campaigned for the educational rights and opportunities of women, who established private schools for young women (most notably, the Hartford Female Seminary in Connecticut in 1824), who persuasively championed calisthenic programs for women (which rejected German gymnastics, which included resisted and unresisted exercises without apparatus, and which also included some sporting games, but neither indulgences, dancing, dangerous games, games of chance, nor games entailing the suffering of animals), and who wrote the first American manual of physical education, A Course of Calisthenics for Young Ladies in 1832; Beecher's work and example had a profound influence on the expansion of educational franchise for women, on softening opposition to vigorous physical activity for women, on disproving false prejudices against vigorous physical activity for women, and on reforming women's fashion in ways that made vigorous physical activity more liberating;

- Diocletian "Dio" Lewis (1823-86), who was a renowned temperance and health lecturer, abolitionist, and advocate of women's rights, who was especially much influenced by Beecher, who was mainly concerned with exercise as a form of preventive medicine, who opposed German gymnastics and devised instead a formal system of light, musically accompanied gymnastics for schools called new gymnastics (comprised not of movements on heavy apparatus, but of non-sporting movements with small hand implements such as balls, clubs, dumbbells, rings, and wands, as well as of dancing, bowling, and walking), who organized the first normal school instruction in physical education in the United States at the Normal Institute of Physical Education in Boston in 1861 (-68), who established the first American periodical devoted to physical education in the United States (the short-lived Gymnastic Monthly and Journal of Physical Culture) in 1861, and who wrote among the most influential books in nineteenth-century American physical education (New Gymnastics for Men, Women and Children) in 1862;

- Edward Hitchcock (1828-1911), a physician, who was mainly concerned with exercise as a means to good health, who favored the new gymnastics of Dio Lewis and sporting games, who established the first college department of physical education in the United States at Amherst College (Massachusetts) in 1861 (where he served until his death in 1911), who was the first to hold the rank of Professor (of Hygiene and Physical Education) in the subject in the United States, who did the first authentically scientific studies concerning physical education in the United States (anthropometric studies revealing the structural consequences of exercise), and who was instrumental in founding and directing the earliest professional organizations concerning physical education in the United States (the American Association for the Advancement of Physical Education in 1885 and the Society of College Gymnasium Directors in 1897);

- Dudley Allen Sargent (1849-1924), a professional acrobat and physician, who was born to poverty and made himself arguably the most influential American physical educator of the nineteenth century; who directed physical education programs at Bowdoin College (Brunswick, Maine; 1869-75), Yale University (New Haven, Connecticut; 1873-78), and Harvard University (1879-1919); who founded and directed two of the earliest and most significant professional preparation centers for gymnastics teachers in the United States (Sargent Normal School for Physical Education, Cambridge, 1881, and Harvard Summer School of Physical Education, 1887-1932); who developed a natural system of gymnastics for men and women which rejected German gymnastics, Swedish gymnastics, and light gymnastics, which included extensive activities on innovative apparatus (much of it invented by Sargent himself), dancing, and sporting games (most notably, baseball, basketball, bowling, boxing, canoeing, cycling, fencing, field hockey, ice hockey, ice skating, rowing, soccer, swimming, tennis, track and field, and wrestling), and which was comprised mainly of individualized exercises (neither in the form of established regimens nor in the form of massed circumstance) framed according to physical need; who greatly advanced the science of physical education, principally through anthropometry, photography, and persuasive appeals for academic recognition of the subject; and who campaigned tirelessly for the reform of intercollegiate athletics (he attempted to emphasize the educational and cultural, not the competitive, values of sport, to bring sport under faculty control, and to discourage the excesses of specialization and commercialization);

- Luther Halsey Gulick (1865-1918), a physician, who did undergraduate studies with Thomas Denison Wood at Oberlin (Ohio) College in a program directed from 1886 to 1920 by Delphine Hanna (1854-1941) and who developed a very broad view of the significance of sport (in the context of play, education, and the spiritual, intellectual, and bodily unity of authentically human experience) which was expressed most memorably in his journal, Physical Education (1892-96), in his seminal work concerning the philosophy of sport, A Philosophy of Play (1918-20), and in his many administrative achievements:

- taught and later directed physical training (1887-1900) in the newly established Young Men's Christian Association (YMCA) Training School in Springfield, Massachusetts (later, Springfield College), formed in 1887; in which capacity he championed amateur sporting activity in the context of religious experience, devised the first athletic achievement test ("Pentathlon Test of the Athletic League of the YMCAs of North America," 1890), and created the famous emblem of the YMCA (the inverted triangle of spirit, mind, and body, 1890);
- directed physical education in the New York City public schools (1903-08); in which capacity he established the Public Schools Athletic League (for all boys and later [1905] for all girls as well) in 1903;
- founded and directed (1906-10) the Playground Association of America (later, the National Park and Recreation Association) in 1906; and
- founded and later directed (1910-18) the Camp Fire Girls (an outdoor recreation association for girls) in 1910.
- R. Tait McKenzie, the Canadian-American physician, educator, and sportsman, who is primarily remembered for his engaging aesthetic vision of physical education and sport, a vision in which ancient Greek sporting and artistic inclinations were brought into the relief of modern amateur sporting practice and a vision in which modern physical education and sport are connected to the full scope of the medical and art worlds, largely through the most accomplished athletic sculpture of the twentieth century, through Exercise in Education and Medicine (1909), among the most notable twentieth-century volumes concerning physical education, and through the pedagogical and administrative work he did in physical education and medicine at McGill University (Montreal; 1891-1904) and the University of Pennsylvania (Philadelphia; 1904-31).

The seminal transformation of American physical education from its domination by gymnastic systems in the nineteenth century to its domination by sporting and dancing activity in the twentieth was most conspicuously embodied in the "natural gymnastics," or "new physical education," of the early twentieth century. The "new physical education" was based on the fundamental skills of occupational, athletic, and dance movements, was play-oriented, was opposed to calisthenic regimens in general and the European gymnastic systems in particular, and was consonant with the broad aims of progressive education. The earliest major advocate of this tendency was Thomas Denison Wood (1865-1951), a physician, who (with Luther Halsey Gulick among many others of this persuasion) did undergraduate studies at Oberlin College, who taught at Stanford University (Palo Alto, California; 1891-1901) and at Teachers College, Columbia University (New York City; 1901-32), who was greatly influenced by the pragmatism and democratic progressivism of John Dewey (who also taught at Columbia University in this time, 1904-30), who embraced wide educational objectives for physical education (biological fitness, social character, agreeable recreation, and distinctly human fulfillment), and who authored (with Rosalind E. Cassidy [1895-1980]) the defining canon of the movement, The New Physical Education (1927). The other leading exponents of the "new physical education" were Clark Wilson Hetherington (1870-1942), Jay Bryan Nash (1886-1965), Jesse Feiring Williams (1886-1966), and Earle Frederick Zeigler (1919-).

The twentieth-century interest of American physical education in dancing activity (and fundamental forms of movement education) was most favorably affected by the work of Luther Halsey Gulick and Elizabeth Burchenal (1876-1959) in folk dancing, by the establishment of the American Folk-Dance Society in 1916, and by the contributions of Margaret N. H'Doubler (1889-1982) in modern, interpretive dance. The twentieth-century interest of American physical education in sporting activity as such first took the form of Play Days in which (male and female) physical education students from the same or different schools participated together in sport-like forms of game-playing. Formalization of the (fairly long-standing) **intramural sport movement** followed, first at the college and university levels, then in the elementary and secondary schools. The earliest formal programs of intramural sport were established at the University of Chicago (1912), University of Michigan (Ann Arbor; 1915), and Ohio State University (Columbus; 1915). The inter-school sport movement, which had begun in the mid-nineteenth century, came full blown in the twentieth; it formed a major chapter in the broad development of American sport in this time; and its practice also came into increasing conflict with the ideals of physical education as they had been customarily proposed to that time.

The broadening of American physical education in the nineteenth and twentieth centuries was significantly augmented by the establishment of public and college gymnasia, of professional preparation centers and laboratories for physical education, and of professional organizations and conferences concerning physical education. The principal advocate for the establishment of **public and college gymnasia** was the renowned physician and Harvard professor, John C. Warren (1778-1856), who also wrote among the first contemporary modern apologies of physical education, The Importance of Physical Education (1831). The earliest of numerous public gymnasia was the Boston Gymnasium (1826-32), first directed by Charles Follen, the German political refugee, friend of Charles Beck, and devoted acquaintance of Friedrich Ludwig Jahn. The earliest of numerous college gymnasia was the Harvard Gymnasium (1826), also first directed by Follen (with assistance from Beck). Follen was succeeded in both cases (in 1827) by the political philosopher, Francis Lieber (1800-72), also a German political refugee and devoted acquaintance of Jahn. The first **professional preparation centers for physical education** in the United States were Dio Lewis' Normal Institute for Physical Education in Boston (1861), the Normal School of the North American Gymnastics Union in New York City (1866), and the Sargent Normal School for Physical Education in Cambridge (1881). The first baccalaureate degree program in physical education (Bachelor of Science in Anatomy, Physiology, and Physical Training) was established by Harvard University in 1891; the first Master's degree program in physical education (Master of Arts) was established by Columbia University in 1901; and the first Doctor's degree in physical education (Doctor of Philosophy) was established by Columbia University in 1925. The first College of Physical Education in a university was established by the Pennsylvania State University (University Park) in 1930. And the first formal laboratory devoted to physical education (Physiological Laboratory) was established at Harvard University in 1892 by George Wells Fritz (1860-1934), a research-oriented physician tellingly influenced by Dudley Allen Sargent. The earliest of the (national) **professional organizations concerning physical education** in the United States was the American Association for the Advancement of Physical Education (later, the American Alliance of Health, Physical Education, Recreation, and Dance [AAHPERD]), established in an organizational meeting convened by William Gilbert Anderson (1860-1947) in Brooklyn, New York in 1885. Edward Hitchcock served as this organization's first president. The earliest of the (national) **conferences concerning physical education** in the United States was the first annual convention of this organization in 1886. Among the earliest and most influential periodicals in American physical education were the official organs of this organization, The American Physical Education Review (first published in 1896 and continuing throughout the twentieth century, mainly as the Journal of Physical Education, Recreation, and Dance) and The Research Quarterly (first published in 1930 and continuing throughout the twentieth century, mainly as the Research Quarterly for Exercise and Sport). Other (national) organizations and conferences followed; most notably:

- Conference in the Interest of Physical Training (also known as the Physical Training Conference of 1889) in Boston in 1889; devoted to the promotion of Swedish gymnastics; organized by Mary Hemenway (1820-94), the philanthropist who was also instrumental in the establishment of the Boston Normal School of Gymnastics, and Amy Morris Homans (1848-1933), who directed the Boston Normal School of Gymnastics from its founding in 1889 to 1918;
- Society of College Gymnasium Directors, established in an organizational meeting convened by William G. Anderson and Edward Mussey Hartwell in New York City in 1897 (later, the National College Physical Education Association for Men [NCPEAM], then merged with the National Association of Physical Education for College Women [NAPECW] to become the National Association for Physical Education in Higher Education [NAPEHE] in 1978); published among the leading periodicals in contemporary modern physical education, Quest, from 1963; Edward Hitchcock served as this organization's first president;
- Athletic Research Society, formed by Dudley Allen Sargent, Luther Halsey Gulick, and Clark Wilson Hetherington in 1907 (-24);
- National Association of Directors of Physical Education for College Women, established informally in 1909; established formally as the National Association of Physical Education for College Women (NAPECW) in 1924; merged with the National College Physical Education Association for Men (NCPEAM) to become the National Association for Physical Education in Higher Education (NAPEHE) in 1978; and
- American Academy of Kinesiology and Physical Education, formed mainly by Clark Wilson Hetherington, Jay Bryan Nash, and R. Tait McKenzie in 1926; devoted to honoring distinguished work in, and to advancing the interests of physical education.

Excepting those previously cited, these are the earliest such gymnasia, centers, laboratories, organizations, and conferences in the world. Similar institutions were later established in most of the world's other developed nations and in many of the world's developing nations. **International institutions concerning physical education** were also later and importantly formed; most notably, the International Federation of

Physical Education (1923), the International Council for Health, Physical Education, Recreation, Sport, and Dance (1958), the International Council of Sport Science and Physical Education (ICSSPE; 1958; published among the leading periodicals in contemporary modern physical education, Gymnasion/International Journal of Physical Education, from 1963), and the first International United Nations Educational, Scientific, and Cultural Organization Conference on Physical Education in Paris (1976). Throughout the twentieth century there too developed **national, continental, and world societies devoted to the scholarly study of sport** (as well as their associated conferences) in rigorous biological, psychological, sociological, artistic, historical, and philosophical terms. The most notable of these societies devoted to biological research (together with their associated journals) were the:

- German Imperial Committee for the Scientific Investigation of Physical Training (1912);
- International Federation of Sports Medicine (1928); published the Bulletin from 1934 and the Journal of Sports Medicine and Physical Fitness from 1961;
- British Association of Sport and Exercise Medicine (1953);
- American College of Sports Medicine (1954); published the American Journal of Sports Medicine/Medicine and Science in Sports and Exercise from 1954;
- Australian Sports Medicine Association (1955);
- International Society of Electrophysiology and Kinesiology (1965); published the Journal of Electromyography and Kinesiology from 1993;
- International Society of Biomechanics in Sports (1967);
- International Society of Biomechanics (1973); published the Journal of Biomechanics from 1968 (antedated the organization itself);
- American Society of Biomechanics (1977);
- International Federation of Adapted Physical Activity (1973); published the Adapted Physical Activity Quarterly from 1984;
- British Association for Sport and Exercise Sciences (1984), a confederation of scholarly subjects and organizations concerning sport; and
- North American Federation of Adapted Physical Activity (1994).

The most notable of these societies devoted to psycho-social research (together with their associated journals) were the:

- International Society of Sport Psychology (1965); published the Journal of Sport Psychology/Journal of Sport and Exercise Psychology from 1979;
- North American Society for the Psychology of Sport and Physical Activity (1966); published the Sport Psychology Bulletin from 1966 and the Journal of Motor Behavior from 1969;
- Association for the Advancement of Applied Sport Psychology (1985);
- International Committee for the Sociology of Sport (1964); published the International Review of Sport Sociology from 1966;
- North American Society for the Sociology of Sport (1978); published the Sociology of Sport Journal from 1984;
- Sports Place International (1991); published Sport Place: International Journal of Sports Geography from 1987 (antedated the organization itself); and
- North American Society for Sport Management (1985); published the Journal of Sport Management from 1987.

And the most notable of these societies devoted to humanistic research (together with their associated journals) were the:

- Sport Literature Association (1983); published Arete: Journal of Sport Literature/Aethlon: The Journal of Sport Literature from 1983;
- International Committee for History of Sport and Physical Education (1967); merged with the International Association for the History of Physical Education and Sport in 1989 to form the International Society for the History of Physical Education and Sport;
- International Association for the History of Physical Education and Sport (1973); merged with the International Committee for History of Sport and Physical Education in 1989 to form the International Society for the History of Physical Education and Sport; published the Bulletin from 1973 and Stadion: International Journal of the History of Sport from 1975;
- North American Society for Sport History (1973); published the Journal of Sport History from 1974;

- Association for the Anthropological Study of Play/Association for the Study of Play (1974); published Play and Culture from 1988;
- International Society on Comparative Physical Education and Sport (1978); published the Journal of Comparative Physical Education and Sport from 1979;
- Philosophic Society for the Study of Sport/International Association for the Philosophy of Sport (1972); published the Journal of the Philosophy of Sport from 1974; and
- International Committee of Sport Philosophy (1979).

The creation of these societies was also importantly accompanied by (in some cases preceded by) the development of a **distinguished professional research literature concerning physical education and sport**. This literature began with anthropometric and strength studies, cardio-respiratory assessments, and physical fitness indices; it progressed to work of a deeply sophisticated sort. Its earliest champions were Per Henrik Ling, Archibald Maclaren, Edward Hitchcock, and Dudley Allen Sargent, who were succeeded by accomplished physicians, educators, and scholars of virtually all manner of stripe, none more fervent nor more influential than American physiologists, Charles Harold McCloy (1886-1959) and Thomas K. Cureton, Jr. (1901-92). The earliest kinesiological-biomechanical accounts of systematic note were Baron Nils Posse's The Special Kinesiology of Educational Gymnastics (1890), William Skarstrom's Gymnastic Kinesiology (1909), and Wilbur P. Bowen's Action of Muscles (1912). The earliest exercise physiology texts of systematic note were A.V. Hill's Muscular Movement in Man (1927) and James H. McCurdy's Physiology of Exercise (1924). The earliest systematic text of note concerning motor learning was C.E. Ragsdale's The Psychology of Motor Learning (1930); concerning the psychology of sport was Coleman R. Griffith's Psychology and Athletics (1928); concerning the sociology of sport was Heinz Risse's Sociology of Sports (1921); concerning the history of sport were E. Norman Gardiner's Greek Athletic Sports and Festivals (1910) and Fred E. Leonard's Pioneers of Modern Physical Training (1910) and History of Physical Education (1923); and concerning the philosophy of sport was Luther Halsey Gulick's A Philosophy of Play (1920). From these modest, but nonetheless impressive, beginnings developed a voluminous and searching literature in essay, book, thesis, and dissertation forms concerning all aspects of physical education and sport. The periodical literature has too expanded exponentially from the modest efforts of the nineteenth century; that is, from Dio Lewis' Gymnastic Monthly and Journal of Physical Culture (1861), Luther Halsey Gulick's Physical Education (1892-96), Baron Nils Posse's Posse Gymnastic Journal (1892-1915), the North American Gymnastic Union's Mind and Body (1894-1935), and the American Association for the Advancement of Physical Education's The American Physical Education Review (1896-). Most of this literature was developed in the context of leading national, continental, and world societies devoted to the scholarly study of a major aspect of sport as has been said. Some of it, however, developed outside this context; most notably, Arbeitphysiologie (Germany, 1928), Journal of Applied Physiology (United States, 1948), Perceptual and Motor Skills (North America, 1967), Canadian Journal of History of Sport and Physical Education/Sport History Review (Canada, 1970), Review of Sport and Leisure (United States, 1976), Journal of Sport and Social Issues (United States, 1977), Journal of Teaching in Physical Education (United States, 1981), Journal of Sport Sciences (Great Britain, 1983), International Journal of Sport Biomechanics/Journal of Applied Biomechanics (United States, 1985), and Journal of Sports Economics (United States, 2000).

Likewise accompanying the development of a distinguished research literature concerning physical education and sport was the establishment of **research-oriented departments and institutes of sport studies** in higher education; most notably, in the Soviet Union, the Germanies, the People's Republic of China, the United States, Canada, Great Britain, and Australia. In the Soviet Union, the Lesgaft Institute of Physical Culture (Leningrad/St. Petersburg) was established in 1919 and the Central Institute for Physical Culture (Moscow), in 1920. In the Germanies, Die Deutsche Sporthochschule (Cologne) was re-established (from 1920-34) in 1947 and the Deutsche Hochschule fur Koerperkultur (Leipzig) was formed in 1950. In the People's Republic of China, the Shanghai Institute of Physical Culture was established in 1952 and the Beijing Institute of Physical Culture, in 1953. In the United States, many distinguished such departments were variously established or re-formed after the Second World War; most significantly, at the University of California (Berkeley), University of Illinois (Champaign), University of Iowa (Iowa City), University of Maryland (College Park), University of Massachusetts (Amherst), University of Michigan (Ann Arbor), Ohio State University (Columbus), University of Oregon (Eugene), and Pennsylvania State University (University Park); the United States Olympic Committee also came to do distinguished research concerning sport. In Canada, several outstanding such departments were too variously established after the Second World War; most significantly, at the University of Alberta (Edmonton) and the University of Western Ontario (London). In Great

Britain, the most exceptional, early such department was fashioned at the University of Loughborough in 1975. And in Australia, the most memorable development of this type was the establishment of the Australian Institute of Sport (Canberra) in 1981. Similar organizations have been since created virtually throughout the world.

As the physical education and sporting enthusiasms of western Europe eventually made their way to the Americas and beyond in the west, these enthusiasms were also eventually passed on to eastern Europe and beyond in the east; most importantly in this latter respect to Bohemia and Russia. Both the Bohemian and the Russian cases, like the main western European instances, tended to a highly nationalistic emphasis, albeit a Slavic such emphasis. The Bohemian development, **Bohemian gymnastics**, resembled the German Turner's movement in several pivotal respects. For one, it stood in political opposition to foreign oppression (that of Austria-Hungary) and thus often ran afoul of governing authority. For a second, it evoked a sense of national pride as well as an ambition for democratic reforms and for national independence; it eventually played a role in achieving Czech independence from the Austro-Hungarian Empire in 1918. And for a third, it took the principal form of gymnastic clubs devoted to moral, aesthetic, intellectual, and physical development and it was centered in the culture's most notable city (Prague). This, the Sokol (falcon) movement was first established by Miroslav Tyrs (1832-84) in 1862 (came to include women in 1869). It organized large, mass demonstrations of gymnastic skills performed in unison with and without apparatus, known as slets, which also sometimes included combative sports and folk dancing. This movement staged its first national, All-Sokol Festival in Prague in 1882; established the Bohemian Sokol Union in 1889; organized international festivals in 1891, 1895, 1901, 1907, 1912, and at irregular intervals since; formed the Slavic Sokol Association in 1912; and came, in the late nineteenth and early twentieth centuries particularly, to have a wide influence virtually throughout eastern Europe (most tellingly, in Bulgaria, Croatia, Hungary, Poland, Russia, Serbia, Slovenia, and Ukraine) as well as among Czech immigrants in Netherlands, United States, and Canada.

The leading figure in the early development of modern Russian physical education, of **Russian gymnastics**, was the noted teacher and physician, Pyotr Franzevich Lesgaft (1837-1909). Lesgaft, like many of the foremost educational and gymnastic reformers of the nineteenth and twentieth centuries, advocated a nationalistic and a liberal transformation of government and education, a transformation that was to significantly include gymnastics. Lesgaft was predictably opposed in these aims by the conservative, tsarist state in which he lived and was prevented by official authority from teaching both early and late in his career. Although unfavorably disposed to organized, competitive sport on social grounds and to the use of apparatus on scientific grounds, he was most influenced by the salutary health benefits characteristic of Swedish gymnastic exercise and British outdoor team sport. Lesgaft is best remembered, however, for his establishment of:

- the earliest professional preparation centers for men and women gymnastic teachers in Russia; the celebrated Lesgaft Institute of Physical Culture was established in his honor in Leningrad after the Bolshevik Revolution (of 1917) in 1919; and
- the scientific basis of modern Russian physical education in his two major volumes on the subject, Relationship of Anatomy to Physical Education and the Major Purpose of Physical Education in the Schools (1877) and Teaching Physical Education to School Children (1888).

The nationalistic, populist, and scientific emphasis in Russian physical education that continued after Lesgaft was owed in its original formulation to him. This formulation was deepened by the popular emphasis of the Office of the General Supervisor for the Physical Development of the People of Russia (established by the provisional government after the First Russian Revolution [of 1905] in 1913) and it was very significantly transfigured by the First World War, the Revolution of 1917, and subsequent events. In the Soviet Union, not altogether unlike other leading twentieth-century nations, physical education and sport were not merely to serve the ends of patriotic pride and to act as a means of unifying citizens in a common legacy, they were to become utter instruments of the (new) national state; they were to explicitly serve the policies of the new government. They were to be practiced by all social classes and to aim at a universal fitness, itself devoted to the efficient performance of daily labors; i.e., military, industrial, agricultural, professional, educational, and domestic labors. From 1917 to 1923, military themes dominated Russian physical culture, largely under the direction of the Department of Physical Development and Sport, which was itself a part of the Central Board of Universal Military Training (both established in 1918). After 1923, however, mainly under the direction of the first central government ministry of physical education and sport in the world (the Supreme Council of Physical Culture of the Russian Soviet Federated Socialist Republic, established in 1923; later, the All-Union Council of Physical Culture and Sports Affairs), the Soviet Union emphasized socialization agendas and, from

1929-36, began its long and impressive journey to world sporting supremacy. The form of this journey also had a profound affect on (was a virtual model for) the physical culture and sporting programs of the other major communist nations, most particularly since the Second World War. Many of these nations likewise counted themselves among the foremost sporting states in the world: Bulgaria, People's Republic of China, Cuba, Czechoslovakia, Ethiopia, East Germany, Hungary, North Korea, Poland, and Romania.

The broadening of contemporary modern physical education from gymnastic regimens to sport-like forms of game-playing was also greatly influenced by three as-yet-unmentioned, non-school developments closely related to physical education and sport: 1) muscular religiosity; 2) the playground, recreation, and camping movement; and 3) the health, hygiene, fitness, and strength movement. **Muscular religiosity** entailed the cultivation by organized religion of sporting (and other vigorous secular) activities for the purpose of promoting religious values, moral character, and socially edifying behavior. It was mainly aimed at combating delinquency and discouraging unsavory sexual practices among youth; it constituted a significant reversal of religion's earlier antipathy for sport; it tended to nationalistic, Darwinist, and amateur perspectives; and it was most influential in Christian and Jewish communities (thus, muscular Christianity and muscular Judaism). Many distinguished intellectuals, social reformers, and even religious leaders (such as, Henry Ward Beecher [1813-87], a brother of Catharine Esther Beecher and of Harriet Beecher Stowe) came to enthusiastically advocate the practice of decent physical education and sport in the late nineteenth and early twentieth centuries. The principal organizations embodying this tendency were the Young Men's Christian Association (YMCA), created by George Williams (1821-1905), an English clerk, in Great Britain in 1844; the Young Men's Hebrew Association (YMHA), established in the United States in 1854; the Young Women's Christian Association (YWCA), established in Great Britain in 1855; the Young Women's Hebrew Association (YWHA), established in the United States in 1888; and the Catholic Youth Organization (CYO), established in the United States in 1930. Of these, the YMCAs and the YWCAs had by far the largest affect, achieving a presence virtually throughout the world, but most significantly in Great Britain, Canada, United States, China, Korea, Japan, India, Philippines, Brazil, Czechoslovakia, France, Switzerland, and Greece.

The **playground, recreation, and camping movement** was closely allied with social welfare campaigns of the late nineteenth and early twentieth centuries, campaigns that tended to reinforce conventional values, to fashion a sense of order among the youth of working poor in turbulent cities, and to provoke sharp debate about public finance and land use. The seminal developments of this movement occurred mostly in the United States and took several main forms, all of which actively promoted sporting activity:

- public playgrounds, first in Boston (1872);
- national public parks, the first of which, Yellowstone (in Idaho, Montana, and Wyoming; 1872), was governed by the National Park Service, established by the administration of President Ulysses S. Grant, also in 1872;
- municipal public parks, first in Chicago (Washington Park; 1876);
- settlement houses (community recreation programs), first in New York City (1886) and Chicago (1889); the most notable of these was Hull House, established in Chicago in 1889 by Jane Addams (1860-1935), a prominent American social reformer and co-recipient of the 1931 Nobel Peace Prize;
- the principal national governing body of the movement, the Playground Association of America, formed in 1906, largely by Luther Halsey Gulick with strong support from President Theodore Roosevelt;
- the principal national governing body of the camping phase of the movement, the Camp Directors' Association (later, the American Camping Association), formed in 1910; and
- various private agencies for youth; most notably:
  - the Big Brothers Movement (1904) of Danish-American journalist, social reformer, foremost anti-slum advocate, and legendary photographer, Jacob Riis;
  - the Youth Hostel Movement, which began in Germany in 1904;
  - the Boys' Clubs of America (1906);
  - the Boy Scouts (1908) of British soldier, Robert Stephenson Smyth Baden-Powell (1857-1941);
  - the Outing Clubs (outdoor recreation clubs; 1910);
  - the Camp Fire Girls (1910) of Luther Halsey Gulick; and
  - the Girl Scouts (1912) of American social activist, Juliette Magill Kinzie Gordon "Daisy" Low (1860-1927).

This movement has since had a wide development virtually throughout the world.

The **health, hygiene, fitness, and strength movement** too had a very broad following in the late nineteenth century and throughout the twentieth. Its formative development was most affected by the views of biological science concerning disease, the mechanism of the body, and the restorative-corrective consequences of exercise; by unfavorable military conscription data (particularly in respect to the two World Wars) which demonstrated the broad need for physical fitness and hygiene in respect to military, labor, and children's health issues; and by a fascination with powerful physique (as the most conspicuous expression of health). The documentary canon of the movement was William Blaikie's <u>How to Get Strong and How to Stay So</u> (1879). The movement's earliest champions were also variously implicated in the contemporary modern development of bodybuilding, weightlifting, and wrestling:

- American weightlifting enthusiast and strength advocate, George Barker Winship (1834-76), lectured widely throughout the United States concerning the virtues of heavy strength gymnastics;
- Prussian-English-American strongman, Eugen Sandow/Friedrich Wilhelm Mueller (1867-1925), campaigned extensively in Europe and America for the acceptance of heavy gymnastics, largely by performing astounding feats of strength, and gave fitness instruction to no less than George V of Great Britain; and
- American journalist and physical culturalist, Bernarr Macfadden (1868-1955), greatly advanced the cause of physical fitness among men and women by almost any conventional or exotic means, explicitly opposed light, in favor of strength gymnastics, and began publishing the influential, if specious, periodical, <u>Physical Culture</u>, in 1899 (-1940).

Arguably its main twentieth-century manifestations were the establishment of national organizations concerning physical fitness (such as, the Central Council of Recreative Physical Training, Great Britain, 1935; the National Council for Physical Fitness, Australia, 1941; and the President's Council on Youth Fitness, United States, 1956) and mass participation in virtually all manner of fitness activity, particularly since the Second World War.

Contemporary modern athletics to the First World War

The second of the two main fronts on which the maturation of modern sport unfolded, athletics as such, developed largely, but not entirely, in non-school circumstance. By the rough middle of the nineteenth century, first in Victorian Britain, then in the main colonies/dominions or former colonies/dominions of Great Britain (most notably, Ireland, Australia, Canada, New Zealand, South Africa, India, British West Indies, and United States of America), then in western Continental Europe (mainly, France, Netherlands, Germany, Austria-Hungary, Scandinavia, Italy, and Spain), eastern Europe (mainly Bohemia, Poland, and Russia), South America (mainly, Argentina), the Middle East (mainly, Palestine and Egypt), west Africa (mainly, Nigeria), east Africa (mainly, Kenya), and east Asia (mainly, China and Japan), then elsewhere, the formal conditions of sport's contemporary institutional development were firmly in place. It is at about this time that competitive circumstances were first widely standardized by the uniform codification of sporting rules, sporting facilities, and sporting equipment; that the terms of (much) sporting performance first became technically quantifiable, measurable, and verifiable; and that sport governing bodies of national and international scope were first formed. The organizational triumph of contemporary modern sport itself stands on these developments, albeit developments which diminished the significance of local, regional, and folk practices. It is on the basis of these developments that sport has come to its current form, has become a firmly entrenched social institution, and has become an integral expression of a well disposed person and society. The formalization of sporting rules began in earnest with the establishment of local (written) rules, out of oral reminiscences, by British sporting clubs in the eighteenth century (as has been said) and it was expanded in the nineteenth century under the influence of nationalistic, technological, and commercial tendencies. The vast expansion of national and international sport, of professional sport, of gambling interests in respect to sport, of exertions to bring institutional control over human activities, and of commercial concerns among sporting goods firms required a larger sense of formalization and standardization than had been achieved in the eighteenth century. Technological advances (such as the standardization of measures and the stop-watch) made the precise measurement of sporting performance more reliable as well as more useful for gambling and commercial promotions; these advances also made sport more nearly resemble the alienations of industrial work but they too made it possible to define sporting performance in terms that made it potentially more edifying for humanistic ends (as a more exacting basis for achievement and fulfillment); and they fueled as well the quest for records that characterizes much of contemporary modern sport. National and international sport governing bodies regulated the maintenance and revision of rules (which included eligibility standards for athletic participation), supervised the just, equitable, and uniform administration of rules and of the contests ordered by rules, organized national and international sporting competitions, and validated records.

Sporting practices from the early nineteenth century to the First World War continued to develop, as had earlier formal and informal types of modern sport, in the context and form of class society. These practices are perhaps most profitably spoken of in such a perspective, as aristocratic and bourgeois sport, pedagogical (or student) and proletarian (or worker) sport, professional sport, military sport, and national and international amateur sport. Contemporary modern **aristocratic and bourgeois sport** was dominated by both old and new wealth, but increasingly by those of newly won industrial affluence. The triumphs of capital industrialism produced a class of persons, many of modest origins, who often made quick and very large fortunes in such as the timber, coal, oil, iron-steel, railroad, manufacturing, banking, and publishing industries. These persons were deeply competitive in an adversarial sense; they subscribed to the precepts of social Darwinism in which the strong (and wealthy) justifiably prevail over (as well as reign over) the weak (and poor); and they ardently endorsed the notion of conspicuous consumption. Although the sporting practices of this class would in some respects eventually be passed on to the middle and lower classes, mainly in the twentieth century, the dominant nineteenth-century upper-class tendency was to emphasize sporting activities that were readily available only to itself, only to those of substantial wealth and leisure, and to emphasize a system of sporting values that was likewise available only to those of extraordinary means. Contemporary modern aristocratic and bourgeois sport thereby:

- isolated and insulated itself from the popular sporting games of the lower classes;
- established exclusive athletic clubs (as well as country houses, country clubs, and châteaux) for the purpose of achieving this aim and of demonstrating its superiority over other forms of sport practiced by the lesser classes; the earliest and most notable of these many clubs were the Olympic Club of San Francisco (1863), London Athletic Club (1866), New York Athletic Club (1868), Chicago Athletic Club (1871), Young Men's Gymnastic and Athletic Club of New Orleans (1872), and Hungarian Athletic Club (Budapest, 1875); and
- developed the notion of amateurism in sport which it reserved for itself (and for its school analogs).

The leading upper-class sports of the period were thoroughbred and harness horse racing, polo, blood sports, yachting/sailing, cycling, tennis, golf, croquet, mountain climbing, automobile racing, hydroplane racing, figure and speed skating, and, to a lesser extent, baseball, billiards, bowling, cricket, curling, and shooting. Boxing, rowing, and track and field, although not the distinct prerogative of the ruling classes, were nonetheless also a prominent feature of the sporting recreations of these classes.

The growth of organized sport in educational institutions (so-termed pedagogical, or student, sport) and in athletic organizations for the working class (so-called proletarian, or worker, sport) was also extraordinary throughout the nineteenth century and in the early twentieth century (most particularly from the middle of the nineteenth century to the First World War). This growth occurred first at the (non-school) club, public (preparatory) school, college, and university levels in Great Britain and North America, then elsewhere, and later it occurred at the secondary and elementary school levels in these, then in other countries-regions. It occurred, moreover, under the basically amateur disposition of the upper classes, which were, in turn, often themselves tangibly involved in the conduct of student and working-class sporting activities. The sporting practices and sporting values of aristocratic-bourgeois precinct thus had a powerful, if not altogether dominating, affect on formal types of student and working-class sport, as well as on the typically less formal recreations of inns, taverns, fairs, festivals, streets, sandlots, parks, playgrounds, and municipalities often associated with student and working-class life. In any case, sport with a largely participatory emphasis was made progressively more widely available to both student and working-class persons throughout this period.

Pedagogical sport, which was far more prominent in Great Britain and in the United States than elsewhere in the world, first developed in the form of inter-class contests within English public schools and universities and within North American colleges and universities in the early nineteenth century. It then came to feature inter-school contests in these schools, colleges, and universities, mainly in the form of student-sponsored and alumni-sponsored athletic clubs in cricket-baseball, rugby-football, rowing, track and field, and basketball. In the United States, sport was taken fully into the schools and made a constituent part of them; it was effectively managed as a feature of the (extra-) curriculum. Elsewhere in the world (even in Great Britain), sporting clubs became (or remained) affiliated with the schools (or with communities in which schools were located) but they did not typically become features of the schools themselves in the strong sense. Prospects for the corruption of school sport, it turns out, were far greater in the United States than elsewhere, largely because the schools themselves (as well as their sporting attributes) were less regulated by government authorities in the common interest; the schools were consequently and almost entirely taken over by the dominant commercial emphasis of the culture; and new types of schools devoted to practical concerns (such as agricultural, mining, military, technological, and pedagogical pursuits), to expanding educational opportunities for all classes, races, and genders, and to an elective principle of curriculum were widely established. Sport had become an immensely popular aspect of American college and university life by the 1870s; it had become an integral aspect of such life by the 1880s; and it had become the most important unifying aspect of such life by the 1890s, by which time it was the principal mark of institutional prestige, the principal basis for public support, and a major element in fiscal prosperity. It likewise contributed significantly to the increasing popularity of higher education itself in the late nineteenth and early twentieth centuries.

As the commercial success and the esteem of college and university sport expanded, however, so also did its injury to the central, to the educational, mission of schools. The corruption of American school sport took many unseemly forms; most notably, participation by pseudo-students and pseudo-coaches, rank partisanship, gambling scandals, violence, excessive inducements, alumni interference, distortion of academic principles, amateur-professional disputes, blatant commercialism, excessive travel expenses, and recruiting irregularities. As these abuses accumulated, school sport was brought increasingly and predictably under the supervision of educational authorities, first in the 1870s by athletic associations and athletic managers (the earliest of which were established at Harvard University and Princeton University in 1874 and 1876 respectively), then in the 1880s by the faculty itself. The first attempts to control school sport for men by means of faculty direction (to fashion school sport in accord with distinctly educational prescriptions) were made by the Princeton Committee (1881), the Harvard Committee (1882), and the Intercollegiate Athletic Conference (1883), a meeting of faculty athletic representatives (most notably, those of Princeton [New Jersey], Harvard [Cambridge, Massachusetts], and Cornell [Ithaca, New York]). These efforts attempted to eliminate professional coaches and athletic scholarships, control training and competitive schedules, promote amateurism, monitor athletic eligibility, limit commercialism, and promote winning. They led, in turn, to the establishment of athletic conferences, groups of like-minded and similarly constituted institutions devoted to a responsibly educational administration of all intercollegiate sports. The earliest of these was the New York State Intercollegiate Athletic Association (mainly, Cornell, Rochester, Syracuse, and Union [Schenectady]) of 1885; the most illustrious was the Intercollegiate Conference of Faculty Representatives (later, the Western Conference, then the Big-Ten Conference; mainly, Chicago, Illinois, Michigan, Minnesota, Northwestern, Purdue, and Wisconsin) of 1895. Numerous other attempts were also made before the First World War to reform American intercollegiate sport; most notably, the Brown Conference on Intercollegiate Sports (1898), which failed, and the White House Conference on Football (1905), which led to the formation of the national governing body of American intercollegiate sport, the Intercollegiate Athletic Association (later, the National Collegiate Athletic Association [NCAA]), in 1905. The first serious attempt to control American school sport for women (to fashion it in accord with distinctly educational prescriptions) was achieved by the Women's Athletic Association at Bryn Mawr (Pennsylvania) College in 1891. The earliest attempt to control American interscholastic sport for men (to fashion it in accord with distinctly educational prescriptions) was achieved in Wisconsin in 1896. Although these attempts muted some of the worst abuses, they fell well short of eliminating them. Weak faculties, the dominant influence of alumni (mainly via governing boards), and economic necessities assured that American school sport would continue to profess amateur values (in order to leave the public impression, howsoever false, of educational merit) and to promote commercial-professional orientations. The importunate abuses inherent in school sport of this type and the bitter debate about their less-than-salutary influences on schools have continued to our own time.

Proletarian sport, which was far more prominent in Europe than elsewhere in the world, first developed in such as inns, taverns, fairs, festivals, streets, sandlots, parks, playgrounds, municipal agencies, and industrial organizations. It then established formal clubs and broad governing organizations for approximately the same sports that were of greatest interest to students. The rise of modern labor and contemporary socialism in the late nineteenth and early twentieth centuries spawned the development of a sporting movement explicitly associated with distinctly working-class experience and distinctly working-class values. This movement attempted to distinguish itself from, and to oppose, aristocratic-bourgeois practices and its participants were often the object of severe discrimination by the power elite. Its governing body, the Socialist International of Physical Education (later, the Socialist Workers' Sports International), was established in Belgium in 1913 and the movement was most prominent in Germany (where it came into significant conflict with the Turner's movement), England, Finland, Russia, France, Austria, Palestine, Sweden, Norway, and Canada. Arguably the most telling of these cases before the First World War (particularly in view of what was coming at the end of the War) was the Russian. In the period following the First Russian Revolution (in 1905), the prior domination of Russian sport by the aristocratic-bourgeois classes (the effective exclusion of others from sporting recreation) was slightly modified. In an attempt to improve the broad domestic state of physical culture and the international record of sport performance, the government established the Office of the General Supervisor for the Physical Development of the People of Russia in 1913 and conducted Russian Olympiads in Kiev and Riga in 1913 and 1914 respectively. The most prominent forms of student and working-class sports of the contemporary modern period to the First World War were football (in various forms, including rugby and soccer), rowing, track and field, cricket-baseball, and basketball. Many other sports were nonetheless also played, on a lesser scale, in the schools and working-class organizations of this period; most notably, archery, badminton, billiards, bowling, boxing, cycling, fencing, field hockey, golf, gymnastics, ice hockey, lacrosse, shooting, skiing, swimming, tennis, volleyball, weightlifting, and wrestling.

Professional sport of the contemporary modern variety was likewise becoming firmly established in the period from the middle of the nineteenth century to the First World War. This form of sporting activity grew out of an entrepreneurial interest in sport's commercial possibilities by the capital class and out of rising middle-class wealth and leisure that could support the spectatorial emphasis of the activity. Although they attracted investors from all social classes, early contemporary professional sporting institutions were organized by entrepreneurs and their political allies in government and in crime as cartels for the profit and prestige of the power elite. These institutions were also devoted to gambling associations, given to corruption in the service of private gain, and oriented to the bachelor sub-culture of the time. Most professional athletes had worked for wages; they were thus, by definition, of the working class; they became increasingly specialized and skillful performers; they were tightly controlled by owners in terms of mobility, compensation, and security; and they often "retired" to poverty. Spectators assembled in increasing numbers (up to c. 20,000 in the early-to-mid nineteenth century), were increasingly impractical in terms of the emphasis put on win-loss records, increasingly interfered with and otherwise influenced the results of sporting contests, and increasingly behaved in disorderly and violent ways. The new professionalism (not unlike the pre-industrial variety) was also predictably at significant odds with the new amateurism. The legendary and persistent disputes between professional and amateur sporting institutions most challenged the amateur side of the distinction. The amateur ideal, which was mainly of aristocratic-bourgeois origin, had prospered only in activities requiring imposing resource or in activities unattractive to large numbers of spectators. In any case, amateurism was increasingly and adversely affected by the instrumental (principally the commercial) character of professional sport. Even amateur sport itself gradually took on the ideological clothing of professionalism; broken-time payments (compensation for wages lost due to sporting participation), for prominent instance, were fairly common practice in amateur sport, even in the amateur sport of Great Britain, by the mid-nineteenth century. The two most prominent professional sports of this period (discounting horse racing) were boxing and baseball, although cycling, pedestrianism, wrestling, (American-rules) football, ice hockey, and rugby had also developed notable professional forms by the First World War.

Military and paramilitary organizations likewise increasingly formalized their commitment to sporting activities and increasingly promoted and sponsored such activities throughout the nineteenth and early twentieth centuries, most emphatically in periods of major industrial warfare from the middle of the nineteenth century. The commitment of official resource to sporting programs within the military and the formalization of such programs within the military, effectively **military sport**, expanded by unprecedented degree in this period. Military respect for sport as a means to bodily health, as a diversion from the brutalities of military life, and as a preparation for war (as a form of miniature battlefield) rose very substantially from the middle of the nineteenth century to the First World War. The most widely practiced forms of military sport in this time were cricket-baseball, boxing, fencing, rugby-football, soccer, track and field, and wrestling.

It is also in the contemporary modern period to the First World War that sporting activities, most especially amateur activities, were first organized on a national and international basis. Sport became an immensely powerful influence on national identity and international prestige in this period. The advent of **national and international amateur sport** was most conspicuously signified by the development of national multi-sport governing bodies and international multi-sport competitions. The most significant of the **national multi-sport governing bodies** were the National Association of Amateur Athletes of America (later, the Amateur Athletic Union [AAU]), United States, 1879; the Amateur Athletic Association of Canada (later, the Amateur Athletic Union of Canada), 1884; the Gaelic Athletic Association (GAA), Ireland, 1884; the Union des Sociétés Françaises des Sports Athlétiques, France, 1890; and the German Sports Federation, 1891. The most notable of the **international multi-sport competitions** were the **Nordic Games** (Nordische Spiele), winter celebrations which began in Stockholm in 1901 (-26); the Inter-Empire Games, which were staged in conjunction with the coronation of George V of Great Britain in London in 1911, which were preceded by the unsuccessful proposals of 1891-94 to hold Anglo-Saxon Olympiads, or Pan-Brittanic Gatherings, and which were the precursor of the British Empire and Commonwealth Games; the YMCA-inspired **Far Eastern Games**, the first multi-sport continental championships, which were first staged in Manila in 1913 (-34); the Baltic Games, which were first staged in Malmo, Sweden in 1914; and the Olympic Games. These bodies and competitions were most notably devoted to conducting athletic competition in archery, cycling, fencing, gymnastics, rowing, shooting, soccer, swimming, tennis, track and field, weightlifting, and wrestling.

Of the rich panoply of sporting developments that marked the late nineteenth and the early twentieth centuries, none is more significant to the history of sport than the modern international Olympic movement. There had been many **abortive attempts to revive the ancient Olympic Games**, several of which had an especially profound affect on the successful revival of the Games in the late nineteenth century. The earliest of these were the **Cotswold Games**, or Olympick Games, initiated by Captain Robert Dover at Dover's Hill (near Stratford), England in 1604 and variously carried on until 1857 (revived in 1951). These Games most notably included wrestling, leaping, pitching the bar, throwing the hammer, and tossing the pike as has been said. The other major pre-industrial multi-sport festival that survived into contemporary modern civilization and that also importantly influenced the formation of the modern international Olympic movement were the **Highland Games**. These Games, which began in eleventh-century Scotland and which were significantly implicated in eighteenth-century, nineteenth-century, and twentieth-century Scottish nationalism, were mainly devoted to track and field athletic forms of exertion (principally to various forms of heavy-implement throwing for distance and height, such as weight throwing, hammer throwing, stone putting, and caber tossing). They established their most notable, strictly athletic meeting, the Braemar (Royal Highland Society) Gathering, in 1817 (other such meetings followed shortly thereafter); from c. 1820, they also became prominent outside Scotland (most tellingly, in Canada, United States, Australia, and New Zealand), where they were often known as Caledonian Games; in 1867, they staged a major international club meeting in New York City, the Great International Caledonian Games; and they have continued a vibrant practice to our own time.

Also contributing significantly to the revival of the ancient Games were several early and contemporary modern attempts to conduct **archaeological excavations at ancient Olympia**. The earliest of these were inspired by eighteenth-century Enlightenment classicism/neo-classicism and were largely unsuccessful. French Benedictine scholar, Bernard de Montfaucon (1655-1741) had failed to gain support for excavations in 1723; British archaeologist, Richard Chandler (1738-1810), had done some preliminary work in 1766; and German scholar, Johann Joachim Winckelmann (1717-68), among the leading figures in the seminal development of modern archaeology, was murdered en route to Olympia in 1768. Although periodic British and French visits continued with modest successes into the early nineteenth century, it was not until after the Greek triumph over the Ottoman Empire in the Greek War of Independence (1821-29) that a fervent concern for unearthing the treasures of ancient Greece developed. The fame and sympathy won for Greece in the War, the growing sophistication of archaeological scholarship, and the neo-classical/romantic inclinations of the period conspired to produce an ardent interest in ancient Greek culture (including ancient Greek sport). German scholar, Ernst Curtius (1814-96), did the first systematic excavations of Olympia in 1875. Such excavations have continued sporadically since and have contributed very notably to rekindling interest in the Olympic Games. Among the most prominent educational and cultural leaders of the late eighteenth and early nineteenth centuries (most notably, Jean-Jacques Rousseau, Johann Bernhard Basedow, and Johann Friedrich GutsMuths), also spoke of the ancient Olympic Games; some even advocated their revival.

The fascination with reviving the ancient Olympic Games was greatly advanced by these achievements. In Greece, the poet, Panagiotis Soutsos (1806-66), repeatedly but unsuccessfully attempted, between 1835 and 1861, to reestablish the Games as sporting, intellectual, and artistic contests, largely by appeal to King Otto I. Major Evangelis Zappas (1800-65), a wealthy Greek-Romanian merchant, who had been much influenced by Soutsos, donated immense sums and erected an impressive building ("Zappeion," Athens) for the purpose of reviving the Games. The first celebration of Zappas' efforts, the **Pan-Hellenic Games**, which were endorsed and attended by Otto I, was staged in Athens in 1859. This celebration was, however, open only to Greek citizens, included only four events (the rough equivalent of a 200 yards dash, a two mile run, a triple jump, and a discus throw), and was a disorderly failure. The ancient Panathenaic Stadium, which became the primary stage for the first modern Olympic Games in Athens in 1896, was excavated and partially restored for the second celebration of Zappas' efforts in 1870. Unlike the first spectacle, the 1870 affair was a great success. It included agricultural and industrial contests as well as sporting events (mainly, track and field and gymnastic events); fashioned an Olympic hymn; and awarded cash prizes which were conferred by King George I. The third of these celebrations, in 1875, was a fiasco. It had primarily to do with agricultural and industrial exhibitions; nonetheless included sporting contests in track and field, gymnastics, and wrestling;

and permitted the participation only of upper-class youth, thus prohibiting the participation of working men. The fourth and last of these celebrations, in 1888, was a strictly agricultural and industrial exhibition; it included no sporting contests. The Panhellenic Gymnastic Society, which was formed in 1891, nonetheless conducted Pan-Hellenic Games in 1891 and 1893. The would-be Games of 1892, which were to have been the first quadrennial celebration under formal government auspices (directed by Crown Prince Constantine; later, King Constantine I), were aborted.

Elsewhere, the movement to revive the ancient Games was most incisive in England, principally owing to the ventures of William Penny Brookes (1809-95). Brookes, a physician and philanthropist, organized the Much Wenlock (near Birmingham) Olympian Society in 1850. The Society was devoted to the moral, intellectual, and physical improvement of the working class and it conducted annual **Much Wenlock Olympian Games** from 1850 to 1890. These Games were much influenced by Zappas' efforts in Greece and they would have an enormous (perhaps a formative) affect on Coubertin's views of pedagogical and Olympic sport. They were significantly provoked by the amateur-professional disputes of the period and awarded cash prizes; they were involved in promoting physical education in the schools; and they incited Brookes to propose the revival of international Olympic Games in Athens no later than 1880, very significantly before Coubertin's similar proposals of the 1890s. The Much Wenlock Olympian Games variously included a parade of athletes, victory ceremonies, considerable pageantry associated with ancient Greek cultural and sporting symbols, and non-sporting (for both boys and girls) as well as sporting events, all conspicuous marks of the modern Olympic Games themselves. The most prominent of the sporting events were footraces (of approximately 200, 400, and 1500 meters for adult men, special races for boys under fourteen years of age, and special races for boys under seven years of age), a 50 yards hopping race, jumping contests (long jumping, triple jumping, and high jumping), pole climbing, discus throwing (for distance and height), javelin throwing (for distance and accuracy), tilting, chariot racing, and cricket, football, and quoits matches. Likewise in England in the mid-to-late nineteenth century, the Liverpool Olympic Games were staged in 1862, 1863, 1864, 1865, 1866, and 1867 and the London Olympic Games, in 1866. The London celebration included athletic contests in track and field, gymnastics, swimming, boxing, wrestling, and fencing; the Liverpool celebrations included athletic contests in the same activities save swimming. In North America, the Toronto Olympic Games were staged in 1838, the Montreal Olympic Games were conducted in 1844, and the New York Olympic Games were held in 1853. The lot of the Greek, English, Canadian, and American efforts, however, never gained much larger than local favor and none survived the century.

The principal architect of the movement that succeeded in reviving the ancient Olympic Games in modern, international, and enduring terms, the principal architect of the **modern international Olympic movement**, was the French aristocrat, Baron Pierre de Coubertin (near Versailles). As was fairly typical of wealthy French youth of his time, Coubertin was educated at conservative Catholic and military schools in Paris; he then won baccalaureate degrees in the arts, the sciences, and law from the University of Paris and did post-graduate studies at the Free School of Political Science in Paris. Coubertin was nonetheless unimpressed with the inflexible, dogmatic, and unathletic character of his early education in particular and vowed to connect himself to a great educational reform. This reform was intended to redress the French decline signified by the humiliations of the Franco-Prussian War of 1870-71, to transfigure the archaic French educational system partially responsible for these humiliations, to promote a progressive, national type of compulsory, free, secular, and public education in which the humanities and sport were to count very prominently, and to fashion an international movement aimed at promoting physical education throughout the world and at invigorating the youth of the world. The models for this reform and the models which provided the **ideological groundwork of modern Olympism** were based principally in ancient Greek and in modern British culture, education, and sport. From ancient Greek humanism, Coubertin took the notions of excellence, goodness, virtue, beauty, peace, and harmony as the basis of an educational ideal which included sport as an essential component. By this view, sport must always be practiced to the end of enlightenment; that is, to effect high skill, grace of form and movement, proportionate development of intellectual and physical faculties, and right conduct in all persons. It must be directed to honorable and creative purposes, serve human dignity and progress, and contribute substantially to interpersonal, intercultural, and international accord.

The modern British influence was embodied in the English public school and university system. Coubertin's knowledge of this system came largely from his childhood reading of Thomas Hughes' (1822-96) celebrated Tom Brown's School Days (1857), from his university studies, and from his several English journeys (first in 1884). The Hughes volume depicted the teaching and example of Dr. Thomas Arnold (1795-1842), father of the remarkable English realist poet, essayist, and critic, Matthew Arnold, headmaster of the public school, Rugby (near Birmingham), from 1828 to 1842, and himself an accomplished classical scholar.

Arnold's pedagogy wedded an education in ancient Graeco-Roman studies and modern mathematics, language, and history with muscular Christianity; it aimed at moral and optimistic discipline that was to teach individual responsibility, confidence, loyalty, and sportsmanship; and it thus embodied a character-building view of recreational sport. Coubertin was convinced that the vigor, wealth, and power of Great Britain were due largely to its unique educational system. He was likewise convinced that the French system, not unlike the French state, paled in comparison. Among the principal differences between the English and French circumstances was the commitment of the former to pedagogical sport.

Coubertin's notion of pedagogical sport, which formed the seminal philosophic basis of the modern international Olympic movement, constitutes the single most significant modern association of gymnastics/physical education and sport. Its novel embrace of the nationalistic, evolutionistic, and romantic tendencies of the nineteenth century framed the formative philosophy of modern Olympism. Coubertin portrayed this philosophy (late in his life) as embodying the essential characteristics of religion, peace, and beauty indissolubly united and indissolubly devoted to the perfection of humanity. He was of the view that no religion (or philosophy) teaches more noble human lessons than those taught by the codes of amateur athletic competition, that these codes thereby constitute a form of moral pedagogy, and that the modern international Olympic adoption of these codes brings Olympism to a sense of piety, reverence, inspiration, fulfillment, and vitality reminiscent of religious sentiment at its broad best. He was also of the view that modern Olympism promotes magnanimity and world peace through the cultivation of mutual friendship and mutual understanding among the diverse peoples of the world. And he was too convinced that modern Olympism raises sport to a sense of art and beauty, to an authentic sense of unified harmony among our various intellectual and physical attributes, to a genuine sense of appealing proportion in respect to form, movement, and character, to a dramatic sense of intrinsic excellence embodying aesthetic qualities. The Games themselves have come to include, at Coubertin's insistence and beginning in 1912, competitions and exhibitions in the arts (variously in architecture, sculpture, painting, literature, theater, dance, music, and opera) on sporting subjects; they have embodied an explicit sense of aesthetic appeal in terms of the sports that have been included in them and in terms of the victory ceremonies/rituals associated with distinguished performance in these sports; and they have aimed at aesthetic considerations in their crafting of opening and closing ceremonies/rituals.

The **institutionalization of modern Olympism** was especially much affected by the example of the Highland Games and by the many abortive attempts to revive the ancient Games; most notably, by William Brookes' Much Wenlock Olympian Games (the 1890 version of which was attended by Coubertin), themselves significantly affected by Evangelis Zappas' Pan-Hellenic Games. It was nonetheless mainly Coubertin who marshaled these (and other) inspirations to the end of tangibly establishing the institutional framework of the modern international Olympic movement. Coubertin had been involved in educational and sporting reform for several years before his successful revitalization of Olympism. He had been the Secretary-General (the principal working officer) of the Committee for the Propagation of Physical Exercises in Education and of the first International Congress for the Promotion of Physical Education. The 1888 conference of this Committee in Paris attempted to forge an effective alliance between French sport and French culture, to examine the prospect of introducing Arnoldian pedagogy to French education, and to propose the restoration of French national vitality through physical education and sport. The International Congress of 1889, also in Paris, proposed the internationalization of the principles adopted for French sport, education, and culture at the 1888 conference. Coubertin was, likewise in 1889, dispatched to North America by the Ministry of Public Instruction for the purpose of preparing a report on life (including sporting life) in American colleges and universities. While in North America, he also participated in the Physical Training Conference of 1889 in Boston, where he extolled the virtues of Arnold's teaching and shared information about the Paris meetings of 1888 and 1889. His American journey had convinced him that prosaic commercial, professional, and nationalistic influences were having menacing affects on sporting participation and that there would soon be the greatest need for an organization capable of dominating or at least controlling these influences (while nonetheless preserving their enthusiasm and intensity) and capable of promoting a cosmopolitan and an international perspective concerning sport. Coubertin had also been variously involved in organizing, promoting, and administering sporting clubs for French athletes (he became Secretary-General of the Union des Sociétés des Sports Athlétiques in 1891), in publishing bulletins about French sport, and in arranging national and international contests for French athletes in rowing (such as the England-France race of 1892), soccer (such as the England-France match of 1892), and track and field (such as the dual meeting between the Racing Club of France and the Manhattan Athletic Club in 1892).

Two further meetings set the final stage for the gathering in which the governing body of the modern international Olympic movement was established:

- at a meeting of the Committee for the Propagation of Physical Exercises in Education in Paris in May 1892, the status of physical education in the French schools and the results of the Committee's exacting study of foreign systems (of physical education) were discussed; the conclusion of the meeting led Coubertin to suppose that the leading national systems of physical education and sport were sufficiently well developed to operate as groundwork for an international sporting movement; and

- at a meeting of the Union des Sociétés des Sports Athlétiques in Paris in November 1892, Coubertin took the first concrete steps toward establishing the modern international Olympic movement; in his address ("Les Exercises Physiques dans le Monde Moderne"), he made a dramatic resolution proclaiming the rebirth of the Olympic Games; convinced that this "renaissance athlétique" was among the most urgent needs of his time, Coubertin sought to exhume the spirit of classical antiquity and to work that spirit into the imperatives of modern culture, into the spirit of pure amateur sport; only in the form of such a movement, by Coubertin's view, can sport be other than a merely ephemeral occurrence, can sport fulfill its high educational and cultural calling; the proposal was altogether misunderstood, however (it was widely thought to have advocated ethereal pageants, or theatrical re-creations), and failed to gain favor.

The provincial French orientations of the 1890s and the Continental European commitment to calisthenic gymnastics, which had kept the proposal from being either understood or accepted, persuaded Coubertin that wide support from outside Continental Europe would be necessary to the success of his proposition. Variously throughout 1893, at meetings of the Union des Sociétés des Sports Athlétiques, Coubertin asked the organization to summon an international congress of all major sporting associations in the world for the purpose of discussing athletic rules and regulations, amateurism, and the revival of the Olympic Games. Coubertin and his American colleague, William Milligan Sloane (1850-1928), a distinguished professor of European history at Princeton University who had organized the Princeton Committee to regulate American intercollegiate sport in 1881 and who had assisted Coubertin in arranging the dual track and field meeting between the Racing Club of France and the Manhattan Athletic Club in 1892, were mainly responsible for making the preparations. Prior to the congress, Coubertin again traveled to the United States and to England; he also made a journey to Greece, all for the main purpose of soliciting succor for his Olympic dream. In the end, however, the raging controversy in the United States between the Amateur Athletic Union and rival intercollegiate organizations convinced him that the notion of international athletics was contrary to the sectarian perspectives of the country. The English view tended to conceive of sport as a national province which was not to be shared with others. And the results of the Greek visit were inconclusive. The **International Olympic Congress**, arguably the most significant meeting in the entire history of modern Olympism and among the most significant gatherings in the entire history of sport, nonetheless went forward.

The Congress was staged at the University of Paris from June 16 to June 23, 1894. The representatives to it were among the most influential political and educational authorities of the time; 49 honorary members and 79 delegates from thirteen nations (Australia, Belgium, Bohemia, England, France, Greece, Hungary, Italy, Netherlands, Russia, Spain, Sweden, and United States of America) attended; Greek King George I served as honorary president. The Congress was conducted throughout in a spirit of scholarly and cultural grandeur and in the omnipresent image of ancient Greece. It was steered throughout by Coubertin toward an emphasis on Olympic revival; on its final day, Coubertin formally proposed the revival of quadrennial Olympic Games; the proposal was unanimously accepted. The formation of a twelve-member, self-contained governing body, the **International Olympic Committee** (IOC)/Comité International Olympique (CIO), modeled after the Committee of the Management of Henley Royal Regatta and appointed by Coubertin, also won unanimous approval. Each member of the Committee was to act in a politically independent fashion; the first allegiance of each member was to international Olympic principle, not to national, political, or economic interests; all members were considered representatives of the Committee to the nations of the world, not representatives of national traditions to the Committee; and thus all members were elected only by the Committee and could be expelled only by the Committee. The Committee was to promote the Games, determine where they were to be held, and establish policies and procedures by which they were to be conducted. From the beginning, the Committee created, out of the most prominent athletic activities of the time, a festival devoted to a fundamentally organic ideology in the tangible context of a mechanistic world unsuited to such an ideology and thus in the tangible context of all of the inequalities (particularly, class, gender, and ethnic inequalities) which are at basic odds with organic teaching. Even the early leaders of the modern international Olympic movement itself (and, for that matter, most since) have been virulently opposed to the sort of collective, unified, and democratic political orientation that empowers all people. Among the most conspicuous marks of such inequality was the utter exclusion of women from the International Olympic Committee until 1980.

The International Olympic Committee is governed by a President (chosen by majority vote of all members, currently for an eight-year term with provisions for re-election on a modified schedule), three Vice-Presidents, and a fifteen-member Executive Board chaired by the President. The Committee is importantly advised by its many commissions which deal with special aspects of the Games. It:

- has conducted periodic meetings concerning its own affairs (from 1894), broader sport congresses (which also include National Olympic Committees and international sport federations; also from 1894), and still broader sport studies congresses (concerning scientific and humanistic research in respect to sport; from 1936);
- has published official reports and films for each edition of the Games, the Bulletin of the International Committee of the Olympic Games (from 1894), and Revue Olympique (from 1901); and
- established its first offices in Paris in 1894 (moved to Lausanne, Switzerland in 1915), the Olympic Library and Museum in Lausanne in 1916, and the International Olympic Academy in Olympia, Greece in 1939.

The Committee is most significantly assisted by the **National Olympic Committees** (in the member nations) and by the international sport federations (in respect to the disparate sports comprising the Olympic program). The earliest of the National Olympic Committees were those of France (Comité Olympique et Sportif Français, established by Coubertin in 1894), Australia (Australian Olympic Committee, 1895), Germany (Nationales Olympisches Komitee fur Deutschland, 1895), Greece (Comité Olympique Hellénique, 1895), Hungary (Comité Olympique Hungrois, 1895), United States of America (United States, or American, Olympic Committee, 1895), and Bohemia/Czechoslovakia (Comité Olympique Tchékoslovaque, 1899). Many member nations functioned informally until they established formal organizations in the twentieth century. Most of the international sport federations were formed in the twentieth century after the inaugural editions of the Games had passed.

Coubertin's great triumph was arguably the most significant in the entire history of modern sport and was too likely the most memorable of his exceedingly productive life. In addition to his several colossal administrative successes, he was an avid, if not a thoroughly adept, sportsman (most notably, a pistol shooter); he wrote prolifically on many searching subjects (particularly, education and history) as well as on sport; and he too won many national and international honors. Over an approximately fifty year period (1886-1936), Coubertin published 26 books and many hundreds of essays, brochures, pamphlets, monographs, and speeches, the most notable of which were Une Campagne de Vingt-et-Un Ans 1887-1908 (1908) and Mémoires Olympiques (1931). In 1912, under the German pseudonyms, Georg Hohrod-Martin Eschbach, he won the fine arts competition in literature at the Olympic Games in Stockholm for his poem, "Ode to Sport;" in 1928, he was nominated for the Nobel Peace Prize.

The immediate task ahead, however, was to formulate and to carry out the revival of the Olympic Games. This formidable task fell mainly to Coubertin, who was selected as the principal working officer, the Secretary-General, of the newly formed International Olympic Committee in 1894, and to noted Greek literary scholar, Demetrios Bikelas (1835-1908; r. 1894-96), who became the first President of the International Olympic Committee also in 1894. The Games of the First Modern Olympiad were originally planned to take place in conjunction with the International Exposition of 1900 in Paris although London and Budapest were also briefly considered as plausible sites. On appeal from Bikelas, however, the Games were in the end awarded to Athens and they were held in 1896. There were nonetheless immense difficulties readying Athens for the great event. Coubertin and Bikelas shared deep apprehensions about the Greek capacity to stage the Games, mainly owing to grave economic troubles (foreign trade failures, high currency inflation, and large public debts), civil turmoil and political instability associated with the economic troubles, and continuing territorial disputes with the Ottoman Empire in the Aegean. Coubertin made a long journey to Greece in 1894-95 with the intention of assisting with preparations but met with much official pessimism and intransigence, if also with considerable popular support. Crown Prince Constantine (later, King Constantine I) then took full administrative command of the preparations and, together with overwhelming popular enthusiasm, significant royal and commercial patronage, and the very considerable efforts of Coubertin and Bikelas, was mainly responsible, against long odds, for saving the **1896 Olympic Games**. Among the most intractable difficulties was the construction of a main stadium. Largely through the generosity of wealthy Greek-Egyptian commercialist, Georgios "George" Averoff (1819-99), the Panathenaic Stadium, an alleged restoration of the stadium of Lycurgus (a fourth-century B.C.E. administrative superintendent of Athens) from the fourth century B.C.E. and the stadium of Herodes Atticus (a wealthy second-century C.E. Athenian benefactor, orator, and teacher) from the second century C.E., the stadiums at which the ancient Panathenaean Games had been mainly staged, was effectively completed in time for the opening of the Games. Although little of the original structures had remained, excavations of the site had been done from 1869 to 1878, a partial restoration had been achieved for the 1870 version of Evangelis Zappas' Pan-Hellenic Games as has been said, and the new stadium was constructed on the site of the ancient facilities in 1895-96. The result was the largest and the most impressive athletic stadium in the world; it was done on a colossal scale, was of classical Greek proportion and (symmetric) design, was finished in stunning white marble, and was an aesthetic marvel. Its sharply elongated shape (also an ancient tendency) nonetheless made the turns of the running track too acute for effective performance and the running track itself was only one-third kilometer per lap.

Although Athens' festive preparations were coming to a satisfactory conclusion by the spring of 1896, world support for the Games was not robust even on the eve of their opening. The International Olympic Committee nonetheless staged its second meeting from April 4 to 12 in Athens and the Games themselves were opened at the Panathenaic Stadium by Greek King George I before roughly 50,000 spectators on Monday, April 6 (the Greek Day of Independence), the first Olympic celebration in more than fifteen centuries. The vision of Coubertin (among others) had been realized as c. 311 male athletes representing fourteen nations (Australia, Austria, Bulgaria, Chile, Denmark, France, Germany, Great Britain, Greece, Hungary, Italy, Sweden, Switzerland, and United States of America) contested nine sports (track and field athletics, gymnastics, swimming, cycling, fencing, [lawn] tennis, shooting, weightlifting, and Graeco-Roman wrestling). Of the competing nations, only five participated in every edition of the modern Games to the end of the twentieth century: Australia, France, Great Britain, Greece, and Switzerland. Of the sports contested, only five appeared in all editions of the modern Games to the end of the twentieth century: track and field athletics, swimming, gymnastics, cycling, and fencing.

The Games went forward even though many of the formal provisions necessary for their full success had not yet been established. There was, for prominent instance, no mechanism for the systematic and impartial selection of most athletes and national teams of athletes; most were therefore not formally chosen or designated; many were invited by well-connected Olympic authorities who happened to be aware of them; and still others simply turned up. Few of the world's most distinguished athletes participated; the standards of performance were therefore quite low; no "world records" were so much as approached, let alone surpassed. Unsurprisingly, approximately two-thirds of the participants were Greek and the Greek team won more medals (counting the first three places in each event even though only the first two received tangible medals) than any other contingent. American athletes (numbering only thirteen) won the most events, however; namely, eleven (including nine of twelve track and field events) to the hosts' ten. This began a long-standing tendency in which the host team does notably better than in Games it does not host and in which the American team is among the leading two (or three) teams in the Games. German athletes achieved a broad domination of gymnastic events. And track and field athletics established itself as the most prestigious of Olympic sports, an arrangement that has continued to our own time.

The first champions of the modern Olympic era were determined on the opening day of the Games. The very first was American (Harvard) student, James Brendan Connolly (1868-1957), who won the triple jump (hop, hop, jump) by a convincing margin; the second was American (Princeton) student, Robert Garrett (1875-1961), who narrowly upset the Greek favorite in the discus throw and who later also narrowly won the shot put. The other most notable champions were:

- American sprinter, Thomas Edmund Burke (1875-1929), who won both the 100 meters and 400 meters dashes (the only such double in Olympic history);
- Australian-British middle-distance runner, Edwin Harold Flack (1873-1935), who won both the 800 meters and 1500 meters runs;
- American jumper, Ellery Harding Clark (1874-1949), who won both the high jump and long jump (the only such double in Olympic history);
- Greek shepherd and long-distance runner, Spiridon "Spiro" Loues (1873-1940), who won among the first marathons ever run (there had been two slightly earlier Greek trials races over the Olympic course) in the only time beneath three hours from 25 starters and an unofficial female participant, Melpomene (who finished in approximately 4 ½ hours) on the alleged route from Marathon to Athens over which the ancient Greek messenger ran after the Battle of Marathon in 490 B.C.E., a distance of

approximately 40 kilometers/c. 25 miles; Loues was the most heralded victor of the Games and was acclaimed a national hero;

- American hurdler, Thomas Pelham Curtis (1870-1944), who won the first Olympic hurdle event, the 110 meters high hurdles;
- American jumper, William Welles Hoyt (1875-1954), who won the inaugural Olympic pole vault;
- Hungarian swimmer, Alfred Hajos/Alfred Guttmann (1878-1955), who won both the 100 meters and 1200 meters freestyle events; Hajos was also an exceptional soccer player as well as a renowned architect of sporting facilities; and
- French cyclist, Paul Masson (1874-1945), who won three events, time trial (1/3 kilometer), sprint (2000 meters), and 10,000 meters track race.

The Games of 1896 closed on April 15 with the awarding of silver (not gold) medals and certificates to the victors and bronze (not silver) medals to the second-place performers (no medals were awarded to third-place performers), a parade of champions in the main stadium, and the formal declaration of closing by King George I. The Olympic hymn had been written for these Games (although it was not officially adopted until 1958) by Greek operatic composer, Spyros Samaras (1861-1917), with lyrics by Greek poet, Kostis Palamas (1859-1943). The modern Olympic Games, the first authentically international, multi-sport athletic championships of modern civilization, have been held continuously, since 1896, in the first year of every four-year cycle (known as an olympiad), with the exception of the Games of 1916, 1940, and 1944, all of which were cancelled due to global military conflict.

Coubertin replaced Bikelas as President of the International Olympic Committee in 1896 and held the office until 1925 (but for the duration of the First World War [1914-18]), the longest tenure of any International Olympic Committee President. The major dispute following the 1896 celebrations concerned the site (s) of future Games. For a time, Greece was adamantly opposed to holding the Games anywhere but Athens. Despite the popular and official Greek enthusiasm for the Games, the Greek successes in the Games, and the nationalistic fervor raised by the Games, however, continuing economic, political, and military difficulties soon dissuaded the Greek attempt to insist on a permanent Athenian home for the Games. It was nonetheless agreed that "interim" Games would be staged every four years in Athens, in the even-numbered years between Olympic festivals, beginning in 1906. Coubertin effectively won the 1900 Games themselves for his home city, Paris, and aimed to conduct them in conjunction with the International Exposition of 1900, also in Paris. He later regretted both acts as the Games were deplorable organizational failures and became little other than ancillary features of the Exposition.

Unlike the generally well organized efforts of 1896, the **1900 Olympic Games** were conducted on poor, hastily constructed facilities, were very sparsely attended, went on for an inordinately long period (May 20 to October 28), included no formal opening or closing ceremonies, followed no uniform policy in respect to awards, were marked by long-raging disputes over competitions on the Sabbath, and included some remarkably bizarre events by classical Olympic standard (such as, cannon shooting, automobilism, motorboating, balloon racing, still fishing in the Seine River, leap frogging, underwater swimming, and an obstacle swimming race). There were too special events for professional athletes and it was not in every case clear which events were exhibitions and which others official Olympic activities. Only track and field events were from the beginning designated as Olympic contests; many others have been accepted as official Olympic events post hoc. The French government largely confiscated preparations for the Games from Coubertin for the purpose of making the industrial exhibits the main focus of the gathering. The results were so unbecoming that only memory of the largely splendid Games of Athens saved the modern international Olympic movement from an early demise.

The Games of Paris nonetheless excelled the Athens celebrations in several notable respects: the standard of athletic performance was much improved over Athens as many of the world's finest athletes competed in Paris; there were many more events (even standard sporting events), athletes, and represented nations in Paris than there had been in Athens; and women participated in the Olympic Games for the first time (in croquet, golf , and tennis), although the status of their events, as exhibition or official, was equivocal. Archery, croquet, equestrian, golf, polo, rowing, rugby, soccer, tug-of-war, water polo, and yachting/sailing (in principle open to both men and women) were added to the Olympic program; weightlifting and wrestling were temporarily excluded from the Games; cricket made its only Olympic appearance; and Belgium, Bohemia/Czechoslovakia, Cuba, Haiti, Luxembourg, Mexico, Netherlands, Norway, Russia, and Spain participated in the Games for the first time. Approximately 1206 men and 19 women representing 26 nations contested 17 sports in Paris. The leading teams were the French, American, and British contingents. The

French won more events (28) and more medals than any other team (most notably, in fencing, gymnastics, and rowing); the Americans were next best in both categories, winning 22 events (most notably, the first Olympic 8-oars rowing competition and 17 of 23 track and field events); and the British, next best also in both categories, winning 16 events (most notably, the first Olympic soccer tournament, the first Olympic water polo tournament, and the middle-distance and long-distance runs). The host team thus continued its tendency to disproportionate success and the American team continued its tendency to especially high distinction. Track and field athletics also continued as the dominant athletic program of the Games, adding the 200 meters dash, the 200 meters low hurdles (which was discontinued after the 1904 Games), the 400 meters intermediate hurdles, steeplechasing events, standing jumping events, and the hammer throw to the Olympic schedule.

The track and field events were contested mainly on a very poor, temporary, soft, 500 meters grass running track (and associated facilities) on the grounds of the Racing Club of France in the Bois de Boulogne. The foremost champions of the Games were American track and field athletes:

- Raymond Clarence "Ray" Ewry (1873-1937) of Purdue University and the New York Athletic Club, who had overcome boyhood poliomyelitis to become one of the most accomplished jumpers in the world, won all three standing jumps (standing long jump, standing triple jump, and standing high jump);
- Alvin Christian Kranzlein (1876-1928) of the University of Pennsylvania became the only person to win four individual track and field events in one olympiad (60 meters dash, 110 meters high hurdles, 200 meters low hurdles, and running long jump);
- Irving Knott Baxter (1876-1957) of the University of Pennsylvania won the pole vault and running high jump (the only such double in Olympic history) and was second to Ray Ewry in all three standing jumps;
- John Walter Beardsley "J. Walter" Tewksbury (1878-1968) of the University of Pennsylvania won the inaugural Olympic 400 meters hurdles as well as the inaugural Olympic 200 meters dash; and
- Maxwell Warburn "Maxey" Long (1878-1959) of Columbia University achieved among the finest marks of the Games in his stirring victory in the 400 meters dash.

The other most noteworthy champions of the Games were Charlotte Reinagle Cooper Sterry (1870-1966) of Great Britain, the first women's Olympic champion, who won the singles and mixed doubles titles in tennis; and the Luxembourgois-French runner, Michel Johann Théato (1878-1919), a Parisian gardener, who won the marathon in the only time beneath three hours over a 40,260 meters/c. 25 miles course of disputed distance and patrol against 19 starters (only 7 of whom finished) in brutal heat. The 1900 Olympic Games also included the youngest competitor, medalist, and champion in the history of the Games, an approximately ten-year-old French boy of unknown identity who was hastily recruited as coxswain by the victorious Dutch coxed pairs crew. Norway was the only nation that formally established a National Olympic Committee in the Olympiad of the Second Modern Games; the Norwegian Olympic Committee was created in 1900.

The **1904 Olympic Games** were originally awarded to Chicago but, on appeal from American President Theodore Roosevelt (then also the [honorary] President of the United States, or American, Olympic Committee) and from the leading administrative figure in early twentieth-century American amateur sport, James Edward Sullivan (1860-1914), the Games were staged instead as a feature of the Louisiana Purchase Exposition (centenary celebration) in St. Louis. As in Paris, then, the 1904 Games again became a secondary feature of a world exposition and with similar results. Although not up to the standard of Athens, the Games of St. Louis were nonetheless better organized and better attended than the debacle of Paris. Still at this, the Games of 1904 failed the same aesthetic test as those of Paris. The so-termed Anthropological Days, which included competitions among primitive tribes from throughout the world in such as mud fighting and greased pole climbing, likely contributed most to this impression. Also as in Paris, only the track and field program was uniformly and explicitly designated as Olympic; the official Olympic status of many other events was problematic. Unlike in Paris (more nearly like Athens), however, many of the world's finest athletes, particularly European athletes, did not compete owing to excessive travel expenses. In most events, the Games were thus little more than an American inter-club meeting; as it turned out, between representatives of the New York Athletic Club and the Chicago Athletic Association. Even very few accomplished American intercollegiate athletes competed. The Games were therefore not authentically international championships.

Likewise as in the Paris case, the Games were conducted over an excessively long period, from July 1 to November 23, and lacked a concise and cohesive schedule. Approximately 681 men and 6 women representing 13 nations contested 14 sports. Boxing, diving, lacrosse, freestyle wrestling, and women's archery came onto the Olympic program for the first time; equestrian, shooting, yachting/sailing, and Graeco-Roman wrestling were temporarily excluded from the Games; golf and croquet made their final Olympic appearances; basketball was played as a demonstration sport; and Canada and South Africa participated in the Games for the first time. The Games were opened by David Rowland Francis (1850-1927), a prominent local business and political leader and President of the Exposition. The main stadium, Francis Field, was named for him; it included a one-third mile (c. 536 meters) running track of modest quality and was otherwise unexceptional as well. The American team dominated virtually every phase of the program except fencing (in which Cuba excelled) and swimming (in which German and Hungarian athletes were preeminent). It comprised roughly five-sixths of all athletes and won most events (78) and most medals overall by very wide margins; Canada and Germany each won second-most events (4). Track and field continued as the athletic centerpiece of the Games; American athletes won 22 of 24 track and field events and very nearly swept all other medals in the sport as well. The track and field schedule included the first Olympic 56 lbs. weight throw (which was discontinued after its second appearance in the 1920 Games) and the first Olympic composite event, an all-around competition (ten events in one day), which was won by Thomas Francis Kiely (1869-1951) of Great Britain-Ireland. Four American track and field athletes each won three events:

- Ray Ewry of the New York Athletic Club successfully defended all three standing jumps titles he had won in Paris (standing long jump, standing triple jump, and standing high jump);
- Charles Archibald "Archie" Hahn (1880-1955) of the University of Michigan won the 60 meters, 100 meters, and 200 meters (straight-course) dashes;
- Harry Livingston Hillman, Jr. (1881-1945) of the New York Athletic Club won the 400 meters dash, 200 meters low hurdles, and 400 meters intermediate hurdles (the only flat 400 and 400 hurdles double in Olympic history); third in both the low and intermediate hurdles was George Coleman Poage (1880-1962) of the Milwaukee Athletic Club, the first black American Olympian and the first black Olympic medalist; and
- James Davis Lightbody (1882-1953) of the Chicago Athletic Association won the 800 meters run, 1500 meters run, and (2590 meters) steeplechase.

The magnificent Polish-American horizontal jumper, Myer Prinstein (1880-1925) of Syracuse University, successfully defended the running triple jump title he had won in Paris and also won the running long jump title that had narrowly eluded him in Paris (the only such double in Olympic history).

The marathon was again among the most disputed, grueling, and bizarre events of the Games. The race was run over an extremely taxing, hilly, and dust-covered 40 kilometers (c. 25 miles) course in alarmingly hot and humid conditions among 31 starters (only 14 of whom finished). It included a colorful Cuban postman, Felix Carvajal, who had effectively begged his way to the Games, competed largely in street-clothes, insisted on eating green apples (which made him ill) mid-way through the run, but nonetheless finished fourth. It also included two black South African runners, Lentauw and Yamasini (the first black Africans to compete in the Games), both of whom had also participated in the Anthropological Days. And it too included American Fred Lorz who retired early in the race, was given a ride in an official rescue car until it broke down, whence resumed the run, ostensibly winning the race as a prank, was discovered and disqualified. The race was won by English-American Thomas J. Hicks (1875-1963), who variously walked and ran the last quarter of the distance under the influence of alcohol and other drugs and who finished in delirium in the only Olympic marathon won above three hours. The other most noteworthy champions of the Games were:

- American gymnast, Anton Heida (b. 1878), who won the individual all-around (of four events), team all-around, vaulting horse, horizontal bar, and pommelled horse;
- American cyclist, Marcus Latimer Hurley (1883-1941), who won the ¼ mile, 1/3 mile, ½ mile, and 1 mile track races;
- Cuban fencer, Ramon Fonst Segundo (1883-1959), who successfully defended the individual épée title he had won in Paris and who also won the individual foil and team foil titles;
- American (New York Athletic Club) swimmer, Charles Meldrum Daniels (1885-1973), who won the 220 yards freestyle, 440 yards freestyle, and 4 x 50 yards freestyle relay and who also medaled widely in the 1906 and 1908 Games; his eight medals (including one in the 1906 Games) are among the most in the history of Olympic swimming; and
- Hungarian swimmer, Zoltan von Halmay (1881-1956), who won the 50 yards freestyle and 100 yards freestyle; he also medaled widely in the 1900, 1906, and 1908 Games; his nine medals (including two in the 1906 Games) are among the most in the history of Olympic swimming.

Denmark (Danmarks Olympiske Komite, 1905), Great Britain (British Olympic Association, 1905), Belgium (Comité Olympique et Interfédéral Belgique, 1906), Canada (Canadian Olympic Association, 1907), and Finland (Finnish Olympic Committee, 1907) formally established National Olympic Committees in the Olympiad of the Third Modern Games.

With the somewhat sordid editions of Paris and St. Louis, Coubertin despaired over the dismal state of the modern international Olympic movement. Although unofficial Olympic celebrations, the **1906 Olympic Games**, the "interim" Games of 1906 in Athens, then designated as International Panathenaic Games and since typically referred to as Intercalated (inserted, or added) Games, contributed very significantly to the recovery and the salvation of the movement. These Games, which were to have continued in Athens every four years (in the even-numbered years between Olympic festivals) as per the agreement of 1896, revitalized the Olympic spirit. They were nonetheless discontinued after the Greeks were unable to stage them in 1910. The 1906 affair was marked by efficient organization, splendid attendance, handsome pageantry, and broad and accomplished participation by the major sporting nations of the world; they were marred only by a dispute over the amateur status of an Austrian weightlifter whose main rival was Greek. Egypt and Finland made their original Olympic appearances. The Games were held mainly in the Panathenaic Stadium (the site of the 1896 Games) and were opened by Greek King George I (also as in the 1896 case) in an impressive ceremony that included a stirring demonstration of Danish gymnastics and that also included the first parade of nations (athletes assembled in national teams marching behind national flag-bearers). They went on from April 22 to May 2 among 877 men and 7 women representing 20 nations and contesting 12 sports. The French team won the most events (15) and the most medals (most notably, in fencing, shooting, and tennis); the American team won second-most events (12) and third-most medals; and the Greek team won third-most events (8) and second-most medals. The host and American teams had again won disproportionate distinction.

The track and field events continued as the preeminent aspect of the Olympic program and these events were again dominated by American athletes, who won 11 of 21 such events. The most noteworthy American champions in track and field were:

- Ray Ewry, who again (as in Paris and St. Louis) won all standing jumps (in this case, the standing long jump and standing high jump);
- Paul Harry Pilgrim (1883-1958) of the New York Athletic Club, who surprisingly won both the 400 meters dash and the 800 meters run;
- Martin Joseph Sheridan (1881-1918) of the Irish-American Athletic Club, a New York City policeman, among the earliest of a large cadre of exceptional Irish-American throwers, and arguably the finest all-around athlete in the world in the first decade of the twentieth century, who again (as in St. Louis) won the discus throw, who also won the shot put, and who too medaled in both standing jumps and a stone throwing event;
- Archie Hahn, who again (as in St. Louis) won the 100 meters dash;
- James Lightbody, who again (as in St. Louis) won the 1500 meters run; and
- Myer Prinstein, who again (as in St. Louis) won the running long jump.

The track and field program of 1906 also included the first javelin throwing event and the first race walking events (1500 meters and 3000 meters events) in Olympic history; it, for the only time in Olympic history, conducted all pertinent walking and running events in a clockwise direction (a practice with which most athletes were unfamiliar); it featured the first Olympic champion from Finland (which has since become among the world's foremost athletic nations); and it was (as in 1896) moved by a stunning marathon victory. Verner Jarvinen (1870-1941), a railroad fireman and father of two luminous Olympic track and field medalists, won the discus throw, Greek style (from a stand and an inclined platform) and thus became the first Finnish Olympic champion and thus too sparked great enthusiasm for sport in early twentieth-century Finland. And William John "W.J." Sherring (1878-1964) of Canada won the most acclaimed event of the Games (owing to Loues' 1896 triumph), the marathon, from a field of 73 starters (37 of whom were Greek) over the approximately 40 kilometers (c. 25 miles) course from Marathon to Athens (the same course over which the 1896 Olympic marathon had been run). The other most noteworthy occurrence of the Games was the Italian domination of rowing; the other most noteworthy champions of the Games were:

- Italian cyclist, Francesco Verri (1885-1945), who won the time trial (1/3 kilometer), sprint (1000 meters), and 5000 meters track race;
- Swiss shooter, Konrad Staheli (1866-1931), who added two rifle titles to the three rifle and pistol titles he had won in Paris in 1900; his nine medals and five gold medals are equal second-most and equal-most respectively in the entire history of Olympic shooting; and

- American swimmer, Charles Daniels, who added the 100 meters freestyle title to the three freestyle titles he had won in St. Louis.

The **1908 Olympic Games** were originally awarded to Rome but a 1906 volcanic eruption of Mt. Vesuvius (near Naples) had such a devastating affect on the Italian economy that the nation was unable to stage them. They were held instead in London from April 27 to October 31 among 1999 men and 36 women representing 22 nations and contesting 21 sports. They were the best organized Games to date; they included the most ambitious athletic program and the broadest and most accomplished athletic fields to their time; and they were conducted on the finest Olympic facilities of their era. The main stadium, White City Stadium, had been constructed on a scale befitting amateur orientations; it avoided the impression of both colossal scale and rigid order; and it embodied an excellent, new, three-lap-to-the-mile (c. 536 meters) running track. The 1908 Games were nonetheless plagued by several serious problems (which included several unfortunate controversies):

- They were held over an excessively long period (not unlike the Paris and St. Louis celebrations) and were thus diffuse in aesthetic effect;
- They were held in conjunction with a cultural exposition (not also unlike the Paris and St. Louis celebrations), the Franco-British Exposition, and were thus distracted by non-sporting activities;
- They included some non-classical forms of sporting activity, such as motorboating;
- They were opened by British King Edward VII in an impressive ceremony that was nonetheless marred by several flag disputes:
    - the American and Swedish flags, unlike all others, were not displayed in the stadium; both the Americans and the Swedes protested; the Swedes later withdrew from the Games;
    - in the parade of nations, the American flag, unlike all others, was not deferentially lowered by the flag-bearer in order to salute the British royal family; although this was apparently done unintentionally, offense was taken; and
    - Finnish athletes refused to march under Russian colors in the parade of nations.
- They were visited by numerous disputes between the British and American contingents concerning the large and talented Irish membership of both teams; and
- There was some strictly athletic bickering as well; perhaps most notably, the British-American feud in the 400 meters dash final which resulted in the disqualification (for interference) of an American runner, an order to re-run the final, the refusal of the remaining two Americans in the final to participate in the re-run, and the only walkover (unopposed) victory in Olympic track and field history for the only man left to participate in the re-run, Wyndham Halswelle (1882-1915) of Great Britain.

Despite all of this, the 1908 Olympic Games were, on balance, the best of the four official and one unofficial editions of the Games yet staged. The Olympic creed was crafted by Coubertin from remarks made by Anglican Bishop Ethelbert Talbot in services held for Olympic athletes during the Games: "The important thing in the Olympic Games is not to win but to take part, just as the important thing in life is not the triumph, but the struggle. The essential thing is not to have conquered but to have fought well." Argentina, Iceland, New Zealand, and Turkey made their initial Olympic appearances. Field hockey came for the first time onto the Olympic program; equestrian and weightlifting were temporarily excluded from the Games; lacrosse made its final Olympic appearance as an official sport; motor sport of any type (in this case, motorboat racing) made its only official Olympic appearance; and jeu de paume (or court tennis) also made its only Olympic appearance as a medal sport. The 1908 Games included the first winter sport in Olympic annals, figure skating, an event which produced the first and the only Olympic champion from tsarist Russia; Nikolai Panin-Kolomenkin (b. 1874) of Russia won the special figures competition; Karl Emil Julius Ulrich Salchow (1887-1949) of Sweden, the most accomplished figure skater of the early twentieth century, won the men's singles competition. The oldest individual champion in Olympic history was also crowned in 1908; Oscar Gomer Swahn (1847-1927) of Sweden won the running-deer shooting (single shot) individual and team gold medals at the age of sixty years. The first of the great contemporary modern swimmers too distinguished themselves in these Games:

- Charles Daniels of the United States again won the 100 meters freestyle (as in Athens, 1906), on this occasion in world-record time; he had also won three freestyle events in St. Louis; and
- Henry Taylor (1885-1951) of Great Britain won the 400 meters freestyle in world-record time, 1500 meters freestyle in world-record time, and 4 x 200 meters freestyle relay; he had also won the 1 mile freestyle in Athens, 1906, and later medaled in the 1912 and 1920 Games; his eight medals (including three in the 1906 Games) are among the most in the history of Olympic swimming.

And the long-standing Hungarian hegemony in Olympic sabre fencing began in 1908 (and went on until 1960) with the individual and team victories of Jeno Fuchs (1882-1955), both repeated in 1912.

The British-Irish team was the most successful, winning most events (54) and most medals overall (mainly in boxing, cycling, rowing, shooting, tennis, track and field, and freestyle wrestling); it also won team titles in field hockey, polo, soccer, tug-of-war, and water polo. The Americans won second-most events (23) and second-most medals (most notably, in track and field). The pattern of host-team and American-team preeminence again held. The American domination of track and field, still the most prominent of Olympic sports, also continued; American athletes won 15 of 26 such events; British-Irish athletes won 7. The leading American victories were secured by:

- Ray Ewry, who again won both standing jumps (standing long jump and standing high jump); these were the final triumphs of Ewry's magnificent Olympic career in which he won all standing jumps thusfar held; in sum, from 1900 to1908, Ewry won ten individual gold medals (including two in the 1906 Games), the most of any track and field athlete in modern Olympic history;
- Martin Sheridan, who won the third of his three Olympic discus throw titles (repeating the triumphs of 1904 and 1906), also won the discus throw, Greek style, and again (as in 1906) medaled in the standing long jump; his nine medals and five gold medals are each among the most in the history of Olympic track and field;
- John Jesus Flanagan (1873-1938) of the Irish-American Athletic Club, among the first of the great Irish-American throwers of the early twentieth century, who won the third of his three Olympic hammer throw titles (repeating the triumphs of 1900 and 1904), thus becoming the only person to win three Olympic hammer crowns;
- Ralph Waldo Rose (1885-1913) of the University of Michigan, who won the second of his two Olympic shot put titles (repeating the triumph of 1904), the first of only two such defenses (the other was done by Parry O'Brien);
- Melvin Winfield "Mel" Sheppard (1883-1942) of the Irish-American Athletic Club, who won the 800 meters run in a brilliant world record, the 1500 meters run, and the first Olympic relay (a 1600 meters medley event); and
- John Joseph "Johnny" Hayes (1886-1965), a New York City department-store clerk of the Irish-American Athletic Club, who won what was again the most dramatic and memorable event of the Games, the marathon, over 55 starters and over the first course at what became the standard distance for the event (26 miles 385 yards, or 42,195 meters); this distance resulted from the accommodation of the royal family's interest in witnessing the start of the race at Windsor Castle (the race was run from Windsor to the main stadium in London); in very warm conditions, Dorando Pietri (1885-1942), an Italian candy maker, led the race into the stadium but, staggered by extreme exhaustion, he turned away from (not toward) the finish line, then fell several times before being assisted across the line by British officials; he was disqualified for having been attended, of course, and the victory went to Hayes; a special trophy was nonetheless presented to Pietri by the royal family in the main stadium on the next day; Hayes and Pietri both turned to professional running after the Games and were widely idolized in Europe and North America.

The most notable of the British triumphs were achieved by:

- George Edward Larner (1875-1949), the first great modern race walker, who won both walking events on the program (the 3500 meters and the 10 miles events) by impressively wide margins in impressively fast times; and
- Timothy J. "Tim" Ahearne (1885-1968), among a fairly large and a very accomplished corps of remarkable, early twentieth-century Irish jumpers, who won the triple jump in world-record fashion.

South Africa ([a white] Olympic Committee, 1908), Portugal (Comite Olimpico Portugues, 1909), Egypt (Comité Olympique Egyptien, 1910), and Turkey (Turkiye Milli Olimpiyat Komitesi, 1911) formally established National Olympic Committees in the Olympiad of the Fourth Modern Games.

The last Games of the pre-First World War era were held in Stockholm in 1912. The **1912 Olympic Games** were the most remarkable Olympic celebrations to their time; they were technically extraordinary; the pageantry in them was magnificent; and the standards of competition, performance, officiating, and attendance had not yet been excelled. After the less-than-pleasing memories of earlier Games (by which the future of the movement was made uncertain), the great athletic and aesthetic successes of Stockholm secured the institutional permanence of the modern international Olympic movement, assured the ongoing practice of the movement, and carried the movement through the First World War (through the hiatus of 1916) to the Games of 1920. The 1912 Olympic Games were transacted from May 5 to July 22 among 2490 male and 57 female athletes representing 28 nations and contesting 14 sports. The schedule of the Games was thus more concise than in earlier editions (except for the Greek celebrations of 1896 and 1906), the program was less glutted than in earlier editions (except also for the Greek celebrations of 1896 and 1906), and the international representation was wider than in earlier editions. The Games were opened in an awesome ceremony, which included musical fare and a memorable demonstration of Niels Bukh's Danish gymnastics, by Swedish King Gustavus V. The main stadium, Olympiska Stadion, was among the finest athletic facilities of its day and is yet among the most charming athletic grounds in the world; its sense of proportion, modest dimension, and covered terraces were characteristic marks of the best amateur sport facilities of the early twentieth century; its running track, although only 383 meters per lap, was nonetheless an excellent surface. Japan, Portugal, and Serbia/Yugoslavia made their initial Olympic appearances and Russia participated in the Games for the last time until 1952. Finland dominated Graeco-Roman wrestling and showed very well in track and field; Sweden dominated the equestrian events. The first Olympic fine arts competitions/exhibitions (on sporting subjects) were staged in 1912. The Games of Stockholm crowned the first woman champion in a major Olympic sport; Sarah "Fanny" Durack (1889-1956) of Australia won the 100 meters freestyle swimming event by a decisive margin; women's diving also came onto the Olympic program for the first time in Stockholm. Modern (or military) pentathlon (horse riding, fencing, shooting, swimming, and running), which was invented by Coubertin himself, also came onto the Olympic program for the first time and was swept by Swedish athletes, the beginning of Swedish Olympic domination of this sport which lasted until 1956. Boxing was not held in the 1912 Games because it was prohibited by Swedish law; weightlifting, field hockey, freestyle wrestling, and archery were also temporarily excluded; and American-rules baseball was played in the Olympic Games for the first time (as a demonstration sport). Oscar Swahn of Sweden became the oldest individual medalist in the history of the modern Olympic Games at the age of 64 years (he was third in the running-deer [rifle] shooting [double shot] event); he also became the oldest gold medalist overall (individual or team) in the history of the modern Olympic Games at the age of 64 years (he participated on the victorious running-deer [rifle] shooting [single shot] team). Alfred P. Lane (b. 1891) of the United States won three shooting events in Stockholm (individual rapid-fire pistol, individual free pistol, and team military pistol [50 meters]); in the 1920 Games, he won three additional medals, two of them gold (in team military pistol events); his five gold medals are equal-most in the entire history of Olympic shooting. And the first great contemporary modern gymnast, Alberto Braglia (1883-1954) of Italy, successfully defended his Olympic individual all-around title (from 1908) and also led Italy to the team all-around championship.

The American and the host team were still again the most successful. The United States won the most events, 25, to Sweden's 23, but Sweden won more medals overall than the United States; Great Britain was third-best in both respects. Swedish athletes were most impressive in the equestrian, modern pentathlon, and shooting events. American athletes again prevailed in track and field, winning 16 of 30 such events; Finnish athletes won 6. The most notable track and field athletes in Stockholm, who were also among the most heralded in the entire history of the sport, led the American and Finnish teams. James Francis "Jim" Thorpe (1888-1953), a native American (Sac and Fox), achieved decisive victories in the first Olympic decathlon (with a world-record performance) and also in the first Olympic pentathlon (which was discontinued after the 1924 Games). Thorpe was as well an exceptional intercollegiate athlete in American-rules football (a two-time [1911 and 1912] All-American running back who scored 25 touchdowns and 198 points in 1912 [both records to their time] and who could also kick, pass, and block expertly well), baseball, boxing, lacrosse, and track and field at the Carlisle Indian School (in Carlisle, Pennsylvania; near Harrisburg). He was too highly proficient in archery, basketball, billiards, bowling, canoeing, golf, gymnastics, (court) handball, ice hockey, rowing, rifle shooting, ice skating, swimming, and wrestling. After his time in Carlisle (1905-09, 1911-12) and the 1912 Games, he played professional baseball (from 1913 to 1919), largely the outfield and mainly with the New York Giants, and professional football (from 1913 to 1926), largely as a running back and kicker and mainly with the Canton (Ohio) Bulldogs. Thorpe has been widely considered the finest male athlete of the first half of the twentieth century. When it was nonetheless discovered, in 1913, that he had played semi-professional baseball in North Carolina in 1909 and 1910, he was declared a professional by the Amateur Athletic Union as well as by the International Olympic Committee and was stripped of his victories, medals, and records. After a long and stirring struggle with the IOC by Thorpe's family, however, these distinctions were reinstated and replicas of his medals were returned to his children in 1982, nearly thirty years after the death of the great and impoverished champion.

The leading figure in the Finnish delegation was the most outstanding long-distance runner in the world in the second decade of the twentieth century and among the most remarkable athletes in both Finnish and world athletic history, Johan Pictari "Hannes" Kohlemainen (1889-1966). Kohlemainen, like Verner Jarvinen, was part of a talented athletic family and, also like Jarvinen, was instrumental in greatly popularizing Finnish sport in the early twentieth century; he was too the first of the great Finnish long-distance runners who dominated the sport until after the Second World War. In Stockholm, he won the inaugural Olympic races over both 5000 meters and 10,000 meters; he also won the individual cross-country race run over a c. 12 km course. His victory in the 10,000 meters event was decisive; his victory in the 5000 meters was by the narrowest of margins. The 5000 meters final was among the most moving in the entire record of modern track and field athletics. It developed into a titanic struggle between Kohlemainen and the magnificent French runner, Jean Bouin (1888-1914). Bouin, who was killed tragically by "friendly fire" in the early months of the First World War and who later had a beautiful athletics stadium in Paris constructed in his honor (Stade Jean-Bouin), did most of the hard early work but was beaten in the end by Kohlemainen's withering kick in world-record time. Eight years later in the 1920 Olympic Games in Antwerp, Kohlemainen won the marathon and thus became the first person (of two; the other was Emil Zatopek) to win the Olympic 5000 meters, 10,000 meters, and marathon, among the greatest achievements in modern sport. The other most noteworthy champions of the Games were:

- American sprinter, Ralph Cook Craig (1889-1972) of the University of Michigan, who won the 100 meters and 200 meters dashes;
- American middle-distance runner, James Edwin "Ted" Meredith (1891-1957) of the University of Pennsylvania, who narrowly won the 800 meters run in world-record time (at the conclusion of a memorable duel with defending champion, Mel Sheppard) and who also ran on the victorious American 4 x 400 meters relay quartet which also achieved a world record;
- South African long-distance runner, Kennedy Kenneth "K.K." McArthur (1880-1960), who won the marathon from a field of 68 starters over a 40,200 meters (c. 25 miles) course; and
- Swedish thrower and all-around athlete, Eric Valdemar Lemming (1880-1930), who won the third of his three Olympic javelin throw titles (repeating the triumphs of 1906 and 1908), thus becoming the first of only two to win three Olympic javelin crowns (the other was Jan Zelezny).

The Olympic track and field program of 1912 included the first of what have become the standard Olympic relay events (the 4 x 100 meters and the 4 x 400 meters relays), which themselves made the first use of relay batons (as distinct from exchange by touch); it included standing jumps for the last time in Olympic history; and it included the first use of photo-finish cameras in sport, of timing to the tenths of seconds (as distinct from fifths), and of chalk lines on the track surface (as distinct from posts and ropes) to mark running lanes.

Austria (Osterreichisches Olympisches Komitee, 1912), Japan (Japanese Olympic Committee, 1912), Luxembourg (Comité Olympique et Sportif Luxembourgeois, 1912), Netherlands (Netherlands Olympic Committee, 1912), Switzerland (Comité Olympique Suisse, 1912), Sweden (Swedish Olympic Committee, 1913), Romania (Comité Olympique Roumain, 1914), and Italy (Comitato Olimpico Nazionale Italiano, 1915) formally established National Olympic Committees in the Olympiad of the Fifth Modern Games. The presidency of the International Olympic Committee was passed in this period by Coubertin, on an interim basis, to Baron Godefroy de Blonay (1869-1937) of Switzerland, who discharged the duties of the office throughout the First World War (1914-18). The Games of the Sixth Modern Olympiad, the 1916 Olympic Games, were scheduled for Berlin but were canceled owing to the First World War.

All of the major sports of the nineteenth and the early twentieth centuries developed formal, standard, institutional frameworks (significantly out of prior developments) and began discernible, widely shared traditions in this time as has been said. Among the most prominent of these were the remnants of blood sports, the ongoing expansion of equestrian sports, and the burgeoning development of conquest, or nature, sports. The most widely practiced **blood sports**, the most widely practiced forms of animal blood sport – cock fighting, bullfighting, badger, bear, and bull baiting, dog fighting, fox hunting, gander pulling (which entailed pulling the heads from gander), and ratting (which entailed the slaughter of rats by dogs or weasels) – had been among the most conspicuous types of sport in early modern civilization. Although some have continued to our own time, all forms of such activity came under heavy scrutiny in the nineteenth century; all have declined in prominence throughout contemporary modern civilization; and all have been effectively replaced in the sporting pantheon by at least slightly less violent activities, activities such as boxing. Animal blood sports were increasingly condemned on grounds concerning cruelty to animals and (like blood sports among humans, such as dueling and gouging [which entailed unrestricted fighting, the ultimate goal of which was to gouge the eyes of the opponent from their natural seat]) also on grounds having to do with temperance. The Society for the Prevention of Cruelty to Animals was established in Great Britain in 1824; the Cruelty to

Animals Act was passed, also in Great Britain, in 1835; and the American Society for the Prevention of Cruelty to Animals was formed in 1866. All augured badly for animal blood sport. Cock fighting, for prominent instance, was outlawed altogether in Great Britain in 1849 and all other forms of animal blood sport were also in sharp decline in Great Britain by the late 1840s. Victorian (and related) opposition to gambling, to other unsavory practices associated with blood sports (such as drunkenness, disorderly conduct, and violence), and to the sense of idleness, self-indulgence, and frivolity also associated with blood sport likewise diminished the prestige and the practice of this type of activity. While these initiatives reduced the prominence of blood sport, they clearly did not eradicate it, even in Great Britain and the United States. These activities continued to prosper in some regions of the world, most particularly in parts of Continental Europe (Spain and France most notably), Australasia, central America, South America, and the Caribbean. Bullfighting, which was of Spanish origin, has been arguably the most persistent of these and is yet enormously popular in Spain, central America, and South America.

The equestrian traditions of the Spanish in the Americas were often associated with bullfighting in some form; it was also from these traditions that modern **rodeo** developed. Although rodeo as such is largely a North American phenomenon, it nonetheless had its formative inspiration in the frontier equestrian activities of eighteenth-century and nineteenth-century Mexico and Argentina, where folk contests on mount were common. Such contests also became a part of frontier life in the United States and Canada where rodeo was transformed into a spectator sport (of basically European type) in the late nineteenth and early twentieth centuries. Depending on what counts as an organized rodeo, the earliest such event was held either in Santa Fe, New Mexico (U.S.A.) in 1847, in Pecos, Texas (U.S.A.) in 1883, or in Prescott, Arizona (U.S.A.) in 1883. The Prescott Rodeo of 1888 is nonetheless typically cited as the first formal event in the sport and the most esteemed rodeos, the Calgary (Alberta, Canada) Stampede and the Winnipeg (Manitoba, Canada) Stampede, were first staged in 1912 and 1913 respectively. The other major equestrian sports of contemporary modern civilization were polo, horse racing, and equestrian itself.

Polo had numerous ancient, medieval, and early modern precursors as has been said, but its distinctly contemporary modern form was first developed by British colonials (mainly military officers) in mid-nineteenth-century India; it was then passed on to Great Britain itself and most importantly, in turn, to the United States and Argentina. The first modern polo matches (among the customary four-man teams) were played in India in the early 1860s (c. 1862); the first modern polo clubs, the Silchar (near Dacca) Polo Club and the Calcutta Polo Club, were established in 1859 and 1862 respectively. The game was first played in Great Britain in the late 1860s (c. 1869); the first British polo club, the Hurlingham (London) Polo Club, was established in 1873 (it framed formal rules and functioned as the governing body of the sport in Great Britain); and the earliest major championship competition, the Hurlingham Champion Cup, was first held in 1876. Polo was first played in the United States and Argentina in the mid-1870s (c. 1876). In the United States, the first club, the Westchester (New York) Polo Club, was established in 1876; the first intercollegiate match, between Wesleyan University (Middletown, Connecticut) and the victorious University of Pennsylvania, was played in 1884; the first major international competition, the Westchester Cup (or International Polo Challenge Cup) was played between the victorious British and the host American teams in Newport, Rhode Island in 1886 (it has been played at irregular intervals since); the governing body of American polo, the United States Polo Association, was created in 1890; and the first United States Open Championship was played in 1904. The Westchester Cup functioned as the effective world championship competition throughout this period even though it was very irregularly held; the second Cup was played at Hurlingham in 1902 and was won, like the first, by Great Britain. Great Britain also won the 1914 contest; the United States prevailed in 1909, 1911, and 1913. The principal polo competition in Argentina, the Argentine Open, was first played in 1893. And polo was contested in both the 1900 and 1908 Olympic Games; Great Britain was the champion on both occasions.

Thoroughbred and harness horse racing were among the very most prominent forms of sport in the nineteenth and early twentieth centuries, most particularly in Great Britain and in the main colonies/dominions or former colonies/dominions of Great Britain (principally the United States, South Africa, Australia, Canada, and Ireland). The contemporary modern British racing tradition was, of course, continuing from the eighteenth century. Several of the most notable British thoroughbred races were nonetheless first run in the early nineteenth century: the Ascot Gold Cup, typically for 4-year olds and older over 2 ½ miles (c. 4000 meters) at Royal Ascot, was first run in 1807; the Two Thousand Guineas Stakes, typically for 3-year old colts over 1 mile (c. 1600 meters) at Newmarket (near Cambridge), was first run in 1809 (and later became the first leg in the British triple-crown series, which also included the earlier established St. Leger and English Derby); and the One Thousand Guineas Stakes, typically for 3-year old fillies over 1 mile at Newmarket, was first run in 1814. The practice of steeplechasing developed out of English traditions in cross-country racing and hunting

377

in the 1830s; the most significant of the steeplechase tracks, Aintree (near Liverpool), was established in 1829; the most significant of the steeplechase events, the Grand National Steeplechase, typically for 6-year olds and older over 4 ½ miles (c. 7200 meters) and 30 fences at Aintree, was first run in 1837. And harness horse (or standardbred) racing (in its two major forms, pacing [simultaneous ipsilateral fore and aft leg movements] and trotting [simultaneous contralateral fore and aft leg movements]) was too owed principally in its original modern formulation to early nineteenth-century English practices.

American horse racing likewise continued from the eighteenth century although most of its early champions were British and much of its early energies were devoted to gaining independence from and superiority over British legacies. The most notable achievements of the nineteenth-century and early twen-tieth-century American turf were:

- the establishment of the National Race Course in Washington, D.C. in 1802;
- the establishment of the New York Trotting Club in 1825;
- the victory of the northern thoroughbred, American Eclipse, over the extraordinary southern horse, Sir Henry, in best 2-of-3, 4 miles (c. 6400 meters) match races in Long Island, New York in 1823 (arguably the most significant chapter in the northern state-southern state turf rivalry);
- the 10 miles (c. 16,000 meters) match trotting victory of the American horse, Rattler, over the British horse, Miss Turner, in England in 1829 (arguably the most significant chapter in the American-British turf rivalry);
- the establishment of the oldest major, ongoing thoroughbred stakes race (a race in which all horses carry the same weight) in the country, the Travers Stakes, typically for 3-year olds over 1 ¼ miles (c. 2000 meters) at Saratoga Springs, New York, first run in 1864;
- the establishment of the National Association for the Promotion of the American Trotting Turf, which began to firmly and widely standardize competitive conditions in the sport, in 1870;
- the establishment of the Alabama Stakes, typically for 3-year old thoroughbred fillies over 1 ¼ miles (c. 2000 meters) at Saratoga Springs, first run in 1872;
- the establishment of the triple-crown thoroughbred races for 3-year olds: the Preakness Stakes, typically over 1 3/16 miles (c. 1900 meters) at Pimlico Race Course (near Baltimore), first run in 1873 (became the second leg of the American triple-crown series); the Belmont Stakes, typically over 1 ½ miles (c. 2400 meters) at Belmont Park (Long Island, New York), first run in 1874 (became the third leg of the American triple-crown series); and the Kentucky Derby, typically over 1 ¼ miles at Churchill Downs (Louisville, Kentucky), first run in 1875 (became the first leg of the American triple-crown series);
- the establishment of the Withers Stakes, typically for 3-year old thoroughbreds over 1 mile (c. 1600 meters) at Belmont Park, first run in 1874;
- the establishment of the Kentucky Oaks, typically for 3-year old fillies over 1 1/8 miles (c. 1800 meters) at Churchill Downs, first run in 1875;
- the establishment of the oldest major, ongoing harness race in the country, The Lexington (Kentucky), a trotting mile for 2-year olds, first run in 1875;
- the establishment of the Belmont Futurity, typically for 2-year old thoroughbreds over 6 ½ furlongs (c. 13/16 mile; c. 1300 meters) at Belmont Park, first run in 1888;
- the establishment of the Kentucky Futurity, a trotting mile for 3-year olds at Lexington, Kentucky, first run in 1893; the Kentucky Futurity later became a leg in the trotters' triple-crown series;
- the establishment of The Jockey Club, which began to firmly and widely standardize competitive conditions in thoroughbred racing, in 1894;
- the establishment of the leading American steeplechase events: the Maryland Hunt Cup, typically for 4-year olds and older over 4 miles (c. 6400 meters) and 22 fences at Glyndon, Maryland, first run in 1894; and the United States Grand National Steeplechase, typically for 4-year olds and older over 3 miles (c. 4800 meters) and various fences at Belmont Park, first run in 1899;
- the running of the first 2-minute pacing mile (1:59 ¼) by Star Pointer in 1897;
- the running of the first 2-minute trotting mile (1:58 ½) by Lou Dillon in 1903;
- the magnificent world-record pacing mile of 1:55 ¼ by the legendary Dan Patch (1896-1916) in 1906, a record that stood for c. 32 years; and
- the establishment of the Blue Grass Stakes, typically for 3-year old thoroughbreds over 1 1/8 miles at Keeneland Race Track (near Lexington, Kentucky), first run in 1911.

In the "other colonies," contemporary modern horse racing developed, largely under British influence, from the early nineteenth century. In South Africa, the earliest races were staged and the South African Turf Club was formed in 1802; the South African Jockey Club was established in 1882; and the foremost race in the country, the July Handicap, was first run in 1897. In Australia, the earliest races were staged in 1810; the Australian Racing and Jockey Club was established in 1828; the premier race in the country, the Melbourne Cup, typically for 3-year olds and older over 2 miles (c. 3200 meters) at the Flemington Racecourse (Melbourne), was first run in 1861; and the Australian Jockey Club Derby was first run in 1861, the Caulfield Cup in 1879, and the Australian Oaks in 1885. In Canada, the most storied races were the King's Plate (Quebec), first run in 1836; the Queen's Plate (Ontario), first run in 1860; the Montreal Grand Steeplechase, first run in 1841; the Grand Military Steeplechase, first run in 1843; and the Woodbine (Toronto) Steeplechase Stakes, first run in 1882. And in Ireland, the most renowned race, the Irish Derby Stakes, typically for 3-year olds over 1 ½ miles (c. 2400 meters) at The Curragh (near Dublin), was first run in 1866; the Irish Grand National Steeplechase, typically for 5-year olds and older over 3 5/8 miles (c. 5800 meters) and various fences at Ratoath (near Dublin), was first run in 1870; and the Irish Oaks, typically for 3-year old fillies over 1 ½ miles at The Curragh, was first run in 1895.

Elsewhere in the world, the most notable events occurred in France, Germany, Argentina, Hong Kong, and Italy, again largely under British influence. The Jockey Club of France was established in 1833; the leading race in the country, the French Derby, typically for 3-year olds over 2400 meters (c. 1 ½ miles) at various sites, was first run in 1835; the French Two Thousand Guineas, typically for 3-year old colts and geldings over 1600 meters (c. 1 mile) at Longchamp (Paris), was first run in 1840; the French Oaks, typically for 3-year old and older fillies over 2100 meters (c. 1 ¼ miles) at Chantilly (near Paris), was first run in 1843; the Longchamp Horse Racing Course (L'Hippodrome du Longchamp), the finest in the country and arguably too the finest on the continent, was opened in 1857; the French St. Leger, typically for 3-year olds and older over 3100 meters (c. 1 5/8 miles) at Le Tremblay (near Paris), was first run in 1861; the Grand Prix (Steeple-chase) de Paris, typically for 5-year olds and older over 5800 meters (c. 3 5/8 miles) and various fences at Auteuil (Paris), was first run in 1874; pari-mutuel betting (in which odds are set by wagers placed, not by bookmakers) was invented in France in 1865; and the French One Thousand Guineas, typically for 3-year old fillies over 1600 meters (c. 1 mile) at Longchamp, was first run in 1883. The German development of the period was also especially fecund; the German Two Thousand Guineas, typically for 3-year olds over 1600 meters (c. 1 mile) at Cologne, was first run in 1842; the German Oaks (Preis der Diana), typically for 3-year old fillies over 2200 meters (c. 1 3/8 miles) at Mulheim (near Cologne), was first run in 1857; and the German Derby, typically for 3-year olds over 1 ½ miles (c. 2400 meters) at Hamburg, was first run in 1869. Horse racing in Argentina was most the result of the equestrian traditions of its frontier and of colonial initiatives; the Jockey Club of Buenos Aires was established in 1881; the Gran Premio Jockey Club (the Argentine Derby), typically for 3-year olds over 1 ¼ miles (c. 2000 meters) at San Isidro (Buenos Aires), was first run in 1883; the Gran Premio Carlos Pellegrini, typically for 3-year olds and older over 11 furlongs 205 yards (c. 1 ½ miles; c. 2400 meters) at San Isidro, was first run in 1887; the Gran Premio (the Argentine Oaks), typically for 3-year old fillies over 2200 meters (c. 1 3/8 miles) at Palermo (Buenos Aires), was first run in 1893; the Gran Premio Polla de Potrillas (the Argentine Two Thousand Guineas), typically for 3-year olds over 1 mile (c. 1600 meters) at Palermo, was first run in 1895; and the Gran Premio Polla de Potrancas (the Argentine One Thousand Guineas), typically for 3-year old fillies over 1 mile at San Isidro, was first run in 1895. The Hong Kong Derby was first contested in 1873; and the Italian Derby was first run in Rome in 1900.

The most accomplished jockeys of the nineteenth century were:

- Englishman Fred Archer (1857-86 [suicide]), who raced from the mid-1870s to 1885, who won 2784 (the most victories to his time) of 8004 starts, and who four times won the Two Thousand Guineas, five times won the English Derby, six times won the St. Leger, four times won the Oaks, twice won the One Thousand Guineas, twice won the French Derby, and three times won the Grand Prix de Paris; and

- African-American Isaac Burns Murphy (1861-96), who raced from 1876 to 1895, who won the Kentucky Derby in 1884, 1890, and 1891 and who (like other black American jockeys of the period) suffered notable racial discrimination in the sport.

Other abusive practices were also numerous in nineteenth-century and early twentieth-century horse racing. Gambling (which increased significantly with the development of pari-mutuel betting) and its attendant ills, the doping of race horses, and criminal corruption brought a torrent of criticism down on the sport. Largely on reformist agendas concerning civil rights, temperance, and cruelty to animals, standardized racing codes were eventually established; these codes attempted to correct some of the more unsavory practices common in the horse-racing culture of the period.

Other forms of animal racing were also formalized in the period from the beginning of the nineteenth century to the First World War; most notably, dog racing and dogsled racing. Dog racing grew out of the early modern practice of coursing in which dogs hunted other animals (game animals), principally hares. The first major such competition was the Waterloo (Liverpool, England) Cup Meet of 1837; the first major national organization having to do with coursing, the National Coursing Club, was established in Great Britain in 1858; artificial hares for racing itself were created in England in 1876; and racing in the strict sense (on tracks) was developed in the United States in the first decade of the twentieth century. The earliest dogsled race, the All-Alaska Sweepstakes, from Nome to Candle, a race of 408 miles (c. 645 km), was first held in 1908.

The formative development of contemporary modern **equestrian** as such was also owed to this time. The earliest showjumping activities were practiced in Ireland and Great Britain in the late 1860s but these activities were not much formalized until the late nineteenth and early twentieth centuries. The first major showjumping exhibitions/competitions, the National Horse Show, United States (1883), the Royal International Horse Show, Great Britain (1907), and the King George V Gold Cup, Great Britain (1911), were established in this period. The first modern equestrian competitions of Olympic moment (in principle, of mixed gender) were staged in the Games of 1900 (most notably, an individual jumping event) and 1912 (individual and team jumping, individual dressage, and individual and team 3-day [jumping, dressage, and cross-country riding] events).

Conquest, or nature, sports likewise passed through a burgeoning development in this time; some even began to establish formal institutional groundworks. Hot-air ballooning adventures continued from the eighteenth century; the Aero Club of France, established in 1905, was the first organization to attempt regulation of ballooning; the international governing body of ballooning (as well eventually as other air sports such as parachuting and gliding), the Fédération Aeronautique Internationale (FAI), was established in 1905; and the first international race, an American-inspired event, was conducted in 1906. The first descent by parachute was achieved by the French André Jacques Garnerin (1769-1823) in London in 1802; formal parachuting contests, however, were not done until after the First World War. The first flight of a manned glider (unmotored airplane) was achieved in 1853. Surfing, which had been practiced in Hawaii from at least the late eighteenth century, established its first formal club, the Hui Nalu (Club of the Waves), in Honolulu in 1908; the club and the broader formal development of surfing in the early twentieth century were significantly inspired by the legendary Hawaiian swimmer, thrice Olympic swimming champion, Duke Kahanamoku. Mountaineering/mountain climbing was nonetheless the most prominent of the conquest sports in this period. It had begun in the Alps in the late eighteenth century as has been said. The first formal clubs, the Alpine Club of London and the Deutscher Alpenverein (German Alpine Club) were established in 1857 and 1867 respectively. The first major ascent of the nineteenth century, that of the Matterhorn (4477 meters/14,688 feet; in the Swiss Alps, on the Swiss-Italian border), was achieved in 1865. Others followed; most notably, Kilimanjaro (5895 meters/19,309 feet; in Tanzania, on the Tanzanian-Kenyan border) in 1889 and Mount McKinley (6194 meters/20,361 feet; in south-central Alaska, U.S.A.) in 1906.

The so-termed classical forms of individual sport, track and field athletics, swimming and diving, and gymnastics, experienced an especially prodigious development in the nineteenth and early twentieth centuries. The incipient development of contemporary modern **track and field athletics** was most influenced by the early modern practice of pedestrianism, by the high place accorded track and field exertions in the Highland Games and the Olympic Games, and by the great interest taken in the sport by British, Irish, Canadian, American, and Australian athletic clubs and schools. The continuing practice of pedestrianism was most widely and influentially done in England, Canada, United States, France, Australia, and South Africa and it was most fully developed and most popular between 1830 and 1890. It entailed running and/or walking colossal distances in impressively brief periods and it took mainly professional forms. Athletes were typically dressed in colorful garb; gambling on the results of events was a very prominent feature of them; and major pedestrian events attracted remarkably large numbers of spectators by the standards of the day (as many as 25,000). The most illustrious of the "peds" were:

- Captain Robert Barclay Allardice (1779-1854) of Scotland, who did 1000 miles (c. 1609 km) in 1000 consecutive hours (c. 42 days) in 1809 and 90 miles (c. 145 km) in 21 ½ hours in 1817;
- Mensen Ernst/Mons Monsen Oyri (1799-1843) of Norway, who allegedly ran/walked from Paris to Moscow (c. 1660 miles/c. 2670 km) in 14 days in 1832, from Munich to Nauplion, Greece (c. 1577

miles/c. 2506 km) in 24 days in 1833, and from Constantinople/Istanbul to Calcutta and return (c. 5550 miles/c. 8930 km) in 59 days in 1836; Ernst died on a run from Cairo to Cape Town in 1843;

- Henry Stannard (b. 1811) of the United States, who was said to have been the first to run 10 miles inside 1 hour in 1835;
- William "The American Deer" Jackson/William Howitt (1821-1902) of England, who was the first to do 11 miles (11 miles 40 yards) in 1 hour in 1845 and who did 10 miles in 51:34 in 1852, the best to its time;
- Louis "Deerfoot" Bennett (1828-97), a native American (Senecan), who ran nearly 11 ½ miles in 1 hour in both 1862 (11 miles 720 yards) and 1863 (11 miles 790 yards) and who also ran 10 miles in 51:26 in 1863, all the best to their time; and
- Edward Payson Weston (1839-1929) of the United States, who walked/ran from Boston to Washington, D.C. (c. 442 miles/c. 711 km) in 11 days on the occasion of President Abraham Lincoln's first inauguration in 1861, who walked/ran from Portland, Maine to Chicago (c. 1326 miles/c. 2134 km) in 26 days in 1867 and again in 1906, who walked/ran from New York City to (near) San Francisco (c. 3895 miles/c. 6267 km) in 105 days in 1909 (at the age of 70 years), and who walked/ran from Los Angeles to New York City (c. 3583 miles/c. 5765 km) in 77 days in 1910.

The most illustrious of the pedestrian competitions were the six-day walk-run (or go-as-you-please) contests for men and women that were most prominent between 1870 and 1890. The most prestigious of these, in turn, were the five Sir John Astley (a prominent English statesman and sporting enthusiast who put up the funds for these events) Belt competitions for men of 1878 and 1879, all variously contested in London or New York City. The record for such events (six-day events), an astounding 623 ¾ miles, was done by George Littlefield of England in 1888. The first major six-day go-as-you-please event for women was held in New York City in 1879. Most of the professional walking and running contests of the nineteenth century were over long, flat distances-courses but there were too many such contests staged over sprint and middle-distances and there were as well many such steeplechasing, hurdling, jumping, and throwing competitions; perhaps the most notable of the latter were the Stawell (near Melbourne, Australia) Gift Handicap foot races which began in 1878. Only a semblance of standardization nonetheless prevailed in these events; well into the twentieth century, pre-modern conditions were common, conditions such as suspect handicapping and pacing, sloped surfaces, short courses, erratic timing and measuring, off-sized running tracks (often with irregular turns), assisting wind complications, and sanctioning ambiguities.

The Highland Games were the most significant formal embodiment of amateur track and field exertions from the Middle Ages into the nineteenth century. Although Scottish in origin, they came also to have a very prominent practice in Canada, United States, Australia, and New Zealand, where they were often known as Caledonian Games as has been said. Their influence on the maturation of track and field in North America was especially large. The earliest Caledonian Games on the continent were held in Glengarry, Ontario (near Ottawa) in 1819. Arguably the most consequential such meetings were staged in Boston in 1853, in Montreal in 1856, in New York City (the Great International Caledonian Games) in 1867, and at Princeton University in 1873. These competitions mainly included hammer throwing, shot putting, weight throwing, caber tossing, standing and running long jumping, standing and running high jumping, running triple jumping, pole vaulting, foot racing over flat distances from 100 yards to 1 mile, hurdling, and wrestling events. And they very significantly affected the wider acceptance and practice of track and field athletics. No development had a larger affect on the acceptance and practice of amateur track and field, however, than the modern Olympic Games. Although women's track and field events were not added to the Olympic program until well past the First World War, track and field (for men) is one of only five sports to appear in every edition of the modern Games. The modern international Olympic movement has embraced track and field more fully than any other sport; track and field has been the singularly most significant sport in the Games from their inception; Olympic track and field functioned as the effective world championships of the sport until the 1980s; Olympic track and field has formed among the most storied chapters in the entire history of modern sport; and Olympic track and field has contributed monumentally to the yet broader development of track and field itself as the most widely practiced and among the most heralded of international sporting endeavors.

Also enormously influential in the early formal development of contemporary modern amateur track and field was the deep interest taken in the sport by British, Irish, Canadian, American, and Australian athletic clubs and schools. The earliest of these inclinations were unsurprisingly British. The first contemporary modern track and field club, Necton (near Norwich in southeastern England) Guild, was formed in 1817; amateur races were first held in London at Newmarket Road and Lord's Cricket Ground in 1825; Eton College (near London) was the first of the public schools to establish interclass footraces in 1837 (interclass cross-country, or hare-and-hounds, races were also first staged [at Rugby School] at roughly this time; that is, in the tenure of Dr. Thomas Arnold); the first organized track and field competition as such was conducted at the Royal Military Academy, Woolwich (near London) in 1849; Oxford University was the first of the universities to establish interclass competitions in 1856 (Cambridge University initiated similar contests in 1857); and the West London Rowing Club held competitions in conjunction with rowing events beginning in 1861. The contemporary modern era began in earnest, however, with the first intercollegiate dual competition and the first competition conducted under approximately contemporary standards of regulation, the Cambridge-Oxford meet at Oxford in 1864; each side won four of eight events (100 yards dash, 440 yards dash, 1 mile run, 120 yards high hurdles, 200 yards low hurdles, steeplechase, running high jump, and running long jump). The semblance of the first national championships in the sport in any country, the inaugural English championships, were held under Amateur Athletic Club auspices in London in 1866; and the semblance of the first national championships in cross-country in any country, the inaugural English championships, were staged in 1876. The first authentically national governing body in the sport in any country, the Amateur Athletic Association (AAA), was established in Great Britain in 1880; the Association conducted its first (national) championships in the same year. And the first of the great-city marathons in Europe, the London-Chiswick (Polytechnic Harriers) Marathon, was created in 1909.

Elsewhere in the world, the early development of contemporary modern track and field occurred most significantly in the British ambit. In Ireland, Dublin University established an interclass competition in 1857. In Canada, the first formal track and field competition, the Toronto Athletic Games (which consisted mainly in 100 yards and 400 yards footraces, a steeplechase, running and standing high jumps, running and standing triple jumps, light and heavy stone puttings, hammer throwing, and sack races) were conducted in 1839; the first club devoted to the sport, the Olympic Club of Montreal, was established in 1842 and first conducted track and field competitions in 1843; the Amateur Athletic Association of Canada (which governed track and field, among other sports, in the country) was formed in 1884 and conducted its first (national) championships also in 1884. In Australia, the first club devoted to track and field, the Adelaide Amateur Club, was established in 1864; the first governing body of the sport, the Amateur Athletic Association of New South Wales, was formed in 1887; and the first national championships were staged in 1893. In New Zealand, the governing body of the sport, the New Zealand Amateur Athletics Association, was established in 1887 and conducted its first national championships in 1889.

Great Britain aside, however, it was in the United States that the formative development of contemporary modern track and field athletics achieved its most telling results. The great interest taken in the sport by private athletic clubs and colleges was most responsible for this. Of the clubs, the New York Athletic Club was by far the most influential. It was formed in 1868 as has been said; it staged the first formal competition in the United States, an indoor gathering (at which spiked shoes were first used) in New York City, also in 1868; it constructed the first running cinderpath in the world in 1876; it conducted a semblance of the first national championships (which consisted in a 100 yards dash, 440 yards dash, 880 yards run, 1 mile run, 120 yards high hurdles, running high jump, running long jump, shot put, and hammer throw) in the country too in 1876; and it sponsored among the earliest cross-country (hare-and-hounds) competitions in the Unites States, beginning in 1883. The governance of amateur sport (including track and field) in the broadest sense passed largely to the National Amateur Athletic Association (which was inspired by the New York Athletic Club) at its formation in 1879. The Association staged the first formal composite event (and composed the first scoring tables for composite events) in modern track and field history, the National All-Around Championships (ten events in one day), in 1884; it became the Amateur Athletic Union (AAU) in 1888; and it conducted the first authentically national championships under its auspices also in 1888. The other major achievements of domestic American track and field outside the schools in this time were the establishment of the first of the annual great-city marathons, the Boston Marathon, which is yet among the colossal events of modern sport, in 1897 and the institution of formal Olympic Trials, which is yet among the most exceptional track and field competitions in the world, in 1908.

The earliest American intercollegiate practice of track and field took the form of distance running races for purses conducted in association with rowing regattas. The first of these was a 2 miles run between representatives of three colleges (Amherst, Cornell, and McGill [Canada]) of the eleven participating in the Intercollegiate Crew Regatta at Saratoga, New York in 1873, an event significantly promoted by James Gordon Bennett, Jr. (1841-1918), better known as the hereditary owner of the New York Herald (a corporate newspaper which greatly favored sport) and for his pioneering contributions to the formative development of American sport (most notably, American yachting/sailing and polo). The track and field program associated with the Intercollegiate Crew Regatta was very significantly expanded over the next two years to include also sprinting, hurdling, and walking events. The successes and the promise of these programs led in 1875 to the formation of the first national governing body of intercollegiate track and field in the United States, the Intercollegiate Association of Amateur Athletes of America (IC4A), a student-initiated organization that staged its first track and field championships at Saratoga in 1876 and its first cross-country championships in 1899. The first dual intercollegiate cross-country (hare-and-hounds) competition, Cornell-Pennsylvania, was staged in 1890; the first dual intercollegiate track and field competition, Harvard-Yale, was held in 1891. Among the principal innovative contributions of American track and field to the wider history of the sport, in addition to composite events, were the seminal development of women's competitions and of relay events, both in the collegiate context. A so-termed Field Day (consisting in a 100 yards dash, 220 yards dash, 120 yards hurdles, running high jump, and running long jump) at Vassar College (Poughkeepsie, New York) in 1895 was the first organized women's competition in the sport. Relay events were first done on an intramural basis at the University of Pennsylvania (Philadelphia) in 1893; the practice was greatly expanded into the fabled relay festival, the Pennsylvania Relay Carnival (the Penn Relays), in 1895. The next-most-prominent of the relay festivals, the Drake Relays (Drake University, Des Moines, Iowa), was instituted in 1910. The Intercollegiate Athletic Association (which became the National Collegiate Athletic Association [NCAA] in 1910) has been the governing body of intercollegiate sport (including track and field) from its formation in 1905 even though it was in rather routine dispute (in respect to governance issues) with the IC4A and the AAU until well past the First World War in the former case and well past the Second World War in the latter.

The British influence was also formidable even outside its own immediate ambit; most notably, in France, Germany, and Scandinavia, all of which became early leaders in the sport. The Racing Club of France was established in 1882, the Stade Française, in 1883, and the French national titles were first staged in Paris in 1889. The British influence and the enthusiasm of gymnastic societies for track and field were most responsible for the development of the sport in Germany and Scandinavia. Track and field was a major feature of sporting life in both regions from the 1870s. National governing bodies of track and field were first established in Sweden in 1895 and in Germany in 1898. The principal German and Scandinavian contribution to the programmatic development of contemporary modern track and field, moreover, concerned the creation of composite, or multiple, events. German and Finnish (as well as American and Irish) experiments with such events dated from the 1880s. The most illustrious of such events, the decathlon, was framed by German and Swedish authorities in the early twentieth century; the first formal decathlon competitions were staged in Germany and Sweden in 1911; the first scoring tables for the decathlon, tables which lifted the event from comparative-place scoring, were written also in 1911.

By the late nineteenth century, track and field athletics was being formally and seriously practiced on every continent and in all major athletic nations. It has since become a central feature of the sporting culture of virtually every nation in the world. Unsurprisingly, the incipient development of international track and field was also owed to the nineteenth and early twentieth centuries. The Olympic Games were, of course, the main influence in this respect but there had been as well several prominent international competitions prior to the advent of the Games in 1896; most significantly, the 1888 American participation in the British AAA Championships, the 1892 dual meeting of the Racing Club of France and the Manhattan (New York City) Athletic Club, the 1894 dual meeting of Yale University and victorious Oxford University in London, the 1895 dual meeting of Cambridge University and victorious Yale University in New York City, and the 1895 dual meeting of the London Athletic Club and the victorious New York Athletic Club in New York City. The first international cross-country competition, between England and France, was conducted shortly after the inaugural Games (in 1898). The other most significant international track and field competitions before the First World War were the first International (World) Cross-Country Championships (contested by England, Ireland, Scotland, and Wales) in Glasgow in 1903 and the first multi-sport continental championships (which importantly included track and field), the Far-Eastern Games in Manila in 1913. The original Olympic program, which was representative of the tendencies of the time, included the 100 meters dash, 400 meters dash, 800 meters run, 1500 meters run, marathon, 110 meters high hurdles, running long jump, running triple jump, running high jump, pole vault, shot put, and discus throw. This program was, of course, significantly revised over the next century and came also to (most importantly) include the 200 meters dash, 5000 meters run, 10,000 meters run, steeplechase, 200 meters low hurdles, 400 meters intermediate hurdles, javelin throw, hammer throw, weight throw, and various walking, relay, standing jumping, and composite events, all before the First World War.

The Olympic Games excepted, the singularly most significant development in contemporary modern track and field athletics before the First World War was the establishment of the sport's international governing body, the International Amateur Athletics Federation (IAAF), largely by the initiative of J. Sigfrid Edstrom (1870-1964) of Sweden, who later became the fifth President of the International Olympic Committee. The proposal to institute the Federation was accepted at the 1912 Olympic Games in Stockholm over Coubertin's objections (which argued that the Federation constituted a rival organization to the International Olympic Committee itself). The organization was formally established in Berlin in 1913 and is yet the international governing body of track and field athletics. It has, most notably, standardized competitive conditions and scrutinized world-record performances in the sport. Prior to this time, competitive conditions varied, in some cases widely, and "world records" were nothing other than the "unofficially accepted" best of the national records. The first official register of world-record performances was compiled by the IAAF between 1913 and 1921.

The standards of athletic performance in amateur track and field athletics rose precipitously throughout the nineteenth and early twentieth centuries; by the First World War, they had reached quite remarkable levels. Excepting professional occurrences, which were commonly of suspect authenticity, the most significant figures and achievements of the period in the sprinting events were:

- Charles Absalom of Great Britain and John P. Tennent of Great Britain, who were the first to run 100 yards in 10.0 in 1868;
- Charles H. Sherrill, Jr. of Yale University and the New York Athletic Club (U.S.A.), who was the first to adeptly use the crouch start in 1887 and who equaled the world 100 meters record of 11.2 with it in 1889;
- John Owen of the United States, who ran the first sub-10.0 for 100 yards (9.8) in 1890;
- Luther Cary of the United States, who ran the first sub-11.0 for 100 meters (10.8) in 1891;
- Frank Jarvis (1878-1933) of Princeton University (U.S.A.), the 1900 Olympic 100 meters champion, who equaled the world 100 yards record of 9.8 in 1899 and equaled the world 100 meters record of 10.8 in 1900;
- Bernard J. "Bernie" Wefers (1873-1925) of Georgetown University and the New York Athletic Club (U.S.A.), who equaled the world 100 yards record of 9.8 in 1895 (and again in 1896 and 1897) and who established a stirring world 220 yards (straight-course) record of 21.2 in 1896 that endured for c. 14 years;
- Arthur F. Duffey (1879-1955) of Georgetown University (U.S.A.), who five times equaled the existing world 100 yards record of 9.8 between 1899 and 1902 and who made a new world 100 yards record of 9.6 in 1902 before having been declared a professional;
- Archie Hahn of the University of Michigan (U.S.A.), the 1904 Olympic 60 meters, 100 meters, and 200 meters champion and the 1906 Olympic 100 meters champion, who equaled the world 100 yards record of 9.8 in 1901;
- Howard P. Drew (1890-1957) of the University of Southern California (U.S.A.), who was the first great black sprinter and the first black world-record holder, equaling the world 100 yards record of 9.6 and the world 220 yards (straight-course) record of 21.2, both in 1914;
- Lawrence "Lon" Myers (1858-99) of the Manhattan Athletic Club (U.S.A.), among the sport's most phenomenal early champions, who ran the first sub-50.0 for 440 yards (49.2) in 1879, who later (1881) established an even more exceptional world record of 48.6 for the distance (which he twice tied, in 1881 and 1885), who made seven world 880 yards records from 1880 to 1885 (thrice running 1:55.4 in 1884 and 1885), who equaled the world 100 yards record of 10.0 in 1880, who established a new world 220 yards (turn) record of 22.2 in 1881, who once held every American record from 50 yards to 1 mile, who won fifteen American, ten Canadian, and three English titles, and who was greatly responsible for popularizing American track and field in the late nineteenth century before turning professional; and
- Maxey Long of Columbia University (U.S.A.), the 1900 Olympic 400 meters champion, who established a brilliant world 440 yards record of 47.8 in 1900 that endured for c. 16 years.

The most significant figures and achievements of the period in the middle-distance and long-distance runs were:

- Arthur Pelham of Great Britain, who ran the first sub-2:00 for 880 yards (1:59.8) in 1873;
- Walter Slade of Great Britain, who made three world 880 yards records in 1876 (best of 1:58.2), two world 1 mile records (best of 4:24.5 in 1875), and two world 2 miles records (best of 9:42.0 in 1876);
- Francis H.K. Cross of Great Britain, who ran the first sub-1:55 for 880 yards (1:54.4) in 1888;

- Ted Meredith of the University of Pennsylvania (U.S.A.), the 1912 Olympic 800 meters champion in a world record of 1:51.9 (1:52.5 for 880 yards) that endured for c. 14 years, who made remarkable world records in 1916 over 440 yards (47.4 that endured for c. 16 years; also 47.4 for 400 meters that endured for c. 12 years) and 880 yards (1:52.2 that endured for c. 10 years);
- N.S. Greene of Ireland, who ran the first sub-5:00 for 1 mile (4:46.0) in 1861;
- Walter Chimnery of Great Britain, who ran the first sub-4:30 for 1 mile (4:29.8) in 1868;
- Josef Ternstroem of Sweden, who ran the first sub-10:00 in the 3000 meters steeplechase (9:49.8) in 1914;
- Roland Mitchell of Great Britain, who ran the first sub-10:00 for 2 miles (9:59.0) in 1867;
- James Gibb of Great Britain, who ran the first sub-15:00 for 3 miles (14:46.0) in 1877;
- Walter George (1858-1943) of Great Britain, the finest middle-distance and long-distance runner of the late nineteenth century, who defeated Lon Myers in 2-of-3 match races in New York City in 1882 (among the most celebrated sporting events of the nineteenth century, attended by as many as 50,000 spectators), who thrice between 1880 and 1884 lowered the world 1 mile record (from 4:23.2 to 4:18.4), who ran the first sub-4:20 for 1 mile (4:19.4) in 1882, who made a world record at 2000 meters (5:44.0 in 1882), two world records at 2 miles (best of 9:17.4 in 1884 that endured for c. 19 years), two world records at 3 miles (best of 14:39.0 in 1884), three world records at 6 miles (best of 30:21.5 in 1884), three world records at 10 miles (best of 51:20.0 in 1884 that endured for c. 15 years), and a world record for 1 hour (11 miles 932 yards/18,555 meters in 1884 that endured for c. 20 years), and who then turned professional in which status he ran 1 mile in an astounding 4:12.8 in 1885; and
- Harold Wilson of Great Britain, who ran the first sub-4:00 for 1500 meters (3:59.8) in 1908.

The towering figures of the early twentieth century in long-distance running were Alfred Shrubb (1878-1964) of Great Britain, Jean Bouin of France, and Hannes Kohlemainen of Finland. Shrubb made very long, frequent, and brisk training runs by the standard of the time and thereby revolutionized training methods in the long-distance events. He won the 1903 and 1904 world cross-country titles and eclipsed two of George's longest-standing and most venerable world records: the 2 miles record (9:17.0 in 1903 and 9:09.6 in 1904, a record that itself endured for c. 22 years) and the 1 hour record (11 miles 1137 yards/18,742 meters, also in 1904). He too established new world records in the 2000 meters (5:37.0 in 1904 that endured for c. 12 years), 3 miles (14:17.6 in 1903 that endured for c. 20 years), 6 miles (29:59.4 in 1904 that endured for c. 26 years), 10,000 meters (31:02.4 in 1904), and 10 miles (50:40.6 in 1904 that endured for c. 24 years). Shrubb was declared a professional in 1905 and was thus disqualified from subsequent amateur competition. He participated thereafter in many professional races, the most notable of which were with the widely heralded, native Canadian (Onondagan) runner, Thomas "Tom" Longboat, the 1907 Boston Marathon champion, who had retired from the 1908 Olympic marathon but later participated in stellar professional marathon races with Shrubb and with the heroes of the 1908 Olympic race, Johnny Hayes and Dorando Pietri. Bouin won the 1911, 1912, and 1913 world cross-country titles and made several world records at quite diverse distances: 8:49.6 at 3000 meters in 1911, 30:58.8 at 10,000 meters in 1911 (that endured for c. 10 years), and 11 miles 1442 yards/19,021 meters for 1 hour in 1913 (that endured for c. 15 years). Bouin was very narrowly beaten by Kohlemainen, 14:36.6 to 14:36.7, in what was among the most storied finals in Olympic track and field history, the 1912 Olympic 5000 meters. And Kohlemainen himself, the first of the magnificent Finnish long-distance runners who dominated the sport from 1912 to 1947, also made several world records, at still more diverse distances: two at 3000 meters (best of 8:36.8 in 1912), one at 5000 meters (the 14:36.6 Olympic victory over Bouin in 1912 that was the first sub-15:00 performance in the event and that endured for c. 10 years), two at 25,000 meters (best of 1:25:19.9 in 1922), and one at 30,000 meters (1:47:13.4 in 1922). He was yet more widely acclaimed, however, for his Olympic triumphs at 5000 meters and 10,000 meters in 1912 and his stupendous Olympic marathon victory in 1920.

The unexcelled colossus of race walking prior to the First World War was George Larner of Great Britain, the first great contemporary modern race walker and the 1908 Olympic 3500 meters and 10 miles champion. Larner established six world records from 2 miles to 10 miles, 1904 to 1908; most notably, the stunning 2 miles standard of 13:11.4 in 1904 that endured for c. 39 years (the longest-standing world record in the history of track and field) and the also magnificent 10 miles standard of 1:15:57.4 (that endured for c. 26 years), achieved on the occasion of his 1908 Olympic triumph.

The most significant figures and achievements of the period in the hurdles were:

- Clement Jackson of India-Great Britain, who ran the first sub-17.0 for 120 yards high hurdles (16.0) in 1865;
- Henry Williams of Yale University (U.S.A.), who ran the first sub-16.0 for 120 yards high hurdles (15.8) in 1891;
- Alvin Kranzlein of the University of Pennsylvania (U.S.A.), arguably the finest hurdler of the era, who won the 110 meters high hurdles and the 200 meters low hurdles (as well as the 60 meters dash and running long jump) in the 1900 Olympic Games, who set new world records in the 120 yards high hurdles (15.2) and 220 yards (straight-course) low hurdles (23.6) in 1898 (the latter of which endured for c. 15 years), and who revolutionized hurdling technique with the development of the extended lead-leg;
- the development of movable, inverted T-shaped hurdles (as distinct from various forms of "immovable" barrier) in 1900, a development that allowed hurdlers a significantly more aggressive (and faster) style of hurdle clearance;
- Forrest Custer Smithson (1881-1962) of the University of Oregon (U.S.A.), who won the 1908 Olympic 110 meters high hurdles in a world record (15.0), the first run at 15.0, a mark that endured for c. 12 years, and who further revolutionized hurdling technique with the development of the "independent" trail-leg; and
- Samuel Morris of Great Britain, who ran the first sub-1:00 for 440 yards intermediate hurdles (59.8) in 1886.

Ray Ewry of the United States was among the most accomplished international athletes of the pre-First World War era and the finest standing jumper in the history of contemporary modern track and field athletics. He swept all Olympic titles in the standing jumps from 1900 to 1908, ten in sum (including two in the Intercalated Games of 1906), and yet remained (at the end of the twentieth century) the most decorated individual Olympic victor in track and field. Ewry's records too remained unsurpassed as long as the standing jumps were a standard feature of the sport: 5 feet 5 inches (1.65 meters) in the standing high jump (1900), 34 feet 8 ½ inches (10.58 meters) in the standing triple jump (1900), and 11 feet 4 ¾ inches (3.47 meters) in the standing long jump (1904).

Contemporary modern running-jump competitions took many forms, including a vast array of multiple jumping events and a resurrection of the ancient Greek practice of jumping with hand-weights. The most significant figures and achievements of the period in the standard running horizontal jumps (the running long jump and running triple jump) were:

- John Lane of Ireland, who made the first 23-feet and 7-meters long jump (23 feet 1 ½ inches/7.05 meters) in 1874;
- William J.M. Newburn of Ireland, who, after the advent of the take-off board (which replaced the scratch-line in 1886), made the first 24-feet long jump (24 feet ½ inch/7.33 meters) in 1898;
- Alvin Kranzlein of the University of Pennsylvania (U.S.A.), the 1900 Olympic champion in the long jump (and three other events), who eclipsed the world record in the long jump with a leap of 24 feet 4 ½ inches/7.43 meters in1899;
- Myer Prinstein of Syracuse University (U.S.A.), the 1900 and 1904 Olympic triple jump champion and the 1904 and 1906 Olympic long jump champion, who twice broke the world record in the long jump (best of 24 feet 7 ½ inches/7.50 meters in 1900);
- Peter O'Connor (1874-1957) of Ireland, the 1906 Olympic triple jump champion, who made five world records in the long jump in 1900 and 1901 (best of 24 feet 11 ¾ inches/7.61 meters in 1901 that endured for c. 20 years);
- John Purcell of Ireland, who was the first to achieve distinctly modern distances in the triple jump, who made a precocious world record of 48 feet 3 inches/14.71 meters in 1887 and who, like many others in the late nineteenth century (including the first Olympic champion in the event, James B. Connolly), also leapt in hop, hop, jump (as distinct from hop, step, jump) fashion; he is said to have achieved 49 feet 7 inches/15.11 meters with this style, also in 1887);
- Tim Ahearne of Ireland, the 1908 Olympic champion in the triple jump, who established a memorable world record of 48 feet 11 ¼ inches/14.92 meters on the occasion of his Olympic victory; and
- Daniel F. "Dan" Ahearn (1888-1949) of Ireland-United States, brother of Tim Ahearne, who achieved the first 50-feet and 15-meters triple jump (50 feet 6 inches/15.39 meters) in 1909 and made a second world record of 50 feet 11 inches/15.52 meters in 1911 (that endured for c. 13 years).

The most significant figures and achievements of the period in the running high jump were:

- Marshall Jones Brooks of Great Britain and William Byrd Page of the University of Pennsylvania (U.S.A.), who were the first to achieve distinctly modern heights, both employing the straight scissors style; Brooks was the first to approach 6 feet with a world record of 5 feet 11 inches/1.80 meters in 1874, made the first 6-feet clearance (6 feet/1.83 meters) in 1876, and made another world record of 6 feet 2 ½ inches/1.89 meters, also in 1876; Page made two world records in 1887, 6 feet 3 ¼ inches/ 1.91 meters and 6 feet 4 inches/1.93 meters;
- Michael Francis Sweeney (1872-1947) of Ireland-United States, arguably the most remarkable high jumper prior to the First World War, who made three world records between 1892 and 1895 (6 feet 4 ¼ inches/1.93 meters to 6 feet 5 5/8 inches/1.97 meters [that endured for c. 17 years]) and who created the Eastern cut-off style of jumping; and
- George Leslie Horine (1890-1948) of Stanford University (U.S.A.), who made two world records in 1912, the first of which was the first clearance of 6 feet 6 inches (6 feet 6 1/8 inches/1.98 meters) and the second of which was the first clearance of 2 meters (6 feet 7 inches/2.01 meters), and who created the Western roll style of jumping.

The most significant figures and achievements of the period in the pole vault were:

- J. Wheeler of Great Britain, who made the first 10-feet and 3-meters vault (10 feet/3.05 meters) in 1866 on a heavy (c. 25 lbs./c. 11 kg), hickory pole with a metal tripod (on the plant-end of the pole) for plant;
- Hugh H. Baxter of the New York Athletic Club (U.S.A.), who, like all authentically modern vaulters, rejected the tendency to pole-climbing (moving the hands over one another to higher positions on the pole after take-off), a practice that produced precocious heights in the late nineteenth century (in England particularly) but has been since outlawed, who made the first 11-feet vault (11 feet ½ inch/ 3.37 meters) in 1883, and who twice in 1887 improved the world record to 11 feet 5 inches/3.48 meters, all on a heavy (c. 25 lbs./c. 11 kg), ash pole with a spike (in the plant-end of the pole) for plant;
- Norman Dole of Stanford University (U.S.A.), who made the first 12-feet vault (12 feet 1 ½ inches/3.69 meters) in 1904 on a light (c. 5 lbs./c. 2 kg), bamboo pole;
- Fernand Gonder (1883-1969) of France, the 1906 Intercalated Games champion and the only non-American to win an Olympic vault title until 1972, who made world records of 12 feet 1 ½ inches/ 3.69 meters and 12 feet 3 ¼ inches/3.74 meters in 1904 and 1905 respectively on a bamboo pole;
- Robert Gardner of Yale University (U.S.A.), who, after the advent of the plant box in 1910, made the first 13-feet vault (13 feet 1 inch/3.99 meters) in 1912 on bamboo; and
- Marcus Snowell "Marc" Wright (1890-1975) of Dartmouth College (U.S.A.), who made the first 4-meters vault (13 feet 2 ¼ inches/4.02 meters) in 1912 on bamboo, who fashioned several major innovations in vault technique (including the single-hand release of the pole and the arch style of bar clearance), and who was thus widely considered the first great modern stylist in the event.

The throwing events also passed through especially noteworthy transformations in respect to both technique and performance in the nineteenth and early twentieth centuries. The most significant figures and achievements of the period in the (16 lbs.) shot put (which from 1904 was uniformly thrown from the now-standard 7-feet-diameter circle) were:

- John Stone of Great Britain, who made the first 40-feet put (40 feet 9 ¾ inches/12.44 meters) in 1870;
- George R. Gray (1865-1933) of Canada and the New York Athletic Club, who established seven world records, from 45 feet 1 ¾ inches/13.76 meters in 1889 to 48 feet 4 ¾ inches/14.75 meters in 1898;
- Denis Horgan (1871-1922) of Ireland-United States, who made three world records, from 48 feet ½ inch/14.64 meters in 1897 to 48 feet 9 ¾ inches/14.88 meters in 1904; and
- Ralph Rose of the University of Michigan (U.S.A.), the 1904 and 1908 Olympic shot put champion, who achieved six world records, from 48 feet 7 inches/14.81 meters in 1904 to 51 feet/15.54 meters in 1909 (a mark that endured for c. 19 years), a series that included the first 50-foot put (50 feet 6 inches/15.39 meters) in 1909, and who successfully developed the side-hop style of throwing that was the dominant style until well past the Second World War.

The most significant figures and achievements of the period in the (2 kg) discus throw (which from 1908 was uniformly thrown from the now-standard 2.5-meters-diameter circle) were:

- Carl Erik Oden of Sweden, who made the first 100-feet and 30-meters throw (101 feet 9 ¼ inches/ 31.02 meters) in 1894;
- Martin Sheridan of the Irish-American Athletic Club (U.S.A.), the 1904, 1906, and 1908 Olympic discus throw champion, the 1906 Intercalated Games shot put champion, and among the greatest all-around athletes in the world in the early twentieth century, who established five world records, from 127 feet 8 ½ inches/38.93 meters in 1901 to 144 feet/43.89 meters in 1909, a series that included the first 40-meters throw (133 feet 7 inches/40.72 meters) in 1902, and who successfully developed the one-turn-step style of throwing that was the dominant style for approximately thirty years; and
- James Henry "Jim" Duncan (b. 1887) of the United States, who made two world records (best of 156 feet 1 3/8 inches/47.58 meters in 1912 that was the first 150-feet throw and that endured for c. 12 years).

Eric Lemming of Sweden was the singularly most eminent figure and made the singularly most notable achievements of the period in the (800 grams) javelin throw. Lemming, the 1906, 1908, and 1912 Olympic javelin champion, legendary technical innovator in the event (particularly in respect to the high significance of the approach run), and outstanding all-around athlete, achieved nine world records, from 161 feet 9 ¾ inches/ 49.32 meters in 1899 to 204 feet 5 3/8 inches/62.32 meters in 1912, a series that included the first 50-meters throw (165 feet 5 ¾ inches/50.44 meters) in 1902. The first 40-meters throw (132 feet 5 ¾ inches/40.38 meters), however, had been done by Axel Lindblad of Sweden in 1892; and the first 200-feet and 60-meters throw (201 feet 7 ¼ inches/61.45 meters) was done by Juho Julius Saaristo (1891-1966) of Finland in 1912.

The most significant figures and achievements of the period in the (16 lbs.) hammer throw (which from 1887 was thrown with a flexible metal [as distinct from an inflexible wood] handle and which from 1908 was uniformly thrown from the now-standard 7-feet-diameter circle) were:
- F. Waite of Great Britain, who made the first 100-feet and 30-meters throw (101 feet 5 inches/30.91 meters) in 1869;
- James Sarsfield Mitchel (1864-1921) of Ireland-United States, who established seven world records, from 119 feet 5 inches/36.40 meters in 1886 to 145 feet ½ inch/44.21 meters in 1892, a series that included the first 40-meters throw (133 feet 8 inches/40.74 meters) in 1889;
- John Flanagan of Ireland-United States, the 1900, 1904, and 1908 Olympic champion, who made thirteen world records, from 145 feet 10 ½ inches/44.46 meters in 1895 to 184 feet 4 inches/56.19 meters in 1909, a series that included the first 150-feet throw (150 feet 8 inches/45.92 meters) in 1897 and the first 50-meters throw (164 feet 1 inch/50.01 meters) in 1899, and who successfully developed the first turning technique in the event in 1907 (originally one, then two, toe-jump turns that remained the dominant style for approximately thirty years);
- Matthew J. "Matt" McGrath (1878-1941) of Ireland-United States, the 1912 Olympic champion, who achieved two world records (best of 187 feet 4 inches/57.10 meters in 1911); and
- Patrick James "Pat" Ryan (1883-1964) of Ireland-United States, the 1920 Olympic champion, who set a remarkable world record of 189 feet 6 ½ inches/57.77 meters in 1913, a mark that endured for c. 25 years.

The surpassing talent in the multiple events prior to the First World War was the native American colossus, Jim Thorpe. Arguably the finest male athlete of the first half of the twentieth century, Thorpe won the pentathlon and decathlon titles in the 1912 Olympic Games. In the only decathlon of his illustrious career, he established an imposing world record of 8412 points (in a three-day contest, since reduced to two) on the inaugural scoring tables for the event (written by Swedish authorities in 1911). This utterly magnificent athlete, who excelled in many forms of sporting endeavor as has been said, boasted career bests that approached world standard in virtually all conventional track and field events: 10.0 for 100 yards, 21.8 for 220 yards, 50.8 for 440 yards, 1:57.0 for 880 yards, 4:35.0 for 1 mile, 15.0 in 120 yards high hurdles, 24.0 in 220 yards low hurdles, 23 feet 6 inches/7.16 meters in running long jump, 6 feet 5 inches/1.95 meters in running high jump, 11 feet/3.35 meters in pole vault, 47 feet 9 inches/14.55 meters in shot put, 136 feet/41.45 meters in discus throw, 163 feet/49.68 meters in javelin throw, and 140 feet/42.67 meters in hammer throw.

Swimming and diving, like track and field athletics, too formalized and standardized significantly older practices and thereby established its basic, modern provisions in the nineteenth and early twentieth centuries. The first contemporary modern swimming clubs (and organized races) were established in Japan in 1810 and in England in 1825; the first artificial swimming pool of notable dimension, an indoor, public facility, was constructed in Liverpool, England in 1828; the first national swimming organization, the National Swimming Society of Great Britain, was formed in 1837; the first organized (national) swimming championships were contested in Australia in 1846; and the first international swimming race, between Charles Stedman of Great Britain and the victorious Jo Bennet of Australia, was staged in 1858. The first formal rules were fashioned by the Associated Metropolitan Swimming Clubs, London in 1869; the first men's national championships of England were done in 1871; the first men's national championships of the United States were held in 1877 (under New York Athletic Club auspices); the first continental championships, the European Championships, were first held (albeit in unofficial terms) in Vienna in 1889 (but were not wholly formalized until 1926); the first women's national championships were contested in Scotland in 1892; the first intercollegiate swimming competition, among Columbia University, the victorious University of Pennsylvania, and Yale University, was held in the United States in 1909; and the first formal Oxford-Cambridge dual competition was done in 1908 (although the first informal such competition had occurred in 1892). The earliest national governing bodies were also established in the late nineteenth century: the Amateur Swimming Association, Great Britain, 1874 (which was itself especially much entangled in the amateur-professional disputes and debates that were common in the period); the German Swimming Federation, 1882; the New Zealand Swimming Association, 1890; the Australian Swimming Association, 1891; and the French Swimming Federation, 1899. And the international governing body of the sport, Fédération Internationale de Natation Amateur (FINA), was created in 1908, mainly for the purposes of standardizing competitive conditions in the sport and of scrutinizing world-record performances; this organization is yet the international governing body of swimming (as well as diving, synchronized swimming, and water polo). FINA published its first register of world records in 1908. The seminal development of modern stroke mechanics was also owed to this period:

- The breaststroke (prone position) and sidestroke (side-lying position), both with underwater arm actions and frog kicks, were fashioned out of similar earlier practices in England in c. 1828;
- The sidestroke with scissors kick was developed in England in c. 1840;
- The single-over-arm sidestroke (one-arm recovery out of the water) was created by C.W. Wallis of Australia in 1850 and remained the dominant stroke for approximately fifty years;
- The trudgeon stroke (crawl arms and scissors kick from a prone position) was fashioned by John Arthur Trudgen (1852-1902) of England in 1873 from observations of native South American practices;
- The Australian crawl (freestyle) stroke (crawl arms and two-beat flutter kick from a prone position) was created by Frederick John "Fred" Cavill (1839-1927) of England-Australia and his six sons, principally Richmond Theophilus "Richard" "Dick" Cavill (1884-1938), also of England-Australia, in 1898-1902 from observations of native Pacific Islander practices; Cecil Healy of Australia revised the kick to a four-beat action in 1906;
- The American crawl (freestyle) stroke (crawl arms and six-beat flutter kick from a prone position) was developed by Charles Daniels of the United States in 1906; and
- The backstroke (or back crawl; crawl arms and flutter kick from a supine position) evolved progressively out of a supine breaststroke (simultaneous double-arm recovery out of the water and frog kick) between 1902 and 1912.

The contemporary modern swimming program (for men) likewise took gradual shape in the period immediately preceding the First World War: freestyle (trudgeon stroke) events were contested over 100 meters, 500 meters, and 1200 meters distances in the first modern Olympic Games in 1896 (these events were done in Australian and American crawl styles from 1904), a backstroke event (over a 200 meters distance) was added to the Olympic program in 1900, and breaststroke (over a 440 yards distance) and freestyle relay (in the form of 4 x 50 yards) events came onto the Olympic program in 1904. What has since become the standard program for men took further form in the 1908 Olympic Games when 100 meters freestyle, 400 meters freestyle, 1500 meters freestyle, 100 meters backstroke, 200 meters breaststroke, and 4 x 200 meters freestyle relay events were contested. Swimming (for men) is one of only five sports to appear in every edition of the modern Games. An individual 100 meters freestyle and a 4 x 100 meters freestyle relay for women were added to the Olympic program in 1912. The standards of athletic performance in swimming also rose precipitously throughout the nineteenth and early twentieth centuries. The most significant figures and achievements of this period were:

- Captain Matthew Webb (1848-83) of England, who, in 1875, was the first person to successfully swim the English Channel; on his second attempt, Webb swam by means of breaststroke from England to France, an approximately 38-mile distance, in 21 hours and 45 minutes, a performance that remained the record for the England-to-France direction of the crossing until 1934; no other person achieved the crossing in either direction until 1911; Webb drowned in an attempt to swim across the rapids just above Niagara Falls (North America) in 1883;

- Alfred Hajos of Hungary, who won the 100 meters and 1200 meters freestyle events in the 1896 Olympic Games;
- Richard Cavill of England-Australia, who was the first person to beat one minute for 100 yards (58.6 by means of Australian crawl stroke) in London in 1902; Cavill later (in 1904) improved his world record to 58.0;
- Frederick Claude Vivian "Freddy" Lane (1880-1969) of Australia, who won the 1900 Olympic 200 meters freestyle and 200 meters obstacle swimming events, who achieved two world 100 yards freestyle records (an equaling 1:00.0 in 1902 and 59.6 also in 1902), and who made a world 200 meters freestyle record of 2:28.6 likewise in 1902;
- Charles Daniels of the United States, who won three freestyle events in the 1904 Olympic Games, one in the 1906 Intercalated Games, and the 100 meters freestyle in world-record time (1:05.6) in the 1908 Olympic Games (after swimming a record-equaling 1:05.8 in qualifying); Daniels also equaled the world 100 yards freestyle record of 57.6 in 1906, then thrice lowered it (56.0 in 1906, 55.4 in 1907, and 54.8 in 1910), reduced the world 100 meters freestyle record to 1:02.8 in 1910, and achieved a world 200 meters freestyle record of 2:25.4 in 1909; he too won 33 national AAU freestyle titles over very diverse distances (50 yards to 1 mile) throughout his illustrious career;
- Zoltan von Halmay of Hungary, who won the 50 yards freestyle and the 100 yards freestyle in the 1904 Olympic Games as well as the 4 x 250 meters freestyle relay in the 1906 Intercalated Games, who also medaled widely in the 1900 and 1908 Olympic Games, and who achieved a world 100 meters freestyle record of 1:05.8 in 1905 and a world 200 meters freestyle record of 2:26.8 in 1908;
- Henry Taylor of Great Britain, who won a freestyle event in the 1906 Intercalated Games and the 400 meters freestyle (in a world record, 5:36.8, after swimming a world record in qualifying), 1500 meters freestyle (in a world record, 22:48.4, after swimming two world records in qualifying), and 4 x 200 meters freestyle relay in the 1908 Olympic Games; Taylor also made an 800 meters freestyle record of 11:25.4 in 1906; and
- Fanny Durack of Australia, who became the first female champion in a major modern Olympic sport with her victory in the 100 meters freestyle in the 1912 Olympic Games and who achieved three world records in the 100 meters freestyle (from 1:19.8 in a qualifying heat of the 1912 Games to 1:16.2 in 1915) and a world record in the 200 meters freestyle (2:56.0 in 1915).

Diving, not unlike track and field athletics, was widely practiced in the nineteenth-century German and Swedish gymnastic societies; its contemporary modern form developed there as a modification of acrobatic gymnastics to water. Although the first contemporary modern diving competition was staged in England in 1880, most of the early international champions in the sport, mainly Olympic titlists and medalists, were German or Swedish. An unofficial European Diving Championships for men, a springboard event, was first contested in 1889, although it was not wholly formalized until 1926. The contemporary modern international diving program began to take firm shape in the early twentieth century: men's platform diving (variously combined with a form of springboard diving) came onto the Olympic schedule in 1904; men's springboard diving (variously combined with a form of platform diving) came onto the Olympic schedule in 1908; men's platform and springboard diving became altogether independent events in the 1912 Games; and women's platform diving came onto the Olympic schedule in 1912. Diving, like swimming itself, has been governed internationally by FINA since 1908. The first modern synchronized swimming competition was contested among men only in England in 1892. The earliest suggestion of the sport's distinctly modern version, however, was owed to Annette Kellerman (1887-1975) of Australia, who first made water-ballet exhibitions in New York City in 1907. The sport did nonetheless not gain a large international stature until well after the Second World War, when it was practiced almost exclusively by women.

The seminal development of contemporary modern **gymnastics** was a largely Continental European phenomenon. This development was owed principally to the informal acrobatic practices of early modern inns, taverns, fairs, festivals, streets, and, like that of contemporary modern diving, to the nineteenth-century German and Swedish regimens of calisthenic exercise and physical education. From the German naturalistic gymnastics, effectively the Turner's movement, evolved the main forms of apparatus event: high (or horizontal) bar, parallel bars, (flying and still) rings, pommelled (or side) horse, and vaulting (or long) horse, as well as balls, clubs, hoops, and ropes (the precursors of rhythmic gymnastics), balance beam, and rope climbing. From the Swedish militaristic gymnastics, largely of Per Henrik Ling, evolved the main forms of non-apparatus event: free (or floor) exercise (or calisthenics), tumbling, and acrobatic gymnastics, as well as rhythmic gymnastics, balance beam, and rope climbing. Many of the formative organizations and gatherings devoted to gymnastic activity were most concerned with regimens of calisthenic exercise (and with closely related activities) as distinct from sporting prowess itself. By slightly past mid-century, however, the earliest organizations and competitions devoted to gymnastic sport had begun their long and uneven development. Gymnastic clubs variously to do with exercise as such and to do with sport as well had been maturing, throughout northwestern, central, and eastern Europe in particular, from the early nineteenth century. Gymnastics also played an especially significant role in the workers' sport movement of the late nineteenth and early twentieth centuries (most notably, in Germany), in the women's sport movement of the late nineteenth and early twentieth centuries (most notably, in Germany), and in the Jewish sport movement of the late nineteenth and early twentieth centuries (most notably, also in Germany).

The first national governing body devoted to gymnastic sport, the Belgian Federation of Gymnastics (Fédération Belge de Gymnastique), was established in 1865. Other national federations (and accompanying national exhibitions and competitions) soon followed: Poland (1867), the Germanies (Deutsche Turnerschaft, 1868), Hungary (1868), Netherlands (1868), Switzerland (1869), Sweden (1869), France (1873), Russia (1883), Austria (1885), Great Britain (1888), Bohemia (Bohemian Sokol Union, 1889), and Finland (1896). The international governing body of gymnastics, the European Gymnastics Federation (Fédération Européenne de Gymnastique) was formally established in 1903 out of informal meetings (and agreements) first held (and struck) in 1881 in Belgium. This organization staged the semblance of world championships (international championships) in Antwerp in 1903, conducted similar competitions every approximately two years thereafter, and became the Fédération Internationale de Gymnastique (FIG) in 1921; FIG is yet the international governing body of gymnastic sport. The first major international competitions were held in 1891 and 1894, in Stockholm and Helsinki respectively, between Swedish and Finnish gymnasts. The first intercollegiate competition was done in the United States in 1899 among nineteen teams (mainly, Brown, Columbia, Cornell, Harvard, Pennsylvania, Princeton, Rutgers, and Yale) and was won by Yale University. Gymnastics (for men) is one of only five sports to appear in every edition of the modern Olympic Games. The contemporary modern international gymnastics program for men began to crystallize in the late nineteenth century: the horizontal (high) bar, parallel bars, pommelled horse, rings, vaulting horse, and rope climbing all appeared on the program of the first modern Olympic Games in 1896; the individual all-around came onto the Olympic program in 1900; the team all-around, in 1904; and club swinging, also in 1904. The program of the first World Championships in 1903 included individual and (six-person) team all-around, horizontal (high) bar, parallel bars, rings, and vaulting horse events; the pommelled horse was added in 1911; and free exercise came onto the program in 1913. The international gymnastics program for women did not come to form until well past the Second World War. Before the First World War, international gymnastics was dominated by Continental European athletes; the Olympic team all-around title was won by the United States in 1904 (virtually by default), Norway in 1906, Sweden in 1908, and Italy in 1912; the world team all-around title was won by France in 1903, 1905, and 1909 and by Czechoslovakia in 1907, 1911, and 1913. The most remarkable gymnast of this time was Alberto Braglia of Italy. Braglia, the first great contemporary modern gymnast, won the individual all-around titles in the 1908 and 1912 Olympic Games and also led Italy to the team all-around title in 1912.

Like the so-termed classical forms of individual sport, virtually all other individual, non-winter sports also formalized and standardized their basic, modern provisions in the nineteenth and early twentieth centuries: archery, bowling, canoeing and kayaking, cycling, golf, modern pentathlon, rowing, shooting, weightlifting, and yachting/sailing. The practice of **archery** in this period evolved out of significantly older practices, often included women as well as men, and varied greatly in respect to the nature of targets, their distances from archers, the number of rounds shot at manifold targets and distances, and the manner of scoring. It was most significantly distinguished by the establishment of:

- the United Bowmen of Philadelphia (U.S.A.) in 1828;
- the Grand National Archery Association , Great Britain in 1844;
- the first British national titles in 1844;
- the National Archery Association, United States in 1879;
- the first American national titles in 1879; and
- an Olympic program for men in 1900 (temporarily discontinued in 1912) and for women in 1904 (discontinued after 1908 until 1972).

Contemporary modern **bowling** also grew out of significantly older practices and developed in many forms, mainly varieties of pin bowling and lawn bowling. Pin bowling evolved principally out of German traditions in the Germanies, Netherlands, Austria, and Switzerland, traditions that had their most notable consequences in the United States. These traditions were variously termed (most notably, kegels and skittles) and they did themselves vary extensively in respect to the number, dimension, and shape of the pins, the configurations in which the pins were placed, the dimension, composition, and mass of the balls, the character of the indoor and outdoor surfaces on which the sport was played, and the rules by which the sport was conducted. Lawn bowling was the dominant form of the sport in Great Britain/Ireland, Australia, France, and Italy. In Great Britain/Ireland and Australia, the sport was known as bowls; in France, other significant variations known as la boule and petanque developed; and in Italy, still another significant variation known as la bocce, or boccie, was fashioned. The most notable developments in pin bowling during this period were the establishment of:

- clubs in New York City (U.S.A.) in the 1840s;
- bottle-shaped pins out of candlestick pins in the United States, c. 1850;
- the National Bowling League, United States in 1875;
- the American Bowling Congress (in 1895), which developed 10-big-pin alley bowling out of the 9-pin Dutch game, which brought uniform conditions to the sport, and which conducted its first (national) championships in 1901;
- duck-pin alley bowling in the United States in 1900 under the influence of American-rules baseball legend, John J. McGraw; and
- 5-pin bowling, which developed out of the 10-pin game in Canada in 1909.

The most notable developments in lawn bowling during this period were the establishment of:

- clubs around the activities of inns and taverns in Ireland (Belfast Bowling Club, 1842), Australia, and Scotland in the 1840s;
- standardized rules in Scotland in 1848-49;
- a national association devoted to an associated sport, the Scottish Quoiting Association , in 1880;
- the Scottish Bowling Association in 1892;
- the first international (test) match, between Australia and England, in London in 1901;
- the English Bowling Association in 1903 and the Hong Kong Lawn Bowls Association in 1909;
- an international governing body for bowls, International Bowling Board, in 1905; and
- the semblance of world championships in an associated sport, the World Horseshoe Pitching Championships, in the United States in 1909.

Contemporary modern **canoeing and kayaking** grew out of significantly older practices among native Indian and Eskimo peoples in the Americas and among native Polynesian peoples in the central and south Pacific. The seminal development of canoeing and kayaking as a sport was owed principally to John MacGregor (1825-92) of Great Britain, who fashioned the first sporting craft (kayak-like vessels that were variously sailed and propelled by double-bladed paddles) in the 1860s, who extensively cruised the rivers of Europe and the near Middle East in these vessels, and who was mainly responsible for establishing the first club devoted to the sport, the Royal Canoe Club, London, in 1865. American and Canadian precincts made the other major, early contributions to the development of contemporary modern canoeing and kayaking. The first American club, the New York (City) Canoe Club, was formed in 1871; it crafted (Canadian) canoe-like vessels that were variously sailed and propelled by single-bladed paddles; and it established the first major international competition (for sailing canoes), the International Challenge Trophy, in 1885. The American Canoe Association was created in 1880 (and came to include wild-water as well as flat-water activities for both men and women in 1900) and the Canadian Canoe Association was formed in 1900.

Unlike other major, contemporary modern sports, which formalized activities that had been earlier practiced in some discernible form, **cycling** (or wheeling) was an invention of the industrial age. Although unpolished devices resembling bicycles had been fashioned in France and the Germanies in the seventeenth and eighteenth centuries, these devices were propelled only by variously pushing them. It was not until the nineteenth century, in France, the Germanies, Scotland, and England, that contemporary modern bicycles (or velocipedes) were developed. And it was not until 1870-85 that James K. Starley (1831-81) of England brought all of the major elements of the contemporary modern bicycle together (in the form of the Ariel): the pedals, chain, gears, spoked wheels, inflatable tires, and approximately equally sized front and rear wheels. The sport was enormously popular among men and women in both participatory and professional terms, most significantly in France, North America, and Australia and most especially between 1860 and 1900; it contributed tellingly to the social and sporting emancipation of women in this time; and it contributed very significantly to the "good roads movement" of the late nineteenth century. It declined rather sharply, however, at the end of the nineteenth and the beginning of the twentieth centuries as the cities closed access to the countryside, as the automobile advanced in popularity, and as its popularity waned among women. As an elite sport, nineteenth-century and early twentieth-century cycling was a largely professional affair.

The first club, the Véloce Club of Rennes (in Brittany, France), was formed in 1869. The earliest national federations were established in Great Britain (National Cyclists' Union) in 1878, United States (League of American Wheelmen) in 1880, France (Union Vélocipédique de France) in 1881, Canada (Canadian Wheelmen's Association) in 1882, Netherlands in 1883, and Germany (German Cycling Federation) in 1884. The earliest national titles (in the form of individual road races) were done in Netherlands in 1888, Belgium in 1894, Italy in 1906, and France in 1907. The first international association devoted to cycling, the International Cyclist Association, was formed in 1892; this association was replaced by the principal international governing body of modern cycling, the Union Cycliste Internationale (UCI), in 1900; and cycling conducted its first world championships in 1893. The international governing body of contemporary modern amateur cycling, Fédération Internationale Amateur de Cyclisme (FIAC), was created in 1900.

The earliest major races were often used for testing machines in order to improve their design and their profitable manufacture. The first of these was a 1200 meters/c. ¾ mile race in Paris in 1868. The other most notable early races were annual, one-day, long-distance contests customarily done from one city to another; most notably, Rouen (northwest of Paris)-Paris, c. 133 km/c. 83 miles, first staged in 1869; Bath (due west of London)-London, c. 100 miles/c. 161 km, first staged in 1874; Bordeaux (southwest of Paris)-Paris, c. 600 km/c. 374 miles, first staged in 1891; Liège-Bastogne-Liège (in Belgium), La Doyenne, c. 200 km/c. 125 miles, in 1892; Paris-Brussels, c. 240 km/c. 150 miles, in 1893; Paris-Roubaix (due north of Paris), The Hell of the North, c. 270 km/c. 168 miles, in 1896; Paris-Tours (southwest of Paris), c. 240 km/c. 150 miles, in 1896; the Tour of Lombardy (in Italy), c. 250 km/c. 156 miles, in 1905; Milan-San Remo (southwest of Milan, near Genoa), La Primavera, c. 290 km/c. 180 miles, in 1907; and the Ronde van Vlaanderen/Tour of Flanders (mainly in Belgium), c. 270 km/c. 169 miles, in 1913. Not unlike the pedestrianism of this time, professional six-day, or go-as-you-please, cycling events also commanded great attention. The first of these was held in England in 1878. The first major cycling race for women was a six-day indoor contest in New York City in 1885, won by Frankie Nelson of the United States. The most notable of the six-day events, The International, began as an individual indoor race in New York City in 1891; it became a two-person (team) race in 1899 and continued well past the Second World War. The record for the individual event was 2093 miles by Charlie Miller of the United States in 1898. Cross-continent and around-the-world feats likewise added to the wide sporting acclaim of cycling. Arguably the most remarkable of these feats was that of Thomas Stevens (1854-1935) of England-United States, who was the first to ride a bicycle across the United States (San Francisco to Boston, c. 3700 miles/c. 5950 km) in 1884, an exploit requiring 84 days; Stevens continued around the world, a deed requiring 971 days (-1886). The first intercollegiate cycling match, between Columbia University and victorious Yale University, was staged in 1880 in association with the IC4A track and field championships. The first world championship competitions were all track contests, a sprint event and a 100 km motor-paced event for amateurs instituted in Chicago in 1893 as well as a sprint event and a 100 km motor-paced event for professionals instituted in Cologne in 1895; both the amateur and the professional competitions were conducted on a virtually annual basis thereafter. European track championships were first conducted in Berlin in 1896. And the first Olympic races – principally an individual road race (over 87 km/c. 54 miles but since over various distances from 84 km/c. 52 miles to 320 km/c. 200 miles), a sprint (over 1/3 km/c. 1/5 mile but since 1928 over 1 km), and a time trial (over 2 km but since 1906 over 1 km), all for men – were included in the first Games of the modern era in 1896. Cycling (for men) is one of only five sports that has been a part of every modern Olympic celebration. A (four-person) team pursuit event (over 1810 meters/c. 1 1/8 miles but since 1920 over 4000 meters) was added to the Olympic program in 1908; a (four-person, later became a three-person) team road race (over the same distance and in the same context as the individual road race) was added in 1912, and track races of various distances (or durations) were included from 1896. The Olympic cycling program for women did not take form until well past the Second World War.

The crown of contemporary modern cycling, moreover, the annual, multiple-stage, road races, were likewise first established in the period immediately preceding the First World War. The first, and yet the most prestigious, of these, the Tour de France, was created in 1903 by the editor of a prominent sport newspaper (L'Auto), who was also a renowned cyclist, Henri Desgrange (1865-1940). The Tour was to have enhanced the competitive position of the newspaper vis-à-vis rival journals; it was open to both amateur and professional cyclists; and it was very significantly influenced by commercial sponsors and commercial advertising. Although since typically contested over 21-25 stages and over approximately 2000-3000 miles/c.

3700-5600 km in approximately three to four weeks, the first Tour was done in six days and over a 2428 km/c. 1510 miles distance. The other most prominent of the annual, multi-stage, road races was also established in this period, the Giro d'Italia (Tour of Italy), in 1909; so too was the Vuelta a Catalunya (Tour of Catalonia) in 1911. The most significant cycling figures and achievements of the nineteenth and early twentieth centuries were:

- Charles Terront (1857-1932), the first great, contemporary modern French athlete and the finest (professional) cyclist of the 1870s-1890s;
- Marshall "Major" Taylor (1878-1932), an African-American phenom, the finest (professional) cyclist of the last decade of the nineteenth century and the first decade of the twentieth; the 1899 world professional sprint champion;
- Henri Desgrange of France, an amateur, who established the inaugural world 1-hour record of 21 miles 1674 yards/35,357 meters in 1893;
- Paul Masson of France, an amateur, who won three events in the 1896 Olympic Games, the time trial (1/3 kilometer), sprint (2000 meters), and 10,000 meters track race;
- Francesco Verri, an amateur, the first of the great Italian cyclists, who won three events in the 1906 Intercalated Games, the time trial (1/3 kilometer), sprint (1000 meters), and 5000 meters track race; also the 1906 world amateur sprint champion;
- Oscar Egg (1890-1961) of Switzerland, a professional, who thrice (1912, 1913, and 1914) broke the world 1-hour record; his 27 miles 1450 yards/44,778 meters record of 1914 endured for c. 19 years; Egg also won Paris-Tours in 1914; and
- Philippe Thys (1890-1971), a professional, the first of the great Belgian cyclists, who was also the first to thrice (1913, 1914, and 1920) win the world's premier cycling competition, the Tour de France; Thys also won Paris-Tours in 1917 and the Tour of Lombardy likewise in 1917.

Contemporary modern **golf** was too formalized and standardized out of notably older practices in the nineteenth and early twentieth centuries. As in the case of early modern developments, contemporary modern golf was owed principally to Scottish initiatives. The earliest formal club, the Ancient Golf Club of St. Andrews, and the earliest formal rules were established in eighteenth-century Scotland as has been said. The sport was disseminated elsewhere in the world mainly by Scottish people throughout the nineteenth century: the Calcutta (India) Golf Club was formed in 1829; the Bombay (India) Golf Club, in 1842; the Melbourne (Australia) Golf Club, in 1847; the Montreal (Canada) Golf Club, in 1873; the Belfast (Ireland) Golf Club, in 1881; and the St. Andrews Golf Club of Yonkers, New York (near New York City, U.S.A.), in 1888. The first club for women (Ladies' Golf Club, St. Andrews, 1867), the first great tournament (the British Open), and the first great players were all Scottish as well. The British Open, the earliest of what are yet the so-termed grand-slam, or major, tournaments, began as a local invitational tournament (without respect to amateur-professional distinctions) in Prestwick, Scotland (near Glasgow) in 1860; it has always been conducted in stroke-play format (over 36 holes from 1860 to 1891 and over 72 holes from 1892); it became a fully open tournament in 1865, adopted the Little Claret Jug Trophy (which yet symbolizes victory in the tournament) in 1872, and moved about Scotland (and eventually about Great Britain) after 1872. The most remarkable early players of contemporary modern golf were a Scottish father and son, each of whom won the British Open tournament four times: Tom Morris, Sr. (1821-1908) won in 1861, 1862, 1864, and 1867 and Tom Morris, Jr. (1851-75) won in 1868, 1869, 1870 (with an astounding, record score of 149 for 36 holes), and 1872. Many of the other most notable tournaments in the world were also established in this period, mainly in Great Britain, United States, and Canada. The most significant of these were:

- the British (Men's) Amateur Championship in 1885, originally a grand-slam, or major, tournament;
- the British Ladies' Amateur Championship in 1893; under the auspices of the Ladies' Golfing Union, Great Britain, also established in 1893;
- the United States (Men's) Open in 1895, yet a grand-slam, or major, tournament; under the auspices of the United States Golf Association, formed in 1894; it has always been conducted in stroke-play format (over 9 holes in 1895, over 36 holes in 1896 and 1897, and over 72 holes since 1898);
- the Canadian (Men's) Amateur Championship in 1895; under the auspices of the Royal Canadian Golf Association, created in 1894;
- the United States (Men's) Amateur Championship in 1895, originally a grand-slam, or major, tournament;
- the United States Women's Amateur Championship in 1895;
- the Western (Men's) Open and Western (Men's) Amateur, United States, both in 1899;

- the Canadian Women's Amateur Championship in 1901;
- the Canadian (Men's) Open in 1904; and
- the Canadian (Men's) Professional Championship in 1912.

The first dual intercollegiate golf match, between Columbia University and victorious Yale University, was staged in 1896; American intercollegiate golf came under the jurisdiction of the Intercollegiate Golf Association of America on its establishment in 1897; the Association held its first national individual and team championships also in 1897; these championships were discontinued after 1916. The first dual international golf match, between Canada and United States, was played in 1898. And the first Olympic events in golf, the men's individual competition and the women's individual competition, were held in 1900; the last such events, the men's individual and team competitions, were held in 1904. The level of play in golf tournaments improved dramatically throughout the nineteenth and early twentieth centuries. Much of this was due to vast improvements in golf courses (effectively due to vast improvements in turf management) and in golf equipment. From the wooden balls most widely used in the eighteenth century developed feather and leather balls in the early nineteenth century, gutta percha (resinous gum) balls in 1848, rubber-cored balls in 1899, and cork-rubber balls in the early twentieth century. Clubs of wood were used throughout this time but their design improved steadily. Much of the enhanced level of play most apparent in the period immediately prior to the First World War was also due to the increasingly articulate techniques and skills of increasingly exceptional athletes. The most extraordinary of these athletes was the finest English-British player in the entire history of the game, Harry Vardon (1870-1937). Vardon, who crafted the revolutionary, overlapping grip in the first decade of the twentieth century, won the British Open six times (1896, 1898, 1899, 1903, 1911, and 1914) and the United States Open once (1900). His highly influential tour of the United States in 1900 contributed significantly to the widening popularity of the sport. In 1913, however, he was unexpectedly beaten in a dramatic play-off at the United States Open by a young American player, Francis Ouimet (1893-1967). Ouimet was the first American to achieve a major international victory in golf; he was the first amateur to win the United States Open; he twice won the United States Amateur Championship (1914 and 1931); and, by his humble origins (he had been, for prominent instance, a caddie, effectively a servant by the standard of the day), he implied (in the progressive-tending second decade of the twentieth century) the opening of what had been a largely aristocratic-bourgeois sport to those of working-class station.

The **modern pentathlon**, or military pentathlon, had no pre-twentieth-century correlate but is comprised of activities that had been variously practiced for centuries to millennia. The sport was invented by the principal architect of the modern international Olympic movement, Baron Pierre de Coubertin, in the early twentieth century. It embodies the major skills of military life, horse riding, fencing, shooting, swimming, and running. Although the order of events (and the number of days over which these events are contested) has varied, the events themselves have, until 1996, included a 5000 meters equestrian cross-country steeplechase ride, épée fencing, 25 meters rapid-fire pistol shooting, 300 meters freestyle swimming, and 4000 meters cross-country running. Its first major competition was the inaugural Olympic contest in 1912 where it took the form of an individual (not a team) activity. It was at that time scored in relative terms (as an aggregate of the orders of finish in each event) and it was swept by Swedish athletes, who continued to dominate the sport until the 1950s.

Rowing was among the most prominent of sports in the late nineteenth century and it participated as stridently as any sport in the amateur-professional disputes that characterized the time. The contemporary modern formalization and standardization of rowing grew largely out of eighteenth-century English developments and this standardization and formalization unfolded most tellingly in Great Britain, United States, Canada, and Australasia. Not unlike track and field athletics, with which it was often associated, the early growth of rowing as a sport owed especially much to the interest taken in it by the schools and by the athletic clubs in these countries. Rowing had been practiced in England from at least the early eighteenth century as has been said; the first rowing club, the Leander Club, was established in England in 1818. The sport had been practiced in North America from at least 1811; the first rowing club on the continent, the Castle Garden Boat Club, was established in New York City (U.S.A.) in 1834. And rowing was practiced in Australasia from at least 1827; the earliest rowing club in Australasia was established in Sydney (Australia) in 1835. The earliest national organizations devoted to rowing were fashioned in the United States (National Association of Amateur Oarsmen, 1872), Great Britain (Metropolitan Rowing Association, 1879; Amateur Rowing Association, 1882; and National Amateur Rowing Association, 1890), and Canada (Canadian Association of Amateur Oarsmen, 1880). The international governing body of contemporary modern rowing, Fédération Internationale des Sociétés d'Aviron (FISA), was formed in 1892.

395

Most of the major early nineteenth-century rowing competitions were either professional match races over 1-4 ¼ miles (c. 1600-7000 meters) in which gambling was highly important or they were races without reference to the amateur-professional distinction. Amateur rowing as such did not become highly significant until the 1860s; thereafter, the amateur-professional schism was frequently prosecuted with divisive and discriminatory zeal although it was also invoked as a way to make opportunities for sporting success approximately equal. The Amateur Rowing Association (of Great Britain), for prominent instance, excluded working-class persons; the National Amateur Rowing Association did not.

The English public schools, mainly Eton College and Westminster School (London), and English universities, mainly Oxford and Cambridge Universities, contested informal races from as early as 1815 and formal interclass races from the early 1820s. Eton and Westminster fashioned an interschool race in 1827; Oxford and Cambridge, the University Boat Race (customarily between 8-oared shells over a 4 ¼ mile/c. 7000 meters distance), in 1829. The 1829 race, which was won by Oxford, was the first of a tradition that has continued variously since (usually annually) and that has become among the most storied in contemporary modern sport. Interclass and intercollegiate rowing was also an especially prominent feature of sporting life in the United States. Yale and Harvard Universities established the first college boat clubs – the Yale Boat Club and the Harvard Boat Club – in 1843 and 1844 respectively; both conducted interclass races from the mid-1840s. In 1852, Yale and Harvard met in a dual rowing contest that was the first intercollegiate event in any sport in the United States. This contest was significantly inspired by a railroad executive as a commercial venture; it was staged between two 8-oared shells, one representing Yale and the other, Harvard; it was contested over a 2 miles distance on Lake Winnipesaukee, New Hampshire; it was won by Harvard; and it established a tradition that has continued variously since (usually annually over a 4 miles distance). The first intercollegiate league in any sport, the College Rowing Association, was formed in 1858 and staged the first intercollegiate multi-team contest in any sport, the College Union Regatta, among Harvard University, Yale University, Brown University, and Trinity College (Hartford, Connecticut), also in 1858. Still broader (effectively, national) organizations, that came to include virtually all major American rowing programs, were established in 1871 (the Rowing Association of American Colleges) and 1895 (the Rowing Association, which became the Intercollegiate Rowing Association in 1899). The Rowing Association of American Colleges conducted annual Gala College Rowing Regattas among 6-oared shells from 1871 to 1876, then collapsed due to the withdrawal of Yale and Harvard Universities (both of whom favored their dual meetings); these events were de facto national intercollegiate titles and did much to popularize American intercollegiate sport. The Rowing Association conducted annual Intercollegiate Rowing Association Regattas (for the Varsity Challenge Cup) among 8-oared shells (customarily over 4 miles) from 1895; these events effectively revived the practice of national intercollegiate titles abandoned from 1877 to 1894. The first international, intercollegiate dual rowing competition, between 4-oared shells representing Harvard University and victorious Oxford University, was held in London in 1869. And the first women's collegiate rowing team was formed at Wellesley (Massachusetts) College (near Boston) in 1875.

Rowing also prospered greatly outside the schools in this period. The Wingfield Sculls (on the Thames River, near London), single sculls match races for amateurs over a 4 ¼ miles course, were first held in 1830. The semblance of world professional sculling championships was created in England in 1831. The foremost rowing regatta in the world throughout the nineteenth century (and in a measure since), the Henley-on-Thames (near London) Royal Rowing Regatta, was established in 1839, largely in order to relieve economic depression in the region. Governance of the Henley Regatta was conducted by a uniquely independent body, the Committee of the Management of Henley Royal Regatta, which provided the model on which the International Olympic Committee was framed. The earliest events at Henley were the 8-oars for men and the double sculls for men, both over a distance of 1 mile 550 yards (c. 2000 meters). A 4-oared coxless event for men was added in 1841; a single sculls for men (the Diamond Sculls), in 1844; a coxless pairs for men, in 1845; and an 8-oared event for women, in 1845; many others followed. Henley became an authentically international event with the first American participation in 1878 and the first French participation in 1883. Other nations in the British ambit later established rowing regattas that resembled Henley; most notably, the Royal Canadian Henley Regatta, formed in 1880. The other most significant rowing competitions before the First World War were the Championship of the Mediterranean Sea Rowing Regatta in Cannes, France in 1866; the first American national titles in 1873; the Centennial Rowing Regatta in Philadelphia, U.S.A. in 1876; the first authentic English national titles in 1877; the International Rowing Regatta among Belgium, France, and Germany in Ostend, Belgium in 1885; the English-French dual competition in Paris in 1892; and the European Rowing Championships in 1893 (contested on an irregular schedule until 1973). The modern Olympic program in rowing also began to take discernible shape in this time. The sport was on the

Olympic schedule for the inaugural Games in 1896 but all events were cancelled due to inclement seas. The first Olympic rowing events, all for men only, were thus staged in 1900: single sculls, coxed pairs, coxed fours, and coxed eights. Double sculls, coxless pairs, and coxless fours, all too for men only, were added in 1904. Rowing events for women did not come onto the Olympic program until well past the Second World War.

Like all other contemporary modern sports, rowing was too greatly affected by technical improvements in its equipment, by rising standards of performance, and by the extraordinary athletes who achieved these standards. The development of the contemporary racing shell was a gradual process, of course; it began in earnest in c. 1838 in the United States with the innovative work of George Steers (1820-56), who designed streamlined rowing vessels and yachts (including America, which won the first America's Cup in 1851). By c. 1870, the basic elements of the contemporary racing craft were achieved: the sliding seat, swivel oarlocks, and lacquered, lightweight shells. Rowers were among the greatest and most heralded athletes of the nineteenth and early twentieth centuries; they were among the earliest and most revered of contemporary athletic hero. The most distinguished of these was arguably the first true world champion in any sport, the first Canadian sporting hero of international significance, and among the most decent sportsmen of the nineteenth century. Edward "Ned" "The Boy in Blue" Hanlan (1855-1908), an Irish-Canadian, so dominated amateur rowing in the early-to-mid 1870s that he exhausted its challenges; he then turned to professional competition and dominated its ranks from 1877 to 1884. He was the world professional single sculls champion from 1880 to 1884, during which period he amassed over 300 consecutive victories.

Contemporary modern **shooting** developed out of significantly older practices that were mainly related to military and hunting activities. The formalization and standardization of shooting as a sport was nonetheless principally owed to English, Irish, Scandinavian, and North American initiatives of the nineteenth century. The earliest national organizations devoted to shooting and to the standardization of targets, of their distances from shooters, of the number of rounds shot at manifold targets and distances, of positions taken by shooters (standing, kneeling, and prone lying), of ammunition, and of weapons-events were the: National Rifle Association, Great Britain, 1860; Norwegian Rifle Association, 1861; Danish Rifle Association, 1861; Dominion of Canada Rifle Association, 1868; and National Rifle Association, United States, 1871. The international governing body of contemporary modern shooting, Union Internationale des Fédérations et Associations Nationales de Tir (UIT), was established in 1907. The earliest major competitions attracted large numbers of spectators and brought wide acclaim to leading champions. The most notable of these competitions were the first American titles in 1871, the first noteworthy international matches (Ireland and the victorious United States in the United States in 1871, Great Britain and the victorious United States in England in 1875, and the Wimbledon [near London] Cup in England in 1875), the first intercollegiate match (Yale University and victorious Harvard University in 1877), and the semblance of (first) world shooting championships in Lyon, France in 1897.

The early practice of sport shooting entailed the use of increasingly sophisticated rifles (and ammunition) and, to a lesser extent, pistols for the purpose of striking stationary targets; this form of the sport reached recognizable sophistication by the 1870s. Trapshooting (with shotguns at single moving targets) evolved in England in the 1830s and progressed to its approximate, current state by the 1880s; and skeet shooting (also with shotguns, but at multiple moving targets) evolved in the United States in the 1910s and progressed to its approximate, current state by the 1930s. The modern Olympic program before the First World War was reserved for men; Olympic events for women were not introduced until well past the Second World War. This program began in 1896 with a rapid-fire pistol event and a free pistol event. A running-game target (rifle) event and a trapshooting event were added in 1900; shooting was temporarily discontinued in 1904; and a small-bore rifle (prone) event was added in 1908. Numerous other, since discontinued, events, largely individual and team rifle events, were also contested in the Olympic Games between 1896 and 1912. The world championships, which were conducted on a near-annual basis from their inception in 1897 to 1933, initially included only individual and team 300 meters (distance varied) free rifle events; 50 meters individual and team sport pistol events were added in 1900; and an individual 300 meters (distance varied) military rifle (3 positions) event was added in 1911. The most decorated shooters of the era were Konrad Staheli of Switzerland, Oscar Swahn of Sweden, and Alfred Lane of the United States. Staheli won nine medals in the 1900 and 1906 Olympic Games, five of them gold medals (equal second-most and equal-most respectively in the entire history of Olympic shooting), in both (individual and team) rifle and (individual) pistol events. He also won twenty-one world individual and team rifle titles from 1898 to 1914 and was the 1906 world free pistol champion. His Olympic and world prowess in both rifle and pistol events is unmatched in the annals of shooting history. Swahn won six medals in the 1908, 1912, and 1920 Olympic Games, three of them gold medals, in individual and team running-deer (rifle) events. He is among the most fabled athletes in the entire history of the modern Olympic Games; he is yet (at the end of the twentieth century) the oldest person to participate in the Games (72 years in 1920), the oldest person to win a medal in the Games (72 years in 1920), the oldest person to win an individual medal in the Games (64 years in 1912), the oldest person to win a gold medal in the Games (64 years in 1912), and the oldest person to win an individual gold medal in the Games (60 years in 1908). And Lane also won six medals in the Olympic Games, five of them gold medals (individual rapid-fire pistol, individual free pistol, and team military pistol events in the 1912 Games and two team military pistol events in the 1920 Games); his five gold medals are equal-most in the entire history of Olympic shooting. He was also the 1913 world free pistol team champion.

Contemporary modern **weightlifting** was little formalized and less standardized before the First World War; the now-conventional types of lift and weight categories (or divisions) for lifters were not firmly established until the third decade of the twentieth century. The sport was, in the nineteenth century, mainly associated with the cults of professional bodybuilding and wrestling and with the strength movement in physical culture and popular entertainment (in such as carnival exhibitions). Its principal advocates, in this form, were American strength enthusiast, George Barker Winship; Prussian-English-American strongman, Eugen Sandow; and French-Canadian strongman, Louis Cyr (1863-1912). The feats of Cyr were particularly astounding; he is said to have lifted 3641 lbs./c. 1655 kg (with a harness) in Quebec in 1888 and to have commonly lifted a table (placed on his chest while supine lying) on which people weighing (in sum) more than 3000 lbs./c. 1364 kg stood. His achievements and those of other strongmen and strongladies, which were especially prominent in the last two decades of the nineteenth century, were also largely unverified, however, and likely exaggerated. The seminal development of weightlifting as a definitive sport was owed principally to the late nineteenth-century Germanic cultures of central and northern Europe (that is, to Austria, Germany, Switzerland, and Scandinavia), where it was sometimes associated with the activities of gymnastic societies. The semblance of world championships for men was nonetheless first conducted in London in 1891; such championships were held on an irregular basis until the First World War; they were contested without body-weight distinctions-limits until 1898 when the heavyweight (or unlimited) class was designated, 1905 when the lightweight and light-heavyweight classes were also instituted, and 1910 when the featherweight class was likewise installed; and they included manifold one-hand and two-hand lifts, variously with dumbbells and barbells. Olympic events for men were too first contested without body-weight distinctions-limits from 1896 (temporarily discontinued in 1900, 1908, and 1912) in one-hand and two-hand lifts, variously with dumbbells and barbells. European Championships for men were first held in Rotterdam, Netherlands in 1896 and staged thereafter on a near-annual schedule. And the first international governing body of contemporary modern weightlifting, the International Weightlifting Federation (IWF), was formed in 1905. An international weightlifting program for women was not established until well past the Second World War. Arguably the most decorated weightlifter of this time was Josef Grafl (1872-1915) of Austria, the 1908, 1909, 1910, 1911, and 1913 world champion and the 1908 and 1909 European champion in the unlimited weight-class.

Contemporary modern **yachting/sailing** evolved principally out of seventeenth-century and eighteenth-century Dutch and British practices, most particularly eighteenth-century British practices. Most of the earliest major nineteenth-century clubs devoted to yachting/sailing were British creations: The Yacht Club (Great Britain), which became the Royal Yacht Squadron, was formed in 1812; the Canton (China) Regatta Club, in 1837; the Royal London (Great Britain) Yacht Club, in 1839; the Royal Bermuda Yacht Club, in 1844; the Royal Canadian (Toronto) Yacht Club, in 1852; and the Royal Yacht Club of Victoria (Australia), in 1856. The other most significant clubs of the period were the New York (United States) Yacht Club, formed in 1844, and the Imperial Yacht Club (Russia), formed in 1846. The earliest national governing body, the Yacht Racing Association, was established in Great Britain in 1875. The international governing body of contemporary modern yachting/sailing, the International Yacht Racing Union (IYRU), was created in 1907.

Because the racing yachts of the nineteenth century were enormous and costly, the sport remained an almost exclusively aristocratic-bourgeois activity until the early twentieth century. Since too the design of racing yachts differed greatly until the early twentieth century, distinction in the sport to that time customarily had less to do with sporting skill than with the character (often associated with the cost) of the craft itself. Small, relatively inexpensive, one-design yachts were first developed in 1911 (in the form of the Star class vessels), from which time sporting skill had a much larger role in deciding yachting/sailing contests. It was nonetheless yachts of the largest classes that dominated the main yachting competitions of the nineteenth and early twentieth centuries. The most heralded of these competitions were the America's Cup events that began in 1851. In that year, a yacht designed by George Steers (who had earlier been principally responsible for the design of the first distinctly contemporary rowing shell) and led by Commodore John Cox Stevens (1785-1857), the America, sailed to England where it won the Hundred-Guineas Cup in a 60-miles race among eighteen yachts around the Isle of Wight (in the English Channel, near Southampton). This race-trophy, which was conducted under the auspices of the Royal Yacht Squadron, was subsequently renamed the America's Cup, after the yacht, not the country. It has been since sporadically contested on a challenge basis — before the First World War, in 1870, 1871, 1876, 1881, 1885, 1886, 1887, 1893, 1895, 1899, 1901, and 1903 over a 30-miles course in New York (City) Harbor — and was uniformly retained by the American defender (until 1983). The 1870 and 1871 events entailed a single challenger against a fleet of defenders in a single race (in 1870) and in a best-of-seven format (in 1871). From the 1876 event, the Cup entailed a single challenger against a single defender in a series of races: best two-of-three from 1876 to 1887 and best three-of-five from 1893 to 1903. Great Britain was the unsuccessful challenger in 1870, 1871, 1885, 1886, 1887, 1893, 1895, 1899, 1901, and 1903; Canada was the unsuccessful challenger in 1876 and 1881.

The other major yachting events of this period were either sporadically contested transoceanic races or annual invitational races. The most notable of the former were:

- the Trans-Atlantic Races of 1866, 1870, 1887, and 1905 from the United States to England, the United States to Ireland, or Ireland to the United States; the first of these was contested among three teams and was won by a yacht, the Henrietta, owned by James Gordon Bennett, Jr., the hereditary owner of the New York Herald (a corporate newspaper which greatly favored sport) and a major contributor to the formative development of American polo, track and field, and yachting/sailing;
- the Trans-Pacific Races of 1906, 1908, 1910, and 1912 from California to Hawaii; and
- the Bermuda Races of 1906, 1907, 1908, 1909, and 1910 from the United States to Bermuda.

The most notable of the latter was the King's Cup, established by Edward VII of Great Britain in 1906. Also noteworthy were:

- the daunting achievements of Captain Joshua Slocum, the Canadian-American navigator, who was the first person to sail alone around the world (in 1898); and
- the incipient development of the Olympic yachting/sailing program (in principle, of mixed gender) in the early twentieth century.

The standardization of yachting/sailing has been a more elusive affair than the standardization of most any other contemporary modern sport, likely owing to rapid shifts in technological advancement and in fashion. Among the most significant consequences of this tendency was that all of the many Olympic yachting/sailing events held prior to the First World War, events which began in 1900 (and were temporarily discontinued in 1904 and 1906), have been long since discontinued and long since replaced by other events.

Most major forms of individual winter sport also began to formalize and to standardize their basic, modern provisions in the nineteenth and early twentieth centuries: skeleton, luge, bobsledding, speed skating, figure skating, cross-country skiing, ski jumping, and alpine skiing. **Skeleton, luge, and bobsledding** all evolved out of the mid-to-late nineteenth-century sledding and tobogganing practices of British and American tourists in the Swiss Alps. Skeleton (head-first, prone sledding) was done on snow-covered downhill roads; luge (feet-first, supine sledding) developed out of skeleton; and bobsledding developed out of tobogganing (sledding on boards without runners). **Tobogganing** as a sport was first done in Canada (mainly Quebec) and by British tourists in Switzerland. Canadians established the first club devoted to the sport, the Montreal Tobogganing Club, in 1881; importantly practiced the sport in the Montreal Winter Carnivals (from 1883 to 1889); fashioned the first formal toboggan course, the Sherbrooke Run (Montreal), in 1883; and also constructed the first artificial course, the Tuque Bleue Run (Montreal), in 1883. The British in Switzerland built the first major toboggan course, the Cresta Run (St. Moritz), in 1884, staged the first formal race there in 1885, and established the St. Moritz Tobogganing Club in 1887. In 1895, bobsleighs were crafted by mounting sled-like runners on toboggans; the new sport became one among the activities of the St. Moritz Tobogganing Club also in 1895, then broke independently away to create the St. Moritz Bobsleigh Club in 1897. This club conducted the first formal bobsleigh competition among 5-person (including two women) teams in the context of the 1898 Bobsleigh Festival on the Cresta Run. The great danger of the much faster bobsleighs (as against toboggans) on the Run, however, encouraged construction of the first artificial bobsleigh course in St. Moritz in 1904. The first national bobsledding championships were conducted in Austria in 1908 and Germany in 1910. Skeleton, like tobogganing, was too practiced on the Cresta Run from 1884 and held formal races there from 1885. The first formal luge competition, a variation of skeleton contests, was held in Innsbruck, Austria in 1890. The International Tobogganing Association was established in 1913 and conducted the first European Luge Championships in Liberec, Czechoslovakia in 1914 (in the form of men's singles and doubles events) and the first European Skeleton Championships in Davos, Switzerland also in 1914 (in the form of a men's singles event).

Ice skating (which included speed and figure activities) was practiced in sporting clubs (such as the London Skating Club, formed in 1842, and the Montreal Skating Club, formed in 1859) and in winter carnivals (such as the Montreal Winter Carnivals, 1883-89) before it developed national and international forms. Both speed and figure skating were also significantly affected by the construction of artificial ice-rinks, first in London (1876) and New York City (1879). Contemporary modern **speed skating** evolved principally out of seventeenth-century and eighteenth-century Dutch and Scottish practices. The Dutch race, Elfstedentocht, an 11-city, c. 198 km (c. 123 miles), one-way contest among thousands on frozen canals, was formalized out of notably older practices in 1909 and had an especially large influence; the full race was contested fifteen times before the end of the century (from 1909 to 1997). The earliest contemporary races (and many since), like the Elfstedentocht, were held on natural (not artificial) surfaces and on naturally occurring (not track) courses; these surfaces and courses (natural and artificial, naturally occurring and track) varied greatly in respect to speed thus obscuring the reliability of record performances. The earliest formal track competitions were held in Oslo in 1863.

The first national governing body, the Amateur Athletic Skating Association of Canada, and the first national titles, the Canadian men's championships, were created/held in 1887. Speed skating (together with figure skating) was the first sport to conduct authentic continental championships; the European Speed Skating Championships (for men) were first contested (together with comparable figure skating titles) in Hamburg, Germany in 1891; the semblance of North American Speed Skating Championships (for men) were also instituted in 1891. Speed skating (together with figure skating) was likewise the first sport to establish an authentic international governing body, the International Skating Union (ISU), in 1892. It was also the first sport to stage authentic world championships, the World Speed Skating Championships (for men) under ISU auspices in 1893 in Amsterdam; the semblance of world championships (for men), over various distances from ½ mile to 5 miles, had been nonetheless first attempted in 1889, also in Amsterdam; the World Speed Skating Championships have been conducted on a near-annual schedule since. The Championships of 1893 (and those that followed) were comprised of races over 500 meters, 1500 meters, 5000 meters, and 10,000 meters; they also declared an all-around champion. The earliest towering figure of contemporary modern speed skating, Jaap Eden (1873-1925) of the Netherlands, distinguished himself memorably in these Championships. Eden, who was also among the world's most remarkable late nineteenth-century athletes irrespective of sport and who was the world amateur sprint cycling champion in 1895, won the world 500 meters, 1500 meters, 5000 meters, and all-around titles in 1893. He was too the world 500 meters champion in 1896, the world 1500 meters champion in 1895 and 1896, the world 5000 meters champion in 1895 and 1896, the world 10,000 meters champion in 1894, 1895, and 1896, and the world all-around champion in 1895 and 1896. He also achieved two world records at 1500 meters (2:35.0 in 1893 and 2:28.8 in 1895), a world record at 5000 meters (8:37.6 in 1894, the first sub-9:00), and two world records at 10,000 meters (19:12.4 in 1894 and 17:56.0 in 1895, the first sub-19:00 and sub-18:00). The other most notable speed-skating phenom before the First World War was Oscar Mathisen (1888-1954) of Norway, who won twenty-one world titles from 1908 to 1914. He was the world champion at 500 meters in 1909, 1910, 1912, 1913, and 1914; at 1500 meters in 1908, 1909, 1910, 1912, 1913, and 1914; at 5000 meters in 1908, 1912, and 1914; and at 10,000 meters in 1908 and 1912; he won the all-around title in 1908, 1909, 1912, 1913, and 1914. He was the first of only three male athletes (the others were Ard Schenk and Eric Heiden) to sweep all four races in the World Championships (in 1912); he was also the European all-around champion in 1909, 1912, and 1914; and he established four world records at 500 meters (from 44.2 in1912 to 43.4 in 1914), a world record at 1000 meters (1:31.8 in 1909), four world records at 1500 meters (from 2:20.8 in 1908 to 2:17.4 in 1914), two world records at 5000 meters (8:36.6 in 1914 and 8:36.3 in 1916), and three world records at 10,000 meters (from 17:46.3 in 1912 to 17:22.6 in 1913) over the course of one of the most brilliant careers in the entire history of the sport. The most notable performance milestones of this period were:

- the first sub-50.0 (49.4) for 500 meters by Alfred Naess of Norway in 1893;
- the first sub-9:00 (8:37.6) for 5000 meters by Jaap Eden of the Netherlands in 1894;
- the first sub-20:00 (19:47.4) for 10,000 meters by Halfdan Nielsen of Norway in 1893; and
- the first sub-19:00 and sub-18:00 (17:56.0) for 10,000 meters by Jaap Eden in 1895.

Contemporary modern **figure skating** was owed principally to three major achievements of the mid-to-late nineteenth century: the invention of steel-bladed skates, the introduction of dance-like movement to ice, and the fashioning of refined jumping movements on ice. Edward V. Bushnell (fl. mid-nineteenth century) of the United States first developed steel-bladed skates in 1848; these skates made feasible the intricate movements since associated with figure skating, movements that were not readily possible on bone, wood, or iron blades. Jackson Haines (1840-79), an American ballet master living in Vienna, added the elements of dance and music to figure skating beginning in 1864. And in the late nineteenth century, Axel Paulsen (1855-1938) of Norway, himself an accomplished figure and speed skater, developed articulate jumping movements and integrated them into the broader figure-skating program. The earliest national organizations devoted to the sport were the Amateur Skating Society (Russia), formed in 1864; the National Figure Skating Association (Great Britain), formed in 1876; the National Figure Skating Association (United States), formed in 1886; and the National Figure Skating Association (Canada), formed in 1888. Figure skating (together with speed skating) was the first sport to establish an authentic international governing body, the International Skating Union (ISU), in 1892. Unlike most contemporary modern sports, figure skating instituted major international competitions before it staged national titles in the leading sporting countries. The first international competitions were held in Vienna in 1882 and in Hamburg, Germany in 1885. Figure skating (together with speed skating) was also the first sport to establish authentic continental championships; the European Figure Skating Championships (for men) were first contested (together with comparable speed skating titles) in Hamburg, Germany in 1891. The first World Figure Skating Championships (in men's singles only) were conducted under ISU auspices in St. Petersburg, Russia in 1896; the women's singles event was added to the world championships in 1906 and the pairs event (a woman and a man together), in 1908. Figure skating was too the first winter sport to win a place on the modern international Olympic program. Sixteen years before the advent of Olympic Winter Games themselves, special figures (for men), men's singles, women's singles, and pairs events were included in the 1908 Games. A professional alternative to amateur figure skating was first developed in Germany, also in 1908. The earliest national titles were done in Germany (a men's singles event only) in 1891, in Canada (a pairs event only) in 1905, and in the United States (men's singles, women's singles, and pairs events) in 1914. Although school (or compulsory) figures (strictly defined patterns that skaters are required to trace on the ice), not free skating regimens (much less strictly defined features of performance open to innovative interpretation), was the dominant feature of the sport before the First World War, the period nonetheless boasted among the greatest performers in the entire history of the sport; namely, Ulrich Salchow of Sweden, the 1908 Olympic men's singles champion, eleven times the world men's singles champion (1901-05, 1907-12), and nine times the European men's singles champion (1898, 1899, 1900, 1904, 1906, 1907, 1909, 1910, and 1913).

Contemporary modern skiing developed in several major forms; most notably, Nordic skiing (which in this time included cross-country skiing and ski jumping) and alpine skiing. It was owed principally to seventeenth-century and eighteenth-century Swedish, Norwegian, and Canadian practices as well as to central European (largely Germanic) inclinations of the nineteenth and early twentieth centuries, all of which were themselves significantly related to military and to transportation activities. The formalization and standardization of **Nordic skiing** began in earnest with the Nordic skiing competition in Tromso, (northern) Norway in 1843 and the inaugural Holmenkollen Ski Festival in Oslo in 1860. This Festival staged the first contemporary modern cross-country ski races and also featured the first measured ski jump, the latter by Sondre Norheim (1825-97) of Norway, who is widely recognized as the progenitor of contemporary modern Nordic skiing. The first major club devoted to the sport, the Christiania (Oslo) Ski Club, was formed in 1877. The first national governing bodies of the sport, the Norwegian Ski Association and the Swedish Ski Association, were established in 1883 and 1892 respectively. Cross-country skiing, not unlike track and field athletics and cycling, was likewise favorably affected in the late nineteenth century by extraordinary pedestrian-like feats. The most remarkable and telling of these was done by Fridtjof Nansen (1861-1930) of Norway, the great Arctic explorer, scientist, and 1922 Nobel peace laureate, who was the first to ski across Greenland in 1888. In Canada, cross-country skiing evolved out of snowshoeing; the first snowshoe club, the Montreal Snowshoe Club, was formed in 1843; the first national snowshoe championships were conducted in 1894; and the national governing body of the sport, the Canadian Snow Shoe Union, was established in 1900. Although Sondre Norheim had effectively fashioned the practice of contemporary modern ski jumping with the invention of heel straps (to hold the skis firmly to the feet), with the development of a crouched leaping technique in 1850, and with the recording of the first measured jump of c. 20 meters/c. 66 feet in 1860, the first major ski jumping competition was not held until 1879 (at the Holmenkollen Ski Festival), the first major artificial jumping hill (the Holmenkollen) was not constructed until 1891, and the first widely acknowledged world jump record was not recorded until the early twentieth century. Although the conditions of jumping hills vary greatly, a circumstance that so confounds the comparison of performances on different hills that only hill (not wider) records are officially recognized, the first unofficially acknowledged world jump record, 41 meters/c. 134 feet by Nils Gjestvang of Norway, was achieved in 1902; it is also surmised that Olaf Tandberg of Norway was the first to jump 100 feet (35.5 meters/c. 116 feet) in 1900.

Alpine skiing (in this time, downhill skiing), like Nordic skiing, was also first developed by Norwegians; most significantly, by Sondre Norheim, who crafted a novel heel strap device, unique ski design, and telemark turning techniques in the mid-to-late nineteenth century. Mathias Zdarsky (1856-1940) of Austria refined existing ski and binding design and developed stem turning techniques in the late nineteenth century. And Johannes "Hannes" Schneider (1890-1955) of Austria "completed" the fundamental technical basis of alpine skiing in its approximate, current form with the fashioning of innovative skiing techniques (mainly, the Arlberg turning techniques) in the early twentieth century. The laminated ski, which contributed significantly to articulate performance in alpine skiing, was developed in 1881. The first alpine ski race, the Roberts of Kandahar Challenge Cup, was nonetheless organized by the British in Montana, Switzerland in 1911. Alpine skiing thereafter became a largely Germanic (Swiss, Austrian, and German) sport. It was not until after the Second World War that French, Italian, American, Canadian, Swedish, Norwegian, and Liechtensteinian athletes began to share the sport's highest honors more widely.

All major forms of team field sport, rugby-football, soccer, cricket-baseball-softball, field hockey, and lacrosse, likewise formalized and standardized their basic, modern provisions in the nineteenth and early twentieth centuries. The several major styles in which football was prominently played in this time – rugby-rules, Australian-rules, American-rules, Gaelic-rules, Canadian-rules, and association-rules (or soccer) – all owed their formative inspiration to the elaborate football tournaments of early modern Europe (which far more nearly resembled rugby than any other contemporary variety of the sport) and to the two forms of the game that evolved out of these tournaments in the English public schools of the early nineteenth century. One of these forms was a kicking game, the form from which soccer matured; the other entailed kicking but also permitted handling the ball, the form from which rugby and the manifold derivatives of rugby, Australian-rules, American-rules, Gaelic-rules, and Canadian-rules, developed. The contemporary fashion of carrying the ball forward instead of merely kicking it forward, a fashion allegorically attributed to the iconoclastic act of William Webb Ellis (1807-72) at the Rugby School in 1823, an act that falsely ascribed the origins of such forms of football to nineteenth-century England – that is, **rugby** in the strict sense – was first formalized by rules struck at the Rugby School in 1845 out of practices common from the 1830s, practices entailing continuous play, prohibition of interference blocking, backward passing of the ball, and unrestricted kicking of the ball. A wider codification and a significantly wider practice of the sport were nonetheless not achieved until 1862-63, largely under the influence of game practices and rules formulations at Cambridge University. This was the amateur form of the game widely played among the upper classes that became fifteen-to-a-side rugby union in 1871 and that gradually thereafter added tries (running scores), conversions (kicking scores after tries), and penalty kicks (unopposed kicks outside the course of ongoing play) to the original practice of scoring only by kicking (goals) in the course of ongoing play. The first university clubs devoted to the new sport were the Cambridge University Rugby Club, informally constituted from 1839 and formalized in 1872, and the Oxford University Rugby Club, established in 1869; Cambridge and Oxford played the first intercollegiate match with twenty-to-a-side teams in 1871. The first major non-school clubs were the Old Blackheath (London) Football Club, formed in 1859, the Huddersfield (near Manchester) Rugby Club, formed in 1864, and the Twickenham (near London) Rugby Club (which became the effective center of English rugby union; formally designated as headquarters in 1909), formed in 1867.

The earliest national governing bodies of rugby union were predictably British: Rugby Football Union (England), 1871; Scottish Football Union, 1873; Irish Rugby Union, 1874; and Welsh Rugby Union, 1881. The first international matches were likewise between the British sides: England and victorious Scotland in Edinburgh, 1871 (became the annual Calcutta Cup in 1879); England-Ireland, 1875; and England-Wales, 1881. The fabled Five Nations Tournament, which effectively began in 1882 among England, Wales, Scotland, and Ireland, was first played (in full respects) in 1910 when France joined the competition. The sport was also soon disseminated by the British to its other most notable precincts; that is, to South Africa, Australia, New Zealand, France, Canada, United States, and Fiji, where it was more widely played by the working classes than it had been in England. Rugby was played in South Africa from 1862, mainly among (colonial Dutch) Afrikaners (who adopted it as a prominent expression of national pride and solidarity), but too among colonial Englishmen, and, during and after the Boer War, between Dutch and English populations; there was little interracial (black-white) play until after the First World War. A white rugby federation was established in 1882; a black rugby federation was established in 1896; the South African Rugby Football Board was established in 1889; South Africa established an interprovincial championship, the Currie Cup, in

1889; it played its first (international) test match, with England, in 1891; and it made its first (highly successful) tour of Great Britain in 1906-07. South Africa eventually formed among the most accomplished national sides in the world (the Springboks). Rugby was played in Australia from 1863, mainly among European colonials; the Southern Rugby Football Union was established in 1874; Australia played its first (international) test match, with England, in 1899; it conducted its first provincial titles, the Sydney First-Grade Premiership, in 1900; it made its first tour of Great Britain in 1908; and it won the second Olympic tournament in the sport in 1908. Australia also eventually formed one of the most storied national teams in the world (the Wallabies). Rugby was played in New Zealand from 1870 among both Maori and colonial populations; the New Zealand Rugby Football Union was established in 1892; New Zealand played its first (international) test match, with Australia, in 1903 (the beginning of the fabled rivalry between the two finest national rugby union sides in the world); it conducted its first interprovincial championships, the Ranfurly Shield, in 1904; and it made its first tour of Great Britain in 1905-06, winning 32 of 33 matches, tying the other, and scoring 868 points against 47 (arguably the most remarkable international tour in the entire history of the sport). Like South Africa and Australia, New Zealand too eventually formed among the most innovative and talented national sides in the world (the All Blacks). Rugby was first played in France in 1872; France conducted its first national titles in 1892; it won the first Olympic tournament in the sport in 1900; and it played its first (international) test match, with New Zealand, in 1905. Rugby was also importantly played in Canada (particularly in Quebec, perhaps from as early as 1868), where the semblance of a national championship, the Challenge Cup, was contested (at first under the aegis of the Canadian Football Association) from 1873; a national governing body, the Canadian Rugby Football Union, was established in 1882; an authentic national championship (under the auspices of the Union) was first played in 1884; and an intercollegiate governing body, the Canadian Intercollegiate Rugby Union, was formed in 1897. The Canadians, in turn, took the sport to the United States in the form of intercollegiate matches in 1874-75, but rugby soon thereafter gave largely way in both countries to local transformations of it, American-rules and Canadian-rules football. Rugby was played in Fiji from 1884; the Fijian Rugby Union was formed in 1913. The international governing body of rugby union, the International Rugby Football Board, was established in 1886 and soon thereafter achieved a fully international standardization of rules.

The amateur-professional distinction and disputes associated with this distinction, disputes which have been a virtually characteristic feature of contemporary modern sport and which were an especially prominent feature of nineteenth-century English contexts, had an utterly profound affect on rugby. The predominantly amateur, upper-class, and northern orientation of English rugby union was seriously challenged in 1893 by northern clubs, clubs that argued for broken-time payments to players; that is, payments to compensate for wages lost at work while playing rugby. The twenty-one clubs of the Northern Rugby Football Union, which became known as the Northern Rugby Football League (in 1902) and the Rugby Football League (in 1922), broke with the Rugby Football Union in 1895, played intercounty titles (the War of the Roses between Yorkshire and Lancashire Counties) from 1895, established its annual national championship, the Challenge Cup, in 1897, became openly professional in 1898, began to play (international) test matches in 1904 (England vs. other nations), played county championships from 1905, and adopted a more fluid, thirteen-to-a-side form of the game in 1906. Rugby league was more egalitarian in respect to class and race issues than rugby union; it was a largely working-class, not upper-class, phenomenon; it was more oriented to player prerogatives than rugby union; and it soon gained a place (typically a more prominent place than rugby union) in other major rugby-playing cultures (most notably, in Australia and New Zealand, where rugby league broke conclusively away from rugby union in 1907). The foremost rugby players of the pre-First World War era all competed in the time in which the union-league rupture was being worked out: Arthur Gould (1864-1919) of Wales, who played in the 1880s and 1890s; Jacob Daniel "Japie" Krige (1879-1961) of South Africa, who played centre in the first decade of the twentieth century (5 caps between 1903 and 1906); Dally Messenger (1883-1964) of Australia, who played wing in the first decade of the twentieth century (2 caps in 1907); and Ronald W. "Ronnie" Poulton-Palmer (1889-1915) of England, who played centre in the period immediately preceding the First World War (17 caps, 8 test tries, and 28 test points between 1909 and 1914) and who was killed in the War.

Australian-rules football was invented (out of games played in the English public schools) in Melbourne in 1858 by English-Australian cousins, Thomas Wentworth "Tom" Wills (1835-80 [suicide]), who was an exceptional cricket and football player, and Henry Colden Antill Harrison (1836-1929). The eighteen-to-a-side game, which entailed continuous play on a very large field and which prohibited tackling, more nearly resembled the original version of rugby (in the sense that scoring was achieved only by kick) than subsequent versions of it. The first clubs devoted to the new sport, the Melbourne Football Club and the University of

Sydney Football Club, were established in 1858 and 1863 respectively; the first formal rules were framed in 1859; the first governing body, the Victorian Football Association (which became the Australian National Football Council in 1906), was formed in 1877; and the first formal league, the Victorian Football League (which became the Australian Football League in 1906), was created in 1896 and conducted its first annual championship game, the Grand Final, in Melbourne in 1897. Increasingly influential working-class sentiment and entrepreneurial ambition brought a burgeoning professional orientation to Australian-rules football beginning in the 1880s.

American-rules football evolved progressively out of rugby and soccer. A version of football (more nearly like rugby than soccer) was played in intraclass and interclass terms at Harvard University from 1827 and at Yale University from 1840. The sport became so disruptive at both institutions, however, that it was prohibited from 1860 to 1871. The fabled match of 1869, the first intercollegiate football game, between Princeton University and Rutgers University at Rutgers, more nearly resembled soccer than rugby. In it, carrying or throwing the ball was not permitted; the ball might be nonetheless batted with the hands as well as the feet; and scoring was done only by putting the ball through the goal. The game was played on a very large field (c. 360 feet/c. 110 meters x c. 225 feet/c. 70 meters), between 25-to-a-side teams, and was decided in favor of the first team to amass six goals (Rutgers prevailed, six goals to four). The precise admixture of rugby-like and soccer-like elements in the early development of American-rules football was rarely altogether unambiguous. Columbia University and Cornell University adopted a version of the sport in 1870; the University of Pennsylvania and Harvard University, in 1871; Yale University, in 1872; and the University of Michigan, in 1873. The Harvard form of the game in particular accorded larger prerogatives to carrying the ball than had the 1869 form played by Rutgers and Princeton. Several games in 1874 and 1875 likely marked the earnest beginnings of American-rules football as such, a game distinct from both soccer and rugby. McGill University (Montreal) and Harvard University played a game by Harvard (as distinct from rugby) rules in 1874 at Harvard in which Harvard prevailed; the following day, the two teams played the first authentic intercollegiate rugby match in North America, a match that ended in a scoreless tie. In 1875, Harvard University and Tufts University (Boston) played under Harvard rules, Tufts prevailing, and Harvard and Yale Universities played under Harvard rules, Harvard prevailing. Harvard rules effectively introduced interference blocking of a sort, a provision that characteristically distinguished the new game from both soccer and rugby. American-rules football came thereafter to dominate both rugby and soccer in the United States. The Intercollegiate Football Association, which embodied the new rules, was established by Yale, Harvard, Princeton, Rutgers, and Columbia Universities in 1876 (-95). The Association, which then included fifteen teams, played its first championship game on Thanksgiving Day in 1876, an event that resurrected medieval and early modern associations of holiday consumption and patriotism with sport. Yale defeated Princeton in the championship match.

The rules of the distinctly American game were more strictly standardized in the 1880s; most notably, by the avid social Darwinist, militarist, and corporatist, Walter C. Camp (1859-1925) of Yale University. Camp was arguably more responsible than any other figure for the transformation of rugby into American-rules football and for popularizing the new sport. He had been an exceptional player of football (as well as baseball, rowing, swimming, and track and field) at Yale from 1876 to 1880 (30-1-5 over six football seasons), became the de facto football coach at Yale in 1880, was formally appointed to the post from 1888 to 1892, and remained the de facto coach well into the twentieth century. Yale lost only fourteen games during Camp's tenure of greatest influence, 1876-1909. Beginning in 1880-82, Camp stopped the continuous action of rugby by introducing a system of downs (3 [not unlimited] downs to gain 5 [not indeterminate] yards, lose 10 yards, or lose possession of the ball) and a line of scrimmage and by eliminating the scrum; teams were reduced from 15-to-a-side to 11-to-a-side; the center-snap was instituted; clear distinctions between offensive and defensive play were established; and the contemporary system of scoring (which included touchdowns, extra points, field goals, and safeties) was fashioned, although kick scoring was yet valued above run scoring. In 1906, the forward pass was legalized, the line of scrimmage came to require at least seven players, and a gain of 10 yards in 3 downs was required in order to retain possession of the ball. In 1912, the contemporary dimensions of the playing field were fixed; a gain of 10 yards in 4 downs was required in order to retain possession of the ball; the touchdown (running score) was more highly prized than the kicking score, commanding 6 points to 3 for field goals; and the ball was made narrower and thus more suitable to throwing but less suitable to kicking. Camp was also instrumental in developing the techniques and strategies (most notably, the t-formation) of playing the new game, including mass formations and other very violent and dangerous practices. From 1883, he also selected the national intercollegiate champion in the sport; and from 1889, he chose the All-American team.

By the 1890s, intercollegiate football had become the most prominent form of school sport in the United States and American-rules football was being also played in many of the country's secondary schools. Football's violence and brutality were nonetheless calling its merits as an educational experience into serious question. Harvard, for prominent instance, banned the sport in 1885 for a year and the Army-Navy games of 1894-98 were cancelled as a result. By 1905, the crisis was palpable; some colleges eliminated football, others replaced it briefly with rugby. Injuries, deaths, and moral concerns had so alarmed the progressive American public and President Theodore Roosevelt, himself an ardent advocate of sport in general and of intercollegiate sport and intercollegiate football in particular, that Roosevelt convened a White House Conference on Football to reform and preserve the game. The 1905 Conference led to the establishment of the Intercollegiate Athletic Association in 1905 (became the National Collegiate Athletic Association [NCAA] in 1910) and to notable reforms of football in 1905-06. The NCAA, an organization of university presidents, has since governed intercollegiate sport (most significantly, football) and it has made football a less inherently dangerous activity (mainly by legalizing the forward pass, by prohibiting most forms of mass play, and by better defining and limiting athletic eligibility). The great rivalries, games, players, and coaches of the late nineteenth and early twentieth centuries also contributed very notably to the sport's preservation, recovery, and prosperity. The earlier-cited Yale-Harvard and Yale-Princeton rivalries were the first major traditional matches; the Army-Navy and Army-Notre Dame rivalries began in 1890 and 1913 respectively. The earliest post-season bowl game, a championship game of qualified sorts, was first played in 1902 in Pasadena, California (near Los Angeles) although it was not staged again until it became an annual event in 1916; it was not formally designated the Rose Bowl until 1923. The foremost intercollegiate players of the period were numbered among the leading heroes of American sport:

- William W. "Pudge" Heffelfinger (1867-1954) of Yale University, an All-American guard in 1889, 1890, and 1891;
- William H. "Bill" Lewis (1868-1949) of Harvard University, an All-American center in 1892 and 1893, the first African-American person to win All-American honors, and later an enormously accomplished jurist;
- Thomas Truxton "T. Truxton" Hare (1878-1956) of the University of Pennsylvania, an All-American guard in 1897, 1898, 1899, and 1900 and a medalist in the 1900 Olympic hammer throw as well as the 1904 Olympic (track and field) all-around events;
- Walter H. Eckersall (1886-1930) of the University of Chicago, an All-American quarterback in 1904, 1905, and 1906;
- Jim Thorpe of Carlisle Indian School, an All-American running back in 1911 and 1912, who, in 1912, established new intercollegiate records for touchdowns scored (25) and for points scored (198) in a season and who is widely considered among the greatest athletes in the entire history of the entire world; and
- Edward W. "Eddie" "Ned" Mahan (1892-1975) of Harvard University, an All-American fullback in 1913, 1914, and 1915.

The leading intercollegiate coaches of the period were likewise among the foremost personalities in American sport:

- Amos Alonzo "Lonny" Stagg (1862-1965) had played football (and baseball) for Walter Camp at Yale from 1884 to 1889 (he was among the most accomplished intercollegiate baseball pitchers in the country at this time and achieved All-American selection at end in football in 1889, following the fabled 1888 season in which Yale outscored opponents, 698-0, among the most remarkable records in the entire history of the game); he coached football at the Young Men's Christian Association (YMCA) Training School in Springfield, Massachusetts from 1890 to 1891 (where he was an avid exponent of Christian sport and a colleague of Luther Halsey Gulick and James Naismith, the founder of basketball); he coached football (as well as baseball, basketball, and track and field) at the University of Chicago from 1892 to 1932 (where he also became the first person to direct a combined department of physical education and athletics in 1892, where he was as well implicated in the establishment of the first formal program of intramural sport in 1912, and where he made many of the most influential innovations in the game; most notably, inventive line and backfield shifts); he coached football at the University of Pacific (Stockton, California; near San Francisco) from 1933 to 1946; and he amassed a career coaching record of 314-199-35 in intercollegiate football over 57 seasons;
- Glenn Scobey "Pop" Warner (1871-1954) invented the single-wing and double-wing formations in 44 seasons at seven colleges (Iowa State [Ames], 1895-98; Georgia [Athens], 1895-96; Cornell, 1897-

98, 1904-06; Carlisle [where he also coached baseball, track and field, and Jim Thorpe in all three sports], 1899-1903, 1907-14; Pittsburgh, 1915-23; Stanford, 1924-32; and Temple [Philadelphia], 1933-38); he amassed a career coaching record of 319 (the record to its time)-106-32 in intercollegiate football; and

- Fielding Harris "Hurry Up" Yost (1871-1946) coached 30 seasons (from 1897 to 1926), most memorably at the University of Michigan (1901-26), where his first five teams (1901-05) scored better than a point per minute, won 56 games (including the first bowl game, the 1902 Rose Bowl), lost once, tied once, and scored 2890 points against 42; he amassed a career coaching record of 196-36-12 (a stunning .828 winning percentage).

It was also in this period that the first of the colossal intercollegiate football stadiums was constructed, the storied Yale Bowl in 1914.

The formative ground of professional (American-rules) football was developed in western Pennsylvania (in and near Pittsburgh) in the early 1890s. Pudge Heffelfinger, the legendary Yale guard, is thought to have been the first to sign a professional contract, with the Allegheny Athletic Association in Pittsburgh, in 1892. The sport was soon also being played on a sporadic basis in Ohio and New York but it did not become a national game until after the First World War. Professional football was widely condemned by intercollegiate coaches; it was widely associated with gambling activities; and it was also adversely affected by the practice of raiding talented players from rival teams. A so-termed World Series of Professional Football was nonetheless played in New York City in 1902 and 1903 and African-American players were included in the sport from at least 1904.

Gaelic-rules football was standardized out of significantly older forms of rugby-like football, mainly by Irishmen Maurice Davin (1842-1927) and Michael Cusack (1847-1906), each of whom had been an exceptional track and field athlete and both of whom were mainly responsible for the creation of the Gaelic Athletic Association (GAA). The Gaelic Athletic Association, the governing body of Gaelic-rules football (as well as hurling and camogie), was established in Dublin in 1884, wrote the first formal rules of Gaelic-rules football in 1885, fully standardized these rules in 1887, and conducted the first national titles (among county champions), the annual All-Ireland Gaelic Football Championships, also in 1887. The award to the team winning these Championships, the Sam Maguire Trophy, is the most coveted sporting prize in Ireland. Although unsurprisingly centered in Ireland, Gaelic-rules football has been also widely played in Irish communities in Scotland, western Continental Europe, North America, and Australasia. This 15-to-a-side form of football, not altogether unlike Australian-rules football, entails continuous play and scoring by kick only. The formalization of contemporary modern **hurling** out of significantly older practices antedated that of Gaelic-rules football. The first formal rules of hurling were written by the Dublin University Hurley Club in 1870; the Irish Hurley Union was formed in Dublin in 1879; and Michael Cusack established the highly influential Dublin Hurley Club in 1882. This 15-to-a-side game, in which the ball may be advanced only by striking it with a hurley (an elongated stick) and in which scoring entails striking the ball through goal-like targets, was brought under the auspices of the GAA in 1884, fully standardized its rules in 1885, and conducted its first national championships (among county champions), the annual All-Ireland Hurling Championships, in 1887. The award to the team winning these Championships, the Liam McCarthy Cup, is among the most esteemed in Irish sport. Camogie, the 12-to-a-side women's version of hurling, was crafted in Dublin in c. 1900 and came under the aegis of the GAA shortly thereafter.

Canadian-rules football began to develop as an amalgam of rugby and American-rules from the earlier-cited McGill-Harvard game of 1874. It established the Canadian Rugby Union in 1891, an organization which governed a game that departed somewhat from both classic rugby union and American-rues football; it conducted the first Canadian Football Championships in 1892; and it first contested the annual Grey Cup (effectively, the new Challenge Cup, originally a national, amateur, intercollegiate, rugby-football champion-ship), donated by Albert Henry George Grey/Lord Grey (1851-1917), Governor-General of Canada, in 1909. Canadian-rules football evolved progressively out of rugby into various adaptations of American-rules football, which it came largely to resemble. Like American-rules football, unlike rugby, it is not a game of continuous action; it, not unlike rugby, however, is played on a slightly larger field than American-rules with slightly larger teams (eventually 12-to-a-side teams) and puts a slightly larger emphasis on kicking and lateral passing than American-rules. Canadian-rules nonetheless continued to more nearly resemble rugby than American-rules until the early twentieth century, particularly the 1901-03 period, when a scrimmage line and a downs-system were instituted. The definitive transformation of Canadian-rules from rugby had thus begun, a transformation that was not "completed" until after the Second World War.

The remaining major style in which contemporary modern football has been prominently played, association-football, or **soccer**, evolved out of the earlier forms of football-playing that emphasized kicking and that prohibited various ways of handling the ball, mainly such forms that had been practiced in the English public schools of the early nineteenth century. In any case, it was soccer, not rugby, that departed most emphatically from the pattern of football-playing that had been most pronounced in medieval and early modern civilization. The English public schools fashioned a form of football without the mauling and hacking characteristic of rugby. The first formal rules of soccer were written at Cambridge University in 1848; the rules struck by the English public school alumni of the London Football Association in 1863 confined play wholly to kicking (or at least to not handling) the ball; and the approximate rules by which the 11-to-a-side game is yet played were framed by the Football Association (England) in 1866. An offside rule, provision for corner kicks and throw-ins, and the goalkeeper's handling prerogatives were added in 1871; the free-kick, in 1873; the penalty-kick, in 1891; and current pitch markings, in 1905. Contemporary modern soccer was a British (mainly, an English) creation that was in fairly short order transported about the world; first, to other precincts of the United Kingdom, then to the main colonies/dominions or former colonies/dominions of Great Britain, then to Continental Europe, central and South America, Asia, and Africa, all from the late 1860s. The Dutch, French, and Germans also importantly dispersed the sport to their colonies as soccer began its journey to the most widely played game in the world. The first formal soccer club was established in Sheffield, England (near Manchester) in 1857; the first national governing body, the Football Association (FA), was formed in England in 1863; the first national titles, the Football Association Cup (the FA Cup), was played in England in 1872; and the first league, a professional league, the English Association Football League (First Division), was created in 1888. Soccer clubs were established in Argentina by 1867, India by 1874, South Africa by 1874, Portugal by 1875, Denmark by 1876, Belgium by 1878, Netherlands by 1879, United States by 1879, Hungary by 1885, Hong Kong by 1886, Russia by 1887, China by 1887, Sweden by 1887, Italy by 1889, Uruguay by 1889, Chile by 1889, Singapore by 1889, Bohemia by 1892, France by 1892, Germany by 1892, Austria by 1894, Brazil by 1894, Spain by 1898, Turkey by 1905, Bulgaria by 1909, Uganda by 1910, and Croatia by 1911. Among the leading club teams in the entire history of the sport were established before the First World War; most notably:

- Bayern Munich Football Club, Germany, 1875;
- Tottenham Hotspur Football Club, England, 1882;
- Manchester United Football Club, England, 1885 (won more FA Cups than any other team in the history of the storied competition);
- Arsenal Football Club, England, 1886;
- Dynamo Moscow Football Club, Russia, 1887;
- Celtic Football Club, Scotland, 1888;
- AC Milan, Italy, 1889;
- Nacional Football Club, Uruguay, 1889;
- Penarol Football Club, Uruguay, 1891;
- Liverpool Football Club, England, 1892;
- Juventus Football Club, Italy, 1897;
- Real Madrid Football Club, Spain, 1898;
- Barcelona Football Club, Spain, 1899;
- West Ham United Football Club, England, 1900;
- Ajax Amsterdam Football Club, Netherlands, 1900;
- River Plate Football Club, Argentina, 1901;
- Leeds United Football Club, England, 1904;
- Chelsea Football Club, England, 1905;
- Independiente Football Club, Argentina, 1905;
- Boca Juniors Football Club, Argentina, 1908;
- Bologna Football Club, Italy, 1909;
- Internazionale Football Club, Italy, 1909;
- Corinthians Football Club, Brazil, 1910; and
- Santos Football Club, Brazil, 1912.

National governing bodies of soccer were formed in Scotland (the Scottish Football Association) in 1873; Wales (the Welsh Football Association) in 1876; Ireland (the Irish Football Association) in 1880; and soon thereafter elsewhere: United States (1884), Netherlands (1889), Denmark (1889), New Zealand (1891), (white) South Africa (1892), Argentina (1893), India (1893), Belgium (1895), Switzerland (1895), Chile (1895), Italy (1898), Germany (1900), Uruguay (1900), Czechoslovakia (1901), Hungary (1901), Norway (1902), France (1904), Sweden (1904), Austria (1904), Paraguay (1906), Finland (1907), Romania (1909), Canada (1912), Russia (1912), Spain (1913), Brazil (1914), and Portugal (1914). National titles were first held in Scotland (the Scottish Football Association Cup) in 1874; Wales (the Welsh Football Association Cup) in 1878; Ireland (the Irish Football Association Cup) in 1881; Italy in 1898; Netherlands in 1898; Germany in 1903; Belgium in 1905; and soon thereafter elsewhere. And national leagues were also first established in Scotland (the Scottish Association Football League [First Division]) in 1890, Ireland (the Irish Association Football League) in 1890, Germany (effectively, the fabled Bundesliga) in 1902, Belgium in 1905, and soon thereafter elsewhere. The earliest international matches were likewise between British entities: England-Scotland (1872), England-Ireland (1883), England-Wales (1883), Scotland-Ireland (1883), Scotland-Wales (1883), Ireland-Scotland (1883), and Ireland-Wales (1883). Others followed soon thereafter; most notably, United States-Canada (1886), England-France (1892), England-Austria (1896), England-Bohemia (1896), England-Germany (1896), Uruguay-Argentina (1901), Hungary-Austria (1902), France-Belgium (1904), Belgium-Netherlands (1905), England-Belgium (1908), England-Sweden (1908), and England-Denmark (1910). English amateurs first visited Continental Europe in 1875 (Oxford University to Bohemia); English professionals first visited Continental Europe in 1900 (Southampton to Vienna); and English professionals first visited South America in 1905 (Southampton to Argentina); all of which had a significant affect on the broadening international popularity of the game. A soccer exhibition was included in the inaugural edition of the modern Olympic Games in 1896; the sport came fully onto the Olympic program in 1900; the Olympic tournament before the First World War was unsurprisingly dominated by Great Britain, the Olympic champions in 1900, 1908, and 1912. The international governing body of association football, Fédération Internationale de Football Association (FIFA), was established in 1904 and has since come to include very nearly every nation in the world.

The amateur-professional distinction that had such a telling affect on nineteenth-century and early twentieth-century sport in general also greatly influenced soccer. This distinction first and most importantly played out in English soccer and at roughly the same time that it had wrought the earlier-discussed schism in English rugby. Professional players began to dominate English soccer in the 1880s; professionalism was accepted in English soccer by 1885; a professional league, the English Association Football League (First Division), was created in 1888 as has been said; and a national titles tournament for amateurs only, the Football Association Amateur Cup, was instituted in 1894. Labor-management disputes in professional English soccer were common in the period before the First World War. The most notable of these was the players' strike of 1890 which led to transfer limitations (regulations restricting the prerogatives of players to change teams), ongoing from 1891 (-1962), and to the establishment of players' unions, the National Union of Association Players and the Association Football Players' Union, in 1898 and 1907 respectively. Also common in this time were soccer riots; most significantly, the disturbance that killed 25 people at the England-Scotland match in Glasgow in 1902. It was too the case that, although soccer had been played by all social classes in this period and that it, unlike rugby union, was mainly a working-class sport, there was strident discrimination in some British-inspired circumstances of it; most notably, in South Africa, where white people excluded black people, and in Brazil, where light-skinned people excluded dark-skinned people. Women nonetheless played soccer on an organized basis in England particularly from at least 1890, the year in which the British Ladies Football Club was established.

Cricket had formalized and standardized the seminal groundwork of its basic, modern provisions throughout Great Britain and had been also seriously played in India, North America, Continental Europe, and Pakistan in the eighteenth century as has been said. In the nineteenth and early twentieth centuries, it developed yet more fully; baseball evolved out of it and out of other English bat-and-ball games (such as one old cat, stoolball, and rounders); and softball, in turn, evolved principally out of baseball. Like soccer, cricket was largely an English creation, an 11-to-a-side game played by both men and women at local, national, and international levels. The English public schools (Eton and Harrow; both near London) began interschool play in 1805; the English universities (Oxford and Cambridge) began intercollegiate play (widely considered the oldest of first-class cricket matches) in 1827; county cricket, which became the major form of the sport in England, began to develop in earnest in the 1820s, matured with the further formalization of the practice in Sussex (1839) and Surrey (1844), and was crowned with the establishment of the County Cricket Championship in 1873; and the first authentic English national titles were played in 1864. The amateur-professional distinction had an especially early affect on English cricket and was often also connected, in this context, to distinctions of social class. The first test match between so-termed gentlemen (leading amateurs) and so-termed players (leading professionals) was played in 1806; the distinction was significantly implicated in the development of county cricket; an All-England Eleven, comprised of professional players, was established in 1846; the first professional women's team in the world in any sport, the Original English Ladies Cricketers, was formed in 1890; and the first major players' strike in professional cricket occurred in 1896. The finest and most significant cricket grounds in the world, Lords' Cricket Ground (London), was constructed in 1813 and the approximate current rules of the game were "finalized" in the early-to-mid nineteenth century (the current wicket and play in respect to it were defined in 1817 and overarm, straight-arm bowling [pitching] became fully legal in 1864). The greatest players of the pre-First World War era, players who completed their careers before the War, were likewise English and they were also among the most revered athletes of the period in the world:

- Alfred Mynn (1807-61), who was widely considered the finest all-around player of the first half of the nineteenth century;
- William Gilbert "W.G." Grace (1848-1915), who played first-class cricket from 1864 to 1908, scored c. 100,000 runs and captured (took outs as a bowler) c. 7000 wickets overall, including 54,896 runs and 2876 wickets in first-class play (both records in their time), made 126 centuries (100 or more runs in an inning) in first-class play (also a record in its time), and was the first to make a triple century (300 or more runs in an inning) in first-class play, to score 1000 runs and take 100 wickets in a first-class season, and to score 2000 runs in a first-class season; he also contributed significantly to the development of lawn bowling in England; and
- Frederick R. Spofforth (1853-1926) of England-Australia, who was the most exceptional bowler of the nineteenth century (played mainly from 1873 to 1888); his most astounding achievements were the capture of 764 wickets in the overall season of 1878 and of 763 wickets in the overall season of 1880.

Cricket was dispersed to other major precincts in the British ambit in this period; most notably, to Australia (1800s), Barbados (1800s), South Africa (1800s), South America (1800s), central America (1820s), Ceylon/Sri Lanka (1830s), New Zealand (1840s), Hong Kong (1850s), and Fiji (1870s). Native (east) Indian and Pakistani players began to distinguish themselves in the sport in the late nineteenth century and native British West Indies (mainly Antigua, Barbados, Jamaica, and Trinidad) players, in the early twentieth century; players of these traditions are yet among the most accomplished in the world. In Australia, the first major clubs, the Australian Cricket Club (Sydney) and the Melbourne Cricket Club, were established in 1826 and 1838 respectively; the earliest first-class cricket match was played in 1851; the magnificent Melbourne Cricket Ground was constructed in 1853; the national governing body of the sport, the Australian Cricket Council, was formed in 1892; the first authentic national titles were played in 1893; and the first major organization devoted to women's cricket, the Victorian Women's Cricket Association, was created in 1905. Aboriginal peoples played organized cricket in Australia from the 1830s; a team that included aboriginal players toured England in 1868; aboriginals were nonetheless excluded from white sport altogether in the late nineteenth and early twentieth centuries; and many of the early matches were competitions between Australian-born and British-born populations. In the British West Indies, the first (white) cricket club was fashioned in Barbados in 1806; the national governing body of the sport, the Barbados Cricket Committee, was created in 1893. Racial discrimination in Caribbean cricket abounded; blacks were not permitted to play organized cricket until the 1890s, did not form clubs until well past the First World War, and were systematically excluded from the highest levels of the sport well into the twentieth century. In South Africa, the first (white) cricket club was formed in 1843, the first (black) club, in 1876; the (white) cricket federation, in 1890; and the first "national" titles, also in 1890. In India-Pakistan, the first native cricket club, the Oriental Cricket Club, was established in 1848; native and colonial British teams first played in 1877. The sport also became a major phenomenon in North America where it had flourished since the eighteenth century; the first international club match, between the New York Cricket Club and the Toronto Cricket Club, was played in 1840; the first intercollegiate match outside England, between the University of Pennsylvania and victorious Haverford College (near Philadelphia), was played in 1864; the governing body of the sport in the United States, the Cricketer's Association of the United States, was formed in 1878; and the governing body of the sport in Canada, the Canadian Cricket Association, was established in 1892.

Nineteenth-century international cricket matches were often private arrangements (not publicly sanctioned events) and they also typically included an admixture of amateur and professional players. The oldest series of such matches, the United States-Canada series, began in 1844. The England-Canada and England-United States series began with the first English cricket tour abroad in 1859. The England-Australia series began with the second such tour in 1861-62; the first Australian tour of England occurred in 1868; the first test match between the two countries was played in 1876; and the great series of such matches known as the Ashes was first played in England (and won by Australia) in 1882. The England-South Africa series began with the first English tour of South Africa in 1888. And the England-British West Indies series began with the first English tour of the British West Indies (Barbados) in 1894-95. Cricket made its only appearance in the modern Olympic Games in 1900; the lone Olympic title in the sport was unsurprisingly won by Great Britain. The international governing body of contemporary modern cricket, the Imperial Cricket Conference (later, the International Cricket Council), was established in 1909; it initially included only England, Australia, and South Africa; and it was controlled by the Marylebone Cricket Club until very near the end of the twentieth century.

Baseball first developed in the early nineteenth century in the United States, mainly out of significantly older, English bat-and-ball games such as cricket, one old cat, stoolball, and rounders; most notably, cricket and rounders. Cricket had been fairly widely played in the United States from the eighteenth century as has been said. Rounders, which had been apparently derived from stoolball, had been played extensively from the 1820s in New England, where it was known as town ball. In that form, the game had five irregularly placed stations, any hit ball was in fair territory, the runner was put out by striking him with a thrown ball, one out constituted one-half inning, 100 runs by a team constituted a game, the teams were of indeterminate size (but typically of from 12 to 20 players) and included indeterminate positions, and the matter of hitting in respect to strikes (and such) was neither uniform. In the 1840s, a transformed version of rounders developed in New York City and in the regions subtending New York City. This transformation replaced the stakes previously used as stations with (flat) bases and became known as baseball. The first formally constituted baseball team, the Knickerbockers Base Ball Club of New York, was established in 1845. Alexander J. Cartwright (1820-92), a prominent member of the Club, framed the first formal rules of the sport in 1845-46. These rules established four regularly placed bases, enlarged the infield to 90 feet between bases, limited fair territory, defined teams as 9-to-a-side, designated positions of play, and put the pitcher at 45 feet from the batsman. Pitching was by underhand motion, the batsman requested the placement of pitches, there were no called strikes, and batsmen were put out if the throw to base arrived before they did or if they hit a ball that was caught either on the fly or on the first bounce. Three outs constituted one-half inning and twenty-one runs by a team constituted a game. The first formal game held under these rules, between the New York Knickerbockers Base Ball Club of New York and the New York Nine, was played in Hoboken, New Jersey (near New York City) in 1846; it was umpired by Cartwright himself; and it ended 23-1 after four innings in favor of the New York Nine. A second match under these rules (which in 1848 made tagging base runners required at all bases except first) was not played until 1851. Shortly thereafter, however, the game blossomed; numerous teams were established, most particularly in the region of New York City; and the sport surpassed cricket as the leading team bat-and-ball game in the country by the end of the decade. The game was defined in terms of nine innings, as distinct from twenty-one runs by a team, in 1857.

The first national organization devoted to baseball – effectively, to the New York transformation of rounders – the National Association of Base Ball Players, was formed in 1858 (-72). This organization, like the early form of the sport itself, was exclusively concerned with the amateur form of play that had been practiced to that time, largely by the middle class in urban circumstance. Also in 1858, the first championship games were played in New York City; the first college baseball clubs were formed at Harvard and Princeton Universities; the called strike rule was instituted; and the rule allowing a putout by catching a hit ball on the first bounce was eliminated. In 1859 (-62), bat specifications were instituted (most importantly, a rounded bat was required; the flat bat of cricket was prohibited) and the first intercollegiate game, between Williams College (Williamstown, Massachusetts) and Amherst College (Massachusetts), was played; Amherst prevailed, 73 runs to 32, in a 13-to-a-side, 26-inning affair.

Baseball was much more widely played and much more widely dispersed in the 1860s than before, principally owing to three developments. For one, the Excelsiors Base Ball Club of Brooklyn (New York) made several successful tours of the northeastern United States in 1860 and thereby popularized the game beyond the region of New York City. For a second, although less widely played outside the military during the American Civil War than before, baseball was very widely played in the military during this time (1861-65). It was introduced to soldiers throughout the country during the War and it was too widely played by returning soldiers at war's end, also throughout the country, in rural as well as in urban contexts. And for a third, what was to become the dominant form of the sport in the last approximate one-third of the nineteenth century, professional baseball, was established in the period of enormous capital and nationalist expansion just past the American Civil War. The first openly professional (salaried) team, the Cincinnati Red Stockings, was organized in 1866 and it was led by two remarkable players, the English-American, William Henry "Harry"

Wright (1835-95), and his American-born brother, George Wright (1847-1937), both of whom later played and managed with notable success in the fledgling professional leagues, the National Association of Professional Baseball Players and the National Baseball League. Harry had been a prominent amateur player and an accomplished cricketer; he managed the team and played center field. George was the team's most accomplished player, its captain and shortstop. In the team's 1869 tour of the country, he hit .518 and made 59 home runs in 52 games. The 1869 and 1870 tours of the Cincinnati Red Stockings throughout the United States were colossal successes on all counts, including strictly athletic counts; in 1869, the team won 65 of 66 games, tying the other, and scored 2395 runs against 574; it was not beaten until 1870, not until it had amassed an astounding record of 92-0-1. These tours established the seminal groundwork on which professional baseball developed; they further and greatly popularized the game in general and its professional form in particular; and they effectively ended the preeminence of amateur baseball, which had itself become increasingly influenced by gambling interests and had become increasingly corrupt as well. The rise of professional baseball and the decline of amateur baseball (outside the schools), both of which began in earnest in this period, made the sport most importantly a professional endeavor from this time. Baseball nonetheless remained a highly significant feature of intercollegiate athletics through this and notably later periods. In the intercollegiate context, the amateur-professional controversy and the debate over eligibility rules that accompanied this controversy remained acute. The American College Baseball Association (1879-87) was formed in order to foster the amateur disposition of the college game and to deal with the challenge that semi-professional summer baseball (among college players beginning in 1880) posed to this disposition.

The phenomenal achievements of the Cincinnati Red Stockings in 1869 and 1870 sparked the establishment of the first national organization and the first national league of professional baseball, the National Association of Professional Baseball Players, in 1871. The economic depression of 1873-78 then slowed the expansion of professional sport (including professional baseball) and also framed its subsequent development. The National League of Professional Baseball Clubs was established in 1876 and put an end to the National Association. Its principal architects were William Ambrose Hulbert (1832-82), a successful Chicago merchant, and Albert Goodwill "A.G." Spalding (1850-1915), arguably the greatest pitcher of the early professional game. Spalding played from 1871 to 1878 in the National Association and the National League; twice won more than 50 games in a season (most notably, 56-5 in 1875); twice won better than 40 games in a season; and amassed a career record of 207-56; all in the underarm era. In 1876, he also founded the earliest and most influential sporting goods firm in the world, A.G. Spalding and Brothers. The National League was formed in order to limit the prerogatives of players and to assure profits to owners. The most notorious feature of this strategy, the reserve clause, prevented players from moving at will from a team to another. The legality of the reserve clause was upheld by the federal courts in 1879, more than a decade before the Sherman Anti-Trust Law of 1890 prohibited such practices and the monopolistic cartels they entail. The first professional minor league, the International League, was formed in 1877 and a rival professional major league, the American Baseball Association, was established in 1882 (-91). The National Association had been labor- (player-) dominated and prestige- (sport-) compelled. The new leagues were capital- (owner-) dominated and profit- (business-) compelled; they greatly heightened the nationalistic and commercial ambitions that have become characteristic of the sport; they deepened the sport's association with unsavory gambling interests and corrupt political agendas; they were run through with profane, violent, and scandalous misbehavior; and they practiced systematic forms of racial discrimination. The National Agreements of 1882 and 1885, agreements between players and owners that greatly favored owners on such matters as player salaries and other contractual issues, further deepened the rift between players and owners and compelled the formation of two rival major leagues, both with the reform agenda of restoring some lost prerogatives to players and both short-lived, the Union Association (1884) and the Players' (Brotherhood) League (1890). Both waged emphatic struggles against the National League and the American Association; both were vigorously opposed by the established leagues; and both were overwhelmed after a single season by the more powerful corporate edifices of the older leagues and by banking interests that conspired with these leagues to withhold capital from the upstart organizations.

After the broad economic devastations of the 1870s, great prosperity returned to professional baseball in the decade following and highly significant rules changes adopted in the 1880s effectively brought the game to its current form. These changes, as well as those that were enacted just before and just after, were shaped largely by Henry Chadwick (1824-1908), a prominent English-American journalist and pioneer baseball writer, who had a larger role in fashioning the rules of modern baseball than any other figure since Alexander Cartwright. These changes most importantly included: the current dimension and mass, if not the current composition, of the ball (1872), the current position of home plate (1877), the elimination of all restrictions on the nature of the pitcher's delivery (the rule that allowed overarm pitching, 1884), the elimination of the batsman's prerogative to order the location of pitches (1887), the definition of an out as three strikes (1888), the definition of a walk as four balls (1889), the increase in distance from the pitcher to home plate, first to 50 feet (1881), then to 60 feet 6 inches (1893), and the widening of the strike zone from 12 inches to 17 inches (1901). These changes, taken together, made baseball a much more active and athletic activity and they further ingratiated it as the leading team sport in the country.

The American Association failed after the 1891 season, largely owing to competition for players with the National League and the Players' League. The National League nonetheless continued as the only major baseball league through the economic depression of 1893 and the Spanish-American War of 1898, both of which augured badly for the capital-driven phenomenon of professional sport (including professional baseball). The National League's principal rival, the American League, was established in 1901, mainly by the initiatives of Byron Bancroft "Ban" Johnson (1864-1931), a prominent sport journalist and baseball executive. Johnson scrapped the National Agreements, put an effective end to most of the corruptions then haunting the sport, and brought renewed prosperity to professional baseball. The ensuing conflict between the two leagues ended in 1903 in a truce of co-existence. Although post-season inter-league titles (between the champions of the National League and the champions of the American Association) had been played as early as 1882 (-90), the modern World Series (between the champions of the National and American Leagues) was first played in 1903. Even the economic depression of 1907 failed to substantially impair either the welfare or the popularity of the game. It was not until the sharp rise in costs associated with escalating players' salaries and construction expenditures in the second decade of the twentieth century, the disastrous conflict with the capital-motivated Federal League in 1914-15, and the First World War that the sport again fell into temporary decline. Many of the finest and most expensive baseball stadiums in the country were constructed in this period and they added significantly to the debt burdens of their teams: Shibe Park, Philadelphia, 1909; Comiskey Park, Chicago, 1910; Fenway Park, Boston, 1912; Tiger Stadium, Detroit, 1912; and Wrigley Field, Chicago, 1914. The Federal League was bought off by the other two leagues after the 1914 season and disbanded but the costs were steep. And the First World War had the customary affect of major periods of military conflict on professional sporting pursuits; it drained capital from such pursuits.

Baseball largely, but not entirely, excluded women and racial minorities in the nineteenth and early twentieth centuries. Women and African-American men nonetheless played some amateur baseball, particularly in the colleges, from the 1860s and 1870s, and several African-American men too played professional minor league baseball from the 1870s. Even professional (major league) baseball included a very few black players before they were formally excluded in 1888 (as the game became more profitable); most notably, William Henry "Esteban" Bellan (1850-1932), the first Latin American (Cuban) to play in the major leagues (1871-73, mainly as an infielder in the National Association); Moses Fleetwood "Fleet" Walker (1857-1924), the first African-American to play in the major leagues (1884, as a catcher in the American Association); and Welday Wilberforce Walker (1860-1937), brother of Fleetwood (1884, as an outfielder in the American Association). Native American players were never formally excluded from the game but they nonetheless too suffered systematic discrimination. The most notable native American player of this period was the outstanding pitcher, Charles Albert "Chief" Bender (1883-1954), a Chippewa, who played in the American League (mainly Philadelphia), Federal League, and National League from 1903 to 1917/25 and who amassed a career record of 210-128. Black professional teams and leagues began to form in the 1880s and 1890s. Several of these teams made successful national tours; most notably, the Philadelphia Orions in 1882 and the Cuban (New York City) Giants in 1885. The first post-season championship between professional black teams, the first black World Series, was played in 1888.

Baseball was also widely dispersed to countries other than the United States during this period. The sport had been variously played in Canada and Mexico (principally by way of the Mexican War of 1846-48), mainly by Americans, from the 1840s; it was widely played among Canadians from the 1850s and among Mexicans from the 1880s. Cuban revolutionaries adopted baseball in the 1860s as an expression of their affinity for American culture and their ambition for independence from Spain; it was prohibited by Spanish authorities in 1895 but thrived again after the Spanish-American War of 1898 and the American military occupations of the country in 1898-1902 and 1906-08. The first Cuban professional league, the Cuban Professional Baseball League, an interracial organization, was established in 1878. Largely by means of relationships among sugar plantations, Cubans then introduced baseball to the Dominican Republic in 1880 (an event augmented by the American military occupation of the country that began in 1916 and went on until 1924), Venezuela in 1895, and Puerto Rico in 1898 (an event augmented by the American annexation of the country in 1898). American political and commercial influence in central America brought baseball to Nicaragua in 1889 (an event augmented by the American military occupation of the country that began in 1912 and went on until 1933) and to Honduras and Panama shortly thereafter. American merchants and military authorities gradually introduced baseball (and other western sports) to Japan, China, and Korea after the opening of trade with east Asia in the 1850s and to the Philippines and Guam after the Spanish American War of 1898, phenomena significantly augmented by the subsequent influence of the YMCA in the region. American gold miners introduced the sport to Australia in 1882. The dispersion of baseball outside the United States was also greatly encouraged by the several international baseball tours directed mainly by A.G. Spalding between 1874 and 1914. These tours included Europe, Latin America, Oceania, Asia, and Africa; the most notable of them were the tour of 1874 to Great Britain and the tour of 1888 to Hawaii, Australia, Ceylon/Sri Lanka, Egypt, Italy, France, England, and Ireland. Baseball first appeared on the modern international Olympic program as a demonstration sport in 1912.

Likewise contributing to the near-mythological status of baseball in the United States was the claim that the sport was an entirely American invention and the heroic stature of its most accomplished players. In order to demonstrate the uniquely American origins of the game, a commission (the Mills Commission), financed principally by A.G. Spalding, was established in 1905. The Commission was chaired by Abraham G. Mills (1844-1929), a distinguished lawyer and former President of the National League, and it included no less than American amateur sport mogul, James E. Sullivan. It concluded, contrary to virtually all evidence on the subject, that baseball had been invented by American army general, Abner Doubleday (1819-93), at Cooperstown, New York (in south-central New York) in 1839. The evidence points predominantly instead to the sport's evolution from such as English cricket and rounders as Henry Chadwick had claimed. The great players of the period also did particularly much to popularize baseball and to establish it on an enduring basis. The best of these were among the most talented and admired athletes of the time:

- Adrian Constantine "Cap" Anson (1851-1922), who played in the National Association and the National League (Chicago) from 1871 to 1897, mainly as an infielder and manager; twice hit better than .400 in a season (most notably, .421 in 1887 when walks effectively counted as hits); nineteen more times hit better than .300; made 3524 career hits in 2508 games; and achieved a lifetime batting average of .340;
- Michael Joseph "King" Kelly (1857-94), who played in the National League (mainly Chicago and Boston), Players' League, and American Association from 1878 to 1893, principally as a catcher; nine times hit better than .300 in a season (most notably, .394 in 1887 when walks effectively counted as hits) and stole 84 bases also in 1887;
- Charles G. "Old Hoss" Radbourne (1853-97), who played in the National League (mainly Providence and Boston) and Players' League from 1880 to 1891; arguably the finest pitcher of the nineteenth century (when the pitching distance was 50 feet); once won 60 games in a season (60-12 in 85 games in 1884), once more better than 40 games, once more better than 30 games, and six more times better than 20 games; won all three games in the 1884 World Series; and won 310 of 517 games over his career;
- William B. "Buck" Ewing (1859-1906), who played in the National League (mainly New York) from 1880 to 1897; was the finest catcher of the nineteenth century and eleven times hit better than .300 in a season (most notably, .371 in 1893);
- Denton True "Cy" Young (1867-1955), who played in the National League (mainly Cleveland) and American League (mainly Boston) from 1890 to 1911; among the several greatest pitchers in the history of the game; five times won better than 30 games in a season (most notably, 36-10 in 1892 when the pitching distance was 50 feet); fifteen more times won better than 20 games in a season; threw three no-hitters (including the first perfect game in baseball history, 1904); appeared in 906 games as a pitcher (then a record), 815 as a starting pitcher (yet the record); pitched 749 complete games (yet the record); pitched 7356 innings (yet the record); won 511 games (yet the record), including 76 shutouts; lost 316 games (yet the record); had a career earned-run-average of 2.63; and won the World Series title with Boston in 1903;
- William Henry "Wee Willie" Keeler (1872-1923), who played in the National League (mainly Baltimore and Brooklyn) and American League (New York) from 1892 to 1910, principally as an outfielder; once hit better than .400 in a season (.432 in 1897); sixteen more times hit better than .300; hit safely in 44 consecutive games in 1897 (then a record); and achieved a lifetime batting average of .345;
- Napoleon "Larry" "Nap" Lajoie (1875-1959), who played in the National League (Philadelphia) and American League (mainly Cleveland) from 1896 to 1916; was the finest second baseman to his time;

413

once hit better than .400 in a season (.405 in 1901); fifteen more times hit better than .300; and made 3252 career hits in 2475 games;

- John Peter "Honus" "Hans" "The Flying Dutchman" Wagner (1874-1955), who played in the National League (mainly Pittsburgh) from 1897 to 1917; arguably the finest shortstop in the history of the game and the finest base runner to his time; seventeen times hit better than .300 in a season (most notably, .380 in 1900); won eight league batting titles; made 3430 career hits in 2785 games; achieved a lifetime batting average of .328; stole 720 career bases (then a record); and won the World Series title with Pittsburgh in 1909; and

- Christopher "Christy" "Matty" Mathewson (1880-1925), who played in the National League (mainly New York) from 1900 to 1916; among the several greatest pitchers in the history of the game; among the highest embodiments of the Merriwell persona of heroism owing to his disabling service in the First World War, his work ethic, and his sportsmanship; four times won 30 games or better in a season (most notably, 37-11 in 1908); eight more times won 20 games or better in a season; achieved three shutout victories in the 1905 World Series; made 2499 career strikeouts (then a record); won 373 (equal third-most ever) of 634 games over his career with an astounding .665 win-percentage; and won the World Series title with New York in 1905.

Softball, which was variously known in its original form as kitten ball or playground ball, evolved progressively out of baseball in the United States in the late nineteenth and early twentieth centuries. George W. Hancock (fl. late nineteenth century) invented an indoor version of baseball (for winter play) in Chicago in 1887. This 9-to-a-side version employed a smaller playing space and a larger, less active ball than baseball. The first national governing body of the sport, the National Amateur Playground Ball Association of the United States, was established in 1900; the first softball league was formed in Minneapolis, Minnesota in 1900; and the first standardized rules were written in 1908. The sport was not at all widely played, however, in either an indoor or an outdoor form by either women or men until well past the First World War.

Field hockey also formalized and standardized its basic, contemporary modern provisions in the nineteenth and early twentieth centuries, largely out of similar early modern practices in Ireland and England and out of similar early nineteenth-century practices in England, Scotland, and Netherlands, practices such as bandy and shinty. Both bandy and shinty also themselves eventually codified their rules and formalized their organizational frameworks in the late nineteenth century. Bandy was played predominantly on ice by the 1890s; most notably in the context of the National Bandy Association (England), established in 1891. Shinty was played most notably in the context of the Camanachd Association (Scotland), which was established in 1893 and which began playing the much esteemed Camanachd Cup for men in 1896. The contemporary modern sport of field hockey itself was nonetheless owed, in both men's and women's forms, principally to England and it flourished most tellingly in countries heavily influenced by England; it had reached Ireland, Scotland, Wales, India/Pakistan, and Australia by the 1880s. The English universities and public schools were the first to formalize the recent modern version of the sport, the 11-to-a-side version allowing advancement of the ball by sticks and hands alone; field hockey was played among men at Cambridge University from 1848; it was first played among boys at Eton College in 1868. The first non-school club devoted to the sport, the Wimbledon (near London) Hockey Club, instituted men's programs in 1883 and women's programs in 1887. The first national governing body of men's field hockey, the English Hockey Association, was formed in England in 1882; the first national governing bodies of women's field hockey, the Irish Ladies' Hockey Union and the All-England Women's Field Hockey Association, were established in 1894 and 1895 respectively. The first standardized rules for both men and women were written in 1883. The first intercollegiate game, between the men of Oxford and Cambridge Universities, was played in 1890. The earliest international match for men, between England and Ireland, was played in 1895; the earliest international match for women, also between England and Ireland, was played in 1896. The first of several international governing bodies of contemporary modern field hockey, the International Hockey Board, which included only England, Ireland, Scotland, and Wales, was created in 1900. Although the women's form of the sport was far nearer parity with the men's than almost any other form of nineteenth-century athletic activity, an Olympic tournament for women was not instituted until decades past the Second World War. The first Olympic men's tournament, conversely, was staged in 1908 (temporarily discontinued in 1912); unsurprisingly, it was swept by British teams; England won, Ireland was second, and Scotland and Wales were equal third.

Contemporary modern lacrosse first developed in Quebec, Canada in the mid-nineteenth century out of a significantly older native Canadian (Iroquois) game, baggataway. Most forms of the original activity, which was played very widely among the pre-literate peoples of North America and which took manifold shapes, entailed play between very large (c. 75-c. 1000 member), and not always equal, teams, on very large and frequently shifting fields of play, with the customary sticks for catching, throwing, and carrying the ball, in which scoring was assessed by advancing the ball beyond a specified boundary, amid extensive ceremony, and with the intent to damage opposing players sufficiently to discourage them from continuing the contest. Baggataway was the most thoroughly organized form of this activity; it was played between equal teams of 12-15 players per team, on a pitch approximately 40 yards/37 meters long, with the customary sticks for catching, throwing, and carrying the ball, in a style according to which scoring was assessed by advancing the ball into a goal-like structure, amid extensive ceremony, and in a very combative way. The first game much resembling the contemporary modern sport was played in Montreal in 1834 between teams of Iroquois and Algonquian Indians; the first such game among colonial players was staged in 1844, also in Montreal; and significant games between colonial and native teams were played in 1844, 1848, and 1851, too in Montreal. The earliest club devoted to the new sport, the Montreal Lacrosse Club, was formed in 1856; this Club crafted the first written rules of lacrosse also in 1856. The first national championship of lacrosse, the semblance of a Canadian championship, was played between the Caughnawaga Indians and the Montreal Lacrosse Club in 1866. The first national governing body of the sport, the National Lacrosse Association, was established in Canada in 1867; this organization, largely under the direction of (William) George Beers (1843-1900) of Canada, refined and fully standardized the rules of lacrosse also in 1867. These rules adopted the contemporary rubber ball (as distinct from the hair and deerskin ball used in the Indian games), codified the stick (or crosse), stipulated 12-to-a-side teams, defined positions of play, and allowed advancement of the ball by sticks and feet alone. A Canadian Indian tour of Great Britain and France in 1867 introduced lacrosse to Europe slightly before it was dispersed to the other major, recent centers of the sport, the United States and Australia, in the early-to-mid 1870s. Another Canadian tour of England and Ireland in 1883 further popularized the activity in Great Britain. National governing bodies were established in the United States (the United States Amateur Lacrosse Association) and England (the English Lacrosse Union) in 1879 and 1892 respectively. In the United States, lacrosse developed most notably in colleges and universities; the first intercollegiate match, between Manhattan College (New York City) and New York University (New York City), was played in 1877; the Intercollegiate Lacrosse Association was formed in 1882 and crowned its first (national) champion (Harvard University) also in 1882. In England, national titles (the Iroquois Cup) were instituted in 1890 and intercollegiate play began with the Oxford-Cambridge match of 1903. And the contemporary modern, national amateur titles of Canada (for the coveted Mann Cup) were first conducted in 1910.

The amateur-professional dispute came most emphatically to lacrosse in 1880s Canada; rival organizations were established, the National Amateur Lacrosse Association (1880) and the Canadian Lacrosse Association (1886), to deal with the issues of amateurism, violence, and unsportsmanlike conduct; lacrosse declined in popularity with the triumph of professionalism after 1886; and native Canadian athletes were excluded from amateur lacrosse in the 1880s. The earliest international matches of note were nonetheless played in the early twentieth century: the North American Lacrosse Championship was first staged in conjunction with the Pan-American Exposition in Buffalo, New York in 1901 and the only two Olympic lacrosse tournaments (medal tournaments) were contested in 1904 and 1908; Canada prevailed on all occasions. Women's lacrosse first developed as a 12-to-a-side game with very little body contact (more so akin to the light body contact inherent in field hockey as distinct from the heavy body contact inherent in men's lacrosse, contact which more nearly resembles that of ice hockey than that of field hockey) in the nations where men's lacrosse had prospered. The earliest such major development occurred in the last decade of the nineteenth century and the first decade of the twentieth. The first clubs, the Lacrosse Club (Scotland) and the Southern Lakes Ladies' Lacrosse Club (England), were formed in 1899 and 1905 respectively; the first national governing body, the All-England Ladies' Lacrosse Association, was established in 1912.

The world's leading form of team ice sport, **ice hockey**, likewise formalized and standardized its basic, modern provisions in the nineteenth and early twentieth centuries. Ice hockey likely developed out of several older forms of European (particularly, English, Scottish, and Dutch) field hockey – such as bandy and shinty – which were transposed to an ice surface. It was first played in informal terms in Nova Scotia, Canada in the first two decades of the nineteenth century; in Quebec, Canada from the 1830s; and in Ontario, Canada from the 1850s. It was first played in formal terms either in Kingston, Ontario, Canada (between Toronto and Ottawa) in 1855 or in Montreal, Quebec, Canada in 1875. The subsequent development of the sport was importantly affected by the construction of natural-ice rinks in Canada from 1852 and the construction of artificial-ice rinks in Canada from 1911. The first formal clubs, the Metropolitan Hockey Club of Montreal and the Victoria Hockey Club of Montreal, were established in 1877 and 1882 respectively. The first formal rules of ice hockey effectively combined the tendencies of field hockey and rugby, substituted a puck for a ball, and put the entire matter on ice; they were written for 9-to-a-side teams at McGill University (Montreal) in 1879. The sport was significantly included in the Montreal Winter Festivals of 1883-89. The earliest league was established, without regard to the amateur-professional distinction, among four teams in Kingston in 1885. The first national governing body, the Amateur Hockey Association of Canada, was formed in 1886. And the first national amateur titles, for the coveted Stanley Cup, were played in Canada in 1893. As professional teams increasingly took over the Cup in the early twentieth century, however, a distinctly amateur titles, the Allan Cup, was established in 1908. Ice hockey was first formally played by women in Ottawa in 1891; the first formal all-female game was held in Toronto in 1892. The sport was first played in its other major, pre-World War One precincts, the United States and Continental Europe (Belgium and France) in 1893 and 1907 respectively. Although Oxford and Cambridge Universities played an intercollegiate bandy match as early as 1885, a practice that was later replaced by ice hockey, the earliest intercollegiate ice hockey match in the strict sense, between Harvard University and victorious Brown University, was played in the United States in 1895; the first league in the United States, the Amateur Hockey League, was formed in New York City in 1896; and the first United States national amateur championship was played in 1898. A largely annual European Championships in amateur ice hockey was first conducted in Montreux, Switzerland in 1910 (-91) and the international governing body of amateur ice hockey, the International Ice Hockey Federation (IIHF), or Ligue Internationale de Hockey sur Glace, was created in 1908.

The incipient development of professional ice hockey was also owed to Canadian (and American) initiatives of the late nineteenth and early twentieth centuries. Although some professional ice hockey had been apparently played in Canada on a regional basis in the 1890s, the earliest professional leagues, the International Hockey League (a coalition of American [Michigan] and Canadian [Ontario] teams) and the Ontario Professional League, were not established until 1904 and 1908 respectively. The most significant of the early (pre-World War One) professional ice hockey leagues, however, was the National Hockey Association, created in Canada in 1909. The Association transformed the sport into a 6-to-a-side game in 1912 and introduced the blue line (as well as passing rules in respect to the blue line) in 1913. In 1917, it was disbanded and replaced by another Canadian creation, the National Hockey League (NHL), which has since set the course for ice hockey's ascent as one among the foremost professional sports in the world and which has since itself become one among the most influential professional sporting organizations in the world. The Stanley Cup, which had been donated by Frederick Arthur/Lord Stanley of Preston (1841-1908), Governor-General of Canada, was originally (in 1893) awarded to the national amateur champions of Canada. In the early twentieth century, however, professional teams also variously competed for it; in 1917, National Hockey League teams were included among those that competed for it; in 1926, it became associated solely with the championship of the National Hockey League; and it has since become symbolic of supremacy in professional ice hockey (of the North American variety at least).

Among the leading precursors of ice hockey, **bandy**, which was itself derived from similar early modern practices in England (c. 1800) and which was originally played on fields in a way similar to field hockey, was by the 1890s played most prominently on ice in a way similar to ice hockey. This 11-to-a-side form of the game was most widely played in England (where the National Bandy Association, the first national governing body of the sport, was established in 1891), Sweden, Switzerland, Germany, Netherlands, Russia, Finland, and Norway in the period before the First World War.

The world's leading form of team aquatic sport, **water polo**, also formalized and standardized its basic, modern provisions in the nineteenth and early twentieth centuries, a period in which it was played almost exclusively by men. Its European, or hardball, version (which has since become the standard, 7-to-a-side version throughout the world) was first informally played in England in 1869 at the Bournemouth (near Southampton) Rowing Club, perhaps by players who rode on floating barrels and struck the ball with a stick. Its first formal rules were written by the London Swimming Club in 1870; its first formal match was played in London in 1874; it was further civilized by revised rules and by the use of a soccer ball in Scotland in 1877; it was recognized by the Amateur Swimming Association (Great Britain), its first national governing body, in 1885; and its first intercollegiate match was played between Oxford and Cambridge Universities in 1891. The sport was dispersed to its other major, pre-World War One precincts in the late 1880s, to Canada (Montreal Swim Club) in 1887, to the United States (New York Athletic Club) in 1888, and to Hungary in 1889, then to Austria and Germany in 1894, to France in 1895, and to Belgium in 1900. A somewhat different version of the game was practiced in North America than in Europe, a slower, rougher, and less forthright version, a softball version, that was codified in 1897 but that gave way to the hardball version in 1906. The first American intercollegiate water polo match, between Columbia University and the victorious University of Pennsylvania, was contested in 1899 and the first American national titles were played under Amateur Athletic Union auspices in 1906. Its first international match, between England and victorious Scotland, was staged in 1890; it came onto the modern international Olympic program in 1900 and Olympic tournaments were also held in 1904, 1908, and 1912, all (except 1904 when only the United States participated) were won by Great Britain; and the international governing body of the sport, Fédération Internationale de Natation Amateur (FINA), which also governs swimming and diving, was formed in 1908.

All major forms of team court sport, basketball, volleyball, and team handball, were inventions of the late nineteenth century; they all too formalized and standardized their basic, modern provisions in the late nineteenth and early twentieth centuries. **Basketball** was created by Canadian-American educator and (later) physician, Dr. James A. Naismith (1861-1939), at the Young Men's Christian Association (YMCA) Training School in Springfield, Massachusetts, U.S.A. in 1891. Directed by Luther Halsey Gulick and assisted by Amos Alonzo Stagg, Naismith crafted an indoor game for winter use (to augment gymnastic regimens) in the YMCAs. He affixed peach baskets (as scoring targets) to the gymnasium balcony, employed a soccer ball for play, prohibited body contact and running with (carrying) the ball, and required that the ball be passed and shot entirely with the hands. The original game used a closed basket (that required someone to climb up a ladder to retrieve the ball after each score), was for 9-to-a-side teams, counted three points for field goals, and counted one point for a team suffering three fouls. Although the rules of basketball were not altogether standardized until well past the First World War (until 1934), teams were fairly uniformly defined as 5-to-a-side (after experiments with 9, 8, and 7-to-a-side arrangements) in 1897; backboards were instituted in 1893; free throws (scoring one point) for fouls were introduced and a unique ball (slightly larger than a soccer ball) was adopted in 1894; dribbling was permitted and field goals came to count for two points in 1896; double-dribbling was prohibited in 1898; open baskets were adopted in 1906; and shooting off of a dribble was permitted and the five-personal-foul-disqualification rule was instituted in 1908. Techniques of the game also evolved quickly; pivot play and screening were developed in the first decade of the twentieth century; the bounce pass and fast-break were fashioned in the second.

The rate of dispersion and rising popularity of basketball were meteoric; the sport was first played in the YMCAs as has been said, then in the secondary schools, then the colleges and universities in the United States; and it had become an authentically national game in the United States by the First World War. The first 5-to-a-side intercollegiate game (for men) was played between the University of Iowa and the University of Chicago in 1896. The first national championship (for men), the National Amateur Athletic Union Championship, was played in the United States in 1897. The first intercollegiate conference, the Eastern Intercollegiate League, was formed in 1902 and crowned its first champion (Yale University) also in 1902; Big-Ten Conference play began in 1906. The first unofficial, national intercollegiate title was declared in 1905 and was won by Columbia University. The YMCAs in particular were instrumental in rapidly dispersing the new game throughout the world, to Canada, the Caribbean, Asia, Oceania, Europe, central America, South America, and Africa. Two European variations became themselves fairly prominent in this period:

- netball evolved out of basketball variously as a 5-to-a-side, a 9-to-a-side, and eventually a 7-to-a-side women's sport in England in 1895-1901 and in Sweden in 1901, established a national presence in England by 1902, and soon became an important form of sporting activity throughout the extensive British ambit; and
- korfball evolved out of basketball as an 8-to-a-side, mixed-gender sport in the Netherlands in 1902, established a national governing body (the Royal Dutch Korfball Association) in 1903, and soon became an important form of sporting activity throughout the Dutch ambit.

Basketball made its first international appearance in exhibitions at the Pan-American Exposition in Buffalo, New York, U.S.A. in 1901 and at the 1904 Olympic Games. Basketball was adapted for women by Lithuanian-American educator, Senda Berenson-Abbott (1868-1954), at Smith College (Northampton, Massachusetts, U.S.A.) in 1892. Berenson, who had earlier studied at the Boston Normal School of Gymnastics, who later studied at the Royal Central Institute of Gymnastics in Stockholm, and who became a leading advocate of Swedish gymnastics and physical education for women, fashioned a 6-to-a-side game that was played in three (later in two) zones. The first women's intercollegiate basketball match, between the University of California and victorious Stanford University, was contested in 1896. Although professional basketball did not establish a major league until well past the First World War, its seminal development occurred in the late nineteenth and early twentieth centuries in the United States. The first professional team, the Trenton (New Jersey; near Philadelphia) Basketball Team, was formed in 1896; the first of several pre-World War One professional leagues, the National Basketball League, was created in New Jersey and Pennsylvania in 1898 (-1903).

Volleyball, like basketball, was too an American invention and it was also owed to the YMCAs of western Massachusetts. William G. Morgan (1870-1942), a former student of the YMCA Training School in Springfield, Massachusetts, fashioned the sport at the Holyoke (Massachusetts; near Springfield) YMCA in 1895. It was first known as mintonette and first developed as an indoor sport more suitable for winter use than basketball by other-than-athletically-adept (mostly older) people. The game entailed teams of varying size striking (neither catching nor throwing) the bladder of a soccer ball over an elevated tennis (or badminton) net by means of the hands alone. A match was set at twenty-one points and the top of the net was put at 7 feet 6 inches/2.29 meters from the playing surface in 1900; the size of teams was standardized at 6-to-a-side and the dimensions of the court as well as the rotation of players were standardized in 1912. Volleyball was fairly widely played by both men and women in the period before the First World War, largely under the influence of the YMCA movement, which dispersed it to Cuba in 1906, to Japan in 1908, to China in 1910, to the Philippines in 1910, and to Brazil in 1917. It even made its first appearance in a major international multi-sport competition in this period, the 1913 Far Eastern Games. It did not become deeply popular, however, until played outdoors in the several years just prior to the First World War. Even at this, volleyball did not become an authentically national form of physical recreation, even in the United States, until after the First World War and did not become a genuinely international activity until after the Second World War.

Team handball has taken two main forms, an 11-to-a-side outdoor form played on a large field and a 7-to-a-side indoor form played on a significantly smaller court. In both forms, however, it comes to a rough amalgam of basketball and soccer in which a ball (slightly smaller than a volleyball) is variously dribbled, passed, and thrown, largely with the hands (like basketball) into a target goal that stands on the level of the playing surface (like soccer) with only the sort of body contact characteristic of basketball and soccer permitted. The outdoor version of the sport apparently evolved out of similar Czechoslovakian, Danish, Swedish, and German practices between 1892 and 1898 and was originally known as field handball, or fieldball. The indoor version of the sport, which is now the dominant version, was not much developed until the period between the World Wars.

The leading dual combative sports, boxing, wrestling, the martial arts, and fencing, had all been widely practiced for centuries to millennia before the nineteenth century as has been said. All were nonetheless further formalized and standardized in this period; all came to their contemporary modern forms in the nineteenth and early twentieth centuries. With the arguable exceptions of horse racing and cricket, no modern sport had been more fully institutionalized in the eighteenth century than **boxing**. Professional boxing had been an exceedingly important sport in England from the early eighteenth century as has been also said. After the defeat of Daniel Mendoza by "Gentleman" John Jackson in 1795 and the retirement of Jackson in 1800, the ungloved ("bare knuckle") form of the sport continued in the early nineteenth century under Broughton's Rules, continued in this time to be governed as much by gambling as by sporting interests, continued in this time to be dominated by English fighters, and continued in this time as well through wide shifts in popularity owing to moral concerns. The legality of boxing likewise remained in dispute throughout this, and later periods; bouts were often raided, disrupted, and stopped by police authorities (as well as by spectators and attendants), in some cases deciding their outcomes; and claims to the "world" title were often seriously contested. In 1814, the Pugilistic Society was established in Great Britain and came to exercise considerable influence over professional boxing, most particularly in terms of recognizing worthy champions and credible challengers.

Jem Belcher (1781-1811), a grandson of former champion, Jack Slack, held the world heavyweight title from 1800 to 1805. The most accomplished and memorable figure of the first quarter of the nineteenth century, however, was the first great counter-puncher in modern boxing history, Thomas "Tom" Cribb (1781-1848). Cribb's most notable fights were with two African-American slaves, one of whom he met before becoming world champion and the other of whom he twice met after having become world champion. In 1805 in England, he beat the diminutive (c. 150 lbs.) and talented Georgia slave, Bill Richmond (1763-1829), who was the first of many black persons to fight at the top levels of the sport. Cribb won the world title in 1809 and resigned it in 1822. While champion, he twice faced the resourceful, former Virginia slave, Tom Molineaux (1784-1818), in England. Molineaux outfought Cribb in the first match in 1810 before c. 25,000 spectators but eventually lost in a bizarre turn of concluding fate. Cribb decisively won the second match in 1811 before c. 40,000 spectators. The last two men to hold the world title under Broughton's Rules were Jem Ward (1800-81) and James "Deaf" Burke (1808-45). Ward was the first to regain the championship; he reigned from 1825 to 1827 and again from 1827 to 1832. Burke, an enormously decent, courageous, and popular man, reigned from 1832 to 1839; amassed a career record of 18-2; won the longest heavyweight title fight in boxing history in 1833 (98 rounds in more than three hours) over Simon Byrne of Ireland who died of injuries suffered in the bout; and made the first foreign tour by an established champion, an extended, a largely successful, and a highly influential tour of the United States (1834-38). Burke was beaten for the title in 1839 by "Bendigo" William Thompson (1811-80) in the first match under new rules, the London Prize Ring Rules.

The London Prize Ring Rules supplanted Broughton's Rules in 1838; they standardized the dimensions of the ring; replaced the central square with a scratch line which fighters were required to reach by their own devices (i.e., unassisted by attendants) within eight seconds of having been knocked down; prohibited butting, kicking, kneeing, blows beneath the belt-line, and intentional falls, but continued to allow throwing and other wrestle-like actions; and excluded all attendants from the ring. These Rules made boxing a faster, safer, somewhat less brutal, and potentially more socially acceptable activity. The most illustrious champions of the era governed by the London Prize Ring Rules, the last of the great "bare knuckle" champions, were Ben "Big Ben" Caunt (1815-61), Tom Sayers (1828-65), John C. "Benicia Boy" Heenan (1833-73), and "Gypsy" Jem Mace (1831-1910), all Englishmen save Heenan. Caunt held the title variously between 1842 and 1847 and, like Burke, fought importantly in the United States where he significantly enhanced the popularity of the American ring. Sayers was an unusually small man by boxing standards (c. 150 lbs.) but enormously skilled and unfailingly game, by all accounts among the greatest fighters of the nineteenth century. He held the title from 1858 to 1860; lost only once in his memorable career; and fought the enormous (c. 195 lbs.) American champion, John C. Heenan, to a draw in England in an 1860 bout of epic character and colossal international significance for the sport, then retired. Heenan assumed the title on Sayers' retirement in 1860 and thus became the first American to claim the world heavyweight boxing championship; he was beaten for the title in England by Englishman Tom King in 1863. Although professional boxing was not practiced in the United States until 1816, although the United States did not crown an authentic national champion until 1841, and although there was not an American champion worthy of the world title until 1853 (John C. Morrissey, 1831-78), Heenan's reign, together with the deeply moralistic temperament of English society in the 1860s, began the shift from English to American preeminence in the sport. It would be nonetheless nearly another twenty years before a second American pugilist held the world heavyweight title. The dominant figure in this approximately twenty-year period was Jem Mace, who may have been the most accomplished boxer to his time. Mace was a small man by heavyweight standards (c. 160 lbs.) but an enormously clever and scientific athlete and a very decent fellow. He claimed the title on Tom King's retirement in 1863 and variously possessed it until 1871; campaigned to great effect in Australia and the United States from 1868 to 1871; and importantly promoted the use of gloves in the sport.

The last man to relinquish the world heavyweight boxing title under London Prize Ring Rules was the second American to hold the title, Paddy "The Trojan Giant" Ryan (1853-1900). Ryan, like most of the other major figures in nineteenth-century American heavyweight boxing, was Irish-American and large (c. 220 lbs.). Unlike any other figure in the entire history of modern boxing, however, he won the title in his first recorded professional fight (in 1880) and lost it in his second; he made nine professional fights from 1880 to 1887, won two of these, lost six, had one no decision, and was unable to score a single knockout. Ryan was beaten for the championship by the Irish-American colossus, John Lawrence "John L." Sullivan (1858-1918), in 1882 and a new era in modern boxing history began. Sullivan's enormous popularity did especially much to advance the public acceptance of boxing in the late nineteenth century. He made numerous tours of the United States, Great Britain, and Australia between 1882 and 1898; most notably, the gloved tours of Great Britain (1887-88) and Australia (1891), which significantly and favorably elevated the cultural viability of boxing. Sullivan was too instrumental in the adoption of gloved rules, the Marquis of Queensberry Rules, and in promoting the perception that these Rules further civilized the sport. The Marquis of Queensberry Rules were written in 1865 by John Graham Chambers (1843-83) of Wales-England, a prominent rower and founder of the Amateur Athletic Club in London; they were sponsored and published in 1867 by the eccentric English politician, John Sholto Douglas (1844-1900), (eighth) Marquis of Queensberry (Scotland), under the auspices of the Amateur Athletic Club. These Rules required gloved hands (as distinct from "bare knuckles"); they prohibited throwing and other forms of wrestle-like actions; they defined rounds as three-minute periods and provided one-minute rest intervals between rounds; and they defined a knockout as a knockdown lasting not less than ten seconds. These Rules were first employed at a boxing tournament in London in 1872 and they were variously, but unevenly, embraced from that time until 1889, when Sullivan voluntarily adopted them for all of his subsequent matches. They have functioned as the effective governing regulations of professional boxing since. Although they created a circumstance only ostensibly safer than the one it replaced, the acceptance of these Rules further tranquilized boxing, provided more uniform conditions for gambling in

419

respect to it, mollified claims against it on grounds of immorality and brutality, and contributed significantly to the manifold legalization of the sport in its major centers of practice, beginning in 1889.

Sullivan himself, also an exceptional baseball player, was large by the boxing standards of his time (c. 195 lbs.); he was an imposingly powerful puncher; he made 40 professional matches (and several hundred exhibitions) from 1878 to 1905, won 30 of these, lost one, drew three, had six no decisions (variously defined), and scored 16 knockouts; and he was among the most revered and influential sporting heroes of the nineteenth century. His most memorable fights were the:

- 1882 bare-knuckle triumph in the United States over Ryan that brought him the title;
- 1883 gloved victory in the United States over the talented, little (c. 160 lbs.) Englishman, Charlie Mitchell;
- 1883 bare-knuckle thrashing of Maori (New Zealand) colossus, Herbert A. Slade, in the United States;
- 1888 epic bare-knuckle draw with Charlie Mitchell in France; and
- 1889 victory over American, Jake Kilrain, in the last world heavyweight championship match under London Prize Ring (ungloved) Rules, a match that was contested in the United States, that ended when Kilrain was unable to continue after 75 rounds, that lasted more than two grueling hours, and that resulted in the arrest of both fighters.

Sullivan effectively became the first world heavyweight boxing champion under Marquis of Queensberry Rules when he embraced these Rules after the Kilrain fight. He was thus also the first to relinquish the title under these Rules. James J. "Gentleman Jim" Corbett (1866-1933) knocked out an unfit Sullivan in the twenty-first round of a title fight in New Orleans in 1892 to become the new champion.

It was Sullivan, Corbett, and the subsequent champions of the heavyweight division who dominated public enthusiasm for professional boxing in the late nineteenth and early twentieth centuries. Like Sullivan, Corbett was Irish-American and a fine all-around athlete (an accomplished baseball player, gymnast, and runner); he was smaller than Sullivan (c. 180 lbs.); and, unlike Sullivan, he was not an especially prodigious puncher but was a highly skilled boxer. He fought 27 professional matches from 1886 to 1903, won 13 of these, lost five, drew five, had four no decisions, and scored nine knockouts. His most notable fights were an 1890 gloved victory over Jake Kilrain; an 1891 draw with the great Virgin Islands-Australian black fighter, Peter Jackson, whom Sullivan (among prominent others) had refused to fight for racial reasons; the title victory over Sullivan; a successful title defense against Charlie Mitchell in 1894; and two knockout losses to then-champion James J. Jeffries in 1900 (nearly won by Corbett) and 1903 (decisively won by Jeffries). Corbett, who was the principal subject of the film, "Gentleman Jim," was beaten for the championship by one of the most versatile champions in the history of the ring, Robert L. "Bob" "Fitz" Fitzsimmons (1862-1917), of England-New Zealand-United States. Fitzsimmons, at c. 150 lbs., won the world middleweight title from Jack Dempsey "The Nonpareil" by way of a thirteen-round knockout in New Orleans in 1891; he relinquished this title in 1897. At c. 165 lbs., he won the world heavyweight championship from Corbett by way of a fourteen-round knockout in Carson City, Nevada, U.S.A. in 1897. Fitzsimmons lost the heavyweight title to James J. Jeffries by way of an eleven-round knockout at Coney Island, New York in 1899 and was again narrowly beaten by Jeffries in 1902. Fitzsimmons won the world light-heavyweight title in 1903 and lost this title in 1905. He was thus the first man and one of only two men (the other was Henry Armstrong) to hold as many as three world boxing titles before the vast expansion of weight divisions and governing agencies (that greatly increased the number of available titles) in the last approximate quarter of the twentieth century; he is yet (at the end of the twentieth century) the only man to hold world titles in the middleweight, light-heavyweight, and heavyweight divisions. Fitzsimmons made 65 professional fights (and several hundred exhibitions) from 1880 to 1914, won 53 of these, lost seven, drew one, had four no decisions, and scored 25 knockouts.

The American, James J. "Jim" "Jeff" Jeffries (1875-1953), was significantly larger (c. 220 lbs.) and stronger than his leading contemporaries. His principal claims to distinction before the unexpected triumph over Fitzsimmons in 1899 were promising sparring sessions with Corbett in 1897 and a victory over Peter Jackson in 1898. After gaining the title, Jeffries most importantly defeated American challenger, Tom Sharkey, by decision in 1899; knocked out Jim Corbett in 1900 and 1903; and again knocked out Bob Fitzsimmons in 1902. Lacking serious challengers and motivation to train, Jeffries retired undefeated in 1905. In 1910, he was lured from retirement to fight then-champion Jack Johnson and was soundly beaten. He made 20 professional matches from 1896 to 1910, won 17 of these, lost one, drew two, and scored 13 knockouts. American Marvin Hart (1876-1931) won what amounted to an elimination tournament to determine Jeffries' successor. Hart had beaten future-champion Jack Johnson in a dubious twenty-round decision in 1905, then knocked out former light-heavyweight champion (1903), American Jack Root, in twelve rounds at Reno,

Nevada, also in 1905, for the heavyweight crown. Hart made 47 professional fights from 1899 to 1910, won 28 of these, lost seven, drew four, had eight no decisions, and scored 20 knockouts. He was defeated in his first defense of the title by French-Canadian pugilist, Tommy Burns/Noah Brusso (1881-1955). Burns, who had also been an exceptional ice hockey and lacrosse player, was a fast, skillful, and courageous fighter, a natural light-heavyweight (c. 175 lbs.), but also a good puncher. He defeated Hart for the world heavyweight title by means of a twenty-round decision in Los Angeles in 1906; made fourteen successful defenses of the title in the United States, England, Ireland, France, and Australia; held the world light-heavyweight crown from 1907 to 1912; and lost the heavyweight title to the larger (c. 195-210 lbs.) and vastly superior African-American fighter, Jack Johnson, in a fourteen-round thrashing (stopped by police) in Sydney, Australia in 1908. The Burns-Johnson match produced the first truly modern (i.e., very large) gate and the first truly modern (i.e., very large) purses. Burns made 60 professional fights from 1900 to 1920, won 46 of these, lost five, drew eight, had one no decision, and scored 36 knockouts.

John Arthur "Jack" Johnson (1878-1946) was the first black man to win the world heavyweight boxing championship and he was also arguably the best heavyweight fighter in the history of professional boxing to the First World War. He had exceptional defensive skills, was an outstanding counter-puncher, could hit, and boxed well. His most memorable fights were with Burns; African-Canadian phenom, Sam Langford (1886-1956); world middleweight champion, American Stanley Ketchel; and former world heavyweight champion, James J. Jeffries. Langford was a remarkable athlete who had campaigned widely from the featherweight to the heavyweight divisions, often engaging and beating notably larger opponents, and who made 252 professional fights from 1902 to 1926, won 137 of these, lost 23, drew 31, had 61 no decisions, and scored 117 knockouts. Johnson won a fifteen-round decision over Langford, who then weighed only c. 160 lbs., in 1906 and later denied Langford the opportunity to fight him for the title. Johnson defeated Ketchel, who then weighed only c. 170 lbs., in a twelve-round knockout in 1909. And he soundly defeated an unfit Jeffries in one of the most storied matches in boxing annals. Jeffries was drawn out of retirement in 1910 as the "white hope" to defeat Johnson and regain the title; he was knocked out in the fifteenth round in Reno, Nevada in a fight that also featured the largest purses in the history of the ring to that time. In 1912, Johnson fell out with the American government over vice and tax issues; he married and openly dated white women (with whom he traveled across state lines), a practice that brought contrived morals charges against him, and he was also accused of tax evasion. The deeply controversial Johnson, who also emphatically opposed American patterns of racial discrimination and dared to say as much publicly, fled to Europe and fought outside the United States (in France and Cuba) until after he had lost the title. He later surrendered to American police authorities and served a prison term. During his absence from the country, a tournament was staged, variously in the United States, Canada, and England in 1913-14, to determine the white heavyweight boxing champion of the world. Johnson, unprepared for the fight, lost the championship to colossal (c. 230 lbs.) American, Jess Willard, in a fabled and disputed 26-round knockout in Havana, Cuba in 1915. He made 94 professional matches from 1899 to 1924, won 66 of these, lost five, drew nine, had 14 no decisions, and scored 32 knockouts.

Although the heavyweight division dominated public attention of boxing in this time, the lighter (of the eight classic) divisions were nonetheless all created in the nineteenth and early twentieth centuries. The light-heavyweight division (175 lbs. limit) was established in 1903; the middleweight (158 lbs., later 160 lbs. limit), in 1867; the welterweight (145 lbs., later 147 lbs. limit), variously in 1792, 1795, and 1815; the lightweight (133 lbs., later 135 lbs. limit), in 1868; the featherweight (118 lbs., later 120 lbs., 122 lbs., and 126 lbs. limit), in 1885; the bantamweight (105 lbs., later 112 lbs., 116 lbs., and 118 lbs. limit), in 1885; and the flyweight (108 lbs., later 112 lbs. limit), in 1910. The most accomplished fighters of this period in the lighter divisions were as remarkable as the best of the heavyweights and they were too among the most memorable champions in the entire history of the sport. Heavyweight champions, Bob Fitzsimmons (who also won middleweight and light-heavyweight titles) and Tommy Burns (who also won the light-heavyweight crown), were earlier cited in this respect. The most notable of the others were:

- Irish-American Jack Dempsey "The Nonpareil"/John Kelly (1862-95), the lightweight champion from 1882 to 1884 and the middleweight champion from 1884 to 1891; made 67 professional fights from 1882 to 1895, won 51 of these, lost three, drew nine, had four no decisions, and scored seven knockouts;
- Irish-American Jack McAuliffe (1866-1937), the undefeated lightweight champion from 1884 to 1893; made 52 professional fights from 1884 to 1896, won 42 of these, lost none, drew nine, had one no decision, and scored nine knockouts;

- African-Canadian George Dixon (1870-1909), the bantamweight champion from 1890 to 1894 and the featherweight champion from 1892 to 1899; made 153 professional fights from 1886 to 1906, won 84 of these, lost 22, drew 38, had nine no decisions, and scored 29 knockouts;
- American Joe Gans/Joseph Gaines (1874-1910), the lightweight champion from 1901 to 1908; made 156 professional fights from 1891 to 1909, won 119 of these, lost eight, drew 10, had 19 no decisions, and scored 53 knockouts;
- American Abraham W. "Abe" Attell (1884-1970), the featherweight champion in 1904 and from 1908 to 1912; made 163 professional fights from 1900 to 1915, won 89 of these, lost 10, drew 17, had 47 no decisions, and scored 46 knockouts; and
- American Stanley Ketchel/Stanislaus Kiecal (1887-1910 [murdered]), the middleweight champion in 1907 and from 1908 to 1910; made 61 professional fights from 1903 to 1910, won 49 of these, lost four, drew four, had four no decisions, and scored 46 knockouts.

European professional champions were first declared in 1909.

Amateur boxing was also formalized and standardized in the several decades just prior to the First World War. The first national governing body, the Amateur Boxing Association, was established in Great Britain in 1880; the first national championships were organized by the Amateur Athletic Union in the United States in 1888; and the first Olympic program in the sport was conducted in 1904 (in the flyweight, bantamweight, featherweight, lightweight, welterweight, middleweight, and unlimited weight divisions). The earliest Olympic tournaments, those of 1904 and 1908, were dominated by American and British athletes. Because boxing was illegal in Sweden at the time, the sport was not included in the 1912 Olympic Games.

Contemporary modern **wrestling** developed out of very much older activities and took numerous local forms; most notably, the relatively unrestricted forms in Great Britain, the upright forms in France, and the ground forms in Germany. The standardization of the sport into its two main contemporary modern forms, Graeco-Roman and freestyle, began in the early nineteenth century. Graeco-Roman wrestling of the modern type (which was fashioned on the approximate theme of ancient Greek and Roman wrestling, which limits holds to and by the upper body, and which emphasizes throwing the opponent to the ground/mat) was first developed in this period in France. Freestyle wrestling of the modern type, or catch-as-catch-can wrestling (which permits holds to and by the entire body and emphasizes both taking the opponent to the ground/mat and actions on the ground/mat itself), was largely an American innovation (on British themes) of the mid-to-late nineteenth century. Both styles developed broad weight divisions and also fashioned professional and amateur versions in the mid-to-late nineteenth century; all formal styles and versions were nonetheless almost exclusively reserved for men in this time.

The professional version of the sport did not typically include weight divisions and was thus dominated by large men. This version of the sport was also early on often associated with the strength movement in physical culture and popular entertainment and with tributaries of this movement having to do with weightlifting, bodybuilding, and boxing. The first of the great professional Graeco-Roman wrestlers, American William A. Muldoon (1845-1933), who variously trained and grappled with world heavyweight boxing champion, John L. Sullivan, was widely considered the finest wrestler in the world in the 1880s and did especially much to popularize Graeco-Roman wrestling in the late nineteenth century. Likewise, the first great professional freestyle wrestlers, Estonian-Russian Georges Karl Julius "Hack" "The Russian Lion" Hackenschmidt (1878-1968) and American Frank Gotch (1878-1917), were widely acknowledged as the finest wrestlers of the quarter-century before the First World War and did especially much to popularize catch-as-catch-can wrestling (which then permitted all measure of wrestle-like action except strangling) in the late nineteenth and early twentieth centuries. Hackenschmidt was an exceptional weightlifter as well as an enormously powerful wrestler who nonetheless relied mainly on well-crafted movements; he was also exceedingly adept in both Graeco-Roman and freestyle forms of the sport. He wrestled over 3000 matches between 1900 and 1911, lost only twice (both times to Gotch, in 1908 and 1911), was the European amateur Graeco-Roman heavyweight champion in 1898, and was the world professional Graeco-Roman champion in 1901. Gotch was too exceedingly strong and clever; he was the world professional freestyle champion from 1904 to 1906 and from 1906 to 1913; and he won 154 matches and lost only six over his remarkable career (1903-13). A national governing body of professional wrestling in both its Graeco-Roman and freestyle forms, the National Wrestling Alliance, was established in the United States in 1904. Shortly after Gotch's retirement, however, the professional version of wrestling began to develop tendencies to staged entertainment; it nonetheless remained a largely legitimate sporting enterprise until the period between the World Wars.

Although the New York Athletic Club had staged amateur (freestyle) championships from 1878, the first authentic national amateur titles, a freestyle tournament in four weight classes, was conducted in the United States under Amateur Athletic Union auspices in 1889. The sport's first Olympic appearance, a Graeco-Roman tournament in the unlimited weight class, occurred in 1896; weight classes as such (light-flyweight, flyweight, bantamweight, featherweight, lightweight, welterweight, and unlimited weight divisions) first came into Olympic wrestling in the earliest Olympic freestyle tournament, the tournament of 1904 (a middleweight division was added in the 1908 Games); and weight classes as such (lightweight, middleweight, and unlimited weight divisions) first came into Olympic Graeco-Roman wrestling in 1906 (a light-heavyweight division was added in the 1908 Games and a featherweight division was added in the 1912 Games). Wrestling was temporarily excluded from the Olympic program in 1900; Graeco-Roman wrestling was temporarily excluded from the 1904 Games; and freestyle wrestling was temporarily excluded from the 1912 Games. A semblance of irregularly scheduled, world amateur championships, a Graeco-Roman tournament, was first held in Paris in1898; a semblance of largely annual European amateur Graeco-Roman championships was also first held in 1898 (in Vienna). The World Amateur Graeco-Roman Wrestling Championships, which had begun with only two weight classes (lightweight and heavyweight), expanded to three such classes in 1905, to four in 1910, and to five in 1911. The first intercollegiate match, a freestyle meeting among Columbia University, University of Pennsylvania, Princeton University, and victorious Yale University, was conducted in the United States in 1905. And the international governing body of contemporary modern amateur wrestling, Fédération Internationale de Lutte Amateur (FILA), was established in 1912.

Like boxing and wrestling, contemporary modern forms of the **martial arts** developed out of activities that had been variously practiced for centuries to millennia. These forms nonetheless began, in the nineteenth and early twentieth centuries, to formalize and to standardize themselves in ways that were unique to contemporary modern civilization. The principal influences on this development were related transformations in Asian political, economic, social, and intellectual circumstance and burgeoning Western prerogatives in Asia. The broad practice of martial arts virtually throughout Asia, most significantly in east Asia (Japan, Korea, and China) and in southeast Asia, continued in traditional ways connected mainly to military affairs in the nineteenth and twentieth centuries. By far the most significant developments in this respect, in the nineteenth and early twentieth centuries, occurred in Japan and China.

The warrior cult in Japan (and its devotion to the martial arts) was abolished with the Meiji Restoration of 1868; the largely military significance of the martial arts was thereafter converted to more strictly artistic and sporting orientations. The resumption of trade (and other relations) with the West (with the United States and Europe mainly), which began in 1853-54 and which was accelerated by the rapid subsequent industrialization of Japan, by Japanese successes in the First Sino-Japanese War of 1894-95, and by Japanese successes in the Russo-Japanese War of 1904-05, very significantly enlarged the influence of Western culture (including Western sport) on Japanese life. Western sporting values and practices consequently gained increasing prominence in Japan; most notably, by way of (American and British) YMCA and YWCA influence in the country. The result of these developments on the traditional martial arts of Japan, particularly on sumo, kenjutsu, and jujutsu, was enormous. These activities were transfigured by the shift from feudal to industrial society and by the associated spell of Western authority over them; they were made over in the image of European and American sport, the codified sport of capital industrialism. Sumo, which had been on the wane since the twelfth century, was revived and made more characteristically sport-like; it was more fully standardized and more finely regulated. Kendo, a more characteristically sport-like activity than kenjutsu, was developed out of kenjutsu. And Judo, a more characteristically sport-like activity than jujutsu, was fashioned out of jujutsu. Of these, judo has had the largest presence outside of Japan and has had the most telling affect on modern international sport. It was crafted by Jigoro Kano (1860-1938), a long-time member of the International Olympic Committee, in 1882 in order to maintain a traditional element in modern Japanese sporting culture, in order to divest jujutsu of its feudal, class associations, and in order to invest jujutsu with strictly performance-based criteria of achievement. The sport was transported, principally by Kano, to Great Britain in 1885, to the United States in 1902, and to France in 1905.

A similar development unfolded in the Chinese culture of the nineteenth and early twentieth centuries. The Qing Dynasty was increasingly taken over by foreign interests in this time, largely by way of the Opium War of 1839-42, the Lorcha War of 1856-58, the Taiping Rebellion of 1850-64, the First Sino-Japanese War of 1894-95, the Boxer Uprising of 1898-1900, and the Russo-Japanese War of 1904-05. Despite formal Chinese opposition to Western (and Japanese) domination, including opposition to Western forms of sporting activity, Western sport came to increasing prominence in China, largely (as in Japan) by way of (British and American) YMCA and YWCA influence. The abdication of the Qing in 1911 further diminished the commitment to traditional forms of Chinese physical culture. In Europe, mainly in France, a form of martial art entailing kicking and striking, savate, developed out of boxing and dueling practices between 1820 and 1845.

Contemporary modern **fencing** was also formalized and standardized out of notably older practices in the nineteenth and early twentieth centuries. Increasing uses of gunpowder in military affairs, diminishing uses of archery and swordsmanship in such affairs, and decline in the practice of dueling with swords encouraged the development of fencing as a sport in this time. The three main forms of fencing implement, sabre, épée, and foil, which differ in shape, dimension, and mass, were codified and techniques of their use significantly refined in the nineteenth century, largely by French and Italian adepts. The sabre (which requires touches with the tip, front edge, or last one-third of back edge of the blade on the upper body of the opponent) had developed out of the combat sword in the seventeenth century as has been said and it was standardized as a sporting device in the nineteenth century. The épée (which requires touches with the tip of the blade on any aspect of the opponent's body) developed out of the dueling weapon in the nineteenth century and was standardized as a sporting device also in the nineteenth century. And the foil (which requires touches with the tip of the blade on the torso of the opponent) developed out of the combat-training sword in the nineteenth century and was standardized as a sporting device also in the nineteenth century. The Turner's and Swedish gymnastics movements importantly promoted fencing in Europe and North America in the mid-to-late nineteenth century. The first major modern fencing competition was conducted between French and Italian professional and amateur fencing masters in Paris in 1889. The first national governing body, the Amateur Fencers League of America, was established in the United States in 1891 and conducted its first national titles for men in 1892 (although national titles under Amateur Athletic Union auspices had been held from 1888), for women in 1912. Other major national governing bodies soon followed; most notably, the Amateur Fencing Association in Great Britain in 1902 and Fédération des Salles des Armes et Sociétés d'Escrime in France in 1906. The first intercollegiate competition, between Columbia University and victorious Harvard University, was staged in the United States in 1894. And the first Olympic fencing tournament was organized in 1896; fencing (for men) is one of only five sports to appear in every edition of the modern Olympic Games; an Olympic fencing tournament for women was not established until well past the First World War. Individual foil and sabre events were held in the 1896 Games; individual épée was added in 1900; team foil, in 1904; and team épée and sabre, in 1906. French athletes were the dominant figures in foil and épée; Hungarian athletes, in sabre. The most decorated international fencers in the pre-World War One era were:

- Ramon Fonst of Cuba, who won the individual épée event in the 1900 Olympic Games and the individual épée, individual foil, and team foil events in the 1904 Olympic Games; and
- Jeno Fuchs of Hungary, who won the individual and team sabre events in both the 1908 and 1912 Olympic Games, achievements that began the Hungarian hegemony in Olympic sabre fencing that went on until 1960.

The international governing body of contemporary modern fencing, Fédération Internationale d'Escrime (FIE), was established in 1913.

The leading dual court sports, (court) handball, squash, (lawn) tennis, badminton, and table tennis, likewise formalized and standardized their basic, modern provisions in the nineteenth and early twentieth centuries. The fundamental organizing theme of these sports, a person (or two) opposing another person (or two) in a court of varying character in which a ball of varying sorts is variously struck by the hand or by an implement held in the hand (typically a racquet of varying sorts) had been well known for centuries to millennia prior to the nineteenth century. The distant parent of (lawn) tennis, which is the most prominent of these sports, was **court handball**, or "fives." The modern form of court handball was owed mainly to early modern England and to nineteenth-century Ireland. The English public schools (most notably, Eton College) played court handball as such, likely from the very late eighteenth century, certainly from the very early nineteenth century. The contemporary modern development of the sport in its several main forms (hardball and softball forms on one-wall, four-wall, and three-wall courts of varying dimension) is nonetheless most plausibly attributed to Irish and Irish-American initiatives of the last two decades of the nineteenth century and the first decade of the twentieth. Especially significant were attempts of the Gaelic Athletic Association (Ireland) to standardize rules of the sport in the 1880s. The great Irish-American professional player, Phil Casey (1841-1904), was likely the most notable figure in the early contemporary modern formalization of the game. Casey won the first American professional title in a challenge match in New York City in 1887 and won the first so-termed world professional title by defeating the champion of Ireland in a series of challenge matches in Cork, Ireland and New York City in 1888. Casey was undefeated in singles matches from 1876 to his retirement in 1900 and he also remained the world champion until his retirement in 1900. The last

Irish-American challenge match for the world professional (court) handball championship was played in 1909. The first national amateur titles in (court) handball, the American national titles, were conducted under the auspices of the Amateur Athletic Union (with the influential support of the YMCA movement) in 1897. Handball had been importantly dispersed, in formal terms, also to Australia, Canada, France, and Spain before the First World War.

Several significant forms of dual court sport developed quite directly out of handball; most notably, jai alai, racquets, and court tennis. Jai alai evolved from a type of Basque football-handball, or pelota, which had been played from at least the sixteenth century. In its seminal, contemporary modern, its nineteenth-century, development, it entailed striking a ball with the hand alone, then striking a ball with a flat bat, then catching and throwing a ball with a short basket attached to the hand, and, in the end, catching and throwing a very hard and a very fast ball with a long basket (or cesta) attached to the hand-forearm in a three-wall court. It was dispersed in both singles and doubles forms from Spain to adjoining countries (mainly, France and Italy), to other Spanish-speaking countries (mainly, Mexico, Cuba, and the Philippines), and to the United States in the early twentieth century. It has flourished as a professional, indoor sport in these countries in the twentieth century owing significantly to its associations with gambling activities.

Racquets also evolved out of a form of handball in which a ball was first struck with the hand alone, then with a flat bat, and, in the end, with a stringed racquet in either a one-wall, two-wall, three-wall, or four-wall, enclosed court. Although it had been variously played in eighteenth-century English prisons, its contemporary modern form was apparently developed in early nineteenth-century prison courtyards (most likely in London, c. 1800). It was greatly advanced by its first acknowledged national-world champion, Robert Mackey (fl. early nineteenth century) of England, a former inmate himself, who was crowned in 1820; it was significantly popularized by its practice in the English public schools (most notably, Harrow School) beginning in 1817-22; and it flourished tellingly from the 1840s when the English upper classes constructed especially elaborate (one-wall and four-wall) courts for its play. The sport was dispersed, beginning in the 1820s, to Canada, United States, and India/Pakistan most notably. The first intercollegiate match in racquets, between Oxford and Cambridge Universities, was played in 1858; the first national amateur championships in the sport were conducted in Great Britain in 1888 and in the United States in 1890; and the first national governing body of the sport (which effectively became the sport's international governing body), the Tennis and Racquets Association, was formed in Great Britain in 1907. Racquets was played by men in singles and doubles forms in the 1908 Olympic Games, where it was predictably dominated by British players. It nonetheless declined dramatically in practice after the First World War.

Squash, or squash racquets, evolved directly out of racquets at Harrow School (England) in the 1850s; its first formal rules were written in 1886. The game is played on significantly smaller, less elaborate courts than racquets with softer and slower balls than racquets and it is always played on four-wall, enclosed courts; it is otherwise very similar to racquets in both its singles and doubles forms. The distinction between racquets and squash in this time was not altogether unambiguous, however, as both a hardball version (played on a smaller court) and a softball version (played on a larger court) of squash evolved. The softball version, which less resembled racquets than the hardball version, eventually triumphed but not conclusively until well after the Second World War. From the English public schools, the sport was dispersed to English universities and clubs, then most notably to the United States, Canada, and India/Pakistan, beginning in the 1880s. The first national governing body, the United States Squash Racquets Association, was established in 1907, the first national championships were conducted in the United States (men's singles only) in 1907 and in Canada (also men's singles only) in 1912.

Court tennis (royal, or real, tennis), effectively "le jeu de paume," the form of dual court, racquet sport that had been played for centuries in France and England particularly and the form from which (lawn) tennis was derived, was played with a soft, slow, cloth ball on an elaborate, enclosed, four-wall court divided at the center by a net. The sport was dispersed in the late nineteenth century (c. 1876) to the United States most notably, where the earliest authentically national titles were first contested (in men's singles) in 1892. Although the semblance of so-termed world championships for men had been irregularly staged in France on a challenge basis from 1740, and although these championships were resumed (from the eighteenth century) in 1816 and continued to be held irregularly thereafter, the first authentically international tournament, the World Open, was played (in men's singles) in 1885; the first national governing body, the Tennis and Rackets Association, was formed in England in 1907; and the first (and only) medal practice of the sport in the Olympic Games occurred in 1908 (in the form of men's singles), a competition that was predictably dominated by American and British players. The practice of court tennis declined quite dramatically in the period that followed.

Although there was some tendency to eliminate the walls from court tennis beginning in the 1850s, the modern sport of **lawn tennis**, so termed because it was originally played only on grass (it has since been prominently played on several other types of surface as well), was not formally codified until 1873. A British army officer, Major Walter Clopton Wingfield (1833-1912), invented the game (which he called sphairistike after an ancient Greek activity that he thought resembled lawn tennis) in Wales in that year, largely by eliminating the walls of court tennis. The sport was almost entirely an upper-class and an amateur activity until after the First World War. The ball that has made this predominantly outdoor sport among the most athletic of the racquet games, the hollow rubber ball covered in flannel, was developed in 1876. Lawn tennis for both men and women was quickly dispersed to other leading nations, to Bermuda, Canada, and United States in 1874, then to Australasia, Continental Europe, South Africa, and central and South America well before the end of the nineteenth century. The first national governing bodies, the United States Lawn Tennis Association, the Canadian Lawn Tennis Association, and the Lawn Tennis Association (Great Britain), were established in 1881, 1884, and 1886 respectively. The earliest intercollegiate matches were played between Oxford and Cambridge Universities in England in 1881 and between Amherst College, Brown University, Harvard University, Trinity College, and Yale University in the United States in 1883; the Intercollegiate Lawn Tennis Association was established in the United States and conducted its first (national) titles for men (in singles and doubles), both in 1883. The four leading annual tournaments in the world – the so-termed grand- slam tournaments – were also created in the late nineteenth and early twentieth centuries:

- the All-England (Wimbledon [near London]) Championships in 1877 (men's singles, 1877; men's doubles, 1879; women's singles, 1884; women's doubles, 1899; mixed doubles, 1900);
- the United States Open Championships (various sites: Newport, Rhode Island; Forest Hills [New York City], New York; and Flushing Meadow [New York City], New York) in 1881 (men's singles and doubles, 1881; women's singles, 1887; women's doubles, 1889; mixed doubles, 1887);
- the French Open Championships (Paris, mainly Stade Roland Garros) in 1891 (men's singles, 1891; women's singles, 1897; men's and women's doubles, 1925; mixed doubles, 1925); and
- the Australian Open Championships (mainly Melbourne) in 1905 (men's singles and doubles, 1905; women's singles and doubles, 1922; mixed doubles, 1922).

The other leading national open tournament established in this period was the annual German Open Championships, first played among men in 1892 and among women in 1896.

Lawn tennis was played in every edition of the Olympic Games before the First World War, including the first; men's singles and doubles events were staged in 1896; women's singles and mixed doubles events were added to the Olympic program in 1900; British athletes were the dominant figures in these events. The first female Olympic champion, Charlotte Cooper of Great Britain, was the singles and mixed doubles tennis champion in 1900 as has been said; she was also the Wimbledon singles champion in 1895, 1896, 1898, 1901, and 1908 and among the finest players of her day. The other leading female players of the late nineteenth and early twentieth centuries were also among the most accomplished athletes of the age irrespective of sport and they too did a great deal to advance the practice of women's sport in general and of women's tennis in particular:

- Charlotte "Lottie" Dod (1871-1960) of Great Britain, who won the Wimbledon singles crown in 1887, 1888, 1891, 1892, and 1893, who won the British Ladies' Amateur Golf Championship in 1904, and who was also outstanding in archery (in which she won an Olympic silver medal in 1908), field hockey, and ice skating;
- Hazel Virginia Hotchkiss-Wightman (1886-1974) of the United States, who won United States Open singles titles in 1909, 1910, 1911, and 1919, United States Open doubles titles in 1909, 1910, 1911, 1915, 1924, and 1928, and United States Open mixed doubles titles in 1909, 1910, 1911, 1915, 1918, and 1920, who won the 1924 Wimbledon doubles title, the 1924 Olympic doubles and mixed doubles titles, and the 1930 United States national squash singles title, and who was the sponsoring donor of the Wightman Cup (the female equivalent of the Davis Cup for men); and
- Eleanora R. Sears (1881-1968) of the United States, who won United States Open doubles titles in 1911, 1915, 1916, and 1917 as well as the United States Open mixed doubles title in 1916, who won the United States national squash singles title in 1928, and who was also outstanding in baseball, canoeing, equestrian, golf, pedestrianism, polo, shooting, swimming, yachting/sailing, and automobile and motorboat racing.

The foremost male players of the period were too exemplary, if less versatile, athletes and they likewise contributed much to the burgeoning popularity of the game:

- William Charles "Willie" Renshaw (1861-1904) of England, who won Wimbledon singles titles in 1881, 1882, 1883, 1884, 1885, 1886, and 1889 and Wimbledon doubles titles in 1880, 1881, 1884, 1885, 1886, 1888, and 1889;
- Richard D. Sears (1861-1943) of the United States, no relation to Eleanora, who was the first United States Open singles champion (1881), who also won this title in 1882, 1883, 1884, 1885, 1886, and 1887, who won United States Open doubles titles in 1882, 1883, 1884, 1885, 1886, and 1887, and who won the first United States national court tennis singles title in 1892; and
- Maurice E. "Red" McLaughlin (1890-1957) of the United States, who won United States Open singles titles in 1912 and 1913 and United States Open doubles titles in 1912, 1913, and 1914 and who was the first working-class person to achieve high distinction in tennis, this at the beginning of the second decade of the twentieth century, a time of unusually progressive political, economic, and social tendency.

The major international team titles for men in modern lawn tennis, the annual Davis Cup, was established in 1900. The trophy emblematic of these titles was donated by Dwight Filley Davis (1879-1945) of the United States, himself an accomplished intercollegiate and open amateur player (he won the 1899, 1900, and 1901 United States Open doubles titles) and a significant national political figure (Secretary of War and Governor-General of the Philippines). Davis Cup competition initially included only the United States and Great Britain but gradually came to include virtually all other tennis-playing nations as well; Austria, Belgium, and France joined the competition in 1904, Australia/New Zealand (Australasia) was first included in 1905 for prominent instance. The first such competition was won by the United States; all subsequent titles before the First World War were won by the United States, Great Britain, or Australia. The international governing body of contemporary modern lawn tennis, the International Lawn Tennis Federation (ITF), or Fédération Internationale de Tennis, was formed in 1913.

One of the two remaining, major forms of dual court sport, badminton, was not explicitly linked to tennis, its precursors, or its derivatives; the other, table tennis, was. **Badminton**, or "poona," was first fashioned in India by English army officers in c. 1871 and transported to England, to the Badminton Estates (in southwestern England, near the Welsh border), in 1873. The first formal club, the Bath Badminton Club, was established near Badminton in 1887; it transformed the original Indian game and wrote the first standardized rules, also in 1887. The first national governing body, the Badminton Association, was created in Great Britain in 1895. And the first national championships, the annual All-England Badminton Championships/British Badminton Open were conducted in 1899 (men's and women's doubles and mixed doubles, 1899; men's and women's singles, 1900); it remained the most important tournament in the world until well past the Second World War. The finest player of this period, Ethel Warneford Thomson-Larcombe (1879-1965) of England, won the women's singles event at this tournament ten times (1900, 1901, and 1903-10), won the women's doubles event at this tournament four times (1902, 1904, 1905, and 1906), and won the mixed doubles event at this tournament twice (1903 and 1904); she was also the 1912 Wimbledon singles tennis champion and the 1914 Wimbledon mixed doubles tennis champion. The other most significant tournament of the pre-World War One period was the Scottish Open, first played in 1907. The new sport was dispersed to its other major centers, Australasia, Canada, Denmark, Malaysia, Netherlands, Norway, South Africa, Sweden, and United States, in the 1890s.

The origins of **table tennis**, "indoor tennis," or "ping pong," conversely, are less clear but the sport was likely owed to British army officers serving in India and South Africa in the 1880s and to subsequent and related English practices of the 1890s. It grew out of an attempt to create an indoor version of tennis, a version played on a more modest spatial scale than tennis itself. The distinctive celluloid balls and rubber-covered wooden paddles, which have significantly defined play of the game, were developed in England in 1900 and 1902 respectively. The first national governing body of table tennis, the Ping Pong Association/English Table Tennis Association, was established in 1902. Although table tennis had made its way to North America, Australasia, and Continental Europe before the First World War, it did not become a prominent national and international sport until after the War.

Other major forms of dual sport, billiards, croquet, and curling, also formalized and standardized their basic, modern provisions in the nineteenth and early twentieth centuries. The development of contemporary modern **billiards** (referring generally to cues and caroms) was greatly affected by technical advancements in the table on which it was played and in the equipment with which it was played: leather tips were affixed to the striking end of cues and brass balls were replaced with ivory balls in the first decade of the nineteenth century; chalk was used on cue tips in order to rotate cue balls in creative ways in the second decade of the nineteenth century; wooden tables were replaced with marble-top, then slate-top tables in the 1820s; and felt-covered wooden cushions were replaced by felt-covered rubber cushions in the 1830s. The game itself has been played in a dizzying variety of forms, even in the nineteenth and early twentieth centuries; its most notable forms, however, have been three-cushion, pocket (pool), balkline, and snooker. Three-cushion billiards entails the successive striking of the cue ball in such a way that it contacts two object balls and three cushions before coming to rest. Pocket billiards itself comes in numerous forms, all of which entail successively striking object balls into pockets by way of the cue ball; its main forms are a fifteen-object-ball game (straight pool) sometimes played in stipulated rotations, sometimes not, an eight-object-ball game played in stipulated rotations, and a nine-object-ball game played in stipulated rotations. Balkline billiards, also of manifold types, entails successively striking the cue ball in such a way that it contacts two object balls and drives one of them outside "the" balkline (lines drawn parallel to all four cushions); in its two principal forms, 18.1 and 18.2, balklines are put eighteen inches from each cushion; in 18.1, one shot is permitted in balk; in 18.2, two shots are permitted in balk. And snooker, a distinctive variety of pocket billiards, is played with twenty-one variously colored and valued object balls that must be successively pocketed by way of the cue ball in loosely stipulated rotations.

Before mid-century, billiards was primarily an unstandardized pocket game of varied sorts played in exhibitions and challenge matches in France, Great Britain, Spain, the Germanies, and the United States. The dominant form of billiards in the 1850s and 1860s was a four-ball type of pocket game; in the 1870s and 1880s, three-ball and four-ball types of game emphasizing caroms alone, three-cushion billiards, and snooker became also prominent; balkline games began in the 1880s but were not widely played until the 1890s; the eight-ball form of pocket billiards was developed in c. 1900; and straight pool was fashioned in c. 1910. At the top levels, the sport was primarily professional, not amateur, in basic orientation and it was significantly governed by gambling concerns. The first intercollegiate match was played between Harvard and Yale Universities in the United States in 1860. The first national governing bodies, the American Billiards Players Association, the National American Billiards Association, and the Billiards Association of Great Britain and Ireland, were established in 1865, 1866, and 1885 respectively and they did especially much to standardize the rules of the sport. Although professional challenge matches for so-termed national titles had been played in Great Britain from 1825, the first authentically national professional championships were played in the United States and in Great Britain in 1870. The semblance of (irregularly scheduled) world professional championships in carom and pocket billiards began in 1870; the semblance of (irregularly scheduled) world professional championships in three-cushion billiards began in 1878; 18.1 and 18.2 balkline play conducted (irregularly scheduled) world championships from 1903; and the semblance of (irregularly scheduled) world professional championships in pocket billiards for women began in 1897. Although the incomparable Willie Hoppe played very successfully before the First World War, his career came to full prominence after the War. The other leading players prior to the First World War were:

- Jacob "Jake" Schaefer, Sr. (1855-1910) of the United States, who was the greatest player of the nineteenth century, who competed at the highest levels between 1876 and 1908, who won the world 18.2 balkline title in 1907 and the world 18.1 balkline title in 1908, and whose son, Jacob "Jake" Schaefer, Jr. (1894-1975) of the United States, was also several-times world champion; and
- Alfredo DeOro (1862-1948) of Spain, who won or tied for the world pocket title in 1887-89, 1892-95, 1899-1901, 1903-05, 1908, and 1910-13 and who won or tied for the world three-cushion title in 1908-11, 1913-14, and 1916-19.

Contemporary modern **croquet** (referring generally to a crooked stick) developed mainly out of older French games in nineteenth-century France, Ireland, and England. This form of croquet was first played in France in 1846, passed to Ireland in 1851, and to England in 1852. The first formal clubs devoted to the sport, the Oatlands (near Dublin, Ireland) Croquet Club and the Grand National Croquet Club (England) were established in 1858 and 1867 respectively. The first formal rules were written in England in 1866; the first national titles were played in Ireland (in 1861), in England (in 1867), and in the United States (in 1882); and the first national governing bodies, the National Croquet Association (United States) and the United All-England Croquet Association, were established in 1879 and 1896 respectively. The popularity of croquet among both men and women advanced with that of lawn tennis in the last several decades of the nineteenth century, then declined sharply with the triumph of tennis over it in the 1890s. The seminal development of contemporary modern croquet was nonetheless much associated with that of lawn tennis, largely owing to the reliance of both on extraordinary grass courts and to the exclusive sporting tendencies of the aristo-cratic-bourgeois class (that could uniquely afford to construct and maintain such courts). The most notable organization in the early development of contemporary modern croquet, the All-England Croquet Club, was formed at Wimbledon (near London, England) in 1869 and associated itself with lawn tennis in 1875, becoming the All-England Croquet and Lawn Tennis Club; it is on the grounds of this Club that the fabled Wimbledon Tennis Championships are played.

Croquet's most prestigious competition, the (annual) United All-England Croquet Association Open Championship/British Open Championship, was first played in the form of a singles event in 1897, after the administration of croquet had been separated from that of lawn tennis. The sport was included in both the 1900 and 1904 Olympic Games, then discontinued as an Olympic activity. In the 1900 Games, the European form of the game (croquet in the strict sense) was contested; both the singles and doubles events were open in principle to men and women; and these events were dominated by French men. In the 1904 Games, a faster, more athletic, American version known as roque was contested. This was a version that used smaller and harder mallets than croquet itself, harder balls than croquet, two balls per player instead of one (as in croquet), and smaller wickets (arches, hoops) than croquet, a version that (unlike croquet itself) entailed carom shots off boundary boards, but a version that was otherwise similar to croquet (that is, played with two stakes, nine wickets, and like rules). The only such event on the 1904 Olympic program, a men's singles event, was dominated by American players. The sport did nonetheless not come to its approximate, current form until the several years just prior to the First World War (c. 1912-14) when the width of wickets was standardized at their current dimensions, when the rule concerning the necessity of playing the balls in sequence was abolished, and when the current grip and techniques of play were developed. The major innovations of grip and playing technique were owed principally to three Irishmen who were among the most accomplished players of the pre-World War One era: C.L. O'Callaghan (1875-1942), Cyril Corbally (1881-1946), and Patrick Mathews (1886-1960).

Contemporary modern **curling** (referring generally to the arched path of a well-thrown curling stone) had begun its formal development in eighteenth-century Scotland as has been said. This dual winter sport (it is similar to lawn bowling but played on ice surfaces) with tendencies to team orientation (it is customarily played between four-person male or female teams) was nonetheless standardized in the nineteenth century. Rounded stones with handles replaced irregular cubed stones in c. 1800; the first formal rules were written by the Dudingston Curling Club of Edinburgh (Scotland) in 1803; and these rules and stones were first standardized by the Amateur Curling Club of Scotland in 1834. The earliest national governing body of curling, the Grand (or Royal) Caledonian Curling Club, was established in Scotland in 1838 and became the principal organization for the sport throughout the world. The first national championships, the so-termed Grand Match, were contested in 1847 under the auspices of this Club. The sport was dispersed to its other major centers mainly by Scottish immigrants; it was played formally in Canada by c. 1807, in the United States by c. 1820, and in central and northern Continental Europe by c. 1880. The largest curling tournament in the world prior to the First World War, the Manitoba (or Winnipeg) Bonspiel, was established in Canada in 1889. The first international competitions were: played between Canadian and American clubs (became the near-annual Gordon International Gold Matches, or Gordon International Medal Series) in 1884; the Scotland-Canada (became the Strathcoma Cup) and Scotland-United States matches of 1902-03; and the England-Scotland match of 1903.

Unlike most other major, contemporary modern sports, which formalized activities that had been earlier practiced in some discernible form, **motor sports** were a creation of the industrial age. Before the First World War, these sports were mainly the province of the upper classes; they were governed by a sense of invention, entrepreneurial opportunity, and adventure; they were used as testing grounds for the design and manufacture of salable machinery as well as for publicity and the advertising of such machinery; and they were greatly troubled by frequent and serious accidents and by the safety concerns associated with such accidents. Self-propelled steam-driven devices, effectively cars and boats, had been variously derived from the invention of the steam engine (by Scottish engineer, James Watt) in 1769. A steam car was fashioned in that year and many others were attempted with measured success in England, Italy, and France over the next approximate century. The steamboat was developed in 1807 and was occasionally raced on major American rivers in particular. It was, however, the invention of the internal combustion engine by German engineer, Gottlieb Daimler, in 1884-85 that established the technological groundwork of modern motor sport. Daimler attached his engine to a bicycle in 1885 and thus formed the pioneer motor-driven vehicle. The motorcycle did not receive concentrated attention, however, until 1900 when its distinctive design was worked out in Belgium and the United States. The first formal club devoted to the sport, the Motor Cycling Club of Great Britain, was established in 1901; the first endurance run was done from New York City to Boston in 1902; the first race was conducted in Brooklyn, New York, U.S.A. in 1903; and the first hill climb was staged in Boston in 1904. The first national governing body, the Federation of American Motorcyclists, was established in the

United States in 1903; the international governing body of modern motorcycle racing, Fédération Internationale des Clubs Motocyclistes/Fédération Internationale de Motocycliste/Fédération Internationale de Motocyclisme (FIM), was formed in 1904; and the most notable race before the First World War, the (annual, individual) Tourist Trophy, was first contested on the Isle of Man (in the Irish Sea, between Ireland and England) in 1907. The first world championships in the sport, the (near-annual, national team) FIM World Trophy for the International Six-Day Endurance Race, was first contested in 1913. Likely the most memorable pre-World War One achievement in motorcycling was the first 100-miles-per-hour performance in 1912.

In 1887, Daimler attached his engine also to a rowboat, thus fashioning the first outboard motorboat. The motorboat did not receive concentrated attention, however, until 1896 when its distinctive design and an inboard version of it were worked out in the United States. The first national governing bodies of the sport were established in the early twentieth century: the Marine Motoring Association (Great Britain) in 1902, the Congress of Automobile Boats (France) in 1903, and the American Power Boat Association also in 1903. The first international governing body of modern motorboat racing, the International Motor Yacht Association/Association Internationale du Yachting Automobile, was formed in 1908. The two major competitions before the First World War, the Harmsworth Cup/British International Cup for Motor-Boats (a sporadically scheduled but near-annual, international contest originated by Alfred Charles William Harmsworth Northcliffe [1865-1922] of Ireland and England) and the Gold Challenge Cup Trophy (the annual national championships of the United States), were established in 1903 and 1904 respectively. The other most significant races in this period included a 100km/c. 62 miles circuit race at Meulan, France in 1903, a 370 km/c. 230 miles race from Paris to Trouville, France in 1903, and a 40 km/c. 25 miles English Channel Race (from Dover, England to Calais, France) in 1904. Still other influential races were also staged in the vicinity of New York City from 1903 and in Monte Carlo, Monaco (the Monaco International Regatta) from 1904. Motorboat racing is the only motor activity that has been a medal (or even a formal demonstration) sport in the Olympic Games; its lone Olympic appearance occurred in 1908 and included three events, one in each of three classes of boat, two for three men and one for one man. These events were dominated by British drivers; all major events prior to the First World War were dominated by either British or American drivers. A radical redesign of the boat's hull in 1910 and the replacement of inboard motor designs with hydroplane designs in 1912 brought the fastest speed achieved before the First World War to just beneath one mile per minute (i.e., to c. 58 m.p.h./c. 94 k.p.h. in 1912).

Daimler too experimented briefly with his engine as a means of propelling what could be loosely called an automobile but the distinctive design of the automobile was more notably worked out in France and the United States in 1887-88 and 1892 respectively. The notion of racing automobiles was also a largely French and American invention. The first automobile race, from Paris to Rouen (c. 110 km/c. 78 miles), was conducted in 1894. Many others soon followed; most notably, Paris-Bordeaux-Paris (c. 1170 km/c. 732 miles) in 1895; a race in Chicago (c. 54 miles/c. 87 km) in 1895; Paris-Amsterdam-Paris in 1898; a race in Detroit in 1899; the James Gordon Bennett Trophy races from Paris to Lyons in 1900-05; Paris-Berlin in 1901; Paris-Vienna-Paris in 1902; Paris-Madrid in 1903; the Vanderbilt Cup races in Long Island (New York City) from 1904; Peking/Beijing-Paris in 1907; New York City-Paris (effectively, an around-the-world, east-to-west race of c. 12,427 land miles/c. 19,970 km) in 1908; and a transcontinental race, New York City-Seattle, in 1909. These were mostly stock-car (or slightly modified stock-car) races. The earliest major contest for highly specialized racing vehicles were the first Grand Prix races, the French Grand Prix at Le Mans (southwest of Paris) in 1906 and the American Grand Prix in 1908; the first major, ongoing, long-distance road race, the Targa Florio, in Sicily, Italy in 1906; the first major auto rally, the Monte Carlo Rally, in Monaco in 1911; and the first Indianapolis (Indiana, U.S.A.) 500 on arguably the most fabled automobile race track in the world, the Indianapolis Speedway (constructed in 1906-09), in 1911. The first national governing bodies of automobile racing, the Automobile Club of France and the American Automobile Club/Association, were established in 1895 and 1902 respectively; the first national titles were conducted in the United States in 1909; and the international governing body of modern automobile racing, Fédération Internationale de l'Automobile (FIA), was formed in 1904. Speed records as such also became a significant feature of automobile racing in this period; these records were customarily established over one-mile, straight courses with flying starts; one mile per minute was first achieved in 1899 and 100 miles per hour was first done in 1904. The first person to surpass these barriers on a closed-circuit track (in 1903 and 1910 respectively), American driver, Berna Eli "Barney" Oldfield (1878-1946), was likely the most celebrated figure in motor sports before the First World War and feasibly also the first person of modest origins to achieve high distinction in motor activities. The origins of airplane racing were also owed to this time; the international governing body of air sports, Fédération Aéronautique Internationale (FAI), was established in 1905; the first airplane races were staged in Rheims, France in 1909.